Vermont

AN EXPLORER'S GUIDE

WITHDRAWN

Vermont

Christina Tree & Diane E. Foulds

TWELFTH EDITION

The Countryman Press ✳ Woodstock, Vermont

DEDICATION

To Bill Davis, my companion on the road. C.T.

For Edith C. Foulds—as much a Vermonter as a person can be. D.F.

We welcome your comments and suggestions. Please contact Explorer's Guide Editor, The Countryman Press, P.O. Box 748, Woodstock, Vermont 05091, or e-mail countrymanpress@wwnorton.com.

Twelfth Edition

ISBN-13: 978-0-88150-848-2

Maps by Moore Creative Design, © 2009 The Countryman Press
Cover and interior design by Bodenweber Design
Text composition by PerfecType, Nashville, TN
Cover photograph by Bill Krist/CORBIS

Published by The Countryman Press, P.O. Box 748, Woodstock, Vermont 05091

Distributed by W. W. Norton & Company, Inc., 500 Fifth Avenue, New York, NY 10110

Printed in the United States of America

10 9 8 7 6 5 4 3 2 1

EXPLORE WITH US!

We have been fine-tuning *Vermont: An Explorer's Guide* for the past 26 years, a period in which lodging, dining, and shopping opportunities have more than quadrupled in the state. As we have expanded our guide, we have also been increasingly selective, making recommendations based on years of conscientious research and personal experience. What makes us unique is that we describe the state by locally defined regions, giving you Vermont's communities, not simply its most popular destinations. With this guide you'll feel confident to venture beyond the tourist towns, along roads less traveled, to places of special hospitality and charm.

WHAT'S WHERE

In the beginning of the book you'll find an alphabetical listing of special highlights, with important information and advice on everything from antiques to weather reports.

LODGING

Prices. Please don't hold us or the respective innkeepers responsible for the rates listed as of press time in 2009. Some changes are inevitable. **We do not include state room and meals tax in rates unless stated.** (See *Taxes* in "What's Where.") Many lodging establishments also add a gratuity to their listed rate, something we try to note but do not always catch. It's best to check ahead of time.

    Smoking. State law bars smoking in all places of public accommodation in Vermont, including restaurants and bars.

RESTAURANTS

Note the distinction between *Dining Out* and *Eating Out*. By their nature, restaurants listed in the *Eating Out* group are generally inexpensive.

KEY TO SYMBOLS

⚭   **Weddings**. The wedding-ring symbol appears beside establishments that frequently serve as venues for weddings and civil unions.

⚚   **Special value**. The special-value symbol appears next to lodging and restaurants that combine high quality and moderate prices.

🐾   **Pets**. The dog-paw symbol appears next to lodgings that accept pets (usually with a reservation and deposit) as of press time.

✎   **Child-friendly**. The kids-alert symbol appears next to lodging, restaurants, activities, and shops of special appeal to youngsters.

♿   **Handicapped access**. The wheelchair symbol appears next to lodging, restaurants, and attractions that are partially or fully handicapped accessible.

☏   **Wireless Internet**. This symbol appears beside places offering WiFi or computer access.

We would appreciate your comments and corrections about places you visit or know well in the state. Please e-mail Chris: ctree@traveltree.net.

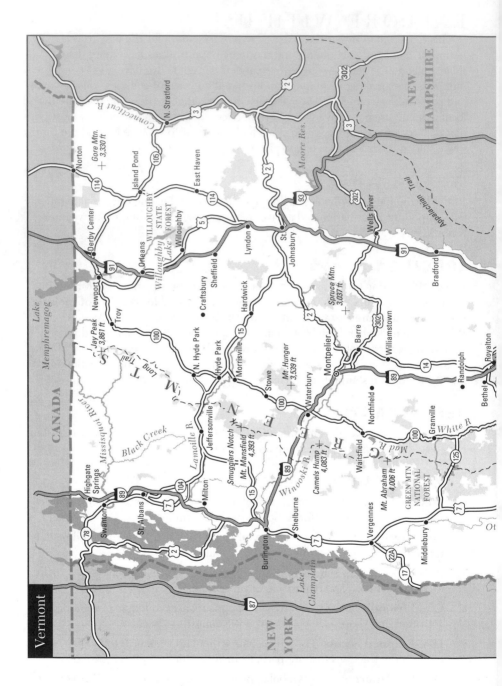

Vermont

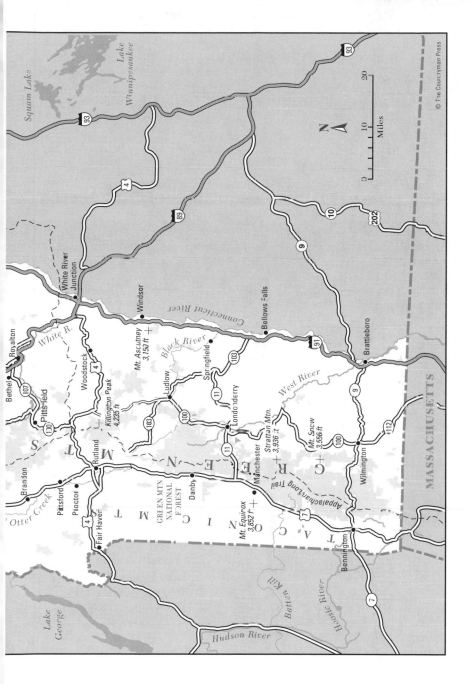

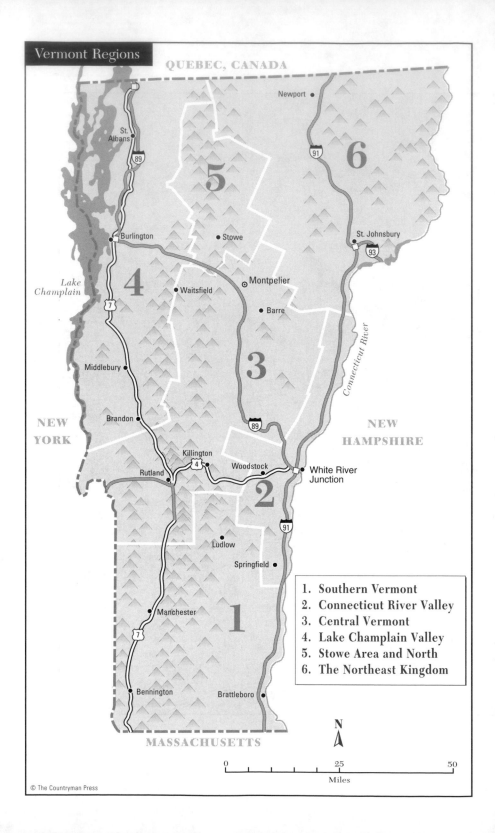

Vermont Regions

QUEBEC, CANADA

Newport

St. Albans

89

5

91

6

Burlington

Stowe

St. Johnsbury

93

Lake Champlain

4

Waitsfield

Montpelier

Barre

3

Middlebury

Connecticut River

NEW YORK

Brandon

Killington

4

Rutland

Woodstock

White River Junction

89

NEW HAMPSHIRE

2

91

Ludlow

Springfield

Manchester

1

7

Bennington

Brattleboro

MASSACHUSETTS

N

1. Southern Vermont
2. Connecticut River Valley
3. Central Vermont
4. Lake Champlain Valley
5. Stowe Area and North
6. The Northeast Kingdom

0   25   50
Miles

© The Countryman Press

CONTENTS

6 The Northeast Kingdom / 559

INTRODUCTION

Welcome to the Green Mountain State and this 12th edition of the most comprehensive guide to its distinctive landscape, character, things to do, and places to see and stay. No other portrait of Vermont gathers so much practical information between two covers—so much that even Vermonters find it useful.

We have divided the guide into generally accepted regions. Each section begins with a verbal snapshot of the area against a historical background, and includes descriptions of just about every legal form of recreation, from skiing and swimming to llama trekking and whitewater rafting.

We describe roughly two-thirds of Vermont's inns, B&Bs, farm stays, and family-owned (but not chain) motels. We are candid about what we like and don't like. We visit regularly and we describe many reasonably priced gems found in no other book.

We critique upscale restaurants (*Dining Out*) and everyday options (*Eating Out*), plus good delis, bakeries, and coffeehouses. Local entertainment, interesting shops, and special events round out coverage of virtually every city and town, and most villages.

Ironically, Vermont's fame as an autumn and winter destination has upstaged its original tourist season. Vermont's summer is soft, still, and deep, almost secretive. While traffic jams New England's coastal resorts, Vermont's roads and widely scattered lodgings remain blissfully quiet. Wooded paths and swimming holes are never far but rarely obvious.

Vermont is not an in-your-face kind of place. Most of the things we like best about it are not obvious. Of course there are the ski resorts, country inns, and "attractions" like Ben & Jerry's, the Shelburne Museum, and the Rock of Ages. Vermont is found, however, along its vast network of unpaved roads and hiking paths, in crafts studios, visiting or staying at a farm, picnicking by a waterfall or covered bridge, eating at a community supper, and shopping at farmer's markets.

A CHURCH IN BROOKFIELD

Christina Tree

Christina Tree

FARM, WEST GLOVER

During the 26-year life of this book Vermont's rural character has changed, but not essentially. Farming and processing locally grown and produced products is a flourishing industry that continues to evolve. Growing and eating locally sourced food has become almost a religion in diners and delis as well as the most expensive restaurants and inns.

As an income source, tourism is, admittedly, outstripping the agriculture that Vermonters so passionately espouse. Twice since 1993 the National Trust for Historic Preservation has placed Vermont on its list of the nation's 11 Most Endangered Places. In 1998 the state launched a program called "Green Hotels in the Green Mountain State." At this writing it has conferred green certification on 82 (out of 985) lodging establishments that meet standards for recycling, composting, and energy conservation. This number includes all the lodging establishments in the town of Chester. The number of those to comply is growing quickly.

True, today's shopping-center culture has made inroads here. Still, for every acre of open land paved for a parking lot, currently at least 10 acres are added to the holdings of the Vermont Land Trust, therefore shielded from development. The administrators of Act 250, the state's pioneering land-use program, also still exercise sensible controls over new commercial development, defeating sporadic efforts to dilute the act's provisions. Vermonters, prudently and in a spirit of thrift, have been loath to tear down the past. Abandoned farmhouses have been restored, and in a score of towns adaptive preservation techniques have been thoughtfully applied.

Contrary to its image, Vermont's landscape varies substantially from north to south and even more from east to west. Rather than following the main tourist routes (east–west Rts. 9 and 4 and north–south Rt. 100), we suggest that (weather permitting) you drive the dramatic but well-paved "gap" roads (see *Gaps, Gulfs, and Gorges* in "What's Where") east or west across the state's relatively narrow width, bundling very different landscapes—mountain valleys and the broad sweep of farmland along Lake Champlain—into a few hours' drive.

While focusing on all the state's regions through the same lens (our format), we fervently hope that this book conveys the full spectrum of Vermont's beauty: the river roads of the Upper Valley, the high rolling farmland around Tunbridge and Chelsea, the glacially carved, haunting hills of the Northeast Kingdom, and the limestone farmsteads of Isle La Motte. Villages range from the elegant, gentrified resorts such as Stowe, Woodstock, and Manchester, to the equally proud but far less traveled villages of Craftsbury Common, Grafton, and Newfane, and the Victorian brick streetscapes of Brattleboro and Burlington.

Vermont has never been a "rich" state. Except for machine tools, the industrial revolution passed it by; as one political scientist noted, Vermonters leaped from "cow chips to microchips." Nevertheless, at least a few 19th-century families made their fortunes from lumber, wool, marble, and railroads. The 14 years that it existed as a sovereign nation (between 1777 and 1791) stamped Vermont with a certain contrariness. Many examples of its free spirit animate its subsequent history, from the years when Ethan Allen's Rabelaisian Green Mountain Boys wrested independence from the grip of Hampshiremen, 'Yorkers, and "The Cruel Minestereal Tools of George ye 3d" to their quashing of British attempts to retake the Champlain Corridor. This autonomous spirit was later responsible for the abolitionist fervor that swept the state in the years before the Civil War and impelled Vermonters to enlist in record numbers when President Lincoln appealed for troops. Vermonters voted their consciences with much the same zeal when, in both world wars, the legislature declared war on Germany, in effect, before the United States did. More recently Vermont was the first state to legalize civil unions between same-sex couples. It boasts one of the nation's highest percentages of women in the legislature and a strict environmental policy, and is always prepared—if push comes to shove—to secede.

The Authors

A flatland author, born in Hawaii, raised in New York City, and living near Boston, Chris Tree claims to be a professional Vermont visitor. Her infatuation with the state began more than 40 years ago in college.

"The college was in Massachusetts, but one of my classmates was a native Vermonter whose father ran a general store and whose mother knows the name of every flower, bird, and mushroom. I jumped at her invitations to come 'home' or to 'camp' and have since spent far more time in Vermont than has my friend. As a travel writer for the *Boston Globe*, I spent more than 35 years writing newspaper stories about Vermont towns, inns, ski areas, and people. I interviewed John Kenneth Galbraith about Newfane, Pearl Buck about Danby. I rode the Vermont Bicentennial Train, froze a toe on one of the first inn-to-inn ski treks, camped on the Long Trail and in state parks, paddled a canoe down the Connecticut, slid over Lake Champlain on an iceboat as well as paddling it in a kayak, soared over the Mad River Valley in a glider, and hovered above the Upper Valley in a hot-air balloon. I have also tramped through the woods collecting sap, led a foliage tour, collided with a tractor, and broken down in a variety of places."

Research for this edition represents the 12th time that Chris has combed regions around the Green Mountain State, traveling back roads to check out B&Bs, craftspeople, cheesemakers, and (yes!) swimming holes. It all seems to take longer than it once did, perhaps because there's more to talk about along the way. Vermont is as much about people as landscape, and both welcome an old friend.

Diane Foulds is an eighth-generation Vermonter. Her father was a forester

TOURISM IN VERMONT

Contrary to common belief, tourism (for lack of a better word to describe the phenomenon of visitors "from away") is an integral part of Vermont's history, one that has affected its landscape—not just since the 1950s but for 150 years.

Before the Civil War, southerners patronized mineral spas in every part of the Green Mountain State, from Brattleboro to Brunswick Springs. You can still see glimpses of these antique establishments in such off-the-beaten-track places as Clarendon Springs. After the war, Vermont's burgeoning railroads teamed up with the state's Board of Agriculture to promote farm vacations. Railroad guides also promoted Newport, with its elegant four-story Lake Memphremagog House ("one of the largest and finest hotels in New England"), and Lake Willoughby ("one of the most remarkable places in the continent"). Carriage roads were built to the top of Jay Peak, Mount Mansfield, and Mount Equinox, and of course there was a summit hotel atop Mount Mansfield (the highest peak in the state) as well as a the Green Mountain Inn in Stowe Village.

In the 1850s the Equinox House was recognized as one of New England's leading hotels. By 1862 the *Manchester Journal* could report that the previous summer, "Every house in the village was as full as a 'Third Avenue car,' almost entirely New Yorkers." Woodstock was equally well known in the right Manhattan circles by the 1890s.

All 19th- and early-20th-century visitors arrived by train (the exception being those who crossed Lake Champlain by ferry), and Vermont was slower than many other states to provide roads suitable to touring. The flood of 1927 washed out a number of major highways and bridges. In 1936 a proposal for building a federally funded, 260-mile Green Mountain Parkway the length of the state—passing just below the crests of Pico, Killington, and several other peaks—was roundly defeated in a public referendum.

After World War II, however, Vermont launched what may be the world's first and most successful campaign to turn off-season into peak season.

"If you can pick and choose, there is no better time for a motor trip through Vermont than in autumn," Abner W. Coleman wrote in the first issue of *Vermont Life*, a state publication. The autumn 1946 article continued: "To the color photographer, Vermont during the autumn months offers delights indescribable. Should film become more plentiful this year, hundreds of camera enthusiasts will be roaming around these hills, knocking themselves out in a happy frenzy of artistic endeavor. For the autumn woods run the entire spectrum's course, from the blazing reds of the maple through the pale yellows of beech and birch to the violet of far-off mountain walls." The story was illustrated with the first of many vividly hued photos for which *Vermont Life* remains famous.

While Vermonters can't claim to have invented skiing, the state does boast America's oldest ski resorts. In the 1930s skiers began riding rope tows up slopes in Woodstock, at Pico, and on Mount Mansfield; after World War II, Stowe became "Ski Capital of the East." Patrons at Mad River Glen built the country's first slope-side lodging, and in the early '60s nearby Sugarbush opened with the East's first bottom-of-the-lifts village. In ensuing decades more than a dozen Vermont ski areas have evolved into year-round resorts, several (Stowe, Sugarbush, and Killington) spawning full-fledged communities. Stowe and Warren were towns before they were resorts.

Vermont's ski communities mirror (in reverse) the story of its mill towns. Whereas mills were positioned on waterfalls—and no longer need the water to generate power—ski resorts have grown around mountains chosen for their good terrain and "dependable" snowfall. Only in recent years has it become apparent that access to enough water—to make snow—is crucial.

The question of whether skiing or any other manifestation of "tourism" (again that inadequate term) contributes to the preservation or destruction of the Vermont character and landscape can be argued interminably. But the fact is that it has been here for 150 years. Today Vermont inns and B&Bs outnumber farms, and Vermont visitors outnumber cows.

Today's visitor is more likely than not to be welcomed by ex-visitors: More than 40 percent of the state's population of 623,908) has come "from away," a post–World War II phenomenon that has profoundly affected the cultural and political landscapes.

Much has been made of the proverbial "Vermont mystique," that indefinable quality of life and character. It is, we are happy to report, alive and well, especially along the back roads and in villages and hamlets where "neighboring" still reigns. While the portrait of the legendary Vermont Yankee—frugal, wary, taciturn, sardonic—has faded somewhat in today's homogenized culture, independent-minded Vermonters (many of them ex-"tourists") take care of one another, tolerate eccentricities, and regard the world with a healthy skepticism.

A NOTE ON LODGING LISTINGS

We do not charge innkeepers to be included in this book. It's worth noting that some guides do impose a "processing fee" in order to be included. Within this edition we supply hundreds of Web sites, but we feel strongly that the Internet has increased rather than obviated the need for an honest, opinionated guidebook based on actual snooping around rather than virtual research. This volume is a useful search engine, but it's also much more: a combination of critical, current sleuthing and a sense of how to convey what's out there, based on decades of exploring and describing the Green Mountain State.

whose frequent travels took her to some of the state's remotest corners. She remembers gazing unseeing from the backseat of the family car, absorbed in childhood fantasies, barely aware of the scenery whizzing by.

After graduating from the University of Vermont with degrees in Russian studies and French, she left for Europe, a hiatus that lasted 20 years. She spent the time interpreting, guiding tours, and working with refugees. In Vienna she took up writing, first for the BBC World Service and then for United Press International and the *Washington Post*. She covered the Middle East for Germany's largest news service and finally spent three years in Prague, where she published a book on Bohemian glass. But "home" was always Vermont.

In 1994 she returned to her native Burlington, more flatlander now than Vermonter, and coauthored *Curious New England*, a guide to eccentric destinations in the Northeast. She also started exploring the state to research stories for the *Boston Globe*.

"It was like seeing Vermont for the first time. It all seemed new."

For this edition of *Vermont: An Explorer's Guide* a family crises confined her to the Greater Burlington area, but her input has been far broader.

Chris is deeply indebted to Peter Jennison, a sixth-generation Vermonter, who coauthored this book during its first eight editions, and many of the best words in it remain his. Peter was born on a dairy farm in Swanton, attended one-room schoolhouses, and graduated from Middlebury College. After 25 years in the publishing business in New York City, he became a "born-again" Vermonter, returning to his native heath in 1972 and founding The Countryman Press.

For help with research during this edition Chris has more people to thank than for help with any project, ever. They include Lucia Osiecki and William Hays in Brattleboro, Don Cole of Bennington, Leslie Brenner of Rutland, Nancy Maxwell of Bridport, Bob Foley of Brandon, Susan Cogley of Arlburg, Deborah Dolby of Milton, Thom and Joan Gorman of Waitsfield, Beth Kennett of Rochester, Jane Doerfer of Brookfield, Paul Heller and Marianne Kotch of Barre, Neil Humphrey, Paula Maynard, and Chris and Ted Sprague of Manchester, Kim and Jeff Seymour of Weston, Anne Weber of East Arlington, Stan Smith of Wilmington, Bud McKeon of Stowe, Barbara Thomke of Smugglers' Notch, Donna Smith of Shrewsbury, Patricia and Paul Dexter of Chester, Lori Webster of North Danville, Nancy Rodgers of West Glover, Lorraine Willy of East Burke, Mim LeBlanc of Newport Center, Joyce Emery of South Newbury, and Joanie Binns of Quimby Country.

Thanks too to those chamber of commerce directors who helped beyond the call of duty—especially to Darcie McCann of the Northeast Kingdom chamber, Susan Roy of the Mad River Valley, Sue Hoxie of Addison County, and Jo Sabel Courtney of the Stowe Area Association—and to regional tourism promoters Maree Bushey of the Northeast Kingdom and Lynn Barrett of the Southern Vermont. Thanks as well to Erica Houskeeper of the Vermont Department of Tourism and Marketing, Elsa Gilbertson of Vermont' s Division of Historic Preservation, Kelly Loftus of the Department of Agriculture, and Diane Beliveau of Tourisme Cantons de-l'Est. Last but not least, a big thank you to my husband Bill Davis, long-suffering companion during much of this research as well as proofreader and researcher during the months of inputting.

Both authors are grateful to Kermit Hummel and Jennifer Thompson for launching this update, and to Lisa Sacks for shepherding it to fruition with the help of our ever-speedy and supportive copy editor, Laura Jorstad.

Christina Tree (ctree@traveltree.net)
Diane Foulds

WHAT'S WHERE IN VERMONT

AREA CODE The area code for all of Vermont is **802**.

AGRICULTURAL FACTS AND FAIRS Some 1.25 million acres of the state's total of 6 million acres are devoted to agriculture. The farmhouse and barn are still a symbol of Vermont, and a Vermont vacation should include a farm visit, whether to buy syrup, cheese, wool, or wine, maybe to pick apples or berries, tour a dairy operation, or to stay for a night or a week. Finding farms can be an excuse to explore unexpectedly beautiful backcountry.

Of course a "farm" isn't what it used

Vermont Department of Agriculture

to be. Fewer than 1,100 of Vermont's 6,400 farms are now dairy, compared with 10,000 dairy farms 40 years ago. Even so, the average size of dairy herds has increased: With just 15 percent as many dairy farms, the state produces more than twice as much milk as it did 45 years ago. Vermont remains New England's largest milk-producing state; gross sales of cheese, ice cream, dips, cream cheese, yogurt, milk, and milk powder total $1.2 billion per year.

Before cows, there were sheep. In the 1830s and '40s, meadowland was far more extensive, and was populated by millions of merino sheep. When the Civil War ended, so did the demand for wool blankets, and a significant number of sheep farms went under. Luckily railroads were expanding to every corner of the state by the 1870s, and railroad companies teamed up with state agriculture departments to promote farms to "summer boarders."

Now farmers are once again looking to visitors as well as to new forms of agriculture to maintain their farms. Vermont farmers raise goats and llamas, beef cattle, miniature donkeys, Christmas trees, flowers, vegetables, fruit, trout, and more. Within "What's Where" we suggest how to find a variety of agricultural products, from apples to wine. Request a packet of brochures from the Vermont Agency of Agriculture (802-828-2416; 116 State St., Drawer 20, Montpelier 05620-2901; vermontagriculture.com) or contact the Vermont Farms! Association (866-348-FARM; vermontfarms.org).

The **Champlain Valley Exposition** (cvfair.com) in Essex (lasting an entire week around Labor Day) is by far the state's largest agricultural fair. **Addison County Fair and Field Days** in early Aug. in New Haven, as well as the **Orleans County Fair** in Barton (orleanscountyfair.com, five days in mid-Aug.) and the **Caledonia County Fair** (vtfair.com), always the following weekend in nearby Lyndonville, all feature ox, pony, and horse pulling as well as a midway, live entertainment, and plenty to please all ages. The **Bondville Fair** (two days in late Aug.) in southern Vermont is also the genuine thing, the **Vermont State Fair** (vermontstatefair.net) in Rutland lasts nine days in early Sept. The **Tunbridge World's Fair** (four days in mid-Sept.) is the oldest and most colorful of them all (tunbridgefair.com). See also in this chapter *Apples, Cheese, Christmas Trees, Farmer's Markets, Farms Open to the Public, Farm Stays, Gardens, Maple Sugaring, Pick Your Own, Sheep and Wool,* and *Wine.*

AIR SERVICE **Burlington International Airport** (802-863-1889; burlingtonintlairport.com) offers by far the most scheduled service in Vermont with flights to Atlanta, Baltimore, Chicago, Cleveland, Detroit, Newark, New York, Orlando, Philadelphia, and Washington, DC. Carriers include **Delta Connection** (Comair), **Continental Express**, **United Airlines**, **US Airways**, and both **JetBlue** and **AirTran**, which offer some good deals. Curiously, at this writing, the only commuter service to Boston is from the **Southern Vermont Regional Airport** (flyrutlandvt.com) in

Rutland and the **Lebanon Municipal Airport** (flyleb.com) in New Hampshire, serving the Upper Connecticut River Valley. For national service to southern Vermont check **Bradley International Airport** in Windsor Locks, Connecticut (bradleyairport .com), and **Albany Airport** (albanyairport.com) in New York , convenient for much of the western part of the state. **Manchester (New Hampshire) Airport** (flymanchester.com) is the largest airport in northern New England, with many domestic and some international flights.

AIRPORTS Click on **airports .vermont.gov** for details about Vermont's 16 airports, just 2 (see above) with scheduled flights, but all accessible to private and some to charter planes. Request a copy of the *Vermont Airport Directory* from the Vermont Agency of Transportation (802 828 2587).

AMTRAK (800-USA-RAIL; amtrak .com). Amtrak's **Vermonter** runs from Washington to St. Albans with stops (at decent hours both north- and southbound) in Brattleboro, Bellows Falls, Claremont (New Hampshire), Windsor, White River Junction, Randolph, Montpelier, Waterbury, and Burlington. The **Adirondack** runs up the western shore of Lake Champlain en route from Manhattan to Montreal and stops at Port Kent, New York, accessible to Burlington by ferry. The **Ethan Allen Express** connects Rutland with New York City via Albany—but it's a long haul. All Vermont trains accept skis (but not bicycles) as baggage.

ANTIQUARIAN BOOKSELLERS The **Vermont Antiquarian Booksellers Association** (VABA) publishes a pamphlet listing its more than 60 member dealers, available in the stores

or online at vermontisbookcountry
.com.

ANTIQUING The pamphlet
Antiquing in Vermont lists 68 of the
state's most prestigious dealers, members of the Vermont Antiques Dealers'
Association (vermontada.com). The
association sponsors an **annual
antiques show** in Sept. Major concentrations of dealers can be found in
Bennington, Burlington, Dorset, Manchester, Middlebury, Woodstock, and
along Rt. 30 in the West River Valley.
The **Weston Antiques Show** (weston
antiquesshow.org), usually the first
weekend in Oct., is the state's oldest
and still one of its best. Look for large
group dealerships in Quechee, Danby,
East Arlington, and East Barre.

APPLES During fall harvest season
the demand is not only for bushel baskets already filled with apples but also
for an empty basket and the chance to
climb a ladder and pick the many varieties grown in Vermont—primarily in
the Champlain Islands, the Champlain
Valley around Shoreham, and the
Lower Connecticut River Valley
between Springfield and Brattleboro.
Listings of orchards and apple festivals
can be found under descriptions of
these areas in this book and by
requesting a map/guide to farms from
the Vermont Apple Marketing Board
(vermontapples.org). From the earliest

Vermont Department of Agriculture

days of settlement through the mid-
1800s, more apples, it's said, were used
for making hard cider and brandy than
for eating and cooking. In 1810 some
125 distilleries were producing more
than 173,000 gallons of apple brandy
annually. Today wineries and cideries
are once more making apple wines
(see *Wine*).

ART GALLERIES Vermont's art collections (painting, sculpture, and decorative arts) are small, diverse, and
widely scattered. See the **Vermont
Museum & Gallery Alliance** Web
site, vmga.org, for an overview. The
Bennington Museum is known for its
works by Grandma Moses; there is also
the **Robert Hull Fleming Museum**
at the University of Vermont, Burlington; the **Middlebury College Museum of Art**; the **St. Johnsbury
Athenaeum and Art Gallery**; the
**Thomas Waterman Wood Art
Gallery** in Montpelier; and the **Shelburne Museum** in Shelburne. While
they lack permanent collections, the
best changing exhibits in the state are
usually found at the **Southern Vermont Arts Center** in Manchester, the
Brattleboro Museum & Art Center,
and the **Helen Day Art Center** in
Stowe; also check out the nonprofit
**Firehouse Center for the Visual
Arts** in Burlington and the **Chaffee
Center for the Visual Arts** in Rutland. Brattleboro, Woodstock, Brandon, and Bellows Falls offer the
greatest number of private galleries.
Burlington and Brattleboro hold open
gallery tours the first Friday of every
month; Bellows Falls, on each third
Friday.

AUCTIONS Most major upcoming
auctions are announced in the Thursday edition of Vermont newspapers,
with a listing of items that will be up

Christina Tree

for bid. Auctions may be scheduled at any time, however, during summer months. Check local chapters for details.

BALLOONING Year-round flights are offered by **Balloons of Vermont** (balloonsofvermont.com), based in Quechee, also the base for **Balloons Over New England** (balloonsovernewengland.com). **Brian Boland** at Post Mills Airport (802-333-9254) offers ascents over the Upper Connecticut River Valley and showcases some 100 balloons in this hot-air **Balloon Museum. Above Reality** (balloonvermont.com) operates year-round over northern Lake Champlain and the Champlain Valley. The **Annual Balloon Festival** in Quechee is held in June during Father's Day weekend, while the **Stoweflake Hot-Air Balloon Festival** (stoweflake.com) is a mid-July event with balloon launch and tethers.

BARNS Many barns along the highways and byways have distinctive touches, such as ornate Victorian cupolas, and still more are connected to farmhouses in the architectural style that served as shelter for the farmers' trips before dawn in deep snow. Just

13 round barns survive in Vermont, all built between 1899 and World War I. The concept of the round barn is thought to have originated with the Shakers in Hancock, Massachusetts, where the original stone barn, built in 1824, is now the centerpiece of a museum. The Vermont survivors include: the **Moore barn** in East Barnet; the **Hastings barn** in Waterford; the **Metcalf barn** (Robillard Flats) in Irasburg; the **Parker barn** in Grand Isle, converted into a housing center for the elderly; two barns in Coventry; the **Powers barn** in Lowell; the **Parker barn** in North Troy; one in Enosburg Falls; and **Southwick's** in East Calais. In Waitsfield the **Joslin round barn** is now a cultural center with a swimming pool in its bowels, attached to the **Inn at Round Barn Farm**; in Strafford the **Round Robin Farm**, a 350-acre working dairy farm with a 10-sided barn, takes guests. The **Welch Barn** on Rt. 12 in Morristown just north of Lake Elmore rises into view as you drive the beautiful stretch north from Montpelier.

Round-barn addicts should check at local general stores for exact location and to secure permission to photograph the structures. Among other Vermont barns open to the public are those at Shelburne Farms, including the vast, five-story, 416-foot-long Norman-style **Farm Barn**, the acre-large **Breeding Barn**, and the handsome **Coach Barn** in Shelburne. The round barn once in Passumpsic has been moved to the Shelburne Museum. Two lively, illustrated guides are *A Field Guide to New England Barns and Farm Buildings* by Thomas Visser and *Big House, Little House, Back House, Barn: The Connected Farm Buildings of New England* by Thomas Hubka (both from the University Press of New England).

BED & BREAKFASTS The hundreds of B&Bs we have personally inspected are listed under their respective locations in this book they range from working farms to historic mansions.

BICYCLE TOURING In Vermont the distance via back roads from swimming hole to antiques shop to the next inn is never far. John Freidin, author of *Backroad Bicycling in Vermont* (The Countryman Press), introduced the whole notion of guided bike tours for adults back in 1972. Woodstock-based **Bike Vermont** (bikevt.com) is the state's largest, most respected inn-to-inn tour outfitter, providing a "sag wagon" (a support vehicle with spare parts and snacks), renting 27-gear hybrid bikes, specializing in small (under 20) groups, and a wide variety of Vermont and foreign destinations. Guided camping tours (with a sag wagon) are offered by **POMG (Peace of Mind Guaranteed) Bike Tours of Vermont** (pomgbike.com). **Vermont Bicycle Touring** (vbt.com) offers inn-

Bike Vermont

to-inn biking tours to several destinations. In southern Vermont, **Diverse Directions** (vtcycling.com) offers self-guided tour packages that include baggage transfer, lodging, and routing, as does **Vermont Inn-to-Inn Walking** (vermontinntoinnwalking.com)—an association of innkeepers whose establishments are a comfortable bike ride (or hike) from one another. Participants are largely on their own, but rental equipment is available and baggage is transferred from inn to inn.

Bicycle paths continue to grow and multiply in Vermont. Stowe's **"Rec" Path** is 5.3 miles with convenient rentals. The **Burlington Bike Path** follows the shore of Lake Champlain for 12 miles (rentals available). It connects six different parks, continuing across the Winooski River on a bike bridge and through Colchester to a (summer weekends only) bike ferry that links it with the Champlain Islands, arguably the most popular corner of Vermont for bicyclists. Check out the **Lake Champlain Bikeways** site (champlainbikeways.org) for an overview of 1,100 miles of routes on both shores of the lake and extending into Canada. The 26-mile **Missisquoi Rail Trail** follows an old railbed from St. Albans to Richford, and the 34-mile **D&H Recreation Trail** follows an abandoned railroad bed almost 20 miles from Castleton to West Rupert, with the remainder in New York State. In central Vermont, the Mad River Valley is the hub of the 100-mile Century Ride (mrvcenturyride.com) in Aug. and the Green Mountain Stage Race (gmsr.org) during the Labor Day weekend.

Within each chapter we have described sources for local bike rentals. Also see *Mountain Biking*.

BIRDING While the hermit thrush, the state bird, is reclusive and not too easy to spot, Vermont offers ample opportunities for observing herons and ducks, as well as raptors like owls, hawks, falcons, ospreys, even bald eagles. It's home to more than 240 species of birds. Stop at the **Missisquoi National Wildlife Refuge** (802-868-4781) in Swanton even if you don't have time to walk the trails. The new visitor center is a must-see with exhibits showcasing local geology and the history of human habitation as well as bird and animal life. Other outstanding birding areas include the **Dead Creek Wildlife Refuge** (802-759-2398) in Vergennes, and the 4,970-acre **Victory Basin** east of St. Johnsbury. The 255-acre **Green Mountain Audubon Nature Center** in Huntington (vt.audubon.org/centers .html) is open year-round; inquire about guided walks and special programs. The neighboring **Birds of Vermont Museum** (birdsofvermont.org) in Huntington features lifelike carvings of over 200 species, showing both male and female plumage, displayed in their natural habitats, all the work of master carver Bob Spear of Colchester. The **Vermont Institute of Natural Science (VINS)** maintains a nature center beside Quechee Gorge (vinsweb .org) open year-round, with owls, hawks, eagles, and other raptors in residence and a full program of naturalist walks and demonstrations.

BOAT EXCURSIONS If you don't own a yacht, there are still plenty of ways to get onto Vermont rivers and lakes. Possible cruises from Burlington include the *Spirit of Ethan Allen II* (soea.com), a 500-passenger excursion boat, and *Moonlight Lady* (vermont discoverycruises.com)—a three-deck converted swamp yacht with eight staterooms (private baths) offering one-, three-, and six-night cruises on Lake Champlain. Farther south the

M/V Carillon (carilloncruises.com) offers narrated cruises from Larrabees Point in Shoreham near Fort Ticonderoga. The *M/V Mountain Mills* (greenmountainflagship.com) sails on Harriman Reservoir near Whitingham. For details, check under respective locations in this book. See also *Ferries*.

BOATING A booklet, *Laws and Regulations Governing the Use and Registration of Motorboats*, is available from the Vermont State Police, Marine Division, in Williston (802-878-7111). Click onto boatsafe.com/vermont. (See also *Canoeing and Kayaking, Connecticut River*, and *Whitewater*.)

BOOKS In addition to the books we mention in specific fields or on particular subjects, here are some of the most useful current titles: *Vermont Atlas and Gazetteer* (DeLorme) and *Vermont Place Names: Footprints in History*, by Esther Swift (Vermont Historical Society). *Hands on the Land: A History of the Vermont Landscape*, by Jan Albers, published by the MIT Press for The Orton Family Foundation, is also essential reading for anyone truly interested in understanding why Vermont looks the way it does. Lovers of natural history should seek out *The Nature of Vermont*, by Charles Johnson (University Press of New England). Basic reference directories include the *Vermont Encyclopedia* (University Press of New England). Civil War buffs will be rewarded by Howard Coffin's *Full Duty: Vermonters in the Civil War*; *Nine Months to Gettysburg: Stannard's Vermonters and the Repulse of Pickett's Charge*; and *The Battered Stars: One State's Civil War Ordeal During Grant's Overland Campaign* (all The Countryman Press). For children, *Vermont: The State with the Storybook Past*, by Cora Cheney (New England Press), is the best.

Our favorite current Vermont fiction writer is unquestionably Howard Frank Mosher of Irasburg, whose evocative novels include *On Kingdom Mountain*, *Disappearances*, *Northern Borders*, *Where the Rivers Flow North*, and *A Stranger in the Kingdom*; the last two are also films. Joseph Citro is the author of several books about occult occurrences and folk legends in the state, including *Green Mountains, Dark Tales* (University Press of New England), and *Ghosts, Ghouls, and Unsolved Mysteries* (Houghton Mifflin). The Brattleboro-based mysteries of Archer Mayor, including *Open Season* and other titles in his Joe Gunther police-procedural series, are gaining momentum. And look for the charming little *Art of the State: Vermont* by Suzanne Mantell (Abrams). For a narrative guide to some off-the-beaten-path attractions, seek out *Off the Leash: Subversive Journeys Around Vermont* by Helen Husher (The Countryman Press). *Northeastern Wilds* (AMC Books), by Stephen Gorman, features stunning photography and includes informative text about Vermont's stretch of the northern forest.

BREWERIES Civil War–era Vermont was New England's leading hops-producing state; in the United States only New York surpassed its output. In the late 19th century, however, temperance movements and other factors virtually eliminated its beer and wine industries. But Vermont brewing is back. Check out vermontbrewers.com. **Magic Hat Brewing Co.** (802-658-2739) in South Burlington, **Otter Creek Brewing** (802-388-0727) in Middlebury, **Long Trail Brewing** (802-672-5011) in West Bridgewater, and **Trout River Brewing Co.** (802-626-9396) in Lyndonville are all widely distributed and draw fans from afar, as does **Harpoon Brewery** (802-674-

Kim Grant

5491) in Windsor, which recently expanded its pub menu and space. Vermont's standout microbrewery pubs includes **Jasper Murdock's Alehouse** at the Norwich Inn (802-649-1143), **The Shed** (802-253-4364) in Stowe, **McNeill's Brewery** (802-254-2553) in Brattleboro, and **The Alchemist** (802-233-4120) in Waterbury.

BUS SERVICE "You can't get there from here" is no joke for would-be transit passengers to, from, and around Vermont. Vermont Transit has been absorbed by **Greyhound** (greyhound .com), which still maintains a Boston–Burlington run via White River Junction and Montpelier (where the station is a dysfunctional trailer) and New York City via Brattleboro and Bellows Falls to White River Junction. Regional bus services are taking up the slack. Bennington-based **Green Mountain Express** (greenmtncn.org) serves Bennington County including Manchester and Pownal with stops between. Rutland-based **Marble Valley Transit** (thebus.com) serves Manchester, Killington, Middlebury, Fair Haven, and points between. See *Getting There* under each destination for the local companies that are taking up the slack. New York City skiers should check **Adventure Northeast Bus Service** (adventurenortheast.com), offering daily service to Mount Snow, Stratton, and Killington from Thanksgiving weekend through April. Check with Okemo for similar services.

CAMPS, FOR CHILDREN For information about more than 50 Vermont summer camps for boys and girls, contact the **Vermont Camping Association** (vermontcamps.org).

CAMPGROUNDS Vermont has over 75 privately owned campgrounds, 40 state campgrounds, and many general areas as well as camping both in designated and general areas within the Green Mountain National Forest. A detailed annual publication, *Vermont Campground Guide*, is published by the Vermont Campground Association and available online (campvermont.com), as well as at the welcome centers on Vermont interstates. Private campgrounds offer creature comforts such as snack bars, stores, playgrounds, electricity, cable TV, and WiFi. For those same reasons, the state parks are quieter.

A list of Vermont's state parks is available from **Vermont State Parks** (802-241-3655; vtstateparks.com). The excellent Web site describes each park in detail with maps of the camping areas. Facilities include furnished cottages, unfurnished cabins, lean-tos, and tent and trailer sites. Fees vary with the class of the area. For reservations 14 days or less beforehand call the park directly (listed online); otherwise reserve online or by phone at 888-409-7579 weekdays 9–4. Trees separate most Vermont state park campsites from neighboring sites, and they are well maintained. Many offer organized programs such as hikes, campfire sings, films, and lectures. Most parks are relatively uncrowded, especially midweek; the most popular are Branbury, Stillwater, Groton Forest, Grand Isle, and Lake St. Catherine. This book describes state parks as they appear geographically.

Within the 400,000-acre **Green Mountain National Forest** seven designated camping areas are available on a first-come, first-served basis for a maximum 14-day period for $10 per night. These areas are **Hapgood Pond Recreational Area** near Peru, **Red Mill Brook Campground** near Woodford, **Grout Pond Recreational Area** (free) near Stratton, **Greendale Campground** north of Weston, **Silver Lake** (free) and **Moosalamoo** near Goshen, and **Chittenden Brook Campground** near Brandon. Camping is also permitted in the wilds without fee or prior permission unless otherwise posted, but before you pitch your tent, visit one of the district ranger offices; see *Green Mountain National Forest*. The **U.S. Army Corps of Engineers**, New England District, also maintains campsites close to flush toilets, showers, and swimming at the **Winhall Brook Camping Area** at Ball Mountain Lake in Jamaica and at **North Hartland Lake** near Quechee. For details click on corps lakes.us. To reserve sites at any of these campgrounds, phone the National Recreation Reservation Service at 877-444-6777 or go to recreation.gov.

CANOEING AND KAYAKING Arlington-based **BattenKill Canoe** (battenkill.com), Vermont's oldest and largest outfitter, offers day trips and inn-to-inn tours throughout the state; **Clearwater Sports** (clearwatersports .com) in Waitsfield offers guided tours, instruction, and special expeditions, as does **Umiak Outdoor Outfitters** (umiak.com) in Stowe. **Vermont Canoe Touring Center** (802-257-5008) in Brattleboro offers canoe rentals, shuttle service, and river camping on the Connecticut. **North Star Canoe Livery** (kayak-canoe

Christina Tree

.com), based in Cornish, New Hampshire, offers rentals and shuttles for the scenic reach between White River Junction and the Cornish–Windsor bridge, one particularly rich in camping spots. **Wilderness Trails** (802-295-7620) in Quechee offers similar trips on the neighboring stretch of the river, also on nearby ponds and on the White River. The stretch of the Lamoille River around Jeffersonville is served by **Green River Canoe** (802-644-8336). For the upper reaches of the Connecticut check out **Hemlock Pete's Canoes & Kayaks** (603-667-5112) in North Haverhill, New Hampshire.

Fish Vermont, a map/guide free from the Vermont Fish and Wildlife Department (vtfishandwildlife.com), notes ponds, lakes, and put-in places. Recommended books: Roioli Schweiker's third edition of *Canoe Camping Vermont and New Hampshire Rivers* (The Countryman Press) is a handy guide, and the *AMC River Guide: Vermont/New Hampshire* (AMC Books) is good for detailed information on canoeable rivers, as is *The Connecticut River Boating Guide, Source to the Sea* (Falcon Press, 3rd edition 2007) published in cooperation with the Connecticut River Watershed Council. See also *Connecticut River* and *Whitewater*. The 740-mile **Northern Forest Canoe Trail** (northernforestcanoetrail.org), which begins in Old Forge, New York, dips in and out of Vermont on its way to Fort Kent, Maine. The organization is headquartered in Waitsfield (802-496-2285).

CHEESE In recent years Vermont's production of cheese has increased to more than 100 million pounds annually in 150 varieties, with sheep and goat as well as cow cheeses winning top national and international honors. Check out the following producers among the 39 **Vermont Cheese Council** members currently listed on

CATAMOUNT TRAIL

(catamounttrail.org). You may not want to ski the 300 miles from Massachusetts to Canada, but it's nice to know you can—along the longest cross-country ski trail in this country. Since 1984, when three young skiers bushwhacked their way the length of Vermont, the Catamount Trail has been evolving. The nonprofit Catamount Trail Association (CTA) now has over 1,800 paying members. Over the years countless permits and dozens of easements have secured use of private and public lands. Bridges have been built, trailhead parking created, and a 9th edition of *The Catamount Trail Guidebook* ($19.95) maps and describes each of the trail's 31 segments. The excellent Web site includes a "trip planning" section with suggested places to stay along the way. Members receive a regular newsletter and discounts at participating touring centers and retailers. Also see *Skiing, Cross-Country*.

the downloadable Vermont Cheese Trail map (vtcheese.com).

A century ago most Vermont towns had a cheesemaker to which farmers brought the day's surplus milk. **Crowley Cheese** (crowleycheese-vermont .com), established in 1882 and billed as "the oldest continuously operated cheese factory in the U.S.," is the only survivor of this era, and welcomes visitors to its wooden factory just west of Ludlow on Rt. 103 in Healdville (open weekdays 8–4). This distinctive cheese is creamier than cheddar and still made the traditional way. **Cabot Creamery** (802-563-2231; cabot creamery.com) in Cabot is the state's largest, most famous producer, a farmer-owned cooperative since 1919 with a modern plant turning out 12 million pounds of cheese a year. Its visitor center is open daily, year-round, and offers plant tours (call ahead for cheesemaking days); its annex in Waterbury Center south of Stowe sells a variety of the dairy products and cheeses that have made market inroads nationwide.

Award-winning **Vermont Shepherd Cheese** (802-387-4473), a rich, tangy sheep's-milk cheese from Westminster, opens its "cave" to visitors at certain times (call). **Grafton Village Cheese Company** (800-472-3866) in Grafton had its beginnings around

Christina Tree

1890 and was resurrected by the Windham Foundation in 1966; visitors view the cheesemaking from outside, through a picture window here and at the company's far larger new plant and retail store in Brattleboro, also showcasing 50 other artisanal cheeses. The **Taylor Farm** (802-824-5690) in Londonderry (southern Vermont) is making a reputation with its Gouda, and **Woodcock Farm** in Weston has won top national honors for its European-style sheep cheese. Also in southern Vermont, **Peaked Hill Farm** in Townshend welcomes visitors at convenient times. In Randolph Center, minutes off I-89, Exit 4, at **Neighborly Farms** (802-728-4700), you can walk down a hallway and view cows on one side and cheesemaking on the other (open Mon.–Sat. 10–5). **Vermont Butter & Cheese Company** in Websterville (800-884-6287) makes a wide variety of tantalizing goat cheeses, and **Blythedale Farm** (802-439-6575) in Corinth produces multiple soft cheeses (a fine Vermont Brie, a Camembert, a Green Mountain Gruyère, and Jersey Blue), but neither is open to visitors. **Sugarbush Farm** (802-457-1757), set high on a hill in Woodstock, smokes and packages several varieties of cheddar cheese and welcomes visitors but beware the road in mud season.

At **Shelburne Farms** (802-985-8686; open daily, year-round), in Shelburne near Burlington, prizewinning cheddar is made from the milk of a single herd of Brown Swiss cows. In New Haven, **Orb Weaver Farm** (802-877-3755) produces a creamy, aged, Colby-type cheese, made in small batches entirely by hand (available in 2-pound wheels and 1-pound waxed wedges). In the northwest corner of the state goat cheese is made at **Willow Hill Farm** (802-893-2963) in Milton. In Highgate Center visitors are welcome at **Green Mountain Blue**

Cheese (802-868-4193). The Northeast Kingdom also has its share of cheesemakers. **Bonnie View Farm** in Craftsbury makes a superb sheep's-milk cheese, and **Jasper Hill Farm** in Greensboro is known for its Bayley-Hazen Blue cheese. Also see *The Vermont Cheese Book* by Ellen Echer Ogden (The Countryman Press).

CHILDREN, ESPECIALLY FOR

Look for the 𝄢 symbol throughout this book; it designates child-friendly attractions as well as lodging and dining. Alpine slides delight children of all ages at **Bromley's** summer **Thrill Zone** (bromley.com). There are also alpine slides at **Stowe** (stowe.com) and at Pico, part of the **Killington/Pico Adventure Center** (killington.com), which includes waterslides, a climbing wall, an in-line skate park, mountain biking, guided hikes, and more. Alpine lifts, which operate in summer, are also a way of hoisting small legs and feet to the top of some of Vermont's most spectacular summits. In Stowe, **Mount Mansfield**, Vermont's highest peak, and **Killington Peak**, second highest in the state, are accessible via gondola on weekdays. **Jay Peak**, commanding as dramatic a view as the others, is

FAIRBANKS MUSEUM IN ST. JOHNSBURY
Liam Davis

accessible on aerial tram (jaypeakresort.com). At **Stratton Ski Resort** in southern Vermont, the gondola runs daily in foliage season.

Santa's Land in Putney is the only commercial attraction geared specifically to children (open late May–late Dec.; santasland.com), but stuffed-animal lovers shouldn't miss the **Vermont Teddy Bear Factory** (vermontteddybear.com) in Shelburne, where tours demonstrate how the toys are made.

The **Shelburne Museum** (shelburnemuseum.org) has many exhibits that please youngsters, as does the **Fairbanks Museum and Planetarium** (fairbanksmuseum.org), St. Johnsbury, which is filled with taxidermied animals, birds, and exhibits from near and far. The **Montshire Museum of Science** (montshire.org) in Norwich is a real standout, with hands-on exhibits explaining many basic scientific mysteries plus a 2-acre outdoor exhibit inviting plenty of water experiments (bring a towel) and a beautiful riverside walk. **ECHO at the Leahy Center for Lake Champlain** (echocenter.org) is a new science center and aquarium featuring 2,200 live fish, amphibians, and reptiles, with hands-on exhibits for kids 3–17. The **Billings Farm & Museum** (billingsfarm.org) and **Vermont Institute of Natural Science** (vinsweb.org), both in the Woodstock area, are child pleasers.

Over the past few years, as ski areas have come to compete for family business, resorts have developed special programs for children. **Smugglers' Notch** (smuggs.com) offers the largest, most extensive and reasonably priced full summer day camp and ski-geared programs for a wide range of ages. The **Tyler Place Family Resort** (tylerplace.com) in Highgate Springs and the **Basin Harbor Club** (basinharbor.com) in Vergennes are family-geared resorts with teens' and children's programs. The **Wildflower Inn** (wildflowerinn.com) in Lyndonville, **Highland Lodge** (highlandlodge.com) in Greensboro, and **Quimby Country** (quimbycountry.com) in the northeastern corner of the state all offer summer half-day programs for children. (See also *Agricultural Facts and Fairs*, *Farms Open to the Public*, *Farm Stays*, *Boat Excursions*, and *Railroad Excursions*.)

CHRISTMAS TREES Vermont's many Christmas tree farms generally open after Thanksgiving, inviting customers to come tag the tree they want, leaving it until the last moment to cut. Check the Web sites vermontchristmas trees.org and vtfarms.org for a list of the more imaginative marketers. These include **Redrock Farm** (866-685-4343; christmastrees.net) in Chelsea and **Elysian Hills** (802-257-0233; elysianhillsfarm.com) in Dummerston, where you can pick out a tree in summer or fall and have it shipped to you at Christmas anywhere in the continental United States the day it's cut. (If you do this, judging from our own experience, schedule delivery for the beginning of the week and at least a week before Christmas.) In recent years bed & breakfasts and inns have teamed up with farms to offer preholiday lodging packages that include a fresh Christmas tree (contact the Vermont Chamber of Commerce: vtchamber.com). For a do-it-yourself experience, contact the **Green Mountain National Forest Service** in Rochester (802-767-4261) and inquire about tagged trees you can cut for a nominal fee.

CIVIL UNIONS The law sanctioning civil unions was passed in July 2000. In the following 12 months 2,479 such ceremonies were performed, with almost twice as many females as males taking vows. Only 479 of the same-sex couples were from Vermont. The post office in the central Vermont village of Gaysville has become a favorite venue for wedding pictures. Throughout this guide, we indicate venues that specialize in weddings and civil unions with the wedding-ring symbol ⚭.

COLLEGES For information about all the state's colleges and universities, contact the **Vermont Higher Education Council** (802-549-2758; vhec.info). Also check out the **Association of Vermont Independent Colleges** Web site: vermont-icolleges.org.

COMMUNITY SUPPERS No Web site serves this elusive but ubiquitous Vermont institution. Check local papers and bulletin boards and try to catch at least one supper for a sense of local communities as well as fine food.

CONNECTICUT RIVER New England's longest river rises near the Canadian–New Hampshire border and forms the boundary between that state and Vermont for some 255 miles. Not far below its source are a series of lakes; five in New Hampshire's North Country town of Pittsburg, and two—Moore and Comerford—near St. Johnsbury. The 145 miles between Barnet and Brattleboro are punctuated by four dams, each creating deeper pools that turn the river into a series of slow-moving, narrow lakes. But of the 275 miles the river runs from its source to the Massachusetts border, 134 miles are free flowing. The entire river is now the centerpiece of the 7.2-million-acre, four-state Silvio O. Conte National Fish and Wildlife Refuge, and the Connecticut River National Scenic Byway. The **Connecticut River Joint Commissions**, the nonprofit organization responsible for establishing bistate information centers in Bellows Falls, White River Junction, and St. Johnsbury, as well as in Lancaster and Colebrook, New Hampshire, maintains two excellent Web sites. Click onto crjc.org for a series of detailed boating maps (also for directions on ordering hard copies) and onto ctrivertravel.net for a historical and cultural guide. Note that we include information about river towns in both states in our Connecticut River Valley chapters.

COVERED BRIDGES The state's 99 surviving covered bridges are marked on the official state map and on our maps and are described in the appropriate chapters of this book under *To See*. Bridge buffs should get a copy of *Covered Bridges of Vermont* by Ed Barna (The Countryman Press). The **Vermont Covered Bridge Museum** in Bennington features a theater production, dioramas, interactive exhibits, and a model railroad with covered railroad bridges (vermontcoveredbridge museum.org).

CRAFTS More than 1,500 Vermonters make their living from crafts. There are also more than 100 retail crafts venues in the state and during Vermont's **Open Studio Tour** (Memorial Day weekend), circa 300 artisans welcome visitors in almost as many locations. Request a copy of the *Vermont Crafts Studio Tour Map*, avail-

Christina Tree

GALLERY IN THE WOODS, BRATTLEBORO

able at information centers and on request from the Vermont Crafts Council (802-223-3380; vermontcrafts .com). It's worth having in the car any time of year, as many craftspeople welcome visitors informally. Within this book we have described studios, galleries, and shops as they appear geographically and have also included major crafts tours and fairs. The outstanding galleries are: **Frog Hollow Vermont State Craft Center** in Middlebury (froghollow.org), **The Artisan's Hand** (artisanshand.com) in Montpelier, **Art on Main** (artonmain .net) in Bristol, **The Collective** (collective-theartofcraft.com) in Woodstock, **Vermont Artisan Designs** (buyvermontart.com) in Brattleboro, and the **Brandon Artist's Guild** (brandonartistsguild.com). Craftspeople also sell at events ranging from farmer's markets and church bazaars to juried shows and festivals. In late Nov. and early Dec. there are many open studios around the state. The **Putney Craft Tour** (putneycrafts.com) has been attracting savvy shoppers for more than 30 years.

CUSTOMS INFORMATION Vermont shares a 90.3-mile border with the Canadian province of Quebec.

Christina Tree

Since the September 11 terrorist attacks, all border crossings have become far stricter. Even in Derby Line (Vermont), where it's tempting to walk the few steps into Stanstead (Quebec) to a restaurant, repercussions can be serious. Travelers must present a picture ID (preferably a passport) and, if they are not American or Canadian, valid tourist visas. Pets are required to have a veterinarian's certificate showing a recent vaccination against rabies. At this writing it's possible to bring in Canadian fruits, vegetables, and some cheese—but check on your entry into Canada. For detailed information contact the U.S. Customs District Office in St. Albans (802-524-6527), in Montreal (514-636-3875), or in Toronto (416-676-2606).

DINERS Vermont will not disappoint diner buffs. Hearty meals at reasonable prices can be found in Burlington at

JOSH LETOURNEAU BLOWS GLASS IN PUTNEY.

Ryan Wonderchuck

Henry's Diner on Bank St. **Libby's Blue Line Diner**, Rt. 7 (perched on a hill with a great view just off I-89, Exit 16), Colchester, is popular. The **Parkway Diner** at 1696 Williston Rd., South Burlington, is known for its Greek specialties, such as homemade pastitsio. The **Miss Lyndonville Diner** on Bond St., Lyndonville, is admired for its pies (a breakfast special). **Anthony's Restaurant** on Railroad St. in St. Johnsbury has expanded and is wheelchair accessible but still offers great food at great prices.

Just off I-91 in Wells River, the **P&H Truck Stop** (open 24 hours but no longer full service at all hours) is a truckers' oasis that serves large, reasonably priced meals and up to 23 flavors of pie. The **Wayside Restaurant and Bakery** (Exit 7; follow signs for Rt. 302 and it's on your left) south of Montpelier has expanded gradually over the years to become Vermont's ultimate family restaurant. **The Blue Benn Diner**, 102 Hunt St. in Bennington, serves imaginative vegetarian as well as standard diner fare. Add to these the **Farmer's Diner**, Rt. 4 in Quechee Gorge Village.

T. J. Buckley's in Brattleboro may look like the battered vintage Worcester diner it is, but inside oak paneling gleams and the fare (dinner only, and only by reservation) is recognized as some of the best in the state. West Brattleboro also offers the **Chelsea Royal Diner**, west on Rt. 9, which, while a bit heavy on diner decor, is still a great family bet (wheelchair accessible). In Chester our pick is **Jack's Diner. Miss Bellows Falls Diner** is on the National Register of Historic Places; the equally historic **Windsor Diner** has been nicely restored. The **Fairlee Diner** in Fairlee is the real thing. Check these establishments out in their respective chapters. (Also see *Highway Road Food.*)

EMERGENCIES Try **911** first. This simple SOS has finally reached most corners of Vermont. For state police phone 802-878-7111, for poison 800-222-1222, and for help with dental emergencies 800-640-5099.

EVENTS Almost every day of the year some special event is happening somewhere in Vermont. Usually it's something relatively small and friendly like a church supper, contra dance, community theatrical production, concert, or crafts fair. We have worked up our own *Special Events* for each region, and listings can also be found in various ways on the state's travel Web site, vermontvacation.com. Still, many of the best events are like fireflies, surfacing only on local bulletin boards and in the Thursday editions of local papers. In Burlington check out the free and information-rich *Seven Days*, a funky weekly listing of local arts and entertainment, available in shops and grocery stores all over town.

FACTORY OUTLETS Within the book we have mentioned only a small fraction of the factory outlets of which we are aware. Our bias has been to favor distinctly made-in-Vermont products. Among our favorites: **Johnson Woolen Mills** (quality wool clothing for all ages) in Johnson; **Bennington Potters** (dinnerware, housewares, and more) in Bennington and Burlington; and **Vermont Marble** in Proctor. **Charles Shackleton and Miranda Thomas** produce outstanding furniture and ceramics in an old mill in Bridgewater. **Copeland Furniture** in Bradford also has some seconds in its showroom. **Simon Pearce** in Quechee and Windsor sells seconds of his gorgeous glassware at affordable prices. **The Outlet Center** just off I-91, Exit 1, in Brattleboro harbors some genuine finds. Manchester merchants refuse to

call the dozens of upscale stores clustered in their town "outlets," but the prices in designer name stores are lower than retail; this is in fact the state's prime destination shopping center.

FARMER'S MARKETS Mid-June–early Oct., count on finding fresh vegetables, fruit, honey, and much more at farm prices in commercial centers throughout the state. Look for listings within each chapter. Click on **vermontagriculture.com** for a complete list.

FARMS OPEN TO THE PUBLIC For a list of farms open to the public for tours, to sell their products, or for farm stays, check on the Vermont Farms Association Web site, **vtfarms .org**.

FARM STAYS A century ago hundreds of Vermont farms took in visitors for weeks at a time. "There is no crop more profitable than the crop from the

Vermont Department of Agriculture

city," an 1890s Vermont Board of Agriculture pamphlet proclaimed, a publication noted by Dona Brown in *Inventing New England* (Smithsonian, 1995). Articles advised farmers on how to decorate, what to serve, and generally how to please and what to expect from city guests—much as B&B literature does today. Our own family found a farm stay so enriching that we returned year after year. Within the book we have listed those farms that we have personally visited. For a fuller listing you can click on the Vermont Farms! Association's Web site, **vtfarms .org**.

   Maple Crest Farm (802-492-3367) in Shrewsbury deserves special mention because it remains in the same family who have been taking in guests on this working farm since the 1860s. Beth Kennett at **Liberty Hill Farm** (802-767-3926) in Rochester has pioneered the resurgence in farm stays by successfully combining a working dairy farm with genuine hospitality and great food. **Allenholm Farm** (802-372-5566) in South Hero offers a B&B in the midst of a major apple orchard. **Round-Robin Farm** (802-763-7025), way off Sharon's beaten track, features a round barn, and **Emergo Farm Bed and Breakfast** (888-383-1185) on the edge of Danville Village is also a picture-perfect but genuine working dairy farm with comfortable rooms and a warm welcome from Lori Webster. In West Glover, **Nancy and Jim Rodgers** (802-525-6677) share meals with guests in their farmhouse, and at **Cliff Haven Farm** (802-334-2401) in Newport Center guests can explore the 300 acres of woods and meadows overlooking Lake Memphremagog. **Hollister Hill Farm** (802-454-7725) in Marshfield invites guests to participate in sugar making and take home the results of their labors. At the other extreme is lakeside **Shelburne**

Vermont Department of Agriculture

Farms, the most beautiful farm in the state—with its most elegant inn, the **Inn at Shelburne Farms** (802-985-8686).

FERRIES A number of car-carrying ferries ply Lake Champlain between the Vermont and New York shores, offering splendid views of both the Green Mountains and the Adirondacks. The northernmost crosses to Plattsburgh, New York, from **Grand Isle**, on Rt. 314 (year-round; 12-minute passage). From **Burlington** they cross to Port Kent, New York (one hour); the **Essex Ferry** travels between Charlotte and Essex, New York (20 minutes). All three are operated by the **Lake Champlain Transportation Company** (802-864-9804; ferries.com), descendant of the line founded in 1828 claiming to be "the oldest steamboat company on earth." Near the southern end of the lake, the car-carrying **Fort Ticonderoga Ferry** (802-897-7999; middlebury.net/tiferry) provides a seasonal, scenic shortcut (seven minutes) between Larrabees Point and Ticonderoga, New York. The Fort Ti Ferry has held a franchise from the New York and Vermont legislatures since circa 1800.

FIDDLING Vermont is the fiddling capital of the East. Fiddlers include concert violinists, rural carpenters, farmers, and heavy-equipment operators who come from throughout the East to gather in beautiful natural settings. The newsletter of the **Northeast Fiddlers Association** (802-476-7798; nefiddlers.org) lists fiddling meets around the state, such as the **Northeast Regional Oldtime Fiddler's Contest and Festival** in Barre (usually the last weekend in Sept.)—which, sadly, has been suspended in 2009 but hopefully not forever. Other annual events include the **Cracker Barrel Bazaar & Fiddle Contest** in Newbury in July and the **Lake Champlain Bluegrass Festival** fiddle and banjo contest mid-Aug. in Alburg (lakecham plainmusic.com). Fiddle festivals tend to start late morning and end around midnight.

FILM A number of Hollywood hits have been filmed in Vermont, including *The Cider House Rules*, *Forrest Gump*, *The Spitfire Grill*, and *What Lies Beneath*. But Vermont filmmakers have produced independent hits of their own in recent years. Jay Craven's dramatizations of Howard Frank Mosher's novels—*Where the Rivers Flow North*, *A Stranger in the Kingdom*, and *Disappearances*—evoke life as it was in the Northeast Kingdom not so long ago. Nora Jacobson's *My Mother's Early Lovers* and *Nothing Like Dreaming* are absorbing narratives. By the same token, John O'Brien's film trilogy, *Vermont Is for Lovers*, *Man with a Plan*, and *Nosey Parker*, goes right to Vermont's still very real rural core. *Man with a Plan* actually launched its hero's real-life political campaign in 1998: To the amazement of the country, retired Tunbridge dairy farmer Fred Tuttle not only defeated a wealthy carpetbagger for the Republican nomination but won a respectable percentage of the vote for a U.S. senatorial seat. Tuttle died in 2003, but O'Brien continues to make films. Sam-

plings of Vermont-made films can be found on the **Vermont Film Commission**'s Web site (vermontfilm.com).

FISHING Almost every Vermont river and pond, certainly any body of water serious enough to call itself a lake, is stocked with fish and has one or more access areas. Brook trout are the most widely distributed game fish. Visitors ages 15 and over must have a 5-day, a 14-day, or a nonresident license good for a year, available at any town clerk's office, from the local fish and game warden, or from assorted commercial outlets. Because these sources may be closed or time consuming to track down on weekends, it's wise to obtain the license in advance from the **Vermont Fish and Wildlife Department** (802-241-3700; vtfishandwildlife .com). Request an application form and ask for a copy of *Vermont Guide to Hunting, Fishing and Trapping*, which details every species of fish and where to find it on a map of the state's rivers and streams, ponds, and lakes. Boat access, fish hatcheries, and canoe routes are also noted on the *Fish Vermont Official Map & Guide*.

The Orvis Company, which has been in the business of making fishing rods and selling them to city people for more than a century, also maintains an outstanding museum in Manchester devoted to fly-fishing. Many inns, notably along Lake Champlain and in the Northeast Kingdom, offer tackle, boats, and advice on where to catch what.

Quimby Country (802-822-5533; quimbycountry.com), with a lodge and cabins on Forest and Great Averill Pond; **Seymour Lake Lodge** (802-895-2752; seymourlakelodge) in Morgan; and **Seyon Ranch** (802-584-3829) on Noyes Pond in Groton State Forest have all catered to serious fishermen since the 19th cen-

Kim Grant

05402); and *Fishing Vermont's Streams and Lakes* by Peter F. Cammann (The Countryman Press). Within this book we have listed shops, outfitters, and guides as they appear within each region. **Vermont Outdoor Guide Association** (800-747-5905) represents qualified guides throughout the state; check out their informative Web sites at voga.org or adventureguidesvt .com.

tury. Landlocked salmon, rainbow trout, brown trout, brookies, and lake trout are all cold-water species plentiful in the Northeast Kingdom's 37,575 acres of public ponds and 3,840 miles of rivers and streams. For guiding services check in those chapters. Warmwater species found elsewhere in the state include smallmouth bass, walleye, northern pike, and yellow perch.

Federal fish hatcheries can be found in **Bethel** (802-234-5241) and **Pittsford** (802-483-6618). State hatcheries are in **West Burke** (802-467-3660), **Bennington** (802-442-4556), **Grand Isle** (802-372-3171), **Roxbury** (802-485-7568), and **Salisbury** (802-352-4471). Ice anglers can legally take every species of fish (trout only in a limited number of designated waters) and can actually hook smelt and some varieties of whitefish that are hard to come by during warmer months; the **Great Benson Fishing Derby** held annually in mid-Feb. on Lake Champlain draws thousands of contestants from throughout New England. The **Lake Champlain International Fishing Derby**, based in Burlington (call 802-862-7777 for details), is a big summer draw. Books to buy include the *Vermont Atlas and Gazetteer* (DeLorme), with details about fishing species and access; the *Atlas of Vermont Trout Ponds* and *Vermont Trout Streams*, both from Northern Cartographics Inc. (Box 133, Burlington

FOLIAGE Vermont is credited with inventing foliage season, first aggressively promoted just after World War II in the initial issues of *Vermont Life*. The Department of Tourism (see *Information*) maintains a foliage "hotline" and sends out weekly bulletins on color progress, which is always earlier than assumed by those of us who live south of Montpelier. Those in the know usually head for northern Vermont in late Sept. and the first week of Oct., a period that coincides with peak color in that area as well as with the **Northeast Kingdom Fall Foliage Festival**. By the following weekend central Vermont is usually ablaze, but visitors should be sure to have a bed reserved long before coming, because organized tours converge on the state. By the Columbus Day weekend the odds of finding a bed are dim. During peak color, we recommend visiting midweek and avoiding Vermont's most congested tourist routes; there is plenty of room on the back roads, especially those unsuited to buses. We strongly suggest exploring the high roads through Vermont's "gaps" (see *Gaps, Gulfs, and Gorges*) during this time of year.

GAPS, GULFS, AND GORGES

Vermont's mountains were much higher before they were pummeled some 100,000 years ago by a mile-high sheet of ice. Glacial forces contoured the landscape we recognize today, notching the mountains with a number of handy "gaps" through which humans inevitably built roads. Gaps frequently offer superb views and access to ridge trails. This is true of the **Appalachian**, **Lincoln**, **Middlebury**, and **Brandon gaps**, all crossing the Long Trail and linking Rt. 100 with the Champlain Valley; and of the Roxbury Gap east of the Mad River Valley. Note, however, that the state's highest and most scenic gap of all is called a *notch* (**Smugglers Notch** between Stowe and Jeffersonville), the New Hampshire name for mountain passes. Gaps at lower elevations are *gulfs*, scenic passes that make ideal picnic sites: Note **Granville Gulf** on Rt. 100, **Brookfield Gulf** on Rt. 12, **Proctorsville Gulf** on Rt. 103 between Proctorsville and Chester, and **Williamstown Gulf** on Rt. 14. The state's outstanding gorges include: 163-foot-deep **Quechee Gorge**, which can be viewed from Rt. 4 east of Woodstock; **Brockway Mills Gorge** in Rockingham (off Rt. 103); **Cavendish Gorge**, Springfield; **Clarendon Gorge**, Shrewsbury (traversed by the Long Trail via footbridge); **Brewster River Gorge**, south of Jeffersonville off Rt. 108; **Jay Branch Gorge** off Rt. 105; and (probably the most photographed of all) the **Brown River** churning through the gorge below the Old Red Mill in Jericho.

GARDENS Vermont's growing season is all the more intense for its brevity. Commercial herb and flower gardens are themselves the fastest-growing form of agriculture in the state, and many inns and B&Bs pride themselves on their gardens. Lodging places with especially noteworthy gardens include **Willow Pond Farm** in Shelburne, **Basin Harbor Club** in Vergennes, the **Inn at Shelburne Farms** in Shelburne, **Blueberry Hill** in Goshen, the

Hidden Gardens B&B in Hinesburg, and the **Jackson House** in Woodstock. **Historic Hildene** in Manchester also features formal gardens with thousands of peonies, and the **Shelburne Museum** holds an annual Lilac Festival in mid- to late May. Within this book we describe our favorite commercial gardens in *Selective Shopping*. For a listing of commercial nurseries log onto vermontagriculture.com/links. Within each chapter we list outstanding nurseries under *Farms*.

GENERAL STORES A distinct species, Vermont country stores are both endangered and evolving to fill the changing needs of the hundreds of villages for which they still serve as hubs. Most now offer hot food and a good deli. Some invite patrons to linger at tables or on couches. Within the book we've lovingly described the state's iconic general stores such as **Floyd's** in Randolph Center, **Currier's** in Glover, **Willy's** in Greensboro, **Hastings** in West Danville, and **Dan & Whit's** in Norwich. We also note variations on the old model with standouts like the **Newbury Village Store**, **South Woodstock Country Store**, and **The Village Store** in Tunbridge with its genuine French chef. For a

FLOYD'S GENERAL STORE, RANDOLPH CENTER

Christina Tree

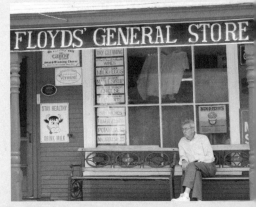

complete list and map check out the **Vermont Alliance of Independent Country Stores** Web site (vaics.org). **The Vermont Country Stores** in Weston and Rockingham publish a thick catalog—a source of long underwear and garter belts and Healthy Feet Cream—and have become tourist destinations. **Farm-Way, Inc.**, in Bradford, is Vermont's L.L. Bean, billed as "complete outfitters for man and beast."

GOLF More than 60 Vermont golf courses are open to the public, and more than half of these have 18 holes, half a dozen of them justly famed throughout the country. A full program of lodging, meals, and lessons is available at Mount Snow, Killington, Okemo, Stratton Mountain, Sugarbush, and Stowe. The Woodstock Inn, Lake Morey Inn, and others also offer golf packages. The Manchester area boasts the greatest concentration of courses. Sixty-seven courses are identified on the *Vermont Attractions Map*; also see vermontvacation.com.

THE GREEN MOUNTAINS Running 160 miles up the spine of this narrow state, the Green Mountains themselves range in width from 20 to 36 miles, with peaks rising to more than 4,000 feet. A part of the Appalachian Mountain chain, which extends from Alabama to Canada's Gaspé Peninsula, they were once far higher. The Long Trail runs the length of the range, and Rt. 100 shadows its eastern base. Also see *Hiking and Walking* and *Gaps, Gulfs, and Gorges*.

GREEN MOUNTAIN CLUB See *Hiking and Walking*.

GREEN MOUNTAIN NATIONAL FOREST The Green Mountain National Forest encompasses more than 400,000 acres spread across nearly two-thirds of Vermont's length, traversed by 900 miles of trails, including the **Appalachian Trail** and the **Long Trail**, which follows the ridgeline of the main range of the Green Mountains (see *Hiking and Walking*). The forest harbors six wilderness areas. Use of off-road recreational vehicles is regulated. Information—printed as well as verbal—about hiking, camping, skiing, berry picking, and bird-watching is available from the ranger stations in **Manchester Center** (802-362-2307), **Middlebury** (802-388-4362), and **Rochester** (802-767-4261). Request a free "mini map" from the **Green Mountain National Forest** (802-747-6700; 231 N. Main St., Rutland 05701). All four offices maintain visitor centers, open weekdays 8–4:30; Rochester is open 8–4 except Sun., weekdays only off-season.

HANDICAPPED ACCESS The wheelchair symbol & indicates lodging and dining places that are handicapped accessible.

HEALTH Almost every Vermont town has a health clinic or local physician. The two largest hospitals are in Burlington and just over the border from White River Junction, in Lebanon, New Hampshire. The **Dartmouth-Hitchcock Medical Center** (1 Medical Center Dr., Lebanon, NH 03756; 603-650-5000; dhmc.org) oversees children's, cancer, spine, and cardiology centers, a medical school, and a level one trauma center. A branch of Dartmouth-Hitchcock is the 201-bed **Veterans Affairs Regional Medical and Office Center** (215 N. Main St., White River Junction 05009-0001; 866-687-8387; visn1.med.va.gov/wrj). **Fletcher Allen Health Care** in Burlington (111 Colchester Ave., Burlington 05401; 802-847-0000;

fletcherallen.org), also a level one trauma center and teaching hospital, has just doubled the size of its emergency room as part of a major expansion.

Other Vermont hospitals include (from south to north) **Brattleboro Memorial Hospital** in Brattleboro (802-257-0341; bmhvt.org); **Southwestern Vermont Health Care** in Bennington (802-442-6361; svhealth care.org); **Grace Cottage Hospital** in Townshend (802-365-7357; otishealth carecenter.org); **Springfield Hospital** in Springfield (802-885-2151; spring fieldhospital.org); **Rutland Regional Medical Center** in Rutland (802-775-7111; rrmc.org); **Porter Medical Center** in Middlebury (802-388-4701; portermedical.org); **Mt. Ascutney Hospital and Health Center** in Windsor (802-674-6711; mtascutney hosp.hitchcock.org); **Gifford Medical Center** in Randolph (802-728-7000; giffordmed.org); **Central Vermont Medical Center** in Barre (802-371-4100; cvmc.hitchcock.org); **Copley Hospital** in Morrisville (802-888-4231; copleyhealthsystems.org); **Northwestern Medical Center** in St. Albans (802-524-5911; northwesternmedical center.org); **Northeastern Vermont Regional Hospital** in St. Johnsbury (802-748-8141; nvrh.org); and **North Country Hospital** in Newport (802-334-7331; nchsi.org). For more general information, contact the **Vermont Association of Hospitals and Health Systems** in Montpelier at (802-223-3461 or vahhs.org). As elsewhere in the country, when faced with a medical emergency, dial 911.

HIGH SEASON "High season" varies from Vermont community to community and even within a community such as Manchester (one side of town is nearer the ski resorts; the other is geared more to summer). While "foliage season" represents peak price as well as color everywhere, a ski condo can easily cost four times as much in Feb. as it does in July. Meanwhile, a country inn may charge half its July price in Feb.

HIGHWAY ROAD FOOD Cruising Vermont's interstates over the years, we have learned where to find good food less than a mile from exits. We strongly favor diners and local eateries over fast-food chains. All the following restaurants are described in their respective chapters.

Along **I-91**, south to north: Just west of *Exit 2* on Rt. 9 is the **Chelsea Royal Diner**. *Exit 4:* The **Putney Inn** is good for all three meals; around the corner is **Curtis' Barbecue**, and just up Rt. 5 is the **Putney Diner**. *Exit 15:* The **Fairlee Diner** is just north. *Exit 16:* The **Bradford Village Store** in the middle of the village serves hot soups and deli sandwiches (try for the window seat), while for dinner there's **Colatina Exit** and **Perfect Pear Café**. *Exit 17:* **P&H Truck Stop** is open 24 hours. *Exit 23:* Turn north onto Rt. 5 to find the **Miss Lyndonville Diner**.

Along **I-89**: *Exit 3:* **Eaton's Sugar House** is right off the exit. *Exit 7:* Follow signs to Rt. 302 and the **Wayside Restaurant and Bakery** is on your left. *Exit 9:* **The Red Hen Café** is a bakery (great breads) and café just west of the exit on Rt. 2, Middlesex. *Exit 10:* Turn left, then left again, and you are in the middle of Waterbury at **Arvad's**. *Exit 14W:* Burlington is just down the hill, worth a detour. *Exit 14E:* Turn east onto Williston Rd. and head away from town to find **The Parkway Diner**. *Exit 16:* **Libby's Blue Line Diner** is right there on the hill, and great. Also see *Diners*.

HIGHWAY TRAVEL INFORMATION See *Information*.

HIKING AND WALKING More than 700 miles of hiking trails Web Vermont—which is 162 miles long as the crow flies but 255 miles long as the hiker trudges, following the **Long Trail** up and down the spine of the Green Mountains. But few hikers are out to set distance records on the Long Trail. The path from Massachusetts to the Canadian border, which was completed in 1930, has a way of slowing people down. It opens up eyes and lungs and drains compulsiveness. Even die-hard backpackers tend to linger on rocky outcrops, looking down on farms and steeples. A total of 98 side trails (175 miles) meander off to wilderness ponds or abandoned villages; these trails are mostly maintained, along with the Long Trail, by the **Green Mountain Club** (802-244-7037; greenmountainclub.org), founded in 1910. The club also maintains about 66 shelters and 70 campsites, many of them staffed by caretakers during summer months. The mission of the GMC is to make the Vermont mountains play a larger part in the lives of the people by protecting and maintaining the Long Trail System and fostering, through education, the stewardship of Vermont's hiking trails and mountains. Check the Web site for current programs and for details about Wheeler Pond Camps rentals near Lake Willoughby. The club publishes the *Long Trail Guide*, which gives details on trails and shelters throughout the system, as well as the *Day Hiker's Guide to Vermont*. These and other guides are sold in the club's new **visitor center** (4711 Waterbury Rd., Waterbury Center 05677; open 9–5 daily, but closed on weekends in the off-season). The **Appalachian Trail Conservancy** (appalachiantrail.org) includes detailed information in its *Appalachian Trail Guide to Vermont and New Hampshire*, and a wide assortment of trails are nicely detailed in *50 Hikes in Vermont* (The Countryman Press).

Backpackers who are hesitant to set out on their own can take a wide variety of guided hikes and walks. **Adventure Guides of Vermont** (adventure guidesvt.com) and **Vermont Outdoor Guide Association** (voga.org) can put you in touch with guides and adventure-geared packages. For who prefer to have their baggage transferred and to combine hiking with fine dining and lodging, **Country Inns Along the Trail** (inntoinn.com) has been offering guided and self-guiding packages since 1975.

Within this book we suggest hiking trails as they appear geographically. Also note the recent proliferation of trail systems: In the Northeast Kingdom check out **Kingdom Trails** (kingdomtails.org) in East Burke, the **Vermont Leadership Center** near Island Pond, and the **Hazen's Notch Association Trails** (hazensnotch.org). We should also note that both Killington and Stowe offer ridge hiking from the top of their lifts. (See also *Birding, State Parks, Mountain Biking,* and *Nature Preserves.*)

HISTORY Vermont is a small state, but it has had a dramatic life. In essence, the whole state is a living history museum, even though most towns were settled after the Revolution. Many often overlapping land grants issued by the royal governors of both New Hampshire and New York were not truly sorted out until 1791, when Congress admitted Vermont as the 14th state, after 14 years as an independent republic.

For an overview visit the outstanding exhibits collectively titled "Freedom and Unity" (the state motto) in the **Vermont Historical Society Museum** (vermonthistory.org), housed

in a replica of the Pavilion Hotel that stands beside the Vermont State House in Montpelier. A pamphlet guide to **Vermont Historic Sites**, operated by the Division for Historic Preservation (historicvermont.org), is available at information centers throughout the state. See also *Historical Societies*.

The Abenaki presence in Vermont is far more pervasive than was acknowedged until recently. **St. Anne's Shrine** on Isle La Motte memorializes Samuel de Champlain's first landfall on the lake that bears his name; the site was an Indian village and by 1666 a mission as well as a French fort, which was abandoned in 1679 but remains an evocative place. Nearby in present-day Swanton, the Indian village of Missisquoi became a mission village, a way stop for Abenaki headed for Canada. Abenaki life is presented in an exhibit at the **Abenaki Tribal Museum and Cultural Center**. Native American settlements are also recorded at Otter Creek, and the 18th-century tavern at **Chimney Point State Historic Site** in Addison has a well-mounted display that explains the territory's Native American and French colonial heritage. In Newport the lakeside state office building displays the **Memphremagog Historical Society**'s

exhibit on northern Vermont's native people, from Paleolithic through current times, and at the **Fort at Number 4** in Charlestown, New Hampshire (see "The Lower Connecticut River Valley")—a community in which settlers and Indians lived side by side—the reconstructed fort exhibits Native American artifacts from the Connecticut River Valley.

Bennington, chartered by the avaricious Governor Benning Wentworth in 1749, the first chartered town west of the Connecticut River in the New Hampshire Grants, became the tinderbox for settlers' resistance to New York's rival claims, confirmed by King George in 1764. The desperate grantees found a champion in the protean Ethan Allen from Connecticut. This frontier rebel—land speculator, firebrand, and philosopher—recruited the boisterous Green Mountain Boys militiamen, who talked rum and rebellion at the Catamount Tavern in **Old Bennington**, pledged defiance of the 'Yorkers, and then fought the British. Ethan's rambunctious life is reflected in the **Ethan Allen Homestead**, the farm north of Burlington where he died in 1789.

In Westminster, on the bank of the Connecticut River, the 1775 **"Massacre"** was thought, incorrectly, to have been the first armed engagement of the Revolution. But the death of William French, shot by a 'Yorker sheriff, galvanized opposition to both New York and England, leading to a convention in Westminster in January 1777, where Vermonters declared their independence of everyone.

Formal independence was declared the following July, upriver in Windsor, where delegates gathered in Elijah West's tavern (now **The Old Constitution House**). They adopted a model constitution, the first to abolish slavery, before rushing off to attack the British, who had retaken Fort Ticonderoga. (While in Windsor, visit the **American Precision Museum**, a landmark showcasing early gun makers and the heyday of the machine tool industry.)

Since its discovery by Samuel de Champlain in 1609, Lake Champlain has been not only one of the nation's most historic waterways but also a strategic corridor in three wars. The French controlled the lake until 1759, when Lord Jeffery Amherst drove them out of Fort Carillon (now **Ticonderoga**) and then captured Montreal. In the American Revolution, the British used the lake as an invasion route to divide the colonies, but were thwarted when Ethan Allen's Green Mountain Boys captured Fort Ticonderoga in 1775.

Facing Ticonderoga across the lake's narrowest channel, the **Mount Independence State Historic Site** near Orwell dramatizes the struggle that ended with the decisive British defeat at Saratoga in 1777. The only battle of the Revolution to have been fought on Vermont soil is commemorated at the **Hubbardton Battlefield** near Castleton, where a small force of Green Mountain Boys under Colonel Seth Warner stopped a far larger British contingent as Burgoyne's British troops marched south. The invaders were soon repulsed again in the battle of Bennington—actually fought in New York—marked by the **Bennington Battle Monument** and by exhibits in the **Bennington Museum**.

The lake also figured in naval warfare when Benedict Arnold and a quickly assembled American flotilla engaged a heavier British squadron off Plattsburgh, New York, in the battle of Valcour Island in October 1776. One of Arnold's small gunboats, the *Philadelphia*, sunk by the British, was salvaged in 1935 and reposes in the Smithsonian. An exact replica is moored at the **Lake Champlain Maritime Museum** at Basin Harbor near Vergennes. A number of ships and other artifacts of that battle have been found buried in the mud on the lake bottom in recent years. In 1814 the British again tried to use Lake Champlain as an invasion route. Thomas McDonough moved his headquarters from Burlington to Vergennes and a shipyard at the mouth of Otter Creek. His small fleet barely managed to defeat British ships at Plattsburgh Bay, a bloody engagement that helped end the War of 1812.

With Vermont in the vanguard of the antislavery movement of the 1840s, the Underground Railroad flourished, notably at **Rokeby**, the home of the Robinson family in Ferrisburg, now a museum. Evidence of the state's extraordinary record in the Civil War and its greater-than-average number of per capita casualties may be seen in the memorials that dot most town and village greens. How Vermonters turned the tide of the battle at Cedar Creek is portrayed in Julian Scott's huge and newly restored painting that hangs in the **State House** in Montpelier. The anniversary of the October 1864 **St. Albans Raid**, the northernmost engagement of the Civil War, is observed annually.

There are few 18th-century structures in the state, but the settlers who poured in after 1791 (the population nearly tripled, from 85,000 to 235,000 in 1820) built sophisticated dwellings and churches. **Dorset**, **Castleton**, **Chester** (Old Stone Village), **Middlebury**, **Brandon**, **Woodstock**, and **Norwich** are architectural showcases of Federal-style houses. Several historic, outstandingly splendid mansions built by 19th-century moguls are open to the public: the **Park-McCullough House**, North Bennington; the **Wilburton Inn** and **Hildene**,

Manchester; **The Castle Inn**, Proctorsville; **Wilson Castle**, West Rutland; the **Marsh-Billings-Rockefeller National Historical Park**, Woodstock; and **The Inn at Shelburne Farms** (built by Lila Vanderbilt Webb and William Seward Webb), Shelburne.

Vermont's congressional delegations, especially in the 19th century, always had more influence in Washington than the state's size might suggest. For example, the **Justin Morrill Homestead** in Strafford, a spacious Gothic Revival house, reminds us of the distinguished career of the originator of the Land Grant Colleges Act, who served in Congress from 1855 to 1898.

The Vermont Historical Society maintains a research library in Barre with changing special exhibits. Arts, crafts, architecture, and transportation are featured in the **Shelburne Museum** in Shelburne. In Woodstock the **Billings Farm & Museum** re-creates a model 1890s stock farm and dairy and the **Marsh-Billings-Rockefeller National Historical Park** traces the state's environmental history. Outstanding collections of the ways people lived and worked can be found in town historical societies, notably the **Farrar Mansur House** in Weston, the **Sheldon Museum** in Middlebury, and the **Dana House** in Woodstock. *Freedom and Unity: A History of Vermont*, published by the Vermont Historical Society (2004), is a readable reference work that complements the society's permanent exhibit.

HISTORICAL SOCIETIES The attics of every town, historical societies are frequently worth seeking out, but because most are staffed by volunteers, they tend to be open just a few hours a week, usually in summer. Of Vermont's 251 towns, 194 have historical societies; we have tried to give accurate, current information on them within each chapter. The **Vermont Historical Society** (vermonthistory.org) publishes a free booklet, *Passport to Vermont History*, listing hours and contact phones. Outstanding local historical societies found are in **Brownington**, **Newfane**, and **Middlebury**, and **Woodstock**.

HORSEBACK RIDING AND EQUESTRIAN SPORTS Horses are as much a part of the Vermont landscape as the famous black-and-white Holsteins. Resorts offering horseback riding include **Topnotch** in Stowe, the **Mountain Top** in Chittenden, and **Hawk Mountain** in Plymouth. Inn-to-inn treks are offered by **Vermont Icelandic Horse Farm** (icelandichorses.com) in Waitsfield and by **Kedron Valley Stables** (kedron.com) in South Woodstock, the state's outstanding place for beginners to learn and for experienced equestrians to ride. Other options for trail rides are listed in almost every chapter. Vermont has three polo clubs: **Sugarbush Polo Club** (802-496-3581), based in the Mad River Valley and Middlebury; **Green Mountain Polo Club** near Manchester (802-375-9491; 802-442-8070; greenmountainpolo.com), which offers a polo school in summer; and **Quechee Polo Club** (802-775-5066.). All hold games on Saturday and Sunday during summer (usually at 1 PM); most games are free or inexpensive. The **Vermont Summer Horse Festival** (vt-summerfestival.com), the largest of several hunter-jumper shows around the state, takes place in the Manchester area, mid-July–mid-Aug. The **Vermont Quarter Horse Association** (vtqha.com) hosts shows around the region in summer. The **Green Mountain Horse Association** in South Woodstock (802-457-1509;

gmhainc.org) holds **Dressage Days** and other events open to spectators. **Miniature horse and donkey farms** are proliferating around the state, and many show their animals by appointment (sites to check: amha.com and nmdaasset.com). Driving is also gaining popularity, and pleasure-driving events can be fun to watch; the Web site is americandrivingsociety.org. (Also see *Morgan Horses*.)

HUNTING The *Vermont Digest of Hunting, Fishing and Trapping Laws* and a useful *State of Vermont Hunting Map* are available from the Vermont Fish and Wildlife Department (802-241-3700; vtfishandwildlife.com). Of special interest to nonresidents: a reasonably priced, five-day small-game license. The ruffed grouse or "partridge" is the state's most abundant game bird, while woodcocks, or "timberdoodles," are found throughout the state. The wild turkey is considered "big game"—as hunters will understand when they try to bag them (in-season in Oct. and May). October is bow-and-arrow season for white-tailed deer, and Nov. is buck season. Black bear and moose populations are both healthy, but hunting regulations vary with the year.

ICE CREAM Vermont's quality milk is used to produce some outstanding ice cream as well as cheese. The big name is, of course, **Ben & Jerry's**, proud producers of what *Time* has billed "the best ice cream in the world." Their plant on Rt. 100 in Waterbury (featuring factory tours, free samples, real cows, and a gift shop full of reproductions in every conceivable shape) is the state's most popular tourist attraction. Other good Vermont ice creams include **Wilcox Brothers** (try "sweet cram") in Manchester, **Ellsworth Ice Cream** in North Springfield, the

Strafford Organic Creamery in Strafford, **Green Mountain Gelato** in Barre, and **Island Homemade** ice cream, sherbet, and sorbets from Grand Isle. Soft-serve maple creamees are the current craze at ice cream stands throughout the state; whatever the source of the soft serve, the maple is local.

INNS It's safe to say that we have visited more Vermont inns, more frequently, than anyone else living today. We do not charge for inclusion in this book, and we attempt to give as accurate and detailed a picture as space permits. We quote 2009 rates—which are, of course, subject to change. Summer rates are generally lower than winter (except, of course, at lake resorts); weekly or ski-week rates run 10–20 percent less than the per diem price quoted. Many inns insist on MAP (Modified American Plan—breakfast and dinner) in winter but not in summer. Some resorts have AP (American Plan—three meals), and we have shown EP (European Plan—no meals) where applicable. We have attempted to note when 15 percent service is added, but you should always ask if it has been included in a quoted rate and whether an additional local tax is added. Always add the 9 percent state tax on rooms and meals. It's prudent to check which, if any, credit cards are accepted. Many lodging places now insist on minimum two- or three-day stays during busy seasons. Within the text, special icons highlight lodging places that specialize in weddings and civil unions ∞ , those that offer exceptional value ✿, those that accept pets ❤, those that appeal to families ✦, those that are handicapped accessible ⓗ, and those with WiFi access ⁰ᵢ⁰ .

LAKES The state famed for green mountains and white villages also

INFORMATION

The Vermont Department of Tourism and Marketing (800-VERMONT) offers vacation planning, information packets, seasonal highlights, and an excellent Web site (vermont vacation.com) with links to every aspect of exploring the state. A Vacation Planning pack-

WAYPOINT VISITORS CENTER, BELLOWS FALLS   Christina Tree

et can be requested through an online form on the Web site, or by calling the toll-free number above. The standard packet includes the *Official Vermont Road Map & Guide to Vermont Attractions* (a detailed road map with symbols locating attractions, covered bridges, golf courses, state parks and historic sites, ski areas, public boat and fishing access ramps, and more), and a seasonal guide, *The Vermont Vacation Guide* (summer/fall) or the *Winter Guide*; both are helpful and current magazine-format guides published by the Vermont Chamber of Commerce (vtchamber.com). You may also want to request the *Vermont Historic Sites Guide*, the handy *Vermont Farms* brochure, or the *Vermont Campground Guide*. All of these publications and more are available at Vermont's numerous welcome and information centers once you arrive in the state.

The **Vermont Information Center Division** maintains highway welcome and information centers with pay phones, WiFi, and bathroom facilities. At the Massachusetts border, northbound at **Guilford** on I-91, the state's largest and most complete **Welcome Center** (802-254-4593; facilities open 24 hours) showcases Vermont products. Other I-91 rest areas open daily, are southbound at **Bradford** and **Lyndon.** Along I-89 your first stop should be the **Sharon Welcome Center** (802-281-5216), which is also the **Vermont Vietnam Veterans Memorial**, an architecturally striking building that tells its story well and also includes an octagonal greenhouse filled with exotic vegetation recycling Sharon's wastewater. Less elaborate rest areas are found southbound at **Williston** and both north- and southbound in **Georgia**. There's also an inviting welcome center just over the state line on I-93 at **Waterford** (802-748-9368), as well as visitor centers at the New York–Canadian border on Rt. 2 in **Alburg** (802-796-3980) and on the New York border on Rt. 4A in **Fair Haven** (802-265-4763). In Montpelier the **Capital Region Visitors Center**, 134 State St. (802-828-5981), is the source of statewide information. Due to state budgetary cuts, at this writing the facilities at four more rest areas are temporarily closed.

Steve Cook

Waypoint Visitors Centers, along the **Connecticut River Scenic Byway** (ctrivertravel .net), serve communities on both sides fo the river. Look for them in **Bellows Falls** (802-463-4280), Windsor (not yet open at this writing), **White River Junction** (802-281-5050), **Wells River** (802-222-5631) and **St. Johnsbury** (802-748-2436). Each is described under "Guidance" in their respective chapters.

AAA Emergency Road Service: 800-222-4357. For road conditions dial 511 or click on 511vt.com. Also see *Highway Road Food* and *Weather Reports.*

First-time visitors may be puzzled by **Vermont's Travel Information System** of directional signs, which replace billboards (banned since 1968, another Vermont first). Stylized symbols for lodging, food, recreation, antiques and crafts, and other services are sited at intersections off major highways.

We have noted local chambers of commerce town by town in each chapter of this book under *Guidance.* In small towns inquiries are welcomed by the town clerk.

WAYPOINT VISITORS CENTER, BELLOWS FALLS

Christina Tree

harbors more than 400 relatively blue lakes: big lakes like **Champlain** (110 miles long) and **Memphremagog** (boasting 88 miles of coastline, but most of it in Canada), and smaller lakes like **Morey**, **Dunmore**, **Willoughby**, **Bomoseen**, and **Seymour**. A century ago there were many more lakeside hotels; today just a handful of these classic summer resorts survive: **Quimby Country** in Averill, **Highland Lodge** in Greensboro, the **Tyler Place** in Highgate Springs, the **Basin Harbor Club** near Vergennes, and the **Lake Morey Inn Resort** in Fairlee. Lakes are particularly plentiful and rentals reasonable in Vermont's Northeast Kingdom. There are also state parks with campsites on **Groton Lake**, **Emerald Lake**, **Island Pond**, **Maidstone Lake**, **Lake Bomoseen**, **Lake Carmi**, **Lake Elmore**, **Lake St. Catherine**, and **Silver Lake** (in Barnard). On Lake Champlain, there are a number of state campgrounds, including those on **Grand Isle** (accessible by car) and **Burton Island** (accessible by public launch from St. Albans Bay). See *Campgrounds* for details about these, private campgrounds (we recommend Harvey's Lake Cabins and Campground) and those maintained by the Army Corps of Engineers on **Ball Mountain Lake** and **North Hartland Lake**. The **Green Mountain Club** (see *Hiking*) maintains two cabins for rental on Wheeler Pond near Lake Willoughby.

Christina Tree

There is public boat access to virtually every Vermont pond and lake of any size. Boat launches are listed on the state map.

LIBRARIES Along with general stores, libraries are central to Vermont communities. The 189 or so libraries in the state range from the one-room cottage at Joe's Pond in West Danville to opulent late-19th-century buildings gifted by wealthy native sons. Notable examples are the **Aldrich Public Library** in Barre, the **Kellogg Hubbard Library** in Montpelier, the **Norman Williams Public Library** in Woodstock, and the **St. Johnsbury Atheneum and Art Gallery**. Some of our favorites are, however, found in very small places. The **Lincoln Library**, destroyed by flood a decade ago, has been replaced with a new building with porch rockers, also the signature of the new **Craftsbury Public Library** with its handsome interior (visitors are requested to remove their shoes). In Peacham the library marks the center of the village and is also an art center. The **Grafton Public Library** is an elegant vintage 1822 house but remarkably homey. The **Tunbridge Pubic Library** is also in a renovated historic brick house, as is **Alice M. Ward Memorial Library** (with historical exhibits upstairs) on the green in **Canaan**. The **Pope Memorial Library** on the common in Danville is said to have ghosts, and the small **Fairlee Public Library** has an excellent collection. For research, the **Vermont Historical Society Library** in Barre is a treasure trove of Vermontiana and genealogical resources; likewise the **Wilbur Collection** of the Bailey-Howe Library at the University of Vermont and the **Russell Collection** in Arlington. Three of the Vermont state colleges—Castleton, Johnson, and Lyndon—have collec-

Diane E. Foulds

tions of Vermontiana in the Vermont Rooms of their libraries. In East Craftsbury there's also the **John Woodruff Memorial Library**, a former general store open just seasonally two days a week but well stocked, especially with children's titles.

LLAMAS AND LLAMA TREKKING

Google the Vermont Llama & Alpaca Association Web site for farms that welcome visitors; we list these within our chapters. Treks are offered by **Applecheek Farm** in Hyde Park (802-888-4482); **Northern Vermont Llama Co.** (802-644-2257) in Waterville; **On the Loose Expeditions** (800-688-1481) in Huntington; **Dream Come True Farm** in Hartland (802-295-1573); and **Woodstock Llama Trekking** (802-457-1500).

MAGAZINES *Vermont Life* (vtlife

.com), the popular and colorful quarterly published by the Agency of Commerce and Community Development, is an outstanding chronicle of Vermont's people and places, featuring distinguished photographers. *Vermont Magazine* (vermontmagazine.com), an upbeat, statewide bimonthly, covers major issues, townscapes, products, and personalities, and reviews inns and restaurants. The new (since 2004) bimonthly *Livin' the Vermont Way* (livinmagazine.com), aimed in-state instead of out, covers issues of local

concern such as the environment, industry, and politics, with smaller features on folklore, food, and recreation. *Seven Days* (sevendaysvt.com), Burlington's free weekly tabloid of area arts and entertainment, is far more than a calendar of events.

MAPLE SUGARING Vermont pro-

duces some 400,000 gallons of maple syrup each year, over a third of the national supply and more than any other state. Approximately 2,000 maple growers tap an average of 1,000 trees each. About a quart of syrup is made per tap; it takes 30 to 40 gallons of sap to make each gallon of syrup. The process of tapping trees and boiling sap is stubbornly known as *sugaring*, rather than *syruping*, because the end product for early settlers was sugar. Syrup was first made in the early 19th century, but production flagged when imported cane sugar became more accessible. The Civil War revived the maple sugar industry: Union supporters were urged to consume sugar made by free men and to plant more and more maples.

We urge visitors to buy syrup direct from the producer, any time of year (finding the farm is half the fun), but also to seriously consider making a special trip to a sugarhouse during sugaring season in March and April. It's then (not in autumn) that sugar maples really perform, and it's a show that can't be seen through a windshield. Sugaring season begins quietly in February as thousands of Vermonters wade, snowshoe, and snowmobile into their woods and begin "tapping," a ritual that has changed since plastic tubing replaced buckets. But the timing is the same. Traditionally, sugaring itself begins on Town Meeting Day (the first Tuesday in March). But sap runs only on those days when temperatures rise to 40 and 50 degrees during the day

Kim Grant

three-day event that includes tours through the local sugarbush (vtmaple festival.org). At **Maple Grove Farm** of Vermont, "the world's largest maple candy factory" in St. Johnsbury, factory tours are offered Mon.–Fri. year-round, and there is a maple museum and gift shop. Videos on maple are also shown in the **New England Maple Museum** in Pittsford. Within this book we list maple producers in the areas in which they are most heavily concentrated. There are many more than found on any formal lists. Ask locally.

MAPS The *Official Vermont Road Map & Guide to Vermont Attractions* (see *Information*) is free and extremely helpful for general motoring but will not suffice for finding your way around the webs of dirt roads that connect some of the most beautiful corners of the state. Among our favorite areas where you will need more detail: the high farming country between Albany, Craftsbury, and West Glover; similar country between Chelsea and Williamstown; south from Plainfield to Orange; and between Plymouth and Healdville. We strongly suggest securing a copy of the *Vermont Atlas and Gazetteer* (DeLorme) if you want to do any serious back-road exploring, or the *Vermont Road Atlas and Guide* (Northern Cartographics); both are widely available at bookstores, gas stations, and general stores. Among the best regional maps for anyone planning to do much hiking or biking are those published by Map Adventures. Also see *Hiking and Walking*.

MARBLE The **Vermont Marble Trail**, described in a glossy booklet (phone 800-VERMONT), focuses on the visual evidence of Vermont's once all-important marble industry. One trail leads from Bennington via Dorset and Danby to Rutland, where the

and drop into the 20s at night. When the sap does run, it must be boiled down quickly. What you want to see is the boiling process: sap churning madly through the large, flat evaporating pan, darkening as you watch. You are enveloped in fragrant steam, listening to the rush of the sap, sampling the end result on snow or in tiny paper cups. Sugaring is Vermont's rite of spring. Don't miss a sugar-on-snow party: plates of snow dribbled with viscous hot syrup, accompanied by doughnuts and dill pickles. Vermont maple syrup is 100 percent pure, no additives.

A *Vermont Ski Resort & Maple Syrup Guide* map, available by phoning 800-VERMONT, lists and pinpoints producers who open their doors to the public on **Maple Open House Weekend** in mid-March. See **vermontmaple.org** for similar information and a list of producers who ship. The **Vermont Maple Festival**, held in late April in St. Albans, is a

nearby **Vermont Marble Museum** in Proctor is a must-see. Here the history and extent of the industry in Vermont are dramatized in exhibits and in a film that depicts, among other things, the ongoing underground quarrying in Danby. The **Dorset Historical Society** also has impressive exhibits and a diorama pinpointing all the onetime quarries in that area, some now popular swimming holes. Additional trails includes the marble works at the center of **Middlebury**, as well as the **Fisk Quarry** preserve and ancient reefs on Isle La Motte, with a film at the Goodsell Ridge Preserve that describes the evolution of limestone.

MONEY Each inn has its own policy about credit cards and checks. Personal checks are frequently more acceptable to craftspeople and small lodging places than credit cards.

MORGAN HORSES The Vermont state animal is a distinctive breed of saddle horse popular throughout America. The first "Morgan" was born in the late 1790s to singing teacher Justin Morgan of Randolph. Colonel Joseph Battell began breeding Morgans on his Weybridge farm in the 1870s and is credited with saving the breed (America's first developed breed of horse) from extinction. The farm is now a breeding and training center operated by the **University of Vermont** (uvm.edu/morgan), open to the public. For more about Morgan horse sites and events, visit vtmorganhorse.com.

MOUNTAIN BIKING In recent years Vermont mountain biking options have dramatically broadened as the potential for the state's hundreds of miles of dirt and Class 4 roads as well as crosscounty trail systems has been recognized. The nonprofit **Kingdom Trails Association** (kingdomtrails.org) in

East Burke maintains a roughly 100-mile mix of trails across woods and meadows that have been rated among the top networks in the country and attract many fans from Canada. The **Craftsbury Outdoor Center** (craftsbury.com), also in the Northeast Kingdom, was the first place to rent mountain bikes and offer guided tours over dirt and abandoned logging roads. A former prep school now devoted to running and rowing as well as biking in summer and cross-country skiing in winter, it's set in high, rolling farm country with mountain views. In East Barre, **Millstone Hill Touring and Recreation Center** (millstonehill.com) offers 70 miles of singletrack trail in 350 acres of wooded terrain, spotted with abandoned granite quarries. The **Three Stallion Inn** (3stallion.com) in Randolph opens its network of trails to the public as well as guests. In Putney the **West Hill Shop** (westhillshop.com) publishes its own map to an extensive network of singletrack trails and forgotten roads. In the Burlington area the **Catamount Family Center** (catamountoutdoor.com) and **Sleepy Hollow Inn, Ski, and Bike Center** (skisleepyhollow.com) both offer extensive cross-country trail networks and bike rentals. **Blueberry Hill Inn** (blueberryhillinn.com) is set high in Goshen with easy access to trails in the Moosalamoo region of the Green Mountain National Forest and to Silver Lake.

Several ski areas offer lift-assisted mountain biking. The **Mount Snow Mountain Bike School** (mountsnow.com) offers 45 miles of trails, some served by lifts Memorial Day to Columbus Day. **Stratton Mountain** (stratton.com) offers more than 100 miles of trail, primarily in its Sun Bowl; lifts accessing trails off the summit run during foliage season. The 45 miles of trails at **Mountain Bike Park at**

Killington (killington.com) are accessed by lift from Rt. 4 July–Columbus Day weekend (weather permitting). **Jay Peak Resort** (jaypeak resort.com) also permits mountain biking on ski trails, accessible via its tramway.

The nominally priced *Topographic Maps & Guides* produced by **Map Adventures** (mapadventures.com) are useful map/guides outlining rides in various parts of Vermont: the Burlington and Stowe areas, the White River Valley, the Upper Valley, and southern Vermont, among others. Also check out **Adventure Guides of Vermont** (adventureguidesvt.com) and *Bicycle Touring*.

MOUNTAINTOPS While Vermont can boast only seven peaks above 4,000 feet, there are 80 mountains that rise more than 3,000 feet and any number of spectacular views, several of them accessible in summer and foliage season to those who prefer riding to walking up mountains. **Mount Mansfield**, which at 4,393 feet is the state's highest summit, can be reached via the Toll Road and a gondola. The mid-19th-century road brings you to the small Summit Station at 4,062 feet, from which the 0.5-mile Tundra Trail brings you to the actual summit. The Mount Mansfield gondola, an eight-passenger, enclosed lift, hoists you from the main base area up to the Cliff House Restaurant, from which a trail also heads up to the Chin. **Killington Peak**, Vermont's second highest peak at 4,241 feet, can be reached via a 1.2-mile ride on a gondola that takes you to a summit restaurant and a nature trail that even small children can negotiate. **Jay Peak**, a 3,861-foot summit towering like a lone sentinel near the Canadian border, is accessible via a 60-passenger tram (daily July–Labor Day, and again mid-Sept.–Columbus Day),

and a "four-state view" from the top of **Stratton Mountain** is accessible via the ski resort's six-passenger gondola, Starship XII (daily in fall). Other toll roads include the Auto Road to the 3,267-foot **Burke Mountain** in East Burke, the Toll Road to the 3,144-foot summit of **Mount Ascutney** in Ascutney State Park, and the Skyline Drive to the top of **Mount Equinox** in Sunderland. There are also chairlift rides to the tops of **Bromley** (you don't have to take the alpine slide down) and **Mount Snow**.

MUD SEASON The period from snowmelt (around the middle of March) through early May (it varies each year) is known throughout the state as mud season for reasons that few visitors want to explore too deeply. Dirt roads can turn quickly into boggy quagmires.

MUSEUMS The variety of this state's museums is immediately apparent when you click onto the **Vermont Museum & Gallery Alliance** Web site, **vmga.org**. Within this book, we have listed museums in their geographic areas. They vary from the immense **Shelburne Museum**—with its 39 buildings, many housing priceless collections of art and Americana, plus assorted exhibits such as a completely restored lake steamer and lighthouse—to the **American Precision Museum** in Windsor, an 1846 brick mill that once produced rifles. They include a number of outstanding historical museums (our favorites are the **Bennington Museum** in Bennington, the **Sheldon Museum** in Middlebury, the **Old Stone House Museum** in Brownington, and the **Dana House** in Woodstock) and some collections that go beyond the purely historical: The **Bennington Museum** is famed for its collection of Grandma Moses paintings as well as early American glass and

Christina Tree

relics from the Revolution, and the **Fairbanks Museum and Planetarium** in St. Johnsbury has vaulted wooden halls filled with taxidermied birds and animals. The **Billings Farm & Museum** in Woodstock shows off its blue-ribbon dairy and has a fascinating, beautifully mounted display of 19th-century farm life and tools.

MUSIC The Green Mountains are filled with the sounds of music each summer, beginning with the **Discover Jazz Festival** (discoverjazz.com), more than 100 concerts held over a week around Burlington in early June. In Putney a late-June-through-July series of three evening chamber music concerts each week is presented in the **Yellow Barn Festival** (yellowbarn .org). In July and Aug. options include the internationally famous **Marlboro Music Festival** (marlboromusic.org) at Marlboro College, presenting chamber music on weekends, and the **Vermont Mozart Festival** (vtmozart.com), a series of 20 concerts performed at a variety of sites ranging from beautiful barns at the University of Vermont and Shelburne Farms to a Lake Champlain ferry and including some striking classic and modern churches and a ski area base lodge. The **Killington Music Festival** (killingtonmusicfestival.org) is a series of Sunday concerts at Rams Head Lodge from late June to early Aug., and the **Manchester Music Festival** (mmfvt.org) brings leading performers to various venues around Manchester. Also well worth noting: the **Central Vermont Chamber Music Festival** (centralvtchamber musicfest.org) at the Chandler Music Hall in Randolph in mid- to late Aug., the **Summer Music School** in Adamant (adamant.org/summer.htm), concerts at the Town House in Hardwick by the **Craftsbury Chamber Players** (craftsburychamberplayers .org), and in Stowe, for a week in late July, at the **Performing Arts Festival** (stowearts.com).

Other concert series are performed at the **Southern Vermont Arts Center** (Thu. and Sun.; svac.org), Castleton State College (csc.vsc.edu), the **Dibden Center for the Arts**, Johnson State College (jsc.edu), and the **Middlebury College Center for the Arts** (middlebury.edu). The **Vermont Symphony Orchestra** (vso.org), the oldest of the state symphonies, figures in a number of the series noted above and also performs at a variety of locations, ranging from Brattleboro's Living Memorial Park and the State House lawn to Wilson Castle, throughout summer. In Weston the **Kinhaven Music School** (kinhaven.org) offers free concerts on summer weekends, and in Brattleboro the **Brattleboro Music Center** (bmcvt.org) brings in world-renowned classical groups for its year-round Chamber Music Series. See also *Fiddling*.

NATIONAL PUBLIC RADIO See *Vermont Public Radio (VPR)*.

NATURE PRESERVES The **Vermont Land Trust** (vlt.org), founded in 1977, is dedicated to preserving

Vermont's traditional landscape of farms as well as forest (it has helped protect more than 400 operating farms), and many local land trusts have acquired numerous parcels of land throughout the state. Many of the most visitor-friendly preserves are owned by **The Nature Conservancy** (802-229-4425; nature.org), a national nonprofit that has preserved close to 7 million acres throughout the United States since its founding in 1951. Its Vermont branch is at 27 State St., Montpelier 05602.

OPERA HOUSES Northern New England opera houses are a turn-of-the-20th-century phenomenon: theaters built as cultural centers for the surrounding area, stages on which lecturers, musicians, and vaudeville acts as well as opera singers performed. Many of these buildings have long since disappeared, but those that survive are worth noting. The **Hyde Park Opera House**, built in 1910, has been restored by the Lamoille County Players, who stage four annual shows—one play, two musicals, and an annual foliage-season run of *The Sound of Music*. The **Barre Opera House**, built in 1899, is an elegant, acoustically outstanding, second-floor theater, home of the Barre Players; productions are staged here year-round. In Derby Line, in the second-floor **Opera House** (a neoclassical structure that also houses the Haskell Free Library), the audience sits in Vermont watching a stage that is in Canada. Tom Thumb and Houdini performed at Rutland's 1914 **Paramount Theater**, which has been restored and now offers a full repertory from cabaret to jazz, comedy, and musicals. The theater company **Northern Stage** has taken up residence at White River Junction's **Briggs Opera House**, offering year-round performances and courses for children and young adults in summer months.

The **Chandler Center for the Arts** in Randolph and the opera houses in **Vergennes** and **Enosburg Falls** have been restored for cultural events. Each of these is described under *Entertainment* within its respective chapter.

PETS We note lodging places that accommodate pets with the symbol 🐾. For a small additional fee, many B&Bs and inns now accommodate dogs as well as their owners. Among the most elegant to do so are the **Inn on the Common** in Craftsbury, **Topnotch** in Stowe, the **Basin Harbor Club** in Vergennes, the **Woodstock Inn and Resort** in Woodstock, and the **Mountain Top Inn and Resort** in Chittenden. **The Paw House Inn** in West Rutland and in West Dover (at Mount Snow) caters to guests with dogs, supplying dog-sitters and off-leash areas as well as equipping each room with dog bowls, beds, and biscuits.

PICK YOUR OWN Strawberry season is mid- to late June. Cherries, plums, raspberries, and blueberries can be picked in July and Aug. Apples ripen by mid-Sept. and can be picked through foliage season. For specifics on where, see *Apples* and *Farms Open to the Public*.

QUILTS A revival of interest in this craft is especially strong in Vermont, where quilting supply and made-to-order stores salt the state. The **Vermont Quilt Festival** (vqf.org) is held for three days in late June in Essex Junction, including exhibits of antique quilts, classes and lectures, vendors, and appraisals. **Shelburne Museum** has an outstanding quilt collection, and the **Billings Farm & Museum** holds an annual show.

RAILROAD EXCURSIONS Trains Around Vermont (rails-vt.com) runs a number of excursion trains around the state. The **Green Mountain Flyer**, named for the fastest train on the old Rutland Railroad, runs between Bellows Falls on the Connecticut River and Chester (13 miles), with special foliage runs for another 14 miles to Ludlow and seasonal Santa Claus runs before Christmas. The **White River Flyer** runs seasonally up along the Connecticut River from White River Junction to the Montshire Museum in Norwich, and the **Champlain Valley Flyer** runs from Burlington to Shelburne, connecting with optional cruises aboard the excursion boat *Ethan Allen II*. Check the Web site for other special trips. We also note rail excursions within respective chapters.

Christina Tree

RESTAURANTS Culinary standards are rising every day, along with the commitment to using local ingredients. You can lunch simply and inexpensively nearly everywhere and dine superbly in a score of places. Further boosting culinary standards is the Vermont Fresh Network; see the entry below. Fixed price menus (prix fixe) have been so noted. We were tempted to try to list our favorites here, but the roster would be too long. Restaurants that appeal to us appear in the text in their respective areas. Note that we divide restaurants in each chapter into *Dining Out* (serious dining experiences) and *Eating Out* (everyday places). See also *Highway Road Food*.

ROCKHOUNDING The most obvious sites are the **Rock of Ages Quarry and Visitor Center** in Barre and the **Vermont Marble Museum** in Proctor, both with interactive exhibits. Vermont fossils, minerals, and rocks (including dinosaur footprints) may be viewed at the **Perkins Museum of Geology** at the University of Vermont, Burlington (uvm.edu/perkins/visitor

.htm), and the **Fairbanks Museum** in St. Johnsbury. The 480-million-year-old coral reef at Fisk Quarry on Isle La Motte is another must-see. And an annual **Rock Swap and Mineral Show** is held in early Aug., sponsored by the Burlington Gem and Mineral Club (burlingtongemandmineralclub .org). Gold, incidentally, can be panned in a number of rivers, notably Broad Brook in Plymouth; the Rock River in Newfane and Dover; the Williams River in Ludlow; the Ottauquechee River in Bridgewater; the White River in Stockbridge and Rochester; the Mad River in Warren, Waitsfield, and Moretown; the Little River in Stowe and Waterbury; and the Missisquoi in Lowell and Troy.

SHEEP AND WOOL Specialty sheep and alpaca farms are numerous in Vermont. A number of farmers specialize in processing wool and fiber. Check vermontsheep.org. The annual **Vermont Sheep and Wool Festival**, featuring sheep shearing, spinning, weaving, and plenty of critters, is held in early Oct.

SHIPWRECKS Well-preserved 19th-century shipwrecks are open to the public (licensed divers) at any of nine underwater historical preserves in Lake Champlain near Burlington. Check with the **Lake Champlain Maritime Museum** (lcmm.org) in Vergennes, which is charting underwater remains. Nondivers can explore the lake's shipwrecks at the museum's Nautical Archaeology Center, which has interactive exhibits, a touch-screen "Virtual Diver," and archaeologists on site.

SKIING, CROSS-COUNTRY The **Vermont Ski Areas Association** (skivermont.com) lists more than 30 cross-country centers on its Web site and profiles them in its useful free *Ski Vermont Alpine and Nordic Directory* and *Ski Vermont Magazine*. Centers are also listed in the *Vermont Winter Guide*, published by the Vermont Chamber of Commerce and available free by phoning 800-VERMONT. Within this book we have described each commercial touring center as it appears geographically. It's important to check conditions before you jump in the car. Vermont's most dependable snow can be found on high-elevation trails in **Stowe**, at **Craftsbury Outdoor Center** in Craftsbury Common, **Hazen's Notch** in Montgomery Center, **Bolton Valley Resort** (between Burlington and Stowe), **Burke Mountain Cross-Country** in East Burke, and **Blueberry Hill** in Goshen. **Mountain Top Inn** in Chittenden and and **Grafton Ponds** in Grafton offer some snowmaking. All the cross-country ski centers mentioned above are located on the 300-mile **Catamount Trail**, a marked ski trail that runs the length of the state (see *Catamount Trail*). Inn-to-inn tours are possible between **Craftsbury Outdoor Center** and the **Highland Lodge and Ski Touring Center** in Greensboro. Also see **inntoinn.com**. **Prospect Mountain Nordic Ski Center** (prospectmountain.com), a former alpine area in the southeastern corner of the state, also tends to have reliable conditions because of its site in the state's highest town. **Mad River Glen** and **Bolton Valley** are two alpine resorts that specialize in telemarking. Also see *State Parks* and *Green Mountain National Forest*.

SKIING, DOWNHILL Since the 1930s, when America's commercial skiing began with a Model T Ford engine pulling skiers up a hill in Woodstock, skiing has been a Vermont specialty. Twenty ski areas are members of the **Vermont Ski Areas Association** and accessible with daily updated snow conditions and weather on the Web site **skivermont.com**. Request a free *Ski Vermont Alpine and Nordic Directory* and a *Ski Vermont Magazine* and/or phone 800-VERMONT for a a glossy *Vermont Winter Guide*. Daily lift tickets are, of course, not the cheapest way to ski. A season's pass aside, there are always deeply discounted multiday lift and lodging packages, and there are frequently discounts for ordering ahead online.

The areas vary widely in size and character. **Killington/Pico** is the largest ski resort in the East. **Mount Snow**, Vermont's second largest area, is the most convenient area to New York City; **Stratton** is a close second (there's daily shuttle service to all three areas from Manhattan). **Stowe** remains the Ski Capital of the East when it comes to the quantity and quality of inns, restaurants, and shops. **Sugarbush**, with a lower profile and almost equal options on and off the slopes, is preferred by many New England skiers, especially given the local option of skiing **Mad River Glen**, a famously

SKI VERMONT

WINTER IN ITS ORIGINAL STATE

Ski Vermont

trails are laced in a system maintained by the **Vermont Association of Snow Travelers** (vast.com). VAST's corridor trails are up to 8 feet wide and are maintained by 140 local snowmobile clubs; for detailed maps and suggestions for routes, activities, and guided tours, check the Web site. Due to insurance laws, snowmobile rentals and tours are relatively few. The Northeast Kingdom in general and Island Pond in particular are best geared to snowmobiling, with storage facilities and a wide choice of lodging handy to trails. The **Northeast Kingdom Chamber of Commerce** (nekchamber.com) publishes a snowmobiling map/guide to the area. Within the book we list snowmobile rentals and tours as they appear geographically.

old-fashioned ski area with minimal snowmaking, a single chair, and a ban (the only one in the East) against snowboarders. **Okemo** is known for its outstanding snow grooming and facilities and **Jay Peak** for its natural conditions, while **Burke** is the "Vermonter's Mountain." We describe these and smaller areas as they appear geographically.

SLEIGH RIDES Sleigh rides are listed under *To Do* as they appear geographically in the book.

SNOWBOARDING An international sport first popularized by Burton Snowboards (born in Manchester, long since moved to Burlington, where we list details about its factory store). Snowboarding lessons, rentals, and special terrain parks are offered at every major Vermont ski area except Mad River Glen.

SNOWMOBILING Vermont's roughly 6,000 miles of well-marked, groomed

SNOWSHOEING Snowshoeing is experiencing a rebirth in Vermont, thanks to the new lightweight equipment. Virtually all ski-touring centers now offer snowshoe rentals, and many inns stock a few pairs for guests.

SOARING **Sugarbush Soaring**, in the Mad River Valley, is known as one of the prime spots in the East for riding thermal and ridge waves. The Sugarbush Airport is a well-established place to take glider lessons or rides or simply to watch the planes come and go. The **Fall Wave Soaring Encampment** held in early Oct. (weather permitting) draws glider pilots from throughout the country. Gliders and airplane rides are also available at the **Stowe-Morrisville Airport** (802-888-7845) and from the **Post Mills Soaring Club** at the Post Mills Airport (802-333-9992), where soaring lessons are also a specialty, along with simply seeing the Connecticut Valley from the air.

SPAS Vermont is home to the lion's share of New England's resort spas. In

SNOWSHOEING AT MAD RIVER GLEN

Stowe both **Topnotch Resort and Spa** (topnotchresort.com) and **Stoweflake Mountain Resort & Spa** (stoweflake.com) can claim to be the region's biggest and best, and the spa at newly opened **Stowe Mountain Lodge** (stowe.com) is in its own class. The recently expanded and rebuilt **Equinox Resort** (equinox.rockresorts .com) in Manchester Center offers a magnificent full-service spa. The **Castle Hill Spa** in Cavendish, near Okemo, is small but lovely (castlehill spa.com). Many more spas have been opened through the state and are described under *To Do* in almost every chapter.

SPIRITUAL CENTERS/RETREATS
Karmê Chöling Shambhala Meditation Center (karmecholing.org) is a long-established retreat in Barnet with many special programs. **Yoga Vermont** in Burlington (yogavermont .com) draws Ashtanga yoga practitioners from throughout the country. The **Green Mountain Dharma Center and Maple Forest Monastery** in Hartland is the scene of a major retreat (families welcome) in July and

throughout winter (greenmountain center.org), and the **Weston Priory** (westonpriory.org) in Weston is a long-time Benedictine monastery known for its music, offering unstructured retreats.

STATE PARKS
Vermont's more than 50 exceptionally well-groomed state parks include camping and/or day-use facilities, and are so diverse an assortment of properties that no one characterization applies. Within this book we attempt to describe each as it appears geographically. Vermont state parks are also detailed in an exceptional Web site (vtstateparks.com) and are part of the **Department of Forests, Parks and Recreation** (vtfpr.org), which manages more than 157,000 acres of state land, offering opportunities for hunting, fishing, cross-country skiing, mountain biking, snowmobiling, and primitive as well as supervised camping. Also see *Campgrounds*.

SUMMER SELF-IMPROVEMENT PROGRAMS
Whether it's improving your game of tennis or golf, learning to take pictures or to weave, cook, identify mushrooms, fish, or bike, or simply to lose weight, there is a summer program for you somewhere in Vermont. See *Tennis, Golf, Canoeing and Kayaking,* and *Fishing* for lodging and lesson packages. Intensive language programs are offered at **Middlebury College** (among the offerings are Arabic and Japanese, as well as more standard ones; middlebury.edu), and a writers' conference is held at its Bread Loaf summer campus. Senior citizens can take advantage of some outstanding courses offered at bargain prices (which include lodging) as part of the **Elderhostel** program (elderhostel .org). The state's oldest, most respected crafts program is offered by the **Fletcher Farm School for the Arts**

and Crafts (fletcherfarm.com) in Ludlow: off-loom weaving, wooden-spoon carving, quilting, pottery, bookbinding, gourd or birch-bark vessel design, virtually every craft imaginable, including meals and lodging (minimum age 18, except for Young Artists programs). The nonprofit **Shelburne Art Center** (shelburneartcenter.org) offers similar courses though on a smaller scale, and the **Vermont Studio Center** in Johnson (vermontstudiocenter.org) has a national reputation. Working visual artists and writers come to renew their creative wellsprings or to explore completely new directions during intensive sessions that feature guidance and criticism by some of the country's premier artists. **Craftsbury Outdoor Center** in Craftsbury (craftsbury.com) has summer programs for all ages in running, bicycling, and sculling.

SWIMMING On the *Official Vermont Road Map & Guide to Vermont Attractions*, you can pick out the day-use areas that offer swimming, most with changing facilities, maintained by the Vermont State Department of Forests, Parks and Recreation (vtstateparks.com). Similar facilities are provided by the Green Mountain National Forest at Hapgood Pond in Peru, and the U.S. Army Corps of Engineers has tidied corners of its dam projects for public use in Townshend and North Springfield. There are also public beaches on roughly one-third of Vermont's 400 lakes and ponds (but note that swimming is prohibited at designated "Fishing Access Areas") and plenty on Lake Champlain (in Burlington, Charlotte, Colchester, Georgia, and Swanton). Add to these all the town recreation areas and myriad pools available to visitors and you still haven't gone swimming Vermont-style until you've sampled a Vermont swimming hole. These range from deep

spots in the state's ubiquitous streams to 100-foot-deep quarries (**Dorset Quarry** near Manchester and **Chapman Quarry** in West Rutland are famous) and freezing pools between waterfalls. We have included some of our favorite swimming holes under *Swimming* in each section but could not bring ourselves to share them all. Look for cars along the road on a hot day and ask in local general stores. You won't be disappointed.

TAXES Vermont's lodging and meals tax has recently become more complicated and cumbersome. Until recently it was simply 9 percent statewide, but in 2008 many communities adopted an optional 1 percent meals and alcoholic beverage tax and/or a local option rooms tax. In Burlington it's 11 percent rooms and meals and 12 percent alcohol. In Rutland it's 10 percent rooms and meals. It can all add up. Our recent tab for three people lodging and two meals was $300 + $27 (9 percent tax) plus a bottle of wine ($30) + 10 percent alcohol tax = $360. This didn't include service, which is frequently added as 15–18 percent of the total.

TENNIS Vermont claims as many tennis courts per capita as any other state in the Union. These include town recreation facilities and sports centers as well as private facilities. For a listing of both public and private facilities see **ustavermont.com**. Summer tennis programs, combining lessons, lodging, and meals, are offered at **Bolton Valley**, **Killington**, the **Village at Smugglers' Notch**, **Stratton**, **Topnotch Resort** in Stowe, and the **Bridges Family Resort and Tennis Club** at Sugarbush. Check *Tennis* in each area.

THEATER Vermont's two long-established summer theaters are both in the Manchester area: the **Dorset**

Playhouse and the **Weston Playhouse**. Other summer theater can be found in Castleton, in Saxtons River, in Waitsfield (the **Valley Players**), in Warren (**Phantom Theater**), in Stowe (the **Stowe Playhouse** and the **Lamoille County Players** in Hyde Park), and **Northern Stage** at the Briggs Opera House in White River Junction. There's also the **Lost Nation Theater** in Montpelier, and in Brattleboro there is the **New England Youth Theatre** and the **Vermont Theatre Company**. The **Flynn Theater** in Burlington and the **Paramount Theater** in Rutland are the scene of year-round film as well as live entertainment.

TRAINS See *Amtrak* and *Railroad Excursions*.

VACATION RENTALS There are plenty to choose from; Google "vacation rentals" + "Vermont."

VERMONT FRESH NETWORK (802-229-4706; vermontfresh.net), 116 State St., Montpelier 05620. Vermont's better restaurants share more than an interest in fine cuisine. Increasingly, they display a distinctive green sign flaunting their affiliation to an exclusive club: Vermont Fresh Network, a nonprofit that partners chefs with local farmers. The idea came to Pam Knights in 1994, while she was public relations director at the New England Culinary Institute. Such a network, she felt, would not only provide restaurateurs with the freshest ingredients— from venison to just-picked berries— but also keep local producers in business, which in turn would help preserve Vermont's rural landscape. With the help of Roger Clapp, then deputy commissioner of agricultural development, Knights founded VFN in 1996. Today Vermont's finest dining establishments are members, and the little green sign has come to be regarded as a prestigious badge of culinary savvy.

VERMONT PUBLIC RADIO Stations for those addicted to National Public Radio can be found throughout the state on the FM dial (click onto vpr.net). Recently VPR Classical has been added to the VPR World Channel, a collaboration with St. Michael's College. For this news channel in the Burlington area, tune in to WVPS (107.9); in the Windsor area WVPR (89.5); in the Rutland area WRVT (88.7); in St. Johnsbury WVPA (88.5); in Manchester 92.5; in Brattleboro 94.5; in Bennington WBTN (94.3); in Middlebury 95.3; in Montpelier 94.1; and in Rupert 101.1.

WATERFALLS Those most accessible and worth seeing include (north to south): the falls at **Brewster River Gorge**, Rt. 108 in Jeffersonville and, farther south off Rt. 108 (the Mountain Road) in Stowe. At **Bingham Falls** (an unmarked pull-off on the north side of the road), a trail leads downhill to the falls and gorge, recently conserved and deeded to the state. In Stowe also look for **Moss Glen Falls**, a 125-foot drop off Rt. 100. (About 3 miles north of the village, turn right onto Randolph Rd., then right again on Moss Glen Falls Rd.; park at the area on your left just

before a 90-degree turn across from a narrow bridge and look for the well-worn trail.) Beware **Big Falls** in Troy (directions are in our Jay Peak chapter): The top of this series of drops and cascades is a dramatic but rather scary spot; they represent the largest undammed waterfall on any major Vermont river (the Missisquoi). Also in northern Vermont: the **Great Falls of the Clyde River** in Charleston; **Duck Brook Cascades** in Bolton; **Little Otter Creek Falls** in Ferrisburg; the seven falls on the **Huntington River** in Hanksville; **Shelburne Falls** in Shelburne; and **Cadys Falls** in Morrisville.

On the east–west roads linking the Champlain Valley with Rt. 100 (see *Gaps, Gulfs, and Gorges*), several falls are worth noting. On Rt. 17 look for the parking area, picnic table, and a short trail leading to the 45-foot **Bartlett Falls** in Bristol Memorial Park. On Rt. 125 check out **Middlebury Gorge** in East Middlebury; off Dugway Road note the scenic **Huntington Gorge** in Huntington (responsible for at least 20 drowning deaths); and in Hancock you'll find the 35-foot **Texas Falls**. North on Rt. 100 from Hancock also look for 45-foot **Moss Glen Falls** in Granville Gulf; here a boardwalk leads back to the falls, passing **Little Moss Glen Falls**. In the Upper Valley of the Connecticut River look for **Cow Meadows Ledges** in Newbury, the falls on the **Waits River** by Rt. 5 in the village of Bradford, and **Glen Falls**, a 75-foot drop in Fairlee almost opposite the fishing access on Lake Morey Rd.

In southern Vermont look for **Buttermilk Falls** (a popular swimming hole) in Ludlow; **Old City Falls** in Strafford off Old City Falls Rd.; the **East Putney Falls** and **Pot Holes**; and, our favorite of all, 125-foot **Hamilton Falls** in Jamaica, cascading

VDT

down a schist wall with pools (responsible for more than one death over the years). Ask locally for directions to 160-foot **Lye Brook Falls** in Manchester. Most of these sites can be located on the invaluable *Vermont Atlas and Gazetteer* (DeLorme); also check Dean Goss's fact-filled north eastwaterfalls.com and the colorful newenglandwaterfalls.com.

WEATHER REPORTS For serious weather travel information in Vermont, check with the Vermont Agency of Transportation's weather line: Dial 511 or 800-ICY-ROAD, or go to 511vt .com. Listen to *An Eye on the Sky* on Vermont Public Radio (see *Vermont Public Radio* for stations; fairbanks museum.org). The show, produced by the Fairbanks Museum and Planetarium, reports entertainingly as well as informatively on life's most constant variable. **Vermontvacation.com** also carries current weather information.

WEB PAGES In this edition we list hundreds of Web sites within each region. Among the most helpful statewide sites are the following: **vermontvacation.com** is maintained by the Vermont Department of Tourism and Marketing. The Vermont Outdoor Guide Association, **voga.org**, maintains the best overall site for activities of every kind in the state; **vtstateparks.com** includes locator maps and special programs related to state parks. This guide is a search engine in its own right, listing Vermont Web sites with phone numbers throughout the book.

WEDDINGS Destination weddings have become big business in Vermont, so big and so ubiquitous that we use the wedding-ring symbol ∞ to designate establishments that specialize in them. Contact vermontweddingbook .com or weddingevents.com to request a free copy of the promotional *Vermont Wedding Resource Guide* (remember, it's all advertising). One great wedding site that doesn't make these listings is the elegant **Grand Isle Lake House** (grandislelakehouse.com) in the Champlain Islands, a turn-of-the-20th-century summer hotel maintained by the Preservation Trust of Vermont. Also see *Civil Unions*.

WHITEWATER During whitewater season beginning in mid-April, experienced canoeists and kayakers take advantage of stretches on the **White**, the **Lamoille**, and the **West rivers**, among others. **Whitewater rafting** is also available on the **West River** during spring dam releases.

WINE Vermont has traditionally made apple and other fruit wines, but grape has become the fruit of choice. Grape vineyards and wines are proliferating so quickly that it's best to check **vermontgrapeandwinecouncil.com** to keep abreast. The pioneers are two wineries in the northern reaches of the state: **Boyden Valley Winery** in Cambridge, and **Snow Farm Vineyard and Winery** in South Hero. Other newcomers include **Honora Winery and Vineyard** in West Halifax in the southeastern corner of Vermont, with hundreds of acres of vineyards and a Napa Valley–style tasting center, and **Lincoln Peak Vineyard** in New Haven. Among producers who offer tours and tastings are **Shelburne Vineyard**, open daily for tastings, and **Nasbobe River Winery** with tastings in a vintage post-and-beam barn in Brandon. **North River Winery** (northriverwinery.com), Vermont's first vintner, produces fruit wine; the associated **Ottauquechee Valley Winery** (802-295-9463) is in Quechee. **Flag Hill Farm** (flaghillfarm.com) in Vershire produces hard apple cider (the traditional state drink), **Grand View Winery** (grandviewwinery.com) in East Calais near Montpelier offers tastings of a variety of fruit wines (also maintains a tasting room in Waterbury), and **Putney Mountain Winery** makes cider and apple wine and brandy.

WOODWORKERS *Vermont Woodshop & Forest Tours* is a glossy pamphlet guide available from the Vermont Department of Tourism and Marketing (800-VERMONT) and vermontforest heritage.org. It details and locates 60 woodworking concerns, ranging from furniture makers to sculptors, throughout the state.

Marilyn Pastore

Southern Vermont

1

BRATTLEBORO, PUTNEY,
AND THE WEST RIVER VALLEY

THE MOUNT SNOW VALLEY

BENNINGTON AREA

MANCHESTER AND THE MOUNTAINS
(INCLUDING ARLINGTON, DORSET,
WESTON, DANBY, LONDONDERRY,
AND PAWLET)

OKEMO VALLEY REGION
(INCLUDING LUDLOW, CHESTER,
AND PLYMOUTH)

Kim Grant

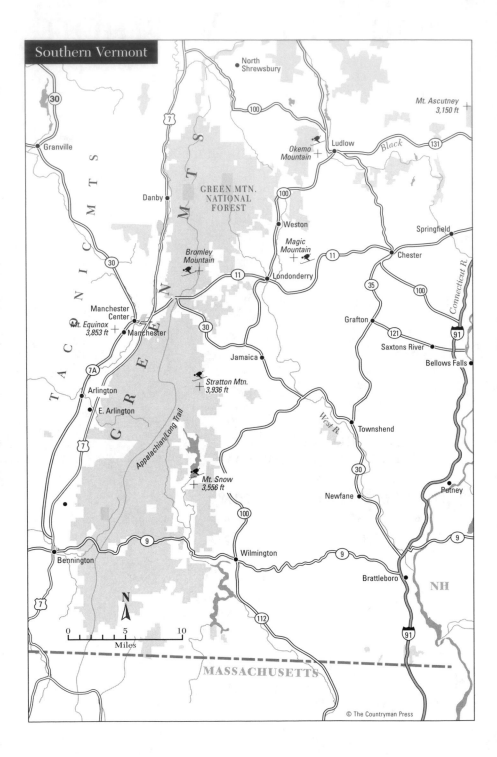

Southern Vermont

BRATTLEBORO, PUTNEY, AND THE WEST RIVER VALLEY

Vermont's southeastern corner is the obvious gateway to the state from points south, and many visitors—a number of them now residents—get no farther. Brattleboro, the area's Victorian brick commercial and cultural hub, contrasts with the classic white-clapboarded, green-shuttered towns of Newfane, Townshend, and Jamaica, which are strung like pearls along the West River, and with equally rural Putney, north on the Connecticut.

Brattleboro is a college town without a college, a vibrant artistic and activist community in which the earnest spirit of the '60s continues to build. A major downtown supermarket is a co-op showcasing Vermont cheeses, the downtown movie house is a restored art deco theater, and several buildings are honeycombed with artists' studios. Downtown is a rich mix of traditional stores and galleries, restaurants and cafés, owner-operated bookstores, boutiques, and counter-counter-cultural shops. Year round, the first Friday of every month is Gallery Walk, show-casing local art and music in some 40 venues.

Despite its accessibility, this is far from the most touristed corner of Vermont. The confluence of the Connecticut and West rivers at Brattleboro is itself a beautiful, placid place to paddle. Beyond the widely scattered country inns, antiques dealers, and crafts studios and shops, swimming holes and hiking trails lead to unexpected vistas. Back roads web the area, connecting villages in sometimes heart-stoppingly beautiful ways.

GUIDANCE Brattleboro Area Chamber of Commerce (802-254-4565; 877-254-4565; brattleborochamber.org), 180 Main St., Brattleboro 05301, is good for walk-in information (open year-round, Mon.–Fri. 9–5). It maintains seasonal information booths staffed by knowledgeable locals just north of the junction with Rts. 30 and 5 and on Western Ave. (Rt. 9, west of I-91) at the Creamery Covered Bridge. Public **restrooms** are at Brooks Memorial Library, 224 Main St. (closed Sun.) and in the River Garden, a weather-proofed public space on Main St., 153 Main St. (at the High St. light), home to A Better Brattleboro (brattleborovt.org).

The **Southern Vermont Regional Market Organization** (southernvermont .com) maintains a Web site for Windham County.

The **Southeast Vermont Welcome Center**, I-91 in Guilford (open daily 7 AM–1

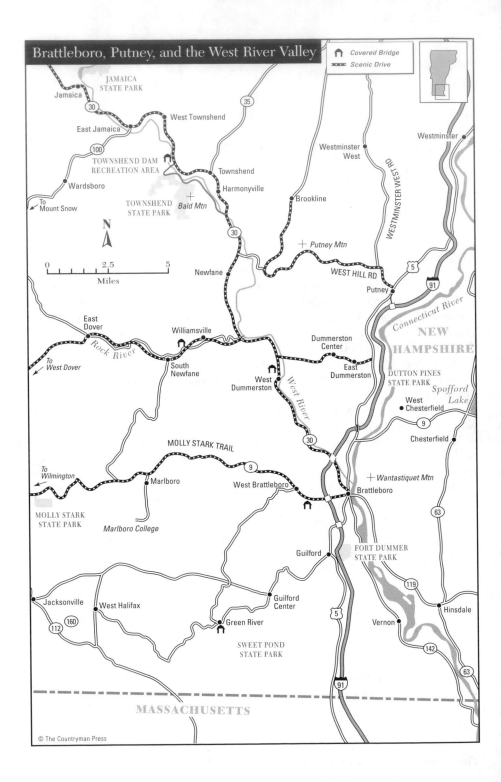

Brattleboro, Putney, and the West River Valley

Covered Bridge
Scenic Drive

JAMICA STATE PARK
Jamica
30
East Jamaica
100
Wardsboro
To Mount Snow
TOWNSHEND DAM RECREATION AREA
TOWNSHEND STATE PARK
Bald Mtn
West Townshend
35
Townshend
Harmonyville
Westminster West
Brookline
Westminster
WESTMINSTER WEST RD
N
0   2.5   5
Miles
Newfane
30
Putney Mtn
WEST HILL RD
Putney
5
91
East Dover
Rock River
To West Dover
Williamsville
South Newfane
West Dummerston
West River
30
Dummerston Center
East Dummerston
Connecticut River
NEW HAMPSHIRE
DUTTON PINES STATE PARK
West Chesterfield
Spofford Lake
Chesterfield
9
MOLLY STARK TRAIL
To Wilmington
Marlboro
9
West Brattleboro
Wantastiquet Mtn
Brattleboro
MOLLY STARK STATE PARK
Marlboro College
Guilford
FORT DUMMER STATE PARK
63
Jacksonville
West Halifax
Green River
Guilford Center
5
Vernon
Hinsdale
112
160
SWEET POND STATE PARK
119
91
142
63

MASSACHUSETTS

© The Countryman Press

AM), is Vermont's most elaborate visitor center, with displays on all parts of the state, featuring local attractions and events. **Restrooms** are open 24 hours.

Newspapers: The *Brattleboro Reformer* (802-254-2311; reformer.com) publishes a special Thursday calendar that's the best source of current arts and entertainment. Also check out *The Original Vermont Observer*, a weekly, and *The Commons*, a monthly.

GETTING THERE *By bus:* **Greyhound Bus Lines** (802-254-6066; greyhound bus.com) offers service from New York and Connecticut, as well as from Boston via Springfield and Northampton. The bus stop is north of town on Rt. 5 at its junction with Rt. 9 west.

By train: **Amtrak** (800-USA-RAIL; amtrak.com) trains from Washington, DC, and New York City stop twice daily at Brattleboro's vintage railroad station, now a museum.

By air: **Bradley International Airport** (bradleyairport.com) in Connecticut offers connections with all parts of the county.

GETTING AROUND **Brattleboro Taxi** (802-254-6446) will meet trains, buses, and airports.

Connecticut River Transit (802-885-5162; 888-869-6287; crtrsnsit.org) offers shuttle service among Brattleboro, Putney, Westminster, and Bellows Falls.

Parking: Main St. has metered parking; side streets are possible. A large parking area (Harmony Place) in the rear of the Brooks House is close to shops on High, Elliot, and Main streets; access is from High St. (Rt. 9). Brattleboro's Transportation Center offers multilevel parking with access from Elliot or Flat streets. Another large lot runs between High and Grove streets.

WHEN TO GO Brattleboro itself is appealing in almost any weather. Summer brings riverside eating and strolling, twice-weekly farmer's markets, hiking, and paddling. Off-season the shops and cafés seem even more inviting. The June **Strolling of the Heifers** up Main St. is a big draw, and the **Brattleboro Literary Festival** attracts book lovers and writers for a weekend in early fall. Foliage brings day-trippers, and it's wise to avoid Rt. 9. Luckily, there are many options (see *Scenic Drives*). Canny shoppers know about the **Putney Craft Tour** on Thanksgiving weekend and December open studios in Brattleboro's Cotton Mill. In summer and winter alike gracious West River Valley inns and B&Bs beckon.

MEDICAL EMERGENCY Call **911**.

Brattleboro Memorial Hospital (802-257-0341), 17 Belmont Ave., Brattleboro. **Grace Cottage Hospital** (802-365-7357), Rt. 35, Townshend.

✳ Towns and Villages

Brattleboro. This largely 1870s brick and cast-iron town is the commercial hub for rural corners of three states, with population swelling from 12,000 at night to 20,000 by day. Brattleboro is also a state of mind. The Web site **brattleboro.com** lists "Activism" and "Meditation" under "Recreation." The present mix of native Vermonters and flatlanders was seeded in the 1970s by former members of

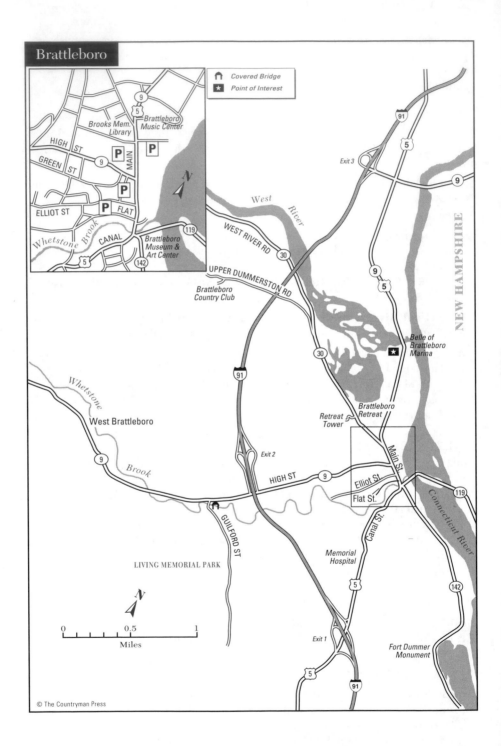

Brattleboro

Covered Bridge
Point of Interest

Brooks Mem. Library
Brattleboro Music Center

HIGH ST
GREEN ST
MAIN
ELLIOT ST
FLAT

Whetstone Brook
CANAL

Brattleboro Museum & Art Center

West River

WEST RIVER RD

UPPER DUMMERSTON RD

Brattleboro Country Club

Belle of Brattleboro Marina

NEW HAMPSHIRE

Whetstone

West Brattleboro

Brook

Brattleboro Retreat

Retreat Tower

Exit 3

Exit 2

HIGH ST

Main St.

Elliot St.
Flat St.

Connecticut River

GUILFORD ST

LIVING MEMORIAL PARK

Memorial Hospital

Canal St.

N

0   0.5   1
Miles

Exit 1

Fort Dummer Monument

© The Countryman Press

communes that flourished in this area. Artists, musicians, and social activists continue to be drawn by local educational institutions, which include the Brattleboro Music Center as well as Marlboro College to the west; World Learning with its SIT Graduate Institute (formerly the School for International Training) just north of town in Dummerston; and, most recently, the New England Center for Circus Arts in the Cotton Mill down by the Connecticut River in Brattleboro itself. The town's old landmark stores like Sam's Outdoor Outfitters, Brown & Roberts Hardware, and Miller Brothers–Newton continue to thrive, but art galleries, crafts stores, and dozens of independently owned, one-of-a-kind enterprises are now the rule, not the

William Hays

BROOKS HOUSE IN DOWNTOWN BRATTLEBORO

exception. Year-round on first Fridays, dozens of restaurants and cafés as well as galleries and studios transform downtown into New England's most successful Gallery Walk (gallerywalk.org).

During its long history, this town has shed many skins. The site of Fort Dummer, built in 1724 just south of town, has been obliterated by the Vernon Dam. Gone, too, is the early-19th-century resort town; no trace remains of the handsome, Federal-style commercial buildings or two elaborate hotels that attracted train-loads of customers who came to take their water cure developed by Dr. Robert Wesselhoeft. The gingerbread wooden casino in Island Park and the fine brick town hall, with its gilded opera house, are also gone. However, the slate-sided sheds in which hundreds of thousands of Estey organs were made are slowly being restored—one houses the new Estey Organ Museum.

Motorists stopped by the lights along Main Street can't help but notice Brooks House, built splendidly in 1872 as an 80-room hotel, once frequented by Rudyard Kipling, now converted to housing, offices, restaurants, and shops. A couple of blocks down, the 1930s art deco Latchis Hotel and Theater remains both a hotel and a theater.

Brattleboro is full of pleasant surprises. The former railroad station is now the outstanding Brattleboro Museum and Art Center. The Connecticut River is accessible by rental canoe and kayak and can be viewed from a hidden downtown park and several restaurants. Whetstone Brook, once the power turning the town's mills, is increasingly visible. In the middle of Main Street the Robert H. Gibson River Garden is a weather-proofed public space with public restrooms. Live theater and children's theater, music, dance, and circus performances are presented without hoopla.

Along Route 30 in the West River Valley
Newfane (newfanevermontusa.com). A columned courthouse, matching Congregational church, and town hall—all grouped on a handsome green—are framed by

dignified, white-clapboard houses, including two elegant inns. When Windham County's court sessions began meeting in Newfane in 1787, the village was about the same size it is now: 20 houses and two hotels. But in 1787, the village was 2 miles up on Newfane Hill. Beams were unpegged and homes moved to the more protected valley by ox-drawn sleighs in the winter of 1824.

Newfane inns have been famous for more than a century, at first because the whitewashed jail accommodated 25 paying guests, feeding them (as an 1848 poem says) "good pies and oyster soup" in the same rooms with inmates. By the time this facility closed (in the 1950s), the Old Newfane Inn—which incorporates much of its original hilltop structure—was beginning to acquire a reputation for gourmet fare. Economist John Kenneth Galbraith, a summer resident in the area since 1947, helped publicize the charms of both the village and the inn—whose onetime chef eventually opened the Four Columns Inn at the rear of the green. Newfane Village is more than a place to dine, sleep, and stroll. It is the site of one of the state's oldest and biggest Sunday flea markets, and the immediate area offers an unusual number of antiques shops. Beyond the stores and the remnants of the railway station (which served the narrow-gauge Brattleboro–Londonderry line from 1880 to 1936) is a fine old cemetery.

Newfane has bred as well as fed famous people. You'll learn about some of them in the exceptional **Historical Society of Windham County** (802-365-4148), Rt. 30, south of the common (open Memorial Day–late Oct., Wed.–Sun. noon–5). It looks like a brick post office, but exhibits fill both the main floor and second-floor gallery; in addition to changing shows, there are permanent displays on the West River Railroad, which operated between Brattleboro and Jamaica (1880s–1927) and is remembered as "36 miles of trouble"; on Porter Thayer's photographs of local turn-of-the-20th-century scenes; and on the saga of John Wilson (see Brookline, below).

NEWFANE VILLAGE

Kim Grant

Brookline (brooklinevt.com). Half as wide as it is long, Brookline is sequestered in a narrow valley bounded by steep hills and the West River. (Turn off Rt. 30 at the Newfane Flea Market.) Its population of 410 is four times what it was 50 years ago but a small fraction of what it was in the 1820s and '30s, when it supported three stores, three schools, two hotels, and a doctor. Those were the decades in which its two landmark brick buildings were constructed. One is a church, but the more famous is a round schoolhouse, said to be the only one in the country—and also probably the only school designed by a crook.

John Wilson never seems to have mentioned his past career as Thunderbolt, an infamous Scottish highwayman. In 1820 the obviously well-educated newcomer designed the circular schoolhouse. He gave it six large windows, the better (it was later noted) to allow him to see whoever approached from any side. Wilson taught for only a term before moving to the neighboring (and more remote) town of Dummerston, just about the time that an Irish felon, "Lightfoot" Martin, was hanged in Cambridge, Massachusetts. In his confession (reprints are sold at the historical society), Martin fingered Wilson as his old accomplice, but with no obvious effect. Not long thereafter, Wilson added "Dr." to his name and practiced medicine in Newfane, then in Brattleboro, where he married, fathering a son before his wife divorced him "because of certain facts she learned." When he died in 1847, scars on Wilson's ankles and neck suggested chains and a rope. Today several of Thunderbolt's pistols are preserved by the HSWC Museum (see Newfane, above) and in Brattleboro's Brooks Library.

Unfortunately, the round schoolhouse is now virtually never open. In 1928 the town's first eight grades moved down the road to the current wooden schoolhouse. As the population dwindled through the '30s, '40s, and '50s, the building was used for town meeting, but that assemblage is now held in the vestry of the Baptist church, Brookline's second landmark. Built in 1836, the church has been beautifully restored.

Townshend (population: 1,133; townshendvermont.org). The next village green north on Rt. 30 is a splendid 2 acres, complete with Victorian style gazebo. It's bordered on one side by a classic white 1790 Congregational church flanked by lovely clapboard houses and a former brick tavern, on others by a columned and tower-topped stucco town hall of the Leland and Gray Union High School (founded as a Baptist seminary in 1834), and by a clapboard commercial block. May through October, the common is the scene of a farmer's market, and on the first Saturday in August it fills with booths and games to benefit Grace Cottage Hospital, which has grown out of the back of a rambling old village home. (Known for the quality of its service, this is Vermont's first hospital to have installed a birthing bed.) West Townshend, farther along Rt. 30, is a three-corners with a photogenic church and post office. The town also harbors a public swimming area, Vermont's largest single-span covered bridge, 15 cemeteries, and several good places to stay and to eat.

Jamaica (population: 911; jamaicavt .com). The village clusters around its white Congregational church (1808) and a recently restored red-clapboard town hall with a painted curtain. Jamaica is the kind of place you can drive through in two minutes, or stay a week. The village buildings are few but proud, and there is swimming and plenty of hiking as well as camping in **Jamaica State Park**. The village, which lies within the bailiwick of Stratton Mountain's resort community, also offers lodging, dining, and exceptional shops.

TOWNSHEND GREEN

Kim Grant

JAMAICA TOWN HALL

Christina Tree

North along Route 5

Putney (population: 2,635; putney.net and iputney.com). This town's riverside fields have been heavily farmed since the mid–18th century, and its hillsides produce more than one-tenth of all the state's apples. Putney is an unusually fertile place for progressive thinking, too. Back in the 1840s it spawned a group who practiced Bible Communism, the sharing of all property, work, and wives. John Humphrey Noyes, the group's leader, was charged with adultery in 1847 and fled with his flock to Oneida, New York, where they founded the famous silverplate company. Known today for experimental education rather than religion, Putney is the home of the Putney School, a coed, college preparatory school founded in 1935, with a regimen that entails helping with chores, including raising animals. Landmark College is a fully accredited college specifically for dyslexic students and those with other learning disabilities. In July the **Yellow Barn Music School and Festival** is housed in a barn behind the library; concerts are staged there and at other local venues throughout the month. The **Sandglass Theater** (serious puppetry) is also based in Putney Village, which offers interesting shopping, augmented by exceptional artisans who welcome visitors. During the three days following Thanksgiving some two dozen local studios are open for the **Putney Artisans Craft Tour** (putneycrafts.com). Putney's scenic roads are also well known to serious bicyclists, and Putney Mountain (see *Hiking*) is beloved by both hikers and mountain bikers.

Putney's native sons include the late George Aiken, who served as governor before going on to Washington as a senator in 1941, a post he held until his retirement in 1975. Frank Wilson, a genuine Yankee trader who was one of the first merchants to enter Red China, built **Basketville**, "The World's Largest Basket Store," in the village. The **Putney Historical Society** (802-387-5862; putneyhistory.org) is housed in the town hall, open when it's open. Sadly, the general store at the heart of the village burned in 2008; plans call for its restoration.

South on Route 5

Guilford (population: 2,046; guilfordvt.org). Backroaded by I-91 (which has no exit between Brattleboro and Bernardston, Massachusetts), this old agricultural town rewards with quiet rural scenery anyone who drives or pedals its roads. Check out **Sweet Pond State Park**, a former 125-acre estate with a large pond, good for swimming and boating, and circled by a nature path. Labor Day weekend is big here, the time for the old-fashioned **Guilford Fair** and for the annual two-day, free concerts sponsored for more than 40 years by **Friends of Music at Guilford** (802-254-3600; fomag.org) in and around the **Organ Barn**. The **Guilford Historical Society**, 236 School Rd., is open Memorial Day–Columbus Day, Tue. and Sat. 10–2 and by appointment (802-257-0147). It maintains exhibits in the 1822 town hall, in the 1837 meetinghouse, and in the 1797 one-room brick schoolhouse.

MUSEUMS

Brattleboro Historical Society (802-258-4957; bratttleborohistoricalsociety.org). Thu. 1–4, Sat. 10–noon; other times by appointment. The society maintains exhibits, including historical prints and artifacts along with multimedia presentations, in a former schoolroom on the third floor of the Municipal Center, 230 Main St. It also offers exhibits, including a model of Fort Dummer, in the parlor room of the Jeremiah Beal House, 974 Western Ave., West Brattleboro. Open mid-July–mid-Oct., Sat.–Sun. 1:30–4.

Brooks Memorial Library (802-254-5290), 224 Main St. (open daily except Sun.), mounts changing exhibits of regional art and has a fine collection of 19th-century paintings and sculpture, including works by Larkin G. Mead, the Brattleboro boy who first won recognition by sculpting an 8-foot-high angel from snow one night and placing it at the junction of Rts. 30 and 5.

Also see the **Historical Society of Windham County** in Newfane under *Towns and Villages*.

COVERED BRIDGES In Brattleboro the reconstructed **Creamery Bridge** forms the entrance to Living Memorial Park on Rt. 9. North on Rt. 30 in West Dummerston, a Town lattice bridge across the West River is the longest still-used covered bridge in the state (for the best view, jump into the cool waters on either side; this is a popular swimming hole on a hot summer day). The **Scott Bridge**, Vermont's longest single-span bridge, stands by Rt. 30 in West Townshend just below the Townshend Dam, but it's closed to traffic. The region's oldest covered bridge spans the **Rock River** between Williamsville and South Newfane. The **Green River** in Guilford also boasts a covered bridge.

FOR FAMILIES ❧ **Retreat Petting Farm** (802-257-2240; theretreatfarm.com), 350 Linden St., and the neighboring **Grafton Village Cheese Company** (802-246-2221), both at the beginning of Rt. 30 as you head north of Brattleboro. The Farm is open Memorial Day–Oct., Wed.–Sat. 10–4, Sun. noon–4, also holiday Mondays. $5 ages 2–11, $6 ages 12 and over. This was the Brattleboro Retreat's working dairy farm. Currently it's owned by the Grafton-based Windham Foundation, which has replaced the cows with a major cheesemaking facility and shop. There are still plenty of farm animals in residence: llamas, pigs, emus, lambs, sheep, goats, oxen, donkeys, horses, chickens, kittens, shaggy Highland cattle, and more. Next door the new cheese shop includes a window in which to watch cheese

---

& **Brattleboro Museum & Art Center** (802-257-0124; brattleboromuseum.org), 10 Vernon St. (corner of Canal and Rt. 119), Brattleboro. Open early Apr.–late Feb. except Tue., 11–5. $4 adults, $3 seniors, $2 students. The town's 1915 rail station makes a handsome home for increasingly compelling changing exhibits with an emphasis on local and contemporary art. Check the Web site for the current exhibit and a lively calendar of receptions, readings, music, lectures, and more. The gift shop is also worth checking.

Estey Organ Museum
(802-246-8366; estey
organmuseum.org),
108 Birge St. (rear),
Brattleboro (turn off
Canal St. at the Sunoco
station). Open June–
Columbus Day, Sat.
10–5, Sun. 1–5. Visits
are also available by
special arrangement;
call 802-254-8398.
Admission $3. For
many years Brattle-
boro's largest employ-

ORGANISTS IN THE ESTEY ORGAN MUSEUM

er, the Estey Organ Co. produced thousands of organs each year between
1846 and its demise in 1960. This evolving museum, founded in 2002, is
housed in a former engine house, a large, airy, well-lit space in which
exhibits trace the history of organs in general and of Estey organs in particular. There are examples of reed organs from the 1860s and the ornately
carved parlor organs found in countless Victorian homes. There are also the
pipe organs Estey made for small churches throughout the county, and finally
there are electronic organs, highly innovative when they first appeared.
Eventually the museum will include sound as well as visuals and several
more buildings. Inquire about frequent special events.

being made and a big retail store full of Vermont specialty foods and gifts. Also note the adjoining **Retreat Trails**, a 9-mile network with an entrance at the farm.

✪ **Santa's Land** (802-387-5550; santasland.com), Rt. 5, 4 miles north of Putney. Hours 10–5. Open Memorial Day–July 1, Fri.–Sun.; July 2–Labor Day, Thu.–Sun., then weekends, weather permitting, through mid-Dec. $15 adults, $13 children over age 2, $10 seniors. A local fixture since 1957, geared to children ages 2–8, this Christmas theme village includes Christmas shops, Santa's home, reindeer, kiddie rides, a barnyard and unusual animals, a kiddie train, and, of course, Santa.

Also see the **Southern Vermont Natural History Museum** at Hogback Mountain (west of Brattleboro) in "The Mount Snow Valley" and the **Nature Museum** of Grafton in "The Lower Connecticut River Valley."

SCENIC DRIVES The hilly, heavily wooded country between the West and Connecticut river valleys is webbed with roads, most of them dirt. Our favorites include:

Putney Mountain Road to Brookline. From Rt. 5 in the middle of Putney, turn left onto Westminster West Rd. and left again about a mile up the hill onto West Hill Rd. Not far above the Putney School, look for a dirt road on your right. It forks immediately; bear right to Putney Mountain. Trees thicken and sunlight dapples through in a way that it never seems to do on paved roads. Chipmunks scurry ahead on the hard-packed dirt. The few drivers you pass will wave. The road curves up and up—and up—cresting after 2.1 miles. Note the unmarked parking area on your right (see Putney Mountain under *Hiking*). The road then snakes down the other side into Brookline.

West Dummerston to West Dover. Beautiful in a car or on a bike, the 13 miles between Rt. 30 and Rt. 100 form a shortcut from Newfane to Mount Snow. Turn west off Rt. 30, 2 miles north of the covered bridge. Follow the Rock River (in summer, clumps of cars suggest swimming holes) west from West Dummerston and Williamsville, on through the picturesque village of South Newfane (the general store is a source of picnic fare); detour 0.5 mile into the old hill village of Dover, very different from West Dover down on busy Rt. 100.

Route 30 from Brattleboro to Jamaica (you can loop back on Rt. 100 and take either of the two routes sketched above) shadows the West River, passing two covered bridges and going through the exceptionally picturesque villages of Newfane and Townshend, as well as by the Townshend Dam (good for swimming). Both villages offer first-rate crafts and antiques.

East Dummerston to West Dummerston. A handy shortcut from Rt. 5 to Rt. 30 (or vice versa), just 2 miles up one side of a hill to picturesque Dummerston Center and 2 miles down the other. This was long known in our family as the Gnome Road because of the way it winds through the woods to Vermont's longest (refitted) traffic-bearing covered bridge. It's generally known as the East/West Rd.

Brattleboro to Guilford Center to Halifax and back. This can be a 46-mile loop to Wilmington and back; ask locally for shortcuts back up to Rt. 9. Take Rt. 5 south from Brattleboro to the Guilford Country Store (selling sandwiches), then right into Guilford Center. Continue for 0.5 mile and bear right on Stage Rd. to Green River with its covered bridge, church, and recently restored crib dam. Bear right at the church (before the bridge) and then left at the Y; follow Green River

Rd. (along the river) and then Hatch School Rd. into Jacksonville. To complete the loop, see *Scenic Drives* in "The Mount Snow Valley."

The **Molly Stark Scenic Byway**—Rt. 9 between Brattleboro and Bennington—is dedicated to the wife of General John Stark, hero of the battle of Bennington. The 20-mile stretch west from Brattleboro bypasses the village of **Marlboro**, climbing high over **Hogback Mountain** with its **Southern Vermont Natural History Museum** before winding down into Wilmington. For details about Marlboro and Hogback see *Scenic Drives* in the Mount Snow chapter. Note that this route is heavily trafficked during foliage season.

✳ To Do

BICYCLING Some 200 miles of dirt and abandoned roads, along with miles of off-road trails, add up to a well-established mecca for bicyclists. While Amtrak no longer permits you to carry your own bike, it does still stop in Brattleboro where you can rent a hybrid at the **Brattleboro Bicycle Shop** (802-254-8644; 800-BRAT-BIKE; bratbike.com), 178 Main St., and pick up plenty of advice about where to use it. In Putney the **West Hill Shop** (802-387-5718; westhillshop.com), open daily, just off I-91, Exit 4, is under new ownership but still offering mountain and road bike rentals. It's also still home to the **Putney Bicycle Club**, which organizes races and (hard-core) tours. The **Ranney-Crawford House** in Putney (see *Lodging*) is geared to cyclists. **Diverse Directions** (vtcycling.com) offers multiday self-guided inn-to-inn tours in the area, including lodging and baggage transfers.

BOATING Vermont Canoe Touring Center (802-257-5008), 451 Putney Rd., Brattleboro. Located on the West River at the cove at Veterans Memorial Bridge, Rt. 5, just north of the junction with Rt. 30. Open daily Memorial Day weekend–Labor Day weekend 9–dusk, weekends to Columbus Day, weather permitting. John Knickerbocker rents canoes and kayaks, and offers shuttle service, guided trips, and camping on the river. The 32 miles from Bellows Falls to the Vernon Dam is slow-moving water, as is the 6-mile stretch from below the dam to the Massachusetts border.

Whitewater on the West River. Twice a year, once in spring and again in September, the Army Corps of Engineers releases water from the **Ball Mountain Dam** (802-874-4881) in Jamaica, creating whitewater fit for national kayak championships. The races are no longer run here, but commercial whitewater rafters as well as whitewater kayakers and canoeists take advantage of the flow, especially in fall, when many of the region's other whitewater courses are dry.

FISHING In the **Connecticut River** you can catch bass, trout, pike, pickerel, and yellow perch. There is an access on Old Ferry Rd., 2 miles north of Brattleboro on Rt. 5; another is from River Rd. on the New Hampshire shore in Westmoreland (Rt. 9 east, then north on Rt. 63). For fishing boat rentals contact the **Marina Restaurant** (802-257-7563).

The **West River** is a source of trout and smallmouth bass; access is from any number of places along Rt. 30. In Vernon there is a boat access on **Lily Pond**; in Guilford on **Weatherhead Hollow Pond** (see the DeLorme *Vermont Atlas and Gazetteer*).

GOLF Brattleboro Country Club (802-257-7380), Upper Dummerston Rd., offers 18 holes and includes a full driving range, practice areas, and instructional range. The **Tater Hill Golf Club** (802-875-2517), Popple Dungeon Rd. in North Windham, also offers 18 holes. Also see **Mount Snow** and **Stratton** ski resorts under *Downhill Skiing;* both offer golf schools and 27 holes.

HIKING In **Brattleboro** a pleasant path up to the Retreat Tower, a 19th-century overlook, begins beside Linden Lodge on Rt. 30. Another trail follows the West River along the abandoned **West River railroad bed**. Access is off Rt. 5 north of town; take the second left turn after crossing the bridge. **Wantastiquet Mountain**, overlooking Brattleboro from across the Connecticut River in New Hampshire, is a good 1½-hour hike from downtown, great for picnics and views of southeast Vermont. See also Fort Dummer State Park under *Green Space* for a wooded trail south of town overlooking the Connecticut, and Townshend State Forest for a steep trek up Bald Mountain.

Putney Mountain between Putney and Brookline, off Putney Mountain Rd. (see *Scenic Drives*), is one of the most rewarding 1-mile round-trip hikes anywhere. A sign nailed to a tree in the unmarked parking area assures you that this is indeed Putney Mountain. Follow the trail that heads gently uphill through birches and maples, then continues through firs and vegetation that change remarkably quickly to the stunted growth usually found only at higher elevations. Suddenly you emerge on the mountain's broad crown, circled by a deep-down satisfying panorama. The view to the east is of Mount Monadnock, rising in lonely magnificence above the roll of southern New Hampshire, but more spectacular is the spread of Green Mountain peaks to the west. You can pick out the ski trails on Haystack, Mount Snow, and Stratton.

Jamaica State Park offers a choice of three interesting trails. The most intriguing and theoretically the shortest is to **Hamilton Falls**, a 125-foot cascade through a series of wondrous potholes. It's an obvious mile (30-minute) hike up, but the return can be confusing. Beware straying onto Turkey Mountain Rd.

Black Mountain Natural Area, maintained by **The Nature Conservancy of Vermont** (802-229-4425). Cross the covered bridge on Rt. 30 in West Dummerston and turn south on Quarry Rd. for 1.4 miles. The road changes to Rice Farm Rd.; go another 0.5 mile to a pull-off on your right. The marked trail begins across the road and rises abruptly 1,280 feet to a ridge, traversing it before dropping back down, passing a beaver dam on the way back to the river. The loop is best done clockwise. Beautiful in laurel season.

RAILROAD EXCURSION The **Green Mountain Flyer** (802-463-3069; rails-vt .com), based just north of this area in Bellows Falls, offers a 26-mile run in-season. (See "The Lower Connecticut River Valley.")

SWIMMING 𝒮 **Living Memorial Park**, west of downtown Brattleboro on Rt. 9, offers a public pool (mid-June–Labor Day). In the West River Valley at the **Townshend Lake Recreation Area** (802-874-4881) off Rt. 30 in West Townshend you drive across the top of the massive dam, completed in 1961 as a major flood-prevention measure for the southern Connecticut River Valley. Swimming is in the reservoir behind the dam, with a human-made beach and gradual drop-off, good for children. Changing facilities provided; small fee. The **West River** itself offers a few swimming holes, notably under the West Dummerston covered bridge on Rt. 30 and at Salmon Hole in Jamaica State Park. **Hamilton Falls**, accessible from the park, and **Pikes Falls**, also in Jamaica (ask directions locally), are favorite swimming holes, but not advised for children. Just off Rt. 30, a mile or so up (on South Newfane Rd.), the **Rock River** swirls through a series of shallow swimming spots; look for cars. In Guilford there is swimming at **Sweet Pond**, a state-owned former 125-acre estate with a large pond circled by a nature path. Also handy to Brattleboro, **Wares Grove** is across the Connecticut River in Chesterfield, New Hampshire (9 miles east on Rt. 9, the next left after the junction with Rt. 63). This pleasant beach on Spofford Lake is good for children; you'll find a snack bar and makeshift changing facilities.

✳ Winter Sports

CROSS-COUNTRY SKIING **Brattleboro Outing Club Ski Hut** (brattleboro outingclub.com/xcskiing.htm), Upper Dummerston Rd., Brattleboro. Trails through woods and a golf course, more than 20 km of which are machine tracked, plus rentals, lessons, and moonlight ski tours. **West Hill Shop** (802-387-5718), just off I-91, Exit 4, is the source of cross-country ski and snowshoe rentals as well as trail information for the Putney area. **Jamaica State Park** in Jamaica (see *Green Space*) offers marked trails.

See also **Grafton Ponds Recreation Center** in "The Lower Connecticut River Valley."

ICE SKATING **Living Memorial Park Skating Rink** (802-254-6700), Rt. 9 west, Brattleboro. Open late Oct.–mid-Mar. with skate rentals. A seasonal weather-proofed rink. Call for public skate times.

DOWNHILL SKIING The big ski areas are a short drive west into the Green Mountains, either to **Mount Snow** (Rt. 9 from Brattleboro and then up Rt. 100 to West Dover—see "The Mount Snow Valley") or up Rt. 30 to **Stratton** (see "Manchester and the Mountains").

SLEIGH RIDES **Fair Winds Farm** (802-254-9067), Upper Dummerston Rd.

SKI JUMPING

The Harris Hill Jumping Competition (harrishillskijump.org) is strictly a spectator sport but too big a deal to demote to a *Special Events* listing. An annual tradition inaugurated in 1922 by Brattleboro native Fred Harris, founder of the Brattleboro Outing Club, the Dartmouth Winter Carnival and the U.S. Eastern Amateur Ski Association. An entirely new 300-step-high, 90-meter ski jump (the only one in New England) was constructed for the 2009 competition. The FIS-approved event draws competitors from throughout the United States and Europe. Check the Web site for exact dates. Ideally this coincides with the Brattleboro Winter Carnival, but not always.

VAST (Vermont Area Snow Travelers; vtast.org) trail system can be accessed in West Brattleboro.

✳ Green Space

Fort Dummer State Park (802-254-2610), Guilford. Located 2 miles south of Brattleboro (follow S. Main St. to the end). Surrounded by a 217-acre forest, overlooking the site of its namesake fort, built in 1724 to protect settlements along the Connecticut River. It was flooded by the Vernon Dam in 1908. There are 51 tent/trailer sites and 10 lean-tos, hot showers, and a dump station but no hookups. There are also hiking trails and a playing field.

Townshend State Park (802-365-7500), Townshend, marked from Rt. 30 south of town. Open early May–Columbus Day. Up a back road, an attractive, classic '30s Civilian Conservation Corps (CCC) stone-and-wood complex with a picnic pavilion. This is really an 856-acre state forest with 41 acres reserved for the park. The camping area (30 tent/trailer campsites, four lean-tos) is near the start of the 2.7-mile (steep) climb to the summit of Bald Mountain; trail maps are available at the park office.

✔ **Jamaica State Park** (802-874-4600), Jamaica. This 758-acre wooded area offers riverside camping, swimming in a great swimming hole, a picnic area, and an organized program of guided hikes. An old railroad bed along the river serves as a 3-mile trail to the Ball Mountain Dam, and an offshoot mile-long trail leads to Hamilton Falls. A weekend in spring and again in fall is set aside for whitewater canoe races. There are 61 tent/trailer sites and 18 lean-tos. A large picnic shelter is handy to the swimming hole; a playground includes swings, a teeter-totter, and slides.

Ball Mountain Lake (802-874-4881), Jamaica. This 85-acre lake, created and maintained by the U.S. Army Corps of Engineers, is a dramatic sight among the wooded, steep mountains, conveniently viewed from the access road off Rt. 30. Over 100 campsites are available on Winhall Brook at the other end of the reservoir, open mid-May–Columbus Day; it's accessible off Rt. 100 in South Londonderry. For reservations phone 877-444-6777. A controlled release from this flood dam provides outstanding canoeing on the West River below Jamaica each spring and fall (see *Boating*).

✔ **Living Memorial Park** (802-254-5808) just west of Brattleboro on Rt. 9. This 56-acre park includes a swimming pool (mid-June–Labor Day), an enclosed ice-skating rink (see *Ice Skating*), two tennis courts, wooded walking trails (dogs are welcome, but pick up) a playground, ball fields, picnic shelter, and a ski hill serviced by a T-bar.

Dutton Pines State Park (802-254-2277), Brattleboro. On Rt. 5, 5 miles north of town, this is a picnic area with a shelter.

See also *Hiking* and *Swimming*.

✳ Lodging

COUNTRY INNS ⚭ 🐾 ♿ ⁽₁⁾ **Four Columns Inn** (802-365-7713; 800-787-6633; fourcolumnsinn.com), Newfane 05345. This Greek Revival mansion, built in 1830 by General Pardon Kimball to remind his southern wife of her girlhood home, fronts on Newfane's classic green. Innkeepers Bruce and Debbie Pfander offer 15 guest rooms, varying from merely country elegant, to deluxe (with gas fireplace), to extravagant suites (two-person whirlpool or soaking tub, typically with a view of the gas fireplace). The very best suite fills the space above the four columns, formerly a porch, with a Jacuzzi overlooking the green. While it's set in a splendid village, the inn backs onto 150 steep and wooded acres, good for walking or snowshoeing. Dining is a big attraction (see *Dining Out*), and facilities include a seasonal swimming pool. $170–370 per night midweek, $195–370 weekends, $215–390 holidays and foliage season. Breakfast included. $25 extra for pets.

⚭ **Windham Hill Inn** (802-874-4080; 800-944-4080; windhamhill.com), West Townshend 05359. High above the West River Valley, this 1825 brick farmhouse is a luxurious retreat. Several of the 21 guest rooms have soaking tub, private deck, Jacuzzi, fireplace, or gas stove, and all have private bath and phone. All are furnished with antiques and interesting art. Eight are in the White Barn Annex, some with a large deck looking down the valley. Common space in the inn itself includes a living room and an airy sunporch with wicker. Two sitting rooms are country elegant with wood-burning fireplace, Oriental carpets, and wing chairs, and the dining room also has a fireplace, a formal dining table, and tables for two (see *Dining Out*). A nicely landscaped pool overlooks the mountains and tennis court. The 160-acre property also includes an extensive network of hiking paths, groomed as cross-country trails in winter (when the frog pond freezes for skating). Inquire about weddings, both inside (there's a small conference center in the barn) and outside (for up to 75 guests). $215–465 per couple B&B. Check the Web site for packages.

⚭ 🐾 ⁽₁⁾ **Three Mountain Inn** (802-874-4140; 800-532-9399; threemountaininn.com), Rt. 30, P.O. Box 180, Jamaica 05343. Ed and Jennifer Dorta-Duque welcome you to their 1790s inn in the middle of a classic Vermont village. There are 7 upstairs rooms and 7 in neighboring Robinson House, all nicely decorated, several with whirlpool tub and 10 with gas or wood fireplace or stove. Sage Cottage in the garden features a Jacuzzi tub, gas fireplace, two skylights and a stained-glass window, surround sound, and, of course, a TV/DVD. Common space includes the old tavern room with its large hearth and a cozy corner bar. There are two small but elegant dining rooms (see *Dining Out*) and a private gallery/dining room featuring a new artist every six weeks. Jamaica State Park and its trails are a short walk away, and Stratton Mountain, with its 27-hole golf course, is a short drive. From $165 off-season for a small room in the inn to $300 high-season for the ground-floor two-room Jamaica Suite with French doors in the bedroom and sitting rooms opening onto the patio; $325–360 for Sage Cottage; a three-course breakfast is included. Add $20 during foliage season and holidays. $15 less for solo travelers.

🦟 🐾 ✍ ♿ **The Putney Inn** (802-387-5517; 800-653-5517; putneyinn.com), P.O. Box 181, Putney 05346; just off I-91, Exit 4. The inn's centerpiece is an

18th-century red-clapboard farmhouse. In the early 1960s, when the land was divided for construction of I-91, it was sold to local residents, who renovated the farmhouse without disturbing the posts and beams or the central open hearth. It's been owned by the Ziter family for more than 30 years, and there's an easy sense of hospitality. Plants and antiques add to the pleasant setting of the entry and large dining rooms. Twenty-five air-conditioned guest rooms occupy a motel-like wing, each with Queen Anne reproductions, bath, color TV, and phone. Pets are permitted but "must be smaller than a cow and not left alone in the rooms." The complex is set in 13 acres, with views of the river valley and mountains. Staff are helpful, and the restaurant features first-rate New England fare made with local products (see *Dining Out*). At $98–188 per couple (children free under age 14) with a "farmer's breakfast," this is one of the best values around. $10 pet fee.

❀ ❝❞ **Chesterfield Inn** (603-256-3211; 800-365-5515; chesterfieldinn .com), P.O. Box 155, Chesterfield, NH 03443. On Rt. 9, 2 miles east of Brattleboro. The original house served as a tavern from 1798 to 1811 but the present facility is contemporary, with a large attractive dining room, spacious parlor, and 13 guest rooms and two suites divided between the main house and the Guest House. All rooms have sitting area, phone, controlled heat and air-conditioning, optional TV, and wet bar, and some have a working fireplace or Jacuzzi. Innkeepers Phil and Judy Hueber have created a popular dining room and a comfortable, romantic getaway spot that's well positioned for exploring southern Vermont as well as New Hampshire's Monadnock region. $175–345 includes a full breakfast. Inquire about pet packages.

In Brattleboro 05301

❝❞ **The Artist's Loft B&B and Gallery** (802-257-5181; theartistsloft .com), 103 Main St. Artist William Hays and his wife, Patricia Long, offer a third-floor middle-of-town two-room suite that's spacious and colorful, with a private entrance, queen-sized bed, and river view (private bath). This is a great spot if you want to plug into all that Brattleboro offers in the way of art, music, dining, and shopping; Patricia and William delight in sharing their knowledge about their adopted town. Their Web site features an extensive area guide. From $138 with continental breakfast (there are many options within walking distance) and $158 with full breakfast, $20 more in foliage season. No credit cards.

Meadowlark Inn (802-257-4582; 800-616-6359; meadowlarkinnvt.com), Orchard St., P.O. Box 2048. The town of Brattleboro includes some surprisingly rural corners, like this maple-walled ridge road. The large farmhouse, set in lawns with vista views, has been renovated by innkeepers Lucia Osiecki and Deborah Jones. Common space includes a wraparound screened porch as well as a large living room. The yard offers a shady garden with Adirondack chairs, a hammock, and several tables with umbrellas. Rooms are divided between the main house and an 1870s coach barn with its own central area warmed by a hearth and decorated by a rural mural. All rooms have private bath and phone. In the Coach House, two have Jacuzzis and views of the woodland garden and two more feature a king bed, views, and refrigerator. Our favorite, however, is Maple View—the original master bedroom upstairs in the main house— with a queen bed, ample bath, and graceful vanity. The innkeepers are warm hosts and culinary school

RUDYARD KIPLING AND NAULAKHA

Rudyard Kipling first visited Brattleboro in the winter of 1892 and determined to build himself a house high on a hill in Dummerston (just north of the Brattleboro line), on property owned by his wife's family. The young couple then headed for Samoa to see Robert Louis Stevenson but got no farther than Yokohama; at that point their bank failed, taking virtually all their money. Returning to Vermont, they rented a cottage while building Naulakha; the name is a Hindi word meaning "great jewel." The shingled house is 90 feet long but only 22 feet wide, designed to resemble a ship riding the hillside like a wave. Its many windows face east, across the Valley to the New Hampshire hills with a glimpse of the summit of Mount Monadnock.

RUDYARD KIPLING IN HIS STUDY AT NAULAKHA, CIRCA 1895

Landmark Trust USA

Just 26 years old, Kipling was already one of the world's best-known writers, and the two following years here were among the happiest in his life. Here he wrote the *Jungle Books.* Here the local doctor, James Conland, a former fisherman, inspired him to write *Captains Courageous* and also delivered his two daughters. Kipling's guests included Sir Arthur Conan Doyle, who brought with him a pair of Nordic skis, said to be the first in Vermont. Unfortunately, in 1896 a highly publicized falling-out with his dissolute brother-in-law drove the family back to England. They took relatively few belongings from Naulakha, and neither did the property's two subsequent owners, who used it as a summer home.

Happily, in 1992 it was acquired by The Landmark Trust USA, which rewired, repaired, and replumbed it (a new septic system was required) but otherwise preserved every detail of the home as Rudyard and Carrie Kipling knew it. Though the house is not available for functions and rarely for tours, it can be rented for $1,351–2,700 per week and, depending on the season, for a few days at a time ($275–425 per day, three-night minimum). There are

Landmark Trust USA

FROM THE ORIGINAL ARCHITECTURAL DRAWING OF NAULAKHA, WHERE RUDYARD KIPLING LIVED FROM 1893 TO 1896

four bedrooms (three baths). Some 60 percent of the present furnishings are original, including a third-floor pool table. A game of tennis, anyone, on the Kipling court? Or how about curling up with the *Jungle Books* on a sofa by the fire, only a few feet from where they were written? Or stooping in Kipling's own deep tub? For details about renting Naulakha, contact The **Landmark Trust USA** (802-254-6868; landmarktrust.usa), c/o 707 Kipling Rd., Dummerston 05301. *Rudyard Kipling in Vermont: Birthplace of the Jungle Books* by Stuart Murray (Images from the Past) offers an excellent description of Kipling's relation to and portrayal of the area.

Landmark Trust USA has restored two more historic buildings at neighboring 571-acre Scott Farm. **The Sugarhouse**, a classic century-old sugarhouse, has been fitted with radiant floor heating and a gas log stove, a bedroom (sleeping two), and a fully equipped kitchen with a dishwasher and linens ($500 per week, $125–160 per night, three-night minimum). The eight-room **Dutton Farmhouse** is an 1837 Greek Revival white-clapboard homestead set near the highest point of the farm with 30-mile views over the Connecticut River Valley to Mount Monadnock. There are four bedrooms—two doubles and two with twins—two and a half baths, a full kitchen, a living room with gas log fireplace, a dining room, and a fully equipped kitchen ($400–1,750 per week, $275 325 per night, three-night minimum). Both properties offer access to hiking trails on the farm and to the tennis courts at Naulakha.

graduates who enjoy creating a fresh and bountiful breakfast with a choice of hot entrées and freshly baked goods. Guests may want to take advantage of the 3-mile loop walk beginning at the front door, and cross-country ski trails at the nearby Brattleboro Country Club. $145–225 includes breakfast.

&. ⁙ **Forty Putney Road** (802-254-6268; 800-941-2413; frtyptny@sover .net), 40 Putney Rd. Just north of the town common and within walking distance of downtown shops and restaurants, this house with steeply pitched, gabled roof, reminiscent of a French château, was built in 1930 for the director of the neighboring Brattleboro Retreat. Tim and Amy Brady offer five guest rooms, each with phone, TV, and private bath, one with a whirlpool bath and fireplace. There is also a two-room suite with a gas fireplace in the sitting room and garden views. Common space includes a sunny living room and a bar with an unusually wide selection of beers. We would request one of the rear rooms overlooking the gardens, away from Rt. 5 (Putney Rd.), but front rooms are air-conditioned so noise is muted. Common space is plentiful and attractive, and landscaped grounds border the West River. $159–299 includes a full breakfast.

In Putney 05346

✐ ❀ **Hickory Ridge House** (802-387-5709; 800-380-9218; hickoryridge house.com), 53 Hickory Ridge Rd. south. An 1808 brick mansion, complete with Palladian window, set on 12 acres with walking/cross-country ski trails. Gillian and Dennis Petit offer six softly, authentically colored guest rooms in the inn. Pets and children are welcome in the neighboring cottage, available either as two rooms or together. Inn rooms come with and without wood-burning or gas fireplaces, but all have private bath,

phone, and TV/VCR. The original Federal-era bedrooms are large, with Rumford fireplaces, and there's an upstairs sitting room. The cottage consists of a room and a separate suite with its own living room (with fireplace) and kitchen; it can also be rented as a whole. A swimming hole lies within walking distance, and cross-country touring trails are out the back door. $175–215 per couple includes a full breakfast.

✐ **Ranney-Crawford House** (802-387-4150; 800-731-5502; ranney-craw ford.com), 1097 Westminster West Rd. Another handsome brick Federal (1810) homestead on a quiet country road, surrounded by fields. Innkeeper Arnie Glim is an enthusiastic bicyclist who knows all the local possibilities for both touring and mountain biking. Four attractive guest rooms—two spacious front rooms with hearths, along with two smaller back rooms, all with private bath—are $155–190, including a three-course breakfast served in the formal dining room.

In the West River Valley

♠ ⁙ **Boardman House** (802-365-4086; 888-366-7182), village green, Townshend 05353. We like the friendly feel of this 1840s Greek Revival house tucked into a quiet (away from Rt. 30 traffic) corner of one of Vermont's standout commons. Sarah and Paul Messenger offer four attractive guest rooms (one can be a suite) with private bath. There's also a two-bedroom suite, a parlor, and an airy, old-fashioned kitchen. Breakfast usually includes fresh fruit compote and oven-warm muffins with a creative main dish. $80 for rooms, $110–120 for a suite.

The Old Brick Tavern (802-365-7621; oldbricktavern.com), 82 Common Rd. (P.O. Box 568), Townshend 05454. Built solidly of brick in 1791, this elegant home stands on the corner of Townshend's spacious common and Rt. 30. Patty and Barry Galbraith have done a great job of restoring it, elegantly furnishing a library and TV lounge, both with working fireplace, and two luxurious, antiques-furnished upstairs rooms with curved ceilings recalling the tavern's onetime ballroom. $150 with breakfast.

🍁 **Ranney Brook Farm** (802-874-4589; ranneybrookfarm.com), P.O. Box 1108, West Townshend 05359. Set back from Rt. 30 in wooded grounds, this comfortable old red farmhouse is just up the road from boating and swimming at Townshend Dam. It's an informal, relaxing place with a piano in the den, a "great room" in the rear (a former 1790s barn), and a cheerful dining room in which a full breakfast is served family-style. Residents include a dog, two cats, and a parrot. The four rooms are upstairs; two have private bath. Diana Wichland is innkeeper; her husband, John, owns Miller Brothers–Newton, a long-established clothier in Brattleboro. $70–80 (no surcharge for foliage season).

In Guilford 05301

Green River Bridge House (802-257-5771; 800-528-1861; greenriver bridgehouse.com), 2435 Stage Rd., Green River. Joan Seymour has totally rehabbed a vintage-1830 house next to the covered bridge in this classic backroads village. It's full of whimsical touches, like a former confessional as the reception window and specially designed ceilings to display her collection of crystal chandeliers. Amenities range from Jacuzzis to hair dryers. There are three guest rooms with private bath. Gardens and lawn stretch back along the river, with a "meditation garden," a venue for weddings. $165–235 per couple includes a full breakfast, organic by prearrangement. Inquire about spa services.

OTHER LODGING 🍁 "📶" **Latchis Hotel** (802-254-6300; latchis.com), 50 Main St., Brattleboro 05301. This downtown, art-deco-style hotel first opened in 1939 and has been resurrected after a thorough restoration. It remained in the Latchis family until 2003, when it was acquired by the Brattleboro Arts Initiative (BAI), a local group dedicated to turning the hotel's magnificent theater into a performance center. Push open the door into the small but spiffy lobby, with its highly polished terrazzo marble floors. There's an elevator; surprises in the rooms include WiFi, restored 1930s furniture, air-conditioning, and soundproof windows (a real blessing). Rooms are cheerful, brightly decorated, all with private bath, phone, fridge, and coffeemaker. The 27 rooms and 3 two-room suites are accessible by elevator. The rooms to request are on the second and third floors, with views down Main St. and across to Wantastiquet Mountain. The hotel is so solidly built that you don't hear the traffic below. For more about the theater see *Entertainment*. $75–155, $150–180 for suites, includes continental breakfast.

🍁 🐾 ✍ "📶" **Colonial Motel & Spa** (802-257-7733; 800-239-0032; colonial motelspa.com), 0.5 mile south of the I-91, Exit 3 roundabout at Putney Rd. A 70-room (with phones) motel, family owned (since 1975) and geared, with a 75-foot heated lap pool in a glass greenhouse. There's an indoor Jacuzzi and outdoor hot tub and pool. $60–140 includes a continental breakfast.

✍ **Sugar House** (802-365-7573), P.O. Box 480, 47 Radway Hill Rd., Newfane 05345. Beside but entirely separate and private from Lenore and Dennis Salzbrunn's home, this former 18th-century sugarhouse has been nicely converted into a cozy guest house with a queen bed facing a working hearth and twins in a loft above. The fridge is stocked with milk, juice, fruit, and cheese. Fresh muffins arrive in the morning. $200 per night.

CAMPGROUNDS See *Green Space* for information on camping in Fort Dummer State Park, Townshend State Park, Jamaica State Park, and Ball Mountain Lake.

✳ Where to Eat

DINING OUT

In Brattleboro

T. J. Buckley's (802-257-4922), 132 Elliot St. Open Wed.–Sun. 6–9. Reservations suggested. From the outside this small (eight tables) but classic red-and-black 1920s Worcester diner looks unpromising, even battered. Inside, fresh flowers and mismatched settings (gathered from yard sales) brighten the tables, walls are oak paneled, and chef-owner Michael Fuller prepares the night's fish, fowl, and beef (vegetarian is also possible) in the open kitchen behind the counter. Fuller buys all produce locally, and what's offered depends on what's available: The menu might include roasted local rabbit or bluefin tuna with roast lobster stock served with a risotto with a ginger-pheasant stock. The $40 entrée includes salad; appetizer and dessert are extra. The wine list ranges $20–85. No credit cards, but personal checks are accepted.

Peter Havens (802-257-3333), 32 Elliot St. Open from 6 PM Tue.–Sat. Just 10 tables in this nifty restaurant decorated with splashy artwork, and with an inspired menu to match. Chef owned for more than 20 years and a universal favorite. Locals sup at the bar; if you don't know anyone, Tom Dahlin with introduce you. The menu usually includes pasta del mar (a nest of linguine with a creamy pesto sauce

topped with shrimp, scallops, and artichoke hearts) and tenderloin grilled with Jack Daniels and cream and tortellini with Andalusian sausage. Daily specials always include fresh seafood. We dined on butter-tender swordfish with a black bean sauce. Entrées $26–30, including salad. Credit cards accepted.

Adagio Trattoria (802-254-6046), 132 Main St. Open daily for lunch (11:30–3) and dinner (5–10) with the bar open later. Off-season lunch is Mon.–Wed. With its bright decor and fresh, from-scratch food, this is a great addition to downtown dining options. It's housed in a part of what was once the Brooks House hotel lobby, with a long, inviting brick-walled bar room and a contrastingly intimate, warmly colored dining room on Main St. In summer there are café tables. On a rainy winter day we lunched on a pot of tea and light but crispy frittatas, which came with greens. Friends enthused about the from-scratch soup of the day and the "outtanesca" with sautéed tiger shrimp and a spicy marinara sauce, tossed with linguine. Dinner entrées $15–22.

Alici's Bistro (802-254-5600; alicis bistro.com), 51 Harris Place. Tucked off Main St. between the Harris Place parking lot and the river. Open nightly, menu until 10 PM. A river-view patio, martini bar with wine by the half bottle and glass. Chef-owner Musa Alici features Turkish fare. Entrées $14–22, but you can also put together two starters or opt for light fare.

Thirty9 Main (802-254-3999), 39 Main St. Open Thu.–Mon. from 5:30 PM. Chef-owner Matthew Miner offers a zany decor and eclectic dishes. Entrées include tapas-style "small plates" like a three-cheese tart with fig salsa; "bigger plates" from $13 for baked tofu with roasted tomatoes, artichokes, and olives, and $16 for venison chop with cider glaze.

♪ � **Riverview Café** (802-254-9841; riverviewcafe.com), 36 Bridge St. Open daily for lunch and dinner. The big news here is the (seasonal) rooftop seating with the best dining view of the Connecticut River along its 410-mile length; there's also a downstairs deck and, of course, window-side dining. Chef-owner Tristan Toleno has transformed this old standby into an informal but sophisticated restaurant with a mainstream menu, including fish-and-chips, steak, and applewood-smoked spicy pork spareribs. Full liquor license and regional microbrews on tap. Entrées $7–19.95.

Also see **Windham Wine Gallery** under *Wines and Brews.*

Along Rt. 30

The Four Columns Inn (802-365-7713; fourcolumnsinn.com), Rt. 30, Newfane. Serving 5:30–9 nightly except Tue.; reservations suggested. Chef Greg Parks has earned top ratings and awards for his efforts, served in a converted barn with a large brick fireplace as its centerpiece. The emphasis is on herbs (homegrown), stocks made from scratch, and locally raised lamb. While the menu changes frequently, it might include rack of lamb with mushroom rosemary garlic demiglaze, or red snapper with lobster, crabmeat, and tomato finished with a lemon essence. Entrées $25–38.

Old Newfane Inn (802-365-4427), Rt. 30, Newfane Village. Open for dinner except Mon. but closed during slow periods. Reservations requested. The low-beamed old dining room is country formal. Chef-owner Eric Weindl is widely known for his Swiss-accented Continental menu with entrée choices like venison with spaetzle and roast duckling au Cointreau à l'orange ($22–31).

Windham Hill Inn (802-874-4080; 800-944-4080; windhamhill.com), West Townshend. The attractive, candlelit dining room, overlooking a pond, is open to the public for dinner (6–8:30) by reservation. You could opt for the four-course prix fixe dinner for $60, or a tasting menu for $80. Entrées might include roast lamb loin with polenta and port wine glaze, or roasted vegetable and tofu Wellington with a green peppercorn cream.

Three Mountain Inn (802-874-4140), Rt. 30, Jamaica Village. Dinner reservations recommended. While enjoying a candlelit dinner in front of the fireplaces in the two small dining rooms of this 18th-century village house, it's easy to imagine that you're in a colonial tavern. Chef Will Hollinger grew up on a dairy farm, graduated from the New England Culinary Institute, and has worked in French kitchens. His locally sourced four-course menu might feature pan-roasted duck breast with wild rice and haricots verts, or portobello mushroom Wellington with mozzarella, roasted peppers, spinach, and fresh tomato basil sauce. It's $55 prix fixe, but items can be ordered à la carte. Entrées $30–36.

🐾 **Asta's Swiss Restaurant** (802-874-8000), 3894 Main St. (Rt. 30), Jamaica. Open for dinner 5–10 except Wed.; also for Sun. brunch noon–3. Chef-owner Michel de Preux hails from the Swiss canton of Valais and has a sure touch with everything he prepares, from turkey breast snitzel (topped with lemon, caper, and anchovies) and roast half duckling à l'orange (finished with an orange green peppercorn sauce) to filet mignon café de Paris (topped with mustard, herbs, and spice butter, and served with rösti potatoes). There are options for vegetarians, such as falafel with garlic tahini, cucumber salad, hummus, and pita chips; also look for

Swiss specialties like fondue and raclette (both cheese and meat) and choucroute garnie. Sunday brunch offers plenty of egg dishes plus pastas, salads, even grinders. All entrées come with bread and salad. The ambience is warm. $17.95–32.50. Wine and beer.

Elsewhere

🦞 🍴 **The Putney Inn** (802-387-5517; 800-653-5517; putneyinn.com), just off I-91, Exit 4, in Putney. Open for all three meals. The area's oldest 18th-century homestead retains its open hearth and is now an attractive restaurant as well as centerpiece for an inn. The dinner menu features classic but classy New England comfort food with an emphasis on local ingredients. Lunch choices might include macaroni and cheese Vermont-style (with Grafton Village extra-sharp cheddar) and roast (local) turkey potpie. Dinner choices might include roast Vermont lamb with sausage risotto cake, or maple Dijon horseradish glazed prime rib with Vermont cheddar mashed potatoes. Entrées $24–29, but there is also a lighter fare menu, $8.50–14.

EATING OUT

In Brattleboro

🍴 **The Marina Restaurant** (802-257-7563; vermontmarina.com), Rt. 5 just north of the West River bridge. Open daily Apr.–mid-Oct. Situated at the confluence of the West and Connecticut rivers, this place has a great view and maximizes it, with a screened porch and patio as well as a dockside deck; in winter there's fireside dining. The reasonably priced menu includes plenty of seafood and vegetarian choices at both lunch and dinner, but also burgers. Full liquor license. A great place to enjoy a margarita while watching the sunset.

🍴 **Fireworks** (802-254-2073; fireworks restaurant.net), 73 Main St. Open for dinner nightly 5:30–10. Chef-owner Matthew Blau has opened several successful restaurants around town. This latest venture is a storefront featuring a 700-degree stone oven. Good for other dishes as well as pizza—roasted pears with prosciutto and Gorgonzola, for instance. And these are not your ordinary oven-roasted pizzas. "Blue Moon" combines fresh chopped clams, bacon, garlic, onion, herbs, and Parmesan. Pastas and delicacies like miso-roasted salmon are also on the menu. Children's menu available.

Shin La Restaurant (802-257-5226), 57–61 Main St. Open 11–9, closed Sun. Yl'soon Kim is the dynamo behind this attractive Korean restaurant, really a standout that has evolved over its years at this storefront. It's known for homemade soups, dumplings, and other Korean fare, and includes a sushi bar.

Amy's Bakery Arts Café (802-251-1071), 113 Main St. A good lunch spot. There are river views from tables in the back of this attractive storefront café, and the food is appealing, too: spinach and cheese croissants, salads, and sandwiches, some with meat but plenty without.

Back Side Cafe (802-257-5056), Harmony St. parking lot. Open weekdays for breakfast and lunch until 3; first Fridays for dinner; Sunday brunch. A great place for breakfast if you like an omelet with lots of fresh garlic or homemade salsa. Lunch features homemade soups, salads, deli sandwiches, and bagels; dinner runs from burgers to roast chicken, with a full bar featuring Vermont beers. Brunch both Sat. and Sun.

Brattleboro Food Co-op (802-257-0236), 2 Main St., Brookside Plaza. Open Mon.–Sat. 8–9, Sun. 9–9. An outstanding natural food market and deli worth checking out for its stellar choice of Vermont cheese—but while you're there, take advantage of the Café and Juice Bar featuring creative smoothies, first-rate sandwiches, and salads.

India Palace Restaurant, 69 Elliot St. Open daily for lunch and dinner, both reasonably priced for authentic Indian curries, tandoori, and biryani dishes. The list of Indian breads alone is long, and the menu is immense. Dinner specials include multicourse meals.

Sarkis Market DeliCafe (802-258-4906), 50 Elliot St. Open for lunch and dinner (until 8), for take-out and eat-in. A great source of stuffed grape leaves, spinach pies, lamb stew, homemade baklava, and falafel pockets.

Thai Bamboo (802-251-1010; thai bamboovt.com), 7 High St. Open daily for lunch (11:30–3) and dinner (5–10). Sign of the times! This is genuine Thai. Try deep-fried fish cakes served with cucumber sauce topped with crushed peanuts, followed by a wide choice of hot curries or stir-fried duck with black mushrooms and veggies. Wine and beer are served.

Mole's Eye Café (802-257-0771; moleseyecafe.net), corner of Main and High streets. Open Mon.–Thu. 4–midnight, Fri.–Sat. 11:30–1 AM. No food after 9 PM. A popular local gathering place serving soups, chili, and sandwiches, with a full bar and frequent live and lively music until 1 AM.

"ı" **Café Lotus** (802-254-6245), 29 High St. Open Mon.–Fri. 8–5, Sat. 10–5. Walk through the Blue Moose (a gift store) and you are in a lovely space (formerly the Café Beyond) with a long food bar under big old industrial windows and plenty of space to read or work on your laptop. Breakfast on anything from oatmeal to an omelet; lunch on salads, sandwiches, wraps, and daily specials.

⏚ **Brattleboro Farmer's Markets**. If you happen into town around noon on a sunny Sat. or Wed., head for the farmer's market. Saturday is the big day (early May–Oct., 9–2) just west of town by the Creamery Bridge. A live band and crafts, as well as produce vendors, are usually on hand. On Wed. (mid-June–Sept., 10–2) it's downtown off Main St. by the Merchants Bank Building (look for the Harris St. parking lot right there), with food vendors next to a small park overlooking the river.

Common Loaf Bakery (802-246-0677), Harmony Lot, also accessible from 128 Main St. The spelt-flour baked goods are the big draw here, but you'll also find tables and light fare. Open until 7 weekdays except Fri., when it closes at 3. The spelt is raised, ground, and baked at a nearby farm maintained by the Twelve Tribes, the international sect that has won respect in Vermont over the years for the quality of its work. Within the life of this book plans call for the group to reopen the Common Ground Restaurant, a legendary town gathering place. Worth checking.

Along Putney Rd. and in Putney
🍖 ⏚ **Top of the Hill Grill** (802-258-9178), 632 Putney Rd. Open mid-Apr.–Oct., 11–9. You have to be looking for this unusual BBQ place. It comes up fast after the bridge, heading north on Rt. 5 out of town. You order, get a card, take in the view of the river and "Retreat Meadows," and sit at a picnic table or in the screened deckhouse (muffling traffic noise, including restrooms) until your card is called (could be the Queen of Hearts). Indiana-born Julian Johnson hickory smokes his brisket and pork ribs, and apple-smokes his turkey. He also makes corn bread and coleslaw from scratch. You can also get a tempeh

burger, Cajun dishes, a salad, or a hot dog. Sides include red beans and rice, garden greens, and garlic-rosemary potatoes.

✿ **Curtis' Barbeque** (802-387-5474). Summer through fall, Tue.–Sun. 10–dusk. Follow your nose to the blue school bus parked behind the Mobil station on Rt. 5 in Putney, just off I-91, Exit 4. Curtis Tuff cooks up pork ribs and chicken, seasoned with his secret barbecue sauce; also foil-wrapped potatoes, grilled corn, and beans flavored with Vermont maple syrup. There are picnic tables and a weather-proofed pavilion.

Front Porch Café (802-387-2200), 133 Main St. Open except Mon. for breakfast (7–11), lunch (11:30–3), and Sunday brunch (10–2). Also for Friday dinner, 8–9. The rambling old white tavern on Putney's green is once more the village gathering place thanks to Jeremy Burrell and Steven Griffiths, former owners of the Saxtons River Inn. Fresh-baked muffins, scrambled egg wraps, soups, sandwiches, and daily specials along with coffees and teas are ordered and served up in a small corner space adjoining the informal café space with a hearth (also adjoining Putney Books).

✿ ✿ **Putney Diner** (802-387-5433), Main St. Open 6 AM–8 PM daily. Another pleasant option in the middle of Putney Village, open for all three meals. Good for Belgian waffles, Philly cheese steak, and homemade vegetable lasagna, super sandwich plates, salads, chicken-fried steak, grilled liver and onions, even burritos and tacos. Pastries made daily. Children's menu.

Putney Food Co-op (802-387-5866), Rt. 5 just south of the village. Open for lunch at 11. This is a great, quick lunch stop at a supermarket-sized cooperative with a pleasant café area: daily soups, salads, and deli.

Putney Village Pizza (802-387-2203), 84 Main St. These are Turkish-style pies, hand made by Erhan Oge and Tugce Okumus with all the toppings; also subs, salads, and pastas; beer and wine.

Along Rt. 30
Newfane Café (802-365-4442), 550 Rt. 30, south of Newfane Village. Open except Mon. 7–7. Nothing here is what you expect: It's all far more imaginative and tasty. The printed menu lists specialty paninis, sandwiches, and pre-pared foods such as the "tortilla critter" we feasted on: layers of tortillas, onions, peppers, corn, black beans, cheese, and salsa. Yum! Everything comes with mixed greens. At this writing expanded hours and space, along with beer and wine, are planned.

Rick's Tavern (802-365-4310), south of Newfane Village. Open daily for lunch and dinner, live jazz Thu., and acoustic music Sat. night. The bar was built around 1890 in Bismark, North Dakota, but the draft beers are Vermont microbrews. Daily blackboard specials, pizza, homemade desserts.

Townshend Pizza (802-365-4800), junction of Rts. 30 and 35, Townshend green. Hours vary. John and Nancy Papadopoulos serve Greek-style pizza plus calzones, subs, gyros, salads, and pastas. Beer and wine.

✿ ✿ **The Townshend Dam Diner** (802-874-4107), Rt. 30, 2 miles north of the Townshend Dam. Open daily 5 AM–8 PM. Breakfast all day. There's a big U-shaped counter and plenty of table seating, the greenery is genuine, and the waitresses are friendly. Specialties include homemade French toast, home fries, muffins and biscuits, the "best dam chili," soups, and bison burgers (from the nearby East Hill Bison Farm). Dinner staples include roast turkey, spaghetti, and garlic bread; daily specials. Peanut butter and jelly comes with chips and pickle.

Along Rt. 9 west

♪ **Chelsea Royal Diner** (802-254-8399; chelsearoyaldiner.com), Rt. 9, West Brattleboro. Open 6 AM–9 PM. A genuine '30s diner that's been moved a few miles west of its original site (it's a mile west of I-91, Exit 2). Plenty of parking and diner decor. Serving breakfast all day as part of a big menu that includes pizza, burgers, platters, daily blue plate specials, and great ice cream.

WINE AND BREWS ⁹₁⁹ **Windham Wine Gallery** (802 246-6400; windhamwines.com), 30 Main St., Brattleboro. Open Wed.–Sat. from 5. A delightful surprise. Long windows on the back overlook the tumbling falls of Whetstone Brook at this sophisticated wine bar (with artisanal beers on tap). Tables are nicely placed. The menu changes daily: from salad, soup, tapas, oven-roasted veggies, and quiche to serious dinner entrées like chèvre-crusted lamb ($18). Upward of 20 wines are usually available by the glass.

McNeill's Brewery (802-254-2553), 90 Elliot St., Brattleboro. Open at 4 Mon.–Thu. and at 2 Fri. and Sat. This brewery was once the town firehouse/offices/police station/jail. Ray McNeill was working on a graduate degree in music when he decided to focus instead on his second passion. This mecca for beer and ale lovers has medals to show for its variety of 35 brews, including lagers, traditional cask-conditioned real ales, and barley wines. A dozen are usually on tap. The rustic bar features communal tables, a horseshoe bar, a dartboard, and enchanting (local) art. Occasionally you will find McNeill playing his cello.

Flat Street Brew Pub (802-257-1911), 6 Flat St. Open 4–1 all week. There are 20 select microbrews on tap, including 10 from Berkshire Brewing Company, based in South Deerfield, MA, as well as a full bar with wine list. Pub fare ranges from a ploughman's platter and quesadillas to paninis and burgers; top it all off with a slice of sumptuous chocolate cake. Opened in 2005 by Brit Steve Pardoe, Flat Street has quickly become a hot spot for locals, a great place for meeting friends or just stopping after a movie or concert at the Latchis Theatre next door. The true flavor of a homey English pub in southern Vermont.

Mocha Joe's (802-257-7794), 82 Main St., Brattleboro. Coffee is taken seriously here, roasted as well as brewed. Live music on weekends.

Twilight Tea Lounge (802-254-8887), under 51 Main St., Brattleboro. Open Wed.–Sun., noon to varying hours. A barbershop for 75 years, this pleasant space is filled with mismatched tables and chairs and the aroma of rare teas. A cooperative, the venue for poetry and music.

Putney Mountain Winery (802-387-5925). Music professor and composer Charles Dodge has established a reputation for the quality of his sparkling apple wines. Tastings and tours are offered daily at Basketville (see *Special Stores*) in Putney.

⁹₁⁹ **Jamaica Coffee House** (802-874-4643), 3863 Rt. 30, Jamaica. Closed Wed.; otherwise open 7–5, until noon Tue. Fair-trade coffee, teas, ice cream, and baked goods. Ask about live music.

✳ Entertainment

The Latchis Theater (802-254-6300; latchis.com), 50 Main St., Brattleboro, shows first-run and art films, also live performances. For film buffs, this 900-seat art deco movie house with three screens is itself a destination. Apollo still drives his chariot through the firmament on the ceiling; walls are graced with Doric columns, and the lobby floor bears the zodiac signs in multicolored terrazzo. Along with the Latchis Hotel in which it's housed, the theater is owned by the Brattleboro Arts Initiative; there's also an art gallery.

New England Youth Theatre (802-246-6398; neyt.org), 100 Flat St. Fabulous year-round productions of children's and all-time classics in a beautiful new theater. New England Youth Theatre is a state-of-the-art acting school for children age 6 to 18; its performance space seats 125. Theater, music, dance, and circus performances occur frequently at this and other venues in the Brattleboro area. Not just the actors but the set builders, costumers, stage managers, and technicians in the light and sound booth are youth. The vintage 2007 theater with 150 to 190 state-of-the-art seats also contains classrooms. Check the Web site for current productions.

Sandglass Theater (802-387-4051; sandglasstheater.org), Kimball Hill, Putney. A resident theater company performs original work combining live theater with puppetry performances. When not on tour they perform in a 60- seat renovated barn theater in Putney Village.

Sanctuary: Hooker-Dunham Theater (802-254-9276; hookerdunham.org), 139 Main St., Brattleboro. Check out what's going on at this middle-of-town venue: theater, music, classic films, and lectures.

Whittemore Theater and other performance venues at Marlboro College (802-257-4333; marlboro.edu), in Marlboro Village (10 miles west of Brattleboro) are the setting for frequent presentations.

Actors Theatre Playhouse (877-233-7905; actorsplay.org), corner of Brook and Main streets, West Chesterfield, New Hampshire. Ten minutes from Brattleboro, seasonal performances, reasonably priced. With a diverse variety of plays and exceptional performances by local actors, this is not your run-of-the-mill community theater.

SUMMER MUSIC FESTIVALS

Marlboro Music, Persons Auditorium, Marlboro College. (marlboromusic .org), 10 miles west of Brattleboro off Rt. 9. This internationally famous series of chamber music concerts has been performed Fri.–Sun., early July–mid-Aug., for more than five decades. The festival is a seven-week gathering of 70 or so world-class musicians who come to work together. It is held on this rural campus because Rudolf Serkin, one of its founders, owned a nearby farm. Pablo Casals came every year from 1960 to 1973. Some concerts are sold out in advance, but you can frequently find good seats before the performance (chairs are metal, and regulars bring cushions). There are (almost) always bargain-priced seats in the tent just outside the auditorium's sliding glass doors (tickets are $15–35, with last-minute, unsold seats $5).
Yellow Barn Music Festival (802-387-6637; 800-639-3819; yellowbarn.org), Putney. Begun in 1969, this is a series of chamber music concerts in July and early Aug., staged in a 150-seat barn in Putney Village. Artists include both well-known professionals and 40 students chosen each summer from leading conservatories.

The New England Center for Circus Arts (802-254-9780; necenterfor cicrcusarts.org), 76 Cotton Mill Hill, #300, Brattleboro. A full program of circus arts is offered year-round in the Cotton Mill; check the Web site for performances.

Kipling Cinemas (at Fairfield Plaza, Rt. 5 north of Brattleboro), a multiplex, also shows first-run films.

Brattleboro Music Center (802-257-4523; bmcvt.org), 38 Walnut St., Brattleboro. Housed in a former convent, this burgeoning music school sponsors a wide variety of local musical events and festivals as well as a fall-through-spring Chamber Music Series.

Vermont Jazz Center (802-254-9088; vtjazz.org), 72 Cotton Mill Hill, Studio 222, S. Main St., Brattleboro, stages frequent musical, vocal, and jazz happenings.

Friends of Music at Guilford (802-254-3600; fomag.org), Guilford. A series of concerts throughout the year at various locations. Note the free Labor Day weekend concerts under *Special Events*.

Also see the Mole's Eye Café and Rick's Tavern under *Eating Out*.

✳ Selective Shopping
ANTIQUES

In Brattleboro
Twice Upon a Time (802-254-2261; twicetime.com), 63 Main St. Open Mon.–Wed. 10–6, Thu.–Sat. 10–7, Sun. 11–6. Auctions are held 6 PM Wed. at Brookside Plaza, Rt. 9, West Brattleboro. "I always wanted a consignment shop that would be able to display anything that anyone wanted to give me," says Randi Crouse, proprietor of this truly amazing shop that now fills the entire three-level space created in 1906 for the E. J. Fenton

Department Store. In the '50s it was chopped into smaller storefronts, but the two-story-high Corinthian columns, bubble glass, and wooden gallery are back, a setting for clothing, antique furniture, and furnishings. The markdown schedule is patterned on that of Filene's Basement. More than 100 dealers and thousands of consignors are represented.

Along Rt. 30
Newfane Flea Market (802-365-4000), just north of Newfane Village. Sundays, May–Oct. Billed as the largest open-air market in the state; usually 100 tables with assorted junk and treasure.

Jack Winner Antiques (802-365-7215; winnerantiques.com), Rt. 30, Newfane. Open Thu.–Mon. 10–5. Specializing for over 30 years in 18th- and 19th-century formal and country furniture, equestrian antiques, Spode china, brass, and hunting prints.

Auntie M's Attic (802-365-9796), Rt. 30, south of Newfane Village. Open May–Oct., Thu.–Mon. A nice selection of antique china, furniture, glass, lamps, linens, and prints.

Riverdale Antiques (802-365-4616), Rt. 30, Harmonyville (between Newfane and Townshend). Open year-round, daily 10–5. More than 70 dealers selling quality antiques and collectibles.

Townshend Auction Gallery (802-365-4388), Rt. 30, Townshend. Over 30 years Kit Martin and Art Monette have established a solid reputation for their frequent auctions, usually Sat. mornings.

Also see Old Corkers Emporium in Jamaica under "Art and Crafts Galleries."

ART AND CRAFTS GALLERIES
Note: The first Friday of each month is Gallery Walk in Brattleboro: open

house with refreshments and music at dozens of downtown businesses that hang works by local artists and at studios as well as at formal galleries, usually 5:30–8:30; a special brochure is prepared for each walk. Check out gallerywalk.org.

Windham Art Gallery (802-257-1881; windhamartgallery.com), 69 Main St., Brattleboro. Open Wed.– Sun. noon–5, weekends until 7:30. Exhibits by members of an outstanding artists' cooperative. This is also the source of the Arts Council of Windham County's quarterly publication *Arts in the Season*, which lists current theater, poetry readings, and gallery shows throughout southeastern Vermont.

Vermont Artisan Designs (802-257-7044; buyvermontart.com), 106 Main St., Brattleboro. Open daily. A must-visit, this is a Brattleboro phenomenon. Least obvious and best of all is Gallery 2 on the second floor, displaying 50 to 60 of Vermont's best artists. Special exhibits change with every Gallery Walk (first Fri.), when there are opening receptions with live music. The store's main floor is an outstanding contemporary crafts gallery displaying the well-chosen work of hundreds of artisans. There's also a kitchen store—and in the basement you can rent a tux. This was the town's department store when Greg Worden acquired a portion of the space more than 15 years ago and established the town's first quality gallery. It continues to evolve.

Gallery in the Woods (802-257-4777; galleryinthewoods.com), 143 Main St., Brattleboro. For decades Dante and Suzanne Corsano's gallery has been a standout, featuring folk art, finely crafted furniture, and known painters and artists in a variety of media from throughout the world. Don't miss the changing exhibits on the basement level.

Artist's Loft Gallery (phone/fax 802-257-5181; theartistsloft.com), 103 Main St., Brattleboro. Realistic landscapes as well as portraits and other worth-checking oils by William Hays.

Vermont Center for Photography (802-251-6051; vcphoto.org), 49 Flat St. Squirreled back in a corner beside the Transportation Center. Open Fri. 2–7, Sat.–Sun. noon–5. Quality changing exhibits. Worth checking.

Borter's Jewelry Studio (802-254-3452; bortersjewelry.com), 103 Main St., Brattleboro. Tue.–Fri. noon–5:30, Sat. noon–4, and by appointment. Gemstones; silver and gold jewelry handcrafted into stunning settings on the premises.

Altiplano (802-257-1562), 42 Elliot St. Open daily. The shop features contemporary clothing and other crafted products, some with the store's own widely distributed label, designed in-house but made in Guatemala.

Neumann Studios (802-251-9901; neumannstudios.com), 80 Strand Ave. By chance and appointment. Custom stained glass, lamps, architectural accents.

In Putney
Note: **The Putney Craft Tour** (putneycrafts.com), held for more than 30 years for three days after Thanksgiving, showcases the work of craftspeople within a dozen miles of Putney. However, many of these—and the craftspeople listed on the town Web site (putney.net)—do not hold regular hours. The exceptions are:

Penelope Wurr Glass (802-387-5607; penelopewurr.com), 12 Kimball Hill. Open Thu.–Sun. noon–5. Trained as a printmaker, this English-born designer who has operated studios in London and SoHo (NYC) showcases her glass, distinctive for the way it's patterned, suggesting textiles more than art glass—which it is. Other crafts and gifts are also carried.

Edel Byrne Stained Glass (802-387-2115), 88 Main St. Open by chance or appointment. Dublin-born Byrne specializes in "lace leadwork," creating medieval-inspired geometric patterns in windows and lamps.

Brandywine Glassworks (802-387-4032; robertburchglass.com), Fort Hill Rd. (off Rt. 5 north). Robert Burch, a pioneer in art glass, hand-blows his signature cobalt perfume bottles and vases, veiled with delicate silver bubbles, and amber and ruby swirling paperweights in a 200-year-old barn beside his home. He supplies some 200 shops and galleries across the country and is also a respected teacher of his craft, drawing students regularly from Boston. Phone before you stop by. Seconds are available.

Lilli Crites Pottery (802-387-2222), 2888 Westminster West Rd. Visitors welcome; call ahead. Lilli Crites Flesher crafts wheel-thrown, functional, but decorative and brilliantly glazed pottery.

GREEN MOUNTAIN SPINNERY

Christina Tree

Richard Bissell Fine Woodworking (802-387-4416; bissellwoodworking.com), Signal Pine Rd. Open Mon.–Fri. 9–5. Exceptional Shaker-inspired furniture, cabinetry, Windsor chairs.

Green Mountain Spinnery (802-387-4528; 800-321-9665; spinnery.com), just off I-91, Exit 4. Open Mon.–Fri. Founded as a cooperative more than 30 years ago and now worker owned, this is a real spinning mill in which undyed, unbleached fibers—alpaca, mohair, wool, and organic cotton—are carded, spun, skeined, and labeled. You can buy the resulting yarn in various plies in natural and dyed colors. Many original patterns are shown in the catalog. The store also carries buttons and knitting supplies.

Along Rt. 30

Newfane Country Store (802-365-7916; newfanecountrystore.com), Newfane. Open daily, year-round. Owner Marilyn Distelberg is herself a quilter—and quilts, many locally handmade, are the big reason to stop. Also gifts, pottery, books, and more.

Taft Hill (802-865-4200; tafthill.com), Harmonyville (Townshend). Open daily 10–5. A fine art gallery within a gift shop, featuring West River Valley artists and hand-painted glass and china created here at Crest Studio.

Dunberry Hill Designs (802-874-7288; dunberryhilldesigns.com). The studio is usually open, but call. Just off Rt. 30 near Townshend Dam, Cameron Howard creates durable and distinctive cotton canvas floorcloths with geometric and folk art designs.

Jennie Blue (802-874-4222; jennieblue.com), Jamaica Village. Hours vary. Susan Leader's bright, irresistible plates, vases, and pots with cheerful designs and Jennie's personalized wedding and other special-occasion plates and bowls are featured.

MARGIE'S MUSE HANDWEAVING IN JAMAICA

Margie's Muse Handweaving & Gallery (802-874-7201; margiesmuse .com), Rt. 30, Jamaica Village. Open Thu.–Mon. Handwoven wool blankets, chenille throws and scarves, hand-dyed and -spun natural yarns, changing artwork and work from hundreds of craftspeople, also yarn supplies, bath products, and more; classes in felting and knitting are offered.

Elaine Beckwith Gallery (802-874-7234; beckwithgallery.com), Rt. 30/100, Jamaica Village. Open daily except Tue. This is a long-established,

SKIP WOODRUFF CRAFTS RUSTIC FURNITURE IN JAMAICA.

destination gallery with a strong contemporary collection, representing some 30 artists in a variety of styles and media, a third from Vermont artists. Superb artist-printmaker Joel Beckwith is also featured. A must for art lovers.

Skip Woodruff, Rustic Furniture Maker (802-874-4172; oldcorkers antiques.com), Rt. 30, Jamaica. Open year-round. Hours vary. Skip and Maureen Woodruff began by selling Adirondack lodge-style camp furniture and furnishings; Skip now handcrafts a line of his own: tables, servers, mirrors, frames, and more. Skip gives new meaning to *rustic*, with each piece individually crafted. A great stop!

Monsoon Vermont (888-874-4643; monsoonvt.com), open sporadically weekdays beside the Jamaica Post Office; products also available in the Jamaica Coffee House (see *Brews*) and online. Julia Genatossio, formerly of Save the Children, UK, designs distinctive tote bags, laptops, shower curtains, travel bags, and much more. She then orders them from a small company in Jakarta, Indonesia, that gathers nonrecyclable plastic trash, triplewashes it, and uses it to create the items, all featuring a collage of products in English and Basha (Indonesian).

BOOKSTORES The Book Cellar (802-254-6026; vtbookcellar.com), 120 Main St., Brattleboro. An outstanding, long-established, full-service bookstore, particularly strong on Vermont and New England titles.

Everyone's Books (802-254-8160; everyonesbks.com), 25 Elliot St., Brattleboro. This is an earnest and interesting alternative bookstore, specializing in women's books; also a great selection of children's and multicultural titles.

Old & New England Books (802-365-7074), 47 West St., Newfane. Open May–Oct., Thu.–Mon. 10:30–6. A delightful browsing place with an interesting stock of books old and new.

Putney Books (802-387-4800), at the junction of Rt. 5 and West Hill Rd. in Putney. Open daily 10–6. Housed in the restored old tavern at the center of Putney Village, a full-service bookstore that also carries used books, cards, and toys and invites browsing, with a frequently working hearth in the adjacent Front Porch Café.

Brattleboro Books (802-257-0777), 34 Elliot St., Brattleboro. Open 10 6 daily except Sun. An extensive selection of used and out-of-print books; over 60,000 titles fill two storefronts and the basement. Browsing strongly encouraged.

SPECIAL SHOPS

In Brattleboro

Sam's Outdoor Outfitters (802-254-2933; samsoutfitters.com), 74 Main St. Open daily, varying hours. The business that Sam Borofsky started in 1934 now fills two floors of two buildings with a full stock of hunting, camping, and sports equipment. Prices are reasonable, but people don't shop here for bargains. The big thing is the service—skilled help in selecting the right fishing rod, tennis racket, or gun. There are also name-brand sports clothes and standard army and navy gear. Fishing and hunting licenses are sold. *Tip:* There's free popcorn every day, all day.

Delectable Mountain (802-257-4456), 125 Main St. Fine-fabric lovers make pilgrimages to Jan Norris's store, widely known for its selection of fine silks, all-natural imported laces, velvets, cottons, and upholstery jacquards. It also offers a wide selection of unusual buttons.

Brattleboro Food Co-op (802-257-0236), 2 Main St., Brookside Plaza. Open Mon.–Sat. 8–9, Sun. 9–9; deli and fresh-baked products. The cheese counter could just be the best showcase for Vermont cheese in the state; cheeses from around the world are also knowledgeably selected and presented (note the "cheese of the week"), and there's local produce, grains, wines, and a café.

Adavasi Imports (802-258-2231), 8 Flat St. Shram and Elissa Bhanti keep prices low because they are also wholesalers, traveling to northwest India to buy their fabrics: linens and clothing hand blocked with natural vegetable dyes; silk saris for $25; cotton rugs; and a wide variety of crafted items and jewelry. It's an exotic, fragrant emporium that keeps expanding.

Tom & Sally's Handmade Chocolates (802-254-4200), Rt. 30. Locally made and worth a taste.

A Candle in the Night (802-257-0471), 181 Main St. Donna and Larry Simons have built up a vast knowledge as well as inventory of Oriental and other handcrafted rugs over the decades.

Save the Corporations from Themselves (802-254-4847; savethecorporations.com), 169 Main St. Hemp clothing is the specialty here, but don't miss the "activists' attic."

Beadniks (802-257-5114), 115 Main St. Beads, baubles, and whimsical wonders.

Turn It Up (802-251-6015; turnitup .com), 2 Elliot St. Open Mon.–Thu. 10–9, Fri.–Sat. 10–10, Sun. 11–7. Discounted new, rare, and overstock compact discs, records, and more. In-store listening available. Will order for you at no extra charge.

In Putney

Basketville (802-387-5509; basketville
.com), Rt. 5. Open daily 9–6. Founded
by Frank Wilson, an enterprising Yankee trader in the real sense, this is a
family-run business. The vast store features woodenware, wicker furniture
(filling the entire upstairs), wooden
toys, and exquisite artificial flowers as
well as traditional baskets and myriad
other things, large and small. *Note:*
Check out the Columbus Day weekend Basketville Seconds Sale. This is
also the venue for **Putney Mountain
Winery** tastings.

Silver Forest of Vermont (802-387-
4149), 14 Kimball Hill (middle of the
village). A must-stop for clothing,
accessories, and silver jewelry, with
Indonesian teak furniture upstairs.

Offerings (802-387-4566; offerings
jewelry.com), middle of the village.
Featuring handmade silver jewelry
with semiprecious stones, unusual gold
jewelry, watches, and cards.

Along Rt. 30

Lawrence's Smoke House (802-365-
7751), Newfane. Corncob-smoked
hams, bacon, poultry, fish, meats, and
cheese are the specialties of the house.
Catalog and mail order.

FARMS TO VISIT One of the state's
concentrations of farms and orchards is
here in the Lower Connecticut River
Valley, some offering "pick your own,"
others welcoming visitors to their farm
stands, sugaring houses, or barns. Call
before coming.

Note: Also see Farmer's Markets under
Eating Out and vtfarms.org for details
and directions for many of the following.

Cheese

Grafton Village Cheese (802-254-
2201; graftonvillagecheese.com), 400
Linden St. , Brattleboro. Open Mon.-
Sat. 10-6; Sin. 10-5. This big, new facility for the Grafton-based cheese

Christina Tree

GRAFTON VILLAGE CHEESE

company is beside the Retreat Farm
(see For Families) at the beginning of
Rt. 30. It's a must stop. While the store
features its own handcrafted cheeses,
more than 80 varieties are available,
along with Vermont microbrews, fresh
bread, and Vermont specialty foods
and gifts. Cheese making can be
viewed and samples are offered.

Vermont Shepherd (802-387-4473;
vermontshepherd.com), Patch Rd.,
Westminster West. Vermont Shepherd
holds one of the country's top awards
for its distinctive, hand-pressed, sweet
creamy sheep's-milk cheese. It's made
Apr.–Oct., then aged four to eight
months and available mid-Aug. until
the year's supply runs out in spring.
Call for appropriate visiting times. A
self-serve shop is open daily.

Peaked Mountain Farm (802-365-
4502), 1541 Peaked Mountain Rd.,
Townshend. Call first. In an idyllic
locale high above the West River Valley, Ann and Bob Works make sheep's-
milk cheese, combination sheep/cow's-
milk "Ewe Jersey," and a sheep/goat
cheese.

Other

Robb Family Farm (802-258-9087;
888-318-9087; robbfamilyfarm.com),
827 Ames Hill Rd., Brattleboro. This
420-acre dairy farm has been in the
same family since 1907, and visitors
are welcomed here in a number of
ways and in all seasons. In spring the
sugarhouse is a fragrant, steamy place;

year-round it's also the Country Shop (open Mon.–Sat. 10–5, Sun. 1–5, closed Wed.), stocked with maple products and floral items. Visitors are also welcome in the barn, moved here from Halifax in 1912 (50 of the 100-head herd are presently milked).

Olallie Daylily Gardens (802-348-6614; daylilygarden.com), 129 Augur Hole Rd., South Newfane. Open early May–Labor Day weekend, daily 10–5 except Tue. No charge for self guided tours, but a two-hour guided tour is $5. Pink irises in mid-June; daylilies June–Sept. PYO organic blueberries in July and Aug. Garden shop and potted plant nursery. Inquire about the Daylily Festival.

Dutton Berry Farm and Stand (802-365-4168), farm stand on Rt. 30, Newfane. Open year-round. This is a large, varied stand featuring varied fruit and other produce from Paul and Wendy Dutton's family farm, Christmas trees, much more.

Hickin's Mountain Mowings Farm (802-254-2146), 1999 Black Mountain Rd., Dummerston. Retail shop open Apr.–Dec. Selling raspberries July–Oct., other farm-fresh fruit in-season, also jams, jellies, and preserves, maple pickles, fruitcake, syrup, cheese, and honey. Marked off the East/West Rd. between Putney and Rt. 30 (see *Scenic Drives*).

Dwight Miller & Son Orchards (802-254-9158), 581 Miller Rd., East Dummerston. Open daily year-round. One of Vermont's oldest family farms. A retail stand with the farm's own organic fruit and vegetables, preserves, pickles, and syrup; seasonal pick-your-own apples and varied fruit in-season.

Elysian Hills Tree Farm (802-257-0233; elysianhillsfarm.com), 209 Knapp Rd., Dummerston. Bill and Mary Lou Schmidt maintain this 100-acre tree farm. Trees are available for tagging from July on, but the tradition-

al "Tag Days" are Columbus Day weekend and the two following weekends: wagon rides, pumpkins, and marked hiking trails. Tagged trees, wreaths, and other decorations are also shipped UPS and FedEx in Dec. Retail sales of ready-cut Christmas trees begin the Saturday after Thanksgiving and end at 4 PM Dec. 24.

Green Mountain Orchards (802-387-5851; greenmtorchards.com), 130 West Hill Rd., Putney Open daily in-season. Pick-your-own apples and blueberries; cider available in-season. Christmas trees, local crafts, and produce also sold, gift shop, horse-drawn wagon rides on fall weekends, wedding sites.

The Scott Farm (802-254-6868; landmarktrustusa.org), 707 Kipling Rd., Dummerston. Turn off busy Putney Rd. (Rt. 5) at the sign for WORLD LEARNING AND SCHOOL FOR INTERNATIONAL TRAINING and follow it up beyond the hardtop to this historic gentleman's farm currently under restoration by the Landmark Trust USA (see *Lodging*) The farm stand carries its peaches, pears, cherries, grapes, berries, and quince, but heirloom apples are the specialty, with more than 70 varieties.

Walker Farm (802-254-2051; walkerfarm.com), Rt. 5, Dummerston. A 200-year-old farm and garden center (open Apr. 15–fall, 10–6), specializing in hard-to-find annuals and perennials and garden books by local authors. Jack and Karen Mannix have made this a destination for serious gardeners. Choose from 30 kinds of heirloom peppers and 50 kinds of tomatoes as well as a peerless selection of flowers (30 varieties of pansies and 1,200 other annuals and perennials started from seed, plus 700 other plants nurtured in 17 greenhouses) and a full line of produce June–Thanksgiving, featuring the Mannixes' own organic vegetables and local fruit. Display gardens.

Christina Tree

HARLOW'S SUGAR HOUSE

Harlow's Sugar House (802-387-5852; harlowssugarhouse.com), Rt. 5 north of Putney Village. Open Mar.–late Dec., Harlow's is one of the most visitor-oriented operations. The Sugar House lets you watch maple production in-season, and there's a film and maple museum; the big store sells their own syrup and honey and offers pick-your-own apples, blueberries, and strawberries. The produce stand features a wide variety of apples in-season.

FACTORY OUTLETS Big Black Bear Shop at Mary Meyer (802-365-4160; 888-758-BEAR; bigblackbear .com), Rt. 30, Townshend, west of the village. Open daily. The original location of Vermont's oldest stuffed-toy company. More than 500 designs, 20–70 percent off.

The Outlet Center (802-254-4594), 580 Canal St., Brattleboro; Exit 1 off I-91. Open daily 9:30–8 except Sun. 10–6. This former factory building that once produced handbags is an old-fashioned factory outlet center with 15 varied stores worth checking, one being **Winterset Designs** (802-246-1471), which features locally made laundry bag holders (ingenious but dif-

ficult to describe), solidly built furniture, and Bennington Pottery. Other stores include Carter's, Dress Barn, and locally based **Northeast Mountain Footwear**.

✳ Special Events

Note: **Gallery Walk** (gallerywalk.org) in Brattleboro is the first Friday of every month.

February: **Brattleboro Winter Carnival**, a full week of celebrations, climaxed by the Washington's birthday cross-country ski race. **The annual Harris Hill Jumping Competition** (harrishillskijump.org) may or may not coincide with the carnival.

March: **Affair of the Arts**, a daylong collaboration showcasing many Brattleboro arts organizations.

May through October: **Farmer's markets** are held in **Brattleboro** on Sat. on Rt. 9 at the Creamery Covered Bridge and on Wed. downtown; in **Townshend** Thu. 4–7.

Third Saturday of May: **Jamaica Fiber Festival** (jamaicafiberfestival.org).

May: **Salmagundi,** a weeklong festival of the performing arts, offering a vari-

**THE WINDHAM GALLERY DURING
BRATTLEBORO'S MONTHLY GALLERY WALK**

ety of classes, workshops, and lectures for youth and adults, with performances by theater professionals from across the U.S. and Europe.

Memorial Day: **Dawn Dance**, 8 PM–7 AM in Brattleboro.

First Saturday of June: **Strolling of the Heifers** down Main St., Brattleboro, along with a Dairy Fest and marketplace, Heifer Ball.

Late June: Dummerston Center **Annual Strawberry Supper**, Grange Hall, Dummerston.

July through August: **Marlboro Music** in Marlboro and the **Yellow Barn Music Festival** in Putney (see *Entertainment*).

July 4: A big **parade** winds through Brattleboro at 10 AM; games, exhibits, refreshments in Living Memorial Park; **fireworks** at 9 PM.

Late July: **Rock River Artists Open Studio Tour** (rockriverartists.com)— open studios sponsored by artists in Williamsville and South Newfane.

August: **Free concert** on the Newfane common every Wed. *First Saturday:* **Grace Cottage Hospital Fair Day**— exhibits, booths, games, rides on the green in Townshend.

September: Labor Day weekend in Guilford is observed both with the old-style **Guilford Fair** and with the annual two-day music festival in **Guilford's Organ Barn** (802-257-1961). Concerts are free. **Heritage Festival Benefit** in Newfane, sponsored by the Newfane Congregational Church. **Puppets in the Green Mountains**— more than a week of performances by puppet theaters from near and far in varied venues, mostly in Brattleboro and Putney (802-251-5070; puppetsinthegreenmountains.com).

October: The first weekend marks the **Brattleboro Literary Festival** (brattleboroliteraryfestival.org) with nationally known authors. **Newfane Heritage Fair** (newfaneheritage festival.org) on Columbus Day weekend—crafts, dancing, raffle, sponsored by the Newfane Congregational Church. **Harvest Festival at the Putney School** (putneyschool.org) features music, artisans, and a farm parade.

Mid-October: The **Apple Pie Festival** in Dummerston features hundreds of Dummerston's famous apple pies, also crafts, at the Dummerston Center Congregational Church and Grange. The annual **Pumpkin Festival** on Townshend common features biggest-pumpkin and best-pumpkin-pie contests, plenty of vendors, food.

Weekend after Thanksgiving: **Putney Craft Tour**—some two dozen local studios open to the public (putney crafts.com).

Early December: **Christmas Bazaar** on the common, Newfane. **Community Messiah Sing** at Centre Congregational Church in Brattleboro. **Cotton Mill Open Studio & Holiday Sale** (thecottonmill.org) featuring some 50 resident artists, also in Brattleboro.

December 31: **Last Night Celebrations**, Brattleboro. Fun family day and night with fireworks at the Retreat Meadows about 9 PM.

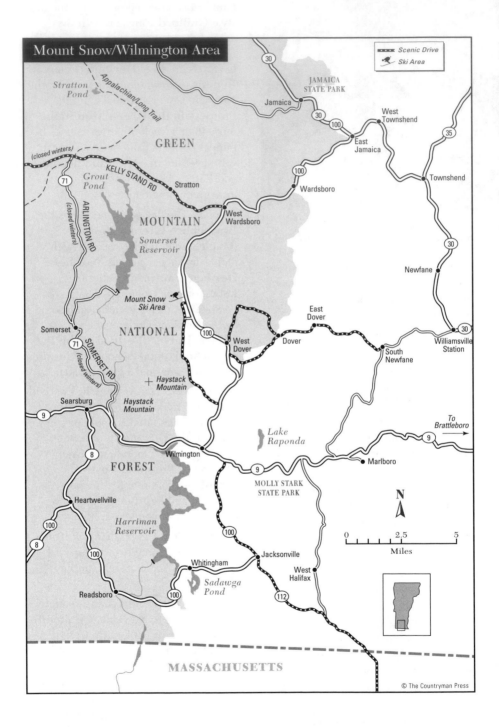

Mount Snow/Wilmington Area

THE MOUNT SNOW VALLEY

Long before this steep-sided valley drew skiers, summer visitors arrived via the Hoosac Tunnel and Wilmington Railroad, staying in hotels at Sadawga Springs in Whitingham and on Lake Raponda in Wilmington. In the 1890s a number of these urbanites transformed local farms into summer homes. The shingle-style Child's Tavern (now the Crafts Inn), designed by no less an architect than Stanford White, opened in the center of the village of Wilmington in 1902 and soon became part of the "Ideal Tour" through New England, widely promoted for "pleasure driving," promising auto travelers "A First Class Hotel at the End of Each Day's Run."

In the 1920s and '30s cars became affordable (between 1908 and 1927, 15 million Ford Model T's were produced) and ordinary folks began motor touring (ergo "tourists"). In 1938 the 48 miles of Rt. 9 between Brattleboro and Bennington was formally pronounced a scenic driving route, the Molly Stark Trail. It's now an official Vermont Scenic Byway, still named for the wife of the New Hampshire general who traveled this route in August 1777 on his way to defeating the British at the battle of Bennington.

The compact village of Wilmington sits at the junction of Rts. 9 and 100 north. Site of one of the state's first rural traffic lights, it's midway between Brattleboro (20 miles) and Bennington (21 miles). West Dover, another picturesque village clustered around its church and tavern, is 6 miles north of Wilmington. The intervening stretch of Rt. 100 is now lined with restaurants, lodges, and shops, reflecting the vagaries of the ski industry since 1954, the year Reuben Snow's farm was transformed by ski lifts and trails, lodges, a skating rink, and an immense, floodlit geyser. Ski lodges soon mushroomed for miles around, varying in style from Tyrolean to 1950s futuristic.

The geyser is gone and Mount Snow has mellowed into one of Vermont's largest family-geared ski resorts, with a loyal following among skiers of all levels. Since local Olympian Kelly Clark's gold in the half-pipe, boarding has grown huge here as well, with Carinthia (once an independently owned ski area) now a 100-acre freestylers' domain.

Over the years the ski resort has spawned a large number of condos, many available for rental. More traditional lodging places are scattered along back roads, an unusual number offering dinner as well as breakfast, perhaps because Mount Snow is the most convenient major ski mountain to New York City, the country's biggest source of car-free skiers.

Beyond this narrow corridor, mountains rise on all sides. The village of Dover is a knot of white-clapboard buildings on the crest of a hill. Rt. 100 is heavily forested north to the classic village of Wardsboro, south to the delightfully backroaded towns of Jacksonville and Whitingham, and east to the college town of Marlboro, site of the world-class Marlboro Music Festival in July and August.

The surrounding hills were once lumbered extensively. Two former logging villages actually lie at the bottom of the sizable Harriman and Somerset reservoirs, which have transformed the Deerfield Valley into one of the most watery parts of Vermont, good for fishing, boating, and swimming as well as hiking and biking.

GUIDANCE Mount Snow Valley Chamber of Commerce (802-464-8092; 877-887-6884; visitvermont.com) maintains a major Vermont Information Center on 21 W. Main St. in Wilmington (Rt. 9 west, seven doors from the junction of Rts. 9 and 100). Pick up the useful *Mount Snow Valley Visitor's Guide.* The *Deerfield Valley News*, the local weekly, is also a good source for current events.

Southern Vermont Regional Marketing Organization (877-887-2378; southern vermont.com) maintains a good Web site and is a source of printed area information.

GETTING THERE The obvious route to Mount Snow from points south and east is I-91 to Brattleboro, then Rt. 9 to Wilmington. There are also **two scenic shortcuts**: (1) Rt. 30 north from Brattleboro 11.1 miles to the marked turnoff for Dover; follow the road through the covered bridge in South Newfane past Dover to West Dover; (2) turn off I-91 onto Rt. 2 in Greenfield, Massachusetts; follow Rt. 2 for 3.6 miles to Colrain Rd. and proceed 17.3 miles to Jacksonville, where you pick up Rt. 100 into Wilmington (under *Scenic Drives* see this route detailed in reverse).

From New York City: **Adventure Northeast Bus Service** (917-861-1800; adventurenortheast.com) goes in both directions daily during ski season, typically Thanksgiving weekend–April. Call for reservations. Vehicles vary from mini vans to buses, depending on demand. Midweek rides are usually timed to arrive around 3 PM. The most popular departures are Friday evening from Manhattan, leaving Mount Snow on Sunday afternoon.

Christina Tree

GETTING AROUND The MOO-ver (802-464-5457; moover.com) is a free community bus service operated by the Deerfield Valley Transit Association (DVTA). It connects points of interest in the valley, along Rt. 100 from the Deerfield Valley Health Center in Wilmington, picking up passengers at DVTA stops 7 AM–10 PM. Look for its Holstein cow logo.

WHEN TO GO High season is Christmas through February; in March snow is less dependable here than in other parts of the state. Golfers arrive in June, and in July and August the Marlboro Music Festival draws a cultured crowd. Summer brings many low-key happenings along with mountain biking at Mount Snow. Foliage usually fills every inn and restaurant during October's first three weekends.

MEDICAL EMERGENCY Emergency service is available by calling **911**.

✳ To See

SCENIC DRIVES **East along the Molly Stark Scenic Byway**. Five miles east of Wilmington on Rt. 9 you come to **Hogback Mountain**. Formerly a ski area, this is now a major overlook, said to offer a 100-mile view (weather dependent) facing south. This is also the site of the **Southern Vermont Natural History Museum** (802-464-0048; vermontmuseum.org; open daily Memorial Day–late Oct., 10–5, Nov.–May most weekends, but call to be sure). Larger than it looks from the outside, it displays mounted specimens of more than 500 New England birds and mammals in 80 dioramas, the collection of taxidermist Luman R. Nelson. Continue along the Molly Stark Trail east some 5 miles to the turnoff to **Marlboro Village**, home of Marlboro College. From mid-July until mid-August its campus is the venue for the Marlboro Music Festival (marlboromusic.org). The **Marlboro Historical Society** (marlboro.vt.us), with its collection of pictures, old farm tools, and antique furniture, is housed in the Newton House and the 1813 one-room schoolhouse on Main St. and is open in July and Aug., Sat. 2–5, or by appointment. See *Selective Shopping* for the studios of notable Marlboro craftspeople. Continue into Brattleboro and return via the Dover Hill Rd. or follow the road past the college to the T, turn right, and you are soon in Jacksonville. See the following tours.

GREEN MOUNTAIN HALL IN WHITINGHAM
Christina Tree

Jacksonville and Whitingham. From Wilmington follow Rt. 100 south 6 miles, past Flames Stable and the turnoff for Ward's Cove, to the village of Jacksonville. Near the junction of Rts. 100 and 112 stop by **Stone Soldier Pottery** (see *Selective Shopping*). In the middle of the village **Valpert's Diner** (802-368-2600; open for lunch until 2 PM except Tue. and Wed.) is good for soups, sandwiches, and daily specials. Just down Rt. 112 is the **North River Winery** (see *To Do*). Follow Rt. 100 another 1.5 miles south and turn left onto Town Hill Rd. (marked for the **Brigham Young Monument**) into Whitingham. At the top of Town Hill a monument commemorates the Mormon prophet who led his people into Utah and is hailed as the founder of Salt Lake City. He was born on a hill farm here, the son of a poor basket maker. The view takes in surrounding hills; there are picnic benches, grills, a playground, and a parking area. Continue down the hill to the Whitingham General Store and turn right onto Stimpson Hill. Look on the right-hand side of the road near the top of this hill for a small marker that proclaims this to be the homestead site of Brigham Young: BORN ON THIS SPOT 1801 . . . A MAN OF MUCH COURAGE AND SUPERB EQUIPMENT. (BRIGHAM YOUNG FATHERED 56 CHILDREN BY 17 OF HIS 52 WIVES.) Before leaving the village, note the 25-acre "floating island" in the middle of Sadawga Pond. Whitingham was once a busy resort, thanks to a mineral spring and its accessibility via the Hoosac Tunnel and Wilmington Railroad. The old railroad bed is now a **12-mile walking trail** along this remote shore of Lake Whitingham. (Continue 1 mile south on Rt. 100 beyond the store, and take a right onto Dam Rd.; park and walk across the dam. Note the "Glory Hole," a large concrete overflow funnel that empties into the Deerfield River.)

Dover Hill Road, accessible from Rt. 100 via either Dorr Fitch Rd. in the village of West Dover or East Dover Rd. farther south (just below Sitzmark). The road climbs steeply past the tiny village center of Dover. Here you could detour onto Cooper Hill Rd. for a few miles to take in the panorama of mountains. On an ordinary day, you can pick out Mount Monadnock in New Hampshire beyond Keene. You can either loop back down to Rt. 100 via Valley View Rd., or continue down the other side of the hill through East Dover to the general store, covered bridge, and picturesque village center in South Newfane, following Augur Hole Rd. back to Rt. 9—or, if you're out for a real ride, continuing to Rt. 30, then south to Brattleboro and back to Wilmington on Rt. 9.

Handle Road runs south from Mount Snow, paralleling Rt. 100, turning into Cold Brook Rd. when it crosses the Wilmington line. The old farmhouses along this high, wooded road were bought up by city people to form a summer colony in the late 1880s. It's still a beautiful road, retaining some of the old houses and views.

Arlington–Kelley Stand Road heads west from West Wardsboro through the tiny village of Stratton. At 6.3 miles the Grout Pond turnoff is clearly marked and leads 1.3 miles to the pond. Hiking trails loop around the pond, through the woods, and continue to Somerset Reservoir. Beyond this turnoff is the monument to Daniel Webster, who spoke here to 1,600 people at an 1840 Whig rally. The hiking trail to Stratton Pond that begins just west of the monument is the most heavily hiked section of the Long Trail. It's possible (your vehicle and conditions permitting) to return to Rt. 9 through the Green Mountain Forest via the Arlington–Somerset Rd. (closed in winter). Roughly halfway down you pass the turnoff for Somerset Reservoir.

Also see the West Dummerston (Rt. 30) road through South Newfane to West Dover under *Getting There*.

✳ To Do

AIRPLANE RIDES Mount Snow Airport (802-464-2196), off Country Club Rd., West Dover, offers scenic air rides.

BIKING Mount Snow Sports adjacent to the Grand Summit Hotel at Mount

Snow (802-464-4040; 800-245-SNOW) offers mountain biking lessons, rentals, and repairs on its 45 miles of trails, with lifts servicing a portion in summer months. Inquire about lodging/biking packages, clinics, and guided tours.

Alpine Trader (802-464-7101; alpinetrader.com), 316 Rt. 100, West Dover. Call for opening hours in summer; open 8–6 in winter. Sales and rentals of Jamis mountain bikes.

Equipe Sport (802-464-2222; equipesport.com), on Mount Snow Access Rd. in West Dover, rents cross-country bikes and helmets.

BOATING Green Mountain Flagship Co. (802-464-2975; greenmountainflag ship.com), 389 Rt. 9 west from Wilmington. Richard Joyce offers seasonal excursions on the Harriman Reservoir (also known as Lake Whitingham) aboard the M/V *Mt. Mills*, a twin-stacked pontoon vessel accommodating 65. Joyce caters to bus groups, but there are usually at least half a dozen seats left over. His narration of the logging history of the area is often accompanied by live music. Canoes, sailboats, and kayaks can be rented, too.

High Country (802-464-2108; 800-627-7533; high-country-tours.com), 2 miles west of Wilmington Center on Rt. 9 and Lake Harriman, rents pontoon boats and Waverunners.

Zoar Outdoor (800-532-7483; zoaroutdoor.com), Charlemont, Massachusetts. The Deerfield River flows south into Massachusetts, where a regular dam releases power whitewater rafting that's exciting enough to satisfy most jocks but still doable for children. This long-established outfitter also rents kayaks and sit-on-top canoes for lower stretches of the river. Charlemont is about 40 minutes south of Wilmington via Rt. 8A.

Equipe Sport (802-464-2222; equipesport.com), on the Mount Snow Access Rd. in West Dover, rents canoes and kayaks.

BOWLING North Star Bowl and Mini Golf (802-464-5148), Rt. 100, Wilmington, open daily 11:30 AM–10 PM for candlepin bowling; also videos and pool tables, with ice cream and pizza parlor.

CHAIRLIFT Mount Snow (800-245-SNOW). The lift operates on weekends in summer and daily through peak foliage season.

DAY CAMPS ✂ Mount Snow Day Camps (802-464-3333), Mount Snow. Mini Camp (ages 6 weeks–12 months), Kids Camp (ages 5–8), and Sports Camp (ages 9–12) run during summer, Mon.–Fri. 9–4. Activities include swimming, chairlift rides, arts and crafts, nature hikes, field trips, and more.

FISHING The **Deerfield River** is known for rainbow and brook trout (the season runs from the second Saturday in April through October). The remote Harriman Bypass Reach, a 4.5-mile stretch of the river between the dam in Whitingham and Readsboro, is a good bet. Fly-anglers can readily find guides: Note **Taddingers/Orvis Fly Fishing School and Guiding Service** (802-464-6263; taddingers.com), Rt. 100 north, Wilmington, and **Hookenum Fishing Tours**, 2 W. Main St., Wilmington (802-368-2945). **Harriman Reservoir** is stocked with trout, bass, perch, and salmon; a boat launch is located off Fairview Ave.

Somerset Reservoir, 6.5 miles west of Wilmington then 10 miles north on Somerset Rd., offers bass, trout, and pike. There is a boat launch at the foot of the 9-mile-long lake. Smaller **Sadawga Pond** in Whitingham and **Lake Raponda** in Wilmington are also good for bass, trout, perch, salmon, pickerel, northern pike, and smelt; there is a boat launch on the former.

Fishing licenses are available in Wilmington at C&S Beverage & Dairy and Taddingers, and in Whitingham at the Whitingham General Store. One-, three-, seven-day, and season licenses are available.

GOLF Mount Snow Country Club (802-464-4254; thegolfschool.com), Country Club Rd., West Dover. Billing itself as "The Original Golf School," this program has been evolving since 1978. Weekend and two- to five-day midweek golf school packages are offered May–Sept.; the 18-hole, Cornish-designed championship golf course is also open on a daily basis.

Haystack (802-464-8301; haystackgolf.com), 17 Spyglass Drive, Wilmington. Eighteen holes designed by Desmond Muirhead with a clubhouse (full-service restaurant and bar) and full pro shop, lessons with PGC professionals, stay-and-play packages.

Sitzmark Golf & Tennis Club (802-464-3384), 54 E. Dover Rd., Wilmington; 18 holes, club and cart rentals. No tee times.

HIKING Along with the trails in **Molly Stark State Park** (see *Green Space*) and a short, self-guided trail atop Mount Snow, there are a number of overgrown roads leading to ghost towns. The Long Trail passes through the former logging town of Glastenbury (261 residents in 1880), and a former colonial highway in **Woodford State Park** (see "Bennington Area") leads to a burying ground and 18th-century homesites. Somerset is another ghost town. The **Hogback Mountain Overlook** on Rt. 9 is the starting point for a hike up the old ski area access road to the Mount Olga fire tower. Inquire at the Mount Snow Valley Chamber of Commerce about accessing the 12-mile trail along the undeveloped shore of **Lake Whitingham**. Also see Grout Pond Recreation Area under *Green Space*.

Forest Care Nature Walks (802-254-4717; heartwoodpress.com). Consulting forester Lynn Levine leads popular nature and animal tracking walks in summer and fall, discussing area ecology and wildlife. Reserve a week ahead.

HORSEBACK RIDING ✔ **Flames Stables** (802-464-8329), Rt. 100 south, Wilmington. Western saddle trail rides, half-hour horse-drawn wagon rides, pony rides for young children.

✔ **Brookside Stables** (802-464-0267; brooksidestables.com), Rt. 100 north of Wilmington. Pony rides for the kids.

SWIMMING There are several beaches on 11-mile-long Harriman Reservoir, also known as Whitingham Lake. **Mountain Mills Beach** is 1 mile from Wilmington Village, posted from Castle Hill Rd. **Ward's Cove Beach** is on Rt. 100 south of Wilmington—turn right at Flames Stables and follow signs. Inquire locally about less publicized places.

Sitzmark Lodge (802-464-3384), north of Wilmington on Rt. 100, has a pool that's open daily to the public 11–6 ($2 adults, $1 children). Snacks and a bar are available poolside.

TENNIS The two municipal courts at **Baker Field** off School St. in Wilmington are open to the public; also eight courts at Sitzmark (see above).

✳ Winter Sports

CROSS-COUNTRY SKIING **Timber Creek Cross Country Ski Area** (802-464-0999; timbercreekxc.com), West Dover. Just across Rt. 100 from the entrance to Mount Snow, a high-elevation, 14 km wooded system of mostly easy trails that hold their snow cover, access to backwoods trails; ski and snowshoe rentals, instruction available. Full- and half-day trail fees and special packages.

The Hermitage Inn (802-464-3511; hermitageinn.com), 25 Handle Rd., West Dover, offers some 45 km of cross-country trails including high elevation and ridgeline, also separate trails for snowshoeing and snowmobiles.

Prospect Mountain Nordic Ski Center (802-442-2575; prospect mountain.com), Rt. 9, Woodford. This former downhill ski area features 35 km of groomed trails with access to backcountry trails and special trails for snowshoeing and a comfortable base lodge with a fireplace, home-cooked food, and baked goods. Rentals. Because of its elevation, Prospect Mountain often has snow when other areas are bare.

DOWNHILL SKIING/SNOWBOARDING 🌤 **Mount Snow** (information 802-464-3333; snow report 802-464-2151; reservations 800-245-SNOW; mountsnow .com), West Dover. Peak Resorts, the mountain's current owner, has invested heavily in snowmaking and brought new energy to this 588-acre area, the Northeast's second largest ski destination (after Killington). Crowning the resort is the sprawling Grand Summit Hotel, 196 rooms plus shops and services. Farther down by a small lake is the more modest Snow Lake Lodge, popular with college students and young families for its inexpensive (though basic) rooms. But the vast majority of the area's 2,100 "on-mountain" beds are rentals and condos in the boxy residential communities spread out around the foot of the mountain. As for skiing, there are four distinct areas: the Main Mountain, the expert North Face, and the Sunbrook and Carinthia slopes (now a series of 12 terrain parks and pipes). Mount Snow's vertical drop is 1,700 feet. Base area facilities include three lodges, rental/repair shops, retail, and restaurants, plus the Ski and Snowboard School at the Discovery Center, an instruction area with a learning slope and special lifts where beginners can get their feet wet. See the chapter introduction for the resort's history.

Lifts: 20 chairlifts—3 high-speed and 1 fixed quad, 7 triples, 4 doubles. There is also 1 surface lift and 4 Magic Carpets.

Ski/snowboard trails: 102, including 33 "easier," 65 "more difficult," 25 "advanced," and 2 "double black diamonds." You'll also find 100 acres of hand-cleared "Tree Terrain."

Snowmaking: 80 percent of the mountain.

Facilities: 4 base lodges, an upper lodge near the summit, the Snow Barn (night-club with entertainment, dancing), and the Grand Summit Resort spa.

Ski school: Over 200 instructors and dozens of clinics.

For children: Ski and Snowboard School: Cub Camp (3-year-olds), Snow Camp (4- to 6-year-olds), and Mountain Camp and Mountain Riders (7- to 14-year-olds).

Rates: Midweek adults $69 (weekends $75), young adults (ages 13–18) $56 (weekends $64), juniors (6–12) and seniors (ages 65 and over) $45 (weekends $52). Kids 5 and under ski free. See **mountsnow.com** for a full schedule of events.

SLEIGH RIDES Sleigh rides are offered at **Adams Farm** (802-464-3762), Wilmington, with a refreshment stop at a cabin in the woods. They are also offered at **Flames Stables** (802-464-8329) on Rt. 100, south of Wilmington.

SNOWMOBILING High Country Snowmobile Tours (802-464-2108; 800-627-SLED) in Wilmington and **Twin Brooks Snowmobile Tours** (802-442-4054; 888-616-4054) in Woodford, both on Rt. 9 west, offer rentals and guided tours. **Sitzmark** (802-464-3384), Rt. 100 north of Wilmington, registers and garages sleds for use on the VAST trails.

✳ Green Space

Molly Stark State Park (802-464-5460), Rt. 9 east of Wilmington Village. This 158-acre preserve features a hiking trail through the forest to the Mount Olga fire tower, at 2,415 feet, from which there is a panoramic view. The 34 campsites include 11 lean-tos. Open May 26–Oct. 15. See *Campgrounds* in "What's Where" for state park fees and reservations.

Grout Pond Recreation Area (802-362-2307), west of West Wardsboro, off the Arlington (aka Kelley Stand) Rd. A 1,600-acre piece of the Green Mountain National Forest designated for hiking, picnicking, fishing, boating, and camping. In summer a ranger resides at the Grout Pond Cabin, and campsites are available on a first-come, first-served basis (6 vehicle sites, 11 walk-in campsites, and 4 sites accessible by canoe). Twelve miles of trails, which circle the pond and connect with Somerset Reservoir, are open in winter for skiing (they are not groomed). At the north end of the pond there are five picnic sites.

Lake Raponda. This hidden treasure, a town-owned 200-acre pond, is accessed by Stowe Hill Rd. from Rt. 100, and via Lake Raponda Rd. from Rt. 9 west of Molly Stark State Park. Good for fishing and paddle boats.

FARMS, ORCHARDS, AND VINEYARDS TO VISIT 🐾 **Adams Farm** (802-464-3762; adamsfamilyfarm.com), 15 Higley Hill Rd., off Rt. 100, Wilmington. Check the Web site for hours and frequent special events. Admission. A sixth-generation, exceptionally visitor-friendly farm. The livestock barn holds a variety of animals to pet and feed, including kittens, calves, horses, goats, sheep, donkeys, llamas, alpacas, chickens, pigs, and rabbits. Visitors can ride a wagon around the farm in summer. In winter there are sleigh rides to a cabin for hot chocolate. The **Farm Store** and **Quilt & Fiber Arts Loft** feature homespun yarns and locally crafted gifts.

Boyd Family Farm (802-464-5618; boydfamilyfarm.com), 125 E. Dover Rd., Wilmington. A fifth-generation working hillside farm, with pick-your-own flowers, raspberries, and blueberries June–Sept., then pumpkins, gourds, and Christmas wreaths.

Wheeler Farm (802-464-5225), marked from Rt. 100 north of Wilmington Village. A third-generation working farm with Jersey and Dutch belted cows, part of the cooperative that produces Cabot Cheese. Maple syrup is produced and sold, along with maple cream and sugar.

& **North River Winery** (802-368-7557; northriverwinery.com) 201 Rt. 112. Open daily year-round, 10–5. In 1985 this was the state's first bonded winery, turning locally grown fruit into 11 different wines, ranging from very dry to very sweet and including a 100 percent organic rhubarb wine. There are tours of the winery, and tastings are free. The winery maintains tasting rooms at several locations, including the Hogback Mountain Gift Shop on Rt. 9 east of Wilmington. See *To See* for directions.

∞ **Honora Winery & Vineyard** (802-368-2930; honorawinery.com), West Halifax. Check the Web site for directions to the vineyard on a 200-acre property with a nicely designed events center with a four-sided stone fireplace and two hand-crafted bars, accommodating 200 guests. At this writing the venue has been used for weddings but isn't yet open for tours. This and a rebabbed barn on Rt. 9 in Wilmington are due to open for tastings in 2009. Honora (grape) wines are made from cold-weather varietals. Check the Web site for current details.

Farmer's markets are Sat., 10–3 (Memorial Day weekend–late Oct.), 17 W. Main St., Wilmington.

✳ Lodging

This area offers a choice of mountainside inns, condominiums, and ski lodges. The **Mount Snow Valley Chamber of Commerce** keeps track of vacancies and refers callers; it also maintains a Web site with direct links to lodging places, and you can reserve online (877-887-6884; visitvermont .com). **Mount Snow Vermont Rentals** (800-451-6876; mountsnow vermontrentals.com) offers one- to four-bedroom condos to rent for short- or long-term stays. Our listings focus on the inns and B&Bs.

RESORT ✐ **The Grand Summit Resort Hotel at Mount Snow** (802-464-6600; 800-498-0479; mountsnow .com/summer/grandsummit.html), 1 Grand Summit Way, West Dover 05356. At the base of the ski lifts, this 196-room, ski-in, ski-out condo hotel and conference center, built in 1998 to look something like an Austrian chalet, features one- to three-bedroom suites (many with kitchen) as well as the usual hotel rooms. Amenities include a year-round heated outdoor pool and hot tubs, child care and arcade, spa and fitness center, and, of course, ski lifts. In summer there are golf and mountain biking programs and schools. Moderately priced **Harriman's Restaurant** is open for breakfast and dinner; the **Grand Country Deli & Convenience Store** offers take-out. Rates vary seasonally as well as for midweek and weekend stays: Rooms can be anything from a basic two-person studio to a two-bedroom deluxe suite. The ritziest option is the three-bedroom, three-bath penthouse on the top floor. This two-level, 2,000-square-foot suite sleeps 12 and has a full kitchen, a fireplace, and a bird's-eye view of the mountain ($337 in low season, $1,237 in high). The standard rooms and the one-bedroom suites (consisting of a bedroom, bath, living room, and galley kitchen) range $179–520, including continental breakfast.

SOUTHERN VERMONT

In Wilmington/West Dover

⚇ 🐾 ♿ "⊤" **The Inn at Sawmill Farm** (802-464-8131; 800-493-1133; theinnatsawmillfarm.com), on Crosstown Rd. just off Rt. 100, West Dover 05356. Closed early Apr.–mid-May. This world-class inn was the creation of Rod Williams, an Atlantic City architect, and his wife, Ione, an interior designer, who discovered the old farm during a ski vacation and bought it on a whim. Over 40 years they have turned it into a vision of country luxury: rough wooden beams over plush furniture, Oriental carpets and old brick, fresh bouquets and antique portraits. The side of a barn and hayloft form a wall of the library. Management has now passed to the Williams's children. Brill, their son, has won awards for his superlative cuisine (see *Dining Out*). Each of the 20 guest rooms (including 3 cottages) is different, all with phones, most with king-sized bed, some with jetted tubs, each individually decorated with an eye to comfort and detail. With the exception of those in the main house, all have TV and most have wood-burning fireplace; several cottages overlook the trout-stocked ponds. There's a resident blue heron and lawns that slope to the edge of a pine forest. You'll also find a tennis court, a heated pool, a workout room, and wide floorboards that creak underfoot. The multicourse breakfasts include fresh-squeezed juices, white truffle butter, and attentive, black-tie service. $475–750 per room MAP; there's a $50-per-night charge for pets.

⚇ "⊤" **The Hermitage Inn** (802-464-3511; 877-464-3511; hermitageinn .com), 25 Handle Rd., West Dover 05356. *Seclusion* is the operative word in this inn, built in the 1840s as a farmhouse and for some years the summer home of an editor of the Social Regis-

ter. An inn since the 1960s, it's recently been entirely revamped by new owners Jim and Donna Barnes, who have installed a solar-powered photovoltaic system for their electrical needs and used environmentally sensitive materials throughout, reopening late in 2008. Rooms are all fitted with gas fireplace, flat-screen TV, phone, coffeemaker, and fridge, furnished with antiques and reproductions. At this writing there are just 11 guest rooms in the main house and Wine Wing, but a total of 50 plus a spa are planned. There's a game room, fitness room, and massage rooms; outdoors you'll find a hot tub, stocked trout pond, and three separate networks of trails on the inn's 100 acres, groomed for cross-country skiing, snowshoeing, and snowmobiling (machines are available for guests). The classy, spacious dining room is open to the public by reservation for all three meals (see *Dining Out*). Rates vary seasonally, $195–395 plus 18 percent service.

⚇ ♿ "⊤" **The White House of Wilmington** (802-464-2135; 800-541-2135; whitehouseinn.com), 178 Rt. 9 east, Wilmington 05363. Built in 1915 on a knoll overlooking Rt. 9 as a summer residence for Martin Brown, founder of Brown Paper Company, the interior of this gorgeous Colonial Revival mansion lives up to its elegant facade. Common rooms are huge, light, and atmospheric, but also stay warm in winter—with the help of 14 yawning hearths. At the front is an inviting sunken bar overlooking the valley (recently dubbed Baxter's Tavern). Otherwise the decor is Old World, including genuine French wallpaper (the detail that hooked current innkeeper Stan Smith). There are hand-carved mahogany mantelpieces and marble-topped antiques in a total of 16 rooms, 9 with fireplace, some with two-person whirlpool tub, terrace,

Christina Tree

THE WHITE HOUSE INN OF WILMINGTON

or balcony. A 60-foot outdoor pool lies next to a formal garden; a small, cozy indoor pool on the lower level has a sauna and steambath. There are views from every window. Breakfast and Sunday brunch are served in the parlor (ask to see the secret staircase); dinner (see *Dining Out*) is served in a romantic candlelit dining room by a roaring fire. From $148–208 per room in low season to $160–255 in high.

⊕ ♿ **Deerhill Inn** (802-464-3100; 800-993-3379; deerhill.com), 14 Valley View Rd., P.O. Box 136, West Dover 05356. Chef-owner Michael Allen has won raves for his dining room (guests only) as well as for his 14 luxurious rooms and suites, some in the old farmhouse, others in a newer wing. Eight have a fireplace, seven have whirlpool tub and French doors opening onto a deck with mountain views. One comfortable sitting room adjoins the tiny bar and two spacious dining rooms, walled with the work of local artists; upstairs is another lounge for guests, plus a library nook. In summer, flowers abound inside and out and around the patio of the swimming pool. $126–355, including a full-service breakfast; add $82–89 for MAP.

⁰₁⁰ **Nutmeg Inn** (802-464-7400; 800-277-5402; nutmeginn.com), P.O. Box

1899, Wilmington 05363. This delightful 1777 roadside farmhouse on Rt. 9 west is a restaurant and bakery as well as a B&B. Situated on the western edge of Wilmington, it offers 14 guest rooms, 6 with fireplace. There are four suites, all with hourglass-shaped two-person whirlpool and wood-burning fireplace. All rooms have central air-conditioning and private bath; they're decorated with quilts, botanical prints, and braided rugs. There is a cozy antiques-filled living room, library, and BYOB bar, plus three intimate dining rooms for breakfasts that might include caramelized pear stuffed French toast topped with a caramel pear syrup and bacon sausage. Fresh pastries are legion. The **Steak House Grill** here is open on a seasonal basis, also available for groups of six or more. Summer $109–159 for rooms, $189–215 double for suites; winter $89–149 for rooms, $179–234 for suites.

🐾 ♫ **The Red Shutter Inn** (802-464-3768; 800-845-7548; redshutterinn .com), Rt. 9, P.O. Box 636, Wilmington 05363. Amie and Hannah Waller preside over this big, gracious 1894 house on the edge of the village within walking distance of shops and restaurants. The nine nicely furnished guest rooms include two suites with fireplace. The dining room, furnished with an assortment of old oak tables and antique tools, has a good reputation and is open to the public. In winter from $125 for a cozy room in the carriage house to $295 during holidays for the spacious two-room Courtemanche Suite in the main house; country breakfast included. In summer the range is $110–195.

Doveberry Inn (802-464-5652; 800-722-3204; doveberryinn.com), Rt. 100, P.O. Box 1736, West Dover 05356. A spacious, well-built lodge on Rt. 100 near the Mount Snow access. There's a comfortable, large living room with fireplace and wine bar. The 11 rooms have private bath and cable TV; newer rooms offer fireplace, whirlpool tub, and balcony, some with A/C in summer. Request a back room overlooking the woods. Innkeepers Michael and Christine Fayette are culinary school graduates and prepare all the northern Italian cuisine (see *Dining Out*). $115–215 in winter, $79–175 in summer. MAP is available on request.

West Dover Inn (802-464-5207; westdoverinn.com), P.O. Box 1208, 108 Rt. 100, West Dover 05356. Built in 1846 as the village inn and now on the National Register of Historic Places, Phil and Kathy Gilpin's handsome inn includes modern amenities and country-style appointments in each of its 12 guest rooms, some fireplace suites with jetted tubs. All rooms have doubles or queen beds, private bath, and cable TV. Guests enjoy a homey common room with a fireplace, as well as a cocktail lounge and casual restaurant (see *Dining Out*). B&B rates: $125–195 per room in summer and late fall; $158–285 in foliage and ski season. Some minimum stays required

THE WEST DOVER INN IN WILMINGTON
Joe Citro

during holidays. Children welcome (pets not).

Trail's End & Wellness Spa (802-464-2055; 866-629-9634; trailsendvt.com), 5 Trail's End Lane, Wilmington 05363, off East Dover Rd. Unusual spaces in this '50s ski lodge include a library and game room, a large living room with a two-story, fieldstone fireplace, and a dining space. The 14 rooms all have private bath, TV and include a large family suite; several have a wood-burning fireplace. Lois Smith and her family specialize in spa packages with "detoxification" and restorative massages, Reiki, and more. Yoga classes and day-spa treatments are also offered. A two-night spa package ($249–419; $299–469 weekends) includes breakfasts and dinner; week-long packages run $749–1,520.

🐾 🐕 **Whetstone Inn** (802-254-2500; whetstoneinn.com), 550 South Rd., Marlboro 05344. Handy to the Marlboro Music Festival, this is a 1786 tavern with a Palladian window, part of the cluster of white-clapboard buildings—including the church and post office—that form the village core. Innkeepers Jean and Harry Boardman have been here 30 years, and there's a casually comfortable feel to the place. Most guests have been here before and have their own favorite rooms, of which there are 11, 7 with private bath and 2 with kitchen. Singles with private bath run $50–80; doubles, $80–125. Breakfast, served daily, is $10 extra, as is dinner, which is served on Saturdays and selected weekdays. There's swimming in a spring-fed pond.

BED & BREAKFAST ⊗ 🐾 ♪ "1"
Cooper Hill Inn (802-348-6333; 800-783-3229; cooperhillinn.com), P.O. Box 146, 117 Cooper Hill Rd., East Dorset 05341. High on a hilltop on a quiet

country road with one of the most spectacular mountain panoramas in New England, this spacious white farmhouse has 10 bright, tastefully decorated guest rooms, all with private bath. At the heart of the house, dating from 1797, is a gracious living room with a fireplace and piano. Lee and Charles Wheeler have reserved one wing of the house for families, creating kid-friendly suites, and the other for romantic getaways, featuring rooms with fireplace, king beds, Jacuzzi, and balcony. There's a large dining room, game room, deck, and covered porch as well as spacious grounds, with fields for softball, tag, and long walks. Lee has also created formal flower gardens and a landscaped hollow for weddings. The house can hold 24 and is frequently rented in its entirety. You can watch the sun rise on one side of the house and see it set on the other. The Wheelers lived 12 years in Singapore, which explains the Asian antiques throughout. $110–210 per room, depending on the season, includes breakfast.

🐾 ✂ ⁰ᵀ⁰ **Austin Hill Inn** (802-464-5281; 800-332-7352; austinhillinn .com), Box 859, Rt. 100, West Dover 05356. Up a short dirt drive from Rt. 100, hosts John and Debbie Bailey offer 11 rooms in this contemporary home, each with private bath, some with balcony, fireplace, and hand stenciling. Six have fireplace, and three are large enough to accommodate more than two. Their specialties are fall and winter Murder Mystery Weekends including a welcome reception, four-course Saturday-evening dinner meal, a mystery character packet, and drama: $475 for two. Regular B&B rates are $125–165 in low season, $135–195 in high. $25 fee for pets.

🍴 🐾 ✂ ♿ **Gray Ghost Inn** (802-464-2474; 800-745-3615; grayghostinn .com), 290 Rt. 100 north, West Dover

Christina Tree

THE VIEW FROM THE COOPER HILL INN

05356. Closed Apr. Swedish-born Carina and Magnus Thorsson are avid bikers, and this family-friendly '50s-era ski lodge is geared in warm-weather months to motorcyclists. It's also minutes from Mount Snow. There's a large basement game room, hot tub, play area, and outdoor pool. Dogs are welcome in summer and fall (there are two in residence). Each of the 26 rooms has private bath; one is a three-room suite. The third floor has rustic pine interiors and terrific views. From $88 in summer and $154 in winter, including breakfast.

The Paw House Inn (802-464-8303; 866-729-4687; pawhouse.com), 145 Rt. 100, West Dover 05456. Formerly the Four Seasons Inn, this village dog owners' oasis offer 12 comfortable rooms with private bath in which dogs are welcome (but not alone); dog amenities include a temperature-appropriate Playhouse with Animal Planet on TV. Staff also provide "dog services" (staff will walk and feed), and there's a separate dog run for each canine guest. Guests are asked to bring their own doggy beds and prior to coming to complete a "dog profile form." Pampering services also include a full menu of body treatments and massage for dog owners. Rates are based on double human occupancy plus two dogs and breakfast. $145–245; more at peak times.

🐾 **Shearer Hill Farm** (802-464-3253; 800-437-3104; shearerhillfarm.com), 297 Shearer Hill Rd., P.O. Box 1453, Wilmington 05363. Off Rt. 9, 2 miles southeast of Wilmington, turn right onto Shearer Hill Road, bearing left at the fork to Bill and Patti Pusey's restored 200-year-old farmhouse. Three rooms in the main house have private bath; there is an annex with a ground-floor room and kitchenette, plus two bedrooms and a sitting room upstairs, all with private bath. The pleasant large living room in the farmhouse has a VCR library. $105–120 double, $80 single with full breakfast buffet. Cross-country skiing on the grounds, and maple sugaring in spring.

♿ **The Candlelight Bed & Breakfast** (802-368-2004; 866-429-1702; candlelightbandb.com), 3358 Rt. 100, Jacksonville 05342. Fran and Peter Madden run this attractive three-room B&B set above a rural stretch of Rt. 100; two guest rooms feature fireplace. $110–125 per couple includes breakfast. Two-night minimum on weekends.

CONDOS AND LODGES Mount Snow Condominiums (802-464-7768; 800-451-4211; mountsnow.com/lodging .html). A general reservation service that includes condos at the base of the mountain from studios to three-bedroom units with full kitchens and access to pools, saunas, and fitness rooms.

Mountain Resort Rentals (802-464-1445; 888-336-1445, mountainresort rentals.com). Rentals ranging from the humble to the sublime for short- or long-term stays. Open daily, year-round.

CAMPGROUNDS See Molly Stark State Park and Grout Pond Recreation Area in *Green Space*.

OTHER The Amos Brown House, the oldest house in the back-road town of Whitingham, has been meticulously restored by the nonprofit Landmark Trust USA. The brick Cape-style farmhouse, built around 1800 with connected barn and sheds, is set in 30 acres of meadow on a quiet dirt road and features a pantry and modern amenities as well as an old wooden four-holer privy in the adjacent barn. For details about renting the house, contact Landmark at 802-254-6868 (landmarktrust usa.org).

✳ Where to Eat

DINING OUT The Inn at Sawmill Farm (802-464-8131), Rt. 100, West Dover. Open for dinner only, 6–9:30. Chef-owner Brill Williams regularly earns top awards for his cuisine. The main dining room is the interior of a former barn, with lush chintz and 18th-century oil portraits. The linen-covered tables are set with sterling and fresh flowers; there is also a smaller, sun- and plant-filled dining room. The 34,000-bottle wine cellar has earned the Grand Award from *Wine Spectator*. On a summer evening you might begin with Maine crabmeat salad with avocado mousse ($15) and dine on sliced duck breast with homemade spaetzle and bordelaise sauce ($38). Desserts are irresistible. Casual business attire required (no jeans). À la carte entrées $35–46.

The Hermitage Inn (802-464-3511; hermitageinn.com), 21 Handle Rd., Wilmington. Open daily for lunch 11:30–3, dinner from 5, and Sunday brunch 11–3. Reserve. Recently reopened after a total renovation, the casually elegant, many-windowed inn dining rooms are more attractive than ever, still hung with distinctive artwork. Chef James Bennett comes most recently from the Spruce Point Inn in Boothbay Harbor. At dinner you might begin with Vermont goat cheese and artichoke heart fritters ($8), followed by choices ranging from fish-and-chips to Cavendish Farm–raised pheasant with spiced apple cider, apple brandy, and sweet potato gnocchi. Entrées $14–38. Lighter fare is also served in the smaller dining room and in the pub.

Ravello (802-464-8437; ravellovt .com), 840 Rt. 100 north of Wilmington. Open 5:30 till closing, Fri.–Mon., but call; hours vary with the season. The former Le Petit Chef is now a fine Italian trattoria in four rooms of this 250 year old white clapboard farmhouse. Chef-owners Douglas and Carolyn Sanzone offer a palette of Italian classics, making their pastas, breads, sorbets, and gelati from scratch. The signature dishes are osso buco and the constantly changing pastas, which you can order in half portions or whole. There are multiple coffees and desserts (like warm chocolate soup with whipped cream), and a three-page list of Italian wines, many available by the glass. Entrées $18–33. Reservations suggested.

Doveberry Inn (802-464-5652), Rt. 100, West Dover. Closed Tue. This elegant inn is chef owned, and the accent is authentic northern Italian. The à la carte menu might include stuffed zucchini blossoms with red pepper drizzle, and rack of venison with Chianti demiglaze. Extensive wine list. Entrées $25–40.

West Dover Inn (802-464-7264), Rt. 100, West Dover. The dining room at the West Dover Inn is low-lit and romantic with a fireplace and seasonally changing menu that usually includes crabcakes and jumbo shrimp cocktail among starters, plus the popular applewood-smoked pork tenderloin and handmade ravioli. Entrées $26–32; both crabcakes and ravioli are also on the more economical Tavern menu. Jazz piano on Sundays.

Two Tannery Road (802-464-2707), 2 Tannery Rd., Rt. 100, West Dover. Open Tue.–Sun. The building itself is said to date in part from the late 1700s, when it stood in Marlboro, Massachusetts, and has moved several times within this valley, serving for a while as a summer home for Theodore Roosevelt's son. The bar began service in the original Waldorf-Astoria (present site of the Empire State Building). The food is highly rated, with a large à la carte menu that might include Tannery country pâté, pecan-stuffed shrimp, or the Nutty Vermonter, a ham-and-cheese-stuffed chicken breast with an almond crust. Entrées $28–35. Nightly specials.

The White House of Wilmington (802-464-2135), Rt. 9 east, Wilmington. Open for lunch, dinner, and Sunday brunch. Hours vary with the season. The elegant wood-paneled dining room is warmed by a glowing hearth in this mansion atop a hill, and the gourmet menu is extensive and skillfully prepared. You might find pan-seared Parmesan-encrusted sea scallops on the menu, along with filet mignon or semi-boneless roasted Vermont duckling with mandarin orange and wild blueberry melba. Entrées $27–33. Solo diners may want to cozy up to the wide, three-sided sunken bar, now known as Baxter's Tavern. The view is down the valley, and the menu ranges from chili with cheddar to macaroni and cheese with lobster ($8–14). There's also a great, reasonably priced Sunday brunch, with a children's menu.

Breakfast and lunch

🐾 🍴 **Dot's Restaurant** (802-464-7284; 802-464-6476), Wilmington, is open 5:30 AM–8 PM, until 9 PM Fri. and Sat. This cheerful, pine-sided diner is a local institution and the most popular breakfast place in town. There's a long Formica counter as well as tables, a fireplace in back, and wine by the glass. Stop by for a bowl of Jailhouse Chili, the hottest in New England. The soup and muffins are homemade, and the Reubens are first-rate.

🍴 ⁙ᵀ⁙ **Dots of Dover** (802-464-6476; dotsofdover.com), 3 Mountain Park Plaza, Rt. 100, West Dover. Open 5:30–3, also dinner on winter weekends. A spacious offshoot of the Wilmington Village landmark (see above) with WiFi and a flat-screen TV (a gift from a patron). Berry-berry pancakes at breakfast and flame-grilled burgers at lunch are big sellers, but there are plenty of choices. Soups are from scratch; grilled meat loaf, salads, and much more. This is a great place for kids, who have a special menu.

Jezebel's Eatery (802-464-7774), 26 W. Main St., Wilmington Village. Lunch specials include paninis, soups, and salads, with fresh-baked desserts a specialty; also dinner Friday and Saturday.

Mildred's Fine Foods Deli (802-464-1224), Rt. 9, Wilmington Village. Open 11–5. A source of standout deli sandwiches and wraps; eat in or take on a picnic.

Bean Heads Cafe (802-464-1208), Main and River streets, Wilmington. Espresso, cappuccino, bagelry, soup, and sandwiches. Open daily 6–4.

Dinner

🐾 **Maple Leaf** (802-464-9900), 3 N. Main St., Wilmington. Open daily noon–closing. No longer a brewpub since since changing hands in 2008, this place is better than ever, offering a wide choice of crafted microbrews and a large, reasonably priced all-day pub menu with the likes of ribs, pesto chicken, beer-battered fish, and specials. We felt lucky to land a seat.

The Vermont House (802-464-9360; thevermonthouse.com), 15 W. Main St., Wilmington. Brenda and Charley Waldron, who also own the bakery (802-464-9600) down the street, offer a menu varied both in price and quantity, from breaded artichoke hearts with garlic butter sauce to steaks, meat loaf, burgers, and Yankee pot roast. This is where the locals go. There is a bar in the next room and 10 tastefully decorated rooms upstairs in this 1850 stagecoach stop.

Anchor Seafood House & Grille (802-464-2112; anchorseafood.com), 8 S. Main St., Wilmington. Daily lunch and dinner, Sunday brunch. An intimate, upscale spot with a marble and oak bar. Daily specials like Parmesanbaked tilapia, fresh Maine lobsters, and horseradish-encrusted salmon. Lunch $6–15, dinner $14–20.

Jerry's at Old Red Mill (877-733-6455; oldredmill.com), Rt. 100 north on the edge of Wilmington. Check hours, varying with the season. Jerry Osler has owned this converted 1828 sawmill for more than 35 years. The large, rustic restaurant and tavern features fascinating antique fixtures dating to the mill's early days and offers plenty of atmosphere. We especially recommend the riverside deck in summer but like the choice of menus (regular) and "deck" year-round.

TC's Family Restaurant (802-464-5900), 178 Rt. 100, West Dover (2 miles south of Mount Snow). Open for dinner nightly, lunch on weekends. Owned by Olympic gold medalist Kelly Clark's family, a casual, affordable place for burgers, pizza and pastas, steaks, nightly specials. Outdoor riverside dining in summer.

✳ Entertainment

Note: Be sure to check out the **Marlboro Music Festival** under *Entertainment* in the Brattleboro chapter.

Memorial Hall Center for the Arts (802-464-8411; memhall.org), lodged in the McKim, Mead & White–designed theater next door to the historic Crafts Inn, Wilmington. This nonprofit center hosts community theater productions as well as films, a range of live musical performances, and community events.

Mountain Park Cinema (802-464-6447), Mountain Park Plaza, Rt. 100, about 5 miles north of Wilmington in West Dover, has three movie theaters for first-run films; matinees on rainy weekends.

✳ Selective Shopping

ANTIQUES Wilmington Antique & Flea Market (802-464-3345), junction of Rts. 9 and 100. Open May–Oct., Sat. and Sun. Bills itself as southern Vermont's largest outdoor flea market.

ARTISANS AND CRAFTS Quaigh Designs (802-464-2780), Main St., Wilmington. Open daily late June–late Oct.; Fri.–Sun. late May–late June and Nov.–Dec. This is a long-established showcase for top Vermont crafts; imported Scottish woolens are also a specialty. Lilias MacBean Hart, the owner, has produced a Vermont tartan. There's also many woodcuts by Vermont artist Mary Azarian. The art gallery is on the second floor.

The Vermont Bowl Company (802-464-8175; vermontbowl.com), 103 W. Main St., Rt. 9, Wilmington. Adjacent to the John McLeod Ltd. Store and

factory. A Scottish engineer, McLeod fell in love with the state and decided to settle here and make a living from woodturning. Hardwood bowls, clocks, mirrors, cutting boards, and furniture on the western edge of the village; open daily.

Young & Constantin Gallery (802-464-2515; ycgallery.com), 10 S. Main St., Wilmington. Chinese antique furniture, fine art, and a superb collection of art glass in what used to be the town's Unitarian church, with its stained-glass windows compounding the shimmering effect. Open daily 10–5.

Gallery Wright Sticks & Stones Studio (802-464-9922; gallerywright .com), 7 N. Main St., Wilmington. In summer open daily 11–6; in winter Tue. and Wed. or by appointment. The area's finest selection of fine art, including landscapes, figures, and still lifes in oil, pastels, and prints. The artisan jewelry of gallery director Mary Therese Wright is also featured.

Stone Soldier Pottery (802-368-7077; stonesoldier.com), Jacksonville Village. Connie Burnell is the second generation of her family to handcraft functional stoneware pottery in this classic pottery shed/showroom. Connie's work differs somewhat from that of her father, the late Robert Burnell,

AT STONE SOLDIER POTTERY IN JACKSONVILLE

Christina Tree

who created the iconic stone soldier that still resides in the shop—which is large, displaying dinnerware, mugs, vases, bakeware, and more, most pieces hand decorated and all hand glazed, some deeply colored. Check the Web site.

Applewoods (802-254-2908), 8 miles east of Wilmington on Rt. 9, in Marlboro. Open in summer Thu.–Mon. 10–4, or by appointment. David and Michelle Holzapfel create amazing tables, benches, and vessels from burls and other wood forms.

Ann Coleman Gallery (802-368-7090; artistanncoleman.com), 22 W. Main St. (second floor), Wilmington. Open daily 9–5. Vermont landscapes and images.

BOOKSTORES Bartleby's Books and Music (802-464-5425; bartlebysvt .com), N. Main St., Wilmington, an independent bookstore offering new books (mostly paperbacks), greeting cards, cassettes, art supplies, stationery, games, and music.

Austin's Antiquarian Books (802-464-8438; 800-556-3727; austinsbooks .com), 123 W. Main St. on Rt. 9, 0.5 mile west of downtown Wilmington. Open daily 10–6. Maps, prints, and 15,000 used, rare, and out-of-print books, many with leather bindings.

R&S Kurland Fine Books (802-464-9670), 59 Davis Dr., Wilmington. Mid-May–mid-Oct, usually noon–7. Please phone. Used and antiquarian books. First editions, New Englandiana, Americana, Civil War. Call before coming.

SPECIAL SHOPS Taddingers (802-464-6263; 800-528-3961; taddingers .com), Rt. 100, Wilmington. Seven specialty shops under one roof: antiques and fine prints, exclusive decorative accessories, Christmas Room, Nature Room, Vermont Country Food Store, and an Orvis dealership, with gear for fly-fishing, fly-tying, and shooting, plus sponsorship of one- and two-day fly-fishing schools.

Manyu's Boutique (802-464-8880), 4 N. Main St., Wilmington, has casual, contemporary clothes and accessories for women. Open daily 10–6, Sun. 10–5.

Down in the Valley (802-464-2211), 7 W. Main St., Wilmington. A long-established, genuinely discount ski- and sportswear shop, featuring fleece outerwear.

Hundredth Monkey (802-464-4640), Rt. 9 W., 17 W. Main St., Wilmington. A holistic health food store offering vitamins, supplements, homeopathic remedies, organic foods, an array of books, organic bulk herbs and spices, and fair-trade food, clothing, and gifts. Upstairs there are yoga classes, holistic workshops, plus reflexology, massage therapy, and nutritional coaching.

1836 Country Store Village (802-464-5102), W. Main St., Wilmington, has an eclectic stock of decorative brasses, pierced-tin lanterns, toys and games, Vermont specialty foods, and the usual souvenirs. Note the amazing old floors.

Norton House (802-464-7213; norquilt.com), adjacent to the 1836 Country Store at 30 W. Main St., Wilmington, was pulled here by oxen in the 1830s and dates from 1760, making it Wilmington's oldest structure. A quilter's paradise with over 3,000 fabrics and every quilting accessory. Note the yawning brick hearth and the historical objects upstairs in the windowed closet.

Pickwell's Barn (802-464-3198; pick wellsbarn.com), 22 W. Main St., Wilmington, has pottery, clocks, prints, colorful glassware, Vermont wines, and specialty foods.

SweDenNor Ltd. (802-464-2788), Rt. 100, West Dover. Established in 1972, this store features a wide selection of country and casual furniture; also lamps, paintings, and gifts.

✳ Special Events

Late January: **Harriman Ice Fishing Derby** on Lake Whitingham (802-368-2773).

Easter weekend: Nondenominational **sunrise service** on Mount Snow's summit with continental breakfast. Eggs hidden all over the mountain, good for prizes.

Memorial Day: **The Great Duck Race**—over 1,500 rubber ducks are released at noon at Wilmington's bridge. BBQ, games, prizes, duck quacking contest.

July 4 weekend: A very big celebration in these parts with fireworks, parades, et cetera.

Late July through mid-August: **Marlboro Music Festival** (802-254-2394; see the Brattleboro chapter).

July 4 weekend through August: **Saturday Village Walking Tours** are offered by the Historical Society of Wilmington beginning at 12:30 at the Mount Snow Chamber of Commerce office (see *Guidance*). They end at the Historical Society (5 Lilse Hill; 802-464-3004; wilmingtonvermont.us), open 1–3 those Saturdays or by appointment.

August: **Southern Vermont Blueberry Festival**, a happening throughout the valley (visitvermont.com).

September: **Taste of the Deerfield Valley** under the tent at Mount Snow (celebratethevalley.com). *Last weekend:* **Vermont Life Wine and Harvest Festival** (thevermontfestival .com).

October: **Octoberfest and Craft Fair** (mountsnow.com).

December: **Walk of the Santas** (celebratethevalley.com).

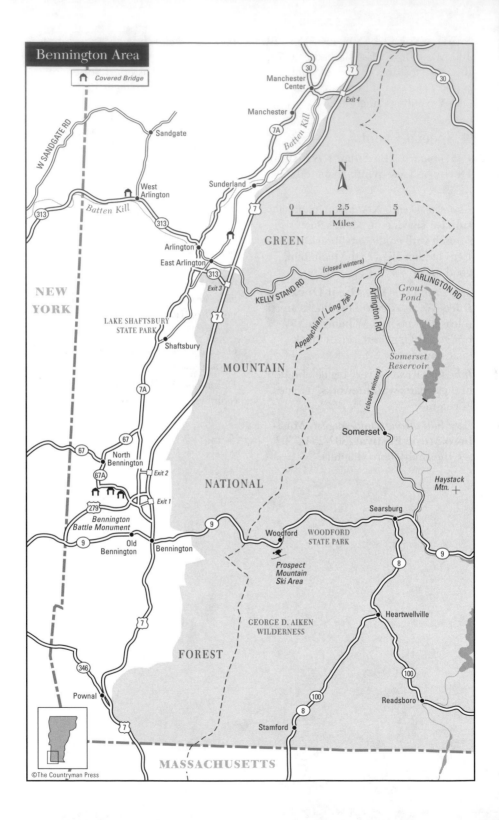

Bennington Area

Covered Bridge

NEW YORK

MASSACHUSETTS

©The Countryman Press

BENNINGTON AND SOUTH SHIRE

Bennington is the name both of Vermont's southwesternmost town, and of its southwesternmost county. It's the only county divided into North and South "shires," each with a venerable courthouse, one in Manchester and one in the town of Bennington. The name honors Benning Wentworth, the avaricious governor of the New Hampshire Grants. The town, settled in 1749, was the first he designated west of the Connecticut River. In 1770 Bennington became a hotbed of sedition when the "Bennington Mob"—also known as the Green Mountain Boys—formed at Fay's Catamount Tavern, choosing Seth Warner and Ethan Allen as their leaders and vowing to expel the "Yorkers" (who claimed the territory) and, later, the British.

The August 16, 1777, battle of Bennington—more precisely, the battle for Bennington—deflected General Burgoyne's occupation of the area, thanks to New Hampshire general John Stark's hastily mobilized militiamen. They beat the tar out of Colonel Baum's overdressed Hessians on high ground near the Walloomsac River, across the New York border. The story is memorialized in the Bennington Battle Monument, a 306-foot high obelisk that towers over Old Bennington and the surrounding countryside. The story is dramatized through paintings and memorabilia in the nearby Bennington Museum.

THE JUNCTION OF ROUTES 7 AND 9 IN DOWNTOWN BENNINGTON

Christina Tree

Major old north–south and east–west highways (Historic Rt. 7A and Rt. 9) cross at downtown Bennington's "Four Corners." However, limited-access highways (Rts. 7 and 279) now circumvent the town. Along with outlying commercial strips and loop roads, these have backroaded the community's three distinctive centers—Old Bennington, North Bennington, and downtown. All are worth finding.

North Bennington is a gem of a former mill village with mansions hidden down leafy side roads. The most ornate of these, the Park-McCullough

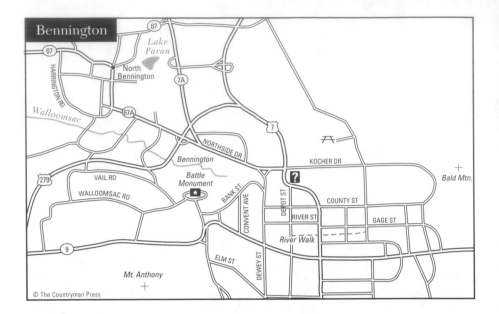

House, is open to visitors; and another estate forms the core of Bennington College campus. The town also offers a choice of B&Bs, fine and casual dining, three of the county's five covered bridges, several waterfalls, extensive walking paths, and Lake Parlin

GUIDANCE The **Bennington Area Chamber of Commerce** (802-447-3311; 800-229-0252; bennington.com), 100 Veterans Memorial Dr., maintains a cheerfully staffed, well-stocked information center, open year-round Mon.–Fri. 10–5, Sat. 10–4; also open Sun. 10–4 mid-May–mid-Oct. Their free Bennington guide is excellent and their fold-out map/guide is the best we've seen, an almost essential tool for finding your way around town.

Downtown Welcome Center (802-442-5758; betterbennington.com), 215 South St., corner of Rt. 7 and Elm St. Open year-round weekdays 9–5, staffed by volunteers seasonally Mon.–Sat. 9–5. A 19th-century stone building, originally a smithy, then a police station, now an information center with comfortable seating and rest rooms.

Also check the **Shires of Vermont** regional tourism Web site: thegreenmountains .com.

GETTING THERE *By car:* From New York City/New Jersey: Take I-87 to Exit 23, then I-787 to Exit 9E ; continue to Rt. 7 east to Bennington and Rt. 279.

From Boston: Rt. 90 to I-95 to Brattleboro and Rt. 9 (the Molly Stark Scenic Byway).

GETTING AROUND Going north can be confusing; watch the signs carefully to choose between the limited-access Rt. 7 to Manchester and the more interesting but slower Historic Rt. 7A to Shaftsbury and Arlington.

Southwestern Vermont Medical Center (802-442-6361; svhealthcare.org), 100 Hospital Dr., Bennington.

✳ To See

Old Bennington and the Bennington Battle Monument (802-447-0550; historicvermont.org), Old Bennington. Open mid-Apr.–Oct., daily 9–5, $2 adults, $1 children. Parking area at its base, just off Rt. 9 west. There's an elevator to the observation floor, with a three-state view. The focal point in Old Bennington, this 306-foot, blue limestone shaft was dedicated in 1891 and remains the tallest man-made structure in Vermont. It commemorates the battle in which General John Stark defeated invading British and Hessian forces at Walloomsac Heights, 5 miles to the northwest, on August 16, 1777. Given the busy traffic pattern, it's wise to keep your car parked at the monument and stroll down Monument Ave., by the fine early houses and the Old Academy to the imposing **Old First Church** with its triple-decker belfry and Palladian windows, built in 1806; five Vermont governors and Robert Frost repose in its burying ground; the vintage Walloomsac Inn is now private.

MUSEUMS ♿ **Bennington Museum** (802-447-1571; benningtonmuseum.org), 75 Main St., Rt. 9, Bennington. Open daily except Wed. and holidays, 9–5. This top-notch collection features memorabilia from the battle of Bennington, including one of the oldest American Revolutionary flags in existence, plus early American furniture, dolls, tools, a spectacular two-room collection of American glass (including iridescent Tiffany and Loetz pieces), and historic Bennington Pottery, notably an extraordinary 10-foot ceramic piece created for the 1853 Crystal Palace Exhibition in London. In a separate room is a luxury 1925 Wasp touring car, the only surviving model of the rare automobiles made by Karl Martin in Bennington. The one-room schoolhouse that Grandma Moses (Anna Mary Robertson, 1860–1961) attended as a child now houses the country's largest collection of her paintings, along with some of her personal possessions. There's a gift shop (featuring Grandma Moses prints and cards), café, genealogical library, and changing exhibitions. Give yourself a few hours to absorb it all. $9 adults, $8 students/seniors, under 12 free.

Bennington Center for the Arts and the **Vermont Covered Bridge Museum** (802-442-7158; benningtoncenterforthearts.org; vermontcoveredbridgemuseum.org), Rt. 9 west of town at Gypsy Lane. Open May–Christmas,

THE BENNINGTON BATTLE MONUMENT
Christina Tree

THE BENNINGTON MUSEUM

Tue.–Sun. 10–5; weekends only in winter. Adults $8, seniors/students $7, families $20, children under 12 free. These are two adjoining but distinct, very different museums. The Bennington Center offers has four fine art galleries, including Native American arts and fine art bird carvings, changing exhibits, and a perform-ance area for the Oldcastle Theatre Company (see *Entertainment*). The second museum presents Vermont's covered bridges and their lore, delivered through videos, dioramas, and interactive exhibits, part of the Bennington Center for the Arts.

In North Bennington

∞ **The Park-McCullough House** (802-442-5441; parkmccullough.org), 1 Park St., just off Main St. Open for one-hour tours mid-May–mid-Oct.; group tours off-season. Last tour at 3 PM. $10 adults, $8 seniors, $5 students. A splendid 35-room Victorian mansion built in 1865 by Trenor W. Park. Born poor, Park was a self-educated lawyer who married the daughter of a former governor at age 23. In 1852 he took his young family to California, where he made a fortune in the gold rush. Back in Vermont, he bought his father-in-law's farm and built this three-story,

PARK-MCCULLOUGH HOUSE AND DOLL-
HOUSE IN NORTH BENNINGTON

mansard-roofed mansion with a grand staircase and hall, stained-glass sky-light, and richly paneled woodwork. Park's son-in-law, John G. McCullough, became governor of Vermont in 1902 and raised his family in this capacious house. It has been open to the public since 1965 and is on the National Reg-ister of Historic Places, functioning as a community arts center. The house is filled with artwork, furniture, artifacts, clothing, and toys, more than 100,000 items belonging to the Hall-Park-McCullough family. There's an appeal-ing children's playhouse replica of the mansion; also a gift shop. Afternoon tea on the side veranda by reservation. The **Carriage Barn** houses a collection of carriages and has been recently renovated as an events and reception site. Inquire about concerts, lectures, and other special events.

In Shaftsbury

Robert Frost Stone House Museum (802-447-6200; frostfriends.org), 121 Rt. 7A. Open May–Dec., Tue.–Sun. 10–5. $5 adults, $2.50 ages 18 and under; 6 and under free. The poet lived and worked for a time in the 1920s in this stone-house-turned-museum; it was here that he wrote "Stopping by Woods on a Snowy Evening." From the windows you can still see the apple trees, stone walls, and country lanes that inspired him. Biographical exhibits and a few of his personal belongings are on display.

The Shaftsbury Historical Society (802-375-6376), Rt. 7A. Open May–Oct., weekends 2–4 PM. This gradually developing cluster of historic buildings includes two schools and an 1846 Baptist meetinghouse. Free.

SCENIC DRIVES **Bennington County's five covered bridges**. The **Silk Road Bridge** (1840), the **Paper Mill Village Bridge** (1840s), and the **Henry Bridge** (rebuilt 1989) are all within a couple of miles just off Rt. 67A, south of the village of North Bennington. Continue north on Rt. 67A as it turns into Main St., then left on Rt. 67 to Rt. 7A and follow it north, past the Robert Frost House and Lake Shaftsbury State Park to the village of Arlington. Note the historic marker in front of the home of writer Dorothy Canfield Fisher. Turn left onto Rt. 313 and follow the Battenkill for 4.4 miles through woods and farmland to West Arlington to find the frequently photographed tableau of the classic green-shuttered church with a spiky steeple, farmhouse (painter Norman Rockwell's home from 1939 until 1953) and the red **West Arlington Bridge** (1872). Return to Arlington Village and, at the sign for East Arlington, turn north on the East Arlington Rd., following it 1.9 miles to the **Chiselville Bridge**, built high above Roaring Branch Brook in 1879. Continue along this road until it veers to join Rt. 7A in Sunderland, near the toll road to the top of Mount Equinox.

Readsboro. This road less taken is our favorite way to Bennington from Massachusetts. Follow Rt. 2 west from Greenfield, Massachusetts, for 3.6 miles to Colrain Rd. Continue for 17.3 scenic miles through Colrain, Massachusetts, to **Jacksonville**, Vermont. Here Rt. 100 splits, the more traveled road heading north to Rt. 9 (see below) at Wilmington, the other branch meandering west through **Whitingham** and on 14 miles to Readsboro—arguably the most remote town in southern Vermont and one that's recently become a center for artists and crafts-people. It was its proximity to the Hoosac Tunnel and its status as a roundhouse for the Wilmington Railroad that spawned this late-19th-century mill village (population: 809), which was later known for its large chair factory. The **Readsboro Inn** (802-423-5048; readsboroinn.com) marks the center of town with its lounge and cheerful, reasonably priced dining room. **Always Emma's Café & Bakery** (open for breakfast and lunch) is another draw, along with the Glass Works (see *Selective Shopping*). Several more studios are open periodically (readsboroarts .com). The **Readsboro Historical Society** (802-423-56301; 7009 Main St.) is open by appointment. It's 11 more miles northwest through high backcountry to Rt. 9 at Searsburg 14 miles east of Bennington.

Molly Stark Byway. For a map and details about the 48 miles of Rt. 9 between Bennington and Brattleboro, see the the introduction to "Southern Vermont" and *Scenic Byways* in the Mount Snow chapter.

✳ To Do

CANOEING BattenKill Canoe Ltd. (802-362-2800; 800-421-5268; battenkill .com), River Rd., off Rt. 7A, Arlington, is the center for day trips—with van service—canoe camping, instruction, rentals, and equipment. Customized inn-to-inn tours with hiking as well as paddling.

GOLF AND TENNIS Mount Anthony Country Club (802-447-2617; mtanthonycc.com), 180 Country Club Dr. (just below the Battle Monument): 18-hole golf course, tennis and paddle courts, pool, lunch and dinner. See *Dining Out*.

HIKING/WALKING The Appalachian Trail crosses Rt. 9 several miles east of Bennington. There's a parking area and an easy hike south to Harmon Hill for a 360-degree view. Allow three to four hours round-trip.

Mile-Around Woods (northbenningtonfund.org), Park St., North Bennington. West of the Park-McCullough House, look for the break in the stone wall and the marked entrance to this foot and bridle path across lovely woods and meadows, part of the original estate.

HORSEBACK RIDING Kimberly Farms Riding Stables (802-442-5454; kimberlyfarms.org), 1214 Cross Hill Rd., Shaftsbury, offers trail rides, lessons, and an overnight horse camp on its 60-acre farm.

Lively's Livery (802-447-7612; 802-379-1299; livelyslivery.com), 193 Crossover Rd., Bennington. Horse-drawn carriage service, wagon rides, trail rides, sleigh rides, bridge tours.

White Birch Horse & Carriage (802-558-9991), 2837 Rt. 7A, Shaftsbury. Horse, wagon, and foliage rides.

NORTH BENNINGTON'S MILE-AROUND WOODS PATH

SWIMMING Lake Parlin, Rt. 67, North Bennington. This hidden gem, a town recreation area centered on a small lake with facilities for swimming, also has good fishing.

Also see Lake Shaftsbury State Park and Woodbury State Park under *Green Space*.

SKIING ⚡ **Prospect Mountain Nordic Ski Center** (802-442-2575; prospectmountain.com), Rt. 9, Woodford, 7 miles east of Bennington. Open daily 9–5, as long as there's snow. Little Woodford has the highest elevation of any town in the state. The base at this cross-country skiing area is 2,250 feet, increasing the odds for consistent snow. Frequently it's snowing here when it's raining (literally) down the road. Phone or check the Web site for conditions. A former downhill family ski area, the focus is now on 30 km of cross-country trails groomed for skating and classic skiing plus extensive backcountry connecting with the Green Mountain National Forest trails. The base lodge has a big stone hearth, a woodstove, and a restaurant good for complete meals and snacks.

SNOWMOBILING Twinbrooks Tours (802-442-4054; 888-616-4054; twin brookstours.com) in Woodford (see above) offers snowmobile rentals, sled storage, trail maps, and guided tours.

✳ Green Space

✔ **Lake Shaftsbury State Park** (802-375-9978; vtstateparks.com), 10.5 miles north of Bennington on Rt. 7A. Open Memorial Day weekend–Labor Day weekend. A private resort until 1974, this 84-acre area surrounding Lake Shaftsbury offers swimming, picnicking, rental kayaks, rowboats and pedal boats, a concession stand, a lakefront cottage rental sleeping six, and 15 lean-tos for group camping. The Healing Spring Nature Trail circles the lake.

✔ **Woodford State Park** (802-447-7169; vtstateparks.com), Rt. 9, 10 miles east of Bennington. This 400-acre heavily wooded area includes 103 camping sites, 20 with lean-tos; swimming in Adams Reservoir from a small beach; a children's playground; picnic spots; and canoe, kayak, and rowboat rentals.

✳ Lodging

INNS The Four Chimneys Inn (802-447-3500; fourchimneys.com), 21 West Rd. (Rt. 9), Old Bennington 05201. This stately, 1910 Colonial Revival home, once the estate of Phillip Jennings, offers 11 luxurious rooms, all spacious with private bath, TV, and phone, most with fireplace and Jacuzzi, and two with glassed-in porch. Firewood provided. The owners, Peter and Lynn Green, keep the grounds beautifully landscaped. Two are appropriate for families of four, but the inn is not suited to pets or children under age 12. $110–230 per room, including full breakfast. (See also *Dining Out*.)

In Bennington 05201
"I" South Shire Inn (802-447-3839; 888-201-2250; southshire.com), 124 Elm St. This attractive turn-of-the-20th-century mansion features 10-foot ceilings with plaster moldings, a library with a massive mahogany fireplace, an Italianate formal dining room, and comfortable bedrooms furnished with antiques. Three of the nine guest rooms have a fireplace, and all have a private bath; two can be joined as a suite. Four newer rooms have been added in the old carriage house, each with whirlpool tub, fireplace, and TV. Tea is served 4–6 PM. $125–265 with breakfast; children 12 and older.

Samuel Safford Inne (802-442-5934; samuelsaffordinne.com), 722 Main St. This is one of the eoldest house in Bennington Village, built by Lieutenant Colonel Samuel John Safford in 1774; it was restored and expanded during the Victorian period. Sandy Redding offers rooms with and without private bath, a full breakfast. And a warm welcome $88–145, from $58 single.

Alexandra B&B (802-442-5619; 888-207-9386; alexandrainn.com), 916

Orchard Rd. (at Rt. 7A south). Daniel and Amanda Tarquino offer 12 spacious rooms in this newly refurbished 1859 farmhouse, each with private bath, king or queen four-poster bed, fireplace, and fine linens. The six newest rooms in the attached addition have sitting area and water jets in the tub. Guests can relax in the sunroom or sitting room, sit out on the terrace, or wander the garden. A four-course, candlelit dinner for guests and their friends is available by reservation. Breakfast is included in $105–185. Single and corporate rates. Two-night minimums on most weekends and holidays.

In North Bennington
🦞 ⁙¶⁙ **The Eddington House** (802-42-1511; 800-941-1857; eddington houseinn.com), 21 Main St., North Benninton 05257. This sunny, elegantly comfortable vintage 1857 manse is in the middle of a picturesque village, within walking distance of a waterfall and some of the best dining choices in South Shire, also handy to walking paths and swimming. Patti and Steve Eddington offer three tastefully furnished, unfussy rooms with private bath and boast "the best beds anywhere." A full breakfast is included in $99–139. Patti is a font of local information, which she delights in sharing.

∞ ⅗ **The Henry House** (802-442-7045; 888-442-7045; henryhouseinn .com), 1338 Murphy Rd., North Bennington 05257. Closed in winter. Don and Judy Cole have five beautiful guest rooms, four with private bath and four common rooms, built in 1769 (it's on the National Register of Historic Places), set in a quarter acre. Among the guest rooms, the Ballroom, with its vaulted 14-foot ceiling, four-poster canopy bed, and a sitting area with working fireplace, is the most notable ($145). The others are also distinctive:

$90–145, including breakfast. Pets may be kept in the garage or crated. Children over 12 are welcome. With its gracious rooms and expansive grounds, this is a great venue for weddings.

∞ ⁙¶⁙ **Taraden** (802-447-3434; taraden.com), 183 Park St., North Bennington 05247. The Tudor-style manor of a former 500-acre estate that still retains 19 acres, its barn (horses are welcome), and a guest cottage. Bob and Nan Lowary offer three suites: The two-room "Night Pasture" upstairs sleeps four and has a fridge, microwave, and TV; the West Wing suite sleeps three (fridge and TV); and the Cottage sleeps two with French doors opening onto a deck (fridge and microwave). $150–175 per couple, $35 per extra person, includes a full breakfast.

MOTOR INNS *Note:* Bennington has an unusual number of independently owned, reasonably priced motels.

In Bennington 05201
☂ ✎ **Vermonter Motor Lodge** (802-442-2529; thevermontermotorlodge .com), Rt. 9 (2968 West Rd.). This motel, 2 miles west of Old Bennington, is an attractive mini resort with nicely decorated rooms and cabins, cable TV, room phone, swimming, boating, bass pond; from $55 in winter to $129 per room in fall; children under 12 stay free.

⁙¶⁙ **Paradise Motor Inn** (802-442-8351; theparadisemotorinn.com), 141 W. Main St., close to the Bennington Museum, has 77 air-conditioned rooms, a pool, and a tennis court, set in 8 landscaped acres on a knoll above Rt. 9. The Bean and Leaf Café (see *Eating Out*) is next door. From $70 for a standard room (two king beds) off-season to $220 for s suite with living room and kitchen in foliage season.

🐾 **Knotty Pine Motel** (802-442-5487; knottypinemotel.com), 130 Northside Dr. (Rt. 7A). The locals use this family-owned motel to put up their guests, which is always a good sign. There's a pool and an adjacent diner, and pets are welcome as long as they are not left alone. The clean, well-kept rooms range $63–77 in summer, $79–95 in fall.

🐾 **Kirkside Motor Lodge** (802-447-7596; kirksidemotorlodge.com), 250 W. Main St. (Rt. 9 west). The Kirkside offers 25 pleasant, individually decorated guest rooms (and morning coffee) in a downtown setting. $59–119.

🐾 **Harwood Hill Motel** (802-442-6278; 877-442-6200;), 864 Harwood Hill Rd. Perched on a hilltop north of Bennington, this motel "with the million dollar view" offers eight deluxe rooms, three cottages, and three economy units, all with air-conditioning, refrigerator, and cable TV. The deluxe rooms have microwave and phone; **Hunter's American Grill** is within walking distance. $73–95; pets (with restrictions) $8 per night.

✳ Where to Eat

DINING OUT **Pangaea** (802-442-7171; lounge 802-442-4466; vermont finedining.com), 1 Prospect St., North Bennington. Open Tue.–Sat. 5–9. **Pangea Lounge** is open nightly, 5–10. This chef-owned eatery in the center of tiny North Bennington is southern Vermont's culinary star. William Scully aims to draw the best from every continent, and it shows in his menu. His wine cellar has won *Wine Spectator* awards, and beers include imports from India and the Czech Republic. Scully offers two distinct dining options side by side. Crispy fried oysters or a wild mushroom crêpe over heirloom tomato confit might be a prelude to grilled swordfish on warm spinach salad or proscuitto-wrapped veal loin. Entrées $18–37 in the dining room, $9–22 in the lounge. Simpler fare, including sandwiches and burgers, is served in the lounge, with summer seating extending to an outdoor terrace overlooking the river. You might dine on an eggplant and mozzarella napoleon ($13) or a Cobb salad with Danish blue cheese ($10).

⚭ **The Four Chimneys Inn** (802-447-3500; fourchimneys.com), 21 West Rd. (Rt. 9), Old Bennington. Open for dinner Tue.–Sun. (closed Tue.–Wed., Dec.–May). The setting is a casually elegant dining room and an enclosed porch. Dinner could begin with Brie en croute for two ($12) or cured salmon on blini ($7) and continue with pan-seared Chilean sea bass ($32), or filet mignon with a bourbon sauce ($36). Full bar, fresh flowers, white linen. Entrées $19–36.

⚭ **The Grille at Mount Anthony Club** (802-442-2617; mtanthonycc-com), 180 Country Club Dr. Open year-round for lunch and dinner. With a winter hearth and seasonal terrace, the setting is delightful, golf or no golf It's just below the Bennington Monument; take Convent Ave. off Rt. 9. Chef Marcel Holland is a Culinary Institute of America grad with more than 25 years' experience. For lunch try a wrap, panini, or burger. Dinner choices range from pastas to prime rib. Entrées $13–20.

EATING OUT

In Bennington
Allegro Ristorante (802-442-0990), 520 Main St. Open nightly for dinner. This gets high mark as a sophisticated trattoria with a colorful decor and fresh, fabulously prepared seafood like pan-seared scallops served on fried polenta in an anchovy, caper, and lemon sauce (that's an appetizer!), and

delicacies such as wild boar and porcini mushrooms with grilled seasonal vegetables in a spicy roasted tomato cream sauce. Service can be slow. Entrées $14–21. Italian wines and beers are featured.

Izabella's Eatery (802-447-4949), 351 W. Main St. Open for breakfast and lunch Tue.–Fri. 7:30–4, Sat. 8:30–4. Order at the counter from the overhead menu, then take a seat and people-watch. This sunny, urbane downtown spot is wildly popular for its creative sandwiches made from fresh, local, and organic ingredients. A panini might combine goat cheese, avocado, tempeh, and free-range chicken; in summer you can eat outside (if you can snag a seat at all).

🦞 **Blue Benn Diner** (802-442-5140), 314 North St. (Rt. 7). Open daily except Sun. from 6 AM; Mon.–Tue. until 5, Wed.–Fri. until 8 PM, Sat. until 4, Sun. 7–4. This 1940s diner combines "road fare" with more esoteric items like eggs Benedict, tabouli, falafel, and herb teas. A 10-minute wait for a seat is not uncommon.

Alldays & Onions (802-447-0043), 519 Main St. Open Tue.–Sat. for breakfast, lunch, and dinner; Sun. brunch. Choices range from bakery items and full breakfasts to gourmet pastas, deli sandwiches, and dinner entrées. There's outdoor seating in warm weather and live weekly entertainment. Sunday brunch includes a basket of warm scones.

✔ **Carmody's Restaurant** (802-447-5748; carmodysisishpub.com), 421 Main St. Open daily 11 AM–10 PM, the bar later. An Irish pub with family dining and take-out. A wide variety of sandwiches, pastas, chicken, seafood, and nightly specials.

❝ℸ❞ **Bean & Leaf Café** (802-442-8822; beanandleafcafevt.com), 139 Main St. Set atop a knoll beside Paradise Inn

with easy parking, this is a relaxing spot for a caffeine boost or herbal tea and a quiche, salad, or sandwich. The blackboard menu includes vegetarian specials and fresh-made soups.

Rattlesnake Cafe (802-447-7018; rattlesnakecafe.com), 230 North St. Open Tue.–Sun., 4:30–9. Choose your margarita, pardner. You can have a Cadillac, a Snake Bite, a Gold, a Bennington Blue, a Frozen Raspberry, or an Over the Top. Also lots of beer and Mexican food, including plenty of nachos to accompany drinks.

✔ **Peppermills of Bennington** (802-447-9900), 716 Main St. Open daily at 4 PM. A cozy, chef-owned, family-geared restaurant with a large, reasonably priced menu featuring Italian veal and pasta classics, also fried and broiled seafood, dinner salads, and famously good burgers with sweet potato fries. Children's menu.

In North Bennington

Note: For a reasonably priced dinner we recommend Pangaea Lounge (see *Dining Out*).

Kevin's Sports Pub & Restaurant (802-442-0122), 27 Main St. Open daily 11 AM–midnight. Live entertainment Fri., Sat. The community gathering spot, frequently packed for dinner—but you can always find space at the bar. Lunch is served until 4; dinner choices include Mike's famous marinated steak and fried flounder. Nightly specials, large servings.

❝ℸ❞ **Powers Market** (802-442-6821; powersmarket.com), 9 Main St. (Rt. 67A). Open daily 7–6. Sited on the village's triangular square, this columned establishment was built in 1833 as a company store for the local paper mill. An oasis for Bennington College students with comfortable seating, tables, WiFi, and a choice of vegetarian as well as deli salads and sandwiches.

Marigold Kitchen (802-445-4545), 25 Main St. Open daily except Mon. from 4:30. A storefront with pleasant atmosphere, organic freshly made pizzas and salads.

✻ Entertainment

Oldcastle Theatre Company (802-447-0564; oldcastle.org), Box 1555, Bennington. This accomplished theater company offers early June–mid-Oct. performances in the Bennington Center for the Arts. Comedy, drama, and musicals.

Also check **bennington.edu/cal** for concerts and other events at Bennington College, open to the public.

✻ Selective Shopping

ART AND CRAFT GALLERIES

Hawkins House (802-447-0488; hawkinshouse.net), 262 North St. (Rt. 7), Bennington, is a crafts market complex for the work of some 400 artisans in silver and gold, unusual textiles, handblown glass, pottery, quilts, cards, books, music, prints and woodcuts, stained glass, candles, and more. Open daily except Christmas and New Year's.

Bennington Arts Guild (802-442-7838; benningtonartsguild.com), 103 South St., Bennington. Open daily (except Tue.) 10–5, Sun. noon–4. Showcasing the work of more than two dozen local artists, photographers, and craftspeople; changing exhibits.

Fiddlehead at Four Corners (802-447-1000), 338 Main St., Bennington. Open 10–5, Sun. 11–3. Closed Wed. A downtown gallery featuring fine art and contemporary crafts housed in a former bank with marble walls, high ceilings, and brass chandeliers. Former teacher Joel Lentzner and his wife, Nina, themselves produce one-of-a-kind hand-painted furniture. Dr. Seuss art, glass, sculpture, jewelry, ceramics.

Mt. Nebo Gallery (800-328-6326; willmoses.com), 60 Grandma Moses Rd., Eagle Bridge, New York. Open daily. Off Rt. 67, less than a dozen miles west of North Bennington, the original white frame farmhouse that was home for Grandma Moses is now home to Will Moses, whose well-known rural scenes are reminiscent of his great-grandmother's. Numbered and signed prints, cards, and other products.

Readsboro Glassworks (802-423-7706), 6954 Main St. (lower level), Readsboro. Open during Open Studio events and by chance. The showroom for the town's former chair factory makes a fine studio for Mary Angus and K. William LeQuier. The couple are usually here, working and willing to chat with visitors. LeQuier's hand-blown, sandblast-carved sculptures are true works of art, while Angus shapes gloriously graceful perfume bottles and small gift items.

McAdoo Rugs (802-442-3563; mcadoorugs.com), 1 Pleasant St., North Bennington. Open weekdays 9–4. We missed this because we were looking for a shop instead of a red wooden mill (two doors down from Pangaea Restaurant). Primarily sold wholesale, these brightly colored and imaginatively designed hand-hooked rugs are made here, and a limited number are sold. Tours are offered.

BOOKSTORES Bennington Bookshop (802-442-5059), 467 Main St., Bennington. Open daily 9–5:30, Fri. till 9 PM, Sun. noon–4. A full-service, independent bookstore specializing in Vermont books, adult and children's titles, and greeting cards.

Now and Then Books (802-442-5566; nowandthenbooksvt.com), 439 Main St., 2nd floor, Bennington. Open Sun. and Mon. noon–5:30, Wed.–Sat. 11:30–

5:30. Closed Tue. except by chance. The oldest used- and collectible-book shop in the area, with an emphasis on fiction, cookbooks, and Vermont. Over 50,000 tomes.

FARMS AND FARMER'S MARKETS

The Apple Barn and Country Bake Shop (802-447-7780; 888-8APPLES; theapplebarn.com), Rt. 7 south, Bennington. Open daily. Up to 30 varieties of apples to pick, a corn maze for the kids, and plenty of candy, cheese, pies, and food specialties in the farm store.

Shaftsbury Alpacas (802-447-3992; shaftsburyalpacas.com), 12 S. Stateline Rd., Shaftsbury. Sandy and Johan Harder invite you to spend a day as an alpaca farmer—or just to shop in the Alpaca Shack for throws, slippers, outerwear, and more.

Walloomsac farmer's markets, behind Bennington Station at Riverwalk Park. Open Mid-May–mid-Oct., Tue. 3:30–5:30, Sat. 10–1.

SPECIAL SHOPS

Hemmings Old-Fashioned Filling Station (802-442-3101; hemmings

---

Bennington Potters Yard (802-447-7531; benningtonpotters.com), 324 County St., Bennington. Open year-round, Mon.–Sat. 9:30–6, Sun. 10–5. Bennington was known for its stoneware pottery in the early and mid-1800s. Ornate samples can be viewed in the Bennington Museum, but this distinctive, handcrafted, simply lined stoneware, pottery, bakeware, and tableware began with David Gil in 1964. It later expanded into its present home, once a business supply outlet for coal, firewood, ice, and lumber. Over the years the company has grown, but it retains its quality, design, and a dozen full-time potters. This flagship factory store also stocks specialty foods, housewares, and gifts; tours are offered.

BENNINGTON POTTERS

Christina Tree

.com), 216 Main St., Bennington. Open daily 7 AM–8 PM. A full-service classic Sunoco filling station and convenience store—and the home of *Hemmings Motor News*. Vintage vehicle displays include a 1937 Hudson and a 1910 Buick; there's also a quasi-museum selling auto-related memorabilia. Open seasonally or by appointment. Check the Web site for frequent cruise-ins.

Mahican Moccasin Factory (802-823 5294; mahicanmoc.com), 2970 Rt. 7 in Pownal, 6 miles south of Bennington on the right. Open Memorial Day–Christmas, daily (except Wed.) 9:30–4:30; in winter, Fri.–Mon. 10–4. Closed Mar. Charles Gray crafts handmade footwear from deerskin, elk, cow, and buffalo hide, crafting them to fit.

Camelot Village (theshopsatcamelot village.com), located in a string of renovated 18th-century barns just west of the Old First Church on Rt. 9 in Bennington. Open 9:30–5:30 daily. The **Antique Center** (802-447-0039) displays antiques and collectibles from more than 140 dealers, and the **Craft Center** (802-447-0228) represents the work of more than 100 artisans. **The Country Store and Wine Shop** (802 442-3997) sells Vermont cheese, specialty foods, maple products, and its own homemade fudge. **Occasional Flowers** (802-442-61291) specializes in folk art and home decor, while **North River Winery** (802-442-9463; northriverwinery.com) offers tastings and sells fruit-based wines from nearby Jacksonville.

The Chocolate Barn (802-375-6928; the chocolatebarn.net), 5055 Historic Rt. 7A north in North Shaftsbury, sells more than 65 varieties of hand-dipped chocolates from over 800 antique candy molds. Open daily 9:30–5.

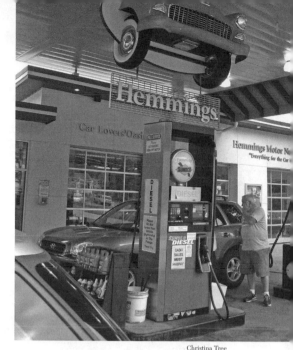

Christina Tree

A GAS STATION/VINTAGE CAR MUSEUM IS HOME TO *HEMMINGS MOTOR NEWS.*

✳ Special Events

May 1: **Annual Bennington Road Race**—the local marathon, at the Park-McCullough House, North Bennington.

Late May: **Bennington Mayfest**—a 10–5 street festival downtown with crafts and entertainment.

May through October: **Funky Friday**. The second Friday of each month, galleries all over the area are open 5–8 PM with receptions, special sales, and an opportunity to meet the artists.

June weekends: **Bennington June ARTS**—art, music, dance, and street performances downtown on the first three weekends in June.

July 4: **Annual 4th of July Celebration** with evening fireworks, Willow Park.

July: **Annual Bennington Museum Antique Show** (see *Museums*). **Pownal Valley Fair** (802-823-5683)—exhibits, antique tractor pull, bingo,

134

SOUTHERN VERMONT

music, fireworks, petting zoo, and more.

Mid-July through mid-August: **Summer in the Park**—free concerts 7–9 PM at the corner of North and Pleasant streets, downtown Bennington.

Mid-August: **Bennington Battle Day Week of Celebrations**, with the annual fire department's Sunday parade. Battle reenactments, special museum events, family activities. **Tri-State Fair**, Green Mountain Racetrack, Pownal.

Labor Day weekend: **Southern Vermont Garlic & Herb Festival** (love garlic.com), Camelot Village. Sample garlic jelly and ice cream, pickled and roasted garlic, garlic golf, also crafts and music.

September 7: **Grandma Moses Birthday Party** at the Bennington Museum (802-447-1571).

Mid-September: **Annual Bennington-Hemmings Car Show & Swap Meet** at Green Mountain Racetrack, Pownal (802-447-33114). Crafts fair, flea market, tractor pull, motorcycle show, food, and entertainment. **Annual Bennington Quilt Fest** (bennington quiltfest.com)—an exhibit of statewide quilts, plus lectures and demonstrations.

Late September: **Casino at the Castle** at the Edward Everett Mansion, Southern Vermont College (802-442-6323). Blackjack, roulette, bingo, craps, slot machines, a chocolate fountain, and fireworks. Admission.

Late November through mid-December: **Festival of the Trees**, Bennington Museum. Silent auction, food, and tour of decorated trees and wreaths throughout the museum's galleries (802-447-1571).

MANCHESTER AND
THE MOUNTAINS

INCLUDING ARLINGTON, DORSET, WESTON, DANBY, LONDONDERRY, PERU, AND PAWLET

Manchester has been a summer resort since the Civil War. The nearby Green Mountains have drawn skiers since 1939 when Bromley opened, augmented in the 1960s by Stratton and Magic and by several dependably snowy cross-country centers.

Manchester itself is an up-and-down town consisting of two villages that once varied in status with their altitude. Hilltop Manchester Village is a gathering of mansions along marble sidewalks around the Congregational Church, the gold-domed North Bennington Shire County courthouse, and the white-columned, tower-topped Equinox Resort. Mrs. Abraham Lincoln and her sons spent two seasons here, booking a third for the entire family for the summer of 1865; the president, unfortunately, never made it.

Other presidents Taft, Grant, Theodore Roosevelt, and Benjamin Harrison—came to stay at the Equinox, but it was Lincoln's family who adopted the village. Robert Todd Lincoln, president of the Pullman Palace Car Company, selected Manchester Village as his summer home, building Hildene, the lavish mansion that's now such an interesting place to visit. Other opulent "summer cottages" are sequestered off River Road and nearby country lanes. Several are now B&Bs.

In the 19th century the opulence of Manchester Village contrasted sharply with the poverty of neighboring "Factory Point" down the hill, home to sawmills, marble works, and a tannery. The era is memorialized in Sarah Cleghorn's 1917 quatrain:

> The golf links lie so near the mill
> That almost every day
> The laboring child can look out
> And see the men at play.

Today Manchester Center (alias Factory Point) is the bustling, attractive center of town, a walkable mix of factory outlets and specialty stores. While the villages retain separate zip codes and zoning, the lines between have been blurred by the lineup of shops and restaurants along Rt. 7A. Some 30 top brand outlets fill old homes and house-sized compounds, blending nicely with shopping landmarks like

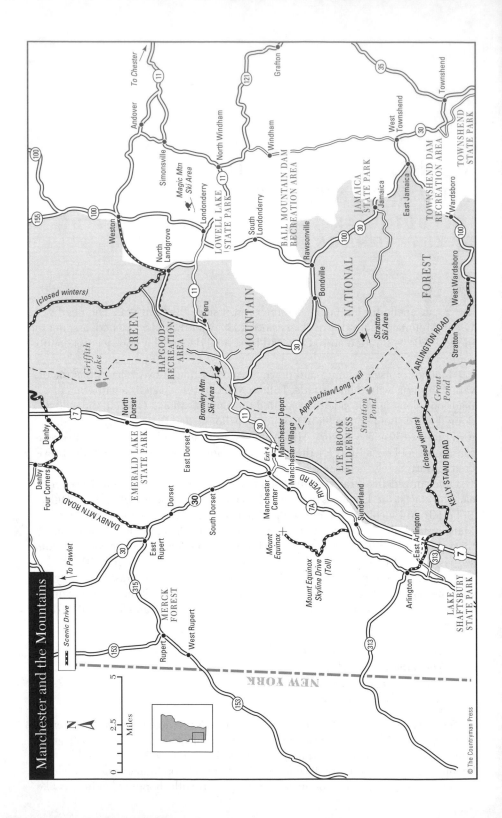

Manchester and the Mountains

Scenic Drive

N

Miles
0   2.5   5

NEW YORK

To Pawlet

To Chester

100

155

100

Andover

Simonsville

11

Magic Mtn Ski Area

Londonderry

North Windham

11

121

Windham

Grafton

35

Townshend

West Townshend

30

TOWNSHEND STATE PARK

Weston

North Landgrove

LOWELL LAKE STATE PARK

South Londonderry

BALL MOUNTAIN DAM RECREATION AREA

Rawsonville

Bondville

100

30

JAMAICA STATE PARK

Jamaica

East Jamaica

Wardsboro

TOWNSHEND DAM RECREATION AREA

100

(closed winters)

Griffith Lake

GREEN

HAPGOOD RECREATION AREA

11

Peru

MOUNTAIN

NATIONAL

Stratton Ski Area

FOREST

West Wardsboro

ARLINGTON ROAD

Stratton

KELLY STAND ROAD

7

North Dorset

Bromley Mtn Ski Area

Manchester Depot

11

30

Appalachian/Long Trail

Stratton Pond

Crout Pond

Danby

Danby Four Corners

EMERALD LAKE STATE PARK

East Dorset

Dorset

Exit 4

Manchester Village

LYE BROOK WILDERNESS

DANBY MTN ROAD

30

South Dorset

Manchester Center

RIVER RD

7A

Sunderland

(closed winters)

East Arlington

7

East Rupert

Mount Equinox

Mount Equinox Skyline Drive (Toll)

Arlington

313

315

MERCK FOREST

West Rupert

Rupert

153

153

313

LAKE SHAFTSBURY STATE PARK

7

© The Countryman Press

the Orvis Retail Store, which has been supplying the needs of fishermen and other sporting folk since 1856.

Luckily the 1930s Work Progress Administration plan to carve ski trails on Mount Equinox never panned out, and Manchester Village retains its serene, white-clapboard good looks, at least for the time being. A stray peak from the Taconic range, Mount Equinox thrusts up 3,800 feet from behind its namesake hotel. Much of it now owned by the Carthusian monks, it's accessible by hiking trail and by a toll road from Rt. 7A in Sunderland, south of town.

The Battenkill, beloved by fishermen and canoeists, runs south from Manchester through Sunderland and Arlington, one of Vermont's oldest towns with more than its share of covered bridges, antiques stores, and genuine beauty.

To the east the Green Mountains rise even within Manchester town limits to 3,100 feet, rolling off into heavily forested uplands punctuated along Rt. 11 by picturesque villages like Peru and Landgrove, Weston and Londonderry. In winter there's skiing at Bromley and Magic Mountains and at a choice of cross-country centers. In summer there's summer music and theater in Weston. Rt. 30 climbs southwest to Bondville, home to 3,900-foot-high Stratton Mountain, the area's largest ski resort.

Manchester Center is sited at the confluence of major roads north and south, east and west. From Manchester, Rt. 30 leads to the elegant village of Dorset, known for its year-round playhouse and destination dining. It then veers northeast through the lovely, long-farmed Mettawee River Valley to the intriguing village of Pawlet and beyond. Heading directly north, Rt. 7 follows the Otter Creek from North Dorset to Danby through a steep-sided, heavily wooded, and lonely valley, a hiking haven.

Manchester itself remains a cultural as well as shopping center, home to the Southern Vermont Arts Center and the Manchester Music Festival, as well as to the monthlong Vermont Summer Festival Horse Show.

GUIDANCE Manchester and the Mountains Regional Chamber of Commerce (802-362-2100; 800-362-4144; manchestervermont.net), 5046 Main St., Manchester Center. The chamber of commerce information booth is walled with pamphlets, good for general walk-in information. The chamber does not make reservations but does keep a running tally on space in member lodging places.

Stratton Mountain maintains a reservation and information service (in-state 802-297-4000; 800-STRATTON; 800-787-2886; stratton.com) and serves over 20 lodges, condo clusters, and inns on and around Stratton.

Londonderry Chamber of Commerce (802-824-8178) maintains an information booth and office in the Mountain Marketplace, junction of Rts. 11 and 100.

GETTING THERE *By car:* From Bennington, US 7 to Manchester is a

MOUNT EQUINOX RISES BEHIND MANCHESTER VILLAGE.

Joe Citro

limited-access highway that's speedy but dull, except for viewing Mount Equinox. You get a more interesting taste of the area, especially around Arlington, by clinging to Historic Rt. 7A. From the southeast, the obvious access is I-91 to Brattleboro, then Rt. 30 north.

From New York City, take I-87 to Exit 23, then I-787 to Exit 9E to Rt. 7 east to Bennington; continue on Rt. 279 to Rt. 7 north to Exit 4, or follow Historic Rt. 7A from Bennington.

MEDICAL EMERGENCY Emergency service is available by calling **911**.

Northshire Medical Center (802-362-4440), Manchester Center. **Manchester Medical Center** (802-362-1263), Rt. 7A, Manchester. **Mountain Valley Medical Clinic** (802-824-6901), Rt. 11, opposite the Flood Brook School, 2 miles west of Londonderry, 3 miles east of Peru. **Carlos Otis Clinic** (802-297-2300), at Stratton Mountain. **Tri Mountain Rescue Squad** (802-824-3166) serves Bondville, Landgrove, Peru, and Stratton.

✳ Villages

In addition to Manchester, the area's picturesque places include Arlington, 7 miles south along Rt. 7A; Weston, 15 miles to the northeast; Dorset, 8 miles to the northwest; Pawlet, another 7 miles to the north on Rt. 30; and Danby, 8 miles north of Dorset and 10 miles east of Pawlet.

Arlington (population: 2,400). Although never formally the capital of Vermont, this was the de facto seat of government during most of the Revolutionary period. Fearing British attacks in the north, Vermont's first governor, Thomas Chittenden, moved south from Williston, liberated a Tory property in Arlington (the area known as Tory Hollow), and conducted affairs of state from there, making it one of Vermont's most historic villages.

Many older visitors to Arlington fondly remember Dorothy Canfield Fisher, the author of 50 immensely popular, warmhearted novels and a Book-of-the-Month Club judge for 25 years. Another famous resident was artist Norman Rockwell, who lived in West Arlington from 1939 to 1953 and incorporated local scenes into his paintings of small-town Americana. One of his models was Dr. George A. Russell, the country doctor immortalized in the Rockwell print that hangs in thousands of doctors' offices. Russell amassed an important collection of Vermontiana (including S. C. Fisher materials, works by Norman Rockwell, and many photographs dating from 1860–1890), now on view by arrangement in the **Martha Canfield Memorial Free Library** (802-375-6153), 528 East Arlington Rd. Turn east off Rt. 7A to find antiques shops and the way along the Battenkill to the Chiselville Covered Bridge.

NORMAN ROCKWELL LIVED HERE IN WEST ARLINGTON, WITHIN SIGHT OF THE CHURCH AND COVERED BRIDGE.

Christina Tree

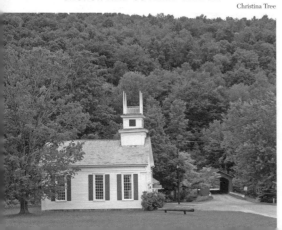

Dorset (dorsetvt.com). This pristine village of 2,000 souls is visible evidence that it takes money to "prevent the future." A fashionable summer refuge for years, few signs of commerce mar its carefully manicured nature. Today's tranquility, making it a haven for artists, writers, and the affluent, contrasts sharply with the hotheaded days of its youth. In 1776 the Green Mountain Boys gathered in Cephas Kent's tavern and issued their first declaration of independence from the New Hampshire Grants, signed by Thomas Chittenden, Ira Allen, Matthew Lyon, Seth Warner, and other Founding Fathers of Vermont. Today the Dorset Inn, said to be the state's oldest continuously operating hostelry, is the village focal point, along with the Dorset Playhouse (see *Entertainment*), one of New England's most venerable summer theaters, and the private Dorset Field Club, an 18-hole golf course billed as the state's oldest. The first marble to be quarried in North America came from Dorset, and one quarry—now a popular swimming hole—supplied the marble for New York City's Public Library. The newly expanded **Bley House Museum** (802-867-0331; dorsethistory.com) at the junction of Main St. and Rt. 30 offers exceptional displays about the history of local marble quarrying. Maintained by the Dorset Historical Society, it is also worth a visit to see landscapes of the Mettawee Valley by painter John Willie (1867–1942) and works by other artists who painted here during Dorset's golden age as an art center. It's open Apr. 15–Oct. 15, Wed. 10–noon, Thu.–Sat. 10–2; otherwise Wed., Fri., Sat. 10–noon.

Pawlet (pawletvt.com). Not far north of Dorset, this hamlet on Rt. 30 is an unexpected delight, with a mix of architectural styles in buildings that cling to the rather steep slopes leading up from Flower Brook, over which Johnny Mach's General Store extends. Gib Mach harnessed the rushing brook to a turbine that generated his electricity and built a glass-topped counter at the end of a store aisle through which you can still peer down at the water surging through the narrow gorge below. Next door, a former railroad station is now a restaurant; the clutch of shops is worth investigating.

Danby. A bypassed hamlet on Rt. 7 between Dorset and Wallingford, Danby is an village known for its marble quarries, including Vermont's only still-active underground quarry. It was home base for Silas Griffith, an 1850s lumber baron who was Vermont's first millionaire. In the 1960s novelist Pearl Buck bought seven local buildings and began to renovate them; the village offers several antiques shops along with a general store, B&B, and café.

THE WESTON PRIORY

Christina Tree

Weston. A mountain crossroads that's a logical hub for exploring all of southern Vermont, this village of just 630 souls looms large on tourist maps. It's the home of one of the **Weston Playhouse**, one of the country's oldest and best summer theaters, and the **Vermont Country Store**, New England's number one nostalgia outlet. The oval common is shaded with majestic maples, and a band plays regularly in

HILDENE, THE LINCOLN HOME

(802-362-1788; hildene.org), Rt. 7A, Manchester Village. Open year-round 9:30–4:30. $12.50 adults, $5 ages 6–14. Members and children under 6, free. Limited handicapped accessibility. A standout among Vermont's historic houses, this 24-room Georgian Revival manor is set on 412 acres, including formal gardens and an observatory to the side with mountain views. Bring a picnic lunch and plan to stay half the day. A grounds and walking trail pass only is $5 adults, $3 ages 6–14; under 6 are free.

ROBERT TODD LINCOLN

Historic Hildene

The 90-minute tour begins at the Carriage Barn, now a sophisticated welcome center with a museum store and a film about Robert Todd Lincoln and the Hildene experience. You learn that Robert, the eldest and only child of President Abraham and Mary Todd Lincoln to survive to adulthood, first came to the village as a boy with his mother for a stay at the Equinox House; his father was assassinated before the family could return, as they had intended, the following summer. Forty years later, following a successful career as a lawyer and statesman and while he was president of the Pullman Company, Robert returned to Manchester to build the place he called his ancestral home, Hildene, a name chosen for its meaning: "hill and valley." Robert died here

HILDENE'S GARDENS AS SEEN FROM THE PERGOLA

Historic Hildene

in 1926, and members of the family, three generations of Lincolns, lived at Hildene until 1975, some 70 years. Guides are familiar with the true character of the house, which is furnished almost entirely with the family's belongings.

Tours include the restored formal gardens, where the family's original peonies have survived for

Historic Hildene

THE DINING ROOM AT HILDENE

100 years, producing more than 1,000 blooms each June. Returned to its former splendor, Hildene's garden restoration effort earned it the Victorian Society in America's Preservation Award. Guests may also expect to see exhibits, including one of Abraham Lincoln's rare stovepipe hats, and hear a brief concert by the 1,000-pipe aeolian organ, which was once playable both manually and with one of 240 player rolls. Picnic tables outside command a view of the valley below, and there are numerous trails to stroll or to explore on skis or snowshoes in winter.

The new **Rowland Agricultural Center**, set on the picturesque 10 Acre Meadow, features a 40-by-100-foot timber-frame barn, designed specifically to house Hildene's goat herd and for viewing cheesemaking from the milking of the goats to the processing of a signature Hildene Farm cheese. **Wagon rides** along the Farm Loop Trail begin at the welcome center on weekends from summer through foliage.

ONE OF LINCOLN'S STOVEPIPE HATS IS ON DISPLAY AT THE HILDENE LIBRARY.
Historic Hildene

Check the Web site for frequent special events throughout the year, among them concerts, outdoor Shakespeare productions, and arts and crafts festivals. These take place both on the grounds of the mansion and on Hildene's meadows, located on the lower elevation of the property—which includes 0.5 mile along the Battenkill.

the bandstand. Free summer concerts are presented by the **Kinhaven Music School**; Weston was actually one of the first villages in Vermont to be consciously preserved. The theater, the unusually fine historical collection in the **Farrar Mansur House**, and (indirectly) the Vermont Country Store all date from the "Weston Revival" of the 1930s. The village also it offers lodging and dining. Visitors are also welcome at **Weston Priory** (802-824-5409; westonpriory.org), a community of Benedictine monks, nationally known for the Gregorian chant in their daily common prayer and other music sung and played at Sunday liturgies; there's also a gift shop, retreat house, and rare sense of peace both in and outside the monastery.

✳ To See

&. **Southern Vermont Arts Center** (802-362-1405; svac.org), West Rd., 1 mile north of the Equinox, Manchester Center. Open all year, Tue.–Sat. 10–5, Sun. noon–5. $8 nonmembers, $3 students; free for members and children under 13. The Elizabeth de C. Wilson Museum, opened in 2000, is a work of art in itself with its soaring, light-filled galleries that house some first-class touring shows of paintings, sculpture, prints, and photography. Concerts, including the summer Manchester Music Festival series, ballet performances, and lectures, are held in the adjacent, 430-seat Arkell Pavilion; there are other special events throughout the year. Light lunches are served in the Garden Café (see *Eating Out*). Extensive trails run through the woods, among them a botany trail (past outdoor sculpture) featuring rock formations, 67 varieties of wildflowers, and birches. Limited handicapped accessibility.

The American Museum of Fly Fishing (802-362-3300; amff.com), next to the Orvis Company's flagship store on Rt. 7A, Manchester Village. Open daily 10–4 (closed major holidays; also Sun.–Mon off-season); $5 adults, $3 ages 6–14; free for students and children under 6. Manchester native Charles Orvis perfected the ventilated reel, accelerating the drying of fishing line on a fishing reel. He opened his first store in 1856. The museum displays the beautiful flies of Mary Orvis Marbury as well as hundreds of rods and reels made by famous rod builders and owned by such luminaries as Daniel Webster, Bing Crosby, Ernest Hemingway, and Presidents Hoover and Eisenhower. The private research library upstairs (admission $20) is open by appointment.

Museums of Weston (802-824-5294; 802-824-6624), village green, Weston. Open for tours and demonstrations late June–mid-Oct., Sat. and Sun. afternoons, also Wed. through Aug. Even if you have never set foot inside a historic house, make an exception for the **Farrar Mansur House**, built in 1797 as a tavern with a classic old taproom. Thanks to 1930s Work Progress Administration (WPA) artists, murals of Weston in its prime cover the living room walls, and a number of primitive portraits hang in the adjacent rooms over period furniture and furnishings donated by Weston families. The upstairs ballroom displays magnificent 1820s stenciling. In the attic a rendition of townspeople dancing—each face is painted to resemble a specific resident—conjures the spirit of a town that knew how to have fun. Next door the reproduction 1780 **Old Mill** stands by a dam and waterfall. Grain is ground, and there are many vintage tools. David Claggett, a skilled tinsmith, regularly works here, using 18th-century methods to create exceptional chandeliers, lanterns, sconces, and folk art.

Also see Dorset's **Bley House Museum** under *Villages*.

SCENIC DRIVES Mount Equinox (802-362-1114; equinoxmountain.com). The summit of Mount Equinox is 3,848 feet high. Most of the mountain is owned by the Carthusian monks who occupy the monastery that you can see from the top. A toll road (open May–Oct., 9 AM–dusk; $12 per car and driver; $2 per passenger; $10 per motorcycle) climbs more than 5 miles from Rt. 7 to the top. This can be a spectacular ride on a clear day, even more dramatic if the mountain is in the clouds and the road keeps disappearing in front of you. Be sure to drive back down in low gear and total sobriety.

Green Mountain National Forest Road Number 10, Danby to Landgrove. Closed in winter. The longest (14 miles) and most isolated of these byways, the road (beginning in Danby) climbs through the White Rocks Recreation Area, crossing a number of tempting hiking paths as well as the Long Trail. There are some fine views as you continue along. You might want to picnic somewhere in the middle of the forest, as we did by a beaver pond. The road follows Tabor Brook down into Landgrove, itself a tiny, picturesque village.

Peru to Weston. From the village of Peru, an enticing wooded road is paved as far as Hapgood Pond, then continues smoothly through Landgrove, a minuscule village with an outstanding inn (open to the public for dinner) set in rolling fields. The way to Weston is clearly marked.

East Rupert to Danby. Danby Mountain Rd. is the logical shortcut from Dorset to Danby, and it's quite beautiful, winding up and over a saddle between Woodlawn Mountain and Dorset Peak. Well-surfaced dirt, with long views in places. If you're coming from East Rupert, be sure to turn right at Danby Four Corners and follow Mill Brook into Danby.

Kelley Stand Road. From Rt. 7A, follow East Arlington Rd. past Candle Mill Village and continue until you cross a one-lane bridge. Turn right onto Kelley Stand Rd., which is a great foliage-viewing trip all the way to Stratton. Closed in winter.

Also see *Scenic Tours* in the Bennington chapter.

✳ To Do

BICYCLING In Manchester, mountain bike, hybrid bike, and touring bike rentals and touring information are available from **Battenkill Sports Cycle Shop** (802-362-2734; 800-340-2734; battenkillbicycle.com), open daily 9:30–5:30, at 1240 Depot St., in the Stone House at the junction of Rts. 7 and 11/30.

First Run Ski Shop (802-297-4321) at Stratton Mountain rents mountain bikes and offers off-mountain guided tours (with five days' prearrangement). Open Mon.–Fri. 9–5, Memorial Day weekend–July 4; then daily 9–5.

Equipe Sport and Mountain Riders (800-282-6665; equipesport.com),

A BICYCLISTS NEGOTIATES DOWNTOWN MANCHESTER.

Christina Tree

junction of Rts. 30 and 100 in Rawsonville; also on Mount Snow Access Rd. in West Dover (802-464-2222) and in the Village Square at Stratton Mountain (802-297-3460). The Equipe Outdoor Activity Center offers sales, rentals, free bike maps, and guided tours.

CANOEING The **Battenkill** makes for satisfying canoeing in spring; the Manchester-to-Arlington section is relatively flat water, but it gets difficult a mile above Arlington.

BattenKill Canoe Ltd. (802-362-2800; battenkill.com), Rt. 7A in Arlington. An outfitter offering inn-to-inn canoe trips throughout the state but specializing in this area with combination hiking-and-paddling tours. Canoe rentals and shuttle service on the Battenkill are also offered.

First Run Ski Shop (802-297-4321), on Stratton Mountain. Canoe and kayak tours, rentals, and sales. **Equipe Sport** (800-282-6665; equipsport.com), at the junction of Rts. 30 and 11 in Rawsonville, also offers kayak rentals and tours.

DRIVING TOURS Off-road School at the Equinox Resort (802-362-4700; equinoxresort.com), Manchester Village, at the Equinox. Equinox Resort offers off-road Land Rover driving courses, with junior off-road for the 5-to-12 age set (summer months only). Expert instructors offer tips at the school's 80-acre course. Extra passengers are welcome; drivers must have a valid license. The junior course, in the woods behind the hotel, features mini Land Rovers the size of go-carts, which have brake and gas pedals and max out at about 5 mph.

Backroad Discovery Tours (802-362-4997; backroaddiscovery.com). Sharon O'Connor drives six to eight guests in her special touring vehicles through the back roads and byways of southern Vermont, stopping along the way to give you a taste of local history. She also knows the best places to watch sunsets and view fall foliage. Daily, June–Oct.

FISHING Fly-fishing has been serious business on the Battenkill since the mid–19th century. The Orvis Company began manufacturing bamboo rods in Manchester Village near the spot where they are still produced.

The **Battenkill** is generally recognized as Vermont's best wild trout stream; access is available at a number of places off Rt. 7A. Brown trout can also be found in **Gale Meadows Pond**, accessible via gravel road from Rt. 30 at Bondville. **Emerald Lake** in North Dorset is stocked with pike, bass, and perch; rental boats are available at the state park facility.

Orvis Fishing Schools (800-235-9763; orvis.com), *the* name in fly-fishing instruction as well as equipment; two-day courses are offered two to three times weekly, Apr.–Oct. There are six other schools around the country and others in foreign locales.

Upland Outfitters (802-297-1780), Rt. 30, Bondville. Fly-fishing equipment and guided trips.

Chuck Kashner's Guide Service (800-682-0103; vermontfishingtrips.com). Chuck will take care of the tackle, rods, flies, bait, and gear and will provide a hot meal on full-day trips. Four-hour, six-hour, or full-day (eight-hour) trips available, fly- or spin fishing.

GOLF The 18-hole **Golf Club at Equinox** (802-362-7879; playequinox.com), 108 Union St., Manchester Village, was established in the 1920s for guests of the Equinox House, expanded and redesigned in 1991 by Rees Jones. The Dormy Grill here (see *Eating Out*) offers pleasant noontime dining with a beautiful view of the course.

The Stratton Golf School (802-297-2200; 800-843-6867) offers weekend and midweek sessions, including professional instruction, use of the 27-hole course at the Stratton Mountain Country Club, and a special 22-acre "training site." A good and reasonably priced seasonal lunch is available at the club.

The Practice Tee (802-362-3100), Rt. 7A, Manchester Center. A 335-yard driving range offering group and individual lessons. Open in-season, weather permitting, weekdays 9–7, weekends and holidays 8–7.

HIKING From the Green Mountain National Forest District Office (802-362-2307), request hiking maps for **Lye Brook Wilderness**, a 14,600-acre preserve south of Manchester with a 2.3-mile trail to the Lye Brook Waterfalls and the **Long Trail**. This Massachusetts-to-Quebec path doubles as the Appalachian Trail throughout the area; portions of the trail make good day hikes, either north over Bromley Mountain or south over Spruce Peak from Rt. 11/30. Another popular route is the Stratton Pond Trail, which starts at Kelley Stand Rd. and stretches to Stratton Pond; there is one shelter in the immediate area, and swimming is permitted. **Griffith Lake**, accessible from Peru and Danby, is a less crowded swimming and camping site on the trail. For details, consult the Green Mountain Club's *Long Trail Guide.*

Mount Equinox. Details about the rewarding, 6-mile Burr and Burton Trail from Manchester Village to the summit are available in *Day Hiker's Guide to Vermont* (Green Mountain Club). At 3,825 feet, this is the highest mountain in the state that is not traversed by the Long Trail. See also *Green Space.*

HORSEBACK RIDING, ETC. ✍ **Horses for Hire** (802-297-1468; horsesforhire .net), Rt. 30, Bondville. Deb Hodis and Ron Amedon offer one- and two-hour and half-day trail rides, sleigh rides, and riding lessons for individuals and groups, even in winter, weather permitting.

Karl Pfister Farm (802-824-4663; 802-824-6320; sover.net/~npfister), Landgrove. Fall foliage carriage and wagon rides available by reservation.

Mountain View Ranch (802-293-5837; mountvainviewranch.com) at 502 Easy St. in Danby. Horse and pony rides.

✍ **Chipman Stables** (802-293-5242; chipmanstables.com), and at Danby Four Corners. Year-round horse and pony rides, hayrides, and kids' camp by the day or week, Western-style. Sleigh rides.

HUNTING Orvis Manchester Shooting School (802-362-3622; 800-548-9548) of Manchester offers one- and two-day wingshooting courses July–Oct. Tuition includes guns, ammo, and lunch, but not lodging.

The **British School of Falconry** and **The Archery School at the Equinox** (802-362-4700) at the Equinox Resort, Manchester Village, offer introductory lessons, hawk walks, and pheasant hunting with hawks and falcons.

MOUNTAIN RIDES *&* **Bromley Mountain** (802-824-5522; bromley.com), Rt. 11, Peru (6 miles east of Manchester). This 3,284-foot-high mountain offers excellent views of Stratton and Equinox mountains. It's traversed by the Long Trail and also accessible by hiking the ski trails from the midpoint exit on the chairlift. This lift, serving the alpine slide, is open Memorial Day–mid-Oct., weather permitting, on weekends 10–5 and daily July–Labor Day 9:30–6 (fee). The Bromley Alpine Slide, the longest in this country, is a great ride with fabulous views whatever your age. The Big Splash waterslide (biggest in Vermont) and the Giant Swing are huge draws for the teen set. You'll also find miniature golf, a 24-foot climbing wall, space bikes, a parabounce, the "trampoline things," and an extreme zipline. Lunch, snacks, and drinks are available at the base lodge.

& **Stratton Mountain** (802-297-2200; 800-STRATTON; stratton.com) offers a four-state view from its summit, accessible by gondola from the ski resort (Rt. 30, Bondville). The gondolas run 10–5, Sept. 23–Oct. 10. And there's lots of summer action in its Adventure Zone—a skate park, a climbing wall, boulders, and a cave.

NATURE WALKS AND WORKSHOPS *&* **Vermont Institute of Natural Science** (VINS), in partnership with the Equinox Preservation Trust (802-362-4374; vinsweb.org), offers natural history walks and programs for adults, families, and children. The fee-based programs run year-round, geared to the season.

SWIMMING *&* **Dana L. Thompson Recreation Area** (802-362-1439), Rt. 30 north, 340 Recreation Park Rd., Manchester Center, is open daily in summer, but hours for general swimming are limited; nominal fee.

& **Dorset Quarry**, aka Norcross-West Quarry, off Rt. 30 on Kelly Rd. between Manchester and Dorset (turn at the historic marker), is a deep, satisfying pool but lacks easy access, making it unsafe for small children. Though the land is private property, the owners allow access by members of the public who treat it respectfully.

THE ALPINE SLIDE AT BROMLEY MOUNTAIN
Bromley Mountain

& **Hapgood Pond** in Peru, with its sand and calm, shallow drop-off, is favored by families with young children.

& **Emerald Lake State Park** (802-362-1655), Rt. 7, North Dorset, offers clear lake swimming.

See also *Green Space.*

TENNIS *&* **Gunterman Tennis Schools at Stratton Mountain** (802-297-4230; 800-787-2886; greattennis .com). Tennis pro Kelly Gunterman offers instruction for adults both midweek and on weekends on 15 outdoor and four indoor courts. *Note:* Stratton Mountain offers free "KidsKamp" supervision for two children ages 4–12 whose parents are enrolled in the golf and tennis programs, late June–early Sept. The Junior Tennis Day Camp runs weekdays for children 6–15.

Dana L. Thompson Recreation Area, Manchester. Public courts are available with weekly memberships or on a per-hour basis.

Equinox Hotel Tennis (802-362-4700), Rt. 7A, Manchester Village. Three Har-Tru courts are open to the public for a $65 hourly fee.

Kim Grant

THE DORSET QUARRY

✳ Winter Sports

✒ CROSS-COUNTRY SKIING AND SNOWSHOEING **Viking Nordic Centre** (802-824-3933; vikingnordic.com), 615 Little Pond Rd., Londonderry. Trail fee. The Viking trail system includes 35 km of groomed trails, 3 km lighted for night skiing on Sat. and holidays, and dedicated snowshoe trails. You'll also find instruction, rentals, a retail shop, on-snow kid-sitters (by reservation), and a café serving drinks, light breakfasts, and lunches. The **Viking Nordic House**, a home with a library, hearth, and four bedrooms that sleeps 10, is available for rental by the weekend or week.

Wild Wings Ski Touring Center (802-824-3933; wildwingsski.com), North Rd., Peru. Tracy and Chuck Black run a family-oriented touring center located within the Green Mountain National Forest, 2.5 miles north of Peru. Trails are narrow, geared to beginning and intermediate skiers. This area tends to get a heavier snowfall than other local touring centers; the 28 km of groomed one-way trails are at elevations between 1,650 and 2,040 feet. Instruction and rentals; no skate skiing or dogs.

Stratton Mountain Nordic Center (802-297-2200), Stratton Mountain. Based at the Sun Bowl, a 30 km series of groomed loops plus adjoining backcountry trails. Guided backcountry tours as well as a variety of other tours are offered. Hot lunch and snacks available at the Sun Bowl Base Lodge.

Equinox Ski Touring Center (802-362-3223) has 35 km of groomed trails and tracked terrain, snowshoeing, instruction, a lounge, tours, vacation camps, and rentals. This network includes trails on the golf course, up through the forests of the Equinox Preservation Trust, and around Equinox Pond.

DOWNHILL SKIING **✒ Bromley** (802-824-5522; bromley.com), 3984 Rt. 11 in Peru, 6 miles east of Manchester. In winter there's a reservations service for condominiums. Founded in 1936 by Fred Pabst of the Milwaukee brewing family, this is among the oldest ski areas in the country. The only southern-facing ski mountain in Vermont, it was also one of the first to develop snowmaking, a slope-side nursery, chairlifts, and condominiums. Pabst set up a rope tow in what is now the parking lot. Later he invented the J-bar, which allowed skiers to be pulled up the mountain rather than having to clutch a rope. Fred sold the area to Stig Albertsson in 1971, but remained president until his death in 1977. Albertsson brought the first alpine slide to North America, helping Bromley develop into more than just a winter destination. Today the resort is owned by Boston-based Joe O'Donnell, who made extensive renovations, adding a snowboarding park and half-pipe, a high-speed quad chairlift that gets skiers from base to summit in six minutes, and a new lodge. The Halo Terrain Park is wired for sound and has its own T-bar, tabletops, glades, gaps. spines, quarter-pipes, and dedicated groomer. There are three more terrain parks: Exhibition Park for intermediates, focusing on rails and boxes; the Unforgiven Boardercross Park, featuring tons of higher-speed terrain with whoops, gaps, and banked tours; and the Bonanza Park, a progression for beginner board-ers. This is a popular family mountain, with many trails suited to beginners and intermediates, but there are a number of challenging runs on the mountain's east side, particularly Stargazer, Blue Ribbon, Avalanche, Havoc, and Pabst Peril.

Lifts: 10: 1 high-speed detachable quad, 1 fixed-grip quad, 4 doubles, 1 T-bar, 2 Mighty-Mites, and Magic Carpet.

Trails: 45 trails—evenly divided among intermediate, beginner, and expert.

Vertical drop: 1,334 feet.

Snowmaking: 85 percent of terrain from base to summit.

Facilities: The base lodge offers two cafeterias as well as more formal tavern upstairs. Skiers unload right at the base lodge; the driver then parks in an area across Rt. 11 and rides back on a shuttle bus. Valet parking is another option.

Ski school: Ski and snowboard schools are a particular pride, rated number one in North America for Family Programs by *Ski Magazine.*

For children: The Bromley Thrill Zone is one of the largest summer amusement parks in the state. It includes the Giant Swing—which looms as tall as a four-story building—an 18-hole mini golf course, a 0.7-mile triple-track alpine slide, DévalKarts (gravity-driven mountain go-carts), a 24-foot climbing wall, and a vari-ety of spinning, splashing rides. For the youngest set there's PigDog's Fun Park, with a 24-foot inflated slide, Bounce House, and bumper boats. Adults can settle in with a snack at the Sun Café and enjoy the view.

Lift tickets: $39 adults midweek, $63–66 weekends, $55 teen, $39 junior, substan-tially less for two days ($52–22 weekends); half days are available.

🏂 **Stratton** (800-STRATTON; ski report 802-297-4211). Located atop a 4-mile access road from Rt. 30 in Bondville, Stratton is a popular, well-groomed moun-tain. It was here that Jake Burton invented the snowboard, an event the mountain has made the most of with weekly races, not to mention the hosting of the U.S. Open Snowboarding Championships. Stratton keeps a loyal following by harvest-ing a steady crop of snow for what are predominantly intermediate-level runs, but there are also plenty of opportunities for advanced skiers along its 90 trails, including some good moguls and long top-to-bottom runs of 2,000 vertical feet. As one of Vermont's youngest ski areas (it was established in 1961, a year after Killington and five after Mount Snow), it is among the most modern, with a vibrant après-ski scene in winter and a well-known golf and tennis school. During the off-season, the slope-side population shrinks to 150 (although in 1960, its resi-dents numbered a mere 24). Acquired by the Canadian resort company Intrawest in 1994, Stratton is respected statewide for its environmental policies; it has relin-quished development rights on nearly a third of its acreage to protect bear, deer, and thrush habitat.

The mountain itself rises to 3,936 feet, with two separate areas: the original North Face, otherwise known as Stratton Village, and the distinctly sunnier Sun Bowl, the newer of the two. Thanks to the quantity of lifts, skiers are generally dispersed over the trail network. Stratton Village, a complex that includes a variety of shops, a dozen restaurants, a 120-room inn, a 90-room lodge, and 300 condominiums, dwarfs the base facility. A sports center includes a 25-yard-long pool, whirlpool, indoor tennis courts, racquetball courts, exercise equipment, and a lounge.

A lot happens here in summer, too. There's a 27-hole golf course, hiking, mountain biking, hiking, paintball, fishing, kayaking, scenic gondola rides, and tennis and golf schools, and kids ages 6 weeks–12 years can attend KidsKamp for half or full days, late June–early Sept.

Lifts: 16: a 12-passenger gondola, four 6-passenger high-speed detachable, 4 quads, 1 triple, 1 double chair, 2 surface lifts, and 3 Magic Carpets.

Trails and slopes: 92.

Terrain parks: Four, including the pro Power Park and Power Superpipe, designed and built with the stamp of approval from Stratton snowboarder and Olympic medalist Ross Powers. The superpipe is 420 feet long, with walls of 17–22 feet. Skiers and riders must earn access to Stratton's biggest park by completing a safety awareness session.

Vertical drop: 2,003 feet.

Snowmaking: 95 percent.

Facilities: Restaurant and cafeteria in the base lodge; also cafeterias midmountain and in Sun Bowl Ranch. Chapel of the Snows at the parking lot, a little Bavarian-style church, has frequent nondenominational and Roman Catholic services. A shuttle bus brings skiers from inns on the mountain to the base lodge. You'll also find a clinic, sports center, and shops and restaurants in the base area Village Square.

Ski school: Ski and snowboard lessons.

For children: Childcare Center for ages 6 weeks–3 years; Mountain Riders 5–8 and 9–18. A separate base lodge and new slope-side meeting place for KidsKamp; combined ski and play programs are offered—Little Cubs (ages 4–6), Big Cubs (7–12), Junior Newcomers (7–12).

Rates: $69 per adult midweek, $78 weekends and holidays; less for young adults and seniors. Many special multiday packages. Ski and stay from $79.

 Magic Mountain Ski Area (802-824-5645; magicmtn.com), south of Londonderry off Rt. 11, 18 miles east of Manchester. The smallest of southern Vermont's ski areas, Magic Mountain may also be its most challenging. Its 34 trails are twisty and narrow, and almost half of its 1,600 vertical feet are steep drops. The 108-acre area was developed in 1960 by Swiss ski instructor Hans Thorner, who hoped to re-create the atmosphere of a Swiss Alpine village. He chose this mountain for the sheer drama of its terrain. Magic remains relatively overlooked, making it a perfect destination for those out to escape the crowds (and expense) of the larger resorts. Though the advanced trails are the real draw here, there is still plenty of good, well-groomed terrain for beginners and intermediates. The two chairlifts, the red double and the black triple, are long and comparatively slow, reminding you of what it was like to ski before high-speed detachable chairs were invented.

Beginners should turn left at the top and follow the Magic Carpet trail a third of the way down, then choose a blue or green route to the bottom. Intermediate-level skiers and riders should take the red double lift to Whiteout or Betwixt. Advanced skiers will want to go straight down Redline and turn a little right from the red chair to try Twilight Zone and Goniff Glade, which are steep and dotted with numerous surprises, among them trees, rocks, bushes, and other natural obstacles. Magic Mountain is good for families, as the central base lodge is easy to find yet spacious enough to spread out in. Though it lacks the indulgences and amenities of the larger resorts, the commercial hype and sprawling condos are refreshingly absent. Kids will enjoy the Ala Kazaam Tubing Park, which is illuminated Saturday and holiday nights until 8; it's the only tubing park in the region with its own tow. Summer activities are gearing up at Magic Mountain, with a mountain biking program and a skateboard ramp in the base lodge.

Lifts: 4: 1 triple chair, 1 double, and 2 surface.

Trails and slopes: 40.

Vertical drop: 1,700 feet.

Facilities: Cafeteria in the base lodge.

Ski school: Ski and snowboard lessons. Ask about special events and lift packages.

Tickets: $56 adult on weekends, $39 midweek ($30 half-day); multiday, teen, senior, and junior rates.

ICE SKATING **Riley Rink at Hunter Park** (802-362-0150; 866-866-2086; rileyrink.com) is an Olympic-sized ice-skating rink on Rt. 7A, 1.4 miles north of its junction with Rt. 11/30. Check the Web site for public skating hours and fees; rentals available.

SLEIGH RIDES **Karl Pfister Farm** (802-824-6320) in Landgrove offers the most remote, romantic sleigh rides around. At **Taylor Farm** (802-824-5960; taylor farmvermont.com), box-style sleighs are pulled by Belgian draft horses courtesy of cheesemakers Jon and Kate Wright, on Rt. 11 in Londonderry. (The benefit here is that you can buy some of their wonderful cheese at the same time.)

Other options include the **Equinox** hotel (802-362-4700) and the **Merck Forest and Farmland Center** (802-394-7836).

SNOWMOBILING A *Winter Recreation Map*, available free from the Green Mountain National Forest District Ranger Office (802-362-2307), Manchester, shows trails presently maintained in this area by the Vermont Association of Snow Travelers.

Equinox Snowmobile Tours (802-824-6628), Rt. 11/30 just west of Bromley Mountain, offers guided snowmobile tours on state-of-the-art vehicles. Helmets are provided; boots and clothing can be rented.

Twin Brooks Tours (802-442-4054; 888-616-4054; twinbrookstours.com) in nearby Woodford has guided tours by the hour, half day, or full day.

✷ Green Space

✍ **Equinox Preservation Trust** (802-362-4374), Manchester Village. A not-for-profit organization created in 1993 by Equinox Resort Associates and administered through the Vermont Land Trust and The Nature Conservancy. Some 855 acres on Mount Equinox are now a user-friendly preserve. Secure a map/guide to the trail system (a portion is open to cross-country skiers) and inquire about the nature walks and seminars offered year-round, some geared to children, in conjunction with the Vermont Institute of Natural Science. Horseback riding and mountain biking are also permitted on the ski trails in summer and fall. Be sure at least to walk the 1.2-mile loop through the hardwoods around Equinox Pond. *Note:* All parking for access to the trust property is at the parking lot of the Equinox hotel.

✎ **Merck Forest and Farmland Center** (802-394-7836; merckforest.org), P.O. Box 86, 3270 Rt. 315, Rupert 05768. Open year-round, dawn to dusk; free. This 3,150-acre forest and farming area, set aside in the 1950s to serve as a model for conservation and sustainable land use, is a nonprofit environmental education organization reliant solely on donations. Workshops and nature programs are offered year-round, and there is an organic farm, an organic sugarbush, and Friends of the Forest, a gift shop selling farm products. The forest contains 28 miles of trails for walking, hiking, skiing, snowshoeing, and horseback riding, and a spring-fed swimming pond at the end of a 2-mile hike. Six rustic but fully enclosed cabins accommodating anywhere from 6 to 15 campers are available year round (by reservation) for a modest fee, each with a wood-burning stove, wooden bunks, and a nearby outhouse. Shelters and tent sites are also available. The **Stewardship Field Program** offers educational day programs and camping trips for children ages 4–20. Open year-round.

Grout Pond Recreation Area (802-362-2307), west of the village of Stratton, marked from Kelley Stand Rd. Deep in the Green Mountain National Forest, this remote, forest-encircled lake is a great spot to bird-watch or picnic, complete with grills and a small beach. Tables and fireplaces overlook the shore, and there is a launch for canoes. Short hikes lead around the pond, and one of them wanders 2 miles through the Green Mountain National Forest, emerging at the Somerset Reservoir. Campsites available on a first-come, first-served basis.

Lowell Lake State Park (vtstateparks.com), Londonderry, off Rt. 11 east of Magic Mountain. More than 460 acres surround this pristine lake with a 3.5-mile loop hiking trail. A former summer camp with a rustic lodge, it's currently undeveloped with no facilities. Fishermen drifted in on the evening we stopped by, but we didn't see any swimming access.

Also see Emerald Lake State Park and Hapgood Pond in *Campgrounds*.

LOWELL LAKE STATE PARK IN LONDONDERRY
Christina Tree

✳ Lodging

RESORTS ⊚ 👣 ᶑ ⁹ᵀ⁹ **The Equinox Resort & Spa** (802-362-4700; 800-362-4747; equinoxresort.com), 3567 Main St., Manchester Village 05254. This is Vermont's most historic hotel. It's grown incrementally over the centuries, beginning as a pre–Revolutionary War tavern and becoming a premier summer resort by

1863, the year that Mrs. Abraham Lincoln and her two sons vacationed here. It's the white-columned centerpiece of an aristocratic village that includes a domed courthouse and lineup of 19th-century clapboard mansions. Placed on the National Register of Historic Places in the 1980s, it was renovated from the foundations up. In the 1990s it received another infusion of life from British investors who also added off-road Range Rover driving, falconry, and archery to its exceptional choice of resort activities—which include a world-famous fly-fishing school and use of a private, 18-hole golf course. A spa was also added and the Equinox Preservation Trust formed to preserve the trout pond and nearly 900 aces on and around Mount Equinox, which rises majestically behind the hotel.

In 2008 another $20 million makeover by current owners HEI Hotels & Resorts has revamped the spa and dramatically altered the interior look of the hotel. Replacing the old, low-beamed lobby as its focal entry, designer Geoffrey Bradfield has created an imposing "Great Room" featuring sculpture by Diego Giacometti and a contemporary feel. Guest rooms are furnished with heavy, dark, custom-made beds and wardrobes and fabrics in blue and dark brown stripes on beige; they're also fitted with obtrusively placed large, flat-screen TVs. It's a decor that overstuffs the many smaller rooms designed for a simpler era and one that clashes with a sense of place. Even in the largest and most luxurious suites this is a decor that would seem more appropriate for an urban hotel.

There are now a total of 195 rooms in four buildings, including two-bedroom housekeeping suites in the neighboring Charles Orvis Inn (built in the 19th century as a residence for the founder of the Orvis fly-fishing empire) and in the Townhouses (10 suites with fireplaces and kitchens). There are also 13 traditionally furnished rooms, many with wood-burning fireplaces (and now all with flat-screen TVs) in the 1811 House, a magnificent building dating from the American Revolution and an inn since 1811, except for the few years when it was owned by President Lincoln's granddaughter, Mary Lincoln Isham. Until recently this was an independent bed & breakfast, and it's now marketed as a venue for weddings.

THE EQUINOX RESORT & SPA

Diane E. Foulds

The resort includes the **Falcon Bar**, the **Chop House**, the **Marsh Tavern**, the **Dormy Grill**, and the **Colonnade Dining Room**. The superb **Spa at Equinox** is in a separate building with a fitness center, outdoor and indoor pools, and a full menu of services. You'll also find touring bikes, a 14-acre stocked trout pond, tennis courts, a cross-country ski network, and snowmobiling. Guests enjoy a full concierge service. Rates are $149–599 EP per night, plus a $25 resort fee.

INNS AND BED & BREAKFASTS

In Manchester

& "I" **The Inn at Ormsby Hill** (802-362-1163; 800-670-2841; ormsbyhill .com), 1842 Main St., Manchester Center 05255. The inn is 2 miles southwest of Manchester Village on Rt. 7A, set in 2.5 acres of rolling lawns with spectacular mountain views. This gracious, elegant manor was the home of Edward Isham—Robert Todd Lincoln's law partner—and his family for 100 years. Its connection to Hildene is strong, spiritually and aesthetically. Innkeepers Chris and Ted Sprague offer eight guest rooms and two suites that they obviously enjoyed distinctively decorating some in Waverly prints, all with exceptional antiques. Each has a fireplace and two-person Jacuzzi; some come with two-person steam sauna. The spacious Frances Suite affords views of the Green Mountains and is fitted with a wet bar, two fireplaces, and his-and-hers bathrooms. The Taft Suite, with its wood-burning fireplace and huge four-poster, is the unofficial honeymoon suite, but every one of the rooms is romantic enough to qualify. The downstairs Library Room is handicapped accessible. Common space includes a formal parlor and an inviting library lined with bookshelves that hold many of Isham's personal volumes. The huge, many-windowed dining room with ornately carved hearth is the scene of bountiful breakfasts featuring Chris's famous breakfast dessert, a specialty of the house. Ask to see the prison cell in the basement; it may be Manchester's earliest jail. Room rates ($195–315 midweek, $235–415 weekends, more on holidays) include breakfast and gratuities.

"I" **The Inn at Manchester** (802-362-1793; 800-273-1793; innatman chester.com), 3967 Main St., Rt. 7A, Box 41, Manchester Village 05254. A gracious old home set back from Main Street with an expansive front porch, big windows, gables, and three floors. Frank and Julie Hanes have upgraded its 18 rooms, which include 5 suites (4 rooms are in the restored, vintage-1867 carriage house out back). All have full private bath, TV, and air-conditioning, and four have working fireplace. The dining room and parlors are imaginatively and comfortably furnished with a mix of modern and 19th-century art under high ceilings. The tapestries and Oriental carpets give the common areas a worldly, sophisticated feel. There's a fully licensed bar, a secluded pool in the back meadow, and plenty of rocking chairs on the rear porch. Breakfasts are full and hearty, including homemade breads and such treats as cottage cakes—a cottage cheese concoction served with hot apricot sauce. Children over 13 are welcome. Rates are $155–295 per room, including a full breakfast and self-service pantry with drinks and fresh-baked goods.

∞ & "I" **Reluctant Panther Inn & Restaurant** (802-362-2568; 800-822-2331; reluctantpanther.com), 17–39 West Rd., Manchester 05254. This gray, purple-shuttered home, a village landmark, burned to the ground in

September 2005, only a month after it changed hands. Innkeepers Liz and Jerry Lavalley and their son Matt have rebuilt and then some, adding an elevator, restaurant, and wine cellar and improving the 20 guest rooms while retaining some of the inn's historic look. The suites in the adjacent Porter House, which the fire missed, have been redecorated with fine linens and antiques. Several rooms and all the suites have a fireplace. Many suites feature two wood-burning fireplaces— one in front of the two-person whirlpool bath and a second in the bedroom. All have private bath, room phone, and cable TV, and two rooms are wheelchair accessible. Breakfast is served in-house to guests only, but the sophisticated dining room, the tavern, and a more casual bottle-lined eatery, The Wine Cellar, are accessible to all (see *Dining Out*). Open year-round; $259–659 per room includes breakfast.

⊙ ♪ よ **Wilburton Inn** (802-362-2500; 800-648-4944; wilburton.com), River Rd., Manchester 05254. This secluded Tudor brick mansion, once home to a stockbroker, is set in 20 acres of manicured, sculpture-spotted gardens. Common rooms are richly paneled; the large living room has a piano, comfortable window seats and couches, and Oriental rugs. There are 4 suites and 5 bedrooms in the main house, plus another 25 rooms in outlying cottages. The grounds include a pool and tennis courts. Dinner is served in the clublike Billiard Room. Psychiatrist Albert Levis, the inn's owner since 1987, has opened a holistic center on the property and offers massage, clinics, and workshops on mind–body harmony. $135–325 per couple (plus a 10 percent service charge) includes a full breakfast and afternoon tea. Weddings are a specialty.

The Inn at Willow Pond (802-362-4733; outside Vermont 800-533-3533; innatwillowpond.com), Box 1429, Manchester Center 05255. Located 2.3 miles north on Rt. 7A and owned by the Bauer family, this inn offers 40 spacious guest rooms and suites in three separate, contemporary buildings on a hillside overlooking the Manchester Country Club's golf course. The 18th-century Meeting House reception building contains the lofty main lounge, conference facilities, a fitness center with exercise equipment, two saunas, and a library. There's also an outdoor lap pool and a restaurant (northern Italian cuisine) in a renovated 1770 house. The suites feature a living room with a wood-burning fireplace. $198–218 for a standard room, $248–288 for a one-bedroom fireplace suite, $428–468 for a two-bedroom fireplace suite. Full breakfast is served in the restaurant on weekends and holidays. Many packages available.

♞ ⁗¶⁗ **Seth Warner Inn** (802-362-3830; sethwarnerinn.com), P.O. Box 281, 2353 Main St., Manchester Center 05255. This imposing vintage-1800 house is set back from Rt. 7A southwest of Manchester Village, and it's a beauty—carefully restored by Stasia and Richard Carter. Ask to see the thank-you note that Robert Todd Lincoln wrote after staying here in 1911. Rooms with open beams and stenciling are furnished in antiques and curtained in lace. Five bright guest rooms have country quilts, queen canopy bed, and private bath. Common space includes a gracious living room, a small library, and the dining room, in which guests gather for a full breakfast. There is also a deck outside overlooking the brook-fed duck pond. $135–145 per room includes breakfast. Children 12 and over.

♪ **Ira Allen House** (802-362-2284; 877-362-2283; iraallenhouse.com), 6311 Rt. 7A, Sunderland (mailing address: P.O. Box 251, Manchester 05254). Maria and Ed Jones are the innkeepers in this nicely renovated and expanded roadside tavern built by Ethan Allen (his brother Ira was the surveyor) in 1779 with a "new" wing added in 1846. There are five suites, some set up for families. It's a mile south of Manchester and 3 miles north of Arlington, near the entrance to the Mount Equinox toll road. Across Rt. 7A, the property includes lovely river frontage with Adirondack chairs set out under a big willow tree. The Battenkill is good for trout fishing; for the warm-blooded, there's a 10-foot-deep swimming hole here. $125–275 per room with full breakfast.

In Arlington 05250
∞ "1" **The Arlington Inn** (802-375-6532; 800-443-9442; arlingtoninn .com), 3904 Rt. 7A in the center of Arlington, occupies the stunning 1848 Greek Revival mansion built by Martin Chester Deming, a Vermont railroad magnate, and has been used as an inn off and on since 1889. Owners Eric (a noted chef) and Elizabeth Berger offer 18 rooms: 6 suites in the main house, 6 in the carriage house, and 6 in the adjacent 1830 parsonage. Most are spacious and furnished with Victorian antiques, and there's a formal parlor. Sylvester's Study on the ground floor of the main building is particularly impressive. The units in the parsonage have Drexel cherry four-posters and sleigh beds, TV, and air-conditioning. The inn is also a popular spot for dinner (see *Dining Out*), and the gardens make this a great spot for weddings or civil unions. Rates per room are $129–319, including a full breakfast. MAP also available. Open all year. Value season packages.

∞ 🐾 🐕 ♿ "1" **West Mountain Inn** (802-375-6516; westmountaininn.com), 144 West Mountain Inn Rd. at the jct.

of Rt. 313 and River Rd. west of Arlington. Open year-round. A very special place with the easy warmth and comfort that comes with longtime ownership. Overlooking splendid views of Mount Equinox and the Battenkill Valley, the Carlson family converted this rambling, century-old white-clapboard hillside home to an inn in 1978. Current innkeeper Amie Emmons (a Carlson) prides herself on her long-time staff. The 22 attractive rooms, 9 of which are suites, are country elegant, named for famous people associated with Arlington; a copy of Dorothy Canfield Fisher's *Vermont Tradition* is in every room. There are also 3 two-bedroom town houses with cooking facilities at the Historic Mill on the property. There are paneled, many-windowed common rooms with fireplaces and a children's playroom. Breakfast and dinner are served daily; Sunday brunch seasonally (see *Dining Out*). The inn's 150-acre property includes walking and snowshoeing trails, gardens, and llamas in residence. A number of special events are featured, such as a St. Lucia Festival of Lights in early December, Maple Weekend in early May, and Ethan Allen Days over Father's Day weekend. $165–310 B&B for two, $240–368 MAP. Pets are $30 per day.

🌷 "1" **Country Willows B&B** (802-375-0019; 800-796-2585; country willows.com), 332 East Arlington Rd. Longtime area innkeepers Anne and Ron Weber offer true hospitality in this 1850s village historic landmark with four spacious, comfortable guest rooms, all with private bath, decorated in Victoriana. The West Mountain Room has a fine view, a fireplace, and a sitting area. The Dorset Suite is a two-bedroom, one-bath suite that can accommodate parents with school-aged children. The Manchester Room has a king-sized four-poster, a gas fireplace, and a deep claw-foot tub plus separate stall shower. There is a wraparound porch and a hammock for two. (The Webers also offer a two-bedroom, self-catered Manchester cottage.) Rates of $146–195 per double include full country breakfast—possibly an omelet with fresh tarragon, basil, and veggies from Anne's garden, served with Ron's secret-recipe apple compote and French press coffee.

✿ ♿ ⁗⁗ **Hill Farm Inn** (802-375-2269; 800-882-2545; hillfarminn.com), 458 Hill Farm Rd. Located off Rt. 7A north of the village, this historic farmstead, owned and managed by Al and Lisa Gray, is set on 50 acres of land with walking trails bordering the Battenkill. The 1830 main building, 1790 guest house, and four seasonal cabins hold a total of 15 rooms, some of them suites or cottages, all with private bath. Double rooms are $110–235, including full country breakfast. Children are welcome at special rates.

🐾 ✿ **The Inn on Covered Bridge Green** (802-375-9489; 800-726-9480; coveredbridgegreen.com), 3587 River Rd. Fans of Norman Rockwell can now actually stay in his former home, built in 1792 across from a red covered bridge and the village green where Ethan Allen mustered his Green Mountain Boys. The inn offers four guest rooms, all with private bath, gas fireplace, and air-conditioning. Pets are accepted in the two housekeeping cottages, one of which was the studio where Rockwell painted. There's swimming, canoeing, and fly-fishing in the Battenkill just a few hundred feet from the inn, and the setting is quintessentially Vermont. $175–225 includes a full country breakfast.

∞ ✿ ⁗⁗ **Green River Inn** (802-375-2272; 888-648-2212; greenriverinn .com), 3402 Sandgate Rd., Sandgate 05250. Three miles off Rt. 313 from New York State and 7.5 miles west from Rt. 7A in Arlington. Sixteen renovated guest rooms, all with private bath, some with whirlpool bath, balcony, and fireplace, others geared to families. There are quilts, down comforters, Waverly prints, and antiques, and the rooms have river or mountain views. Guests are also welcome in the sunroom, on the outdoor deck, and in the special children's room. Bob and Carol Potozney specialize in weddings, reunions, and special events. $100–205 with breakfast, plus 15 percent gratuity.

In Dorset 05251

∞ 🐾 ♿ **The Barrows House** (802-867-4455; 800-639-1620; barrows house.com), 3156 Main St., Box 98. This exceptional mini resort on Rt. 30, now owned by Linda and Jim McGinnis, features attractive, flexibly arranged accommodations: 18 rooms, 10 suites. The 1796 house, Dorset's first parsonage, is a short walk from the center of this historic village, but there is an out-in-the-country feel to the 11-acre grounds, which include organic gardens, a gazebo, a heated outdoor swimming pool, and two tennis courts. In summer bikes are available; golf and hiking are nearby. In winter cross-country ski equipment is available. There are comfortable sitting rooms in the main house and the larger cottages, where large families or groups can be lodged. A convivial bar is wallpapered to resemble a private library. The dining room and a guest room in one of the outer buildings are wheelchair accessible. The dining room is outstanding (see *Dining Out*). $165–340 per couple, including breakfast and dinner; B&B rates also available.

🐚 🐾 **Dovetail Inn** (802-867-5747; 888-867-5747; dovetailinn.com), Rt. 30. This unpretentiously gracious 1800s inn faces Dorset's green. The 10 guest rooms (all with private bath) range from cozy to luxurious (Hearth-side has a fireplace, wet bar, and deck), all with private bath and A/C. Jean and Jim Kingston are hospitable hosts. Guests have access to a butler's pantry with a fridge, mircrowave and sink. An expanded continental breakfast is served in the Keeping Room or in guest rooms. From $89 midweek and $115 on weekends for the smallest double room to $250 for a two-room suite with a fireplace and TV, sleeping up to four. There's no WiFi, but the library is across the way.

♂ & **Inn at West View Farm** (802-867-5715; 800-769-4903; innatwest viewfarm.com), Rt. 30, just south of Dorset, is a small, well-groomed lodge with an appealing personality, once the focus of a 200-acre farm, now known especially for its exceptional cuisine. (Under the direction of chef Raymond Chen, the dining room—see *Dining Out*—remains the focal point of the inn.) Christal Siewertsen is the innkeeper. The inn has a large, cozy living room with a wood-burning fire-place, common space also includes an inviting, wicker-filled sunporch. One downstairs room has been fitted for handicapped access, and the 10 upstairs rooms are all furnished comfortably with cheerful paper, private bath, and bright, crisp fabrics; all rooms are air-conditioned. Rates are $110–200, including full breakfast. Children over 12.

& **The Dorset Inn** (802-867-5500; 877-367-7389; dorsetinn.com), 8 Church St. A national historic site and the state's most venerable hostelry (in continuous operation since 1796) faces Dorset's pristine town green. Known for its cuisine (see *Dining Out*) and relaxing atmosphere, the inn has 30 guest rooms, all newly renovated with air-conditioning and private bath. It's

within walking distance of the theater and offers a fireplace in the parlor as well as a lineup of front-porch rockers from which you might not want to stir. $195–250 includes breakfast; $385–500 MAP.

❀ ♂ **Marble West Inn** (802-867-4155; 800-453-7629; marblewestinn .com), out Dorset West Rd. This Greek Revival house has seven marble columns on its marble front porches, and there are marble walkways and three marble fireplaces. It offers eight well-decorated guest rooms (one a two-room suite with fireplace), an inviting living room, and a music room. The stencil work in the entrance hall-way and on stairway walls is exceptional, and the high ceilings and bull's-eye moldings are pleasant reminders of an earlier era. Guests mingle in the library for drinks and conversation. Rates are $125–225 per couple, including a candlelit, gourmet breakfast and afternoon tea. Pets by prearrangement.

In Danby 05739
❀ "ŧ" **The Quail's Nest** (802-293-5099; 800-599-6444; quailsnestbandb .com), 81 S. Main St., is a homey, pleasant B&B in an 1835 house in the middle of this small village, handy to the Appalachian and Long trails. The four guest rooms, all with private bath, are furnished with antiques and country quilts. Four have king-sized beds. There's a comfy living room with a wood-burning fireplace, hardwood floors, and a library where guests can browse the titles or choose a movie to play on the VCR. In summer months breakfast is served on a back deck with views of the Green Mountains. Children 16 and over welcome. $96 includes a full breakfast. Reservations required.

In Weston 05161
∞ ❀ & "ŧ" **Inn at Weston** (802-824-

6789; innweston.com), P.O. Box 66, Rt. 100. Innkeepers Bob and Linda Aldrich have made this truly one of Vermont's outstanding inns. A doctor who has taken early retirement, Bob nurtures his collection of more than 1,000 orchids in a greenhouse in cooler months, distributing them through the rooms and in summer around the inn's terrace and gazebo. Linda, an enthusiastic gardener, has overseen the fabulous flowering of the 6 acres surrounding this vintage 1848 inn on the edge of Weston Village. The 13 guest rooms are divided among the main inn, the Coleman House (with its own library/sitting room) across the road, and the Carriage House, with the most luxurious suites. All have private bath and are delightfully furnished in antiques, fitted with phone, A/C, and TV; some have deck, whirlpool tub, and fireplace. The dining room (see *Dining Out*) is open to the public and justifiably popular, especially in summer when the Weston Playhouse is a big draw. The common room here is the library, inviting guests to relax by hearth with a well-chosen book. Given the landscaped grounds, fine dining, and luxurious lodging, this is a popular place for weddings. $225–285 in the main inn, $185–205 in the Coleman House, $325 in the Carriage House. Add $50 per room on holidays.

Colonial House Inn & Motel (802-824-6286; 800-639-5033; cohoinn.com), 287 Rt. 100. A rare and delightful combination of nine motel units and six traditional inn rooms (shared baths), connected by a pleasant dining room, a comfortable, sunken sitting room with dried flowers hanging from the rafters, and a solarium overlooking the lawn. Innkeepers Kim and Jeff Seymour (Kim is the daughter of former owners John and Betty Nunnikhoven) make all ages feel welcome, and most guests are repeats. Rates include memorable, multicourse breakfasts. Dinner is served family-style ($19.95) on weekends. The inn is 2 miles south of the village, with lawn chairs facing a classic farmscape across the road; most guest rooms overlook a meadow. Rooms are $73–123 double occupancy (B&B), from $58.50 off-season; extra charges for children, singles, pets ($10 per day), and service. Ramp available for wheelchairs.

In Peru 05152

Johnny Seesaw's (802-824-5533; 800-424-CSAW; johnnyseesaw .com), 3574 Rt. 11. Built as a dance hall in 1920 and converted into one of Vermont's first ski lodges, this is a wonderfully weathered, comfortable place. Within walking distance of the slopes in winter, it offers tennis and an Olympic-sized pool in summer. There are 25 air-conditioned rooms—doubles, master bedrooms with fireplace in the main house, and family suites—as well as four cottages with fireplace, good for large families and small groups. There is a licensed pub (see *Dining Out*); "Yankee cuisine" dinners are à la carte and have a French accent. The living room boasts Vermont's first circular fireplace. Rates are $80–140 per room in the lodge, cottages $110–360, including a full breakfast. Add 15 percent service charge, and $5–6, depending on season, for children staying in a room with parent. $10 nightly for pets.

The Wiley Inn (802-824-6600; 888-843-6600), P.O. Box 7, 2759 Rt. 11, just 1 mile from Bromley. Its core is an 1835 farmhouse containing a delightful living room with fireplace, library, and dining room. A six-room motel-like wing, now refurbished, includes one room with a fireplace and a two-person whirlpool tub. A room with the same amenities is available in the main house. Jerry and Judy Goodman extend a special welcome to families with the configuration of a number of rooms, as well as a game room with a TV, videos, a piano, and toys. Couples, on the other hand, may prefer the suitably quiet and romantic rooms in the original part of this rambling inn. Altogether there are 14 rooms, 3 two-bedroom suites, and several family rooms, all with private bath. Summer facilities include a backyard heated pool and play area; there's also a hot tub in the woods that holds eight. Summer rates are $95–165; $135–205 for family rooms and suites. In winter it's $115–195 for rooms, $185–235 for suites. Children stay free in parent's room.

In Landgrove 05148

∞ 🍴 👻 🐾 ♂ 🔷 **The Landgrove Inn** (802-824-6673; 800-669-8466; landgroveinn.com), 132 Landgrove Rd. Innkeepers Tom and Maureen Checchia have improved this red-clapboard building that rambles back and around, beginning with the 1810 house, ending an acre or two away. The "Vermont continuous architecture" draws guests through a handsome lobby, past 18 air-conditioned rooms (16 with private bath) that meander off in all directions, through the inviting Rafter Room Lounge (huge, filled with games and books), to the attractive dining room in the original house. Its serene location and multiple wings make it an ideal place for a writing workshop or retreat. Check the Web site for frequent workshops in art, writing, and dance based at the new InView Center for the Arts, a post-and-beam studio by the pond. Our favorite rooms are tucked up under the eaves in the oldest part of the inn, papered in floral prints and furnished with carefully chosen antiques but with new baths. Many rooms are well suited to families, who

also will appreciate the heated pool, the stocked trout pond (catch and release), lawn games, and the two tennis courts. In winter you can take a sleigh ride or step out onto the 10 km groomed cross-country trail system that leads to the picturesque village of Landgrove (just a church, a former school, and a salting of homes cupped in a hollow). You can ski on into the surrounding Green Mountain National Forest. Bromley Ski Area is just 6 miles away, and Stratton is a 20-minute drive. Breakfast is an event here, served on oak tables in the wood-beamed dining room with a many-windowed wall overlooking the garden. The dining room is open to the public five nights a week. Dining is by candlelight, with a choice of entrées prepared by a well-respected local chef (see *Dining Out*). $130–175 per couple with full breakfast, less for the two rooms with shared bath, more for the two deluxe rooms with sitting areas, fireplaces and Jacuzzis; pet fee.

In and around Londonderry

🍴 ♂ 🔷 "♦" **The Londonderry Inn** (802-824-5226; 800-644-5226; londonderryinn.com), 8 Melendy Hill Rd., South Londonderry 05155. On a knoll overlooking the West River, this large historic home has been a country inn since 1941. Innkeepers Maya Kearn and Brian Drummond have decorated the 22 guest rooms with folk-art-painted furniture and walls, as well as patchwork quilts and teddy bears on every bed. Room 6 (on the third floor) sleeps eight. The bright common rooms include a huge stone fireplace, tropical bird aviary, billiards room, movie room, and Maya's antique bell collection. Fresh-baked cookies are served every afternoon. Continental breakfast and afternoon tea are included. Maya has won state recognition for running an environmentally conscious inn. Children will enjoy the resident dogs and cats, thriving gardens, spring-fed outdoor swimming pool, and the many nooks to explore. Gift shop on premises. $136–156 for double rooms, $186–276 for larger family rooms, includes breakfast.

MOTELS & **Palmer House Resort** (802-362-3600; 800-917-6245; palmer house.com), P.O. Box 1964, 5383 Main St., Manchester Center 05255. A family-owned luxury motel with 50 rooms/suites with fireplace and Jacuzzi, all with cable TV, refrigerator, in-room coffee, and phone. Facilities include indoor and outdoor pools, fit-ness center, stocked trout pond, tennis courts, and nine-hole golf course, all on 22 acres adjacent to the Green Mountain National Forest. The vener-able Ye Olde Tavern restaurant (see *Dining Out*) is right next door. Rooms $95–185, suites $190–300, depending on season. Children 12 and over.

✔ & **The Manchester View** (802-362-2739; 800-548-4141; manchester view.com), P.O. Box 1268, Rt. 7A, Manchester Center 05255. Tom and Pat Barnett own this place just north of town with marvelous views. Thirty-five rooms with fridge, cable TV, VCR, and wireless Internet, plus 3 two-bed-room suites and 7 one-bedroom suites (most with fireplace, living room, and two-person Jacuzzi); also handicapped-accessible units. Facilities include a heated outdoor pool in summer. Golf and tennis available at nearby Man-chester Country Club. Summer: $115–180 for standard rooms, $195–300 for suites. From $85 in win-ter because this is the side of town far-thest from the ski areas.

🐾 ✔ ⁞¶⁞ **The Barnstead Inn** (802-362-1619; 800-331-1619; barnstead inn.com), Box 998, 349 Bonnet St., Manchester Center 05255. This isn't a motel, but it doesn't quite fit into any category—and it's a gem. Just up Bon-net St. (Rt. 30), two blocks from the amenities of town, Vermonter Neil Humphrey has converted an 1830s hay barn into 14 attractive rooms with cable TV, A/C, individual thermostats, and lovely baths. It's all been done with consummate grace and charm, with many small touches like braided rugs, rockers, bedside lighting, and exposed old beams. There is also an attractive, secluded outdoor pool and a pond, plus an attractive pub (no food or drink but a nice place to sit). $99–290. The high-end rates are for spacious suites with fireplace and Jacuzzi. No meals, but an easy walk to good breakfast places.

✔ **The Weathervane Motel** (802-362-2444; 800-262-1317), Rt. 7A, 2212 Main St., Manchester 05254. Set back from the road with two picture windows in each of its 22 large units, this is a motel with class. Each air-conditioned room has TV, free coffee, and full or queen-sized beds, many with linens as fine as any upscale inn. Some of the rooms connect. There is a common area with Oriental carpets, antiques, and an outdoor deck. Out back you'll find a volleyball court, a trampoline, and a heated pool. Kids are welcome, pets not. $75–150 includes breakfast in summer.

⁞¶⁞ **Brandmeyer's Mountainside Lodge** (802-824-5851; brandmeyers lodge.com), 913 Rt. 100, Weston 05161. Located north of town, as Rt. 100 begins its climb up heavily wooded Terrible Mountain to Ludlow. Bob and Lisa Brandmeyer operate a cheery motel, some family units with double beds, all with fridge and TV. The Moose Lounge, with a reasonably priced menu, is open Thu.–Sat. $109–139 includes breakfast.

CONDOMINIUMS AND SKI LODGES

At Stratton Mountain Resort 05155

The complex at the top of Stratton's 4-mile access road includes two large wooden inns and some 300 condominiums. There's a central reservations/check-in desk and Web site for all: in-state 802-297-4000; 800-787-2886; stratton.com.

"1" Long Trail House The newest Stratton lodge is a five-minute walk from the lifts. Amenities include a concierge desk, heated year-round outdoor pool, hot tubs, and a sauna. Winter rates: from $110 for a weekday in a studio to $769 for a two-bedroom unit during peak season.

Stratton Mountain Inn. All 122 rooms and suites have private bath, phone, and TV, and facilities include a large dining room, saunas, whirlpools, and an outdoor pool. Winter rates are $69–309 per night, including continental breakfast.

Stratton Condominiums. The number of the resort's privately owned condominium units in the rental pool varies at any given time, as do the range of sizes and shapes. All resort guests have access to the sports center and its indoor pool, exercise machines, and racquetball and tennis courts (a fee is charged).

Liftline Lodge. This older, Austrian-style 70-room lodge is close to Stratton's lifts and village shops and restaurants. At $59 ski-and-stay per person midweek, this is the best deal at Stratton and handy to the lifts. Don't expect to find a staffed front desk, however, and note that the walls are thin, carpets worn, and so on. Once upon a time it was privately owned, well tended.

Elsewhere

✔ Bromley Village (802-824-5458; 800-865-4786; bromley.com), P.O. Box 1130, Manchester Center 05255, is a complex of 50 attractive one- to four-bedroom condo units adjacent to the ski area. Summer facilities include a pool and tennis courts. In winter you can walk to the trails; there is also a shuttle bus. Call for rates.

❀ ✿ ✔ "1" Swiss Inn (802-824-3442; 800-847-9477; swissinn.com), 249 Rt. 11, Londonderry 05148. Handy to Magic Mountain and to Bromley, this is a family-geared lodge with 19 basic but spacious rooms, all with private bath. Public space includes a library as well as a sitting room and bar. Joe and Pat Donahue feature Swiss dishes in their dining room (see *Dining Out*). There's also an outdoor pool. $75–150 per room includes a full breakfast.

CAMPGROUNDS Green Mountain National Forest (802-362-2307), District Ranger Office, Manchester. A public information office serving the southern half of the 400,000-acre Green Mountain National Forest is located on Rt. 30/11 east of Manchester at 2538 Depot St.; open year-round, Mon.–Fri. 8–4:30. Maps and details are available about where to fish, hike, cross-country ski, and camp. All national forest campsites are available on a first-come, first-served basis.

Emerald Lake State Park (802-362-1655; vtstateparks.com), 65 Emerald Lake Lane, East Dorset, just off Rt. 7. Open Memorial Day–Columbus Day weekend. This 430-ace park surrounds Emerald Lake, named for the color of its water. There's a small beach, a snack bar, and a hillside picnic area; also paddle- and pedal-boat rentals. There's good fishing, and 67 campsites and 37 lean-tos are sited on a headily wooded ridge about the lake. Facilities include flush toilets, hot showers, and a dump station. Hiking and nature trails.

& **Hapgood Pond Recreation Area** (802-362-2307; recreation.gov), Hapgood Pond Rd. (off Rt. 11) Peru. Acquired in 1931, this was the beginning of the Green Mountain National Forest. There is swimming, fishing, and limited (but wheelchair-accessible) boating on the 7-acre pond. Removed from the picnic ground and beach are 28 campsites (first come, first served). A pleasant 8-mile forest trail threads through the woods.

🐾 **Dorset RV Park** (802-867-5754 ; dorsetrvpark.com), Rt. 30, Dorset. Open May–Nov. A family-run area offering 13 sites with hot showers, flush toilets, rec room and outdoor games, electric and water hookups, laundry, and camp store. Dogs must be leashed.

✳ Where to Eat

DINING OUT

In Manchester

Mistral's at Toll Gate (802-362-1779), off Rt. 11/30, 10 Tollgate Rd. Open for dinner daily except Wed. in summer; Thu.–Mon. in winter. Reservations recommended. Chef Dana Markey and his wife, Cheryl, maintain this longtime dining landmark, housed in the old tollhouse once serving the Boston-to-Saratoga road. During warm-weather months a brook rushes along just under the windows. The menu might include tournedos of veal lyonnaise, seared diver scallops with mushroom cream, or stuffed chateaubriand. All are accompanied by a *Wine Spectator*–recognized wine list. Entrées $27–40. Seatings begins at 6 PM.

The Perfect Wife (802-362-2817; perfectwife.com), Rt. 11/30, 1 mile east of the Rt. 7 overpass. Open

Tue.–Sun. 5–10 for dinner. Closed Sun. in winter except for holiday weeks. Manchester native Amy Chamberlain was single when she opened this popular restaurant in 1996, but there was an obvious solution: She married her first bartender, Geoff Chamberlain, now the business manager. Amy credits her stint at Arrows in Ogunquit, Maine, for two of her specialties, sautéed crabcakes served with rémoulade on mixed greens as an appetizer ($12) and sesame-crusted yellowfin tuna, seared medium rare and served over stir-fried vegetables ($27) as an entrée. Others range from Howling Wolf (steamed veggies with brown rice pilaf and sweet potato hash for $20) to grilled filet mignon with a wild mushroom, roasted garlic, and Guinness Stout demiglaze ($30). Dining is either in the cobble-walled dining room or the nicely lit greenhouse terrace. It's also possible to dine as we did on an two appetizers (those crabcakes and the yummy Peking duck with Mandarin pancakes). The tavern here is a totally different and equally inviting scene, a lively local gathering place with music on weekends and a pub menu ranging from salads, sandwiches, and burgers to grilled strip steak.

Reluctant Panther (802-362-2568; reluctantpanther.com), 39 West Rd. (Rt. 7A), Manchester Village. Open for dinner Tue.–Sat. The relatively formal (jacket required for men), sleek, Main House Dining Room of the inn features two fireplaces and many windows with views of Mount Equinox and a landscaped backyard with a pond, gardens, and a gazebo. The cuisine is "Northeast regional" with an ever-changing menu, and the wine list is extensive. You might dine on spinach-and-garlic stuffed crispy chicken with lemon and chive risotto, or butter-poached Maine lobster with fresh fettuccine pasta. Entrées $31–43. There's also a more intimate pub with full bar.

The Equinox Resort & Spa (802-362-4700; equinoxresort.com), 3567 Main St., Manchester Village. The hotel offers several dining options. **The Chop House** is decorated in browns, burgundies, and reds with leather banquettes. It features steaks broiled at 1,700 degrees and finished with herb butter ($37–49); sides are extra. **The Marsh Tavern**, occupying the shell of the 1769 tavern by the same name, is open for breakfast, lunch, and dinner daily with live music on weekends. You might dine on hot smoked Scottish salmon or seared beef medallions with Vermont blue cheese gratin potatoes, local morels, and asparagus (entrées $24–45). The elegant **Colonnade Dining Room** is also open seasonally and some holidays for traditional brunch.

🍴 **Ye Olde Tavern** (802-362-0611; yeoldetavern.net), 214 N. Main St., Manchester Center. Open daily for dinner from 5. A genuine 1790 tavern theoretically specializing in "authentic American" dinner dishes like roast tom turkey and pot roast, but steak au poivre and bouillabaisse are also on the menu. One of the better values in town with entrées from $17 (for chicken potpie) to $30. Early-bird menu before 6 PM.

Bistro Henry (802-362-4982; bistro henry.com), 1942 Rt. 11/30. Open for dinner daily except Mon. Dina and Henry Bronson run this Mediterranean-style dining room with a casual atmosphere, a full bar. Mixed reviews lately. You might dine on Merlot-braised lamb shank or linguine with lobster, shrimp, crab, and sea scallops in a brandy tomato cream. Dina's desserts have their own following, particularly the Grand Marnier crème brûlée. Entrées $24–30.

In Dorset

Chantecleer (802-362-1616), Rt. 7A, East Dorset. Open daily except Tue. (Mon. and Tue. in winter, except on holidays) 6–closing. Long regarded as one of Vermont's top restaurants, Swiss chef Michael Baumann's establishment is known for nightly game specials, whole Dover sole Chantecleer ($36), and Australian roast rack of lamb ($38). Leave room for profiterole de maison or coupe Matterhorn. The setting is an elegantly remodeled old dairy barn with a massive fieldstone fireplace. There is an extensive wine list. Reservations essential.

Inn at West View Farm (802-867-5715; innatwestviewfarm.com), 2928 Rt. 30. Open for dinner Thu.–Mon. The main dining room is exceptionally attractive, and the food is dependably good. Chef Raymond Chen describes his cuisine as contemporary American with French influences. Entrées ($27–34) might include coriander-crusted venison with asparagus and basil gnocchi, or sautéed skate with baby spinach and potato puree. Asian-inspired "little dishes" are served in the tavern.

The Barrows House (802-867-4455), Rt. 30. Open for dinner nightly from 5:30. The Dorset Room, a spacious, somewhat formal country dining room, is walled with primitive murals showing how this village looked in the 19th century. In an adjacent room you can watch the snow fall from behind glass walls. On the wall beside the full bar is an autograph collection discovered in an old shoe box; signatures include U.S. presidents and such personalities as P. T. Barnum, Brigham Young, and Jefferson Davis. Diners can select from an à la carte menu that changes seasonally. In autumn, for instance, you might begin with carrot ginger soup, then dine on crisp Long Island duckling with apricot sauce and wild rice. Entrées $17–35.

The Dorset Inn (802-867-5500), 8 Church St. Open daily for all three meals. Popular for pretheater dining, within walking distance of the Dorset Playhouse. Under new ownership, the locally sourced menu in this venerable dining room might include pan-seared free-range duck with a confit leg, white beans, and roasted asparagus, or spinach gnocchi with wild mushrooms, asparagus, and roasted garlic. Entrées $18–30; lighter fare is available from $15.

Nearby
Inn at Weston (802-824-6789; inn weston.com), Rt. 100, Weston. Open from 5:30 nightly. The candlelit dining room and adjacent pub are delightful in any season—and summer dining on the deck and orchid-filled gazebo with its table for six is an added draw. Chef Cassidy Warren uses local ingredients whenever possible. You might begin with maple-smoked Gouda from nearby Taylor Farm followed by a salad of local greens, then dine on pork osso buco from Northeast Family Farms, with house-smoked bacon and Vermont white and green beans. Entrées $28–37.

Café at the Falls (802-824-5288), Weston Playhouse, on the green in Weston. Open for dinner on theater nights beginning at 5:30; 5 on Sun. Currently run by the Inn at Weston, this is a pleasant dining room with windows overlooking a waterfall. It's less formal dining than at the inn; full bar and cabaret performances with light fare and dessert after the performance. Reserve. (See also *Entertainment.*)

Three Clock Inn (802-824-6327; threeclockinn.com), 95 Middletown Rd., South Londonderry. Dinner daily except Mon. Reserve and request directions. Owner Serge Roche works magic in a rustic dining space with low

beams and glowing hearths on a back street in this little-visited hamlet. The menu changes frequently but the dozen appetizers might include foie gras, oysters on the half shell, and $175 caviar. Specialties include Maine lobster potpie with root vegetables and cream, roasted Vermont farm rabbit, and aged New York strip sirloin au poivre. This is not a place to pass up desserts like crème caramel à L'orange or warm Valrhona chocolate cake. $50–72 for a complete dinner, entrées $28–44 à la carte. There is an extensive wine cellar.

Mio Bistro (802-325-3041; miobistro .net), Rt. 30, Pawlet Village. Open Wed.–Sun. 5–9; Thu.–Sun. in winter. The former rail station in this tiny, picturesque village now houses a Mediterranean-inspired country bistro with an open kitchen and terrace. The focus is on from-scratch meals with fresh ingredients. The à la carte menu might include vodka penne with seafood, fresh basil, and prosciutto ($18), or Black Angus strip steak with french fries ($26).

♪ **Johnny Seesaw's** (802-824-5533; 800-424-CSAW; johnnyseesaw.com), 3574 Rt. 11, Peru. A Prohibition-era dance hall, then one of New England's first ski lodges, this atmospheric inn with its central round fireplace is well worth a dinnertime visit even if you don't happen to be staying there. The extensive French-influenced menu usually includes a choice of veal and seafood dishes and pork chops Vermont-style, but huge prime rib of beef is the house special (children can always get hamburgers or pasta as well as half-sized portions). Adult entrées $19–34. Soft music played live on weekends.

♪ **The Landgrove Inn** (802-824-6673), 132 Landgrove Rd., Landgrove. Dinner by reservation Wed.–Sun. This fine old inn is off by itself up dirt roads at the edge of a tiny village. Meals are by candlelight in a delightful old dining room with windows overlooking the garden. You might begin with Elise's famous crab and shrimp cake, then dine on crispy roast duckling (entrées $24–30). Three-course prix fixe "Vermont night" dinners are offered year-round on Wed. and Sun. (nonholiday periods) for $28.

The Arlington Inn (802-375-6532; arlingtoninn.com), 3904 Rt. 7A in the center of Arlington. Chef Eric Berger has a reputation for serving reliably fine food in his magnificent 1848 mansion. There's a mauve-walled formal dining room, or you can dine in the more casual **Deming Tavern**. The Arlington Inn mixed grill, with petit mignon, duck breast, and loin lamb chop, is the house special. There's always a vegetarian dish, maybe grilled vegetable ravioli. Entrées $24–32.

West Mountain Inn (802-375-6516; westmountaininn.com), at the junction of Rt. 313 and River Rd. west of Arlington. Open daily by reservation 6–8:30 PM. Hidden away on up on a hillside, overlooking the Battenkill Valley and Mount Equinox, this is a gracious inn that's well worth seeking out. Fruit and cheese are served in the bar, followed by chef Jeff Scott's five-course ($44 prix fixe) dinners, served in the many-windowed and paneled dining room. The menu changes nightly but appetizers might include caramelized leek puree with Gouda crisps or sautéed sea scallops with a smoked bacon and maple cream sauce, followed by a salad and sorbet. The choice of entrées might range from grilled sirloin with local blue cheese flan, artichokes, and wine to vegetarian soba noodles with tofu, mushrooms, scallions, and roasted peppers in lime ginger broth.

In and around Manchester: breakfast/lunch

The Dormy Grill (802-362-4700, ext. 833; equinox.com), in the Golf Club at the Equinox on Union St., serves lunch outside daily mid-May–mid-Oct., 11:30–4, on the back deck. Never mind the food; feast your eyes on the spectacular mountain vistas here at one of the best views in town. Tasty soups, salads, burgers, and wraps. Dinners till Labor Day weekend, Thu.–Sun. 5:30–8. Reservations are wise, as the best seats fill up fast.

Garden Café at the Southern Vermont Arts Center (802-366-8298; svac.org), West Rd., 1 mile north of the Equinox, Manchester Village. Open May–Oct., Tue.–Sat. Dinner is served on performance nights, when reservations are strongly recommended. The food is fine and the setting is superb: a pleasant indoor room or the outside terrace, both featuring views over the sculpture garden and down the mountain to Manchester Village.

Al Ducci's Italian Pantry (802-362-4449;), Elm St., one block up Highland

THE DORMY GRILL AT THE EQUINOX RESORT & SPA

Diane E. Foulds

Ave. from Rt. 11/30, Manchester Center. Open daily till 6 PM, except closed Mon. Eat in or take out at this authentic Italian deli. Daily specials, plus the best supply of specialty cheeses and artisan breads in the region.

& **Little Rooster Cafe** (802-362-3496), Rt. 7A south, 4645 Main St., Manchester Center. Breakfast and lunch 7:30–2:30; closed Wed. This cheerful midtown café is probably the hottest lunch spot in town. Full liquor. If you come at noon, be prepared to wait. No credit cards.

❧ **Gourmet Café and Deli**, Rt. 7A, Manchester Center. Open daily 7:30–5. Tucked back into Manchester Center's Green Mountain Village shopping center, this café is a real find with a pleasant atmosphere and service, reasonable prices, great salads and sandwiches. Save room for Phyllis's French silk pie. A pleasant terrace in warm weather; beer, wine, and mimosas.

The Lawyer and the Baker (802-366-8018), 32 Bonnet St. Great breads and pastries, soups, salads, and immense sandwiches. Limited but sunny seating. A particularly good breakfast bet.

Zoey's Deli & Bakery, Rt. 11/30, Manchester Center. Serving lunch only, 11:30–2:30. Fresh-baked breads and from-scratch soups and desserts make this a good bet.

◦Ⴒ◦ **Spiral Press Café** (802-362-9944; spiralpresscafe.com), 15 Bonnet St., at the Northshire Bookstore. Open daily 8–7, Tue.–Sat. until 9 PM. A pleasant oasis for book lovers with teas and specialty coffees, good sandwiches.

Up for Breakfast (802-362-4204), 4235 Main St. Breakfast Mon.–Fri. 7–noon, weekends 7–1. Bright, artdecked space with tables and a counter, an open kitchen, and blackboard menu specials—trout with eggs and hash browns, or wild turkey hash. Still worth climbing the stairs but on our most recent visit service was sluggish, portions smaller, and prices higher.

❀ **Sherrie's Cafe** (802-362-3468), Rt. 11/30, 709A Depot St. Open 8–3, this café serves great breakfasts, homemade soups, sandwiches, salads, and desserts. Outdoor seating.

In and around Manchester: dinner
Also see Ye Olde Tavern under *Dining Out*, arguably the best value in town.

❀ **Candeleros** (802-362-0836), Main St., Manchester Center, is a Tex-Mex cantina and grill open daily for lunch and dinner. Chips and salsa when you sit down, 36 tequilas, children's menu, and a pleasant outdoor patio in summer. Margaritas are half price on Thursday.

❀ **Mulligan's Manchester** (802-362-3663), Rt. 7A, Manchester Village. Open daily for lunch and dinner. A convenient, moderately priced, family-geared place featuring flame-grilled steaks, seafood, and pastas. Children's menu.

❀ **Laney's Restaurant** (802-362-4456; laneysrestaurant.com), Rt. 11/30, Manchester Center. Open from 5 PM, this is a festive, kid-friendly spot, specializing in exotic pizzas from a wood-fired brick oven, Adam's Ribs (baby back pork ribs), Gone with the Wind (pork and beef ribs), and Oliver Twist (pasta primavera); draft beer in frosted mugs.

❀ **Bob's Diner** (802-362-8171), Rt. 11/30, 2279 Depot St., Manchester Depot. Open daily for breakfast, lunch, and dinner. A shining chrome diner with very good food (the milk shakes are literally the best) at good prices in this upscale part of the world. Give it a try, especially with kids.

Zoey's Double Hex Restaurant (802-362-4600), Rt. 11/30. Open 11–9.

Just what you may be looking for: a cheery informal atmosphere with roomy booths and famous burgers—but plenty of other choices as well, from meat loaf and chicken potpie to sage-rubbed grilled rib eye. Full liquor license.

Depot Café (366-8181), 515 Depot St. Open 11:30–9. Open for lunch and dinner inside the Turkish rug and furniture store Depot 62, definitely a hidden treasure. We've heard from a number of sources that the fresh, organic, vegetarian food and brick-oven pizzas are outstanding. Meals are served at a long table with mismatched chairs in the center of the store.

In Arlington
Jonathon's Table (802-375-1021), Rt. 7A. Open May–Dec. Keep your eyes peeled for the sign; the place is worth your trouble. Cheerful and done in lots of natural wood, Jonathon's Table is attracting both a local and a tourist crowd. Jonathon serves Veal Jonathon with a sherry and mushroom sauce and Vermont rainbow trout as well as steak, ribs, and pasta. The prices are moderate, and the food is good.

✔ **South Arlington Café & Restaurant** (802-375-9900), Rt. 7A. Open Tue.–Sat. 11–2 and 5–9. Less well known than the competition. Chef-owner Dave Ingison offers a low-key atmosphere and the kind of food that can hit the spot after a day on the road. We can vouch for the chicken potpie in puff pastry with a full salad bar.

In Danby
White Dog Tavern (802-293-5477), 1759 Rt. 7, 3 miles north of Danby. Open for dinner at 5 Wed.–Sun.; closed Sun. in winter. This is an 1812 farmhouse with a central chimney and three fireplaces, each serving as the focal point of a dining room. Tom and Lisa Musso have created a genial atmosphere. There's a cheery bar, and an outdoor deck in summer. The blackboard menu includes clams, shrimp, and the house special—chicken breasts à la Tom, served up with herbs, garlic, and melted cheese over spaghetti. Options might include blackened catfish and clams zuppa ($14–20).

Alice's Someday Café (802-293-5040), 34 South Main St. Open except Tue. for breakfast (from 6:30) and lunch, weekends until 5. A delightful café in the middle of this village halfway between Manchester and Rutland. Many egg dishes available all day plus salads, grilled and deli sandwiches for lunch, pizza and deep-dish apple pie.

In Weston/Londonderry
✤ ✔ **The New American Grill** (802-824-9844), Mountain Marketplace, Londonderry. Open daily for all three meals (dinner 4:30–9). Chef-owner Max Turner has put this cheerful, booth-filled eatery with friendly service and decent prices on the culinary map. It's a big, varied, reasonably priced menu. Starters includes venison chili and mussels steamed in lemon broth, white wine, and lemon. There are salads, pastas, and barbecue, roast duck and steak poutine, jambalaya (seafood, sausage, and veggies in a Cajun broth), veggie stir-fry, grilled sandwiches (available at dinner), a kids' menu, and desserts (all $5.95) that usually include mango-passionfruit cheesecake and apple crisp served warm with a scoop of Wilcox ice cream. Daily specials.

The Bryant House (802-824-6287), Rt. 100, Weston. Owned by the neighboring Vermont Country Store, this fine old house belonged to one family—the Bryants—from the time it was built in 1827 until the family line petered out. Upstairs, a special room is set aside to look as it did in the 1890s. There are plenty of salads, sandwiches, and Vermont-style chicken pie. Lunch served 11:30–3. Closed Sun.

Jake's (802-824-6614), Mountain Marketplace at the junction of Rts. 100 and 11, Londonderry. Open daily for lunch and dinner (lunch on weekends only in winter). A local institution with a sports lounge, a lunch counter, and a pleasant pink dining room. Overstuffed sandwiches, salads, homemade soups, burgers. Pasta, steak, fish, and personal pizzas.

Gran'ma Frisby's (802-824-5931), Rt. 11 east of Londonderry. Open daily except Tue. for lunch and dinner. When Magic Mountain Ski Area is open, you're lucky to get in the door of this wonderfully pubby place. Known for its fries and fresh-dough pizza, this is a friendly, reasonably priced find any time of year.

Swiss Inn (802-824-3442), Rt. 11, Londonderry. Open to the public for dinner daily except Wed., the Swiss Inn has a strong local following. While ownership is no longer Swiss, the current owner-chef seems to have the right touch with such dishes as Geschnetzeltes (veal à la Swiss), beef fondue, and chicken Lugano (chicken breast dipped in a Gruyère cheese batter); also Continental dishes like shrimp à la Marseilles and veal Marsala. Fondues are a specialty. Entrées run $13–23.

Elsewhere

🍴 ✍ **The Barn** (802-325-3088; barn restaurant.com) Rt. 30, Pawlet. Open for dinner June–Oct. at 5 PM. This is a genuine old barn with a huge stone hearth and a view of the Mettawee River. There's plenty of atmosphere— and it's casual. The menu is large with something for everyone, but best known for burgers and steaks. There's a salad bar and children's menu.

✍ **Mulligans** (802-297-9293) at Stratton Mountain also has a Manchester Village locale (802-362-3663). This spacious restaurant is open daily for lunch and dinner; good for burgers, sandwiches, salads, and dinner options. Children's specials include a Ninja Turtle Burger and Gorilla Cheese. No plate sharing.

✍ **Out Back at Winhall River** (802-297-FOOD), Rt. 30, Bondville. Dinner daily from 5 PM, with lunch on weekends. This is a great spot, set back from the road down by the river with views from the dining room and deck. Special family-geared BBQ nights with dining at picnic tables and live music. Beer on tap, a lengthy wine list, a children's menu, pool table, and game room.

Village Pantry du Logis (802-824-9800), 1 Main St., South Londonderry. Open daily, 7 AM–8 PM. This superb French deli camouflaged as a Vermont country store is a culinary gem, with a smorgasbord of entrées and salads, cheeses, wines, and fresh-baked desserts. Owner Serge Roche owns the Three Clock restaurant just up the hill.

BETWEEN MEALS Wilcox Brothers Dairy (802-362-1223), 4367 Main St., Manchester. Some of the creamiest, most delectable flavors in Vermont are made in this family-owned and -run dairy, available at the grocery store and in a variety of local restaurants. The ice cream stand, open only in summer, is 7 miles south of the blinking light in Manchester on the west side of the road.

Mother Myrick's Confectionary (802-362-1560; mothermyricks.com), 4367 Main St. (Rt. 7A), Manchester. Open Sun.–Fri. 10–5:30, Sat. 9–6. Sumptuous baked goods, handmade chocolates, and fudge.

Village Peddler Chocolate Shop (802-375-6037) 261 Old Mill Rd., East

Arlington. In the middle of a picturesque village just off Rt. 7A, this is a colorful as well as tasty shop, known for a "Chocolatorium" in which visitors, for a small fee, can sample many chocolate in its many forms, learn its history and processing. Demonstrations as well as tastings plus the world's largest chocolate teddy bear.

⚫¶ The Village Green Gallery (802-824-3669), 661 Main St., Weston. A delightful coffee bar with comfortable seating to gather your thoughts and/or check e-mail surrounded by art and fine crafts.

✳ Entertainment

MUSIC Vermont Symphony Orchestra (800-VSO-9293; vso.org). When it's not on tour, especially around the Fourth of July weekend, the symphony's concerts in the arena are major events. Concerts are held at the Hildene Meadowlands.

Strattonfest (802-297-0100), Stratton Mountain, July and Aug. This series usually includes folk, jazz, classical, and country-western music on successive weeks.

Manchester Music Festival (802-362-1956; 800-639-5868; manchester musicfestival.org), early July–mid-Aug. at the Arkell Pavilion at the Southern Vermont Arts Center, and mid-July–mid-Aug. at the Riley Center for the Performing Arts, Burr and Burton Academy. A seven-week series of evening chamber music concerts. Also fall and winter performances in Manchester and Dorset.

Kinhaven Music School (802-824-4332; 610-868-9200; kinhaven.org), Lawrence Hill Rd., Weston, a nationally recognized summer camp for musicians ages 10–19, presents free concerts by students in July, usually Fridays at 4 and on selected Sundays

at 2:30. Faculty perform Saturdays at 8 PM. Performances are in the Concert Hall, high in the meadow of the school's 31-acre campus. It still looks more like a farm than a school. Picnics are encouraged.

Sundays on the Hill Concerts (vtchurchonthehill.org), Lawrence Hill Rd., Weston. On summer Sundays through mid-Sept., 4–5 PM, mostly chamber music concerts are held in a vintage-1838 church, now nondenominational.

THEATER Dorset Playhouse (802-867-5777; 802-867-5570; dorsetplayers .org). The Dorset Players, a community theater group formed in 1927, actually owns the beautiful playhouse in the center of Dorset and produces winter performances there. In summer the Dorset Theatre Festival stages new plays as well as classics, performed by a resident professional group six days a week June–early Sept.

Weston Playhouse Theatre Company (802-824-5288; westonplayhouse .org), 703 Main St., Weston. Not long after the Civil War, townspeople built a second floor in their oldest church on the green and turned the lower level into a theater, producing ambitious plays such as Richard Sheridan's *The Rivals*. Theatrics remained a part of community life, and in the 1930s a summer resident financed the remodeling of the defunct church into a real theater. Now billed as "the oldest professional theater in Vermont," the Weston Playhouse has a company composed largely of professional Equity actors and routinely draws rave reviews. Quality aside, Weston couldn't be more off-Broadway. The pillared theater (the facade is that of the old church) fronts on a classic village common and backs on the West River, complete with a waterfall and

Joe Citro

THE WESTON PLAYHOUSE

Holsteins grazing in the meadow beyond. Many patrons come early to dine at Café at the Falls and linger after the show to join cast members at the **Weston Playhouse's Act IV Cabaret** (reservations required; $9–10). Performances are every night except Mon. (plus Wed. and Sat. matinees), late June–Labor Day weekend, plus a fall production. Main stage tickets run $28–55. A second, smaller stage, **Other Stages**, offers more avant-garde productions.

FILM Village Picture Shows (802-362-4771; villagepictureshows.com), 263 Depot St., Rt. 30/11, Manchester Center.

✳ Selective Shopping

ANTIQUES SHOPS See *Special Events* for area antiques shows and festivals.

In Arlington
East Arlington Antiques Center (802-375-6144), just off Rt. 7A on East Arlington Rd. Open daily 10–5. In a vintage former movie theater on a scenic byway, John Maynard maintains this amazing space with 70 dealers selling everything from linens to silver, furniture, and art. Continue along this

road to the Chiselville Covered Bridge, built in 1870 and named for the chisel factory that once stood nearby. It spans Roaring Branch brook. The road eventually crosses the Battenkill in Sunderland, joining Rt. 7A near the base of the Mount Equinox toll road.

Gristmill Antiques (802-375-2500), 316 Old Mill Rd., East Arlington. Open daily July–Oct. Ethan Allen's cousin, Remember Baker, built a gristmill on Peter's Brook in 1764. Two hundred years later it became a candle factory. Now the building on Peter's Brook is an inviting shop representing several area dealers with an emphasis on 1800s and early-1900s period antiques.

In Danby
1820 House of Antiques (802-293-5990), 82 S. Main St. Open year-round, daily 10–5. A multidealer shop featuring American country and formal furniture and accessories. The former Danby Antiques Center has been revived by Carol Wehner and now houses eight dealers.

The Vermont Wreath Company (802-293-5333), Rt. 7. This is a large, two-story space representing 25 dealers. In winter it's also the source of wreaths and garlands.

In the Manchester area
Equinox Antiques and Fine Art (802-362-3540; equinoxantiques.com), 3568 Rt. 7A, Manchester Village. Open daily 10–5. Fine 18th-, 19th-, and 20th-century American furniture and art. Customers receive a discount at the Equinox Resort across the way.

Judy Pascal Antiques (802-362-2004), 145 Elm St., Manchester Center. Antique clothing, fabrics, linens, architectural salvage, painted and garden furniture, ironstone, quilts, hooked and rag rugs, American and English silver, tableware, mirrors, and garden ornaments. Open year-round.

Marie Miller Antique Quilts (802-867-5969; antiquequilts.com), 1489 Rt. 30, Dorset. Over 200 antique quilts, all in superb condition, plus hooked rugs, Quimper, and other faience. Open 10–5.

Comollo Antiques (802-362-7188; vtantiques.com), 4686 Main St., Manchester Center. Open daily (except Wed.) 10–5. Furniture, paintings, and accessories.

ART GALLERIES Southern Vermont Arts Center (see *Museums*). In addition to solo shows held throughout the year, the SVAC hosts a Members' Show in early summer and a National Fall Exhibition. There are also outdoor sculpture shows May–Oct., and other special exhibits in winter.

"1" The Village Green Gallery (802-824-3669), 661 Main St., Weston. Open daily 9–5. An unusually inviting gallery that includes a small café, this features the work of co-owner and exceptional photojournalist W. Nobushi T. Fiji'I. Also a variety of artwork, fine jewelry, selective crafts, and cards.

Tilting at Windmills Gallery (802-362-3022; tilting.com), 24 Highland Ave., Rt. 11/30, Manchester Center. Open daily 10–5, Sun. 10–4. An unusually large gallery with national and international works in oils and egg tempera, mostly realism and impressionism.

Whales of Vermont Gallery (802-824-3604; wickahrens.com), 9 Mill Lane, Weston (behind the inn). Artist Wick Ahrens is known for his carvings of whales (also of their outdoor placement against a backdrop of Vermont hills, suggesting waves). His work and that of other nationally known sculptors is displayed at his studio/home.

Pawlet Art Collective (PAC), Pawlet Village (off Rt. 30). Open in summer Thu.–Sun. 11–5, until 8 on Sat. Otherwise call ahead. Featuring work by George Bouret, Matt Solon, and friends.

BOOKS ✒ **The Northshire Bookstore** (802-362-2200; 800-437-3700; northshirebookstore.com), 4869 Main St., Manchester Center. Open Tue.–Sat. 10–9, Sun. and Mon. 10–7. One of Vermont's most browse-worthy bookstores. The Morrows have stocked the venerable Colburn House with a wide range of volumes, including used and antiquarian. A broad selection of adult titles, children's books, and records, along with current hits and classics. They schedule frequent author lectures, book signings, and co-sponsored events, and offer breakfast, lunch, and snacks in their Spiral Press Café (see *Eating Out*).

CRAFTS The Porter House of Fine Crafts (802-362-4789), Green Mountain Village Shops, Manchester Center. Open daily 10–6. Unusual jewelry and handcrafts, clothing, toys, fabric art, kitchenware, alternative music.

Flower Brook Pottery (802-867-2409), 3210 Rt. 30, Dorset. Open in summer, daily 10–5 except Tue.; also closed Sun. in winter. A showroom for hand-painted pottery, baby clothes, candles, cards, whimsical slippers, and more.

D. Lasser Ceramics (802-824-6183; 888-824-6183; lasserceramics.com), 6405 Rt. 100, Londonderry. Open daily 9–6. A studio showroom with potters doing their thing, and shelves—inside and out—filled with bright pitchers and platters, bowls and vases, mugs and plates, all highly original and affordable. We're delighted with the multicolored "stix" we bought that hold either candles or flowers.

FACTORY OUTLETS The contemporary cluster of designer discount stores in Manchester Center evokes mixed feelings from Vermonters. Some chafe at what they consider corporate intrusion into a once quiet village. Others welcome the increased exposure, not to mention the acres of quality goods. In general, the prices are not rock bottom, but better than you'd find in the city. Most are open 10–6 daily, later in summer.

Manchester Designer Outlets (800-955-SHOP; manchesterdesigneroutlets .com). The glass-and-wood anchor complex at and near the junction of Rts. 7A and 11/30 in Manchester Center presently houses Giorgio Armani, J. Crew, Brooks Brothers, Coach, Anichini, Crabtree & Evelyn, Movado, Polo/Ralph Lauren, Reed & Barton, and many others.

LASSER CERAMICS IN LONDONDERRY
Christina Tree

Battenkill and Highridge Outlet Centers (914-949-5030; outletfind .com) houses Tommy Hilfiger, Bose, Dana Buchman, Liz Claiborne, Ellen Tracy, Van Heusen, Natori, DF&C Co., Lancome, Jockey, PacSun, Farberware, Nine West, and more.

Equinox Square (Rt. 11/30) includes Coldwater Creek, Burberry's, Garnet Hill, Carter's, et cetera.

Manchester Marketplace Outlet Shops (next to the Super Shoes Factory Store) harbors more shops.

J. K. Adams Co. and **The Kitchen Store**, Rt. 30. Open daily 9–5:30. A three-floor cornucopia of top-quality kitchen gear, from butcher blocks to knife racks, tableware, and cookbooks, with an observation deck over the woodworking factory. Everything a foodie could want.

FARMS AND FARM STANDS

Dutton Farm Stand (362-3083), Rt. 11/30, Manchester. This is one of two super farm stands (the original is in Newfane) featuring local produce, much it grown in 14 greenhouses on Paul Dutton's farms in the West River Valley. In winter it's a good spot for locally grown Christmas trees and wreaths.

Taylor Farm (802-824-5690), 825 Rt. 11 west of Bromely Moutain (1 mile east of Londonderry). Some 40 Holstein and Jersey milk cows provide the milk for the farm's famous Gouda cheeses. The shop is open daily 10–5.

Equinox Nursery (802-362-2610; equinoxvalleynursery.com), Rt. 7A, south of Manchester. Open daily 8–5, Sun. 9–4. An outstanding farm stand and nursery managed by three generations of the Preuss family; good for picking vegetables, berries in-season. Especially famous in fall for the 100,000 pounds of pumpkins it produces, also for its display of scarecrows and pumpkin faces. Sells pumpkin bread, pie, ice cream, and marmalade, along with other farm stand staples, annuals, perennials, and shrubs. In Jan. and Feb. the family cultivates a tropical conservatory with birds and indoor flowering plants.

Mad Tom Orchard (802-366-8107; madtomorhard.com), 2615 Mad Tom Rd., East Dorset. Raspberries in July and Sept., apples mid-Sept.–mid-Oct. Farm stand and PYO.

FARMER'S MARKETS

Memorial to Columbus Day weekends

In Dorset (dorsetfarmersmarket.com), Sun. 10–2 at H. N. Williams hardware store, Rt. 30—the place to buy Consider Bardwell goat cheeses, produced in West Pawlet.

In Manchester (manchestermarket .org), Thu. 3–6, Dana Thompson Rec. Center, Rt. 30.

In Londonderry, West River Farmers Market, Sat. 9–1, Mountain Marketplace, at the junction of Rts. 100, 30, and 11.

GENERAL STORES **The Vermont Country Store** (802-824-3184), Rt. 100, Weston Village. Open year-round, Mon.–Sat. 9–6. Established by Vrest Orton in 1946 and billed as America's first restored country store, this pioneer nostalgia venture included one of the country's first mail-order catalogs. The original store (actually an old Masonic temple) has since quintupled in size and spilled into four adjacent buildings. The specialty of both the catalog (which accounts for 75 percent of the company's business) and the store is the functional item that makes life easy, especially anything that's difficult to find nowadays—jumbo metal hairpins, hardwood coat hangers,

Christina Tree

THE VERMONT COUNTRY STORE IN WESTON

slippery-elm throat lozenges, garter belts. Lyman, the present Orton-in-charge, has a penchant for newfangled gadgets, such as a plastic frame to hold baseball caps in dishwashers. He's a zealot when it comes to basics that seem to have disappeared, and he frequently finds someone to replicate them, as in the case of the perfect potato masher. The store's own line of edibles features the Vermont Common Cracker, unchanged since 1812, still stamped out in a patented 19th-century machine.

The Weston Village Store (802-824-5477; westonvillagestore.com), Rt. 100, Weston. Open daily. A country emporium catering to visitors, boasting the state's largest collection of weather vanes.

J. J. Hapgood Store (802-824-5911), off Rt. 11, Peru. Daily 8–8. A genuine general store that has a potbellied stove, old-fashioned counters covered with food, and some clothing staples; geared to locals as well as tourists.

H. N. Williams General Store (802-867-5353), 2691 Rt. 30, about 2 miles south of Dorset. Open daily. A large white barn of a store housed in what started out as an 1840 harness shop. You can still see the steep staircase to the second floor, where the help lived in the old days. In the same family for six generations, the store sells everything from yard equipment to clothing, fertilizer, tools, and furniture.

Dorset Union Store (802-867-4400), Dorset Village, opposite the Dorset Inn. Daily 7–8. A village landmark since 1816, formerly Peletier's: staples and then some, including gourmet dinners to go, baking to order, and an extensive selection of wines, cheeses, and Vermont products. Because there are no lunch spots in Dorset, this also serves the purpose; good for picnic fare.

Mach's General Store (802-325-3405), Rt. 30, Pawlet Village. Daily 6 AM–8 PM. The focal point of this genuine old emporium is described under Pawlet (see *Villages*), but the charm of this family-run place goes beyond its water view. Built as a hotel in 1818, it's filled with a wide variety of locally useful merchandise.

SPECIAL SHOPS Orvis Retail Store (802-362-3750; orvis.com), 4200 Rt. 7A, Manchester Center, supplying the needs of anglers and other sportsmen since 1856. Known widely for its mail-order catalog and retails shops throughout the United States and UK, the Orvis flagship store is styled as a luxury country lodge but still specializes in the fishing rods made in the factory out back. There's also fishing tackle and gear, country clothes, and other small luxury items—from silk underwear to welcome mats—that make the difference in country, or would-be country, living.

Susan Sargent Designs (802-366-8017; susansargent.com) 3609 Main St., Manchester Village. Open daily

10–6, Sun. 10–5. Housed in a historic little brick building beside the Equinox, this brilliant store features Sargent's striking colors and designs woven into rugs, pillows, and throws, fabrics, ceramics, and a line of paints among other household items including books, stationery, and Simon Pierce glass.

Lake's Lampshades (802-325-6308), School St., Pawlet. Judi Sawyer Lake's studio/shop is a riot of fabrics and colors, all shaped into lampshades. If you can't find something here to brighten a corner of your life, Judi will make it to order.

Long Ago & Far Away (802-362-3435), Green Mountain Village Shops, Manchester Center. This is an extensive shop showcasing Native American craftsmanship, specializing in Canadian Inuit and Native Alaskan sculpture.

Vermont Country Bird Houses (802-293-5991), 12 N. Main St., Danby. Imaginatively handcrafted birdhouses in various architectural styles, with steeples, cupolas, bell towers, and the like, by Jim Kardas. Open daily 9–4:30.

Bob Gasperetti (802-293-5195; gasperetti.com), **Dan Mosheim** (802-

JUDI SAWYER LAKE MAKES LAMP SHADES IN HER PAWLET SHOP.

Christina Tree

867-5541; dorsetcustomfurniture.com), **Bill Laberge** (802-325-2117; williamlaberge.com), **David Spero** (802-824-4550; vermontwindsorchairs.com), and **Joe Breznik** (802-824-3263; finewoodenfurniture.com) produce handmade, heirloom-quality furniture in the Dorset area, and welcome visitors to their showrooms.

The Mountain Goat (802-362-5159), 4886 Main St., Manchester Center. Quality outdoor clothing and gear are the hallmarks of this and other Mountain Goats (in Williamstown and Northampton, Massachusetts)—but owner Ron Houser really knows feet and what shoe is good for your foot. Houser specializes in orthotics "for athletes, hikers and everyday victims of gravity."

✳ Special Events

March: Spring skiing, sugaring. **Vermont Maple Open House Weekend** (*last weekend*) with sugaring off at Merk Forest and Farmland Center (802-394-7836)

April: Trout season opens; Easter parades and egg hunts at ski areas. Whitewater canoeing on the West River.

Memorial Day weekend: **Vermont Studio Tours** (vermontcrafts.com); season opens for weekly **farmers markets** (through Columbus Day weekend). See *Selective Shopping.*

June: **Antique and Classic Car Show in Manchester** (800-362-4144) and **vintage sports car climb** to Equinox Summit; **Hildene Peony Festival**, and the annual **Stratton Quilt Festival. Ethan Allen Days** with Revolutionary War reenactments in Hildene Meadows (802-362-1788).

Mid-June through early August: Summer theater seasons at **Dorset Playhouse** and **Weston Playhouse**.

Fourth of July: Manchester and Dorset host an **old-fashioned Fourth**, a day-long celebration that culminates in fireworks.

July through mid-August: The **Vermont Summer Festival Horse Show** comes to Manchester for six weeks. **Kinhaven Music School** concert series. **Manchester Music Festival**— a series of concerts at the Southern Vermont Art Center (800-639-5868). **Strattonfest** at Stratton Mountain Resort. **Summer concerts on the Manchester town green**, Friday evenings 7–8:30, begin mid-July.

August: **Southern Vermont Crafts Fair**—juried exhibitors, entertainment, food, and music at Hildene. **Norman's Attic** in Arlington is a town-wide tag sale, and the **Manchester Sidewalk Sale** is a garage sale of designer goods. **Annual Bondville Fair** (*third weekend*; 802-297-2927), one of Vermont's oldest and most colorful country fairs.

September: The month is chock-full of antiques shows around the area; the biggest is the annual **Vermont Antiques Dealers Association Show** at Riley Rink in Hunter Park, but there's also one at Hildene. **Peru Fair**—just one day (*fourth Saturday*), considered one of Vermont's most colorful (and crowded), it includes a pig roast, crafts, food, and entertainment (parking is at Bromley).

October: **Hildene Foliage Art & Craft Festival** (*first week*) at Hildene Meadows. The **Weston Antiques Show** (*first weekend*), one of the state's oldest and most respected, staged in the Weston Playhouse, features more than 200 dealers, coinciding with the **Antiques in Vermont** show (with around 80 exhibitors) at Riley Rink, Manchester Center. The **Weston Crafts Fair** (*second week*; westoncraftsshow.com).

November: Harvest dinners and wild game suppers abound; check local papers and bulletin boards.

December: A **tour of the historic inns** of Manchester Village takes place the first two Saturdays of December.

Hildene Holiday Evenings (*between Christmas and New Year's*)—cider, carolers, a bonfire on the front lawn, and tours through the mansion, decorated for Christmas.

OKEMO VALLEY REGION

INCLUDING LUDLOW, CHESTER, TYSON, AND PLYMOUTH

Okemo is the name of a mountain, not a valley, but it's a major ski mountain with a golf course and year-round appeal—and this is the era of "branding." Okemo towers 3,300 feet above Ludlow, a lively village on the eastern edge of the Green Mountains. It is, in fact, in the valley named for the Black River, which rises in the chain of ponds and lakes north of town and here joins Jewell Brook, forming the power source for the 19th-century mills around which the town was built. Calvin Coolidge grew up a dozen miles north of town in the village of Plymouth Notch, now preserved as a state historic site to look much the way it did on August 3, 1923, when he was sworn in as the 30th president of the United States by his father in his kerosene-lit home. Coolidge attended Ludlow's Black River Academy in a building that's now a great little museum.

East of town Rt. 131 follows the Black River through the smaller mill villages of Proctorsville and Cavendish. Rt. 103 branches south, following the Williams River to Chester, a handsome old crossroads community at the confluence of five roads and comprising three distinctive villages, all within walking distance and adding up to a livable town that styles itself as "The Vermont You've Been Hoping to Find." Chester offers a wide choice of lodging, dining, and shopping as well as easy access to much of southern and central Vermont.

GUIDANCE Okemo Valley Regional Chamber of Commerce (802-228-5830; 866-216-8722; yourplacein vermont.org), P.O. Box 333, Ludlow 05149. Open except Sun. This walk-in information office in the Marketplace,

OLD ACADEMY BUILDING ON
THE CHESTER GREEN

Christina Tree

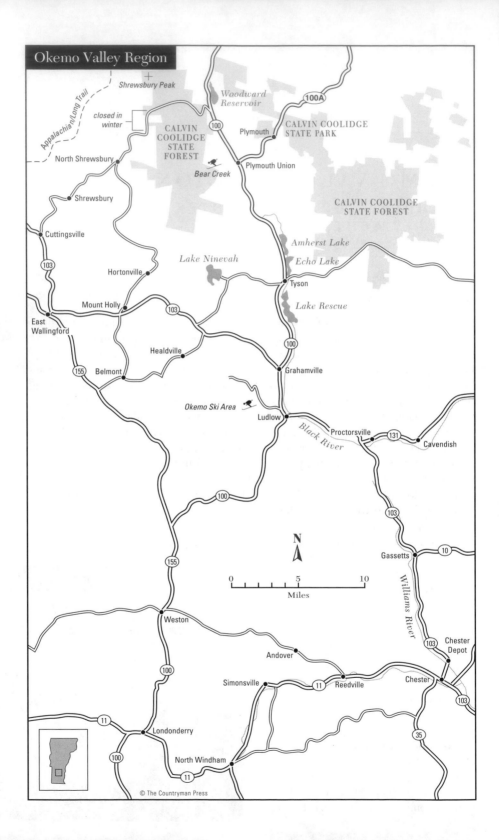

Okemo Valley Region

Shrewsbury Peak

Appalachian/Long Trail

closed in winter

CALVIN COOLIDGE STATE FOREST

North Shrewsbury

Shrewsbury

Cuttingsville

103

Hortonville

Mount Holly

East Wallingford

155

Belmont

Healdville

Woodward Reservoir

100A

100

Plymouth

CALVIN COOLIDGE STATE PARK

Plymouth Union

Bear Creek

CALVIN COOLIDGE STATE FOREST

Lake Ninevah

Amherst Lake

Echo Lake

Tyson

Lake Rescue

103

100

Grahamville

Okemo Ski Area

Ludlow

Black River

Proctorsville

131

Cavendish

100

103

Gassetts

10

N

Williams River

0   5   10
Miles

155

Weston

Andover

Simonsville

11

Reedville

103

Chester Depot

Chester

103

100

11

Londonderry

North Windham

11

100

35

© The Countryman Press

across from Okemo Mountain Access Rd. on Rt. 103 (look for the clock tower), has menus, events listings, and lodging brochures. The chamber maintains information for towns throughout this area and a seasonal information booth on the green in Chester (802-875-2939) (no restrooms). Request the current issue of the *Okemo Valley Regional Guide.*

GETTING THERE *By air:* The Albany, Hartford, and Burlington airports are all a two-hour drive.

By car: From points south, take I-91 to Vermont Exit 6 to Rt. 103 north, which leads you to Chester and on to Ludlow. The area can also be accessed from I-91, Exits 7 and 8.

GETTING AROUND **George's Shuttle Service** (800-208-3933), based in Weathersfield, provides transport by reservation to and from the railroad stations in Bellows Falls and Rutland, as well as airports throughout New England.

Okemo Mountain Resort (802-228-4041) offers a free shuttle to the village during peak times in ski season.

Ludlow Transport is a free shuttle service that runs several routes throughout Ludlow and the surrounding area. The service operates Mon.–Fri. Pick up the schedule at the chamber of commerce.

WHEN TO GO The chain of lakes north of Ludlow and the classic countryside around Chester draw summer and fall visitors. In winter Okemo is the big draw; cross-country skiing and snowmobile trails crisscross the region.

MEDICAL EMERGENCY Service is available by calling **911**.

✳ Towns and Villages

Ludlow (population: 2,640) boomed with the production of "shoddy" (fabric made from reworked wool) after the Civil War, a period frozen in the red brick of its commercial block, Victorian mansions, magnificent library, and academy (now the Black River Museum). In the wake of the wool boom, the General Electric Company moved into the picturesque mill at the heart of town and kept people employed making small-aircraft engine parts until 1977. Okemo opened in 1956, but for years it was a sleeper—a big mountain with antiquated lifts on the edge of a former mill town. Ski clubs nested in the Victorian homes, and just a few inns catered to serious skiers. Tim and Diane Mueller bought the ski

BLACK RIVER ACADEMY HISTORICAL MUSEUM IN LUDLOW

Christina Tree

area in 1982, and it has been evolving ever since as one of New England's most popular ski resorts, known for the quality of its snowmaking, grooming, and on-mountain lodging and other facilities. A major golf course doubles as a full-service cross-country ski center. The effect on Ludlow has been dramatic. The old General Electric plant has been turned into condominiums. Other lodging options as well as restaurants have multiplied. For a sense of Ludlow in its pre-skiing era visit the **Fletcher Library** (802-228-8921) with its reading rooms with fireplaces; old-style, green-shaded lights; and 19th-century paintings of local landscapes. The **Black River Academy Historical Museum** (802-228-5050), 14 High St., is open Memorial Day–Columbus Day, Tue.–Sat. noon–4. Built in 1889, the academy's reputation drew students from throughout New England. President Calvin Coolidge was a member of the class of 1890. Exhibits about "Main Street" circa 1900 and the third-floor classroom offer a sense of what it meant (and still means) to live in the Black River Valley. North of town off Rt. 100, rental cottages can be found on all four lakes, as well as on Lake Ninevah in nearby Mount Holly. Given its central location and lodging both on and off the mountain, Ludlow is a good base from which to explore in all directions.

Chester (ourchester.org) is sited at the confluence of three branches of the Williams River and of five major roads. Its string-bean-shaped village green is lined with shops, restaurants, and lodging places, including the double-porched old Fullerton Inn. Across the street (Rt. 11) is the early-19th-century brick Academy building is now occupied by the **Chester Historical Society** (802-875-5459), open May–Columbus Day, Sat.–Sun. 2–4. It presents the town's colorful history, including the story of Clarence Adams, a prominent citizen who broke into more than 50 businesses and homes between 1886 and 1902 before being apprehended. Rt. 103 forks north from the village center to **Chester Depot**, a cluster of homes and public buildings around the well-kept Victorian depot, now the northern terminus for the **Green Mountain Flyer** excursion train from Bellows Falls. The town hall is here along with Lisai's Market, a well-stocked general store. Follow Rt.

VERMONT COUNTRY ROAD SIGN

Christina Tree

103 up past the vintage 1879s red wooden Yosemite Fire House with its two towers (one for the bell and the tall one for drying hoses) to the **Stone Village**, a double line of early-19th-century houses built from locally quarried granite. Cool in summer, warm in winter, stone houses are a rarity in New England. All of these are said to have been built by two brothers in the pre–Civil War decade, with hiding spaces enough to make them a significant stop on the Underground Railroad. Chester offers more than its share of local lodging, dining, and shopping. It's handy to skiing at Magic Mountain and Bromley as well as Okemo, and to cross-country at Grafton Ponds.

✳ Must-See

SCENIC DRIVES Okemo Mountain Road in downtown Ludlow (off Rt. 100/103) follows the Okemo Mountain Access Rd. beyond the base lodge (stay left). This is a ski trail in winter, but in summer and fall it offers a hard-topped 2.5-mile route to the summit. There's a small parking lot and a 0.5-mile trail through the woods to a former fire tower that boasts (on a clear day) 360-degree views.

Shrewsbury Loop. From Ludlow head north 2 miles on Rt. 100, then northwest on Rt. 103 for 5 miles to

Christina Tree

EXTERIOR OF CROWLEY CHEESE FACTORY IN HEALDVILLE

Healdville and the sign for the **Crowley Cheese Factory**. In the 1880s every Vermont town had its cheese factory to process surplus milk, but Crowley Cheese, which the family had begun making in the 1820s, was distributed up and down the East Coast. The three-story wooden building, built in 1882 by Winfield Crowley, is now billed as America's oldest cheese factory. It's a 2-mile detour down a side road but well worth the effort. Visitors are welcome weekdays 8–4, but cheese is actually made Tue.–Fri., and the best time to come is around 1 PM when the cheese is being "drained." The shower-capped employees also hand cut and rake the curd, rinsing it with springwater, draining 75 percent of the whey. This is a Colby cheese, which is moister and ages more quickly than cheddar. It takes 5,000 pounds of fresh milk to make 500 pounds of Crowley Cheese. Needless to say, you can pick up samples and reasonably priced "ends." Rt. 103 climbs on to **Mount Holly**, then continues another 5 miles to Cuttingsville. Turn up the road ("Town Hill") posted for Shrewsbury, and right again at the T. **Shrewsbury Center** is marked by a white wooden church set back on a knoll beside two face-to-face taverns, now both B&Bs. One of these, **Maple Crest Farm**, remains in the same family that built it in 1808 and has been taking in guests since the 1860s.

Although the dairy herd is gone, this is still a working farm with more than 30 head of beef cattle and some 300 acres in hay. Stop and take in the view and the quiet and long vistas. In **North Shrewsbury**, 2 more miles up the hill, is the **W. E. Pierce General Store**—a 19th-century building restored by the Preservation Trust of Vermont and at this writing scheduled to reopen as a community-backed cooperative store selling baked goods and local products. Check out the signs tacked to the a big old fir tree nearby. They point west to Rutland and east to Plymouth Union, confirming the impression that you are standing on the peaked roof of this

CHEESEMAKERS AT CROWLEY CHEESE FACTORY

Christina Tree

CALVIN COOLIDGE AND PLYMOUTH NOTCH

Calvin Coolidge (1872–1933) is best remembered for his dry wit and thrift, his integrity and common sense, all famously Vermont virtues. The village of Plymouth Notch—in which Coolidge was born, assumed the presidency, briefly governed the country (in the summer of 1924), and is buried—is said to be the best-preserved presidential birthplace in the nation. It may also be the best-preserved Vermont village, offering an in-depth sense of the people who lived there.

In the spirit of Coolidge himself, the village remains low-key: no 1920s-costumed interpreters, no multimedia displays. The cheese factory built by the president's father, John Coolidge, showcases the history of Vermont cheesemaking and produces its own granular curd cheese. The square-steepled Union Christian Church, with its acoustically superb interior, is the setting for frequent concerts and lectures. The general store sells pickles, afghans, and some Vermont specialty foods like dilled carrots and Moxie—reportedly President Coolidge's favorite drink (it was, after all, Prohibition).

"Colonel" John Coolidge became storekeeper here in 1868, and his son Calvin was born on the Fourth of July, 1872, in the modest attached house. The family moved across the street to the larger Coolidge Homestead when he was four years old, and it was there, because he happened to be home helping with the haying, that Vice President Calvin Coolidge learned of President Warren Harding's unexpected death. At 2:47 AM on August 3, 1923, he was sworn in, by his father, as 30th president of the United States.

"I didn't know I couldn't" was the reply Coolidge Sr. gave when reporters asked how he knew he could administer the presidential oath of office. "Colonel John" was a former state senator, a

THE CALVIN COOLIDGE STATE HISTORIC SITE

Diane E. Foulds

notary public, and the village sheriff as well as shopkeeper. His terse response typifies the dry wit for which his son would later become known.

Vermont Division for Historic Preservation

PRESIDENT CALVIN COOLIDGE

It should come as no surprise that in this classic Vermont village you encounter a classic Vermont family. The Coolidges were hard-working (up before dawn for chores), self-sufficient (you see an intricate quilt that was stitched by Cal at age 10 and a graceful carriage built by his father), and close-ly linked to the land. Coolidge is buried with seven generations of his family in the small graveyard across the road from the village. Village residents numbered 29 during Coolidge's presidency, and a high percentage of these formed the Old-Time Dance Orchestra, which played in the dance hall above the general store. This same room served as the office of the Summer White House for a dozen days in 1924. At the time Calvin and his wife, Grace, were grieving the death of their son Calvin Jr., a promising 16-year-old who had died due to a complication from an infected blister he acquired while playing tennis at the White House.

Plymouth resident Ruth ("Midge") Aldrich opened several tourist cabins (prefab jobs brought up from Boston) to accommodate the Secret Service and a Top of the Notch Tea Room to serve a steady stream of the Coolidge-curious. Plymouth Notch, however, never really hit the big time as a tourist attraction, perhaps because, while he continued to visit "The Notch," President Coolidge himself retired to private life not here but in his adopted home, Northampton, Massachusetts. After graduating from nearby Amherst College, Coolidge had opened a law practice in Northampton, and it was there that he met his wife (fellow Vermonter Grace Anna Goodhue, who was teaching there at the Clarke School for the Deaf) and served as mayor. He represented Northampton in the Massachusetts Legislature before becoming governor of the Bay State, and he died in Northampton.

It was Aurora Pierce, the family housekeeper, who fiercely preserved the Coolidge Homestead, adamantly opposing even minor changes, like plumbing and electricity. Not until Aurora's death in 1956 did Vermont's

Historic Sites Commission assume management of the house and its contents (which Grace Coolidge had deeded to them). The state had already purchased the 1840s village tavern that had also been Calvin's mother's home, turning it into a lunchroom and information center.

The President Calvin Coolidge State Historic Site presently encompasses 25 buildings, the majority of the village. The site includes a cheese factory, still making cheese in the 19th century style, and a general store selling, among other things, cold cans of Moxie, the president's favorite soft drink; its upstairs hall is restored to look just as it did as the office of the Summer White House. There is also an 1840s church and the reconstructed Wilder Barn, housing farm implements, horse-drawn vehicles, and the **Wilder House Restaurant** (open daily 10–3 for breakfast and lunch)—a pine-walled café with exposed beams in what was once the home of Calvin Coolidge's mother. The visitor center is itself a mini museum with changing exhibits. Power lines have been buried (electricity actually didn't reach Plymouth until after Calvin's death), and roads have been paved. Otherwise the village looks about as it did in the 1920s, sitting quietly at the foot of East Mountain. It's set in 580 acres presently owned by the Vermont Division for Historic Preservation, surrounded by the 500-acre Coolidge State Park, in turn abutting the 16,000-acre Calvin Coolidge State Forest. The President Coolidge State Historic Site (802-672-3773; historicvermont.org/coolidge) is open late May–mid-Oct., daily 9:30–5. $7.50 adults, $2 ages 6–14; 5 and under are free. During the off-season the Aldrich House, which doubles as an office and exhibit space, is open weekdays (no charge)—but call ahead.

THE VISITOR CENTER AT THE CALVIN COOLIDGE STATE HISTORIC SITE

Diane E. Foulds

entire region. Fasten your seat belt and (conditions permitting) plunge east down the vintage-1930s **CCC Road**, one of Vermont's steepest and most scenic routes. It's 6 miles seemingly straight down—with superlative mountain and valley views—to Rt. 100 in Plymouth. Note the pullout for **Shrewsbury Peak**, the trailhead for a steep 1.2-mile path connecting with the Long Trail here. Remarkably enough, this was the site of Vermont's second rope tow, installed in 1935 by the Rutland Ski Club. According to the write-up, some 2,400 spectators came up this road (brand new then, it's closed now in snow season) to watch the skiers come down. Continue down to Rt. 100A to **Plymouth Union**, perhaps the first rural Vermont village to appear in publications throughout the world—on August 2, 1923. (See the box on page 183.) Make your way back to Rt. 100; from Plymouth it's a scenic 9-mile ride south past a chain of lakes to Ludlow.

✳ To Do

ADVENTURE SPORTS **Extreme Adventures of Vermont** (802-875-5626; extremeadventuresvt.com). This Andover-based outfitter offers year-round guided tours: rock climbing, whitewater rafting, fishing, kayaking, mountain biking, hiking, and orienteering in summer and fall; ice climbing, winter caving, mountaineering, snowshoeing, and cross-country skiing in winter.

ARTS AND CRAFTS **Fletcher Farm School for the Arts and Crafts** (802-228-8770; fletcherfarm.org), 611 Rt. 103 south, Ludlow. Operated since 1947 by the Society of Vermont Craftsmen, headquartered in an old farmstead on the eastern edge of town. More than 200 courses in a wide variety of crafts are offered in summer and more than 100 in fall and winter in traditional crafts, contemporary crafts, and fine art. In summer lodging and meals are available on campus; fall through spring, multiday workshops are offered at area inns. Crafts include fiber arts, basketry, theorem painting, glass, weaving, woodcarving, quilting, oil and watercolor painting, spinning, rug hooking and braiding, and more. Open to all ages.

BIKING **Mountain Cycology** (802-228-2722), 5 Lamere Square, Ludlow. No rentals but equipment, repair, guidebooks, and local advice as well as sales. Rentals are available from **Joe Jones Sports** (802-228-5440), 57 Pond St., Ludlow. **Bike Vermont** (800-257-2226; bikevermont.com) offers a choice of inn-to-inn tours in this area.

BOATING **Echo Lake Inn** (802-228-8602), Rt. 100, Tyson, rents canoes and other boats to guests only. **Camp Plymouth State Park** (802-228-2025) off Rt. 100 in Tyson also offers seasonal canoe, kayak, and rowboat rentals (see *Swimming* for directions). Nearby **Lake Ninevah** (turn off Rt. 103 just past Harry's Café onto Shunpike Rd., then right again onto Ninevah Rd.) is quieter, with some beautiful marshes and woods. **Hawk Inn and Mountain Resort** (802-672-3811) in Plymouth also rents boats. For paddling sites, see okemovalleyvt.org/activities/paddle.html.

FISHING Public access has been provided to Lake Rescue, Echo Lake, Lake Ninevah, Woodward Reservoir, and Amherst Lake. Fishing licenses are required except under age 16. The catch includes rainbow trout, bass, and pickerel. There is also fly-fishing in the Black River along Rt. 131 in Cavendish, and the 6-mile stretch from the covered bridge in Downers down to a second covered bridge is a trophy-trout section, stocked each spring with 1.5-pound brown trout and 18-inch rainbows.

FITNESS CENTERS AND SPAS Castle Hill Spa (802-226-7419; castlehill resortandspa.com), junction of Rts. 103 and 131, Cavendish. An aesthetically pleasing center set apart from the inn and open to the public. The outdoor pool and whirlpool are heated for year-round use, the workout room offers aerobics classes as well as Nautilus equipment, and the Aveda spa offers a variety of wraps and massages; there's also a salon and Har-Tru tennis courts.

The Spring House at Okemo Mountain Resort (802-228-1418; okemo.com), Rt. 103, Ludlow. At Jackson Gore Lodge a two-level fitness and aquatic center offers year-round swimming, racquetball, fitness classes, weights and cardio equipment, hot tub, and sauna. The Ice House sports pavilion transitions from a winter skating rink to a warm-weather complex with tennis courts, basketball courts, and jogging track. A full massage menu is offered. Day passes available.

GOLF The **Okemo Valley Golf Club** (802-228-1396; golf.okemo.com), Fox Lane, Ludlow. An 18-hole championship "heathland-style" course featuring wide fairways with dips, ripples, rolls, and hollows said to suggest Scottish links. The **Okemo Valley Golf Academy** also utilizes an 18-acre outdoor Golf Learning Center with a 370-yard-long driving range, four practice greens, a 6,000-square-foot indoor practice area, a computerized virtual golf program, classrooms, and changing rooms with showers. The clubhouse includes a fully stocked pro shop and Willie Dunne's Grille (see *Eating Out*).

Tater Hill Golf Club (802-875-2517), 6802 Popple Dungeon Rd., North Windham (off Rt. 11, not far from Chester). A recently renovated 18-hole course with a pro shop and practice range, now owned by Okemo.

PLYMOUTH NOTCH

Christina Tree

HORSEBACK RIDING AND HORSE-DRAWN RIDES

Cavendish Trail /Horse Rides (802-226-7821), Twenty Mile Stream Rd., Proctorsville, offers guided tours and pony and wagon rides through fields and hills. Sleigh rides in-season.

Hawk Inn and Mountain Resort on Rt. 100 in Plymouth (see "Killington/Rutland Area") also offers trail rides.

RAILROAD EXCURSIONS See Trains Around Vermont (rails-vt.com) in the Lower Connecticut River chapter.

SWIMMING ✍ **West Hill Recreation Area** (802-228-2849), West Hill off Rt. 103 in Ludlow, includes a beach (with lifeguard) on a small, spring-fed reservoir; also a snack bar and playground/picnic area. Fee charged.

Buttermilk Falls, near the junction of Rts. 100 and 103. This is a swimming hole and a series of small but beautiful falls (turn at the VFW post just west of the intersection).

✿ **Camp Plymouth State Park** (802-228-2025). Turn east over the bridge off Rt. 100 across from the Echo Lake Inn at Tyson. Continue 1 mile to the crossroads, then turn left onto Boy Scout Camp Rd. There's a sandy beach on Echo Lake, picnic area, boat rentals, volleyball, horseshoes, and playground. Try panning for gold in Buffalo Brook. **Star Lake** in the village of Belmont in Mount Holly is also a great place for a swim.

WALKING Vermont Inn to Inn Walking, Hiking & Biking (800-728-0842; vermontinntoinnwalking.com). Four-night, inn-to-inn walking tours (3 to 10 miles per day) are offered among four area inns (Rowell's Inn, the Combes Family Inn, the Inn Victoria, and Old Town Farm). Luggage is transported for you and a trail snack is provided, along with lodging, breakfast, and dinner.

✳ Winter Sports

DOWNHILL SKIING ✿ **Okemo** (information 802-228-1600; snow report 802-228-5222; reservations 800-78-OKEMO; okemo.com). A big mountain with southern Vermont's highest vertical drop, Okemo is a destination ski and snowboard resort with a small-resort, family feel. This is a ski area of many parts—in fact five distinct areas: Jackson Gore Peak, Solitude Peak, South Face, Glades Peak, and South Ridge. Jackson Gore, added in 2006, brought a whole new face to the resort, one with its own entrance, base area, lodging, and restaurants. Off around the corner of the mountain from the main access, Jackson Gore remains a bit of a secret, the rear door to the slopes on busy weekends.

Family owned and operated since 1982 by Tim and Diane Mueller, Okemo is far larger than it looks from its base. Surprises begin at the top of the initial chairlifts, where you meet a wall of three-story condominiums and find your way down to the spacious Sugar House base lodge—from which the true size of the mountain becomes apparent. From the summit, beginners can actually run a full 4.5 miles to the base; there are also a number of wide,

DOWNHILL SKIING AT OKEMO

Okemo Mountain

central fallline runs down the face of Okemo. World Cup is a long and steep but forgiving run with sweeping views down the Black River Valley to the Connecticut River.

Lifts: 19, including 5 high-speed quads.

Trails and slopes: 119 slopes trails and glades—32 percent novice, 36 percent intermediate, 32 percent advanced expert. five mountain areas: Jackson Gore Peak, Solitude Peak, South Face, Glades Peak, South Ridge.

Vertical drop: 2,200 feet (highest in southern Vermont).

Snowmaking: Covers 96 percent of trails (605 acres).

Facilities: Base lodge with cafeteria; midmountain Sugar House base lodge with café, Smokey Jo's BBQ, Vermont Pizza Co., deli; Summit Lodge with café, Sky Bar, Jump (Asian specialties); Solitude Day Lodge with Epic restaurant, snack bar, and outdoor BBQ (open 11–3). At Jackson Gore you'll find the Roundhouse, Siena, and Coleman Brook Tavern (see *Dining Out*); Waffle House is at the bottom of the Black Ridge Triple.

Ski school: Okemo's Ski + Ride School is staffed by 450 instructors. Children's programs include Mini Stars (ages 3–4), Snow Stars (ages 4–7), Mountain Explorers (7–14). Ski and snowboard programs include Women's Alpine Adventures (2- to 5-day intensive programs) and Snowboard Camps. Senior discounts are available on group lessons. The state-approved Penguin Day Care Center serves children 6 months to 6 years and offers supervised indoor and outdoor activities. Inquire about Kids' Night Out programs, available 6–10 PM in-season.

Lift tickets: Adult $72 midweek, $77 weekend and holiday. Kids 6 and under ski free. Savings on multiday tickets are substantial, even more so when packaged into stays at area inns and B&Bs as well as slope-side lodging.

CROSS-COUNTRY SKIING AND SNOWSHOEING Okemo Valley Nordic Center (802-228-1396; okemo.com), junction of Rts. 100 and 103, Ludlow. A café and a rental shop are surrounded by the open roll of the golf course; there are also wooded and mountain trails adding up to 22 km (including 22 km of skating lanes), plus 10 km of dedicated snowshoe trails. The clubhouse offers a fireplace, changing rooms, rentals, and showers.

Also see Grafton Ponds Recreation Center in Grafton (in "Lower Connecticut River Valley") and Viking Nordic Centre in Londonderry (in "Manchester and the Mountains").

SNOWMOBILE RIDES Okemo Snowmobile Tours (802-422-2121; 800-FAT-TRAK; snowmobilevermont.com) at Okemo Mountain Resort. The "Mountain Tour" is a one-hour tour through the woods, while the "Back Country Tour" is a 25-mile ride into the Calvin Coolidge State Forest for beginner through expert.

✳ Lodging

RESORTS Okemo Mountain Resort (802-228-5571; 800-78-OKEMO; okemo.com), Ludlow 05149. Open year-round, featuring winter skiing and summer golf, with lodging options that include nearly 700 condominium units, along with **Jackson Gore Inn**, with 245 condo-style units at the Jackson Gore Base Area including restaurants, a reception area, health club, and underground parking. This complex includes the Adams and Bixby lodging annexes and the Spring House, a two-level fitness and aquatic center with year-round swimming, racquetball, fitness classes, weights and cardio equipment, hot tub, and sauna. The Ice House sports pavilion transitions from a winter skating rink to a warm-weather complex with tennis courts, basketball courts, and jogging track.

There is also **Okemo Mountain Lodge**, a three-story hotel at the entrance to the resort that's really a cluster of 55 one-bedroom condos, each with a sleeping couch in the living room. There's a compact kitchen with eating counter and a fireplace; enough space for a couple and two children. **Kettle Brook** has one-, two-, and three-bedroom units, all nicely built, salted along trails. **Winterplace**, set high on a mountain shelf, consists of 17 buildings with a total of 250 units ranging in size from two bedrooms to three bedrooms plus a loft. Residents have access to a fitness center with indoor pool. **Solitude Village** is a ski-in/ski out complex of one- to five-unit condos and town houses plus a lodge with indoor/outdoor heated pool and a service area with a restaurant, ski shop, and children's learning center. **Ledgewood Condominiums** are three- and four-bedroom units with garages accessed by their own trail. Rentals also are available through **Strictly Rentals** (800-776-5149; strictlyrentals .com) in downtown Ludlow. See *Condominiums* (below) and *Downhill Skiing* (above).

Also see Hawk Inn and Mountain Resort in Plymouth, described in "Killington/Rutland Area."

INNS ∞ **The Castle Hill Resort and Spa** (802-226-7361; 800-438-7908; thecastle-vt.com), P.O. Box 525, Proctorsville 05149. Quarry and timber baron Allen Fletcher, elected governor of Vermont in 1913, built this imposing neo-Jacobean stone manor on a knoll, importing European artisans in 1901 for the oak and mahogany woodwork and detailed cast-plaster ceilings. The 10 rooms are regal. Rates $249–300; ask about spa, ski, and a variety of other packages. Also inquire about lodging in "resort homes" currently under development on the inn's property. See the day spa under *To Do* and the restaurant under *Dining Out.* Weddings and civil union celebrations for up to 200 are a specialty, with facilities to accommodate many guests in the neighboring resort homes and motor inn (see *Motels*).

🐾 ⁞Ⅰ⁞ **The Andrie Rose Inn** (802-228-4846; 800-223-4846; andrierose inn.com), 13 Pleasant St., Ludlow 05149. Michael and Irene Maston preside over this complex on a quiet back street with unexpectedly luxurious rooms and suites and a reputation for fine dining. The inn itself is a 19th-century house in which the old detailing has been carefully preserved, but the feel—thanks to skillful decor and skylights—is light-filled, cheerful, and informal. Guests check in at the

CASTLE HILL RESORT IN PROCTORSVILLE
Christina Tree

kitchen counter. Five of the nine upstairs guest rooms have whirlpool tub, and all are furnished with antiques and designer linens. Summit View features a skylight framing the summit of the mountain. Next door is Solitude, an 1840s Greek Revival building with seven luxury suites featuring bedside whirlpool tub for two facing a gas fireplace. See *Dining Out* for details about dinner. Guests in the main house breakfast in the dining room, while those without kitchen facilities in the neighboring buildings receive breakfast in a basket. Amenities include shuttle service to and from Okemo. Rates from $110 in low season, $140 in high season.

🌂 **Echo Lake Inn** (802-228-8602; 800-356-6844; echolakeinn.com), Rt. 100 in Tyson, but the mailing address is P.O. Box 154, Ludlow 05149. One of the few survivors among the many 19th-century summer hotels that once graced Vermont lakes, this is a gem, a white-clapboard, four-story inn, rambling on from its 1820 core, through the 1840s, finishing with Victorian-style dormers and a long porch, lined in summer with pink geraniums and vintage red rockers. Now winterized, it offers 23 rooms, all with private bath, and seven condo units in the adjacent

ECHO LAKE INN

Christina Tree

Cheese Factory and Carriage House With good taste and carpentry skills innkeepers Laurence Jeffery and Peter Modisette have brought it back up a notch or two. The living room with its hearth and richly upholstered couches is once more elegant as well as comfortable, and there's an inviting pub along with a low-beamed dining room that's been recognized as outstanding (see *Dining Out*). Guest rooms vary far more widely than in most inns, from country traditional (iron bedstead, small-print wallpaper, and genuine 19th-century cottage furnishings), to romantic come-ons with king-sized beds and jetted tubs in the room, to spacious family suites with several beds. Amenities include a spa room, tennis courts, an outdoor pool, and a dock on Echo Lake across the road, with rowboats and canoes. Rates also vary widely: $89–229 per couple in summer, $149–259 in fall, full breakfast included. Inquire about MAP rates and special packages.

The Inn at Water's Edge (802-228-8143; 800-706-9736; innatwatersedge.com), 45 Kingdom Rd., Ludlow 05149. The aforementioned water is Echo Lake, and Bruce and Tina Verdrager have taken full advantage of the location, offering canoeing and flyfishing as well as bicycles for guests. The expansive, 150-year-old home has 11 smallish but well-appointed rooms and suites with jetted tubs and gas fireplaces. Doc's English Pub is a good spot for lounging, and guests sit down to a four-course candlelit dinner. Rates are $175–300 plus 15 percent gratuity, including breakfast and dinner; $125–250 for B&B; midweek specials.

∞ **The Fullerton Inn** (802-875-2444; 866-884-8578; fullertoninn.com), 40 The Common, P.O. Box 968, Chester 05143. Bret and Nancy Rugg are the innkeepers of this big, old-fashioned inn on the Chester green. The Ruggs have renovated all 21 guest rooms (private baths), decorating each individually, adding country quilts and fabrics, sitting rooms, and ceiling fans. Common space includes the inviting seating in the handsome lobby around the stone hearth, a lounge, a formal, consistently good dining room (see *Dining Out*), and a sunny breakfast room. $114–164 per couple for rooms in summer and fall, $129–169 during ski season; suites are $179–209; rates include continental breakfast.

BED & BREAKFASTS

In the Ludlow area

¶ **The Governor's Inn** (802-228-8830; 800-GOVERNOR; thegovernors inn.com), 86 Main St., Ludlow 05149. Open year-round except Dec. 23–26. William Wallace Stickney, governor of Vermont 1900–1902, built this Victorian house with its ornate slate, hand-painted fireplaces. Now it's owned by Jim and Cathy Kubec. The seven upstairs guest rooms are furnished with antiques, and an inviting suite in the rear of the third floor features a jetted tub for two and a sitting room. Jessica's Room has a jetted tub for two; six rooms have gas fireplace. The living room is small but elegant. Beer and wine are available to guests in the den. For a minimum of six guests Cathy prepares a six-course dinner that might begin with artichoke hearts in puff pasty pockets with a Vermont cheese custard, feature crispy duckling, and end with Kentucky bourbon pecan pie. A three-course breakfast is served in a cheery back room, warmed by the sun and a woodstove. A serious tea is served in the front parlor. Cathy also offers cooking classes and will pack picnic baskets with a little prior notice. $165–315 B&B double in fall and winter, $149–249 in regular season,

$189–299 during foliage and ski seasons; add $100 per couple MAP plus 18 percent dinner gratuity.

❧ **The Okemo Inn** (802-228-8834; out of state 800-328-8834; okemoinn .com), junction of Rts. 100 north and 103, Ludlow 05149. Open year-round except for two weeks in April and November. Ron Parry has been the innkeeper here since 1972, and his 1810 home has the feeling of a well-kept lodge, effortlessly welcoming. There are 11 nicely furnished guest rooms, 2 on the ground level, most with kings and queens, all with private bath. In the living room a table in front of the hearth is made from old bellows, and the dining room has low, notched beams; there's also a TV room, a sauna, and in summertime a pool. $120–200 per day B&B per couple includes a full breakfast. Inquire about ski, golf, and crafts packages; from $70 off-season.

& **Golden Stage Inn** (802-226-7744; 800-253-8226; goldenstageinn.com), P.O. Box 218, 399 Depot St., Proctorsville 05153. Sandy and Peter Gregg are at the helm of this handsome, historic house. An inn in the 18th century, it belonged to the Skinner family for 100 years, beginning in 1830. There are eight guest rooms and one suite, one named for the writer and performer Cornelia Otis Skinner. Dining areas include the solarium and the inn's greenhouse. The inn is centrally air-conditioned and wheelchair accessible; a swimming pool is set in gardens. $79–250 B&B includes a full breakfast, afternoon tea, and a bottomless cookie jar, MAP available. Ski packages begin at $89 per person.

🐾 ✄ ¶ **The Combes Family Inn** (802-228-8799; 800-822-8799), 953 East Lake Rd., Ludlow 05149. Ruth and Bill Combes have celebrated their 30th anniversary as innkeepers, welcoming families to their peaceful 1891 former dairy farm home. There are 11 guest rooms, all with private bath—6 in the farmhouse and 5 in an attached unit (where pets are allowed). B&B double rates are $76 spring, $100 summer, $130–176 winter. Ruth's delicious Vermont country dinners are available nightly by reservation at $18 per adult and $9 for kids.

In Chester

Note: The **Chester Innkeepers Association** (chesterlodging.com), the first in the state to achieve status as a Green Hotels association, maintains an excellent Web site.

&. **Inn Victoria** (802-875-4288; 800-732-4288; innvictoria.com), 321 Main St., Chester 05143. Yellow brick with purple shutters, a mansard roof, and columned porch, this showy Victorian on the Chester green has seven antiques-furnished guest rooms and a suite. All rooms have queen-sized bed, three have Jacuzzi, and the first-floor garden room is handicapped accessible. The Princess Victoria Room fills almost the entire third floor and features a queen-sized bed in front of a gas fireplace, a separate sitting room, a mini fridge, and a deluxe bath with the works ($225–295). Innkeepers Jon and Julie Pierce hail from Cambridge, England, and their Vermont connection is unusual—a story you should get them to tell. They are enthusiastic and thoughtful hosts (there's a stocked guest fridge), serving a full breakfast at the dining room table. No children under 15, please. Request a room with access to hot tub on the back deck. From $115 for a small room off-season to $255 for a suite, breakfast included.

🦞 🖉 **Henry Farm Inn** (802-875-2674; 800-723-8213; henryfarminn.com), 2206 Green Mountain Turnpike, Chester 05143. We love this place! There's a nice out-in-the-country feel to the old tavern, set in 56 rolling acres. Larger than other farmhouses of the period, it was built in 1760 as a stagecoach stop on the Green Mountain Turnpike, which is now a quiet dirt road but minutes from the edge of the Chester green. It retains its pine floors, beehive oven, paneling, and sense of pleasant, uncluttered comfort. The nine rooms are large, with private bath. Two of the rooms are suites with kitchen, accommodating three or four. What you notice are the quilts and the views. A path leads to the spring-fed pond up the hill, and a swimming hole in the Williams River is just across the road. In winter you can ski out the back door and up around through the woods and meadow. Inquire about frequent quilting workshop weekends. Your hosts are Patricia and Paul Dexter and their brilliant son Joseph. Children welcome. $90–100 per couple for rooms in summer, $115–125 in winter, $110–135 for the suites, more during foliage and holidays. Rates include a full country breakfast, served in the country dining room.

🦞 **Stone Cottage Collectables** (802-875-6211; stonecottagebb.net), 196 North St., Chester 05143. Chris and Ann Curran are your hosts at this 1840 stone house in Chester's Stone Village historic district. Three sitting rooms are furnished with antiques and collectibles; you'll also find a pleasant patio, deck, and garden. There are two guest rooms with private bath, but the find here is a glorious queen-bedded room with window seats and a working fireplace plus a great bath with soaking tub. It was all created by the late owner, best-selling author Olivia Goldsmith (*The First Wives Club*). It's $125; the adjoining Cozy Corner room is $100. Both rooms access a sitting room with a sofa bed; the three-rooms (two-bath) setup is $230 for three, $275 for six. Rates include a full breakfast. The Currans also operate a shop here, featuring radios and tubes, cameras, and stamps as well as antiques.

○○ **Williams River House B&B**
(802-875-1790; williamsriverhouse
.com), 397 Peck Rd., Chester 05143.
This classic 1780 brick farmhouse
(long since turned gentleman's farm)
and innkeepers Geoffrey Brown and
Mark Martins are a good match. The
home and neighboring greenhouse are
set in 46 genuinely secluded acres off
by the Williams River. The innkeepers
are interior and exterior designers who
have created an unusually luxurious
retreat. There are 10 suites in the
house, 3 with working fireplace. Common spaces—including hot tub, tavern,
and greenhouse—feature all the comforts. A screen in the living room pulls
down to create a home theater. The
kitchen is the centerpiece of the inn,
with dinners available for groups of six
or more. $195–225 includes a full
breakfast; the entire house can be
rented. Weddings are a specialty.

✍ **Hugging Bear Inn & Shoppe**
(802-875-2412; 800-325-0519; hugging
bear.com), 244 Main St., Chester
05143. A teddy bear lover's haven with
bears on the beds of eight guest rooms
(private bath). The place teems with
them: teddy bear wallpaper, teddy bear
sheets and shower curtains, and more
than 1,000 stuffed bears in the shop
behind the kitchen. Georgette Thomas
believes that people don't hug enough.
Everyone is invited to hug any bear in
the house, and the atmosphere here is
contagiously friendly. Rates are
$125–145 double, $150–180 in foliage.
Full breakfast is included.

Rowell's Inn (802-875-3658; 800-728-
0842; rowellsinn.com), 1834
Simonsville Rd. (Rt. 11), Andover
05143. Open year-round. This distinctive, double-porched, brick stage stop
has been serving the public off and on
since 1820. Its most colorful era,

according to innkeeper Michael Brengolini, was that of early auto touring,
which happened to overlap with Prohibition. Photos show patrons of the day
arriving with their chauffeurs, and
Rowell's looms large on an "Ideal
Tour" map, with few other stops in
Vermont. Located midway among Londonderry, Weston, and Chester, the inn
is off by itself with some fine walks and
cross-country skiing out the back door.
Mike and wife Susan McNulty (who
offers acupuncture and Reiki) have
seven comfortable guest rooms with
private bath, one with a working fireplace. Two roomy spaces on the third
floor have been carved from the old
ballroom, furnished grandly with
antiques and Oriental rugs. Ample
common space includes an English-
style pub. Mike, the former owner of a
San Francisco restaurant, offers a four-
course, single-entrée dinner Friday
and Saturday nights (24-hour reservations required) and for groups of six or
more midweek. A $25 four-course
meal might begin with cheese pie, featuring cognac-glazed Cornish hens as
the entrée. Inquire about "Mad Mike's
Hot Sauce." $90–175 per couple
includes a full country breakfast.

Popple Fields (802-875-4219; popple
fields.com), P.O. Box 636, 1300 Popple
Dungeon Rd., Chester 05143. It took
Conrad Delia 10 years (1989–1999) to
build this amazing reproduction 18th-
century house, and it's a beauty,
remarkable for its detailing, right down
to a Colonial-style bar. It's on a back
road, set in 18 rolling acres. There are
four guest rooms, two with private
bath, and Conrad has made much of
the furniture, too (he operates a Windsor chair and cabinet shop on the
premises). Marylin Delia serves a full
buffet breakfast in the large country
kitchen. No children under 15, please.
$125–160. Inquire about the property's
two-bedroom cottage, a real gem.

⊙ 🐾 🐾 🖊 **Old Town Farm Inn** (802-875-2346; 888-232-1089; otfi.com), 665 Rt. 10, Chester 05143. This former "Town Farm" is in Gassetts, a village midway between Chester and Ludlow. Long known to families as a reasonably priced ski lodge, the old place with its wide-board floors has been nicely rehabbed by Michiko and Alex Hunter. There are now seven comfortable guest rooms, all with private bath. It's set in 11 acres with a pond. $119–139 with breakfast; $10 per extra person. Okemo ski packages $79–119 per person including lift ticket. Given Michiko's fame as a chef (see *Dining Out*), the comfortable size of the inn, and the attractive grounds—including a pondside BBQ—it's becoming a popular place for weddings and reunions.

MOTELS 🖊 **The Pointe at Castle Hill Resort & Spa** (802-226-7688; 800-438-7908; cavendishpointe.com), Rt. 103, Cavendish 05142. This contemporary motor inn has an inviting lobby with fireplace. Facilities include an indoor pool, hot tub/spa room, business and fitness centers, and game room. The 70 fairly large rooms come equipped with cable TV, speakerphone, fridge, and coffeemaker; there are also 26 suites, some with full kitchen and sitting room with gas fireplace. This is also the check-in point for Castle Hill (see *Inns*), and guests have easy access (for a fee) to its full-service spa. Breakfast year-round. From $99 in summer, $119 in winter when there's complementary shuttle service to Okemo.

🐾 🖊 **Timber Inn Motel** (802-228-8666; timberinn.com), 112 Rt. 103, Ludlow 05149. This 17-room cedar and knotty-pine motel on the Black River is on the eastern fringe of town with surprisingly good views, a winter shuttle-bus stop for Okemo. Hot tub

and sauna in winter, heated outdoor pool in summer, rooms with phone, A/C, and cable TV; there's a two-bedroom unit as well as a two-bedroom apartment with full kitchen. Dogs are accepted by reservation ($10 per night). $69–229 includes morning coffee and teas.

🐾 🐾 🖊 "🍴" **Motel in the Meadow** (802-875-2626; 888-668-3514; motelinthemeadow.com), 936 Rt. 11 West, Chester 05143. Pat Budnick offers nine rooms with country quilts and decor. Two have kitchenettes, another pair feature two queen-sized beds, and one room has two queens and two bunk beds. $69–85 for rooms, $110 for the big family room, includes a continental breakfast. A former nurse, Pat is accustomed to caring for people—as guests will attest. Inquire about Music in the Meadow, held on a Saturday in July.

❄ Where to Eat

DINING OUT **Echo Lake Inn** (802-228-8602; 800-356-6844; echolakeinn.com), Rt. 100 north in Tyson. Open to the public for dinner. The dining room, with print wallpaper and shades of mauve, is attractive. Chef Kevin Barnes has established an enviable reputation over the past 20 years. The à la carte menu offers genuine choice and usually includes a freshly made vegetarian pasta dish such as roasted vegetable ravioli; pan-seared duck breast served with the day's sauce; and sautéed veal medallion. Entrées $19–28.

The Castle Hill Resort and Spa (802-226-7361), intersection of Rts. 131 and 103, Proctorsville. Open for dinner by reservation nightly. The interior of this stone mansion is a rich blend of American oak, Mexican mahogany, and French marble. The $45–59 prix fixe four-course menu is priced according to your choice of several entrées, usually including roast rack of lamb and the Castle Beef Wellington.

The Andrie Rose Inn (802-228-4846; andrieroseinn.com). Open to the public by reservation (before 3 PM) Fri.–Sat. with a three- or four-course dinner menu ($39/$46 per person). Chef-owner Irene Maston's menu on a summer evening included a choice of three appetizers and five entrées. Cavendish Farm quail is usually an option, along with a tempting veggie option. You might begin with prosciutto, onion jam, and tomato tart, then dine on Maine Jonah crabcakes, with apple slaw and red pepper vinaigrette.

Tokai-Tei Japanese Restaurant at the Old Town Farm Inn (802-875-2346; 888-232-1089), 665 Vermont Rt. 10, Chester. Open Wed.–Sun. 5–9 by reservation. Halfway between Chester and Ludlow isn't exactly where you expect to find a first-rate Japanese restaurant, but that's where Michiko Hunter presides over the kitchen of this old family-geared lodge, turning out tantalizing and reasonably priced sushi and such entrées as *gyu-aspara maki* (beef asparagus roll), *buta niku no shoga yaki* (gingered pork), and a choice of tempura dishes. It's BYOB, and desserts include green tea or red bean ice cream, made in house. Entrées $15–26, including miso soup and garden salad.

☙ **Bella Luna Ristorante** (802-228-6666), 68 Rt. 100 north, Ludlow. Open from 5 PM Wed.–Sun. There's more than a little fantasy to the decor in this Italian restaurant that features a fiber-optic ski ceiling, complete with shooting stars and a comet. The menu is classic Italian with plenty of pasta options, but entrées include house specials like oven-roasted duck, maple bourbon salmon, and seafood stuffed chicken. There's a children's menu and a pub menu that includes a bruschetta burger. Entrées $13.95–17.95.

Coleman Brook Tavern (802-228-1435), Jackson Gore Inn, Rt. 103, Ludlow. This is the signature restaurant in Okemo's new base complex and it's sleekly comfortable, with sofas, wing chairs, and dim lighting to mitigate its size. The cherrywood-paneled Wine Room is the most intimate setting. The menu ranges from vegetarian strudel to steak, pan-seared with a green peppercorn sauce. Entrées $15–22. A Wednesday "Lobster Fest" with steamers, mussels, and all the fixings is $14.95.

☙ **Harry's Cafe** (802-259-2996; harryscafe.com), 3621 Rt. 103, Mount Holly. Open daily 5–10; closed Mon.–Tue. off-season. Trip Pierce took the funky old Backside Restaurant and turned it into the nicest kind of a light, airy space with a bar, tables and booths, good art, and a woodstove. Best of all is the food: Begin with a salade Niçoise or corn and shrimp bisque with fresh dill. It's a big menu ranging from hot smoked salmon with ginger sauce, to Jamaican jerk pork, to roast half duck with all the trimmings. You can also get fish-and-chips or pizza; "For Kids," there's also plenty of choice and curly fries. Every Thursday a $20 three-course Thai meal is featured. Entrées $13–20. Reservations accepted.

Cappuccino's Restaurant (802-228-7566; cappuccinosrestaurant.com), 41 Depot St., Ludlow, serves dinner Tue.–Sun.; reservations suggested. Longtime chef-owner Steve Degnan and his wife, Dawna, have created a pleasant ambience and a varied menu of pasta, seafood, beef, chicken, and nightly specials; full bar. You might dine on duck dressed with apricot Grand Marnier sauce ($20.95) or New York strip steak ($21.95); pastas from $10.95.

Panarello's Italian Restaurant (802-228-7222; panarellos.com), 31 Rt. 103 south, Ludlow. Open Tue.–Sat. for dinner. Another Italian dining option in Ludlow. Interesting pasta options include butternut squash ravioli with sage butter sauce and baked penne pasta with white sauce, sausage, and broccoli rabe. Entrées ($16–32) include classic dishes such as osso buco.

♪ **Sam's Steakhouse** (802-228-2087; sams-steakhouse.com), 91 Rt. 103, just east of downtown Ludlow. Open for dinner nightly with midweek specials. Known for filet mignon you can cut with a butter knife, excellent seafood, a good salad bar, and sinful desserts. Entrées $16–38. Children's menu.

In Chester

Fullerton Inn (802-875-2444; fullertoninn.com), 40 The Common. Open nightly except Sun. This classic old inn dining room is surprisingly casual with a varied menu and reliably good food, ranging from pizza to schnitzel Fullerton (breaded veal sautéed with mushrooms and Dijon cream sauce) and pan-roasted New Zealand venison. Inquire about live music. Entrées $10–24.

Also see the Inn at Weathersfield ("The Lower Connecticut River Valley") and the River Tavern at Hawk Inn and Mountain Resort in Plymouth ("Killington/Rutland Area"). Rowell's Inn (see *Lodging*) is open to the public by reservation with 24 hours' notice.

EATING OUT

In and around Ludlow

Willie Dunne's Grille (802-228-1387), at the Okemo Valley Golf Club & Nordic Center, Rt. 100. Open year-round for lunch and dinner, serving surprisingly affordable and good food. Two windowed walls are open to views of the pond and the 18th green. All entrées are served with greens.

♪ **Pot Belly Restaurant and Pub** (802-228-8989), 130 Main St., Ludlow. Open for dinner nightly and lunch most days. Since 1974, a pleasant atmosphere with live music (swing and blues bands, jug band music, and rock and roll) on weekends. At lunch try a Belly Burger or the Cajun chicken sandwich. The dinner menu is large.

⁜ **Java Baba's Slow Food Café** (802-228-4131), at the base of the Okemo Access Rd., features overstuffed chairs and couches. It serves fresh-baked muffins and pastries, homemade soups, sandwiches, salads, desserts, and a variety of coffee drinks. WiFi.

Crows Bakery and Opera House Café (802-226-7007), 73 Depot St., Proctorsville. Off Rt. 103. Open Tue.–Fri. 6–2, weekends 7–2. An attractive café serving full breakfasts and exotic wraps such as Veggie Wrap-sody and Tuna Kahuna, plus a choice of veggie sandwiches as well as ham and Swiss. The bakery is open until 6 most nights. Known for its from-scratch pastries and breads.

In Chester

♪ **Heritage Deli & Bakery** (802-875-3550; heritagedeliandbakery.com), Rt. 103 south of the green. Open daily 7–5. A café/gourmet food and wine shop, this is a terrific road-food stop. All the baked goods and soups are made from scratch daily. Co-owner Claire Hoser is the baker and with Michele Wilcox has created a warmly attractive café with Provençal print tablecloths, bright colors, booths, and fresh flowers whenever possible. You order off the blackboard and settle into a booth. Breakfast options range from pancakes to steak and eggs. At lunch try a soup or salad combo with one of more than a dozen signature sandwich-

es named for Vermonters. We usually agonize between Grandma Moses (tarragon turkey salad on a croissant) and Ira Allen (turkey, sun-dried tomato cream cheese, and lettuce on a baguette). Box lunches; wine and beer served.

Curtis's All American Restaurant (802-875-6999; curtisbbqvt.com), 908 Rt. 103. Open Wed.–Sun year-round with all-you can-eat weekend buffets. A genuine offshoot of the popular Curtis's BBQ in Putney. Sarah Tuff, daughter of the original Curtis, and Chris Parker are the proud owners of this tantalizing new road-food option just east of Chester. It's all about BBQ ribs and chicken.

The Phoenix Café at Baba-A-Louis Bakery (802-875-4666), Rt. 11 west. Closed Apr. and the first part of Nov., as well as Sun. and Mon., but otherwise open 7 AM–6 PM. This long-established bakery (see *Special Shops*) is the setting for an independent café, serving made-from-scratch soups and sandwiches in a soaring, attractive space just west of the green.

Moon Dog Café (802-875-4966), on the green. Open 10–8 daily. Healthy food is cooked up in the middle of this combination health food store, crafts shop, and café, with plenty of comfortable seating. On a winter day we lunched at a deal table in the sunny, plant-filled dining area in the rear of the shop. The Turkish lentil soup was steaming hot, served in a china bowl.

Jack's Diner (802-875-1062), 521 Main St. Open 5 AM–9 PM daily. Under relatively new ownership, Jack's is the place for straightforward diner food, although there are those hot pan crêpes at breakfast; eggs Benedict too. Local favorites are sausage gravy and buttermilk biscuits as well as sides of corned beef hash, grilled sandwiches, burger plates, and pies.

Bradford Tavern (802-875-2444), at the Fullerton Inn, 40 on the Common. Open for lunch Thu.–Sat. Yet another middle-of-the-village source of hot sandwiches like fish fillet or beer-battered fried portobello mushroom with tomatoes and provolone in a bulky roll. This casual lounge (full bar) is open evenings but closed for lunch midweek.

Rose Arbour Tea Room (802-875-4767), 55 School St., just off the green. Open seasonally 11–5, closed most Tuesdays. A combination B&B, gift store, and tearoom. Specializing in two-course high teas but also good for salads, sandwiches, and quiche. Chef-owner Suzanne Nielson is known for her scones and pastries.

Stone Hearth Inn (802-875-2525; stonehearthinnvermont.com), 698 Rt. 11. Restaurant and tavern open Thu.–Mon, from 4 PM; lunch is served on weekends noon–3. Chef owned with some French Canadian specialties and ambience, comfort foods, salads, beers on tap.

Ø **Zachary's Pizza House** (802-875-5466), 319 S. Main St. Open for lunch through dinner. Set back from the street, this is an easy-to-miss town staple. We discovered it out of desperation late one midweek evening when no other source of comfort food was open. A classic Greek gyro and Magic Hat beer hit the spot.

MacLaomainn's Scottish Pub in Chester (802-722-4855), 52 Main St. Open for lunch and dinner, closed Tue. Scotsman Alan Brown and Chester resident Deb Brown met playing cribbage online, met, built this cozy pub, and were married in it. Haggis, a dish so peculiarly Scottish it's a national symbol, has been a big hit (don't ask what's in it besides oatmeal!), along with steak pie. The bar is fully licensed and offers a variety of Scottish beers as well as whiskeys.

SOUTHERN VERMONT

✳ Selective Shopping

ANTIQUES SHOPS Stone House Antiques (802-875-4477), Rt. 103 south, Chester, is an antiques mall with 250 dealers and a touristy collection of country crafts. Open daily 10–5.

William Austin's Antiques (802-875-3032; wmaustin.con), 42 Maple St., Chester. A full line (more than 500 pieces) of antique country furniture and collectibles.

Stone Cottage Collectables (802-875-6211), 196 North St., Chester. Antiques and collectibles, stamps and philatelic supplies. Also see *Bed & Breakfasts.*

ART GALLERIES Crow Hill Gallery (802-875-3763) 729 Flamstead Rd., Chester. Open Wed.–Sat. 10–5, Sun. by appointment. Watercolorist Jeanne Carbonetti welcomes visitors to the many-windowed home and studio/gallery that she and her husband designed and built on a rise above the meadows. It's an ideal setting for her richly colored paintings. The author of several books, she also offers group and private instruction in painting and the creative process.

Reed Gallery (802-875-6225), on the green, Chester. Open Thu.–Sun. 10–5. Featuring local artwork and offering workshops and demonstrations, the gallery is owned and operated by Bob and watercolorist Elaine Reed.

BOOKS AND MAPS Misty Valley Books (802-875-3400; mvbooks.com), on the green, Chester. Open daily. Lynne and Bill Reed maintain an unusually friendly, well-stocked bookshop; browsing is encouraged, and author readings are frequent. Their "New Voices" weekend in January features first-time novelists drawn from throughout the country. Past flyers for this event paper the store's "archives" (the bathroom), and they picture a number of current best-selling authors. The store also sells Persian carpets and offers French classes (Bill Reed has taught in Africa and France as well as Vermont schools).

The Book Nook (802-228-3238), 136 Main St., Ludlow. An independent bookstore with a wide selection of primarily contemporary books.

CRAFTS Depot Street Gallery, Home of the Silver Spoon (802-228-4753), 44 Depot St., Ludlow. Steve Manning fashions an amazing variety of things—from bracelets (including watches) to decorative trees and fish. Local artists and sculptors are also featured in the first-rate adjoining gallery.

Bonnie's Bundles (802-875-2114; bonniesboundlesdolls.com), Stone Village, Rt. 103, Chester. Look for the OPEN flag in this 1814 house in the middle of Chester's Stone Village. It's usually out. Bonnie Waters doesn't like to sell her handmade cloth dolls to retails shops. "I want to meet the people who buy my dolls," explains Waters, who welcomes visitors to her parlor, home to roughly 100 one-of-a-kind dolls. Many people request portrait dolls, supplying a photo of a child or friend.

Gallery 103 (802-875-7400), Rt. 103, Chester. Open Thu.–Mon. 10–5. Just east of town, a sizable gallery featuring wrought iron and metalwork by owners Elise and Payne Junker, also showcasing pottery, blown glass, jewelry, prints, clothing, and more.

Tsuga Studios (802-875-1825; tsuga studios.com), 678 Goldswaite Rd., Chester. Squirreled up a back road on the western edge of town, usually open only by appointment—but check the Web site for periodic open houses, such as the early-December weekend when hand-blown Christmas ornaments festoon the rafters and seconds draw fans from afar. Glassmaker Nicholas Kekic's deeply colored, elegantly simple pitchers and bowls can be found in most of the country's top crafts and glass galleries.

Six Loose Ladies (802-226-7373; fiberartsinvermont.org), 7 Depot St., Proctorsville. Open Wed.–Sun. 10–6, Tue. until 9. The unlikely name for this totally wholesome store comes from the 19th-century practice of teaching streetwalkers to spin, weave, and knit as an alternative to their lifestyles. Local fleece, yarns, and woven products, pottery, and more are carried on consignment.

Craft Shop at Fletcher Farm (802-228-4348), 611 Rt. 103, east of Ludlow. Open late June–early Sept., 9:30–5, and weekends from Memorial Day. Work by members of the Society of Vermont Craftsmen (see *To Do*).

SPECIAL SHOPS **Baba-A-Louis Bakery** (802-875-4666), Rt. 11 west. Closed Apr. and the first part of Nov., as well as Sun. and Mon., but otherwise open 7 AM–6 PM. John McClure's sticky buns, croissants, French loaves, and peasant breads are distributed throughout New England, but here you'll also find his French pastries. The octagonal building, which McLure designed and built, features arches soaring 30 feet. Also see *Eating Out*.

Chapter XIV (802-228-4438; chapter xiv.com), 126 Main St., Ludlow. This is a totally eclectic and thoroughly chic (as in female) shop: clothes, books, adornments of all kinds, as much a delight as ever under new proprietor Willow Monika Feller. Bargains are upstairs.

Conrad Delia, Windsor Chair Maker (802-875-4219), Popple Dungeon Rd., Chester. After a long career as a home builder on Long Island, Conrad Delia studied with several New England chair makers before opening his own shop. Call to schedule a visit.

Hugging Bear Shoppe (802-875-2412; 800-325-0519; huggingbear .com), 244 Main St., Chester. Georgette Thomas has filled four rooms at the rear of her middle-of-town Victorian house with more than 10,000 teddy bears, plus plush animals and collectibles. It's a phenomenon.

F O O D **Crowley Cheese Factory** (802-259-2340; 800-683-2606; crowley cheese.com), Rt. 103, 5 miles northwest of Ludlow. Check for hours. See *Scenic Drive* for the history of this exceptional cheese, which is sharper and creamier than cheddar.

Green Mountain Sugar House (802-228-7151), Rt. 100, 4 miles north of Ludlow. You can watch syrup being produced in March and April; maple candy is made throughout the year on a weekly basis. This is also a place to find freshly pressed cider in September. The gift and produce shop is open daily 9–6 "most of the time."

Mitch's Maples (802-228-5242), 240 Green Mountain Turnpike, just off Rt. 11 in Chester. Open during sugaring season. We can vouch for this syrup, which we bought on the honor system in the combination sugarhouse/store.

Singletons' Store (802-226-7666), Rt. 131, Proctorsville. Best known for its smoked meats. This much-expanded family-run (for three generations) grocery store has kept abreast of the demands of the area's condo owners while continuing to cover the basics:

a Vermont liquor store, fishing and hunting licenses, rods and reels, guns and ammo, sporting goods, Johnson Woolen Mills and other sturdy outdoor wear and boots, plus fine wines, choice meats, a standout deli, and Vermont products. An average of 350 pounds of meat is sold per day. Note the antique guns running like a frieze above the shelves, and the stuffed trophies. But why the camel?

Wine & Cheese Depot (802-228-4128), 46 Depot St., Ludlow. A serious wine store but also showcasing local cheeses; the only place in town you can buy Crowley, a real amenity if you don't want to schlep up to the factory (see above) for this outstanding local product.

Farmer's Markets: Chester (Memorial Day–Columbus Day weekends), Sun. 11–3, Rt. 103 south at Zachary's Pizza. In Gassetts (between Chester and Ludlow), Rt. 103 at jct. of Rt. 10, most days June–Oct.

Also see the **Vermont Country Store** in Weston and Rockingham.

SINGLETONS' STORE IN PROCTORSVILLE
Christina Tree

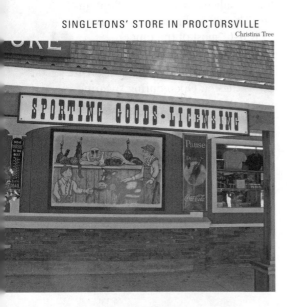

✳ Special Events

January through February: **Winter Carnival**, Ludlow (yourplacein vermont.com)—snow sculptures, parade, a bonfire and fireworks.

Second weekend of February: **Chester Winter Carnival**, genuine old-fashioned fun.

Last weekend of March: **Vermont Maple Open House Weekend** (vermontmaple.org).

April: **Okemo's Annual SlushHuck Weekend-Wacky Spring Celebration** (okemo.com).

Memorial Day weekend: Townwide tag sale and Open Studio tour.

July 1: **Fletcher Farm Arts and Crafts Fair**, Rt. 103, Ludlow; **St. Joseph's Carnival**; **horse show and community picnic**, Chester.

July 4: Fireworks, West Hill Park, Ludlow. **Calvin Coolidge Birthday Memorial**, Plymouth.

Late July **Annual Music in the Meadow Festival**, Chester. **Plymouth Old Home Day** (historic vermont.org).

Late July through August: **Okemo Valley Music Festival**—free concerts in Ludlow, Cavendish, and Chester (yourplaceinvermont.org).

August: **Chester Outdoor Art Show**. **Vermont State Zucchini Festival**, Ludlow—four days of "zucchini madness," including a costume parade. **Thursday-evening concerts** on the Chester green all month.

Late September: **Civil War Expo Chester** (18thvt.com), Chester. **Fall Fair on the Green**, Chester. **Plymouth Cheese and Harvest Festival** (historicvermont.org).

October: **Historical Society Halloween Cemetery Tour**.

November through January: **Green Mountain Festival Series** of performances in Chester (greenmountain festivalseries.com).

December: **Overture to Christmas** (*first and second Saturdays*; see okemovalleyvt.org), Chester. Events include a Children's Day the first Saturday, with Santa and Mrs. Claus arriving by fire engine; tree lighting and candlelight caroling the second; the Polar Express runs from Bellows Falls to Chester Depot both days. **Torchlight Parade and Fireworks Display** at Okemo.

The Connecticut River Valley

Christina Tree

INTRODUCTION

The Connecticut River flows 410 miles from its high source on the New Hampshire–Quebec border to Long Island Sound in the state of Connecticut. What concerns us here are its 270 miles as a boundary—and bond—between the states of New Hampshire and Vermont. Defying state lines, it forms one of New England's most beautiful and distinctive regions, shaped by a shared history.

Judging from more than 130 archaeological sites along this stretch of the river, its banks have been peopled for many thousands of years. Evidence of Western Abenaki villages have been found at Newbury, at Claremont (New Hampshire), and at the Great Falls at present-day Bellows Falls. Unfortunately, these people were decimated by disease contracted from English traders.

By the late 17th century English settlements had spread from the mouth of the Connecticut up to Deerfield, Massachusetts, just below the present New Hampshire–Vermont border. In 1704 Deerfield was attacked by French and Indians, who killed 40 villagers and carried off more than 100 as captives to St. Francis, a full 300 miles to the northwest. This was one in a series of bloody incidents generally lumped together as "the French and Indian Wars."

Recent and ongoing scholarship is deepening our sense of relationships among Frenchmen, Western Abenaki tribespeople, and Englishmen during the first half of the 18th century. By 1700 many settlers had adopted the canoe as a standard mode of travel and, according to Dartmouth professor Colin G. Calloway in *Dawnland Encounters*, in 1704 New Hampshire passed a law requiring all householders to keep "one good pair of snow shoes and moqueshens moccasins." Settlers and Abenaki traded with each other. Beaver remained the prime source of revenue for the settlers, and the Indians were becoming increasingly dependent on manufactured goods and alcohol. Both at Fort Dummer—built in 1724 in what, at the time, was Massachusetts (now Vernon, Vermont)—and at the Fort at No. 4, built 50 miles upriver in 1743 in present Charlestown, New Hampshire, settlers and Indians lived side by side. However, during this period former friends and neighbors also frequently faced each other in battles to the death.

At the reconstructed Fort at No. 4 you learn that five adults and three children were abducted by a band of Abenaki in 1754 (all survived), and that in 1759 Major Robert Rodgers and his Rangers retaliated for the many raids from the Indian village of St. Francis (near Montreal) by killing many more than 100 residents, including many women and children. The suffering of "Rodgers' Rangers" on their winter return home is legendary. A historic marker on Rt. 10 in Haverhill (New Hampshire) offers a sobering description.

After the 1763 Peace of Paris, France withdrew its claims to New France and English settlers surged up the Connecticut River, naming their new communities for their old towns in Connecticut and Massachusetts: Walpole, Plainfield, Lebanon, Haverhill, Windsor, Norwich, and more.

This was, however, no-man's-land.

In 1749 New Hampshire governor Benning Wenworth had begun granting land on both sides of the river (present-day Vermont was known as "The New Hampshire Grants"), a policy that New York's Governor George Clinton refused to recognize. In 1777, when Vermont declared itself a republic, 16 towns on the New Hampshire side opted to join it. In December 1778, at a meeting in Cornish, New Hampshire, towns from both sides of the river voted to form their own state of "New Connecticut," but neither burgeoning state was about to lose so rich a region. In 1779 New Hampshire claimed all Vermont.

In 1781 delegates from both sides of the river met in Charlestown (New Hampshire) and agreed to stick together. Vermont's Governor Chittendon wrote to General Washington asking to be admitted to the Union, incorporating towns contested both by New Hampshire and New York. Washington replied: Yes, but without the contested baggage.

In 1782 New Hampshire sent 1,000 soldiers to enforce their jurisdiction. Not long thereafter Washington asked Vermont to give in—and it did. Needless to say, the river towns were unhappy about this verdict.

The Valley itself prospered in the late 18th and early 19th centuries, as evidenced by the exquisite Federal-era (1790s–1830s) meetinghouses and mansions still to be seen in river towns. With New Hampshire's Dartmouth College (established 1769) at its heart and rich floodplain farmland stretching its length, this valley differed far more dramatically than today from the unsettled mountainous regions walling it in on either side.

The river remained the Valley's highway in the early 19th century. A transportation canal was built to circumvent the Great Falls at present-day Bellows Falls, and Samuel Morey of Orford (New Hampshire) built a steamboat in 1793. Unfortunately Robert Fulton scooped his invention, but the upshot was increased river transport—at least until the 1840s, when railroads changed everything.

"It is an extraordinary era in which we live," Daniel Webster remarked in 1847, watching the first train roll into Lebanon, New Hampshire, the first rail link between the Connecticut River and the Atlantic. "It is altogether new," he continued. "The world has seen nothing like it before."

In this "anything's possible" era, the Valley boomed. At the Robbins,

THE WINDSOR–CORNISH COVERED BRIDGE IS AMONG THE LONGEST IN THE U.S.

Christina Tree

Kendall & Lawrence Armory in Windsor, gun makers developed machines to do the repetitive tasks required to produce each part of a gun. This meant that for the first time an army could buy a shipment of guns and know that if one was damaged, it could be repaired with similar parts. In the vintage-1846 armory, now the American Precision Museum, you learn that this novel production of interchangeable parts became known as the American System of precision manufacturing. Springfield too became known for precision tool making. Until recently this area was known as Precision Valley.

In places the railroad totally transformed the landscape, creating towns where there had been none, shifting populations from high old town centers like Rockingham and Walpole (New Hampshire) to the riverside. This shift was most dramatic in the town of Hartford, where White River Junction became the hub of north–south and east–west rail traffic.

The river itself was put to new uses. It became a sluiceway down which logs were floated from the northern forest to paper mills in Bellows Falls and farther downriver. Its falls had long powered small mills, but now a series of hydro dams were constructed, including the massive dam between Barnet, Vermont, and Monroe, New Hampshire, in 1930. This flooded several communities to create both Comerford Reservoir—and the visual illusion that the Connecticut River stops there. At present 16 dams stagger the river's flow between the Second Connecticut Lake above Pittsburg, New Hampshire, and Enfield, Connecticut, harnessing the river to provide power for much of the Northeast.

By the 1950s the river was compared to an open sewer and towns turned their backs to it, depositing refuse along its banks.

Still, beyond towns, the river slid by fields of corn and meadows filled with cows. In 1952 the nonprofit Connecticut River Watershed Council was founded to "promote and protect wise use of the Connecticut Valley's resources." Thanks to the 1970s Clean Water Act and to acquisitions, green-ups, and cleanups by numerous conservation groups, the river itself began to enjoy a genuine renewal. Visitors and residents alike discovered its beauty; campsites for canoeists were spaced along the shore. At present kayaks as well as canoes can be rented along several stretches.

The cultural fabric of towns on either side of the river has remained close knit and, although many bridges were destroyed by the hurricane of 1927, the 21 that survive include one of the longest covered bridges in the United States (connecting Windsor, Vermont, and Cornish, New Hampshire). It's only because tourism promotional budgets are financed by individual state taxes that this stretch of the river valley itself has not, until recently, been recognized as a destination by either New Hampshire or Vermont.

A bistate group, the Connecticut River Joint Commissions—founded in 1989 to foster bistate cooperation and represent 53 riverfront towns—stepped into this breach, with dramatic results. It has now spawned the Connecticut River Scenic Byway Council dedicated to, among other things, creating an infrastructure to identify appropriate places in which to promote tourism and the cultural heritage.

At this writing nine "waypoint" information centers are salted along the river. These include Bellows Falls, White River Junction, Wells River, Haverhill (New Hampshire), Lancaster (New Hampshire), St. Johnsbury, and Claremont and Colebrook, both in New Hampshire. All are serving visitors well and in the process reestablishing the Connecticut at its rightful place as the centerpiece of a genuine region. A similar center in Windsor is planned. Their work has been enhanced by the federally funded Silvio O. Conte National Fish and Wildlife Refuge, which seeks to preserve the quality of the natural environment within the entire Connecticut River watershed. For a sense of wildlife and habitat in this area, stop by the Montshire Museum (the name melds both states) in Norwich, Vermont.

The Connecticut River corridor is now officially "the Connecticut River National Scenic Byway." We are proud to note that for more than 20 years both our New Hampshire and Vermont Explorer's Guides have included both sides of the river.

Visually visitors see a river, not state lines. Interstate 91 on the Vermont side has backroaded Rt. 5, as it has Rt. 10 on the New Hampshire side. Following these "byways" travelers can explore historic towns, farm stands, and local scenic spots, finding their way to quiet river roads along both riverbanks. Access to the river via canoe and kayak has increased in recent years, thanks to both outfitters and conservation groups that maintain launch areas and campsites.

Within each chapter prime sights to see shift from one side of the river to the other; the same holds true for places to eat, stay, hike, and generally explore this very distinctive region. Of course in this book we focus in more detail on Vermont, while in *New Hampshire: An Explorer's Guide* the focus is more detailed on that state.

GUIDANCE **ctrivertravel.net**, an excellent, noncommercial Web site covering the entire stretch of the Connecticut shared by Vermont and New Hampshire, is maintained by the Connecticut River Scenic Byway Council. Also look for "way-point" information centers serving both sides of the river, described under *Guidance* in ensuing chapters.

Helpful pamphlet guides available from the Connecticut River Joint Commissions (603-826-4800; ctrivertravel.net) include:

Explorations Along the Connecticut River Byway of New Hampshire and Vermont (a map/guide).

Connecticut River Heritage Trail (a 77-mile driving/biking tour for the historically and architecturally minded).

Connecticut River Birding Trail map/guides (two): *Northern Section* and *Upper Valley.*

RECOMMENDED READING *Proud to Live Here in the Connecticut River Valley of Vermont and New Hampshire* by Richard J. Ewald with Adair D. Mulligan, published by the Connecticut River Joint Commissions (crjc.org).

Confluence: A River, Politics, and the Fate of All Humanity by Nathaniel Tripp (Steerforth Press, Hanover, New Hampshire).

This American River: Five Centuries of Writing About the Connecticut by Walter Wetherell (University Press of New England, Hanover, New Hampshire).

The Connecticut River Boating Guide, Source to the Sea (Falcon Press, 3rd edition 2007), published in cooperation with the Connecticut River Watershed Council.

Where the Great River Rises: An Atlas of the Connecticut River in Vermont and New Hampshire by the Connecticut River Joint Commissions (University Press of New England, Hanover, New Hampshire).

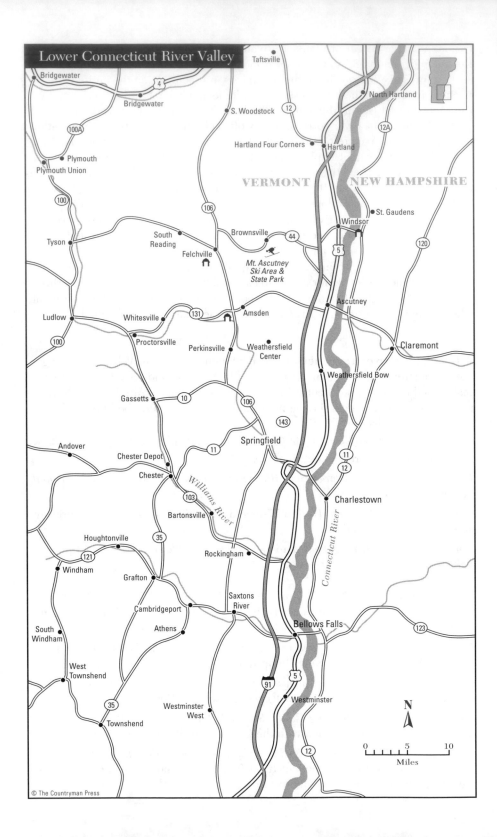

Lower Connecticut River Valley

THE LOWER CONNECTICUT RIVER VALLEY

INCLUDING BELLOWS FALLS, SAXTONS RIVER, GRAFTON, SPRINGFIELD, WEATHERSFIELD, AND WINDSOR

The story here is water, gravity and time.

—*Richard Ewald*

As the River Flows, an excellent film on view in the Bellows Falls Waypoint Visitors Center, is a great introduction to this 40-mile stretch of the Connecticut River. It details the area's strikingly visible historic layerings. Within walking distance you can inspect Indian petroglyphs, an 1802 canal, and a late-19th-century brick mill and railroad center.

Sited at one of the largest drops in the entire length of the river, Bellows Falls itself cascades down glacial terraces so steep that steps connect the brick downtown with Victorian homes above and with surviving riverside mill buildings. All this bustle contrasts with the haunting stillness of the town's original settlement, gathered around the exquisite 18th-century Rockingham Meeting House a few miles north.

In Windsor the layerings are even more compressed along a Main Street that includes the 18th-century "Constitution House" (the official birthplace of Vermont), a 1950s diner, and a white-pillared 1790s Asher Benjamin church. South of the covered bridge is an 1846 brick armory in which inventors are credited with introducing the concept of interchangeable parts, a process that revolutionized the gun and tool industry globally. Locally it spawned some significant tool companies, the reason this area is still known as the Precision Valley.

Water and gravity have combined along this stretch of the Connecticut River and its tributaries—the Saxtons, Williams, and Black rivers in Vermont and the Sugar River in New Hampshire—to power a variety of 19th-century mills. Around these the communities of Bellows Falls, Springfield, Windsor, and Claremont, New Hampshire, have all evolved.

While waterfalls no longer power mills, gravity still plays a part in the local economy—on more than 50 ski trails on Mount Ascutney, a lone monadnock that looms 3,144 feet above the Connecticut River. Like the mills before it, this ski area is not large enough to affect the quintessential back-roads Vermont feel of the surrounding area with its scattered inns and B&Bs.

We include Grafton in this chapter because it's most closely associated with Saxtons River and Bellows Falls (7 and 10 miles east, respectively.) A classic old crossroads village, Grafton is also handy to several other areas in southern Vermont. Restored and preserved by the Windham Foundation, this is a "village beautiful," complete with gracious inn, cheesemaking factory, low-key museums, shops and galleries, and a vintage covered bridge.

New England's longest and most famous covered bridge links the communities of Windsor and Cornish, New Hampshire, site of the 19th-century summer home of sculptor Augustus Saint-Gaudens. Now a national historic site, the estate evokes the era (1885–1935) in which prominent artists, with the help of pioneering landscape architects, transformed many of the Valley's oldest farms into summer homes. They commuted from New York on the train line that still stops in Windsor and Bellows Falls en route from Manhattan to Montreal. Bellows Falls is also departure point for an excursion train, running along the Black River to Chester.

Today I-91, with exits for Bellows Falls, Springfield, Ascutney, and Windsor, is the quick way up and down this "Precision Valley." It's a stretch of river well worth savoring as slowly as possible, preferably from a kayak or canoe in the center of the region's original highway.

GUIDANCE Great Falls Regional Chamber of Commerce (802-463-4280; gfrcc.org), housed in the handsome **Waypoint Visitors Center** (restrooms) on Depot St. (near the Amtrak station), is open daily 10–4. It serves Walpole (New Hampshire), Bellows Falls, and the surrounding area.

The **Springfield Area Chamber Commerce** (802-885-2779; springfieldvt.com), 56 Main St., answers phone queries year-round (weekdays 8–5) and maintains the 18th-century Eureka Schoolhouse (Rt. 11, near I-91) as a seasonal information booth.

In Grafton the **Daniels House Gift Shop/Café** (802-843-2255; windham -foundation.org), behind the Old Tavern, is open daily, year-round except Mar. and Apr., and doubles as a town information center with public restrooms. Pick up a walking tour brochure.

The **Windsor–Mount Ascutney Area Chamber of Commerce** (802-674-5910; windsorvt.com) is open varying hours. A Waypoint Center has been completed beside the railroad station and will hopefully open soon with staffing. Also check tourwindsorvermont.com (802-484-7283).

The **Southern Vermont Regional Market Organization** (southernvermont .com) also covers much of this area.

GETTING THERE *By bus:* **Greyhound** (800-552-8737; greyhound.com) buses from points in Connecticut and Massachusetts stop in Bellows Falls at the rail station.

By train: **Amtrak** (800-USA-RAIL; amtrak.com). The Vermonter stops at Bellows Falls, Claremont (New Hampshire), and Windsor en route from New York City and Washington to Essex Junction and St. Albans (with connecting bus service to Montreal).

MEDICAL EMERGENCY Call **911**.

☀ Villages and Towns

Bellows Falls (a village, population: 3,165 within the town of Rockingham, total population: 5,309). Viewed from above the dam here, the river resembles a glassy, narrow lake. The view from below the village, however, is very different. Instead of thundering falls, what you usually see is a power station between two narrow water channels and several bridges. The Bellows Falls Canal Co. was the first in the country to obtain a charter, and it was an amazing feat easing flatboats through a series of locks, substantially expanding navigation up the Connecticut. The creation of the canal also formed the island separating the village from the Connecticut River, which for much of the year is now reduced to a modest cascade, dropping through the 0.5-mile gorge beneath the dam. It's on the island that the 1920s railroad station stands, serving **Amtrak** and the **Green Mountain Flyer**.

Christina Tree

A MURAL IN DOWNTOWN BELLOWS FALLS

In 1869 William Russell developed the novel idea of making paper from wood pulp, using logs floated down from both sides of the river. He went on to found International Paper. The canal was put to work powering mills, and it still powers turbines generating electricity. Despite major fires, much of the village architecture dates from the 1890s, the period depicted in a building-sized mural just south of the square. Rockingham Town Hall, with its Florentine-style tower, includes a recently restored, town-owned 500-seat **Opera House** used for frequent live performances as well as films. The surrounding square is lined with a lively mix of shops and restaurants.

Little more than a decade ago this wasn't the case. The paper and machine mills were long gone, and storefronts stood empty. When a low-level nuclear dump and a prison were proposed as economic boosters, a cadre of longtime residents and newcomers joined forces to restore the long-silent town hall clock. Then painter Robert McBride hit on what seemed an unlikely way to jump-start the economy: art.

McBride founded the Rockingham Arts and Museum Project (RAMP) and secured grants to transform the **Exner Block**, just off the village square, into housing, studios, and shops for artists. It also funded public art and generally served as a catalyst for what has come to be known as "Creative Economy." **The Great River Arts Institute**, founded across the river in Walpole, has since moved to Bellows Falls and there are open studios and galleries, music and theater, good places to eat, a lively independent bookstore, and ambitious developments in the offing.

Bellows Falls is also known as the home of Hetty Green (1835–1916), who parlayed a substantial inheritance into a $100 million fortune; she was called the Witch of Wall Street, to which she traveled by day coach, looking like a bag lady in threadbare bombazine. The **Bellows Falls Historical Society** is housed in the vintage-1831 Adams Grist Mill; it's open June–Oct., Sat. and Sun. 1–4. The **Rockingham Free Library** (802-463-4270), 65 Westminster St. (open Mon.–Wed. 11–7, Thu.–Fri. 11–5:30, Sat. 11–2) has archival photos and genealogical archives. At this writing a history museum that includes Hetty Green memorabilia is closed for renovation.

Geologists tell us that 400 to 600 million years ago two continents collided and separated at this site, one of the narrowest points with one of the greatest single drops in the entire length of the Connecticut River. This has long been a sacred place for Native Americans, as evidenced by petroglyphs visible from the Vilas Bridge: a series of round heads, said to date in age anywhere from 300 to 2,000 years. (Unfortunately they have been eroded by logging and railroad blasting, and years ago were painted bright yellow to make them easier to see.)

Saxtons River, like Bellows Falls, is a village in the town of Rockingham. Said to be named for a surveyor who fell into the river and drowned, it's best known as the home of the Vermont Academy (founded in 1876, a private prep school since 1932). This village of 541 souls is also a good place to stay, eat, and shop. The **Saxtons River Historical Museum** (802-869-2566; open summer Sundays 2–4:30) is housed in a former Congregational church built in 1836 at the western end of the village. Its collection includes art, tinware, toys, Civil War memorabilia, and a furnished Victorian parlor and kitchen.

Grafton (population: circa 650; graftonvermont.org). Prior to the Civil War, Grafton boasted more than 1,480 residents and 10,000 sheep. Wool was turned into 75,000 yards of Grafton cloth annually; soapstone from 13 local quarries left town in the shape of sinks, stoves, inkwells, and foot warmers. But then one in three of Grafton's men marched off to the Civil War, and few returned. Sheep farming, too, "went west." An 1869 flood destroyed the town's six dams and its

GRAFTON POST OFFICE

Christina Tree

road. The new highway bypassed Grafton. The town's tavern, however, built in 1801, entered a golden era. Innkeeper Harlan Phelps invested his entire California gold rush fortune in adding a third floor and double porches, and his brother Francis organized a still-extant cornet band. Guests included Emerson, Thoreau, and Kipling; later both Woodrow Wilson and Teddy Roosevelt visited. However, the Tavern was sagging, and nearly all the 80-some houses in town were selling cheap with plenty of acreage in the 1960s when the Windham Foundation, funded by a resident summer family, bought much of the town and set about restoring it. The **Old Tavern** itself was renovated, cheesemaking was revived, the village wiring was buried, and **Grafton Ponds**, a cross-country ski center, was established, doubling as a mountain biking center in warm-weather months.

In the **Daniels House** behind the Old Tavern, pick up a pamphlet *Walking Tour of Grafton.* The **Nature Museum** (open weekends) and the **Grafton Village Cheese Company** are alone each worth a detour. Within its few streets, Grafton can pleasantly fill a pleasant day. The vintage-1811 Butterfield House is now the inviting **Grafton Public Library** (open daily except Sun.); the **Blacksmith Shop** (open seasonally Wed.–Sun.) is a working forge, demonstrating and selling wrought-iron work; and the **Grafton Historical Society Museum** (802-843-1010; graftonhistory.org; open daily during foliage season, weekends and holidays Memorial Day–Columbus Day 10–noon and 2–4 and whenever Eli Prouty is there) has an extensive collection of memorabilia as well as changing exhibits. There are also several quality art galleries. The Windham Foundation continues to own nearly half the buildings in the central village as well as 1,500 acres, which include walking trails, meadows to pasture its flock of sheep, vegetable gardens for the inn, and a greenhouse that, among other things, furnishes some 250 wreaths and 2,000 yards of evergreen roping to decorate the town for Christmas. The largest foundation chartered in Vermont, it funds a variety of philanthropic programs across the state and a series of conferences based at the inn. The town's cornet band, founded in 1867, performs on the village green in good weather and in the White Church if it's raining.

Springfield (population: 3,938; springfieldvt.com). Sited near the confluence of the Connecticut and Black rivers, Springfield boomed with Vermont's tool industry in the 19th and first half of the 20th centuries—and has suffered as that industry has atrophied. Beyond the defunct factories and the powerful falls, the town's compact downtown offers several places to eat and shop. Gracious 19th-century mansions in residential neighborhoods terraced above the historic district include the **Springfield Historical Society** and **Miller Art Center** at 9 Elm St. (802-885-2415; millerartcenter.org). It's open May–Oct., Wed.–Sat., with collections of pewter, Bennington Pottery, toys and dolls, primitive paintings, and costumes as well as changing art exhibits. Straight uphill from the village square, **Hartness House**, the town's elegant inn, is well known to astronomers. An inventor, James Hartness patented 120 machines. An aviator, he held one of the first 100 pilot's licenses in the United States and built Vermont's first airport. President of Jones Lamson, the town's leading tool company, and a Vermont governor (1920–1922), Hartness was also an astronomer who installed one of the first tracking telescopes in the country (tours by reservation). It was designed by fellow Springfield native Russell W. Porter and sits at the end of an underground corridor connected to the mansion. Porter also organized the country's first group of amateur telescope makers, and his **Stellafane Observatory** on Breezy Hill is home base for an annual convention during the week of the July/August new moon. It routinely attracts 3,000 amateur astronomers (stellafane.com). See *Biking* for the Toonerville Trail along the Black River. The 18th-century Eureka School House on Rt. 11 exhibits vintage books and school materials, and serves as a seasonal information center.

Weathersfield Center (weathersfield.org). On a scenic old north–south road between Springfield and Rt. 131 stands this gem of a hamlet with its brick 1821 Meeting House and Civil War memorial, a particularly sobering reminder of how many young Vermonters served and died (12 boys from just this small village) in that war. The **Weathersfield Historical Society** (802-263-5230; housed in the Reverend Dan Foster House, 2656 Weathersfield Center Rd. (open by appointment), displays Civil War memorabilia, archival photos, an old forge, and the last wildcat killed in Weathersfield (1867). It was Weathersfield native William Jarvis who transformed the economy of Vermont—and the rest of northern New England—by smuggling 4,000 sheep out of Spain during his term as U.S. consul in Lisbon. That was in 1810. By 1840 there were upward of two million sheep in Vermont.

Windsor (population: 3,759; windsorvt.com). In *Roadside History of Vermont*, Peter Jennison notes that while it is known as the "Birthplace of Vermont," Windsor can also claim to be the midwife of the state's machine tool industry. Windsor resident Lemuel Hedge devised a machine for ruling paper in 1815 and dividing scales in 1827. Asahel Hubbard produced a revolving pump in 1828, and Niconar Kendall designed an "under hammer" rifle, the first use of interchangeable parts, in the 1830s in the picturesque old mill that's now the **American Precision Museum**. Windsor's mid-19th-century prosperity is reflected in the handsome lines of the columned Windsor House, once considered the best public house between Boston and Montreal. The Italianate building across the street was designed in 1850 by Ammi Young as a post office (the oldest federal post office in continuous use in the United States) with an upstairs courthouse that served as Woodrow Wilson's summer White House from 1913 to 1915; the president spent his summers in Cornish, just across the **Windsor–Cornish Covered Bridge**. Cornish was at the time an artists' and writers' colony that had evolved around sculptor Augustus Saint-Gaudens. The colony nurtured artist Maxfield Parrish; his painting *Templed Hills* hangs in the Vermont National Bank branch that is next to Windsor House (Parrish left it in perpetua to the bank's tellers for "keeping my account balanced"). It depicts a mountain that resembles Mount Ascutney, towering above water that resembles Lake Runnemede. The lake is now the town-owned conservation area **Paradise Park**. The **Cornish Colony Museum** (802-674-6008; cornishmuseum.com), housed in the old firehouse at 147 Main St. (open Memorial Day–Oct., daily except Mon; Fri.–Sun. year-round) showcases prints and original work by Maxfield Parrish and other members of the art colony that flourished in this area 1885–1935 (admission: $6 adults, $4 children) around sculptor Augustus Saint-Gaudens. Across Main St. stands the 1798 Old South Congregational Church designed by Asher Benjamin. Also worth noting: the contemporary St. Francis of Assisi Roman Catholic Church and its panels depicting the *Seven Sacraments*, donated by noted American painter George Tooker. On the common (off Main St.), St. Paul's, built in 1832, is Vermont's oldest Episcopal church. Townsend Cottage, across the square, is a striking example of 1840s Carpenter Gothic style. North of town a riverside, visitor-geared industrial park features the **Simon Pearce Glass** factory and **Harpoon Brewery**. Note the neighboring Path of Life Garden.

Across the river

Walpole, New Hampshire (population: 3,697). Along the length of the Connecticut River, few communities are more closely historically and physically linked (by two bridges), yet more different, than Walpole and Bellows Falls. Walpole's village is a white wooden New England classic, set high above Rt. 12, graced by fine old churches and dozens of mansions, some dating from the late 18th century, more from the early and mid–19th century, when it was a popular summer haven with several large inns. Louisa May Alcott summered here; Emily Dickinson visited. In the 20th century James Michener came here to research the opening chapter of *Hawaii*—the one about the New England–born missionaries and their families. Current creative residents include filmmaker Ken Burns and chocolate maker Lawrence Burdick. Together they have transformed the Post Office Block in the middle of town into destination dining and shopping. **Burdick Chocolate Shop and Café** draws day-trippers from Boston. The **Walpole Historical Society** (603-756-3308, open May–Sept., Wed. and Sat. 2–4) displays a significant collection of paintings, photographs, furniture, and other local memorabilia. It's housed on three floors of the tower-topped Academy Building in the middle of the village and includes a large research library. Walpole's big hotels have vanished, but a vintage golf course remain. The town offers some of the area's best lodging as well as dining.

Charlestown, New Hampshire (population: 4,929), was a stockaded outpost during the French and Indian Wars. Its Main Street was laid out in 1763, 200 feet wide and a mile long, with more than five dozen structures that now make up a National Historic District; 10 buildings predate 1800. Note the 1840s Congregational church; the former Charlestown Inn (1817), now a commercial building; the vintage-1800 Stephen Hassam House, built by the great-grandfather of impressionist painter Childe Hassam; and the Foundation for Biblical Research, housed in a 1770s mansion. *Historic Charlestown Walkabout*, a nominally priced guide, is available in most town stores. Also see the **Fort at No. 4** under *To See.*

Claremont, New Hampshire (population: 13,344). Massive textile mills and machine shops line the Sugar River as it drops 300 feet from the city's compact core around Tremont Square. At this writing the mills are being rehabbed. Tremont Square retains some magnificent 1890s buildings, notably the massive Italian Renaissance Revival–style city hall with its magnificent and well-used second-floor Opera House, and the Moody Building, built originally as a hotel in 1892. Adjoining Pleasant Street is now lined with antiques shops. The mammoth brick Monadnock Mills on Water Street (off Broad and Main) on the Sugar River are among the best-preserved small 19th-century urban mills in New Hampshire; note the 1840s gambrel-roofed brick Sunapee Mill across the river and the small brick overseers' cottages (also 1840s) on Crescent Street. The railroad was an essential contributor to Claremont's industrial and cultural heyday. It remains an Amtrak stop. The **Claremont Historical Society** (603-543-1400), 26 Mulberry St., is open seasonally. A walking tour is available from the chamber of commerce. West Claremont (3 miles west on Rt. 103) is a vanished village graced by New Hampshire's oldest Episcopal and Catholic churches. It seems that the Catholic priest who founded St. Mary's parish in 1824 was the son of the Episcopal rector who built St. John's across the street. Both buildings are interesting architecturally. The only sign of the congregations that both men taught and served is the West Part Burying Ground adjoining the churches. Note the waypoint visitors center on Rt. 11/10. The **Greater Claremont Chamber of Commerce** (603-543-1296) maintains a walk-in office in the Moody Building, 24 Opera House Square.

✳ To See

Listed from south to north.

⚓ **Fort at No. 4** (603-826-5700; fortat4.com), Rt. 11, 1 mile north of Charlestown Village. Open June–late Oct., Wed.–Sun. 10–4:30; gift shop 10–5. $8 adults, $6 seniors, $5 children. This living history museum, set in 20 acres on the Connecticut River, conjures an otherwise almost forgotten chapter in New England history. The stockaded village exactly replicates the way the settlement looked in the 1740s. It served first as a trading post in which Natives and newcomers lived together peaceably until the outbreak of the French and Indian Wars. A full 50 miles north of any other town on the Connecticut River, the original fort fell once but then withstood repeated attacks. The complex includes the Great Hall, cow barns, and furnished living quarters; there is also an audiovisual program, and costumed interpreters prepare meals, perform chores, and staff a blacksmith forge. Inquire about frequent battle reenactments and special programs for children throughout summer. A small museum displays authentic local Native American artifacts, and the gift store carries historical books for all ages. Check the Web site for frequent reenactments and other events.

THE AMERICAN PRECISION MUSEUM IN WINDSOR

Kim Grant

The American Precision Museum (802-674-5781; americanprecision.org), 196 S. Main St., Windsor. Open Memorial Day–Oct., 10–5 daily; $6 admission. The 1846 Robbins & Lawrence Armory, a National Historic Landmark, holds the largest collection of historically significant machine tools in the nation. The American Society of Mechanical Engineers has designated the museum an International Heritage Site and Collection. At the 1851 Great Exposition in London's Crystal Palace, the firm demonstrated machine tools and rifles made with interchangeable parts. The British army ordered 25,000 rifles and 141 metal-working machines on the spot and coined the term *the American System* for this revolutionary approach to gun making. Excellent special exhibits feature machine tools from the collection, tracing their impact on today's world.

View from Mount Ascutney in Mount Ascutney State Park, Windsor. Open late May–mid-Oct.; day-use fee. A 3.8-mile summit road from Rt. 44A (off Rt. 5) between Ascutney and Weathersfield winds steeply up through mixed hardwoods to a parking lot in the saddle between the mountain's south peak and summit. A 0.8-mile foot trail takes you the additional 344 vertical feet to the summit. It's well worth the effort for an overview of the Valley. A former fire tower has been shortened and transformed into an observation platform. Local history traces the road to a trail cleared in 1825 for the Marquis de Lafayette's visit—but the marquis was a day behind schedule and came no closer than a coffee shop on Main Street. The present road was built in the '30s by the CCC.

Old Constitution House (802-674-6628; historicvermont.org), N. Main St., Windsor. Open mid-May–mid-Oct., weekends 11–5. Nominal admission. This is Elijah West's tavern (but not in its original location), where delegates gathered on July 2, 1777, to adopt Vermont's constitution, America's first to prohibit slavery,

Rockingham Meeting House. Vermont's oldest unchanged public building is off Rt. 103 between Chester and Bellows Falls, and open Memorial Day–Columbus Day, 10–4. Built as a combination church and town hall in 1787, this Federal-style structure stands quietly above its graveyard. It's striking inside and out. Inside, "pigpen"-style pews each accommodate 10 to 15 people, some with their backs to the minister. The old burying ground is filled with thin old markers bearing readable epitaphs. An annual pilgrimage is held the first Sunday in August, with a 3 PM historical program.

ROCKINGHAM MEETING HOUSE

Kim Grant

establish universal voting rights for all males, and authorize a public school system. Excellent first-floor displays trace the history of the formation of the Republic of Vermont; upstairs is the town's collection of antiques, prints, documents, tools and cooking utensils, tableware, toys, and early fabrics. Special exhibits vary each year. A path out the back door leads to Lake Runnemede.

The Saint-Gaudens National Historic Site (603-675-2175; nps.gov/saga), Rt. 12A, Cornish, New Hampshire. Grounds open daily, dawn–dusk. Buildings open 9–4:30 daily late May–Oct. $5 adults (good for a week); free under age 16. This glorious property with a view of Mount Ascutney includes the sculptor's summer home and studio, sculpture court, and formal gardens, which he developed and occupied between 1885 and his death in 1907. A visitor center features a 28-minute film about the artist and his work. Augustus Saint-Gaudens (1848–1907) is remembered primarily for public pieces: the Shaw memorial on Boston Common, the statue of Admiral Farragut in New York's Madison Square, the equestrian statue of General William T. Sherman at the Fifth Avenue entrance to Central Park, and the *Standing Lincoln* in Chicago's Lincoln Park. He was also the first sculptor to design an American coin (the $10 and $20 gold pieces of 1907). His home, Aspet, is furnished much as it was when he lived there. Augustus Saint-Gaudens loved the Ravine Trail, a 0.25-mile cart path to Blow-Me-Up Brook, now marked for visitors, and other walks laid out through the woodlands and wetlands of the Blow-Me-Down Natural Area. Saint-Gaudens was the center of the "Cornish Colony," a group of poets, artists, landscape artists, actors, architects, and writers who included Ethel Barrymore, Charles Dana Gibson, Finley Peter Dunne, and Maxfield Parrish; President Woodrow Wilson's wife was drawn into this circle, and the president summered at a nearby home from 1913 to 1915. *Note:* Bring a picnic lunch for Sunday-afternoon chamber music concerts, at 2 PM in July and August.

✍ **The Nature Museum** (802-843-2111; nature-museum.org), 186 Townshend Rd., Grafton. Open weekends year-round 10–4. $4 adults, $2 children. Housed in the town grange, the exhibits here are extensive and fascinating, focusing on local flora and fauna. Stuffed animals include such elusive forest residents as a catamount, a fox, a bobcat, and a fisher. Children can dig for fossils and explore a simulated underground tunnel; also family programs during vacation periods. Nature trails lead from here lead through meadow and woods to the green up to Rocky Cliff Junction.

COVERED BRIDGES At 460 feet the **Cornish–Windsor covered bridge**, linking Rt. 5, Windsor, and Rt. 12A, Cornish, is one of the country's longest covered bridges and is certainly the most photographed in New England. A lattice truss design, built in 1866, it was rebuilt in 1989. There are three more covered bridges in Cornish, all dating from the early 1880s: Two span Mill Brook—one in Cornish City and the other in Cornish Mills between Rts. 12A and 120—and the third spans Blow-Me-Down Brook (off Rt. 12A). For the best view, turn left on Rt. 12A and look of the marked boat launch area a short way upstream.

Also look for two covered bridges in **Bartonsville** (one is 1.5 miles north of Rt. 103; the other, east off Rt. 103) north of Rockingham (not far from the Vermont Country Store); one in **Grafton village**; and one in **Saxtons River** off Rt. 121, noteworthy for its "flying buttresses" (replaced in 1982).

BICYCLING **Grafton Ponds** (802-843-2400; graftonponds.com) in Grafton rents mountain bikes for use on dirt roads radiating from the village and on its cross-country trails.

Orange Lake Ascutney Resort (802-484-3511) in Brownsville rents mountain bikes and offers 32 km of trails.

Paradise Sports (802-674-6742; paradisesportsshop.com), 20 State St., Windsor. Bikes sold and fixed; some for rent, also a source of cross-country skis and snow-shoes.

In Springfield the **Toonerville Trail**, a 10-foot-wide, paved recreation path good for bicycling and walking, follows the Black River along an old trolley line from the trailhead on Rt. 11 (behind the Robert Jones Industrial Center) 3 miles to another parking area on Rt. 5, just north of the Cheshire Bridge across the Connecticut.

Road biking is popular in this area thanks to the many interlinking back roads and river roads.

BIRDING Outstanding areas include town-owned **Lake Runnemede** in Windsor, **North Springfield Lake** (thanks to the local Audubon chapter there are trails and an observatory at the northern end of the lake), **Mount Ascutney** (hawks in Sept.), and **Herricks Cove** in Rockingham.

BOATING With its placid water and lovely scenery, the Connecticut River through much of the Lower Valley is ideal for easygoing canoeists.

🖎 **North Star Livery** (603-542-6929; kayak-canoe.com), Rt. 12A in Cornish, New Hampshire, will shuttle patrons to put-ins either 3 or 12 miles above the Cornish–Windsor covered bridge. North Star itself is New England's most pictur-esque canoe livery: The check-in desk is in the barn of a working farm, redolent of bales of hay; the canoes and kayaks are stacked behind the farmhouse. Full-day, half-day, and multiday trips are offered. With over 90 boats, including 30 kayaks, this is the largest, oldest, and best-loved commercial rental service on the Con-necticut River. Tubes too.

Still River Outfitters (802-674-6767; stillriveroutfitters.com), 36 Park Rd. (next to Harpoon Brewery), Windsor. Guided canoe and kayak trips, shuttle service, raft-ing and novice whitewater and recre-ational kayak clinics are offered.

Boat access to the Connecticut River

Herricks Cove. Picnic area, boat landing, and bird sanctuary, a good picnic spot off Rt. 5 near I-91, Exit 6, in Rockingham, above Bellows Falls.

Hoyt's Landing. Off Rt. 11 and I-91, Exit 7, in Springfield, a recently upgraded put-in that's also good for fishing and picnicking.

MOUNTAIN BIKING AT ASCUTNEY MOUN-TAIN RESORT

Ascutney Mountain Resort

Ashley Ferry Boat Landing. Off River Rd. (parallel to Rt. 11/12), about 2 miles south of Claremont, New Hampshire. A boat landing and park at a bend in the river.

Also see "Upper Valley River Towns."

Other boat access

North Springfield Lake and **Stoughton Recreation Area**, Reservoir Rd. between Springfield and Weathersfield, are maintained by the U.S. Army Corps of Engineers and offer boat launches.

CAMPING See Wilgus and Mount Ascutney State Parks under *Green Space*. The Vermont State Parks reservation line operates weekdays: 888-409-7549.

CAR RACING Claremont Speedway (603-543-3160; twinstatespeedway.net), Thrasher Rd., 4 miles east of I-91, Claremont, New Hampshire. May–Sept.

FISHING NL Wilson Outfitters (888-FLY-CAST; nlwilson.com), 7 State St., Windsor. Guided fly-fishing lessons, wading and float trips.

GOLF Bellows Falls Country Club (802-463-9809), Rt. 103, Rockingham. Scenic nine-hole course; clubhouse with bar and lunchroom.

Tater Hill Golf (802-875-2517), 6802 Popple Dungeon Rd., North Windham. Now owned by Okemo, newly renovated, 18 holes with a pro shop.

Crown Point Country Club (802-885-1010), Weathersfield Center Rd., Springfield. A gem of an 18-hole course with pro shop, golf lessons, driving range, restaurant, and banquet facilities.

Hooper Golf Club (603-756-4020) Prospect Hill, Walpole. This vintage course offers nine holes and a clubhouse serving lunch.

HANG GLIDING Mount Ascutney State Park, Rt. 44A off Rt. 5, Windsor. Brownsville Rock, less than a mile by trail northwest of the Mount Ascutney summit, is a popular launch site. Note that a paved summit road accesses the trail.

Morningside Recreation Area (603-542-4416; flymorningside.com), Rt. 12 in Claremont, New Hampshire, is the site of events on weekends. Lessons in hang gliding and paragliding are offered along with a repair service, sales, swimming, and hiking.

HIKING Mount Ascutney offers the area's most dramatic hiking. Of the four trails to the summit, we recommend the 2.9-mile ascent from Weathersfield with an 84-foot waterfall about halfway (the trailhead is on Cascade Falls Rd., 3.5 miles north off Rt. 131). The 3.2-mile Brownsville Trail begins on Rt. 44 between Windsor and Brownsville; the 2.7-mile Windsor Trail starts on Rt. 44A in Windsor. The 4.4-mile Futures Trail begins in Windsor State Park and links up with the Windsor Trail.

RAILROAD EXCURSIONS *✎* **Trains Around Vermont** (802-463-3069; 800-707-3530; rails-vt.com), 54 Depot St., Bellows Falls. Round-trips on the Green Mountain Flyer are available Tue.–Sun. in summer; daily during foliage season.

This 13-mile (one-way) route follows the Connecticut River past covered bridges, then heads up the Williams River and through wooded rock cuts, which include the spectacular Brockway Mills gorge. Inquire about special runs.

SWIMMING ✐ **Grafton Swimming Pond**, Rt. 121, 1 mile west of the village, is an oasis for children. **Stoughton Pond Recreation Area** (802-886-2775), Stoughton Pond Rd. off Rt. 106 in Weathersfield, offers pond swimming, and in the village of Perkinsville the **Black River** cascades into delicious pools at an old power site. **Kennedy Pond** (Rt. 44 west) in Windsor has a small beach, great for kids. Inquire locally about numerous other swimming holes in the Black and Williams rivers and about Twenty-Foot Hole (a series of cataracts and pools in a wooded gorge) in Reading.

✳ Winter Sports

CROSS-COUNTRY SKIING AND SNOWSHOEING **Grafton Ponds Outdoor Center** (802-843-2400; graftonponds.com), Townshend Rd., Grafton. Thirty km of trails groomed both for skating and classic strides, meandering off from a log cabin warming hut, over meadows, and into the woods on Bear Hill. Snowmaking on 5 km, rentals, and instruction, plus ice skating, snow tubing, and trails specifically for snowshoeing.

Orange Lake Ascutney Resort (802-484-7711; 800-243-0011), Rt. 44, Brownsville. A touring center with instruction, rentals, 30 km of trails (25 km machine-tracked, 15 km for skaters), with separate loops for snowshoers.

DOWNHILL SKIING AND SNOWBOARDING **Ascutney Mountain Resort** (802-484-7711; 800-243-0011; ascutney.com), Rt. 44, Brownsville (I-91, Exit 8 or 9). Current owners Steve and Susan Plausteiner have increased snowmaking and added the North Peak Area, substantially increasing expert trails, served by a mile-long quad chair. Take Gateway to Cloudspin for a nearly 3-mile-long run (intermediate to beginner). Still, the mountain is best known for its black diamond and double diamonds on the Sunrise side of the ski area. In 2008 the self-contained, family lodging and sports complex at the base of the mountain was sold; see below.

Trails: 57.

Lifts: 6.

Vertical drop: 1,800 feet.

Snowmaking: 95 percent.

For children: Nursery/child care from 6 weeks; Young Olympians program for 1- to 12-year-olds.

Features: 9 double-diamond advanced trails, expert tree skiing, 2 terrain parks, a tubing slope, a separate lift-served Learning Park, and a strong children's program.

Rates: $62 adults weekend, $45 seniors/juniors; $60/$44 midweek. Half-day tickets and many special packages are offered.

✳ Green Space

✐ **Wilgus State Park** (802-674-5422; 802-773-2657), 1.5 miles south of I-91, Exit 8, Rt. 5, Windsor. Open Memorial Day–Columbus Day. This small, quiet campground

Christina Tree

THE PATH OF LIFE GARDEN

on the Connecticut River is ideal for canoeists—the 17 tent sites, six lean-tos, and two cabins are on the riverbank. Car shuttle service available (see *Boating*); playground, picnic tables, hiking trails, also canoe, kayak, and rowboat rentals.

Ascutney State Park (802-674-2060). Open mid-May–mid-Oct., Windsor. Rising out of the Valley to an elevation of 3,144 feet, Mount Ascutney represents some 3,000 acres of woodland. The 3.8-mile paved Summit Road begins on Rt. 44A, off Rt. 5, between Ascutney and Windsor (see View from Mount Ascutney, above). Granite was quarried here as early as 1808. A total of 49 tent sites, trailer sites, and lean-tos can be reserved. The ski slopes and self-contained Ascutney Mountain Resort (not on state land) are accessed from Rt. 44 in Brownsville. Also see *Hiking*.

Paradise Park. Lake Runnemede in the heart of Windsor is circled by a 5.5-mile path set in this 177-acre preserve. It's best accessed from the Old Constitution House (see *To See*).

Path of Life Garden (802-674-6789; pathoflifegarden.com), 36 Park Way, Windsor. Open year-round. $5 adult, $2 ages 4–12. Walk from the visitor-geared industrial park that's home to Simon Pearce and Harpoon Brewery—through a tunnel beneath the railroad tracks—and you are in a 14-acre meadow like no other. The path leads you through 18 distinct "rooms"—some resembling sculpture gardens but including a maze lined with 800 hemlock trees and a 90-foot rock labyrinth, huge dream catchers, a driftwood band, a granite Buddha, and more. A natural amphitheater is used for summer bonfires and drumming. A side path leads to the Connectiut River. For $75 you can spend the night in one of the two tepees. The creation of Norwich therapist Terry McDonnell, the garden is all about the circle of life and making life's decisions.

✳ Lodging

RESORT ✎ Orange Lake Ascutney Resort (802-484-7711; 888-657-3529; orangelake.com), Rt. 44, Brownsville 05037. In 2008 the contemporary, 215-unit wooden condo hotel and flanking condominiums at the base of Mount Ascutney were acquired by Orlando-based Orange Lake Resorts. Accommodations range from standard hotel rooms to three-bedroom units with kitchen, fireplace, and deck, all nicely furnished with reproduction antiques. In winter there are both alpine and cross-country trails; facilities include indoor and outdoor pools and a spa with massage services. An extensive summer adventure program for adults (mountain biking, road biking, and kayaking/canoeing) as well as kids. Call the central reservations center for pricing.

INNS *Listed from south to north.*

⊙ ⅙ ⁹⫯⁹ **The Old Tavern** (802-843-2231; 800-843-1801; oldtavern.com), 92 Main St., Grafton 05146, where Rts. 35 and 121 intersect. The brick core of this splendid building dates from 1801, but the double-porched facade is mid–19th century. The early-19th-century-style interior is country elegant but unstuffy and comfortable (a discreet elevator accesses the second and third floors). In recent years more than $1 million has been invested in reducing the number of rooms from 66 to 45, 11 (including 3 suites) in the Tavern itself, the remainder divided between the Windham and Homestead cottages. Four rental houses with full kitchens and common space, some with working fireplace, sleep between 6 and 10 people apiece. In total the inn can accommodate 90. All guest rooms have private bath, many have air-conditioning, and all are individually decorated with antiques and country papers and fabrics. Candlelit dining is in the formal dining room (see *Dining Out*); there's a sunny breakfast room and an informal bar with a fireplace—and occasional dining and live music—in the Phelps Barn, attached to the inn. And you'll find a Ping-Pong table and game room in a neighboring house. In summer heated platform tennis courts, cross-country biking trails, and a sand-bottomed swimming pond are all nearby; in winter there's cross-country skiing, tubing, and ice skating at Grafton Ponds. Youngsters ages 8 and older are welcome in all rooms, younger in some cottages. Pets are not permitted, but you can bring your horse (there's a stable). $160–245 for rooms, $215–360 for suites. $45 for a third person, depending on the room, day (weekends are more expensive than weekdays), and season. Inquire about houses ($750–950). A full country breakfast and afternoon tea are included.

⁹⫯⁹ **Inn at Saxtons River** (802-869-2110; innsaxtonsriver.com), 27 Main St., Saxtons River 05154. This vintage-1903 inn with a distinctive square, five-story tower has an attractive streetside pub and a large dining room (see *Dining Out*). Geared to Saxton's River Academy parents, there are 16 pleasant rooms (all with private bath). $109–150 per couple includes continental breakfast. Inquire about packages.

⊙ **Hartness House** (802-885-2115; 800-732-4789; hartnesshouse.com), 30 Orchard St., Springfield 05156. In 1904 James Hartness (see Springfield under *Villages and Towns*) built himself a stone-and-shingle mansion set above town on a parklike bluff; since 1939 it's been an inn. There are 45 guest rooms, 11 in the main house, the remainder in connecting tasteful motel-like annexes. All rooms have private bath, phone, and color TV/DVD player. There's a formal feel to the large lobby, with its traditional check-in desk, and to the pub and dining room (see *Dining Out*). Facilities include a swimming pool and nature trails. $130–240 per couple in the main house includes breakfast, $99–129 in the annexes doesn't. Inquire about numerous packages.

ⓧ ⁊ **The Inn at Weathersfield** (802-263-9217; weathersfieldinn.com), 1342 Rt. 106, Weathersfield 05151. Set way back from quiet Rt. 106, just south of the village of Perkinsville, this handsome inn dates in part from 1792, but columns give it an antebellum facade. This is one of Vermont's most distinctive and romantic inns, as well as one of its best places for fine dining. Jane and David Sandelman seem to be doing everything right. Each of the nine guest rooms and three suites is different. All have phone and private bath (ranging from powerful shower to Jacuzzi) and amenities such as slippers and plush robes; seven have a fireplace (some gas, some wood burning). Some have TV and DVD. Wireless Internet access throughout. The setting is 21 wooded acres with hiking/snowshoeing trails and an amphitheater used as a wedding venue. Hiking and ski trails

on Mount Ascutney, a web of back roads good for biking, and a glorious swimming hole are all handy. Guests enjoy their own common room in the opposite side of the inn from the long, tiered dining room and pub. See *Dining Out* for more about the inn's legendary dining, thanks to executive chef Jason Tostrup. $179–290 in high seasons, $149–259 in low, includes a full breakfast and afternoon refreshments. Inquire about special packages.

ⓧ ✧ **Juniper Hill Inn** (802-674-5273; 800-359-2541; juniperhillinn .com), off Rt. 5 on Juniper Hill Rd., Windsor 05089. Set high on a hill above its impressive drive, with a magnificent view of Mount Ascutney and the Connecticut River Valley, this splendid 28-room Colonial Revival mansion, built by Maxwell Evarts in 1901, combines Edwardian grandeur with the informal hospitality of innkeepers Robert Dean and Ari Nikki. Relax by the hearth in the huge main hall, in a second living room (with TV), or in the library with its leather armchairs and unusual hearth. One of Vermont's most romantic getaways, the inn offers no fewer than 11 guest rooms with fireplace (all but 4 are wood burning). All 16 guest rooms have private bath and are furnished with flair and genuinely interesting antiques. Guests gather for meals in the dining room, with floor-to-ceiling fireplace. Reserve for candlelit dinners. We could easily spend a day by the pool or walking around Lake Runnemede, a hidden conservation area within walking distance that's great for birding. Rates $135–265 per room, full breakfast included; add $30 for an additional person. Inquire about the **Vermont Culinary Arts Center**, a program of cooking classes taught by outstanding area chefs, geared to improving home cooking skills.

JUNIPER HILL INN IN WINDSOR

Christina Tree

BED & BREAKFASTS
Listed from south to north.

In Grafton 05146

☙ **The Inn at Woodchuck Hill Farm** (802-843-2398; woodchuckhill .com), Woodchuck Hill Rd. Open most of the year, but the main house is open only seasonally. It's a 1780s farmhouse, high on a hill, off a back road. The porch, well stocked with comfortable wicker, has a peaceful, top-of-the-world feel, and there are views from the living room and dining room, too. Operated as an inn by the Gabriel family for more than 30 years, it offers five rooms, three with private bath. By the pond, the old barn has been revamped to offer suites, one with two bedrooms, bath, kitchen, and living/dining area with fireplace; a smaller unit has sitting room, fridge, and microwave. Spruce Cottage offers privacy and seclusion. Furnished in antiques, it's fully equipped and sleeps up to seven people ($375 per day). There's a sauna in the woods next to the pond, which is good for swimming, fishing, and canoeing, and the 200 rolling acres are laced with walking trails. No smoking. $99–280 B&B.

⁽ᵀ⁾ **By the River Bed & Breakfast** (802-843-2886), 460 Rt. 121. Bill Brooks is a master cabinetmaker, and his wife, Elise, is a yoga instructor. Their (shoes-off) home is comfortably, unstuffily elegant, with choice contemporary furnishings, hung with striking art and with windows overlooking the gardens and river. There are two guest rooms with private bath. We just stopped by but would have liked to linger by the fire. $135–145 per couple includes breakfast. The entire three-bedroom, three-bath house is available for rent in winter.

In Bellows Falls/Saxtons River
Readmore Bed, Breakfast & Books (802-463-9415; readmoreinn.com), 1 Hapgood St., Bellows Falls 05101. The most elegant B&B in the area, a 19th-century mansion on the National Register with five guest rooms, each themed with appropriate books (for sale), most with fireplace and whirlpool bath. $150–270.

☙ **River Mist B&B** (802-463-9023; 888-463-9023; river-mist.com), 7 Burt St., Bellows Falls 05101. On a quiet street, this 1895 "painted lady" is high Victorian inside and out, reflecting the way the town's onetime mill owners lived. Michael and Roger offer four lacy guest rooms with private bath, plenty of personal attention, and a very full breakfast—perhaps quiche and baked apples or stuffed French toast. $100–150.

🌿 **Moore's Inn** (802-869-2020; moores inn.com), P.O. Box 424, 57 Main St. (Rt. 121), Saxtons River 05154. Dave Moore is a sixth-generation Vermonter who grew up in this Victorian house with its fine woodwork and spacious veranda. It remains very much Dave and Carol's family home and a guest house (as opposed to B&B). The spacious guest rooms—six on the second floor and three on the third—are all self-contained, six with private bath, TV, fridge, coffeemaker, and breakfast cereals. The three third-floor guest rooms share a living room and can, of course, be rented as a whole. $89–125 based on a two-night stay. $10 more for just one night. Several rooms easily accommodate three people. Bicyclists are especially welcome and will find maps and plenty of advice.

∞ **Inn at Cranberry Farm** (800-854-2208; cranberryfarminn.com), 61 Williams River Rd. (off Rt. 103), Chester 05143. Despite the postal address, this appealing inn is in the town of Rockingham not far from the Rockingham Meeting House, with property that extends to the Williams River. Built as an inn in the 1990s with 11 guest rooms and 3 two-room suites (with whirlpool tub and fireplace). The airy design of the inn, with its spacious common areas, lends itself to groups and weddings (there's a pond outside the door). $145–225.

☙ **The Pond House at Shattuck Hill Farm** (802-484-0011; pondhouse inn.com), P.O. Box 234, Brownsville 05037. This 1830s Cape sits beside its barn on a steeply rising back road near Mount Ascutney, with views across its pond and fields to mountains. There are three guest rooms, sparely, tastefully furnished, each with private bath. Gretel Schuck is an avid cook; breakfast might feature orange French toast, and dinner (selective nights) might include tuna with artichoke hearts or wild mushroom risotto. Guests dine together in the square dining room with its pumpkin pine floors and original six-over-six window. Gretel is also an avid cyclist and delights in tuning guests to local back roads, also good for horseback riding. Horses and polite dogs can be accommodated. $115–135 in summer, $95–140 per couple in winter includes breakfast; dinner $50 per couple. Inquire about bargain three-night weekend packages. Beware the strict cancellation policy.

Also see **Bailey's Mills Bed & Breakfast** in Reading in the "Woodstock/Quechee" chapter.

Across the river

The Walpole Inn (603-756-3320; walpoleinn.com), RR 1, Box 762, 297 Main St., Walpole, NH 03608. Originally this distinguished colonial was home to Colonel Benjamin Bellows, commander of a strategic garrison along the Connecticut River during the French and Indian Wars. Now, in another life, it offers a restaurant that's among the best in the area (see *Dining*

Out) and eight sparely elegant guest rooms, each furnished with a pencil-post, queen-sized bed and tailored linens. Four have walk-in shower; the others feature a luxurious soaking tub with shower. You can choose among chess in the paneled parlor, tennis on the grounds, or golf at the nearby Hooper Golf Course. A full breakfast comes with an artist's view of meadows and hills, and is included in the $90–175 rate.

✐ **The Inn at Valley Farms** (603-756-2855; 877-327-2855; innatvalley farms.com), 633 Wentworth Rd., Walpole, NH 03608. Set in 105 acres bordering an apple orchard, this circa-1774 house offers exceptionally handsome, antiques-filled guest rooms along with lovely common rooms, including a formal parlor and dining room, and a sunroom overlooking a lovely perennial garden. Upstairs in the main house there is a two-bedroom suite with bath, along with two other bedrooms, each with four-poster bed, private bath, phone, and dataport. Niceties include fresh flowers, plush robes, and Burdick chocolates. Families can choose one of two cottages, each with three bedrooms, kitchen, and living area. Innkeeper Jacqueline Caserta is a serious organic farmer/gardener; she uses fresh eggs as well as her organic vegetable harvest creatively to make a breakfast that's both good and good for you. Inn rates: $175–215 per couple with full breakfast. Cottages, which sleep six, are $220 for two. A basket of homemade breads and muffins is delivered each morning to the door. Inquire about Sunnyside, a renovated, three-bedroom, three-bath farmhouse a short walk from the inn, available by the week.

Dutch Treat (603-826-5565; the dutchtreat.com), P.O. Box 1004, Charlestown, NH 03603. Open year-round. Formerly Maple Hedge, this handsome, 1820s Main Street house has been completely refurbished by Dob and Eric Lutze, natives of Holland who have also lived in Canada, England, and Austria and speak French and German. There's a Dutch theme to guest rooms with names like the Tulip Suite (our favorite) and the Delft Room, both big, sunny guest rooms in the front of the house. Smaller rooms—the Lace Maker (honoring the Dutch painter Vermeer), the twin-bedded Tasman Room (named for a Dutch explorer who discovered New Zealand and Tasmania), and the Generals Room (with a picture of a forefather who fought under both Napoleon and Wellington)—are also inviting. The sunny, square dining room is elegant. There's a big comfortable parlor, wicker on the porch, and an outdoor hot tub. Dob and Eric are delighted to help guests explore the best of the area. $109–159.

✳ Where to Eat

DINING OUT **The Inn at Weathersfield** (802-263-9217; weathersfield inn.com), 1342 Rt. 106, just south of Perkinsville. Open for dinner Wed.–Sun. in winter, Tue.–Sun. in summer. Reserve. The dining room is a former carriage house, candlelit with windows overlooking the garden and a floor-to-ceiling hearth. Historically this is one of the best restaurants in Vermont, a tradition as alive as ever with executive chef Jason Tostrup, who has come to Weathersfield via New York City, Aspen, and Napa and works directly with local farmers and producers to shape a menu that changes weekly. He continues to win top awards. On an early-December night you might begin with Valley Brook Farms autumn squash soup ($8), or a salad with Cider House herb vinai-

grette and local goat cheese ($8). Entrées include Atlantic monkfish and calamari with cannelloni beans, rice, and a caper salad; locally raised veal with herb-crusted rutabaga lasagna and rapini; and local Highlander beef hash with potato-celery root ($25–28). For dessert: a cinnamon brioche bread pudding or dark chocolate ganache ($7). The chef's tasting menu ($57 per person) features crab and basil cannelloni, Champlain Valley rabbit risotto, and duck confit, with accompanying wines. A pub menu is also offered at Lucy's Tavern. Inquire about special events such as "foraging" or a local farms dinner; also about the prize-winning wine list.

The Old Tavern (802-843-2231), Main St., Grafton, serves breakfast and dinner daily. Candlelit dinner is served in the formal old dining room amid fine portraits and Chippendale chairs—with music, if you're lucky, by assistant innkeeper Bill Toomey on the lute. Chef David Smith works to utilize local ingredients. A fall menu might begin with a salad of heirloom beets tossed with candied pecans, Vermont goat cheese, and local mesclun greens; entrée choices could include pan-seared Vermont chicken breast with wild mushrooms, and braised lamb shank served with mashed potatoes and seasoned vegetables ($22–33). Innkeeper Kevin O'Donnell takes special pride in the wine list, good value. In winter the tavern opens at 5 PM to complement the concert series in the Phelps Barn.

Inn at Saxtons River (802-869-2110), Main St., Saxtons River. Open for dinner nightly. The à la carte menu might include scallops and fresh mussels in a garlic marinara sauce served with fettuccine, or New York strip steak. Entrées $10.95–23.95. Pub fare is also offered. This is the obvious spot to dine before Main Street Arts productions.

𝒮 **Leslie's** (802-463-4929; lesliestavern .com), Rockingham, Rt. 5 just south of I-91, Exit 6. Open nightly except Tue. Reservations appreciated. John Marston opened his restaurant in a 1790s tavern back in 1986 and continues to create new and eclectic dishes, fusing many influences with experience and using as much home-grown produce as possible. Certified Black Angus beef and free-range chicken are served a variety of ways, and there's always a vegetarian plate and seafood—maybe Alaskan king crab stuffed sole, or "pescatora" (large shrimp and scallops sautéed with tomatoes and garlic over sun-dried tomato ravioli). Leave room for dessert. Entrées $18–28; bistro specials $13–19.

𝒮 **Windsor Station Pub** (802-674-2052; windsorstation.com), Depot Ave., Windsor. Open nightly for dinner. Built as a passenger train station (it remains an Amtrak stop), now decorated in natural wood plus velvet and brass. A locally sourced varied menu ranges from a BBQ pulled-pork sandwich to roast duck and short ribs. Entrées $12–23. Good luck getting a seat on half-price margarita and martini nights.

Juniper Hill Inn (802-674-5273; juniperhillinn.com), 153 Pembroke Rd., Windsor. Open for dinner Thu.–Mon. A lovely dining room with large windows, burgundy-colored walls, and a large hearth is the setting for gracious dining following cocktail specials on the bar/patio. You might begin with mission figs with Vermont blue cheese or Vermont apple ginger soup, then dine on pumpkin-stuffed ravioli or pecan-crusted New England pork chop. Entrées $17–32.

Hartness House (802-885-2115; hart nesshouse.com), 30 Orchard St.,

Springfield. Open for dinner; closed Mon. The dining room in this venerable landmark is a popular special-occasion place for local residents and generally has a good reputation. The dinner menu might include mussels in tomato saffron broth for an appetizer, and pomegranate-roasted duck as a main course. Entrées $16–36.

𝒮 **Penelope's** (802-885-9186), on the square, 30 Main St., Springfield. Closed due to fire at this writing but expected to reopen in 2009. Polished woods, stained glass, and greenery, an attractive setting for dining from a large menu.

Also see **Boccelli's** under *Eating Out*.

Worth crossing the river for

& **The Walpole Inn** (603-756-3320; walpoleinn.com), 297 Main St., Walpole, New Hampshire. Open for dinner: in summer Wed.–Sun., in winter Thu.–Sun. Reservations recommended. The menu changes weekly. The dining room, overlooking a painterly scene of rolling meadows, is simple but elegant with celery-toned paneling, exposed brick, white linen, and appealing art. The menu ranges from house pizza or Angus burger to herb-crusted rack of lamb or grilled Black Angus New York strip steak. Entrées $10–32.

& **Burdick's Bistro and Café** (603-756-2882; burdickchocolate.com), 47 Main St. (next to the post office), Walpole, New Hampshire. Open Tue.–Sat. 11:30–2:30 for lunch; 5:30–9 for dinner; Sun. brunch 10–2. Chocolatier extraordinaire Larry Burdick and his friend, filmmaker Ken Burns, have transformed the town's former IGA into a chic dining spot. With its warm yellow walls, soft lighting, and artfully placed mirrors and paintings, this is as close to a Paris brasserie as you can get in New Hampshire. You order from the same menu all day, but around 5 PM the ambience shifts. White tablecloths appear, and the café morphs into a more formal restaurant. You might lunch or dine on house sausage, Provençal beef stew, sole meunière, or oven-roasted chicken. The bread is crusty; the wine list, top-notch; the chocolate desserts, to die for. Entrées are $11–23; for two, figure $50 with wine.

EATING OUT
Listed from south to north.

Café Loco at Harlow Farm Stand (802-722-3515), Rt. 4 north of I-91, Exit 5, Westminster. Open Mon.–Sat., 7–5, Sun. 8–4., May–Dec. The farm stand is a standout, but it's easy to miss this delightful café featuring fresh-made soups, sandwiches, homemade pies, and daily specials.

Father's Restaurant (802-463-3909), Rt. 5, 1 mile south of Bellows Falls. Open Sun. 7–3, Mon. 6–3, Tue.–Thu. 6–9, Fri.–Sat. 6 AM–9 PM. An attractive family restaurant with a salad bar, kids' menu, prime rib for $11.95, wine and beer.

Boccelli's Café & Specialty Shop (802-460-1190; boccellisonthe canal.com), 46 Canal St., Bellows Falls. Open Wed.–Sat. for lunch and dinner. Some of the freshest, tastiest food in the Valley can be found in this cheery restaurant with its very open kitchen, original art, and windows by the canal. Sharon Boccelli was a successful auctioneer in Cambridge (Massachusetts) for many years before moving into this remarkable space. The adjoining space is still her auction hall (estates) but frequently doubles as an extension of the restaurant and performance (music; see *Entertainment*) space. Boccelli grew up cooking in a large extended Italian American family, and the menu includes bruschetta, antipasto, soups of the day, and plenty of pasta and artisan garlic bread. Try the "chewy gooey

sandwich" (melted Grafton cheddar on an open-faced garlic ciabatta with artisan mustard and avocado). Local produce, Italian deli meats, and cheeses are also sold. Dinner entrées are mostly under $15, but the lobster ravioli made with real lobster and served with the day's cream sauce is $18.50. Between meals this is a great spot to sit with a book or laptop and espresso.

Hraefnwood Café (802-299-7429; hraefnwoodcafe.com), 23 Canal St. Open 7 AM–8 PM most nights, until 11 Sat., 9–5 Sun. "Great coffee, evermore," is the motto of this enticing oasis. The name is Old English for "ravenwood." Eric and Kirsten Jette specialize in an artisan fair-trade coffee and carefully selected pastries, also soups and grilled paninis. Microbrews and wines, live music or poetry the third Friday of each month.

Fat Frank's (802-463-4388), 92 Rockinghm St., Bellows Falls. Open except Mon. from 11 to dinner hours. A small place with a big following, strictly sausages, skinny as well as fat franks, and "the best of the wurst," including lamb sausage, andouille sausage, and kielbasa. Self-serve toppings.

Vermont Pretzel & Cookie (802-460-2424; vermontpretzel.com), 24 Rockingham St., Bellows Falls. The pretzels are locally made. This is also a good bet for sandwiches, salads, and pastries.

Miss Bellows Falls Diner (802-463-9800), 90 Rockingham St., Bellows Falls. Open daily from 6 AM through dinner. Inside and out this Worcester Diner (#771) is still pure, unhokey 1920s.

Joy Wah (802-463-9761), Rockingham Rd. (Rt. 5), Bellows Falls. Full-service Chinese fare in a Victorian farmhouse high on a knoll overlooking the Connecticut River; all the usual dishes on its lengthy menu. Open daily for lunch and dinner. Sunday brunch is a local favorite.

The Golden Egg (802-869-2380), 37 Main St., Saxtons River. Open Tue.–Sun. 7–2:30, Wed.–Sat. 5–8:30. In addition to the breakfast and lunch basics are plenty of Mexican offerings: breakfast burritos, huevos rancheros, tacos, quesadillas, and more. Mexican night Friday.

Daniels House Café (802-843-2255), Townshend Rd., Grafton. Just behind the Old Tavern and attached to the village's information center/gift shop. Open 11–4 for lunch with soups, salads, wraps, and sandwiches.

𝒮 **56 Main Street** (802-885-6987; fiftysixmainstreet.com), 56 Main St., Springfield. Open for lunch and dinner Mon.–Sat. Cozy, casual restaurant with a varied menu that includes Mexican, Italian, and vegetarian dishes as well as standard American fare. Entrées $7.99–18.99. Full liquor license.

𝒮 **Country Creemee Restaurant**, Downers Corner (junction of Rts. 131 and 106), Amsden. Seasonal. Locals will tell you that everything tastes good here; we always get the super-long hot dog to consume at a picnic table under the trees.

Brownsville General Store (802-484-7480), Rt. 44 just west of the entrance to Ascutney Mountain Resort. A regular general store with busy gas pumps but also with a big red Aga cookstove behind the lunch counter, a clue to the quality of soups and daily specials like chicken and biscuits. Bread is fresh baked, and there's a full deli.

❝1❞ No Name Café (802-674-2888) 131 Main St. Open at 7 daily for breakfast and lunch. Worth checking the nights that are open for dinner. Comfy chairs, booths, daily soups,

from-scratch dinners $10–18; beer and wine served.

𝒮 **Windsor Diner** (802-674-5555), 135 Main St., Windsor. Open daily 6 AM–8 PM. This spiffed-up 1952 classic Worcester diner (#835) serves good, honest diner food: meat loaf, liver and onions, and macaroni and cheese, along with omelets, burger baskets, pies, and more.

Harpoon Brewery Beer Garden (1-802-674-4591, ext. 221; harpoon brewery.com), south of Exit 9, north of Windsor on Rt. 5. Open May–Aug., Sun.–Wed. 10–6, Thu.–Sat. 10–9; Nov.–Apr., Tue.–Sun. 10–6. Founded in Boston in 1986 and still Boston based, Harpoon purchased this, the former Catamount Brewery, in 2000. The recently expanded Beer Garden offers a full pub menu and a bar with 24 (Harpoon) beers on tap, each served in its signature glass. Patrons (over 21 years) are welcome to sample up to four kinds. A glass wall overlooks the lawn and picnic tables. There's a fireplace, and table as well as bar seating. Check the Web site for special events. Tours offered Fri. and Sat. at 3 PM.

Worth crossing the river for
Charlestown Heritage Diner (603-826-3110), 122 Main St., Charlestown, New Hampshire. Open daily 6 AM–2 PM; Wed.–Sun. 4–9 PM for fresh seafood and beef specialties. This authentic 1920s Worcester diner is attached to an 1820s brick building that expands its space (there are two small dining rooms in the older building), offering a choice of atmospheres but the same blackboard menu. There's also a tavern upstairs—and the liquor license extends to the diner. The breakfast menu is huge, while "the Live Free or Die Burger" with multiple toppings is a lunch specialty.

✳ Entertainment

Bellows Falls Opera House (802-463-4766), on the square in Bellows Falls, operated by the town of Rockingham. Formerly the New Falls Cinema, this vintage theater in the town hall has recently been refurbished with new seating, flooring, screen, and sound system. First-run and classic movies are shown Mon.–Tue., Sat.–Sun. Tickets $4 ($2.50 on Tue. night). This fine old vaudeville house is also the venue for live performances.

Stone Church Arts (802-463-3100), 20 Church St. Immanual Episcopal Church is the venue for a series of classical music performances.

More music and performance in Bellows Falls: **Boccelli's** (802-463-9595), 46 Canal St., is the venue for a monthly series of "**Vermont Festivals**" with varied live music. See flyingunderradar.com for details about this and the annual four-day music extravaganza held every June and for other folk music by nationally known and local artists in Bellows Falls. Also check the **Village Square Booksellers** Web site (villagesquarebooks.com) for readings and for the **Front Porch Series** of free, summer Sunday-afternoon performances and concerts on Bellows Falls porches. There's also generally music during Art Walk on the third Friday (5–8) of each month.

Main Street Arts (802-869-2960; mainstreetarts.org), Main St., Saxtons River. This local arts council sponsors dance and musical performances, parades, cabarets, recitals, as well as art classes and the Jelly Bean crafts shop.

Springfield Theater (802-885-2929), 26 Main St., downtown Springfield. First-run films.

The **Grafton Cornet Band** performs in either Grafton or Chester (sometimes in Townshend) on summer weekends.

✳ Selective Shopping

ANTIQUES SHOPS **Grafton Gathering Places Antiques** (802-875-2309), 748 Eastman Rd., open year-round daily except Tue. A two-story country barn filled with early country and period furniture and accessories.

Also see Three Seasons in Windsor (under *Crafts*) and Boccelli's (in *Eating Out*).

ART GALLERIES

In Bellows Falls

Note: **Arts Walk** the third Friday evening of each month features art and music in venues around town.

The Framery of Vermont (802-463-3295; theframeryofvermont.com), 22 Bridge St. The particular focus here is the Connecticut River Valley, its landscape, flora, and fauna, featuring Sabra Fields and Will Moses prints.

Great River Arts Institute (802-463-3330; greatriverarts.org), 33 Bridge St. Workshops in writing and a variety of visual arts are offered. Check the current calendar for lectures, special events. Changing art exhibits.

Also see *Crafts*.

In Grafton

Gallery North Star (802-843-2465; gnsgrafton.com), 151 Townshend Rd. Open daily except Tue. 10–5. Six rooms in this 19th-century Grafton Village house are hung with landscapes and graphic prints, oils, watercolors, and sculpture.

Jud Hartmann Gallery (802-843-2018; judhartmanngallery.com), 6 Main St., by the Brick Church on Main St.

Open mid-Sept.–foliage season 10–5 and again in Dec.–Memorial Day by chance or appoitment. Hartmann began his career as a sculptor in Grafton and has since won national acclaim for his bronze portrayals of Native Americans, specifically a series of limited-edition sculptures titled The Woodland Tribes of the Northeast. He is working on increasingly complex historical renditions. He divides his time among studios here, Maine, and the Virgin Islands. In Grafton he divides his time between his studio and cross-country skiing at Grafton Ponds, which he actually founded many years ago. The studio also displays paintings by various other artists.

Hunter Gallery (802-843-1440) 74 Main St., Grafton. Open May–Nov., daily 9:30–6:30. Original paintings, pastels, and sculptures by East Coast artists are displayed in this, the studio of watercolorist Peter Jeziorski. Artwork, crafts, and furniture are also displayed (10–5 daily, year-round) at 56 Townshend Rd., behind the Old Tavern in the Daniels House, which serves as an information center and houses a café (see *Eating Out*).

Elsewhere

Gallery at the Vault (802-885-7111; galleryatthevault.com), 65 Main St., Springfield. This quality crafts store is all about Visual Art Using Local Talent (hence its name) and is definitely worth checking out.

Cider Hill Gardens & Art Gallery (802-674-5293; ciderhillgardens.com), Hunt Rd., 2.5 miles west of State St., Windsor. Open May–Oct., Thu.–Mon 10–6; weekends Nov., Dec. Sarah Milek's commercial display garden is the setting for Gary Milek's studio, displaying his striking Vermont landscapes done in egg tempera, botanically correct floral prints, and stunning cards made from them.

BOOKSTORES "┬" **Village Square Booksellers and Wireless Café** (802-463-9404; villagesquarebooks .com), 32 The Square, Bellows Falls. Open Mon.–Sat. 9–6, Fri. until 7, and Sun. 10–3. Patricia Fowler's independent, full-service bookstore is an inviting place to linger with coffee and your laptop. This is a local cultural center with regular poetry and authors' readings and other special programs, and also features local photography by Alan Fowler and changing work by local artists. Specialties include local authors and books on barging in Europe; you can also book a barge. There's a sitting area and café in the rear of the store.

Arch Bridge Bookshop (802-463-2098), 14 Village Square. Open Wed.–Sat. 9:30–5. An antiquarian bookstore specializing in difficult-to-find titles, also the Civil War, American West, fishing/hunting, railroads, and Vermontiana.

BLACKSMITH IAN EDDY IN HIS SAXTONS RIVER FORGE

Christina Tree

Ray Boas, Bookseller (603-756-9900; rayboasbookseller.com), 44 Elm St., Walpole, New Hampshire. Open most days, but it's best to call ahead if you're traveling a distance. More than 13,000 titles with an emphasis on nonfiction in a lovely old Colonial home. Decorative arts and antiques a specialty.

CRAFTS **Jelly Bean Tree** (802-869-2326), Main St., Saxtons River. Open May–Dec., daily noon–5. A crafts cooperative run by local artisans and carrying the work of many more on consignment: pottery, macramé, leather, weaving, batik, and hand-sewn, -knit, and -crocheted items.

Ian Eddy Blacksmith Studio (802 869-2828; ianeddyblacksmith.com), 14 Pleasant Valley Rd. (off Rt. 121), Saxtons River. A great selection of functional and decorative items include lighting, bathroom and kitchen accessories, fireplace tools, and door hardware. Eddy works in his forge (a former auto body shop) most days, but call ahead.

Coyote Moon Jewelry & Imports (802 (802 463-9529), 22 Rockingham St., Bellows Falls. Open daily except Sun. Intriguing gifts from throughout the world with an emphasis on Mexico, and sterling-silver jewelry.

Maplewing Artisans (802-460-4161), 7 Village Square, Bellows Falls. Open May–Dec. daily 10–6, Jan.–Apr. 11–6. Erin and Hilaire Hennessy represent 28 area artists and craftspeople, featuring woodwork but also with a selection of pottery, basketry, photography, sculpture, paintings, and much more.

Sherwin Art Glass (802-376-5744; sherwinartglass.com), 33 Bridge St. Housed in the Great River Arts Institute. On most days Chris Sherwin can be found creating colored art glass, and visitors are welcome.

Three Seasons (802-674-6400), 85 Main St., Windsor. Jill Crowley has an eye both for craftsmanship and antiques. She has created an exceptional shop, showcasing work by 40 carefully selected artisans and quality antiques.

Walpole Artisans Cooperative (603-756-3020; walpoleartisans.org), 52 Main St., Walpole (across from Burdick's Café). Open Wed.–Sat. 11–6, Sun. 11–3. A new cooperative showcasing local craftspeople.

FOOD, FLOWERS, AND FARM STANDS

Boggy Meadow Farm (877-541-3953; boggymeadowfarm.com), 13 Boggy Meadow Lane, Walpole, New Hampshire; location marked from Rt. 12. The 620-acre Boggy Meadow Farm has been in the Cabot family since 1820. Powell Cabot produces Fanny Mason Farmstead Swiss Cheeses, all made with raw milk and vegetable rennet that pasteurizes naturally during the 60-day curing process. Call to

The Grafton Village Cheese Company (802-843-2221; graftonvillage cheese.com) Townshend Rd., Grafton. Open Mon.–Fri. 9–5, Sat.–Sun. 10–5; cheesemaking weekdays 8–11. The source of some of Vermont's best prizewinning cheddars. Visitors are welcome to learn how 6,000 to 10,000 gallons of buttery milk from Jersey cows is processed daily, from cutting the curds to waxing the wheels and blocks of cheese. Different colors connote age and flavor, and visitors are welcome to sample.

make sure the retail shop and cheese plant are open. The drive along the river to the shop is a treat in itself.

Allen Brothers Farms & Orchards (802-722-3395), 6–23 Rt. 5, 2 miles south of Bellows Falls. Open year-round, daily, 6 AM–9 PM. Offers pick-your-own apples and potatoes in-season, also sells vegetables, plants and seeds, honey, syrup, and Vermont gifts.

Alyson's Orchard (603-756-9800; 800-856-0549; alysonsorchard.com), Wentworth Rd., Walpole, New Hampshire. Some 28,000 trees cover this beautiful hilltop overlooking the Connecticut River Valley. Heritage-variety apples, peaches, pears, blueberries, raspberries, hops.

Harlow Farmstand (802-722-3515), Rt. 4, less than a mile north of I-91, Exit 5. Open May–Dec., daily 9–6. Organic produce, bedding plants, flowers, and baked goods. Also see Café Loco under *Eating Out.*

Plummer's Sugar House (802-843-2207; plummerssugarhouse.com), 3 miles south of Grafton Village on Townshend Rd. Open all year. A third-generation maple producer, making pure syrup for more than 30 years; also maple candy, sugar, and more. Will ship anywhere in the United States.

Morning Star Perennials (802-463-3433; morningstarflowers.com), 221 Darby Hill Rd., Rockingham (off Rt. 5). More than 300 varieties of organically grown perennials, including many rare ones.

Wellwood Orchards (802-263-5200), 529 Wellwood Orchard Rd., Springfield. Pick your own strawberries (June and July), then raspberries and blueberries (mid- to late July), and finally apples (mid-Aug.–Oct.). Farm tours, farm stand.

Farmer's markets are held the third week of May through the third week of October in **Bellows Falls** on Fridays, 4–7, at the Waypoint Center (beside the railroad station). They take place mid-June through late September in **Springfield**, Wed. 3–6.

SPECIAL SHOPS Vermont Country Store (vermontcountrystore.com), Rt. 103, Rockingham Village. An offshoot of the famous Vermont Country

MAPLEWING ARTISANS, A GALLERY ON THE BELLOWS FALLS VILLAGE SQUARE

Christina Tree

Store in Weston, this is also owned by Lyman Orton and houses a Common Cracker machine, which visitors can watch as it stamps out the hard round biscuits. The store also sells whole-grain breads and cookies baked here, along with a line of calico material, soapstone griddles, woodenware gadgets, natural-fiber clothing, and much more. There's also an upstairs bargain room.

Sam's Outdoor Outfitters (802-463-3500; samsoutdoor.com), 78 The Square, Bellows Falls, bills itself as "the biggest little store in the world." A branch of the Brattleboro store but still big.

Simon Pearce Glass (802-674-6280; simonpearce.com), Rt. 5, north of Windsor. Open daily 9–5. Pearce operated his own glassworks in Ireland for a decade and moved here in 1981, acquiring the venerable Downer's Mill in Quechee and harnessing the dam's hydropower for the glass furnace (see "Woodstock/Quechee Area"). He subsequently built this additional, 32,000-square-foot facility down by the Connecticut River. Designed to be visitor-friendly, it includes a catwalk above the factory floor—a fascinating place from which you can watch glass blown and shaped. Of course there's a big showroom/shop featuring seconds as well as first-quality glass and pottery. The pottery shed next door is also open to visitors.

Windsor Vermont Mercantile (802-230-4261), 59 Main St., Windsor. This former department store has had many lives and now carries an eclectic mix of staples and gifts, from wool pants to toys and puzzles.

Also see **Harpoon Brewery** under *Eating Out.*

✳ Special Events

Note: Check bellowsfalls.org for current happenings, and see Art Gallery Walk under *Art Galleries.*

June: **Roots on the River** (flying underradar.com). A four-day folk/rock/country music festival in Bellows Falls that's gaining national recognition.

July through August: Sunday-afternoon (2 PM) **lawn concerts** at the Saint-Gaudens National Historic Site (603-675-2175) in Cornish, New Hampshire; free with admission to the grounds. Bring a picnic.

July 4 weekend: A big **parade in Saxtons River** and fireworks. **Windsor Heritage Days** (*weekend following July 4*) celebrate Vermont's birthplace as a republic. **Windsor County Agricultural Fair** (802-886-1322), Barlow's Field, Eureka Rd., Springfield.

August: Rockingham **Old Home Days**, Bellows Falls (gfrcc.org). A full weekend of events—railroad excursions, live entertainment, art show, Rockingham Meeting House Pilgrimage, fireworks. Annual **Stellafane Convention of Amateur Telescope Makers** (stellafane.com), Springfield.

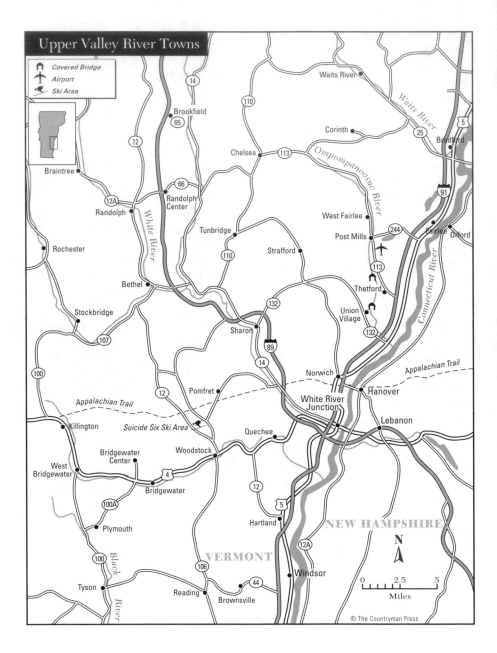

Upper Valley River Towns

Covered Bridge
Airport
Ski Area

© The Countryman Press

UPPER VALLEY RIVER TOWNS

T he Upper Valley ignores state lines to form one of New England's most rewarding and distinctive regions.

Upper Valley is a name coined in the 1950s by a local daily, the *Valley News*, to define its two-state circulation area. The label has stuck, interestingly enough, to the group of towns that back in the 1770s tried to form the state of "New Connecticut." The Dartmouth-based, pro–New Connecticut party was, however, thwarted (see the introduction to "The Connecticut River Valley").

In 1769 Eleazar Wheelock had moved his Indian school—which had been funded through appeals made by Mohegan preacher Samson Occum in England and Scotland to "spread Christian knowledge among the Savages"—from Lebanon, Connecticut, to Hanover, New Hampshire. Initially Dartmouth College recruited Indian students, many from St. Francis, but the school also served white students and the percentage of Indians quickly dwindled.

The Valley itself prospered in the late 18th and early 19th centuries, as evidenced by the exquisite Federal-era meetinghouses and mansions still salted throughout this area. The river was the area's only highway in the 18th and early 19th centuries and was still a popular steamboat route in the years before the Civil War.

The Upper Valley phone book includes towns on both sides of the river, and Hanover's Dresden School District reaches into Vermont (this was the first bistate school district in the United States). Several Independence Day parades start in one state and finish across the bridge in the other. The Montshire Museum, founded in Hanover, New Hampshire, but now in Norwich, combines the two states in its very name.

Dartmouth College in Hanover, New Hampshire, remains the cultural center of the Upper Valley. With the nearby Dartmouth-Hitchcock medical complex and West Lebanon shopping strip, this area forms the region's commercial hub, handy to the highways radiating, the way rail lines once did, from White River Junction.

The Connecticut and White rivers converge at White River Junction, an obvious stop for the area's first travelers, who arrived by canoe, then by raft and steamboat. Like an evolving species, they continued on land with the advent of the railroad, which spawned a brick village. In the mid-19th century, some 100 steam locomotives chugged into this station each day, bringing railcars full of tired, hungry passengers.

However, like a noose looping loosely around White River Junction, the inter-states (I-89 and I-91) have since channeled traffic away from this 19th-century village, slowly draining its lifeblood. Happily, the downtown commercial blocks here are presently evolving as an arts and dining center, still with the vintage rail depot—now a combination visitor center and transportation museum—at its core. Once more it even offers canoe access to the Connecticut River.

GUIDANCE White River Junction Welcome Center (802-281-5050; hartford vtchamber.com), 100 Railroad Row in the Amtrak station, White River Junction. Open 10–4 except Sun. This information-packed center is staffed by the Hartford Chamber of Commerce and offers friendly, knowledgeable advice, and restrooms. From I-91 exit to Rt. 5 and follow the blue WELCOME CENTER signs.

GETTING THERE *By car:* Interstates 91 and 89 intersect in the White River Junction (Vermont)–Lebanon (New Hampshire) area, where they also meet Rt. 5 north and south on the Vermont side; Rt. 4, the main east–west highway through central Vermont; and Rt. 10, the river road on the New Hampshire side.

By bus: White River Junction is a hub for **Greyhound** (800-552-8737; greyhound .com) with service to Boston and Burlington, New York, and Montreal. **Dartmouth Coach** (603-228-3300; concordcoachlines.com) offers aggressively competitive service from Boston and Logan Airport to Hanover, New Hampshire.

By air: The **Lebanon Regional Airport** (603-298-8878); flyleb.com, West Lebanon (marked from the junction of I-89 and Rt. 10), has frequent service to Boston via Cape Air (flycapeair.com). Rental cars are available from Avis, Hertz, and Alamo; the airport is also served by **Big Yellow Taxi** (603-643-8294).

By train: **Amtrak** (800-872-7245) serves White River Junction, en route to and from New York/Washington and Essex Junction, Vermont.

MEDICAL EMERGENCY Dartmouth-Hitchcock Medical Center (603-650-5000), off Rt. 120 between Hanover and Lebanon, is generally considered the best hospital in northern New England.
Call **911**.

✳ Communities

AMTRAK'S VERMONTER PULLS INTO WHITE RIVER JUNCTION
Chris McKinley

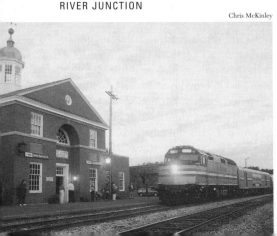

Listed from south to north.

White River Junction (population: 2,569; whiteriverjunction.org) is one of five villages within the town of Hartford. As noted in this chapter's introduction, downtown White River—which at its peak saw 100 steam locomotives chug into the station daily—is now a bit of cul-de-sac. Still, it's well worth finding. **Northern Stage**, a professional theater company, performs year-round in the old Briggs Opera House. The Tip Top building, a former commercial bakery, is honeycombed with artists' studios. You'll also find a natural food co-op, some interesting shops, a choice of restaurants, and the groundbreaking **Center for Cartoon Studies** (a two-year program with a library endowed by Charles M. Schulz, creator of *Peanuts*). There are also several shops worth a detour in their own right. Museum exhibits span the Valley's river and air history as well as rail. The station itself is a seasonal departure point for the **White River Flyer** (see *To Do*). Follow the walkway along the tracks to the free **Main Street Museum** (802-356-2776; mainstreetmuseum.org), open Thu.–Sat. 1–6. Housed in a former firehouse, this "cabinet of curiosities" seems a parody of the museum genre. Owner David Fairbanks (as in St. Johnsbury's Fairbanks Museum) Ford's exhibits include Elvis Presley's gallstones and an eclectic range of stuffed and "found" objects. Check the Web site for ongoing events.

At the center of the village is the **Hotel Coolidge**, one of the last of New England's railroad hotels. In its former incarnation as the Junction House, the hotel's clientele included Lillian Gish and President Calvin Coolidge, for whose father it is named. Ask to see the hand-painted murals in the Vermont Room, depicting the state's history from wilderness to the 1940s. Lovingly preserved by its present owners, the Coolidge is rich in character, something conspicuously absent from the interstate-geared, brand-name motels and fast-food stops along the village periphery. Horace Wells of White River Junction was, incidentally, the first person to use laughing gas as an anesthetic for pulling teeth. The other villages in the town of Hartford are Quechee (see the Woodstock/Quechee chapter), Hartford Village, Wilder, and West Hartford.

Norwich (population: 3,800; norwichvt.us), one of the prettiest towns in Vermont, was settled in 1761 by a group from Marshfield, Connecticut. It has always had close ties to Hanover (just across the bridge) and was itself the original home of Norwich University (founded 1819), which moved to Northfield after the Civil War. The village is an architectural showcase for fine brick and frame Federal homes. Note the Seven Nations House, built in 1832 as a commercial "tenement." **The Norwich Historical Society** (802-649-0124), housed in the newly renovated vintage 1807 Lewis House, 277 Main St., is open Wed. 2–4:30 and Sat. 9–noon. Across the way is the **Norwich Inn**, dating back to 1797 and with a popular brewpub as well as dining room, the hospitable heart of town. Sequestered down by the river (east of I-91), the recently expanded **Montshire Museum** offers insights into ways the world and universe go 'round as well as into how the river shapes the immediate environment; it also offers trails through its 110 acres. **King Arthur Flour Company**'s flagship Baker's Store and Baking Education Center on Rt. 5, south of town, draw devotees from throughout the county.

Hanover, New Hampshire, is synonymous with Ivy League **Dartmouth College** (dartmouth.edu), chartered in 1769 and one of the most prestigious colleges in the country. Dartmouth's student population averages 4,300 undergraduate men and women and 1,700 graduate students. Its handsome buildings frame three sides of an elm- and maple-lined green, and the fourth side includes a large inn, an arts center, and an outstanding art museum. The information booth on the green open June–Sept.) is the starting point for historical and architectural tours of the campus. **Baker Memorial Library**, a 1920s version of Philadelphia's Independence Hall, dominates the northern side of the green. Visitors are welcome to see a set of murals, *The Epic of American Civilization*, by José Clemente Orozco, painted between 1932 and 1934 while he was teaching at Dartmouth. (Some alumni once demanded these be removed or covered because of the Mexican artist's left-wing politics.) In the Treasure Room (near the western stair hall on the main floor), Daniel Webster's copies of the double elephant folio first edition of John Audubon's *Birds of America* are permanently displayed. The **Hopkins Center for the Arts** (*Entertainment*) was designed by Wallace Harrison a few years before he designed New York's Lincoln Center (which it resembles). It contains three theaters, a recital hall, and art galleries for permanent and year-round programs of plays, concerts, and films. It's also home base for the Dartmouth Symphony Orchestra. **Dartmouth Row**, a file of four striking white Colonial buildings on the rise along the eastern side of the green, represents all there was to Dartmouth College until 1845. You might also want to find Webster Cottage, maintained as a museum by the Hanover Historical Society, and the vintage-1843 **Shattuck Observatory** (open for observations at various times during the year; for schedules call 603-646-9100 or visit Dartmouth.edu/physics). Also see the **Hood Museum of Art**, below.

Lyme, New Hampshire, is known for its splendid **Congregational church**, completed in 1812, a Federal-style meetinghouse complete with Palladian window, an unusual tower (three cubical stages and an octagonal dome), and no fewer than 27 numbered horse stalls. The gathering of buildings, including the inn, fine old houses, and general stores, is one of New Hampshire's most stately. Take **River Road** north by old farms and cemeteries, through an 1880s covered bridge.

Thetford has an unusual number of post offices per capita: There are six villages in all. Thetford Center has a friendly general store and handsome brick Methodist church. Thetford Hill is a beauty, the site of Thetford Academy, the Parish Players, and the **Thetford Historical Society** (open Aug., Sun. 2–5) and its **Historic Library** (open year-round, Mon. and Thu. 2–4 and Tue. 10–noon).

Fairlee Village, shelved between the Palisades and a bend in the Connecticut River, is a plain cousin to aristocratic Orford, New Hampshire (well known for its lineup of elegant Federal-era houses), just across the river. But we like it better. Check out Chapman's, a 19th-century pharmacy that has expanded in unusual directions. Summer camps and inns line nearby **Lake Morey**. Samuel Morey, a resident of Orford and a lumberman in Fairlee, was the inventor of the first steamboat: In 1793, 14 years before Fulton launched his *Clermont*, Morey was puffing up and down the river in a primitive craft barely big enough to hold him and his firewood. The remains of the little steamer are believed to lie at the bottom of Lake Morey, scuttled by its builder when the $100,000 in stock offered him by Robert Fulton turned out to be worthless. Morey also patented an internal combustion engine in 1825. Lake Fairlee, lined with children's camps and with a public swim beach, straddles the town line and is best accessed from Rt. 244 west of Ely.

Orford, New Hampshire, is known for its **Ridge Houses**, a center-of-town lineup of seven houses so strikingly handsome that Charles Bulfinch has been (erroneously) credited as their architect. They were built instead by skilled local craftsmen using designs from Connecticut Valley architect Asher Benjamin's do-it-yourself guide to Federal styles, *The Country Builder's Apprentice*. These houses testify to the prosperity of this valley in the post–Revolutionary War era. Each was built by an Orford resident—with money earned in Orford—between 1773 and

1839. The **Samuel Morey House** is the oldest of the seven, a centerpiece for the
others. Its owner, credited with inventing the steamboat, heated and lighted his
house with gas, and in 1826 he patented a gas-powered internal combustion engine.

✳ Must-See

Hood Museum of Art (603-646-2808; hoodmuseum.dartmouth.edu), Dartmouth
green, Hanover, New Hampshire. Open Tue.–Sat. 10–5, until 9 on Wed.; Sun.
noon–5. Free. An outstanding collection of world-class art from almost every geographic area of the world and historical period. Featuring ninth-century Assyrian
reliefs from the Palace of Ashurnarsipal II at Nimrod (present-day Iraq); European
Old Master prints and paintings; two centuries of American paintings, portraits,
drawings, and watercolors; American decorative arts; ancient and Asian objects;
traditional and contemporary African, Oceanic, and Native American collections;
cutting-edge contemporary art; and a stunning set of murals by José Clemente
Orozco. Two floors of galleries, permanent collections, traveling exhibitions.
Explore on your own or arrange for a tour by calling (603-646-1469. Hood Museum of Art Shop has something for all ages and budgets.

✳ To Do

BALLOONING **Boland Balloons** (802-333-9254), Post Mills Airport, West Fairlee, Vermont Mid-May–mid-Nov., Brian Boland offers morning and sunset balloon
rides. On the summer evening we tried it, the balloon hovered above hidden pockets in the hills, and we saw a herd of what looked like brown and white goats that,
on closer inspection, proved to be deer (yes, some were white!). After an hour or
so we settled down gently in a farmyard and broke out the champagne. Boland
builds as well as flies hot-air balloons and maintains a **private museum** of balloons, airships, and antique cars. He also maintains rustic cabins on the premises
for patrons ($60 per night) and offers packages in conjunction with nearby Silver
Maple Lodge (see *Bed & Breakfasts*). Balloon rides are $260.

Also see **Balloons of Vermont** and **Balloons over New England** in the "Wood-
stock/Quechee Area" chapter.

BICYCLING Given its unusually flat and scenic roads and well-spaced inns, this
area is beloved by bicyclists. Search out the river roads: from Rt. 12A (just north of
the Saint-Gaudens site) on through Plainfield, New Hampshire, until it rejoins Rt.
12A; from Rt. 10 north of Hanover, New Hampshire (just north of the Chieftain
Motel), through Lyme, New Hampshire, rejoining Rt. 10 in Orford, New Hampshire. A classic, 36-mile loop is Hanover to Orford on Rt. 10 and back on the river
road. The loop to Lyme and back is 22 miles. For inn-to-inn guided tours in this
area, contact **Bike Vermont** (802-457-3553; 800-257-2226; bikevermont.com).

BOATING With its usually placid water and scenery, the Connecticut River
through much of the Upper Valley is ideal for easygoing canoeists. **The Ledyard
Canoe Club** (603-643-6709) in Hanover, New Hampshire, is Dartmouth's mellow,
student-run canoeing and kayaking center; rentals but no shuttle service.

Fairlee Marine (802-333-9745), Rt. 5 in Fairlee, rents pontoons, canoes, rowboats, and small motors for use on the Connecticut and two local lakes.

✔ **Montshire Museum of Science** (802-649-2200; montshire.org), 1 Montshire Rd., Norwich. Open daily 10–5 except Thanksgiving, Christmas, and New Year's Day; $10 adults, $8 ages 2–17. Use of the trails is included with admission. Few cities have a science museum of this quality. Happily this hands-on science center with more than 100 exhibits is sited on 110 trail-webbed acres beside the Connecticut River. The name *Montshire* derives from blending Ver*mont* and New Hamp*shire*. The focus is on demystifying scientific phenomena in the world in general and the Upper Valley in particular. The elaborate 2.5-acre Science Park features water bubbling from a 7-foot Barre granite boulder, and from this "headwater" a 250-foot "rill" flows downhill, snaking over a series of terraces, inviting you to manipulate dams and sluices to change its flow and direction (visitors are advised to bring towels). You can also shape fountains, cast shadows to tell time, and push a button to identify the call of birds and insects within actual

THE MONTSHIRE MUSEUM IN NORWICH

John Douglas

Information on seven primitive campsites along this stretch of the Connecticut River can be found on the **Upper Valley Land Trust**'s Web site: uvlt.org.

FISHING You can eat the fish you catch in the Connecticut River—it yields brown and rainbow trout above Orford. There's a boat launch on the Vermont side at the Wilder Dam, another just north of Hanover, New Hampshire, and another across the river in North Thetford. Lake Mascoma (look for boat launches along Rt. 4A in Enfield, New Hampshire) and Post Pond in Lyme, New Hampshire, are other popular angling spots.

hearing. Note Ed Kahn's *Wind Wall*, a billboard-sized sheet attached to the museum's tower, composed of thousands of silver flutter disks that shimmer in the breeze, resembling patterns on a pond riffled by wind.

The Montshire also serves as a visitor information center for the the Silvio O. Conte National Fish and Wildlife Refuge; exhibits include a giant moose and tanks of gleaming local fish. The museum theater features *ViewSpace*, a program showing the latest images, movies, and animations from the Hubble Space Telescope and other NASA observatories. Some of our favorite exhibits: the fog machine up in the tower, the

Gilbert Fox

THE MONTSHIRE MUSEUM IN NORWICH HAS DOZENS OF FASCINATING EXHIBITS FOR CHILDREN.

see-through beehive, displays illustrating which vegetables and fruits float, and the physics of bubbles. There are also astounding displays on moths, insects, and birds. Most exhibits, even the boa constrictors (at designated times), are hands-on. While there's a corner for toddlers, an outside playground, and many demonstrations geared to youngsters, this is as stimulating a place for adults as for their offspring. The museum shop alone is worth stopping for. Inquire about special events, programs, summer camp, and changing exhibits. In summer and fall the excursion train **White River Flyer** (800-707-3530) offers round-trip jaunts from Union Depot in White River Junction up along the Connecticut River to the Museum.

FITNESS CENTER **Upper Valley Aquatic Center** (802-296-2850; uvac-swim .org), 100 Arboretum Lane, junction of Rts. 89 and 91, White River Junction. Featuring a 25-meter competition training pool, three-lane lap pool, splash park with children's area, fitness center, and café. Open to the public.

GOLF **Hanover Country Club** (603-646-2000), Rope Ferry Rd., off Rt. 10, Hanover. Open May–Oct. Founded in 1899, an 18-hole facility with 4 practice holes, pro shop, PGA instructors. **Carter Golf Club** (603-448-4483), Rt. 4, Lebanon. Nine holes, par 36. **Lake Morey Country Club** (802-333-4800; 800-423-1211), Fairlee, has 18 holes.

RAILROAD EXCURSION ✔ **Trains Around Vermont** (802-463-3069; 800-707-3530; rails-vt.com), Union Depot, 100 Railroad Row, White River Junction. Take a round-trip along the Connecticut River to the Montshire Museum and Thetford on the White River Flyer. Frequent round-trips mid-June–Labor Day and weekends in foliage season (mid-June–mid-Oct.), plus the Polar Express in Dec. $10–14 adults, $18–19 adults, $14–15 children.

SWIMMING Ask locally about swimming holes in the Connecticut River.

✔ **Storrs Pond Recreation Area** (603-643-2134), off Rt. 10 north of Hanover, New Hampshire (Reservoir Rd., then left). Open June–Labor Day, 10–8. Bathhouse with showers and lockers, lifeguards at both the (unheated) Olympic-sized pool and 15-acre pond. Fee for nonmembers.

🐾 ✔ **Treasure Island** (802-333-9615), on Lake Fairlee, Thetford. This fabulous town swimming area is on Rt. 244 (follow Rt. 113 north of town). Open late June–Labor Day, 10–8 weekends, noon–8 weekdays. Sand beach, picnic tables, playground, tennis. Nominal admission.

Union Village Dam Recreation Area (802-649-1606), Thetford. Open Memorial Day–mid-Sept.; five swimming areas along the Ompompanoosuc River. Also walking and cross-country skiing trails, picnic tables, and grills.

Also see *Fitness Center*.

❋ Winter Sports

CROSS-COUNTRY SKIING AND SNOWSHOEING **Dartmouth Cross Country Ski Center** (603-643-6534), Rope Ferry Rd. (off Rt. 10 just before the country club), Hanover, New Hampshire. Open in snow season Mon.–Fri. 9–7, weekends 9–5. $10 pass. Twenty-five km of varied trails, some geared to skating, through the Storrs Pond and Oak Hill areas; rental skis, skates, and snowshoes.

Lake Morey Inn Resort (802-333-4800; 800-423-1211), Fairlee. Turns the golf course into a touring center in winter; rentals, instruction.

Also see **Thetford Hill State Park** under *Green Space*.

DOWNHILL SKIING ✔ **Dartmouth Skiway** (603-795-2143; skiway.dartmouth .edu), 39 Grafton Turnpike, Lyme Center, New Hampshire. An amenity for families as well as the college, with a snazzy 16,000-square-foot timber base lodge. Open 9–4 daily in-season; rentals and ski school. More than 100 skiable acres spread over two mountains: 1 quad chair, 1 double chair, a beginners' J-bar. *Vertical drop:* 968 feet. *Snowmaking:* 65 percent. Reasonable rates.

Whaleback (603-448-1489; whaleback.com), I-89, Exit 16, Enfield, New Hampshire. Zero Gravity Skate Park open year-round, winter hours with skiing/snowboarding: noon–9 weekdays, 9–9 Sat., 9–4:30 Sun. This beloved family mountain, just off I-89, is now an "action sports center." It offers 35 trails served by a double chair, four surface lifts (with 80 percent snowmaking), and night skiing. What's new: a renovated base lodge, indoor and outdoor skate parks, and seasonal mountain biking, BMX, and pit bikes plus paintball. Staff are headed by two-time Olympian Evan Dybvig, and it's all about teaching action sports. Reasonable ski/snowboard rates.

Also see **Ascutney Mountain Resort** in the previous chapter.

✳ Green Space

Pine Park, just north of the Dartmouth campus between the Hanover Country Club and the Connecticut River, Hanover, New Hampshire. Take N. Main St. to Rope Ferry Rd. Park at the trail sign above the clubhouse. These tall pines are one of the beauty spots of the Valley. The 125-year-old trees were saved from the Diamond Match Company in 1900 by a group of local citizens. The walk is 1.5 miles.

& **Montshire Museum of Science Trails**, Norwich. The museum's 110 acres include a 12-acre promontory between the Connecticut River and the marshy bay at the mouth of Bloody Brook. The 0.25-mile trail leading down through tall white pines to the bay is quite magical. The 1.5-mile Hazen Trail runs all the way to Wilder Village. These trails are hard packed, accessible to strollers and wheelchairs.

Thetford Hill State Park (802-785-2266; vtstateparks.com), 622 Academy Rd., Thetford Center. Open Memorial Day–Labor Day. Developed by the Civilian Conservation Corps in the 1930s, 177 acres with a **campground** (14 tent/trailer sites, two lean-tos, hot showers), hiking and cross-country trails (maintained by Thetford Academy).

See also **Quechee Gorge State Park** in "Woodstock/Quechee Area."

✳ Lodging

HOTELS 🐾 & **The Hanover Inn** (603-643-4300; 800-443-7024; hanoverinn.com), corner of Maine and S. Wheelock streets, Hanover, NH 03755. This is the Ritz of the North Country. A four-story, 92-room, neo-Georgian building owned and operated by Dartmouth College, the "inn" traces itself back to an 1780 tavern. It remains the heart of Hanover. In summer the front terrace is crowded with faculty, visitors, and residents enjoying a light lunch or beer. Both Zins Wine Bistro and the more formal Daniel Webster Room draw patrons from throughout the Upper Valley. Rates range from $260 for a standard room to $310 for a junior suite, no charge for children under age 12; senior citizens' discount; honeymoon, ski, golf, and seasonal packages. Handicapped accessible and pets accepted.

🦞 ✐ **The Hotel Coolidge** (802-295-3118; 800-622-1124; hotelcoolidge .com), White River Junction 05001. Not luxurious but a beloved icon as New England's last railroad hotel. It's also comfortable, clean, and reasonably priced. All 30 elevator-served guest rooms have private bath, phone, and TV. Some back rooms are dark, but others are quite roomy and attractive, and the family suites (two rooms connected by a bath) are a good value. The hotel sits across from the Amtrak station, adjacent to the Briggs Opera House. Local buses to Hanover and Lebanon stop at the door, and rental cars can be arranged. Search out the splendid Peter Michael Gish murals in the Vermont Room, painted in 1949 in exchange for room and board while the artist was studying with Paul Sample at Dartmouth. Owner-manager David Briggs, a seventh-generation Vermonter, takes his role as innkeeper seriously and will arrange for special needs. From $89 single; $109 for most double rooms, $169 for a suite.

INNS *Listed from south to north.*

& **Home Hill Country Inn** (603-675-6165; homehillinn.com), 703 River Rd.,

Plainfield, NH 03781. Built in 1818, this is one of those magnificent, four-square mansions spaced along the Connecticut River. The main house offers three elegant guest rooms and a two-room suite; there are also six guest rooms in the Carriage House. A small cottage with a bedroom and sitting room is beside the pool. $188–275 per couple includes breakfast and after-noon refreshments. Lovely as it is oth-erwise, this inn is all about outstanding food; check *Dining Out.*

❦ "❦" **Moose Mountain Lodge** (603-643-3529; themoosemountainlodge .com), P.O. Box 272, Moose Mountain Hwy., Etna, NH 03750. Open June–Sept., Oct. (Wed.–Mon.), Jan., and Feb. Just 7 miles from the Dart-mouth green, the feel is remote, and the view, spectacular. This is a classic "lodge," built from stones and logs cleared from these hills, walled in pine. The roomy porch (filled with flowers in summer) is like a balcony seat above the Valley, commanding a view of Ver-mont mountains from Ascutney to Sugarbush, with Killington center stage, beyond lower hills. This is also the view from the sitting room, with its window seats, baby grand piano, and massive stone fireplace. Upstairs the 12 rooms are small but inviting (with spruce log bedsteads made by

THE NORWICH INN

Christina Tree

innkeeper Kay Shumway); the five shared baths are immaculate. Kay is a cookbook author who continues to pre-pare feasts for hikers (the inn is just off the Appalachian Trail), bikers, and cross-country skiers. Innkeepers since 1975, Kay and Peter Shumway still welcome each new guest with enthusi-asm and interest. The 350 acres include a beaver pond, ample woods, meadows, and access to 50 miles of dependably snowy cross-country ski trails. In summer/fall MAP rates are $150 per adult single, $120 per person double; in winter lunch is also included in $155 single, $130 per person dou-ble; $70 year-round for children under 14. Dinner is a must, both because the food is good and because you probably won't want to drive up and down this hill at night—but if you don't want it, deduct $20 per adult, $10 per child.

❦ 🐾 "❦" **Norwich Inn** (802-649-1143; norwichinn.com), 325 Main St., Nor-wich 05055. Just across the river from Hanover and less formal and expensive than the Hanover Inn, this is very much a gathering place for Dartmouth parents, faculty, and students. The present three-story, tower-topped inn dates from 1889 (when its predecessor burned). Joe and Jill Lavin are the cur-rent owners. The 27 rooms are divided among the main building, the Vestry, and a backyard motel. All have private bath, telephone, and cable TV. A brew-pub, Jasper Murdock's Alehouse, fea-tures 15 varieties of inn-made brews (see *Eating Out*). The dining rooms are open for breakfast, lunch, and din-ner. Rates run from $99 in the off-season in the motel and $149–209 in the inn to $154–239 for a two-bed-room suite in the Vestry. All three meals are served but not included. Dogs are permitted in one twin-bed-ded room in the motel and in a two-room unit in the Vestry.

⊗ ✒ ♿ **Lake Morey Resort** (802-333-4311; 800-423-1211; lakemorey resort.com), Club House Rd., Fairlee 05045. On the shore of Lake Morey, this sprawling, lakeside landmark best known for its golf course is also a winter getaway for cross-country skiers, snowshoers, and ice skaters. In summer supervised children's programs are included in with MAP. Given the landscaped grounds and reception areas, this is a wedding venue as well. The resort dates from the early 1900s and was owned by the Avery family for some 20 years beginning in the 1970s, then sold and reclaimed several years ago. It has since been completely renovated. There are 130 rooms and suites. The splendid lake view remains key, along with a player-friendly 18-hole golf course. Facilities include an indoor swimming pool, Jacuzzi, sauna, fitness center, and the Waters Spa with a full menu of treatments. There are also tennis courts, plus cross-country ski and snowmobile trails. All three meals are served. Winter EP rates are per room and include up to two children sharing a room with parent: $105–149 per room and $172–217 for suites. MAP per-person summer and fall rates are $123–279 with a $35–54 charge for children, depending on age. Inquire about golf and other packages, and about cottage rentals.

BED & BREAKFASTS *Listed from south to north.*

🐾 ✒ **Norwich Bed and Breakfast at Shear Luck Farm** (802-649-3800; norwichbnb.com), 229 Bradley Hill Rd., Norwich 05055. A newly renovated, 125-year-old farmhouse on Bradley Hill offers two guest rooms, one of them a suite, both with king bed and private bath. Just 4 miles from Dartmouth College, this 20-acre farm offers sheep, chickens, and mountain

views. $100–180 includes breakfast; dinner on request.

White Goose Inn (603-353-4812; 800-358-4267; whitegooseinn.com), P.O. Box 17, Rt. 10, Orford, NH 03777. This is as a handsome 1830s brick house—four chimneyed and green shuttered, with the original 1766 clapboard home now an ell at the back. Marshall and Renee Ivey have lightened and brightened this inn, expanding the common spaces. There are eight antiques-furnished guest rooms with private bath and two that share. $89 (shared bath)–149 includes a full breakfast. Inquire about floorcloth workshops. Guests can take advantage of Peyton Place (see *Dining Out*), housed in the neighboring Federal-era tavern, one of the best places to dine in the Upper Valley.

🐾 💰 ✒ ♿ **Silver Maple Lodge & Cottages** (802-333-4326; 800-666-1946; silvermaplelodge.com), 520 Rt. 5 south, Fairlee 05045. Situated just south of the village on Rt. 5, Silver Maple was built as a farmhouse in 1855 and has been welcoming travelers for more than 80 years. Now run by Scott and Sharon Wright, it has seven nicely appointed guest rooms in the lodge and eight separate, pine-paneled, shaded cottages. The farmhouse has cheerful sitting rooms with exposed 200-year-old hand-hewn beams in the living room and dining room, where fresh breads appear with other continental breakfast goodies. The newest cottages with kitchenette and working fireplace are real beauties. Play horseshoes, croquet, badminton, or shuffleboard on the lawn, or rent a bike or canoe. Scott will also arrange a ride in a hot-air balloon for you at neighboring Post Mills Airport. He grew up on a Tunbridge farm and takes pride in introducing visitors to Vermont. $79–109 per couple. Pets are accepted in the cottages, one of which has wheelchair access.

HOSTEL 🌸 🐾 **The Hotel Coolidge** (802-295-3118). A wing of the Coolidge, described under *Hotels*, is a Hostelling International facility with dorm-style beds and access to a self-service kitchen and laundry. Private family rooms are also available by reservation. $25–40 per person for HI members, $35–55 for nonmembers.

Note: Chain hotels in White River Junction include **Holiday Inn** (800-465-4329; 121 Ballardvale Dr.), **Comfort Inn** (800-465-4329; 56 Ralph Lehman Drive), and **Hampton Inn** (802-296-2800; 104 Ballardville Dr.).

✳ Where to Eat

DINING OUT Carpenter and Main (802-649-2922; carpenterandmain .com), 326 Main St., Norwich. Open for dinner except Tue. and Wed.; tavern 5:30–10, dining room 6–9; reservations suggested. Chef-owner Bruce MacLeod is known for locally sourced, seasonal food with a French accent. On a winter night you might begin with a house pâté with cornichons or house-cured salmon, then dine on pan-roasted local chicken breast with a leek-potato gratin and celery root slaw,

THE HOTEL COOLIDGE IN WHITE RIVER JUNCTION

Christina Tree

with blue cheese and port wine. Entrées $10–19 in the bistro and $24–37 in the formal dining rooms.

Norwich Inn (802-649-1143; norwich inn.com), 325 Main St., Norwich. Open for breakfast, lunch, and dinner, also Sun. brunch; closed Mon. Across the river from Hanover, the dining room in this classic inn is popular with Dartmouth faculty and local residents, good for vegetarian as well as wide variety of entrées ($24–34). Jasper Murdock's Alehouse (see *Eating Out*), open nightly, is beloved for its hand-crafted brews (sold only here) as well as for its atmosphere and pub food.

Across the river (south to north)
Home Hill Country Inn (603-675-6165; homehillinn.com), River Rd., Plainfield, New Hampshire. Open for dinner Wed.–Sun. 5–9, Sun. brunch 9–2. Reservations suggested. The dining room in this four-square 1820s mansion by the river is bathed in light from floor-to-ceiling French doors, with warmly colored walls, white-draped tables, specially deigned chandeliers and furnishings, and a working (not gas) hearth. Chef-innkeeper Paula Snow is a passionate believer in locally sourced produce; the inn also creates its own breads, sausages, cured salmon, mozzarella cheese, pasta, and ice cream. On an autumn evening half a dozen appetizers might include handmade crayfish ravioli with smoky local sweet corn and andouille sausage. For an entrée, you could try veal with slow-roasted tomato, Fontina cheese, grilled polenta, and broccolini. Entrées $16–24; there are also less pricey daily specials such as (local) chicken potpie. Reasonably priced Sunday brunch is a great excuse to drive to this lovely spot. (Also see *Lodging*.)

Canoe Club Bistro and Music (603-643-9660; canoeclub.us), 27 S. Main St., Hanover, New Hampshire. Open daily for lunch and dinner with light fare between meals (2–5) and late-night menus Thu.–Sat. Reservations suggested for dinner. Acoustic music nightly, also Sunday jazz brunch. "Sensational" is the way local residents describe this attractive addition to Hanover's dining options. The lunch may include wild mushroom stroganoff, pulled pork quesadilla, and warm smoked sausage with port-braised cabbage, a grilled baguette, and ale mustard. The dinner menu might include house-made ravioli (ingredients change daily) and Vermont lamb with Swiss chard, sun-dried tomato pesto, parsnips, sweet potatoes, and brussels sprout leaves. Dinner entrées $10–25.

Peyton Place (603-353-9100; peyton placerestaurant.com), Rt. 10, Orford, New Hampshire. Open for dinner Wed.–Sun. 5:30–10:30; in the off-season, Thu.–Sat. Reservations a must. Destination dining, this restaurant (named for owners Jim, Heidi, Sophie, and Shamus Peyton) is housed in a 1773 tavern with a genuine old pub room and a genuinely interesting pub menu—as well as more formal dining rooms. Dinner entrées might range from house-made vegetarian ravioli, Asian shrimp stir-fry, and steak fritters to rack of lamb with wild mushrooms. Ice creams and sorbets are handmade as well. Wine and spirits are served. The pub menu might include house-made duck and chorizo dumplings, and quesadillas with tortillas made in-house. Dinner entrées $15.50–26.50. Inquire about cooking classes.

EATING OUT

In Hartland Four Corners
🍴 **Skunk Hollow Tavern** (802-436-2139), Hartland Four Corners, off Rt. 12 south of Rt. 4, north of I-91, Exit 9. Dinner Wed.–Sun., more days during

peak periods. Reservations suggested. Carlos Ocasio's split-personality restaurant, hidden away in a small village, is a local favorite. Patrons gather downstairs in the pub to play darts and backgammon and to munch on fish-and-chips, mussels, or pizza; the more formal dining is upstairs in the inn's original parlor. The menu changes every few months, but staples include Chicken Carlos. Variables might be red pepper shrimp with Oriental pasta, or shiitake chicken; always salad of the day and homemade soups. Open-mike night Wed. and entertainment Fri. nights.

In White River Junction
The Tip Top Café (802-295-3312), 85 N. Main St. Open Tue.–Sat. 11:30–2 and 5–9. Reserve on theater nights (see Northern Stage under *Entertainment*). Chef-owner Eric Hartling (creator of the Perfect Pear) now presides in this glass-fronted bistro on the ground floor of a former commercial bakery. The decor incorporates industrial ducts, hanging lamps, and the polished cement floor. Walls are hung with big, splashy (changing) paintings, and tables are dressed with brown paper. Order from the blackboard

ERIC HARTLING PRESIDES AT THE TIP TOP CAFÉ IN WHITE RIVER JUNCTION.

Christina Tree

menu at lunch; dinner is full service. Lunches include soups, salads, and unusual sandwiches such as balsamic figs with spinach and Gorgonzola on rosemary focaccia. Dinner might be a pork and ginger meat loaf, or sesame-crusted tilapia with mango salsa and mixed greens.

⁰₁⁰ **Tucker Box**, 15 Main St. Open Mon.–Sat. 7–5, closed Sun. A café with casual seating and a light-fare menu of soups and salads, breads, pastries, and coffees.

Junction House Buffet (802-295-1778), 39 Main St. Open for lunch Mon.–Sat. 11–1; for dinner Mon.–Sat. 5–9; Sunday brunch 10–3. This is strictly a buffet—all you can eat. At this writing $7.05 for lunch, $12.95 for brunch, and $15.95 for dinner. We haven't tried it yet but the promise is "fresh & delicious." Well placed for theater and serving Hotel Coolidge guests.

In Lebanon/West Lebanon, New Hampshire

Three Tomatoes Trattoria (603-448-1711), 1 Court St., Lebanon. Open for lunch Mon.–Fri. 11:30–2, and nightly for dinner. A trendy trattoria with a sleek decor, wood-fired oven and grill, and a reasonably priced menu: plenty of pasta creations like penne con car-ciofi—sautéed mushrooms, spinach, roasted garlic, and olive oil tossed with *penne ziti regate*. There are also grilled dishes like *pollo cacciatora alla gorgo-lia*—boneless chicken topped with tomato basil sauce, mozzarella, and Romano cheese, and served with lin-guine—and no less than 16 very differ-ent pizzas from the wood-fired oven. Wine and beer are served.

Gusanoz (603-448-1408; gusanoz.com), 410 Miracle Mile, Lebanon. Open Mon.–Sat. 11–9, Sun. 10–3. The Upper Valley's hottest Mexican restau-rant is squirreled away in a Lebanon

mini mall (off I-89, Exit 19; look for a movie theater and the DMV). Maria Limon and Nick Yager have already tripled their seating in answer to demand since their 2005 opening. Spe-cialties include chicken mole, carnitas, tamales, and pork asado—staples of Limon's girlhood in Durango, Mexico. On Sunday it's a dazzling "all you can eat" brunch. The only problem still may be getting in.

✎ **West Lebanon fast-food strip**. Rt. 12A just south of I-89, Exit 20, is lined with representatives of every major fast-food chain in New England—a godsend to families with cars full of kids.

In Norwich

Jasper Murdock's Alehouse in the Norwich Inn (802-649-1143), 225 Main St. Open 5:30–9. The house brew comes in many varieties. The Alehouse is a green-walled, comfort-able pub; the bill of fare changes fre-quently but usually represents some of the best "bar food" in the Valley. The menu might include Vermont venison burger, a grilled ahi tuna BLT, and Chinese noodles with stir-fried veggies. The big attractions here are the varied and widely respected house brews, available nowhere else.

Alléchante Patisserie and Cafe (802-649-2846), Main and Elm streets. Open Mon.–Fri. 7:30–6; until 5 Sat. Nicky Barraclough's shop is in a small shopping complex, easy to miss but well known to local residents who drop by for a morning brioche and latte and to check the daily sandwich board. This might include freshly roasted beef with homemade horseradish cream on white sourdough, and imported fresh goat cheese with sliced tomatoes and green olive spread on a baguette. There are also daily baked artisan breads and pastries, plus a full deli with a weekly changing take-out dinner menu. It might include chicken pot-pies, roast skate with peas and mash and a variety of vegetables, plus a choice of meat and fish. This is also a place to pick up farmstead cheeses. The new name is French for "mouth-watering."

Note: **The Norwich Farmer's Market** (norwichfarmersmarket.org) is Sat. 9–1, May–Oct. on Rt. 5, 1 mile south of the village. It's unusually big and colorful with 50 vendors, many baked goods. Winter markets are indoors at Norwich Grange or Tracy Hall, the first Sat. of each month.

In Hanover, New Hampshire
Lou's Restaurant and Bakery (603-643-3321), 30 S. Main St. Open for breakfast weekdays from 6 AM, Sat. from 7, and Sun. from 8. Lunch Mon.–Sat. until 3 PM. Since 1947 this has been a student and local hangout and it's great: a long Formica counter, tables and booths, fast, friendly service, good soups, sandwiches, daily specials, and irresistible peanut butter cookies at the register.

Molly's (603-643-2570), 43 Main St. Open daily for lunch and dinner. The greenhouse up front shelters a big, inviting bar that encourages single dining. The menu is immense and reasonably priced: big salads, enchiladas, elaborate burgers at lunch, pasta to steak at dinner.

In Fairlee
The Third Rail (802-333-9126), Rt. 5, south of the bridge. Open for dinner except Sunday. A family find. Entrées might include roast salmon teriyaki and veal marinara but also a variety of burgers, fish-and-chips, and children's menu.

Fairlee Diner (802-333-3569), Rt. 5. Closed Tue., otherwise 5:30 AM–2 PM; until 7 PM Thu. and 8 PM Fri. Turn left (north) on Rt. 5 if you are coming

off I-91. This is a classic wooden diner built in the 1930s (across the road from where it stands), with wooden booths, worn-shiny wooden stool tops, and good food. The mashed potato doughnuts are special, and both the soup and the pie are dependably good. Daily specials.

Leda's Restaurant & Pizza (802-333-4773), Rt. 5. Open Wed.–Sun. for lunch and dinner. This is a friendly standby for Greek specialties like moussaka, gyros, and feta cheese pie along with burgers, pizza, and even rib-eye steak.

Holy Mackerel, (802-333-9286), Rt. 5 south across from Fairlee Marine. Open Mon.–Sat. 6–9. Peg DeGoosh and Jim Macdonald have turned a former Citgo station into a destination fish market and café with deli sandwiches, fish-and-chips, clams, lobster rolls, scallop dinners, as well as burgers and fries, and fresh baked goods. Peg, a Bradford native, was co-owner of a fishing business in Port Judith, Rhode Island, for 24 years. Jim, a Woodsville native, has a real flair for grilling and marinades. Peg drives to Boston twice weekly for the fish. Beer and wine are served.

Note: See the **Fairlee Drive-In** under *Entertainment* for the best burgers in town.

✳ Entertainment

MUSIC AND THEATER Hopkins Center (box office 603-646-2422; hop.dartmouth.edu), on the Dartmouth green, Hanover, New Hampshire. Sponsors some 150 musical and 20 theater productions per year, plus 200 films, all open to the public.

Lebanon Opera House (603-448-0400), town hall, Coburn Park, Lebanon, New Hampshire. This 800-seat, turn-of-the-20th-century theater hosts frequent concerts, lectures, and performances by the North Country Community Players. Throughout the month of August, **Opera North** (operanorth.org) stages excellent performances featuring soloists from major opera companies.

⊘ **Northern Stage** (802-296-7000; northernstage.org), Briggs Opera House, White River Junction. Northern Stage is a professional nonprofit regional theater company that produces six main-stage shows Oct.–May in a theater with a three-quarter-thrust stage and 245 seats. Productions include dramas, comedies, musicals, as well as brilliant, lesser-known works and new plays fresh from Broadway and London's West End. Prices range $27–69, depending on seat and day of the week.

The Parish Players (802-785-4344), based in the Eclipse Grange Hall on Thetford Hill, is the oldest community theater company in the Upper Valley; its Sept.–May repertoire includes classic pieces and original works; summer presentations vary.

FILM *⊘* **Fairlee Drive-In** (802-333-9192), Rt. 5, Fairlee. Summer only; check local papers for listings. This is a beloved icon, the last of the Valley's seasonal drive-ins. It's attached to the Fairlee Motel and has a famously good snack bar featuring "thunderburgers," made from beef on the family's farm across the river in Piermont. The gates open nightly at 7; films begin at dusk.

Dartmouth Film Society at the Hopkins Center (603-646-2576), Hanover, New Hampshire. Frequent showings of classic, contemporary, and experimental films in two theaters.

Nugget Theaters (603-643-2769), S. Main St., Hanover, New Hampshire. Four current films nightly, surround sound.

✳ Selective Shopping

Note: First Fridays of every month, galleries and a number of other venues im White River Junction and Lebanon, New Hampshire, host music, refreshments, and general good cheer.

Cooler Gallery (802-285-8008; coolergallery.biz), Tip Top Café Building, White River Junction, showcases international artworks.

Lampscapes (802-295-8044; lampscapes.com), 77 Gates St., White River Junction. Open Tue.–Sat. 10–5. Kenneth Blaisdell is a former engineer and a serious landscape artist whose combination studio/shop is one of the more exciting shopping finds in town. The metal floor and table lamps themselves are simple but artistic; the shades ($30–150) are definitely works of art, each one of a kind and ranging from luminescent literal to semi-abstract, truly striking landscapes, priced within reasonable reach.

Revolution, Vintage & Urban Used Clothing (802-295-6487), 25 N. Main St., White River Junction. Kim Sousa offers an eclectic, funky selection of vintage, used, and handmade clothing plus jewelry and accessories.

Tip Top Media & Arts Building, 85 North St., White River Junction. A warren of 40 studios and changing galleries, worth a look.

King Arthur Flour Baker's Store (802-649-3361; 800-827-6836; kingarthurflour.com), 135 Rt. 5, Norwich. Open Mon.–Sat. 8:30–6, Sun. until 4. Home as well as prime outlet for the country's oldest family-owned flour company (since 1790), this store draws serious bakers and would-be bakers from throughout several time zones. The vast store is a marvel, its shelves stocked with every conceivable kind of flour, baking ingredient, and a selection of equipment and cookbooks, not

Christina Tree

KENNETH BLAISDELL HARD AT WORK IN HIS LAMPSCAPES SHOP IN WHITE RIVER JUNC-TION

to mention bread and pastries made in the adjacent bakery (with a glass connector allowing visitors to watch the hands and skills of the bakers). Next door too is the **King Arthur Baking Education Center**, offering baking classes ranging from beginner to expert, from making piecrust to braided breads and elegant pastries.

Dan & Whit's General Store (802-649-1602), Main St., Norwich. The quintessential Vermont country store. Hardware, groceries, housewares, boots and clothing, farm and garden supplies, and a great community bulletin board: If they don't have it, you don't need it.

The Norwich Bookstore (802-649-1114), Main St., Norwich, next to the post office. This is a light, airy store with well-selected titles and comfortable places to sit. Staff are very knowledgeable. Frequent readings, and a good children's section.

Pompanoosuc Mills (802-785-4851;

pompy.com), Rt. 5, East Thetford. Showroom open daily 9–6, Sat. 9–5, Sun. noon–5. Dartmouth graduate Dwight Sargeant began building furniture in this riverside house, a cottage industry that has evolved into a riverside factory with showrooms throughout New England.

Chapman's (802-333-9709), Fairlee. Open daily 8–6, 7–5 on Sun. Since 1924 members of the Chapman family have expanded the stock of this old pharmacy to include 10,000 hand-tied flies, wines, Mexican silver and Indonesian jewelry, used books, maple syrup, and an unusual selection of toys.

✳ Special Events

For details about any of these events, phone the town clerk, listed with information.

Mid-February: **Dartmouth Winter Carnival**, Hanover, New Hampshire. Thu.–Sun. Ice sculptures, sports events, ski jumping.

Fourth of July: **Independence Day Open Fields Circus**, Thetford. A takeoff on a real circus by the Parish Players. **Fourth of July celebration**, Plainfield, New Hampshire. Community breakfast, footraces, parade, firemen's roast beef dinner. Lebanon, New Hampshire, stages the largest fireworks display in the area.

Mid-July: **Norwich Fair**. Mix of old-time country fair and honky-tonk carnival. Lobster dinner, parade, ox pulling.

Early August: **Thetford Hill Fair**, Thetford Hill. Small but special: a rummage sale, food and plant booths, barbecue.

Saturday after Labor Day: **Glory Days of Railroad celebration** in White River Junction (glorydaysofthe railroad.org)—railroad excursions, music, sponsored by the **New England Transportation Institute and Museum** (603-252-9703; newengland transportationmuseum.org).

Saturday of Columbus Day weekend: **Horse Sheds Crafts Fair**, at the Lyme Congregational Church, Lyme, New Hampshire, 10–4; also a **Fall Festival** lunch at the church.

Mid-December through Christmas: **Christmas Pageants** in Norwich and Lyme, New Hampshire. **Revels North**, in the Hopkins Center, New Hampshire. Song and dance.

WOODSTOCK/QUECHEE AREA

Cradled between Mount Peg and Mount Tom and moated by the Ottauquechee (pronounced *otto-KWEE-chee*) River, Woodstock is repeatedly named among the prettiest towns in America. The story behind its good looks, which include the surrounding landscape as well as historic buildings, is told at the Marsh-Billings-Rockefeller National Historical Park, the country's only national park to focus on the concept of conservation.

The Ottauquechee River flows east through Woodstock along Rt. 4 toward the Connecticut River, generating electricity as it tumbles over falls beneath the covered bridge at Taftsville and powering Simon Pearce's glass factory a few miles downstream in Quechee Village. Below Quechee the river has carved Vermont's "Grand Canyon," Quechee Gorge, spanned by Rt. 4 and by a high, spidery railroad bridge.

The Woodstock Railroad carried passengers and freight the 20 miles between Woodstock and White River Junction between 1875 and 1933. How to ease current traffic congestion, which includes 18 wheelers headed for Rutland as well as tour buses and tourists in summer and fall and skiers in winter, remains a very real challenge. Rt. 4 is the shortest way across "Vermont's waist," and an ever-growing stream of vehicles continues to wind up the valley, filing through the middle of Woodstock, around its exquisite green, and on through the village of West Woodstock, following the river west into Bridgewater.

Our advice: Walk. Park at the picnic area just beyond Quechee Gorge and savor the view of the river churning far below between 163-foot-high walls. Walk the path down to the water's edge or around VINS, the neighboring raptor and nature sanctuary. In Woodstock Village stroll the streets, then walk Mountain Avenue through Faulkner Park, on up to the top of Mount Tom, then back down the Pogue Carriage Road to Billings Farm.

Like most of the world's famously beautiful and heavily touristed areas, especially those that are also home to sophisticated people who could live anywhere, the Ottauquechee River Valley offers visitors plenty to see and do superficially and still more, the more you explore.

GUIDANCE **The Woodstock Area Chamber of Commerce** (802-457-3555; 888-496-6378; woodstockvt.com) maintains a friendly, staffed information center (802-457-1042) with restrooms on Mechanic St., marked from Central St. (the main shopping block), open weekdays, year-round, 9–5. The chamber publishes

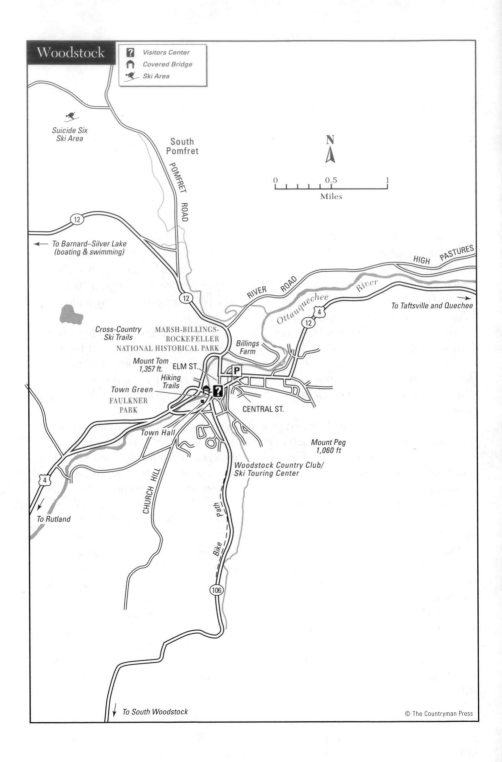

Woodstock

?	Visitors Center
⌂	Covered Bridge
🎿	Ski Area

Suicide Six
Ski Area

South
Pomfret

POMFRET ROAD

N

0   0.5   1
Miles

12

← To Barnard–Silver Lake
(boating & swimming)

HIGH PASTURES

12

RIVER ROAD

Ottauquechee River

12 4

→ To Taftsville and Quechee

Cross-Country
Ski Trails

MARSH-BILLINGS-
ROCKEFELLER
NATIONAL HISTORICAL PARK

Billings
Farm

Mount Tom
1,357 ft.

ELM ST.

Hiking
Trails

P

Town Green

FAULKNER
PARK

CENTRAL ST.

Town Hall

Mount Peg
1,060 ft

Woodstock Country Club/
Ski Touring Center

4

CHURCH HILL

To Rutland

Bike Path

106

To South Woodstock

© The Countryman Press

Window on Woodstock, a useful free pamphlet guide. Lodging places post available rooms on the Web site of the chamber, which has been known to find beds during foliage season for stranded leaf-peepers. Restrooms are also available weekdays in the town hall, west of the green. Check the **Town Crier** blackboard at the corner of Elm and Central streets for current happenings.

The Quechee Gorge Visitors Information Center (802-295-6852; 800-295-5451; hartfordvtchamber.com) is maintained by the Hartford Area Chamber of Commerce, Rt. 4 at Quechee Gorge. Open year-round, 9–5 May–Oct., 10–4 off-season. This is a lovely, well-stocked center with helpful staff and restrooms.

GETTING THERE *By car:* Rt. 4 west from I-91 and I-89.

By train: **Amtrak** to White River Junction or to Rutland. **Woodstock Transportation** (802-770-0416) offers shuttle service from the train to Woodstock in a seven-person van by reservation.

By bus: **Greyhound** (800-552-8737; greyhound.com) with service to Boston and Burlington, New York and Montreal, stops in White River Junction.

MEDICAL EMERGENCY Emergency service is available by calling **911**.

PARKING This is a walk-around town in which the first thing you do is park. Two-hour meters on Central and Elm streets and four-hour meters on Mechanic off Central are closely monitored 10–4, Mon.–Sat.: 25¢ per half hour. Red drop boxes in front of the town's two pharmacies are provided to pay fines. There are free lots by the river on Pleasant St., behind the Norman Williams Public Library, and—on weekends only—at the elementary school on Rt. 106.

WHEN TO COME This area is as genuinely year-round as Vermont gets. Marsh-Billings-Rockefeller National Historical Park and the Billings Farm & Museum are open May through mid-October, but Woodstock's early-December Wassail Weekend is its most colorful happening, and January through March bring cross-country and alpine skiing. The Quechee Hot Air Balloon Festival is the area's most famous event.

✳ Villages

Woodstock. In the 1790s, when it became the shire town of Windsor County, Woodstock began attracting prosperous professionals, who, with local merchants and bankers, built the concentration of distinguished Federal houses that surround the elliptical green, forming an architectural showcase that has been meticulously preserved. In the 19th century it produced more than its share of celebrities, including Hiram Powers, the sculptor whose nude *Greek Slave* scandalized the nation in 1847, and

A VIEW OF THE OTTAUQUECHEE VALLEY FROM THE APPLEHILL INN

Christina Tree

Christina Tree

WOODSTOCK'S MAIN STREET

Senator Jacob Collamer (1791–1865), President Lincoln's confidant, who declared, "The good people of Woodstock have less incentive than others to yearn for heaven."

Three eminent residents in particular—all of whom lived in the same house but in different eras—helped shape the current Woodstock (see the box on page 260).

"Innkeeping has always been the backbone of Woodstock's economy, most importantly since 1892 when the town's business leaders and bankers decided to build a new hotel grand enough to rival the White Mountain resorts," Peter Jennison writes in *Woodstock's Heritage.* By the turn of the 20th century, in addition to several inns, Woodstock had an elaborate mineral water spa and golf links, and it had become Vermont's first winter resort, drawing guests from Boston and New York for snowshoeing and skating. In 1934 America's first rope tow was installed here, marking the real advent of downhill skiing.

By the early 1960s, however, the beloved Woodstock Inn was creaky, the town's ski areas had been upstaged, and the hills were sprouting condos. Laurance Rockefeller acquired the two ski areas (upgrading Suicide Six and closing Mount Tom) and had the 18-hole golf course redesigned by Robert Trent Jones Sr. In 1969 he replaced the old inn. Rockefeller also created the Woodstock Foundation, a nonprofit umbrella for such village projects as acquiring and restoring dozens of historic homes, burying power lines, and building a new covered bridge by the green. In 1992 it opened the Billings Farm & Museum. The Marsh-Billings-Rockefeller National Historical Park, which includes the neighboring Rockefeller mansion and the 550 surrounding forested acres on Mount Tom, opened in 1998.

Woodstock itself remains a real town with a lot going on. Events chalked on the Town Crier blackboard at the corner of Elm and Central streets are likely to include a supper at one of the town's several churches (four boast Paul Revere bells), the current film at the theater in town hall, as well as events at the historical society and guided walks.

Note: The Woodstock Historical Society has published detailed pamphlets and guides available at Dana House (see *Also See*).

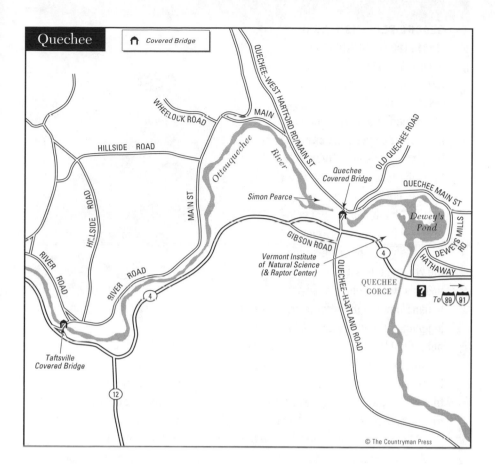

Quechee, on Rt. 4, some 6 miles east of Woodstock, is one of five villages in the township of Hartford. In the mid- and late 19th century life revolved around the J. C. Parker and Co. mill, which produced a soft baby flannel made from "shoddy" (reworked rags). A neighboring mill village surrounded the Deweys Mill, which made baseball uniforms for the Boston Red Sox and the New York Yankees. In the 1950s, however, both mills shut down. In the '60s the Deweys Mill virtually disappeared beneath a flood-control project, and 6,000 acres straddling both villages was acquired by the Quechee Lakes Corporation, the largest second-home and condominium development in the state. Thanks in good part to Act 250, Vermont's land-use statute, the end result is unobtrusive. Most homes are sequestered in woods; open space includes two (private) 18-hole golf courses. In Quechee Village the mill is now Simon Pearce's famous glass factory and restaurant, and the former mill owner's mansion is the Parker House Inn. Dramatic Quechee Gorge is visible from Rt. 4 but is best appreciated if you follow the trail to the bottom. The VINS Quechee Nature Center is also here. Tourist-geared shops and eateries continue to proliferate along Rt. 4, but, along back roads, so does village conservation land.

GEORGE PERKINS MARSH (1801–1882), FREDERICK BILLINGS (1823–1890), AND LAURANCE ROCKEFELLER (1910–2005)

Three men in particular have helped shape Woodstock's landscape. The first, George Perkins Marsh, born and raised here, had damaged his eyesight by age 7 by devouring encyclopedias and books on Greek and Latin. Sent outdoors, he studied the woods, fields, birds, and animals with equal intensity. As a man he noted the effects of logging on the landscape (60 percent of Vermont's virgin forest was harvested in the first half of the 19th century) and the resulting floods and destruction of fisheries. Later, traveling in the Middle East as the U.S. ambassador to Turkey, Marsh noted how once fertile land had become desert. He wrote: "I fear man has brought the face of the earth to a devastation almost as complete as that of the moon."

Courtesy Billings Farm Museum

FREDERICK BILLINGS BY KURTZ, C. 1873

Marsh wrote *Man and Nature* at age 63, while U.S. ambassador to Italy. Published in 1864, it is widely recognized as the first book to acknowledge civilization's effect on the environment, and the first to suggest solutions. In contrast with Henry David Thoreau (*Walden* appeared in 1854), Marsh doesn't idealize wilderness. Instead, he attempts to address the interdependence of the environment and society as a whole.

Man and Nature isn't an easy read, but it greatly influenced this country's nascent sciences of forestry and agriculture as well as many of the era's movers and shakers, among them Frederick Billings. Raised in Woodstock, Billings departed at age 25 for San Francisco. That city's first lawyer, he made a fortune registering land claims and speculating in land during the

✳ Must-See

Listed from east to west.

Quechee Gorge, Rt. 4, is one of Vermont's natural wonders, a 3,000-foot-long, 163-foot-deep chasm sculpted 13,000 years ago. Visible from the highway, it is now encompassed by a state park that includes hiking trails along the rim and down into the gorge. See *Green Space*.

gold rush. As a returning son who had "made good," Billings spoke at the 1864 Windsor County Fair, remarking on the rawness of the local landscape, the hills denuded by logging and sheep grazing. In 1869 he bought the old Marsh farm and transformed the vintage 1805 house into a mansion. On Mount Tom he planted more than 100,000 trees, turned a bog into Pogue Pond, and created the carriage roads. Billings's primary home was in New York, and as president of the Northern Pacific Railroad (the reason Billings, Montana, is named for him) he toured the country

Courtesy Billings Family Archives

GEORGE PERKINS MARSH
BY G. P. A. HEALY, C. 1820

extensively. He continued, however, to retreat to Woodstock, creating a model dairy farm on his property, a project sustained after his death, through thick and thin, by his wife and two successive generations of Billings women.

In 1934 Frederick Billings's granddaughter Mary French (1910–1997) married Laurance Rockefeller in Woodstock. John D. Rockefeller Jr. had been largely responsible for creating more than 20 state and national parks and historic sites; Laurance inherited his father's commitment to conservation and quickly became an effective advocate of ecotourism. In the 1950s Mary Rockefeller inherited the Billings estate in Woodstock and Laurance bought and replaced the old Woodstock Inn, incorporating the golf course and Suicide Six ski area into one resort. It's now owned by his Woodstock Foundation, a nonprofit umbrella for numerous village projects (see *Villages*) and for collecting local antique farm tools and oral histories, opening the Billings Farm & Museum in 1983. In 1992 the Marsh-Billings-Rockefeller National Historical Park was created. It opened in 1998.

The Vermont Institute of Natural Science/Vermont Raptor Center (802-FLY-5000; vinsweb.org), Rt. 4, Quechee. Open daily May–Oct., 10–5; Nov.–Apr., Wed.–Sun. 10–4; also open holidays and school vacations. $8 adults, $7.20 seniors, $6.50 children. A beloved institution devoted to rehabilitating birds of prey, VINS occupies 47 acres of rolling forestland just west of Quechee Gorge. Resident raptors include bald eagles, peregrine falcons, snowy owls, hawks, and other birds of prey that have been injured. They are displayed in huge outdoor flight enclosures.

VINS

A RED-TAILED HAWK MEETS THE PUBLIC
THANKS TO VINS.

There are outdoor interpretive exhibits, nature trails, and a nature shop. Inquire about naturalist-led walks, and twice-daily flight programs.

Visitor Center for Billings Farm & Museum and the Marsh-Billings-Rockefeller National Historical Park, Rt. 12 north of Woodstock Village. Open May–Oct., daily 10–5. The parking lot and visitor center at Billings Farm serve both the farm and national park with displays on Marsh, Billings, and Rockefeller and a theater showing *A Place in the Land*, Charles Guggenheim's award-winning documentary dramatizing the story of all three men. (There's no admission fee for the restrooms and gift shop, but a nominal fee is charged to see the film if you aren't visiting the farm or museum.)

Note: A combination ticket to the Billings Farm & Museum and programs at Marsh-Billings-Rockefeller National Historical Park is offered: $16 adults, $12 seniors.

Marsh-Billings-Rockefeller National Historical Park (802-457-3368; nps.gov/mabi), Rt. 12 north of Woodstock Village. Mount Tom carriage roads and forest trails (see *Green Space*) are open year-round, free in summer (for winter use see *Cross-Country Skiing*). The Queen Anne mansion, the centerpiece of this estate, is notable for its antiques, Tiffany glass, and American art, and for a sense of the amazing individuals who lived there. Guided hour-plus tours, offered Memorial Day–Oct., are limited to a dozen visitors at a time; reservations are advised ($8 adults, $4 seniors and ages 6–15). These depart from the **Carriage Barn** (open late May–Oct., 10–5; free), an elegant space with dark bead board walls and the feel of a library, with exhibits that position Marsh, Billings, and Rockefeller within the time line of America's conservation history. A multimedia exhibit, People Taking Care of Places, profiles individuals practicing conservation around the world. Visitors are invited to record their own conservation stories on computers and to take advantage of the reading area with its conference-sized table (crafted from wood harvested on Mount Tom) and relevant books, including children's stories.

The Dana House (home of the Woodstock Historical Society, 802-457-1822; woodstockhistorical.org), 26 Elm St., Woodstock. Open May–Oct., Wed.–Sun. 11–4. Office and research library open year-round. Admission $5 (free under age 12); 40-minute tours on the hour. John Cotton Dana was an eminent early-20th-century librarian and museum director whose innovations made books and art more accessible to the public. Completed in 1807 and occupied for the next 140 years by the Dana family, this historic house has an interesting permanent exhibit portraying the town's economic heritage and an admirable collection of antiques, locally wrought coin silver, portraits, porcelains, fabrics, costumes, and toys. The John Cotton Dana Library is a research and reference center. There is also an exhibit gallery.

✪ **The Norman Williams Public Library** (802-457-2295), on the Woodstock green. Open daily 10–5 except Sun. and holidays. A Romanesque gem, donated

✍ ☂ **Billings Farm & Museum** (802-457-2355; billingsfarm.org). Open May–Oct., daily 10–5; weekends Nov.–Feb. 10–4. $11 adults, $10 seniors 62 and over, $6 ages 5–15, $3 ages 3–4; 2 and under, free. Billed as the "Gateway to Vermont's Rural Heritage," this is one of the finest Jersey farms in America and a museum dedicated to telling the story of Vermont's rural past. Established as a model farm by Frederick Billings in 1871, it became a museum unter the stewardship of his granddaughter Mary French Rockefeller and her husband, Laurance Rockefeller. Exhibits demonstrate traditional ways of plowing, seeding, cultivating, harvesting, and storing crops; making cheese and butter; woodcutting and sugaring. The restored 1890 farm manager's house reflects the farm as it was in Billings's day. Visitors can also observe what happens on a modern dairy farm with a prizewinning Jersey herd. The farm's Percheron workhorses—Jim, Joe, Purse, and Daisy—welcome visitors. Almost every day activities are geared to kids, from toddlers on up. Cows are milked daily at 3:30 PM. Inquire about special events, like Pumpkin & Apple Celebration and Harvest Weekend in fall; Thanksgiving weekend and Christmas week celebrations; sleigh ride weekends in Jan. and Feb.; and periodic demonstrations and crafts exhibits. Their annual quilt exhibit in Aug.–Sept. is worth a special trip.

PATIENT COWS AT BILLINGS FARM AND MUSEUM IN WOODSTOCK

Billings Farm and Museum

and endowed in 1883 by Dr. Edward H. Williams, general manager of the Pennsylvania Railroad and later head of Baldwin Locomotives. It offers children's story hours, poetry readings, and brown-bag summer concerts on the lawn; also Internet access for a small fee.

✳ Also See

COVERED BRIDGES There are three in the town of Woodstock—the **Lincoln Bridge** (1865), Rt. 4, West Woodstock, Vermont's only Pratt-type truss; the **Middle Bridge**, in the center of the village, built in 1969 by Milton Graton, "last of the covered-bridge builders," in the Town lattice style (partially destroyed by vandalism and rebuilt); and the notable red **Taftsville Bridge** (1836), Rt. 4 east, utilizing multiple king- and queenposts and an unusual mongrel truss. This is the second oldest bridge in Vermont and overlooks a hydroelectric dam, still in use.

SCENIC DRIVES The whole area offers delightful vistas; one of the most scenic shortcuts is North Rd., which leaves Rt. 12 next to Silver Lake in Barnard and leads to Bethel. Also be sure to drive Rt. 106 to South Woodstock.

✳ To Do

BALLOONING Balloons of Vermont (802-291-4887; balloonsofvermont.com), based in Quechee, operates year-round (the two-person basket has a seat) and will launch from your home or inn (conditions permitting). **Balloons Over New England** (800-788-5562; balloonsovernewengland.com) operates seasonally from Quechee, which is also the scene of the **Quechee Hot Air Balloon Festival** on Father's Day weekend in June, New England's premier balloon festival, featuring rides as well as live entertainment and crafts (see *Special Events*).

BICYCLING Bike Vermont (802-457-3553; 800-257-2226; bikevt.com), Box 207, Woodstock. Vermont's most experienced, most personalized, and altogether best inn-to-inn tour service, offering weekend, five-, and seven-day trips through much of Vermont. Twenty-one-speed Trek and Cannondale hybrids are available for rent. Tours are also offered to Ireland.

Wilderness Trails (802-295-7620), Clubhouse Rd. at the Quechee Inn. Bike rentals for the whole family, plus maps.

Woodstock Sports (802-457-1568), 30 Central St., Woodstock, has mountain and hybrid bike rentals; offers repairs and clothing; and rents snowshoes, skates, and sleds.

WOODSTOCK COVERED BRIDGE

Christina Tree

The Start House (802-457-3377), 28 Central St., Woodstock. Open daily. A full-service ski and bike shop with rentals.

BOATING Wilderness Trails (802-295-7620), Clubhouse Rd. at the Quechee Inn, offers guided canoe and kayak trips; also rentals and shuttle service on the Connecticut, White, and Ottauquechee rivers, as well as in the Deweys Mills Waterfowl Sanctuary. Inquire about island camping.

Silver Lake State Park (802-234-9451) in Barnard rents rowboats, canoes, and kayaks.

FISHING Vermont Fly Fishing School (802-295-7620), the Quechee

Inn at Marshland Farm. Marty Banak offers lessons as well as providing tackle and guided fishing on Deweys Pond and the Connecticut, White, and Ottauquechee rivers.

GOLF Woodstock Inn and Resort Golf Club (802-457-2114; woodstockinn .com), part of the Woodstock Inn and Resort, offers one of Vermont's oldest (1895) and most prestigious 18-hole golf courses, scenic and compact, redesigned by Robert Trent Jones Sr. in 1961. Be warned that it crosses water 11 times. Tee times can be made just 24 hours in advance of play. Facilities include a pro shop, putting green and practice range, lessons, electric carts, restaurant, and lounge.

FITNESS CENTER AND TENNIS Woodstock Resort Racquet & Fitness Center (802-457-6656), part of the Woodstock Inn and Resort, Rt. 106. Indoor tennis and racquetball, lap pool, whirlpool, aerobic and state-of-the-art fitness equipment; spa treatments, facials, massage, manicure and pedicure; flexible memberships and day-use options; pro shop. There are 10 outdoor courts (4 deco turf and 6 clay) that can be rented; also lessons and equipment rental.

✍ **Vail Field**, Woodstock. Two public tennis courts and a children's playground.

HORSEBACK RIDING Woodstock has been an equestrian center for generations, especially for the hardy Morgans, which are making a local comeback in South Woodstock.

Kedron Valley Stables (802-457-1480; kedron.com), Rt. 106, South Woodstock. Generally recognized as one of the best places to ride horseback—if you know how but don't happen to own a horse—in New England. Learn to ride or spiff up your skills in the ring, or take a guided trail ride, a weekend vacation, a six-day riding clinic (with accommodations at Kendall Homestead), or a four-day inn-to-inn tour that averages 20 miles a day, five hours in the saddle. Over the years Paul and Barbara Kendall have pieced together a network of paths to link appealing inns. They lead riders over hiking and recreation trails, dirt roads, and meadows. Inquire about carriage, wagon, and sleigh rides.

The Green Mountain Horse Association (802-457-1509; gmhainc.org), Rt. 106, South Woodstock, sponsors events throughout the year including sleigh rallies, long-distance rides, and jumping and dressage competitions. Visitors are welcome at shows and other events.

POLO Quechee Polo Club. Matches are held most Saturdays at 2 PM in July and Aug. on the field near Quechee Gorge.

ROCK CLIMBING ✍ **The Wall** (802-457-2221; vermontrocks.com), just east of the intersection of Rts. 4 and 12, Quechee. Open daily. Weekday rates are adults $16, under 18 years $15; weekends $20 and $18. This indoor rock-climbing gym and bouldering cave draws serious local climbers year-round. Equipment rentals and instruction for adults and children; birthday parties a specialty. Also includes an outdoor golf driving range.

SWIMMING Silver Lake State Park (802-234-9451; vermontstateparks.com), 10 miles north on Rt. 12 in Barnard, has a nice beach. Open Memorial Day weekend–Columbus Day weekend. Another smaller beach is right next to the general store.

⚓ **The Woodstock Recreation Center** (802-457-1502), 54 River St., has two public pools, mostly for youngsters.

For **indoor pools** see *Fitness Center* above and in "Upper Valley River Towns."

✳ Winter Sports

CROSS-COUNTRY SKIING AND SNOWSHOEING **Woodstock Inn and Resort Nordic Center** (802-457-6674; woodstockinn.com), Rt. 106. A total of 60 km of some of the most varied and scenic trails for skiing and snowshoeing in New England. It utilizes the 30-km system of 1880s carriage roads on Mount Tom, climbing gently from the valley floor (700 feet) to the summit (1,250 feet), skirting a pond, and finally commanding a view of the village below and down the Ottauquechee Valley. The center itself, source of tickets, a map, ski (skating and classic stride) and snowshoe rentals (also poles), lockers and lessons, is at the Woodstock Inn and Resort Golf Club, with 10 km of gentle, meadow skiing out the door on the golf course, connecting with another 20 km of woodland trails on Mount Peg as well as snowshoe trails. Group and individual lessons; rentals; salesroom; lockers; soup and sandwiches.

Wilderness Trails (802-295-7620; quecheeinn.com), Clubhouse Rd. at the Quechee Inn, has 18 km of track-set trails, including easy loops through the woods and meadows around Quechee Gorge, offering fine views of its waterfalls, also harder trails down into the gorge. Snowshoe rentals are offered.

DOWNHILL SKIING ⚓ **Suicide Six Ski Area** (802-457-6661; woodstockinn .com), South Pomfret, 5 miles north of Woodstock on Pomfret Rd. Heir to the first ski tow in the United States, which was cranked up in 1934 but on the other side of this hill. Suicide Six is now part of the Woodstock Inn and Resort complex and has a base lodge finished with native woodwork. Its beginners' area has a J-bar; two double chairlifts climb 655 vertical feet to reach 23 trails ranging from easy to the Show Off and Pomfret Plunge, plus a half-pipe for snowboarders. Lessons, rentals, restaurant. Weekend/holiday lift rates are $57 for adults and $42 for seniors and children; weekdays (with just the big chair running) it's $38 adults, $32 seniors and children. Half-day and single-ride rates; free lifts and rentals midweek (nonholiday) to Woodstock Inn guests.

ICE SKATING **Silver Lake**, by the general store in Barnard. **Union Area**, at Woodstock Union High School, Rt. 4 west, occasionally has night skating for families. **Woodstock Sports** (802-457-1568), 30 Central St., Woodstock, offers skate and ski rentals. **Wilderness Trails** (see *Cross-Country Skiing*) in Quechee also rents skates and clears the pond on its property and across the road.

SLEIGH RIDES **Kedron Valley Stables** (802-457-1480; kedron.com), Rt. 106, South Woodstock. Weather permitting, sleigh rides are offered daily.

Three Brothers Farm (802-457-4934). Peter and Beth Mantello offer sleigh rides, tours, and carriage rides.

✳ Green Space

Mount Tom's 1,250-foot summit towers above the village of Woodstock. It's one of Vermont's most walked and walkable mountains. From Mountain Ave. in the village itself **Faulkner Park** (donated by Mrs. Edward Faulkner, one of Woodstock's most thoughtful philanthropists) features a trail patterned on Baden-Baden's "cardiac" walks. A marked, 1.6-mile path zigzags up to the summit (bring a picnic; a bench overlooks the village). The **Marsh-Billings-Rockefeller National Historical Park** encompasses more than 500 acres on the back side of Mount Tom, with 30 miles of footpaths that were originally carriage roads, including a trail to Pogue Pond. Enter on Rt. 12 at the park (follow signs) or at the trailhead on Prosper Rd., just off Rt. 12. Inquire about frequent seasonal programs offered by the national park (802-457-3368). Also see *Cross-Country Skiing* for winter use.

Mount Peg Trails begin on Golf Ave. behind the Woodstock Inn. Open May–Oct. One is roughly 5 miles round-trip, a peaceful walk up along easy switchbacks beneath pines with a picnic bench at the summit, with views west down the valley to Killington.

Quechee Gorge State Park (802-295-2990; vtstateparks.com), off Rt. 4, Quechee. This 611-acre preserve encompasses the gorge (see *Must-See*), and trails from the rim lead gently down (south of Rt. 4) into the gorge, which should be approached carefully. On a hot day it's tempting to wade into the shallow water at the south end of the gorge—but beware sudden water releases that have been known to sweep swimmers away. Ditto for the rockbound swimming hole at the north end of the gorge under the spillway. Look for picnic tables under the pines on Deweys Mills Rd. The campground (open mid-May–Oct. 15) offers 47 tent/trailer sites, seven lean-tos, and a dump station. This property belonged to a local woolen mill until the 1950s when it was acquired by the U.S. Army Corps of Engineers as part of the Hartland Dam flood-control project.

North Hartland Lake Recreation Area (802-295-2855) is a 1,711-acre preserve created by the U.S. Army Corps of Engineers to control the confluence of the Ottauquechee and Connecticut rivers. It offers a sandy beach, wooded picnic area with grills, and nature trail. Access is poorly marked, so ask directions at the Quechee information booth.

Silver Lake State Park (802-234-9451; Jan.–May 800-299-3071; vtstateparks), Rt. 12, Barnard. Campground open Memorial Day–Labor Day. On Silver Lake, good for fishing, swimming, and boating (rentals available). The park offers a snack bar and wooded campground with 40 tent/trailer sites and seven lean-tos. Hot showers.

Teagle Landing is Woodstock's vest-pocket park, a magical oasis below the bridge in the middle of town (Central St.). Landscaping and benches invite sitting a spell by the river, a tribute to Frank Teagle (1945–1997), one of Woodstock's most dedicated residents.

Dewey Pond Wildlife Sanctuary, Deweys Mills Rd., Quechee. Originally a millpond, this is a beautiful spot with nature trails and a boat launch, good for bird-watching and fishing.

Hurricane Forest, Rt. 5, White River Junction. This 500-acre town forest harbors a pond and many miles of trails. Ask directions at the Quechee information booth.

Eshqua Bog, off Hartland Hill Rd., Woodstock. A 40-acre sanctuary managed by the New England Wild Flower Society and The Nature Conservancy with a white-blazed loop trail circling through 8 acres of wetlands, with orchids blooming in summer. Ask directions locally.

Also see **Vermont Institute of Natural Science** under *Must-See.*

✳ Lodging

RESORTS ⊚ ✈ "🌴" **The Woodstock Inn and Resort** (802-457-1100; 800-448-7900; woodstockinn.com), on the green, Woodstock 05091, is the lineal descendant of the 18th-century Eagle Tavern and the famous "old" Woodstock Inn that flourished between 1893 and 1969, putting the town on the year-round resort map. Today's 142-room, air-conditioned, Colonial-style 1970s edition was created by Laurance S. Rockefeller and has been recently, thoroughly, and tastefully remodeled. The comfortably furnished main lobby is dominated by a stone hearth where 5-foot birch logs blaze late fall through spring, the glowing heart of this sociable town .A book-lined library with games and a computer and sunny Garden Room also invite guests to linger.

Vermont's best-known craftspeople have contributed to the most recent remake of guest rooms, which vary substantially in look and feel but are all fitted with marble bathrooms, down comforters, and flat-screen TVs. Among the more moderately priced rooms we prefer those in the front of the inn, overlooking the green. The most luxurious are the Tavern Rooms, with fireplace or sunroom overlooking inner garden, and two-room suites with one full bath and one half bath (sleeping two to four).

The grounds include a landscaped swimming pool, and resort facilties are spread all around the village they encompass. See *To Do* for details about the outstanding 18-hole Golf Club, the Racquet and Fitness Club, Suicide Six Ski Area, and the Nordic Center with 60 km of trails meandering out over the golf course and on Mount Tom.

The Red Rooster off the lobby is now the inn's casually elegant restaurant. Beyond a small, sleek bar, the bright space is nicely divided. Windows overlook the garden, and a there's a soothing fountain in the middle (see *Dining Out*). The formal main dining room is reserved for breakfast and functions while richly paneled Richardson's Tavern with its deep leather chairs is open evenings for drinks.

All in all the creature comforts of these pearly precincts, beautifully appointed and managed, make this one of Vermont's premier places to stay and play. Current regular-season rates are $175–680; children under 12 are free when staying in the same room with an adult. MAP available. Check out the many packages.

Twin Farms (802-234-9999; 800-894-6327; 802-234-9990 fax; twinfarms .com), Barnard 05031. There's luxury and then there's luxury. From its opening 15 years ago, Twin Farms has ranked among the world's very top resorts. Peter Jennison, for many years this book's coauthor, has noted how ironic it is that this—the former country home of Sinclair Lewis, whose novels satirized the materialism of American life in the '20s, and Dorothy Thompson, the acerbic foreign correspondent—is now a 300-acre Shangri-la for "corporate CEOs, heads of government, royalty, and celebrities," who are "welcome to unwind, frolic, and be rich together in sybaritic privacy." That said, this is authentically a place apart, with each room and cottage an amazingly crafted creation.

For instance: "The Studio," set beyond a meadow on the edge of the woods, features a two-story window and sitting room decorated with original art by the likes of Frank Stella and David Hockney. The Treehouse is squirreled in the pines and decorated in amazing twig furniture; hand-carved birds peer down on you from the top of the spiral-posted ebony bed. Of course there are fireplaces, luxurious baths, and amenities everywhere you turn. Before dinner guests gather for cocktails in the living room of the Main House and (a puzzling detail) dine off a set menu in the rustic dining room. (It's possible, however, to order almost anything you want and advisable to ask ahead of time what's being served.) The tone throughout the resort is casual, relaxed, and friendly. Of the four stylish rooms in the main house, Red's is only $1,200 a day; Dorothy's, $1,350. The 16 cottages range from $1,850 to $3,000 including meals, two bars, and the use of all recreational amenities, including the former Sonnenberg ski area, a fully equipped fitness center, Japanese furo, croquet, tennis, a pond, and mountain bikes. There are minimum stays on weekends and holidays, and an 18 percent service charge. The entire enclave can be yours for $38,000 a day. Check the Web site for current rates—which, given the economy, may include almost affordable specials.

🦐 ♂ **The Quechee Inn at Marshland Farm** (802-295-3133; 800-235-3133; quecheeinn.com), P.O. Box 747, Quechee Main St., Quechee 05059. Off by itself on a quiet side road east of Quechee Village, just up from Deweys Mills Pond and Quechee Gorge, this historic farm is a comfortable and attractive inn with 25 guest rooms. Look closely in the oldest rooms and you'll see the rough-hewn beams of the original Georgian-style house built here by Colonel Joseph Marsh in 1793. With successive centuries and owners it expanded to include a distinctive, two-story, double-porched ell. In 1954 it was actually forced to move to higher ground to escape the rising waters created by the Hartland Dam. In 1968 it became the first headquarters and accommodations for the Quechee Lakes Corporation; a decade later it was acquired by an energetic couple who established its present looks and reputation, which subsequent owners have preserved.

Rooms vary in size and feel. Three are suites; all have private bath and phone and are furnished with antiques. The brick-floored, raftered lounge with its piano, books, and games opens onto a big, sunny dining room in which breakfast and dinner (see *Dining Out*) are served. The inn is home to the Vermont Fly Fishing School and also offers canoeing and kayaking tours on the Connecticut, White, and Ottauquechee rivers, along with mountain bike rentals. In winter it maintains 18 km of groomed cross-country ski trails. Guests also enjoy privileges at the nearby Quechee Club with its 18-hole golf course, tennis courts, health center, and pools. Rates range $90–250 and include full breakfast. Inquire about packages.

I N N S 🐾 ♂ "🐕" **The Kedron Valley Inn** (802-457-1473; 800-836-1193; kedronvalleyinn.com), P.O. Box 145, Rt. 106, South Woodstock 05071. This mellow brick centerpiece of South Woodstock has been welcoming visitors since 1828 and served as a stop on the Underground Railroad. Seasoned innkeepers Tom and Cindy List are now the enthusiastic owners of this special inn, offering 27 varied guest

Christina Tree

THE KEDRON VALLEY INN

rooms divided among the main inn, the Tavern Building (vintage 1822), and the log lodge motel. The 12-acre property includes a 2-acre swim pond with sandy beach. All guest rooms have TV, A/C, and private bath; most have a fireplace. Both the pub-style Tavern and the inn dining room are gathering places for local residents as well as guests. Room rates are $125–335 double for rooms, $250 for suites, B&B. Discounts are available for May–June and for midweek, off-peak periods year-round. The inn can host receptions for up to 200. Also see *Dining Out*. The Green Mountain Horse Association and Kedron Valley Stables are within strolling distance.

☀ **Parker House Inn** (802-295-6077; theparkerhouseinn.com), 1792 Main St., Quechee 05059. A redbrick mansion built in 1857 by Vermont senator Joseph Parker beside his flannel mill on the Ottauquechee River, this inn is best known for food (see *Dining Out*) but is also a comfortable place to stay. Since acquiring it, chef Alexandra Adler and husband, Adam, have installed new baths and revamped the

rooms. The downstairs parlors are now dining rooms, but there is a small second-floor sitting room with a TV, a sunny downstairs reading nook, a breakfast room, and a riverside deck. $145–325 includes a full breakfast. Add 15 percent for service. Dogs are $30. Guests have access to Quechee Club facilities.

The Jackson House Inn (802-457-2065; 800-448-1890; jacksonhouse .com), 37 Old Rt. 4, West Woodstock 05091. This luxuriously appointed and equipped 1890 farmhouse has been expanded to include nine air-conditioned rooms and six single-room suites furnished in period antiques (from several different periods). It's all set amid 5 acres of manicured grounds and gardens, with a spring-fed pond. Rates begin at $170 in low season for the Josephine Bonaparte Room on the ground floor, furnished in the French Empire style, and at $300 for one of the four new mini suites, three of which have a thermal massage tub for two; more in foliage season. One mini suite, the Christine Jackson on the first floor, has a Brazilian mahogany four-poster queen bed, a gas fireplace, and French doors to the brick patio and garden. Rates include breakfast and a pre-dinner glass of wine and hors d'oeuvres. Also see *Dining Out*.

BED & BREAKFASTS

In Woodstock 05091

Note: Parking can be tough, hence the advantage of the many in-town B&Bs described below. All face major thoroughfares, however, you might want to request back- or side-facing rooms.

ⁱⁱ **The Charleston House** (802-457-3843; 888-475-3800; charlestonhouse .com), 21 Pleasant St. This luxurious Federal brick town house (vintage 1835) in the middle of the village is especially appealing, with period furniture in nine guest rooms, all with private bath and air-conditioning, several with fireplace and Jacuzzi. Rates are $135–290 (higher during foliage season) and include full breakfast in the dining room. Your genial hosts are Willa and Dixi Nohl (Dixi for many years managed Burke Mountain ski area in the Northeast Kingdom).

ⁱⁱ **Canterbury House** (802-457-3077; 800-390-3077; thecanterbury house.com), 43 Pleasant St. Bob and Sue Frost's village Victorian has seven air-conditioned rooms with private bath (our favorites are the original second-floor bedrooms in the front) and air-conditioning. Guests meet around the hearth in the large, gracious living room. From $160 for a back room overlooking the parking lot to $220 for Chaucer's Garret, which has a fireplace and cable TV ($135–175 in low seasons). Full breakfast.

ⁱⁱ **Ardmore Inn** (802-457-3887; 800-497-9652; ardmoreinn.com), 23 Pleasant St. A meticulously restored 1867 Greek Revival that offers five spacious rooms, each with private marble bath. The room we like best here is Tully,

with its tall four-poster, eyebrow windows, and marble bathroom. Guests breakfast around the antique Nantucket dining room table and relax in the attractive library or on the large, screened veranda overlooking the back garden. $125–225, less off-season, includes a three-course breakfast (at 8:30 sharp) and afternoon refreshments. Innkeepers Cary and Charlotte Hollingsworth are from Pasadena.

ⁱⁱ **The Woodstocker** (802-457-3896; woodstockervt.com), 61 River St. (corner of Rt. 4). Brits Dora Foschi and David Livesly have painted the exterior of this 1830s house neon yellow and decorated most of the nine rooms are both colored and decorated boldly with contemporary flare, fitted with flat screen TVs. Rooms are pictured on the website but it's bathrooms deserve closer coverage. "Westminster" features two claw foot slipper tubs and "Chelsea's" sink and tub are both a luminous ruby color that's illuminated from within. There are also traditional rooms and baths. Common space includes a well-stocked library and attractive dining room with a woodstove, the setting for generous organic breakfasts. The Inn fronts on busy Rt. 4 but rambles back along quiet River St. and is near the entrance to Faulkner Park with its walking trails up Mount Tom. Rates are $110–250 in low season, $195–340 in peak periods.

The Village Inn of Woodstock (802-457-1255; 800-722-4571; villageinnof woodstock.com), 41 Pleasant St., is a romantic pink Victorian manse with fireplaces, oak wainscoting, a fully staffed tavern (guests only), and pressed-tin ceilings. David and Evelyn Brey offer eight comfortable rooms, all with private bath and several with fireplace. Pasta dinners available Jan.–Mar. $185–320 in high season, $150–275 in low with three-course

🛏 "1" **The 1830 Shire Town Inn**
(802-457-1830; 866-286-1830;
1830shiretowninn.com), 31 South St.
Arlene Gibson is a natural host, and
her 1830 home, within walking distance of the green, has three comfortable rooms with private bath. Our
favorite is the downstairs, very private
Woodstock Room, set into the rocks
with a leafy view. The common rooms
feature wide-pine floors, hand-hewn
beams, a fireplace, and good art.
$95–170 includes a hearty country
breakfast.

Beyond the village

🐾 🛏 "1" **Deer Brook Inn** (802-672-
3713; deerbrookinn.com), 535 Woodstock Rd. (Rt. 4), Woodstock 05091.
Five miles west of Woodstock and 10
miles east of Killington's Skyeship
Gondola, George DeFina and David
Kanal have added some great decorating touches to this restored 1820 farmhouse, set back in fields across the
road from the Ottauquechee River.
The floors are wide honey-colored
pine, and each of the five rooms has a
full bath and climate-controlled heat,
radio/CD player, and air-conditioning.
A ground-floor two-room suite with a
sitting room is a delight and good for
families. Our favorite of the four second-floor rooms is Room 1, with skylights above the bed and in the
bathroom. $115–185 includes a full
breakfast served at either a common or
an individual table in the light-filled
dining room or on the stone patio
overlooking the grounds.

👶 🛏 ♿ "1" **Apple Hill Inn Bed &
Breakfast** (802-457-9135; applehill
inn.com), P.O. Box 24, 2301 Hartwood
Way, Woodstock 05091. This renovated
Vermont Cape—good for families and
pet owners—has been expanded to
maximize the spectacular 30-mile view
of the Ottauquechee and surrounding

hills, which can be enjoyed from the
big country kitchen, from the spacious
common rooms and deck, and from
two of the three guest rooms (one is a
suite with private entrance, fireplace,
and kitchenette). Eighteenth-century
antiques and Oriental rugs add a rich-
ness to light-filled spaces, as do the
surrounding fruit and vegetable gardens. An avid (organic-geared) cook
and baker, Beverlee Cook caters receptions and wedding receptions and
serves afternoon teas to outside guests
in the solarium. The vintage barn is a
venue for wedding receptions.
$135–205; $10 per extra person
includes a full, healthy buffet breakfast. There's a $15 charge for pets.

"1" **Applebutter Inn** (802-457-4158;
800-486-1734; applebutterinn.com),
P.O. Box 395, Happy Valley Rd.,
Woodstock 05091. This is a graceful
1850s Federal with wide-pine floors, a
bright, spacious dining area/library,
and an elegantly comfortable living
room with a fireplace. The six guest
rooms, each named for a different variety of apple, have private bath, A/C,
and wireless; four have working wood
fireplace or stove. Your hosts are Barbara Barry and Michael Pacht.
$100–225 per couple includes a full
breakfast and afternoon refreshments.

🛏 **Shepherd's Hill Farm** (802-457-
3087; shepherdshillfarm.com), P.O.
Box 34, 25 Hartwood Way, Taftsville
05073. High on the hill above the
Taftsville General Store, Ellen Terie
raises Polypay sheep, a breed developed in Idaho in 1976 and good for
both wool and high-quality meat. This
contemporary house on 36 acres features an open kitchen and eclectically
furnished two-story living room overlooking the valley and its hemming
hills. Ellen, an artist and psychothera-
pist, has covered the walls with varied
art. Two guest rooms share a bath and

a ground floor efficiency suite works for families. Guests are invited to collect eggs from the henhouse for their breakfast and to help with as many farm chores as they wish. These include herding sheep, picking fruit and vegetables and feeding farm animals.

🐾 ✎ **Top Acres Farm** (802-457-2135; topacresfarm@aol.com), 3615 Fletcher Hill Rd., South Woodstock 05071. This is a fabulous find for families. Milton and Pat Fullerton's 1850s gabled white-clapboard, hilltop farmhouse has been in the family—and known for the quality of its maple syrup—for four generations. There is an upstairs apartment with a fully equipped kitchen, three bedrooms, a large living and dining room, laundry facilities, TV, and VCR. Fridges are stocked for your first morning's breakfast. $125–150.

🐾 ✎ "🍴" **Inn at Chelsea Farm** (802-234-9888; innatchelseafarm.com), P.O. Box 127, Rt. 12, Barnard 05031. Some places just click the moment you walk in, and for us this classic white Cape, set back from Rt. 12 and surrounded by gardens, was one of those places. Inside spaces flow from the living room with its fireplace and are filled with quiet light, nicely decorated with original art. The three guest rooms, each named for a season (there's no "winter"), are also bright and comfortable without being fussy, and fitted with fine linens and down comforters. A large ground-floor suite has a cherry four-poster, a sofa, armchairs, a coffee table, and a TV if requested. Host Emmy Fox spent much of her life managing a prestigious Bermuda inn, and hospitality comes naturally. Children are welcome. Silver Lake State Park and its beach are just up the road. $140–180 per couple includes a full breakfast.

"🍴" **The Fan House** (802-234-9096; thefanhouse.com), P.O. Box 294, Rt.

12 north, Barnard 05031. This distinguished, 1840s clapboard house is filled with light, decorated with heirloom tapestries and antique furnishings to create the feel of an Italian farmhouse. The three artfully furnished guest rooms have private bath and are appointed with high-thread-count linens and Turkish bath sheets. Silver Lake and the Barnard General Store are within walking distance. $180–210 includes a full breakfast Inquire about Avonly Hill, the family's second B&B, with three guest rooms high on a hillside in Bethel ($180–220).

🐾 🐕 ✎ "🍴" **Bailey's Mills Bed & Breakfast** (802-484-7809; 800 639-3437; baileysmills.com), 1347 Bailey's Mills Rd., Reading 05062. As happens so often in Vermont, surprises lurk at the end of a back road, especially in the case of this venerable guest house, a few miles west of Rt. 106. With a two-story porch and fluted columns, Bailey's Mills resembles a southern antebellum mansion. The 17-room brick home includes 11 fireplaces, two

TOP ACRES FARM B&B IN SOUTH WOODSTOCK

Christina Tree

beehive ovens, a dance hall, and an 1829 general store, all part of an ambitious manufacturing complex established by Levi Bailey (1766–1850) and operated by his family for a century. Today Barbara Thaeder offers several comfortable rooms, two with working fireplace, each with a cozy sitting area and private bath, tastefully furnished with antiques. A spacious solarium makes the Honeymoon Suite especially appealing. The library with its Rumford fireplace has a large collection of fascinating books and is furnished, as is the dining room, with family antiques and "old stuff." Paths lead off across the meadows into the woods and to a swim pond. Barbara is an avid conservationist, a member of Green Hotels of Vermont. $135–189 with breakfast. (Ask about the adjacent Spite Cemetery.) Justly popular Keepers Cafe (see *Dining Out*) is minutes away.

&. "T" **Maple Leaf Inn** (802-234-5342; 800-516-2753; mapleleafinn.com), P.O. Box 273, 5890 Rt. 12, Barnard 05031. Mike and Nancy Boyle are the innkeepers in this reproduced turn-of-the-20th-century Victorian farmhouse, designed specifically as a B&B. Stenciling, stitchery, and Nancy's handmade quilts decorate the seven air-conditioned guest rooms, each with a capacious private bath, king-sized bed, sitting area, telephone, and TV/VCR. Most guest rooms have wood-burning fireplace and whirlpool bath. The parlor, library, and dining room are bright and inviting. Rates are $230–290 in high seasons, $160–220 in low, with full breakfast. The Country Garden Room on the main floor has easy access for anyone who needs special assistance, plus a whirlpool bath.

Farmhouse Inn (802-672-5433; farmhouseinnvt.com), 543 Woodstock Rd., Woodstock 05091. Six miles west of Woodstock Village, this imposing white-clapboard farmhouse sits back from the road, across the river from the Ottauquechee River and backed by a striking five-story red barn. Barry and Tory Milstone offer five second- and third-floor guest rooms with private bath and temperature control, furnished in antiques. Children are welcome, and there's a family suite with a sitting room. $135–195 includes a full breakfast. Inquire about packages ranging from romance to knitting.

Also see the October Country Inn in "Killington/Rutland Region."

MOTELS 🐾 𝒮 **Pond Ridge** (802-457-1667; pondridgemotel.com), 506 Rt. 4, West Woodstock 05091. Set way back from Rt. 4, 1.5 miles west of Woodstock Village, in 6 landscaped acres with a pond and picnic/barbecue area bordering the Ottauquechee River (swimming, fishing), this family-run motel is a real find. The 14 units are fitted with two double beds or one queen as well as air-conditioning, cable TV, and coffee machines. There are also six apartments with full kitchens, great for families. Rooms from $79 weekdays in midseason (from $110 in foliage); a two-bedroom apartment is $109–165. Children 6 and under are free.

𝒮 &. **Shire Riverview Motel** (802-457-2211; shiremotel.com), 46 Pleasant St., Woodstock 05091. Location, location. This two-story, independently owned 42-unit motel is within walking distance of downtown, and while it fronts on Pleasant St. (Rt. 4), it backs on the river and many rooms have river views and deck access. A separate new building with six upscale suites is also in back; another recently refurbished building houses three more high-end rooms. All rooms are comfortable with phone and computer hookup, furnished with two queens, two doubles, or a king. Most have a fridge, and some have gas fireplace and Jacuzzi. From $88 off-season for a standard "village view" room and $148 for a river-view room to $228 for a luxury river-view room with a gas fireplace and/or Jacuzzi.

🦌 ♨ **Farmbrook Motel** (802-672-3621; farmbrookmotel.net), Rt. 100A, Plymouth 05056. Open last week of May–third week of Oct. An unusually attractive 12-unit motel with a babbling brook and working waterwheel. Two rooms come with kitchenette; many have balcony, and some sleep five. It's a mere 3 miles from Coolidge's birthplace and handy to Killington. The beautifully landscaped grounds have outdoor fireplaces and picnic tables for summer use. $60–125 per couple; children under 12, free.

OTHER LODGING ♨ At **Quechee Lakes Resort** (quecheelakes.com) rental units range from small condos to six-bedroom houses, all with access to resort facilities, which include the golf courses and clubhouse with its indoor pool and squash courts. These can be rented through local Realtors, such as **Quechee Lakes Rentals** (802-295-1970; 800-745-0042; quecheelakes rentals.com) and **Care-free Quechee** (802-295-9500; 800-537-3962; carefree quecheevacations.com).

Note: For camping at the area's two state parks, see *Green Space.*

✳ Where to Eat

DINING OUT **The Prince and the Pauper** (802-457-1818; princeand pauper.com), 24 Elm St., Woodstock. Open daily for dinner (reservations advised). One of the state's best; "worth every calorie and dollar," we said in the first edition of this book, and we have had no reason to change our minds. For more than 25 years, owner-chef Chris Balcer's genuinely Continental cuisine has been consistently superior. Given the number of regular patrons, the $48 prix fixe changes nightly, but there are always half a dozen appetizers and entrées from which to choose. The house pâté of pork, veal, and chicken livers with sun-dried cherries and pistachios is a fixture; boneless rack of lamb in puff pastry is also always on the menu. The dining room is candlelit, elegantly rustic. In the more casual wine bar a bistro menu ($14–25) usually includes Maine crabcakes and hearth-baked pizzas.

Parker House Inn (802-295-6077; theparkerhouseinn.com), 1792 Main St., Quechee. Open for dinner daily (reservations, please); also for lunch summer weekends. Chef Alexandra Adler has brought a new look and menu to the dining rooms in this classic brick Victorian mill owner's mansion. Lace has been replaced by elegant bistro colors and napery; the taste is French. You might begin with brandy-spiked onion soup or a warm goat cheese tart, followed Moroccan lamb stew or duck cassoulet. Entrées $16–20. Light fare and cocktails are served in the riverside back bar. Lunch, when served, is on the river side deck.

Simon Pearce Restaurant (802-295-1470; simonpearce.com), The Mill, Quechee. Open for lunch (11:30–2:45) and dinner (6–9; reservations advised) daily. This is a cheerful, upbeat, contemporary place for consistently superior food, served on its own pottery and glass, overlooking the waterfall. Despite its high profile as a tourist stop (with a store that remains open through the dinner hours), it gets raves from locals for the wine list and service as well as the food. The patio is open in summer, and the Ballymaloe brown bread alone is worth a visit. Lunch

THE DINING ROOM AT SIMON PEARCE
OVERLOOKS THE OTTAUQUECHEE RIVER.

entrées could be spinach and endive salad with cheddar and apple fritters, spiced nuts, and apple vinaigrette, or beef and Guinness stew; at dinner you might begin with a Sullivan Harbor smoked trio of salmon, trout, and char, followed by crisp roast duckling with mango chutney. Dinner entrées range from $20 for ravioli to $38 for grilled filet mignon.

The Jackson House Restaurant (802-457-2065), Rt. 4 west, Woodstock. Open Wed.–Mon. Highly rated and priced. A sleekly contemporary dining room with a floor-to-ceiling double hearth and windows opening on gardens is the setting for locally sourced cuisine. The menu might include red wine braised boneless short ribs, grilled black Berkshire pork tenderloin, and locally raised chicken with grilled asparagus and caramelized onions. Entrées $25–29.

The Meadows at the Quechee Inn at Marshland Farm (802-295-3133; 800-235-3133; quecheeinn.com), Club-

house Rd., Quechee. Open nightly at 6, this country-elegant dining room is just enough off the beaten track to be a discovery, the quiet setting for dependably good food. You might dine on slow-roasted crispy duck with orange apricot demiglaze, or maple stout braised short ribs. Entrées $23–32.

∞ **The Barnard Inn Restaurant & Tavern** (802-234-9961; barnardinn restaurant.com), 10 miles north of Woodstock on Rt. 12, Barnard. Max's Tavern is open Tue.–Sat. from 5; the dining room is open Fri.–Sat. Reservations advised. Chef-owners Ruth Schimmelpfennig and Will Dodson operate this 1796 brick house with nicely appointed formal rooms. A three-course $55 prix fixe menu includes a choice of soups, salads, and appetizers such as mussels steamed in saffron and orange white wine fumé, or applewood-smoked salmon with horseradish crème fraîche. Entrées might include roast lamb with wild mushrooms and rosemary-roasted potatoes, or pork loin with roasted garlic mashed potatoes and apple-pear chutney. In the less formal Max's Tavern, the menu might range from pasta primavera with prosciutto to roast lamb top round with "fixin's." A large selection of wines and beers is available by the glass.

The Red Rooster at The Woodstock Inn and Resort (802-457-1100; woodstockinn.com), 14 the Green, Woodstock. Open daily noon–10. This casually elegant restaurant (a makeover and expansion of the former Eagle Café) is airy and inviting, decorated in light woods and bright fabrics, divided in way that permits privacy. A wall of windows overlooks the garden, a small fountain provides a soothing undertone, and a sleek bar divides the dining area from the lobby. The menu stress-es locally sourced products and produce. Lunch options feature specialty sandwiches and salads. The à la carte dinner menu includes a plate of regional cheeses. Entrées range from the inn's chicken burger to rack of lamb ($13–33). A children's menu is $12.50.

✦ **The Kedron Valley Inn** (802-457-1473; kedronvalleyinn), Rt. 106, 5 miles south of Woodstock. Open for dinner Thu.–Sun. The large, low-beamed dining room is still country elegant but more casual than in past years. You might begin with goat cheese or Brie en croute. Entrées range from locally sourced turkey burgers and sirloin burgers to chili-crusted rib eye; slow-roasted pork spare ribs with house baked beans are a specialty. Outside dining in the summer, also in the inviting pub. Entrées $11–24.

Mangowood Cafe (802-457-3312; mangowood.com), 530 Woodstock Rd. (Rt. 4), West Woodstock. Open Tue.–Sat. 6–9. Chef-owner Teresa Tan grew up in Malaysia and is a graduate of the Cordon Bleu. Be prepared for new taste combinations such as pan-seared duck breast with maple tamarind sauce and citrus almond rice, or a crispy whole fish with udon noodles and ginger scallion sauce. Don't pass up the maple ginger crème brûlée. Mango's Tavern with its fireplace is a pleasant place to begin or cap off an evening. During summer months there's dining on the terrace overlooking the Ottauquechee. A four-course prix fixe dinner is $36; à la carte entrées are $19.50.

Osteria Pane e Salute (802-457-4882; osteriapaneesalute.com), 61 Central St. (upstairs), Woodstock. Closed Nov. and Apr.; otherwise, open for dinner Thu.–Sun. (reservations recommended). Over the past dozen years Deirdre Heekin and Caleb Barber have acquired a passionate following for their commitment to slow and regional food and to authentically regional Tuscan fare, expanding from a small street-level café to a full dining room upstairs. The locally sourced menu changes daily. In autumn you might begin with a home-grown tomato salad, then dine on house-made fresh noodles served with local rabbit ragout ($16) or halibut roasted with parsley, garlic, anchovy, and capers $19). A prix fixe four-course menu is $42, but courses are also available à la carte (main courses for $18). There's also Tuscan pizza and a wine bar featuring 100 labels, all Italian

✦ **Keepers Cafe** (802-484-9090), Rt. 106 at Baileys Mill Rd., Reading. Open Tue.–Sat. 5–9, until 9:30 Fri. and Sat. The former Hammondsville Store is now one of the most popular restaurants around. Totally rebuilt, its three connecting rooms are a warm green, with finished wood floors, good-sized pedestal tables, and hardy wooden office chairs. The feel is Shaker and the food is fresh, simply presented on white ironstone, and outstanding. Choose from several salads as well as starters, then dine on the likes of herb-rubbed half chicken with mashed potatoes, Swiss chard, and a sherry-caper sauce; or grilled marinated sirloin in a green peppercorn demiglaze. Desserts might include ginger crème brûlée and an old-fashioned Bavarian layer cake. Entrées $14–21, but there's also always a "Stump's burger" ($9). The downside: no reservations for fewer than six people.

Also see **Norwich Inn**, **Carpenter and Main**, and **Skunk Hollow Tavern** in "Upper Valley River Towns," and **The Corners Inn and Restaurant** in "Killington/Rutland Area."

In Woodstock

Bentley's Restaurant (802-457-3232), Elm St., Woodstock. Open daily for lunch and dinner. The original restaurant here, an oasis of Victoriana and plants, has been expanded to include a café/ice cream parlor. A lifesaver in the middle of town, good for everything from brawny hamburgers and croissant sandwiches to veal Marsala and Jack Daniels steak. Frequent live entertainment.

Alléchante Bakery (802-457-3300), 61 Central St., Woodstock. Open weekdays 8–5, weekends 7:30–5. As in Norwich, this is a great spot for breakfast, lunch, and pastries between. The artisanal bakery offers yummy savory ham-and-cheese croissants and fabulous breads, house-made yogurt with granola for breakfast. The Sunday brunch menu includes corned beef hash with organic eggs, and a Gruyère omelet with organic salad and toasted sourdough; sandwiches might include Brie and cucumber on a baguette or avocado with Vermont extra-sharp cheddar. Inquire about Saturday Supper Club.

✿ **EastEnder Restaurant** (802-457-9800; eastendervt.com), 442 Woodstock Rd. (Rt. 4), Woodstock. Open seasonally for lunch Fri.–Sat. 11:30–2:30, dinner Tue.–Sun. (Wed. is burgers-and-margaritas night). Pleasant, casual atmosphere with a menu that changes seasonally but usually includes dishes such as chicken schnitzel, fettuccine with bay shrimp, and sirloin of lamb. Entrées $17–29, but also lighter-fare options.

Fairways Grill (802-457-6672), Woodstock Inn and Resort Golf Club, Rt. 106 south, Woodstock. Open in summer for lunch 11:30–3. This is a Woodstock insider's meeting spot for lunch but open to the public, especially appealing on sunny days when you can dine on the deck. Designer sandwiches and salads, burgers, a good grilled Reuben. During ski season hot chili and snacks are available for cross-country skiers in the fireside lounge.

Woodstock Coffee & Tea (802-457-9268), 43 Central St., Woodstock. Open Mon.–Thu. 7–5, Fri.–Sat. 7–6, Sun. 9–5. This comfortably furnished café is a village gathering center. A variety of free-trade and organic coffee roasts as well as an extensive selection of teas and fruit smoothies are offered. Exceptional corn muffins, also locally made pastries, and "quick bites" for lunch.

✿ **Mountain Creamery** (802-457-1715), Central St., Woodstock, serves breakfast daily 7–11:30, lunch until 3, pastry and espresso until 6. This is the local meeting place but less friendly to visitors than it used to be. Soups, sandwiches, salads, daily specials, and their own handmade ice cream as well as apple pie. Pies and cakes are also for sale.

In Quechee

✿ **FireStones** (802-295-1600), Rt. 4, Waterman Place, Quechee. Open daily for lunch, dinner, and Sun. brunch. Live piano music Fri. and Sat. evenings; open mike Thu. The proprietors of Bentley's (see above) also help operate this rustic, lodgelike restaurant, with a big wood-fired oven as its centerpiece, featuring made-to-order flatbreads, fire-roasted shrimp marinated in Long Trail Ale, fire-roasted chicken, and steaks. You'll also find pastas, soups, sandwiches, and salads; BBQ baby back ribs and good daily specials; and a friendly barman. Children's menu; outdoor rooftop deck.

Farmer's Diner (802-295-4600; farmersdiner.com), Quechee Gorge Village, Rt. 4. Open Mon.–Tue. 6:30–3, Wed.–Sun. till 8 PM. Locally sourced diner food, milk from local cows, cheesy fries (local potatoes, local cheese), hush puppies using local organic cornmeal. Lunch all day on the likes of a "sappy squealer" (pulled Vermont pork in house maple BBQ sauce), or a cheeseburger with freshly ground local beef, cheese, and more.

Dana's By the Gorge (802-295-6066), Rt. 4, Quechee. Open May–Nov., daily 7–11:15 and 11:45–2:45. This family-geared eatery sits smack dab in the area's single most touristed spot. Try Vermont rarebit for breakfast (an open-faced English muffin topped with Canadian bacon, Vermont cheddar, and sliced fresh tomatoes). The lunch menu features a wide selection of salads and sandwiches.

Ott Dog Snack Bar (802-295-1088), Rt. 4, Quechee Gorge. Open mid-May–mid-Oct. Family owned with the motto "Not fast food. Good food fast." Fresh soups and five different kinds of hot dogs are the specialties.

Elsewhere
Barnard General Store (802-234-9688), Rt. 12, Barnard Village. A classic general store (established 1832) but with a 1950s lunch counter serving standout breakfasts, ice cream, soups, and sandwiches as well as pizza all day. Handy to Silver Lake.

South Woodstock Country Store (802-457-3050), Rt. 106, South Woodstock. Open Mon.–Fri. 6–6, Sat. 7–6, Sun. 8–4. The only general store we know that has its own chef. Under owner Dan Noble, the store stacks staples and local specialties. Stop by for homemade muffins, omelets, or breakfast sandwiches; soups, sandwiches, and pizzas at lunch.

PICNICS On a beautiful summer or fall day the best place to lunch is outside. In Woodstock itself there's Teagle's Landing, right on Central St. by

Kim Grant

BARNARD GENERAL STORE

the river, and Faulkner Park on Monument Ave. See *Green Space* for other ideas.

The Village Butcher (802-457-2756), 18 Elm St., Woodstock. A superb butcher and a deli with sandwiches, soups, and specials to go, along with its top-flight meats, wines, and baked goods, plus homemade fudge.

SOUTH WOODSTOCK COUNTRY STORE
Christina Tree

Woodstock Farmers' Market (802-457-3658), Rt. 4 west, has a thoughtful deli case, plus soups and an outstanding selection of sandwiches, fresh fish, free-range chicken, local produce, meals to go, and Baba à Louis bread and cookies.

✳ Entertainment

Pentangle Council on the Arts (802-457-3981; pentanglearts.org), Town Hall Theater, 31 The Green, Woodstock. First-run films are shown Fri.–Mon. evenings at 7:30 in the Town Hall Theater. Live presentations at town hall and at the Woodstock Union High School include a variety of musical and other live entertainment. Check the **Town Crier** blackboard at the corner of Elm and Central streets for current happenings. Inquire about the Woodstock Film Society.

Also see *Entertainment* in "Upper Valley River Towns."

✳ Selective Shopping

ANTIQUES SHOPS The Woodstock area is mecca for antiques buffs. There are two big group galleries. **Quechee Gorge Village Antique Mall** (802-295-1550), Rt. 4, east of Quechee Gorge, open daily, is one of New England's largest antiques collectives, with two floors full of dealers. The **Antiques Collaborative** (802-296-5858; antiquescollaborative.com), Waterman Place, Rt. 4 at the blinking light in Quechee, is also open daily (10–5) and shows representative stock from more than 150 upscale dealers: period furniture usually in good condition, silver, Oriental rugs, and more.

Among the more than dozen individual dealers: **Wigren & Barlow** (802-457-2453; wigrenandbarlow.com), 29 Pleasant St., is Woodstock's most elegant antiques shop, with a large selection of fine country and formal furniture, dec-

orative accessories, and garden appointments (open daily 10–5); **Pleasant Street Books** (802-457-4050; pleasantstreetbooks.com), 48 Pleasant St., Woodstock, carries 10,000 selected titles in all fields (open daily 11–5 in summer and fall, by appointment off-season); **Fraser's Antiques** (802-457-3437), Happy Valley Rd., just off Rt. 4 in Taftsville, has a good stock of early American furniture and accessories; **Mill Brook Antiques** (802-484-5942), Rt. 106, Reading (11 miles south of Woodstock), has a shop and barn full of early American furniture, primitives, stoneware, china, quilts, and more (open year-round, but call ahead).

ART GALLERIES **Woodstock Folk Art, Prints & Antiques** (802-457-2012), 8 Elm St., specializes in contemporary carvings, prints, and antiquities. **Gallery on the Green** (802-457-4956), corner of Elm St., features original art, limited-edition prints, photography, and occasionally sculpture, from New England artists. **Polonaise Art Gallery** (802-457-5180), 15 Central St., features contemporary and traditional styles in paintings and sculpture.

ARTISANS **Simon Pearce Glass** (802-295-2711; simonpearce.com), The Mill, 1760 Main St., Quechee. The brick mill by the falls in the Ottauquechee was the 19th-century home of J. C. Parker and Co., producing "shoddy": wool reworked from soft rags. Parker was known for fine baby flannel. It closed for a spell, then served as offices for Quechee Lakes Resort. In 1981 Simon Pearce opened it as a glass factory, harnessing the dam's hydropower for his glass furnace. Pearce had already been making his original glass for a decade in Ireland, and here he quickly established a reputation for his distinctive production pieces: tableware, vases, lamps, candlesticks, and more. Visitors can watch glass being blown and can shop for individual pieces from the retail shop, along with Simon Pearce pottery. The shop (802-295-2711) is open 9–9 daily; pottery throwing can be viewed daily 9–4, glassblowing 9–9. The **Simon Pearce Restaurant** (see *Dining Out*), overlooking the falls, is justifiably one of Vermont's most popular. Simon Pearce now also operates a large, visitor-friendly glass and pottery factory in nearby Windsor (see "Upper Valley River Towns") as well as in Maryland and Pennsylvania. His glass and pottery are sold in over 300 stores throughout the country.

Charles Shackleton Furniture and **Miranda Thomas Pottery** (802-672-5175; shackletonthomas.com), The Mill, Rt. 4, Bridgewater. Open daily 10–5:30 at both places; inquire about mill tours. This couple met at art school in England and again at Simon Pearce Glass. Charles was an apprentice glassblower before he switched to furniture making; Miranda founded the pottery studio there, and the showroom carried both their work. But no longer. They have since acquired much of the Bridgewater Mill, and Charles works with more than two dozen fellow crafters to produce exquisite furniture. It's made to order, but models are displayed (along with seconds at the mill), complemented by Miranda's distinctive pottery, hand thrown and carved with traditional designs, such as rabbits, fish, and trees. Her pottery is housed in a former worker's cottage in the mill's parking lot.

Collective (802-457-1298; collective-theartofcraft.com), 47 Central St., Woodstock. An outstanding artisan-owned and cooperatively run gallery showcasing the art of some of Vermont's truly fine artisans.

David Crandall (802-672-5475), Bridgewater Mill, Rt. 4, Bridgewater. Superb, custom-styled gem and 18-karat gold jewelry.

BOOKSTORES **The Yankee Bookshop** (802-457-2411; yankeebookshop.com), 12 Central St. Established in 1935, this is Vermont's oldest continuously operated independent bookshop. It carries an unusually large stock of hardbound and paperback books for adults and children, plus cards; it features the work of local authors and publishers. It also carries toys and learning tools, kites and spinners.

Shiretown Books (802-457-2996; shiretownbooks.com), 9 Central St., Woodstock, is an intimate, very personalized shop that has a carefully selected stock of books for adults and children.

SPECIAL SHOPS

In Woodstock Village
F. H. Gillingham & Sons (802-457-2100, 800-344-6668), Elm St., owned and run by the same family since 1886, is something of an institution, retaining a lot of its old-fashioned general store flavor. You'll find plain and fancy groceries, wine, housewares, and hardware for home, garden, and farm. Mail-order catalog.

✧ **Woodstock Pharmacy** (802-457-1306), Central St. Open daily 8–6, Sun. until 1 PM. Another Woodstock institution that has branched out well beyond the basics, especially good for stationery and (downstairs) for children's toys and books.

Unicorn (802-457-2480), 15 Central St., is a treasure trove of unusual gifts, cards, games, toys, and unclassifiable finds.

Arjuna (802-457-3350), 20 Central St., is a small cornucopia of unusual collectibles and items from around the world, plus funky jewelry.

Who Is Sylvia? (802-457-1110), 26 Central St., in the old village firehouse, houses two floors of great vintage clothing and accessories for men as well as women.

Red Wagon Toy Co. Children's Shop (802-457-9300), 41 Central St., specializes in creative toys and children's clothing, from infant to size 16.

Whippletree Yarn Shop (802-457-1325), 7 Central St., has yarns, knitting patterns, sample sweaters, and gifts. Inquire about knitting classes.

In and near Quechee

F. H. Clothing Co. (802-296-6646; fathat.com), corner of Rt. 4 and Clubhouse Rd., Quechee. A business that has evolved over more than 27 years from making floppy "fat hats" to a variety of comfortable, colorful clothing. Check out the markdowns upstairs.

New England Specialties Shoppe (802-295-6163), Rt. 4, Quechee. The Laros's store, east of the gorge, has an especially large and carefully selected stock of Vermont products, from cheese, syrup, and preserves to sweatshirts and toys.

✔ **Quechee Gorge Village** (802-295-1550; 800-438-5565; quecheegorge .com), Rt. 4 at Quechee Gorge. The most elaborate of several Rt. 4 shopping complexes, it includes the **Antique Center** (see *Antiques Shops*) and **Farmer's Diner** (see *Eating Out*), a Danforth pewter shop and Cabot cheese outlet as well as the **Vermont Toy & Train Museum and Gift Shop**.

Taftsville Country Store (802-457-1135; taftsville.com), Rt. 4 east, Taftsville. Refurbished and restocked, this 1840 landmark is also still the post office and carries carefully chosen Ver-

mont gifts as well as a good selection of cheeses, maple products, jams, jellies, smoked ham, and bacon, plus staples, wine, and books. Mail-order catalog.

Scotland by the Yard (802-295-5351), Rt. 4, 3 miles east of Woodstock, imports tartans and tweeds, kilts, capes, coats, sweaters, skirts, canes, books, records, oatcakes, and shortbreads.

The Fool on the Hill (802-457-3641; thefoolonthehill.com), Rt. 4 west of Quechee Gorge. Open daily 9–5, later in fall. Closed Jan.–mud season. Ed and Debbie Kerwin's unabashed tourist trap sells pottery, gifts, and Vermont specialty foods. Memorial Day–Oct., it features corn roasting on an open flame.

Elsewhere

FARMS Sugarbush Farm (802-457-1757; 800-281-1757; sugarbushfarm .com), RR 1, Box 568, Woodstock, but located in Pomfret: Take Rt. 4 to Taftsville, cross the covered bridge, go up the hill, turn left onto Hillside Rd., then follow signs. *Warning:* It's steep. Beware in mud season, but it's well worth the effort: Sample seven Vermont cheeses, all packaged here along with gift boxes, geared to sending products to far corners of the world. In-season you can watch maple sugaring, walk the maple and nature trail, or visit with their farm animals.

On the Edge Farm (802-457-4510), 49 Rt. 12, Woodstock (2.5 miles north of Woodstock Village). An outstanding farm stand open year-round but just Fri.–Sun. in Jan. Locally raised and smoked meat as well as seasonal fruit and veggies, fresh eggs, jams, pickles, pies, and flowers.

Talbot's Herb & Perennial Farm (802-436-2085; talbotsfarm.com),

The Bridgewater Mill, Rt. 4, Bridgewater. Open daily 10–5:30. The core of this vast, yellow wooden mill dates back to the 1820s, when it worked cotton, switching to wool in the 1840s, supplying uniforms and blankets for the troops in several wars. In the 1970s when it closed, the building was saved by a local bootstrap effort and became a hive of small shops. It has had its ups and downs since, but continues to serve as an incubator for interesting enterprises, worth checking. Shackleton Thomas maintain their workspace as well as showroom here, as does David Crandall (for both of these, see *Artisans*). Randy Eysyk also makes and sells his Whisper Hill (whisperhill soaps.com) fine soaps and body oils here.

CHARLES SHACKLETON FURNITURE AND MIRANDA THOMAS POTTERY ARE BASED AT THE MILL AT BRIDGEWATER CORNERS.

Charles Shackleton Furniture/Miranda Thomas Pottery

Hartland–Quechee Rd., 3 miles south of the Rt. 4 blinker. Open mid-Apr.–Oct., daily 9–5 except Mon. Patty and David Talbot have been a popular source of local herbs, perennials, and annuals since 1971. Inquire about gardening courses.

Seasonal farmer's markets in Woodstock are Wed. on the green.

✳ Special Events

Note: Check the **Town Crier** blackboard on Elm St. for Woodstock weekly happenings.

Washington's birthday: **Winter Carnival** events sponsored by the Woodstock Recreation Center (802-457-1502).

Christina Tree

WASSAIL WEEKEND IN WOODSTOCK

March: **Home Grown Vermont**—sugaring and festival of Vermont foods.

May: **Plowing Match** (*first weekend*) among dozens of teamsters and draft horses and oxen at Billings Farm & Museum, also the scene of **Sheep Shearing**. In downtown Woodstock the **Memorial Day Parade** is worth a trip to see.

First Sunday of June: **Covered Bridge Quechee/Woodstock Half Marathon**.

Father's Day weekend: **Quechee Hot Air Balloon Festival** (802-295-7900)—a gathering of more than two dozen balloons with ascensions, flights, races, crafts show, entertainment.

July 4: **An Old Fashioned 4th** at Billings Farm & Museum includes a noon reading of the Declaration of Independence, 19th-century-style debates, games, and wagon rides.

August: **Quechee Scottish Festival** (*third Saturday*)—pipe bands, sheepdog trials, Highland dancing, more than 50 clans. **Billings Farm Quilt Show** (*all month*). Also at the farm: **Antique Tractor Parade** (*first Sunday*).

September: **Annual Vermont Fine Furniture & Woodworking Festival** at Woodstock's Union Arena (vermont woodfstival.org).

Mid-October: Quechee **antiques and crafts festivals**. **Apple & Crafts Fair** (*Columbus Day weekend*), Woodstock—more than 100 juried craftspeople and specialty food producers.

Second weekend of December: **Christmas Wassail Weekend** includes a grand parade of carriages around the Woodstock green, yule log lighting, concerts.

LOWER COHASE

*C*ohase is an Abenaki word meaning "wide valley." That's according to the chamber of commerce by that name that now embraces this gloriously little-touristed 15-mile stretch of the Connecticut River north of the Upper Valley.

Its southernmost towns are sleepy Piermont, New Hampshire, and (relatively) bustling Bradford, built on terraced land at the confluence of the Waits River and the Connecticut. Bradford is a 19th-century mill village producing plows, paper, and James Wilson, an ingenious farmer who made America's first geographic globes. Low's Grist Mill survives across from the falls, now housing a popular restaurant, and a golf course spreads below the business block across the flood-plain. From Bradford the view across the river encompasses Mount Moosilauke, easternmost of the White Mountains.

Moving upriver, Haverhill, New Hampshire, and Newbury, two of northern New England's most handsome and historic towns, face each other across the river.

Haverhill is immense, comprising seven very distinct villages, including classic examples of both Federal-era and railroad villages. Thanks to a fertile floodplain, this is an old and prosperous farming community, even now. Haverhill Corner, New Hampshire, was founded in 1763 at the western terminus of the Coos Turn-pike that wound its way up the Baker Valley and over the mountains from Ply-mouth. It became the Grafton County seat in 1773; a graceful 19th-century courthouse has recently been restored as a performance and information center. The village itself is a gem: a grouping of Federal-era and Greek Revival homes and public buildings around a double, white-fenced common.

Just north of Haverhill Corner (but south of the junction of Rts. 10 and 25) a sign points the way down through a cornfield and along the river to the site of the Bedell Bridge. Built in 1866, this was one of the largest surviving examples of a two-span covered bridge, until it was destroyed by a violent September windstorm in 1979. The site is still worth finding because it's a peaceful riverside spot, ideal for a picnic.

In North Haverhill, New Hampshire, you come unexpectedly to a lineup of modern county buildings—the courthouse, a county home, and a jail—and then you are in downtown Woodsville, New Hampshire, a 19th-century rail hub with an ornate 1890s brick Opera Block and three-story, mustard-colored railroad station. The Haverhill–Bath covered bridge, built in 1829 and billed as the oldest covered bridge in New England, is just beyond the railroad underpass (Rt. 135 north).

Newbury is one of Vermont's oldest towns, founded in 1761 by Jacob Bailey,

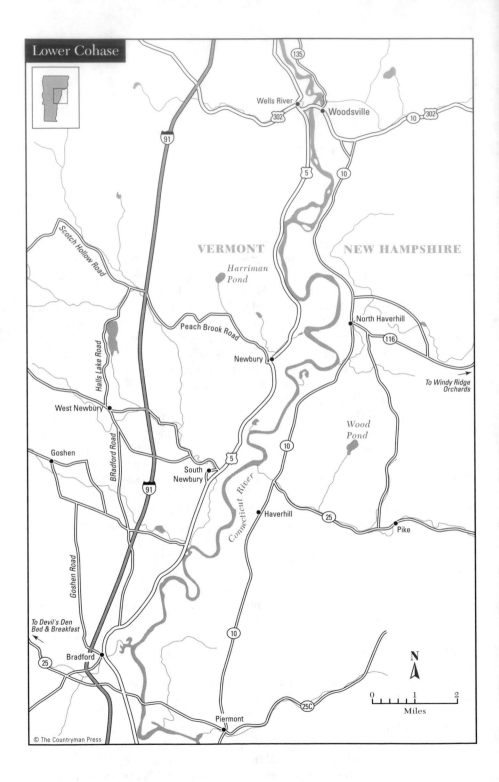

Lower Cohase

VERMONT

NEW HAMPSHIRE

Scotch Hollow Road

Harriman Pond

Peach Brook Road

Newbury

North Haverhill

To Windy Ridge Orchards

Wells River

Woodsville

Halls Lake Road

West Newbury

Wood Pond

Goshen

South Newbury

BRadford Road

Connecticut River

Haverhill

Pike

Goshen Road

To Devil's Den Bed & Breakfast

Bradford

Piermont

N

0   1   2
Miles

© The Countryman Press

a Revolutionary War general still remembered as the force behind the Bayley-Hazen Road, conceived as an invasion route northwest to Canada. It was abandoned two-thirds of the way along, but after the Revolution it served as a prime settlement route. A plaque at the northern end of the business block in Wells River (a village in Newbury) notes the beginning of the trail, while another in Hazen's Notch marks its terminus. Newbury was the site of a Native American village for many thousands of years, and its mineral springs drew travelers as early as 1800. Wells River marked the head of navigation on the Connecticut through the 1830s. In the 1840s river traffic was upstaged by the railroad, which transformed Woodsville. Wells River and Woodsville (the two are linked by a brief bridge) still represent a major highway junction (east–west Rt. 302 meets north–south Rt. 5, Rt. 10, and I-91), and some seriously good road food.

GUIDANCE Lower Cohase Regional Chamber of Commerce (802-757-2549; 866-526-4273; cohase.org) publishes a helpful map/guide and maintains a seasonal welcome center in Wells River, just west of the bridge on Rt. 302.

Alumni Hall (603-989-5500), Court St., Haverhill Corner, New Hampshire. Open mid-June–mid-Oct., Tue.–Sun. noon–4. Built gracefully in brick in 1846 as the Grafton County courthouse, later part of Haverhill Academy, and restored as a venue for performances, art shows, and the like and as a Connecticut River Scenic Byway interpretive center. Cultural map/guides and books published by the Joint River Commissions are featured, along with local information.

✳ To Do

BALLOONING See **Boland Balloons** in the "Upper Valley River Towns."

BICYCLING Given the beauty of the landscape and the little-trafficked, level nature of Rt. 10 and of this stretch of Rt. 5, the appeal to bicyclists is obvious. Less obvious are the long-distance routes that draw serious cyclists up over the White Mountains on Rts. 116 and 25.

BOATING Hemlock Pete's Canoes & Kayaks (603-667-5112) Rt. 10, North Haverhill, New Hampshire. Scott Edwards teaches at the local high school and actually makes as well as rents canoes and kayaks; guided tours, too. His shop is the barn beside Union House B&B (stay two nights and get a free rental), across from the fairgrounds.

GOLF Bradford Golf Club (802-222-5207), Bradford. Nine holes down by the river. **Blackmount Country Club** (603-787-6564; blackmountcountryclub.com), 400 Clark Rd., North Haverhill, New Hampshire Cart rentals, driving range, practice green. A par 36, nine-hole golf course.

SWIMMING Lake Tarleton State Park, Rt. 25C in Piermont, Warren, and Benton, New Hampshire. More than 5,000 acres surrounding Lake Tarleton, smaller Lakes Katherine and Constance, and much of Lake Armington are now public land divided between White Mountain National Forest conservation trusts and a state park featuring the sand beach on Lake Tarleton (part of a onetime resort). The property was slated for major development in 1994 when preservation forces, spearheaded by the Trust for Public Land, raised more than $7 million to preserve this magnificent woodland with its views of Mount Moosilauke. The lake is stocked with trout and also beautiful for canoeing and kayaking (public boat launch). Hiking trails are taking shape, including a connector to the Appalachian Trail, which passes through the property 0.5 mile from the lake.

✳ Lodging

Listed from south to north.

❧ ♿ **Piermont Inn** (603-272-4820), 1 Old Church St., Piermont, NH 03779. A 1790s stagecoach stop with six rooms, four in the adjacent carriage house (only the two in the inn are available year-round), all with private bath. The two in the main house are outstanding rooms, both carved from the tavern's original ballroom, high ceilinged and spacious, with writing desks and appropriate antiques. The carriage house rooms are simple but cheery; one is handicapped accessible. Common space includes a living room with a fireplace, TV, wing chairs, and a nifty grandfather clock. Charlie and Karen Brown are longtime Piermont residents who enjoy tuning guests in to the many ways of exploring this upper (less touristed) part of the Valley, especially canoeing the river. Rooms in the main house are $135, and in the carriage house $95. A full breakfast is available in winter for $8.

⊙ ❧ **The Gibson House** (603-989-3125; gibsonhousebb.com), RR 1, Box 193, Haverhill, NH 03765. Open June–Oct. New innkeepers Susie Klein and Marty Cohen offer imaginatively decorated rooms in one of the Valley's finest Greek Revival homes, built in 1850 on the green in Haverhill Corner. The eight guest rooms, especially the four big second-floor rooms, are artistic creations, each very different from the next. Taj North is the most opulent and exotic with its faux balcony, rich colors, and glowing stained-glass moon. We enjoyed the golden, Asian-themed Bamboo Room, but our favorite is "A Day on the Beach," sunny, blue and white with a garden view. While the house fronts on Rt. 10, the 50-foot-long sunny back porch with wicker seats and swing takes full advantage of the splendid view west across the terraced garden and the Connecticut River. A full breakfast is served in the fanciful dining room or, weather permitting, on the first-floor screened porch. $135 weekdays, $150–175 weekends includes a full breakfast.

❧ **Peach Brook Inn** (802-866-3389; peachtree@netzero.com), Doe Hill, off Rt. 5, South Newbury 05051. Joyce Emery has opened her spacious 1837 home with its splendid view of the Connecticut River. What a special place! Common space includes two nicely furnished parlors with exposed beams and a fireplace, an open kitchen, and a screened porch with a view of Mount Moosilauke across the river. The house is on a country lane in the almost vanished village of South Newbury, once connected to Haverhill, New Hampshire, across the river by a long-gone covered bridge. Plenty of farm animals are within walking distance. There are three comfortable guest rooms; $70–75 with shared bath, $80–85 with private, including full breakfast. No smoking. No children under 10, please; under 18 are $10.

⁰1⁰ **The Hayloft Inn at Blackmount** (603-787-2367; prfctlie@earthlink.net), 440 Clark Pond Rd., North Haverhill, NH 03774. The plain exterior of this house belies its airy, open post-and-beam interior. Innkeeper Joyce Read is

a native of Plainfield, New Hampshire, where her mother modeled as a young girl for painter Maxfield Parrish. Read has been collecting the artist's distinctive prints all her life and displays them in a special gallery room. There are two bright, tastefully furnished upstairs guest rooms ($85) and a ground-floor room with a king bed and sitting area. All rooms have A/C and TVs. A hearty breakfast is served at 8 AM. The golf links at Blackmount Country Club is next door.

✿ ᕐ ⁿᛏⁿ **The Whipple-Tree Bed & Breakfast** (802-429-2076; 800-466-4097; whipple-tree.com), 487 Stevens Place, Wells River 05081. High on a wooded slope with views across the valley to the White Mountains, William Bailey has built a splendid home designed as a bed & breakfast with six spacious guest rooms, all with private bath. Carol Bailey's decor throughout is casual, country elegant. Amenities include A/C and TVs, a guest fridge, a game room, and a big outdoor hot tub. Bill Bailey is, incidentally, the great-great-great-great-grandson of General Jacob Bailey, the Revolutionary War hero responsible for the Bayley-Hazen Road (see chapter introduction). While the feel is remote, the house is just over 2 miles up country roads from Rt. 302 and little more than that from I-91, Exit 17. A full country breakfast is included in rates of $140–190; $15 per extra person.

🐾 ✿ ᕐ ⁿᛏⁿ **Nootka Lodge** (603-747-2418; 800-626-9105), 4982 Dartmouth College Hwy. (junction of Rts. 10 and 302), Woodsville, NH 03785. This attractive 34-unit log motor inn offers efficiencies, connecting rooms for families and two-bedroom suites with Jacuzzi and fireplace. Amenities include TV, A/C, a pool, indoor whirlpool, and game room.

Also see **South Road Pottery** under *Selective Shopping*, and **Silver Maple Lodge** in "Upper Valley River Towns."

✳ Where to Eat

DINING OUT **The Perfect Pear Café** (802-222-5912; theperfectpearcafe.com), the Bradford Mill, Main St., Bradford. Open for lunch Tue.–Sat. 11:30–3, dinner Tue.–Sun. 5–8:45. Jan.–Apr., closed for dinner Mon.–Wed. Dinner reservations recommended. Chef-owner Adam Coulter's charming bistro is housed in a historic brick mill by a falls. It's especially appealing in summer when there's dining on the flower-decked patio overlooking the Waits River, churning along because the big falls are just across the road. Lunch is reasonably priced with choices like Gorgonzola and candied walnut salad with maple balsamic vinaigrette, and a lamb and rosemary sausage sandwich on whole grain with honey mustard. Dinner entrées might include crabmeat-stuffed rainbow trout with a pesto cream, or house-smoked pork loin with sauerkraut, pomegranate glaze, and roasted corn salsa. Dinner entrées $14.99–21.99.

🦞 ✿ **Warners Gallery Restaurant** (802-429-2120), just off I-91, Exit 17, 2284 Rt. 302, Wells River. Open Tue.–Sat. 5–9 PM, Sun. 11–8 with brunch 11–2. This is a find, a dependable all-American family restaurant with an eating-out, candlelit atmosphere. Entrées usually include twin stuffed lobster tails, a fisherman's platter, and roast prime beef au jus. Dinner entrées run $13–23 and include the generous salad bar. On Tuesdays the sirloin, haddock, and BBQ chicken are all $10 (we took advantage of this!); Wednesday is "bring a friend" (half price on the second dinner), and on Friday kids eat free. The Sunday buffet draws folks from throughout the North Country. Full liquor license.

EATING OUT For lunch in Bradford/Piermont, check **Perfect Pear** under *Dining Out.*

Colatina Exit (802-222-9008), Main St., Bradford. Open daily from 11. Vincent and Angela Windell's expansive trattoria features a wood-fired pizza oven. We still like the original dining room best: candles in Chianti bottles, Italian scenes on the walls, checked (green in summer, red in winter) tablecloths, and a few tables in back with a view of the river. The big menu offers plenty of antipasto and insalata choices and traditional Italian dishes like chicken Marsala. The specialty is campfire steak di Costello (fire seared with crispy onions). Plenty of pizza choices, paninis, and calzones. There's also an upstairs pub with river views.

Bliss Village Store and Deli (802-222-4617), Main St., Bradford. Housed in a former 19th-century hotel, this is a classic general store but with Crock-Pots full of soup, chili, or stew-fried chicken and a deli with daily specials. Tables are in the back—including a booth with the best river view in town.

Newbury Village Store (802-866-5681), 4991 Rt. 5, Newbury. Open 6 AM–8 PM weekdays, Sat. 7–8, Sun. 8–6. This is the new breed of general store. Gary and Maggie Hatch have added comfortable seating near the periodicals and expanded the deli to feature sandwiches named for local landmarks like "The Oxbow" ("basil herb-roasted turkey breast with Vermont cheddar, ripe tomatoes, leaf lettuce and the house garlic cream cheese spread on multi grain bread"). There's also a hummus wrap and "The Flatlander" ("shaved black pastrami warmed and piled high on rye and pumpernickel swirl bread, topped with swiss cheese

NEWBURY VILLAGE STORE

Christina Tree

and deli mustard"). There are staple groceries, also a selection of wine and Vermont products. Locals tells us these are the best sandwiches around. Creative pizzas are a specialty. Tables in the back, overlooking the Connecticut, within earshot of a town carillon that plays "Come Let Us Gather at the River."

⌀ **The Happy Hour Restaurant** (802-757-3466), Rt. 5, Wells River. Open daily 11:30–8, later in summer. This large, pine-paneled family restaurant in the middle of town has been lightened and brightened in recent years and hums with a sense of friendly service and satisfied patrons. Most entrées include the salad bar—and servings are generous. We couldn't finish a tender sirloin topped with red wine mushroom sauce, with baked potato and good coleslaw (a $12.99 special). Dinner entrées $11.99–17.99. "Pub Fare" is less. Children's menu.

Shiloh's Cabin Cooking (603-747-2525), 202 Central St., Woodsville. Open 7 AM–9 PM, closing Sun. at 8 PM. Nicole and Miranda Fenoff fill the need for good road food in Woodsville. The beef and as many ingredients as possible are local.

P&H Truck Stop (802-429-2141), just off I-91, Exit 17, on Rt. 302, Wells River. Now open just 6 AM–10 PM for hot meals but still 24 hours for to-go premade sandwiches, pies, and the like. Dozens of rigs are usually parked on one side, and the range of license plates on cars in the other lot is often broad. This is a classic truck stop with speedy service, friendly waitresses, and heaping portions at amazing prices. Plus, the bread is homemade; ATM and phone are available (cell phones don't tend to work around here, and pay phones are scarce).

ICE CREAM Mountain Scoops, Rt. 10, North Haverhill, New Hampshire. Open Memorial Day–Columbus Day 11–9. This colorful stand in the middle of town is the source of Rhonda Abrams's homemade ice cream.

✳ Entertainment

Old Church Community Theater (802-222-3322; oldchurchtheater.org), 137 Main St., Bradford. For more than 20 years this community theater has presented seasonal, family-geared productions.

Alumni Hall (603-989-5500), Court St., Haverhill Corner, New Hampshire. Open mid-June–mid-Oct., 10–4. Built gracefully in brick in 1846 as the Grafton County courthouse, later part of Haverhill Academy and recently restored as a venue for concerts and other performances, art shows, and the like. Call for current schedule.

Summer band concerts can be found in Bradford, Woodsville, and Haverhill; for details see cohase.org.

✳ Selective Shopping

SPECIAL SHOPS Copeland Furniture (802-222-5300; copelandfurniture .com), 64 Main St., Bradford. Open Mon.–Fri. 10–6, Sat. 10–5. Contemporary, cleanly lined, locally made furni-

BRUCE MURRAY IS A POTTER IN BRADFORD.

Christina Tree

ture in native hardwoods displayed in a handsome showroom in the converted 19th-century brick mill across from Bradford Falls. Seconds.

Farm-Way, Inc. (800-222-9316), Rt. 25, Bradford. One mile east of I-91, Exit 16. Open Mon.–Sat. until 8 PM. Billed as "complete outfitters for man and beast," this is a phenomenon: a family-run source of work boots and rugged clothing that now includes a stock of more than two million products spread over 5 acres: tack, furniture, pet supplies, syrup, whatever. Recently expanded: Shoes and boots remain a specialty, from size 4E to 16; 25,000 shoes, boots, clogs, sandals, and sneakers in stock; also kayaks, sporting equipment, furnishings, and gifts.

South Road Pottery (802-222-5798; brucemurraypotter.com), 3458 South Rd., Bradford. Open May–Oct., 10–5. Bruce Murray is a long-established, nationally known potter whose stu-

dio/showroom is in a timber-frame 18th-century barn surrounded by farm fields. It's well worth the scenic drive to this exceptional, long-established studio with its wide variety of hand-made and hand-decorated stoneware, both functional (lamps, vases, unusual butter dishes—really mini crocks that keep butter soft) and decorative (wall tiles and plaques). Inquire about workshops and about the **Barn Bridge Guest Room**, an attractive guest unit with a private deck, bath, and galley kitchen ($150 per night).

Round Barn Shoppe (603-272-9026), 430 Rt. 10, Piermont, New Hampshire. Open May 2–Christmas, Thu.–Mon. 9–5; Jan.–May 1, Fri.–Sun. This 1990s post-and-beam round barn replicates the authentic 1906 barn across the road. It houses a shop selling New England products ranging from baskets and dolls to local dairy milk and fresh pies, ice cream, fudge, and cheese.

FOUR CORNERS FARM IN SOUTH NEWBURY

Christina Tree

Woodsville Bookstore (603-747-3811), 91 Central St., Woodsville, New Hampshire. Dave Major's friendly, well-stocked bookstore is an unexpected oasis, fully stocked and totally independent. One room of new, one of used books.

FARMS Four Corners Farm (802-866-3342; 4cornersfarm.com), 306 Doe Hill Rd., just off Rt. 5, South Newbury. Bob and Kim Gray sell their own produce and flowers. An exceptionally pretty farm, just off but up above the highway, with a big farm stand. Known for strawberries, but always a trove of seasonal fruits and vegetables with year-round produce from their greenhouses, Christmas trees, PYO berries in-season.

Windy Ridge Orchard (603-787-6377; windyridgeorchard.com), Rt. 116, North Haverhill, New Hampshire. Open daily Labor Day–Thanksgiving, 9–6; weekends Thanksgiving to Christmas, 9–4. Pick your own apples and pumpkins, farm animals, kids' corral playground, nature trails, picnic tables, Cider House Café, gift shop. Apple picking begins in mid-August and lasts through mid-October depending on the variety. There are 3,500 apple trees on 20 acres, overlooking the Valley and Green Mountains; also cut-your-own Christmas trees.

Flag Hill Farm/Vermont Hard Cyder (802-685-7724; flaghillfarm.com), Vershire. Vermont Hard Cyder is produced on this 250-acre hilltop, organic family farm with panoramic views. Sabra and Sebastian Ewing welcome visitors but need warning to dispense directions (MapQuest seems to have it wrong). Check out their sparkling Hard Cyder, Still Cyder, and Pomme-de-Vie at stores throughout Vermont.

Look for seasonal **farmer's markets** in **Bradford** (Sat. 9–1), **Piermont** (Tue. 3–6), and **Woodsville** (Fri. 4–7).

✳ Special Events

Memorial Day weekend: Open studio tours (cohase.org and vermontcrafts.com).

July: **4th of July Parade and celebration** in Woodsville and Wells River—marching bands, floats, horses, chicken barbecue, dancing, fireworks. **Connecticut Valley Fair** (*mid-month*), Bradford. Ox and horse pulling, sheep show, midway, demolition derby. **Cracker Barrel Bazaar** (*third or final weekend*), Newbury, includes fiddlers' contest, antiques show, quilt show, sheepdog trials, church suppers. The **North Haverhill (New Hampshire) Fair** (*last weekend*) is an old-style fair with ox and tractor pulls, pig races, and more.

Last weekend of September: **Whole Hog Blues & BBQ Festival**—blues music by leading bands, roast pig cook-off, arts and crafts.

Weekend before Columbus Day: **Vermont North by Hand**—25 crafts and art studios hold open house (cohase.org).

Central Vermont 3

THE WHITE RIVER VALLEYS

SUGARBUSH/MAD RIVER VALLEY

BARRE/MONTPELIER AREA

KILLINGTON/RUTLAND AREA

Christina Tree

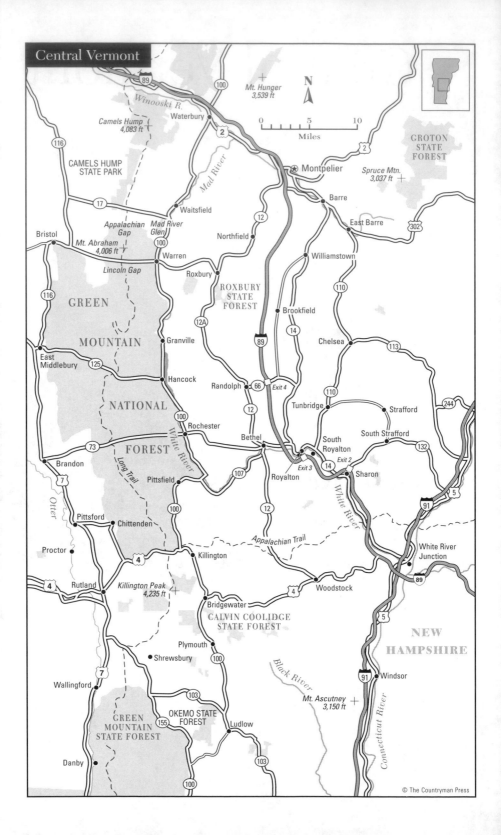

THE WHITE RIVER VALLEYS

"Vanishing Vermont" could be the subtitle for this chapter. As I-89 sweeps up through central Vermont in a grand 52-mile arc—from White River Junction to Montpelier—it yields a series of panoramas. Motorists see the high wall of the Green Mountains beyond the Braintree Range on the west and catch glimpses of an occasional valley village. What they don't see is one of Vermont's best-kept secrets: the classic old villages, abrupt valleys, and hill farms along the White River and its three branches.

The White River rises high in the Green Mountains above Granville Gulf and rushes down through Hancock, widening and slowing among farms in Rochester, keeping company with Rt. 100 until Stockbridge, where its course dictates a dog-leg in the highway. Turning sharply east and carving a narrow valley for Rt. 107 (the Gaysville reach is an especially challenging one for kayakers during spring freshets), the river reaches Bethel and begins to parallel Rt. 14 and I-89. As it courses through the Royaltons and Sharon, it's joined by the three northern branches; both tubing and fishing possibilities increase.

Each of these streams, rising some 20 miles north of the main stem of the river, has carved its own valley. The First Branch, shadowed by Rt. 110, threads six covered bridges, lush farmland, and the unself-consciously beautiful villages of Chelsea and Tunbridge. The Second Branch begins above pictur-esque Pond Village in Brookfield, known for its floating bridge, and flows south along Rt. 14. The Third Branch rises in Roxbury, conveniently near a fish hatchery, and flows south through a lonely valley (along Rt. 12A) to Randolph, one of the area's few I-89 exits and an Amtrak stop as well as the only commercial center of any size in this entire area.

Beautiful as these valleys are, the high east–west roads that connect them, climbing up over the hills and

CHELSEA VILLAGE

Christina Tree

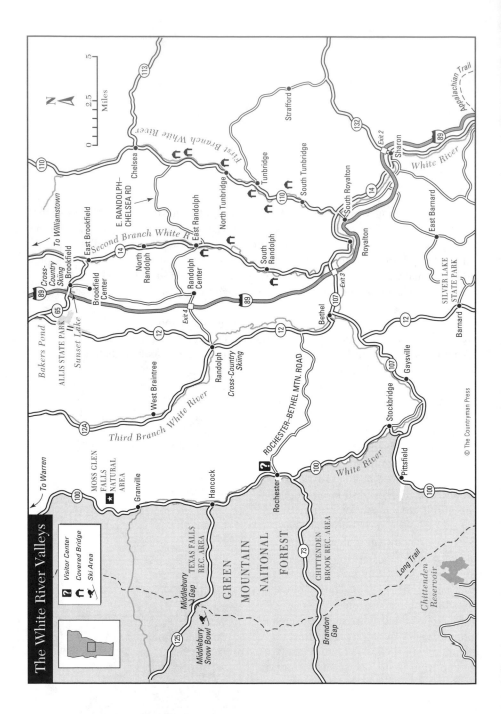

The White River Valleys

Legend:
- ? Visitor Center
- ⊏ Covered Bridge
- Ski Area

© The Countryman Press

5
2.5
0
Miles

N

Appalachian Trail

89
Exit 2
Sharon
White River
132
Strafford

East Barnard

SILVER LAKE STATE PARK
Barnard

14
South Royalton
Royalton
Exit 3
107
Bethel
12
Gaysville
107
Stockbridge
White River
Pittsfield
100

South Tunbridge
Tunbridge
North Tunbridge
110
South Randolph
East Randolph
Randolph Center
North Randolph
Second Branch White R.
14
East Brookfield
To Williamstown

Chelsea
110
First Branch White River
E. RANDOLPH–CHELSEA RD

89
Exit 4
89
65
Cross-Country Skiing
Brookfield
Brookfield Center
ALLIS STATE PARK
Sunset Lake
Bakers Pond

12
West Braintree
Randolph Cross-Country Skiing
12A
Third Branch White River

113

ROCHESTER–BETHEL MTN. ROAD

To Warren
100
MOSS GLEN FALLS NATURAL AREA
Granville
Hancock
? Rochester
100

Middlebury Gap
TEXAS FALLS REC. AREA
125
Middlebury Snow Bowl

GREEN MOUNTAIN NAITONAL FOREST

73
CHITTENDEN BROOK REC. AREA

Brandon Gap

Long Trail
Chittenden Reservoir

down into the next valley, are more rewarding still. To begin exploring this backroaded and unresortified heart of Vermont, you might exit in Sharon and climb through the Straffords to Tunbridge and north to Chelsea, west to Brookfield, then south to Randolph, on down Rt. 12, and west over Rochester Mountain. See *Scenic Drives* for tours that can pleasantly fill many days.

GUIDANCE Randolph Area Chamber of Commerce (802-728-9027; 877-772-6365; randolphvt.com), 31 Rt. 66, Randolph 05060. Phone answered and office open year-round, weekdays 8:30–4; information center maintained Memorial Day–mid-Oct. at State Plaza just off I-89, Exit 4 (next to the Mobil station).

Christina Tree

WILL'S STORE IN CHELSEA

♿ **Sharon Northbound Information Center and Vermont Vietnam Veterans' Memorial** (802-281-5216), I-89, Sharon. Open 7 AM–11 PM. Not what you expect to find at a roadside rest area. The 7,000 names on the memorial itself represent all the Vermonters who served in the Vietnam War, which is recalled through exhibits that include a time line and film clips. Also unexpected here: a "living greenhouse" filled with plants and descriptions of how they recycle waste. The center is staffed, a good source of local information. The restrooms, incidentally, are outstanding.

Green Mountain National Forest Ranger District Office and Visitor Center (802-767-4261), Rt. 100 in Rochester. Open 8–4 daily (except Sun.) Memorial Day–Columbus Day, weekdays off-season. A magnificent center (restrooms) with detailed information on hiking, biking, picnicking, bird-watching, camping, and other recreation in this part of the GMNF.

The *Herald of Randolph* (802-728-3232), Box 309, Randolph, a weekly published on Thursday, carries local news and events for Orange and northern Windsor counties.

GETTING THERE *By train:* **Amtrak's** Vermonter (800-USA-RAIL; amtrak .com). Randolph and White River Junction (see "Upper Valley River Towns") are stops for trains from Washington, DC, and New York City via Springfield and Amherst, MA.

By bus: **Stagecoach Transportation Services** (802-728-3773; stagecoach-rides .org) offers service from the Randolph train depot to Bethel, Randolph, Rochester, and Hancock.

By car: This area covers a wide, hilly swath of Vermont. I-89 runs diagonally across it, but with only three exits (Sharon, Bethel/Royalton, and Randolph).

GETTING AROUND *By taxi:* **JT's Taxi & Courier** (802-728-6209) is based in Randolph.

By rental car: **Especially Imports** (802-728-4455), Rt. 66, Randolph, can arrange to meet you at the train.

WHEN TO GO Rochester offers winter cross-country skiing, and Tunbridge draws Vermonters for the Vermont History Expo in June and the World's Fair in September. March brings sugaring; in May there's kayaking and in summer, tubing along the lower reaches of the White River. In July there are old-fashioned Independence Day parades, the biggest one in Randolph. Labor Day weekend, that same town is the site of the New World Festival, with performances by more than 100 old-time northern New England and Canadian musicians. Given its scattering of appealing places to stay, its farms, and its back-road scenery, this is a rewarding getaway area anytime except mud season (April and early May).

MEDICAL EMERGENCY Call **911** or **Gifford Medical Center** (802-728-4441), 44 S. Main St., Randolph.

✳ Villages

Sharon Village. An old commercial center at the junction of the river road (Rt. 14) and the high road (to Strafford), this remains a cluster of services just off I-89. The columned **Sharon Trading Post** is a classic general store with a serious meat department, also selling local maple products. The **Sharon Historical Society**, also at this crossroads, is open summer Sundays (1–3) and in early August on Old Home Day—a lively event at which guests over 70 can eat free at the chicken pie supper.

South Royalton Village. On a bend in the river and off Rt. 14, this classic railroad village frames an outsized green with two bandstands and a Civil War cannon. A granite arch recalls the 1780 raid on Royalton by more than 300 Native Americans commanded by an English lieutenant. The railroad hotel, an 1887 brick Queen Anne–style commercial block, the train depot, and many of the clapboard buildings within eyeshot have all received a new lease on life thanks to the presence of Vermont Law School. Founded in 1972 and headquartered in a tower-topped old school building, this draws students from around the country. In the village of **Royalton**, north on Rt. 14, most buildings predate the Civil War.

Tunbridge. Some 20,000 people jam into this village of 400 for four days each September. They come for the **Tunbridge World's Fair**, first held in 1867. Sited in a grassy, natural bowl by a bend in the river, it has everything an agricultural fair should have: a midway, livestock displays and contests, a Floral Hall, collections of old-time relics, dancing, sulky racing, a fiddling contest, horse pulls, a grandstand, and more. Known as the "Drunkards Reunion" during a prolonged era when it was claimed that anyone found sober after 3 PM was expelled as a nuisance, it's now a family event. In June the fairgrounds are also the site of the wonderfully colorful annual **Vermont History Expo**, showcasing Vermont historical societies from around the state with displays, reenactments, music, and much more. Tunbridge boasts four covered bridges (see our map), a fishing hole, and a photogenic brick Methodist church (in South Tunbridge).

Strafford. If it were any nearer a highway, this quietly spectacular village would be mobbed with tourists. Happily, it's 9 miles north of I-89, and not on the way to anywhere except Tunbridge. Coming *from* Tunbridge, the road climbs steeply through woods and fields, finally cresting and beginning its downhill run through beautifully restored farms with ponds out back (pools would be too garish), stables, and other signs of wealth not evident on the western side of the mountain. Aristocratic homes—which include the Gothic Revival **Justin Morrill Homestead**—cluster near the common, at the head of which stands the churchlike white-clapboard Town House, built in 1799, so classic it's a staple of New England photo books.

Chelsea. A village with not just one but two picturesque commons and twin brick 1818 general stores. Noteworthy buildings also include a steepled church, the Orange County Courthouse, a brick library, a bank (since 1822), and many Federal-era homes. An amazing number of services—post office, restaurants, barber, and fish and wildlife office—are compressed into a small space.

Brookfield. "Pond Village," as it's known, easily ranks among the most picturesque four-corners in all New England. It boasts the state's oldest continuously operating library (established in 1791) and Sunset Lake, traversed by a floating bridge, buoyed by barrels (the lake is too deep to support a pillared span) but frequently sagging in the middle. During summer much of its traffic stops midway to fish, and on the last Saturday in January it's a coveted viewing point for one of New England's last ice-harvest festivals. At the center of the village are Green Trails Inn and Ariel's Restaurant, which draws diners from a 50-mile radius. **Allis State Park**, a few miles west, offers camping, picnicking, and a sweeping view. The **Marvin Newton House**, Ridge Rd. in Brookfield Center, is an eight-room home built in 1835, now housing local historical exhibits (open Sundays in July and Aug., 2–5; $2; 802-276-3927).

POND VILLAGE, BROOKFIELD

Christina Tree

Bethel (population: 1,968). At the confluence of the White River and its Third Branch as well as of Rts. 107 and 12, this was once a major source of white granite used to face such buildings as Washington, DC's, Union Station. An eight-sided former school, now a community center, stands on Rt. 14 in West Bethel.

Randolph (population: 4,800). **Randolph Center** (east on Rt. 66 from I-89, Exit 4) is clearly the oldest of the five Randolphs. It's a lineup of brick and clapboard Federal-era mansions along a main street that was cut unusually wide with the idea that this might be the state capital. Instead it's now a quiet village in which life centers on **Floyd's General Store** and the nearby complex of **Vermont Technical College**, grown from the grammar school built here in 1806. According to a historical marker, musician and schoolmaster Justin Morgan brought a young stallion from Massachusetts to his home here in 1789 (Justin Morgan the man lies buried in the nearby cemetery; the grave of Justin Morgan the horse is marked by a simple stone off Rt. 110 in Chelsea). Randolph remains a horsey community, but with the arrival of the railroad in the mid–19th century, population shifted from the center down to the valley, 3 miles west (now the other side of I-89). It's here that Amtrak now stops, at the station steps from the **Chandler Center for the Arts**, a lively town-owned performance center. The **Randolph Historical Society Museum** (802-728-6677), upstairs in the police station, exhibits memorabilia, with the emphasis on railroading; three rooms are furnished in circa-1900 style. (Open third Sun. in May–Oct., 2–4; also July 4.) On Main Street check out Belmains, a well-stocked representative of that vanishing breed: "the five-and-dime." Randolph's **Independence Day parade** is one of the biggest around.

Rochester (population: 1,200) straddles Rt. 100 in a quiet valley between the Green Mountains and the Braintree Range. The village centerpiece is 4-acre Rochester Park, a classic green with a bandstand, the scene of Sunday concerts. Just north of the park a walkable lineup of mismatched buildings is full of surprises. There's a locally owned supermarket (Mac's), a heavy-duty hardware store/laundry, a serious bike shop, two major galleries, a bookstore, plus your choice of cafés and dining options. Lodging ranges from an upscale inn and luxurious hideaways to a family-geared working dairy farm. The approach over Rochester Mountain provides panoramic views and a delightful alternation of field and forest. North of the village on Rt. 100 the **Green Mountain National Forest Visitor Center** orients sportsmen, picnickers, and hikers to the largely uninhabited western portion of the town that lies within the GMNF. The Bingo area, in particular, offers swimming holes, abandoned town roads, cellar holes, and Civil War–era cemeteries. Rochester also has a nine-hole golf course and serves as a center for mountain biking and for backcountry

DOWNTOWN ROCHESTER

Christina Tree

cross-country skiing. The **Rochester Historical Society** (802-767-4453) is upstairs in the library. Summer brings a variety of music, inside and out, but everything about Rochester is very low-key.

✳ To See

Justin Morrill Homestead (802-828-3051; morrillhomestead.org), Rt. 132, Strafford Village. Open Memorial Day–Columbus Day, Sat.– Sun. 11–5; tours on the hour, $5. Justin Morrill never went to college but is remembered as the congressman who sponsored the Land Grant Colleges Acts

JUSTIN MORRILL HOMESTEAD IN STRAFFORD

(one in 1862 and another in 1890) that created more than 76 present institutions, currently enrolling some 2.9 million students. Many have evolved into state universities. The son of a Strafford blacksmith, Morrill made enough money as a country storekeeper (which he parlayed into a chain of stores) to retire at age 38 and enter politics on an antislavery and temperance platform. He served in Congress for 44 years (1855–98), never finding much time to spend in his striking, 17-room Gothic Revival mansion because he kept getting reelected. A man who was instrumental in the design and construction of the Washington Monument and the Library of Congress, Justin Morrill helped design his own house and (now restored) gardens and orchard. The icehouse and carriage barn are fitted with interpretive panels about Morrill and the many national events in which he played a role. Inside and out, this is a fascinating house, well maintained by the Vermont Division for Historic Preservation and Friends of the Morrill Homestead. Inquire about frequent events including the Heritage Crafts Weekend and 19th-century apple festival, along with programs such as painting, landscape gardening, village walks, and more.

Floating Bridge at Sunset Lake, Brookfield Village. First built in 1820 and replaced six times since, this is the only heavily used bridge of its kind in the country. It's quite picturesque. On our last visit it was sagging badly.

Joseph Smith Memorial and Birthplace (802-763-7742), Dairy Hill Rd., South Royalton. Open year-round: May–Oct. 9–7 daily, 1:30–7 Sun.; otherwise closing at 5. A marker on Rt. 14 (1 mile southeast of the village) points you up a steep, 2-mile hill to a complex maintained by the Church of Jesus Christ of the Latter-day Saints. The property itself begins with a steep hill of maples leading to a hilltop

THE JOSEPH SMITH MEMORIAL AND BIRTHPLACE, SOUTH ROYALTON

Christina Tree

visitor center with paintings, sculpture, exhibits, and a film housed in two buildings. A 38.5-foot-high shaft, cut from Barre granite in 1908, marks the site of the farm on which the founder of the Church of Jesus Christ of Latter-day Saints was born in 1805 and lived until he was 10. Each foot on the shaft marks a year in the life of the prophet, who was murdered by a mob in Carthage, Illinois, in 1844. The 360 well-maintained acres include picnic tables.

Porter Music Box Museum & Gift Shop (802-728-9694; 800-811-7087; porter musicbox.com), Rt. 66 between I-89 and downtown Randolph. Open May–Dec. (call for hours). Small admission. The former home and office of Dwight and Mary Porter and the Porter Music Box Company. A large collection of music boxes is displayed, and both boxes and recordings are sold.

Texas Falls, Hancock. On Rt. 125 west of Rt. 100 in Hancock; a sign points to the road to the falls. It's 0.25 mile. The falls are an exceptional series of shoots and pools, rimmed by interesting rock formations and spanned—until a flood in 2008—by footbridges. A short, steep (be careful) trail still leads down to the falls. A quarter mile farther up the road (also damaged in '08) is a picnic area with grills and outhouses. At this writing repairs are planned. The falls are not far off Rt. 125, worth walking in if you have to.

TEXAS FALLS

Kim Grant

SCENIC DRIVES **The Quickie Tour**: Sharon to South Royalton via Strafford and Tunbridge (22 miles). Take I-89 to Exit 2, Sharon, and climb Rt. 132 to Strafford, site of the Justin Morrill Homestead and the Town House. Continue up and over the hills and down into Tunbridge. If time permits, turn north on Rt. 110 for 5 miles and past three covered bridges (see the sidebar) to Chelsea. Otherwise turn south on Rt. 110 for the 5 scenic miles back (past one covered bridge) to Rt. 14 at South Royalton and pick up I-89 again at Exit 3 in Royalton, or turn back down Rt. 14 to Sharon. En route you pass the turnoff for the Joseph Smith Memorial.

Royalton to Randolph via Granville Gulf (117 miles). Take I-89 to Exit 3, just west of Eaton's Sugar House. The low road west (Rt. 107) follows the White River to Rt. 100, but the high road over **Rochester Mountain** saves 11 miles and is beautiful besides. At the junction in Bethel take Rt. 12 north a little more than 2 miles and turn left onto Camp Brook Rd. At the height-of-land the view is a panorama of the

Green Mountains ahead. Keep to the main road (the one with the line down the middle) until a T, and turn left (it's marked) for the descent into Rochester. Turn north on Rt. 100 and, 4 miles up, note the Hancock Hotel and the turnoff for Middlebury Gap, Rt. 125. Continuing north on Rt. 100, the mountain walls close in as you near **Granville Gulf** and **Moss Glen Falls**. Turn off Rt. 100 into **Warren Village** and follow signs 2 miles to East Warren, where you turn onto the **Roxbury Gap Road**. Be sure to pull out near the top for a look back down the valley. It's a popular soaring center, and you may see a glider or hawks riding the thermal waves. Continue downhill to Rt. 12A and turn south, following the railroad tracks and the Third Branch of the White River past the turnoff for Braintree Hill to Randolph and back to I-89, Exit 4.

Randolph Center, **Brookfield**, **Chelsea** (27 miles). Take I-89 to Exit 4 and turn east into Randolph Center, then north along a glorious ridge road (marked TO BROOKFIELD) to Brookfield with its floating bridge across Sunset Lake, leading to Allis State Park. Addicted as we are to shortcuts, we still recommend passing up

COVERED BRIDGES

There are five covered bridges in Tunbridge: the **Cilley Bridge**, south of the junction of Rt. 110 with Strafford Rd. and built in 1883; the **Howe Bridge** (1879), east off Rt. 110 in South Tunbridge; and in North Tunbridge, the 1845 **Flint Bridge** and 1902 **Larkin Bridge**, both east of Rt. 110. The **Mill Bridge** (1883), crushed by ice in the winter of 1999, has been rebuilt. In Randolph two multiple kingpost bridges, both built in 1904, are just off Rt. 14 between East Randolph and South Randolph. In Chelsea there is the **Moxley** or **Guy Bridge**, an 1886 queenpost, east off Rt. 110.

DOWNTOWN TUNBRIDGE'S MILL BRIDGE

Christina Tree

the gravel road from East Brookfield to Chelsea; go around through East Randolph (6 miles south on Rt. 14, then turn onto the road marked for Chelsea; it's 6 more miles). Return on Rt. 110 and Rt. 14 to I-89, passing six covered bridges.

Middlebury Gap. Robert Frost Memorial Drive is too glorious a stretch of road to pass by. From Rt. 100 in Hancock, turn onto Rt. 125 west and take the short detour into **Texas Falls**. Rt. 125 continues to climb through Middlebury Gap (the Long Trail crosses at an altitude of 2,149 feet). Then it's on through the Green Mountain National Forest until the rambling yellow Bread Loaf Inn and its annexes unexpectedly appear, banked in hydrangeas. Owned by Middlebury College, this 1860s hotel is nationally known for its summer literary programs. Just west, a dirt road leads to the Homer Noble farm; a short way past the farm is the **Robert Frost Cabin**, in which Frost spent 23 summers. Continue to the Robert Frost Wayside. Return the way you came or continue to Middlebury and return to Rt. 100 via Brandon Gap (Rt. 73), Appalachian Gap (Rt. 17), or Lincoln Gap.

✳ To Do

BIKING In Randolph the **Three Stallion Inn** offers its own 35 km network of mountain biking trails and offers maps to other local possibilities.

Green Mountain Bikes (802-767-4464; 800-767-7882; greenmountainbikes .com), Rt. 100 in Rochester Village. Doon Hinderyckx is a fount of information about local trails in and beyond the national forest. He offers guided tours and rents and sells mountain and cross bikes.

Also check with the **Green Mountain National Forest Visitor Center** (see *Guidance*), and see this chapter's *Scenic Drives*.

BOATING AND TUBING While most of the White River is navigable in high water (May–July), the 20-mile stretch from Rochester to Bethel is especially popular with canoeists, tubers, and kayakers. A good place to put in is at the cement bridge just south of Rochester. Tubing on the White River is so popular that you can rent tubes at a number of places along the stretch from Gaysville to South Royalton.

Christina Tree

FARMS TO VISIT ✑ **Neighborly Farms of Vermont** (802-728-4700; 888-212-6898; neighborlyfarms.com), 1362 Curtis Rd., Randolph Center. Open Mon.–Sat. 9–4. Rob and Linda Dimmick and their three children run an organic dairy and make organic cheeses that they sell at the farm store and through area stores. Visitors are welcome to see the cows and watch cheesemaking (call ahead for days/hours) through the viewing window in the store, which also features honey products from Brookfield (the bees are raised on several local farms) and fresh goat cheese, lamb, eggs, four

flavors of goat's-milk caramel from Fat Toad Farm in Brookfield, and floral wreaths
and baskets from Spruce Lake Farm (also in Brookfield).

❧ **Vermont Technical College Farm** (802-728-3395) Rt. 66 east off I-89 Exit 4.
Tour the sugarhouse, apple orchard (pick your own in-season), and dairy barn.

Maple Ridge Sheep Farm (802-728-3081; mrsf.com) in Braintree, said to be the
oldest and largest Shetland sheep farm in the country, produces fleece, machine-
washable sheepskin, yarn, knit and woven items, meat. Call first.

❧ **Marge's B&B at Round Robin Farm** (802-763-7025), RR 1, Box 52, Fay
Brook Rd., Strafford. This is a 350-acre working dairy farm with one of Vermont's
famous 10-sided round barns (built in 1917). It's been in the family for six generations. The 60 cows are milked between 5 and 7 PM; visitors are welcome. There's
also a sugarhouse and a B&B (see *Lodging*).

FISHING Trout abound at the junction of the Tweed and White rivers, downstream of Bethel, above Randolph, and below Royalton. Fly-fishing enthusiasts
find the Bethel area good for large rainbow and brown trout, while below Royalton
there are bass, spring walleye, and trout. Fishing licenses are available at **Tracy's
Midway**, a convenience store and gas station on N. Main St. in Sharon; at **Hubbard's General Store** in Hancock; and elsewhere.

Bakers Pond on Rt. 12 in Brookfield has a parking area and boat launch, good for
trout fishing. There is a boat access on **Rood Pond** in Williamstown and a canoe
access on **Sunset Lake** in Brookfield, also stocked with trout. The floating bridge
is a popular fishing spot.

White River National Fish Hatchery, Gaysville (Bethel), Rts. 12/107 west of
Bethel Village, raises imprint salmon for the Connecticut River restoration program.

Roxbury State Fish Hatchery, Rt. 12A in Roxbury, raises brookies and Atlantic
salmon, over 350,000 fish per year. It abuts the Third Branch of the White River,
and the fishing downstream can be amazing.

GOLF **Montague Golf Club** (802-728-3806), Randolph. One of the oldest courses in Vermont, 18 holes. The Second Branch of the White River winds through it.
Light fare is served in the clubhouse; lessons offered. *Note:* A driving range maintained by the Three Stallion Inn is just west on Rt. 66.

The White River Golf Club (802-767-GOLF), Rt. 100, Rochester. Nine holes,
clubhouse with a restaurant serving lunch (dinner by arrangement). Open
May–Oct. Affordable, great for families, a historic and beautiful course. Next to it
is a driving range (802-767-3211).

HIKING The **Green Mountain National Forest** (see *Guidance*) harbors
numerous trails. On Rt. 100 itself in Granville Gulf there are two short nature
trails. At Moss Glen Falls, the 0.5-mile loop on the west side of the road is more
rugged than the 1-mile loop on the east side.

In **Allis State Park**, Brookfield (off Rt. 12; see *Green Space*), a 2.5-mile trail circles down through meadows and back up through woods. A trail leads from the
picnic area to a fire tower with one of the best views in central Vermont (on a clear
day, from Killington–Pico to Mount Mansfield to Ascutney). The Bear Hill Nature
Trail is another reason for finding this special place.

PICNICKING **Brookfield Gulf**, Rt. 12 west of Brookfield. Picnic facility, nature trail.

Braintree Hill, Braintree Hill Rd. (off Rt. 12A just west of downtown Randolph). A great picnic spot with an early cemetery and sweeping views to the White Mountains. The handsome Braintree Meeting House here is open by appointment and on Old Home Day (first Sun. in Aug.).

Bingo Brook in Rochester off Rt. 73 in the national forest. Picnic sites with grills by a mountain stream, good for fishing and swimming.

Also see Allis State Park in *Green Space*, Texas Falls in *To See*, and the Robert Frost Wayside in *Scenic Drives*.

SWIMMING Ask locally about various swimming holes in the First, Second, and Third branches and the main stem of the White River. In Randolph Center there is a human-made beach, bathhouse, and picnic area. There is also a pool at the recreational park in Randolph.

✳ Winter Sports

CROSS-COUNTRY SKIING AND SNOWSHOEING

Three Stallion Inn Ski Touring Center (802-728-5656; threestallioninn.com), Stock Farm Rd., off Rt. 66, Randolph. Twenty km of groomed trails weave through woods and meadows; there are also trails and equipment for snowshoeing. Rentals and instruction are available, and both lunch and dinner are open to the public next door at the inn.

Nordic Adventures (802-767-3272; vt-nordicadventures.com), Rt. 100, Rochester Village. Dean Mendell offers a full line of cross-country equipment and snowshoes, lessons, rentals and guided tours into the heart of the Green Mountain National Forest and from inn to inn. His slogan is "ski everywhere."

Green Mountain National Forest (see *Guidance*) maintains trails in Rochester on Liberty Hill and at Chittenden Brook.

✳ Green Space

Allis State Park (802-276-3175), Brookfield. Open May 30–Sept. 15. A camping area with 18 tent sites, 8 with lean-tos (no hookups), each on a wooded loop road separate from the picnic area, in which you can choose tables on a windy hilltop or under a pavilion. A hiking trail (see *To Do*) accesses a fire tower with an outstanding view.

Green Mountain National Forest (GMNF). Among the highlights of the Rochester district of the GMNF are the Long Trail and the Texas Falls Recreation Area. A good short hike is from Brandon Gap north 0.6 mile to the cliffs of Mount Horrid, where there are views to the east. Because of the abundance of other things to do in this area, be sure to drop in the new GMNF Visitor Center 2 miles north of the Rochester green on Rt. 100 (802-767-4261).

✳ Lodging

INNS ⊕ ✎ ⓣ **Three Stallion Inn**
(802-728-5575; 800-424-5575; three
stallioninn.com), Lower Stock Farm
Rd., off Rt. 66, Randolph 05060. The
setting is the 1,300-acre Green Mountain Stock Farm, a mix of pasture and
woodland. From 1927 to 1962 this was
one of Vermont's major centers for
Morgan horses. In 1971, when real
estate developer Sam Sammis bought
the property, it was zoned for 2,600
building sites. In the decades since,
fewer than a dozen have been built,
each on no less than 10 wooded acres.
The inn occupies a handsome farmhouse and has featured cross-country
skiing from the start (its first resident
innkeepers were Olympic skiers). In
winter groomed trails continue to draw
skiers, and in summer the network is
popular with mountain bikers. The
property adjoins the 18-hole Montague
Golf Club, and the inn maintains a
driving range. There's also swimming
and fishing in the Third Branch of the
White River, which runs through the
property; a trout pond invites catch-
and-release. Facilities include a fitness
room, a whirlpool and sauna, two tennis courts, and an outdoor lap pool.

There are seven guest rooms on the
second and third floors in the main
house, all with recently renovated
bath, most with heated floors and marble countertops. The remaining seven
rooms—including several suites—are
in the Morgan House across the road,
overlooking the golf course. Three are
on the ground floor. The entire house
is frequently rented for weddings and
reunions. Rooms in the main house
are $215 in regular season, $245 in
foliage and holidays; in the Morgan
House they vary from $125 for the two
upstairs rooms with (shared bath) to
$225 for a two-room suite, breakfast
buffet included. The inn's popular

Morgan's Pub and Lippitt's Restaurant
(see *Dining Out*) are set apart from the
inn proper, which offers ample common space for its guests.

ⓣ **The Huntington House Inn**
(802-767-91400; huntingtonhouseinn
.com), 19 Huntington Place, Rochester
05767. Sited on Rochester's large, leafy
Central Park, this handsome home has
been an inn for many years. From 1819
until 1964, however, it served as a combination home and office for four generations of Huntingtons, all of them
doctors—hence the pub known as
Doc's Tavern. Since the present owners
took over in 2003 the inn has been
totally renovated. Six guest rooms are
crisply, comfortably, unfussily furnished
with crafted beds, quilts, and simple
window treatments; they're equipped
with private bath, air-conditioning,
phones, and TV. $125–150 includes a
full country breakfast. Next door a former general store has been transformed into The Steven's Suites, three
unusually luxurious two-bedroom
condo units accessed by elevator, each
with a full kitchen, two baths, and a living room furnished with Oriental rugs

THREE STALLION INN

Christina Tree

and antiques, gas fireplace, and large-screen TV ($375 per night, with a two-night minimum). Also see *Dining Out.*

BED & BREAKFAST Green Trails Inn (802-276-3412; greentrailsinn .com), P.O. Box 494, Brookfield 05036. Open June–Dec. full service; Jan.–May for longer stays. This handsome house at the heart of Pond Village has welcomed visitors since Jessie Fiske, a Brookfield native who became one of the first women professors at Rutgers University, began renting rooms to her students and associates. Jane Doerfer, the present innkeeper, is an accomplished cook and cookbook author. She offers eight attractive rooms with and without private bath, one with its own entrance. Beds have high-quality mattresses and linens, and the guest rooms all have well-chosen antiques and books. A buffet-style breakfast usually includes fresh fruit, smoked salmon, local cheeses, and a hot dish such as sausage apple cobbler. It's served in the big, sunny dining area with a stone hearth and view of Sunset Lake (where guests have access to a small beach). $95–145, $25 per extra person. Inquire about cooking classes, solo rates, and whole-house rental (it sleeps 18). Ariel's Restaurant (see *Dining Out*) is across the street.

GREEN TRAILS INN

Christina Tree

The Gathering Inn (802-767-3734; gatheringinnathancock.com), 1295 Rt. 100, Hancock 05748. There are five owners and six rooms in this pleasant, environmentally conscious B&B, geared to individual and group retreats and workshops. $100–125 B&B plus $25 for dinner, available Fri. and Sat.

FARMS

🏅 🌿 **Devil's Den Farm Homestay Bed & Breakfast** (802-685-4582), 296 Rt. 110, Chelsea 05038. We passed the big rambling farmhouse and red barn a couple of times before realizing that this was what we were looking for. With a school bus and serious wood-pile, it isn't your ordinary B&B. The welcome from Rhoda and Bill (who drives the bus) Ackerman was, however, hospitality itself. The farmhouse was built in 1921 by Rhoda's grandparents, and the family (both sides) is rooted six generations deep in Chelsea. There's plenty of sitting space inside and out (on the flower- and rocker-lined porch). Upstairs are two double-bedded rooms and a suite, all furnished with family antiques, quilts, and handwoven rag rugs on polished hardwood floors. You'll also enjoy 65 acres of fields, pastures, and woods, access to the First Branch of the White River, and a trail to the Devil's Den cave in the ledge behind the farm. Downtown Chelsea is a mile back beyond the bend. $70 includes a full breakfast.

🏅 🌿 **Marge's B&B at Round Robin Farm** (802-763-7025), RR 1, Box 52, Fay Brook Rd., Strafford 05072. This is a 350-acre working dairy farm with one of Vermont's famous 10-sided round barns (built in 1917). It's been in the family for seven generations. What's offered is the homey, clean, and cheerful farmhouse with its Mission-style dining room and sitting room with a

TV/VCR, or rooms therein (two rooms with double bed and two with twins, sharing one bath), plus a fridge with the fixings for making your own breakfast in the big country kitchen. Marge Robinson lives within call in the adjacent house. Cross-country ski or walk woods and meadows. No smoking and no pets, please. A double room is $40 per person per night. Inquire about the price for the whole house. Snowmobile trails run right through the property.

Four Springs Farm, Campground and Learning Center (802-763-7296; fourspringsfarm.com), 776 Gee Rd., Royalton 05068. Jinny Cleland raises organic vegetables, chickens, and flowers on her 70-acre farm and invites visitors to tag along on chores. Programs are also offered to the families and groups who stay here, either taking advantage of eight secluded campsites ($25) or the four-bunk cabin with mountain views ($75). There's a central washhouse and a picnic pavilion.

SECOND HOMES AND COTTAGES

⌁ **Hawk North, Vermont's Mountain Hideaway** (800-832-8007; vthideaway.com). Two- to four-bedroom contemporary hilltop chalets with superb mountain and valley views in the Stockbridge/Rochester area, privately owned but splendidly built by the same developer, all with signature fieldstone fireplace, living room deck, and fully equipped kitchen. Rates vary with the season: $200–375 per night, third night free. Weekly, monthly rentals.

🐾 ⌁ **Birch Meadow Farm** (802-276-3156; bbhost.com/birchmeadow), 597 Birch Meadow Dr., Brookfield 05036 (East St. off Rt. 65 south). This is Mary and Matt Comerford's woodsy hideaway, with three modern, air-conditioned log cabins equipped for housekeeping. There are TVs and

woodstoves, plus a B&B suite in the main house, which sits high on a hill with splendid views and a swim pond. $120–125 per couple, $15 each additional adult, $5 per child. Rates include the initial morning's breakfast in the cabins.

Placidia Farm Bed & Breakfast (802-728-9883; placidia.com), 1470 Bent Hill Rd., Braintree 05060. This is an apartment in a hand-hewn log home (deck, kitchen, bedroom, and living room) on a large Christmas tree farm with its own pond. A full breakfast in Viola Frost-Latinen's plant-filled sunporch is included. $125 per couple; $45 each additional person. Not appropriate for children under age 13.

CAMPGROUNDS **Lake Champagne Campground** (802-728-5298), P.O. Box C, Randolph 05061. Open Memorial Day weekend–mid-Oct. A 150-acre property with fields, a 3-acre swim lake, hot showers, mountain views, and facilities for tents through full-sized RVs.

Limehurst Lake Campground (802-433-6662; limehurstlake.com), 4101 Rt. 14, Williamstown 05679. This family-geared campground offers 76 sites with full hookups for RVs, a separate area for lean-tos and tents, modern restrooms, hot showers, a waterslide, a sandy swim beach, boat rentals and fishing (no license required), and a game room.

Chittenden Brook Campground in the Green Mountain National Forest (802-767-4261), 5.3 miles west of Rochester on Rt. 73. The 17 campsites are fitted with picnic tables and grills; there are hand-operated water pumps and vault toilets. The surrounding forest provides good fishing, hiking, and birding. No trailers over 18 feet. No hookups or showers.

LIBERTY HILLS FARM

Christina Tree

🐾 ✎ **Liberty Hill Farm** (802-767-3926; libertyhillfarm.com), 511 Liberty Hill Rd., Rochester 05767. This is the real thing: a working, 150-head dairy farm set in a broad meadow, backed by mountains. Its 1890s red barn with cupola is one of the most photographed and painted in Vermont (Woody Jackson has printed it on silk screens that, we're told, sell by the thousands in Japan). There's a capacious white-clapboard 1825 farmhouse and, best of all, there is farmwife-

Note: Primitive camping is permitted almost everywhere in the Green Mountain National Forest.

Allis State Park (802-276-3175; vtstateparks.com). Open mid-May–Labor Day. Named for Wallace Allis, who deeded his Bear Mountain Farm to the state as a campground and recreational area. Sited on the summit of Bear Mountain, it includes a picnic area and trail to the fire tower, as well as 18 tent and 8 lean-to sites, each with a picnic table and fireplace. Hot showers but no hookups. Handy to Sunset Lake and several other good fishing ponds.

✳ Where to Eat

DINING OUT ✎ **Ariel's Restaurant** (802-276-3939; arielsrestaurant.com), 29 Stone Rd., Brookfield. Open May–Oct. Fri.–Wed. Reservations advised. Overlooking Sunset Lake in the middle of Pond Village, this destination dining room is known as one of the best places to eat in Vermont. Lee Duberman and Richard Fink are longtime chef-owners who specialize in Mediterranean and Pacific Rim dishes, using local ingredients whenever possible. On a summer day you might begin with a crabcake in kataifi pastry, then dine on grilled boneless Cavendish

host par excellence Beth Kennett. Beth's own family's farming history dates back to the 17th century in Maine, and "farmer" Bob Kennett's roots run deep into New Hampshire soil. Both families were horrified when Beth and Bob moved "west" in 1979 to this 230-acre spread in a magnificent Vermont valley. Since 1984 they've been welcoming guests. Their sons are now grown and involved with the work, but visitors of all ages are treated to a sense of how much fun (and work if they so desire) living on a farm can be.

Meals are served family-style, and Beth makes everything from scratch. Dinner is at 6 (BYOB) and as delicious as it is prodigious: maybe incredibly moist sliced turkey, a zucchini casserole, cucumber salad, a garden salad with tomatoes, pumpkin muffins, mashed potatoes, fresh-picked sweet corn, a choice of homemade dressings and stuffings—all set in the middle of a table seating eight adults and at least as many children. The kids disappear after the main course, and adults linger over blueberry pie with homemade (from the farm's own milk) raspberry ice cream.

There's plenty of common space, including two sittings rooms and two pianos, but in summer adults seem to congregate on the porch. There are seven guest rooms (five with double beds, one with two single beds, and a room with five single beds) and four shared baths; families can spread into two rooms sharing a sitting room and bath. In summer you can hear the gurgle of the White River (good for trout fishing as well as swimming), and in winter you can ski or snowshoe up into the woods and off into the village across the meadows. $110 per adult, $50 per child under 12, MAP.

Farm quail with fig, honey, and balsamic vinaigrette, topped off with a lemon napoleon with raspberry coulis. Entrées $13 (for a Vermont natural beef burger with a choice of Vermont cheese)–$27. Children are welcome. Also see Ariel's Riverside in Montpelier.

Stone Soup Restaurant (802-765-4301), on the green, Strafford. Open for dinner Thu.–Sun. 6–9. Reservations strongly suggested. There is no sign for this elegantly rustic restaurant, which has acquired a strong following over more than two decades. You step from Strafford's handsome green into a

LEE DUBERMAN, CHEF AND CO-OWNER OF ARIEL'S IN BROOKFIELD

Christina Tree

cheery tavern room with a large hearth. The candlelit, low-beamed dining rooms are beyond. On our last visit, the blackboard menu included Portuguese kale and fish stew, and veal with red pepper butter. Note the attractive herb garden. Personal checks, but no credit cards. Entrées $23.95–28.95.

♂ & **Morgan's Pub and Lippitt's Restaurant at the Three Stallion Inn** (802-728-5575; threestallioninn .com), off Rt. 66 (just off I-89), Randolph. Open for dinner Tue.–Sun. year-round. Two adjoining spaces—a casual, congenial pub area and a more formal dining room—with summer patio dining overlooking a green meadow and wooded hill. On a summer evening it's possible to dine splendidly on Prince Edward Island mussels steamed in tomato, fennel, and saffron, followed by honey-glazed pork shanks with bok choy and sesame wonton crisps. Executive chef Bob Hildebrand and his sister Carol have coauthored two cookbooks, *500 Three Ingredient Recipes* and *500 Five Ingredient Desserts.* Entrées $18.95–22.50. You can also dine off the pub menu on the likes of a beer-batter-fried haddock sandwich.

SUNSET LAKE IN BROOKFIELD

Christina Tree

Huntington House Inn (802-767-9140; huntingtonhouseinn.com), 19 Huntington Place, Rochester. Open nightly for dinner from 5. This attractive dining room has white linens and candles, windows overlooking the green, and a romantic feel. Chef Daniel Wallace uses local ingredients as much as possible to create entrées such as vegetable Wellington, beef tenderloin with baby fingerlings and bordelaise sauce, and grilled and stuffed pork loin. Entrées $20–30. In the adjoining **Doc's Tavern** you can slide into a booth and sup on pizza, paninis, pastas, and comfort food like shepherd's pie or blue-cheese-stuffed meat loaf, also available to go.

The Village Porch Bar and Bistro (802-767-3126), Main St. (Rt. 100), Rochester Village. Open Thu.–Sun. from 4 PM. Geared to the local community, this is a delightful restaurant with an open kitchen and seasonal porch seats, also pleasant inside space. Appetizers might include butternut squash bisque, or spinach and heirloom tomato tarts. Entrées, priced generally from $9.95 for a Porch burger through $13.95 for house-smoked baby back rib, include several $19.95 options, like lemon chicken schnitzel and smoked and grilled flank steak over black bean and corn salad.

EATING OUT *Road food, listed geographically from south to north, off I-89.*

At I-89, Exit 2
Dixie's Country Kitchen (802-763-8721), Rt. 14 in Sharon on the way to South Royalton. Open for lunch and dinner. Good road food, seafood, steak, and specials.

Chelsea Station (802-763-8685) on the green, South Royalton. Booths, a counter, breakfast from 6 AM, a friendly atmosphere, and a basic menu.

ᵀ 5 Olde Tavern & Grill (802-763-8600), 192 Chelsea St., South Royalton. Open daily 11–11. The original eatery by this name is at 5 Olde Nugget Alley (hence the name) in Hanover, New Hampshire, and this too is a sleek, student-geared coffeehouse/pub with a menu ranging from pizza, burgers, and quesadillas to reasonably priced dinner entrées such as veggie stir-fry and ribs.

South Royalton Market (802-763-2400; soromarket.com), on the village green, South Royalton. Open daily. A co-op style store featuring local and organic and Equal Grounds Café.

At I-89, Exit 3

Eaton's Sugar House, Inc. (802-763-8809). Located at the junction of Rts. 14 and 107 in Royalton, just off I-89, Exit 3. Open daily 7–3. A good old-fashioned family restaurant featuring pancakes and local syrup, sandwiches, burgers, and reasonably priced daily specials. Try the turkey club made with fresh-carved turkey on homemade bread. Vermont maple syrup, cheese, and other products are also sold.

Along Route 110 in Tunbridge and Chelsea

ᵀ The Village Store (802-889-9888; tunbridgevillagestore.com), Tunbridge. Open weekdays 6:30 AM–7 PM, Sat. 7–7, Sun. 8–1. From the outside this store looks pretty much the way it did in 1840, but the cheerful man at the counter, Frenchman Jean-Pierre Debeuf, happens to be a five-star chef. You'll find fresh breads and croissants, homemade pastas and ice cream, blueberry gelato, and JP's signature crispy cheesecake. Luckily there are also four "quad" tables at which patrons can feast on eggs Benedict for breakfast, blackboard specials like veggie wraps with avocado, jalapeño, cheddar, fresh onions, spinach, black beans, roasted

Christina Tree

JOHN PIERRE DEBEUF AT THE VILLAGE STORE IN TUNBRIDGE HAPPENS TO BE A FIVE-STAR CHEF.

red peppers, and Cajun mayo. There are also grocery staples and local produce. While we can think of several "nouveau" general stores that seem out of place in this bastion of old Vermont, JP and his hardworking co-owner, wife Judi, have created a genuine gathering place for the town. Lucky Tunbridge!

Chelsea Diner (802-685-3000), Main St. (Rt. 110), Chelsea Village. Open 5–2, until 8 on Friday. Closed when we came through but it looks inviting and the word is that it's a good spot for soup and greens.

Dixie's II (802-685-7802), Main St. (Rt. 110), Chelsea Village. Open daily from 6 AM, until 7:30 PM Thu.–Sat., closing at 1:30 Mon.–Wed. The same menu all day with blackboard specials, BYOB at dinner. This is a 19th-century brick bank building with a nice atmosphere, standard menu.

Along Route 107

⌇ Peavine Family Restaurant & Thirsty Bull Brew Pub (802-234-9434; peavinerestaurant.com), 3657 Rt. 107 east of Stockbridge. Open Wed.–Sun. for dinner year-round; in summer, open daily for dinner and for

Sunday lunch. This is a special place with a patio overlooking the river and a zany kid-geared decor with a train running around the open rafters. The name and train, along with photos and memorabilia, recall the 19-mile White River Valley Railroad (1900–1933), known as the Peavine line because the narrow valleys forced it to thread along beside the winding White River, reminding some witty gardener of a peavine's wandering coils. The '27 flood pretty well crippled this railroad, as well as wiping out the woolen mills in the neighboring village of Gaysville. Fresh seafood, handcut steaks, and slow-cooked ribs are staples, along with brick-oven-baked pizza. Live music on weekends. Kids' menu and a computer corner for their use.

Tozier's Restaurant (802-234-9400), west of Bethel. Open May–Oct., in summer 11–8, limited hours in shoulder seasons. Looking tired but still a classic road-food stop with pine paneling and a river view. Seafood (mostly fried, some broiled) is a dinner specialty, along with marinated steak tips and turkey dinner.

Creek House Diner (802-234-9191), junction of Rts. 107 and 12, Locust Creek. Open year-round, daily 7 AM–8 PM. A clean, handy road-food stop with booths, a salad bar, liver and onions, prime rib, beer and wine.

In Bethel and along Route 12 north

⁰Ⲓ⁰ Cockadoodle Pizza Café (802-234-9666; cockadoodlepizza.com), 269 Main St., Bethel. Open Mon.–Thu. 11–8, Fri.–Sat. 11–9, Sun. noon–8. A welcome addition to this reawakening downtown: a wide choice of mouthwatering signature pizzas plus panini and sandwiches on "rustic rolls," each named for a different Vermont town. No credit cards.

⁰Ⲓ⁰ Three Bean Café (802-728-3533), 22 Pleasant St., Randolph. Open 6:30–5. Closed Sun. The in gathering place for many miles around. Adjacent to the food co-op, it offers from-scratch croissants and baked goods, then nourishing soups and veggie sandwiches plus a variety of coffees and teas, the day's papers, and comfortable seating.

Patrick's Place (802-728-4405), 2 Merchants Row. Open for breakfast and lunch. Known for omelets, specialty pancakes, and Belgian waffles for breakfast; at lunch for salads, the soup-and-sandwich combo, and Patrick's corned beef Reuben.

⁰Ⲓ⁰ Randolph Depot (728-3333), 2 Salisbury St. Open Mon.–Sat. 7–4. Housed in the town's Victorian-style brick train depot (an Amtrak stop), this attractive restaurant features an unusual choice of salads as well as panini sandwiches and wraps.

Morgan's Pub at the Three Stallion Inn (800-424-5575), off Rt. 66 (just off I-89, Exit 4). Open except Mon. for dinner. This is a popular local gathering place with a tavern menu that usually includes char-grilled Vermont Black Angus burgers and a wide choice of reasonably priced "small plates" as well as the same menu as the inn's more formal restaurant.

Randolph Village Pizza (802-728-9677), 1 S. Main St. Open daily 11–9, until 10 in summer and on weekends year-round. A wide variety of better-than-average pizzas and calzones; also salads, grinders, and pasta.

Along Route 100

Rochester Café & Country Store (802-767-4302), Rt. 100, Rochester Village. Breakfast 7–11:30, lunch until 4. Good fries and burgers, pleasant atmosphere.

Christina Tree

BREAD AT THE SEASONED BOOKS AND
BAKERY, ROCHESTER

ᵗ¹ Seasoned Books and Bakery
(802-767-4258), 30 N. Main St. (Rt.
100), Rochester. Open 7:30–6. Just
north of the gas pumps. Good in the
morning for espresso, fresh-made
whole-grain breads and muffins, and at
lunch for soups, salads, and sandwiches, vegetarian choices, cookies all day,
beer and wine. Light dinner served but
only until 6.

Hubbard's General Store (802-767-
9030), 38 Rt. 125, at the junction with
Rt. 100 in Hancock. A community center since 1840, good for gas, staples,
wildlife licenses, and good deli sandwiches to take for a picnic to nearby
Texas Falls or one of the pullout areas
down by the White River.

✳ Entertainment

**Chandler Music Hall Chandler
Center for the Arts** (802-728-9133;
chandlermusichall.org), 71–73 Main
St., Randolph. A fine, acoustically outstanding music hall built in 1907 and
restored to mint condition. It's open

year-round for musical and theatrical
performances: chamber music, blues,
jazz, opera, folksingers, the Vermont
Symphony, and Mud Season Talent
Show. The annual **New World Festival** on the Sunday of Labor Day weekend features 100 musicians performing
northern New England and Canadian
music here and in other local, weather-
proofed venues.

In August the **Central Vermont
Chamber Music Festival** (central
vtchambermusicfest.org) includes performances in the area.

**Rochester Chamber Music Society
Concert Series** (802-767-9234;
rcmsvt.org) during June and July in
Rochester and Hancock village venues.

**Summer Park Concert Series
Rochester**, summer Sunday evenings.

The Playhouse Movie Theatre,
Main St., Randolph, is the oldest
movie house in the state. Shows first-
run flicks.

Randall Drive-In Movie Theatre,
Rt. 12 in Bethel, operates in summer
only.

The White River Valley Players
(wrvp.org), a major community theater

MICHAEL EGAN AT WORK AT PLUSH
QUARTZ ART GLASS

Kim Grant

in Rochester, performs a spring musical and fall production in the high school.

✻ Selective Shopping

ART/CRAFTS STUDIOS AND GALLERIES Plush Quartz Art Glass (802-767-4547), Rt. 100, Granville. Open Wed.–Mon. 9–5 most of the year. Don't pass up this exceptional roadside studio and gallery. Vermont natives Michael and Angela Egan shape Venetian-style freehand blown glass into spectacular vases, pitchers, and a variety of art glass.

Judy Jensen Clay Studio (802-767-3271), Rt. 100 back behind the Rochester Café. Open daily. Jensen's pottery ranges from tiny vases to large urns, tile to chess sets, sculpture, handmade cards, and plenty of highly

BETHEL'S BRICK STORE

Christina Tree

decorative functional ware. She also displays work in fiber, wood, glass, iron, and paper.

BigTown Gallery (802-767-9670; bigtowngallery.com), 99 N. Main St., Rochester Village. Open Wed.–Sat. 10–5, Sun. 11–4. Anni Mackay designs and makes wearable art, but her studio showcases an eclectic mix of paintings, sculpture, and furniture as well as yarns and one-of-a-kind hats and scarves. The gallery features local artists with exhibits changing monthly. It's also a setting for piano rehearsals and plays performed in the backyard amphitheater.

SPECIAL STORES The Bowl Mill (802-767-4711; outside Vermont 800-828-1005), Rt. 100, Granville. Open 9–5 daily, year-round. Decorative wooden bowls are no longer made here but still sold at this writing, along with toys, crafts, cards, books, baskets, maple products, specialty foods.

Cover to Cover Books (802-728-5509), 27 N. Main St., Randolph. A friendly, full-service store, also cards, gifts. Inquire about author signings.

⁰ᵀ⁰ **Seasoned Booksellers** (802-767-4258; seasonedbooks.com), 30 N. Main St., Rochester. Librarian Sandy Lincoln specializes in sustainable lifestyles, wilderness tales, and renewable energy; the store is also a café (see *Eating Out*) and sells a full line of Vermont Soap Organics (Sandy's husband's venture) as well as crafted items, fresh flowers, and more.

GENERAL STORES Floyd's General Store (802-725-5333), Rt. 66, Randolph Center, 1 mile from I-89. Exit 4. Open daily 7:30–7. The store's vintage-1912 cash register is here, Al Floyd assures us, not for tourists but because it works. The vintage Sylvan Acorn potbellied stove is no longer hooked

Christina Tree

up, but locals as well as visitors like to sit around it anyway. The store, which offers veterinarian supplies, a full line of groceries, penny candy, and a magazine swap shelf, remains essentially the same village center that Floyd inherited from his father.

Snowsville General Store (802-728-5252; snowsville.com), Rt. 12, East Braintree. Owner Gene Booska, an avid hunter, stocks more than 400 guns, from handguns to rifles, new and used, and U.S.-manufactured outdoor clothing such as Johnson Woolen Mill jackets and pants; wood and used cars are also sold along with groceries and a selection of papers, just not *The New York Times*. The Round Oak stove here burns away most of the year, the centerpiece for this village gathering spot.

Also see the Village Store in Tunbridge and Hubbard's General Store in Hancock under *Eating Out*, and the Original General Store in Pittsfield in "Killington/Rutland Area."

FARMER'S MARKETS are held in **Randolph**, Rt. 66, mid-May–Oct. Sat. 9–2. **Chelsea**, late May–Columbus Day weekend, Wed. 3–5:30. **South Royalton Common**, Memorial Day–Columbus Day, Thu. 3–6:30.

FARMS AND SUGARHOUSES
Note: These maple producers sell syrup year-round and welcome visitors into their sugar shacks during the March production period.

Blair's Berry Farm (802-767-3989), Rt. 100 north, Rochester. Organic blueberries and raspberries, pre-picked or PYO, mid-July–Sept., Mon.–Thu. 9–5, Sun. 9–6.

Redrock Farm (802-685-2282; 866-685-4343; christmastrees.net), 2 Redrock Lane (off Jenkins Brook Rd., which is off Rt. 110), Chelsea. Pick out your Christmas tree any time of year and have it shipped to you—anywhere in the contiguous 48 states—at Christmas. You can also order by mail but you miss half the fun. Fish in the pond and paddle the boat.

North Hollow Farm (802-767-4255), Rt. 100, Rochester. Maple syrup, gift baskets.

Also see Neighborly Farms under *Farms to Visit*.

❊ Special Events

Last Saturday of January: **Brookfield Ice Harvest Festival**—ice cutting, ice sculpting, hot food, sledding, skating, skiing.

February: **Strafford Winter Carnival**.

March: **Open sugarhouses. Casino Night** (*late March*) at Vermont Technical College, Randolph Center, sponsored by the Randolph Area Chamber of Commerce (802-728-9027).

Mid-June: **Vermont History Expo**, a two-day gathering of Vermont historical societies from throughout the state, bringing their exhibits to fill the Tunbridge Fairgrounds—historic reenactments and demonstrations, music, grandstand, and many varied events.

July: **July 4 parades** in Strafford and Rochester, a bigger one in Randolph (usually over 5,000 spectators), with food and crafts. **Family Farm Festival**, Randolph Center. **Chandler Players** perform at Chandler Center for the Arts, Randolph. **Chelsea Flea Market**—150 dealers cover both greens. **Summer Night**, a community-wide celebration in Rochester.

July–August: **Randolph Gazebo Series** (802-728-3010)—Tuesday-evening music. **Summer music school**—workshops at the Mountain School, Vershire. **Huntington Farm Show**, Strafford. **Brookfield Blues Festival** (August), off Rt. 65 in Brookfield. The **South Royalton Town Band**, in business for more than a century, gives free concerts on the green Thursday evenings. **Sharon Old Home Day**.

September: **New World Festival** (*Sunday before Labor Day*; newworldfestival.com) at the Chandler Music Hall in Randolph features northern New England and Celtic music, in addition to food and crafts. **White River Valley Festival**, Bethel. **Tunbridge World's Fair** (tunbridgefair.com), Tunbridge, four days mid-month, ongoing for more than 130 years in a superb setting, definitely one of the country's most colorful agricultural fairs with horse and oxen pulling, contra dancing, sheepdog trials, livestock and produce judging, horse racing, amusement rides, pig races, pony rides, and more. **Harvest Fair on the Park** in Rochester.

Columbus Day weekend: **Lord's Acre Supper**—sale and auction, Barrett Hall, Strafford.

November: **Annual Hunters' Supper**, Barrett Hall, Strafford.

SUGARBUSH/MAD RIVER VALLEY

There were farms and lumber mills in this magnificent valley before Mad River Glen began attracting skiers in 1948, but the look and lifestyle of the present community center on its ski areas. The '60s brought an influx of ski-struck urban ites to Sugarbush and Mad River Glen (the two have long since merged). They played polo, built an airport, a gliding school, specialty shops, and fine restaurants. Young architects eager to test new theories of solar heating and cluster housing designed New England's first trailside homes and condominiums.

Physically just 4 miles apart, philosophically Sugarbush and Mad River Glen seemed at opposite poles of the ski world in the 1990s. By then it was painfully clear that northern New England's natural snow is too fickle a base for the big business that skiing had become, and that to make snow you need water. The two ski areas faced this challenge in their own ways. Mad River Glen, the "ski it if you can" mountain, kept its demands modest, becoming the country's first cooperatively owned ski area (divided among upward of 2,000 shareholders). It also remains the only area in the East that bars snowboarders, featuring telemarking and animal tracking instead.

Thanks to the American Ski Company, Sugarbush installed a much-needed (and ecologically acceptable) snowmaking pond and other major improvements, but when the multi-resort-owner proposed to build one of its signature "grand" hotels at the base of Lincoln Peak, the community balked. Sugarbush Resort is currently owned by Summit Ventures, a locally based partnership, and the newly completed Lincoln Peak Village features the relatively modest-sized red Clay Brook Hotel and Residences, styled to suggest a barn, complete with a silver silo and round barn housing the restaurant.

Not so long ago the very question of what to call this valley (Mad River? Sugarbush?) would have sparked a debate, but residents now agree: It's the Mad River Valley, named for the river down its center. Seven miles wide, the valley is magnificent, with meadows stretching to the Roxbury Range on the east. In summer and fall there is hiking on the Long Trail over some of the highest peaks in the Green Mountains, soaring in gliders above the Valley, mountain biking on ski trails and high woods roads, horseback riding, fishing and swimming in the Mad River, plus outstanding golf, tennis, and polo. In August the monthlong Vermont Festival of the Arts offers daily happenings.

With direct links to the Champlain Valley via the scenic roads through the Appalachian and Lincoln gaps on the west, this is a logical lodging and dining hub

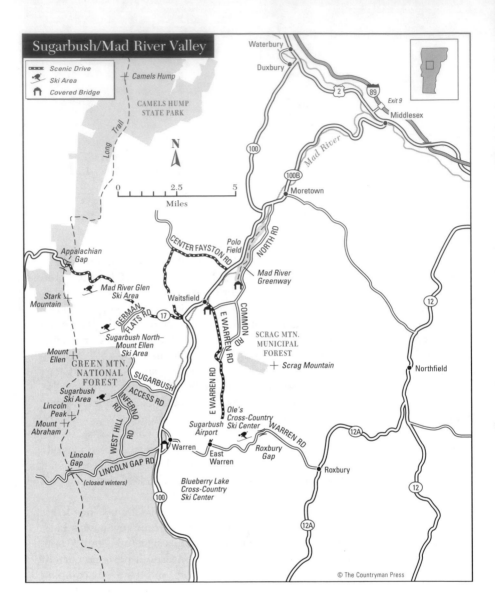

Sugarbush/Mad River Valley

Scenic Drive
Ski Area
Covered Bridge

Camels Hump

CAMELS HUMP
STATE PARK

Long Trail

N

0   2.5   5
Miles

Waterbury
Duxbury

2   89
Exit 9
Middlesex

Mad River

100

100B

Moretown

CENTER FAYSTON RD

Polo
Field

NORTH RD

Mad River
Greenway

Appalachian
Gap

Mad River Glen
Ski Area

Waitsfield

12

Stark
Mountain

GERMAN FLATS RD

17

COMMON RD

E WARREN RD

SCRAG MTN.
MUNICIPAL
FOREST

Scrag Mountain

Northfield

Sugarbush North–
Mount Ellen
Ski Area

Mount
Ellen

GREEN MTN.
NATIONAL
FOREST

SUGARBUSH

Sugarbush
Ski Area

ACCESS RD

INFERNO RD

E WARREN RD

Lincoln
Peak

Mount
Abraham

WEST HILL RD

Ole's
Cross-Country
Ski Center

Sugarbush
Airport

WARREN RD

12A

Lincoln
Gap

Warren

East
Warren

Roxbury
Gap

Roxbury

LINCOLN GAP RD

(closed winters)

100

Blueberry Lake
Cross-Country
Ski Center

12

12A

12

© The Countryman Press

from which to explore some of Vermont's most magnificent and varied landscapes. Dining and shopping are outstanding but uncrowded. Several thousand visitors can bed down here on any given night, but it's far from obvious where. You can drive right through the Valley on Rt. 100, noticing nothing more than some roadside shops in Waitsfield, entirely missing Warren Village (6 miles south, just off Rt. 100). This Valley lacks the high-profile images enjoyed by Stowe to the north and Killington to the south—which is fine by residents and regulars.

GUIDANCE **Mad River Valley Chamber of Commerce** (802-496-3409; lodging: 800-82-VISIT; madrivervalley.com), Box 173, Waitsfield 05673. A walk-in visitor center in the General Wait House, Rt. 100, Waitsfield, is open year-round weekdays 9–5, Sat. 9–1. During crunch times, vacancies are posted after 5 PM in the lobby by the courtesy phone (available 24 hours). Request the helpful, free guide.

Green Mountain National Forest Ranger District Office and Visitor Center (802-767-4261), Rt. 100 in Rochester. Open 8–4. While this magnificent information center is 25 miles south of Warren, it's worth knowing it's there (see "White River Valleys") as a resource for exploring much of the area immediately west and south of the Valley.

GETTING THERE *By bus and train:* Montpelier is the nearest Vermont Transit/Greyhound stop. Waterbury, 12 miles north of Waitsfield, is the closest Amtrak station.

By air: Burlington International Airport is 45 miles away; see "Burlington Region" for carriers.

By car: Valley residents will tell you that the quickest route from points south is I-89 to Randolph, 15 miles up Rt. 12A to Roxbury, then 8 miles over the Roxbury Gap to Warren. This is also the most scenic way (the view from the top of the gap is spectacular), but be forewarned: This high road can be treacherous in winter. In snow, play it safe and take I-89 to Middlesex, Exit 9, then Rt. 100B the 13 miles south to Waitsfield.

GETTING AROUND During ski season the **Mad Bus** fleet circles among condos at the top of the access road and restaurants and nightspots. These are free 26-passenger buses that link the Valley floor to all three mountain base areas, running daily and until 1:30 AM on Saturday night.

Mad Cab (802-793-2320), **C&L Taxi** (802-496-4056), and **Morf Transit** (802-864-5588; 800-696-7433) offer local and long-distance service.

Note: Waitsfield–Champlain Valley Telecom offers free local calls on some pay phones (but not all, so check) scattered around the Valley. Wireless Internet service is widely available in local lodgings.

WHEN TO GO Christmas week through February is high season, high volume, especially in a snowy season when Mad River Glen is wide open. Midweek during this same period is cheaper and far quieter. Ditto for March, when the human-made snow base at Sugarbush is deep and weekend crowds have eased. By mid-April it's all over. May and June appeal to birders (spring migration before trees are in full leaf). Warren's Fourth of July parade, small but famous, kicks off a series of summer events. As noted above, thanks to the gap roads this is an ideal hub for foliage. After the leaves fall it's dead until mid-December.

MEDICAL EMERGENCY Emergency service is available by calling **911**.

Ambulance (802-496-3600). **Mad River Valley Health Center** (802-496-3838), Rt. 100, Waitsfield. **Mad River Integrative Medicine** (802-496-2202).

✳ Villages

The Mad River Valley includes Moretown (population: 1,653) to the north and Fayston (population: 1,140), an elusive town without a center that produced potatoes in the 1860s and was an important lumbering presence into the early 20th century. It's home to Mount Ellen and Mad River Glen ski areas and to inns along Rt. 17 and the German Flats Rd.

Warren Village. The village center of the long-established farm town of Warren (population: 1,700) is a compact clapboard cluster of town hall, steepled church, and bandstand, with a double-porched general store by a waterfall across from an inn. At first glance the village doesn't look much different from the way it did in the 1950s when Rt. 100 passed through its center, but the effect of Sugarbush, the ski resort that's way up an access road at the other end of town, has been total. The Pitcher Inn's self-consciously plain face masks an elegant restaurant and some of the most elaborate (and expensive) themed rooms in Vermont; the Warren Store (once a stagecoach inn itself) stocks a mix of gourmet food and upscale clothing and gifts. Arts, antiques, crafts, and a full-service spa are within an easy walk, and a covered bridge spans the Mad River. The village is the setting for one of Vermont's most colorful July 4 parades.

Waitsfield (population: 1,659) is the Valley's commercial center, with two small, tasteful shopping malls flanking Rt. 100 on land that was farmed until the 1960s. This area is also known as Irasville, but don't let the highway signs confuse you: It's still the center of Waitsfield. The historic district is 0.5 mile up Rt. 100, a gathering of 18th- and 19th-century buildings, including a library and steepled church, on and around Bridge St. (it leads to a covered bridge). Much larger and denser than it first looks, the village offers a sophisticated mix of boutiques and services and several first-rate restaurants. Changing historical exhibits are displayed in the General Wait House. Benjamin Wait, you learn, had been a member of Vermont's famed Rodgers' Rangers and weathered dozens of French and Indian Wars battles, as well as serving in the Revolution before founding the town at age 53 in 1789.

WARREN VILLAGE WITH THE SLOPES OF SUGARBUSH IN THE BACKGROUND

Sugarbush Resort/David Brownell

He later was pitted against his fellow settlers on the question of where to put the common. He wanted it just about where the commercial center is today (the original common has been left high and dry out on Joslin Hill Rd.). Largely denuded of its woods during its era as a logging and sheep-farming community, the town is now mostly wooded and home to more people than ever.

✳ To Do

In winter the Valley's magnets are its alpine and cross-country ski areas, but in summer there are an unusual number of activities to pursue. Check the following list!

BICYCLING The Valley's wide variety of terrain, from smooth dirt roads to technical singletrack, lends itself to mountain biking. It's the hub of the 100-mile Mad River Valley Century Ride (mrvcenturyride.com) in Aug. and the Green Mountain Stage Race (gmsr.org) during the Labor Day weekend.

For rentals and service, check **Clearwater Sports** (802-496-2708), **Inverness Ski Shop** (802-496-3343), **Stark Mountain Bike Works** (802-496-4800), and **Mad River Bike Shop** (802-496-9500), all on Rt. 100 in Waitsfield. The routes listed under *Scenic Drives* are also popular bike routes. Rentals and tours are available.

Lift-served mountain biking at the Sugarbush Summer Adventure Center (802-583-6530; sugarbush.com), top of the Sugerbush Access Rd., Warren. Bring a bike or rent one; a $30 lift ticket accesses 15 miles of singletrack, cross-country, and downhill runs. Lessons and multiday programs for ages 7–70. **Blueberry Lake Cross Country Center** (802-496-6687) in Warren also opens its trails to mountain bikers.

CANOEING AND KAYAKING ♦ **Clearwater Sports** (802-496-2708; clear watersports.com), Rt. 100, Waitsfield. Barry Bender offers learn-to-canoe and -kayak programs, full-moon canoe cruises on Waterbury Reservoir, camping excursions, also a children's day program (ages 9–13) and a five-day wilderness camp program for 9- to 13-year-olds.

FARM TO VISIT **Mountain Valley Farm** (802-496-9255; vermontexperience .com), 1719 Common Rd., Waitsfield 05673. Set high on an open shoulder of the valley with a classic red cupolaed barn, the farm welcomes visitors for wagon and sleigh rides, weddings, birthday parties, or simply to meet the barnyard animals and walk or cross-country ski. Inquire about the guest suite.

FISHING Numerous streams offer good fly-fishing. The chamber of commerce keeps a list of half a dozen guide services. Vermont fishing licenses are required and can be obtained at the Village Grocery, Rt. 100, Waitsfield.

Fly Fish Vermont Service (802-253-3964). Rob Shannon, based at the Fly Rod Shop in Stowe (flyrodshop.com), offers year-round instructional, guided tours. Licenses are available at Moretown Store (802-496-6580).

FITNESS CENTERS **Sugarbush Health & Racquet Club** (802-583-6700; sugarbush.com), Sugarbush Village, Warren. An outstanding complex with indoor and outdoor pools, indoor and outdoor Jacuzzis, whirlpool, sauna, steam room, exercise room, indoor squash, tennis, and racquetball courts, massage room, aerobics studio, 11-station Nautilus, and a full range of cardiovascular equipment. Massage also available.

Bridges Family Resort and Tennis Club (802-583-2922; bridgesresort.com), Sugarbush Access Rd., Warren. A year-round health and tennis club with indoor and outdoor tennis, heated pools, fitness center, hot tub, and sauna.

FOR FAMILIES *✶* **Sugarbush Summer Adventure Center** (802-583-6300; sugarbush.com), Sugarbush Village Plaza, top of the Access Rd. Open seasonally. An 800-foot zipline; two disk golf courses, including the Peak Course (chairlift access); and mountain biking with kids' programs and instruction for all ages.

GOLF Sugarbush Golf Course (802-583-6725), Warren, at the Sugarbush Inn. An 18-hole, Robert Trent Jones Sr. course, PGA rated 42, par 72; cart and club rentals, lessons, practice range, café. Inquire about golf/lodging packages.

HIKING *Trails, Paths & Long Trail Hikes Guide*, available at the chamber of commerce, unlocks the area's many superb hiking secrets.

The **Long Trail** runs along the ridge of the Green Mountains here and is easily accessible from three places: the two gap roads and the Sugarbush Bravo chairlift. From the Lincoln Gap Rd. (the gap itself is 4.7 miles west of Rt. 100) you can hike a short way south to Sunset Ledge for a view of the Champlain Valley and Adirondacks. The more popular hike, however, is north from the gap (be advised to start early; parking is limited) to the Battell Shelter and on to Mount Abraham (5 miles round-trip), a 4,052-foot summit with spectacular views west, south as far as Killington Peak, and north as far as Belvidere Mountain. From Mount Abraham north to Lincoln Peak (accessible by Sugarbush chairlift) and on to Mount Ellen (4,135 feet) is largely above tree line; 3,600-foot General Stark Mountain to the north is best accessed (still a steep 2.6-mile hike) from Rt. 17 at Appalachian Gap. For details about the two shelters, contact the **Green Mountain Club** (802-244-7037; greenmountainclub.org). Mill Brook Inn's Joan Gorman also recommends beginning 2.1 miles up Tucker Hill Rd. at the small parking area (on the left) at the CAMEL'S HUMP STATE FOREST sign. Follow the blue blazes through the stand of pines known as "the Enchanted Forest" to the top of Dana Hill Rd. (approximately a one-hour round trip, good for skiing and snowshoeing).

VERMONT ICELANDIC HORSE FARM, WAITSFIELD

Christina Tree

Mad River Glen (802-496-3551; madriverglen.com) offers a full schedule of guided backcountry trips and bird-watching tours. Also see *Walking and Running* for the Mad River Path Association trails.

HORSEBACK RIDING Vermont Icelandic Horse Farm (802-496-7141; icelandichorses.com), N. Fayston Rd., Waitsfield. Year-round. These strong, pony-sized mounts were brought to Iceland by the Vikings, but are still relatively rare. Karen Winhold uses her stable of around 20 mounts for one- and two-hour, half- and full-day trail rides and (seasonal) inn-to-inn treks from her stable. The horses have an unusually smooth gait (faster than a walk, gentler than a trot).

POLO Sugarbush Polo Club (802-496-8938). The oldest and most active polo club in Vermont holds matches Thu., Sat., and Sun. during summer months. Polo fields are in Waitsfield Village near the Health Center and at the junction of the East Warren and Roxbury Gap Rds. Spectators welcome.

ROCK CLIMBING The **Valley Rock Gym** (802-583-6754), part of the Sugarbush Health & Racquet Club, Sugarbush Village, features an indoor climbing wall. Open to anyone over age 6 but no experience necessary. Instruction offered.

SCENIC DRIVES East Warren Road. If you miss this road, you miss the heart of the Valley. From Bridge St. in Waitsfield Village, cross the covered bridge, bear right onto East Warren Rd., and continue the 6 miles to East Warren. The views are of the Green Mountains set back across open farmland. For an overview of the Valley, take the Roxbury Gap Rd. up to the pullout (be careful, because there aren't many places to turn around). From East Warren, loop back the 2 miles through Warren Village to Rt. 100.

Bragg Hill Road. The views from this peerless old farm road are magnificent: down across pastures and the narrow valley cut by the Mill Brook to Mount Ellen. Begin at Bragg Hill Rd. (off Rt. 100 just north of the Rt. 17 junction) and drive uphill, continue as it turns to dirt, and follow it around (bearing left); it turns into Number 9 Rd. and rejoins Rt. 17.

Granville Gulf (see the map in "The White River Valleys"). Drive Rt. 100 south from Warren and the Valley quickly disappears, replaced by a dark, narrow, and twisty pass, part of the Granville Gulf State Reservation. At the height-of-land, the Mad River begins its north-flowing course toward the Gulf of St. Lawrence and the White River rises, flowing south to eventually empty into Long Island Sound. A few miles south **Moss Glen Falls** spill down a steep cliff by the road. To turn this 20-mile drive into a day trip, continue to Hancock and across the Middlebury Gap to Middlebury, then back across Appalachian or Lincoln gap (see the box) to the Mad River Valley.

SOARING Sugarbush-Warren Airport (802-496-2290; sugarbush.org), Warren. Open daily May–Oct. Respected as one of the East's prime spots for riding thermal and ridge waves. Solo and private glider lessons,

BRAGG HILL ROAD

Christina Tree

GAP DRIVES

Appalachian Gap. Even if you aren't continuing down the other side, be sure to drive up Rt. 17 past the Mad River Glen base area to its high point (there's parking at the trailhead for the Long Trail) and look down across the Champlain Valley, across the lake, to the Adirondacks in the distance. This is a great sunset ride.

Lincoln Gap is the steepest of Vermont's east–west gap roads (nothing allowed in tow, good brakes required, closed in winter), and the most spectacular. It begins on Rt. 100 just below Warren Village and climbs for 3 miles, seemingly straight up to the top of the 2,424-foot-high Lincoln Gap, where there's a pullout, a trailhead for the Long Trail. Next come magnificent vistas south, across farm fields (this stretch of road is unpaved in wide places and paved when it narrows). The village of Lincoln, clustered around a good general store, is about as quiet as Vermont gets. Continue through West Lincoln and down to Bartlett Falls in Rocky Dale (see "Addison County").

For the **ultimate foliage loop** drive west over the Appalachian Gap (Rt. 17) 16 miles from Waitsfield to Rt. 116, then 2 miles south on Rt. 116 to the Lincoln Gap Rd. and head back east 14 miles to Warren.

rides, vacations available for all ages. Come just to see who's gliding in and out. There's a café.

SPAS **Alta Day Spa** (802-495-2582; altadayspa.com), 242 Main St., Warren Village. Adjacent to the Pitcher Inn, with which it shares ownership and patrons. A full menu of spa services is offered, from massage to aromatherapy to facials and salon services.

MadRiver Massage (802-496-5638; madrivermassage.com), Starch House overlooking the Mill Brook, Rt. 100, Waitsfield (just north of the Rt. 17 junction). Open daily 10–5, Sunday seasonally. A full range of massage, also shiatsu, reflexology, Reiki, and "stress-diffuser," plus body and bath products.

SUMMER DAY CAMPS *Sugarbush Resort* (802-583-2381), the **Bridges Family Resort and Tennis Club** (802-583-2922; 800-453-2922) in Warren, and **Clearwater Sports** (802-496-2708) in Waitsfield all offer summer day camps. For ages 13 and up there's even a weeklong **Junior Soaring Camp** (802-492-2708) at the Sugarbush Airport (see *Soaring*). **Mad River Glen** also offers nature-geared day camps in summer.

SWIMMING South of Warren Village, the Mad River becomes a series of dramatic falls and whirlpools cascading through a gorge. The most secluded swimming hole is by the **Bobbin Mill** (the first right off Rt. 100 after Lincoln Gap Rd., heading south); park by the gravel pit and follow the path through the pines to a series of pools, all icy cold. Ask locally about **Warren Falls** and the best spot for skinny-dipping. The **Lareau Farm swimming hole** (now a town park) in the

Mad River, south of Waitsfield on Rt. 100, is best for kids. **Blueberry Lake** in Warren is now owned by the Green Mountain National Forest; the **Ward Fishing Access area** on Rt. 100B in Moretown is another good bet. **Bristol Falls** is just about 10 miles from Warren via the Lincoln Gap Rd. The **Sugarbush Sports Center** features a large, L-shaped outdoor pool with adjacent changing facilities, café, bar, and Jacuzzi; the **Bridges Family Resort and Tennis Club** offers indoor and outdoor pools and swimming lessons. Many inns also have outdoor pools. Inquire about the Punch Bowl (clothing optional).

TENNIS The **Bridges Family Resort and Tennis Club** (802-583-2922; 800-453-2922), Sugarbush Access Rd., Warren, offers indoor and outdoor courts and year-round tennis clinics for both adults and juniors.

WALKING AND RUNNING The **Mad River Path Association** (madriver path.com) maintains several evolving recreation paths in the Valley, namely: the Warren Path, beginning near Brooks Field at Warren Elementary School (Brook Rd., Warren); the Millbrook Path in Fayston, running along the hill through the woods (blue blazes) between Millbrook Inn and Tucker Hill Lodge, on up across German Flats Rd. to the Inn at Mad River Barn; the Mad River Greenway, following he Mad River from a parking area on Tremblay Rd. (urn off Rt. 100 north of Waitsfield at the sign for the Mad River Inn); and the Village Path, which begins at Fiddlers' Green and heads south to the Irasville Cemetery and beyond. See also *Hiking* and *Scenic Drives*.

☾ **WEDDINGS** Many inns and resorts throughout Vermont specialize in weddings—but those in the Valley were among the first to do so. Indeed, the area probably still represents the state's single largest concentration of venues and related services. Begin with the chamber—VermontWeddings.com—and look for our weddings symbol throughout this chapter.

✳ Winter Sports

CROSS-COUNTRY, TELEMARK SKIING, AND SNOWSHOEING **Ole's Cross-Country Center** (802-496-3430; 877-863-3001; olesxc.com), at the airport, Warren. Fifty km of machine-tracked trails radiate out across the meadows and into the woods with elevations ranging from 1,120 to 1,640 feet. This is a hidden treasure at the heart of the valley, with views of the mountains on both sides. Rentals and instruction. Breakfast and lunch served weekends 10–3, otherwise soups and sandwiches 9–5 at the Diner Soar Deli.

Blueberry Lake Cross-Country Ski Center (802-496-6687), 424 Robinson Rd., Warren. On the scenic east side of the Valley, a total of 60 km of secluded and protected trails.

Clearwater Sports (802-496-2708), Rt. 100, Waitsfield, offers rentals, along with custom and group tours, backcountry skis, and "skins" for attempting local stretches of the Catamount Trail (below).

Local trails

Puddledock in Granville Gulf State Reservation on Rt. 100, south of Warren, has 3.5 miles of ungroomed trails marked with red metal triangles; a map is available at the registration box.

Catamount Trail (catamounttrail.org). Check the guidebook (see "What's Where") and Web site for stretches of the trail in the Valley. The most popular begins at the Battleground (see *Lodging*) on Rt. 17 and climbs steadily uphill to the Beaver Ponds in the Phenn Basin Wilderness area.

DOWNHILL SKIING ✍ **Sugarbush Resort** (802-583-6300; 800-53-SUGAR; sugarbush.com), 1840 Sugarbush Access Rd., Warren. Two separate trail systems on two major peaks—3,975-foot Lincoln Peak at Sugarbush South and 4,135-foot Mount Ellen at Sugarbush North, originally two different ski areas—were linked in 1995 by a 2-mile (9½-minute) quad chair traversing the undeveloped Slide Brook Basin that separates them (newly accessible to skiers via a 12-passenger Pisten Bully cat). Sugarbush skiers will tell you how fortunate their resort was to be side-lined during the era in which a large percentage of New England's best ski trails were smoothed, widened, and generally homogenized. In particular they are thankful that the Castle Rock trails, recognized throughout the country as some of the meanest, most natural, and most interesting expert terrain at any major American ski resort, survive. Skiers of all abilities find plenty to please here.

Lifts: 17—7 quads, 3 triples, 4 doubles, and 3 surface. All operate 9–4, 8:30–4 weekends and holidays.

Trails: 111; 20 acres of patrolled tree skiing; 508 skiable acres.

Vertical drop: 2,650 feet.

Snowmaking: 285.5 acres overall.

Facilities: The new Gate House lodge, cafeterias, lounges, ski shops, rentals, restaurants, sports center, the slopeside Clay Brook Hotel and Residences, condominiums, Pisten Bully access to Allyn's Lodge on Lincoln Peak for specialty dinners.

Sugarbush Ski and Snowboarding School: Headed by Olympian Doug Lewis and extreme skier John Egan, the emphasis is on learning by doing. Clinics, special

VIEW OF SUGARBUSH'S LINCOLN PEAK AND MOUNT ELLEN TRAILS

Courtesy Sugarbush Resort/Dennis Curran

teen program; women's clinics, guided backcountry skiing are offered.

Snowboarding: Rentals, lessons, terrain parks.

For children: Nursery from infancy; Sugarbush Adventure Leaning Center for special morning and afternoon programs for older kids.

Rates: In 2008–09, $72 adults, $60 ages 7–18; $48 seniors 70+, $58 afternoon, savings with multiday rates, lodging packages.

✎ **Mad River Glen** (802-496-3551; in-state snow reports: 800-696-2001; outstanding Web site: madriverglen

Mad River Glen

THE NEW SINGLE CHAIR AT MAD RIVER GLEN

.com). The ubiquitous red-and-white bumper sticker challenges MAD RIVER GLEN: SKI IT IF YOU CAN, but the mountain is one of the friendliest as well as the most challenging places to ski. It's also the only one in New England to prohibit snowboarding. One of the region's oldest major ski areas (the first to offer slope-side lodging), in 1995 it became the first to be owned cooperatively by its skiers, who are dedicated to preserving its narrow, continuously vertical trails, cut to the contours of the mountain. Access to the summit of Stark Mountain (3,637 feet) is via the vintage-1948 single chair, the only one left in the country, rehabbed rather than replaced in 2007. All trails funnel into the central base lodge area, the better for families, many of whom are now third-generation Mad River skiers. Another matter of Mad River fact: Some long-popular woods trails are off the ski map, a phenomenon that has since been aped by many other ski areas. This is also a favored place for telemarking and the only major ski mountain with a serious snowshoe trail system and full program of snowshoeing/nature treks. On a good snow day it's the region's best ski buy.

Lifts: 4 chairs, including the single, plus the Callie's Corner Handle Tow.

Trails and slopes: 21 expert, 8 intermediate, 16 novice, a total of 800 skiable acres.

Vertical drop: 2,037 feet.

Snowmaking: 15 percent, which includes top-to-bottom on the Practice Slope, also other high-volume, low-elevation areas.

Facilities: Base lodge, cafeteria, and pub; also the newly rehabbed Birdcage, halfway up the mountain, serving sandwiches, drinks; ski shop, rentals, ski school.

For children: Cricket Club Nursery for 6 weeks–6 years; programs for ages 3–17 include Junior Racing and Junior Mogul.

Rates: $60 adults, $64 holidays, $39 midweek; less for juniors (14 and under) and seniors (65–69); half-day, multiday rates. Under 6 and over 70 ski free.

ICE SKATING **The Skatium** at Mad River Green Shopping Center in Waitsfield (lighted) offers rentals, also available from neighboring **Inverness Ski Shop** (802-496-3343); free day and night skating on the groomed hockey rink at Brooks Recreation Field off Brook Rd. in Warren.

AN INTERPRETIVE TRIP UP STARK
MOUNTAIN BY SNOWSHOE

Christina Tree

SLEIGH RIDES Mountain Valley Farm (802-496-9255) in Waitsfield offers sleigh rides.

Stark Mountain by Snowshoe (Mad River Glen: 802-496-33551; madriver glen.com), Warren. Half a dozen trails ranging in length from a short spur to 2.2 miles are marked, and Mad River's resident naturalist Sean Lawson offers a full program of guided **tracking treks**, including two-hour **Nighttime Nature Rambles** every Friday and Saturday during ski season. An on-mountain nature center has been recently rehabbed and expanded. **Tele-marking** is also a longtime specialty at **Mad River Glen**. Inquire about rentals, lesson and lift packages, and special events.

SNOWMOBILING Eighty miles of local trails are maintained by the Mad River Ridge Runners; snowmobile registration can be purchased at **Kenyon's Store**, Rt. 100, Waitsfield. No rentals.

✳ Lodging

Note: The Sugarbush-based (800-53-SUGAR) reservation service is open 9–5 daily, 8–8 during high ski season, serving roughly half the Valley's condos and 21 inns and B&Bs.

Note also: Many lodging places in the Valley charge an extra 4 percent community fee, used to fund Valley-wide marketing and events, in addition to the usual 9 percent state tax. Most also request a two-night minimum stay on winter and other popular weekends.

RESORTS Sugarbush Resort (800-53-SUGAR; sugarbush.com), 1840 Sugarbush Access Rd., Warren 05674, maintains the two following properties.

∞ 🐾 🔌 ⁽ᵀ⁾ **Claybrook at Sugarbush**, 104 Forest Dr., Warren 05674. This new, full-service, 110-room condo hotel lies at the hub of the Sugarbush lifts. Red with a central silver silo, it's an improvement on the standard box

hotels built recently at many ski mountains, with units ranging from studios to five rooms, all with Shaker-style decor, fireplace, and granite-topped kitchen; 61 units are in the rental pool; those in the South Wing are pet-friendly. Facilities include an outdoor

CLAYBROOK AT SUGARBUSH

Christina Tree

pool and whirlpools, a fitness room, a garage, and Timbers Restaurant (see *Dining Out*). In winter you are steps from the lifts; in summer there's golf, mountain biking, and more. $200–1,699; from $365 per night in winter.

❝❞ Sugarbush Inn (802-583-6100; 800-537-8427; sugarbush.com), Warren 05674. Handy (via shuttle and car) to lifts at both Lincoln Peak and Sugarbush North and across the road from the golf course, this is an inviting 42-room inn, owned by the same company that owns the mountain. Amenities include use of the Sports and Racket Club, room phones, air-conditioning, a library and sitting room, and an outdoor pool. $99–180, breakfast included; from $114 per couple in ski season. Under age 3, free.

✥ ❝❞ The Bridges Family Resort and Tennis Club (802-583-2922; 800-453-2922; bridgesresort.com), 202 Bridges Circle, Warren 05674. A self-contained, family-geared resort just down the access road from the Sugarbush main lifts and base lodge. Tennis is the name of the game here. Facilities include indoor tennis and outdoor courts, an indoor pool, saunas, hot tub and fitness room, and 100 attractive condo-style units ranging from one to three bedrooms, each with fireplace, sundeck, TV, and phone, some with washer/dryer. $180 for a one-bedroom midweek to $965 for two nights (the minimum) for a three-bedroom on a weekend. Cheaper off-season and the longer you stay; inquire about ski and tennis packages.

INNS The inns listed below serve dinner as a matter of course; B&Bs may serve dinner on occasion.

Pitcher Inn (802-496-6350; 888-TO-PITCH; pitcherinn.com), Warren 05674. Designed by architect David Sellers to look like it's been sitting in the middle of Warren Village for a century, the white-clapboard inn opened in the 1997–1998 winter season, replacing a building that had burned. A member of Relais & Châteaux, this is the Valley's most luxurious inn. Common spaces include a small library with books and a hearth, far from the large, elegant dining room (see *Dining Out*), and the downstairs pub. Each nine guest rooms in the inn itself was designed by a different architect to convey a different aspect of local history. The Lodges suggests a Masonic lodge (once a major social force in the Valley), with a ceiling painted midnight blue and delicately studded with stars, and obelisk-shaped posts on the king-sized bed. From a bedside switch in the Mountain Room, you can make the sun rise and set over the mountains painted on the facing wall. Bathrooms are splendid. The Alta spa, adjacent to the inn, offers massage, facials, and a variety of spa therapies. $425–650 for rooms, $800 for each of the two suites in the neighboring annex, includes breakfast, afternoon tea, and (Sun.–Thu., off-peak only) a three-course dinner; a 13 percent service charge is added. Deduct $75 for single occupancy but add $75 per extra person.

⚑ 🐾 ❝❞ Millbrook Inn & Restaurant (802-496-2405; 800-477-2809; millbrookinn.com), Rt. 17, Waitsfield 05673. Open year-round except Apr., May, and mid-Oct.–mid-Dec. This 19th-century farmhouse is a gem. The two living rooms, one with a fireplace, invite you to sit down. The heart of the ground floor, however, is the dining room, well known locally as one of the best places to dine in the Valley (see *Dining Out*). Each of the seven guest rooms is different enough to deserve its own name, but all have stenciled walls, bureaus, antique beds with firm, queen- or king-sized mattresses, and private bath. Our favorite is the Wedding Ring Room with a wedding-ring-patterned quilt on the antique queen bed with its shell-shaped inlaid headboard, a bentwood rocker, dormer window, and a picture of Thom's grandparents on the wall. A ski lodge since 1948, Millbrook has been a true country inn since Joan and Thom Gorman took over in 1979. They are constantly redecorating and landscaping the garden (breakfast is served on the patio, weather permitting), sustaining their enthusiasm with spectacularly adventurous, low-budget travels (Mount Kilimanjaro, South Africa, the Milford Track, Patagonia, and more) during the four months that they close. Guests can peruse the ever-growing stacks of photo albums chronicling these trips. They travel lightly and so there are remarkably few souvenirs, just new dishes on the menu and an ever-expanding wine list. Winter and summer per-couple rates are $110 B&B midweek, $130 on weekends; MAP is $170 midweek, $190 on weekends; foliage season is $130 B&B, $190 MAP. Inquire about the two-bedroom Octagon House on the wooded hillside across the brook (minimum three days). Children ages 6 and older are welcome.

1824 House Inn (802-496-7555; 800-426-3986; 1824house.com), 2150 Main St. (Rt. 100), Waitsfield 05673. North of the village, the gabled house is a beauty, decorated with an eye to room colors, Oriental rugs, and well-chosen antiques, in addition to comfort. The eight guest rooms vary, but all have private bath and featherbed. There are gracious drawing and dining rooms with fireplaces. The 15-acre property invites walking and cross-country skiing. There's also a good swimming hole in the Mad River just across the road. Inkeeper John Lum-

bra is an accomplished chef. The 1870s post-and-beam barn is a frequent wedding venue as well as a restaurant (see *Dining Out*). $88–175 per room includes a full breakfast. Two-day minimum on weekends, three on winter holidays.

The Waitsfield Inn (800-758-2801; 800-758-3801; waitsfieldinn.com), P.O. Box 969, Rt. 100, Waitsfield 05673. Innkeepers Ronda and Mike Kelley seem equal to the task of managing this middle-of-the-village inn, an 1825 parsonage with a "great room"—offering plenty of space to relax in front of the hearth—in the (former) attached carriage and horse barn. The dining rooms (open to the public) are well away from the several comfortable spaces reserved for guests. The 14 guest rooms (all with private bath) vary from cozy doubles to family rooms with lofts. Appropriate for children ages 6 and older. $129–169 during regular summer and winter seasons includes a full breakfast. Lunch and brunch are also served.

Weathertop Mountain Inn (802-496-4909; 800-800-3625; weather topmountaininn.com), 755 Mill Brook Rd., Waitsfield 05673. Deceptively plain on the outside, inside Weathertop is filled with light—and also with Asian art, Persian carpets, and souvenirs from the several years innkeepers Lisa and Michael Lang spent traveling while based in Singapore. More surprises: In addition to a full breakfast, they offer guests an optional full dinner menu with a dozen entrée choices ($14–18), such as spiced minced lamb with yogurt and mint sauce, or venison medallions in black pepper. Common space includes a large, comfortable living room with fieldstone fireplace and piano as well as TV with DVD/video player and a library of old movies, plus a fourth-floor game room with a fireplace.

Down off the patio there's a hot tub and sauna. The eight air-conditioned rooms have either two quilt-covered double beds, a queen, or a king. All have fridge and full bath. $105–165 per room includes breakfast. Inquire about a slope-side condominium.

🦚 𝒮 **Inn at Mad River Barn** (802-496-3310; madriverbarn.com), 2849 Mill Brook Rd., Waitsfield 05673. Betsy Pratt, former owner of Mad River Glen Ski Area, preserves the special atmosphere of this classic 1940s ski lodge, with its massive stone fireplace and deep leather chairs, and a dining room filled with mismatched oak tables and original 1930s art. At this writing, the future plans for lodge are uncertain—but it's worth checking.

BED & BREAKFASTS ⌾ **The Inn at Round Barn Farm** (802-496-2276; theroundbarn.com), East Warren Rd., Waitsfield 05673. Named for its remarkable round (12-sided) barn built in 1910 and now housing the Green Mountain Cultural Center (see *Entertainment*), with a lap pool and greenhouse on its ground floor, this old farmhouse is one of New England's most elegant bed & breakfasts. Innkeeper Anne Marie DeFreest offers 12 antiques-furnished rooms, 7

with gas fireplace, several with steam shower and/or Jacuzzi, all overlooking the meadows and mountains. Guests who come in winter are asked to leave their shoes at the door and don slippers to protect the hardwood floors. Common space includes a sun-filled breakfast room, a stone terrace, a book-lined library, and a lower-level game room with pool table, TV, VCR, and a fridge stocked with complimentary soda and juices. From $165 midweek for a double room with a regular shower to $315 on weekends in high season for a suite with marble fireplace, canopy king bed, Jacuzzi, and steam shower. Midweek packages start at $99 per room. Prices include gourmet breakfast and afternoon edibles. Weddings are a specialty of the barn, which also serves as a venue for summer concerts and opera. In winter the inn maintains extensive snowshoe trails (snowshoes are complimentary to guests). Appropriate for children 15 and older. The inn hosts an Opera Festival in June, a photo exhibit in August, and a juried art show in foliage season.

ʰⁱ **West Hill House** (802-496-7162; 800-898-1427; westhillbb.com), 1496 West Hill Rd., Warren 05674. A gabled farmhouse off in a far corner of the golf course but convenient both to the

THE INN AT ROUND BARN FARM

Christina Tree

Sugarbush lifts and to the village of Warren. Susan and Peter MacLaren offer eight guest rooms, including two suites, all with private bath with either a Jacuzzi tub and shower or steam bath/tub/shower combo, and all with gas fireplace and direct phone. The house offers an unusual amount of common space: a living room, library with fireplace and pool table, and sunroom with views to the mountains and spectacular gardens. Step out the front door to cross-country ski or play golf, out the back into 9 wooded acres. $140–200 per couple B&B midweek, $150–235 weekends with a two-night minimum.

⊙ ₺ ⁽ↂ⁾ **Tucker Hill Inn** (phone/fax 802-496-3983; 800-543-7841; tucker hill.com), 65 Marble Hill Rd., Waitsfield 05673. A classic 1940s ski lodge with a fieldstone hearth in the pine-paneled living room. Phil and Alison Truckle offer 12 rooms and six suites, all with private bath, phone, TV. Most rooms have queen or king bed and are accessed off one hall in the main house. Most suites are in the newer Courtyard Building, but a two-room on the lower level of the main house—with a Jacuzzi, gas fireplace, and private entrance—can accommodate a family (no children under 6, please). A full breakfast is included in $109–299 in high season, $109–269 in low.

⚘ ✇ ⁽ↂ⁾ **Mountain View Inn** (802-496-2426; mountainview.com), 1912 Mill Brook Rd. (Rt. 17), Waitsfield 05673. This very Vermont house is bigger than it looks, with seven nicely decorated guest rooms (private baths). It's been geared to guests since it became one of the Valley's first ski lodges in 1948. Since 1978, under ownership by Fred and Susan Spencer, its year-round feel has been that of an unusually hospitable small country inn. Rooms are furnished with antiques

(our favorite is the 1840s "rolling pin" tiger maple bed) and bright quilts. Guests gather around the wood-burning stove in the living room and at the long, three-centuriy-old pumpkin pine harvest table for breakfast. Handy to Sugarbush, Mad River Glen, and the Mill Brook Path. $100–140 per couple B&B.

⊙ ✇ ⁽ↂ⁾ **The Featherbed Inn** (802-496-7151; featherbedinn.com), 5864 Main St. (Rt. 100), Waitsfield 05673. Tom and Linda Gardner are the new innkeepers in this nicely restored 1806 inn, with exposed beams, pine floors, and a formal living room as well as an informal "lodge room" with a field-stone fireplace, games, and books. It's set far back from Rt. 100, overlooking flower gardens and fields. Ten guest rooms are divided between the main house, which includes two family-friendly suites, and a garden cottage with three more rooms, all with feath-erbed mattresses. $110–215 (depending on room and season) includes a full breakfast; the cottage is $225.

Beaver Pond Farm (800-685-8285; beaverpondfarminn.com), 1225 Golf Course Rd., Warren 05674. There's a welcoming feel to Kim and Bob Sexton's beautifully renovated 1840s farmhouse, overlooking a beaver pond and set in the rolling expanse of the Sugar-bush Golf Course. The four guest rooms all have private bath, fine linens, and down comforters; also spa robes to ease your way to the outside hot tub. Breakfast is an event, and the 24-hour wet bar includes complimentary coffee and tea, honor-system wine and beer. $159–179. Ski & Stay from $117 per person.

✇ ⁽ↂ⁾ **The Mad River Inn** (802-496-7900; 800-832-8278; madriverinn .com), P.O. Box 75, Tremblay Rd. off Rt. 100, Waitsfield 05673. An 1860s house with fine woodwork and large picture windows overlooking meadows that invite snowshoeing in winter. It's also steps from the recreation path and a good swimming hole and serves as lodging base for the Vermont Icelandic Horse Farm. The seven guest rooms and a single two-bedroom suite all have featherbed and private bath. Facilities include an outdoor hot tub and a downstairs game room with a pool table. Rates from $105 for the smallest room with a private but hall bath, to $160 for the largest with private bath on a weekend; a three-course breakfast and afternoon tea are included. Children 5 years and older are welcome. Inquire about two- to five-day riding packages.

The Sugartree Inn (802-583-3211; 800-666-8907; sugartree.com), 2440 Sugarbush Access Rd., Warren 05674. This contemporary ski lodge, with a country inn interior, stands near the very top of the access road. Brits Graham Hewison and Maxine Longmuir pride themselves on their Aga cook stove—but there are plenty of other reasons to stay here. The nine rooms have quilts, canopy and brass beds, also air-conditioning and private bath. A ground-floor suite with a gas fireplace can sleep a family of four. There's also a fireplace in the living room. In the dining room a two-course (sweet or savory) breakfast, with specials like stuffed pears and three-cheese soufflé, is included in the $110–180 per couple rate; so is afternoon tea.

⊗ **Belding House B & B** (802-496-7420; beldinghouse.com), 746 Rt. 100, Moretown. Innkeepers Clif Thompson and Larry Richichi have totally revamped this 1810 home, creating five imaginatively and tastefully decorated queen-bedded guest rooms, two on the first floor, each with private bath, luxury linens, and down com-

forter. Common rooms are hung with original art; patio and porch invite sitting outside. The restored 1840s barn and gardens are a venue for weddings and civil unions. $149–169 includes breakfast (an event).

❝❞ **Yellow Farmhouse Inn** (802-496-4263; 800-400-5169; yellowfarmhouse-inn.com), P.O. Box 345, 550 Old County Rd., Waitsfield 05673. This 1850s farmhouse sits off above meadows, minutes from the middle of Waitsfield. Minke and Sandi Ansatos have improved the decor and comfort of the seven guest rooms and a suite (all with private bath); several rooms have gas or electric Vermont Castings stove, some a whirlpool tub. $109–239 (the high end is for the two-room suite with Jacuzzi and kitchenette, sleeping four).

Camel's Hump View Farm (802-496-3614), Rt. 100B, Moretown. The Maynards have been welcoming guests for decades in their lovely 1830s farmhouse with its big country kitchen. The two guest rooms are removed from the rest of the house. $90 per couple B&B, $150 with family dining. Wilma Maynard makes jams from the farm's blueberries, raspberries, and peaches.

⊗ **Inn at Lareau Farm** (802-496-4949; 800-833-0766; lareaufarm.com), 48 Lareau Road at Rt. 100. This classic old farm adjoins the American Flatbread (pizza) Company, which now owns it. The 12-room inn has spacious grounds stretching to a swimming hole and back to a wooded hill and including an outdoor pavilion, a popular site for weddings.

🦞 🐾 ✎ ❝❞ **Hyde Away Inn** (802-2322), 1428 Millbrook Rd. (Rt. 17), Waitsfield. One of Mad River's original ski lodges, the Hyde Away offers reasonably priced accommodations geared to families and hard-skiing singles alike. The justly famed tavern (see *Après-Ski*) is literally tucked away at the back with a separate entrance from the inn. Guests have their own living room with a fireplace; there's also a popular, family-geared restaurant (see *Eating Out*). Rooms range from two "over the bar" with shared bath ($59–89), to recently added suites with whirlpool bath or fireplace, to family rooms sleeping up to five, $109–199 during ski season. Cheaper in summer. Request a quiet room. Innkeeper Bruce Hyde is an avid bicyclist and this is headquarters for the Mad River Valley Century Ride in August.

CONDOMINIUMS The Valley harbors more than 400 rental condominium units, many clustered around Sugarbush (Lincoln Peak), more scattered along the access road, and some squirreled away in the woods. No one reservation service represents them all. **Sugarbush Resort Condos** (802-583-6100; 800-537-8427; sugarbush.com). The number of resort-managed units available varies and usually averages around 100—some slope-side, most walk-to-the-slopes—with health club access. From $99 for a one-bedroom to $750 for a four-bedroom. Prices vary with season. **Sugarbush Village Condominiums** (800-451-4326; sugar bushvillage.com) represents a similar range of condos and homes around Sugarbush, including Clay Brook Residences. **Sugarbush Real Estate Rentals** (802-496-2591; sugarbush rentals.com) offers nightly, weekly, and monthly rentals in a variety of local condos and homes.

⚘ **The Battleground** (802-496-2288; 800-248-2102; battlegroundcondos .com), Rt. 17, Fayston 05673. An attractive cluster of town houses, each designed to face the brook or a piece of greenery, backing into one another and thus preserving most of the 60 acres for walking or ski touring (the area's 60 km network of trails is accessible). In summer there's a pool, tennis and paddle tennis courts, and a play area for children. Mad River Glen is just up Rt. 17. Rates (two-night minimum) for two-, three-, and four-bedroom units.

🍴 ⛄ ⚘ **PowderHound** (802-496-5100; 800-548-4022; powderhoundinn .com), P.O. Box 135 (Rt. 100), Warren 05674. The old roadside farmstead now serves as reception and dining rooms for condo-style apartments clustered in back. Each of these consists of two rooms, one with two beds and another lounging/dining space with daybeds or pull-out couches and a TV; token cooking facilities. It's all nicely designed and maintained, nothing fancy but a good deal for families and couples who like the privacy of their own space with an option to mix with fellow guests. Summer facilities include a swimming pool; there's a hot tub for year-round use, plus a winter shuttle to the mountain. $89–179 in winter, with many two- and three-day (also midweek) ski packages; less off-season. Small charge for pets.

✳ Where to Eat

DINING OUT *Note:* The Valley restaurants are unusual in both quality and longevity. Most have been around for quite some time and, like most culinary landmarks, have their good and bad days.

Pitcher Inn (802-496-6350; pitcher inn.com), 275 Main St., Warren Village. Open for dinner. The elegant inn dining room features an à la carte menu orchestrated by chef Sue Schickler. It changes seasonally and is frequently dictated by what's available locally that day. On a July evening you might begin with chilled gazpacho, then dine on veal medallions with grilled figs, Swiss chard, sauce verte, and mustard spaetzle. Entrées $29–40. The choice of wines by the glass is large, and the wine list itself is long and widely priced.

Chez Henri (802-583-2600), Sugarbush Village. Open only during ski season from 11:30 for a bistro/bar menu and from 5:30 for dinner. A genuine bistro, opened in 1964 by Henri Borel, former food controller for Air France. It's a snug, inviting café with a fireplace, marble bar (imported from a Barre soda fountain), and terrace for dining out front in summer. Dinner entrées usually include roast duck with a fruit and pepper sauce and bouillabaisse, but items change frequently. Come early to get one of the coveted booths in the bar. Entrées $15–26.

🐚 Millbrook Inn & Restaurant (802-496-2405; millbrookinn.com), Rt. 17, Waitsfield. Open for dinner except Apr., May, and late Oct.–mid-Dec. Thom Gorman is the chef and Joan Gorman the pastry chef, hostess, and waitress in their attractive dining room, a double parlor with hearth and French doors opening onto a garden. This is, in fact, one of the most unusual and best-value restaurants in New England. Thom and Joan reenergize during the months they close by hiking, backpacking, kayaking, and camping in the world's far corners, bringing back new flavors (and wines) to share. They offer an eclectic, changing menu that might range from hand-rolled three-cheese spinach fettuccine to five-peppercorn beef, but always includes a fish of the day and an "innkeeper's choice," along with a few Indian dishes, a legacy of Thom's Peace Corps days. We recommend the badami rogan josh, a wonderfully spiced (local) lamb dish. All dinners include Joan's anadama bread, as well as salad and starch—but save room for one of her freshly made pies, cakes, or

ice creams. The wine list is varied and reasonably priced, especially interesting discoveries from small vineyards in Argentina, South Africa, and Australia. Beer is also served. Entrées $15.95–22.95.

The Common Man Restaurant (802-583-2800; commonmanrestaurant .com), German Flats Rd., Warren. Dinner Tue.–Sat. Reservations suggested. A mid-19th-century barn hung with chandeliers and warmed by an open hearth, this Vermont dining landmark is now owned by chef Keith and Julia Paxman. The menu is varied with an emphasis on local ingredients. Starters might include beggar's purse (phyllo-wrapped escargots and blue cheese with garlic cream sauce). Entrées could include sautéed quail with Vermont smoked bacon and duck confit cassoulet. Entrées $21.50–24.75 with the option of bistro plates like panko-crusted pork tenderloin ($14.50–18.75).

1824 House Inn (802-496-7555; 800-426-3986; 1824house.com), 2150 Main St. (Rt. 100), Waitsfield. Dinner by reservation Thu.–Mon. in summer, Wed.–Sun in winter—but check, because the restaurant sometimes closes for private receptions. North of the village, the inn is a classic white

PERIPATETIC CHEF THOM GORMAN AT THE MILLBROOK INN

Christina Tree

farmhouse turned elegant inn, and the restaurant is an open-timbered barn. Innkeeper John Lumbra, a graduate and former faculty member of Johnson & Wales culinary school, prepares various feasts: "Barn-B-Qs" featuring slow-smoked barbecued ribs, chicken, and steak. Entrées include salad, sides, and corn bread, $16.95–22.95). " Sunday Supper" (the $26 prix fixe menu might feature prime rib, cod, and a vegetarian option) and classic dining from the à la carte menu (entrées $23–32). Reservations appreciated.

Sweetwood Grill & Bar at The Powderhoud (802-496-4552; sweet woodgrill.com), Rt. 100, Warren. Open seasonally. Owner-chef Jeff Lynn serves up classics with a twist, like porter-house steak but with sautéed sweet potato, parsnip, and sweet peach brandy, or pan-blackened Carolina grouper with smoky collard greens, grilled polenta, and roasted corn and poblano salsa. Entrées $26–30. You can also have a burger or panini at the bar.

Timbers Restaurant (802-583-6800) at Lincoln Peak Village, Sugarbush Resort, Warren. Vermont's newest post-and-beam round barn at the base of the Sugarbush lifts is a full-service restaurant serving three squares including a serious dinner menu with a commitment to fresh and local. The menu might include pork & peaches (local pork with grilled peach, frisée salad, and sweet potato hay ($23). The bar menu includes fish-and-chips and burgers

EATING OUT ❦ ✑ **Easy Street Café** (802-496-7234), Rt. 100, 0.5 mile south of the junction of Rts. 100 and 17 (next to the Catholic church). Open daily for breakfast and lunch 8–4; for dinner (except Mon.) 5:30–9:30. A winner! The kitchen is wide open, and the aromas are irresistible. On the

damp day we visited, we had a choice of freshly made soups and chilis, sandwiches on still-warm bread, and freshly made pastries, along with self-serve coffees and teas. The dinner menu is surprisingly varied: You might begin with roasted littlenecks with cob-smoked bacon or vegetable tempura, then dine on vegetable timbales with grilled portobello mushrooms; shellfish in Thai-style curried broth with noodles, scallions, mushrooms, and sprouts; or rosemary-marinated rack of lamb. Kids 12 and under can have a hamburger or grilled cheese with fries. This is also a source of take-out meals. The adjacent Purple Moon Pub (see *Après-Ski*) also features comfortable seating and good food as well as live music on weekends.

✑ **"Ψ" Big Picture Café** (802-496-8996; bigpicturetheater.info), 48 Carroll Rd., off Rt. 100, Waitsfield. Open Wed.–Sun. 7 AM–10 PM. Bavaria-born Claudia Becker has orchestrated a real winner here—both the adjacent Big Picture Theater and this cheery space that's become an all-day community gathering spot, from huevos rancheros through croque monsieur to homemade shepherd's pie. There's also an espresso bar with Italian and French sodas, a Biergarten in summer, a full bar, and an authentic soda fountain.

✑ **The Spotted Cow** (802-496-5151), Bridge St. Marketplace, Waitsfield. Open Wed.–Sun. 7:30–2, also for Italian dinners Fri.–Sat. 5:30–8. This pretty restaurant (the decor survives from its previous life as a bistro) is now the setting for great breakfasts and "country's style meals": burgers, salads, from-scratch soups, and daily specials. Kids' menu. Wine and beer served.

Green Cup Café & Bakery (802-496-4963), 40 Bridge St., Waitsfield. Open 7–2 except Wed.; for dinner Sat.–Mon. We happened to be in town on a Wednesday so we only know the buzz: good for fair-trade coffee, local and organic ingredients; so popular for dinner that reservations are essential (wine and beer served).

American Flatbread Restaurant (802-496-8856), 40 Lareau Rd., Rt. 100, Waitsfield. Open Fri. and Sat. 5:30–9:30, year-round (more or less). George Schenk's distinctive pizza is baked in a primitive, wood-fired oven heated to 800 degrees; the results are distributed to stores from Florida to Chicago. On weekends the kitchen becomes an informal dining space featuring flatbread (toppings include cheese and herbs, sun-dried tomatoes, homemade sausage with mushrooms) and exceptional salads whose dressing boasts homemade fruit vinegar. Also specials such as grilled vegetables with garlic-herb sauce and oven-roasted chicken. Dine in or take out. Beer served. Each night Schenk writes a dedication, always food for thought.

Terra Rossa Ristorante (802-583-7676), Sugarbush Access Rd., Waitsfield. Open Tue.–Sat. for dinner. A new, moderately priced Italian restaurant with a brick pizza oven. Good feedback. No reservations.

Egan's Big World Pub and Grill (802-496-3033), junction of Rts. 100 and 17. Open nightly from 5; also Sunday brunch. Named for local extreme skier John Egan (who skis the world), this local gathering place has moved up in size and pricing from its old quarters down Rt. 100. Still the same chef. Brews and good hearty dishes like Hungarian goulash ($15.75) and New York sirloin ($18.25) are the specialty, but you can also dine on Chinese tofu, "mushroom love" (wild mushroom ravioli), or a burger.

Jay's (802-496-8282), Mad River Green Shopping Center, Rt. 100, Waitsfield. Open for breakfast until noon daily, for lunch and dinner Tue.–Sat. A family restaurant, bright and spacious. Dinner might be chicken pesto, pasta, or pizza. Children's menu; full liquor license.

Hyde-Away Restaurant (802-496-2322), Rt. 17, Open nightly 5:30–9:30 (9 midweek). An informal, affordable restaurant with plenty of appetizers and soups, sandwiches, and burgers. The dinner menu might include crabcakes served with homemade roasted red pepper aioli, Vermont maple chicken with garlic mashed potatoes, and vegetable pasta. All entrées come with salad and homemade bread. Seasonal outdoor deck dining. Children's menu and toy area. Full liquor.

Michael's Good to Go (802-496-3832), Village Square Shopping Center (a few doors down from Mehuron's Market), Waitsfield. Open Tue.–Fri. for lunch, Thu.–Sat. 5–8 for dinner. Michael Flannagan, one of the Valley's favorite chefs, offers condo dwellers and local residents a great take-out menu ranging from Asian fusion to Vermont turkey potpie and Baja-style fish tacos plus the likes of a cheesy cheese pizza for kids.

Warren Store (802-496-3864), Warren Village. Open daily 8–7, Sun. until

WARREN STORE

Christina Tree

6. Year-round the bakery produces French and health breads, plus croissants and great deli food and sandwiches; in summer a deck overlooks the small waterfall.

Sweet Pea Natural Foods (802-496-7763), Village Square Shopping Center, Rt. 100, Waitsfield. Back behind Tempest Book Shop, a source of vegetarian soups and sandwiches as well as body care products, organic produce, healthy drinks, and more.

Village Grocery, Mobil & Deli (802-496-4477), 4348 Main St., Waitsfield. Pick up a really good, reasonably priced (they aren't called "designer") sandwich and head for the picnic tables a miles or so north under the pines (junction of Rt. 100 and Tremblay Rd.).

✳ Entertainment

The Big Picture Theater & Café (802-496-8994; bigpicturetheater.info), Rt. 100, Waitsfield. Mainstream and independent films.

Green Mountain Cultural Center (802-496-7722; theroundbarn.com/ gmcc.htm) at the Joslyn Round Barn, East Warren Rd., Waitsfield. This con-

BIG PICTURE THEATER IN WAITSFIELD
Christina Tree

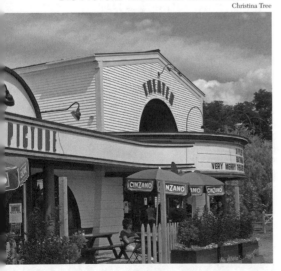

cert and exhibit space in a classic round barn is the setting for a series of summer concerts and opera, along with workshops and a major foliage-season art exhibit.

The **Valley Players** (802-583-1674; valleyplayers.com), a community theater company, housed in the Waitsfield Odd Fellows Building, produces three or four plays a year in its own theater just north of Waitsfield Village, Rt. 100.

The **Phantom Theater** (802-496-5997 in summer), a local group with New York City theater community members, presents original plays and improvisational performances for children and adults at Edgecomb Barn in Warren.

Bundy Center for the Arts (802-496-4781; bundycfa.org), off Rt. 100, Waitsfield. A contemporary arts center with a gallery, the venue for concerts, live performances, weddings, and events.

The Commons Group (802-496-4422; theskinnerbarn.com), the Skinner Barn, 609 Common Rd., Waitsfield. Founded by Broadway and TV performer Peer Boynton, presenting theater, concerts, and a cabaret series.

Also note **Mad River Chorale** performances in June and December (check with the chamber of commerce: 802-496-7907).

APRÈS-SKI The Hyde-Away (802-496-2322) is the hot spot near Mad River Glen (Rt. 17). Literally hidden away behind the inn (see *Lodging*), the tavern offers a fireplace, big friendly bar, and pool table, as well as dimly lit corners for pub food or the inn's full menu (see *Eating Out*). Many microbrews and nightly specials.

The Purple Moon (802-496-3400; purplemoonpub.com), Rt. 100 south of the Rt. 17 junction, features a fireplace, a mahogany bar, couches, and atypical late-night pub food like Vermont goat-cheese fondue; live music Saturday nights.

Localfolk Smokehouse (802-496-5623), junction of Rts. 17 and 100. Open Thu.–Sat. A wide choice of draft beers, known for hickory-smoked barbecued ribs and live music; there's a pool table and an outdoor deck.

✳ Selective Shopping

ANTIQUES Warren Antiques (802-496-4025), Warren Village. Open daily 10–5, May–Oct., then by appointment. Victoriana, furniture, ephemera.

ART GALLERIES Artisans Gallery (802-496-6256), Bridge St., Waitsfield. Open daily 10–5. A highly selective collection of furniture, baskets, canes, rugs, glass, decoys, ornaments, photography, and much more. The fine art and furniture galleries are in the rear.

Parade Gallery (802-496-5445) in Warren Village is a long-standing and widely respected source of affordable prints and original art, sculpture, and photography, featuring Gary Eckhart watercolors and Sabra Field prints.

CRAFTS SHOPS AND GALLERIES Cabin Fever Quilts (802-496-2287; cabinfeverquiltsvt.com), the Old Church, Waitsfield. Closed Tue., otherwise open 10–5. Vee Lowell offers a selection of machine-sewn, hand-tied quilts in a range of sizes and patterns, priced $200–1,600; also 1,400 bolts of quilting fabrics plus pillows and gifts.

Waitsfield Pottery (802-496-7155; waitsfieldpottery.com), Rt. 100 across from Bridge St. Ulrike Tesmer makes functional, hand-thrown stoneware pieces, well worth a stop.

Luminosity Stained Glass Studio (802-496-2231; luminositystudios.com), the Old Church, Rt. 100, Waitsfield.

Christina Tree

MAD RIVER GLASS

Open except Tue. This is a very special shop. Since 1975 this former church has served as the studio in which Barry Friedman fashions Tiffany lamp shades and a variety of designs in leaded and stained glass. Now he devotes most of his time to custom work but keeps a selection of opulent lighting, also showcases Arroyo craftsmen and mica lamps.

Mad River Glass Gallery (802-496-9388), 4237 Main St. (Rt. 100), Waitsfield Village. Melanie and Dave Leppia's handsome gallery is a must-stop. The glass is deeply colored, highly original, and created (blown and cast) on the premises.

Bradley House in Warren Village showcases work by an amazing variety of local craftspeople. It's a trove of mostly Vermont hand-loomed rugs, woven baskets, quilts and pillows, wooden bowls, metalwork, furniture, fabric art, pottery, hand-blown glass, and more. Open daily.

The outstanding **Plush Quartz Art Glass** studio is in Granville, south of Warren on Rt. 100; see "The White River Valleys."

SPECIAL SHOPS Warren Store and More, Warren Village. Staples, wines, and the deli and bakery are downstairs (see *Eating Out*); upstairs is one of Vermont's best-kept secrets, an eclectic selection of clothing, jewelry, and gifts. We treasure everything we have bought here, from earrings to a winter coat.

All Things Bright and Beautiful (802-496-3397), Bridge St., Waitsfield. You'll find an incredible number of stuffed animals and unusual toys on two floors of this old village house.

The Store (802-496-4465), Rt. 100, Waitsfield. Since its 1965 opening, this exceptional shop has grown tenfold, now filling two floors of an 1834 former Methodist meetinghouse with superb early American, French, and English antiques, cookware, tabletop gifts, collectibles, lifestyle books, Vermont gourmet products, and children's toys and books from around the world.

Tempest Book Shop (802-496-2022), Village Square, Waitsfield. This family-run bookstore is a trove of titles in most categories, including children's books. We like their motto: "A house without books is like a room without windows" (Horace Mann). CDs, cassettes, posters.

Alpine Options (802-583-1763; 888-888-9131), with locations at Sugarbush (on the access road) and at Mad River Glen. Open daily, Fri. until 11 during ski season. Ski and snowboard rentals, demos and repair: the best-quality all-around service, according to locals.

SUGARHOUSES Eastman Long & Sons (802-496-3448), Tucker Hill Rd., Waitsfield. "Sonny" Long sets 6,000 taps on 100 high wooded acres that have been in his family for generations. He maintains that the higher the elevation, the better the syrup, and he welcomes visitors to his roadside sugarhouse during sugaring season. On summer weekends he sells from his van at the junction of Rts. 100 and 17.

Palmer's Maple Products (802-496-3696), East Warren Rd., Waitsfield. Delbert and Sharlia Palmer sell syrup from their farm on this scenic road.

✳ Special Events

Note: Check with the chamber of commerce (see *Guidance*) and its Web site (madrivervalley.com) for weekly listings of special events.

March: **Annual New England Telemark Festival**, Mad River Glen.

April: **Vermont Adventure Games**, featuring the Sugarbush Triathlon—canoe, kayak, bicycle, cross-country ski races (more than 600 competitors), Sugarbush.

May–June: Paddling the Mad River; guided bird walks.

Mid-May–early October: **Farmer's Market**, Sat. 9–1 at Mad River Green, Rt. 100, Waitsfield (waitfieldfarmers market.com).

July 4: Outstanding **parade**, Warren Village.

July–August: **Summer productions** by the Valley Players and by the Phantom Theater (see *Entertainment*). **Green Mountain Polo Tournament**, Warren.

August: **Vermont Festival of the Arts** (vermontartfest.com) throughout the Valley: daily happenings **Century Ride** (*third Saturday;* mrvcenturyride.com)—a 100-mile ride through central Vermont based at the Hyde-Away Inn/Restaurant.

Labor Day weekend: Two-day **crafts exhibits**. **Green Mountain Stage Race** (gmsr.org).

Early October: **Soaring Encampment** throughout the Valley. **Peak Foliage Celebration Day**, weekend chairlifts.

December: **Holiday events** throughout the Valley.

BARRE/MONTPELIER AREA

Any serious attempt to understand the character of Vermont entails a visit to Montpelier: a stroll through the exceptional Vermont Historical Society Museum and into the ornate but informal statehouse built of Vermont granite and marble, and still heated with wood. Montpelier itself is a vibrant college town with colorful shops, restaurants along State and Main streets, which are as charming as the Hollywood film they inspired (*State and Main*). The back streets are a jumble of bridges, narrow lanes, and mansard roofs.

An exit on I-89, Montpelier is also at the hub of old roads radiating off into the hills, including Rt. 2, which runs all the way to Bangor, Maine, and Rt. 302 to Portland, which begins here as central Vermont's big commercial strip, "the Barre–Montpelier Road."

Billed as "the granite capital of the world," Barre (pronounced *Barry*) continues to quarry, cut, and sculpt its high-quality gray granite, now used primarily for memorial stones. The big attraction is the Rock of Ages Quarry in Graniteville, southeast of town, but its two cemeteries are the prime showcase for the work— ranging from quirky to spectacular—of generations of mostly Italian and Irish Barre sculptors. The Vermont History Center (headquarters of the Vermont Historical Society) and the Barre Opera House, one of Vermont's most beautiful and active theaters, are right downtown.

Southwest of Montpelier is the proud old town of Northfield, home of Norwich University and of no fewer than five covered bridges. East Barre and East Montpelier are both rural hamlets. As Rt. 2 climbs northeast through Plainfield and Marshfield, it accesses enticing lodging, shopping, and dining, spin-offs from liberal (writ large) Goddard College.

GUIDANCE The Capital Region Visitor Center (802-828-5981), 134 State St., Montpelier, is open 6:30–6 weekdays, 10–6 weekends. Housed in a redbrick house across the street from the capitol with a flag out front, it has knowledgeable, friendly staff and a restroom.

Central Vermont Chamber of Commerce (877-887-3678; central-vt.com) publishes a helpful booklet guide to the area.

GETTING THERE *By bus:* **Vermont Transit** (802-229-9220; 800-451-3292) from Boston to Montreal, connecting with New York and Connecticut service, stops in Montpelier at a disgraceful trailer at 1 Taylor St., off State St.

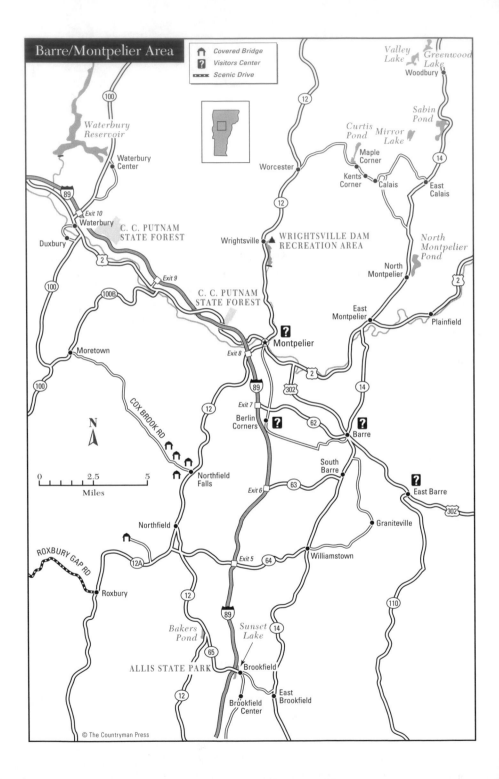

Barre/Montpelier Area

Covered Bridge
Visitors Center
Scenic Drive

Valley Lake
Greenwood Lake
Woodbury

100

Waterbury Reservoir

Waterbury Center

Sabin Pond

Curtis Pond

Mirror Lake

12

Worcester

Maple Corner

14

Kents Corner

Calais

East Calais

89

Exit 10
Waterbury

C. C. PUTNAM STATE FOREST

Duxbury

100

2

Exit 9

12

Wrightsville

WRIGHTSVILLE DAM RECREATION AREA

North Montpelier Pond

North Montpelier

2

100B

C. C. PUTNAM STATE FOREST

East Montpelier

Plainfield

Moretown

100

Montpelier

Exit 8

2

302

14

COX BROOK RD

89

Exit 7

302

Berlin Corners

62

Barre

12

South Barre

N

0   2.5   5
Miles

Northfield Falls

Exit 6

63

East Barre

302

Graniteville

Northfield

ROXBURY GAP RD

12A

Exit 5

64

Williamstown

110

Roxbury

12

89

Bakers Pond

Sunset Lake

14

ALLIS STATE PARK

65

Brookfield

12

Brookfield Center

East Brookfield

© The Countryman Press

By train: **Amtrak** (800-USA-RAIL; amtrak.com) stops in Montpelier Junction, a mile west of town on the other side of I-89.

By car: For **Montpelier** take I-89, Exit 8. At the second traffic light, make a left, crossing the river on Bailey Ave. At the light, turn right onto State St. The redbrick building that houses the information center is on your right, a good place to park. The capitol and Vermont Historical Society are a short way up across the street.

To reach **Barre** take I-89 to Exit 7 and follow signs for Rt. 62, a divided highway, to Main St.

WHEN TO GO Never come on a Monday when the Vermont Historical Society Museum is closed. Otherwise this is a rare corner of Vermont that varies little from season to season. Come Jan.–Apr. to see the Vermont Legislature in action.

MEDICAL EMERGENCY Emergency service is available by calling **911**.

Central Vermont Medical Center (802-371-4100; cvmc.hitchcock.org) is in Berlin off Rt. 62; Exit 7 off I-89.

✳ Towns

Montpelier. The smallest and possibly the most livable of the nation's state capitals, Montpelier is a town of little more than 8,000 people, with band concerts on summer Wednesdays, high school playing fields just a few blocks from the capitol. The gold dome of the State House itself is appropriately crowned by a green hill rising steeply behind it. A path leads right up that hill into **Hubbard Park**, 185 leafy acres with winding roads, good for biking and jogging. Stone Cutters Way down along the Winooski River is also a pleasant bike or jog. The **State House**, the **Vermont Historical Society Museum**, and the **T. W. Wood Art Gallery** are all must-see sights. Montpelier, moreover, is home base for the New England Culinary Institute (NECI).

Precisely why this narrow floodplain of the Winooski was selected as Vermont's statehouse site in 1805 is uncertain, as is why it was named for a small city in the Languedoc region of France. The fact is, however, that Vermont's first legislators picked a town noted for its unusual number of whiskey distilleries and named it for a town known for its wine and brandy. It's also true that Montpelier is unusually accessible, by roads both old and new, from every corner of central and northern Vermont.

Barre. This is a city of 9,300 people, surrounded by a town of 7,600. Motorists caught in Main Street's perpetual traffic may ponder the facades of the commercial buildings. Most

DETAILS OF A SCULPTED MONUMENT IN BARRE

Christina Tree

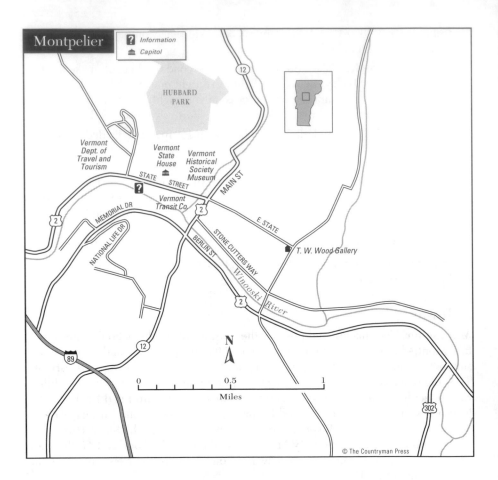

date from 1880–1910, during which the community's population jumped from 2,000 to 12,000, swollen by stonecutters and craftsmen from Scotland, Eastern Europe, Italy, and French Canada, not to mention England, Scandinavia, Spain, Germany, and the Middle East. This volatile mix of largely underpaid workers who elected a socialist mayor were not afraid to strike for their rights or to shelter victims of strikes elsewhere. In the World War I era, many famous anarchists and socialists spoke here. The **Old Labor Hall** (vintage 1900) at 46 Granite St. (off N. Main), the focal point of this struggle, has been partially restored and currently houses the city's best historical exhibits; it can be rented or toured (phone: 802-476-7550 or 802-476-8777). The quarries continue to employ some 2,000 people to produce one-third of the country's memorial stones—for which **Hope Cemetery** and **Elmwood Cemetery** serve as museums of stonecarving virtuosity. A formal **Vermont Granite Museum and Stone Arts School** (802-476-4605; granitemuseum.com) is taking shape in a 25,000-square-foot former granite shed on the Barre–Montpelier Rd., open seasonally by appointment. Check the Web site for progress and workshops.

The quarries themselves are southeast of town, primarily in Graniteville, where Millstone Hill has been chipped and chiseled since 1812, when the bedrock was turned into millstones, door stoops, and posts. In the 1830s huge slabs were hauled by oxen to build the State House, but it was only after the Civil War that the railway and a series of inventions enabled Barre to make its mark. The memorial stone business escalated after 1888, when the branch railroad finally linked the quarries to finishing sheds in the valley and to outlets beyond. All but one of the major quarries are now owned by **Rock of Ages**. This company has long made its operations a showcase for visitors, who can view the unforgettable, surrealistic landscape of the quarries themselves, hear the roar of the drills, and watch ant-sized men chip away at the giant pits. See *To Do* for mountain biking and cross-country skiing around the quarry pits on Millstone Hill.

Northfield (population: 5,748). This town's mid-19th-century commercial blocks suggest the prosperity that it enjoyed while native son Charles Paine served as governor. Paine actually railroaded the Vermont Central through his hometown instead of the more logical Barre. The old depot, now a bank, stands at one end of the handsome common. Today the town's pride is Norwich University, a private, coed college of 1,000 cadets, which bills itself as "the oldest private military college in the United States." In the Norwich University Museum in White Memorial Chapel, you learn that this institution sent more than 300 officers into the Civil War. It wasn't until 1867, however, that the college moved to Northfield from its original site in Norwich. More Northfield memorabilia as well as changing exhibits can be seen in the **Northfield Historical Society Museum** housed at 75 S. Main St. (open Sat.–Sun. 1–4 or by appointment; 802-485-6228). Northfield also boasts six covered bridges, five of which are in publicly accessible areas.

✻ To See

In Montpelier

♪ ఉ **The Vermont Historical Society Museum** (802-828-2291; vermonthistory .org), 109 State St., Montpelier. Open year-round, Tue.–Sat. 10–4; Sunday from May–Oct. only, noon–4; closed Mon.
$5 adults, $3 ages 6–17, students with ID cards, and seniors. This outstanding state museum, maintained by the Vermont Historical Society, occupies the ground floor of the replica of the Pavilion Hotel, a five-story, mansard-roofed landmark that occupied this site between 1870 and 1966. Freedom & Unity: One Ideal Many Stories—the permanent exhibition—tells the story of Vermonters from the year 1600 to the present time. ("Freedom in Unity" is the state motto.) Beginning with Vermont's geological history, it then dramatizes Abenaki Indian life; draws visitors into Bennington's Catamount Tavern to explore the state's beginnings; and

THE VERMONT HISTORICAL SOCIETY MUSEUM IN MONTPELIER

Christina Tree

Vermont State House (802-828-2228), 115 State St., Montpelier. Open Mon.–Fri. 8–4, closed holidays. Friends of the Vermont State House offers free guided tours each half hour, Mon.–Fri. 10–3:30, Sat. 11–2:30, July–mid-Oct.; otherwise Mon.–Fri. 9–3. Groups should call in advance (802-828-1411). Self-guided audio tours are also available. Visitors are welcome to watch the legislature in action, Jan.–mid-Apr.

Vermont's government was homeless from its founding in 1777 until 1805, when Montpelier was chosen as the "permanent seat of the legislature for holding all their sessions," on the condition that the town muster the land and get the capitol erected by 1808. The resulting three-story building was nine sided, with a single cupola, and warmed by a two-story stove. Legislators sat on plank seats at pine desks that were said to have been "whittled out of use" by the representatives' jackknives. The whole building had to be demolished in 1836 and was replaced by a granite Grecian temple designed by the Federal-era architect Ammi Young. After it was virtually destroyed by fire in 1857, it was rebuilt along the same but larger lines and completed in 1859.

While several chambers are quite opulent, there is noticeable informality in the way the 150 state representatives and senators talk with their constituents while standing in the Hall of Flags or seated on the black walnut sofas (which cost $60 apiece in 1859) at either end. The statue of Ethan Allen on the steps is Danby marble, and the handsome black-and-white floor of the lobby was quarried on Isle La Motte and in Proctor. The lobby is lined with portraits of Vermont-born heroes including Admiral George Dewey, Admiral Charles Clark (like Dewey, a hero of the Spanish-American War), and Calvin Coolidge, 30th president of the United States. Upstairs note the enormous oil painting by Julian Scott, *The Battle of Cedar Creek, 1864*. The cannon on the front steps was captured from the Hessians at the battle of Bennington in 1777. The Roman lady atop the gold-leafed dome is Ceres, goddess of agriculture.

THE GOLD DOME OF THE VERMONT STATE HOUSE

Christina Tree

explores life in the 19th century through interactive exhibits and re-created buildings: a general store, creamery, marble shed, train station, and more. It includes exhibits on tourism (1900–1940s), World War II, the changing landscapes of the late 19th century, and a "hall of voices."

T. W. Wood Art Gallery and Arts Center (802-828-8743; twwoodgallery.org) at Vermont College, 36 College St. (corner of E. State St.), Montpelier, open Tue.–Sun. noon–4. Free. The gallery features work by displays Thomas Waterman Wood (1823–1903), known for his genre paintings, portraits, and landscapes. The collection also contains works by his contemporaries and Depression-era art commissioned in Vermont by the WPA, including work by Reginald Marsh, Joseph Stella, and Paul Sample. Excellent changing exhibits feature contemporary Vermont artists and craftspeople.

USS *Montpelier* Museum (802-223-9502; montpelier-vt.org), city hall, at 39 Main St. Tucked upstairs in a few back rooms of the city hall is this unexpected display of ship models, uniforms, medals, and diaries documenting the life of Admiral George Dewey, a native son who inspired the christening of at least three U.S. Navy ships after his hometown, the most recent a 1993 nuclear attack submarine. Open weekdays when city hall is, 8–4:30. Free.

Kellogg-Hubbard Library (802-223-3338; kellogghubbard.lib.vt.us), 135 Main St., Montpelier. Open weekdays 10–8, Fri. and Sat. till 5:30 (earlier in summer). This lovely Italianate structure, built in 1895 of rough granite blocks, is as palatial inside as out. Behind its two-story columned entrance is a second-floor balcony, ornate fireplaces, a fine oak-and-marble staircase, classical friezes, and a central skylight that fills the hall with light. New York City real estate tycoon Martin Kellogg and his wife, Montpelier native Fanny Hubbard, both died in 1889, leaving their estate to the town for the construction of cemetery gates and a public library. But Fanny's nephew contested the will. The probate court ruled in his favor, and the town countersued in a battle that lasted three years and left Montpelier split in two. The nephew offered a truce, to build the library if the town would drop the dispute. He paid dearly: The structure cost $30,000 more than the amount set aside in the will.

In and near Barre

🎗 **Rock of Ages Visitor Center and Tours** (802-476-3119; 877-225-7627; rockofages.com), 560 Main St., Graniteville. The visitor center is open May–Oct., Mon.–Sat. 8:30–5 and Sun. 10–5 (closed July 4); tours June–mid-Oct. There's also a narrated shuttle tour to a working, 50-acre, 600-foot-deep quarry farther up the hill. Tours last 35 minutes, the first starting at 9:15, the last at 3:35. $4.50 adults, $2.50 ages 6–12. From the observation deck of the Manufacturing Division, you'll see the granite being polished and sculpted by master sculptors. We

ROCK OF AGES QUARRY IN BARRE

Joe Citro

wished that the film in the visitor center focused more on the human history of quarrying granite in Barre. The center also features interactive exhibits and a retail store with granite gifts. There is an extensive display of tombstones; many people come specifically to select one. The easiest way to get there, even from Montpelier, is via I-89, Exit 6, to Rt. 63. At the light, go straight and follow signs.

Vermont History Center (802-479-8500; vermonthistory.org), 60 Washington St. Open Tue.–Fri., 9–4:30 (closed state holidays), second Sat. 9-4. $5 users fee. Housed in the splendid Spaulding School, designed in 1891 by Lambert Packard—the architect of St. Johnsbury's Fairbanks Museum—the Vermont Historical Society headquarters includes a gallery with changing exhibits.

Hope Cemetery, Rt. 14 just north of downtown Barre. If you're coming in off I-89 on Rt. 62, continue straight ahead up Maple St. (Rt. 14); if you're on N. Main St. (Rt. 302), turn up Maple. The impressive main gates are a ways up on your left; you can drive in. The 6,000 memorials here range from classic tableaux (a replica of Michelangelo's *Pietà*) to the more whimsical, including an armchair, a Civil Air Patrol plane, a half-scale racing car, a tractor-trailer truck, a perfectly executed cube resting on one corner, and a married couple in bed, holding hands. All were sculpted by stonecutters for themselves and their families, and they rank among the most elaborate to be found anywhere in the world. **Elmwood Cemetery**, at the opposite end of downtown (Rt. 302 turns into Washington St. as it heads east; take Hill St. at the first Y and it's right there), also has many striking memorials. Tours of Barre cemeteries can be arranged through the Old Labor Hall (802-476-0567).

COVERED BRIDGES

In Northfield
Off Rt. 12 in Northfield Falls (turn at the general store) stand three covered bridges: the **Station Bridge**, spanning 100 feet, and the **Newell Bridge** are within sight of each other; farther along Cox Brook Rd. is the **Upper Bridge**, with a span of 42 feet. Another bridge is just south off Rt. 12 on Slaughter House Rd.

SCENIC DRIVES Roxbury to Warren. The road through Roxbury Gap, while not recommended in winter, is spectacular in summer and fall, commanding a breathtaking view of the Green Mountains from the crest of the Roxbury Range. Do not resist the urge to stop, get out, and enjoy this panorama. Ask locally about the hiking trail that follows the ridgeline from the road's highest point.

Northfield to Moretown. Cox Brook Rd. (marked on our map) connects Northfield Falls with the village of Moretown. It's dirt part of the way, offering views in both directions near the crest and passing through three covered bridges at the Northfield Falls end. In Northfield, Turkey Hill Rd. begins across from Depot Square and climbs up to panoramic views.

✳ To Do

BIKING Check out the Central Vermont Chamber of Commerce Web site (central-vt.com) for suggested routes through this area. **Onion River Sports** (802-229-9409; onionriver.com), 20 Langdon St., Montpelier, is the source of local bike maps and rentals (mountain bikes and hybrids).

A superb biking destination is the **Millstone Hill Touring and Recreation Center** (802-479-1000; millstonehill .com), 422 Websterville Rd., East Barre. Seventy miles of singletrack trail web 350 acres of wooded terrain, spotted with dozens of abandoned quarries. A century ago this resembled a harsh moonscape, but the quarries have since filled with water; birch, maple, and aspen have sprouted between cast-off granite boulders. Trails are clearly marked. Open seasonally 9–5. Pierre Couture offers bike rentals and repair, also lodging in the converted barn that serves as the center. Trail fee.

Christina Tree

MOUNTAIN BIKERS AT MILLSTONE HILL IN EAST BARRE

BOATING AND FISHING

Wrightsville Dam, just north of Montpelier; **North Montpelier Pond**, with a fishing access off Rt. 14; and **Curtis Pond** and **Mirror Lake** in Calais (pronounced *CAL-lus*). **Nelson Pond** and **Sabin Pond** in Woodbury are both accessible from Rt. 14, as are **Valley Lake** and **Greenwood Lake** (good for bass and pike). The **Stevens Branch** south of Barre and the Dog River in Northfield offer brook trout.

✔ **East Roxbury Fish Hatchery**, 2 miles south of Roxbury on Rt. 12A. This is a state hatchery in which salmon species are raised; children are allowed to feed the fish.

R&L Archery (802-479-9151; 800-269-9151; randlarchery.com), 70 Smith St., Barre. Open daily. Local source of fishing and hunting licenses, also fishing, bird-watching, archery, kayak, even gold prospecting gear.

GOLF Montpelier Elks Country Club (802-223-7457), 1 Country Club Rd., Montpelier, nine holes. **Barre Country Club** (802-476-7658), 142 Drake Rd., Plainfield, 18 holes. **Northfield Country Club** (802-485-4515), 2066 Roxbury Rd., Northfield, nine holes.

HIKING/WALKING *Guidance:* **The Green Mountain Club** (802-244-7037; greenmountainclub.org), RR 1, Box 650, Rt. 100, Waterbury Center 05677. The club encourages general inquiries and trail description updates (see *Hiking and Walking* in "What's Where").

Spruce Mountain, Plainfield. An unusually undeveloped state holding of 500 acres, rich in bird life. The trail begins in Jones State Forest, 4.2 miles south of the village; the three-hour hike is described in *50 Hikes in Vermont* (The Countryman Press) and in *Day Hiker's Guide to Vermont* (Green Mountain Club).

Worcester Range, north of Montpelier. There are several popular hikes described in the books listed under Spruce Mountain (above), notably **Elmore Mountain** in Elmore State Park (a 3-mile trek yielding a panorama of lakes, farms, and rolling hills), **Mount Worcester** (approached from the village of Worcester), and **Mount Hunger**.

Groton State Forest, east of Montpelier. This 25,000-acre forest offers an extensive year-round trail system. See "St. Johnsbury, Craftsbury, and Burke Mountain."

Hubbard Park and **North Branch River Park** in Montpelier are both accessible from the Vermont Institute of Natural Science (VINS) **North Branch Nature Center** (802-229-6206; vinsweb.org), 713 Elm St. (Rt. 12 north). Hubbard Park, also accessible from the State House, is 200 acres webbed with trails and a stone observation tower; North Branch offers gentle trails along this fork of the Winooski as well as more challenging, higher-altitude trails. Both parks are used for cross-country skiing and snowshoeing. The nature center offers a year-round program of birding and other events.

HORSEBACK RIDING T-N-T Stables (802-476-3097; central-vt.com/web/tnt), 75 Pine Hill Rd., Barre. Tina and Tiffany Poulin offer hour-long trail rides, pony rides, and instruction for those 8 years and over. Helmets provided. Open weekdays 4:30–7, weekends 8–7 or until dark.

STOCK CAR RACING Thunder Road International Speed Bowl (thunderroadspeedbowl.com), marked from Quarry St., Barre. Check the Web site for frequent races and other events.

SWIMMING Wrightsville Dam Recreation Area, Rt. 12 north; also numerous swimming holes in the Kents Corner area.

✳ Winter Sports

CROSS-COUNTRY SKIING Morse Farm Ski Touring Center (802-223-2740; 800-242-2740; skimorsefarm.com), 1168 County Rd., Montpelier (3 miles north of downtown). Open weather dependent 9–5 daily, 8–5 Fri.–Sun. and holidays. At an elevation of 1,200 feet, the farm offers a series of loops ranging from 0.7 to 3.9 km—over 25 km of trails in all. Rentals (on weekends and holidays), lessons, and a warming hut hitched to the gift shop; snacks available. Separate snowshoe trails.

Millstone Hill (802-479-1000; millstonehill.com), 422 Websterville Rd., East Barre, has trails that weave around some 30 old quarries, many with spectacular long-distance views of the surrounding mountains. Stop for trail maps at the Bike Touring Center on the ground floor of the red barn, open 9–5 daily.

Onion River Sports (802-229-9409; onionriver.com), 20 Langdon St., Montpelier, rents cross-country skis and snowshoes. Open daily, year-round, 9:30–6.

ICE SKATING The Central Vermont Civic Center (802-229-5900) at 268 Gallison Hill Rd. in Montpelier, open to the public Sat. 1:30–2:45 and Sun. 4–5:15.

DOWNTOWN NORTHFIELD

Christina Tree

Barre City B.O.R. Rink (802-476-0258; ci.barre.vt.us), 25 Auditorium Hill, Barre, open for public skating mid-Oct.–mid-Mar.

355

BARRE/MONTPELIER AREA

Note: For more on winter sports, see "Sugarbush/Mad River Valley."

✳ Lodging

In Montpelier 05602

✐ ⚬ᵀ⚬ **The Inn at Montpelier** (802-223-2727; innatmontpelier.com), 147 Main St. Two of the town's most stately (adjacent) Federal-style manses, renovated and furnished with antiques, Oriental carpets, and fine linens. Both belonged to James Langdon, a prominent local businessman. A marvelous Greek Revival porch, added around 1900, wraps around the yellow-clapboard Lamb-Langdon house, its wicker chairs a perfect place to rest after an afternoon stroll. Of the 19 rooms, the 7 deluxe chambers (all but one with wood-burning fireplace) are the most handsome in town. Number 27 has a huge private deck; the smaller king-, queen-, and twin-bedded rooms are also lovely. Each comes with private bath and a breakfast of homemade cereals and jams, lemon curd, fresh-baked breads, and coffee or tea. Amenities include central air-conditioning, downstairs guest pantries for coffee and tea at any hour, in-room cable TV, phone, a sunroom on the second floor, and a beautifully appointed parlor and living room with period furnishings. Innkeepers Rita and Rick Rizza have hosted the likes of Laura Bush and Martha Stewart. $142–218. Children under 6, free.

Capitol Plaza (802-223-5252; 800-274-5252; capitolplaza.com), 100 State St. The former landmark tavern is now a four-story downtown hotel with room service, a two-tiered café, and **J. Morgans**, a steak house featuring Sunday brunch, jazz nights, and weekend entertainment as well as conference and reception facilities. The 56 rooms

vary from the standard two double and queen beds with comforters to individually decorated "colonial guest rooms" with bathrobes, eyelet sheets, and Ralph Lauren linens. There are three suites with jet tub, sofa, and refrigerator, and the Executive Suite opens into a large optional living room. All have air-conditioning, cable TV, and modem jack. From $110 for a standard double to $209 for a suite (higher in foliage season).

✐ ⚬ᵀ⚬ **Betsy's Bed & Breakfast** (802-229-0466; betsysbnb.com), 74 E. State St. Betsy and Jon Anderson are warm, helpful hosts who offer 12 attractive rooms and suites (nine of the rooms are suites) in adjacent Queen Anne and Victorian houses and a carriage house in a quiet hillside neighborhood, a short walk from Vermont College and the middle of town. Rooms have private bath, cable TV, air-conditioning, and phone (with voice mail and dataports); eight rooms share full kitchen. $70–100 in low season, $90–130 in high ($10 more in foliage season), includes a generous breakfast. Discounts for three nights or more.

In and around Barre

🐾 ✐ ⚬ᵀ⚬ **Maplecroft Bed & Breakfast** (802-476-0760; maplecroftvermont.com), 70 Washington St., Barre 05641. Convenient for anyone researching Vermont history or genealogy next door at the Vermont History Center (originally a rather grand high school), this striking Victorian house is on Rt. 302 just above downtown and the small city park. Built by a granite sculptor in 1887, it is now home to local librarians Paul Heller, who also happens to be a magician, and Marianne Kotch. They offer five guest rooms, all with private bath and with beds featuring quilts made by Marianne (quilters, librarians, and magicians get a 10 percent discount). The Robert Burns Suite can nicely accommodate a family (a bedroom with queen-sized bed and a studio room with daybed and kitchen facilities). The Amish Suite also has a queen bed in one room and a daybed in the other. Needless to say there are plenty of good books around, as well as comfortable seating to read in the living room with its gas fireplace. $88 per couple ($35 extra includes a breakfast with homemade jams and scones or popovers).

🌸 ✍ **The Lodge at Millstone Hill** (802-479-1000; millstonehill.com), 59 Little John Rd., Websterville 05678. About 4 miles east of downtown Barre, this contemporary lodge is a converted barn, moved here from Warren. The interior is all open lofts, barnboard walls, exposed beams, and views. There are five guest rooms: three with private bath, one with a king-sized bed, and a couple of two-room suites. The William Barkley Suite has a loftlike sitting room, granite-backed shower, and queen-sized bed. Breakfast is served family-style. There are multilevel living rooms and a secluded game room, all with Oriental carpets, mounted trophies, and leather armchairs. The whole house, which sleeps 12, can be rented for special events. Innkeeper Pierre Couture, who grew up next door, is a walking encyclopedia when it comes to the 70 historic granite quarries that stretch from one a few yards away to Millstone Hill a mile or so up above, now part of a trail-webbed recreation area he has developed for mountain biking and cross-country skiing (see *To Do*). $95–125 includes breakfast.

Beyond

✍ "ⓣ" **The Comstock House** (802-272-2693; 802-479-9898; comstock housebb.com), 1620 Middle Rd., Plainfield 05667. A beautifully restored 1891 home on 175 acres with large-windowed, immaculate rooms, utter quiet, and spectacular mountain views on a dirt road 2 miles southwest of Plainfield, handy to Goddard College. Innkeepers Warren Hathaway, a social worker, and journalist Ross Sneyd offer two comfortable rooms, one on the ground floor and a two-room suite upstairs, both with queen-sized bed, private bath, and radiant-heat flooring that visitors can adjust to keep toes warm. The upstairs room has a gas fireplace and wide-pine floors and connects to a second room with a king or two single beds, ideal for groups or families (children 12 and over). There is an antiques-filled parlor where guests can mingle, and the dining room table overlooks a mountain panorama (and sunsets). Afternoon tea, full breakfasts, outdoor patio in warmer months. No pets. $115–135; $165 for a two-room suite.

🌸 ✍ **The Northfield Inn** (802-485-8558; thenorthfieldinn.com), 228 Highland Ave., Northfield 05663. Aglaia Stalb has renovated a grand old 1901 hillside mansion, nicely landscaped with a gazebo overlooking the village. Aglaia is a motherly, hospitable host who makes sure her guests are well fed and well oriented to her handsome town and its scenic surroundings (which include five covered bridges). There are 10 spacious and comfortable guest rooms, 8 with private bath (several combine into family suites), furnished with antiques, brass or carved-wood beds, and European feather bedding. It's delightfully easy to get lost in this rambling old house with its scattered common spaces, including a library, parlor, game room, and comfy third-floor TV room. $139–179, including a multicourse breakfast, snacks throughout the day, and an evening nightcap. Well-behaved children welcome.

🐾 🐱 **Marshfield Inn & Motel** (802-426-3383; marshfieldinn.com), 5630 Rt. 2, Marshfield. Diana Batzel and Tracey Hambleton's big Victorian, flat-roofed farmhouse is set back and above Rt. 2 and forms the centerpiece of this friendly complex. Lodging is in the 10 neighboring motel units with queen or two double beds. A nominally priced breakfast (there's a full menu) is served in the main house 8–9 AM. Halfway between Montpelier and St. Johnsbury, it's a good hub from which to explore in many directions, and there's a riverside path through the extensive property. $68 double in summer, $98 in foliage season. Pets are welcome for an extra $10 per night.

🐱 🎣 **Hollister Hill Farm B&B** (802-454-7725; hollisterhillfarm.com), 2193 Hollister Hill Rd., Marshfield 05658. Technically in Marshfield but less than 2 miles uphill from Plainfield Village, this is a splendid 1825 farmhouse set in 204 acres with three guest rooms, all with private bath. Bob and Lee Light fled New Jersey for Vermont in 1972 and milked cows for 25 years, eventually replacing them with beefalo, pigs, chickens, and turkeys, all of which they sell from the farm store in the barn, along with honey from their hives and their own maple syrup. One guest room has a red cedar sauna; the other two have fireplaces (one can be a family suite by adding an adjoining room). In winter guests are invited to bring cross-country skis, and they will find snowshoes here; VAST trails also run through the property. The price range of $95–115 ($165–175 for the family suite) includes a full, homegrown and -hatched as well as homemade breakfast. Pets by prior arrangement.

♾ 🐱 **Pie-in-the-Sky Farm Bed & Breakfast and Retreat** (802-426-3777; pieinsky.com), Dwinell Rd., Marshfield 05658. This rambling Civil War–era farmhouse was home for a time to the Pie-in-Sky commune; it's since been a dairy and sheep farm and home for Jay Moore, Judy Sargent, and their two cats for many years. Three upstairs rooms can be rented as a suite, with or without living room and kitchen facilities, or as individual double and single rooms. There's common space, a guest kitchen with fridge and snacks, a sunroom with a large tiled hot tub, and 120 acres with a beaver pond and a barn (the cows are gone, and guest horses are welcome), as well as access to VAST trails on the property. Groton State Forest with hiking trails and swimming is nearby. From $95 (for a double), $150–175 for the full six-room apartment, $650 by the week. Pets by prior arrangement.

🎣 **Country Cottage B&B** (802-426-3655), 3314 Rt. 232, Marshfield 05658. Dan and Judy Lloyd, who used to run the Creamery Inn in Cabot, now own and operate this establishment in Marshfield near Groton State Forest. They have two guest rooms with private bath. Children are welcome, but no pets, please. $75–85 includes full breakfast.

✳ Where to Eat

DINING OUT 🐾 **Sarducci's** (802-223-0229; sarduccisrestaruant.com), 3 Main St., Montpelier. Open for lunch Mon.–Sat.; dinner nightly in summer, Fri.–Sat. in winter. This spacious, yellow-walled restaurant with an open wood-fired oven is extremely popular, and because it takes no reservations, on weekends there's a line out the door. Come early and leave your name on the list, then stroll the downtown. Even if they've passed you on the list, you'll get the next free table. Many daily specials, plus antipasti, customized pizzas, salads, and 18 pasta choices, such as shrimp with angel hair, tomatoes, and garlic. At dinner try the saltimbocca (sautéed veal with prosciutto and fresh sage in a portobello mushroom sauce, served with risotto). Entrées are surprisingly reasonable, given the quality and atmosphere: $10.99–18.99.

✏ Ariel's Riverside Café and Bar (802-229-2295; arielsriverside.com), 186 River St., Montpelier. Dinner Tue.–Sun. 5–9. Chef Lee Duberman and her husband, Richard Fink, continue to draw savvy diners to the small, seasonal restaurant attached to their home in Brookfield's Pond Village (see "The White River Valleys"). Now they also serve in this former warehouse (formerly their BBQ venue), where they offer an appealing menu that Lee describes as "the type of food I like to eat." Starters include house-made hummus; light, spinach-filled spanakopita; and Lee's famous chicken and sausage gumbo. Entrées range from steamed mussels Provençal or grass-fed beef steak with *herbes frites* to Moroccan chicken spiced with cinnamon and coriander, served with apricots and almonds on pearl couscous. Entrées $15.95–18.95; a Boyden Farm burger is always an option.

Restaurant Phoebe (802-262-3500; restaurantphoebe.com), 52 State St., Montpelier. Open weekdays for lunch, Mon.–Sat. for dinner. Billed as modern American cuisine with Italian roots and local ingredients. Chef-owners Debbie and Aaron Milton have created a casually sophisticated and welcoming ambience and a reputation for reliably delicious food. A summer lunch menu includes creative salads. Dinner choices range from vegetable fettuccine to seafood paella with shellfish, andouille sausage, house-preserved tomatoes, asparagus, fennel, and chervil. Entrées $17–27, but you can always order a Wood Creek farm hamburger ($12). Creative cocktails are a specialty.

The Main Street Bar and Grill (802-223-3188), 118 Main St. Open for lunch and dinner daily, as well as Sunday brunch. Montpelier-based New England Culinary Institute's signature eatery, a multilevel restaurant and pub with seasonal outdoor seating and a viewing window into the kitchen. Lunch on poached pear and Stilton salad with ginger bisque, or sausage and mussel stew. At dinner begin with a warm beef short rib terrine, and then choose between New England leg of venison and pan-seared rainbow trout. Entrées $11.95–19.95.

EATING OUT

In Montpelier
The Black Door (802-223-7070; blackdoorvt.com), 44 Main St. Bar opens daily at 4, kitchen at 5. A romantic, dimly lit, upstairs hideaway with brick walls, art deco lamps, and an illuminated stained-glass bar in the space where Julio's got its start in 1981. Owner Phil Gentile, who sold the Mexican eatery in 2001, aims this time for a European feel. Chef David Nielsen serves creative, fresh entrées ($14–19) as well as bistro fare ($9–12) and several desserts. Appetizers might include salmon cakes or steamed venison dumplings with pomegranate soy reduction; for entrées you might have mustard seed crusted salmon or five-spice marinated chicken with a shiitake mushroom sauce and wasabi mashed potatoes. Live music Thu.–Sat., daily drink specials.

Thrush Tavern (802-223-2030), 107 State St. Open weekdays for lunch and dinner 11–9, Sat. 4–9. Long a local hangout, this moderately priced spot serves basic, reliable fare in the 1826 brick Federal that was once the home of Silas French, who built the Pavilion Hotel next door (a replica of which is now the Vermont Historical Museum). One of its two rooms has a full bar, and there's outdoor seating in summer months.

Kismet (223-8646), 207 Barre St. Open Wed.–Sun. 8–3. This immensely popular breakfast and lunch place features healthy, largely but not all vegetarian meals using local ingredients, plus an extensive choice of nonalcoholic drinks from smoothies to dandelion latte. Soups, greens, sides of root veggies, and the huevos rancheros are famous. The space is small, so weekend reservations are a good idea. No plastic.

La Brioche Bakery & Cafe (802-229-0443), 89 Main St. Open daily except Sun., 7 AM–5 PM. The source of pastries and bread for all New England Culinary Institute Montpelier restaurants. Order at the counter from among a delectable assortment of French-inspired pastries, freshly made salads, and made-to-order sandwiches. Eat in the dining room or on the patio or take out breakfast and sandwiches.

Coffee Corner, corner of Main and State. Open 6:30–3. A lively little chef-owned diner in the thick of things that's been here forever and specializes in fresh produce, fresh-baked bread, cozy booths, and fast, friendly service.

☞ **Hunger Mountain Food Co-op** (802-223-8000; hungermountain.com), 623 Stone Cutters Way. Open daily 8–8. Hidden away in a corner of this supermarket-style cooperative is an expanded deli with many vegetarian choices and a very attractive glass-sided café area overlooking the river.

Capitol Grounds (802-223-8411), 45 State St. Open Mon.–Thu. 6 AM–7 PM, Fri. and Sat. till 9, Sun. 8–5. An inviting self-service coffeehouse in a former bank, filled with the aroma of roasting brews and comfortable corners in which to sip them. Inquire about jazz, country, and blues nights.

☞ **Positive Pie 2** (802-454-0133; positivepie.com), 69 Main St. Open for lunch, dinner, and later for music. Far bigger and more ambitious than its Plainfield namesake, this is a full-service restaurant featuring house-made pasta and bread, specialty pizzas.

Langdon Street Café (802-233-8667; langdonstreetcafe.com), 4 Langdon St. Open weekdays 8 AM–11 PM, Fri. until 12:30 AM; Sat. 9 AM–12:30 AM, Sun. 9–11. Full breakfast menu (try the green omelet), then crunchy sandwiches, soups, and salads all day. This is a gathering place for nightly poetry, live music, open mike Mon. nights. Teas, coffees, microbrews.

& **National Life Cafeteria** (802-229-3397), 1 National Life Dr. Open for breakfast 7–9, for lunch 11:30–1:30. Some say the best lunch spot in Montpelier is high in the state's largest office building. The cafeteria here partners with the New England Culinary Institute (NECI). Views are through plate glass windows to the mountains. Pick up a dining room pass at the lobby. There's a big salad bar, a choice of made-to-order sandwiches, grill items, specials like eggs Benedict with steak, locally raised barbecued pork over pasta with Cabot cheddar, and a wide choice of delectable desserts.

On the Barre–Montpelier Rd.

☆ ☞ **Wayside Restaurant and Bakery** (802-223-6611), Barre–Montpelier Rd. (Rt. 302). Open daily 6:30 AM–9:30 PM. Vermont's ultimate, a 90-year-old family restaurant featuring "home

cooking away from home." Breakfast on corned beef hash and eggs (with home fries and toast), sausage gravy on a biscuit, or baked oatmeal. Lunch on the soup of the day and maple cream pie; dine on pork liver and bacon or rib-eye steak with fiddlehead ferns. There are over 200 menu items to choose from plus at least four daily specials at country diner prices, and they're fully licensed. Children's menu.

In Barre

Hilltop House Restaurant (802-479-2129), Websterville, on Quarry Hill Rd., a mile from the Rock of Ages visitor center. Open daily for lunch and dinner, 11–1:30 and 5–9; closed Sun. This classic eatery has been in the Reilly/Conti family for three generations and perpetuates Barre's tradition of genuine Italian home cooking. The Rotary Club and Kiwanis hobnob here, along with almost everyone in town. Salad bar, children's menu, cocktails, and moderately priced fare. Homemade lasagna and the salad bar for lunch was $6.25.

In Plainfield

River Run Restaurant (802-454-1246), Main St. (off Rt. 2). Open Wed.–Sun. 7–2 and 5–9. Mississippi-born Jimmy Kennedy and his wife, Maya, dish up soul food to die for: biscuits and sausage, grits and jalapeños, as well as buttermilk pancakes for breakfast, fried catfish and BBQ ribs, pulled pork and grilled steak salad for lunch, and some BBQ at dinner along with "fancy southern" items like roast duck, pork tenderloin, and pan-seared shrimp. They've expanded into a new space with wood-paneled walls, a hodgepodge of wooden tables, and a wooden slab bar serving wine and beer. It's a blackboard menu, and there's a lounge area with toys for kids. The place can be packed at breakfast on weekends, so come early.

Positive Pie (802-454-0133; positive pie.com), Main St. (off Rt. 2). Open daily 11–2 and 4–8; Sun., from 4 only. A small, lively gathering spot featuring homemade pasta and bread as well as pizza.

In Marshfield

Rainbow Sweets (802-426-3531), 1689 Rt. 2. Closed Tue., otherwise open weekdays 9–6, Fri. and Sat. 9–9, Sun. 9–3. Bill Tecosky and Patricia Halloran's colorful café has been a destination in its own right for going on 30 years. Stop by in the morning for empanadas and espresso, or lunch a little later on a brioche filled with warm spinach and walnuts; dine on Moroccan-style shredded chicken in phyllo or real pizza. Come anytime for a St. Honore (a profiterole filled with custard, dipped in caramel with cream on puff pastry) or to pick up some butter cookies.

In Northfield

ΨΙΨ Depot Square Pizzeria (802-485-5500), Depot Square. Open Tue.–Sat. 11:30–9. A pleasant little restaurant with bentwood chairs and a menu that includes reasonably priced Italian specialties as well as pizza; beer and wine.

In Middlesex

The Red Hen Café (802-223-5200; redhenbaking.com). A fabulous road-food stop just off I-89 Exit 9; turn left onto Rt. 2, Middlesex. Open Mon.–Sat. 7–4, Sun. 9–4. Husband-and-wife team Randy George and Liza Cain were already widely known for their many forms of crusty organic bread when they expanded into these larger, more accessible quarters (formerly Camp Mead) and added a café. The blackboard menu lists soups and deli sandwiches; there are also freshly baked delicacies such as brioche tarts topped with caramelized onions and Jasper Hill blue cheese. For breakfast grab an espresso and maple-glazed bun.

❋ Entertainment

THEATER Barre Opera House (802-476-8188; barreoperahouse.org), corner of Prospect and Main Sts., Barre. Built in 1899, after fire destroyed its predecessor, this elegant, acoustically outstanding, recently restored 650-seat theater occupies the second and third floors of the city hall. The Barre Players, a community theater, perform spring through fall, and this is also a venue for year-round music, dance, and other theater productions.

Lost Nation Theater Company (802-229-0492; lostnationtheater.org), Montpelier City Hall Arts Center, 128 Elm St., Montpelier. First-rate productions of contemporary plays, classics, and original works year-round by a professional troupe. The Summer Theater Series features five different shows, June–Oct., five nights a week.

Farmer's Night (802-828-2228). Free concerts given at the State House Jan.–Apr., when the legislature is in session. The series began in the 19th century for lawmakers who found themselves far from home with little to do in the evening after a day's session. At first the men performed for one another. Over the years the offerings have included everything from lectures to a high-wire act. Today they comprise a variety of mostly musical performances.

Capital City Concerts (capitalcity concerts.org), a classical chamber music series in Montpelier, stages seven concerts per year; they have an almost cultlike following here in the capital city.

Also see **Langdon Street Café**, **Back Door**, and **Positive Pie 2** under *Eating Out* for live music.

FILM The Savoy (802-229-0598; recording: 802-229-0509 or 800-676-0509; savoytheater.com), 26 Main St.,

Montpelier. Vermont's premier theater for independent and international art films, with an impressive video shop underneath at **Downstairs Video** (802-223-0050, open Sat. 10–9, Sun.–Fri. noon–9). Two daily showings, occasional speakers, and special events.

The Capitol (802-229-0343), 93 State St., Montpelier, and **The Paramount** (802-479-9621), 241 N. Main St., Barre, are both classic old movie houses showing first-run feature films.

❋ Selective Shopping

ANTIQUES East Barre Antique Mall (802-479-5190), 133 Mill St., East Barre. Open daily 10–5. Closed Mon. and the third week in Oct. In the middle of this one-street village sandwiched between Rts. 302 and 110 is this sprawling former furniture store housing central Vermont's largest group shop: some 400 consignees and dealers on three floors with plenty of furniture, glass, and china and a whole room of kitchenware. Former innkeeper Bob Somaini prides himself on the cleanliness as well as the size and depth of the store. He also prides himself on the spread he puts out for customers during his huge Super Bowl Sale (Super Bowl weekend).

ART STUDIOS AND GALLERIES *Note:* Check the Montpelier Downtown Community organization Web site (mdca.org) for the scheduled **Art Walk** with music and art throughout downtown.

The Artisans' Hand (802-229-9492; artisanshand.com), 229 Main St. at City Center, Montpelier. Open Mon.–Sat. 10–6, Fri. until 8, Sun. noon–4. An exceptional variety of quality Vermont craftwork by a cooperative of some 125 artisans in many media.

The Lazy Pear Gallery (802-223-7680; lazypear.com), 154 Main St.,

Montpelier. Open Wed.–Sun. noon–6, closed Wed. off-season. Located a couple of blocks from downtown (at the roundabout), this is a contemporary gallery in a Victorian house. Sixteen painters, sculptors, and photographers are represented. Frequently changing shows.

River Street Potters (802-224-7000), 141 River St., Montpelier. Some 20 individual potters share this studio producing stoneware and porcelain, whimsical and functional.

Green Mountain Hooked Rugs (802-223-1333; greenmountainhooked rugs.com), 2858 County Rd., Montpelier (out near Morse Farm). Open Tue.–Sat. 10–5. Stephanie Ashworth Krauss comes from four generations of rug hookers and sells colorful examples of the craft at this gallery. Inquire about June workshops at the Green Mountain Rug School, the nation's largest.

SPA (Studio Place Arts) (802-479-7069; studioplacearts.com), 201 N. Main St., Barre. Open Tue.–Fri. 10–5, Sat. noon–4. This art center offering classes for both adults and children maintains the Studio Place Arts Gallery.

Thistle Hill Pottery (802-223-8926; thistlehillpottery.com), 95 Powder Horn Glen Rd., in the hills north of Montpelier. Call ahead. Jennifer Boyer's handmade functional stone pottery—dinnerware, vases, lamps, and more—is carried in one of Vermont's best galleries. Her studio near Morse Farm is a source of bargains, seconds.

Blackthorn Forge (802-426-3369), 3821 Rt. 2, Marshfield (between Plainfield and Marshfield). Call ahead. Working in a red barn, Steve Bronstein makes functional and sculptural ironwork.

Also see **vermontcrafts.com**. This area is particularly rich in studios that open to visitors over the Memorial Day weekend and may or may not be accessible on a regular basis. Worth checking.

BOOKSTORES ♪ **Bear Pond Books** (802-229-0774), 77 Main St., Montpelier. Open Mon.–Thu. 9–6, until 9 on Fri. and Sat., Sun. 10–5. One of the state's best bookstores, heavy on literature, art, and children's books; author readings.

Rivendell Books (802-223-3928), 100 Main St., Montpelier. Open Mon.–Thu. 9–7, Fri. and Sat. till 8, Sun. 10–6. A delightful selection of primarily used but also new books, remainders, and bargain-priced best sellers.

Black Sheep Books (802-225-8906; blacksheepbooks.org), 5 State St., Montpelier. This all-volunteer workers' collective store specializes in radical and scholarly books and stages political discussions and other events.

Barre Books (802-476-3114), 158 N. Main St., Barre. Open until 6. A full-service independent bookstore with an array of general books and a good bargain section.

Capitol Stationers (802-223-2393), 54 Main St., Montpelier, includes new books, with a strong Vermont and New England section.

The Country Bookshop (802-454-0187; thecountrybookshop.com), 35 Mill St. (off Rt. 2 at the blinker), Plainfield. Open daily 10–5. Some 30,000 books, plus postcards and paper ephemera; Ben Koenig's specialties include folk music, folklore, and books on bells.

The Northfield Bookstore (802-485-4588), 56 Depot Square, Northfield. Open Mon.–Fri. 10–5:30, Sat. 10–3. "Affable books and knowledgeable service" is the mission statement for this pleasant store stocking primarily used books with some best sellers, also cards, a children's section, and comfortable seating. Coffee, too.

FARMS ✒ **Morse Farm Maple Sugarworks** (802-223-2740; 800-242-2740; morsefarm.com), 1168 County Rd., Montpelier. (Go up Main St., turn right at the roundabout, continue up the hill 2.7 miles). Open year-round, daily except holidays. Sugar-on-snow Mar.–Apr. weekends, noon–4. The farm has been in the same family for eight generations. The store features its own syrup and maple products, including a "maple creemee" cone; Vermont crafts; and a sugarhouse tour with tastings, exhibits, nature trails, and an outdoor Vermont farm life museum. Also see *Cross-Country Skiing*.

✒ **Bragg Farm Sugarhouse & Gift Shop** (802-223-5757; 800-376-5757; braggfarm.com), Rt. 14 north, East Montpelier. Open daily, 8:30–8 (till 6 after Labor Day). Serving sugar-on-snow Mar.–Apr. noon–5. This fifth-generation farm still collects sap the traditional way (in 2,500 buckets) and boils it over wood fires. The shop carries a variety of maple and other Vermont crafts and specialty foods and includes a museum and a maple ice cream parlor.

Grand View Winery (802-456-7012; grandviewwinery.com), East Calais. Open Memorial Day weekend–Oct.; call ahead. Take Rt. 14 north 4 miles from East Montpelier, turn right onto Max Gray Rd., continue 2.3 miles. The tasting room at the farm is set in gardens amid works by Vermont artists. The wine selection is extensive, from rhubarb, dandelion, and blueberry to French grape blends; hard cider, too. Winemaker Phil Tonks has been growing fruit here for 30 years and estab-

lished the winery in 1997. There's also a tasting room at the Cold Hollow Cider Mill on Rt. 100 in Waterbury Center (open daily 11–5)—but this is more rewarding.

✒ **Knight's Spider Web Farm** (802-433-5568; spiderwebfarm.com), off Rt. 14 at 124 Spider Web Rd., at the south end of Williamstown Village. Open 9–6 daily June 15–Oct. 15, then weekends till Christmas; Jan.–Mar. by appointment. The weirdest farm you ever will see: Artists Will and Terry Knight grow and harvest spiderwebs in their own barn, then mount them onto wood. Will can tell you all about the little critters, and there's a gift store.

SPECIAL SHOPS **Zutano** (802-223-2229; zutano.com), 79 Main St., Montpelier. Open Mon.–Sat. 10–6, Sun. noon–4. With offices in nearby Cabot, Manhattan artists Uli and Michael Belenky, who didn't give a thought to baby clothes until their daughter Sophie arrived in 1989, produce a delightful collection of soft, whimsical baby clothes that defy the tired maxim that blue is for boys and pink for girls. Now known nationwide, this is the duo's flagship boutique.

Onion River Sports (802-229-9409), 20 Langdon St., Montpelier. An outstanding sporting goods store specializing in camping, cross-country, and biking gear, with cross-country and bike rentals.

Gesine's Confectionary (802-224-9930; gesine.com), 279 Elm St., Montpelier. Open daily. This gourmet market and confectionary is known for cookies, sticky buns, desserts, and specialty macaroons.

Woodbury Mountain Toys (802-223-4272), 24 State St., Montpelier. Open daily. The motto is "toys with a purpose." This independent toy store carries many locally made and hard-to-find items as well as major lines.

Buch Spieler Music (802-229-0449; bsmusic.com), 27 Langdon St., Montpelier. Open Mon.–Thu. 10–6, Fri. until 8, Sat. until 5, Sun. 11–4. An independent music store specializing in cards, novelties, and all kinds of music from around the world, since 1973.

Ndakinna Cultural Center and Museum and Gift Shop (802-456-8884; ndakinna.org), 34 Moscow Rd., East Calais. Just off Rt. 14. Open Tue.–Fri. 9–5, Sat. 9–3. Todd Hebert celebrates his Abenaki heritage with this new and worthwhile center/gift shop. The museum (donations appreciated) displays 19th-century black ash baskets and ceremonial dress. The gift shop is a co-op for genuine Native American items: sun catchers, beaded necklaces, assorted herbs, botanicals, and Native American–inspired jewelry. Inquire about drumming and other workshops.

✳ Special Events

Early March: **Rotten Sneaker Contest**, Montpelier Recreation Department (802-223-5141).

April: **Earth Day at the State House** with music, games, displays (802-229-1833).

Memorial Day weekend: **Open Studios weekend** throughout Vermont (vermontcrafts.com).

March–April: Sugaring throughout the region; sugar-on-snow at Morse and Bragg farms.

May–October: **Capitol City Farmer's Market**. Saturday 9–1 at the parking

lot next to Christ Church, State St., Montpelier.

June–July: **Vermont Mountaineers Baseball** (802-223-5224; thevermontmountaineers.com), New England intercollegiate baseball games at the Recreation Field, Elm St., Montpelier, 6:30.

June–August: **Montpelier City Band Concerts**, State House lawn, Wednesdays at 4 PM.

July: **Montpelier's Independence Day Celebration**, sponsored by the Montpelier Downtown Community Association (802-223-9604; mdca.org) —pancake breakfast, games, performances, and a giant fireworks display July 3. **Barre Homecoming Days** (*last weekend*)—music, fireworks, street dance, art exhibit.

Labor Day weekend: In Northfield, a pageant, parade of floats, and Norwich cadets.

September: **Old Time Fiddlers' Contest**, Barre Auditorium, one of New England's oldest contests.

Early October: **Vermont Apple Celebration**, State House lawn, Montpelier.

Mid-October: **Cabot Apple Pie Festival**, Cabot.

Late October: **Festival of Vermont Crafts**, Montpelier High School (call Central Vermont Chamber of Commerce, 802-229-5711).

November: **Greater Barre Crafts Fair**.

December 31: **First Night** celebrations, Montpelier—music, readings, and performances.

KILLINGTON/RUTLAND AREA

K illington is the largest ski resort in the East. It boasts seven mountains and the most extensive snowmaking system in the world. Killington Peak, the second highest summit in the state, is flanked by four other mountains and faces another big majestic range across Sherburne Pass.

Although the road through this upland village has been heavily traveled since the settling of Rutland (11 miles to the west) and Woodstock (20 miles to the east), there was never much of anything here. In 1924 an elaborate, rustic-style inn was built at the junction of Rt. 4, the Appalachian Trail, and the new Long Trail. A winter annex across the road was added in 1938, when Pico Mountain (now part of Killington) installed one of the country's first T-bars. But the logging village of Sherburne Center (now the town of Killington) was practically a ghost town on December 13, 1958, when Killington opened.

Condominiums cluster at higher elevations, while lodges, inns, and motels are strung along the 5-mile length of Killington Rd. and west along Rt. 4 as it slopes ever downward through Mendon to Rutland. Ski lodges are also salted along Rt. 100 north to the pleasant old town of Pittsfield, and in the village of Chittenden, sequestered up a back road from Rt. 4, near a mountain-backed reservoir.

Vermont's second largest city, Rutland is the business and shopping center for a large rural radius. Stolid, early-Victorian mansions and streets crisscrossed with railroad tracks testify to its 19th-century prosperity—when Rutland was known as "the marble city." The long-established shops along Merchants Row and Center Street, among the state's best-preserved commercial blocks, have held their own in recent years.

Rutland lies in a broad, gently rolling corridor between New York State and the Green Mountains. It's broad enough to require two major north–south routes. Rt. 7, the busier highway, hugs the Green Mountains and, with the exception of the heavily trafficked strip around Rutland, is a scenic ride. Rt. 30 to the west is a far quieter ride through farm country and by two major lakes, Lake Bomoseen and Lake St. Catherine, both popular summer meccas.

Rt. 4 is the major east–west road, a mountain-rimmed four-lane highway from Fair Haven, at the New York line, to Rutland, where it angles north through the middle of town before turning east again, heading uphill to Killington. Rt. 140 from Wallingford to Poultney is the other old east–west road here, a scenic byway through Middletown Springs, where old mineral water springs form the core of a pleasant park. Bed & breakfasts are salted through this rolling farm country and

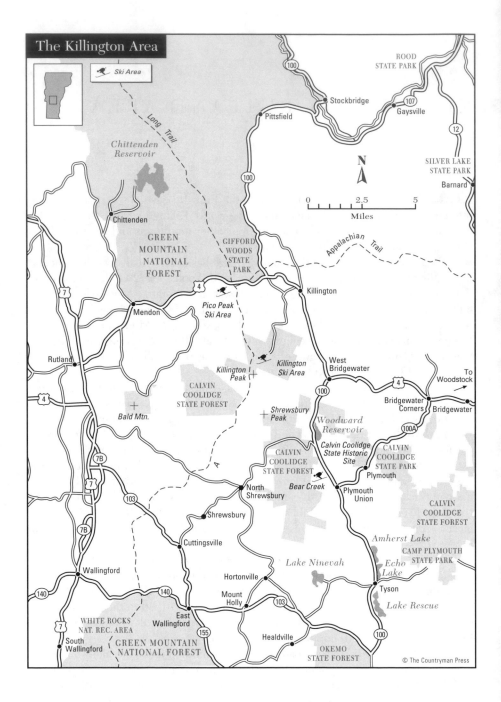

The Killington Area

Ski Area

ROOD STATE PARK

100

Stockbridge

107

Gaysville

Pittsfield

12

Long Trail

Chittenden Reservoir

N

SILVER LAKE STATE PARK

Barnard

0   2.5   5
Miles

Chittenden

GREEN MOUNTAIN NATIONAL FOREST

GIFFORD WOODS STATE PARK

Appalachian Trail

4

Killington

Mendon

Pico Peak Ski Area

Rutland

Killington Peak

Killington Ski Area

West Bridgewater

To Woodstock

4

CALVIN COOLIDGE STATE FOREST

Shrewsbury Peak

100

Bridgewater Corners

Bridgewater

Bald Mtn.

Woodward Reservoir

100A

7B

Calvin Coolidge State Historic Site

CALVIN COOLIDGE STATE PARK

Plymouth

7

CALVIN COOLIDGE STATE FOREST

Bear Creek

Plymouth Union

CALVIN COOLIDGE STATE FOREST

103

North Shrewsbury

7B

Shrewsbury

Amherst Lake

CAMP PLYMOUTH STATE PARK

Cuttingsville

Lake Ninevah

Echo Lake

Wallingford

Hortonville

Tyson

Lake Rescue

140

Mount Holly

103

140

7

WHITE ROCKS NAT. REC. AREA

East Wallingford

155

Healdville

100

7

South Wallingford

GREEN MOUNTAIN NATIONAL FOREST

OKEMO STATE FOREST

© The Countryman Press

the high hamlets of Shrewsbury and North Shrewsbury, tucked up on along the spine of the Green Mountains, still less than 10 miles from Rutland.

GUIDANCE **The Rutland Region Chamber of Commerce** (802-773-2747; 800-756-8880) maintains a Web site (rutlandvermont.com) and an unstaffed **visitor center** in Main Street Park at the junction of Rts. 7 and 4, open late May–mid-Oct Also see rutlanddowntown.com.

Killington Chamber of Commerce (802-773-4181; 800-337-1928; killington chamber.com) is a source of year-round information about the area and maintains a visitor-geared office on Route 4 just west of the Killington access road, staffed weekdays.

The Fair Haven Welcome Center (802-265-4763) on Rt. 4 near the New York line is open every day 7 AM–9 PM.

GETTING THERE *By train:* **Amtrak** (800-USA-RAIL). Daily service to and from New York City on the Ethan Allen Express to Rutland.

By air: **Rutland Southern Vermont Regional Airport** (flyrutlandvt.com) is served by Cape Air (800-352-0714) with frequent flights to Boston. Rental cars and taxis are available at the airport, 5 miles south of town.

By bus: **Marble Valley Regional Transit District** (802-773-3244; thebus.com), operator of "**The Bus**," connects Rutland with Killington, the Rutland airport, Manchester, Fairhaven, and Middlebury as well as points within the city.

In winter shuttle buses run from the Amtrak station in Rutland to several Killington points, from Pico Resort on Rt. 4 to the Skyship Base Station on Rt. 4, and up and down the length of Killington Rd.

MEDICAL EMERGENCY Emergency service is available by calling **911**.

Rutland Regional Medical Center Fast Track Emergency Service (802-747-3601; rrmc.org), 160 Allen St., Rutland.

✳ Villages

Poultney (population: 3,600; poultneyvt.com), on Rt. 30 near the New York border and just north of Lake St. Catherine. Poultney is home to Green Mountain College, a four-year coed liberal arts college focusing on environmental studies. It also has significant journalistic associations: Horace Greeley, founder of the *New York Tribune*, lived at the venerable Eagle Tavern in East Poultney (now a private home) while he was learning the printing trade at the East Poultney *National Spectator* in the 1820s (and organizing a local temperance society). Working with him was George Jones, who helped found the *New York Times* in 1851. Attracted by the slate quarries, Vermont's first Jewish community settled here during the Civil War, and Welsh immigrants poured in to take up quarrymen jobs. Welsh was spoken here until the 1950s in what was one of the largest Welsh communities in the country. Green Mountain College has an extensive Welsh archive, teaches Welsh heritage, and maintains the only choir in the country that sings Welsh songs at each of its performances.

East Poultney is a picturesque village worth detouring to see. The fine white Baptist church, built in 1805, is the centerpiece, standing on a small green

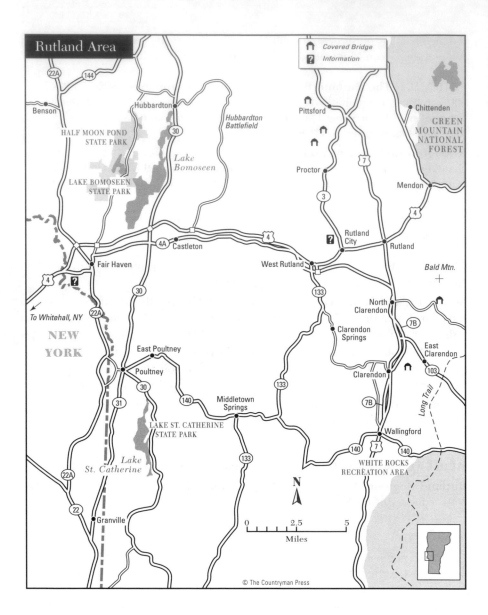

Covered Bridge

Information

22A
144

Benson

Hubbardton

Hubbardton
Battlefield

Pittsford

Chittenden

GREEN
MOUNTAIN
NATIONAL
FOREST

HALF MOON POND
STATE PARK

30

Lake
Bomoseen

7

Proctor

Mendon

LAKE BOMOSEEN
STATE PARK

3

4

4A Castleton

4

Rutland
City

Rutland

Fair Haven

West Rutland

Bald Mtn.

4

30

133

NEW
YORK

To Whitehall, NY

22A

North
Clarendon

7B

East Poultney

Clarendon
Springs

East
Clarendon

Poultney

133

Clarendon

103

30

31

140

Middletown
Springs

7B

LAKE ST. CATHERINE
STATE PARK

133

Wallingford

Long Trail

22A

Lake
St. Catherine

140

7

140

WHITE ROCKS
RECREATION AREA

N

22

Granville

0   2.5   5

Miles

© The Countryman Press

surrounded by a cluster of historic buildings—the Melodeon Factory, Union Academy, and the Old School House—all open June–Aug., Sun. 1–4 and by appointment (802-287-9760; poultneyhistoricalsociety.org). The general store is also a classic and a source of good deli sandwiches. Its picnic benches are within earshot of the Poultney River, here a fast-flowing stream.

Castleton (population: 4,372) at Rts. 4A and 30, is home to **Castleton College**, the oldest member of Vermont's state college system. It was also here in Remington Tavern that Ethan Allen and Seth Warner planned the capture of Ticonderoga. As an offshoot off this conspiratorial meeting, blacksmith Samuel Beach—

Vermont's own Paul Revere—reputedly ran some 60 miles in 24 hours to recruit more men for the raid. The town itself grew rapidly after the Revolution and is a showcase of pillared Greek Revival houses, most designed by Thomas Royal Dake. Main St. is a showcase for his workmanship; note the **Ransom-Rehlen mansion**, with its 17 Ionic columns, and Congregational Meeting House, now the **Federated Church**, with the lovely pulpit that Dake completed with his own funds. Between 1850 and 1870 the West Castleton Railroad and Slate Company was the largest marble plant in the country.

Fair Haven (population: 2,952), located where Rts. 4, 4A, and 22A intersect, is at the core of Vermont's slate industry. One of its earliest developers in the 1780s was the controversial Matthew Lyon, who started an ironworks and published a newspaper called *The Scourge of Aristocracy*, in which he lambasted the Federalists. Elected to Congress in 1796, Lyon had scuffles on the floor of the House and criticized President Adams so vehemently that he was arrested and jailed under the Alien and Sedition Act. Lyon's case caused such a national uproar that this patently unconstitutional censorship law was soon rescinded. Lyon was reelected to Congress while still in jail and took his seat in time to cast the tie-breaking vote that made Thomas Jefferson president instead of Aaron Burr.

Around the spacious green are three Victorian mansions (two faced with marble) built by descendants of Ira Allen, founder of the University of Vermont.

Benson, west of Rt. 22A, 8 miles north of Fair Haven, is one of those tiny proverbial villages "that time forgot" except as a scenic photo op, but in recent years it has developed a creative personality with its artisans and special shops.

✳ Must-See

Vermont Marble Exhibit (800-427-1396; vermont-marble.com), 52 Main St., Proctor. From Business Rt. 4 in West Rutland follow Rt. 3 north. Open mid-May–Oct., daily 9–5. $7 adults, $5 seniors, $4 teens, children free. The first commercial marble deposit was discovered and quarried in Vermont in 1784. This is a privately, superbly maintained museum housed in one of the vast old marble sheds on Otter Creek. The approach is across a multiarched marble bridge built in 1915

KILLINGTON PEAK

On a clear day the view from the summit of the state's second highest mountain (4,241 feet) encompasses five states. It sweeps northwest to the Adirondacks, east to the White Mountains, and north along the spine of the Green Mountains. It's the spot on which the Reverend Samuel Peters in 1763 is said to have christened all that he could see "Verd Monts." The K1 Express Gondola (daily July–Labor Day, then mid-Sept.–Columbus Day; 802-422-6200) hoists visitors up from the K-1 Lodge to the Peak Restaurant (cafeteria lunch menu and special dinners in foliage season) just below the summit, and a nature trail leads to the peak. No matter how hot it is down on Rt. 4, chances are you will need a jacket on top. Bring a picnic and stay awhile. This is one of those special places.

Christina Tree

MARBLE BRIDGE AT THE VERMONT MARBLE EXHIBIT

as a memorial to Fletcher D. Proctor, a scion of the family who formed The Vermont Marble Company in 1870. The entrance to the museum is through a monolithic marble arch and across railroad tracks, then up marble steps to a grand marble hall. A film relates the story of Vermont's marble industry. Marble from Proctor and Danby was used for the U.S. Supreme Court building, the Lincoln Memorial, and the Beinecke Library at Yale. The Proctor family was Vermont's major political dynasty, filling state and national offices for nearly a century. The company continued to thrive until World War II, employing 5,000 workers at its height. It has since been acquired by the Swiss-based Pleuss-Staufer Industries, and the company as such no longer exists. Marble quarrying, however, continues in Vermont on a small scale and includes a subterranean quarry in Danby. The museum includes a number of exhibits, notably a gallery of bas-reliefs of American presidents by local sculptor Renzo Palmerrini. You'll also find replicas of the *Pietà* and the *Last Supper*, a sculptor in residence, and a factory viewing site from which to watch the various stages of transformation from rough-cut blocks to polished slabs. There is an extensive gift shop. A quarter-mile walkway leads to the old Sutherland Falls Quarry. Pick up a sandwich or deli takeout from Proctor's general store.

Note: **The Carving Studio and Sculpture Center** (802-438-2097; carvingstudio .org), 636 Marble St., West Rutland. Open to visitors Sat. and Sun. 1–4 PM or by appointment. Sited at the head of a 200-acre former quarrying and manufacturing site, the center offers workshops. There are changing exhibits and a sculpture garden.

✴ Also See

MUSEUMS **The New England Maple Museum** (802-483-9414; maplemuseum .com), Rt. 7 north of Pittsford. Open June–Oct., daily 8:30–5:30, then 10–4 through Dec. 23 and mid-Mar.–May. $2.50 adults, 75 cents children. The museum has an attractive display of the history, production, and consumption of maple syrup, once called "sweet water," and its by-products. You can view the Danforth

Collection of antique equipment, murals, and a 10-minute slide show, and there is a tasting area and gift shop. Mail-order service.

Norman Rockwell Museum (802-773-6095; 877-773-6095; normanrockwellvt .com), Rt. 4 east, Rutland. Open June–Nov., daily 9–4. $5 adults, $4 seniors, $2.50 ages 8–17. Geared to Rockwell buffs, this is a chronological display of thousands of Rockwell's magazine covers, ads, posters, portraits, and other published illustrations, displayed chronologically with small, almost unreadable typed captions. The introductory video can be heard repeating itself throughout the exhibit area. Still, it's an interesting profile of the artist (1898–1978) and an a documentary of changing American culture and graphic styles. The gift shop, with its many Rockwell prints and cards, is large.

Chaffee Art Center (802-775-0356; chaffeeartcenter.org), 16 S. Main St., Rutland. Closed Tue., otherwise open 10–5, Sun. noon–4. Galleries are housed in an 1896 Queen Anne Victorian listed on the National Register of Historic Places. Permanent and periodic exhibits and a youth gallery for school displays. Traditional and contemporary paintings, sculpture, crafts, graphics, and photography are included. Donation expected.

Slate Valley Museum (518-642-1417; slatevalleymuseum.org), 17 Water St., Granville, NY 12832. Open year-round, Memorial Day–Columbus Day Tue.–Sat. 10–5, Sun. 1–5; otherwise Tue.–Fri. 1–5, Sat. 10–4. Admission $5 per person; children 12 and under are free. Just across the New York border from Poultney in the heart of the slate industry's historic base, on a site where immigrant quarry workers once lived in tenements, this 19th-century Dutch barn reflects the many colors and shapes of slate. It includes a quarry shanty, tools, a mural, paintings, photographs, family artifacts, and a gift shop.

◌ **Wilson Castle** (802-773-3284; wilsoncastle.com), on W. Proctor Rd. between West Rutland and Proctor. This 19th-century turreted mansion was built in 1867 for the English bride of a Vermont physician, John Johnson, no expense spared. Almost everything was imported, including the exterior brick. The opulent furnishings include Venetian tapestries, 400-year-old Chinese scrolls, a Louis XIV French onyx-covered table, and a gallery of classic sculpture, not to mention 84 stained-glass windows. But the seclusion was too much for the aristocratic Mrs. Johnson; she returned to England two years later, and the house was sold. In 1939 it was acquired by pioneering radio engineer Herbert Lee Wilson, who established AM radio towers around the world. It's been in the Wilson family ever since and is open for guided tours daily, late May–late Oct., 9–6. Frankly,

WILSON CASTLE

Christina Tree

we don't think it's worth the price ($10 adults, $9.50 seniors, $5 children), but we would love to attend one of the frequent events staged here. Inquire about special Saturday-night murder mystery dinners, poker evenings, and Halloween and Christmas tours. The mansion can also be rented as a party or wedding venue.

HISTORIC SITE The Hubbardton Battlefield (802-273-2282; historicvermont .org/hubbardton) is on Monument Rd. in East Hubbardton, 7 scenic miles north of the posted Rt. 4 exit. Battle buffs won't want to miss the diorama and narrated 3-D map of this 1777 Revolutionary War site, when Colonels Seth Warner, Ebenezer Francis, and Nathan Hale led Vermont, Massachusetts, and New Hampshire soldiers in a successful rear-guard action against British and German troops. They saved the main American army, which was retreating from Mount Independence and Fort Ticonderoga. Of all American battlefields, this one looks most the way it did on the day of the battle. Paths lead to signs describing the events that unfolded, and the views are spectacular, with sweeping vistas of the Taconic Mountains to the south, Pittsford Ridge to the east, and the Adirondacks to the west. A hilltop visitor center is open late May–Columbus Day, Wed.–Sun. 9:30–5. Admission $2. *Note:* If you want to continue north to Brandon from here, be sure to get careful directions.

COVERED BRIDGES There are six in the area: the 1836 **Kingsley** or **Mill River Bridge**, East Rd., off Airport Rd., East Clarendon; the 1880 **Brown Bridge**, off Cold River Rd., Shrewsbury; the 1840 **Depot Bridge**, off Rt. 7 north, Pittsford; the 1849 **Cooley Bridge**, Elm St., Pittsford; the 1843 **Gorham** or **Goodnough Bridge**, Gorham Bridge Rd., off Rt. 3, Pittsford; and the 1830 **Twin Bridge**, East Pittsford Rd., off Rt. 7 north, Rutland.

FISH HATCHERY Pittsford National Fish Hatchery (802-483-6618; fws.gov/ r5pnfh), 4 Holden Rd., North Chittenden, VT 05763. Open 8–4 daily. The Fish and Wildlife Service raises landlocked salmon and lake trout here.

✳ To Do

AERIAL RIDES The **Killington K1 Express** (802-422-6200; killington.com) runs mid-Sept.–Columbus Day from K-1 Lodge to the top of Killington Peak.

HUBBARDTON BATTLEFIELD

Christina Tree

BIKING There's a lot of great bike riding in this area.

Mountain Bike Park at Killington (802-422-6232; killngton.com). The K-1 Express Gondola operates July–Columbus Day (weather permitting) hoisting bicyclists and their bikes from Rt. 4 up to Killington Peak, accessing 45 miles of trails and a 1,700-foot vertical drop spread across five mountain areas. Guided tours, instruction, bike rentals, and packages.

Bicycle touring

Bike Vermont (800-257-2226), based in Woodstock, offers weekend and five-day tours that include the Lake St. Catherine and Middletown Springs areas.

Escape Routes from Casa Bella Inn, Pittsfield (877-746-8943; casabellainn .com). Self-guided tours with detailed maps and descriptions available with reasonably priced lodging and meals.

Note: Little-trafficked roads wind through the gently rolling countryside around Lake St. Catherine and Mid-dletown Springs. Rentals are available from the **Great Outdoors Trading Company** (802-775-9989) at 219 Woodstock Ave. (Rt. 4) and from the **Sports Peddler** (802-775-0101) at 158 N. Main St., both in Rutland.

Christina Tree

MERCHANT'S ROW, RUTLAND

Also see the **Delaware Hudson Rail Trail**, Poultney–Castleton, under *Hiking*.

BOATING Rentals are available from **Lake Bomoseen Marina** (802-273-2061; 802-265-4611; lakebomoseenmarina.com), and nearby **Woodard Marine, Inc.** (802-265-3690; woodardmarine.com).

CANOEING AND KAYAKING **Chittenden Reservoir** is a sublime place to canoe or kayak, an expansive 674 acres backed by mountains. Boat access is at the end of Chittenden Dam Rd. **Woodford Reservoir** on Rt. 100 south is another beautiful spot to paddle. Kayak rentals for use on **Kent Pond** in Killington are available at nearby **Base Camp Outfitters** (802-775-0166).

FISHING Licenses are available from the Killington town clerk, River Rd., and also from sporting goods stores and state park rangers. Landlocked salmon and trout can be had in Chittenden Reservoir; trout are the catch in Mendon Brook. There also is fishing in Kent and Colton ponds, and the White, Tweed, and Ottauquechee rivers. Woodward Reservoir on Rt. 100 south and Echo Lake in Tyson (accessible from Plymouth Camp State Park) are also good fishing. **Stream & Brook Fly-Fishing** (802-989-0398; streamandbrook.com) offers beginners pro-grams and full- and half-day guided trips. Rod Start, a Vermonter with over 25 years of fishing experience, offers **Green Mountain Fishing Guide Service** (802-446-3375), based in Tinmouth.

FITNESS CENTERS AND SPAS **Pico Sports Center** (802-747-0564; pico mountain.com), 4763 Rt. 4, Killington. Open daily. A 75-foot Olympic lap pool, aerobics area, fitness and cardiovascular room, Jacuzzi, saunas, tanning, massage, fitness evaluations. Day passes and short-term memberships available.

The Spa at the Woods (802-422-3139; spaatthewoods.com), 53 Woods Lane, Killington. Built as the heart of a deluxe condo complex but open to drop-ins, an unusually attractive, full-service spa with pool, Jacuzzi, and a full massage and body treatment menu.

Mountain Green Health Spa (802-422-3113), center of Killington Village at 133 East Mountain Rd. Located in the Mountain Green complex, a club with a 54-foot indoor lap pool, Jacuzzi, aerobics classes, steam rooms, sauna, facials, massage.

New Life Hiking Spa (newlifehikingspa.com), based at the Inn of the Six Mountains. Mid-May–Sept. Since 1978 Jimmy LeSage has been refining and fine-tuning fitness programs (2 to 11 days and longer) that combine sensible eating and moderate exercise. The daily regimen begins with a pre-breakfast walk and includes body conditioning, yoga, and hiking (all levels). Meals are varied, and the focus is on increasing energy and stamina (a good solo vacation).

The Gymnasium (802-773-5333), 11 Cottage St., Rutland. A complete wellness and cardiovascular center, open Mon.–Fri. 5:30 AM–8 PM, Sat. 7–5, Sun. 9–2. Day passes.

Vermont Sport & Fitness Club (802-775-9916), 40 Curtis Ave., Rutland. Outdoor pool, indoor/outdoor tennis, racquetball, cardio equipment. Open daily. Day passes.

FOR FAMILIES ✍ **Killington/Pico Adventure Center** (802-422-6200; killington .com) is physically divided between the base areas of Pico, down on Rt. 4, and of Killington Resort itself. Open late June–July on weekends, then daily through Labor Day, 10–5. An Adventure Center Pass covers everything; passes are also available for single activities.

✍ **The Alpine Slide**, Pico. Patrons ride a triple chairlift up and then slide down a total of 3,410 feet; the slide begins halfway up the mountain with a sweeping view

CHITTENDEN RESERVOIR

Christina Tree

of the valley to the west. Lunch and snacks are served at a snack bar. "Endless Activities" here also include miniature golf (19 holes) and chairlift rides.

GOLF Killington Resort (802-422-6700; killington.com), Killington Rd., Killington, has its own 18-hole, 6,326-yard, par-72 course designed by Geoffrey Cornish. Weekend clinics and golf packages. PGA professional instruction, rental clubs. The **Mountain Golf School** (800-343-0762), at the Killington Resort, features two-day weekend and three-day midweek instructional programs.

Green Mountain National Golf Course (802-422-4653; gmngc.com), Barrows–Towne Rd. and Rt. 100, Killington. This highly rated 18-hole course includes a clubhouse, three practice teeing areas, four target greens, and an 8,000-square-foot putting green.

The Rutland Country Club (802-773-3254), a mile north of the business section on N. Grove St., Rutland. An 18-hole golf course on rolling terrain; restaurant.

Proctor-Pittsford Country Club (802-483-9379), Corn Hill Rd., Pittsford. Eighteen holes, lounge, and restaurant.

Lake St. Catherine Country Club (802-287-9341), Rt. 30, south of Poultney. Eighteen holes, lounge, and restaurant.

The Prospect Bay Country Club (802-468-5581) in Castleton offers nine holes.

Stonehedge Golf (802-773-2666), Rt. 103 west, North Clarendon, is a nine-hole, par-3 public course.

HIKING Deer Leap Trail, off Rt. 4 behind the Inn at Long Trail, is the most popular short hike: a 45-minute one-way trek up a winding, moderately steep path that yields a southerly panoramic view from the top of a tall cliff. For a whole-day hike, you can continue along the Long Trail to Chittenden Reservoir or branch east at the Maine Junction onto the Appalachian Trail. This trail also connects with Gifford Woods State Park. Plant a car at the other end and be sure to bring a hiking map.

The Appalachian Trail (appalahciantrail.org) and the **Long Trail** (greenmountainclub.org), accessed north and south from Rt. 4 in Killington, offer endless possibilities. For guided hikes check out Killington-based **Appalachian Trail Adventures** (888-855-8655; appalachiantrailadventures.com).

Bald Mountain. This 3-mile, three-hour round-trip hike is in Aiken State Forest, off Notch Rd. from Rt. 4 in Mendon. The blue-blazed circle trail begins just past the intersection with Wheelerville Rd.

& **Thundering Falls Trail**, Killington. Off River Rd., a 900-foot boardwalk and path through floodplain and forest lead to a platform at the base of Thundering Falls, a sheer rock face with water pouring down it, part of the Appalachian Trail.

Fox Creek Inn shuttles hikers to the Long Trail as part of the **Country Inns Along the Trail** program (802-326-2072; 800-838-330; inntoinn.com).

Killington Hiking Center (800-621-MTS; killington.com). The K-1 Express Gondola offers easy access to 50-plus miles of trails.

White Rocks Recreation Area, Rt. 140 off Rt. 7 in Wallingford. Follow signs from the White Rocks Picnic Area. The big feature here is a 2,600-foot, conical white peak surrounded by quartzite boulders that retain ice and snow into summer. We advise picking up a hiking guidebook (see *Hiking and Walking* in "What's Where") before starting out.

Delaware Hudson Rail Trail, Poultney–Castleton. A rail-trail enjoyed by hikers, snowmobilers, walkers, bikers, equestrians, and cross-country skiers. A guide is available from the Department of Forest and Parks in Pittsford.

Helen W. Buckner Memorial Preserve (802-229-4425), West Haven. Hiking trails and nature exploration in this Nature Conservancy tract.

HORSEBACK RIDING **Mountain Top Inn & Resort Equestrian Program** (802-483-2311; mountaintopinn.com) offers horseback riding geared to every level from beginner to experienced, one- and two-hour guided trail rides, both English and Western. Jumping, dressage, cross-country, and children's instruction are available.

Hawk Inn & Mountain Resort (802-672-3811; hawkresort.com), at Salt Ash, Rt. 100, in Plymouth. The Stables at Hawk offers lessons, trail rides for ages 10 and over, and pony rides. Open Memorial Day weekend–Labor Day.

🖋 **Pond Hill Ranch** (802-468-2449; pondhillranch.com), 1683 Pond Hill Rd., Castleton, a 200-acre family-owned ranch offering trail rides, lessons, and pony rides for children. Saturday-night **rodeos** are also staged here all summer long and into fall.

Chipman Stables (802-293-5242), Danby Four Corners. This family-run stable offers trail rides, hayrides, and pony rides in the easily accessible hills.

ROCK CLIMBING **Green Mountain Rock Climbing Center** (802-773-3343; vermontclimbing.com). Based in Rutland at 223 Woodstock Ave. and at the Killington Snowshed Lodge, the center offers lessons and climbs for all abilities, from age 4 up. Inquire about winter ice climbing.

SWIMMING **Elfin Lake Beach**, off Rt. 140 west, 2 miles southeast of Wallingford, and **Crystal Beach**, a municipally owned white sand beach on the eastern shore of Lake Bomoseen. Also see *Green Space*.

TENNIS **Summit Lodge** (802-422-3535), Killington Rd., Killington. Four clay outdoor courts are available to the public if not in use by members. **Vermont Sport & Fitness Club** (802-775-9916) in Rutland has three indoor and eight outdoor courts. Public courts are also maintained by the city of Rutland and the towns of Chittenden, Killington, Castleton, Fairhaven, Poultney, and Proctor.

❋ Winter Sports

CROSS-COUNTRY SKIING AND SNOWSHOEING 🐾 🖋 **Mountain Meadows Cross Country Ski and Snowshoe Area** (802-775-7077; 802-775-0166; xcskiing.net), 2363 Rt. 4, Killington, behind Base Camp Outfitters, just east of the main Killington access road. Open daily (conditions permitting) 9–5. This is one of Vermont's oldest and most serious touring centers, operated for more than 20 years by Mike and Diane Miller. The 57 km of trails are still in the same place, but the touring center itself has moved as of the winter of 2008–09 to a new facility behind owner Mike and Diane's Rt. 4 shops. Trails are groomed for skating and classic stride. There are separate snowshoeing trails, plus backcountry terrain. Some instruction, rentals, kids' programs. Call for telemark rentals and for Nordic and snowshoe tours of the backcountry. **Mountain Meadows Lodge** offers hot soup and sandwich lunches for skiers, five minutes down the wooded trail.

Mountain Top Nordic Ski & Snowshoe Center (802-483-6089; mountaintop inn.com), Mountain Top Rd., Chittenden. Sixty km of trails, 40 km of which are groomed, begin at the Nordic Center, one of the country's oldest commercial cross-country ski centers and an ideal location at 1,495–2,165 feet, with sweeping views of the mountains and of Chittenden Reservoir; rentals, lessons, and limited snowmaking.

Hawk Inn & Mountain Resort (802-672-3811; hawkresort.com), Rt. 100 south, Plymouth, offers rentals, lessons, and groomed trails meandering along a brook.

DOGSLEDDING Nordic Center of the Mountain Top Inn & Resort (802-483-2311) offers half-hour ride by reservation. Passengers must be 5 years or older. $75 per person

SLEIGH RIDES Mountain Top Inn & Resort (802-483-2311; mountaintopinn .com). Thirty-minute horse-drawn sleigh rides daily. $25 adults, $15 children under 14. Private rides can be arranged.

Pond Hill Ranch (802-468-2449; pondhillranch.com), Castleton. One- to three-hour rides.

SNOWMOBILING Killington Snowmobile Tours (802-422-2121; snowmobile vermont.com). One- and two-hour mountain and backcountry tours, plus snow-cross track for kids ages 4–11. Rental helmets, clothing, and boots. This is also a source of info about local clubs.

✳ Green Space

Note: For more information about both of the following, see **vtstateparks.com**.

Calvin Coolidge State Forest. This 16,000-acre preserve, which actually includes Killington and Shrewsbury peaks, is scattered through seven local towns and divided by Rt. 100 into two districts. The recreational center is **Coolidge State Park** (802-672-3612), Rt. 100A east of Plymouth Notch. Open late May–mid-Oct., these 500 acres include a campground (60 campsites including 35 lean-tos, a dump station, picnic area, and restrooms with hot showers), picnic shelters (but no hookups), and hiking and snowmobile trails. In another part of the forest, **Camp Plymouth State Park**, off Rt. 100 in Tyson, served as a Civilian Conservation Corps (CCC) camp in 1933 and offers a beach on Echo Lake (picnic area, food concession). Inquire about gold panning and trails into the abandoned village of Plymouth Five Corners. North of the turnoff for Rt. 100A, the steep CCC Rd. (marked for Meadowsweet Farm) climbs away from Rt. 100 into the western swatch of the forest, with beautiful views back down the valley. It's unfortunate (but sensible) that this road is closed in winter, because it harbors some of the area's snowiest cross-country trails, accessible only by going the long way around through Shrewsbury (see *Scenic Drive* in "Okemo Valley Region").

DOWNHILL SKIING AND SNOWBOARDING

✒ **Killington Resort** (800-621-MTNS; killington.com), 4763 Killington Rd., Killington. With six interconnected mountains—plus Pico—and the longest snowboard terrain park in the East, Killington is just plain immense. For many of its 50 years, the resort has been all about superlatives—the world's most and best snowmaking, the East's biggest and best ski school (in 1964 it was the first to introduce the "Graduated Length Method"), and the region's longest ski season (Oct.–May).

The current owner—Powder Corporation of Park City, Utah—has, however, been making changes aimed at quality rather than quantity. The season has been shortened to Nov.–May, and the lifts at Pico now just operate just Thu.–Mon. Ski school class sizes have been cut. Improvements for the 2008–09 season include a new Skye Peak Express chair, speeding access to Bear Mountain's long, intermediate cruising trails and to The Stash, an all-natural terrain park.

SKIING AT KILLINGTON

Killington Resort

With 1,003 acres of slopes, Killington does have something to please everyone, including high-elevation views and 16 gladed trails. It still boasts the tallest summit in the East accessible by lift, the K-1 Express Gondola, which hoists you 4,215 feet to the summit of Killington, the highest of the seven peaks. A quarter of its 191 trails are easy; a third are moderate, and about 40 percent are difficult. The longest, the so-called Juggernaut, runs 6.2 miles.

Thanks to Killington's four entry points, six base lodges, and far-flung network of lifts and trails, the crowds are dispersed throughout the area. Each base lodges offers extensive services. Ramshead is great for kids, with a family center for rentals, a skier development program, child care, a food court, and Snow Play Park.

Given its size and high profile, Killington attracts more ski-weekers than most New England areas, enough for a lively midweek atmosphere in the shops, eateries, and lounges along Killington Rd., but still leaving ample room on the slopes.

Lifts: 30, including 11 quads (7 high-speed) plus the Skyeship and K1 Express Gondolas, 4 doubles, 6 triples, 6 surface lifts (carrying 43,446 riders per hour).

Trails and slopes: 199, with 1,215 skiable acres including 87 miles of trails.

Vertical drop: 3,050 feet.

Snowmaking: 715 acres of terrain, with 1,435 snowguns.

Snowboarding: Superpipe with 18-foot walls, six terrain parks, and the new Stash, an "all-natural" terrain park with 34 features such as rock-wall rides, log jibs, and cliff drops, designed to challenge intermediate and advanced riders.
Facilities: 6 base lodges, 5 ski rental shops, 1 mountaintop lodge, 5 lounges.
Special programs: More than 50 ski and snowboard school instructors; a Ramshead Family Center with a children's Ski and Snowboard School divided into five levels of programs with a maximum of three student per instructor.
Rates: $82 adults at the ticket window but no one in their right mind pays that. Check the Web site or phone Killington's Central Reservations (800-621-MTNS; killington.com) for the many options. The best value is always the five-day lifts/lodging package, available at most local inns, lodges, and condo rental offices.

Pico Mountain (802-422-3333; picomountain.com). One of Vermont's first mountain resorts, Pico opened in 1937 with a tow hooked up to the engine of a Hudson auto. Currently under the same ownership as Killington, the winter lifts at this family-friendly resort are only open Thu.–Mon. and holiday weeks.

Vertical drop: 1, 967 feet.

Skiable acres: 214, with 50 trails adding up to 17 miles, the largest percentage intermediate, all funneling to the base lodge.

Lifts: 2 express quads, 2 triples, and 2 doubles.

Snowmaking: 161 acres.

Facilities: Rentals, instruction, sport center, and condo lodging (see killington .com).

Rates are the same as Killington.

Gifford Woods State Park (summer 802-775-5354), 0.5 mile north of Rt. 4 on Rt. 100, Killington. The campground (27 tent/trailer and 21 lean-to sites, restrooms, and hot showers) is patronized by hikers on the Appalachian Trail, which runs through the park. Across the road is the Gifford Woods Natural Area, a 7-acre stand of virgin hardwoods (sugar maple, yellow birch, basswood, white ash, and hemlock). Trails lead up to Deer Leap Mountain and to the lovely waterfalls where Kent Brook enters Kent Pond. In winter cross-country trails connect with Mountain Meadows.

LAKES AND PONDS **Lake Bomoseen**, just north of Castleton, is a popular local summer colony. The lake gained notoriety in the 1930s because of Alexander Woollcott's summer retreat on Neshobe Island. The portly "Town Crier," a nationally known newspaper columnist, entertained such cronies as Harpo Marx, who was known to repel curious interlopers by capering along the shore naked and painted blue.

Lake Bomoseen State Park (802-265-4242; 802-786-0060), Rt. 4 west of Rutland, Exit 3, 5 miles north on Town Rd. Its 66 campsites, including 10 lean-tos, are set in a lovely wildlife refuge; beach, picnic area, nature program, trails, boat ramp, and rentals.

Half Moon State Park (802-273-2848; 802-786-0060), between Fair Haven and Rutland on Rt. 4; take Exit 4, go 6.5 miles north on Rt. 30, left on Hortonia Rd. and continue 2 miles, then go left on Black Pond Rd. for 2 miles. Wooded campsites (59 tent sites; 10 lean-tos) around a secluded pond; rental canoes; hikes to **High Pond**, a remote body of water in the hills.

Lake St. Catherine State Park (802-287-9158; 802-786-0060), 3 miles south of Poultney on Rt. 30. Fifty tent or trailer campsites and 11 lean-tos, plus sandy beaches, fishing, boat rentals, nature trails.

* Lodging

At and around Killington

Killington Central Reservations (800-621-6867; killington.com) Open daily 8 AM–9 PM, the bureau keeps a tally on vacancies and makes reservations. A wide variety of two- to five-day ski and summer packages are available.

Note: Killington's Skyeship Gondola on Rt. 4 also puts the inns of Plymouth (to the southeast) within easy reach, and lodging in both Woodstock (see "Woodstock/Quechee Area") and Ludlow (see "Okemo Valley Region") is within 14 miles. See *Guidance* for central reservations numbers.

RESORTS **The Killington Grand Resort Hotel** (888-64-GRAND; killington.com), 228 East Mountain Rd., Killington 05751. At the base of the lifts, this 200-room, vintage-1997 facility offers standard hotel rooms, also studios and one-, two-, and three-bedroom suites (with kitchen). It's immense, with endless corridors and Vermont's biggest meeting space (the Grand Ballroom)—ergo conventions. The rooms are irreproachably comfortable. Amenities include an outdoor heated pool, health club, on-site day care, Ovations Restaurant (see *Dining Out*), and a café. It's close not only to the base lodge, but in summer to the golf course as well. $125–500. Best values year-round if combined with a sports package.

☙ ♂ ♿ Mountain Top Inn & Resort
(802-483-2311; 800-445-2100;
mountaintopinn.com), 195 Mountain
Top Rd., Chittenden 05737. Set high
on a hill with a spectacular view of
Chittenden Reservoir against a mountain backdrop, this self-contained
resort has been operating as an inn
since the 1940s. It hosted President
Dwight Eisenhower and his entourage
in 1955 when he arrived for a fishing
expedition (he stayed in what is now
called Ike's View, a corner room with a
terrific view). Today it is one of the few
Vermont resorts to offer both horseback riding and a cross-country skiing
center (both open to the public). Each
of the 30 rooms/suites in the main inn
has been redecorated; 7 on the lake
side are luxuriously appointed with
fabulous linens, a TV hidden in an
armoire, and whirlpool bath or steam
shower. Many have themes: Stags Run,
for instance, features a huge rough-
hewn log bed. Our favorite was the
Angler's Retreat, whose balcony affords
a bird's-eye view of the stunning Green
Mountain National Forest below.
There are also five cabins and several
private "resort chalets" available for
larger groups. In addition to riding,
summer activities include swimming in
both the lake and a heated pool, tennis, lawn games, canoeing and kayaking, claybird shooting, fly-fishing, and
scenic pontoon boat rides on the lake,
where moose sightings are not unusual. There's a horsemanship summer
camp for kids, and any number of winter activities: 80 km of cross-country
ski trails, snowshoeing, horse-drawn
sleigh rides, dogsledding, ice skating,
snowmobiling, a billiards table, and
massage therapy. Rooms and suites in
the inn are $160–545 including break-
fast (add 15 percent service). Two-
night minimum on weekends. Be sure
to request a room with a lake view.
Pets are $25 per night (they receive a
dog bed, bowls, and a welcome treat).
Inquire about the many packages.

**☙ ♂ ♿ Hawk Inn and Mountain
Resort** (802-672-3811; 800-685-4295;
hawkresort.com), Rt. 100, HCR 70,
Box 64, Plymouth 05056. Set on 1,200
acres and owned by longtime residents
Brenda and Jack Geishecker, this ranks
among Vermont's most luxurious modern resorts. Lodging options include
freestanding "mountain villas" salted
away on hillsides with splendid views,
as well as the townhouse-style Ledges
Villas high above the Black River Valley and the 50-room Hawk Inn and
River Tavern (see *Dining Out*). Situated halfway between Killington and
Okemo (basically 10 minutes from
each) and 3 miles from the trails at
Bear Creek Mountain Club, the resort
is well positioned for alpine skiers and
offers its own extensive cross-country
trail network as well as a heated outdoor pool, a spa, ice skating and sleigh
rides, and its own 70-acre nature preserve. In summer there's tennis, horseback riding, swimming, mountain
biking, and fly-fishing, as well as
canoeing, kayaking, sailing, and rowing
on Lake Amherst. The heart of the inn
itself is a 19th-century farmhouse, and
rooms are in modern wings. Each is
decorated differently. Some have
whirlpool bath; all are equipped with
down comforter, featherbed, and large-
screen TV. The spa has a large
indoor/outdoor pool, massage and spa
therapy services, and a salon. In summer and fall, $270–570 per couple in
the inn and $490–980 in the Ledges
Villas (two-night minimum), including
full breakfast. Lunch is served poolside
during summer.

**INNS ⚭ ♿ Mountain Meadows
Lodge** (802-775-1010; 800-370-4567;
mtmeadowslodge.com), Thundering
Brook Rd., Killington 05751. The
main building is an 1856 barn, nicely

converted into a classic lodge with an informal dining room, a game room, a spacious sunken living room with a beautiful lake view, and tons of atmosphere. Anne and Bill Mercier gear the year-round inn to families and AT hikers, catering to people who like the outdoors in warm-weather months as well as in winter. This is also the kind of place that lends itself to renting as a whole for weddings, family reunions, and retreats. There are 17 guest rooms, many of them great for families, all with private bath. A sauna and outdoor Jacuzzi are among the amenities. In summer there is a swimming pool and 100-acre Kent Lake, which abuts the property and is good for fishing and canoeing as well as swimming. In winter it adjoins a major ski-touring center. Year-round residents include Alice, the miniature potbellied pig, a pony, and sheep. The lake is stocked with trout and bass. Low seasons $98 per couple B&B; $178–340 for a family room.

♦ ♪ **The October Country Inn** (802-672-3412; 800-648-8421; october countryinn.com), junction of Rts. 4 and 100A, Bridgewater Corners 05035. Handy to Killington and Woodstock (8 miles) as well as most of the things to do and see in this chapter, yet sequestered up a back road with hiking trails that lead past the swimming pool to the top of a hill for a sweeping, peaceful view. This old farmhouse has a large, comfortable living room with inviting places to sit around the hearth and at the big round table in the dining room—not to be confused with the other cheery dining room in which guests gather around long tables for memorable meals. Innkeepers Edie and Chuck Janisse offer gourmet candlelit dinners with wine and all-fresh local produce served family-style, prix fixe, for $30. Breakfasts are equally creative and ambitious, geared to fuel

bikers in summer and skiers in winter. The 10 guest rooms (with private bath) vary in size; most have queen-sized bed, many with Edie's handmade quilts. $165–195 includes breakfast. Open most of the year.

🐾 ♪ ♿ "I" **Fox Creek Inn** (802-483-6213; 800-707-0017; foxcreekinn.com), 49 Chittenden Dam Rd., Chittenden 05737. This is backwoods luxury in a superb house owned at one time by the inventor William Barstow, who summered here after selling his various holdings for $40 million right before the 1929 stock market crash. Jim and Sandy Robertson offer nine carefully furnished guest rooms, all with private bath, most with Jacuzzi, and five with gas fireplace. The Honeymoon Suite has two fireplaces and a two-person Jacuzzi. Guests gather around the big stone fireplace in the paneled den, in the comfortable living room, and at the cozy bar. The four-course candlelight dinners are a point of pride. There is swimming, canoeing, and fishing in the Chittenden Reservoir just down the road, and in winter you can cross-country ski or just lounge around. The Robertsons also shuttle guests to hiking trails. $195–295 B&B, $210–325 MAP ($260–400 during foliage season). Call ahead about pets and children.

FOX CREEK INN

Christina Tree

🦞 🗡 ⚲ "₁" **The Vermont Inn** (802-775-0708; 800-541-7795; vermontinn.com), Killington 05751. Set above Rt. 4 with a view of Killington and Pico, this 19th-century farmhouse has a homey feel to its public rooms—the living room with woodstove, the pub/lounge with fireplace, a game room, and an upstairs reading room, a sanctuary in the evening when the dining room is open to the public (see *Dining Out*). Summer facilities include a pool, a tennis court, and lawn games. The sauna and hot tub are available year-round. Innkeepers Jennifer and Michael Duffy offer 16 guest rooms, ranging from smallish to spacious, all bright with brass and antique or canopy bedstead and private bath. Five have a fireplace. Facilities include a fitness center and a kids' TV room; $110–305 per couple MAP. B&B rates available. Less for midweek and longer stays. Inquire about golf, fishing, and other packages.

⚲ **Red Clover Inn** (802-775-2290; 800-752-0571, redcloverinn.com), 7 Woodward Rd., Mendon 05701. Set on 13 secluded acres with a pond but minutes from Pico and from the Killington access road, this 1840s farmhouse has been transformed over the years into a top-notch inn and restaurant. As we go to press it's reopening under new ownership as a sister property to Tyler Place, a long-established family-geared summer resort up in Highgate Springs. It's received a thorough renovation from carpets to roof. Rates are $175–375; midweek, this includes breakfast and dinner during regular season. Spa treatments are featured.

⊙ 🗡 **Casa Bella Inn & Restaurant** (802-746-8943; 877-746-8943; casabellainn.com), 3911 Main St. (Rt. 100), Pittsfield 05762. Located 8 miles north of Killington in the center of the vil-

lage on a handsome green, this double-porched old inn has been welcoming guests since 1835. Innkeeper Susan Cacozza is from Britain and her husband, Franco, is a chef from Tuscany. The restaurant is important here and open to the public (see *Dining Out*), but the feel is very much that of a village country inn in the center of this classic Vermont town that's removed from, but still handy to, Killington. The eight guest rooms, all with private bath, are $95–150, including a delicious breakfast. Children over 10 welcome.

LODGES ⊙ 🦞 🗡 "₁" **The Summit Lodge** (802-422-3535; 800-635-6343; summitlodgevermont.com), P.O. Box 119, Killington Rd., Killington 05751. Sited on a knoll just off Killington Road. This is an expansive lodge with fieldstone fireplaces, hand-hewn beams, a cozy library, and two Saint Bernard greeters. Amenities include a large indoor hot tub, saunas, an outdoor heated pool, a game room, and massage therapy. In summer there are also red clay tennis courts, racquetball, bocce, and horseshoes. The Saint's Pub is open nightly for dinner in winter, serving comfort food with flair; the Gristmill (see *Eating Out*), open for lunch and dinner year-round, is also on the grounds. The 45 guest rooms vary, all with private bath, cable TV, king and queen beds (the family rooms sleep up to six). $79–250 in summer.

🗡 ⚲ **Inn of the Six Mountains** (802-422-4302; 800-228-4676; sixmountains.com), Killington Rd., Killington 05751. A 103-room, four-story, Adirondack-style hotel with gabled ceilings, skylights, balconies, and a two-story lobby with a fieldstone fireplace. There is also a spa with lap pool, Jacuzzis, and exercise room, plus a seasonal dining room. In summer $79–159 per room, fall $199–249, winter $149–309, depending on the day and week, continental breakfast included. In winter check on the two-day packages that include skiing, lodging, and breakfast. Children are free with two adults but $17 if over 12. Inquire about Jimmy LeSage's New Life Hiking Spa (newlife hikingspa.com), a program based here early May–Oct.

🐾 **The Inn at Long Trail** (802-775-7181; 800-325-2540; innatlongtrail .com), 709 Rt. 4, Killington 05751. Closed in shoulder seasons. This is the first building in New England specifically built to serve as a ski lodge. It began in 1938 as an annex to a splendid summer inn that has since burned. Designed to resemble the inside of the forest as much as possible, the interior incorporates parts of trees and boulders and is a casual place. The inn caters to through-hikers on the Appalachian and Long Trails and outdoors people of all sorts. The 22-foot-long bar is made from a single log, and a protruding toe of the backyard cliff can be seen in both the pub and the dining room. The 14 rooms are small but cheery (2 are family suites); there are 5 two-room suites with fireplace. The hot tub is used in fall and winter. Dinner is served varying nights in the restaurant, but you can usually count on McGrath's Irish Pub (see *Eating Out*). Summer $75–105 per room B&B. Gratuity is 10 percent. Pets by advance arrangement.

🍴 🏠 **Salt Ash Inn** (802-672-3748; 800-SALT-ASH; saltashinn.com), 4758 Rt. 100A, Plymouth 05056. Built in the 1830s, this historic structure was a stagecoach stop when Salt Ash was the town's name (it was later changed to Plymouth). It also did a stint as a general store. The pub area retains the original grocery counter and the old post boxes where the Coolidge family fetched their mail. It's now an inviting

common space with a circular hearth, exuding warmth and atmosphere. Karla and Naz Jenulevich offer 17 guest rooms, all with private bath, TV, and wireless. There's a nicely landscaped, heated pool. The entire place can be rented by groups of up to 45. $100–250 B&B, depending on the room (from economy to deluxe with fireplace), the season, and the day of the week; less for weekdays and longer stays.

CONDOMINIUMS Killington Central Reservations (800-621-6867; killington.com) serves many hundreds of condo units ranging from **Sunrise Condominiums**, high on the mountain, to **Pico Resort Hotel** on Rt. 4 beside the Pico base lodge. The Web site also list local Realtors specializing in condo and private home rentals.

In Rutland and west
SUMMER RESORT 🏠 ⚓ **Edgewater Resort** (802 468-5251; 888-475-6664); 2551 Rt. 30, 2 miles north of Rt. 4, at Lake Bomoseen, 05732. This 9-mile lake was a celebrity playground in the big-band era. There were five major hotels and a dance pavilion; Benny Goodman and Glenn Miller played. Now all the hotels are gone except this summer-camp-like resort, which the Poremski family has nurtured from a cluster of cabins they bought in the 1950s. It includes the 150-year-old 9-room Edgewater Inn with its huge porch and pine paneling, an 8-room chalet, a 12-unit motel, 14 one- and two-bedroom condo apartments, 4 cottages, and 12 efficiencies. Though not luxurious, all are clean and moderately priced. Most have cooking facilities and lake views; some are right on the water. The Trak-In Restaurant (see *Eating Out*) serves breakfasts and dinner, and there is a beach, boating, fishing, an outdoor pool, an adjacent

nine-hole golf course, a game room, and a playground. Most of the guests return year after year. MAP rates (double occupancy) range $105–130 per day, $700–850 per week. Rooms only $60–85 per day, double occupancy, $385–535 per week; two-bedroom poolside condos $125 per night, $750 per week; two-bedroom cottage, $700 per week; three-bedroom lakeside cottages, $950–1,000 per week.

BED & BREAKFASTS

In Rutland 05071

❝❞ The Inn at Rutland (802-773-0575; 800-808-0575; innatrutland.com), 70 N. Main St. This 1880s-era Victorian mansion with its oak detailing and high ceilings is on Rt. 7 just north of the center of town. Innkeepers Leslie and Steven Brenner offer eight distinctive guest rooms on two upstairs floors, each with phone, private bath, antiques, and color TV. One includes a fireplace, two have private porch, and two have air-jetted tub. The woodwork in the dining room is exceptional, and the fireplaced living room is attractive, with space to work on your computer or play an evening game. An especially welcoming place for solo travelers, who are placed together (if they don't mind) at breakfast. $119–229 (depending on room and timing) includes a delicious three-course breakfast.

In Shewsbury 05738, up in the hills 10 miles southeast of Rutland

❝❞ Maple Crest Farm (802-492-3367; maplecrestfarm.com), 2512 Lincoln Hill Rd. Open year-round except Jan.–Feb. This handsome white-brick farmhouse sits high on a ridge in the old hilltop center of Shrewsbury. It was built in 1808 as Gleason's Tavern and is still in the same family—they began

taking in guests in the 1860s and have done so off and on ever since. The Smiths offer three antiques-filled rooms (the front ground-floor room with a half bath is our favorite) sharing two baths, and two charming apartments that can accommodate small families. "Every piece of furniture has a story," says Donna Smith—and she knows each one. Ask about a rocking chair or spool bed, and you'll begin to sense who has lived in this unusual house down through the years. Books and magazines are everywhere, focusing on local and Vermont tales and history. The Smiths raise beef cattle and hay, and are noted for the quality of their maple syrup, produced in the sugarhouse at the peak of the hill; the same sweeping view can be enjoyed in winter on cross-country skis. You can walk off in any number of directions. $65–100 per room. Breakfast is included. Inquire about theorem painting workshops. No credit cards.

❝❞ Crisanver House (802-492-3589; 800-492-8089; crisanver.com), 1434 Crown Point Rd. Set high on 120 acres of woods and meadows, this is a find—but it's frequently booked weekends for weddings. The 1802 portion of the house offers eight attractive guest rooms, all with down comforters and pillows, exposed beams, original art, robes, and individual heat control. The living room, with a fireplace and grand piano, adjoins a spacious, sunny conservatory maximizing the panoramic view. A downstairs game room has table tennis and a pool table. The building was a summer inn, the Tip Top House, when Carol and Michael Calotta bought it in 1971, along with friends who were looking for a ski house. It's since been totally renovated. We prefer the upstairs front rooms with a view west to the valley, but the most luxurious are two deluxe rooms with Jacuzzi and heated towel rack in the bathroom. A barn has been designed to accommodate 120 people for weddings and parties. In summer there's a heated pool and an all-weather tennis court; in winter, cross-country skiing and snowshoeing; Okemo and Killington are also within striking distance. A five-course dinner can be arranged at $42.50 per person. Rates, including a full breakfast, tea, and transfers to bus, train, and airport, are $155–195 for rooms, $230–325 for suites, less midweek and single. Minimum two-night stay on weekends.

🐾 ❝❞ **The Buckmaster Inn** (802-492-3720; buckmasterinn.com), 20 Lottery Rd. Built as the three-story Buckmaster Tavern beside the Shrewsbury church in 1801, the house is owned by Richard and Elizabeth Davis, who have lightened and brightened its decor. Eight to 10 guests can be accommodated in four rooms (two queen beds, two doubles, all with private bath). There is a spacious living room, a library with fireplace and TV/DVD player, and a long, screened-in porch that's especially inviting in summer and fall. These are enthusiastic hosts who can tell you what to see and do. $95–125 double includes a full breakfast featuring home-baked goodies. No credit cards.

In Fairhaven 05743

🐾 🐾 **Maplewood Inn** (802-265-8039; 800-253-7729; maplewoodinn.net), 1108 S. Main St., Rt. 22A south. Paul Stagg and Scott Rose's historic 1843 Greek Revival home (on the National Register of Historic Places) is decorated in period style with a stately dining room, a long lounging porch, a rear patio, and a parlor with a fireplace and complimentary cordials. The five air-conditioned rooms include two suites with fireplace and sitting area (one is suitable for families with both a queen

and double). All have private bath, cable TV, and DVD player; guests can choose from a 1,400-title DVD library. Rates are $130–160, including a full made-to-order breakfast.

❝❞ **The Haven Guest House Bed & Breakfast** (802-265-8882; havenguesthousevt.com), 1 4th St. (near Rt. 4). Gisela and Werner Baumann are your hosts in this early-20th-century renovated Colonial with its wooden floors and expansive, curving porch. The four comfortable suites each have private bath, TV, and wireless access. The Apple Blossom Room has a king-sized bed, the Rosewood two twins, and there are queens in the other two. Guests can sit by a crackling fire in the living room, play chess at a dining room table, or sit in the parlor. There is a breakfast menu, and Gisela's hearty offerings include fresh breads and pastries. $99–129 includes breakfast. Children over 6; no pets.

Elsewhere

❝❞ **Twin Mountains Farm** (802-235-3700; twinmoutainsfarmbb.com), 549 Coy Hill Rd., Middletown Springs 05757. This 1830 farmhouse with modern comforts is secluded on a long dirt road about 2 miles south of the village on 150 acres stretching from the ridgeline of Coy Mountain on the north to Morgan Mountain on the south. It's not far from Lake St. Catherine. Guests are greeted by two friendly Alaskan malamutes and by Walt and Annie Pepperman. There are three air-conditioned guest rooms with private bath and guest robes. The deluxe Deer Room has a queen-sized sleigh bed, a sofa, and a view of the swimming/skating pond. Each of the smaller Moose and Bear rooms contains two twins. Guests can lounge by the fireplace in the comfortable living room or relax on the screened-in porch. Cross-country skiing, snowshoeing, and a mapped system of hiking trails are steps away (Walt, a retired lawyer, is a nature guide). Breakfast—perhaps baked apples, pancakes with a maple-banana glaze, or eggs Benedict over fried tomatoes—is served by wood-stove in winter, on the patio in summer. The stars pop out in the night sky, and the silence is deafening. $95–150 includes breakfast. Closed in Apr.

♋ ✓ **White Rocks Inn** (802-446-2077; whiterocksinn.com), 1774 Rt. 7 south, Wallingford 05773. Malcolm and Rita Swogger's elegantly furnished, antiques-filled farmhouse and its land-mark barn are on the National Register of Historic Places. The property includes a hilltop gazebo, a rose arbor, a pond with Adirondack chairs, and hik-ing paths that lead to views of the Green Mountains and the White Rocks Recreation Area. It's a popular place to get married; the 15,000-square-foot Gothic-style barn, one of the largest in southern Vermont, is ideal for recep-tions, and guests can be chauffeured to dinner in Malcolm's vintage 1939 Cadil-lac limousine. (Ask about the wedding and elopement packages.) The five guest rooms, each with private bath, have either king, queen, or double canopy beds and go for $139–219 dou-ble occupancy, including full breakfast. The Milk House Cottage (with a whirlpool bath, living room, and full kitchen) is EP or B&B by the day ($249–279) and the Nest Cottage (king canopy bed, air-jet tub, deck, loft with twin beds, farmhouse kitchen, fireplace) is $269–299); both are cheaper by the week. Children over 12 are welcome in the house, any age in the cottage.

🐾 "🐾" **The Paw House Inn** (866-729-4687; pawhouseinn.com), 1376 Claren-don Ave., Rutland 05777. This is all about dogs. Each of the eight guest rooms has a private bath, TV, VCR, a dog water bowl, and a dog bed. On Rt. 133 just south of West Rutland (handy to Rt. 4), this is a handsome old house with ample common space. Humans are required to take their shoes off at the door. Facilities include an off-location dog park. $165–215 includes breakfast served on hand-painted plates picturing dogs.

MOTOR INNS
In Rutland 05071
🐾 ✓ **Mendon Mountain Orchards** (802-775-5477; mendonorchards.com), 16 Rt. 4, Mendon, isn't really a motel but rather a series of pleasant, very reasonably priced old-fashioned cabins, surrounded by orchards, with a pool and a shop for homemade goodies, apples in-season, cider, and flowers. **Holiday Inn Rutland/Killington** (800-462-4810; hivermont.com), Rts. 7 and 4 south, is a downtown landmark that includes **Paynter's Restaurant**, an indoor pool, sauna and exercise room, and **Centre Stage** lounge. The 112-room **Best Western** (866-229-6188; bestwestern-rutland.com) is the former Hog Penny and features one- and two-bedroom condo suites, an out-door pool, tennis court, and game room. Choices also include a **Ramada Limited** (888-818-3297), a **Red Roof Inn** (802-775-4303), and the **Comfort Inn at Trolley Square** (800-432-6788).

CAMPGROUNDS See *Green Space* for information on campgrounds in Lake Bomoseen State Park, Half Moon Pond State Park, and Lake St. Cather-ine State Park.

See *Green Space* for information on camping in Calvin Coolidge and Gif-ford Woods State Parks.

✳ Where to Eat
DINING OUT **The Corners Inn and Restaurant** (802-672-9968; cornersinn.com), Rt. 4, Bridgewater

DESTINATION DINING WORTH A DRIVE

Hemingway's (802-422-3886; hemingwaysrestaurant.com), 4988 Rt. 4, Sherburne Flats, east of Killington. Closed Mon. and Tue. Between Linda's eye for detail in the decor and service and Ted's concern for freshness, preparation, and presentation, the Fondulas have created one of the most exceptional dining experiences in New England. They first opened the restaurant in 1982, but show no sign of sitting on their many laurels. Chandeliers, fresh flowers, and floor-length table linens grace the peach-colored, vaulted main room, while a less formal atmosphere prevails in the garden room and stone-walled wine cellar. It's billed as "regional, classic cuisine," but whatever name you give it, it's divine. You might begin with wood-roasted Vermont quail or a fallen soufflé of Vermont goat cheese with local greens, then dine on morel-crusted veal with fava beans and corn cake or wild striped bass with chive and vanilla. Dinner entrées range $32–38. There is a four-course $62 prix fixe menu, $85 if matched with wine samplings; a four-course vegetarian menu is available for $55, which can be made totally vegan with advance notice. Reservations are a must.

The Victorian Inn at Wallingford (802-446-2099; thevictorianinn.com), 55 N. Main St., Rt. 7, Wallingford, serves dinner Tue.–Sat., and a gourmet Sunday brunch buffet 10–2; closed in Nov. until Thanksgiving. Swiss-born chef-owner Konstantin Schonbachler, formerly executive chef at the Kennedy Center in Washington, DC, brought his European culinary talents with him when he moved to this French Second Empire home in the center of Wallingford. Guests eat in one of three downstairs rooms in a casually elegant ambience; this is very simply one of Vermont's best restaurants. Entrées $19.95–36.95.

Redbrick Grill (802-287-2323; redbrickgrillvt.com), 23 Depot St., Poultney. Open for dinner Wed.–Sun. (Thu.–Sun. in winter), from 5:30 PM. Reservations accepted. Housed in Poultney's former (brick) railroad station, Frank Rhodes and Wendy Jackson have created a destination dining spot to please the fussiest foodies. Local ingredients and a wood-fired oven are the constants in a menu that's printed daily. On an August evening you could begin with handmade ravioli stuffed with house-made ricotta, spinach, and cream, then dine on a salad Niçoise (including olive oil poached tuna, all-local greens, beans, and new potatoes) or house-cured duck confit, among many mouthwatering choices . . . including the wood-fired pizza of the day. Desserts include homemade sorbets and ice cream. Entrées $12–28.

Corners. Open for dinner Wed.–Sun. except Apr. and the first two weeks in Nov. Reservations suggested. Known for the unusual ways he uses fresh, local ingredients, chef-owner Brad Pirkey has created an informal, stand-out small restaurant in an 1890 farmhouse. In winter request a table near the fireplace, and in summer on the terrace with its forested views. There's also a friendly bar. Specials on a summer night included beef Wellington and lobster spring rolls, and the menu ranged from homemade pastas with sweet Italian sausage, prosciutto, mushrooms, garlic, and roasted red peppers to veal with wild mushrooms and artichoke hearts. Entrées ($14.95–19.95) come with daily homemade cheese spread and fresh-baked bread and you can sup for less from the bar menu.

Red Clover Inn (802-775-2290; 800-752-0571; redcloverinn.com), 7 Woodward Ave. (off Rt. 4), Mendon. Open for dinner nightly in-season. A meld of comfort food and fine dining in an elegant inn ambience. You might begin with a squash and apple bisque and dine on braised osso buco or seared Maple Leaf Farm duck breast with port-poached pears and marinated dried fruits. Entrée prices from the teens to $30s.

The Countryman's Pleasure (802-773-7141; countrymanspleasure.com), just off Rt. 4, Mendon. Open 5–9 daily. Chef-owner Hans Entinger, a native of Austria, is known for top-drawer Austrian-German specialties: veal schnitzel, Bavarian sauerbraten, veal à la Holstein, also classics like roast half duckling and rack of lamb. Vegetarian fare is available. The attractive dining rooms occupy the first floor of a charming house. There's a long wine list, and beers as well as international coffees and nonalcoholic wines

and beers are served. The atmosphere is cozy and informal with an open fireplace. Early-bird specials (5–6 PM) are under $14. Otherwise entrées are $18.95–31.95. Senior and kids' menu.

The Vermont Inn (802-775-0708; 800-541-7795; vermontinn.com), Rt. 4, Killington. Open for dinner Thu.–Mon. Chef Stephen Hatch has captured first place three times in the Killington-Champagne Dine Around Contest. It's a pleasant inn dining room with a huge fieldstone fireplace and a varied menu that changes nightly. Entrées might range from Vermont roast turkey to rack of lamb roasted with parsley, rosemary, garlic, and black pepper; $16.95–22.95.

River Tavern (802-672-3811; hawkresort.com/dining) at Hawk Inn and Resort, Rt. 100, Plymouth. Open daily for breakfast, lunch, and dinner nightly, Thu.–Sat. in low season, and for lunch in summer. Dinner reservations essential. The restaurant itself is country elegant, with windowed walls framing the landscape and a deck where you can sit out under the stars in warm weather. A summer à la carte menu might feature lobster ravioli steeped in brandy and tomato blush sauce. Dinner entrées $14–42.

Choices Restaurant (802-422-4030), Glazebrook Center, 3 miles up Killington Rd., Killington. Open in summer Wed.–Sun from 5 PM, more days in high winter season. This combination bistro/brasserie/pub has a huge menu of savory appetizers, salads, soups, raw bar, sandwiches, and pastas, not to mention entrées ranging from curried vegetables with couscous to filet mignon. Dinner entrées $17.95–26.95.

The Highlands Dining Room at the Mountain Top Inn and Resort (802-483-2311; mountaintopinn.com), 195 Mountain Top Rd., Chittenden.

Open for dinner (and breakfast) by reservation to nonguests. The lower-level dining room is large and formal with linen tablecloths, a stone fireplace, and views of the lake and mountains. The à la carte menu changes seasonally. It might include prosciutto and melon and a crab martini as appetizers, diver scallops and rack of veal as entrées. There's a choice of salads and desserts, an impressive wine list, and a kids' menu. Entrées $24–35. The adjacent, casual **Highlands Tavern** is open daily for lunch and dinner. The menu features wraps, burgers, paninis, and a full bar, also maybe pad Thai and grilled flatbread pizza.

Peppino's Ristorante Italiano (802-422-3293), 1 mile up Killington Rd., Killington. Open nightly 5–10 in summer and ski season. A traditional, reasonably priced, reliable Italian restaurant with a dining-out decor, a large choice of pastas ($14.95–17.95), and all the classics, from linguine with clams to sirloin pizzaiola ($19.95–23.95).

✔ ⌖ **Ovations Restaurant at the Killington Grand Resort** (802-422-6111), 228 East Mountain Rd., Killington, is open nightly 5–9. This is a family-geared hotel dining room with soups and salads served all day and dinner selections ranging from burgers and pasta to fine steaks. Entrées $13–28.

Casa Bella Inn (802-746-8943; 877-746-8943; casabellainn.com), 3911 Main St., Rt. 100, Pittsfield. Franco Cacozza is the chef-owner of this pleasant restaurant in the former Pittsfield Inn, a classic old stage stop in the classic village 8 miles north of Killington. The menu is traditional, too, and authentic. Try the linguine *al pescatore* (sautéed with shrimp, squid, and clams in a light tomato sauce) or the *Ravioli al Funghi* (ravioli filled with wild mushrooms in a butter sage sauce).

Superb selection of Italian wines and scrumptious homemade desserts. Entrées $15.25–21.

The Garlic (802-422-5055; thegarlic inkillington.com), 1724 Killington Rd. (midway up). Open nightly, with a broad range of tapas at the bar. A cozy, informal setting for hearty Italian fare, with a choice of pasta dishes and entrées featuring the namesake ingredient. From $17 for "The Puttanesca" (linguine with the house sauce) to $27 for garlic-marinated char-grilled rack of lamb.

In Rutland

Little Harry's (802-747-4848), 121 West St. Open daily 5–10. This offspring of the popular Harry's Cafe in Mount Holly is romantically lit and decorated. Owners Harrison Pearce and Jack Mangan call their venture the "general store of ethnic eating." Besides pad Thai, a "signature" noodle dish, Little Harry's offers such fare as Jamaican jerk pork, shrimp sauté, New York sirloin, shrimp in crisp skins, and lively Spanish dishes plus burritos and steak sandwiches from what Pearce calls a "user-friendly" menu. Entrées $14.95–20.

✔ **The Palms** (802-773-2367), 36 Strongs Ave. Open 4:30–10 daily except Sunday. Italian cooking is a specialty in Rutland because of all the Italians who came to work in the marble quarries. The Palms opened its doors on Palm Sunday, 1933, and in 1948 it served the first pizza in Vermont. Now operated by the fourth generation of the Sabataso family, it's a thoroughly pleasant, family-geared place that can hit the spot if you are traveling. Neopolitan-style pizza remains a specialty, along with antipasto, pastas and veal, chicken and eggplant parmigiana. You can also dine on scallop and calamari Fra Diablo or surf and turf. Most entrées are under $20.

Table 24 (802-775-2424), 24 Wales St. Open Mon.–Sat. 5–midnight. A welcome addition to downtown dining options. The decor is contemporary, and the stress on fresh and local. A wood-fired rotisserie slow-roasts chicken. Prime rib, macaroni and cheese, and meat loaf are all on the menu, along with the day's grilled rib eye and fish. Entrées $11–28, and you can always get a sandwich.

Tokyo House (802-786-8080), 106 West St. Open daily for lunch 11–3, dinner 4:30–10. Owner Ming Li is known for sushi, sashimi, and bento boxes. Eat in or take out; beer and wine. Entrées $9–15.

Elsewhere

Lakehouse Pub & Grill (802-273-3000), 3569 Rt. 30 north, on Lake Bomoseen. Open May–Oct., daily for lunch and dinner. This popular place features a wooden hillside stairway leading down to umbrella-shaded waterside tables, spectacular sunset views from the air-conditioned indoor dining room, and an appealing menu with seafood specials and a full bar with live music on summer evenings. Freddie Field and Brad Burns have added panache to the menu. Light fare might include Thai sesame-tossed noodles; entrées range from fresh lobster to salmon poached in white wine with braised spinach, tomatoes, and artichoke hearts. Dinner entrées $18.50–27.

⊂⊃ ♂ **The Fair Haven Inn** (802-265-4907; 800-325-7074; fairhaveninn .com), 5 Adams St., Fair Haven. In a spacious, neo-Colonial setting, the Lemnotis family serves Greek American fare for lunch and dinner daily. Entrées might include veal Florentine ($18.95), moussaka ($12.95), and seafood medley ($21.95). Other specials include spanakopita and seafood souvlakia. Early-bird special prices are available the first hour; a full Greek menu is offered on Sundays, from *tzatziki* and *skorthia* to baked lamb ($12.95–19.95).

EATING OUT

In and around Killington

McGrath's Irish Pub at the Inn at Long Trail (802-775-7181; innatlong trail.com), Rt. 4 at the Inn at Long Trail, Killington. Open nightly for dinner and drinks. The 22-foot-long bar is made from a single log, and a protruding boulder can be seen in both the pub and the dining room. The first place to serve Guinness on tap in Vermont, the pub boasts the state's largest selection of Irish whiskey and features Irish country and folk music in the pub on weekends. The house specialties are Guinness stew and shepherd's pie. There's serious fare in the adjoining dining room, but it's the pub that's truly special.

♂ **Grist Mill** (802-422-3970; gristmill killington.com), Killington Rd. on the Summit Lodge grounds. Open for lunch and dinner, Sunday brunch; also for breakfast on weekends and holidays. The building is designed to look like a gristmill that has always stood on Summit Pond (there's a 90-year-old waterwheel). The interior is airy and pleasing, dominated by a huge stone hearth. There's an all-day menu of soups, salads, and light fare but after 5 PM there's an extensive dinner menu, also a children's menu and blackboard specials. Full liquor.

♂ **Casey's Caboose** (802-422-3795), halfway up Killington Rd., Killington. Open nightly for dinner in-season. The building incorporates a circa-1900 snowplow car and a great caboose to house the coveted tables, but you really can't lose: The atmosphere throughout rates high on our short list of family dining spots. Pot stickers, fresh calamari, a great seafood selection, and free Buffalo wings 3–6 PM. Children's menu.

🍴 *☙* **Charity's 1887 Saloon-Restaurant** (802-422-3800), midway up Killington Rd., Killington. Open daily in-season for lunch and dinner. Happy hour (free wings) 3–6. Tiffany shades, 1880s saloon decor, and wooden booths—this is the place for French onion soup, a Reuben, or a vegetarian casserole at lunch. Steak is a good dinner choice. Informal, satisfying.

☙ **Back Behind Saloon** (802-422-9907), junction of Rts. 4 and 100 south, West Bridgewater. Open from 4 in the tavern, at 5 for dinner nightly during ski season and summer, less in the off-season. A zany atmosphere (look for the red caboose and antique Mobil gas pump), barnboard, stained glass, a big hearth. Specialties like venison and saloon roast duck augment basic American fare: steaks and chicken, generous portions. Entrées on the

SIDEWALK TABLES AT BACK HOME AGAIN IN RUTLAND

Christina Tree

high side ($14.95–26). Children's menu.

Sugar & Spice (802-773-7832), Rt. 4, Mendon. Open daily 7–2. A pancake restaurant housed in a large replica of a classic sugarhouse surrounded by a 50-acre sugarbush. Besides dining on a variety of pancake, egg, and omelet dishes, along with soups and sandwiches, you can watch both maple candy and cheese being made several days a week. Gift shop.

In downtown Rutland

Three Tomatoes (802-747-7747), 88 Merchants Row, has the same northern Italian flair as its siblings in Burlington and in Lebanon, New Hampshire—wood-fired pizzas and all. Open for dinner nightly from 5. Shrimp sautéed with tomatoes, Greek olives, basil, garlic, crushed red chiles, and white wine, tossed with linguine, is but one sample dish. Entrées $10.95–16.95.

🍴 **Back Home Again** (802-775-9800), 23 Center St. Open Mon.–Thu. 11–9, Fri. 11–3, closed weekends. Operated by the Twelve Tribes (see "Island Pond"), imaginatively decorated with wood slab tables and intimate booths, a sidewalk café in summer. The stress is on wholesome food: sandwiches, salads, soups, and wraps, homemade breads, muffins, and raw juices, smoothies and desserts, also coffees, herbal teas, and maté. No alcohol.

Clem & Company (802-747-3340), 3 Center St. Open 7–1:30, closing at 1 on weekends. A fast, friendly local eatery. Breakfast until closing, also great soups, salads, and sandwiches for lunch (after 11:15). Clem's Café, around the corner at 101 Merchants Row, shares the same kitchen but is open all day.

Gill's Delicatessen (802-773-7414), 68 Strongs Ave. Open daily except Sun., 8 AM–9 PM (until 8 in winter).

Gill's is short for "Gilligan's," and Kathy Gilligan Phillips is the second generation to run this peerless eat-in bakery-deli, the oldest in Rutland. The hot Italian grinders come in four sizes with innumerable fillings (including real Maine crabmeat) and are, hands down, the best in Vermont. There are 10 tables, but most people grab and go.

Costantino's Italian Imports (802-747-0777), 10 Terrill St. Former antiques dealer Dan Costantino has renovated the former Bartlett's Studio building to create a shop that features shelves of imported Italian meats, cheeses, pasta, and olive oil. In the back a deli offers Italian sandwiches and pasta salads.

In Rutland along Route 7 south
🍴 🦌 **Midway Diner & Steak House** (802-775-9901), 120 S. Main St. Open daily, 6:30 AM–9 PM. Judging from its faded neon sign, you might dismiss this aptly named Rt. 7 eatery as just another truck stop. But the Midway is a friendly, air-conditioned community spot with good food, good prices, a broad menu, and decor that is pure Americana. Set back off Rt. 7 beside the municipal pool.

South Station (802-775-1736), at the Trolley Barn, 170 S. Main St. Open daily for lunch and dinner, specializing in prime rib of beef and such munchies as fried potato skins, stuffed mushrooms, chicken wings, hearty soups, salads, burgers, and teriyaki chicken.

Elsewhere
Birdseye Diner (802-468-5817), Main St., Castleton. This restored 1940s Silk City diner, open all day, is a justifiably popular spot for college students and local residents alike.

Trak-In Restaurant (802-468-3212), Rt. 30 on Lake Bomoseen. Open daily

for breakfast and dinner Mother's Day–Oct. Red and Val Poremski have owned this lakeside resort for over 40 years, attracting a large following to their simple air-conditioned eatery by serving large portions of fresh, delicious food to the many guests staying at the adjacent Edgewater Inn and to those passersby lucky enough to find it.

Tinmouth Snack Bar (802-446-3310), Rt. 140, Timouth. Open May–Nov., 11–9. A country diner with all the basics, including fresh-baked pies, Wilcox Ice Cream, and soft serve. A good way stop on a scenic drive.

Wheel Inn (802-537-2755), Lake Rd. at Stage Rd., Benson. Open daily from 7 AM (Sun. from 8) until 9 PM, 10 on Fri., Sat. This family-friendly place in a former carriage house has a loyal following and reasonable prices. Specials usually include chicken and biscuits on Wed. nights and fresh seafood on weekends. Entrées include salads and sides, and everything is homemade but the hot dog buns.

PIZZA **Outback Pizza** (802-422-9885), at the Tabu Nightclub on Killington Rd., Killington. Open from 3 in winter and spring, from 5 in summer and fall. Features wood-fired brick-oven pizza with outdoor patio seating and live music.

Pizza Jerks (802-422-4111; pizzajerks .com), 1307 Killington Rd., Killington. Open daily from 11 AM. A local favorite, part of a virtual café with Internet access. Pizza, calzones, subs.

Sal's South (802-446-2935), 15 S. Main St., Wallingford. Nice outdoor patio. Pizza and Italian specialties. Entrées $11.95–18.95.

BREWS **Long Trail Brewing Company** (802-672-5011; longtrail.com), Rt. 4 west at Bridgewater Corners (near Rt. 100A), produces Long Trail

Ale as well as Hibernator, India Pale Ale, Hit the Trail, Blackberry, Wheat, and Harvest. Pub fare daily 11–5 with riverside seating (in summer); gift shop, taproom, and self-guided tours daily 10–6.

✳ Entertainment

Paramount Theatre (802-775-0570; paramountvt.org), 30 Center St., Rutland. After years of a concerted community effort, this historic 1914 theater has been brought back to life with dance, music, drama, even magic and juggling acts. Call for tickets and schedules of events.

Movieplex 9 (802-775-5500), downtown Rutland Shopping Plaza, Merchants Row, and **Westway 1-2-3-4** (802-438-2888), Rt. 4A in West Rutland, show first-run flicks.

The **Killington Music Festival** (802-773-4003), a series of mostly chamber

music concerts in Snowshed Lodge and at a scattering of other local sites; weekends in July and Aug.

APRÈS-SKI The Wobbly Barn Steakhouse (802-422-6171; wobbly barn.com), 2229 Killington Rd., Killington. A steak and BBQ house (with a children's menu) offering live music, dancing, blues, rock and roll. Ski season only.

McGrath's Irish Pub at the Inn at Long Trail (802-775-7181), Rt. 4, Killington. Live Irish music on weekends to go with the Gaelic atmosphere and Guinness on tap. It's a great pub with a 22-foot-long bar made from a single log and a boulder protruding from the back wall.

Pickle Barrel (802-422-3035; pickle barrelnightclub.com), Killington Rd., Killington. "Some of the finest rock 'n' roll bands in the East." Purchase tickets online for the best prices.

✳ Selective Shopping

BOOKSTORES The Book King (802-773-9232), 94 Merchants Row, Rutland, is a bright, well-stocked store for new trade and children's books, paperbacks, cards, periodicals, and show tickets.

✐ **Annie's Book Stop** (802-775-6993), Trolley Square, 120 S. Main St., Rutland. Annie's has a large selection of new and used books; specializes in children's books and books on tape, plus educational puzzles and games.

The Book Shed (802-537-2010; bensonvermont.com), at the corner of Lake and Stage Rds., Benson. Open Wed.–Sun. 10–6; in winter, call ahead. Housed in what used to be the town clerk's office, this used- and antiquarian-book store with 30,000 volumes is just where you wouldn't expect to find it. The village is tiny.

RUTLAND'S PARAMOUNT THEATRE

Christina Tree

SPECIAL SHOPS Handmade in Vermont (802-446-2400; handmadein vermont.com), 205 S. Main St., Wallingford. Open daily 11–6 except Tue.–Wed., when it's open by appointment. Housed in America's first pitchfork factory (built 1791), this marble structure is now owned by White Rocks Land Trust and operated by a consortium of artists and craftspeople. Ironwork, especially lighting fixtures, is featured, along with Danforth Pewter and a wide selection of Vermont-crafted glass, pottery, furniture, and jewelry.

Michael's Toys, Signs and Carvings (803-677-3765; michaelstoys.com), 64 Merchants Row. Open Mon.–Sat. year-round. It's like stepping into Santa's workshop. Every inch of the store is

Christina Tree

MICHAEL'S TOYS RESEMBLES SANTA'S WORKSHOP.

filled with wooden toys, all sizes and shapes, from tiny puzzles to huge rocking cows. With his white whiskers, Michael certainly resembles the jolly old elf, and he is usually working on something new behind the counter, atop which his cat lounges. It comes as no surprise that he also writes children's stories. We came away with some amazing stocking stuffers and wish we had bought more.

The Great Outdoors Trading Center (802-775-9989; joejonessports.com), Woodstock Ave. (Rt. 4), Rutland, is a vast, complete sporting goods store, with a bike shop, gun shop, and fly-rod department, among others. Open daily 9–6, Sun. 10–5, till 8 PM Fri.

Base Camp Outfitters ands Cabin Fever Gifts (802-775-0166; basecampvt .com), 2363 Rt. 4, Killington. In winter this is the area's best source of "free heel"—cross-country, snowshoes, telemark, et cetera—gear and clothing. Owner Mike Miller and his wife, Diane, also operates the Mountain Meadows Ski Touring Center. In summer Mike's part of the store (Bear Camp Outfitters) is all about hiking and paddling. Diane's adjoining area (Cabin Fever Gifts) is a year-round source of Vermont products, art, crafts, jewelry, and much more.

Farrow Gallery & Studio (802-468-5683; farrowgallery.com), Old Yellow Church, 835 Main St., Castleton. Open daily except Tue. 10–5; in winter, call ahead. Patrick Farrow's limited-edition, award-winning bronze sculptures and wearable artworks are featured, along with the work of other Vermont artists.

Peter Huntoon Studio (802-235-2328; peterhuntoon.com), 17 Studio Lane, Middletown Springs, 05757. Open by appointment. Huntoon is one of Vermont's premier watercolorists, who also teaches and conducts workshops at his studio. His work is available for viewing and for sale.

✳ Special Events

January–March: Frequent **alpine ski and snowboard events** at Killington and Pico.

Late February: **Great Benson Fishing Derby**, sponsored by the Fair Haven Rotary Club—many prizes in several categories. Tickets for the derby: P.O. Box 131, Bomoseen 05732.

May-October: **Farmer's market**, Tuesday and Saturday 9–2, Depot Park, Rutland.

Memorial Day weekend: **Open Studio Weekend** (vermontcrafts.com) for studios throughout the region.

June–August: Sunday-evening **concerts in the park**, Rutland, 7:30 (802-773-1822), and Tuesday **Castleton College's Concerts on the Green**, Castleton.

June–September: **Farmer's market**, Main St., Poultney, Thursday (polutney vt.com).

Late June–August: **Friday Night Live**, 6–10. Downtown Rutland streets become a stage for live entertainment, open-air shopping, and dining (rutland downtown.com). **Killington Music Festival** (killingtonmusicfestival.org), Saturdays at 7 at Rams Head Lodge— a series of classical music concerts.

July 4: **Fireworks Extravaganza**, Vermont State Fairgrounds, Rutland (rutlandvermont.com); **Poultney Fourth of July Parade** and fireworks (poultney.com); **Independence Day Parade**, Killington.

Mid-July: **Annual Killington Wine Festival** (killingtonchamber.com).

Late July: **Ethnic Festival** and sidewalk sale, with dining, theater, and demonstrations, Merchants Row (rutlanddowntown.com).

Early August: **Art in the Park Summer Arts Festival**, Rutland, sponsored by the Chaffee Center (802-775-8836), in Main Street Park, junction of Rts. 7 and 4 east.

Early September: **Vermont State Fair** (vermontstatefair.com)—midway, exhibits, races, demolition derby, and tractor pulls animate the old fairgrounds on Rt. 7 south, Rutland.

First weekend of October: **Killington Mountain Resort's Annual BrewFest** (killington.com).

Columbus Day weekend: **Art in the Park Fall Foliage Festival**, Rutland, sponsored by the Chaffee Center (802-775-0356).

October 31: Rutland City's **Halloween parade**, one of the oldest and best.

Early December: **Vermont Holiday Festival** at Killington's Grand Resort Hotel—over 100 decorated trees, sleigh rides, workshops, and more.

December 31: Rutland's **First Night** celebration, 5 PM–midnight (802-773-9380).

Lake Champlain Valley

THE LOWER CHAMPLAIN VALLEY

BURLINGTON REGION

THE NORTHWEST CORNER

Christina Tree

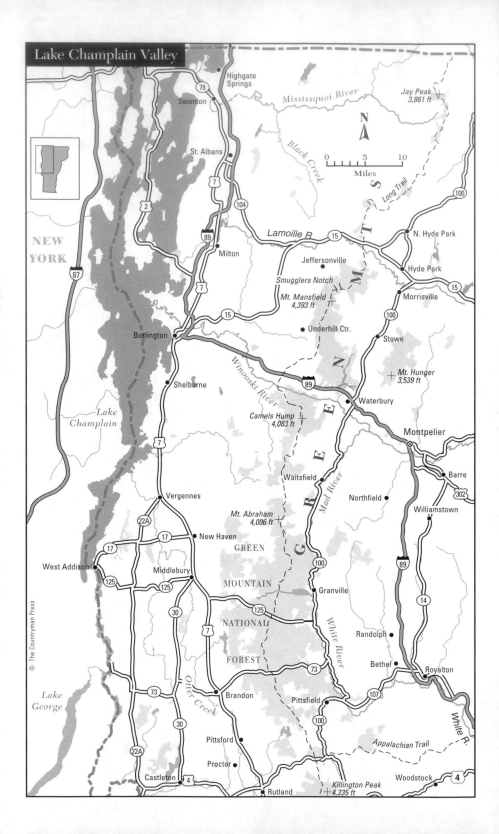

LAKE CHAMPLAIN

L ake Champlain begins in New York and flows north to Canada. For much of its 110 miles, the New York–Vermont border runs down its center. Still, the country's sixth largest lake belongs to Vermont in all the important ways, beginning 20,000 years ago. That's when the glacial waters receded, revealing islands and a wide valley on its eastern shores as opposed to rocky hills rising to mountains—the Adirondacks—on the west.

Traces of human habitation in this fertile valley date back 7,500 years. Archaeological finds of pottery and trading beads suggest both domestic life and distant travel for valley residents by 1000 BC.

In 1609 Samuel de Champlain, the first European to set foot in present-day Vermont, sailed south on the lake, guided by Native allies, to the site of an Indian village. A colossal granite statue of the explorer marks this still-evocative spot, now part of St. Anne's Shrine on Isle La Motte.

In the 18th and early 19th centuries Lake Champlain served as a strategic military corridor. Ethan Allen and the Green Mountain Boys captured Fort Ticonderoga on the New York shore from the British in 1775. During the following winter the fort's heavy cannons were dragged on sleds through thick snow and forest to

LAKE CHAMPLAIN FROM SOUTH BURLINGTON

Joe Citro

Boston, where they were mounted above the harbor, ultimately forcing the British to evacuate the city.

In 1776 the British moved south on the lake from Canada but were delayed by a surprise attack off Valcour Island by a fleet of gunboats commanded by Benedict Arnold. The British won the battle but, confronted with equally fierce resistance from the colonial troops in Forts Ticonderoga and Independence farther south at a narrow in the lake, they turned back. Returning in force the next year, they recaptured Fort Ticonderoga, finally surrendering it for good in 1780.

During the War of 1812 the defeat of a British naval squadron at the Battle of Plattsburgh (also called the Battle of Lake Champlain) in 1814 thwarted an attempt to annex part of northern New England to Canada and effectively ended the war.

The Valley's historic sites that dramatize these events are all within an easy, scenic drive of one another, with those on the New York shore linked by the "Fort Ti" ferry and the Champlain Bridge.

Chimney Point, an 18th-century tavern in West Addison beside the bridge, offers tantalizing glimpses into the layering of life in this Valley. The "Chimney" here alludes to all that was left in 1759 of the French colony here during the French and Indian Wars. Exhibits suggest what life was like in this short-lived corner of New France and in the long-lived Native settlements that preceded it. For many years this was, moreover, a popular Revolutionary War site: the place that Ethan Allen and Seth Warner were said to have planned the siege on Fort Ticonderoga. After the state acquired the site, however, it became apparent that the tavern hadn't been built until after the Revolution. Its previous owner, an excellent promoter, had also expanded the tavern into a summer resort, one of many to be found in this area and in the islands during the late 19th and early 20th centuries.

Early in the 19th century Burlington boomed into a metropolis as a lumbering port. It remains by far Vermont's largest and most dynamic city, one squarely facing Lake Champlain and offering access points for sailing, paddling, and swimming. Burlington is also home to several colleges and to the University of Vermont. In the Lower Valley, Middlebury—home to a prestigious college—is another cultural, dining, and lodging center.

The Champlain Valley remains, however, essentially rural, one of the state's richest agricultural areas, now with more than its share of vineyards as well as apple orchards and every conceivable kind of farm.

Twelve miles wide at its widest, less than a mile at its narrows, Lake Champlain is 400 feet deep in places, deep enough to harbor the monster Champ (mascot of Burlington's minor-league baseball team, the Vermont Lake Monsters). Long and thin like the state itself, this is Vermont's West Coast, especially beloved by birders (lakechamplainbirding.org) and bicyclists (champlainbikeways.org).

LOWER CHAMPLAIN VALLEY
INCLUDING MIDDLEBURY, VERGENNES, BRANDON, AND BRISTOL

Addison County packs as much contrasting scenery within its borders as any county in the country. On the east it includes the high, western wall of the Green Mountains, laced with hiking trails and pierced by four of the state's highest, most dramatic "gaps" (passes). The mountains drop abruptly through widely scattered hill towns—Lincoln, Ripton, and Goshen—into a 30-mile-wide, farm-filled valley, a former ocean floor that now contains Vermont's largest concentration of dairy farms and orchards. Lake Champlain is far narrower here than up around Burlington, and the Adirondacks in New York seem higher and nearer, forming an improbable but spectacular backdrop to cows, water, red barns, and apple trees.

This stretch of the Champlain Valley is particularly popular with bicyclists, not only because it's the flattest piece of Vermont, but also because its quiet old farm roads wind through orchards to discoveries like the "Fort Ti Ferry" ("serving people and their vehicles since Mozart was three months old") and "the world's smallest bank" in Orwell.

Middlebury, the hub of Addison County, is among New England's most sophisticated towns, the home of one of its most prestigious private colleges, several museums, many interesting shops, and restaurants. Brandon, a particularly spirited and visitor-friendly community 15 miles south of Middlebury, is the southern gateway to the Lower Champlain Valley.

We hope that this book will lure visitors to explore the entire Valley: the Lake Champlain shoreline notched at regular intervals with quiet and accessible bays, from Mount Independence across from Fort Ticonderoga to Chimney Point (across from New York's Crown Point) and on up to Basin Harbor and Kingsland Bay State Park. Thanks to widely scattered lodging, it's possible to stay in the heart of farm (Addison and Bridport) and orchard (Shoreham) country, in historic towns like Bristol and Vergennes (actually the country's smallest city), and up in the Green Mountain towns of Ripton and Goshen, close to wooded walking/biking and ski trails, with occasional but spectacular lake and valley views.

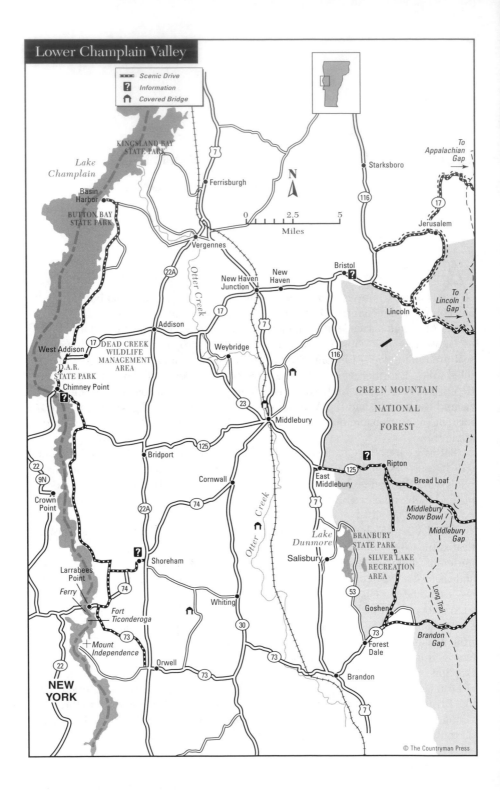

Lower Champlain Valley

Scenic Drive
Information
Covered Bridge

KINGSLAND BAY STATE PARK

Lake Champlain

Basin Harbor

BUTTON BAY STATE PARK

Ferrisburgh

Starksboro

To Appalachian Gap

N

7

116

0   2.5   5
Miles

Vergennes

22A

Otter Creek

New Haven Junction

New Haven

Bristol

Jerusalem

17

To Lincoln Gap

West Addison

17

Addison

17

DEAD CREEK WILDLIFE MANAGEMENT AREA

D.A.R. STATE PARK

Chimney Point

Weybridge

7

116

Lincoln

GREEN MOUNTAIN

NATIONAL

FOREST

23

Middlebury

125

Bridport

125

Ripton

Bread Loaf

22

9N

Crown Point

22A

Cornwall

74

East Middlebury

7

Lake Dunmore

Middlebury Snow Bowl

Middlebury Gap

BRANBURY STATE PARK

SILVER LAKE RECREATION AREA

Larrabees Point

Ferry

74

Shoreham

Whiting

Salisbury

53

Long Trail

Fort Ticonderoga

30

Goshen

73

Mount Independence

73

Orwell

73

73

Forest Dale

Brandon Gap

22

NEW YORK

Brandon

7

© The Countryman Press

GUIDANCE **Addison County Chamber of Commerce** (802-388-7951; 800-SEE-VERMONT; midvermont.com), 2 Court St., Middlebury 05753, in the Painter House, offers information about every corner of its domain, from Vergennes and Bristol in the north to Orwell in the south (but not Brandon). Open Mon. 10:30–5, Tue.–Fri. 9–5. This unusually large walk-in information center publishes a map/guide, stocks brochures, and refers visitors to a wide variety of lodgings, from inns and bed & breakfasts to seasonal cottages on Lake Dunmore. During foliage season it is unusually resourceful in finding lodging for all comers. The chamber also maintains an unstaffed information booth on the common in Vergennes.

Brandon Area Chamber of Commerce (802-247-6401; brandon.org). The unstaffed visitors booth on Park St. (in front of the library, across from the Brandon Inn) is open daily, year-round. It's well stocked with brochures, including an informative walking tour guide to the town's rich architectural heritage.

Moosalamoo, from an Abenaki word possibly meaning "the moose departs" or "he trails the moose," is a dandy map and guide, with site signage, to the trails and other natural features of some 20,000 acres of Green Mountain National Forest, published and distributed by the Moosalamoo Partnership, available at chambers of commerce, the Catamount Trail Association, other outdoor recreation organizations, and several inns. Or call 802-247-6735; 800-448-0707.

GETTING THERE *By car:* The major north–south highway is Rt. 7, but we advise anyone from Boston to approach through the Middlebury or Brandon Gaps (see *Scenic Drives*). From the west you can take the Champlain Bridge in Corwn Point, New York, year-round or the seasonal ferries described below.

By ferry: **Lake Champlain Ferry** (802-864-9804; ferries.com) from Essex, New York, to Charlotte operates spring through fall, takes 20 minutes, and puts you just above Vergennes.

Fort Ticonderoga Ferry (802-897-7999), Larrabees Point to Fort Ticonderoga. Mid-May–July 3, 8–5:45 daily; July 4–Labor Day 8–6:45, then 8–5:45 through mid-Oct. Cars $8 one-way, $14 round-trip. This ferry makes the crossing in six minutes.

FORT TI FERRY

Christina Tree

MEDICAL EMERGENCY
Emergency service is available by calling **911**.

Porter Memorial Center (802-388-4701), 115 Porter Dr., Middlebury.

✳ Villages

Middlebury (population: 8,300) is the county seat, the hub of Addison County, and home to one of the nation's most sought-after private colleges. Inns and restaurants serve visitors as

A VIEW OF THE MIDDLEBURY FALLS

well as potential students and their parents, and in recent years it has become a great place to shop. Middlebury College was founded in 1800 by Gamaliel Painter, a surveyor who settled here before the Revolution. Painter accompanied Ethan Allen on the Fort Ticonderoga raid and returned to Middlebury to become the town's principal landowner, sheriff, judge, and assemblyman. The fine mansion on Court Street, presently housing the information center, belonged to Painter. Another benefactor was Joseph Battell (see the box), who owned thousands of acres of forest and mountain land that he left to the college and the state when he died in 1915. He was the proprietor of the famous old summit house, the Bread Loaf Inn, now the nucleus of the summer Bread Loaf School of English and the Bread Loaf Writers Conference. Battell also owned a weekly newspaper in which he fulminated against the invasion of motorcars. Emma Hart Willard, who pioneered in the education of women, was another Middlebury luminary. The town's proudest buildings—the courthouse, the Middlebury Inn, the Battell House, and the fine Congregational church—are grouped, along with compact business blocks, around the green. It's a short walk down Main Street to the churning Otter Creek falls, a centerpiece for dozens of shops (including the Vermont State Crafts Center) in the old mills and marbleworks on both banks of the river, connected by a footbridge. The distinctive Middlebury College (middlebury.edu) campus rises impressively in tiers as you approach town from the west on Rt. 125.

Brandon (populaton: 3,917; brandon.org) is rich in historic architecture, from Federal style to Queen Anne; its entire center, some 230 homes, is on the National Register of Historic Places. Luckily, several Brandon manses are open to the public as bed & breakfasts. Sited in Rutland County (it's just over the southern border of Addison County) between Otter Creek and the Neshobe River, Brandon (and the adjacent town of Forest Dale) was the home of Thomas Davenport, who invented and patented an electric motor in 1838, and the birthplace of Stephen A. Douglas (1813–61), the "Little Giant" of the famous debates with Abraham Lincoln in 1858, when Douglas was a senator from Illinois. Brandon has blossomed in recent years with the addition of art galleries, antiques shops, bookstores, and some of the region's best dining.

Bristol (population: 3,788). Billing itself as the "Gateway to the Green Mountains," Bristol is nestled at the foot of Lincoln Gap, at the junctions of north–south Rt. 116 (less heavily trafficked than Rt. 7) and east–west Rt. 17. Its broad Main Street is lined with a delightful mix of stores and restaurants, housed in a western-style 19th-century block that leads to a square green, complete with fountain, park benches, and a gazebo. Its pride is the elaborately hand-painted stagecoach in front of the historical society at 19 West St. and the **Lord's Prayer Rock** (on the south side of Rt. 17 entering Bristol from the east), which is inscribed with the Lord's Prayer. A physician named Joseph C. Greene commissioned the inscription in 1891, presumably because he was thankful for having reached this point safely when, as a youth, he was hauling logs over steep, slippery roads.

Vergennes (population: 2,800; vergennes.org) has long claimed to be the smallest city in the country and it's the oldest in Vermont, incorporated as a city in 1788 and named by Ethan Allen for Charles Gravier, comte de Vergennes, the French minister of foreign affairs who was a strong supporter of the American Revolutionary cause. Vergennes's site on an impressive set of falls and its handsome, early-19th-century commercial buildings include the glass-domed 1Upstairs in the **Bixby Memorial Library** (bixbylibrary.org) with its display of Plains Indian artifacts including baskets, clothing, and beadwork, along with local memorabilia and an oustanding archive of of Vermontiana.

In 1811–12 Thomas Macdonough used the Otter Creek Basin just below the falls to build—in record time—three ships, including the 734-ton, 26-gun *Saratoga*. He also equipped nine gunboats, using them all to defeat the British fleet in Lake Champlain off Plattsburgh in 1814. Otter Creek winds from the city to the lake, and the road leads to Basin Harbor, site of the area's premier resort and the Lake Champlain Maritime Museum. We recommend the lake road south from Basin Harbor, by Button Bay State Park. It leads to the State Historic Site at Chimney Point with the ruins of the 18th-century fort at Crown Point, New York, just across the Lake Champlain Bridge. **Shoreham** (population: 1,222) is known for its many orchards. Shoreham Village is a beauty, with a classic Congregational church (1846), a Masonic temple (built in 1852 as the Universalist church), and the graceful St. Genevieve Catholic Church (1873), as well as the old inn and general store. Follow Rt. 74 southwest from the village through the orchards; or continue straight on Witherell Rd. where 74 jogs south, then turn south (left) onto Smith St. along the lake. Either way, you get to Larrabees Point, the site of the small, car-carrying "Fort Ti" cable ferry, which makes the crossing to the fort itself in six minutes flat. It has held the franchise from the Vermont and New York legislatures since 1799, but records indicate the service was initiated by Lord Jeffery Amherst in 1757 for use by his soldiers in the campaigns against the French. Next door Teachout's Store, built in 1836, serves as departure point or excursion boat M/V *Carillon*. Continue south on Rt. 73 to the turnoff for Mount Independence.

COWS CROSS THE ROAD IN SHOREHAM.

Christina Tree

Orwell (population: 1,185). Best known for Mount Independence, the small village at the center of this orchard and dairying community circles a long, sloping green with a brick Congregational church (1843) on a rise by the white-clapboard town hall (built in 1810 as the Baptist church). It all overlooks a brief line of shops with the First National Bank of Orwell, billed as "the world's smallest bank," in the middle. Chartered in 1863 (but known as the Farmers Bank for many years), the bank remains a real center of town, with notices of upcoming events tacked to the authentic old tellers' cages. The other village nerve center is **Buxton's General Store**, the genuine article.

✳ Must-See

Note: The four following historic sites form a pleasant loop tour.

✦ ♿ **Mount Independence State Historic Site** (802-948-2000; 802-759-2412; historicvermont.org/mountindependence), 497 Mount Independence Rd., on the shore of Lake Champlain, 7 miles west of the junction of Rts. 73 and 22A near Orwell. Grounds open year-round with a handicapped-accessible trail; museum open Memorial Day weekend–Columbus Day, daily 9:30–5. $5; ages 14 and under, free. This National Historic Landmark is one of America's best-preserved Revolutionary War sites. A state-of-the-art visitor center tells the story of the 12,000 men who built a massive fort here in 1776 to fend off the British, many of them freezing to death the following winter. An exhibit displays the musket balls, grenades, shovels, knives, forks, bottles, cuff links, dishes, and even the fish bones they left behind on this rocky peninsula across the lake from Fort Ticonderoga. Six miles of marked hiking trails start at the visitor center, weaving past the remains of the hospital, batteries, blockhouses, and barracks of this once bustling fort.

✦ **Fort Ticonderoga** (518-585-2821; fort-ticonderoga.org), Ticonderoga, New York. Open mid-May–late Oct., daily 9–5. $15 adults, $13.50 ages 65 and up, $7 ages 7–12. Accessible via the Fort Ti Ferry from Larrabees Point in Shoreham (see *Getting There*). The 18th-century stone fort has been restored and includes a museum displaying weapons, uniforms, and historical artifacts. Built by the French (who named it Fort Carillon), it was captured by English general Jeffery Amherst and held by the British until 1775, when Ethan Allen and his Green Mountain Boys took the fort by surprise, capturing the guns that eventually helped free Boston. The **Log House** restaurant is open 9–5. No dogs.

THE BRIDGE AT CROWN POINT

Christina Tree

Crown Point State Historic Site (518-597-4666), 739 Bridge Rd., Crown Point, New York. Open May–Oct., Wed.–Mon. 9–5, or by appointment. $3 adults, $2 seniors (over 62) and students, free ages 12 and under. Just across the Lake Champlain Bridge from Chimney Point, West Addison, Vermont. Fifteen miles north of Fort Ticonderoga, Crown Point started out as the French-built "Fort St. Frederic." The British struggled to capture it and succeeded in

1759. But in 1775, on the eve of the Revolution, American colonists overtook it and hauled its cannons and heavy ordnance off to Boston for use in fighting the British. The complex includes 18th-century ruins and a visitor center with a museum.

♿ **Chimney Point State Historic Site** (802-759-2412; historicvermont.org/chimneypoint), at the Vermont end of the Lake Champlain Bridge, junction of Rts. 125 and 17. Open Memorial Day–Columbus Day, Wed.–Sun. 9:30–5. The "chimney" here alludes to what was left of the French colony on this site after Lord Jeffery Amherst burned a French colony consisting of a fort and 21 houses in 1759. The present 18th-century tavern on this site houses an exhibit exploring three of Vermont's early cultures: the Abenaki, French, and early American. Each settled at this lakeside spot, recognizing its strategic importance. The area is still sparsely settled, making it easy to imagine what they experienced. Displays include Native American archaeological treasures and an overview of 19th-century Abenaki weavings and basketry. An extensive new display is devoted to this once promising but isolated corner of New France. A separate room houses changing exhibits of contemporary Abenaki crafts, illustrating the extent to which these skills have survived. In September this is the site of an atlatle competition. (The atlatle is an ancient arrow launcher that's enjoyed a recent revival in Vermont.) Sit a spell in the rockers on the porch, added by innkeeper Millard Barnes in 1897, about the time he began promoting this as the tavern in which Ethan Allen and Seth Warner planned the siege of Fort Ticonderoga (see the Champlain chapter introduction).

⚓ **Lake Champlain Maritime Museum** (802-475-2022; lcmm.org), 4472 Basin Harbor Rd., 7 miles west of Vergennes at the entrance to the Basin Harbor Club off Panton Rd. Open May–late Oct., daily 10–5; $10 adults, $9 seniors, $6 ages 5–17. This museum began in a local schoolhouse constructed from native limestone in 1818, moved stone by stone (2,000 of them) and reconstructed to serve as an exhibit gallery. Today the museum's 12 buildings, spread over 3 acres, contain Revolutionary War artifacts, a working blacksmith shop, and dozens of small craft built around the lake over a period of 150 years. Exhibits reveal the lake's dramatic role in history, colorful characters, and the stories of hundreds of shipwrecks still beneath the surface. Attempts to raise them began in the 1930s but have been abandoned because wood that's been submerged in fresh water quickly disintegrates when exposed to air. Instead, watch nautical archaeologists in LCMM's conservation lab work to preserve artifacts and learn about the lake's Underwater Historic Preserves designated by Vermont and New York. Inquire about on-water shipwreck tours using ROV (remote-operated vehicle), special lectures, boatbuilding and blacksmithing

EXHIBIT OF THE CHATEAUGAY LAKE STEAMER AT THE LAKE CHAMPLAIN MARITIME MUSEUM

Christina Tree

courses, field trips, and demonstrations. A working replica of Benedict Arnold's 1776 gunboat *Philadelphia II*, built on the spot, is open to visitors, and LCMM's full-sized replica 1862 canal schooner *Lois McClure* can be explored at ports of call throughout the region—view her itinerary and Ship's Log at lcmm.org. The museum store carries maritime-related books, prints, gifts, toys, and clothing.

ALSO SEE

In and around Middlebury

& **Middlebury College Museum of Art** (802-443-5007; museum.middlebury .edu, Rt. 30 south. Open Tue.–Fri. 10–5, and select Saturdays noon–5. Free. The college's distinguished permanent collection ranges from the decorative arts through modern painting, with emphasis on photography, 19th-century European and American sculpture, and contemporary prints. Permanent and changing exhibits are displayed in galleries within the multi-tiered arts center, which also includes a café and several performance areas.

The Henry Sheldon Museum of Vermont History (802-388-2117; henry sheldonmuseum.org), 1 Park St. Open June–Columbus Day, Tue.–Sat. 10–5, Sun. 1–5, otherwise closed Sun. Research Center open Tue.–Fri. 1–5, Thu. until 8. $5 adults, $4.50 seniors, $3 ages 6–18; $12 family. One of America's oldest history museums. This 1829 marble merchant's house has no fewer than six black marble mantels and holds an intimate collection of furnishings, tools, household articles, clothes, books, games, and other artifacts portraying Vermont culture, all displayed in period rooms. There are changing exhibits in the Cerf Gallery, a gift shop, and special events.

The **Vermont Folklife Center** (802-388-4964; vermontfolklifecenter.org), 88 Main St. Open Tue.–Sat. 10–5. This growing organization (founded in 1984) collects and preserves the traditional arts and heritage of Vermont, primarily through taped interviews (its archive contains over 3,800). It mounts changing exhibits and maintains an excellent on-site gift shop.

✔ **The UVM Morgan Horse Farm** (802-388-2011; uvm.edu/morgan), 74 Battell Dr., Weybridge. Go through downtown Middlebury, heading west on Rt. 125, then turn right onto Rt. 23 (Weybridge St.) and follow signs. Open May–Oct., daily 9–4. $5 adults, $4 teens, $2 ages 5–12. The first "Morgan" was born in the late 1790s and is recognized as the sire of an entire breed of Vermont horse. Colonel Joseph Battell began breeding Morgans on this farm in the 1870s and is credited with saving the breed (America's first developed breed of horse) from extinction. The farm is now a breeding and training center operated by the University of Vermont. Guided tours of the stables and paddocks are available, along with an audiovisual presentation about the Morgan horse and farm.

In the Vergennes area

Rokeby Museum (802-877-3406), 3 miles north of Vergennes on Rt. 7 in Ferrisburg. Open for guided tours Memorial Day–Columbus Day., Thu.–Sun. at 11, 12:30, and 2, and by appointment year-round. $6 adults, $4 students and seniors, $2 ages 12 and under. A period-furnished home and nine outbuildings evoke the lives of four generations of a Quaker abolitionist family whose members included pioneers, farmers, and Rowland E. Robinson, the 19th-century author, illustrator, and naturalist. Rokeby was one of several merino sheep farms that dotted the Vermont landscape in the early 19th century. More important, it was a destination for

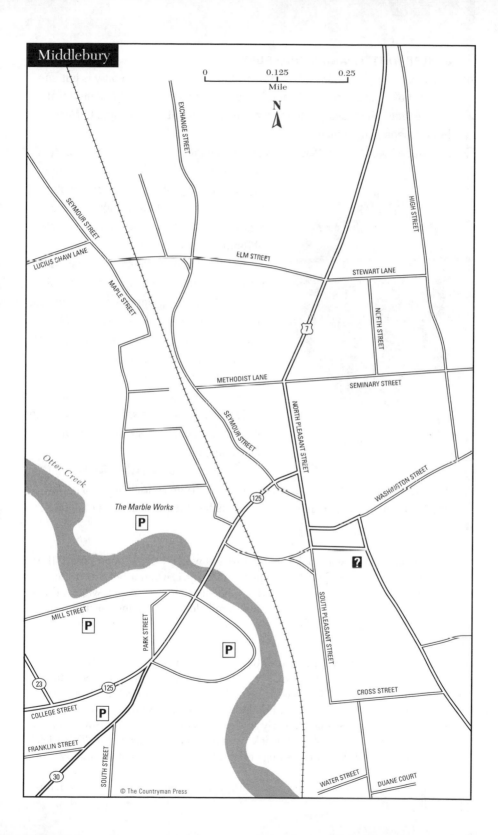

JOSEPH BATTELL AND MIDDLEBURY

The stone bridge that Joseph Battell built in downtown Middlebury is but one element of an enormous and enduring legacy of mountaintops and mortar that this eccentric bachelor left to the state of Vermont as a whole and to Middlebury College in particular.

Battell was born in 1839 to a wealthy and influential Vermont family. He

Henry Sheldon Museum of Vermont History

JOSEPH BATTELL

attended Middlebury College, but ill health kept him from finishing his degree. Instead, he went off to travel the world; upon his return he bought land in the mountain town of Ripton, where he ran an inn, mainly for his friends. Today that land and those buildings house two of the college's most highly regarded summer programs: the Bread Loaf School of English and the Bread Loaf Writers Conference. In addition to being publisher of the *Middlebury Register*, a local newspaper, Battell was also an author. One of his oddest efforts was a book titled *Ellen, or, The Whisperings of an Old Pine*, a dense tome that is seldom read but much wondered about.

Battell was a man who loved mountains and woods and hated cars, so much so that he refused to allow cars on the road that ran up to his Ripton inn. Yet it was because of Battell that the stone

freedom-seeking slaves who took refuge here and worked in the open before the Civil War. The family occupied the property until 1961, when it became a museum. Frugal by nature, they kept every diary, receipt, and newspaper, which added up to an immense library (including 10,000 family letters), making this the best-documented Underground Railroad site in the country.

Elsewhere

The John Strong D.A.R. Mansion (802-759-2309; vmga.org), 6656 Rt. 17W, West Addison, 05491, open Memorial Day–Labor Day, weekends 9–5. $5 adults, $3 seniors and students. This is one of several historic structures built from stone taken from the ruins of Fort Crown Point and skidded across frozen Lake Champlain by oxen. General Strong, an early settler and Green Mountain Boy, built his (third) residence here in 1796 with brick from his own clay pits on the "Salt Lick" where he first hunted deer. Furnishings reflect five generations of the family.

COVERED BRIDGES ✒ *Note:* These bridges are marked on our Lower Champlain Valley map.

bridge spanning Otter Creek in downtown Middlebury is still, a century later, a key to the transportation infrastructure in Addison County. The original wooden bridge that carried traffic across the creek burned down a century ago. Middlebury's town fathers, in a fit of economy, decided to build an iron bridge on the site, but Battell was opposed, arguing that a stone bridge would last significantly longer than an iron one. So determined was he that he is said to have paid the difference out of his own pocket.

A pioneering conservationist, Battell used to send his hired man into the woods, armed with blank deeds and instructions to buy as much acreage as he could from any farmer or logger he came across. Over time he acquired about 35,000 acres, including Camels Hump, which he donated to the state of Vermont for use as a state park. His landholdings also reached over Bread Loaf Mountain from East Middlebury to Hancock, Granville, and Rochester, along Rt. 100, and followed the spine of the Green Mountains from Mount Ellen south to Brandon Gap. When he died in 1915, most of this land was bequeathed to Middlebury College, which has sold off much of it over the years, keeping only a few hundred acres.

Battell is also the father of the University of Vermont's Morgan Horse Farm. He began breeding Morgans on his farm in the latter 1800s, an interest that would prove instrumental in saving America's first breed of horse from extinction. He hired architect Clinton Smith to build the beautiful white farm buildings that still stand in Weybridge. With typical Battell intensity, he spent years tracing out the pedigrees published in the first volume of the *Morgan Horse Register* in 1894. Then in 1906 he gave his farm and his Morgan horses to the U.S. government. It remains a working horse farm to this day, supplying stock to Morgan breeders across the country.

The **Pulp Mill Covered Bridge**, between Middlebury and Weybridge, spanning Otter Creek near the Morgan Horse Farm, is the oldest in the state (1808–20) and the last two-lane span still in use.

Halpin Bridge (1824), Middlebury, 2 miles east of Rt. 7, off Halpin Rd., is Vermont's highest bridge above the streambed.

Station (or Salisbury) Bridge, across Otter Creek in Cornwall (2 miles east of Rt. 30 on Swamp Rd.), is a 136-foot Town lattice bridge built in 1865.

Shoreham Covered Railroad Bridge, East Shoreham off the Whiting–Shoreham Rd. (turn south onto Shoreham Depot Rd.); the bridge is marked on area maps. A Howe bridge built in 1897 by the Rutland Railroad, spanning the Lemon Fair River, one of the few remaining railroad covered bridges left in Vermont. A designated state historic site.

Spade Farm Covered Bridge, located along Rt. 7 in Ferrisburg, is now on the property of the Artisans Guild and Starry Night Café. It was built in 1824 and moved 3 miles to its present location in 1959.

SCENIC DRIVES Middlebury Gap. This is our favorite approach to Addison County from the southeast, and this stretch of Rt. 125 is more dramatic driving east to west. Begin in Hancock and stop at Texas Falls (see our map on page 304). The road quickly crests at its junction with the Long Trail, near the Middlebury Snow Bowl. Then it's all downhill through the woods until the huge, wooden Bread Loaf Inn (now part of Middlebury College) improbably appears. The Robert Frost Wayside Picnic Area and the Interpretive Trail are a short way beyond. We also like to stop in the small, 19th-century cemetery a bit farther down, where a wind chime strikes softly in a row of maples. The picturesque hill town of Ripton is just below, and as the road continues to plunge into the valley, you glimpse the Adirondacks in the distance.

Brandon Gap. Rt. 73 is a high road over Goshen Mountain and through Brandon Gap. At the height-of-land, several wooded hiking trails are posted, and a rest area has been sited to catch the full majesty of Mount Horrid's Great Cliff. The road then rushes downhill with Brandon Brook, joining Rt. 100 and the White River below Rochester.

Note: A well-surfaced woods road (Goshen Rd.) runs south from Ripton through the national forest, past the turnoffs for Silver Lake and past Blueberry Hill to Rt. 73 in the Brandon Gap.

Appalachian Gap. East from Bristol, Rt. 17 climbs steadily for 4 miles (past the Jerusalem General Store), eases off for a couple of miles, and then zigzags steeply to crest at more than 3,000 feet, yielding some spectacular views before dropping into the Mad River Valley. It's even more spectacular heading west.

Lincoln/Appalachian Gap Loop. From Bristol, follow Rt. 17/116 to the turnoff for Lincoln 2 miles east of Bristol, past Bartlett Falls (be sure to stop) to Lincoln and out Downingsville Rd. to Jerusalem, back down on Rt. 116 to Rt. 17.

Lincoln Gap. Follow Rt. 17/116 east from Bristol, as above, but from Lincoln continue on the narrow Gap Rd., unpaved in sections. Again there are beautiful views, and you are quickly down in Warren. *Note:* Unsuitable for trailers and RVs. Closed in winter.

Along Lake Champlain. See *Villages* for Shoreham and Orwell.

✳ To Do

BICYCLING It's no coincidence that the country's first bicycle touring company was founded in this area. The Champlain Valley, with its relatively flat terrain and mountain views, holds a wealth of back roads leading through covered bridges, connecting historic sites and comfortable inns with ample swimming holes, ice cream, and antiquing stops en route. But beware deceptively quiet but narrow, truck-trafficked roads like Rt. 22A and Rt. 30. The area's bicycling info clearinghouse is **champlainhikeways.org**.

Bike Vermont (800-257-2226; bikevermont.com), based in Woodstock, gets good reviews for guided, small-group inn-to-inn tours in this area.

Vermont Bicycle Touring (VBT) (800-245-3681; vbt.com), 614 Monkton Rd., Bristol, the state's oldest bike tour company, offers guided group inn-to-inn tours.

The Bike Center (802-388-6666; bikecentermid.com), 74 Main St., Middlebury, is a source off rental hybrid and road bikes.

Country Inns Along the Trail (800-838-3301; inntoinn.com), P.O. Box 55,
Forestdale 05745. Bike tours begin and end in Brandon, visiting a number of inns
along the way. Bikes available for rent. Hiking and skiing tours available as well.

Mountain Biking at Blueberry Hill (802-247-6735), Goshen. An extensive network of ski trails and woods roads that is well suited to mountain biking; rentals,
lessons.

BIRDING **Otter Creek**, near Lake Champlain in Vergennes, and the **Dead
Creek Wildlife Management Area** in Addison (off Rt. 17) are particularly rich
in bird life, especially during migration seasons in spring and fall. Mount Independence is another popular birding area. Birders should secure the free
map/guide to the **Lake Champlain Birding Trail** (802-287-4284; lakechamplain
birding.org).

BOATING **Carillon Cruises** (802-897-5331; carilloncursies.com). A 60-foot, 49-
passenger replica of a 1920s Thousand Islands luxury motor yacht operates daily
(except Mon.) Father's Day–Labor Day. Geared to groups in spring and fall but walk-
ons accepted (call ahead), from the vintage 1824 Teachout's Lakehouse Store and
Wharf at Larrabees Point. Call for departure times for the hour-and-a-half cruises.

Waterhouse's (802-352-4433; waterhouses.com), 937 West Shore Rd., Salisbury
(Lake Dunmore), rents paddleboats, canoes, and motorboats; fuel station, fishing
supplies, and a game room in the boathouse. **Champlain Bridge Marina** (802-
759-2049; sayahoy.com), 7724 Rt. 17, West Addison. Boat access, pump-out station
for boats.

Chipman Point Marina & Campground (802-948-2288), Chipman Point Rd.,
Orwell. Dockage for 60 boats, pump-out station, game room, swimming; this is
also the base for **Champlain Houseboat Charters** (802-948-2740; champlain
houseboatcharters.com).

Lake Dunmore Kampersville (802-352-4501; kampersville.com), in Salisbury,
also rents rowboats, canoes, sailboats, and paddleboats.

FISHING **Otter Creek** is a warm-water stream good for smallmouth bass and
northern pike. The cooler **Neshobe River**, especially in Forest Dale, is better for
trout, and rainbows can be found in the **Middlebury River** just below Ripton.
The **New Haven River** between Lincoln and Bristol and south of New Haven
Mills also offers good trout fishing.

FITNESS CENTERS **Vermont Sun** (802-388-6888; vermontsun.com), 812
Exchange St., Middlebury, is a spacious indoor sports and fitness center with training equipment, an Olympic-sized pool, and racquetball courts. Open daily for
members; guests by the day or week.

Middlebury Fitness (802-388-3744; middleburyfitness.com), Wilson Rd. off Rt. 7
south, Middlebury, features state-of-the-art equipment. Guests by the day or by
the week.

Waterfalls Day Spa (802-388-0311; middleburyspa.com), 14 Court House
Square. A full menu of spa services featuring the "Waterfalls Stone Relaxer" using
warm stones and massage, focusing on the shoulders and feet.

GOLF **Ralph Myhre Golf Course** (802-443-5125), Rt. 30 just south of the Middlebury campus, is owned and operated by the college; 18 holes. Open mid-Apr.–Nov.

The Basin Harbor Club (802-475-2309), Vergennes, 18 holes. Open early May–mid-Oct.

Neshobe Golf Club (802-247-3611; neshobe.com), 224 Town Farm Rd. (just off Rt. 73), Brandon. Open Apr.–Oct. A full-service club; 18 holes.

HIKING **The Green Mountain National Forest District Office** (802-388-4362), 1007 Rt. 7 south, Middlebury 05753, offers a free pamphlet guide to 28 day hikes. Open year-round, weekdays 8–4:30.

Country Inns Along the Trail (802-326-2072; 800-838-3301; inntoinn.com). A dozen inns collaborate to provide lodging along an 80-mile stretch of the Long Trail and some of its side trails, including the section over Mount Mansfield.

Trail Around Middlebury (802-388-1007). The local Middlebury Area Land Trust has created this remarkable 18-mile loop that circles the town and strings together two parks and half a dozen woodland paths. The most scenic segment is the Otter Creek Gorge Trail, which runs riverside and traverses meadows, forests, and wilderness areas. The Land Trust publishes *The Trail Around Middlebury* (*TAM*), a free map/guide (P.O. Box 804, Middlebury 05753; 802-388-1007), and organizes monthly hikes May–Oct.

Snake Mountain, Bridport. From Rt. 22A, take Rt. 17 east; turn right after a mile onto Mountain Rd. Park about 2 miles up on your right in the designated area. The trail begins on Mountain Rd., about 300 feet south. The first half of this popular hike is easy, but it gets steeper and rockier as you reach the summit. The reward is the stunning lake and Adirondack view. A great afternoon hike.

Mount Abraham (802-388-4362), Lincoln. At over 4,000 feet above sea level, this is Vermont's fifth highest peak, its summit above the tree line, so the open views are magnificent. There are two trails, both strenuous. From the top of Lincoln Gap, you can park at the TV tower and follow the Long Trail (plan three and a half hours round-trip, and remember that the Lincoln Gap is not plowed in winter). You can also take the Battell Trail, a 5.8-mile loop that takes about four hours total. For this route, go to Lincoln Village and turn north onto Quaker St.; after 0.7 mile turn right onto Elder Hill Rd. The parking area is 2 miles ahead. Bring water, a detailed map, a sweater, and insect repellent.

Moosalamoo, an Abenaki word meaning "he trails the moose" or "the moose departs," is a 22,000-acre tract within the Green Mountain National Forest that is prime moose habitat. It is also crisscrossed with hiking routes and a 10-mile spur of the Long Trail, which begins at the parking area atop Brandon Gap on Rt. 73 and threads north for a steep 0.1 mile to a trail to Mount Horrid Cliffs, a rocky outcropping with memorable Adirondack views. The Long Trail stretch ends at a parking area on Rt. 125. Free trail guides are available from the conservation-minded **Moosalamoo Association** (800-448-0707; moosalamoo.org), P.O. Box 108, Forest Dale 05745-0108.

HORSEBACK RIDING ✔ **Deerfield Farm Icelandics** (802-453-3247; deerfieldfarmvt.com), 542 Geary Rd. north, Lincoln. One-hour to half-day treks over 85 pristine acres. Lessons, summer camp, weekend horseback-riding treks from inn to inn.

SWIMMING **Middlebury Gorge**, East Middlebury, off Rt. 125 just above the Waybury Inn, where the road suddenly steepens beyond the bridge. Paths lead down to the river.

Dog Team Tavern Hole, 3.1 miles north of Middlebury, off Dog Team Tavern Rd. Park by the site of the former restaurant and walk along the riverbank until you find an appealing spot in the bends of the New Haven River. Small beach area, gentle current.

Lake Pleiad, behind the Middlebury College Snow Bowl about 8 miles from Middlebury on Rt. 125 east. Park in the lot past the entrance near the Long Trail and walk it south 0.5 mile, turning right onto Lake Pleiad Trail. A truly idyllic setting, perfect for swimming and picnics. The large rocks on the western end provide a perfect perch from which to take in the pristine surroundings.

Bartlett Falls, Bristol. Near the beginning of Lincoln Gap Rd. (off Rt. 116 in Rocky Dale) there's a pull-off for this popular swimming hole with its 20-foot cliffs. A bronze plaque explains that the land is a gift from Irving Wesley Sr., in memory of his son who died at 19 fighting a 1943 forest fire in British Columbia. It's a beautiful spot by a stream with shallow falls dropping into pools. Swimming shoes are a good idea.

♪ **Lake Dunmore** (see *Green Space*), a scenic lake with a firm, sandy bottom and extensive sand beach, with plenty of space for running, game playing, and picnics. See also *Green Space*.

✳ Winter Sports

CROSS-COUNTRY SKIING **Carroll and Jane Rikert Ski Touring Center** at the Bread Loaf Campus of Middlebury College (802-443-2744), Rt. 125, Ripton, 12 miles from the main campus, is owned and operated by Middlebury College. It has 42 km of groomed trails in the area of the Robert Frost Farm and the college ski bowl. Elevations range from 975 to 1,500 feet. Rentals, accessories, lessons, and repairs.

Blueberry Hill Inn (802-247-6735), 1307 Goshen–Ripton Rd., Goshen, has 50 km of tracked and groomed trails plus another 20 km of outlying trails on elevations of 1,400–3,100 feet. This is a surefire cross-country mecca during even marginal seasons. The ski center has retail and rental equipment, waxing, and repairs; a pass gets you free soup noon–2.

DOWNHILL SKIING **Middlebury College Snow Bowl** (802-388-4356), 15 miles east of Middlebury on Rt. 125, at Bread Loaf. A throwback to a less commercial era of skiing: well-maintained, winding trails with a library in the base lodge! Two double chairs, one triple, a total of 15 trails, two glades, and a large terrain park; 40 percent covered by snowmaking. It also offers a ski school, rentals, cafeteria. Closed Dec. 25. Adults $42 weekends, $28 weekdays.

✳ Green Space

Note: Public preserves are clustered on the eastern and western fringes of the valley.

On or near Lake Champlain
Button Bay State Park (802-475-2377; 802-241-3655; vtstateparks.com), 5 Button

Bay State Park Rd., off Panton Rd. just below Basin Harbor. Open late May–mid-Oct. Named for the unusual, buttonlike clay formations found along its shore, this 253-acre area overlooks splendid scenery of the lake and Adirondacks; 73 campsites (including 13 lean-tos), picnic areas, swimming, fishing, nature museum, and trails. Rocky Point juts into Lake Champlain like the prow of a ship.

Kingsland Bay State Park (802-877-3445; 888-409-7579; vtstateparks.com), 787 Kingsland Bay State Park Rd., Ferrisburg. Marked from Rt. 7. Facilities include a picnic area on Lake Champlain, tennis courts, and hiking trails. This is a particularly lovely overlook of Kingsland Bay with lawns that roll down to the lakeside shaded by old maples. Weddings and summer get-togethers are very popular here.

Dead Creek Wildlife Management Area (802-759-2397; vtfishandwildlife .com), 1 mile west of Rt. 22A on Rt. 17, is a 2,800-acre, semi-wilderness tract with a parking area and posted visitor information about the many species of birds that congregate here, including herds of snow and Canada geese that can number up to 20,000 during spring and fall migrations.

D.A.R. State Park (802-759-2354; vtstateparks.com), 6750 Rt. 17 west, 8 miles west of Addison, a 95-acre park comprising the 1765 stone foundations of the area's first colonial structures (in the picnic area). A grassy field contains 70 campsites, including 24 lean-tos; flush toilets and hot showers. Steps lead down to a smooth shale beach for swimming.

In or near the Green Mountain National Forest

⚓ **Lake Dunmore**, in Salisbury between Brandon and Middlebury on Rt. 53 off Rt. 7, is a tranquil, 1,000-acre lake that has licked its once infamous mosquito problem. It is lined with summer cottages at the foot of Mount Moosalamoo and along its hiking trails. On the east shore road is **Branbury State Park** (802-247-5925; vtstateparks.com), with a natural sandy beach, vast grassy areas, 39 tent sites, six lean-tos, boating, snack bar, picnic grove, museum nature trail, and hiking to the Falls of Lana. The trail begins just south of the Branbury Park entrance, and it's just 0.5 mile to the picnic area and falls. From Rt. 53 it's 1.6 miles past these falls up to secluded **Silver Lake**, once the site of religious camp meetings in the 1880s; a large hotel (actually constructed as a seminary) occupied the spot of the present picnic area and stood until around 1940, when it was destroyed by fire. About a mile long, it is now part of the Green Mountain National Forest, accessible only by foot and mountain bike (0.6 mile via the Goshen Trail from the second parking lot on Forest Rd. 27, off Goshen Rd.). There are 31 primitive campsites and a nature trail around the lake; swimming is permitted.

"Robert Frost Country" in the Green Mountain National Forest is a title bestowed in 1983 on a wooded piece of the town of Ripton because it was here, in a log cabin, that the poet summered for 39 years. This section of Rt. 125, between the old Bread Loaf Inn (part of the Middlebury College campus) and the village, has been designated the Robert Frost Memorial Highway; there is also a Robert Frost Interpretive Trail and a Robert Frost Wayside picnic area near the road leading to the farm and cabin. The picnic area has grills and drinking water, and it's shaded by red pines that were pruned by Frost himself. Just east of the wayside, a dirt road leads to the Homer Noble Farm, which Frost bought in 1939. Park in the lot provided and walk past the farm to Frost's cabin (it's not open to the public). The Robert Frost Interpretive Trail, a bit west on the opposite side of Rt. 125, is an easy walk, just 0.75 mile. It begins with a bridge across Beaver Pond (we actually saw a beaver here once) and winds through woods and meadow, past seven Frost poems mounted along the way. This trail is popular with cross-country skiers and snowshoers, and with July and August blueberry pickers.

Texas Falls, in Hancock, is easily accessible from the marked road, 3 miles east of the Middlebury Gap. It's a short drive to the parking area, and the succession of falls is just across the road, visible from a series of paths and bridges. There's also a picnic area.

✳ Lodging

INNS

In the Middlebury area

∞ ✺ ✆ ♿ ⁅ᵀ⁆ **Swift House Inn** (802-388-9925; 802-388-9927; 866-388-9925; swifthouseinn.com), 25 Stewart Lane, Middlebury 05753. Formerly the family estate of the legendary philanthropist Jessica Stewart Swift, who lived to be over 100, the Swift House is now under the ownership of Dan and Michele Brown. Antiques, elaborately carved marble fireplaces, formal gardens, and extravagant wallpaper and upholstery add to the charm of this 1814 mansion. (Ask to see the vintage elevator.) Common space in the inn itself includes a cozy bar as well as two attractive living rooms. Meals (and full breakfasts) are served in the cherry-paneled main dining room, the library, or on the window-ringed sunporch. There are nine guest rooms in the main house, five in the Victorian gatehouse on Rt. 7, and six contemporary-styled ones in the renovated 1886 carriage house. One room is wheelchair accessible, as is the dining room. Some suites have working fireplaces, a sitting area, whirlpool tub, and cable TV. $110–265 in high season, $100–235 in low. The dining room serves some of the best food in town (see *Dining Out*). Pets housed for $25 per day.

∞ ✺ ✆ ⁅ᵀ⁆ **The Middlebury Inn** (802-388-4961; 800-842-4666; middleburyinn.com), 14 Courthouse Square, Middlebury 05753, has been the town's imposing chief hostelry since 1827. Since 2007 new owners Steven and Michael Dopp have given this grande dame a thorough and sensitive face-lift. The vast, comfortable lobby with a formal check-in desk and portraits of the Battell family and Robert Frost suvive. Elegant afternoon tea is available in the Willard Room; buffet breakfast in the pillared, Founder's Room. Lunch and dinner are served in the Morgan Tavern (see *Dining Out*) and on the front porch in summer and early fall. Thoughtful touches still include readable books on shelves near guest rooms and umbrellas next to the door for guests to use. The 70 guest rooms are divided among four adjoining buildings. Those in the main inn are on two floors (there's a 1926 Otis elevator) and are furnished in reproduction antiques. They have private bath, cable TV, air conditioner/heater, and direct-dial phone. The vintage 1825 Porter Mansion, with handsome architectural details and a lovely curved staircase, has been renovated with special care and an eye to housing wedding parties; it includes a luxury suite and eight rooms. The remaining rooms, in the motel-style Courtyard Annex, are also tastefully fitted with inn-style furnishings. Rates run $119–259 double, including afternoon tea. Inquire about packages. Children 18 years old and

BASIN HARBOR CLUB

Christina Tree

RESORT

🐾 ✄ ♿ ⍓ **Basin Harbor Club** (802-475-2311; 800-622-4000; basinharbor.com), 4800 Basin Harbor Rd., Vergennes 05491, located on Lake Champlain 5 miles west of town, off Panton Rd. Open mid-May–mid-Oct. This is Vermont's premier lakeside resort. The 700-acre retreat offers 136 rooms in the main lodge, two guest houses, and cottages scattered along the shore. Since 1886, when they first began taking in summer boarders, members of the Beach family have

younger stay free in parent's room. Pets are welcome in the motel units for a daily fee, and arrangements for babysitting can be made. Guests have access to the nearby Vermont Sun (see *Fitness Centers*) and the new Waterfalls Day Spa in the inn itself.

∞ ⍓ **Waybury Inn** (802-388-4015; 800-348-1810; wayburyinn.com), Rt. 125, East Middlebury 05740. A historic former stagecoach stop that exudes character in each of the 14 imaginatively furnished rooms on its two upper floors. Our favorites are the Nautical Room with its maritime theme, and

the Pineapple Room with its unusual plaid walls. The grandest is the Robert Frost Room, with red walls and a king-sized bed. The Waybury was indeed a favorite of Robert Frost's when he lived up the hill in Ripton, and its exterior was used in Bob Newhart's 1982–90 TV series *Newhart* to represent the quintessential New England inn. There are two dining rooms, and you can dine on the porch in summer; a swimmin' hole under the nearby bridge can be used to cool off. In winter you can warm up by the fire in the pub downstairs. Dinner and Sunday

assiduously kept up with the times. Over the years a large swimming pool, an 18-hole golf course, a wellness center and even an airstrip have been added. Still, the handsome old farmhouse has been preserved. In summer Dutchman's-pipe climbs as it always has around the porch pillars, and three grand old maples shade the lawn, which slopes to flower gardens and the round harbor beyond. There are 18 rooms in the inn, 13 more in the attractive stone Harbor Homestead. The 74 cottages, geared to families (and well-behaved pets), vary in rate depending on size and location. All have phone, fridge, and wet bar; many have fireplace. Eight cottages are handicapped accessible, with ramps and bathrooms, as are all public areas. The lakeside units are worth the little extra, with views of the lake and the Adirondacks so extraordinary that it's difficult to tear yourself away from the window or deck, especially at sunset.

Basin Harbor manages to please both children and elderly couples. Youngsters can take advantage of the beach, elaborate playground, and lively, supervised (complimentary) children's program available 9:30 AM–1:30 PM for ages 3–15, and younger children can also dine together and play until 9 PM. For those 10–15, there are golf and tennis clinics, movies, mixers, and video games in the Red Mill, the resort's informal restaurant off by the airstrip. Those who like to dress for dinner have ample opportunity; at the main restaurant, men and boys over 12 must wear jackets and ties. The food is fine (see *Dining Out*). Daily rates per couple with a full American plan (the only plan available June 13–Sept. 1), $180 per adult and $112 per child; add 15 percent gratuity. Daily rate extra for children 3 and older, depending on age. There are also golf, tennis, and fall foliage packages; inquire about kayaking, horticultural workshops, and birding and nature treks.

brunch are served year-round. $110–250 double occupancy includes a full hot breakfast. Two-night minimum stay on busy weekends and holidays.

Chipman Inn (802-388-2390; 800-890-2390; chipmaninn.com), P.O. Box 115, Rt. 125, Ripton 05766. On the way to or from Bread Loaf and the Middlebury College Snow Bowl, this 1828 inn sits in the center of the tiny village of Ripton, which consists of a schoolhouse, community meeting-house, church, and general store. It's also within striking distance of Robert Frost's house and cabin and the Robert Frost Trail. The house has eight guest rooms of varying sizes, all with private bath. Guests can gather in the bar, around a very large old hearth, in the sunny sitting room near the woodstove, and elsewhere in this roomy house. There's a TV and plenty of books to peruse. Innkeepers Joyce Henderson and Bill Pierce serve breakfast at large tables in the dining room. $115–170 in-season, from $90 off-season, includes full breakfast. Children 12 and older; no pets.

LAKE CHAMPLAIN VALLEY

In Brandon 05733

ㅇㅇ & **Lilac Inn** (802-247-5463; 800-221-0720; ilacinn.com), 53 Park St. (Rt. 73 east). One of New England's most romantic inns, this grand old mansion has been totally restored. Built with an imposing five-arched facade in 1909 by a Brandon-born financier, and currently owned by Shelly and Doug Sawyer, it has some splendid common spaces (a glassed-in ballroom with its crystal chandelier is the scene of wedding receptions), glorious antiques, and a wide entrance hallway with a grand staircase. There is also a formal garden with a gazebo and cobbled patio, a small living room with a fireplace and floor-to-ceiling bookcases, and a copper-topped bar with comfortable seating. The nine ample guest rooms all have luxurious bathrooms with deep, claw-foot tubs; each is furnished in antiques and has a hidden TV. The bridal suite (the original master bedroom) has a whirlpool bath, fireplace, and dressing area. There is one handicapped-accessible room. Weddings are a specialty. Rates include

DOWNTOWN BRANDON, INCLUDING THE BRANDON INN

Christina Tree

a three-course breakfast served in the sun-filled garden room; dinner can be arranged. $175–320 in high season, otherwise $155–285, less midweek. Inquire about MAP, winter weekends featuring music or dramatic readings, and the cottage for four. Children must be over 12, and pets require prior approval.

ㅇㅇ ❦ ✿ & **The Brandon Inn** (802-247-5766; 800-639-8685; historic brandoninn.com), 20 Park St. A large brick landmark overlooking the village green, this inn dates from 1892 and is on the National Register of Historic Places. Innkeepers since 1988, Sarah and Louis Pattis have scaled down the number of guest rooms from 46 to 39, refurbishing them nicely. The inn caters to groups—bus tours, Elderhostel, weddings, and nonprofits—but everyone feels welcome here, especially families. Each room is individually decorated, fitted with a phone, clock radio, and A/C. There are several family suites and two suites with Jacuzzi (one is palatial). There are TV rooms upstairs as well as large living rooms downstairs, and some of the 19th-century furniture and a good deal of the atmosphere survive. The inn's 5 landscaped acres include a swimming pool (with Jacuzzi) and a stretch of the Neshobe River, good for trout fishing. An 18-hole golf course is just up the way. Meals are served but only to guests. Low-season B&B rates are $110–165 per room; high season, $145–200. Children's rates.

❝↑❞ **Churchill House Inn** (802-247-3078; 877-248-7444; churchillhouse inn.com), 3128 Forest Dale Rd. (Rt. 73). Located west of the Brandon Gap on Rt. 73. Seth and Olya Hopkins welcome you to their old farmhouse inn with its eight cheery guest rooms, each named for a different place in the world (your hosts are widely traveled, and Olya hails from Russia), all furnished in 19th-century style. Some have whirlpool or Jacuzzi tub, but no phone or TV. Inquire about inn-to-inn hiking, walking, biking, and ski packages. Breakfasts are big, and four-course dinners ($30 per person plus service charges) can be arranged with advance notice. B&B rates are $100–180 per room, double occupancy, depending on room and sesaon; add $50 for a third adult, $25 for each child 5–12 sharing room with parent. No children under 5.

Elsewhere

👤 ☕ ♪ **The Shoreham Inn** (802-897-5081; from out of state 800-255-5081; shorehaminn.com), Rt. 74 west, Shoreham 05770. Closed in Nov. This friendly, comfortable place is old-time Vermont with an English touch. The 10 air-conditioned guest rooms are whimsically decorated, most with king-sized beds and some with daybeds for the many families and bicyclists who pass through this old stagecoach stop. Seven come with in room bath, while three have a private bath in the hall. The age of this 1790 structure is felt in the floorboards, exposed beams, and steep, creaking stairs. At the center of a quaint village surrounded by apple country, it is not far from Lake Champlain and the college town of Middlebury. The common rooms have plenty of sofas and easy chairs, along with chess and backgammon boards, a wood-burning fireplace, British antiques, and, frequently, the aroma of coffee or some other culinary temptation emanating from the kitchen (see *Eating Out*). Rates range from $110 for a single in low season to $170 for a double, and include a full hot breakfast. Pets accepted with conditions.

⊗ ☕ ♪ ♿ **Blueberry Hill Inn** (802-247-6735; 802-247-6535; 800-448-0707; blueberryhillinn.com), Goshen 05733, on Forest Rd. 32 in Ripton. Over the past three decades Tony Clark has turned this blue 1813 farmhouse on a high, remote back road into one of New England's most famous country inns. The lures are gourmet cuisine, peace and quiet, hiking and mountain biking, and, in winter, cross-country skiing. But there is more to it: a sure touch. The 12 rooms—some with loft, all with full bath—have antiques, handmade botanicals, and fine decor, and the common areas are cozy and inviting, with roses and geraniums blooming in the indoor greenhouse off the kitchen, and a stone fireplace in the dining room. Guests tend to mingle, from morning coffee to evening hors d'oeuvres and dinner, served family-style at long wooden tables. This inn has long been known for its extraordinary food, and British-born chef Tim Cheevers more than deserves the reputation, producing elaborate, creative dinners featuring fresh ingredients, many of them straight from the garden. The cross-country ski center, with 70 km of tracked and groomed trails in the Moosalamoo region of the Green Mountain National Forest, tends to be snowy, thanks to its elevation. In midsummer the blueberry crop ripens and you can graze at leisure, provided half your take makes it to the kitchen. There's swimming in the pristine reflecting pond out back, gorgeous gardens, and a sauna. MAP $140–180 per person (double occupancy); service charges extra. Four rooms can accommodate a family group, with special rates for children 12 and under in room with parent. BYOB.

⊗ ♪ **The Inn at Baldwin Creek** (802-453-2432; 888-424-2432; innatbaldwincreek.com), 1868 N. Rt. 116, Bristol 05443. Open year-round. A classic 1787 Vermont farmhouse inn set on 25 acres including a perennial garden with paths down to Baldwin Creek. Mary's Restaurant, attached to the inn, is a favorite regional dining spot (see *Dining Out*). Five guest rooms with private bath include a couple of two-room suites, which work well for families. Weddings and catered events for up to 200 people. Heated outdoor swimming pool. Innkeeper Linda Harmon and chef Doug Mack are founding members of Vermont Fresh Network; in summer they host special farmhouse dinners featuring local farmers, cooking classes, and music and theater performances in their barn. $95–195 depending on room and season, including a three-course breakfast and afternoon refreshments; children 16 and under are free in the same room, otherwise $25 per extra adult. Guests receive a 15 percent discount on dinner at Mary's.

BED & BREAKFASTS

In and around Middlebury 05753

♦ ♿ **The Inn on the Green** (802-388-7512; 888-244-7512; innonthe green.com), 71 S. Pleasant St. An attractive 1803 Federal town house has two colorfully decorated suites in the main house, plus eight other spacious rooms, each with private bath, phone, cable TV, and high-speed Internet access. There's also a more contemporary carriage house, same amenities. $129–329, breakfast included.

🐾 ♦ **Fairhill** (802-388-3044), 724 E. Munger St., 4 miles east of Middlebury, on 75 acres of woodland, marsh, and meadows. Russell and Fleur Laslocky's 1825 center-chimney Cape has three guest rooms, one with an antique four-poster double bed and private bath; the other two share a bath. The breakfast area is in an 18th-century granary. Rates $85–110.

♦ ♿ **Cornwall Orchards** (802-462-2272; cornwallorchards.com), 1364 Rt. 30, Cornwall 05753, about 2 miles south of the Middlebury golf course. English-born Juliet Gerlin and her husband, Bob, a recovering lawyer, have turned this 1784 Cape into an airy, comfortable place with hardwood floors, antique linens, Oriental carpets, and a spacious living room with a wood-burning fireplace. There's an antique cast-iron cookstove in the open kitchen and a cozy sitting nook that overlooks an outdoor deck and lovely orchard views. Of the five guest rooms, four have queen-sized bed, and one has two twins tucked under the eaves; all have private bath. The ground-floor Governor Room is wheelchair accessible, and the cozy Turner Room upstairs has a skylight and a trapezoid-shaped bathroom door. $120–125 includes a fresh, full breakfast served family-style in the light-drenched dining room. Two-day minimum during foliage season and on summer and holiday weekends.

By the Way B&B (802-388-6291), 407 E. Main St., East Middlebury 05740. Barbara Simoes provides two spacious guest rooms with private bath and air-conditioning. The 1850s village house is furnished with country antiques and original artwork. The wraparound veranda is appealing, and an in-ground swimming pool is set in the orchard. $95–150 per room with breakfast; children 8 and older; no credit cards.

South and west of Middlebury

♿ 🍴 **Fairy Tale Farm** (802-758-3065; fairytalefarmvt.com), 1183 Rt. 125, Bridport 05734. Nancy and Tom Maxwell fled TV careers in Los Angeles for this 1804 farmhouse with its 115 acres, barn, cows, two donkeys, chickens, and mountain views. Guests are greeted with refreshments in the sofa-filled great room with a wood-burning fireplace. The two guest rooms are both on the ground floor and have king-sized beds. We settled contentedly into a (wheelchair-accessible) back room with a views all the way west to the Adirondacks. There's a private deck and a comfortable sitting area, stocked with good reading material. The other guest room has a large claw-foot bathtub in a window-edged nook, the perfect place to soak as the sun sets. $125 includes a full breakfast that usually features freshly laid eggs. Inquire about pets and children.

Quiet Valley Bed & Breakfast (802-897-7887), 1467 Quiet Valley Rd., Shoreham 05770. A new house whose stressed-pine floors make it feel old, this Cape is down a dirt road on 48 acres of hay fields along the Lemon Fair River. The living room includes a shallow, Rumford-style fireplace, and interesting antiques abound. Two of the four guest rooms have four-poster double bed, woodstove, and private bath. Another two have twin singles and share a bath. Bruce and Jane Lustgarten serve up fortifying breakfasts at a table overlooking inspiring mountain views. Guests are welcome to hike the trails or take the canoe for a run up the river. B&B $105–125.

Inn at Lovers Lane (802-758-2185; theinnatloverslane.com), 3740 Rt. 125, Bridport 05734. A two-dog welcoming committee meets guests in the driveway of this 1835 Greek Revival. The two rooms downstairs are a good place to lounge, but the three guest rooms (one is a suite) are the chief attraction with their beautiful pine floors, air-conditioning, and private baths. One has its own sitting room with a sofa that folds out into a double bed. John and Pam Freilich make substantial breakfasts, served on the sunporch outside deck in summer

months. Snowmobile trails nearby. $100–150. Children 9 and older; no pets.

Buckswood Bed & Breakfast (802-948-2054), 633 Rt. 73, P.O. Box 9, Orwell 05760. Open year-round. Linda and Bob Martin offer two guest rooms (private baths) and ample common space in their 1814 home, located in a pleasant country setting just east of Orwell Village. Dinner by reservation. $75–85 per couple includes breakfast. Polite pets accepted.

In and around Brandon 05733

Old Mill Inn (802-247-8002; 800-599-0341; oldmillbb.com), 79 Stone Mill Dam Rd. (Rt. 73 east). This attractive 1786 farmhouse set in 5 acres above the Neshobe River adjoins the 18-hole Neshobe Golf Club. Unusually helpful innkeepers Bob and Rhonda Foley offer four spacious, comfortable, and tastefully furnished guest rooms with private bath, some with air-conditioning. The Trillium Room with a deck overlooking meadows and golf course is a real beauty. Guests can lounge in the two art-filled living rooms, relax on the wicker porch chairs in warm weather, or stroll through the barnyard (with turkeys) and vineyard. The barn houses a meditation space and the **Neshobe River Winery**, due to open in summer 2009. The neighboring river contains a good swimming hole. $109–169 per couple (depending on room and season) includes a full breakfast, maybe a fritatta with fresh herbs, veggies, and cheese, and a spelt scone. Children over 10; no pets.

The Inn on Park Street (802-247-3843; 800-394-7239; theinnonparkstreet.com), 69 Park St. Park Street is Brandon's Park Avenue: It is lined with the town's finest homes, most of them on the National Historic Register. Judy Bunde, a professional pastry chef, offers six guest rooms in this delightful

Queen Anne Victorian, five with private bath and the sixth part of a two-room suite. The Theresa Room comes with cable TV, a choice of videos, double sinks, and a two-person Jacuzzi on a marble floor. The bedding is down filled and hand pressed, rooms come with robes and fine toiletries, and in the morning fresh coffee appears outside the door. In winter months a fire crackles in the tastefully furnished parlor with its baby grand piano; in summer you can dine on the spacious porch. A masterful dessert buffet is prepared each evening, and Bunde's breakfasts are scrumptious: fruits, juices, and fresh-baked breads, plus a choice of dishes that might include pecan-maple waffles or omelets with squash and tomatoes. Ask about the weekend cooking packages with visiting chefs. $125–200.

Rosebelle's Victorian Inn (802-247-0098; 888-767-3235; rosebelles.com), 31 Franklin St., P.O. Box 370, Rt. 7. This nicely restored, mansard-roofed house has a high-ceilinged living room with fireplace and TV and a large dining room—the setting for afternoon tea and full breakfasts. Guests with small musical instruments are especially welcome. Hostess Ginette Milot speaks French. All but one of the five guest rooms have private bath, and two rooms can be joined to form a suite for four. $135 per double in high season, $110 in low. Children must be over 12 and have a separate room. A good place for solo travelers. Two-night minimum stays are required on holiday weekends and during foliage season.

In and around Vergennes 05491

ⓓ ♿ ⑪ **The Strong House Inn** (802-877-3337; stronghouseinn.com), 94 W. Main St. (Rt. 22A). Built in the 1830s by Samuel Paddock Strong in the graceful Federal style, this roomy old house features fine detailing, such as curly maple railings on the free-standing main staircase. Mary and Hugh Bargiel offer 14 guest rooms, all with private bath, cable TV, and telephone. The rooms are in the main house as well as in Rabbit Ridge Country House, a newer building in back. Rates of $105–195 for most rooms, $295 for a suite with Adirondack furnishings—king-sized Adirondack canopied four-poster, private deck, wet bar, and double Jacuzzi tub—include full breakfast and afternoon refreshments. Inquire about quilting, crafting, and other special weekends. Children 8 and over; no pets.

✐ ⑪ **Emerson Guest House** (802-877-3293; emersonhouse.com), 82 Main St. There are five bright, high-ceilinged guest rooms and a suite in this 1850 French Second Empire mansion once owned by a prominent local judge. Susan (an artist) and Bill (a professional musician) Walsh serve delicious breakfasts in a beautiful downstairs nook bordered by stained glass that looks the backyard. On the edge of Vergennes, the house is set in 4 aces of land with walking trails, gardens, and apple trees. Common space includes a library (with TV) and a living room with a vintage 1927 Steinway. Room with private bath are $85–105; with shared bath, $55–65; and the Willard Suite, $140.

In Addison 05491

ⓓ 🐾 ✐ **Whitford House** (802-758-2704; 800-746-2704; whitfordhouse inn.com), 912 Grandey Rd. Between Nortontown and Townline roads, 3.5 miles off Rt. 22A. Situated east of the lake on rich farmland, this idyllic 1790 farmhouse is set among flower gardens on acres of fields and grazing sheep, with gorgeous views of the Adirondacks. Tranquility and warm hospitality are the hallmarks of Bruce and Barbara Carson's exceptional inn, which they share with a cat and two beagles. The two cozy upstairs rooms have king or twin beds, and a first-floor room comes with a four-poster double bed. There's also a cottage ($250–275 per couple) with a king-sized bed, a sitting room with sofa bed, and a full bath (with radiant-heated floor) that can accommodate a family of four. All have private bath. The great room, with its wood-burning fireplace made from local Panton stone, is a wonderful place to unwind. There's a book-lined library, plenty of art and antiques, wide-plank floors, and exposed beams. Rates run $125–250, $25 more in high season, and include afternoon refreshments, a superb candlelit breakfast, and loan of the Carsons' canoe and bicycles. Pets upon prior arrangement ($10 per night).

♪ **Barsen House Inn** (802-759-2646; 888-819-6103; barsenhouseinn.com), 53 TriTown Rd. Innkeeper Peter Jensen, a skilled woodworker, built this house and most of its furniture. He and his wife, Daphne, host guests in three rooms with private bath, one with a king-sized bed and two with queen. Two of them form a suite with a sitting room, TV, and private bath. Kids will find plenty to do here: gathering eggs, picking berries, catching frogs, or roasting marshmallows in the fire pit. There's also swimming and boating at a 3-acre beach nearby. $110–190 includes full breakfast.

In the Bristol area 05443
♪ **Crystal Palace Victorian B&B** (802-453-7609; 888-674-4131; crystalpalacebb.com), 48 North St., Bristol. Stephen and Stacie Ayotte are the hosts at this impressive 1897 turreted mansion. There are 11 stained-glass windows, along with a grand staircase and vintage woodwork throughout. The three guest rooms all come with air-conditioning and private bath. One

has its own dressing room, another a whirlpool bath; $90–135 with full breakfast. No pets; children by prior arrangement.

◯ "1" **Dream House Country Inn** (802-453-2805; dreamhousecountryinn.com), 382 Hewitt Rd., Bristol. A classic Gothic Revival cottage set on 6 acres with three guest rooms, one a bridal suite, all with private bath, TV/DVD, temperature control, and luxury linens. The grounds include a gazebo, perennial gardens, and plenty of space for a tent. $110–185 depending on room and season.

🐾 ♪ **The Old Hotel** (802-453-2567; oldhotel.net), 233 East River Rd., Lincoln. This rambling 1840s gabled building, serving for many years as a hotel for the mill across the street, sits high in the small village near the height of Lincoln Gap. It's funky and comfortable with an eat-in kitchen, common space with a gas fireplace and a screened porch, and seven basic guest rooms of varying sizes sharing three baths. From $65 single, $75 double, $95–105 double—or rent the whole for $495 a day, $2,000 a week. The feel is that of a place geared to groups, good for family reunions.

MOTELS *♪ "1"* **Courtyard by Marriott** (800-388-7775; middleburycourtyard.com), 309 Court St. (Rt. 7 south), Middlebury 05753. Just south of Middlebury Village, this is an 89-room clapboard, gabled New England–style structure with all the amenities (blow dryers, TV, HBO, and house movie rentals). There are 11 suites with whirlpool tub and fireplace. Facilities include an indoor pool, exercise room, and the Courtyard Café, serving breakfast daily. $135–199 in low season, 139–325 in peak-demand periods.

🌸 🐾 ♪ **Cozy Cottages** (802-247-6644; 800-568-5971; maplegrovecottages

.com), 1246 Franklin St. (Rt. 7 south), Brandon 05733. Open early May–mid-Oct. Located on Rt. 7, 1 mile south of Brandon, this is a shady campus of 20 well-spaced one- and two-room cottages well built in the 1930s by Ethan Allan Furniture Company. All have TV, fridge, and coffeemaker; many have fireplace and A/C. Grounds include shuffleboard, a stocked trout pond, and a swimming pool. $89–189 includes continental breakfast. $15 charge for pets.

❦ **North Cove Cottages** (summer 802-352-4236; winter 617-354-0124; northcovecottages.com), 1958 Lake Dunmore Rd., Salisbury 05769. Nine seasonal housekeeping cottages, all with bath and fully equipped kitchen. Sandy beach, free rowboats. $70–105 per night, $386–601 per week, also in winter. Pets sometimes welcome; ask about fees.

Note: The Addison County Chamber of Commerce (802-388-7951) lists rental cottages on both Lake Dunmore and Lake Champlain.

CAMPGROUNDS See *Green Space.*

✳ Where to Eat

DINING OUT

In the Middlebury area

The Storm Café (802-388-1063; thestormcafe.com), 3 Mill St., Frog Hollow, Middlebury. Lunch Mon.–Sat. 11:30–2:30, dinner nightly 5–close . This intimate, casual spot overlooking the river below the falls from an old stone mill building is considered by many to serve the most imaginative food in town. Lunch on soup and salad or half a sandwich like "The Dude": applewood-smoked bacon with sharp cheddar, baby spinach, and tomato on toasted ciabatta bread with chipotle-ranch aioli. Dinner entrées ($16–25)

might range from sautéed potato and scallion pancakes served over wild mushroom and asparagus stew, topped with braised red cabbage and apples, to "Cuban Storm": pork shank in mustard, tomato, pickle, and cabbage slaw, served with potatoes and French beans.

♪ **Fire & Ice Restaurant** (802-388-7166; 800-367-7166; fireandice restaurant.com), 26 Seymour St., Middlebury. Open Mon.–Thu. at 5, Fri. and Sat. at noon, Sun. at 1. This is not so much a restaurant as a dine-in museum, with its stained-glass and mahogany nooks, its library, and a 1921 Hackercraft motorboat that serves as a salad bar. A local favorite since 1974, specializing in steaks, prime rib, and chicken dishes like fresh boneless breast sautéed in a champagne and mushroom cream sauce; there's also a 55-item salad bar. The name was inspired by a Robert Frost poem. Entrées $11–31.

∞ **Roland's Place** (802-453-6309; rolands1796house.com), 3629 Ethan Allen Highway (Rt. 7), New Haven. Open for dinner Fri.–Sat., for Sun. brunch. Reservations recommended. Five miles north of Middlebury, a grand old cupola-topped stagecoach inn, also known as the 1796 House, is the setting. French owner-chef Roland Gaujac has literally cooked his way around the world on cruise ships and in a Club Med in Senegal as well as restaurants in France and the Four Seasons in California (where he met his wife, Lisa). His menu combines a sure touch with sauces with fresh off nearby farms. Order à la carte or "Roland's Inspiration": an appetizer, entrée, and dessert for $32. You might begin with mussels steamed with candied ginger or a goat cheese soufflé and cured salmon, then dine on spiced wild salmon in maple soy and champagne broth. Weddings and events are a specialty. There are also three air-conditioned **guest rooms** upstairs ($95–110.)

Swift House Inn (802-388-9925; swifthouseinn.com), 25 Stewart Lane, Middlebury. Dinner at this popular inn is served Thu.–Sun.(also Wed. in summer) in three atmospheric rooms: a dining area with a working fireplace, a book-filled library, and a converted porch. You might begin with a smoked salmon napoleon ($10) and dine on pan-roasted duck breast with confit duck leg, caramelized apples, and wild rice. Entrées are $18–22. Pub snacks at the bar. Gluten-free and vegan dishes available with prior notice.

The Waybury Inn (802-388-4015; wayburyinn.com), Rt. 125, East Middlebury. Open daily for dinner and Sunday brunch. The center of action in tiny East Middlebury is the Waybury Inn, where moderately priced steaks and seafood are served on the lower level in a warm, trophy-mounted pub. Finer dining happens upstairs in the Coach Room, where garlic sautéed shrimp might be featured along with tenderloin of venison in mushroom and lingonberry-brandy sauce, or filet mignon served with a sherry-lobster sauce and crispy shiitake mushrooms (entrées $15.95–29.50). In summer the pub menu is also is also available on the porch and terrace.

Tully and Marie's (802-388-4182; tullyandmaries.com), 5 Bakery Lane, Middlebury, open daily 11–3, 5–9, and Sunday brunch 10:30–3. You have the sense of being wined and dined on a small, three-decker art deco ship beached on the bank of Otter Creek. In summer you might lunch on a turkey avocado sandwich on the deck. Service can be slow, but you can watch the water flow at every level as you await your meal. You might dine on

lamb kebabs skewered with red pepper and cantaloupe with spiced sauce, basmati rice, and summer vegetables, or on Thai basil shrimp. Desserts are delectable, and there's a full bar. Entrées run $11–27. Good wine list, local beers.

Morgan's Tavern at the Middlebury Inn (800-942-4666; middleburyinn.com), 14 Court Square. Lunch weekdays, dinner Wed.–Sun. This inviting space off the inn lobby has been expanded as the inn's prime restaurant (the Founder's Room, its traditional dining room, is now reserved for breakfast and functions). The menu might include a pork chop stuffed with prosciutto, spinach, and Fontina cheese ($21.95), or grilled yellowfin tuna with lime ginger wasabi sauce ($19.95).

Doria's (802-388-3624), 22 Merchants Row, Middlebury. Open Tue.–Sun. 11–11, brunch Sat.–Sun. 11–3. The Dorias are an Italian family of chefs (father and son), and the menu features pastas as well as chicken Parmesan, Marsala, and Piccata, and seafood diavolo. The restaurant fills two deep old storefronts, one with a long, inviting eat-in bar. Italian specialty drinks and wines. Dinner entrées $11.95–19.95.

In Brandon

Café Provence (802-247-9993; cafeprovencevt.com), 11 Center St. Open Tue.–Fri for lunch 11:30–2, "bistro" 2–4:30, dinner 5–9; Sat. and Sun. for brunch 9–3, bistro 3–4:30, dinner 5–9:30; also open Mon. in summer. Hidden above a shop in the center of downtown Brandon, this celebrated eatery doubles as pizza parlor and French country bistro. Chef-owner Robert Barral earned his stripes cooking for the Four Seasons restaurant chain, subsequently teaching for several years at Vermont's New England

Culinary Institute. The dining room is small but tasteful, the open kitchen gleaming with polished chrome and hanging pans. What emerges is worth traveling long distances for: lobster consommé en croute, by way of example, or pan-seared scallops wrapped in smoked salmon on a bed of wilted spinach and warm tomato salad. Enjoy the outdoor terrace in summer. Dinner entrées $16–25, but also hearth-baked pizzas, $10.

In the Vergennes area

Black Sheep Bistro (802-877-9991), 253 Main St., Vergennes. Open nightly 5–9:30, this intimate place has been wildly popular ever since chef Michel Mahé started serving his innovative French-inspired dishes. You feel as if you're on a side street in Paris, except that the service is first-rate. A specialty is garlic mashed potatoes on the plate, plus french fries delivered in paper cones and served with ketchup and two flavored dips. You might dine on bacon and Brie stuffed chicken breast or mole-rubbed pork chop with black bean sauce. All appetizers $7, entrées $19, salads and desserts $5; it simplifies the math. Terrace seating in summer months. Reservations essential.

Basin Harbor Club (802-475-2311; basinharbor.com), Basin Harbor, off Panton Rd., 5 miles west of Vergennes. Open mid-May–mid-Oct. If you don't stay at Basin Harbor, there's all the more reason to drive out for lunch or dinner, to see the lakeside setting and savor the atmosphere. The dining room is large and the menu changes frequently, but at dinner (reserve) you might begin with a choice of soups, salad, and then enjoy seared breast of ginger soy marinated duck. The prix fixe is $42 plus 15 percent service charge. The wine list is extensive and excellent. Jacket and tie required.

In Bristol

Mary's Restaurant at Baldwin Creek (802-453-2432; 888-424-2432; innatbaldwincreek.com), junction of Rts. 116 and 17. Open Wed.–Sun. 5:30–9:30; Sun. breakfast 8:30–10:30. Chef Doug Mack was an early proponent of using produce from local farmers and the first president of the Vermont Fresh Network. Every Wednesday in July and August "Farmhouse Dinners" showcase the products or produce of specific farmers; off-season there are monthly "Table Talks" own local food topics. Recently Mack has been growing his own vegetables. Three attractive dining rooms in a country inn on the banks of Baldwin Creek are the setting for dining that might begin with grilled fennel or griddled crabcakes served with lobster sorrel sauce. Entrées might include thinly sliced swordfish rolled with citrus, bread crumbs, and herbs, served on tomato salad and Boydon Farm beef tenderloin parcini with spicy sweet potatoes. Entrées are $19.75–26.70; bistro small plates are $5.75–10.95. Inquire about cooking classes.

Bobcat Café & Brewery (802-453-3311), 5 Main St. Open daily from 5 PM. This friendly local eatery began as a community effort and in 2008 came under the same ownership as the Black Sheep Bistro in Vergennes. It's an atmospheric place with an enormous wooden bar scavenged from a warehouse across the lake. Favorites include roasted garlic potato ale soup with Jasper Hill Blue Cheese crostini to start, and Vermont-raised venison and chorizo meat loaf. Entrées $14–10. Pub fare also available.

Elsewhere but worth the drive

✍ **Starry Night Café** (802-877-6316; starrynightcafe.com), 5371 Rt. 7, North Ferrisburg. Open Wed.–Sun.

5:30–9 (reserve). Chef-owner David Hugo grew up working on Vermont farms and is a Culinary Institute of America grad known for his imaginative flavor combinations. The intimate front dining room with its art-covered walls is a former cider mill featuring an antique bar with locally crafted stools, tables, and chairs. There's a larger octagonal dining room, also with locally crafted furnishings, an outdoor deck, and changing art by local artistis. Appetizers might include house-made goat cheese ravioli with local fresh tomato and basil sauce. For entrées, perhaps grilled portobello mushroom stroganoff or seafood and corn paella. The menu reflects what's seasonally, locally available. Entrées $19–26. Inquire about live music.

🦐 **The Shoreham Inn** (802-897-5081; 800-255-5081; shorehaminn.com), Rt. 74 west, Shoreham. Open Wed.–Sun. from 5. Closed Nov. Dominic and Molly Francis have transformed the downstairs of this old Vermont hostelry into a British-style "gastropub" serving such English standards as bangers and mash with a pint of Guinness. They installed a copper-topped bar and a mantel mirror from Greenwich, England, and serve excellent informal dinners on long wooden tables. The menu might include boeuf au poivre, grilled salmon, or penne with Gorgonzola sauce. Entrées $7–18.

EATING OUT

In the Middlebury area

Mister Up's (802-388-6724), 25 Bakery Lane. Open daily lunch–midnight; Sunday brunch buffet 11–2. Dine outdoors on the riverside deck or in the brick-walled, stained-glass, oak-and-greenery setting inside. The menu is equally colorful, ranging from the unlimited soup, salad, and bread board and pizza to grilled Texas barbecue

steaks and a pound of ribs. Try Mister Up's "Famous Thumbs and Toes."

Noonie's Deli (802-388-0014), 2 Maple St., at the Marble Works. Open Mon.–Sat. 8–8, Sun. 11–7. Good soups, the best sandwiches in Addison County (a half sandwich is plenty)—on homemade bread, you design it. Eat in or take out.

American Flatbread (802-388-3300; americanflatbread.com), 137 Maple St., at the Marble Works. Serving Fri. and Sat. evenings 5–9 year-round, with outdoor seating when possible. The company started in the Mad River Valley but has spread like a well-turned pizza crust. The all-natural pizza is made with organic flour and toppings and baked in a wood-fired oven.

Otter Creek Bakery (802-388-3371; ottercreekbakery.com), 14 College St. Open daily 7–5:30, Sun. in summer 7–3. Hugely popular at lunchtime for soups, salads, and deli sandwiches ranging from homemade hummus with veggies in a pita pocket to fresh crabmeat salad. Breads are the specialty, baked from scratch with no preservatives, in a dozen varieties, like wheat berry and onion Asiago. Many kinds of fresh, flakey croissants too, plus dozens of kinds of munchies, tarts, and cakes.

🐟 **Rosie's Restaurant** (802-388-7052), 1 mile south of Middlebury on Rt. 7, is open daily (6 AM–9 PM in winter, until 10 May–Nov.) and serves a lot of good, inexpensive food. This much-expanded family restaurant has a counter and three large, cheerful dining rooms. We lunched on a superb beef and barley soup and turkey salad on wheat. Dinner choices run from fish-and-chips to Smitty's top sirloin, and there are always stir-fries.

A & W Drive-in (802-388-2876), Rt. 7 south, a few miles from Middlebury. Vermont's last surviving carhop, open in summer months. The 1960s road-side spot still dispenses its root beer the old-fashioned way, in frosted mugs by girls on in-line skates. The usual burgers and fries. Flash your head-lights for service.

In Brandon

♪ ⁎ℸ⁎ **Watershed Tavern & Restaurant** (802-247-0100; watershedtavren .com), 31 Center St. Open daily except Tue. for lunch and dinner. Reserve a table by the waterfall. We love this place! This long, narrow 1820s building in the middle of the village has brick walls, a long, gleaming bar, front win-dows set with stained glass, and a back space with tables over overlooking the big falls in the Neshobe River. A find whether you want a family night out, a romantic place for a drink or dessert (after the dinner crowd), or a solo meal. We dined happily on a ham-and-cheese strudel with mixed greens and a microbrew. Inquire about live music.

🦞 ♪ **Cattails** (802-247-9300), 2146 Grove St. (Rt. 7, just north of Bran-don). Open Tue.–Sun. 11–9 and for breakfast Sat.–Sun. 7–1. Closed Mon. Lance and Stephanie Chicoine run a great, family eatery with large portions of southern comfort food, friendly service, and attractive prices. The lunch menu is varied and tasty. Din-ners are surprisingly good, with such things as Mississippi Steak (house-made maple marinated shoulder ten-derloin grilled and topped with Jack Daniels butter). Children's menu. Early-bird dinner specials.

Gourmet Provence (802-247-3002), 37 Center St. Down the street from its parent restaurant (see Café Provence in *Dining Out*, also good for a reason-ably priced and memorable lunch), this is primarily a bakery but with café tables, a great spot for a quick sand-wich on freshly made bread or an exceptionally creamy quiche.

Patricia's Restaurant (802-247-3223), 18 Center St. Open daily from 11 for lunch and dinner; Sunday brunch, when there's a senior citizen discount on complete dinners. Also known as "Sully's Place," this is a local gathering, eating, and drinking place. Traditional fare like grilled pork chops, fried haddock, and Italian dishes rang-ing from cheese ravioli to spaghetti with hot sausage.

In Vergennes

♿ **3 Squares Café** (802-877-2772), 221 Main St. Open daily 8–8. A popu-lar meeting place in the center of Ver-gennes, this is a gourmet café with a huge blackboard menu and a deli case featuring local cheeses. It was formerly known as "Eat Good Food," and while ownership has changed, the same qual-ity and atmosphere persist, with the welcome addition of more seating. Offerings change with the seasons, but breakfast could be challah French toast with strawberries or an egg panini with cheddar and bacon. Hot pressed paninis are a specialty—maybe savory focaccia with roast beef with Swiss cheese, sweet caramelized onions, mushrooms, and spinach. Sit at the bar next to the picture windows or on the patio in summer.

Red Mill Restaurant at Basin Harbor (802-475-2317; basinharbor.com), Basin Harbor, off Panton Rd., 5 miles west of Vergennes. A former sawmill with a rough-hewn interior and antique farm equipment on the walls. Open seasonally for lunch and dinner; children's menu. This is both a handy and pleasant place to lunch when you are visiting the Lake Champlain Mar-itime Museum.

In Bristol

♿ ⁎ℸ⁎ **Bristol Bakery & Café** (802-453-3280), 16 Main St. Open weekdays 6:30–5, Sat. 8–5, Sun. 8–3. This invit-ing storefront is filled with the aroma of coffee and breads, hung with local art, and furnished with chairs by the coffeepot. It's a great spot to pause with a muffin and your paper or laptop or to sample the crabcakes, soups, and specialty salads or design your own sandwich. Breads are baked fresh each morning.

✦ **Snap's** (802-453-2525), 24 Main St. Open daily 6 AM–9 PM, Sun. 7–3. A cheery pine-walled café with booths, family-sized tables, and a fine pressed-tin ceiling; serving breakfast all day plus lunch, dinner, and Sunday brunch. Daily fresh soups, sandwiches, wraps, and salads. Special menu selections for kids and seniors.

Mountain Greens Market & Deli (802-453-8538), 25 Mountain View St. Open daily 9 AM–7 PM. A delightful small-town deli with organic foods, fair-trade fruits, wines, delicious coffee, and eat-in, tasty takeout. A great place to browse.

Almost Home (802-453-5775; almosthomemarket.net), 28 North St. A former general store specializing in gifty items and take-out dinners like turkey meat loaf or grilled salmon. Also sandwiches, soups, and salads.

Elsewhere

♦ **The Bridge** (802-759-2152), 17 Rt. 17, West Addison. Open daily (except Tue.) at 6:30 for steaming breakfasts, plus lunch and dinner till 9 PM (8 in winter). A genuine diner that hits the spot if you find yourself at the Crown Point Bridge and Chimney Point State Historic Site (one adjoins the other)— or anywhere else in the glorious but eatery-scarce farm and lake country south of Vergennes and west of Middlebury. Service is quick and friendly and prices are amazing, but we recommend ordering basic comfort food like homemade meat lasagna rather than the teriyaki stir-fry (which we did).

Regulars also come for the fresh-baked pies (try the Vermont maple cream)

SCOOPS AND BREWS Otter Creek Brewing (800-473-0727), 793 Exchange St., Middlebury. Open Mon.–Sat. 10–6. Free guided tours at 1, 3, and 5 PM. Ales and other beers can be sampled in the Tasting Room.

Carol's Hungry Mind Café (802-388-0101), 24 Merchants Row, Middlebury. Open Mon.–Sat. 7 AM–11 PM, Sun. 8–4. A riverside coffeehouse with yellow- and merlot-colored walls that offers soft music, art, pastries, and plenty of spots to settle into with a book. Live music on weekends.

Antidote (802-877-2555), 3 N. Green St., Vergennes, in the Stevens House over Christophe's. Open 5 PM. Harper Michael and Michel Mahé's solution to the Monday blues is this lounge with its artistically illuminated back bar and high-definition TV. In warm weather you can sit outside on the balcony overlooking the park. Full bar menu with tapas, cheeses, wines, and imported beers.

The Inside Scoop (802-247-6600), 22 Park St., Brandon. Open 10–9 summer and fall. A combination antiques shop and vintage-1950s soda fountain, serving Vermont's own Wilcox Ice Cream from an old marble counter and marble-topped tables.

✳ **Entertainment**

Middlebury College Center for the Arts (802-443-3168; box office 802-443-6433 weekdays noon–5; middlebury.edu/cfa). The stunning 370-seat concert hall in this dramatic building on the southern edge of the college campus (Rt. 30 south) offers a full series of concerts, recitals, plays, dance performances, and films.

Town Hall Theater (802-388-1436, box office 802-382-9222; townhall theater.org), 52 Main St., Middlebury. Open May–Oct. Box office open weekdays noon–5 and an hour before performances. This restored 1884 town hall on the green stages music, dramatic performances, and children's events. It's summer home to the **Opera Company of Middlebury** (ocmvermont .org).

After Dark Music Series (802-388-0216; afterdarkmusicseries.com). A variety of musical offerings performed at the United Methodist Church, on Rt. 7 and Seminary St. in Middlebury. Come an hour early for a light meal and homemade dessert.

Vergennes Opera House (802-877-6737; vergennesoperahouse.org), 120 Main St., Vergennes. A renovated, century-old theater that once rang with

---

MIDDLEBURY'S EXCHANGE STREET: FACTORY TOURS AND SHOPPING
Downtown Middlebury offers plenty of shopping/browsing, but a number of local ventures have outgrown their downtown digs, migrating to this northern fringe of town on and around Exchange St. (see the map), where they remain visitor-friendly. Here **Otter Creek Brewing** (800-473-0727; ottercreek brewing.com), 793 Exchange St., is the big draw, open daily (except Sun.) for free guided tours, free samples, and sales of its Otter Creek craft beers and Wolaver's organic ales. Otter Creek first opened in 1991, in the plant presently occupied by **Vermont Country Soap** (616 Exchange St.; vtsoap .com), now the largest manufacturer of natural handmade soaps in North America. Visitors can take a "Soap Tour," view the soap museum, and shop the factory outlet (open weekdays 9–5, Sat. 10–4). At **Maple Landmark Woodcraft** (802-388-0627; 800-897-7031),1297 Exchange St., one of the country's largest wooden toy manufacturers—known for "Name Trains" and "Montgomery Schoolhouse" lines—visitors can view toymakers through plate glass windows (call ahead for a factory tour; shop open weekdays 9–5; Sat. 9–4, Sun. seasonally). **Danforth Pewters** (802-388-8666; danforth-pewter.com), Middlebury's best-known artisan brand, recently expanded into a workshop and store at 52 Seymour St. (same area) with a similar setup that permits visitors to view craftsmen spinning "holloware" and shaping pewter plates, jewelry, and ornaments, then purchase the results (Mon.–Sat. 10–5; May–Dec., also open Sun. 11–4). Turn off Exchange St. onto Manelli to find **Geiger of Austria** (800-2-GEIGER; geiger-fashion.com), known for its classic felted jackets. Middlebury has been the company's only American base, and the factory store (Mon.–Sat. 10–5) is well worth checking for bargains. Around the corner is **Beau Ties Ltd.** (802-388-0108; 800-488-8437; beauties ltd.com), 69 Industrial Ave. This is a mainly catalog business but there's always always someone on hand in the store to knot ties for beau tie novices. Choose from seemingly every fabric imaginable; also ascots, scarves, and accessories (open weekdays 10–4:30; tours by appointment.)

the sounds of vaudeville now offers a spicy variety of music and theater in addition to "Friday Flicks"—silent movies on the first Friday of each month.

Bristol Band Concerts are held Wed. evenings at 6:30, June–Aug., in Central Park.

Two Brothers Stage and Lounge (802-388-0002; twobrotherstavern .com), 86 Main St., Middlebury, From 10 nightly. Live music most nights in a spacious lounge with a crescent-shaped mahogany bar, leather coaches and coffee tables, a pool table.

❋ Selective Shopping
ART AND CRAFTS GALLERIES

In Middlebury
The Vermont State Craft Center at Frog Hollow (802-388-3177; frog hollow.org). Open year-round, Mon.–Sat. 10–5:30, as well as Sun. afternoon. Check in the off-season. This is the prime gallery for this statewide nonprofit visual arts organization. It combines the natural beauty of Otter Creek falls, just outside its windows, with the best art and crafts in Vermont. More than 200 artisans are represented; you can come away with anything from a 50-cent postcard to a magnificent $14,000 harpsichord. A feast for the eyes, it's also a serious shopping source with outstanding selections of glass, pottery, woven clothing, wall hangings, jewelry, and woodwork, to name just a few.

Sweet Cecily (802-388-3353; sweet cecily.com), 44 Main St. Nancie Dunn's bright eclectic shop is a mix of ceramics, folk art, hooked rugs, and other items from numerous craftspeople worldwide. The shop's back porch offers the best view in town of Otter Creek falls.

Vermont Folk Life Center Heritage Shop (802-388-4964; vermont

Christina Tree

THE VERMONT STATE CRAFT CENTER AT FROG HOLLOW, MIDDLEBURY

folklifecenter.org), 88 Main St. Open Tue.–Sat. 11–4. One-of-a-kind, hand-made crafts and traditional art from Vermont and the world, including baskets, hand-hooked rugs, art photography, hearth brooms, wooden rakes, apple-head dolls, and whirligigs, plus books and recordings.

Note: **Woody Jackson** (woodyjackson art.com), probably Middlebury's best-known artist, has closed his Main St. studio. Best known for his Holstein cows, immortalized on Ben & Jerry's ice cream cartons, Jackson's landscapes continue to evolve. His studio, 1801 Cider Mill Rd., Cornwall, is open by appointment (802-233-6027).

In Brandon
Brandon Artists Guild (802-247-4956; brandonartistsguild.org), 7 Center St. Open daily year-round, 10–5. A standout nonprofit gallery representing more than 50 local artists and artisans.

Liza Myers Gallery (802-247-5229; lizamyers.com), 22 Center St. The work of folk artist Warren Kimble is featured along with that of Liza Myers and photographer Pete Myers.

Gallery-in-the-Field (802-247-0125; galleryinthefield.com) presents contemporary and provocative visual art and music, installations, and improvisations. Call for directions.

In Bristol

Art on Main (802-453-4032; arton main.net) 25 Main St. Open daily 10–6, Sun. seasonally, noon–4. An exceptional nonprofit community art and crafts center and gallery displaying a changing exhibit of weavings, jewelry, glass, ceramics, kaleidoscopes, leather, and more.

Worth a detour

⚓ **Norton's Gallery** (802-948-2552; nortonsgallery.com), Rt. 73 in Shoreham, 1 mile south of the car ferry to Fort Ticonderoga. Worth a trip—but call beforehand to make sure they're open. The small red gallery overlooking Lake Champlain houses an amazing menagerie of dogs, cats, rabbits, birds, and fish, along with flowers and vegetables—all the work of nature lover Norton Latourelle, sculpted from wood in unexpected sizes, unquestionably works of art and a visual delight for children and adults alike. Sculpture dog portraits are a specialty.

ANTIQUES SHOPS Middlebury Antique Center (802-388-6229; in Vermont 800-339-6229), Rt. 7 at the junction of Rt. 116 in East Middlebury. Daily 9–6. A fascinating variety of fur-

AT NORTON'S GALLERY IN SHOREHAM
Christina Tree

Christina Tree

IN SUMMER BROUGHTON AUCTIONS ARE USUALLY THURSDAY NIGHTS IN BRIDPORT.

niture and furnishings representing 50 dealers. Air-conditioned.

Branford House Antiques (802-483-2971), 6691 Rt. 7 south of Brandon. A large, handsome farmhouse and barn filled with a variety of antiques, a good selection of furniture.

Broughton Auctions (802-758-2494; tombroughtonauctions.com), at the junction of Rts. 22A and 125, Bridport. Throughout the summer (usually Thu.), auctions are held under the blue and white tents (Broughton also rents tents) at the Auction Barn, once the home of the Bridport Cheese Factory and a later a milk plant for H. P. Hood. Check the Web site for on-site auctions. Even if you aren't looking to buy anything, it's worth coming just to hear Broughton hold forth.

Antiques by the Falls is several rooms full of antiques and collectables in Brandon; see The Inside Scoop under *Eating Out.*

BOOKSTORES Vermont Book Shop (802-388-2061; vermontbook shop.com), 38 Main St., Middlebury, was opened in 1947 by Robert Dike Blair, who retired several years ago as one of New England's best-known booksellers and the publisher of Vermont Books, an imprint for the poems of Walter Hard. Robert Frost was a frequent customer for more than two decades, and the shop has sold many autographed Frost poetry collections. It remains a first-rate independent bookstore.

Briggs Carriage Bookstore (802-247-0050; briggscarriage.com), 16 Park St., Brandon. Open daily 9–6, later on weekends. A well-stocked independent bookstore in the heart of town, with an upstairs café, **Ball and Chain**, and frequent evening events.

Otter Creek Used Books (802-388-3241), 20 Main St., Middlebury, Open Mon.–Sat. 11–5; Sun. by chance. A book browser's delight: 25,000 very general titles.

 Monroe Street Books (802-398-2200; monroestreetbooks.com), 1485 Rt. 7, 2 miles north of downtown Middlebury. Open daily, but it's a good idea to call. Dick and Flanzy Chodkowski have some 80,000 volume. Specialties include children's books; cartoon, comic, and graphic art books; and Vermontiana.

 Bulwagga Books & Gallery (802-623-6800; 877-206-1357; bulwagga books.net), 3 S. Main St., Whiting, at the Whiting Post Office. Open Tue.–Sat. noon–6, Sun. and Mon. by appointment. More than 10,000 titles plus an art gallery, handcrafted furniture, and a reading room with mountain views and coffee.

CRAFTS PEOPLE **Robert Compton Pottery** (802-453-3778; robert comptonpottery.com), 2662 N. Rt. 116, just north of Bristol. Showroom open mid-May–mid-Oct., daily 10–6 and by appointment. A complex of kilns, studios, and gallery space has evolved out of a former farmhouse and now contains the work space of this seasoned

potter, who uses salt glazes and Japanese wood-firing techniques to produce everything from water fountains to crockery to sinks. Compton throws his pots in winter and glazes them outdoors in summer.

Lincoln Pottery (802-453-2073), 220 W. River Rd., Lincoln. Open daily noon–5. Judith Bryant creates wheel-thrown stoneware. Her studio and showroom are located in an old dairy barn.

FARMS AND FARMER'S MARKETS

Seasonal farmer's markets are held in Middlebury, Wed. and Sat. 9:30–12:30 at the Marbleworks. In Brandon, Fri. 9–2 in Central Park Village. In Bristol, Wed. 3–6 on the green. In Vergennes, Mon. 3–7 on the green. In Orwell, Fri. 3–6 on the green.

Champlain Orchards (802-897-2777) 2944 Rte. 74, Shoreham. A scenic orchard overlooking Lake Champlain, the scene of free concerts in Sept. and a pig roast in Oct. Retail and PYO raspberries in July, apples Aug. 15 through Oct., plums in Sept., pumpkins in Oct.

Douglas Orchards (802-897-5043), 1 mile west of the village of Shoreham at 1050 Rt. 74, has PYO berries, cherries mid-June–July. and apples Sept. till Thanksgiving, as well as a cider mill, a retail store, and hand-knit felt hats designed by Betty Douglas.

Moonlit Alpacas (802-462-3510; moonlitalpacas.com), 2170 Rte. 125, Cornwall. Wed.–Sun. 1–4. Just south of Middlebury in Cornwall. A visitor-geared working alpaca farm with mini horses, angora rabbits, and mini donkeys too. A farm store sells yarn, sweaters, throws, slippers, and teddy bears.

Monument Farms Dairy (802-545-2119), 2107 James Rd., Weybridge.

Open for tours Tue. and Thu. morning by appointment. The store is open weekdays 8:30–5:30. One of the few surviving milk producer-handlers in Vermont. Try the chocolate milk.

Champlain Valley Alpaca Boutique & Guest Ranch (802-758-3276), 152 Merino Lake, Bridport. A 200-acre alpaca ranch in the state with a variety of animals. Visitors welcome but call ahead.

Golden Russet Farm (802-877-7031), 1329 Lapham Bay Rd., Shoreham. A certified-organic farm raising variety of animals, perennials, vegetables, and herbs, wholesaled to stores and restaurants, also sold at their farm stand, open weekdays 1–6, Sat. 9–2.

Maple View Farm (802-247-5412; mapleviewfarmalpacas.com) 185 Adams Rd., Brandon. Deb and Ed Bratton raise alpacas at and invite tourists to see their animals.

GARDENS **Rocky Dale Gardens** (802-453-2782, 220 West River Rd., Lincoln. Open Apr.–Oct. except Tue. Extensive display gardens on 3 acres with dramatic rock outcroppings and unusual plantings as well as staple perennials, shrubs, and trees.

Pinewood Gardens (802-247-3388; pinewoodgardencenter.com), 2473 Franklin St., Rt. 7 south, Brandon. Excellent perennials and annuals for sale. Display gardens open daily May–Oct.

Pine Tree Gardens (802-453-7555), 140 North St., Bristol. Apr.–July, open Mon.–Sat. 9–6, Sun. 10–4. Aug.–Oct., open Fri.–Mon. 10–6. Greenhouses, display gardens, and a retail nursery with fancy-leaved geraniums and other unusual plants.

SPECIAL SHOPS **Kennedy Brothers Marketplace** (802-877-2975), 11 N. Main St. (Rt. 22A), Vergennes.

Open daily 9:30–5:30. This large brick mill no longer produces its own oak and pine woodenware, but a factory marketplace serves as cooperative space for craftspeople, antiques, cheese, and more.

Dakin Farm (800-425-3971; dakin farn.com), Rt. 7, Ferrisburg. Open Jan.–Apr. daily 8–5; May–Dec. 8–6. Now distributed nationally via stores and catalog, this is the original farm store selling cob-smoked ham, maple syrup, aged cheddar, and much more.

Daily Chocolate (802-877-0087; daily chocolate.net), 7 Green St., Vergennes. Open weekdays 11–6, Sat. 10–3. Some 25 varieties of handcrafted chocolates made from locally produced cream, butter, and maple syrup, packed into sumptuous gift boxes.

Wood Ware (802-388-6297), Rt. 7 south of Middlebury, is the home of good values in furniture, beds, lamps, solid butternut door harps, and dozens of other items. Interesting gift items as well. Open daily (closed Sun. in winter).

Vermont HoneyLights (802-453-3952; 800-322-2660; vermonthoney lights.com), 9 Main St., Bristol. Open daily. An assortment of hand-poured and rolled beeswax candles are produced in this small building. Worth a look.

✳ Special Events

Note: For current happenings check the *Addison Independent* (addison indpendent.com) Calendar of Events.

Late February: **Middlebury College Winter Carnival** (802-388-4356)—ice show, concerts, snow sculpture.

Mid-March: **The Pig Race** winds up with a pork barbecue. Information from Blueberry Hill Inn, Goshen.

Memorial Day weekend: Middlebury's **Memorial Day parade** is a popular annual event featuring lots of school marching bands, Scouts, Little Leaguers, politicians, floats, and fire trucks. It starts at 9 AM (not sharp), but you can catch the same parade two hours later in **Vergennes** if you prefer to sleep in.

Early June: **Annual Ladies Car Rally** (802-877-6737). This is a special—and very popular—fund-raiser for the Vergennes Opera House. If you happen to have a wonderful antique car (the driver must be female, but the navigator needn't be), you could call ahead to register. If not, come catch the finish of the rally with festivities on the Vergennes green.

July 4: **Bristol** hosts one of the most colorful **Independence Day parades** around with its comic Outhouse Race, crafts fair, and parade. Brandon's parade is the day before. **Brandon** claims "the largest independence day parade in Vermont." Fireworks at dusk

Early July: A six-day **Festival on the Green**, Middlebury, features individual performers and groups such as the Bread & Puppet Theater as well as a potpourri of music from folk to jazz to exotic international talent. No charge for admission. In Ferrisburg, Rokeby Museum holds an **Annual Pie and Ice Cream Social** with music and house tours (802-877-3406; rokeby .org).

Mid-July: **French Heritage Day** (frenchheritageday.com) in Vergennes. **Annual Basin Bluegrass Festival**—a weekend of food and music (brandon .org). The **Goshen Gallop** is billed as "one of the toughest 10ks in New England." The race is held over rural roads and wilderness trails (blueberryhill .com).

Late July/early August: **Annual Lake Champlain Folk Festival** (cvfest .org), held in Kingsland Bay State Park on Lake Champlain, Ferrisburg. Three days of music.

Early August: **Addison County Field Days** (802-545-2257), New Haven— livestock and produce fair, horse pull, tractor pull, lumberjacks, demolition derby, and other events. There's also a **Taste of Vermont** dinner one night that requires reservations, but the food is worth the small effort.

Fourth Saturday in August: **Vergennes Day** (vergennesday.com).

Fourth Saturday in September: **Bristol Harvest Festival** (bristolharvestfestival .com).

Early October: **Dead Creek Wildlife Day** (802-241-3700)—wildlife demonstrations, nature walks, crafts, and food. **Vergennes Fiddlers' Contest** at the Vergennes Opera House (802-877-6737).

Mid-December: **Holiday Open House at the Henry Sheldon Museum** (802-388-2117), Park St., Middlebury. Come take a look at Christmas as it used to be with holiday traditions, activities, and decorations.

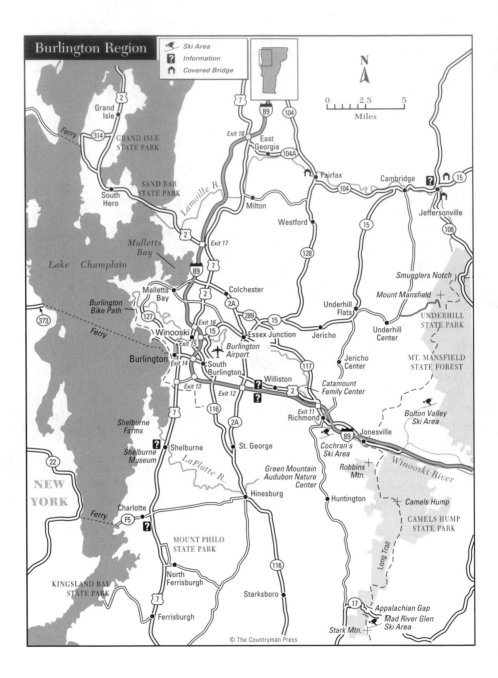

BURLINGTON REGION

Superbly sited on a slope overlooking Lake Champlain and the Adirondack Mountains, Burlington is Vermont's financial, educational, medical, and cultural center. While its fringes continue to spread over recent farmland (the core population hovers around 40,000, but the metro count is now more than 150,000), its heart beats ever faster. Few American cities this size offer as lively a downtown, as many interesting shops and excellent restaurants, or as easy an access to boats, bike paths, and ski trails.

"Downtown Vermont" may sound like a contradiction, but that's just what Burlington is. Vermont is known for mountains, white-steepled churches, and cows, for rural beauty and independent-spirited residents. Its only real city is backed by and overlooks mountains, has more steeples than high-rises, and offers plenty of green space (more about the cows later). Burlington actually pushes the possibilities of the sophisticated, urban good life the ecological, healthy, responsible good life, that is.

The community was chartered in 1763, four years after the French were evicted from the Champlain Valley. Ethan Allen, his three brothers, and a cousin were awarded large grants of choice lots along the Onion (now Winooski) River. In 1791 Ira Allen secured the legislative charter for the University of Vermont (UVM), from which the first class, of four, was graduated in 1804. UVM now enrolls more than 9,000; it's the largest of the city's three colleges.

Ethan and Ira would have little trouble finding their way around the city today. Main streets run much as they did in the 1780s—from the waterfront uphill past shops to the school Ira founded and on to Winooski Falls, site of Ira's own grist- and sawmills.

Along the waterfront, Federal-style commercial buildings house shops, businesses, and restaurants. The ferry terminal and neighboring Union Station, built during the city's late-19th-century boom period as a lumbering port—when the lakeside trains connected with myriad steamers and barges—are now the summer venue for excursion trains, ferries, and cruise boats. The neo-Victorian Burlington Boathouse is everyone's window on Lake Champlain, a place to rent a row- or sailboat, to sit sipping a morning coffee or sunset aperitif, or to lunch or dine on the water. The adjacent Waterfront Park and promenade are linked by bike paths to a series of other lakeside parks (bike and in-line skate rentals abound), which include swimmable beaches.

Halfway up the hill, the graceful Unitarian Church, designed in 1815 by Peter

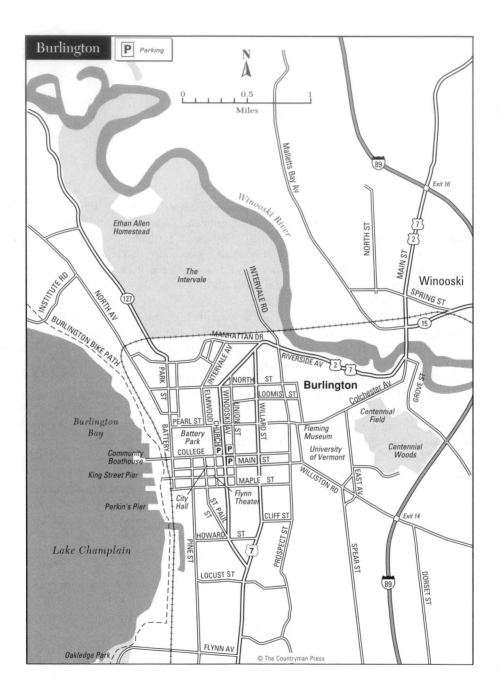

Banner, stands at the head of Church Street—now a bricked, traffic-free market-place for four long blocks, a promenade that's become a 21st-century-style common, the place everyone comes to graze.

Theater and music are constants, but Burlington is best when winter winds soften to cool breezes. The city celebrates summer with an exuberance literally trumpeted from the rooftops in its opening salvo to summer: the Discover Jazz Festival. The weeklong celebration includes some 200 performances. Stars perform at the Flynn Center for the Performing Arts, but jazz venues include buses and ferries, street corners, parks, rooftops, and restaurants. This festival is followed by the Mozart Festival (also in varied venues), a Latino Festival, a folk festival, and other musical shindigs, both indoor and out, all summer.

Burlington in the 1950s and '60s was a different place. Docks and waterside railyards had become privately owned wastelands, overgrown with weeds and rusting debris. The few public beaches were closed due to pollution, and the solution was seen as "urban renewal." In the '70s some 300 homes and 40 small businesses were demolished, and large luxury condo/retail development was planned. Then in 1981, Burlington elected as mayor Bernie Sanders, who had campaigned on the slogan, "The Waterfront Is Not for Sale."

Today that waterfront includes several new parks, such as Oakledge (formerly a General Electric property), just south of downtown, and Leddy (site of a former rendering plant) in the North End. The waterside green space is linked by a 12-mile recreational path that now extends across the Winooski River into Colchester and across Lake Champlain to the Champlain Islands on the bed of the old Rutland Railroad.

Downtown lodging options are expanding. It is possible to walk from two high-rise hotels and several pleasant B&Bs to sights and water excursions, dining and shopping. Of course it's also appealing to bed down in the real countryside that's still within minutes of the city, so we have included B&Bs in nearby Jericho, Williston, Richmond, and Shelburne.

A couple of decades ago the Shelburne Museum, 6 miles south of the city, was the big must-see in the area. Today this "collection of collections" has been

VIEW OF CAMELS HUMP

Joe Citro

upstaged by Burlington itself. Still, the museum draws visitors like a magnet, with treasures ranging from a vintage Champlain Lake steamship and lighthouse to world-class paintings and folk art. Neighboring Shelburne Farms is quite simply New England's most fabulous estate, with prize-winning cows (and cheese), miles of lakeside walks, and a mansion in which you should dine, sleep, or at least breakfast.

GUIDANCE The Lake Champlain Regional Chamber of Commerce (802-863-3489; 877-686-5253; vermont.org), 60 Main St., Burlington 05401. Request brochure guides. Open Mon.–Fri. 8:30–5 year-round, also weekends 10–2 Memorial Day–Labor Day. Not the most obvious place for an information center: It's housed in the former motor vehicles building, halfway between Church St. and the waterfront. The site is augmented by a staffed information booth at the airport that is open daily. This is also the regional marketing organization.

Newspapers: The daily *Burlington Free Press.* For current entertainment happenings, pick up *Seven Days*, a fat, free weekly published Wed. and stacked in the entryways of many shops, supermarkets, and cafés.

GETTING THERE *Note:* Burlington is Vermont's single most car-free destination, accessible by bus from Boston and Montreal and by train from New York City and Montreal, blessed with good local public transport and little need to use it.

By air: **Burlington International Airport** (802-863-1889; 802-863-2874) is just 3 miles from downtown, served by Continental Express, United Airlines, US Airways, and Delta Connection (Comair). JetBlue and AirTran are the new airlines serving Burlington; JetBlue and AirTran have led the way in discounting ticket prices, so there are good deals to be had (jetblue.com; airtran.com). The airport boasts half a dozen car rental firms.

By bus: **Greyhound** (800-552-8737; greyhound.com) offers service to Albany, Boston, New York City, Montreal, Portland, and many points between. Buses depart from 345 Pine St., a 10-minute walk south of Main St.; plenty of parking.

SUNSET AT PERKIN'S PIER IN BURLINGTON
Kim Grant

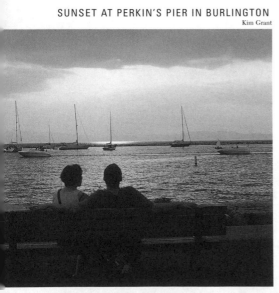

By car: I-89, Rts. 7 and 2.

By ferry: **The Lake Champlain Transportation Company** (802-864-9804; ferries.com), King Street Dock, Burlington. Descended from the world's oldest steamboat company, LCTC offers three local car-ferry services. Between mid-May and mid-Oct. the car ferries make the 75-minute crossing between Burlington and Port Kent, New York. April through early Jan. they also ply between Charlotte, just south of Burlington, and Essex, New York. Year-round service is offered on the 15-minute run between Grand Isle (see "The Northwest Corner") and Plattsburgh, New York.

By train: **Amtrak** (800-872-7245; in Canada 800-4-AMTRAK; amtrak.com). The
Vermonter (Washington to St. Albans via New York and Springfield, Massachusetts) stops at Essex Junction, 5 miles north of Burlington. (The station is served by
two cab companies and by Burlington CCTA buses; see *Getting Around.*) Faster,
more scenic service from New York City is available via the Adirondack to Port
Kent, New York, which connects with the ferry to Burlington, and its free bus up
College St.

GETTING AROUND *By bus:* **Chittenden County Transportation Authority**
(802-864-2282, CCTAride.org). CCTA bus routes radiate from the corner of Cherry and Church streets (hub of the Church Street Marketplace), serving the Shelburne Museum, the airport, the ferry, and the Champlain Mill in Winooski as well
as all the colleges and shopping areas. The fare is $1.25 (60 cents for ages 5–17,
disabled, and seniors 60 and over). Transfers are free. Buses run daily, 6 AM–9 PM,
though not on Sunday except for airport runs. The CCTA also operates weekday
commuter (LINK Express) buses to Middlebury, St. Albans, and Montpelier, and
the College Street Shuttle, a free trolley on wheels that runs up and down the
length of College St. four times per hour, from the medical complex and UVM at
the top of the hill to Union Station and the ferry dock on the lake (daily in summer, weekdays in winter).

MEDICAL EMERGENCY Emergency service is available by calling **911**.

Fletcher Allen Health Care (802-847-0000, fahc.org) on the UVM campus, 111
Colchester Avenue, Burlington, has a 24-hour emergency room.

✳ Nearby Villages

Jericho. Northeast of Burlington, Jericho is best known for the **Old Red Mill**
(jerichohistoricalsociety.org; 802-899-3225), on Rt. 15 at Jericho Corners (open
Mon.–Sat. 10–5, Sun. 11:30–4, except Jan.–Mar., when it's open only Wed., Sat.,
and Sun.). This tower-topped, 1800s red mill set above a gorge is one of the most
photographed buildings in Vermont and appropriately houses prints and mementos
relating to one of the state's most famous photographers, Wilson A. "Snowflake"
Bentley. A Jericho farmer who was the first person in the world to photograph
individual snowflakes, Bentley collected more than 5,000 microphotos. A basement
museum also tells the story of the many mills that once lined six sets of falls. Sales
from the crafts store benefit the preservation of the building, which is owned by
the Jericho Historical Society. A 20-acre park behind the mill, along the river,
offers picnic tables and hiking trails. Ask directions to nearby Jericho Center, with
its oval village common and **Jericho Center Country Store** (802-899-3313), a
genuine, old-fashioned market that's been operating since 1807. Linda St. Amour
and her family carry the usual fresh, frozen, and canned produce, plus socks, mittens, gloves, boots, and so on. The syrup and beans (which, we can attest, bake up
nicely) are local.

Richmond. East of Burlington on Rt. 2 (I-89, Exit 11) and the Winooski River,
Richmond was badly damaged in the flood of 1927 but still has a brief, architecturally interesting downtown. Turn down Bridge St. and drive by the old Blue Seal
grain store (now a restaurant; see *Dining Out*) and the library (a former church) to
the **Old Round Church**. This 16-sided building, one of the most unusual in the

Joe Citro

OLD ROUND CHURCH IN RICHMOND

state, was constructed in 1812–13 as a community meetinghouse to serve five denominations; in the winter, its illuminated windows are a vision of Christmas past (open daily July 4–Labor Day 10–4, also weekends in spring and fall; oldroundchurch.com).

Shelburne. Beyond the commercial sprawl of Shelburne Rd. (Rt. 7 south from Burlington) lie two of Vermont's greatest treasures, both the legacy of 19th-century railroad heirs William and Lila Vanderbilt Webb. In the 1880s the couple hired Frederick Law Olmsted to landscape their 4,000-acre lakeside model farm, and in 1946 their daughter-in-law founded a major museum of Americana. Today 1,400 acres of the estate—**Shelburne Farms**—survive as a combination inn and demonstration farm, complementing the exhibits in no fewer than 39 buildings in the nearby **Shelburne Museum**. Inevitably shops and attractions continue to multiply along Rt. 7, including the **Vermont Teddy Bear Company** Factory and Museum, which threatens to draw more visitors than either Shelburne Farms or the Shelburne Museum. (See *To See* for details about all three.)

Winooski is just across the 32-foot Winooski Falls from Burlington. Ira Allen was the first to harness the water that subsequently powered several mammoth brick 19th-century mills, attracting workers from Ireland, Canada, and Eastern Europe who settled in the cottages that line its streets. The falls, with an art deco bridge, and the common, framed by the vintage-1867 Winooski Block and the handsome Champlain Mill (now a shopping/dining complex), still form the center of town, which gained a roundabout in 2005. St. Michael's College, with its Playhouse (presenting a variety of stage performances) and art gallery (802-654-2535) is just up Allen St. (Rt. 15).

✳ To See

MUSEUMS AND ATTRACTIONS 🔗 ♿ **Shelburne Museum** (802-985-3346; shelburnemuseum.org), Rt. 7, 6000 Shelburne Rd., Shelburne (6 miles south of Burlington), is open late May–late Oct., daily 10–5. $18 adults, $13 teachers and students over 18, $9 ages 6–18. Family cap: $48. Tickets are good for two consecutive days, and parking is free. This fascinating "collection of collections" features American folk art but also includes paintings by Rembrandt, Degas, Monet, and Manet. More than three dozen buildings, many of them historic transplants from around New England, each house a different collection. They are set in 45 landscaped acres that include flower and herb gardens, an apple orchard, and more than 90 varieties of lilacs (the annual Lilac Festival is usually the third weekend in May).

An adequate description of the collections (more than 150,000 objects) would fill a separate chapter. Highlights include a 1915 steam locomotive and a vintage-1890 private Palace Car; the side-wheeler *Ticonderoga*, in her basin near the Colchester Reef Lighthouse; the amazing folk art in the Stagecoach Inn (weather vanes, cigar-store figures, trade signs, and figureheads); the American paintings (Fitz Hugh Lane, Winslow Homer, and many other lesser-known but superb 19th-century New England painters); the Webb Memorial Building, with its elegant rooms (moved from their Manhattan penthouse) hung with impressionist paintings (including a portrait of the museum's founder, Electra Havemeyer Webb, by Mary Cassatt); and the heirloom quilts (the collection includes some 900 American quilts). There are also the Horseshoe Barn's marvelous carriages; the Castleton Slate Jail; Shaker Shed; Dorset House and its decoys, Audubon game bird prints, and fowling pieces; a general store; an up-and-down sawmill; an old-fashioned carousel; and much more. The ticket is good for two days because you may well want to allow time to absorb it all.

Acquisitions continue, but this is still substantially the collection of one woman, gathered at a time when few people were interested in Americana. Electra Have-meyer was 18 in 1910 when she bought her first cigar-store figure. Three years later she married James Watson Webb of Shelburne (son of the wealthy couple who had built Shelburne Farms; see below). Over the next 30 years she raised five children, traveled widely, and managed homes on Long Island and in Manhattan and a 50,000-acre "camp" in the Adirondacks, as well as the Shelburne estate. Gradually she filled all her holdings (even her indoor tennis court) with her treasures, founding the museum in 1947 when her husband retired to Shelburne. Both died in 1960, but their vision for the museum was fulfilled by their son, the late J. Watson Webb Jr. The **Owl Cottage Family Activity Center** gives kids some hands-on time; a number of displays, such as a model circus parade, are also geared to children. There's a museum shop and cafeteria, picnic areas, and a shuttle for the disabled or just footsore. The visitor center is a rare round barn. Inquire about gallery talks and special events.

✿ **Shelburne Farms** (802-985-8686; shelburnefarms.org), at 1611 Harbor Rd., Shelburne, just west of Rt. 7. The Farm Store and Visitor Center (802-985-8442), with an exceptional introductory film, is open daily year-round, 9–5:30 (10–5 in the off-season). Mid-May–mid-Oct., general admission for the walking trails, children's farmyard, and cheesemaking operation on the 1,400-acre lakeside property costs $9 adults, $8 seniors, $7 ages 3–17; full hour-and-a-half open wagon tours are

INN AT SHELBURNE FARMS

Diane E. Foulds

offered four times daily mid-May–mid-Oct. Guided tours cost $9 adults, $8 seniors, $7 ages 3–17. There is no charge to use the walking trails the rest of the year. Inquire about house and garden tea tours, Breeding Barn tours, and special events. This grand 1880s lakeside estate is now a nonprofit experimental farm whose mission is to cultivate a conservation ethic. Founded by railroad magnate William Seward Webb and his wife, Lila Vanderbilt Webb, who built it to be a model agricultural estate, it initially comprised 3,800 acres. Its magnificent setting was landscaped by Frederick Law Olmsted (who also designed New York's Central Park) with the help of America's pioneer forester Gifford Pinchot. Manhattan architect Robert Henderson Robertson designed the magnificent Norman-style barns and the 100-room summer "cottage," known then as Shelburne House, on a bluff overlooking Lake Champlain.

The mansion is now the Inn at Shelburne Farms (open mid-May–mid-Oct.; see *Lodging* and *Dining Out*). The immense, five-story, 416-foot **Farm Barn**, where livestock were kept, is now a place for children to collect eggs, learn to milk a cow, or enjoy a tractor-drawn wagon ride. It also houses the cheesemaking facility. The **Coach Barn,** once the family stable, now hosts weddings, special events, art exhibits, and workshops. The massive **Breeding Barn,** where Dr. Webb's English Hackneys were bred, is now used for large-scale events; guided tours are given Mon. afternoons. The farm's prize-winning cheddar cheese, made from its own herd of Brown Swiss cows, is sold, along with other Vermont products, in the Farm Store. Eight miles of walking trails wind from the Visitor Center, networking the farm and providing sweeping views of Lake Champlain and the Adirondacks. Inquire about naturalist-led bird walks and special events.

Tip: The Inn at Shelburne Farms is open to the public by reservation for breakfast as well as dinner. (No admission fee.) Enjoy the most elegant breakfast in New England, or dine on local delicacies as you watch the sun set over the lake. Before you go, get a glimpse of the spectacular library and stroll the lakeside perennial, herb, and rose gardens.

Burlington waterfront (enjoyburlington.com). As noted in the chapter introduction, Burlington's revived waterfront affords dramatic views and is accessible to the public. The handsome (vintage-1915) **Union Station** at the base of Main St. is now public space (changing art exhibits), and the King Street Dock remains home to the **Lake Champlain Transportation Company** (LCTC), established in 1826. At the base of College St. at the College Street Pier, the (1991) **Community Boathouse** echoes the design of the Lake Champlain Yacht Club, a prestigious gentlemen's domain built on this site in 1889. **The ECHO Lake Aquarium and Science Center**, operated by the Champlain Basin Science Program, doubles as a research facility and science museum. *ECHO*, which stands for "ecology, culture, history, and opportunity," is becoming a world-class museum irresistible to kids (see *For Families*). The 12.5-mile **Burlington Bike Path** links these sites with the nearby **Waterfront Park** to the north (which includes a stroller-friendly fishing pier and a boardwalk promenade with swings) and with **Perkin's Pier** (parking, boat launch, picnic area, canal boat exhibit, and waterfront benches) just to the south. Farther south is **Oakledge Park** with two picnic shelters, a beach, and a wheelchair-accessible tree house. Several more beaches and parks stretch in both directions. Not surprisingly, shops and restaurants have proliferated along neighboring Battery St.; **Battery Park** is the visually majestic setting for free summer concerts Thu. and Sun. and for frequent special events.

CHURCH STREET MARKETPLACE

The city's shopping and dining hub, the Church Street Marketplace extends four car-free blocks, from the graceful Unitarian Church, designed in 1815 by Peter Banner, to City Hall at the corner of Main St. A fanciful fountain plays at its head, and the

BURLINGTON'S CHURCH STREET MARKETPLACE

Joe Citro

bricked promenade is spotted with benches and boulders from different parts of the state. The marketplace buildings themselves, a mix of 19th-century and art deco styles, house more than 100 shops and an ever-increasing number of restaurants. Walk through a storefront at 49 Church St. and you are in the **Burlington Town Center**, a multilevel (stepped into the hillside), multishop complex resembling many in Montreal but few in New England. Unlike Boston's Quincy Market, Church Street is a public thoroughfare, open daily and geared as much to residents as to tourists.

Joe Citro

&. **Robert Hull Fleming Museum** (802-656-0750; uvm.edu/~fleming), 61 Colchester Ave., on the University of Vermont campus. Open weekdays 9–4 (summer months noon–4), Sat.–Sun. 1–5; closed Mon. Limited parking. $5 adults, $3 students and seniors, $10 per family. Vermont's largest collection of international treasures. Varied collections of early to postmodern art, natural history, archaeology, and geology. Holdings include ancient primitive art from several cultures and continents, a collection of American portraits and landscapes (from the 18th century to contemporary works), a Native American collection, and frequent special exhibits showcasing everything from Picasso to the history of shoes. Gift shop and café. The building was designed by the renowned firm of McKim, Mead & White, which also designed UVM's Ira Allen Chapel (1927) and Burlington's City Hall.

Fire House Art Gallery (802-865-7165; burlingtoncityarts.com/firehousegallery), 135 Church St., Burlington, next to City Hall. Open Tue.–Thu. (and Sun.) noon–5, noon–8 on Fri., and 9–8 on Sat. Closed Mon. A nonprofit community space showcasing cutting-edge work by top Vermont artists. Inquire about First Friday Art Walk, free guided tours of local art galleries the first Friday of every month, Apr.–Nov. (5–8 PM: the last tour leaves at 7).

The Ethan Allen Homestead (802-865-4556; ethanallenhomestead.org), off Rt. 127 just north of the downtown Burlington waterfront (take the North Avenue Beaches exit off Rt. 127, the Northern Connector). Open May–Oct., Fri.–Sat. 10–4, Sun. 1–4. Vermont's godfather is memorialized here in the timber farmhouse in which he lived out the last years of his turbulent life; he died in 1789. The visitor center offers a film, interesting descriptive and multimedia exhibits, and a gift shop. The setting is a working garden and an extensive park with some 4 miles of walking trails along the Winooski River. $5 adults, $4 seniors and AAA members. Children 6 and under, free.

FOR FAMILIES ⊙ 𝄢 &. **ECHO Lake Champlain Aquarium** (802-864-1848; echovermont.org), 1 College St., open daily year-round, 10–5. Closed Thanksgiving, Christmas Eve, and Christmas Day. Admission is $9.50 adults, $8 for students and seniors 62 and over, and $7 ages 3–17 (ask about annual passes and group rates). This is the place to see (and handle) what's swimming in the lake (not only the fish, but a display on "Champ," the local Loch Ness monster). Changing exhibits range from dinosaur eggs to bloodsuckers. An environmental-themed café, Think!, offers lunch 11–3, and the gift shop teems with science-minded toys and collectibles.

𝄢 **Vermont Teddy Bear Company Factory and Museum** (802-985-3001; 800-829-BEAR, vermontteddybear.com), 6655 Shelburne Rd., Rt. 7 at the south end of Shelburne Village. Open daily 9:30–5; Oct. 26–June, open 10–4. A phenomenon in its own right, the huge, fanciful birthplace of well over 100,000 teddy bears a year now includes a museum depicting teddy bear history; visitors are also invited to make their own teddy bear ($19.99), to take the highly entertaining 30-minute tour ($2 adults, free for children under 12), and to have a snack at the Hungry Bear Café. There is, of course, a huge teddy bear store.

&. 𝄢 **National Museum of the Morgan Horse** (802-985-8665; morganmuseum .org), 122 Bostwick Rd. near Rt. 7, Shelburne, next to the Shelburne Museum. Open weekdays (except Wed.) 1–4, Sat. 10–2. Closed Sun. A small museum depicts the history of the Morgan horse in America, with changing exhibits. Guided tours can be arranged with advance notice. Admission by donation. (Also see the UVM Morgan Horse Farm in "Lower Champlain Valley.")

*❖ **Lake Champlain Chocolates** (802-864-1808; lakechamplainchocolates.com), 750 Pine St. near Flynn Ave. Tours weekdays on the hour, 9–2. Vermont's premier chocolate company offers free tours (and samples) at its Burlington factory, plus a delectable souvenir selection, including seconds. The café serves hot chocolate and more (another is at 63 Church St.).

✴ To Do

ARTS VACATIONS **Shelburne Art Center** (802-985-3648; shelburneartcenter .org), P.O. Box 52, 64 Harbor Rd., Shelburne 05482. This nonprofit complex, the former Shelburne Craft School, has been holding classes for children and adults for over 60 years. It offers year-round workshops of varying length in pottery, woodworking, fiber, metal, stained glass, and all the fine arts, and shows local work in the on-site gallery, a former library. Summer camp programs for children. Classes and summer programs are also offered at the **Firehouse Center for the Visual Arts** (802-865-7166, burlingtoncityarts.com/classes) in Burlington at 149 Church St.

BICYCLING The **Burlington Bike Path** (802-864-0123; enjoyburlington.com) runs for 12 miles along the waterfront, connecting six different parks, beginning with Oakledge Park in the south. A bike bridge spans the Winooski River, continuing the path through Colchester to a bike ferry that links it with the Champlain Islands. Fun side trips include Ethan Allen Park with its stone lookout tower, the Ethan Allen Homestead, Intervale Community Farms, and the Salmon Hole Fishing Area near the Winooski bridge. **Rental bikes** (including tandems, trailers, and trail-a-bikes) are available from **Local Motion's Trailside Center** (802-652-2453; localmotion.org), on the Burlington waterfront stretch of the Bike Path at 1 Steele St., #103, and at the **SkiRack** (802-658-3313; skirack.com), 85 Main St. The path is used for walking, running, and in-line skating as well as biking. Note that CCTA buses have bicycle racks. For serious bicyclists, we recommend the *Greater Burlington Hiking and Biking Map*, published by Map Adventures (mapadventures .com), which details several Burlington-area loops and longer tours on both sides of Lake Champlain, using ferries. You can also download a free Burlington biking map at localmotion.org. Mountain bikers should check out the 500-acre **Catamount Family Center** (802-879-6001; catamountoutdoor.com), 592 Governor Chittenden Rd., Williston: a 35 km groomed trail system, plus rentals and food in the nearby 1796 house built by Vermont's first governor, now the three-guest-room **Catamount's B&B** (802-878-2180).

*❖ **Sleepy Hollow Inn, Ski, and Bike Center** (802-434-2283; skisleepyhollow .com), 1805 Sherman Hollow Rd., Huntington, features over 10 miles of single-track plus another 20 miles of converted ski trails linking to the Catamount Family Center Mountain Bike Trail. The bike shop rents equipment, and you can take a dip in the on-site pond. Adults $6 per day, $4 ages 6–12; kids under 6, free. Open daily, late May–late Oct.

There is also the **Essex Transportation Trail**, a 3-mile rail-trail from the Essex Police Station to Rt. 15 (Lang Farm); the **Shelburne Recreation Trail**, from Bay Rd. through Shelburne Bay Park to Harbor Rd.; and the unpaved **Intervale**

Bikepath, from Gardener's Supply on Intervale Ave. to the Ethan Allen Homestead. **Bolton Valley** (see *Winter Sports*) also offers mountain biking on its cross-country and alpine trails.

BOATING **Burlington Community Boathouse** (802-865-3377), foot of College St., Burlington. Rowboats, Rhodes and Laser sailboat rentals, captained day sails, sailing lessons, fishing charters, June–Oct. **Winds of Ireland** (802-863-5090; 800-458-9301; windsofireland.net), based here, offers day and sunset sails, bare-boat charters, and instruction.

Spirit of Ethan Allen III (802-862-8300; soea.com). Seasonal, daily scenic cruises as well as dinner cruises aboard a triple-deck, 500-passenger excursion boat, departing from the Burlington Community Boathouse (see above) mid-May–mid-Oct. Narrated sightseeing, plus sunset cruises, dinner, lunch, and brunch cruises, murder mystery cruises, and fifties' night cruises. Specialty cruises include a lobster fest, a night of big-band music, and an Elvis show on the lake. Sightseeing cruise $11.99 adults, $5.99 ages 3–11.

Moonlight Lady (802-863-3350; vermontdiscoverycruises.com). Seasonal one-, three-, and six-night cruises on a three-deck converted swamp yacht with open-air dining and eight staterooms, each with private bath. Themed cruises include wine tastings and watercolor painting; destinations include Vergennes, Basin Harbor, and Montreal. May–Oct. $299 per person per night, double occupancy, meals included (tips, taxes, and port charges extra).

Lake Champlain Cruises (802-864-9669; ferries.com/cruise), King Street Dock, Burlington. The *Adirondack*, the *Champlain*, and now a third cruise boat, the *Northern Lights*, regularly sail the waters of Lake Champlain, offering brunch, lunch, dinner, scenic, and entertainment cruises of all sorts. The caterer runs two local seafood restaurants. The supper club and special entertainment cruises cost about $35 per person, less for the daytime outings.

✍ **Lake Champlain Shipwrecks** (802-578-6120; shipwrecktour.com) Perkins Pier, Burlington. Over 300 vessels cover Lake Champlain's floor, from scattered fragments to fully rigged ships. Husband-and-wife sailing instructors Rachael Miller and James Line offer one-hour tours late June–Oct., using a camera-tipped robot to home in on two wrecks near Burlington's breakwater. Participants see the images on a computer screen on deck. $18 per person, by appointment. Wear sunscreen, rubber-soled shoes, and sunglasses, and bring a windbreaker.

✍ **Lake Champlain Community Sailing Center** (802-864-2499; comunity sailingcenter.org), located along the Burlington Bike Path, is a nonprofit, public-access sailing center with a host of learn-to-sail and learn-to-canoe programs for kids, adults, and families, as well as rentals. Keel boat rentals cost $50 per hour (ask about rental passes), kayaks and canoes, $15 per hour. LCCSC also offers adaptive programs for the disabled.

Also note: Day sails and local marinas are listed with the Lake Champlain Regional Chamber of Commerce (see *Guidance*).

DIVING **Lake Champlain Historic Underwater Preserves** (802-457-2022). The Vermont Division for Historic Preservation (historicvermont.org) maintains seven shipwrecks, identified by yellow Coast Guard–approved buoys, at various points on Lake Champlain; all are open to scuba divers. The *Horse Ferry*, the *Coal Barge*, the *O. J. Walker* canal boat, and the *General Butler* are off Burlington. The *Phoenix* and the *Diamond Island Stone Boat* are in Colchester and Vergennes, respectively, and the *Champlain II*, a passenger ship, lies on the New York side across from Basin Harbor. Register at the **Waterfront Diving Center** (802-865-2771; waterfrontdiving.com), 214 Battery St., Burlington, which provides equipment rentals and repair; instruction in snorkeling, underwater archaeology, photography, and scuba; and charters to historic preserved shipwrecks. See also *Boating*.

FISHING **Schirmer's Fly Shop** (802-863-6105, schirmersflyshop.com), 34 Mills Ave., South Burlington, specializing in Ed Schirmer's own flies, tackle, accessories, guided trips, and instruction. For more fishing guides, contact the Vermont Outdoor Guide Association (800-425-8747, voga.org). The **Salmon Hole fishing area** off Riverside Ave., just west of the Winooski bridge, is a popular local spot, as is the **Fishing Pier** on the Burlington waterfront behind the Water Department Building next to the Coast Guard station.

FOR BIRDERS ✍ **The Birds of Vermont Museum** (802-434-2167; birdsof vermont.org), adjacent to the Green Mountain Audubon Center at 900 Sherman Hollow Rd., Huntington. Open May–Oct., daily 10–4; by appointment in winter. Amazingly lifelike carvings of more than 200 species of birds by Robert Spear Jr.; also nature trails, recorded birdsongs. $6 adults, $5 seniors, $3 ages 3–17, $15 families.

GOLF **Vermont National Country Club** (802-864-7770; vnccgolf.com), 1227 Dorset St., South Burlington, an 18-hole, Jack Nicklaus–designed championship course; **Rocky Ridge Golf Club** (802-482-2191; rockyridge.com), St. George (5 miles south on Rt. 2A from Exit 12 off I 89), 18 holes; **Kwiniaska** (802-985-3672; kwiniaska.com), 5531 Spear St., Shelburne, 18 holes, Vermont's longest course; **Williston Golf Club** (802-878-3747; willistongolfclub.com), 424 Golf Course Rd., Williston, 18 holes; **Essex Country Club** (802-879-3232; essexccvt.com), 332 Old Stage Rd., Essex Junction, 18 holes; **Cedar Knoll Country Club** (802-482-3186; cedarknollgolf.com), 13020 Rt. 116, Hinesburg, 27 holes; **Links at the Lang Farm** (802-878-0298; linksatlangfarm.com), 39 Essex Way, Essex, 18 holes.

HIKING See Camels Hump State Park and Mount Philo State Park under *Green Space*.

HORSEBACK RIDING See Pond Hill Ranch in Castleton under "Killington/Rutland Area."

KAYAKING **Champlain Kayak Club** (ckayak.com) and the **Lake Champlain Maritime Museum** (lcmm.org) are both excellent sources of information.
True North Kayak Tours (802-860-1910; vermontkayak.com). Mother-and-son team Jane and Dovid Yagoda offer instruction and guided tours from a variety of locations on Lake Champlain. Inquire about multiday paddles through the Champlain Islands with B&B lodging.

PaddleWays (802-238-0674; paddleways.com). Burlington-based Kevin and Michele Rose offer custom-designed camping or paddling trips for 4 to 12, tents and food included, on Lake Champlain.

The Kayak Center at North Beach (802-865-6777; 802-658760; canoeimports .com), run by Canoe Imports at 370 Dorset St. in South Burlington, offers weekend courses and rents canoes, kayaks, and equipment. Open daily, weather permitting, June–Labor Day.

Umiak Outdoor Outfitters (802-253-2317; umiak.com). Based in Stowe, Umiak offers self-guided kayaking on the Winooski and Lamoille rivers, plus rentals and instruction. Kayak and canoe rentals are also available from **Waterfront Boat Rentals** (802-864-4858; 877-964-4858; waterfrontboatrentals.com) at Perkin's Pier, at the bottom of King St. in Burlington. Open daily, May–Oct., 10 AM–dusk.

SPECTATOR SPORTS *❧* **The Vermont Lake Monsters** (802-655-4200; vermontlakemonsters.com). Formerly known as the Expos, Burlington's minor-league baseball team plays at Centennial Field (off Colchester Ave.) all summer. There is free parking at the Trinity Campus parking lot at the northern end of East Ave. The field is a few minutes' walk away. The season is mid-June–Sept. 1, tickets are cheap, the park is lovely, the concession food is pretty good, and there's a giant Day-Glo dancing Champ mascot for the kids. All in all, a great time—and the baseball isn't bad. The Lake Monsters operate a souvenir shop and "creamee" (soft-serve) stand at the King Street Ferry Dock on the Burlington waterfront (802-655-4200).

SWIMMING **North Beach** (802-862-0942), off North Ave. at 60 Institute Rd., Burlington (turn at Burlington High School), is the city's longest (and most crowded), providing tent and trailer sites, picnic tables, a snack bar and change room, and swimming from a long, sandy beach, late May–early Sept.; vehicle charge, pedestrians and bicyclists free. (Just before the park is the entrance to Rock Point, where the Episcopal Diocese of Vermont maintains Bishop Hopkins' Hall School, the bishop's residence, a conference center, and an outdoor chapel.)

Other beaches: **Leddy Park** (802-865-5399; enjoyburlington.com/leddypark.cfm), a more secluded, tree-lined beach with picnic areas, grills, and tables (farther north off North Ave. from North Beach, turn left before the shopping mall onto Leddy Park Rd. and drive to the end). **Oakledge Park** (802-865-7247), a tiny yet cozy beach with a rocky spit, plus sheltered picnic area and numerous open-air picnic tables with grills, three tennis courts, a two softball fields, volleyball courts, and walking trails. At the southern end of the bike path off Rt. 7, at the end of Flynn Ave. Fee for vehicles, pedestrians and bicyclists free. **Red Rocks Park** (802-864-4108), Lyons Rd. South Burlington's small but serviceable public beach is valued mostly for its forested hiking trails, with a few picnic tables overlooking the lake. Open mid-June–late Aug. Fee.

✳ Winter Sports

CROSS-COUNTRY SKIING *Northern Vermont Nordic Skiing and Snowshoe*, a weather-proofed map ($6.95) detailing cross-country and snowshoeing trails throughout the region, is available at local outlets and from Map Adventures (mapadventures.com).

Bolton Valley (802-434-3444, boltonvalley.com), Bolton. Ranging in elevation from 1,600 to 3,200 feet, this 100 km network is Vermont's highest cross-country system, with snow that usually lasts well into April. About 35 km are machine groomed. There is a wide and gently sloping 3.6-mile Broadway and a few short trails for beginners, but most of the terrain is backwoods, much of it splendidly high wilderness country. You can take an alpine lift to the peak of Ricker Mountain and ski Old Turnpike, then keep going on cross-country trails for a total of 7 miles. There's a ski school, rentals are available in the cross-country center, and experienced skiers are welcome to stay in the area's high huts by reservation. Telemarking is a specialty here, along with guided tours. Trail fee.

The legendary 12-mile **Bolton-to-Trapp trail** originates here (this is by far the preferred direction to ski it), but requires spotting a car at the other end or on Moscow Rd. Inquire about the exciting new telemark/backcountry trail beginning at the top of Bolton's Wilderness Chair and meandering down into Little River State Park in Waterbury–Stowe. Again, a car needs to be spotted at the other end.

✦ **Catamount Outdoor Family Center** (802-879-6001; catamountoutdoor.com), 421 Governor Chittenden Rd., Williston. The 35 km of groomed trails at this 500-acre nonprofit, family-owned recreation area include a 3-km loop that's lit 5–8:30 on Tue., Wed., and Thu. for night skiing. All of it radiates over rolling terrain, both wooded and open. Geared to all abilities. Guided tours, rentals, instruction, sledding hill, snowshoe trails, and warming hut. Trail fee.

✦ **Sleepy Hollow Inn, Ski, and Bike Center** (802-434-2283; skisleepyhollow.com), 1805 Sherman Hollow Rd., Huntington. Dave, Sandy, Molly, and Eli Enman offer 35 km of well-groomed cross-country ski trails that weave through an 870-acre tract up to the elevated Butternut Cabin (which can be rented all year) with its gorgeous views of Camels Hump. Another 20 km are good for snowshoeing, and there are rentals, lessons, and a warm-up lodge with accommodations (see *Bed & Breakfasts*). Popular with the locals, Sleepy Hollow also offers night skating on its pond, and skiing on a 2 km loop each Mon., Wed., and Fri., sunset–9 PM.

Note: See *Green Space* for more about local parks with trails that lend themselves to cross-country skiing.

DOWNHILL SKIING Bolton Valley Resort (802-434-3444; 877-926-5866; boltonvalley.com), Bolton. This mountain is smaller and less commercial than the state's better-known ski areas, but has advantages the others lack. For one thing, it has the highest base elevation of any winter resort in Vermont, meaning lots of natural snow. The mini village is cozy and Alpine-like, keeping everything within walking distance. A fitness center furnishes muscle-building (and muscle-soothing) facilities, including a sauna, pool, multiperson Jacuzzi, massages, and more. Sixty-four trails cover 165 skiable acres, about half of them geared to intermediate-level skiers, a quarter to beginners, and a quarter to experts. At night the lights go on over 12 trails and three lifts, making Bolton the state's largest night-skiing destination. There's something for everyone: snowshoeing, lots of Nordic trails, and three terrain parks with jumps. Since Vermonters Larry Williams and Doug Neddy took over in 2007, some $2.3 million has been invested in snowmaking equipment. Bolton has a wood-fired pizzeria, a fine-dining restaurant (see *Dining Out*), new glades and backcountry trails for the more adventuresome, and a quad chairlift that runs from the base lodge to Vista Mountain's 3,150-foot summit, the most

Anthony Marnora

SNOWBOARD INSTRUCTION AT BOLTON VALLEY

ambitious improvements in 20 years. Set atop a winding, 4-mile road that is bliss-fully free of the junk-food and chain hotel establishments that plague other ski areas, the spot is refreshingly scenic while still being accessible to Richmond, a 10-minute drive, and to Burlington Airport, some 20 miles away. Prices are another attraction. Lift tickets are considerably lower than in southern Vermont, with plen-ty of enticements: a reduced rate for women on Wed., deals for the locals, and ski packages that include overnights and breakfast at the resort's ski-in, ski-out hotel. In summer the trails fill with hikers and mountain bikers. Residents of the 200 pri-vate condos have the mountain largely to themselves much of the time, though vacationers are gradually discovering the Adventure Center, with its fitness room and pool, along with an outdoor ropes course, zipline, and high wire, plus kayak-ing, rappelling, caving, and bike races. The Ponds is becoming a popular spot for scenic mountaintop weddings. More activities for summer visitors are in the works. Until then, the resort will remain an unspoiled natural area teeming with wildlife and terrific alpine views. With its steep access road veering off a lonely stretch of Rt. 2 between Montpelier and Burlington, this is a genuinely self-contained resort whose atmosphere is guaranteed to make you want to stay put for a while.

Vertical drop: 1,704 feet.

Trails: 64; 6 lifts: 2 quads, 3 double chairlifts, 1 surface.

Base elevation: 2,100 feet.

Snowmaking: 60%.

Full season, half-day, night-skiing, and package ticket options.

✔ **Cochran Ski Area** (802-434-2479; cochranskiarea.com), Cochran Rd., Rich-mond. When Mickey and Ginny Cochran bought this hillside farm in 1961, little did they know that in 1998 it would become the nation's first nonprofit ski area and the incubator of Olympic champions. Two generations of Cochrans have joined the U.S. Ski Team; two have won top trophies. What started as a single backyard slope with a 400-foot rope tow has stretched into a good-sized racing mountain with six trails and three lifts, including a rope tow, a T-bar, and a handle.

This is the state's best children's and instructional spot. Olympic gold medalist Barbara Ann Cochran runs "Ski Tots," teaching parents to instruct their own 3- to 5-year-olds. The lodge serves hot snacks and rents equipment, there's a ski school, and free Lollipop races are held each Sunday; winners receive lollipops. Open on weekends and during holiday weeks 9–4; otherwise Tue., Thu., and Fri. 2:30–5 PM. Full-season family pass $330 if purchased before Dec., $440 thereafter. Day passes $20 adults, $14 students, and $12 half days.

Note: See also Smugglers' Notch Resort in "North of the Notch and the Lamoille Valley," "Stowe and Waterbury," and "Sugarbush/Mad River Valley." Five major alpine areas are within easy striking distance of Burlington.

ICE SKATING 🐾 ♪ **Gordon H. Paquette Arena at Leddy Park** (802-862-8869; enjoyburlington.com/leddypark.cfm), an Olympic-sized rink offering public skating along with hockey and figure-skating instruction. Snack bar, rentals, skate sales. Adults $4, students $3, skate rentals $3. Closed six weeks for maintenance in May and June.

♪ The **Catamount Outdoor Family Center** (802-879-6001; catamountoutdoor .com) floods a 250-meter skating oval, which is illuminated at night. And skating on Lake Champlain from **Waterfront Park** is a special rite of winter on those ever rarer occasions when the lake freezes over; flags indicate ice safety.

SLEIGH RIDES **Shelburne Farms** (802-985-8442; shelburnefarm.org) offers rides in 12-passenger sleighs through a 19th-century-esque landscape of sculpted forests and snow-covered fields, with visions of opulent barns in the distance. Daily late Dec.–Jan. 1 (except Christmas), then weekends through Feb., 11–2. $8 adults, $6 ages 3–17.

✳ Green Space

Burlington Parks and Recreation (802-865-7247; enjoyburlington.com). Request a copy of the Burlington *Bike Paths & Parks* map or pick it up at the chamber of commerce. Burlington's lakeside parks are superb. **Oakledge Park**

OAKLEDGE PARK IN BURLINGTON

Joe Citro

(take Flynn Ave. off Pine St. or Rt. 7) offers swimming and picnicking, and sports a wheelchair-accessible tree house (parking fee, but you can bike or walk in). **Red Rocks Park** just south, occupying the peninsula that divides Burlington from South Burlington (take Queen City Park Rd. off Rt. 7), offers walking and cross-country ski trails (no bikes allowed) as well as a beach. **Ethan Allen Park** (North Ave., past the high school) is a 67-acre preserve, once part of Ethan's farm (it's near the Homestead) and webbed with trails that climb to the Pinnacle and to a Norman-style stone tower built on Indian Rock in 1905 (open Memorial Day–Labor Day, Wed.–Sun. noon–8); both high points offer panoramic views of Lake Champlain.

Winooski Valley Park District (802-863-5744; wvpd.org) consists of 17 parks, one a wetlands, one landlocked, and most maintained as nature preserves. A few contain canoe launches and bike paths. **The Intervale** (entrance on the corner of Riverside Ave. and N. Prospect St.) along the Winooski River offers walking as well as bike trails; it includes the Intervale Community Farm (802-658-2919) and Gardener's Supply (a retail and catalog outlet). Also along the Winooski: a children's discovery garden and walking trails in the 67-acre park around the Ethan Allen Homestead (park headquarters), at **Macrea Farm Park**, and at **Half Moon Cove Park**. **Delta Park** at the mouth of the Winooski River is a magical place with a sandy trail traversing woods to a wetland observation platform. **Centennial Woods** offers nature trails; access is from East Ave.

Bayside Park (802-264-5641), off Blakely Rd. in Colchester. The site of a 1920s resort, this 22-acre park now offers a playground, beach, shuffleboard and tennis courts, sports facilities, and walking trails. In winter this is also a popular spot for ice fishing, sailboarding, and ice skating.

For **Sand Bar State Park** and other green space to the north, see "The Islands" in "The Northwest Corner."

To the east

Underhill State Park (802-899-3022, vtstateparks.com), on the western edge of 4,300-foot Mount Mansfield, the state's highest peak, lies within the 34,000-acre Mount Mansfield State Forest. Camping mid-May–mid-Oct., a Civilian Conservation Corps log picnic pavilion, and four trails to the summit ridge of Mount Mansfield. It's accessed from the Pleasant Valley Rd. west of Underhill Center.

The Green Mountain Audubon Nature Center (802-434-3068; http://vt .audubon.org/centers.html), Huntington. (Turn right at Round Church in Richmond; go 5 miles south to Sherman Hollow Rd.) Trails wind through 230 acres of representative habitats (beaver ponds, orchards, and woodlands). Interpretive classes offered. Groups are welcome to watch (and help in) the wood-fired sugaring conducted each year. Open all year, but call ahead to confirm.

Camels Hump State Park. Vermont's most distinctive and third highest mountain (4,083 feet) is best accessed from Huntington via East St., then East St. to Camels Hump Rd. Request a free map and permission for primitive camping (at lower elevations) from the Vermont State Parks in Waterbury (802-241-3655; 800-VERMONT; vtstateparks.com). The **Green Mountain Club** (802-244-7037; greenmountainclub.org) at 4711 Waterbury-Stowe Rd. (Rt. 100) in Waterbury Center also has maps and maintains shelters, lodging, and the Hump Brook Tenting Area. Camping facilities are available on the reservoir in nearby Little River

To the south

LaPlatte River Marsh Natural Area, Shelburne; parking on Bay Rd. Managed by The Nature Conservancy of Vermont, this 211-acre preserve at the mouth of the LaPlatte River is rich in bird life. It is traversed by an easy trail (45 minutes round-trip).

Shelburne Bay Park, Shelburne. (Park on Bay Rd., across from the entrance to the Shelburne Farms Visitor Center.) The Shelburne Recreation Department maintains a blue-blazed trail along the bay through mixed woods.

Shelburne Farms. Eight miles of easy trails on 1,400 acres landscaped by Frederick Law Olmsted, who designed New York's Central Park. Check in at the Visitor Center.

H. Lawrence Achilles Natural Area, Shelburne, access off Pond Rd. A short hiking trail leads to Shelburne Pond.

Mount Philo State Park (802-425-2390; 802-372-5060), 5425 Mount Philo Rd., Charlotte. Founded in 1924, Vermont's oldest state park has a small, intimate, mountaintop picnic area and campground, with spectacular views of the valley, lake, and Adirondacks. A short but steep ascent off Rt. 7 (not recommended for trailers or large RVs); 10 campsites; admission fee.

Kingsland Bay State Park (802-877-3445; 888-409-7579), 787 Kingsland Bay State Park Rd., Ferrisburg. Take Little Chicago Rd. 1.5 miles west from Rt. 7; turn north onto Hawkins Rd. for 3 miles, then right onto Kingsland Bay State Park Rd. The site of a former girls' camp, Ecole Champlain, this expanded park is good for picnics, swimming, boating, fishing, and scenic shoreline trails. The 1790 Hawley House is the historic centerpiece of this 264-acre park.

✳ Lodging

In Burlington 05401

HOTELS ⊙ ♂ ⅙ "¶" **Hilton Burlington** (802-658-6500; 800-445-8667; hilton.com), 60 Battery St. The former Radisson, this 258-room hotel's recent $16 million makeover has transformed it into the city's most upscale, with a two-story lobby, room service, and a ballroom and convention center. Half the units boast glorious lake views. The lobby-level café, **60 Battery** (802-658-6500), offers three beautifully presented meals a day, with a mix of prices. Most rooms contain the standard two double beds, though lakeside rooms on the sixth and seventh floors furnish robes and cherry headboards;

three family-friendly rooms open onto the indoor pool. Want to splurge? Ask for a corner deluxe king room with its panoramic views, or go for the Presidential Suite, a penthouse-like extravaganza on the top (seventh) floor with views to die for. There are meeting rooms of every size, a fitness center on the second floor with lake views, an attached parking garage, and a free airport shuttle (though the WiFi comes with a $9.95 per day price tag). Rates run $120–600. Twelve rooms are wheelchair accessible.

♂ ⅙ "¶" **Courtyard Burlington Harbor** (802-864-4700; 800-321-2211; marriott.com), 25 Cherry St. Burlington's newest addition to the lakefront stands right beside the larger Hilton on Battery St., both with breathtaking views. Of the Courtyard's 116 rooms, 44 face west, 14 with direct vistas across the waves to the Adirondacks. Some boast stone-lined walk-in showers. All feature flat-screen TVs and WiFi. Downstairs is a bar and breakfast buffet area with a two-sided fireplace, though you'll have to go out for lunch and dinner. A fitness center and indoor pool are on the ground level; the business center even has iMacs. $169–295.

☘ ♂ ♿ **The Sheraton-Burlington** (802-865-6600; 800-325-3535; sheraton .com), 870 Williston Rd. With 309 rooms, this is Vermont's largest hotel and the city's convention and trade center. It's set on campuslike grounds in South Burlington at the top of the hill by the UVM campus and the medical center, near the I-89 (Exit 14W)–Route 2 interchange with easy bus access to downtown. $139–299 per room, depending on season. Pluses include an indoor pool, fitness center, 10 wheelchair-accessible rooms, conference rooms, pub, free parking, and **G's Restaurant**, which serves three meals daily in a four-story atrium filled with lush vegetation. Small pets okay.

BED & BREAKFASTS ∞ ♂ ⁢⁣🍴
Willard Street Inn (802-658710; 800-577-8712; willardstreetinn.com), 349 S. Willard St. Burlington's most elegant inn, this 1881 brick mansion built grandly in the upscale hill section (a few blocks from Champlain College) offers 14 guest rooms, all with private bath. Guests enter an elaborate cherry-paneled foyer and are drawn to the many-windowed, palm-filled solarium with its checkered marble floor and baby grand piano. The living room has a hearth, a tiny gift shop, and vintage portraits. Breakfast starts with coffee in the dining room, followed by a chef-prepared breakfast served in the solarium. Guest rooms are decorated individually and range in size and detailing from spacious master bedrooms and suites to smaller rooms on the third floor. All are tastefully done and equipped with phone, flat-screen TV, WiFi, and air-conditioning. Our favorites were the Tower Room and the Champlain Lookout, both of which have small sitting areas with lake views. The home was built by Charles Woodhouse, a state senator and prosperous merchant whose portrait graces the walls; nowadays the Davis family are your hosts in this certified-green establishment. $140–250 includes a full breakfast. Children 12 and over.

♂ ♿ **Lang House** (802-652-2500; 877-919-9799; langhouse.com), 360 Main St. Innkeeper Kim Borsavage offers 11 rooms with private bath in this lovely restored 1881 Eastlake Victorian, done in period furnishings, antiques, and lush fabrics. One has a gas stove; another is accessibly on the ground floor. The third-floor rooms have lake views, and the former carriage house out back contains a suite with a queen and a double futon. Our favorites were the Van Ness room with its turret and lake vista, and the Captain Lyon room, which has a pineapple four-poster, gold-tinted walls, a hidden TV, and a turret nook with a table and chairs. Common areas include a comfortable living room, a sunroom, and a breakfast area with historic images of Burlington as it looked a century ago. City attractions are within walking distance; rooms on the lower level have kitchen facilities for those seeking long-term stays. $165–245 includes full breakfast, and there are off-season specials. Dog in residence.

♂ ⁢⁣🍴 **Howard Street Guest House** (802-864-4668; howardstreetguest house.com), 153 Howard St. Two bright, spacious suites in a detached carriage barn surrounded by a patio and flower beds. The one downstairs is colorful and contemporary with an airy, open living area and kitchenette, a queen, and a twin. The upstairs is similar, with skylights and gorgeous wooden floors, furnished with flair. Besides the queen bed, it has a pullout sofa and a "secret" closet cot for Harry Potter fans. Air-conditioning and WiFi, though no breakfast; guests can help themselves to the coffee, cereal, and juice. Andrea Gray's house is on a quiet street, about a 15-minute walk from the waterfront and Church St. shopping. Good for a romantic getaway, a family reunion (both suites can be rented at once), or a businessperson needing space to spread out. $160–170 per night, double occupancy. Two-night minimum on most dates.

❦ **Sunset House** (802-864-3790, sunsethousebb.com), 78 Main St. Paul and Nancy Boileau have thoroughly renovated this 1854 Queen Anne–style home, a former boardinghouse, which is just two short blocks from the waterfront. The four air-conditioned guest rooms share two baths and are decorated with family antiques; there's a kitchen nook upstairs for visitors' use; the living room has easy chairs, puzzles, games, and a TV. $99–149 includes continental breakfast.

On the Hill (802-598-6552; onthehillvermont.com), 695 S. Prospect St. A tastefully furnished contemporary home on a narrow lane in Burlington's quiet hill section, right opposite the golf course. Of the three antiques-filled rooms, two with double beds share an adjoining bath (or can be rented as a suite for $145); the third has a queen-sized bed with a private bath across the hall. All three look out onto woods. Guests can lounge in an attractive living room, where crackling fires are common on cold nights. Kay McKenzie serves a continental breakfast that includes fresh fruit, pastries, and Vermont cheese. The adjacent Burlington Country Club is great for walks and cross-country skiing. $110. No pets.

One of a Kind (877-479-2736; oneofakindbnb.com), 53 Lakeview Terrace. Talk about views. The garden of Maggie Sherman's modest 1910 house looks out over a stunning lake panorama. Sit in the flower garden or view it from the tree swing. Her second-floor suite has a queen-sized bed, a private bath, and a sunny sitting room with a sofa that opens to a double. Breakfast includes fresh fruit, baked goods, local cheeses, and home-roasted coffee. $150–200, depending on season and number of guests. Extended-stay visitors can rent the adjacent cottage, a converted garage with a double bed, kitchenette, and lake views, for $1,500 per month.

❦ **254 South Union Street Guesthouse** (802-862-7843; 254southunion.com), 254 S. Union. An 1887 gabled Queen Anne in an architecturally picturesque neighborhood about four blocks from Church St. with a tastefully furnished guest room and a suite, both with private entrance and bath. The suite, with its queen-sized bed and full-sized pull-out sofa, has a fully equipped kitchen, dining area, and sitting room. The smaller room, which sleeps two in a queen, has a gas fireplace. Free WiFi and cable TV. No formal breakfast, but owner Cindy Secondi provides snacks and fresh coffee each morning. $140–210.

❦ ❦ **Hartwell House** (888-658-9242; hartwellhouse.com), 170 Ferguson Ave. Linda Hartwell's unassuming Colonial on this quiet residential street south of the downtown area (accessible

SHELBURNE FARMS, VERMONT'S GILDED-AGE JEWEL

THE WEBB FAMILY

Shelburne Farms

When it was completed in 1899, the mansion at Shelburne Farms was the largest residence in Vermont. Surrounded by a model agricultural farm, it was among New England's most spectacular private estates. At a time when most Manhattan glitterati were summering at Newport, Bar Harbor, or Saratoga Springs, Dr. William Seward Webb and his wife, Lila Vanderbilt Webb, opted for Shelburne. They had family ties there, and Webb sensed business opportunities. Not least of all, a good friend and fellow New Yorker LeGrand B. Cannon encouraged them, having built his own huge estate on a hill overlooking Burlington.

Though a trained physician, Webb shelved his medical practice upon his marriage in 1881, and became president of the Vanderbilt's firm, the Wagner Palace Car Company. The couple built their first summer home (now gone) at what is now Oakledge Park, spending winters at their 58-room Fifth Avenue mansion. When Lila inherited $10 million in 1885, Dr. Webb began the acquisition of over 30 small farms, a multiyear project that culminated in the formation of a 3,800-acre gentleman's estate.

Frederick Law Olmsted, the landscape architect who designed New York's Central Park, shaped the consolidated properties into a pastoral vision of curving drives and towering pines. To ride the 15 miles of roads was to be swept away with the splendor of it all: The lake frontage stretched 6 miles. There were 3 acres of steam-heated greenhouses, and on a knoll overlooking the lake lay the house itself, a glorious fusion of gables, towers, soaring chimneys, and conical-roofed porches.

Days were spent playing croquet, lawn tennis, or golf on the nine-hole golf links, driving carriages, hunting, or entertaining a constant stream of house guests with pony rides or fox hunts. It was an idyllic life, though managing such a place required an army of butlers, cooks, valets, parlor maids, coachmen, nannies, and housekeepers, not to mention hundreds of farmhands to tend the livestock, gardens, and greenhouses. More than a gentleman's folly, the Webb estate became an ambitious experiment in enlightened agriculture. Determined to breed a stronger, more versatile hackney that would be better suited to local conditions, Webb put up the massive Breeding Barn, the largest in the country. Before the project could bear fruit, however, the internal combustion engine came along. The Webbs themselves would buy a tractor in 1917.

Webb died in 1926, his wife a decade later. With the Gilded Age and its excesses a thing of the past, the estate entered a period of benign neglect. Faced with subdividing it or losing it, Webb's descendants opted for a third path: transforming it into a nonprofit. Today it is a 1,400-acre, membership-supported working farm dedicated to inspiring a conservation ethic. Thousands of schoolchildren come for field trips, hundreds more for summer camps; even tiny tots come with their parents to cultivate a love of the land. The four-story Farm Barn now houses a bakery and produces award-winning cheddars from the farm's own herd of Brown Swiss cattle. Shelburne Farms hosts a wealth of concerts, weddings, art exhibits, workshops, and special events. Visitors park at the Welcome Center, watch a short film, then take a truck-driven cart on one of the four daily guided tours.

The Webb home, now a National Historic Landmark, became a luxury inn and restaurant in 1987 (see Dining Out and Inns). Guests can take tea in the parlor, wander the rose gardens, sit by the fire, or dine on the terrace watching the setting sun dapple the waves. Despite extensive restoration, the Gilded Age ambience survives, down to the wood-paneled library with its yawning hearth and leather-covered volumes. Much of the furnishings and family portraits are just as they were. Stroll into the elegant dining room or roam the corridors and you feel as if the Gilded Age never left at all. With its graceful pastures, crashing surf, and mountain vistas as a backdrop, there are few places more magnificent.

AT SHELBURNE FARMS

Shelburne Farms

by public bus) is filled with global art treasures. Guests can choose between a queen or two twins with shared bath in small but cozy air-conditioned rooms on the second floor. Lounging areas include a living room, outdoor pool, and breakfast nook. Rates of $70–90 include WiFi and a full breakfast. Friendly dogs on the premises.

Beyond Burlington

RESORTS ⊗ 🍴 ✏ ⚷ "T" **The Essex Resort & Spa** (802-878-1100; 800-727-4295; vtculinaryresort.com), 70 Essex Way (Rt. 15 east), Essex 05452. Set on 18 acres in a suburban area 10 miles northeast of downtown Burlington (handy to IBM), this contemporary, neo-Colonial complex, formerly the Inn at Essex, has grown into the largest resort and spa this side of Stowe. What makes it special is its culinary theme. A miniature whisk is attached to the door on each of its 120 rooms and suites; inside are boldly colored walls and fabrics. Several rooms come with working fireplace, a few with jet bath or kitchen facilities. The gourmet touch results from its partnership with the New England Culinary Institute, whose 150 white-clad chefs and students staff both of its restaurants. Cooking classes and demonstrations abound; fresh herbs grow in the landscaped gardens. You can choose between the formal dining room, Butler's, and the more casual Tavern, both educational laboratories swarming with cooks (see *Dining Out* and *Eating Out*). Besides the first-rate food, the complex boasts conference facilities, a 22,000-square-foot, full-service spa with an indoor pool, a fitness center, a 25-person outdoor hot tub accessible via heated walkways, an 18-hole golf course, and an outdoor heated pool. Fly-fishing enthusiasts will appreciate its on-site casting pond and designation as one of the state's two Orvis-affiliated fishing centers, with guides and instruction. Other activities include tennis courts, year-round hot-air balloon rides, two dual ziplines, a rock- and ice-climbing facility, and, in the winter months, a snowshoe trail and a small cross-country ski loop. The extensive Essex Shoppes & Cinema is right around the corner. Rates of $169–499 include WiFi; no charge for children under 10 or the airport shuttle; pets $25 per night. Inquire about special packages.

✏ **Bolton Valley Resort** (802-434-3444; 877-9-BOLTON; boltonvalley .com), Bolton Valley 05477. A high mountain valley with a cluster of restaurants, shops, condominiums, and an indoor sports center, the Bolton resort comprises 5,000 wooded acres that abound with birds and wildlife. In winter it's snow-minded with slope-side lodging and night skiing; in summer the focus is on hiking, mountain biking, and adventure ropes. Facilities include a five-floor, 60-room hotel, 20 suites, and condominium rentals. Some rooms come with fireplace and kitchenette; most have kings or multiple doubles and balconies with mountain views. The sports center houses an exercise room, pool, tennis courts, game room, and snack bar. The Ponds, a new wedding facility, overlooks a small lake and the Green Mountains. Rooms range $99–439 with continental breakfast, condos higher, depending on size.

INNS ⊗ ✏ **Inn at Shelburne Farms** (802-985-8498; shelburnefarms .org), Shelburne 05482. Open mid-May–mid-Oct. Guests are treated to a peerless taste of Edwardian grandeur in this 45-room, Queen Anne–style mansion built by William Seward and Lila Vanderbilt Webb on a spectacular bluff overlooking Lake Champlain.

Completed in 1899, the house is the centerpiece of a 1,400-acre estate (see *Museums and Attractions*). Perhaps because its transition from mansion to inn in 1987 entailed a $1.6 million restoration but no sale (the Webb family has turned the estate into a non-profit environmental education organization), there is a rare sense of a time as well as place here. Turn-of-the-20th-century furnishings predominate (most are original), and you feel like an invited rather than a paying guest. You can play billiards in the richly paneled game room, leaf through one of the 6,000 leather-bound books, or play the piano in the library. Common space includes the Main Hall, a gorgeous room divided into sitting areas with fireplaces and dominated by a grand staircase. There's also an elegant tea-room (ask about the inn's special Tea Tours) and the Marble Room, a formal dining room with silk damask wall coverings, a marble floor, and long windows overlooking the formal gardens and lake. Don't miss the third-floor playroom, with its dollhouses. Guest rooms vary in size and elegance—from the second-floor master bedroom to servants' quarters to the two secluded cottages and three-bedroom house—which means room prices also vary. The Green Room, in which we slept, was painstakingly but far from fussily decorated; its wallpaper was specially made to echo the mauve-and-green fabric in a splashy '20s screen. With its alcove desk, freestanding old mirror, fresh flowers, vintage turn-of-the-20th-century bath fixtures, and water view, there was a sense of comfort and space. Guests have access to tennis, boating, a swimming beach, sumptuous gardens, and miles of splendid walking trails. Rates for the 24 individualized bedrooms (17 with private bath) run $150–450, including a 15 percent service charge (but not tax). There is a two-night minimum stay on weekends. Breakfast and dinner are extra, and memorable.

⌾ 🐾 𝄞 **Black Bear Inn** (802-434-2126; 800-395-6335; blkbearinn.com), 4010 Bolton Access Rd., Bolton 05477. Built in the '60s as a ski lodge, now very much a hilltop country inn. Owners Jill and Brian Drinkwater offer 25 rooms, all with bath and 11 with private outdoor hot tub. The quaint lobby is dominated by a roaring stone hearth. There's a gift shop, and common areas are festooned with bears, of both the teddy and the taxidermied variety. Rooms range from bare-bones basic to luxuriously appointed chalets, and gas fireplaces abound. An overnight entails free access to the indoor pool at Bolton Valley a mile up the hill, ski-in, ski-out proximity to trails, a discount on ski tickets, and a full breakfast in the skylit dining room. Dinner is an intimate, candlelit experience. This is a favorite place for returning groups and family reunions, when the dining room fills up. Options range from $89 for a no-frills room in low season to $355 in peak season for the Mountaintop Suite, with a living room, two bedrooms, and two baths. Pets are invited to stay at the "Bone & Biscuit Inn" (an unheated outdoor kennel) for $10 per day, or in the room for $20.

BED & BREAKFASTS **Willow Pond Farm** (802-985-8505, virtual cities.com/vt/willow.htm), 133 Cheese-factory Lane, Shelburne 05482. If we had special sections for birders and gardeners, Sawyer and Zita Lee's elegant home would top both lists. Zita inherited the 200-acre farm, and in 1990 the couple designed and built this exceptional house, a blending of old lines and modern spaces. Windows let in the view of vast rose and perennial gardens with over 20 bird feeders, a willow pond, and a lotus pond whose spectacular blossoms open in August. The living and dining rooms overlook the gardens and ponds and convey a sense of light and space. A full breakfast and the Lees' special cappuccino blend are served at an oval table in the dining area. The upstairs master bedroom overlooks the Adirondacks and contains a cozy built-in sleeping loft for kids (12 or older only). That and the two smaller rooms are furnished in exquisite antiques, Oriental carpets, and handmade quilts made for the king- and queen-sized beds. All have private bath. $110–145 with breakfast. There is a two-night minimum.

⌀ & **Barnhouse B&B** (802) 985-3258), urpampered.com), Barnhouse Farm Road, Shelburne 05482. About 7 miles south of Burlington off Mount Philo Rd., just 0.5 mile south of Shelburne's tiny dirt-track airport. Paul and Phyllis Austin have transformed a 100-year-old dairy barn into a light-filled haven of exposed beams, gardens, and in- and outdoor sitting areas. The wheelchair-accessible Water Garden Room has a queen bed and opens onto a private water-fountain garden that used to be the silo; the private bath accessible from the cathedral living room has a shower and sunken tub. A circular stairway leads to the Balcony Hayloft Suite (good for families) with a queen on one end, two twins on the other, a private bath, and an open balcony with a hanging chair under a skylight. Phyllis, a wellness advocate, equips the air-conditioned rooms with air filters, magnetic mattress pads, filtered water, and a free magnetic (hands-free) back massage. A hot homemade breakfast is included in rates that range $99–150 (cash or check). No pets.

⌀ ♞ ♥ ⌀ **Homeplace B&B** (802-899-4694, homeplacebandb.com), P.O. Box 96, 90 Old Pump Rd. (1.5 miles off Rt. 15), Jericho 05465. This intriguing, H-shaped house is secluded in a 100-acre wood at the end of a half-mile driveway. The interior is a maze of hidden nooks and corners filled with scholarly books and European antiques. There's a big, secluded swimming pond in the rear, a duck pond in the front, a screened-in terrace with bucolic views, and a bevy of animals: chickens, horses, sheep, dogs, a donkey, and a cat. The plant-filled living room is artful and eclectically furnished with marble floors, a wood-burning fireplace, walls of books, and interesting knickknacks. There are six guest rooms, four with private bath and two with shared. Our favorite, the "attic," has two twin beds and a wondrous double that is built into a picture window, with curtains that draw shut on both sides. Depending on the season, you might wake up to lilacs, changing foliage, or birds hovering from a feeder on the adjacent apple tree. Innkeeper Mariot Huessy serves up eggs from the hens in the hexagonal barn, Vermont-roasted coffee, fresh fruit, delicious flapjacks or muffins, and fascinating conversation. $100 single, $125 double, including breakfast; $20 for extra person and per pet, by prearrangement. No credit cards.

⌀ ⌀ **Hidden Gardens B&B** (802-482-2118; thehiddengardens.com), 693 Lewis Creek Rd., Hinesburg 05461. This delightful post-and-beam house is surrounded by 250 acres of land trust forest and bordered with exceptional, seemingly tropical gardens that cascade down the side of a hill to a trout-stocked pond and continue the length of a small field. Driving in through the trees, you would never dream that such a botanical paradise awaits. A sunken garden by the house is filled with water lilies, orchids, and large, exotic blossoms, and the grounds are laced with waterfalls, trails, and Japanese-like micro gardens. The two air-conditioned guest rooms, one a double and one a king, feature elegant linens and share a bath (if both are occupied). Rates run $80–145. The common rooms are spacious and sunny with vaulted ceilings, book nooks, fine art, a granite-countered kitchen, ubiquitous windows, and a bevy of Labrador retrievers. Guests can build a bonfire by the pond, fish, swim, stay in the rustic pondside cabin, or hike wooded trails. The gardens are ideal for weddings and civil unions; light winter meals are available with advance notice. Marcia Pierce's breakfasts are scrumptious. Kids 8 and over, no pets.

& "I" **Heart of the Village Inn** (802-985-2800; 877-808-1834; heartofthe village.com), 5347 Shelburne Rd. (Rt. 7), P.O. Box 953, Shelburne 05482-0953. A handsome 1886 home that's truly in the heart of town, just steps from the Shelburne Museum. The two living rooms, dining room, and nine guest rooms (five in the inn, four in the carriage house) are all carefully, comfortably decorated. All have air-conditioning, fine linens, in-room phone, WiFi, and cable TV, as well as private bath. The most deluxe are in the carriage house: the two-room honeymoon or Webb Suite, for example, has two skylights, sofas, and a two-person whirlpool bath. The Barstow Room has wheelchair access. Rates are $150–280, with breakfast and afternoon refreshments included.

∞ & **Sinclair Inn Bed & Breakfast** (802-899-2234; 800-433-4658, sinclair innbb.com), 389 Rt. 15, Jericho 05465. This fully restored 1890 Queen Anne "painted lady" is located in a village setting within easy driving distance of Richmond and Burlington. All six of the redecorated rooms have private bath and air-conditioning, and one is

fully handicapped accessible. The lawns overflow with perennials and water lilies. Nimmie and Don Huber are your hosts. $130–170 per couple includes a full breakfast and afternoon tea. Children over 10 welcome.

∞ 🍴 **The Richmond Victorian Inn** (802-434-4410; 888-242-3362; rich mondvictorianinn.com), 191 E. Main St., P.O. Box 652, Richmond 05477. On Rt. 2 in the village of Richmond (2 miles off I-89), this exceptionally clean and classy house has five comfortable guest rooms, all with private bath, all individually decorated with antiques and equipped with down comforters, bathrobes, and good reading lights. The Hummingbird Room has both a single and double bed, and a ground-floor room has its own Jacuzzi. Children over 6 welcome. Scottish-born Frank Stewart, a former chef and caterer, runs the place with his American wife, Joyce, serving up fresh homemade breads each morning, private dinner parties (advance reservations required), and on Sunday 2–5, a three-course afternoon "cream" tea (scones, sandwiches, and sweets) for $15.95 (Sept.–Mother's Day). $119–169 for a double includes a full gourmet breakfast.

∞ 🍴 "I" **Elliot House** (802-985-2727; 800-860-4405; elliothouse.com), 5779 Dorset St., Shelburne 05482. This updated 1865 Greek Revival farmhouse adjoins 400 acres of Nature Conservancy land with hiking and cross-country ski trails and mountain views both east and west. Anne and George Voland offer three graciously furnished guest rooms, all with WiFi and private bath. Common areas include a library and sitting room with piano. Guests can wander the extensive perennial gardens, relax on the patio, or take a dip in the secluded swimming pool. Rates are $115 per night, with homemade breakfast.

✐ **Inn at Charlotte** (802-425-2934; 800-425-2934; innatcharlotte.com), 32 State Park Rd., Charlotte 05445. A contemporary home on the Rt. 7 turnoff to Mount Philo. Duker and Josefina Bower host guests in four air-conditioned rooms, all with bath, private entrance, and TV. Two have king-sized beds and cathedral ceilings and open out onto an oval pool. The Family Room comes with a queen, two singles, and a mini fridge, and a separate cottage contains a double brass bed and Mexican-tiled floor. There are tennis courts, a basketball net, and leather-sofa filled common areas; breakfast is served family-style. Burlington is a 12-mile drive. Duker's mesmerizing portraits, sculptures, and surrealistic paintings are displayed in the adjacent Mount Philo Gallery. $110–195 includes full breakfast.

✐ °↑° **By the Old Mill Stream** (802-482-3613; bythestream.com), 84 Richmond Rd., Hinesburg 05461. An 1860s farmhouse with wide floorboards and tin ceilings, but with WiFi and central air-conditioning. Kids will appreciate the pool table in the front hall and the outdoor hot tub seating eight. The upstairs and downstairs guest rooms have queen-sized beds and private baths. Grounds include gardens that border a waterfall (it powered the mill for Isaiah Dow, who built the house). $125 includes breakfast.

⊙ ✐ °↑° **Windekind Farm** (802-434-4455; windekindfarms.com), 1425 Bert White Rd., Huntington 05462. Hidden away in a 160-acre upland valley that's seen little development since it was last farmed around 1935, this is a sensational spot, expansive and remote with distant views and total quiet but for a gurgling brook. Camels Hump State Park spreads for miles, providing space for an extensive network of upland trails. Mark Smith and his Dutch-born wife Marijke live in a restored farmhouse and accommodate guests in two contemporary, comfortable, centrally heated cottages. Both are fully equipped with firewood, dishes, pots and pans, laundry, and linens. Guests bring groceries and cook their own meals. The Studio, perfect for two, is a 600-square-foot upstairs apartment that is bright and airy with a queen-sized bed, satellite TV, WiFi, a dishwasher-equipped kitchen, and mountain views. The Breidaclick Cottage, a 1,100-square-foot two-floor converted post-and-beam blacksmith shop, accommodates a family of four or two couples. Outside are numerous gardens and ponds, plus ducks, heifers, friendly dogs, endless hiking and cross-country skiing potential, and Mark's shop, where he builds historically accurate miniature steam locomotives that haul firewood, curious adults, and ecstatic children. The grounds are ideal for weddings and tented receptions. The Studio rents for $315–393 per weekend, $708–914 per week. The Breideblick is $428–620 per weekend for two, $550–750 for four.

⊙ 🐾 ✐ °↑° **Catamount's B&B** (802-878-2180; catamountoutdoor.com) 592 Governor Chittenden Rd., Williston. Built in 1796 by Thomas Chittenden, the state's first governor, this historic brick Federal has been in Lucy and Jim McCullough's family since 1873. Its antique furnishings, including 6-foot carved headboards and sepia photographs, are original to the house. The three guest rooms (one a suite) feature double beds and sleeper sofas (two queens and one twin). The suite, with a queen-sized sleeper sofa in its sitting room, has a private bath and air-conditioning. After an afternoon of hiking, mountain biking, or cross-country skiing at the adjacent Catamount Outdoor Center, guests can warm themselves by the fire or tap the WiFi in the dining room. $85–125, double occupancy, includes breakfast, with an oven-fresh treat.

⊙ 🐾 🐕 ✐ ♿ **Sleepy Hollow Inn, Ski, and Bike Center** (802-434-2283; skisleepyhollow.com), 1805 Sherman Hollow Rd., Huntington. A friendly, family-owned lodge built on 870 private acres deep in the forest off a dirt road between Richmond and Hinesburg. Six of the eight antiques-furnished guest rooms have private bath, and most have a queen-sized bed; two are equipped with two twins, one with four. There is a two-room suite, and a wheelchair-accessible unit with a wide shower, a full-sized Murphy bed, two twins, and a working fireplace. Common areas include two spacious living rooms with throbbing woodstoves, one upstairs, one down, and the fresh, hot breakfasts are served family-style. All guest rooms contain recycle bins, as the Enmans are environmental stewards: A wood pellet stove generates the heat and hot water, and drivers of hybrids, electric, or renewable energy vehicles get a free day pass. The place for parties and weddings is the 17-sided event center and attached pavilion, built in 2006 to resemble Richmond's picturesque Old Round Church. There's a swimming pond (which ices over for skating in winter) and a wood-fired sauna hut. Myriad trails lead through meadows and woods to views of Camels Hump. Closer to home you can wander the 35,000-volume Sleepy Hollow Books in the event center's basement, which specializes in used tomes on New England, Vermont, and railroads. The adventuresome might choose to trek the mile uphill to the Butternut Cabin, a woodstove-heated chalet with mountain views that sleeps 12 (no electricity or running water). $50 per night in summer, $100 in winter (for four) includes firewood and trail passes.

Lodge rooms run $105–155, including breakfast. The Green Mountain Audubon Nature Center and sugarhouse and the Birds of Vermont Museum are just a mile down the road. All ages welcome, but no pets, please.

MOTOR INNS 🐾 ✐ ♿ **Green Mountain Suites** (802-860-1212; 866-337-1616; hawthornsuitesburlington .com), 401 Dorset St. (just off Rt. 2), South Burlington 05403. Opened in 1998 by Chuck and Ralph DesLauriers, who in 2008 changed its name (from Hawthorn Suites) and made $2.5 million in renovations, this clean and airy inn with its open-timbered lobby features suites with fully equipped kitchens, separate living rooms (containing foldout couches) and bedrooms: 104 one-bedroom suites and 8 two-bedroom; some rooms include fireplaces and jet tubs. Facilities include an indoor pool, a spa/Jacuzzi, and fitness machines. Pets are welcome for $25 per night. While it's located in the heart of South Burlington's strip malls, it's just minutes from downtown Burlington, and there's a complimentary airport shuttle. $119–359 (depending on length of stay) includes a hot breakfast buffet.

Similarly equipped, priced, and situated are the **Anchorage Inn** (802-863-7000; vtanchorageinn.com), the **Best Western Windjammer Inn & Conference Center** (802-863-1125; 800-371-1125; bestwestern.com/wind jammerinn), the **Comfort Inn & Suites** (802-863-5541; 800-808-4656; innvermont.com), the **Doubletree Hotel** (802-658-0250; burlington .doubletree.com), **La Quinta Inn & Suites** (802-865-3400; lq.com), and local developer Gabe Handy's family-priced **Handy Suites Essex** at 27 Susie Wilson Rd. in Essex (802-872-5200; handysuites.com), with its 50 family-oriented units. The kids will love the heated (and very warm) indoor pool and waterslide.

♂ ⓑ **Marriott Courtyard** (802-879-0100; 800-321-2211), 177 Hurricane Lane, Williston 05495. At Exit 12 off I-89, this Marriott Courtyard, one of about four within a mile, is a known quantity with a laundry, in-room refrigerators and work desks, HBO, a whirlpool, and an exercise room. Both rooms and suites are available. Rates begin at $149 for a room with two queen beds.

∞ 🐾 ♂ ⓑ **Hampton Inn and Conference Center** (802-655-6177; 800-HAMPTON, hamptoninnburlington .com), 42 Lower Mountain View Dr. (Rt. 7 north), Colchester 05446, Exit 16 off I-89. North of Burlington, the inn offers 187 well-furnished rooms, indoor pool, whirlpool, fitness facilities, free airport shuttle, and hot breakfast buffet. Kids stay free with adult. Rates begin at $109.

🐾 ♂ **G. G. T. Tibet Inn** (802-863-7110, ggttibetinn.com), 1860 Shelburne Rd., South Burlington 05403. At least a dozen 1960s-era motels line Burlington's periphery, but this one stands out. Owner Kalsang G. G. T. (the initials stand for Gangjong Gesar Tsang), a Tibetan refugee, arrived here in 1993. He worked multiple jobs, lived frugally, and bought this two-story lodge. In 1995 the Dalai Lama gave Kalsang's innkeeping aspirations his blessing. The 21 air-conditioned rooms are clean and comfortable, with cable TV, microwave, fridge, and use of the outdoor pool. Prices are low, with discounts for seniors and families. $39–89. For meals, Pauline's is right next door (see *Dining Out*).

CAMPING ♂ **North Beach Campground** (800-571-1198, 802-865-7247; enjoyburlington.com/campground .cfm), 60 Institute Rd., Burlington. 137

shaded campsites for tents or RVs within 45 wooded acres a few minutes' walk from Burlington's largest sandy beach, with its snack bar, change rooms, and grill-equipped picnic tables. Open May–Columbus Day.

♂ 🐾 **On The Loose** (802-434-7257; 800-688-1481; otloose.com) 1035 Carse Rd., Huntington 05462. Trekking guides Beth Whiting and Bruce Hennessey rent two canvas-sided, Mongolian-style yurts year-round on their 150-acre hilltop MapleWind Farm in Huntington, about 35 miles southeast of Burlington. Inside are bunks sleeping 10, a table and chairs, a propane stove, kitchen equipment, and a woodstove. Outside is firewood, miles of nature and hiking trails, and an outhouse. $135 per night buys exclusive use.

Note: Check campvermont.com, the Web site of the Vermont Campground Association, for more information.

✳ Where to Eat

Note: Burlington has the best restaurant scene between Boston and Montreal, though many of the choicest tables are out of the downtown area. Prices given here do not include the 11 percent tax.

DINING OUT ♂ ⓑ **Inn at Shelburne Farms** (802-985-8498; shelburnefarms.org), Shelburne. Open for dinner (and breakfast) by reservation mid-May–late Oct. This turn-of-the-20th-century manor offers imaginative cuisine using home-grown ingredients in a truly magnificent setting: walls covered in fin-de-siècle silk damask from Spain, a black-and-white marble floor, and a stunning view of the sun setting over Lake Champlain and the Adirondacks. You might begin with black bass seviche and dine on grass-fed Vermont beef with charred frisée, heirloom tomato jam, and tarragon aioli ($33) or Vermont rabbit with artichoke panzanella, roasted sungolds, and baby basil ($28). Dessert might be a dark chocolate rum pot de crème with almond macaroon and chantilly cream, a sour cherry clafouti with lemon balm ice cream, or Vermont-made cheeses with poached figs and crostini. Breakfast, open to the public by reservation, is also an event: wild leek frittata with goat cheese, buttermilk pancakes with rhubarb compote and ginger whipped cream, or eggs Benedict with Vermont ham.

Café Shelburne (802-985-3939, cafe shelburne.com), 5573 Shelburne Rd. (Rt. 7), Shelburne. Open for dinner from 5:30 daily except Sun. and Mon. Located across from the Shelburne Museum, this chef-owned and -operated, authentically French bistro serves up a sophisticated European ambience and fabulous food. Quail with mushroom risotto in white wine sauce ($27), filet mignon in port wine with green peppercorn sauce ($28), and rack of lamb with caramelized onion, tomato, and eggplant tian ($28) are examples of the overall superb offerings. Chef Patrick Grangien studied chocolate making in Lyon. The dessert list is long and masterful, making this unquestionably one of the best restaurants in the state. Entrées run $20–30.

Butler's (802-764-1413, necidining .com), at the Essex Resort & Spa, 70 Essex Way (off Rt. 15), Essex Junction. Open daily, dinner only (though closed Sun. night Jan.–Mar). In the deft hands of the New England Culinary Institute, the cuisine in this elegantly informal room with high-backed, upholstered chairs is a visual as well as gustatory treat, and the service is top-notch. Menus change daily, but a typi-

cal four-course, prix fixe dinner (priced at $41–49) might start with porcini mushroom soup, ostrich carpaccio, or Grafton cheddar soufflé, and proceed to crispy skin black bass with wild rice cake, ratatouille, and tomato beurre blanc, or seared duck breast with asparagus, butternut squash mash, and sautéed mushrooms with bacon sherry cream. Elaborate desserts might include a warm pear ginger strudel or chocolate caramel cashew gateau. A *Wine Spectator* award winner with a selection of over 700 wines.

L'Amante (802-863-5200, lamante .com) 126 College St., open for dinner daily except Sun. Truly superior northern Italian cuisine in a spare, low-lit, urban decor of hardwood floors, cream-colored walls, modern art, and fresh flowers. You might start with squash blossom fritters stuffed with Taleggio and drizzled with honey and truffle oil ($11) and proceed to potato-crusted sea bass with sautéed greens and citrus beurre blanc ($25), or a mixed grill of Vermont quail, jumbo shrimp, and sweet sausage, with polenta, green beans, and whole-grain mustard ($26). The bar serves exceptional wines. Entrées $23–26.

A Single Pebble (802-865-5200; asinglepebble.com), 133 Bank St. Open nightly for dinner, weekdays for lunch. This is a rare find: a Chinese restaurant that serves the real thing. Though not himself Chinese, chef-owner Steve Bogart trained in China and returns each year for inspiration. No fried rice, egg rolls, or MSG here. Instead you get authentic Beijing fare. Chop Your Head Off Soup, for example, a savory blend of ground pork, shredded cabbage, and rice cake noodles, or Ants Climbing a Tree, a smoky-tasting blend of cellophane noodles, ground pork, black mushrooms, scallions, and tree ear fungus. All is served on fine china to the strains of classical Chinese music, and sharing is encouraged. There are numerous small dishes to choose from, like dumplings and mock eel. Entrées $16–20. Reservations essential.

Souza's Churrascaria Brazilian Steakhouse (802-864-2433; souzas .org), 131 Main St. Bring an appetite. This authentic all-you-can-eat Brazilian wood-fired barbecue restaurant (in Portuguese, *shoo-ahs-ker-EE-ah*) sends a parade of grilled meats to your table, sliced from long skewers by gaucho-like servers. Chef Kelly Q. Dietrich does supply à la carte options, but for the real thing try the black bean broth appetizer, help yourself to the 18-foot long salad bar with its 45 selections, then sit back for the rodizo, or continuous flow of (about 15) passing skewers. Had enough? Display the NO card. $38.95 includes salad bar, tropical fruit juices, and rodizo. You can have the salad bar alone for $28.95; separate entrées (steak, seafood, and vegetarian dishes) start at $18.95.

Pauline's Café & Restaurant (802-862-1081; paulinescafe.com), 1834 Shelburne Rd. (Rt. 7 south). Open daily for lunch, dinner, and Sunday brunch. It is worth braving the strip development traffic for the elegant simplicity of this longtime favorite with its enclosed outdoor patio. The subtle cuisine often features wild and local edibles, such as mushrooms, cattail shoots, sea beans, and fresh black and white truffles, all artfully presented in sensible portions. Entrées ($16–32) might be Shelburne Farms chicken breasts covered in cheddar, olive oil poached salmon, or lemon garlic chicken filled with chèvre and kissed with a garlic-lemon glaze.

The Kitchen Table Bistro (802-434-8686; thekitchentablebistro.com), 1840 W. Main St., Richmond. Dinner night-ly. Steve and Lara Atkins, both biology majors, met at the New England Culinary Institute and cut their teeth working at restaurants in California's Napa Valley. Now they operate this superlative bistro in a home that once belonged to Vermont's first governor. The offerings are fresh and healthy, the decor brick-walled and tasteful. You're likely to find free-range chicken with herb-smashed new potatoes and baby carrots ($24), grass-fed beef with an herb-Cabernet reduction and Parmesan summer squash gratin ($34), artisanal cheeses, and Vermont wild-flower honey ice cream.

Taste of Burlington (802-658-4844, tasteofburlington.com), 112 Lake St. Open nightly at 5. Chef-owner Rick Benson, a devoted Phish fan, named this spiffy eatery for one of the group's songs and was delighted when the now-disbanded rock group gave him a 200-gallon aquarium full of tropical marine life. Now it's part of the decor. The walls are penny colored, the abstract art his own doing, and the food just as creative: quail confit with arugula and forest mushroom salad, and wild mushroom and butternut squash lasagna with Alfredo sauce, just for starters. Oodles of mixed drinks, a good wine list, and scrumptious desserts. $21–33.

Trattoria Delia (802-864-5253; trattoriadelia.com), 152 St. Paul St. Open nightly 5–10. Exposed wooden beams, a roaring fire, and Italian pottery make this one of Burlington's most romantic restaurants. For over 10 years, owners Thomas and Lori Delia have refined the menu to the point that it is as authentically Italian as possible this far from Europe, introducing such things as house-made pasta, wood-grilled shrimp, and Prosciutto di Parma. Entrées range from $13.50 for spaghetti *con polpette* (veal meatballs) to $29.50 for *filetto al Barbera d'Alba* (filet mignon with white truffle butter from Alba). Reservations.

Starry Night Café (802-877-6316; starrynightcafe.com), 5371 Rt. 7, Ferrisburg. Dinner daily except Mon. and Tue. Chef-owner David Hugo is a Culinary Institute of America grad who has introduced playfully experimental Euro-Asian fare into this handcraft-filled dining room, a former cider press, which seats 26. Entrées, made from local ingredients, range from portobello stroganoff over house-made sun-dried tomato gnocchi, wilted spinach, and fried leek salad ($17) to a grilled lemon-thyme marinated cage-free chicken with local raspberry-Chambord jam, baked Brie, wilted spinach, and buttermilk mashed potatoes ($21). Desserts are all $7.50. Call ahead, because it's a 25-minute drive south of Burlington. Located among a cluster of barns and a covered bridge.

Asiana House (802-651-0818), 191 Pearl St. Superb, authentic Japanese and Korean cuisine. Reserve in advance, as this sushi destination on the corner of Pearl and North Winooski Ave. fills up fast, especially on the weekends. Regulars keep their chopsticks displayed on a wall at the front; inside, you can watch sushi chefs performing miracles with changing varieties of maki, sushi, and sashimi. A variety of artistically presented hot and cold dishes. Entrées $12.95–$17.95.

The Green Room (802-651-9669; greenroomvt.com), 86 St. Paul St. Dinner served nightly. An urban, up-and-coming eatery that uses local, organic produce and meats, if they can get them, and offers $8, $12, or $16 plates, or the larger $24 specials that change nightly. You might find crab-stuffed calamari, fennel-crusted scallops over polenta, or Asian tuna tartar with avocados. You can eat at the bar, in the main dining room, or in the lounge, which has big, comfy chairs.

EATING OUT *Note:* Thanks to Burlington's huge student population and insatiable hunger for novel cuisine, the restaurant scene is a highly varied, ever-expanding thing. Stroll up and down Church St. for an eyeful of the many options.

In Burlington

Leunig's Bistro (802-863-3759), 115 Church St. (near College St.). Open daily for brunch, lunch, and dinner. In classic bistro style, Leunig's has dark wood, gleaming coffee machines, romantic lighting, a full bar, and streetside tables for people-watching, all of which makes it Church Street's most popular establishment. The food is fresh and good, though somewhat pricey. Frequent live entertainment.

The Daily Planet (802-862-9647, dailyplanet15.com), 15 Center St. Open daily. Dinner and lighter late-night menu in the adjacent (and throbbing) bar. The atmosphere is light and airy in this solarium-style bistro on a tiny side street parallel to the main downtown pedestrian area. The All Natural Planet Burger is a favorite, and the vegetarian offerings are numerous, including the citrus caponata, which is eggplant, red plums, blood oranges, figs, and walnuts over a savory, rosemary cracked pepper waffle ($18). The menu changes as often as the art, but is always imaginative. $17–23.

Three Tomatoes Trattoria (802-660-9533, threetomatoestrattoria.com), 83 Church St., in the cellar of the old Howard Opera House on the Church St. marketplace. A busy, low-lit place with an excellent southern Italian menu, plus top-drawer, wood-fired pizzas. You might lunch on the pasta of the day, or dine on veal Marsala ($18.95) or either chicken or veal saltimbocca wrapped in prosciutto and sage and sautéed with spinach, olive oil, lemon, and parsley then topped with provolone ($16.95 for chicken, $18.95 for veal). Bad acoustics, but good atmosphere. Sidewalk tables in summer. Italian mineral water and wines, moderate prices.

Sakura Bana (802-863-1988, sakuravt .com), 2 Church St. Lunch and dinner daily. Vermont's first (but no longer its only) Japanese restaurant is still generally considered the best sushi spot in town. At lunch its soothing ambience is an oasis of calm and an appropriate setting for savoring sushi and sashimi dishes or simply deep-fried salmon served with a tangy sauce. Vegetarians will appreciate dishes like avocado, bean curd, boiled spinach, vegetable tempura, and hijiki (cooked seaweed). Lone diners appreciate the seats lining the long sushi bar; there's also a tatami room where you sit on pillows instead of chairs. Frequent sushi specials.

✒ **Sweetwater's** (802-864-9800, sweat watersvt.com), 120 Church St. (corner of College St.). Open seven days, 11:30 AM–midnight. Housed in a former and splendidly restored 1920s bank building, this is a deservedly popular spot, especially for people-watching, with its central location, airy atrium, and two-story mural. You might lunch on beer-battered fish-and-chips or a rosemary eggplant sandwich,; enjoy a Maryland crabcake, a bison burger, or chicken Gorgonzola salad. The square bar is one of Burlington's prime schmoozing spots, and the streetside tables are glassed in so you can people-watch year-round. Moderate.

🍴 **Parima Restaurant** (802-864-7917; parimathai.com), 185 Pearl St. Open daily for lunch and dinner (dinner only Sat.–Sun.). The peerless polished wood and ornate glass lamps, the legacy of a previous incarnation, Déjà Vu, has sur-

vived to make this the city's most beautiful dining interior. Parima's owners have adapted it into a romantic sanctuary serving an exhaustive selection of Thai and American dishes, with a noodle bar, an acoustic lounge for live music, and a small outdoor patio in summer. Entrées $9–20.

✒ **American Flatbread, Burlington Hearth** (802-861-2999; americanflat bread.com), 115 St. Paul St. Open daily for lunch and dinner. In the dead of winter, the wood-fired oven emanates blissful heat, though this spacious spot is popular year-round, with outdoor seating in the side courtyard. The mostly organic pizzas are made to order in as many varieties as the in-house brews on tap, and are priced $13–20.

Halvorson's Upstreet Cafe (802-658-0278), 16 Church St. Open daily for lunch, dinner, and brunch. A cozy old landmark that's expanded its basic all-American menu and added beer, wine, and nightly specials. Weather permitting, eat in the rose garden out back, or out on Church St. to people-watch. Moderate.

🍴 **Pacific Rim** (802-651-3000), 111 St. Paul St. Open daily except Sun. for lunch and dinner, this café is pan-Asian with an innovative twist. There's a good choice of hot and cold noodles, plus Korean shrimp cakes, orange chicken stir-fry, dumplings, salads, and desserts, like ginger cheesecake. Order and pick up at the counter; everything is fresh, delicious, and inexpensive.

✒ **Stone Soup** (802-862-7616), 211 College St. Open daily except Sun., all three meals. A hugely popular storefront salad bar and deli specializing in vegan and vegetarian dishes; great soups, salads, and gluten-free breads in an eclectic, natural-wood milieu. Moderate.

Cobblestone Deli & Cafe (802-865-3354; cobblestonevt.com), 152 Battery

St. Open daily, weekdays 7–3:30, Sat. 9–3:30, Sun. 10–2. A deli near the waterfront, beside the last patch of cobblestone from the days when this part of town was the city's commercial core. Pick up a breakfast bagel or a sandwich to take on the bike path or to picnic by the lake.

🍴 🍴 **Henry's Diner** (802-862-9010), 155 Bank St., off Church St. In operation since 1925, this classic diner started out in a single railroad car. Today it's expanded into two spiffy rooms with a counter and retro booth and table seating. Pancakes, clubs, burgers, hot turkey sandwiches, and Greek specialties. Breakfast and lunch.

Sadie Katz Delicatessen, (802-864-5308; sadiekatzdeli.com), 189 Bank St. The former Oasis Diner is now a bona fide Jewish deli, complete with pastrami on rye, matzoh ball soup, and footlong hot dogs. Seating is classic booths and counter stools, and limited, so if you come at noon on Saturday, be prepared to wait.

🍴 **Nectar's** (802-658-4771; liveat nectars.com), 188 Main St. A basic meat-and-potatoes supper spot. Phish fans will want to case the dance floor upstairs (Club Metronome), where the group got its start.

🍴 🍴 **Bove's Cafe** (802-864-6651, boves.com), 68 Pearl St. Closed Sun. and Mon. Dinner served Tue.–Sat. till 8:45; lunch Fri.–Sat. Burlington's oldest restaurant, started by an Italian American family after the war and growing into a spaghetti-sauce empire. Narrow booths, Elvis songs on the Wurlitzer, and heaping plates of steaming spaghetti, plus fresh bread, terrific antipasta salads, and some of the lowest prices in town. You won't go hungry here. Full bar.

The Vermont Pub and Brewery (802-865-0500; vermontbrewery.com), 144 College St. Open daily for lunch,

dinner, and bar food. Despite the modern building, there's an old beer-hall atmosphere (tile floor, huge bar, brass), specializing in ales, lagers, and great ginger ale brewed on the premises. The vast menu has something for everyone, including Cornish pasties, cock-a-leekie pie, bratwurst, and fish-and-chips. The prices can't be beat.

India House (802-862-7800), 207 Colchester Ave. Lunch and dinner daily. This warm, reliable restaurant serves traditional curries, tandoori chicken, and the like, plus puffy poori bread, in an out-of-the-way spot near Centennial Park and the University of Vermont campus. Moderate.

Penny Cluse Cafe (802-658834; pennycluse.com), 169 Cherry St. Innovative, healthy, hearty breakfasts and lunches in an atmosphere of art and natural wood. Famous for black beans, polenta, great biscuits. One of Burlington's best breakfast spots, but come early or stand in line.

Magnolia Breakfast and Lunch Bistro (802-846-7446), 1 Lawson Lane near the corner of College and St. Paul streets. A pleasant brick-walled basement space with gleaming woodwork, high ceilings, a brisk bar, and vegetable-rich cuisine, much of it organic and fair trade. Open daily.

🍴 **City Market** (802-863-3659; city-market.coop), 82 S. Winooski Ave., is the city's member-owned and frankly impressive food co-op, located downtown in the former police department. Open daily till 11 PM, its self-serve offerings range from vegan to African samosas, satay, and sushi.

On the waterfront
🍴 **The Ice House** (802-864-1800), 171 Battery St. Open for lunch and dinner daily, with seasonal open-air decks overlooking the ferry slip and marina. This was a pioneer of the city's

upscale restaurant scene, a 19th-century icehouse with massive stone walls and timbers. American regional dishes feature steak, seafood, and Vermont lamb. Kids' menu; brunch served Mother's Day–mid-Oct.

⚓ **Shanty on the Shore** (802-864-0238), 181 Battery St. Open daily 11–11. Handy to the ferry with spectacular lake views; a good place for seafood platters, crabcakes, and sea-sonal crab and lobster specials. Children's menu.

Breakwater Cafe & Grill (802-864-9804), King Street Dock. Part of the LCTC ferry complex, an informal dockside space serving sandwiches, fried baskets, soups, and salads all day and evening in summer; frequent live (and loud) music.

Splash (802-658-2244), at the Boathouse (bottom of College St.). Open

---

WINOOSKI'S ASIAN BOOM

Burlington's restaurant scene has grown exponentially in the 20-odd years since the New England Culinary Institute (known by its acronym, NECI) started turning out trained (and talented) chefs. But the city's culinary direction took an unexpected detour in 2005, when a small Thai eatery opened up in the Essex Shoppes & Cinema mall. Tiny Thai proved so popular that it quickly added a second location in downtown Winooski, the working-class suburb on Burlington's eastern flank. The recipe was simple: Offer fresh ingredients, novel flavors, and rock-bottom prices, and lines will curl out the door. They did; within a year, Asian eateries were popping up on every corner. They filled up Winooski and then started opening in out-of-the-way sections of Burlington. The majority are ultra-casual, takeout-amenable family operations with none of the upscale crystal and linen of the classic NECI-run, Church Street venues, but standing room only on most nights. All but a few serve lunch and dinner seven days a week. These are our favorites:

🍜 ♿ **Tiny Thai** (802-655-4888) at 24 Main St., on the Winooski roundabout. The little place that started the craze. The irrepressibly fresh, often-changing menu is classic Thai and reliably scrumptious.

🍜 ♿ **Pho Hong** (802-865-8031), 325 N. Winooski Ave., Burlington. Sensational spring rolls, soups, rice and noodle plates, stir-fries, and chef's specials in a converted bus depot.

🍜 **Pho Dang** (802-655-0707), 215 Main St., Winooski. A teensy, unpretentious storefront north of the roundabout serving classic Vietnamese noodle soups, entrées, and delectable spring rolls.

🍜 ♿ **Vietnam Restaurant** (802-872-9998), 137 Rt. 15 in Essex Junction. Daily (except Sun.). A dinerlike eatery in a small strip mall, one of the first to serve Vietnamese fare, and expanding like the rest (it has a second location at 62 Church St. in Burlington). Laid-back, inexpensive, delicious.

Memorial Day–Columbus Day, all meals. Sandwiches, burgers, and hefty salads on dockside tables with umbrellas.

The Skinny Pancake (802-540-0188), 60 Lake St., at College St. The inspiration of three Middlebury College grads, this French-style crêperie is a block from the waterfront, with outdoor seating. Sweet and savory crêpes ranging $7–9.

In Winooski

❦ ✎ **Papa Frank's** (802-655-2433), 13 W. Center St. Open for lunch and dinner daily. A red-sauce Italian neighborhood restaurant that caters to families and students. Good for pizza, calzones, and classic dishes. The vegetables are fresh, and garlic bread comes with your order. Just a block west of Main St. (heading north over the Winooski River, take your first left, first right, and park).

Sneakers (802-655-9081; sneakersbistro.com), 36 Main St. Open daily 7–3. This minuscule bistro serves such an exceptional Sunday brunch that the line winds out the door. The eggs Benedict is delectable, the pancakes huge and fluffy; there's lots of fresh fruit and the orange juice is freshly squeezed. Go early, or leave your name and number, and they'll call when a table opens up.

In Essex Junction and Colchester

Libby's Blue Line Diner (802-655-0343), 1 Roosevelt Ave., Rt. 77, Colchester, with its tile floor, marble counters, and great views, Libby's attracts itinerant diner buffs and area fans for breakfast, lunch, and dinner daily. Try the banana bread French toast.

Along Williston Road (Route 2) to Richmond

Silver Palace (802-864-0125), 1216 Williston Rd., South Burlington. Open daily for lunch and dinner (dinner only on Sun.). Hidden behind Burger King in the commercial sprawl that is Williston Rd., this Chinese restaurant is a cut above. The cuisine is artfully prepared, served on white tablecloths with fine glassware by a doting owner. Pricier than other Chinese eateries, but worth it.

✎ ⚅ **Old Brick Café and Bakery** (802-872-9599; oldbrickcafe.com), 7921 Williston Rd. (Rt. 2), center of Williston village. Serves breakfast and lunch daily, and abundant weekend brunches. Closed Mon. Soups, sandwiches, cappuccino, and fresh-baked pastries in a renovated brick home with a sunny interior. Outdoor deck in summer.

❦ **Toscana Café Bistro** (802-434-3148), 27 Bridge St., Richmond. Open daily (except Mon.) for lunch and dinner, Sun. brunch. Chef-owners Jon and Lucie Fath have created an Old World, Mediterranean feel in a small Vermont village, serving crabcakes, crispy artichokes, and wild mushroom ravioli. For dinner, try the maple, onion, and pecan-crusted salmon, or the butternut squash ravioli. Moderate.

❦ **Sonoma Station** (802-434-5949; sonomastation.com), 13 Jolin Court (off Bridge St.), Richmond. Open for dinner Tue.–Sat. Reservations suggested. Chef-owner Monica Lamay, formerly of Leunig's, is fusing new flavors at this casual, pine-floored country bistro housed in a vintage-1854 feed store. You might begin with the crab and avocado napoleon with cilantro vinaigrette ($8.50), then dine on coriander-crusted pork with garlic mashed potatoes, green beans, and bing cherry port demiglaze ($17), or black bean and cheddar ravioli with crispy achiote tempura shrimp, grilled pineapple, baby arugula, and roasted jalapeño cream sauce ($19). Entrées $17–20.

On the Rise Bakery (802-434-7787), 39 Esplanade St. (corner of Bridge St.), Richmond. This big red barnlike building offers daily lunch specials incorporating fresh-baked breads, organic coffee, bagels, pastries, and sweets, all of it local and made from scratch.

Al's French Frys (802-862-9203; alsfrenchfrys.com), 1251 Williston Rd., South Burlington. Really, that's how it's spelled. Open daily 10:30 AM–midnight. Burlington's own bona fide fast-food joint since 1944, a long-enduring, spanking-clean classic in art-deco-inspired, neon-splashed digs. Fries, burgers, dogs, and shakes, with a playground out back, picnic tables, and ice cream cones, sundaes, and creemees dispensed from a side window as long as weather permits.

On Shelburne Road (Route 7 south)

The Bearded Frog (802-985-9877; thebeardedfrog.com) on Rt. 7 at 5247 Shelburne Rd. (the former Shelburne Inn). French-born Michel Mahé's Vergennes eatery (the Black Sheep Bistro) was so successful that he opened a second restaurant here and named it for himself (he wears a beard). The decor is casual and sophisticated; the eclectic and frequently changing menu might include roast duck breast with mushroom bread pudding and rhubarb puree, hangar steak chimichurri, or bok choy wrapped haddock with lemongrass broth and udon noodles. Open daily. Entrées in the $20 range.

Bistro Sauce (802-985-2830; bistrosauce.com), 97 Falls Rd., by the Shelburne Shopping Plaza just east of Rt. 7, open daily for lunch and dinner, Sun. for brunch. Fresh, abundant, tasty fare in a contemporary ambience of celadon-hued walls and natural-wood booths. Recent offerings included braised rabbit with prosciutto, tomatoes, and white wine over tagliatelle, and salmon braised with artichokes, white wine, and tomato sauce. Entrees $18–22.

La Villa (985-2596, lavillabistro.com) on the right, in a tiny mall some 5 miles south of Burlington at 3762 Shelburne Rd., Shelburne. Surprisingly fresh and tasty Mediterranean fare in a cozy, Tuscan atmosphere. Chef-owner Adam Spell is New England Culinary Institute trained, and it shows. Pizza, pasta, sumptuous salads, fresh-baked breads, grilled specialties, and kids' menu, all affordable. Open nightly for dinner; daily (except Sun.) for lunch.

Koto Japanese Steakhouse (802-660-8976), 792 Shelburne Rd. (Rt. 7). Open daily for lunch and dinner. A traditional hibachi house with knife-juggling waiters, sushi bar, goldfish swimming in an aisle-side aquarium, and delicious lunches served in partitioned Japanese boxes. Can be expensive.

Harrington's (802-985-2000; harringtonham.com), 5597 Shelburne Rd. Across from the Shelburne Museum, a good bet if you can snag one of the few tables and don't mind the Styrofoam at the excellent deli here. Daily specialties include the "World's Best Ham Sandwich" (Harrington's is known for its corn-smoked ham); also smoked turkey, quiche, homemade soups, sausage chili made with Harrington's own pork sausages, and chocolate mousse.

In Hinesburg

Papa Nick's (802-482-6050), 10997 Rt. 116, midtown. Open daily, all meals. A friendly, midpriced family restaurant with a diverse menu and Greek accents, including daily specials like moussaka and chicken souvlaki. Homemade pies, ice cream, and creemees in the summer. Kid's menu.

🦞 🍃 **Good Times Café** (802-482-4444) 10805 Main St. (Rt. 116), where the road takes a sharp left. Lunch and dinner daily except Mon., including everything from Cajun to East Indian. Live music on Wed. night (tickets sometimes required). The homemade pizza here is great, as are the soups, stews, salads, lasagnas, and chana masala. Nightly dinner specials. $6–9.

CAFFEINE/SNACKS

In Burlington

Mirabelle's (802-658-3074; mirabelles cafe.com), 198 Main St. Burlington's most delightful bakery and lunch spot, the fruit of two culinary institute graduates who serve up a smorgasbord of teas, coffees, mouthwatering pastries, daily lunch specials, soups, salads, and light fare. Try the Ploughman's Lunch, a sampling of salads with a kaleidoscope of fresh fruit. Open daily, 7 to about 5.

Dobra Tea (802-951-2424; dobratea .com), 80 Church St. (entrance on Bank St.). Open 11–11, Sun. noon–10 The first North American branch of what started as a Czech teahouse chain, this temple to tea connoisseurs offers 60 varieties from 10 countries, all served as they would be in their native land. Savor Ilati, a rich, black tea from Nepal poured into square ceramic cups; or Tung Ting from Taiwan, in small, shallow cups. Each pot is freshly brewed at the precise temperature and time required. In the back you can shed your shoes and lounge on pillows, the way a tea drinker would in Uzbekistan.

⁽ᵀ⁾ **New Moon** (802-383-1505; new moonvt.com), 150 Cherry St. An urban, brick-walled café a block from the north end of Church St., serving the freshest of sandwiches, lattes, and fruit drinks (but no alcohol). WiFi, a working fireplace, and comfy chairs make it a good place to sit over a laptop. Owned by the Schonbek chandelier people, hence the sparkling light fixtures. Weekdays 7:30–7, Sun. 9–5. Closed Sat.

Sapa Coffeehouse (802-318-4888), 9 Center St. Open 8 AM–10 PM Mon.–Sat., 11–6 on Sun. The place to come for Vietnamese-style coffee, with an abundance of loose teas, juices, and desserts ranging from chocolates to dried fruits. Owner Khuyen Tran has turned this former army-navy store into a peaceful sanctuary reminiscent of teahouses in her native Vietnam.

Muddy Waters (802-658-0466), 184 Main St., just up from Church St., open every day, all day. Excellent coffee, homemade desserts, vegan specials, smoothies, beer, and wine by the glass in a dimly lit, brick-walled den with sofas, lots of reading material, and earnest conversation. Bring a book.

Uncommon Grounds (802-865-6227), 42 Church St. They roast their own here, offering the largest selection in town along with teas and Italian-syrup-based drinks. Down a piece of chocolate cake while perusing the day's papers, which are laid out on wooden holders. Outside seating in summer.

Speeder and Earl's (speederand earls.com). A slim counter and coffee bar downstairs at 104 Church St. (802-860-6630), and a zany shop at 412 Pine St. (802-658-6016), same complex as **Fresh Market**, a specialty foods store with its own deli. Try the popular "clockwork orange," mocha with orange zest and almonds.

Drink (802-860-9463; come2drink .com), 135 St. Paul St. Closed Sun.–Mon. The city's sole wine bar, offering several varieties by the glass, plus a full bar, house-infused vodkas, light fare, and leather sofas. The adjacent store, Wineworks, offers wine tastings each Saturday.

Ben & Jerry's (802-862-9620), 36 Church St. This scoop shop isn't the original location, but the world's legendary ice cream makers did get their start a few blocks away (on the southwest corner of St. Paul and College streets).

✳ Entertainment

Note: For current arts and entertainment in Burlington, call the **Burlington City Arts line** at 802-865-7166, or check *Seven Days* (sevendaysvt.com), a free weekly publication that's available everywhere around town.

MUSIC Vermont Mozart Festival performances (802-862-7352; vtmozart.com), 125 College St., Burlington. Summer concerts in various settings—on ferries, at the Shelburne Museum and/or Shelburne Farms, at the Basin Harbor Club, in churches. Winter chamber series.

Vermont Symphony Orchestra (802-864-5741; 800-VSO-9293; vso .org), 2 Church St., Suite 19, Burlington. One of the country's first statewide philharmonics presents a five-concert Chittenden County series at the Flynn Center; outdoor summer pops at Shelburne Farms and elsewhere.

St. Michael's College concerts (802-655-2000), in Colchester, feature jazz, pop, and classical productions.

Burlington Choral Society (802-878-5919). A volunteer, 100-voice choir presents several concerts a year.

The Discover Jazz Festival (Flynn box office: 802-86-FLYNN; discover jazz.com), Burlington, 10 days in early June, a jazz extravaganza that fills city parks, clubs, restaurants, ferries.

Battery Park Summer Concert Series, Burlington, Thu. and Sun. nights.

THEATER Flynn Center for the Performing Arts (802-86-FLYNN; flynncenter.org), 153 Main St., Burlington. The city's prime stage for music and live performance is a refurbished art deco movie house, now home to plays, musical comedies, jazz concerts, and lectures, in addition to movies. Constantly evolving, it houses the Amy Tarrant Art Gallery and several smaller performances spaces as well.

Royall Tyler Theater (802-656-2094; uvmtheater.org), University Place, on the University of Vermont campus, Burlington, stages an eclectic, top-notch seasonal repertory of classic and contemporary plays.

Main Street Landing Performing Arts Center (802-864-7999; main streetlanding.com), 60 Lake St., Burlington. A nonprofit, independently run complex that acts as a forum for local production groups. The neo-Victorian brick complex facing the waterfront houses a 136-seat theater and a film presentation room; a crêperie, The Skinny Pancake, operates downstairs.

St. Michael's College Theater Department (802-654-2000, smcvt .edu), Winooski, presents two major productions, fall and spring; also an excellent summer playhouse series (802-654-2281).

Lane Series (802-656-4455; uvm.edu/laneseries) sponsors major musical and theatrical performances around Burlington fall through spring.

DRIVE-IN ☙ Sunset Drive-In (802-862-1800; sunsetdrivein.com), Porter's Point Rd., Rt. 127 off North Ave.,

Colchester. It's for real: three screens, a snack bar, mini golf, and a kiddie playground.

MUSICAL VENUES For jazz, blues, rock, and dance clubs, check out these nightspots, all in Burlington: **Nectar's** (802-658-4771), 188 Main St., and above it, **Club Metronome** (802-865-4563). **Red Square Bar and Grill** (802-859-8909) offers frequent nightly music. **Ri Ra** (802-860-9401), an Irish bar at 123 Church St. with interiors imported from the Old Country, has live bands Thu. and Sat., karaoke on Mon., The **Thai Bar at Parima** (802-864-7917) has music Thu.–Sat.

Higher Ground (802-654-8888), 1214 Williston Rd., South Burlington, is the place to hit the dance floor.

❋ Selective Shopping

DOWNTOWN MARKETPLACES
The Church Street Marketplace. Nearly 100 stores, restaurants, and services line four blocks of Church Street, nicely paved, landscaped, closed to traffic, and enlivened by seasonal arts shows, weekend festivals, sidewalk cafés, and wandering entertainers. Park at a city-owned garage for a two-hour discount. Parking is free all day Sunday at the Burlington Town Center garage, accessible from Pine and Bank streets or from Cherry Street.

Pine Street area. There's a small yet interesting cluster of businesses on Pine St. between Flynn Ave. and Kilburn St., just south of the Vermont Transit terminal. Parking is never a problem. Highlights include Four Corners of the Earth lunch deli, Fresh Market/Cheese Outlet deli and café, Burlington Futon Co., Great Harvest Bread Company, Speeder and Earl's Coffee Roastery and Espresso Bar,

Speaking Volumes used-book store, Myer's Bagel factory, Ribbecke Stained Glass, Recycle North used household (and construction) goods, and Lake Champlain Chocolates Factory and café. A number of small crafts businesses are tucked behind Speeder and Earl's, and there are two lighting shops, The Lamp Shop and Conant Metal & Light, with its delightful selection of unusual chandeliers, lamps, thermometers, and brass objects.

Burlington Town Center. This vast, mostly underground indoor agora is linked to a parking garage and Macy's; its 80 mostly upscale stores stock just about everything, starting with a minuscule Starbucks café and a few food stands.

Outside Burlington
University Mall (802-863-1066), Dorset St., off Williston Rd. (I-89, Exit 14E), South Burlington. Your basic shopping mall with 70 stores; Kohl's, Sears, Bonton, and JCPenney are the anchors. Across Dorset is the **Blue Mall**, with less well-known shops and restaurant chains. The **Essex Shoppes & Cinema Factory Outlets** (802-657-2777), Rts. 15 and 289 in Essex, includes Polo Ralph Lauren, Jones New York, Levi's, Jockey, and Bali, plus a cinema complex.

ART GALLERIES **Fire House Art Gallery** (802-865-7166; burlingtoncity arts.com/firehousegallery), 149 Church St., Burlington, open weekdays 9–5, weekends noon–5. Pick up a copy of the *First Friday Art Trolley Tours* pamphlet guide. The trolley runs only first Fridays of each summer month, but the map is a good gallery locator any day. In Shelburne, The **Furchgott Sourdiffe Gallery** (802-985-3848), 86 Falls Rd., has rotating shows and does restoration and framing. **Pine Street**

Art Works (802-863-8100; pinestreet artworks.com), 404 Pine St., a mix of fine art, furniture, artifacts, reproductions, and funk, with changing shows. Open Tue.–Sat. 11–5. **215 College** (802-863-3662; 215college.blog spot.com), 215 College St., Suite 201, is an artists' cooperative in an upstairs space a block from Church St. Changing exhibits range from classic landscape to avant-garde; open weekend afternoons. Be sure to check out the iconoclastic exhibits at the **Amy Tarrant Gallery** (open Sat. 10–4) in the lobby of the Flynn Center for the Performing Arts at 153 Main St., and down the hill the **Katharine Montstream Studio and Gallery** (802-862-8752; kmmstudio.com), in Union Station, 1 Main St. Open daily except Sun. More than most, the work of this native-born watercolorist and oil painter perfectly depicts the lake and mountain landscapes of the Burlington waterfront and downtown area in greeting cards, prints, and paintings, as does the architectural stained glass of **Lawrence Ribbecke** (802-658-3425), whose shop at 377 Pine St. features over 500 types of glass (open Tue.–Fri. 10–6, Sat. 10–1). Another favorite is outsider artist **Dug Nap** (802-860-1386; dugnap.com), whose animals and locals evoke a dark humor reminiscent of Gary Larsen's *The Far Side*. Nap shows his work by appointment at his studio, which is only a block south of City Hall at 184 Church St.

ANTIQUES SHOPS Authentica (802-310-0096) in Charlotte (call for directions). Lydia Clemmons sells museum-quality African antiques and crafts drawn from every corner of the continent, ranging from baskets to calabashes, jewelry, woodenware, sculpture, fabrics, drums, and masks. Thu.–Sat. 2–6 PM.

Mason Brothers Architecturals and Antiques (802-879-4221; greatsalvage .com), which merged with Burlington's Architectural Salvage, is at 11 Maple St. in Essex Junction. The place to explore vintage artifacts salvaged from old houses, such as crystal doorknobs, claw-foot tubs, marble sinks, and stained-glass windows. Mon.–Sat. 9–5.

Champlain Valley Antiques Center (802-985-8116), 4067 Shelburne Rd., Shelburne. Tom Cross has an ever-changing collection of Vermont furniture, folk art, crocks and jugs, and historical items. Daily 10–5.

✐ ❀ **Upstairs Antiques** (802-859-8966), 207 Flynn Ave., Burlington. Open daily, 10–6. Dave Robbins offers a hodgepodge of collectibles, from furniture to books to housewares.

BOOKSTORES

In Burlington
Barnes & Noble (802-864-8001), 102 Dorset St., is a two-story book department store in South Burlington, and **Borders Books** (802-865-2711) is at 29 Church St. **Crow Bookshop** (802-862-0848, crowbooks.com), 14 Church St., has a good selection of new and used discounted books. **Speaking Volumes** (802-540-0107; speakingvolumes vt.com) is Austrian-born Norbert Ender's two-story warehouse with over 30,000 used and rare titles, plus a vast vinyl collection, antiques, and collectibles (ask about his 600 paperweights). At 377 Pine St., in the back. Open daily 10–5, Sun. 10–3.

Elsewhere
✐ **Flying Pig Children's Books** (802-985-3999; flyingpigbooks.com). Former teachers Josie Leavitt and Elizabeth Bluemle have created an award-winning bookstore with close to 40,000 titles for kids and adults.

Housed in the former Shelburne Inn at 5247 Shelburne Rd.

Phoenix Books (802-872-7111; phoenixbooks.biz), 21 Essex Way, #407, an independent bookstore with a café, has a fine selection of popular (and kids') titles, and serves wine and cappuccino. In the Essex Shoppes & Cinema mall in Essex. Open 10–8, Sun. 11–6.

Sleepy Hollow Books (802-434-2283), 1805 Sherman Hollow Road, Huntington. Some 35,000 tomes, with emphasis on New England and on railroading, in a replica of an old round barn. By appointment. See page 465.

CRAFTS SHOPS

In Burlington

Frog Hollow on the Marketplace (802-863-6458; froghollow.org), 86 Church St., is a branch of the Vermont State Craft Center of Middlebury, a showcase for fine things crafted in the state, from furniture and art glass to handwoven scarves, sheepskin hats, photography, woodware, and jewelry of every sort.

Jane Koplewitz Collection (802-658-3447; janekoplewitz.com), 34 Church St., beautifully crafted handmade wedding rings and jewelry.

Bennington Potters North (800-205-8033; benningtonpotters.com), 127 College St., sells kitchenware, home furnishings, glass, woodenware, and the ever-enduring Bennington Pottery. A good selection of seconds in the basement.

Outside Burlington

The Vermont Gift Barn (802-658-7684; vermontgiftbarn.com), 1087 Williston Rd., South Burlington. An overview of Vermont-made products, from specialty foods and weavings to jewelry, Bennington Pottery, furniture,

fine art prints, and Simon Pearce glass. Open daily 9–9, Sunday 10–5.

George Scatchard Lamps (800-643-5267, gslamps.com), P.O. Box 71, Underhill. George Scatchard has been making pottery for over 40 years out of a converted barn, now a contemporary, weatherworn showroom for his simple but multiple-shaped, natural-colored lamps. Seconds at reduced prices. Open weekdays 8:30–4:30, Sat. 9:30–4:30, June–Dec. Located between Underhill Flats and Cambridge.

FARMS Vermont Wildflower Farm (802-425-3641), Rt. 7, Charlotte (5 miles south of the Shelburne Museum). Open Apr.–Oct., daily 10–5. Paths lead through 6 acres of wildflowers in fields and woodland settings with flowers and trees labeled. There's a large gift shop and "the largest wildflower seed center in the East."

Charlotte Village Winery (802-425-4599; charlottevillagewinery), 3968 Greenbush Rd., Charlotte (from Rt. 7 go west on Ferry Rd. to the Charlotte village store, then left onto Greenbush Rd.). A newly hatched winemaking operation with a viewing deck overlooking acres of pick-your-own blueberry fields. Free wine tastings daily in summer, 11–5.

Shelburne Vineyard (802-985-8222; shelburnevineyard.com) on Rt. 7 (just south of the Shelburne Museum). Open daily in summer, 11–5. Taste nine wine varieties for a $2 fee that includes the glass. Tours explain the winemaking process; tables and chairs overlook undulating vines with the lake in the distance. The on-site shop includes Vermont edibles and such novelties as wine racks made from antlers.

FOOD AND DRINK Lake Champlain Chocolates (802-864-1807;

lakechamplainchocolates.com), 750 Pine St., Burlington. Open seven days. The home of the American Truffle and other pricey delectables discounts some of its premium chocolates. Tours available weekdays 9–2, on the hour. A café (flavored coffees, hot chocolate drinks, chocolate ice creams, and more) is open daily 9–6, Sun. noon–5. You can also indulge at the **factory store** and café at 63 Church St. (802-862-5185).

Snowflake Chocolates (802-899-3373), 81 Rt. 15A, Jericho Corners. Bob and Martha Pollak's handcrafted chocolates are so good. Try the dark, liqueur-laced truffles. Their downtown shop is at 150 Dorset St. in the Blue Mall in South Burlington (802-863-8306). Open daily 10–5.

Fresh Market (802-863-3968; 800-447-1205), 400 Pine St., Burlington. Formerly the Cheese Outlet, this is the best deli in town. The shelves groan with local and imported cheeses, gourmet jams and chocolates, foodie magazines, wines, fresh-baked pies and pastries, beautiful produce, and a case loaded with scrumptious olive and mozzarella combinations, freshly made gourmet salads and roasted meats, and other tempting concoctions. A dining area provides a self-serve café with hot drinks and made-to-order sandwiches so you can eat your purchases on the spot. Open daily 8–7, Sun. 10–5.

The Great Harvest Bread Company next door at 382 Pine St. (802-660-2733) also provides a sandwich-ordering and eating area for its peerless hearty loaves and fruit-filled pastries. Try the Hi-5 fiber with flax, oat bran, millet, and other healthy grains. Open weekdays 7–6, Sat. 8–5, closed Sun.

Magic Hat Brewing Company (802-658-BREW; magichat.net), 5 Bartlett Bay Rd., South Burlington (turn off Rt. 7 at the Jiffy Lube). An expanding microbrewery offering free tours and samples in summer, daily 10–6 , Sun. noon–5. Retail store on site.

Also see *Farms*.

Note: The **Saturday Farmer's Market** in City Hall Park (8:30–2:30 summer through fall) is a wonderful place to stroll with the kiddies past artful pies, plants, fruits, cheeses, breads, and veggies, along with African samosas, honey meads, and Tibetan takeout. At the back are crafts, jewelry, clothes, and art.

SPORTS STORES Burton Snowboards (802-660-3200; burton.com), 80 Industrial Parkway (near Oakledge Park), Burlington. Open Mon.–Fri. 9–8, Sun. 11–6. The factory's flagship store and factory outlet for Vermont's name-brand snow- and skateboards and gear.

The Outdoor Gear Exchange (802-860-0190; graex.com), 152 Cherry St., Burlington. Used and new outdoor sporting equipment: cross-country skiing, snowshoeing, rock-climbing, hiking, camping. and backpacking gear. It's rock-climbing central.

The Ski Rack (800-882-4530; skirack .com), 85 Main St., Burlington. This combined store features high-performance sailboards, gives lessons, and offers rentals. It's also a major source of cycling, running, in-line skate, and ski gear and wear, plus camping equipment.

Climb High (802-865-0900; climb high.com), 191 Bank St., Burlington. Hiking, biking, rock climbing, camping, cross-country skiing—you name it, this store has the gear for it, plus quick and reasonable repairs.

North Star Sports (802-863-3832, northstarsports.net), 100 Main St., Burlington. Sells, rents, and repairs bikes of all sorts, plus skis, snowshoes, and other sporting equipment.

VINTAGE CLOTHING AND FURNISHINGS Old Gold (802-864-7786), 180 Main St., is a fun and funky store with the most bizarre window displays around. **Pam's Place** (802-863-1461), 77 Main St., stocks classics, and **Battery Street Jeans** (802-865-6223), 7 Marble Ave., offers more grungy but cool clothing. **Recycle North** (appliances, furniture, books) at 266 Pine St., and its salvaged building supplies branch across the street (have someone direct you), is a nonprofit with a huge supply of recycled housewares that also provides job training in appliance repair. All are in downtown Burlington. At **The Exchange** (802-878-3848), 167 Pearl St. (Rt. 15), Essex Junction, you're apt to find Donna Karan and Ralph Lauren. This used clothing shop, probably the best in the state, has fabulous stuff, but it's also higher priced.

MORE SPECIAL STORES

In Burlington
Peace and Justice Store (802-863-8326; pjcvt.org), 21 Church St., run by the city's active Peace and Justice Center, a source of alternative publications and third-world-crafted items—jewelry, cards, clothing—all purchased from wholesalers committed to nonexploitation and social justice. The bulletin board is also worth checking. Open daily 10–6 (later on weekends), Sun. noon–5.

Gardener's Supply (802-660-3505; gardeners.com), 128 Intervale Rd. One of the largest catalog seed and garden suppliers in New England, with a retail store and nursery adjacent to demonstration gardens along the Winooski River in Burlington's Intervale.

Apple Mountain (802-658-6452; applemountain.net), 30 Church St., is a Vermont products gift and food shop; on the touristy side, but fun. Socks,

ceramics, jewelry, scents, books, and more. Open daily 9–9, Sun. 10–6. Will ship.

Purple Shutter Herbs (802-865-4372; purpleshutter.com), 7 W. Canal St. in Winooski. Laura Brown's emporium is the local source for culinary, medicinal, and cosmetic herbs and tinctures, plus gifts, teas, books, cosmetics, and cards with a botanical theme.

In the Charlotte–Shelburne area
Horsford Nursery (802-425-2811;, horsfordnursery.com), 2111 Greenbush Rd., (turn at the sign on Rt. 7), Charlotte. A 100-year-old farm worth a visit just to roam the bounty of blooming flowers, perennials, and the two antique glass greenhouses.

Shelburne Farms Gift Shop and Visitor Center (802-985-8442), open daily year-round 9–5 (10–5 in the off-season; see a full description of what this place is about under *Museums and Attractions*). The store features the prizewinning cheddar cheeses made from the milk of the estate's own Brown Swiss herd. A variety of Vermont products is also stocked.

Harrington's, Rt. 7, across from the Shelburne Museum, Shelburne, has been known for years for its delectable (and expensive) corncob-smoked hams, bacon, turkey, pork chops, and other goodies. The shop also displays cheeses, maple products, griddlecake mixes, jams, fruit butters, relishes, baked goods, wines, and coffees. Harrington's headquarters (Rt. 2, Richmond) include a smaller store.

The Shelburne Country Store (802-985-3657; shelburnecountrystore.com), 29 Falls Rd. (Rt. 7), Shelburne, encloses several gift galleries under the same roof—a sweets shop, cards, foods, housewares, lamp shades, and more.

◊ **The Vermont Teddy Bear Factory Store** (802-985-3001; 800-829-BEAR), 6655 Shelburne Rd. (Rt. 7), Shelburne (see *For Families*), is immense.

✳ Special Events

February: **Burlington Winter Festival**, Waterfront Park—dogsled rides, snow and ice sculptures (802-864-0123). Annual **Burlington Penguin Plunge**, Waterfront Park (penguin plunge.org).

Saturday before Lent: **Magic Hat Mardi Gras**—a parade and block party on the Church Street Marketplace.

March: **Vermont Flower Show** at the Sheraton Hotel in South Burlington—three days of color and fragrance mark the end of winter.

May: **Lilac Sunday** at Shelburne Museum (802-985-3346)—a festival of 19th-century food and games when the museum's many lilac bushes are in peak bloom.

Early June: **Arts Alive Festival of Fine Art** (802-864-1557; artsalivevt .com)—local shops and restaurants fill up with Vermont art. **Discover Jazz Festival** (802-863-7992; discoverjazz .com)—for nine days the entire city of Burlington becomes a stage for more than 200 musicians (see *Entertainment*). **Lake Champlain International Fishing Derby**—for details about registration and prizes, go to lciderby.com.

Late June: **Green Mountain Chew Chew** at Waterfront Park, Burlington—a three-day food festival featuring more than 50 restaurants; continuous family entertainment. **Vermont Quilt Festival** (802-872-0034; vqf.org), New England's oldest and largest quilting event, at the Essex Junction Fairgrounds on Rt. 15.

July 3: Gala **Independence Day celebrations** on the Burlington waterfront—fireworks over the lake with live bands in Battery Park, children's entertainment, a parade of boats, and blessing of the fleet. **Vermont Brewer's Festival**—local microbreweries ply their stuff under tents at Waterfront Park. **Ferrari Street Fest**—Italian sports cars take up position on Church St. for passersby to admire.

Mid-July through mid-August: **Champlain Valley Folk Festival**, a weekend-long concert featuring local and international folk musicians. The **Vermont Mozart Festival** offers performances in various locations, including Shelburne Farms and Lake Champlain ferries (see *Entertainment*).

Late July, early August: **Vermont Quilters Festival**, New England's largest, at the Champlain Valley Fair Exposition grounds in Essex Junction (802-485-7092; vqf.org).

Mid-August: **The Shelburne Craft Fair** at Shelburne Farms features dozens of exhibitors. **Latino Festival** on the Burlington waterfront is a weekend of Latin musical events.

Late August: **Champlain Valley Exposition**, Essex Junction Fairgrounds—a traditional county fair with livestock and produce exhibits, trotting pig races, midway, rides, cotton candy—the works.

September: **Burlington Literary Festival**, three days of readings, lectures, workshops, booksignings, and events, organized by Burlington City Arts, and the **Vermont Sheep & Wool Festival** (802-434-5646; vermontsheep.org), for workshops on knitting, spinning, and shearing, at the Essex Junction Fairgrounds.

Mid-September: **Annual Harvest Festival,** Shelburne Farms (802-985-8686). **South End Art Hop** (802-859-9222; art-hop.com)—a tour of some 400 art studios in downtown Burlington with music, food, workshops, and demonstrations.

Early October: 200 dealers convene for the **Champlain Valley Antiques Festival** (antiquingvermont.com) at the Champlain Valley Exposition in Essex Junction.

Late October: **Annual Halloween Costume Parade and Festival**, at noon, on Church St., Burlington. **Essex Fall Craft & Fine Art Show**, Champlain Valley Exposition, Essex. **Vermont International Film Festival**, a week's worth of independent, documentary, and outsider films, at area cinemas (802-660-2600; vtiff.org).

Early December: **Christmas Weekend** at the Shelburne Museum—a 19th-century festival; call 802-985-3344 for dates and details, plus **Vermont International Festival** (802-863-6713), food, crafts, dance, and music from 40 countries, at the Champlain Valley Exposition fairgrounds on Route 15 in Essex Junction.

December 31: **First Night** (802-863-6005), the end-of-the-year gala—parades, fireworks, music, mimes, and myriad performances that transform downtown Burlington into an alcohol-free "happening."

THE NORTHWEST CORNER

INCLUDING THE ISLANDS, ST. ALBANS, AND SWANTON

Interstate 89 is the quickest but not the most rewarding route from Burlington to the Canadian border. At the very least, motorists should detour for a meal in St. Albans and a sense of the farm country around Swanton. We strongly recommend allowing a few extra hours—or days—for the route up through the Champlain Islands, Vermont's Martha's Vineyard but as yet unspoiled.

THE ISLANDS

The cows and silos, hay fields and mountain views couldn't be more Vermont. But what about those beaches and sailboats? They're part of the picture, too, in this land chain composed of the Alburg peninsula and three islands—Isle La Motte, North Hero, and South Hero.

The Champlain Islands straggle 30 miles south from the Canadian border. Thin and flat, they offer some of the most spectacular views in New England: east to the

OVERLOOKING LAKE CHAMPLAIN IN NORTH HERO

Kim Grant

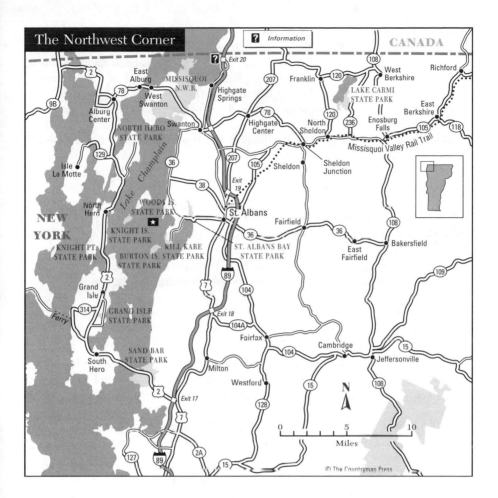

CANADA

? Information

Exit 20

2
East
Alburg
MISSISQUOI
N.W.R.
Highgate
Springs

207
Franklin
120
West
Berkshire
Richford

108

78
West
Swanton

9B

Alburg
Center

NORTH HERO
STATE PARK
Swanton

Highgate
Center

78

North
Sheldon

120

236
Enosburg
Falls

LAKE CARMI
STATE PARK

East
Berkshire

105
118

Isle
La Motte

129

36

207

105

Sheldon

Sheldon
Junction

Missisquoi Valley Rail Trail

NEW
YORK

North
Hero

WOODS IS.
STATE PARK

Lake Champlain

St. Albans

Fairfield

38

Exit
19

36

108

KNIGHT IS.
STATE PARK

KILI KARE

36

Bakersfield

KNIGHT PT.
STATE PARK

BURTON IS. STATE PARK
STATE PARK

ST. ALBANS BAY
STATE PARK

East
Fairfield

2

89

109

Grand
Isle

7

104

GRAND ISLE
STATE PARK

314

Ferry

Exit 18

104A

Fairfax

Cambridge

15

SAND BAR
STATE PARK

104

Jeffersonville

South
Hero

Milton

Westford

15

108

2

Exit 17

128

N

7

0   5   10

127
89
2A

15

Miles

© The Countryman Press

highest of the Green Mountains and west to the Adirondacks. They also divide the
northern reach of the largest lake in the East into two long, skinny arms, freckled
with smaller outer islands. It's a waterscape well known to fishermen and sailors.

This is Grand Isle County, Vermont's smallest, with a small but steadily growing
year-round population. It was homesteaded by Ebenezer Allen in 1783 and has
been a quiet summer retreat since the 1870s.

In the 19th century visitors arrived by lake steamer to stay at farms. Around the
turn of the 20th century a railway spawned several hotels, and with the advent of
automobiles and Prohibition, Rt. 2—the high road down the spine of the islands—
became one of the most popular roads to Montreal, a status it maintained until I-
89 opened in the 1960s.

Happily the decades since, like the interstate, seem to have passed these islands
by. Isle La Motte is the smallest and quietest of the islands, and it's crossed and
circled by narrow roads and linked to the mainland in ways beloved by bicyclists.
St. Anne's Shrine near the northern tip marks the shore on which in 1609 Samuel

de Champlain first set foot in what would be Vermont, cause for major celebrations in the summer of 2009. Near the southern tip of the island Fisk Farm, formerly a major source of the island's distinctive black marble, is now an arts center and a "quarry preserve" with its intriguing fossils; a clue to what's on view a short bike ride away at the Goodsell Ridge Preserve, part of the world's oldest reef. A short and fascinating video explains it all, and you begin to notice fossils embedded in the island's distinctive stone houses.

Viewed primarily as a summer destination, this is actually a great place to visit in September and October when its many apple orchards are being harvested and bicycling is at its best. Bicycling is indeed huge here throughout all the warm-weather months. Innkeepers tell us that up to half their guests are bicyclists.

GUIDANCE **Lake Champlain Islands Chamber of Commerce** (802-372-8400; 800-262-5226; info@champlainislands.com; champlainislands.com), P.O. Box 213, North Hero 05474, next door to the Hero's Welcome General Store, maintains a year-round office and publishes a list of accommodations, restaurants, marinas, campgrounds, and trailer parks. Also see lakechamplainbyway.com.

GETTING THERE *By car:* From New York State and Montreal, Rt. 2 from Rouses Point, and from Vermont, Rt. 78 from Swanton (an exit off I-89). From Vermont on the south, I-89 Exit 17 to Rt. 2, which runs the length of the islands.

By ferry: **Lake Champlain Transportation Company** (802-864-9804; ferries.com) offers year-round, 15-minute ferry crossings between Gordon's Landing, Grand Isle, and Cumberland Head, New York.

MEDICAL EMERGENCY Emergency service is available by calling **911**. *Marine emergencies:* Call 802-372-5590.

ST. ANNE'S SHRINE ON ISLE LA MOTTE
VDT

✳ Must-See

St. Anne's Shrine (802-928-3362; saintannesshrine.org), 92 St. Anne's Rd., Isle La Motte. Open mid-May–mid-Oct., free admission. An open-sided Victorian chapel and 13 shoreside acres mark the site of Vermont's first settlement, a French fort built in 1666. There are daily outdoor Masses in summer and Sunday services as long as weather permits. The shrine is a pleasant and peaceful place with a public beach, and café (open Sun. in July and Aug., 9:30–1, for a breakfast buffet). There's also a picnic area in a large pine grove, presumably descended from what Samuel de Champlain described as "the most beautiful pines I have ever seen" when he stepped ashore in 1609 on this spot. Champlain himself is honored here with a massive granite statue, which was carved in Vermont's Pavilion at Montreal's 1967 Expo. The History Room, which has been upgraded for the 400th anniversary of his arrival, displays artifacts that have washed ashore over the years, among them a tomahawk blade, an old ax head, the remains of pewter cups, and ancient pottery shards. The complex, maintained by the Edmundites, the Roman Catholic order that runs St. Michael's College in Colchester, includes a gift shop with books on the site's history. Mass is Sat. 7 PM, Sun. 9 and 10:30, and daily at 11:15, but check.

✳ Also See

Hyde Log Cabin (802-828-3051; historicvermont.org), Rt. 2, Grand Isle. Open July 4–mid-Oct, Sat.–Sun. 11–5. Nominal admission. Built by Jedediah Hyde in 1783 when the area was a wilderness accessible only by water, the cedar log cabin was restored in 1956. The Grand Isle Historical Society has furnished it with 18th-century artifacts—furniture, kitchenware, toys, tools, clothing, and atmosphere. At age 14 Hyde enlisted in the Revolutionary War. From the spoils, he received a surveyor's compass and theodolite, which he later used to survey Grand Isle and other parts of the state. Ira and Ethan Allen had named the islands "The Two Heroes" in their own honor, and parceled out grants to their fellow Green Mountain Boys. Most of them sold their grants, and Hyde purchased several on what would later become known as Grand Isle. This cabin housed 150 years' worth of Hydes at a spot about 2 miles southwest of where it stands today.

Ed Weed Fish Culture Station (802-372-3171), Bell Hill Rd., Grand Isle. Just beyond the Plattsburgh, New York, ferry on Rt. 314, look for the large hatchery (it's precisely 2 miles up Rt. 314 from Rt. 2), open 8–4 daily. Fish are brought to the facility as freshly spawned eggs (up to 2.2 million eggs at any one time), incubated, then transferred to a series of tanks; well worth checking out.

Christina Tree

THE HEROIC STATUE OF SAMUEL DE CHAMPLAIN, ORIGINALLY CARVED FOR THE MONTREAL EXPO IN 1967

HYDE LOG CABIN IN NORTH HERO

Diane E. Foulds

Joe Citro

THE FISK QUARRY PRESERVE IN ISLE LA MOTTE

THE WORLD'S OLDEST REEF AND ISLE LA MOTTE'S BLACK MARBLE
The Fisk Marble Quarries on West Shore Road, the oldest in the state, were first used by the French in 1664 to make a kiln for Fort St. Anne, Vermont's first colonial settlement. The Fisk family acquired them in the 1780s, working them over four generations. In 1884 the quarries passed to Nelson W. Fisk, who recognized their potential, as a construction boom was under way in America's cities. When polished, this black marble was magnificent, a coveted building material for facades such as New York's Radio City Music Hall and the U.S. Capitol building and Vermont State House. Nelson also shipped boatloads of

✳ To Do

BICYCLING With its flat roads (little trafficked once you are off Rt. 2) and splendid views, the islands are popular biking country. From the chamber of commerce (see *Guidance*) be sure to secure the free *Champlain Islands Bikeways* map/guide, detailing five interpretive theme loops that thread gently rolling terrain. Isle La Motte is especially well suited to bicycling. One of the most dramatic bike trails in Vermont is the 12.5-mile "Island Line" thrusting out across Lake Champlain from Colchester along a former bed of the old Rutland Railroad. Lake views don't get any better than this, and it's flat to boot. Unfortunately, a 200-foot bridge across "the cut" south of South Hero has yet to be built—but on August weekends there's a ferry (localmotion.org).

Rental bikes: Check with **Hero's Welcome General Store** (802-372-4161), North Hero Village; **Loon's Landing Watercraft & Bike Rentals** (802-372-8951), North Hero; **Grand Isle Canoe, Bike & Kayak** (802-782-ISLE) at 300 Rt. 2; or **Bike Shed Rentals** (802-928-3440), 1071 West Shore Rd., Isle La Motte, a mile

apples, lumber, even ice to markets farther south. In 1897, as lieutenant governor, he hosted President William McKinley at the family mansion. It was while Vice President Teddy Roosevelt was visiting in 1901 that McKinley was fatally shot, and it fell upon Fisk to break the news to the next president.

The Fisk mansion burned in 1924. Only its evocative stone ruins and 3 acres of the once-vast estate remained in 1970, when the Fitch family bought it as a summer haven. It's Linda Fitch who has raised awareness of the **Chazy Reef** underlying the southern third of Isle La Motte. Geologists have long recognized it as the world's oldest reef, roughly half a billion years old. Now the **Fisk Quarry** is a 20-acre nature preserve, and the fossilized plants and animals embedded in the grey limestone can be viewed as a vertical time line, evidence that Vermont was once contained within a tropical sea. Coral hardens into limestone that, over millennia, can morph into marble. In the nearby **Isle La Motte Historical Society** (Rt. 129, 4 miles south of the bridge; open July–Aug., Sat. 1–4), an 1840s stone school building and blacksmith shop, displays include a sculpture of local stone that's been partially polished, graphically illustrating that the stone used in many local buildings, is marble. It also displays the cane chair used by President McKinley and Vice President Theodore Roosevelt during their stays at the Fisk mansion, and the industrial looms of weaving entrepreneur Elizabeth Fisk, who, with her prominent husband, acted as their hosts. A left onto Quarry Rd. at the Historical Society and another left at the T brings you to the 81-acre **Goodsell Ridge Preserve**, maintained like Fisk Quarry by the Isle La Motte Preservation Trust (ilmpt.org). Here there are walking trails through woods and meadows with outcroppings of the reef. You'll also find a staffed interpretive center (open seasonally, Wed.–Sun. 1–4) and an excellent video dramatizing the history of the reef. For more about Fisk Farm see *Lodging* and *Entertainment.*

south of St. Anne's Shrine. Both Ruthcliffe Lodge and Terry Lodge (see *Lodging*) offer bikes to their guests. **Mountain Lake Expeditions** (802-777-7646, 1340 Lockhouse Point, North Hero) has instituted a very helpful delivery service that deposits bicycles, kayaks, or canoes right at your front door. In South Hero, **Allenholm Farm** (802-372-5566) offers bike rentals.

BIRDING Located on one of the major flyways, the islands are particularly rich in bird life: Herons, eagles, ospreys, cormorants, among others, migrate through the area. Prime birding sites include the **South Hero Swamp** and **Mud Creek** in Alburg and the **Sand Bar Wildlife Refuge** across from Sand Bar State Park. See also Knight's Island Sate Park under *Green Space.* Just east of Alburg, the **Missisquoi National Wildlife Refuge** (see "St. Albans and Swanton") is the region's prime birding area. An interpretive center features exhibits on local birds, including birdcalls.

BOAT EXCURSIONS **Driftwood Tours** (802-373-0022), North Hero, offers several daytime, sunset, and moonlight cruises in a boat that seats a maximum of six passengers. Captain Holly Poulin offers nature and fishing tours and also does dinner cruises in conjunction with the North Hero House. The trips take two hours and leave from the North Hero House Pier.

Ferry Cruise (802-864-9804; ferries.con), Rt. 314, Grand Isle. If you don't get out on the water any other way, be sure to take the 15-minute ferry to Plattsburgh, New York, and back.

BOATING Rental boats are available in North Hero from **Anchor Island Marina** (802-372-5131); **Hero's Welcome** (802-372-4161) rents kayaks and canoes only. In South Hero, **Apple Tree Bay** (802-372-3922) offers canoes, sailboats, and pontoon boats. **Tudhope Sailing Center and Marina** (802-372-5320), at the bridge in Grand Isle, also offers sailboats, powerboats, boat slips, sailing instruction, and charters. **Mountain Lake Expeditions** (see *Bicycling*) will bring kayaks and canoes right to your door.

FISHING Lake Champlain is considered one of the finest freshwater fisheries in America. With the right bait and a little luck, you can catch trout, salmon, smelt, walleye, bass, pike, muskellunge, and perch.

GOLF AND MINI GOLF **Alburg Country Club** (802-796-3586), Rt. 129, 3 miles west of South Alburg; 18 lakeside holes, gentle, shady terrain, snack bar.

Barcomb Hill Country Club at Apple Tree Bay (802-372-5398), Rt. 2, South Hero. Open May–late Oct. A nine-hole, par-3 executive golf course. Rental carts and clubs.

Wilcox Golf Course (802-372-8343), Rt. 314, Grand Isle, offers nine lakeside holes, golf carts, pro shop, rentals.

⚓ **Beaver Creek Mini Golf** (802-372-5811), Rt. 2, North Hero. Open Memorial Day–Labor Day. An 18-hole miniature golf course.

SWIMMING ⚓ **Alburg Dunes State Park** (802-796-4170; vtstateparks.com), Alburg. This little-trammeled area features the longest sandy beach on Lake Champlain, and its shallowness makes it excellent for swimming with young ones; rare flora and fauna; limited day use only. Call for directions or ask locally.

Sand Bar State Park (802-893-2825; vtstateparks.com) fills to capacity on sunny weekends in summer, but this oasis with its shallow, sandy beach and adjacent 1,000-acre wildlife refuge is a fine place to relax on weekdays. Picnic tables, sailboarding school.

⚓ **Knight Point State Park** (802-372-8389; vtstateparks.com), located on the southern tip of North Hero, is the best place to swim, especially for children. A former farm facing The Gut, a quiet, almost landlocked bay, its grounds include a fine brick house and a nature trail that loops around the point. From the sandy beach you can watch boats pass through the drawbridge between the islands. Canoes and rowboats are available for rent, and there are picnic tables with grills.

✳ Green Space

Mud Creek Wildlife Area, off Rt. 78, Alburg, offers nature trails, a good spot for viewing waterfowl.

Also see the **Missisquoi National Wildlife Refuge** in "St. Albans and Swanton" chapter. Practically in Alburg, this is the area's largest nature preserve and includes a major interpretive center, worth a stop even if you lack time to walk, fish, or boat there.

The **Fisk Quarry Preserve** and **Goodsell Ridge** preserves on Isle La Motte are described in our box about the World's Oldest Coral Reef.

Also see and *Swimming* and *Campgrounds*.

* Lodging

Note: See *Guidance*. The chamber of commerce lists numerous rentals and lakeside cottage clusters. Vermont Lake Sales & Rentals (vermontlakerentals.com) is a prime source.

INNS AND BED & BREAKFASTS

Thomas Mott B&B (802-796-4402; thomas-mott-bb.com), 63 Blue Rock Rd., Alburg 05440. Open May–Oct. This vintage 1830s lakeside farmhouse is splendidly sited on a quiet back road along Alburg's eastern shore, handy to the Missisquoi Nature Reserve and with a dock and sweeping views of the Green Mountains. Hosts Susan and Bob Cogley are delighted to help plan your stay in the area; Susan will prepare dinner on request. The four guest rooms (all with private bath) are furnished with antiques and quilts; three have queen beds and views; one has twins. There's also plenty of common space inside and out. Guests are welcome to use the canoe and the swimming/fishing dock. On a summer evening we wished that we had come prepared with takeout and a bottle of wine to enjoy on the dock (stores in Alburg close at 6 PM). $125–145 includes a great breakfast. Children over 12 welcome.

ꝏ **North Hero House** (802-372-4732; 888-525-3644; northherohouse.com), Rt. 2, North Hero 05474. Open year-round. This century-old summer hotel has become a popular spot for boaters, bikers, and travelers of all sorts. All the rooms—9 upstairs and 17 more across Rt. 2—have private bath. The inn offers a comfortable sitting area, an inviting pub, and a large public dining room beyond (see *Dining Out*). Facilities include a long, grassy dock at which Champlain steamers once moored; canoes, kayaks, power- and pedal boats are available. Our favorite (alas, the most expensive) rooms are in the three buildings that face, even extend out over, the lake—Homestead, Southwind, and Cove House—so that you fall asleep to lapping water. In summer, $125–350 per couple B&B, $14.95 per child. The many specialty weekends include murder mysteries and musical events. Check the Web site for packages.

ꝏ 🐾 ♿ "1" **Fisk Farm** (802-928-3364; fiskfarm.com), 3849 West Shore Rd., Isle La Motte 05463. Owner Linda Fitch offers two lovely guest cottages on the former site of the Fisk family estate. The Stone House, built of wood and stone next to the main house, is a beauty, a place we would like to reserve for a special occasion, but only in warm weather (it has a fireplace but no other heating). There is a rustic Shore Cottage, said to have been built as a playhouse in North Hero and brought across the ice. The ruins of the gray stone Fisk mansion have been preserved in the front garden, currently the scene of Sunday-afternoon teas, and the horse and carriage barn has been preserved as an art gallery. The mansion burned in 1924, but thanks to Fitch, who has dedicated years to restoring the property, it's an exceptionally tranquil place that offers a window into the history not only of Vermont but also of the earth. Rates begin at $700 per week for the Shore Cottage ($110 per day when available) and $900 for the Stone House (both of which have their own kitchens). Grills are available, and guests may help themselves to the herb garden.

✿ *T* **Ruthcliffe Lodge & Restaurant** (802-928-3200; 800-769-8162; ruthcliffe.com), 1002 Quarry Rd., Isle La Motte 05463, open Mother's Day–Columbus Day. Way out at the end of Old Quarry Rd., this lakeside compound includes a small motel and lodge with a total of six rooms, all with private bath and many featuring lakeside panoramas. Mark and Kathy Infante are warm hosts, and the food is well known and highly rated (see *Dining Out*); breakfast and dinner are served. There's a 40-foot water's-edge patio for dining, as well as the cozy knotty-pine dining room in the lodge. Swimming and fishing are out the front door; rental boats and bikes are available. Rates range from $132.50 per couple for a room with a full bath to $142.50 for a two-room adjoining unit with a bath and a half, including a full country breakfast; $15 per extra person. Inquire about the Meadowhouse ($195 per night).

The Ransom Bay Inn (802-796-3393; 802-729-3393), 4 Center Bay Rd., Alburg 05440. A stone house built beautifully in the 1790s, originally a stagecoach stop, set back from Rt. 2 within walking distance of a small beach. On the Vermont Register of Historic Places. Much of the downstairs area is now a seasonal restaurant (see *Dining Out*). Guests are accommodated in two large and airy rooms plus two smaller ones, all nicely furnished with period antiques and private bath. $100–115 year-round includes a choice of breakfast entrées and homemade jams.

Charlie's Northland Lodge (802-372-8822; 802-372-3829; charliesnorthlandlodge.com), 3829 Rt. 2, North Hero 05474, in the heart of the village. Built by Charlie's grandparents early in the 19th century, this year-round lodge contains three guest rooms furnished in country antiques, two with air-conditioning and private bath; all have private entrance, and there's a guest parlor. The lodge is part of a nifty little complex that includes a private beach. $90–115 includes continental breakfast; 10 percent discount for biking and kayaking guests. Housekeeping cottages available.

RUTHCLIFFE LODGE IN ISLE LA MOTTE

Joe Citro

✒ **Terry Lodge** (802-928-3264), 2925 West Shore Rd., Isle La Motte 05463. Open May 15–Oct. 15. Cherie and Matt Bean run a friendly, family kind of place across a quiet road from the lake, with a lakeside deck and swim raft. Most of the seven rooms in the lodge have lake views. Breakfast and dinner (family-style) are served. There's also a four-unit motel ($115–135), a housekeeping cottage ($800 per week), and a housekeeping apartment ($700 per week) in the rear. Lodge rooms are $110 per couple with breakfast, $145 MAP. Request one of the front rooms with a lake view.

✒ **Allenholm Orchards Bed & Breakfast** (802-372-5566; 888-721-56; allenholm.com), 150 South St., South Hero 05486. Pam and Ray Allen offer a guest suite—a bedroom furnished in family antiques, including a queen-sized canopy bed, and a large living room with a TV, VCR, board games, and full-sized pool table, plus a full private bath, patio, rose garden, and private airport. A country breakfast is served upstairs in the dining room or, if you prefer, on your patio. The suite is on the lower level of the Allens' modern home; it opens onto more than 100 acres of apples, billed as Vermont's oldest commercial orchard. Established in the 1870s, it's now owned and operated by the sixth generation of Allens. $98 per couple for the bedroom, $165 for the entire suite.

○○ ✒ **Ferry Watch Inn** (802-372-3935), 121 West Shore Rd., Grand Isle 05458. This wonderfully restored lakefront home, originally built in 1800, overlooks the broad lake with spectacular views of the Adirondacks and the most wonderful sunsets. Janet and Troy Wert offer three guest rooms (two with shared bath; one with private bath) with antique double beds renowned for their comfort. The property is within walking distance of a nine-hole golf course. $100–110 per room with shared bath or $120–130 with private bath includes full country breakfast. Weekly rates from $600.

Adams Landing (802-372-4839; adamslandingvt.com), 1 Adams Landing Rd. Extension, Grand Isle 05458. Year-round. In this lovely big rambling, secluded house on the west shore, Sally Copperswmith and Jack Sartore offer two rooms with shared bath ($120–140) and a suite with private bath, a fridge, and library ($195). Rates include breakfast and afternoon refreshments. Inquire about Kelse House, a fully equipped two-bedroom house.

Crescent Bay Farm (802-372-4807; crescentbaybb.com), South Hero 05486. This restored 1820s farmhouse is a working farm on the quiet, southern end of the island, near Snow Farm Winery. Three guest rooms, two with private bath ($125 includes breakfast) are furnished in country antiques. Dave and Julie Lane have 20 llamas, plus cats, dogs, and Black Angus beef; also flower gardens, lake views, and one of the many miniature stone castles scattered around the Champlain Islands.

OTHER LODGING 🐾 ✒ "†" **Shore Acres Inn & Restaurant** (802-372-8722; shoreacres.com), 237 Shore Acres Dr., North Hero 05474. Motel rooms open May–early Oct. This pleasant motel commands one of the most spectacular views of any lodging place in Vermont. Set in sweeping, peaceful, beautifully groomed grounds, 23 comfortable rooms face the lake and the Green Mountains. There's a bar-lounge; breakfast and dinner are served (see *Dining Out*). Four of the guest rooms are in the garden house, away from the lake. Susan and Mike

Tranby have worked hard to make this an exceptionally friendly as well as comfortable place. Amenities include lawn chairs, two clay tennis courts, a driving range, lawn games, and a 1.5-mile private shore for swimming. All rooms have either a queen, a king, two queens, or two doubles, along with TV and ceiling fan or air conditioner when lake breezes fail. $158.50–206.50 per room. Pets accommodated for $15 the first night, $5 each night thereafter.

🐾 **Wilcox Cove Cottages & Golf Course** (summer 802-372-8343; winter 802-453-3779; wilcoxcove.com), Rt. 314; mailing address: 3 Camp Court, Grand Isle 05458. Open June–mid-Sept. This homey, lakeside cottage colony and nine-hole public golf course, less than a mile from the ferry, is a real find. Each of the seven cottages has a living room, dining area, fully equipped kitchen, one bedroom with twin beds, bathroom with shower, and one or two screened porches. They are completely furnished except for sheets, pillowcases, and bath and kitchen towels, and can be rented for $750 a week including greens fees. Golf is $18 per day, and pets are welcome. Occupancy is limited to two adults unless arrangements are made in advance.

WEDDINGS, NONPROFIT RETREATS, AND EVENTS

Grand Isle Lake House (802-372-5024; grandislakehouse.com), 34 East Shore Rd., Grand Isle. Built on Robinson's Point as the Island Villa Hotel in 1903, this is a classic mansard-roofed 25-room summer hotel with a wraparound porch, set in 55 acres of lawn that sweep to the lake. From 1957 until 1993 it was a summer girls' camp run by the Sisters of Mercy. Since 1997 it has been owned by the Preservation Trust of Vermont, which has restored the upstairs rooms beautifully, as it has

the lobby, kitchen, and dining rooms. It is currently available as a site for conferences and wedding receptions (80 can sit down in the dining room and another 125 guests on the porch; tents on the lawn can accommodate 250 guests).

CAMPGROUNDS The complete rundown on state parks is at **vtstateparks .com** (888-409-7579).

⚓ **North Hero State Park** (802-372-8727) has 99 wooded tent or trailer sites and 18 lean-to sites arranged in three loops, each with a restroom and hot showers (no hookups). They're mostly in lowland forests with access to open fields, a beach, boat launch, boat rentals, and picnic and children's play areas.

Grand Isle State Park (802-372-4300), 36 E. Shore Rd. South, Grand Isle. Open mid-May–mid-Oct. Vermont's second largest (and most visited) state campground has 117 tent/trailer campsites, 36 lean-tos (no hookups), and four cabins on 226 acres, with a beach, playground, nature trail, and recreation building.

Knight Island State Park by way of **Burton Island State Park** (802-524-6353). The *Island Runner* (802-524-

GRAND ISLE LAKE HOUSE

Joe Citro

6353), a ferry operated between Memorial Day and Labor Day by the state, crosses the water to Knight Island on weekends from North Hero as well as Kil Kare and Burton Island every couple of hours, weekdays only from Burton Island. There's even an optional gear delivery service. The seven campsites at Knight Island are primitive (there are no facilities)—even clothing is optional! To maximize privacy, campsites are hidden from public view. Not to be missed is the brochure-guided "Walk of Change" that explores island ecology.

✷ Where to Eat

DINING OUT ♿ **Shore Acres Inn & Restaurant** (802-372-8722), Rt. 2, North Hero. Reservations for dinner are a must much of the time. Also open for breakfast June–Aug. The dining room's large windows command a sweeping view of the lake, with Mount Mansfield and its flanking peaks in the distance. It's a very attractive room with a large fieldstone hearth. You might begin with coconut-beer-battered shrimp ($7.95) or grilled homemade polenta ($6.95), then dine on Apple Island chicken or roast rack of lamb. Entrées ($14.95–32.95) come with home-baked bread, a salad, and seasonal vegetables. The chocolate pie is famous.

Ruthcliffe Lodge & Restaurant (802-928-3200; 800-769-8162; ruthcliffe.com), 1002 Quarry Rd., Isle La Motte. Open mid-May–Columbus Day for dinner. Overnight moorings available for dinner guests. Be sure to reserve for dinner before you drive out to this rustic building, way off the main drag and overlooking the lake. Dine in the pine-paneled dining room or outside on the deck. Owner-chef Mark Infante specializes in Italian dishes like chicken Marsala and veal Sorrentina in homemade marinara sauce, but the menu might also include shrimp scampi Ruthcliffe ($25.95) or broiled scallops ($23.95). Entrée prices include bread, soup, salad, vegetables, and pasta or potato. Leave room for dessert.

North Hero House (802-372-4732; 888-525-3644), Rt. 2, North Hero. Open May–Nov., this historic old inn is famous for its Friday lobster buffet. Dining on the glassed-in veranda with its lake views is popular—or better still, at one of the umbrella covered tables on the lawn; the main dining room adjoins a solarium that's used for private parties. Dine on grilled salmon with peach salsa or pan-seared rack of lamb. Entrées $21–30.

Blue Paddle Bistro (802-372-4814; bluepaddlebistro.com) 316 Rt. 2, South Hero. Open year-round for dinner Wed.–Sun. and Sunday brunch, lunch Thu.–Sat. in summer—but check. This is a cheerful gathering place. To get it off the ground, owners Mandy Hotchkiss and Phoebe Bright gave paddles to investors. Now the paddles cover the walls, and the café hums with activity year-round. Fresh breads, salads, and sandwiches for lunch, full bar, and dinner entrées ($16.50–18.75) such as Gorgonzola-stuffed meat loaf, bourbon-marinated flank steak, and miso-encrusted salmon with shiitake mushrooms and leek risotto. Outdoor deck in summer.

Ransom Bay Inn (802-796-3393; 800 729-3393), 4 Center Bay Rd., Alburg. Open for dinner May 15–Dec. 31; in fall and winter just Thu.–Sun. Longtime innkeepers Richard and Loraine, both culinary school graduates, have created an attractive dining space in the downstairs of their historic stone inn. In summer tables are all set out on a deck, overlooking the garden. In fall there's fireside dining. The meats are all organic. A menu might include pork tenderloin medallions in wine sauce and rib-eye steak with horseradish sauce as well as a choice of pastas. $12.95–22.95.

EATING OUT **Hero's Welcome** (802-372-4161; heroswelcome.com), Rt. 2, North Hero Village. Open daily year-round, an upscale general store with a good deli, a bakery, and a café with waterside seating. "Heroic" sandwiches—think Thomas Jefferson and Gentleman Johnny Burgoyne—and freshly made soups.

North Hero Marina (802-372-5953; northhero.com), 2253 Pelot's Point Rd., North Hero. You eat on the porch, no more than 10 people at a time, and the pool next door invites you in to pass the time between courses. The eating arrangements make it very seasonal. The house specialty is fish of all sorts.

Links on the Lake (802-796-4248), 230 Rt. 129, Alburg. Lunch daily except Mon., dinner Fri. and Sat. 5–9. Good food and reasonable prices in a pretty setting at the Alburg Country Club. There's a good seafood pasta, and the house special is Hungarian goulash. Moderate.

Lakes End Cheeses (802-796-3730; lakesendcheeses.com), 215 West Shore Rd., Alburg. Retail shop, open mid-June–Labor Day 10–7. Shoreline Chocolate and goat cheese are both made here; farmyard animals, hot dogs, ice cream.

Champlain Islands farmer's market is one of the best anywhere, thanks to the abundance of local farm produce. June–mid-Oct. it's Sat. 10–2 at St. Joseph Church, Rt. 2 in Grand Isle; Wed. in the village of South Hero, 4–7.

Island Homemade Ice Cream (802-372-6266; islandhomemadeicecream .com), 205 Rt. 2, Grand Isle. Patty and Gary Sundberg distribute their ice cream widely as well as serving it up on Thursdays during the Snow Farm Vineyard's summer concert series in South Hero.

Note: See also Fisk Farm under *Lodging* and inquire about Tea Garden Art Shows with music on summer Sundays, 1–5.

✳ Entertainment

Music at Snow Farm Vineyard (802-372-9463), West Shore Rd., South Hero. If you fancy meeting the locals, a popular event is the Thursday summer music series beginning at 6:30 PM on the vineyard's lawn. The music ranges, over the course of the season, from classical to rock. It's free, and all you need to bring is a picnic and a chair (bug spray wouldn't be a bad idea, either). You can buy your wine on site.

Arts in the Garden Series concerts at Fisk Farm (802-928-3364), 3849 West Shore Rd., Isle La Motte. Sunday afternoons in July and Aug., 1–5. Music and art exhibits in the carriage barn, free except for refreshments. There is a charge for the Concerts in the Barn—Pro Series: music by professional chamber groups on select Saturdays in June, July, and Aug. Both are sponsored by the Isle La Motte Preservation Trust (ilmpt.org).

✳ Selective Shopping

ANTIQUES The usual count is half a dozen shops, but they are all seasonal and tend to close as one thing, open as another. Standbys include **Blue Heron Antiques**, 288 Rt. 2, South Hero; the **Back Chamber Antiques Store**, North Hero Village; and **Tinker's Barn**, gifts and antiques at 479 Rt. 2, South Hero. Also check with **Alburg Auction House**, Lake St., Alburg, open Sat. 2–6 and 7–midnight.

CRAFTS **McGuire Family Furniture Makers** (802-928-4190; mcguire familyfurnituremakers.com), Isle La Motte. Open year-round 1–5, but call. Two generations of this talented family are involved in the day-to-day production of stunning antique reproduction furniture in spare, heirloom, Shaker, and 18th-century designs: four-poster beds, pegleg tables, grandfather clocks, dressers—anything you want designed, some of it surprisingly affordable.

Island Craft Shop (802-372-5136), a cooperative located behind Hero's Welcome in North Hero Village, open daily mid-May–mid-Oct. Works of local and area artisans.

The Upstairs Gallery, above the Blue Paddle Bistro in South Hero, stocks Harry Wicks's fine wood bowls, jewelry, stained glass, and more.

ORCHARDS ✍ **Allenholm Farm** (802-372-5566; allenholm.com), 111 South St., P.O. Box 300, South Hero 05486. Open July–Dec. 24, 9–5. A sixth-generation, 100-acre apple orchard, Vermont's oldest, with a farmstead selling Vermont cheese, honey and maple syrup, jams and jellies, and Papa Ray's famous homemade pies. There's also a petting paddock with rabbits, chickens, goats, horses, a camel, and a donkey. See also *Special Events* (the Allens are the power behind the October Apple Fest).

Hall's Orchard (802-928-3418; 802-928-3226), 4461 Main St., Isle La Motte 05463. The 1820s brick house sits across from the orchard that has been in the same family since the house was built. The apples we bought here on a crisp October morning are the best we can remember finding anywhere.

✍ **Hackett's Orchard** (802-372-4848), 86 South St., South Hero 05486. Perennials, maple syrup, fruits, berries,

and fresh-picked vegetables in summer; apples, cider, and pumpkins in fall. The farm stand has a family picnic and play area. Fresh cider doughnuts are a specialty, as are the homemade fruit pies.

SPECIAL STORES **Hero's Welcome General Store** (800-372-HERO; heroswelcome.com), Rt. 2, North Hero. Former Pier 1 CEO Bob Camp and his wife, Bev, have transformed this 19th-century landmark into a bright, smart, multilevel emporium: café and bakery, gift shop, art gallery, grocery with a deli, and the island's best takeout as well as Vermont gourmet food products, sports clothes, outdoor toys and sporting goods, wine shop, and bookstore, retaining its flavor as a community gathering spot. They offer canoe, kayak, and bike rentals as well as a boat launch.

Vermont Nut Free Chocolates (802-372-4654; 888-468-8373; vermontnut free.com), 10 Island Circle, Grand Isle, just off Rt. 2. This venture has been so successful, it's moved to the Island Industrial Park—but it's still worth finding. The retail store is open daily, except Sun., 9–5.

WINERY **Snow Farm Vineyard** (802-372-9463; snowfarm.com), 190 West Shore Rd. (follow signs from Rt. 2 or Rt. 314), South Hero 05486. Open Memorial Day–Oct., 10–4:30. Vineyard tours are offered daily at 11 and 2. This pioneering Lake Champlain vineyard is the fruition of several years' hard work by lawyers Molly and Harrison Lebowitz. Visitors enter a barnlike building that is the winery showroom with a tasting counter. There they learn that this is still a relatively new operation (opened in 1997). Initially it processed and bottled wine from grapes grown in New York's Finger Lakes, gradually mixing these with the harvest from vines on Snow Farm's 14 acres. (Also see *Entertainment.*)

✳ Special Events

Note: Check with the chamber of commerce about weekly events. Farmer's market in Grand Isle, Saturdays 10–2. See Fisk Farm under *Lodging*; inquire about Tea Garden Art Shows with music, summer Sundays.

June: **Taste of the Islands: Food & Wine** (*second weekend*), South Hero— local food purveyors show off their culinary creations, accompanied by Snow Farm Vineyard wines. **Celebrate Champlain! Islands Festival** (*third weekend*), Grand Isle—classes and demos on sailboarding, kayaking, sailing, and canoeing; music and BBQ.

July 4: **Parades** and **barbecues** in South Hero and Alburg, and **Island House and Garden Tour** in Grand Isle.

August: **Grand Isle County Art Show & Sale** (*first weekend*). **Lake Champlain Bluegrass Festival** (.lakechamplainmusic.com) Palmers Field, Alburg.

Early September: **Teddy Roosevelt Toast**, Isle La Motte, at the Fisk Farm—a presentation pays tribute to a person or group that has furthered TR's mission with respect to our natural resources and cultural heritage.

Columbus Day weekend: **Apple Fest**—crafts fair, a "press-off," plenty of food and fun (802-372-5566).

ST. ALBANS AND SWANTON

Once an important railroad center, the city of St. Albans (population: 7,305 and surrounded by the town of St. Albans, population: 2,000) is still the Franklin County seat. The community's place in the history books was assured on October 19, 1864, when 22 armed Confederate soldiers, who had infiltrated the town in mufti, held up the three banks, stole horses, and escaped back to Canada with $208,000, making this the northernmost engagement of the Civil War. One of the raiders was wounded and eventually died, as did Elinus J. Morrison, a visiting builder. The surviving Confederates were arrested in Montreal, tried, but never extradited; their leader, Lieutenant Bennett H. Young, rose to the rank of general. When he visited Montreal again in 1911, a group of St. Albans dignitaries paid him a courtesy call at the Ritz-Carlton! It was after the Civil War that St. Albans boomed as headquarters for the Central Vermont Railway. At one time this was the largest railway in New England, employing over 1,700 people just in St. Albans. This and the story of the St. Alban's Raid are dramatized in the St. Albans Historical Museum.

Swanton (population: 6,423) occupies a flat area circled by farmland and intersected by the Missisquoi River. Archaeological digs have unearthed evidence that Algonquian tribes lived here as far back as 8000 BC. The French settled the area about 1748, naming it 15 years later for Thomas Swanton, a British officer in the French and Indian Wars. Due to its proximity to the Canadian border (only 6 miles north), Swanton witnessed a fair bit of smuggling in the 19th century and during Prohibition. During World War I the long-abandoned Robin Hood–Remington Arms plant produced millions of rounds of ammunition for the Allied armies. Today an estimated 20 percent of the population is of Abenaki origin, and the Abenaki Tribal Council and museum are based here. The idyllic village green is home to a pair of swans, a tradition since 1963, when England's Queen Elizabeth II sent the town a pair for its bicentenary, thinking its name had something to do with swans.

GUIDANCE **Franklin County Regional Chamber of Commerce** (802-524-2444; stalbanschamber.com), 2 N. Main St., St. Albans 05478. Open weekdays 8:30–5. Facing Taylor Park, with plenty of easy parking, this is a friendly, staffed office stocked with brochures.

The Swanton Chamber of Commerce (802-868-7200), Merchants Row, Swanton 05488, maintains a seasonal information booth at the north end of the village green.

GETTING THERE **Amtrak** (800-USA-RAIL; amtrak.com) still stops. A ticket office near the corner of Lake and Federal streets marks the northern terminus of the *Vermonter* service from Washington, DC; local taxi service is available. St. Albans is also Exit 19 off I-89.

MEDICAL EMERGENCY Emergency service is available by calling **911**.

Northwestern Medical Center (802-524-5911; 800-696-0321), St. Albans.

✳ Must-See

St. Albans Historical Museum (802-527-7933; stamuseum.com), 9 Church St. (top of Taylor Park), open June–early Oct., weekdays 1–4, or by appointment. $5 adults, $2 ages 6–14. This artifact-rich museum fills a three-story, vintage-1861 brick schoolhouse Exhibits include a fascinating old-time country doctor's office, Civil War artifacts, and period costumes. The century-old waiting room with a ticket office and telegraphic equipment is the setting for models of both a 1923 round-

THE COMMON IN ST. ALBANS

Christina Tree

house and a steam locomotive, as well as plenty of Central Vermont Railroad memorabilia. A diorama of the town uses lights and narration to demonstrate how a group of Confederate soldiers held up three local banks in 1864, making off with $208,000 in loot before setting off makeshift bombs and galloping to Canada. Samples of the stolen bills are on display. The Western Abenaki Exhibit includes a birch-bark canoe, tools, and arrowheads. There's also a children's room and a French heritage exhibit.

✳ Also See

President Chester A. Arthur Historic Site (802-828-3051; historicvermont .org), North Fairfield. A 1950s replica of the little parsonage in which the 21st (and usually underrated) president lived as an infant can be found 10 miles east of Fairfield on Rt. 36 (open July 4–mid-Oct., Sat.–Sun. 11–5). In the visitor center exhibits examine the controversy over the actual site of Arthur's birth, which had an impact on the question of his eligibility to serve as president. Arthur's conduct as president in light of his reputation as a leading New York State political boss is also examined. Note the vintage 1840 brick church northwest of the house, also owned by the state of Vermont and open the same hours as the historic site. It's good for sweeping views, used for weddings and memorials.

Abenaki Tribal Museum and Cultural Center (802-868-2559; abenakination .org), 100 Grand Ave., Swanton. Usually open 9–4 Mon and Wed.–Fri. (call ahead to confirm). For special guided tours, call Fred Wiseman (802-868-3808). A former filling station houses headquarters for the Abenaki Tribal Council and this small museum, with clothing, tools, crafts, and a time line explaining the fur trade and transportation. The stars of this exhibit are the ceremonial headdresses, the birch-bark and dugout canoes, and the intricate handwoven baskets.

Site of former Abenaki Christian mission, on Monument Rd., about a mile north of Swanton off Rt. 7. It's easy to envision a thriving Indian settlement at this riverside spot opening onto Lake Champlain. A granite marker and totem pole commemorate the location of the Jesuit mission on the Mississquoi, established about 1700, and the St. Francis (Abenaki) Indian village that grew up around it until 1775. Unmarked Abenaki burial grounds span the length of Monument Rd. Sadly, houses now encroach on the monument; when we tried to walk down to the river in what appears to be a park, a resident came to his door and screamed, "Private property!" Be forewarned.

⚅ **The Swanton Historical Society Railroad Depot Museum** (802-868-4744; swantonhistoricalsociety.org), 58 S. River St., Swanton. Open May–Oct., Tue.–Sat. 11–3. The first passenger train arrived here in 1863, and by the time this depot was built in 1875, the town was a transportation hub. Note the separate ladies' and men's waiting rooms and the scores of historical photos and artifacts. Now it houses the local historical society and tells the story of the railroad's impact on the area.

🍴 ✎ ⚅ **Enosburg Falls Opera House** (802-933-6171; enosburgoperahouse.org), 123 Depot St., Enosburg Falls. An 1892 structure that fell into decades of disuse until the community mustered the funds to restore it, the intimate stage is the site for year-round events, including Vermont Symphony Orchestra concerts, plays, musicals, and the annual Miss Vermont Pageant. Tickets and schedules online.

CANOEING AND FISHING **The Missisquoi National Wildlife Refuge** (see *Birding*) is a source of walleye, northern pike, largemouth bass, bullhead, white perch, and yellow perch. For rental boats see listing in the "The Islands" section of this chapter.

FARMS AND ORCHARDS TO VISIT 🐾 🦴 **Carman Brook Maple & Dairy Farm** (802-868-2347; 888-84-MAPLE; cbmaplefarm.com), 1275 Fortin Rd., Swanton. Daniel and Karen Fortin run a modern dairy operation that welcomes curious vacationers. Depending on the season, you can tour the cutting-edge barn, watch maple syrup being made, taste a variety of maple products, or take the five-minute hike past the barn to the Abenaki Medicine Caves, known among the locals as the mystical spot where generations of Abenaki gathered medicinal herbs and sought cures. Gift shop, daily tours (call ahead).

West Swanton Orchards and Cider Mill (802-868-9100), Rt. 78 west, West Swanton. Open June–Nov., daily 10–5. A family-owned orchard with 11 varieties of apples, a cider mill, and a gift shop featuring Vermont products and homemade baked goods. Take a walk on the nature trail that winds through the 62 acres of trees.

GOLF **Champlain Country Club** (802-527-1187; champlaincountryclub.com), Rt. 7, 3 miles north of St. Albans. A nine-hole course built in 1915, some holes terraced. Restaurant.

Richford Country Club (802-848-3527), Golf Course Rd., Richford. A hilly, scenic nine holes, just 0.5 mile from the Canadian border. Established 1930.

BIKING

Missisquoi Valley Rail Trail (802-524-5958), 140 S. Main St., St. Albans. This 26.5-mile-long trail has been converted from an abandoned Central Vermont Railroad bed into a path for cross-country skiing, biking, walking, snowmobiling, and just plain strolling—but not for ATVs or dirt bikes. Be sure to secure the excellent free *Bicycling & Walking Guide* to the trail, available from the **Northwest Regional Planning Commission** (802-524-5958) and the Franklin County Regional Chamber (see *Guidance*). The trail runs cross-country from St. Albans to Sheldon Junction, then winds along the Missisquoi River (and Rt. 105) to Enosburg Falls and on up to Richford, at the Canadian border. The map/guide details access, rental sources, and parking along with handy info including where to find phones and ice cream. Most people do the trail in segments, given the round-trip factor. **Porter's Bike Shop** (802-868-7417), 116 Grand Ave., Swanton, is a find for out-of-luck bicyclists. Pauline Porter carries an impressive array of bike parts and can salvage a doomed trek when something on your bike gets broken. Rentals available.

BIRDING

The Missisquoi National Wildlife Refuge (802-868-4781; fws.gov), 371 N. River St. The headquarters/visitor center (open weekdays 8–4:30; Sat. when staffing permits) for this 6,592-acre waterfowl area is 2 miles west of Swanton on Rt. 78. The visitor center is worth a stop even if you can't hike or boat. Exhibits showcase detail local geology and the history of human habitation as well as bird and animal life. The Black Creek and Maquam Creek trails wind through brushland, timberland, and marsh, adding up to about 1.5 miles (a two-hour ramble); both are appropriately marked for the flora and fauna represented. The refuge provides habitat for over 200 species of birds. Hawks, marsh birds, songbirds, and great blue herons are frequent visitors, and migratory birds stop over on their voyage from northern breeding areas to wintering areas farther south. Most of the refuge is accessible only by boat. There are two public boat landings, fishing from the Missisquoi River, and blueberry picking in the bog off Tabor Rd. in July and Aug. The walking trails convert to cross-country ski use in winter; for details, get a copy of the free brochure published by the U.S. Fish and Wildlife Service. Open most of the time, but call ahead to confirm. Dress in light colors and bring insect repellent if you're visiting in the hotter months.

Enosburg Falls Country Club (802-933-2296), Rts. 105 and 108, N. Main St., Enosburg Falls. A hilly, reasonably priced nine-hole course with friendly staff and good views from the restaurant.

✳ Green Space

St. Albans Bay State Park, 4 miles west on Rt. 36, is a good place for picnics, with several tables and grills stretched out along the waterfront, but the water is too shallow and weedy for decent swimming.

Kill Kare State Park (802-524-6021; vtstateparks.com), once a fashionable summer hotel site and then, for years, a famous boys' summer camp; on Point Rd. off Rt. 36, St. Albans Bay. Surrounded on three sides by the lake, it affords beautiful views and can therefore be crowded on weekends, but it's usually blissfully quiet other days; swim beach, playgrounds, boat launch, rowboat rentals, and shuttle (fee) to Burton Island.

Burton Island State Park (802-524-6353; vtstateparks.com), a lovely, 250-acre island reached from Kill Kare by park boat or by your own. Facilities include 17 tent sites, 22 lean-tos, and a 100-slip marina with electrical hookups and 15 moorings. Campers' gear is transported to campsites by park vehicle. Fishing off this beautiful haven is usually excellent. Also accessible for day use; nature center, swim beach, food concession, hiking trails, boat rentals.

Lake Carmi State Park (802-933-8383; vtstateparks.com), at 460 Marsh Farm Rd., Enosburg Falls. Take Exit 19 off I-89 and drive 2 miles on Rt. 104; 1.5 miles

Joe Citro

BURTON ISLAND STATE PARK

north on Rt. 105; 3 miles north on Rt. 108. Set in rolling farmlands, the 482-acre park has 143 tent/trailer sites, the largest camping area in the state. Facilities include two cabins and 35 lean-tos, some on the beach of this sizable lake; nature trails; boat ramp and rentals. Lake Carmi is the state's fourth largest.

Woods Island State Park (802-524-6353), 2 miles north of Burton Island. Primitive camping is available on this mile-long, 0.25-mile wide island of 125 acres. Five widely spaced campsites with no facilities are linked by a trail. The island is unstaffed, although there are daily ranger patrols; reservations for campsites must be made through Burton Island State Park (see above). There is no public transportation to the island; the best boat access is from Kill Kare.

✳ Lodging

RESORT ✐ & **The Tyler Place Family Resort** (802-868-4000; 802-868-3301; tylerplace.com), Box 901, Rt. 7, Old Dock Rd., Highgate Springs 05460. Open late May–mid-Sept. One of the country's oldest and most popular family resorts (since 1933) continues to thrive on 165 acres of woods, meadows, and a mile of undeveloped lakeshore. Faithful partisans have been returning year after year for three generations of the Tyler family's management (25 members of the family are currently involved). They provide just about every conceivable form of recreation for adults and children (infants–16 years of age), with separate programs and dining for each group

THE LAKEFRONT AT TYLER PLACE FAMILY RESORT.

Christina Tree

(special arrangements for infants). The children's recreation centers are exceptional. There are heated indoor and outdoor swimming and wading pools, six tennis courts, and equipment for kayaking, fishing, sailboarding, and more. For adults there is yoga, massage, and a variety of workshops; Montreal is less than an hour's drive away. Accommodations vary: You'll find the contemporary inn plus 27 cottages, a farm, and a guest house, for a total of 67 cottages and family suites, over 40 with fireplace. Each unit has two or more bedrooms, air-conditioning, and a pantry or kitchen. The inn has a spacious dining room with good food, and a big lounge with bar. Stays are usually Sat.–Sat. All-inclusive rates begin at $180 per adult and $112 per child. Reduced-rate packages are available at both ends of the summer season.

BED & BREAKFASTS ⚭ **Tabor House Inn** (802-868-7575; tabor houseinn.com), 58 Homestead St., West Swanton 05488. Location! Location! This 1890s mansion is the shores of Maquam Bay, an arm of Lake Champlain, and borders the 6,700-acre Missisquoi Wildlife Refuge. Innkeeper Jennifer Bright came to an auction held by the previous owners, never meaning to buy the place, but here she is on Tabor Point with four guest rooms including the vast (600 square feet) Lake Shore Suite with a private balcony and Jacuzzi, upstairs above the well-named "Great Room." There is also a 60-foot screened-in porch overlooking the lawn and lake. A full meal is included in the rates ($90–155). Dinner can be arranged, not a bad idea as you probably won't want to stir once you are here. It's a great place for a wedding.

⚭ 🐾 🌿 **Back Inn Time** (802-527-5116; backinntime.us), 68 Fairfield St., St. Albans 05478. A handsome Victori-

an with sloping lawns, gardens, and four outdoor porches. Pauline Cray and Paul Ralston have spent three years restoring its interior to look the way it might have in the 1860s. The living room, chandeliered dining room, and library are done in mauves, russets, and burgundies, with flowing drapes, Oriental carpets, and shining hardwood floors. Antiques abound, as do fine details, like the dark fireplace marble and intricate tiling. Four of the six guest rooms are smallish, with shared bath, and there are two master bedrooms with fireplace, one with private bath. Built by Victor Atwood, a railroad magnate during the Civil War, the house is an easy walk from the center of town. $99–139 includes a full breakfast. Candlelit dinners available with advance notice; inquire about ghosts, packages, murder mystery dinners, and a lakeside cottage.

🕯 🐾 "🍴" **Sampler House Bed & Breakfast** (802-893-2724; 888-508775; samplerhouse.com), 22 Main St., Milton 05468, handy to I-89 exits about halfway between Burlington and St. Albans. Peter Martin and Deborah Dolby have brilliantly restored and expanded their 1830 brick Cape. On a quiet street off Rt. 7, they offer guests two comfortable, tastefully furnished air-conditioned rooms (one upstairs and one ground level), each with private bath and wireless Internet. Peter has also added a bright, dual-level suite to the rear of the house, with a full kitchen, sofa, and satellite TV in its sitting room and an upstairs bedroom whose glorious bath includes a jetted tub and overhead rain shower. $85–125 includes breakfast. In each room the detailing, especially in the baths, reveals Peter's woodworking skill. Breakfast is Deborah's domain and includes something freshly baked as well a hot dish and cheese plate. Dinner can be prearranged.

∞ ♂ "↑" **Grey Gables Mansion** (802-848-3625; 800-299-2117; grey gablesmansion.com), 122 River St., Richford 05476. A turreted mansion built around 1890 by local lumber baron Sheldon Boright, this is a Queen Anne Victorian with hardwood floors, period wallpapers, stained glass, gardens, a wraparound porch, and a widow's walk. Guests enter past the carved walnut-and-mahogany staircase, and can linger in the fireplaced living room or in the library. Tim and Debby Green (and their pet collie) offer five antiques-filled guest rooms, all with full bath, cable TV, and wireless Internet. Hot meals are available at the downstairs pub, and candlelit dinners are available by prearrangement. This is a terrific place for weddings or civil unions, and bikers will be interested in the Missisquoi Valley Rail Trail connecting to St. Albans. The VAST snowmobile trail passes right outside, and there are numerous packages. It's also just a 20-minute drive to skiing at Jay Peak. $99–139 includes a full breakfast. Inquire about murder mystery weekends. Weddings are another specialty.

♦ ♣ ♂ "↑" **Buck Hollow Farm** (802-849-2400; 800-849-7985; buckhollow .com), 2150 Buck Hollow Rd., Fairfax 05454. Way off in rolling farm county some 10 miles southwest of St. Albans, this is a beautifully renovated 1790s carriage house set on 400 acres. Brad Schwartz has decorated each of the four rooms with antiques, queen-sized four-poster, and TV. Guests are encouraged to use the four-person outdoor hot tub and the heated pool or browse the antiques shop. In winter there's cross-country skiing on the property. $83 single, $93–114 per room for two or more, including full country breakfast.

♦ **Tetreault's Hillside View Farm** (802-827-4480), 143 South Rd., Fairfield 05455, is a warm, hospitable farmhouse with a lovely red barn in a quiet village east of St. Albans. There's a fireplace in the family room, antiques, and braided rugs. French spoken. $65–75 per double. No pets; kids over 9 welcome.

♂ **Country Essence B&B** (802-868-4247;), 641 Rt. 7, Box 95, Swanton 05488, 1.5 miles north of the village on Rt. 7. Cheryl Messier provides two pretty rooms with private bath, reached by a private staircase entrance in an 1850s homestead on 12 groomed acres with a playground. $85 per room with country breakfast. French is spoken.

Parent Farmhouse B&B (802-524-4201; 888-603-7135), 854 Pattee Hill Rd., Georgia 05468. Lucy and Roger Parent offer three rooms with shared bath. The handsome 19th-century brick farmhouse with distinctive oval windows is near Lake Champlain, with plenty of walking and biking opportunities. $100 includes continental breakfast. No credit cards.

OTHER LODGING Comfort Inn & Suites (802-524-3300; 800-228-5150; vtcomfortinn.com), 813 Fairfax Rd., Rt. 104, at Exit 19 off I-89, St. Albans 05478. Several of the 81 guest rooms are suites; complimentary continental breakfast, indoor pool, and fitness room, rates for families, seniors, and business groups.

CAMPGROUNDS See Burton Island State Park, Lake Carmi State Park, and Woods Island State Park under *Green Space*.

Homestead Campground (802-524-2356), 864 Ethan Allen Hwy., Exit 18 off I-89 in Georgia, offers 160 shaded campsites with water and electric hookups, laundry facilities, hot showers, cabin and camper rentals, a playground, and two swimming pools. The season is May 1–Oct. 15.

✳ Where to Eat

Chow!Bella (802-524-1405; chow bella.us), 28 N. Main St., St. Albans. Open daily (except Sun.) for lunch and dinner. Reserve for dinner. This intimate, sophisticated wine bar fills two downtown storefronts with its Mediterranean style and freshly prepared food along with a brick-walled low-lit ambience. The emphasis is on steaks, pasta, and flatbread pizza baked in an open hearth. We didn't have a reservation but staff were welcoming and the reasonably priced wine was good. Dinner options range from salads and soups and flatbreads to filet mignon and molasses-brined double pork chops, $8.50–24. Full bar, frequent live music.

Jeff's Bar, Grill, Restaurant (802-524-6135), 65 N. Main St., St. Albans. Open daily (except Sun.) for lunch, Tue.–Sat. for dinner. This obviously began as a fish shop (still next door) and has expanded into an attractive restaurant with specialties like pecan-crusted salmon ($19.95) and a New York strip steak with Jack Daniel's BBQ sauce ($21.95). Pastas are another option, like Boyden Valley beer bolognese over penne pasta ($16.95). Jeff's is housed in a Civil War–era building with a striped awning and views of the adjacent park.

🍴 **Bayside Pavilion** (802-524-0909), 15 Georgia Shore Rd., St. Albans. Open daily for lunch and dinner. Drive from Taylor Park down Lake St. 4 miles until it dead-ends at Lake Champlain; this 1920s roadhouse is on the corner. The daily special we enjoyed—grilled tuna with spinach, cheese, and veggies ($6.95)—was great, and we would love to come back for dinner. Full bar, moderate prices, kids' menu, live music on Fri.; Thu. is karaoke. Dinner entrées $14.95–21.95.

Park Cafe (802-527-0669), 84 N. Main St., St. Albans. Cappuccino, sandwiches, and baked goods, with specialty salads, signature breakfast wraps, and pancakes. Open daily except Sun., 7–3.

Sweet Nothings (802-527-5118), 94 Main St., St. Albans. Open daily. Julie Ludko and Linda Carrol sell Vermont-made chocolate and candy by the pound in this gift shop and soda fountain. In the back is an ice cream parlor where you can snag a sundae, float, milk shake, or more traditional sweets, like homemade cookies, pies, and cake.

Foothills Bakery (802-849-6601), 1123 Main St., Fairfax. Open daily except Sun. for breakfast and lunch. This bakery, housed in the old post office and much beloved by a local clientele, serves freshly baked muffins, scones, Danishes, cinnamon buns, and frittatas early on, then sandwiches on fat slices of homemade bread.

🍴 🗙 ♿ **K. J.'s Diner** (802-527-7340), 51 S. Main St., St. Albans. Open daily 6 AM–9 PM. Americana in tasty, generous portions in an air-conditioned diner serving breakfast all day, plus lunch and dinner. Great salads, pasta, wraps, and BBQ. Kids' menu.

Jacob's Restaurant (802-868-3190), 73 1st St. (Rt. 78), Swanton. Open for lunch and dinner except Tue. This is the place to eat in Swanton. Daily specials. Wed. is all-you-can-eat pasta ($6.99 includes soup and salad); Fri. and Sun. it's prime rib with soup and salad from $12.95. A wide choice of draft beers.

🍴 🗙 **My-T-Fine Creamery Restaurant** (802-868-4616), 159 Rt. 7, Swanton. Open daily for home-style breakfast, lunch, and dinner.

* Selective Shopping

As the Crow Flies (802-524-2800; asthecrowfliesvt.com), 58 N. Main St., St. Albans. Open weekdays and Sat., plus Sun. noon–4. A spiffy kitchen shop in a former hardware store, with specialty foods, wines, cookbooks, gourmet-related gifts, gadgets, housewares, and sundries.

Better Planet Books, Toys & Hobbies (802-524-6835), 44 N. Main St., St. Albans, is a bright place for books, toys, games, puzzles, hobby kits, and art supplies.

The Eloquent Page (802-527-PAGE), 23 Catherine St., a block west of Rt. 7 in downtown St. Albans. Donna Howard stocks over 35,000 used and collectible books, with a big section on Vermont and a wide variety of doll, dollhouse, and children's titles.

BEC Enterprises (802-849-2706), 148 Main St. (Rt. 104), Fairfax. Open May–Oct., 10–4:30, Sun. noon–5. A huge 1850 barn loaded with vintage kitchenware, dishes, glassware, and everything imaginable. Upstairs, Bridget Morgan presides over a surprisingly good collection of vintage books, academic and otherwise, at terrific prices, though a bit musty (the barn is not heated in winter).

Richford Antique and Craft Center (802-848-3836), 66 Main St., Richford.

Open daily 10–5. Twenty rooms filled with antiques, crafts, and collectibles, plus Vermont folk art and vintage clothing.

* Special Events

Late April: **Maple Festival**, St. Albans (802-524-5800; vtmaplefestival .org). For three days the town turns into a nearly nonstop "sugarin' off" party, courtesy of the local maple producers, augmented by a parade, crafts and antiques shows, a pancake breakfast, specialty food show and sale, footrace, and other events.

Late May: **Abenaki Heritage Celebration** (802-868-2559), on the green, Swanton—a powwow with costumed dancing, Native music, foods, books, and crafts.

First weekend in June: **Vermont Dairy Festival** (802-933-8891), Enosburg Falls. Milking contest, baking contest, midway rides, cow plop contest, crafts fair, horse pulling, animal barn, and more.

Early August: **Franklin County Field Days** (802-868-2514), Airport Rd., Highgate. Classic old-time country fair with cattle exhibits, crafts fair, games, rides, musical entertainment, tractor, horse, and oxen pulls, cattle judging, draft horse show.

Stowe Area and North of the Notch

5

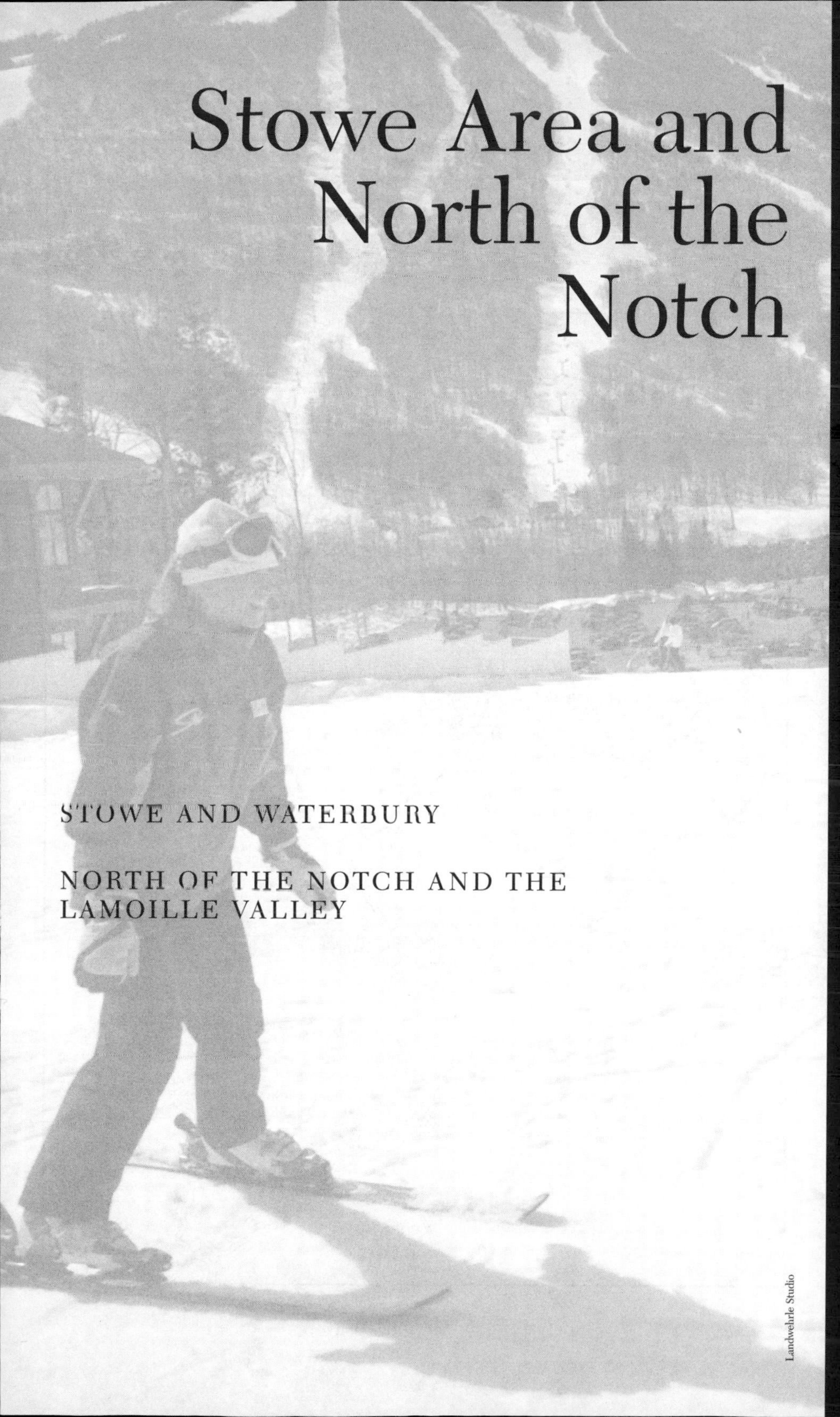

STOWE AND WATERBURY

NORTH OF THE NOTCH AND THE
LAMOILLE VALLEY

Landwehrle Studio

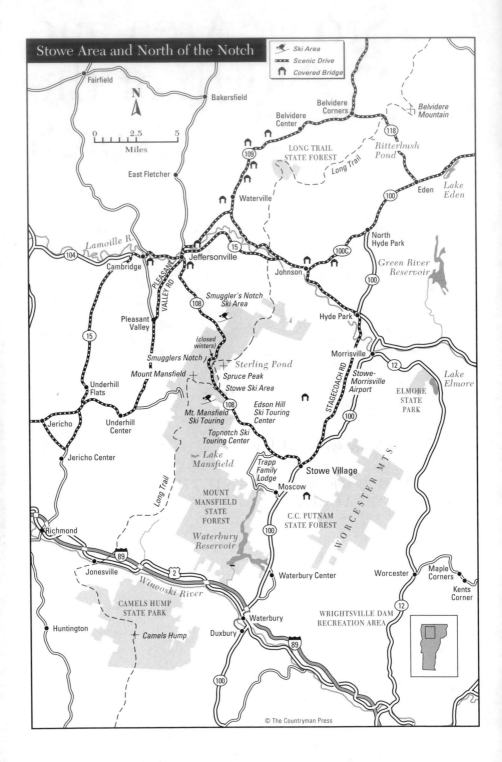

Stowe Area and North of the Notch

Ski Area
Scenic Drive
Covered Bridge

Fairfield

Bakersfield

N

0   2.5   5
Miles

Belvidere Corners

Belvidere Center

Belvidere Mountain

East Fletcher

118

LONG TRAIL STATE FOREST

Ritterbush Pond

Long Trail

109

Waterville

100

Eden

Lake Eden

Lamoille R.

104

Cambridge

15

Jeffersonville

100C

North Hyde Park

Green River Reservoir

Johnson

100

PLEASANT VALLEY RD

108

Smuggler's Notch Ski Area

Hyde Park

Pleasant Valley

(closed winters)

Sterling Pond

Morrisville

12

Lake Elmore

15

Smugglers Notch

Mount Mansfield

Spruce Peak
Stowe Ski Area

STAGECOACH RD

Stowe-Morrisville Airport

ELMORE STATE PARK

Underhill Flats

108

Mt. Mansfield Ski Touring

Edson Hill Ski Touring Center

100

Jericho

Underhill Center

Topnotch Ski Touring Center

Lake Mansfield

Trapp Family Lodge

Stowe Village

Jericho Center

Long Trail

MOUNT MANSFIELD STATE FOREST

Moscow

C.C. PUTNAM STATE FOREST

W O R C E S T E R   M T S.

100

Richmond

Waterbury Reservoir

89

Jonesville

2

Winooski River

Waterbury Center

Worcester

Maple Corners

Kents Corner

12

CAMELS HUMP STATE PARK

Huntington

Camels Hump

Duxbury

Waterbury

89

WRIGHTSVILLE DAM RECREATION AREA

100

© The Countryman Press

STOWE AND WATERBURY

K nown as the "ski capital of the East," Stowe is the state's premier summer and year-round spa resort as well. A 200-year-old village that looks like a classic Vermont village should look, it's set against the massive backdrop of Mount Mansfield, which looks just like Vermont's highest mountain should look.

By the mid–19th century, men were already taxing their imaginations and funds to entice visitors up onto the heights of Mount Mansfield—which bears an uncanny resemblance to the upturned profile of a rather jowly man. In 1858 an inn was built under the Nose, a project that entailed constructing a 100-yard log trestle above a chasm and several miles of corduroy road made from hemlock. In Stowe Village at that time, a hotel, the Mansfield House, accommodated 600 guests.

Swedish families moved into Stowe in 1912 and began using their skis to get around. Then, in 1914, the Dartmouth College librarian skied down the Toll Road. Serious skiing, however, didn't begin until 1933, when the Civilian Conservation Corps cut a 4-mile-plus trail for just that purpose. The following year the town formed its own Mount Mansfield Ski Club, setting up basic lodging near the bottom of the ski trail in a former logging camp. By 1937 a rope tow had been rigged from the camp to the top of the trail, powered by a Cadillac engine. Lift tickets cost 50¢ per day, $5 per season.

Stowe Mountain Resort is still the same outfit formed in 1951 from the various small concerns that had evolved in the 1930s and '40s to serve skiers, and it's still owned by the same insurance company, AIG (American International Group). The good news is continuity and an immense sense of pride and history. Sometimes slow to respond to the demands of this quickly changing industry, the company has become much more aggressive over the past decade with its building and expansion plans.

What Stowe Mountain Resort does, it always does first-class. Just as it was a Cadillac engine, not the Ford used in Woodstock, that first towed Stowe skiers, the eight-passenger gondola, installed in 1991, is one of the world's fastest, and the Cliff House in the summit Octagon offers meals with spectacular alpine views. While the 1950s base lodge, expanded and renovated a couple of times, still serves Mount Mansfield trails, the 2008–09 ski season marked the completion of a 10-year, $400 million improvement and expansion plan that shifted the resort center to Spruce Peak, now linked to the Mount Mansfield trails by the "Over Easy" transfer gondola. The handsome new Spruce Base Camp , adjoining the Alpine Slide and "summer adventure" activities, is now the resort's prime base lodge,

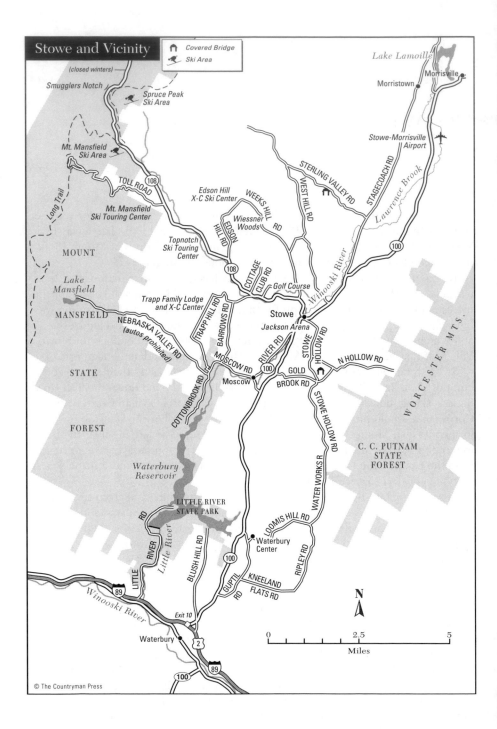

Stowe and Vicinity

Covered Bridge
Ski Area

(closed winters)

Lake Lamoille

Smugglers Notch

Spruce Peak
Ski Area

Morristown

Morrisville

Mt. Mansfield
Ski Area

Stowe-Morrisville
Airport

TOLL ROAD

108

Edson Hill
X-C Ski Center

STERLING VALLEY RD

WEST HILL RD

STAGECOACH RD

Long Trail

Mt. Mansfield
Ski Touring Center

WEEKS HILL RD

Lawrence Brook

Wiessner
Woods

EDSON HILL RD

100

Topnotch
Ski Touring
Center

108

MOUNT

COTTAGE CLUB RD

Golf Course

Winooski River

Lake
Mansfield

Trapp Family Lodge
and X-C Center

Stowe

Jackson Arena

MANSFIELD

NEBRASKA VALLEY RD
(autos prohibited)

TRAPP HILL RD

BARROWS RD

STOWE HOLLOW RD

N HOLLOW RD

RIVER RD

STATE

MOSCOW RD

100

GOLD
BROOK RD

Moscow

COTTONBROOK RD

STOWE HOLLOW RD

WORCESTER MTS.

FOREST

Waterbury
Reservoir

WATER WORKS R

C. C. PUTNAM
STATE
FOREST

RD

LITTLE RIVER
STATE PARK

LOOMIS HILL RD

Little River

BLUSH HILL RD

Waterbury
Center

RIPLEY RD

LITTLE RIVER RD

100

GUPTIL RD

KNEELAND
FLATS RD

89

Winooski River

N

Exit 10

0   2.5   5

Miles

Waterbury

2

100

89

© The Countryman Press

Here there's also a new pedestrian plaza with shops and restaurants and the luxurious six-story shingled "Vermont-Alpine" style Stowe Mountain Lodge with a restaurant and full-service spa. "Mountain cabins" (rustically luxurious condos), a performance center, and a new 18-hole golf course complete this Spruce Peak at Stowe "community."

The actual quality of alpine skiing and snowboarding at Stowe continues to be outstanding. The cross-country ski network totals more than 150 km, with many trails meandering off the high walls of the cul-de-sac in which the resort nestles.

Truth to tell, however, Stowe attracts more visitors in summer and fall than it does in winter. From June through mid-October it offers superb golf, tennis, theater, as well as hiking, biking, fishing, and special events every week. You can ride the lift to the top of Spruce Peak and climb into the alpine slide, a concrete channel that whisks you 2,300 feet down the mountainside. No one should leave without taking a gondola ride; the whole area—peaks, valleys, and fields—opens up before you. Alternatively, you can drive your own car up the 4.5-mile Toll Road, park, and clamber around the summit; hiking paths connect to the Long Trail.

What's most amazing about Stowe is the way it has managed to keep its commercial side low-key and tasteful, a sideshow to the natural beauty of the place. Even in nonskiing months, most visitors are lured from their cars and onto their feet and bicycles, at least onto the 5.5-mile Stowe Recreation Path, which parallels the Mountain Road from the village (albeit at a more forgiving grade) to Mount Mansfield, through cornfields, wildflowers, and raspberry patches.

In warm-weather months Stowe is also an excellent pivot from which to explore northern Vermont: 30 miles from Burlington, just over the Notch from the little-touristed Lamoille Valley, and a short drive from both Montpelier and Barre on the one hand and the Northeast Kingdom on the other.

In mud and stick seasons, when lodging rates are lowest, Stowe remains an inviting spa oasis. Stoweflake Mountain Resort bills itself as New England's largest, but Topnotch Resort is its equal in staffing and services. Trapp Family Lodge and Stowe Mountain Lodge also both offers their guests full spa services; visitors can choose from several other day spas in this town of less than 5,000. Stowe also has almost 50 different lodging establishments, accommodating a total of 10,000 visitors on any given night, along with some 40 restaurants and 70 shops.

Lodging options range from funky to fabulous, including a number of self-contained resorts as well as inns, lodges, motels, and condominiums. The Stowe Area Association has been in business since 1936, matching visitors with lodgings they can afford and enjoy.

Most Stowe-bound visitors know Waterbury, 10 miles down Rt. 100, simply as an I-89 exit; they know the strip just to the north as the home of the Ben & Jerry's ice cream factory, one of the state's most popular attractions. The old town itself lies along a southward bend in the Winooski River, and several interesting shops and restaurants are housed in the brief downtown between the traffic light and the railroad station. Waterbury Reservoir, accessible from Waterbury Center, is the obvious place in this area to swim and paddle a canoe or kayak.

GUIDANCE **The Stowe Area Association** (802-253-7321; 877-247-8693; gostowe .com), 51 Main St., Stowe 05672. The SAA publishes seasonal guides, makes lodging reservations and maintains an expansive, professionally staffed welcome center, open daily 9–5, Sun. 11–5, frequently later.

The **Waterbury Tourism Council** maintains an excellent Web site, waterbury .org.

GETTING THERE *By bus:* **Vermont Transit/Greyhound** (800-552-8737) stops in Montpelier with connections from Boston, New York, and points south.

By train: **Amtrak** from Washington, DC; New York City; and Springfield, Massachusetts, stops in Waterbury.

By plane: The **Stowe-Morrisville Airport**, 7 miles north, provides private plane services and charters. **Burlington International Airport**, 34 miles away, is served by major carriers (see "Burlington Region").

By taxi: **Peg's Pickup/Stowe Taxi** (800-370-9490). **Blazer Transportation Taxi** (802-253-0013).

By car: From most points, I-89 Exit 10, and 15 minutes north on Rt. 100.

GETTING AROUND During winter season **Stowe Mountain Road Shuttle** (802-223-7BUS; gmtaride.org) circles the 7 miles between the village and the mountain. Pick up a schedule at the SAA welcome center (see *Guidance*).

MEDICAL EMERGENCY Emergency service is available by calling **911**.

Copley Hospital (802-888-4231), Morrisville.

✳ Must-See

Mount Mansfield (802-253-3500; stowe.com), the highest point in Vermont— 4,395 feet (it gained 2 feet when it was remeasured in 1998) at the Chin—yields a truly spectacular view, accessible primarily in summer, unless you can clamber up to the summit from the Cliff House restaurant at the top of the gondola over ice and snow. In summer there are two easy ways up: the Toll Road and an eight-passenger gondola.

Mount Mansfield Auto Toll Road (802-253-3000) begins 7 miles up Rt. 108 from the village of Stowe; look for the sign on your left just before the Inn at the Mountain. Open late mid-May–mid-Oct. 9–4, weather permitting. $23 per car. Motorcycles and bikes are no longer permitted. First laid in the mid–19th century, this steep, winding road led to a hotel that served the public until 1957. (It was demolished in the mid-1960s.) The road also serves as a ski trail in winter. It climbs to the Mount Mansfield Summit Station, just below the Nose (4,062 feet). A 0.5-mile Tundra Trail follows the Long Trail (red-and-white blazes on the rocks) north to Drift Rock (the trek should take 20 minutes); another mile along the trail brings you to the summit of Mount Mansfield (4,395 feet). The round trip takes two hours.

Gondola Skyride (802-253-3000; stowe.com) at Stowe operates mid-June–mid-Oct. at Mount Mansfield, weather permitting, 10–5. $22 adults, $14 ages 6–12, $18 ages 65 and older; $48 for a family of four round-trip. The eight-passenger gondola runs from Midway Lodge to the Cliff House; half an hour's trek brings you up to the Chin. However you get there, the view from the summit (the Chin) is spectacular on a clear day: west across 20 miles of farmland to Lake Champlain; east to the Worcester Range across the Stowe Valley; north to Jay Peak (35 miles distant) across the Lamoille Valley; and south, back along the Green Mountains, to Camels

Hump. Mount Washington is visible to the east, Whiteface to the west. Be sure to catch the 5 PM gondola unless you fancy a long walk down.

Stowe Village. A classic, early-19th-century Vermont village with a spired white meetinghouse at one end of Main Street and a brick stagecoach inn at the other, Stowe offers a satisfying variety of stores and restaurants all within an easy stroll. The former wooden high school (one block up School St. from Main) is now the **Helen Day Art Center** (802-253-8358; helenday.com), open in summer daily noon–5 except Mon., closed Sun. too in winter. The changing art exhibits are frequently well worth checking out, and the **Stowe Free Library** offers free computer access and WiFi. The mid-19th-century Bloody Brook Schoolhouse museum next door is open on request in summer months.

Smugglers Notch is the high (elevation: 2,162 feet), extremely winding and narrow stretch of Rt. 108 just north of Mount Mansfield, with 1,000-foot cliffs towering on either side. The first carriage road through this pass wasn't opened until 1894, but the name reflects its heavy use as a route to smuggle cattle down from Canada during the War of 1812, not to mention hooch during Prohibition. One of two formally designated State Scenic Roads in Vermont, Smugglers Notch is known for rock formations: Smugglers Head, Elephant Head, the Hunter and His Dog, the Big Spring, Smugglers Cave, and the Natural Refrigerator. The Notch is closed in winter, inviting cross-country skiing and snowshoeing. See also *To See* in "North of the Notch."

Note: For Ben & Jerry's Ice Cream Factory Tours see *To Do—For Families.*

MOUNT MANSFIELD'S PROFILE, SEEN FROM THE GARDEN AT TOPNOTCH RESORT.

Christina Tree

✳ Also See

Vermont Ski Museum (802-253-9911; vermontskimuseum.org), Old Town Hall, 1 S. Main St., Stowe. Open except Tue. See the actual lifts that carried the first skiers up the Vermont mountains and the ski equipment they used to come down. Discover how dozens of tiny ski areas grew into the handful of mega resorts that dominate the industry today. Watch old ski movies and vintage ski footage on a giant plasma screen. The museum shop sells ski-related gifts. Admission by donation.

COVERED BRIDGES The **Gold Brook Bridge** in Stowe Hollow, also known as Emily's Bridge because Emily is said to have hanged herself from it (due, so the story goes, to unrequited love), remains the most haunted structure in the state (take School St. about 8 miles to Covered Bridge Rd.). There is another picturesque bridge spanning Sterling Brook off Stagecoach Rd., north of the village.

SCENIC DRIVES Not only is Stowe pleasantly situated for touring in all directions, but it is also organized to offer visitors well-researched printed tours. Pick up a copy of *Roads and Tours* from the **Stowe Area Association** (see *Guidance*; gostowe). A summer drive through Smugglers Notch is a must.

✳ To Do

AIR RIDES For **hot-air ballooning**, inquire at Stoweflake Mountain Resort and Spa (802-253-7355; stoweflake.com). Whitcomb Aviation's **Stowe Soaring**, based at the Stowe-Morrisville State Airport (802-888-7845; 800-898-7845), offers **glider rides**, instruction, and rentals. Also see *Gondola Skyride* under *Must-See*.

ALPINE SLIDE Stowe's alpine slide (802-253-3000) is accessed from the Spruce Peak Base Lodge, Mountain Rd., Stowe. Open late June–early Sept., 10–5, then on weekends through Columbus Day. $14 adults, $10 juniors and seniors; discounts for multiple-ride packages.

BIKING The equipage here is a mountain bike, and the rental sources are **AJ's Ski & Sports** (802-253-4593; 800-226-6257; ajsports.com), **Pinnacle Ski & Sports** (802-253-7222; 800-458-9996; pinnacleskisports.com), **Boots 'N Boards** (802-253-4225), the **Nordic Barn** (802-253-6433), and **Skier Shop** (802-253-7919; 800-996-8398; skiershop.com) in Stowe. Neophytes usually head for the 5.5-mile **Stowe Recreation Path** (see *Hiking and Walking*); next there's a 10-mile loop through part of the Mount Mansfield State Forest and into the Cottonbrook Basin. **Green Mountain Bike Tours** (802-279-1619) offers mountain biking tours. Pick up a copy of *Northern Vermont—Mountain Biking* published by Map Adventures of Portland, Maine (207-879-4777; mapadventures.com); it maps and describes over 30 local mountain bike trail and road rides.

BIRDING Fin & Feathers (802-730-4393; finandfeathervt.com). Naturalist-guide Jan Axtell is an expert birder offering hikes throughout northern Vermont.

BOATING Canoes and kayaks can be rented from **AJ's Ski & Sports** (802-253-4593; ajsports.com) and **Umiak Outfitters** (802-253-2317; umiak.com), Stowe.

Umiak also offers river trips, lessons, and guided trips on the Winooski and Lamoille rivers, on Lake Champlain, and throughout the state. **Bert's Boats** (802-644-8189; bertsboats.com) also offers a variety of group tours.

CARRIAGE RIDES **Gentle Giants Sleigh, Carriage, and Wagon Rides at Topnotch** (802-253-2216) in Stowe offers carriage and wagon rides, as does the **Trapp Family Lodge** (802-353-5813).

FISHING The Little River in Stowe is a favorite for brook trout, along with Sterling Pond on top of Spruce Peak and Sterling Brook. Contact **Reel Vermont** (802-223-1869; reelvt.com), geared to guiding everyone (families included) from neophytes to pros. **Catamount Fishing Adventures** (802-253-8500; catamountfishing.com), run by Willy Dietrich, is located in Stowe. It offers year-round guide service, including ice fishing. **Fly Fish Vermont** (802-253-3964; 800-535-9763; flyrodshop.com) is another Stowe resource. **Fin & Feathers** (see *Birding*) offers fly- and spin-fishing expeditions throughout northern Vermont. The **Fly Rod Shop** (802-253-7346; flyrodshop.com), 2703 Waterbury Rd. (Rt. 100), Stowe, carries a full line of gear and offers full- and half-day guided tours.

FITNESS CENTERS AND SPAS **The Spa at Topnotch** (802-253-8585) and the **Stoweflake Spa & Sports Club** (802-253-7355) both offer over-the-top service. "This is not your everyday spa" is something we heard repeatedly during our day at Topnotch, from guests as well as members of the 90-person spa staff. The 120-item spa menu ranges from a Vermont river rocks massage and wrap with local herbs and wildflowers to ayurvedic body balancing and includes any number of dermatological treatments as well as facials. Salon and fitness services are also offered. At Stoweflake facilities include 31 treatment rooms, a Hungarian mineral soaking pool, an aqua solarium, and a 102-degree massaging waterfall. Treatments include a maple facial. Both spas are open to nonguests with spa packages. The **Golden Eagle Resort** (802-253-4811) offers a modest facility, **Trapp Family Lodge** (802-253-8511) has a new fitness center for its guests, and the new Spa and Cooper Wellness at **Stowe Mountain Lodge** (888-478-0938) is also just for guests; it includes a "healing sanctuary with a herbal steam chamber," Jacuzzi pool, and steam shower, also two "harmony rooms." The fitness center and the **Green Mountain Inn** (802-253-7301) offers massage services. The **Stowe Gym** (802-253-2176) on Mountain Rd. has state-of-the-art machines, aerobics and Spinning classes, and more. The **Swimming Hole** (802-253-9229) on Weeks Hill Rd. has a lap pool and fitness center, aqua aerobics, personal training, swimming instruction, a children's pool, and a waterslide.

FOR FAMILIES **Ben & Jerry's Ice Cream Factory Tours** (802-882-1260; 866-BJ-TOURS; benjerry.com), 1281 Waterbury Stowe Rd. (Rt. 100), Waterbury. Take Exit 10 off I-89 and go north 1 mile. No American ice cream has a story, let alone a taste, to match that of the totally Vermont-made sweet and creamy stuff concocted by high school buddies Ben Cohen and Jerry Greenfield, whose personalities linger though they have sold the company to Unilever. More than two decades ago they began churning out Dastardly Mash and Heath Bar Crunch in a Burlington garage; they have now outgrown this seemingly mammoth plant, Vermont's number one attraction. Ice cream is made Mon.–Thu. but a half-hour tour of the plant is offered daily 10–6 (9–8 in July and Aug.), except Thanksgiving, Christmas, and New Year's Day. The gift store, selling an amazing number of things relating to cows and Vermont, is open 10–7, as is the Scoop Shop. The tour includes a multimedia show, a look (from an observation platform) at the production room, and a free sample of one of the many "euphoric flavors." The grounds include picnic facilities and some sample black-and-white cows. $3 adults, $2 seniors, ages 12 and under free.

❦ **Kid's Summer Mountain Adventure Camps** (802-253-3685), based at Spruce Peak, offer age-appropriate activities beginning with "Cubs Daycare" for 3 month- to 3-year-olds and continuing to rock climbing, mountain biking, and the Extreme Obstacle Course for 7- to 14-year-olds. Available on a daily and weekly basis. The Bungee Trampolines, Obstacle Course, and Climbing Wall are also open to kids of all ages (6 to 65+) on a per-ticket basis.

❦ **Stowe Golfpark** (802-253-9951) at the Sun & Ski Inn, Mountain Road, offers 18 holes of miniature golf (May–Oct., 10–9:30).

GOLF **Stowe Country Club & Vermont Golf Academy** (802-253-4893; stowe .com), an 18-hole course with a 40-acre driving range, putting green, restaurant, bar, pro shop, and school. **Stoweflake Mountain Resort and Spa** (802-253-7355; stoweflake.com), adjacent to the Stowe Country Club, also offers instruction. The **Farm Resort** (802-888-3525; 866-888-5810; farmresortlodging.com), Rt. 100, 6 miles north of Stowe in Morrisville, offers nine holes, a driving range, putting green, rentals, and snack bar. **Blush Hill Country Club** (802-244-8974), a nine- hole course in Waterbury, has marvelous views. **Country Club of Vermont** (802- 244-1800), Waterbury, 18 holes, gets rave reviews.

Note: The new **Stowe Mountain Club** is open only to members and guests at Stowe Resort lodging properties.

HIKING AND WALKING **Green Mountain Club (GMC)** (802-244-7037; greenmountainclub.org), a few miles south of Stowe Village on Rt. 100 in Water- bury Center, maintains a Hiker's Center stocked with hiking maps, guides, and gear. Inquire about workshops and special events.

Stowe Recreation Path is a 5.5-mile paved path that begins in Stowe Village behind the Community Church, winds up through cornfields, wildflowers, and raspberry patches, and parallels Mountain Rd. (but at a more forgiving pitch). It's open to walkers, joggers, bicyclists, and more. Note the **Quiet Path** along the West Branch River, a mile loop off the main path (it begins across from the Gold- en Eagle) reserved for walkers (no mountain bikers or in-line skaters).

Mount Mansfield. See the introduction to this section and *To See* for a general description of Vermont's highest mountain. For walkers (as opposed to hikers), it's best to take the Toll Road or gondola up and follow the Tundra Trail. Serious hik- ers should at least purchase the weather-proofed map of the Mount Mansfield region and can profit from the *Long Trail Guide*, both published by the Green Mountain Club. A naturalist is on hand May–Nov. along the heavily traveled 2.5- mile section of the Long Trail between the Forehead and the Chin; the Green Mountain Club maintains Butler Lodge, 0.5 mile south of the Forehead, and Taft Lodge, below the Chin, as shelters for hikers.

Smugglers Notch. The Long Trail North, clearly marked, provides an easy, mile-plus hike to Sterling Pond, a beautiful spot at 3,000 feet, and fish-stocked, too. Elephant Head can be reached from the state picnic area on Rt. 108; a 2-mile trail leads to this landmark—from which you can also continue on to Sterling Pond and thence out to Rt. 108 only a couple of miles above the picnic area. No one should drive through Smugglers Notch without stopping to see the Smugglers Cave and to clamber around on the rocks.

Other local hikes are detailed in *Day Hiker's Guide to Vermont*, which is published by the Green Mountain Club and available from the Stowe Area Association: **Stowe Pinnacle** is a popular 2.8-mile climb; **Mount Hunger** (4 miles) is the highest peak in the Worcester Range; **Taft Lodge** (3.4 miles) is steep but takes you to the oldest lodge on the Long Trail; **Belvidere Mountain** in Eden is a three-and-a-half-hour trek yielding good views in all directions; **Ritterbush Pond** and **Devil's Gulch**, also in Eden, are about two and a half hours round-trip; and **Elmore Mountain** in Elmore State Park is a two- to three-hour hike with spectacular views.

Camels Hump, from Waterbury. See "Burlington Region" for details. This trail is also detailed in *50 Hikes in Vermont* (Backcountry Publications). One trail starts from Crouching Lion Farm in Duxbury; it's a six-and-a-half-hour round-trip hike to the unspoiled summit of Vermont's third highest mountain. Pick up a map at the GMC Hiker's Center (see above).

Little River Trail System, Mount Mansfield State Forest, Waterbury. There are seven beautiful trails through the Ricker Basin and Cotton Brook area, once a settlement for 50 families who left behind cellar holes, stone fences, cemeteries, lilacs, and apple trees. Accessible from both Stowe and Waterbury. Pick up the self-guiding booklet from the Vermont State Department of Forests, Parks and Recreation in Waterbury (802-241-3678).

See also "Barre/Montpelier Area" for hiking in the Worcester Range.

Note: Northern Vermont—Hiking Trails, published by Map Adventures of Portland, Maine (207-879-4777; mapadventures.com), is worth picking up.

HORSEBACK RIDING **Edson Hill Manor Stables** (802-253-8954), Stowe, offers guided trail rides (also pony rides) through its upland wilds and fields, geared to various levels, also lessons. **Nordic Barn Riding Stables** (802-253-6433) at **Topnotch Resort**, Mountain Rd., also offers trail rides and lessons. **Windy Willows Farm** (802-635-7300) and **Vermont Icelandic Horse Farm** (802-496-7141) offer trail rides all year long.

ROCK CLIMBING Check with **Umiak Outfitters** (802-253-2317) in Stowe for instruction and ropes course. Warm up on the **Climbing Wall** at Spruce Peak (stowe.com).

EVEN THE HORSES ARE PAMPERED AT TOPNOTCH RESORT.

Christina Tree

SOARING **Stowe Soaring** (802-888-7845; 800-898-7845; stowesoaring.com), 2305 Laporte Rd., Rt. 100, Morrisville (6 miles north of Stowe Village), offers instruction, rentals, and rides.

*SWIMMING **Waterbury Reservoir**, the best local beach, is accessible from Little River State Park (see *Campgrounds*). **Forest Pool** on Notchbrook Rd., **Sterling Falls**, and the swimming holes in **Ranch Valley** are all worth checking; ask locally for directions. The nonprofit community pool is **The Swimming Hole** (802-253-9119), featuring a competition-sized pool in a barn with a toddler and child swimming area. Many lodging places also have their own pools that nonguests may use for a fee.

TENNIS **The Topnotch Tennis Center** (802-253-9649), Stowe. Four indoor and six outdoor courts, pro shop, instruction, ball machines, videotape, round robins; open daily (hours vary).

Inn at the Mountain Tennis Club (802-253-7311), six well-maintained clay courts adjacent to the Inn at the Mountain, 8–6, available by the hour (dress: whites required).

Free public courts can be found at the town recreation area off School St. A number of inns have courts available to the public; inquire at the Stowe Area Association (802-253-7321).

✳ Winter Sports

CROSS-COUNTRY SKIING A 150-km network of trails that connects ski centers in this area adds up to some of the best ski touring in New England. Given the high elevation of much of this terrain, the trails tend to have snow when few other areas do, and on windy, icy days, cross-country can be better in Stowe than downhill. All four touring centers (in Stowe) honor the others' trail tickets (if you ski, not drive, from one to the next).

Trapp Family Lodge Cross-Country Ski Center (802-253-8511; trappfamily .com). Located on Trapp Hill Rd., off by itself in the upper reaches of the valley, this is one of the oldest and most beautiful commercial trail systems—40 km of set trails and a total of 85 km of trails at elevations of 1,100–3,000 feet. The basic route here is up and up to a cabin in the woods, a source of homemade soups and chili. Start early enough in the day and you can continue along ridge trails or connect with the Mount Mansfield system. Lessons, equipment rental and sales, and outstanding pastries are all available, as well as guided tours.

Stowe Mountain Resort Cross-Country Center (802-253-3688; stowe.com), Mountain Rd. Located near the Inn at the Mountain, this center offers 35 km of set trails, plus 45 km of backcountry trails, at elevations of 1,200–2,800 feet. Trail fees are $16 adults, $9 for juniors and seniors. It's possible to take the Toll House lift partway up the Toll Road and ski down (a good place to practice telemarking). You can also take the quad close enough to the summit to enable you to climb to the very top (via the Toll Road) for a spectacular view out across Lake Champlain; the descent via the Toll Road is relatively easy. Another beautiful trail circles Sterling Pond high in the saddle between Spruce and Madonna mountains (accessible via chairlift). Connecting trails link this system with the Trapp Family Lodge trails (see previous page) along some of Stowe's oldest ski trails, such as Ranch Camp and Steeple, dating to the 1920s, as well as new backcountry trails winding along the curved inner face of the mountain.

Edson Hill Manor Ski Touring Center (802-253-7371; edsonhillmanor.com), Edson Hill Rd. Relatively uncrowded on the uplands north of the Mountain Rd., the area offers 30 miles of set trails, 25 more on outlying trails at elevations between 1,200 and 2,150 feet; instruction, rental, sales, full lunches, and guided tours available.

Topnotch Touring Center (802-253-8585; topnotchresort.com), Mountain Rd., Stowe. Novice to expert, a total of 20 km of groomed trails on 120 private acres; instruction, equipment rental, café, and restaurant available, also changing rooms.

Backcountry tours are offered by the **Stowe Mountain Resort** (802-253-3688), **Trapp Family Lodge** (802-253-8511), and **Umiak Outfitters** (802-253-2317; umiak.com)

Remember: Backcountry skiing is best done with a guide if you don't know the area.

DOWNHILL SKIING ✍ **Stowe Mountain Resort** (800-253-4SKI; stowe.com for information, snow reports, and slope-side lodging). The 2008–09 season marked the completion of a 15-year plan to upgrade, expand, and link facilities at Stowe's two neighboring mountains, Mount Mansfield and Spruce Peak.

Stowe regulars ski Mount Mansfield in the morning, switching after lunch to south-facing Spruce Peak across Rt. 108, now connected by the skis-on "Over Easy" transfer gondola. The new Spruce Camp base lodge is now the resort's central base, with restaurants, shops, rentals, indoor and outdoor fireplaces. It adjoins a new pedestrian plaza with more shops and restaurants and the dramatic new six-story Spruce Mountain Lodge and spa, plus "mountain cabins" (posh condos) and private homes. Spruce Peak has also gained a high-speed quad, a new beginner

SKIING AT THE MAIN MOUNTAIN, STOWE

Landwehrle Studio

Stowe Mountain Resort

THE NEW BASE COMPLEX AT SPRUCE PEAK

slope, and New England's first fully automated snowmaking system to keep the slopes dusted top-to-bottom. Extensive trail work has opened up little-explored backcountry stretches, while the central Main Street trail has been widened and contoured for easier navigation. The Children's Adventure Center, connected by free shuttles every 10 minutes, serves as home to the Ski and Snowboard School and children's programs, and lifts access extensive novice trails. All told, about a fifth of Stowe's nearly 50 (predominantly intermediate-level) trails have been refurbished. Mount Mansfield, whose famous Front Four trails plunge almost vertically down its legendary face, has a quad and double to get you to the top (wear a neck warmer, goggles, and sunscreen). Under the Octagon Café, these expert slopes feature tree-shaded glades and some of the longest trails in the East, though you also have the option of half a dozen intermediate trails that snake down at more forgiving angles. It's an easy traverse from this side of the mountain to the trails served by the eight-person, high-speed gondola to the elevated Cliff House, from which long, ego-building runs like Perry Merrill sweep to the valley floor. The daredevil set gravitates to the Mansfield Triple, with its two new terrain parks, superpipe, and freestyle. Those seeking something tamer can head for the southern-facing Toll House, a double chair with a slow, easy descent through tranquil hardwoods.

Lifts: 8-passenger gondola, intermountain transfer gondola, 3 high-speed quad chairlifts, 4 double and 2 triple chairlifts, 2 surface.

Trails: 116, also glade skiing; 25 percent expert, 59 percent intermediate, 16 percent beginner.

Vertical drop: 2,360 feet on Mount Mansfield, 1,550 feet on Spruce Peak.

Snowmaking: Covers 80 percent of the terrain trails served by all of the 12 lifts.

Facilities: 8 restaurants, including those in the Inn at the Mountain, 3 base lodges, plus the Octagon Café & Gallery (you can send free e-mail postcards) and the newly renovated Cliff House at the top of the busiest lifts; cafeterias, rentals, ski shops, shuttle bus.

Ski school: 200 instructors; a lift especially designed for beginners at Spruce Peak, where novices learn to make the transition from easy to intermediate trails.

Night skiing: More than 20 acres on Mount Mansfield are lighted Thu.–Sat. nights 5–9.

For children: Day care from 6 weeks in Cubs Infant Daycare. The Children's Learning Center offers day care or a combo of care and lessons at Spruce Peak.

Rates: See stowe.com for current ticket prices.

ICE SKATING Ice skating is available at the Olympic-sized **Jackson Arena** (802-253-6148) in the village. Call for public skating times. There's also skating on the pond at **Commodores Inn** (802-253-7131). The town of Waterbury has a large new skating arena called the **Ice Center** (802-244-4040).

SLEIGH RIDES In Stowe, **Edson Hill Manor** (802-253-7371), and **Trapp Family Lodge** (802-253-5813).

SNOWBOARD RENTALS **Misty Mountain Snowboards** (802-253-3040), top of the Mountain Rd., Stowe, advertises "the fastest snowboard rentals in town"; also check out **Dark Side Snowboards** (877-422-3275).

SNOWMOBILING **Stowe Snowmobile Tours** (802-253-6221; stowesnow mobiletours.com) offers rentals and tours of the Mount Mansfield State Forest, and is also a source of information about local trails. **Smugglers' Notch Snowmobile Tours** (800-451-8752) provides guided daytime and evening tours.

SNOWSHOEING **Umiak Outdoor Outfitters** (802-253-2317; umiak.com) offers guided moonlit snowshoe tours, fondue and gourmet dinner tours, even a package tour at the Ben & Jerry's Factory in Waterbury so you can snowshoe before you eat the ice cream. **Trapp Family Lodge Cross-Country Ski Center** has designated more than 15 km of its trails as snowshoe-only. The **Stowe Mountain Resort Cross-Country Center** has cut 5 km of dedicated trails and permits snowshoers on all 80 km of its cross-country trails. **Topnotch at Stowe Resort** has also designated some snowshoe-recommended routes, and permits snowshoes on all 20 km of its trails.

The obvious place to go is, of course, up the unplowed stretch of Rt. 108 into Smugglers Notch, and the more adventurous can also access more than 40 miles of hiking terrain on and around Mount Mansfield, but it's best to check with the **Green Mountain Club** (see *Hiking and Walking*), which also sponsors a February Snowshoe Festival. Local rental sources are plentiful. Pick up a copy of *Northern Vermont Adventure Skiing*, a weather-proofed map/guide detailing trails throughout the region. It's available at Umiak and other local stores in Stowe.

✳ Green Space

For fees and reservation rules, see *Campgrounds* in "What's Where."

Mount Mansfield State Forest. The largest state forest in Vermont—27,436 acres—much of which lies on the other (western) flank of the mountain. The 10-mile Cottonbrook Trail starts at Cottonbrook Rd. off Nebraska Valley Rd. in Stowe. Follow the blazes.

Smugglers Notch State Park (802-253-4014), Stowe 05672; 10 miles up Mountain Rd. (Rt. 108) from Stowe Village, open mid-May–mid-Oct. Thirty-eight campsites, including 14 lean-tos. A few miles beyond the camping area, just beyond the highest point on this high, winding road—open only late May–early Oct., weather permitting—is a turnoff with parking, toilet, and an information center.

Elmore State Park (802-888-2982), Lake Elmore 05657. Open late May–mid-Oct., 14 miles north of Stowe on Rt. 100, then east to Morrisville, south 5 miles on Rt. 12; 709 acres with a beach, bathhouse, rental boats, 45 sites for tents and trailers including 15 lean-tos, picnicking, hiking trail up Elmore Mountain.

Wiessner Woods (802-253-7221; stowelandtrust.org). An 80-acre preserve with nature trails maintained by the Stowe Land Trust. The entrance is on Edson Hill Rd., the next right after the entrance to Stowehof Inn.

STOWE AREA AND NORTH OF THE NOTCH

✳ Lodging

Most accommodations are found either in Stowe Village or along—or just off—the 7.2-mile Mountain Rd. (Rt. 108), which connects the village with the ski slopes. Unless otherwise noted, all are in Stowe 05672.

RESORTS 🍸 ⅍ **The Trapp Family Lodge** (802-253-8511; 800-826-7000; trappfamily.com), 700 Trapp Hill Rd., is an alpine-modern version of the fabled Austrian schloss once owned by the family of *Sound of Music* fame. Johannes von Trapp lives nearby and remains involved in the property's day-to-day operations. The 96-room lodge includes a 12-suite luxury wing and offers ample common space: a charming greenhouse sitting room, three common rooms with fireplaces, and a library, cocktail lounge, large dining room, and conference facilities. Over 100 guest house "fractionally owned" units and 20 villas (inquire about vacancies) are ranged in tiers on the slope below, commanding sweeping views of the Worcester Range. The inn's 2,700 acres are webbed with cross-country ski trails, also good for

TRAPP FAMILY LODGE

Christina Tree

splendid walks. There are tennis courts and a spring-fed pool as well as an indoor pool, a sauna, and a workout room in the Fitness Center. Come in late March (when the sugarhouse is operating and the sun is warm but there is still snow on the high and wooded trails) or in early December (when there is sometimes snow), and you can pay half as much as you would in foliage season. A two- or three-day minimum is mandatory in peak periods like foliage and Christmas. Inquire about family packages (children 16 and under stay free), and about nature walks, snowshoeing, sleigh rides, and children's, exercise, and cross-country ski programs. $220–640 in summer; $310–1,010 in fall, excluding the Columbus Day weekend.

🐾 🍸 ⅍ **Edson Hill Manor** (802-253-7371; 800-621-0284; edsonhillmanor .com), 1500 Edson Hill Rd. Set on 50 acres on a high slope, the manor was built in the 1940s with brick from the old Sherwood Hotel of Burlington. Most of the living room beams were hewn for Ira and Ethan Allen's barn, which stood in North Burlington for more than a century. In the inn itself the nine guest rooms are each different, most with wood-burning fireplace and hand-painted mural in the bath. The honeymoon suite with a view over the gardens is Room 3, and Room 5 has gables, a canopy bed, and the same view. Four carriage houses, each with three or four units, house 16 more rooms. These have knotty-pine walls, wing chairs and reproduction antiques, fireplaces, books, and a spacious, in-the-woods feel. Under the ownership of William O'Neil and family, the small dining room has acquired an enviable reputation (see *Dining Out*). Living rooms are furnished in antiques, hung with exceptional art. Facilities include a stable and trails for horseback riding, outdoor pool, stocked trout pond, and 40 km of cross-country trails. $159–219 per couple B&B or $50 more with dinner; multiday packages available.

🐾 ♿ **Green Mountain Inn** (802-253-7301; 800-253-7302; greenmountaininn.com), 18 S. Main St. Lowell Thomas, President Chester Arthur, and President Gerald Ford were guests in this brick-and-clapboard landmark, which dates back to 1833, when it was built as a private home. In the 1850s it became a hotel, and it last changed ownership in 1982, when it was acquired by the Canadian Gameroff family, who have tastefully renovated the rooms in the inn itself (which has recently acquired an elevator), outfitting them with special perks such as fireside double Jacuzzi, DVD player with surround sound, marble bath, and original artwork. You'll also find the Annex, Clubhouse, Mill House, Depot Building, Sanborn House, and, most recently, the Mansfield House. The reasonably priced downstairs Whip Bar & Grill is justly famous, with poolside patio in summer and a fire in colder months (see *Eating Out*). Afternoon tea and cookies are served in the living room. $159–339 for rooms (two-night minimum stay on weekends); more for suites, apartments and two- to three-bedroom town houses. Guests enjoy complimentary use of Athletic Club facilities, located just on the other side of the pool.

♿ **Inn at the Mountain and The Townhouse and Lodge Condominiums** (802-253-3656; 800-253-4754; stowe.com), 5781 Mountain Rd. The Stowe Resort Company's 35-room lodge and 35 one- to five-room condominiums are high on the Mountain Road, handy to the Toll House lifts on Mount Mansfield. Facilities include **Fireside Tavern** restaurant, clay tennis courts, swimming pools, and the **Toll House Health Spa**. Off-season, from $85 for a room in the inn to $175 for a one-bedroom condo, $415 for a five-bedroom town house. On winter weekends, $250–695, with many rates in between. Children under 12 stay free. Add 10 percent service; inquire about numerous packages.

🛏 ♿ **Stowehof Inn** (802-253-9722; 800-932-7136; stowehofinn.com), 0.5 mile off Rt. 108 on the road to Edson Hill. This Swiss-chalet-style structure was built in 1949 to be an inn, but an AIG executive quickly grabbed it up as a corporate retreat. Now it's back to being an inn, and it's a good thing, because the place transports you into a fantasy world from the moment you step through its sod-roofed porte-cochere entrance, perched as it is on two tree trunks. The Grimes family are constantly renovating and upgrading. No two of the 46 guest rooms are alike (some are suites; a few are fireplaced

STOWEHOF INN

Joe Citro

demi-suites with optional kitchenette), but all come with private bath and balcony with superlative views. Room 45 is an example of a "classic" with a king-sized four-poster bed and miles of alpine scenery. The main floor is furnished like the inside of a castle, with meandering hallways, fireplaced nooks and libraries, a conference room shaped like a covered bridge, and mementos like the divining rod that located the water source for the building. Windows everywhere let in the view. Facilities include a lower-level pub and game room, fine dining (see *Dining Out*), tennis courts, a triangular pool with mountain views, indoor pool, sauna, fitness room, Jacuzzi, tennis courts, and cross-country ski trails connecting with the larger network. Rates start at $129 in winter midweek and climb to $499 for the best rooms on a holiday weekend, with minimum stays required. All lodging packages include breakfast.

ⓒ 🐾 ✒ ᯓ ⁏ **Topnotch Resort and Spa** (802-253-8585; 800-451-8686; topnotchresort.com), 4000 Mountain Rd. The lap of luxury: uncommonly comfortable rooms, lounging areas with a polo club ambience, professional-quality gardens, and for meals, the convivial **Buttertub Bistro** or the stately, glass-sided Norma's (*see Dining Out*). This upscale health-and-fitness spa, Vermont's most famous, offers everything from standard hotel accommodations to sumptuous resort homes. **Topnotch Spa** provides over 120 fragrant treatments in 34 treatment rooms as well as spacious showers, whirlpools, steam rooms, saunas, and leather-chaired fireplace lounges in superb new facilities, including a 60-foot-long indoor pool with skylights and a throbbing waterfall. The Ledges, recently added family units, come with two or three bedrooms and all the bells and whistles. Contemporary sculpture

abounds, and at the outdoor swimming pool you can snack cabana-style, with formally clad waiters serving you at your poolside table. A red barn down across Mountain Road serves as a cross-country ski center in winter (50 km of groomed trails connect with other trail systems in Stowe) and a riding stable. The Topnotch Tennis Center offers a wide choice of programs for all ages and levels, using six courts (four Har-Tru). Rates are $245–795 in low season, $995–1,225 in summer, fall, and ski seasons. This includes use of pool and Jacuzzi but meals, the exercise program, and spa services are extra. A MAP plan is offered; inquire about spa and tennis packages. Pets welcome in some rooms.

ⓒ ✒ ᯓ ⁏ **Golden Eagle Resort Motor Inn** (802-253-4811; 800-626-1010; goldeneagleresort.com), 511 Mountain Rd. The 12-unit motel that Herb and Ann Hillman bought in 1963 has evolved through two generations into an amazing 80-acre complex with 94 units. Accommodations range from standard hotel rooms to mini suites and one-bedroom suites. Two-bedroom apartments and a full house are available for larger families. Family geared as well as owned, it offers a lot for children. Amenities include a playground as well as an attractive health spa with indoor pool, large whirlpool, sauna, exercise equipment, and massage services. There are also outdoor heated pools (swimming lessons are offered); a clay tennis court; fish-stocked ponds; shuffleboard, badminton, lawn games, and game rooms; and a coffee shop and restaurant. Throughout, you have the sense of a well-run resort. A 50-acre wildlife area with walking trails adjoins the property. $99–414 per room (children 12 and under are free) plus a 4 percent resort fee; fully handicapped-accessible rooms available.

✍ ♿ "†" **Stoweflake Mountain Resort & Spa** (802-253-7355; 800-253-2232; stoweflake.com), 1746 Mountain Rd. The small ski lodge that the Baraw family opened more than 30 years ago has mushroomed into New England's largest spa plus a full-facility, 120-room resort (including 9 luxury suites and 60 town houses of various sizes). There are bright, comfortable, inn-style rooms in the original lodge and many nicely furnished motel rooms in the garden wing (besides its own motel wing, the resort includes the former Nordic Motor Inn). All rooms have cable TV, phone, and private bath; common space includes a library and lobby with fireplaces and sitting area, along with a large living room with a sunken fireplace. The Spa & Sports Club includes a Cybex circuit, racquetball/squash court, indoor pool, Jacuzzis, saunas, 30 treatment rooms, and a glass-roofed Aqua Solarium containing a Hungarian mineral pool and a heated jet-filled "pond" with a 15-foot waterfall made to replicate Stowe's moss-covered Bingham Falls. Separate ladies' and men's lounges feature steam and massage rooms. There are also tennis courts, badminton, volleyball, croquet, horseshoes, a putting green, and a brand-new nine-hole executive par-3 golf course, not to mention the Stowe Country Club right next door. Dining options include **Winfield's Bistro** and the pubby **Charlie B's**. $249–589 per room or suite; $309–1,089 for townhouse units; MAP rates and many packages.

INNS AND BED & BREAKFASTS

⊚ 🐾 ✍ ♿ "†" **The Gables Inn** (802-253-7730; 800-GABLES-1; gablesinn .com), 1457 Mountain Rd. Randy Stern and Annette Monachelli are warm, personable hosts who have created one of Stowe's most relaxing and welcoming inns. Common rooms

include a comfortable living room with fireplace, a solarium, and a downstairs game room/lounge. There's a swimming pool on the landscaped grounds, which angle off from Mountain Road, across from an open stretch of the Stowe Recreation Path. The hot tub is steps from the front door, the better to hop into in winter. Each of the 16 rooms (all with private bath) in the main house is different. Those in the Carriage House (handicapped accessible) feature whirlpool and fireplace; the two river-view suites in the neighboring house across the brook have fridge, microwave, and coffeemaker, as well as fireplace and double Jacuzzi. Pets are fine in some rooms for a $10 nightly charge. The famously good breakfasts are also open to the public and generally considered the best in town (see *Eating Out*). $83–235 B&B in high season, $78–165 in low season.

⊚ 🐾 🐾 ✍ **The Stowe Inn** (802-253-4030; 800-546-4030; stoweinn.com), 123 Mountain Rd. With a sense of comfort and good taste, Jed and Annika Lipsky have totally renovated this rambling old inn, set just above Stowe Village at the base of the Mountain Rd. There are 16 rooms (private baths) in the inn itself and 20 more in the Carriage House, which is more in the motel style (a maximum of two pets can stay in this section for $10 per night). Guests share spacious common areas with fireplaces, a game room with billiards, and a Jacuzzi in the main building. Children under 5 stay free and those 6–12 are an additional $5 per day. Rates in summer and winter range from $119 for a double room in the Carriage House to $309 for the deluxe suite in the main inn, less in off-seasons. All rates include continental breakfast.

⊚ 🐾 ✍ "†" **Fiddler's Green Inn** (802-253-8124; 800-882-5346; fiddlers greeninn.com), 4859 Mountain Rd., 5 miles from the village toward the mountain. Less than a mile from the lifts, this pleasant yellow 1820s farmhouse can sleep no more than 18 guests (making it great for small groups) in six small but comfortable guest rooms. Our favorite is tucked under the eaves within earshot of the stream. Guests gather around the fieldstone hearth in the living room and at the long table off the sunny kitchen. Hammocking is out back by the stream, and hiking or skiing are close by. Longtime owners Bud and Carol McKeon cater to bicyclists and cross-country skiers. $60–125 B&B; dinner possible on request (BYOB). Families welcome.

🌸 🎣 **The Inn at Turner Mill** (802-253-2062; 800-992-0016; turnermill.com), 56 Turner Mill Lane. Sequestered in the pines by Notch Brook, off Mountain Rd. just a mile from the lifts, this complex was splendidly built in the 1930s by an eccentric woman doctor. Its 10 wooded acres include a mountain stream and "refreshing" swimming hole; there's also an outdoor pool. The two guest rooms are nicely decorated with handcrafted log furniture and have cable TV, private bath, fridge, and coffeemaker. Greg and Mitzi Speer are friendly hosts who can find a babysitter and help with transfers from Burlington or Waterbury. Snowshoe rentals are available, and guests get half a day free. They can also ski their way from the quad to the back of the inn. This used to be as high as a car could drive up Mountain Rd., and the old Civilian Conservation Corps ski trails (now cross-country ski trails) are within easy striking distance. $75–110 per room. No meals.

⁜ **Brass Lantern Inn** (802-253-2229; 800-729-2980; brasslanterninn.com), 717 Maple St. (Rt. 100), is a welcoming B&B at the northern edge of the village. Nancy and Joe Beres have nicely renovated this 1800s building with planked floors and comfortable common rooms. The nine guest rooms are furnished with antiques and country quilts; all have private bath, and six have whirlpool tub and gas-burning fireplace. There's also an outdoor hot tub. Guests enjoy gym privileges at the Stowe Gym. A farm breakfast using local ingredients and showcasing Nancy's talents as a baker and afternoon tea are included in the rates: $129–199 in regular winter and summer seasons, less in off-seasons, more in foliage and holiday weeks.

🌸 🎣 ⁜ **Auberge de Stowe** (802-253-7787; 800-387-8789; aubergedestowe.com), 692 S. Main St. This 18th-century brick farmhouse and converted carriage house (formerly called the Bittersweet Inn) is a find. Shawn and Chantal Kerivan offer six rooms, including a pair of two-bedroom suites, all with private bath. The house is right on Rt. 100 along the river, but there is a view and a sense of space in the back. Amenities include a comfortable living room, a BYOB bar, a good-sized swimming pool, a large lawn, and a hot tub. $69–109 includes a substantial continental breakfast with homemade pastries. The owners speak both German and French.

♿ **Ten Acres Lodge** (802-253-7638; 800-327-7357; tenacreslodge.com), 14 Barrows Rd. The red-clapboard inn dates from 1836 and has welcomed guests, one way or another, since the 1950s. Innkeepers Robin and Frank Wilson have lived in the Far East, and decor is a mix of antiques. Rooms in the old inn are classic while those in Hill House Suite, a contemporary annex literally up the hill, are large and airy, many with balconies. There's also a two-bedroom cottage. Amenities include a pool, hot tub, and—the inn's most unusual feature—a cinema (in Hill House) with a 9-foot-wide screen, LCD projection, Dolby digital sound, and a library of 100 films, which can be reserved ahead. Dinner is served Saturday evening. Doubles are $99–299 and include a full breakfast.

🐾 ♿ **Ye Olde England Inn** (802-253-7558; 800-477-3771; englandinn.com), 433 Mountain Rd. Anglophiles can revel in the English accent, decor, and menu. The rooms are unabashedly luxurious, from the 17 Laura Ashley–style rooms in the inn to the 3 two-bedroom English "cottages" beside the swimming pool (each with fireplace, Jacuzzi, and kitchen). There are 10 suites on a rise behind the inn, each with a four-poster bed, Jacuzzi, deck, and lounge with a fireplace, wet bar, fridge, and microwave. A full English breakfast and tea are included in $109–188 for rooms, $169–447 for suites. Cottages are $209–349. Mr. Pickwick's Pub & Restaurant serves lunch and dinner (see *Eating Out*). The extravagant breakfasts are served in **Copperfield's**, the inn's other dining room.

Foxfire Inn (802-253-4887; foxfireinn.com), 1606 Pucker St. (Rt. 100) north of Stowe Village. This early-19th-century farmhouse is set on 70 wooded hillside acres. The five guest rooms have wide-board floors (several have exposed beams) and are furnished with antiques, each with private bath. There's also a four-bedroom house available for short-term rental. Downstairs there is plenty of space for guests away from the large, public dining room, well respected for its Italian fare (see *Dining Out*). $130 per double room in high season, $95 in low season, includes a full breakfast served in the garden room.

🐾 🖉 ♿ ((!)) **Commodores Inn** (802-253-7131; 800-447-8693; commodoresinn.com), 823 S. Main St., P.O. Box 970, Rt. 100 south. Carrie Nourjian runs this establishment with 72 large rooms, all with private bath (request one in the back, overlooking the lake). There's a living room with a fireplace; also three Jacuzzis and saunas and an indoor and outdoor pool. The **Stowe Yacht Club Dining Room** (a popular watering hole and spot for an evening burger) overlooks a 3-acre lake on which model sailboat races are regularly held, not to mention canoeing and kayaking. $98–198, breakfast included, service charges extra. Children 6 and under stay free, 6–12 pay $5 for breakfast; pets are welcome for $10 per stay.

🐾 **Inky Dinky Oink, Ink** (802-253-3046; oinkink.com), 117 Adams Mill Rd., Moscow 05672. The playful name reflects the artwork of innkeeper Liz Le Serviget, who houses guests in two air-conditioned rooms in this renovated 1840s farmhouse. One room has two single beds that can be joined together, the other a double bed with a two-tiered outdoor deck, private entrance, and private bath with Jacuzzi. Art and books are everywhere. $135–155. Pets okay (with restrictions). Check out Liz's art gallery and the organic

THE FARMSTAND AT INKY DINKY OINK, MOSCOW

Christina Tree

farmstand out front. Her produce and other regional products/produce figure in breakfast and afternoon tea.

In Waterbury 05676

🐾 ✂ 🕯 **The Old Stagecoach Inn** (802-244-5056; 800-262-2206; oldstagecoach.com), 18 N. Main St. A classic stagecoach inn built in 1826 with a triple-tiered porch but substantially altered in the 1880s, when a millionaire from Ohio added oak woodwork, ornate fireplaces, and stained glass. Renovated in 1987, the inn is run by John and Jack Barwick. There are 11 guest rooms and three efficiency suites, all tastefully furnished but varying widely—from a queen-bedded room with a sitting area, fireplace, and private bath to small rooms with a shared bath. Two efficiency suites are studios; the other has two bedrooms and a sitting area. Many of the rooms are large enough to accommodate families. Coco, the African gray parrot, sits by the fireplace in the living room adjoining the library, with its fully licensed bar. High-season rates are $70–130 per room, low season $70–130. A full breakfast, including a selection of hot dishes, is included. Pets allowed in some rooms.

⌾ 🐾 ✂ **Grünberg Haus** (802-244-7726; 800-800-7760; grunberghaus

OLD STAGECOACH INN

Joe Citro

.com), 94 Pine St., Rt. 100 south of Waterbury. This secluded, Tyrolean-style chalet with carved balconies has 11 guest rooms, 8 with private bath, and three cottages (open Memorial Day–Oct.) where pets are allowed for $5 per night. Many of the rooms have wood-beamed ceilings. Innkeepers Jeff and Linda Connor serve a full breakfast of homemade breads and baked goods, a fresh fruit creation, and a main dish such as ricotta-stuffed French toast. Facilities include a garden deck and self-serve pub and game room. Hiking and snowshoe trails behind the inn feed into a 20 km cross-country trail system. The dark-wood-beamed common rooms include a large fieldstone fireplace. In winter the inn offers discounts at Stowe, Sugarbush, Bolton, and Mad River Glen (all within easy striking distance). Dog in residence. $95–120 for rooms with shared bath, $135–160 for rooms with private bath, and $155–180 for suites and cabins, breakfast included. Weddings and civil unions for 25 or fewer guests.

⌾ ✂ **Moose Meadow Lodge** (802-244-5378; moosemeadowlodge.com), 607 Crossett Hill. Greg Trulson and Willie Docto have created an enchanting mountain sanctuary with Adirondack touches in this cedar log inn. The spirit is Ernest Hemingway with panache: mounted trophies, exposed wood walls, a wraparound deck with mountain views, a large stone fireplace, and exotica (trophies include a water buffalo from Uganda and a 155-pound black bear). The four guest rooms are rustically luxurious with private bath; two have a two-person steam bath, and the basement hot tub seats five. The 86 acres are blissfully secluded, with a trout-stocked swimming pond, a tree-surrounded bonfire area, and countless trails. Snowshoes are available at no charge. You may choose to tackle the 25-minute uphill hike to the Sky Loft, a glass-enclosed mountaintop gazebo with 360-degree views. Rates of $149–199 include an imaginative gourmet breakfast.

In Waterbury Center 05677

&. **The Birds Nest Inn** (802-244-7490; 800-366-5592; birdsnestinn .com), 5088 Waterbury–Stowe Rd. (Rt. 100). This 1832 three-gabled home, formerly known as the Black Locust Inn, has six rooms with private bath, polished wood floors, and stained-glass transoms. One king-bedded room is handicapped accessible. Len, Nancy, and Valerie Vignola (assisted by golden retriever Lady) get great reviews for hospitality. $135–195 ($20–30 more for deluxe rooms) includes a full, candlelit breakfast and afternoon snack. Closed Apr. and Nov.

MOTELS

In Stowe 05672

Arbor Inn (802-253-4772; 800-543-1293; arborinnstowe.com), 3214 Mountain Rd. This is the former home of Olympian Billy Kidd. The owners offer 12 rooms and suites, all with private bath, recently renovated and furnished in antiques, equipped with TV and a small fridge. Two rooms have fully equipped kitchen; four have a fireplace, and two come with two-person whirlpool tub. Common space includes a game room, pool table, and outdoor pool and Jacuzzi. Amenities include two fieldstone fireplaces, spectacular views of Mount Mansfield, and English gardens in summer. $85–265 per room (service charges extra) with full breakfast.

🦐 ♪ "ᵀ" **Alpenrose** (802-253-7277; 800-962-7002), 2619 Mountain Rd. A pleasant, small motel with just seven rooms, three of which are efficiencies with kitchenettes; one family with an efficiency (sleeps five) and one stan-

dard room. There's direct access to a cross-country network and the Stowe Recreation Path. $75–135; inquire about weekly and holiday rates.

In Waterbury 05676

♪ &. **Best Western Waterbury-Stowe** (802-244-7822; 800-621-7822), 45 Blush Hill Rd., Exit 10 north, I-89. There are 84 rooms with private bath and a restaurant for casual dining. A few luxury suites have whirlpool bath and fireplace. Amenities include a large indoor pool with a glass roof, and a full-sized fitness center with high-end weight and aerobic equipment, hot tub, and sauna. Positioned just off the interstate, this is a popular way stop with family-geared rates and access to Sugarbush as well as Stowe. $139–199 per couple for standard rooms in regular seasons, from $100 in low.

CONDOMINIUMS **Stowe Country Homes** (802-253-8132; 800-639-1990; stowecountryrentals.com) handles condos and houses. **All Seasons Rentals** (802-253-7353; 800-54-STOWE; stowerentals.com) and **Rentals at Stowe** (802-253-9786; 800-848-9120, ext. 624; rentalsatstowe.com) also rent homes and condos.

The Village Green at Stowe (802-253-9705; 800-451-3297; vgasstowe .com), 1003 Cape Cod Rd., Stowe 05672. Seven nicely designed buildings set on 40 acres (surrounded by the Stowe Country Club links) contain 73 two- and three-bedroom town houses, all brightly furnished. A recreation building has a heated indoor pool, Jacuzzi, sauna, game and changing rooms; also an outdoor pool and two tennis courts.

"ᵀ" **Stowe Cabins** (802-244-8533; stowecabins.com), P.O. Box 128, Waterbury Center 05677. Tucked into a pine forest whose logging roads become cross-country ski and snowshoeing trails in winter. Completely furnished one- and two-bedroom units with kitchen and TV. Rates $159 for two, standard; $299 for deluxe (two bedrooms, gas fireplaces).

CAMPGROUNDS **Little River Camping Areas** (802-244-7103; 800-658-6934 off-season reservations), 3444 Little River Rd., Waterbury 05676. Six miles north of Waterbury on the 830-acre Waterbury Reservoir: 81 tent and trailer campsites, including 20 lean-tos, plus swimming beaches, playgrounds, boat launch, boat rentals, ball field, nature museum, hiking, and snowmobile trails in Little River State Park.

See also *Green Space* for information on camping in Smugglers Notch and Elmore State Parks.

✳ Where to Eat

DINING OUT **Hen of the Wood** (802-244-7300; henofthewood.com), 92 Stowe St., Waterbury. Open dinner Mon.–Sat. Reservations a must. Chefs Eric Warnstedt and Craig Tresser first opened this small restaurant in fall 2005, and it's still the hottest dining spot in rural Vermont, perhaps because of consistently rave reviews and the fact that in 2008 *Food & Wine* magazine named Warnstedt one of "the best new chefs in America." Plan to reserve several days or weekends ahead. Just 0.25 mile from the I-89 exit, the restaurant is housed in a vintage 1835 gristmill with seasonal seating on a patio overlooking Thatcher Brook. It's on a side street in an old working-class neighborhood of Waterbury, not the direction Stowe-bound gourmands head. The focus is on local, fresh, and farm-raised produce and many sources are named on the menu, which changes daily. You might start with a

salad of watercress and golden beets with Vermont goat cheese. Entrées could include sheep's-milk gnocchi stuffed with roasted cauliflower, toasted pine nuts, and creamed leeks, or Winding Brook Farm pork loin with parsnips. A plate of more than a dozen, mostly Vermont cheeses is always available. Dessert options might include a triple chocolate tart with caramel sauce and hazelnut cream. Entrées are $16–31; all entrées on the Monday chalkboard menu are $20 or less. The wine list (all domestic) is extensive with many available by the glass and discounted bottles on Tuesdays. Inquire about special wine-tasting events. Wish we could give a mouthwatering account of our own dining experience here, but we couldn't get a weeknight reservation almost a week in advance. Be forewarned.

& **Blue Moon Cafe** (802-253-7006; bluemoonstowe.com), 35 School St., Stowe. Open for dinner daily. A very small, candlelit bistro with a huge reputation. Owner Jim Barton serves "contemporary American" dishes. The menu changes weekly, but appetizers might include a chanterelle and sweet onion tart ($10), followed by corn-crusted halibut with black bean tortilla sauce ($26) or pepper-seared venison with dried cherries, port wine, and blue cheese ($32).

Emily's at Stowehof Inn (802-253-9722; stowehoffinn.com), secluded on a hillside 0.5 mile off Rt. 108, Stowe. Innovative American cuisine in a small, definitely romantic dining room. Appetizers range $9–13 and include Brie wrapped in puff pastry or poached shrimp with cocktail sauce and Absolut citron. The entrées ($22–32) might include pan-seared duck in a crêpe with fresh arugula, grilled peaches, and Wiener schnitzel with spaetzle. **Coslin's Pub** downstairs offers less formal fare and a fabulous atmosphere all its own. Inquire about predinner sleigh rides around the 29-acre property before your meal; also about a frequent special: $59 for two entrées and a bottle of wine.

Solstice at Stowe Mountain Lodge (802-760-4735; stowe.com), 7412 Mountain Rd. Open for breakfast, lunch, and dinner daily. A soaring, open space with an open kitchen and contemporary feel, specially and crafted furnishings, polished wood and stone, murals and textured decor. Ingredients are as local as possible. You might lunch on a Vermont sharp cheese plate ($16) or a Vermont Burger (with Vermont bacon, cheese, tomato, pickled onion, ramp aioli, and hand-cut fries, $17). At dinner the four-course chef's tasting menu is $75. A choice of entrées might include locally raised duck tagliatelle ($28) and apple-brined pork loin with smoked apple butter ($31). Dinner reservations requested.

✍ & **Norma's at Topnotch Resort & Spa** (802-253-6445), 4000 Mountain Rd. Open for all three meals. A new option on Stowe's dining scene that might work better at lunchtime, given its curving wall of windows maximizing the superb view of Mount Mansfield and, weather permitting, its attractive patio dining. Part of a recent $25 million renovation, it's sleekly contemporary with a dining bar facing an open kitchen. The food is ambitious. You might begin with "fruta del mar" (shrimp, calamari, and scallops) and dine on "Tuna Two Ways" (sashimi-style ahi tuna, seared with ginger and peanuts, over seaweed salad and tempura-fried maki roll), or lunch on a soup and sandwich: a crab pancetta, bacon, and chèvre panini with spicy tomato gazpacho. We haven't eaten here, but our favorite Vermont reviewer notes that the noise factor is high. Lunch entrées $15–21, dinner entrées $29–45, but burgers and pastas are available all day.

✍ **Harrison's** (802-283-7773), Carlson Building, Stowe Village. Open nightly for dinner. This is a bit of an insider's place because, while it's right in the middle of the village, the entrance is up an alley and the restaurant itself is basement level, but loaded with atmosphere, especially in winter when a fire burns in the hearth. From pasta dishes like goat cheese ravioli (lemon basil ravioli stuffed with fresh goat cheese and red peppers, $15.95) to the sautéed seafood medley ($19.95), this is a real winner, especially if you can snag a booth. Singles eat at the horseshoe-shaped bar. Children's menu.

Foxfire Inn and Italian Restaurant (802-253-4887), Rt. 100, north of Stowe Village. Dinner nightly. Favored by local residents for a predictably good night out. The setting is an 1850s country farmhouse, an inn and restaurant since 1975. The menu is large. You might begin with rolled eggplant (baked with ricotta and prosciutto, mozzarella, and Romano cheese) ($7.95), then dine on veal saltimbocca ($23.95) or chicken stuffed with Gorgonzola cheese, pancetta, and figs sautéed in a creamy Marsala wine sauce ($19.95).

Michael's on the Hill (802-244-7476; michaelsonthehill.com), 4182 Waterbury–Stowe Rd. (Rt. 100). Swiss chef-owner Michael Kloeti describes his cuisine as "locally driven innovative European." The ambience is elegant and the food, reliably delicious. In fall you might begin with roasted squash soup with curried crème fraîche or smoked Grafton cheddar fritters with watercress and harissa aioli. Entrées ($25–43) might include roasted chop and crispy belly of pork pot au feu, or butter-braised Maine lobster with roasted mushroom risotto, cauliflower, and basil. Piano music is offered on Fri. and Sat. nights. Dinner 5–9; closed Tue.

Trapp Family Dining Room (802-253-8511; trappfamily.com), Trapp Hill Rd., Stowe. Open daily, 5:30–9 PM. Reservations required. Noteworthy formal dining (to the strains of live harp music Wed.–Sun.). A fall à la carte menu might include a wild salmon cake with micro greens and grilled asparagus among its starters, and a duet of wild game (wild boar sausage and venison chop on hunter's potatoes with asparagus, chestnuts, and lingonberry demiglaze) in its choice of entrées. Appetizers average $10, entrées $28; slightly less expensive in the less formal lounge. Also see the Austrian Tea Room under *Eating Out.*

Edson Hill Manor (802-253-7371; edsonhillmanor.com), 1500 Edson Hill Rd., Stowe. Open for dinner nightly in-season; reservations required. This is a small, gracious dining room at a low-key resort. The menu changes daily but entrées might include a

THE AUSTRIAN TEA ROOM AT TRAPP FAMILY LODGE

Christina Tree

grilled lamb salad ($19) and grilled New York strip ($25).

Tanglewoods (802-244-7855), 179 Guptil Rd. (going north on Rt. 100, the first right turn after Ben & Jerry's), Waterbury Center. Open Tue.–Sun. for dinner, reservations appreciated. A red barn transformed into a charming, intimate eatery. Chef-owners Carl and Diane Huber whip up a fusion of American favorites, from sesame coriander crusted tuna steak in scallion-ginger sauce with wasabi to seared breast of duck with chipotle demiglaze and papaya relish. There are always handmade innovative pastas, maybe ravioli filled with Maine crabmeat in prosciutto-leek cream. Entrees $17–27; café menu $9–14.

EATING OUT

In Stowe

Whip Bar & Grill (802-253-7301; thewhip.com), Main St. at the Green Mountain Inn. Open daily 11:30–9:30; Sunday brunch is a specialty. For charm and good food at palatable prices, the Whip is hard to beat. The antique buggy whips, brass dumbwaiter, and vintage photos recall the tavern's status. It boasts Stowe's first liquor license, from 1833. In summer there's patio dining and a view of lawns and the pool; in winter the focus is on a roaring hearth. There is a blackboard menu, always a choice of grilled meats or fish, a raw bar, and specials ranging from pan-blackened fish to Montreal smoked meat with hot mustard. Dinner specials might include roast Quebec duckling and sesame-seared yellowfin tuna with citrus-soy reduction. Dinner prices range $10–24.95.Grilled flatbread pizza and burgers are always available.

⌀ **The Stowe Inn Tavern** (802-253-4030), 123 Mountain Road. Open nightly from 5:30. This is a pleasant, expansive dining room in an early-19th-century inn. In summer tables spill out onto the porch and patio, but the focal point remains "Grant's Bar"—a 35-foot-long antique mahogany bar said to come from a stand-up Irish bar near Grant's Tomb in New York's Upper West Side, where it was discovered in numerous pieces by the inn's current owners. Restored by local craftsmen, it's worth a look, and a drink. The Tavern menu includes light fare such as crabcakes or fish-and-chips as well as such entrées as grilled beef tenderloin and sweet potato crusted salmon. Entrées $17–26.

Cliff House (800-253-4SKI; stowe .com), at the top of the gondola on Mount Mansfield's summit. Recent renovations have doubled the floor-to-ceiling window seating, broadening the panoramic view so diners can take in Mount Mansfield, the Worcester Range, even Mount Washington on clear days. The decor is bright and upscale, and dinners are back; inquire about the Summit Series of dinners, for which reservations are required. The menu changes each week, but is resolutely focused on local ingredients, from artisanal cheeses to Vermont breads, brews, and produce, all combined to make meals as memorable as this rarefied spot at 3,625 feet, accessible only by gondola. Lunch is served daily in summer (late June–Columbus Day, 11:30–2:30) and in ski season.

Trapp Family Lodge Austrian Tea Room (802-253-8511; trappfamily .com), Trapp Hill Rd. Open daily for lunch, 11–5. This Stowe landmark continues to please, both with food and with its superb view. Lunch on an Alpine mushroom onion soup and Austrian würst with warm potato salad, leaving room or simply coming for the famous Linzertorte or "appfelstrudel"

with layers of buttery, flaky phyllo dough.

Commodores Inn (802-253-7131), Rt. 100 in Stowe Lower Village. Open nightly 5:30–9. The big attraction here is the generous "New England Country Buffet" featuring clam chowder, baked beans, and plenty of meat, seafood, and veggies for $14.95 adult, $6.95 child, less for just soup and salad.

✍ ও **Gracie's Restaurant** (802-253-6888; gracies.com), 1652 Mountain Rd., Stowe. Open 11:30 AM–10 PM (later on weekends). Sue and Paul Archdeacon's dog-themed pub and gift shop is still a great place to eat, especially when you pull into town late. You can dine on one of chicken jambalaya or on Gracie's signature crabcakes. At lunch we recommend Gracie's famous chicken sandwich served with bacon, mayo, and guacamole ($9.95). Gracie, an Airdale whom the Archdeacons rescued from the pound (his picture hangs at the bottom of the stairs), was a fixture at the Shed all those years Paul worked there as bartender. Dinner entrées $15.95–22.95.

✍ **Trattoria La Festa** (802-253-8480; trattorialafesta.com), 4080 Upper Mountain Rd., Stowe (next to Topnotch Resort). Dinner nightly. On the upper reaches of the Mountain Road with terrace dining in summer, a pleasant spot owned by three experienced chefs, two of them brothers born and raised in Aprilia, a small coastal town not far from Rome. Reliably delicious antipasti, such as carpaccio di carne (thin slices of filet mignon with onions, capers, extra-virgin olive oil; $8.50); pastas (from $14.50) and veal dishes ($21.50) are specialties.

✍ **The Shed Restaurant and Brewery** (802-253-4364), Mountain Rd., open daily for lunch and dinner, also Sunday buffet brunch and a late-night menu (10–midnight). Ken and Kathy Strong's old landmark pub has expanded over the years to include a microbrewery as well as a large, greenhouse-style dining room. The varied menu (with equally varied prices) includes salads, tacos, baked onion soup, zucchini boats, barbecued ribs, seafood strudel, and, of course, Shed burgers. Admittedly, on a 2008 visit we were disappointed in the size of our burger and in the fact "medium rare" came well done. Children's menu.

Mr. Pickwick's Pub & Restaurant at Ye Olde England Inn (802-253-7558), 433 Mountain Rd. Open for lunch, dinner, and Sunday brunch. "A Dickens of a place" offers English-style fish-and-chips ($20) and beef Wellington ($35), as well as fairly exotic dishes such as tequila lime marinated chicken breast ($21). A three-course prix fixe menu is $29. There is also a broad choice of beers, single-malt whiskeys, vintage ports, and martinis.

S **Piecasso Pizzeria & Lounge** (802-253-4411, 1899 Mountain Rd. Open daily 11 AM–close. This is a bright, family-friendly addition to reasonably priced dining options. The pies are thick crusted with plenty of veggie as well as meat toppings; also salads, pastas, paninis, and local organic beef burgers.

S **Depot Street Malt Shoppe** (802-253-4269), 57 Depot St., Stowe Village. Open daily for lunch and dinner. A fun, 1950s decor with a reasonably priced diner-style menu to match, a great lunch stop with old-style fountain treats like malted frappes, egg creams, and banana splits.

Marsala Salsa (802-244-1150), 13–15 Stowe St, Waterbury. Open Mon.–Sat. 5–9:30 PM. An anomaly in these parts: authentic Caribbean fare in an old Vermont storefront. Born in Trinidad and reared on Indian cuisine, chef-owner Jan Chotalal blends those flavors with Mexican for such specialties as shrimp pillows, pot stickers, Baja rellenos, curried chicken, and grilled Island shrimp. On the spicy side. Live music on Fridays; kids' menu. Entrées $10.50–15.95.

Arvad's Grill & Pub (802-244-8973; arvads.com), 3 S. Main St. Waterbury. Open daily 11:30–11:30. A popular (read: frequently crowded) way stop just off I-89, Exit 10, with attractive brick-walls-and-hanging-plants decor, varied lunch and dinner menus, a full bar, and an outdoor veranda in summer.

BREAKFAST *S* **The Gables Inn** (802-253-7730; 800-GABLES-1; gablesinn.com), 1457 Mountain Rd. Breakfast served in summer 8–noon daily, fall 8–10:30 and weekends until noon. Breakfast is an event, served on the porch and under yellow umbrellas in summer, otherwise on the enclosed front porch and in the cheerful dining room. The daily blackboard breakfast specials might include French toast stuffed with cream cheese, walnuts, and molasses ($7.95); a Vermont cheddar cheese omelet with mushrooms, peppers, onions, and garden herbs ($8.95); or portobello mushroom Benedict ($8.95). Mimosas, scrumptious coffee cakes, and mounds of fresh fruit.

S **Dutch Pancake Cafe & The Pub at the Grey Fox Inn** (802-253-5330), 990 Mountain Rd. Open daily 8–11, for brunch until 12:30 on winter weekends and holidays, and for dinner 5:30–8:30. There are about as many types of pancakes (more than 80) served here as you could think of, and then some, ranging from blueberry and cream to shredded potato onion and cheese, all in a decor with Delft tile touches. Kid's menu.

BREAKFAST AND LUNCH 🍴 ♿

McCarthy's Restaurant (802-253-8626), Mountain Rd. next to the Stowe Cinema. Open 6:30–2:30 daily. The local gathering place: quick, cheerful service, an open black-and-white-checked kitchen, oilcloths on the tables, wood skis on the walls, and deep wooden booths. Daily specials for breakfast and lunch, plus a big breakfast menu and a wide selection of soups and sandwiches on homemade breads. Kids' menu, boxed lunches to go. Great all around.

Jamie's on Main (802-253-0077), Depot Building, Main St. Open daily 7–4, until 5 Fri., Sat. Tucked as it is into the middle of Main St. (beside Bear Pond Books), it's easy to miss this walk-through soup 'n' sandwich place—but locals know its quality, augmented by baked goods by Michelle Hines, a former pastry chef at Topnotch.

APRÈS-SKI There are reputedly 50 bars in Stowe. Along Mountain Rd., the landmarks for après-ski are **The Rusty Nail Bar & Grille** (802-253-1821; rustynailbar.com) and the **Matterhorn** (802-253-8198), with live music every weekend during ski season. **Charlie B's**, at Stoweflake, is also usually lively, as is **Mr. Pickwick's Pub**, source of one of Vermont's largest selections of beers (the better to wash down its steak-and-kidney pie). In Waterbury check out **The Alchemist** (802-244-4120; alchemistbeer.com) at 23 S. Main St.: chocolate-colored walls, black tables and ceiling, good bar fare.

✳ Entertainment

The Lamoille County Players (802-888-4507; lamoillecountyplayers.com) stage plays at the Hyde Park Opera House, Hyde Park.

Stowe Theater Guild (802-253-3961; stowetheater.com), staged upstairs at the Akeley Memorial Building in Stowe Village, offers a series of four or more summer musicals and Broadway favorites.

Stowe Performing Arts (802-253-7792; stowearts.com) presents a series of spring and summer concerts in village locations, as well as concerts by distinguished orchestras and performers staged in summer in the natural amphitheater of Trapp Meadow (Meadows hotline 802-253-5720). Patrons are invited to bring a preconcert picnic. The setting is spectacular, with the sun sinking over Nebraska Notch.

Waterbury Festival Players (waterburyfestivalplayers.com), 2933 Waterbury–Stowe Rd. (Rt. 100). This new theater stages "semi-professional" (meaning actors may or may not get paid) summer productions.

Stowe Cinema (802-253-4678), at the Stowe Center, Rt. 108. Standard seats as well as a bar viewing area for first-run films.

✳ Selective Shopping

ARTISANS *Note:* Third Thursdays of each month are Gallery Evenings in Stowe with close to a dozen galleries open until 9 PM (stowegalleries.com).

Stowe Craft Gallery & Design Center (802-253-4693; 877-456-8388; stowecraft.com), 55 Mountain Rd., Stowe. Open 10–6 daily. Outstanding crafts from throughout the country including contemporary glass, furniture, jewelry, and ceramics. The interior design showroom on Main St. features lighting, rugs, hardware, and furniture.

Little River Hotglass Studio & Gallery (802-253-0889; littleriverhotglass.com), 593 Moscow Rd., Moscow.

Open to the public daily except Tue. 10–5, noon–5 on Sun. We are kicking ourselves for not stocking up on the lovely, reasonably priced glass Christmas balls that Michael Trimpol creates in this small and very attractive studio just off Rt. 100. The specialty is exquisite colored glass creations: bowls, balls, paperweights, and perfume bottles.

Ziemke Glass Blowing Studio (802-244-6126; zglassblowing.com), 3033 Rt. 100, Waterbury Center. Studio and showroom open daily 10–6. Glass is usually blown Thu.–Sun.

Stowe Gems (802-253-7000; stowe gems.com), in the village near the Helen Day Art Center at 70 Pond St. Open daily 10–5. Barry Tricker polishes and sets exquisite stones, including tanzanite, tourmaline, Tahitian pearls, and freshwater pearls.

West Branch Gallery & Sculpture Park (802-253-8943), 17 Towne Farm Lane, Stowe, 1 mile up Mountain Rd., behind the Rusty Nail. Open daily 11–6. Contemporary sculpture in glass, oil, steel, stone, and mixed media.

Cotswold Furniture Makers (802-253-3710; cotswoldfurniture.com), 132 Mountain Rd. Open daily 10–6. John Lomas, a graduate of the London College of Furniture, creates classic Shaker and Arts and Crafts furniture by hand, selling it along with Tibetan rugs, Simon Pearce glass, and decorative objects.

Stephen Huneck Gallery in Stowe (802-253-9413), 57 Mountain Rd. Vermont artist and sculptor Stephen Huneck's whimsical creations fill this lively studio, usually with a resident black Lab, at the base of the Mountain Road.

Also see **ShackletonThomas** at the Stowe Mountain Lodge shops. Charles Shackleton is a leading Vermont's furniture maker and his wife, Miranda Thomas, is known for her distinctive pottery.

FLEA MARKETS The **Waterbury Flea Market** (802-244-5916), the biggest in northern Vermont, rolls out its tables every weekend May–Oct., 7–7 (weather permitting), on a grassy, 10-acre roadside spot on Rt. 2 just north of the village (Exit 10W off I-89). Concession stand. The **Charlotte Flea Market** (802-425-2844) is smaller but equally interesting; on weekends, 6 AM–5 PM, Apr.–Oct. The **Stowe Farmers' Market** sells fresh produce and local wares all summer next to the Red Barn Shops on Mountain Rd., weekends 10:30–3:30.

FOOD AND DRINK Cabot Creamery Annex Store (802-244-6334; 800-881-6334; cabotcheese.com/annex .html), 2653 Waterbury–Stowe Rd. (Rt. 100), Waterbury, 1.4 miles north of Ben & Jerry's, in the same complex as Lake Champlain Chocolates (see below). Open year-round, daily 9–6. While the prizewinning cheese isn't made here, this is its major showcase, displaying a full line of dairy products (plenty of samples), along with other Vermont specialty foods and crafts. Also in the annex store are **Lake Champlain Chocolates** (802-241-4150), the chocolate maker that started out in Burlington, and the **Vermont Teddy Bear Co.**, makers of those gift bears.

Cold Hollow Cider Mill (802-244-8771; 800-3-APPLES; coldhollow .com), 3600 Waterbury–Stowe Rd. (Rt. 100), Waterbury, is one of New England's largest producers of fresh apple cider; visitors can watch it being pressed and sample the varieties. We can vouch for the cider doughnuts. The retail stores in this big red barn complex stock every conceivable kind of apple jelly, butters, sauces, natural fruit preserves, honey, pancake mixes, pickles, and mustards, plus Vermont books and other gifts. Try the rhubarb wine at the **Grandview Winery** next door. Open year-round, daily 8–6.

ᵗ¹ᵗ **Green Mountain Coffee Roasters Visitor Center and Café** (877-879-2326; greenmountaincoffee.com), housed in the newly renovated 1867 working Amtrak station, Park Row, Waterbury. Open daily except Thanksgiving and Christmas, 7–5. Displays tell the story of Green Mountain Coffees from around the world, available for a nominal donation along with snacks, inviting tables, and WiFi.

Harvest Market (802-253-3800), 1031 Mountain Rd., Stowe. A high-end takeout featuring fresh-baked country breads and other baked goods as well as house-made granola, an espresso bar, Vermont cheeses, gourmet items, and prepared foods including chicken, salads, pastas, and seasonal dishes.

OTHER Bear Pond Books (802-253-8236; stowebooks.com), Depot Building, Stowe Village. Open daily. An excellent family-owned, independent bookstore; calendars, cassettes, the town's best selection of cards, and an entire section devoted to Vermont books.

Shaw's General Store (802-253-4040), 54 Main St., Stowe Village. Established in 1895 and still a family business, a source of shoelaces and cheap socks as well as expensive ski togs and Vermont souvenirs.

Lackey's Variety Store (802-253-7624), Main St., Stowe Village, open 8:30–8:30 daily. An 1840s building that has housed many enterprises and is now "just a variety store." An anomaly in this resort village, it still stocks nail clippers, india ink, shoe polish, and scissors, not to mention patent medicine and magazines. The walls are

hung with posters for 1930s ocean liners and long-vanished local movie houses and lined with antique bottles, boxes, and other fascinating objects.

Stowe Mercantile (802-253-4554), Depot Building, Stowe. A large, eclectic selection of clothing and gifts.

Stowe Mountain Lodge Shops, 7412 Mountain Rd. In contrast with most hotel boutiques, the shops in Stowe's newest, most dramatic and upscale hotel fill a free-flowing space inviting shoppers to wander. Top Vermont and national retailers represented include Orvis, ShackletonThomas, Ralph Lauren, and N. T. Ferro Jewelers.

Fly Rod Shop (802-253-7346; flyrodshop.com), 2703 Waterbury Rd. (Rt. 100), Stowe, carries a full line of name-brand fishing gear. Full- and half-day instructional tours.

Misty Meadows Herb and Perennial Farm (802-253-8247), 785 Stagecoach Rd., Stowe. Open mid-May–fall, 9–5 daily. Display gardens feature herbs and perennials in a farm setting; also potpourri, everlasting wreaths, seasonings, and herbs. Certified organic.

Nebraska Knoll Sugar Farm (802-253-4655; nebraskaknoll.com), 256 Falls Brook Lane, Stowe. Lewis and Audrey Coty's sugarhouse is open Mar.–Oct., selling maple products at "sugar house prices." Sited up beyond Trapp Meadow, it's a lovely little drive.

Brick House Book Shop (802-888-4300), 632 Morristown Corners Rd., Morrisville. Open Tue.–Sat. 2–5, Sun. and Mon. by appointment. Proprietor Alexandra Heller has amassed 70,000 old books, fiction and nonfiction, hardcover and paperback. She also offers a search and mail service.

See also the **Johnson Woolen Mills** in "North of the Notch"; the short and scenic drive there is certainly worth the effort.

✳ Special Events

Mid-January: **Winter Carnival** is one of the oldest and most gala village winter carnivals in the country—a week of snow sculptures, sled dog races, ski races, public feeds.

Last weekend of February: **Stowe Derby**, the country's oldest downhill/cross-country race—a 10-mile race from the summit of Mount Mansfield to Stowe Village—usually attracts about 300 entrants.

May: Lamoille County Players present **musicals** at the Hyde Park Opera House.

Late June: **Stowe Garden Festival** (800-247-8693)—garden tours, crafts show, speakers.

Summerlong: **Exposed! Outdoor Sculpture Exhibition** (802-253-8358), Helen Day Art Center, tours with the sculptors. Maps available.

July 4: **Stowe Independence Day Celebration** (802-253-7321) starting at 11 AM midtown—parade, food, games, performers, fireworks. Separate festivities in the village of Moscow, too small for its own band, so they parade to the music of radios.

Mid-July: **Stoweflake Hot-Air Balloon Festival** (800-253-2232; stoweflake.com)—annual balloon launch and tethers with live music, food, a beer garden, and kids' activity corner.

Late July: **Stowe Performing Arts Summer Festival**—a week of concerts ranging from chamber to symphony music, including bands and choral groups, presented in a number of places. **Lamoille County Field Days**, a weekend agricultural fair in Morrisville—tractor pulling, crafts, children's rides.

Mid-August: **Antique & Classic Car Show** (802-253-7321). Over 800 models on display, three days, 8–5. Parade, car auction, corral, fashion-judging contest, auto-related flea market, plus a Saturday-night Oldies Street Dance and Block Party.

Late August: Lamoille County Players stage a **musical** in the Hyde Park Opera House.

Mid-September: **Annual British Invasion** (802-253-5320; britishinvasion.com). North America's largest all-British sports car show—contests, food, displays at Mayo Farm Events Field, Weeks Hill Rd., Stowe. **Oktoberfest** (802-253-7321), Jackson Arena—a two-day fest with oompah bands, parade, Bavarian food, microbrews, and children's tent.

Second weekend of October: **Stowe Foliage Art & Craft Festival** (802-253-7321), Stowe Events Field. Three days of juried art and fine crafts from 160 exhibitors, wine tasting, music, magicians, and a special "off the grid" section.

Pre-Halloween: **Lantern Tours**. Carry a candlelit lantern while taking a "ghost walk" through Stowe, hearing tales of the village's resident ghosts. Sept. 15–Oct. 31. Walks begin at the visitor center on Main St. (802-244-1173; stowelanterntours.com).

NORTH OF THE NOTCH AND THE LAMOILLE VALLEY

V ermont's most dramatic road winds up and up from Stowe through narrow, 2,162-foot-high Smugglers Notch, then down and around cliffs and boulders. Just as it straightens and drops through woodland, motorists are startled by the apparition of a condominium town rising out of nowhere (Smugglers' Notch Resort, a self-contained, family-geared village that accommodates some 3,200 people). However, as Rt. 108 continues to descend and finally levels into Jeffersonville on the valley floor, it's clear that this is a totally different place from the tourist-trod turf south of the Notch. This is the Lamoille Valley.

Smugglers Notch, as well as the village of Jeffersonville, is in Cambridge, one of several towns worth exploring along the Lamoille River. Jeffersonville has been a gathering place for artists since the 1930s, and Johnson, 9 miles west along Rt. 15, is also now an art center. It's easy to see why artists like this luminous landscape: open, gently rolling farm country. The Lamoille River itself is beloved by fishermen and canoeists, and bicyclists enthuse about the little-trafficked roads.

While Smugglers Notch is the more dramatic approach, the prime access to the Lamoille Valley region is Rt. 100, the main road north from Stowe, which joins Rt. 15 (the major east–west road) at Morrisville, the commercial center for north-central Vermont. Just west on Rt. 15 is Hyde Park, the picturesque county seat, famed for its summer theater.

North of the Lamoille Valley is the even less-trafficked Missisquoi River Valley, and between the two lies some beautiful, very Vermont country.

GUIDANCE Lamoille Valley Chamber of Commerce (802-888-7607; 800-849-9985, lamoillevalleychamber.com), 34 Pleasant St., Morrisville 05661, covers the area with an office that's open year round. An information booth at the junction of Rts. 15 and 100 at the Morrisville Mobil station is open May–Oct. Also see stowesmugglers.org.

GETTING THERE *By air:* See "Burlington Region." Given 48 hours' notice, Smugglers' Notch Resort arranges transfers for guests.

By train: **Amtrak** stops at Essex Junction (800-872-7245).

By car: When the Notch is closed in winter, the route from Stowe via Morrisville is 26 miles, but in summer via Rt. 108 it's 18 miles from Stowe.

MEDICAL EMERGENCY Emergency service is available by calling **911**.

Copley Hospital (802-888-4231), Morrisville.

✳ To See

Smugglers Notch. During the War of 1812, Vermonters hid cattle and other supplies in the Notch prior to smuggling them into Canada to feed the British army—which was fighting the U.S. Army at the time. A path through the high pass existed centuries before European settlement, but it wasn't until 1910 that the present road was built, which, with its 18 percent grade, is as steep as many ski trails and more winding than most. Realizing that drivers are too engrossed with the challenge of the road to admire the wild and wonderful scenery, the state's Department of Forests and Parks has thoughtfully provided a turnoff just beyond the height-of-land. An information booth here is staffed in warm-weather months; this is a restful spot by a mountain brook where you can picnic, even grill hot dogs. The Big Spring is here and prior to your climb, you can ask about hiking distances to the other local landmarks: the Elephant Head, King Rock, the Hunter and His Dog (an outstanding rock formation), Singing Bird, the Smugglers Cave, Smugglers Face, and the natural reservoir. See the "Stowe and Waterbury" chapter for details about the easy trail to Sterling Pond and about the trail to the Elephant Head.

COVERED BRIDGES *In and around Jeffersonville:* Look for the **Scott Bridge** on Canyon Rd. across the Brewster River near the old mill; the 84-foot-long bridge is 0.1 mile down the road. To find the **Poland Bridge** (1887) from the junction of Rts. 108 and 15, drive north and turn onto Rt. 109, angling off onto the road along the river; the bridge is in 0.2 mile. Heading west on Rt. 15 toward Cambridge Village, look for Lower Valley Rd.; the **Gates Farm Bridge** (1897) is a few hundred feet from where the present road crosses the river.

In Waterville and Belvidere: Back on Rt. 109, continue north to Waterville and, at Waterville Town Hall (on your right), turn left; the **Church Street Bridge** (1877) is in 0.1 mile. Back on Rt. 109, continue north; the **Montgomery Bridge** (1887)

ENTRANCE TO SMUGGLERS' NOTCH RESORT

Diane E. Foulds

is east of the highway, 1.2 miles north of town hall. Go another 0.5 mile north on Rt. 109 and turn right; the **Kissin' Bridge** (1877) is in 0.1 mile. Continue north on Rt. 109, and 1.5 miles from the Waterville Elementary School (just after the bridge over the North Branch), turn left and go 0.5 mile to the **Mill Bridge** (1895) in Belvidere. Back on Rt. 109, continue north 0.9 mile and turn left to find the **Morgan Bridge** (1887). See the "Jay Peak Area" chapter for a description of six more covered bridges another dozen miles north in Montgomery.

In Johnson: Take Rt. 100C north from its junction with Rt. 15 for 2.6 miles and turn right; the **Scribner Bridge** (around 1919) is 0.3 mile on your right.

Note: For detailed descriptions of all these sites, see *Covered Bridges of Vermont* by Ed Barna (The Countryman Press).

GALLERIES **Mary Bryan Memorial Art Gallery** (802-644-5100; bryanmemorial gallery.org), 180 Main St., Jeffersonville. Open daily 10–5 June–Oct., otherwise Thu.–Sat. 10–4. Built by Alden Bryan in memory of his wife and fellow artist, Mary Bryan, this mini museum has changing exhibits featuring artists who have worked in Jeffersonville. Also check out neighboring galleries under *Selective Shopping* and the Vermont Studio Center (802-635-2727; vermontstudiocenter .org), Johnson, under *Entertainment.* Over the past 30 years this nonprofit center has absorbed more than two dozen buildings in the village of Johnson. The lecture hall is a former meetinghouse, and the gallery, exhibiting the work of artists in residence, is in a former grain mill one street back from Main, down by the river. Billed as the largest artists' and writers' residency program in the United States, this unusual campus stages frequent gallery shows, readings, and lectures open to the public.

Dibden Center for the Arts (802-635-1476; johnsonstatecollege), Johnson State College, Johnson. Open weekdays during the academic year, noon–6. Changing solo and group shows

SCENIC DRIVES Four loop routes are especially appealing from Jeffersonville:

Stowe/Hyde Park (44 mile loop). Take Rt. 108 south through Smugglers Notch to Stowe Village, drive up the old Stagecoach Rd. to Hyde Park (be sure to see the old Opera House), and head back through Johnson.

Belvidere/Eden (40-mile loop). From Jeffersonville, Rt. 109 follows the North Branch of the Lamoille River north to Belvidere Corners; here take Rt. 118, which soon crosses the Long Trail and continues to the village of Eden. Lake Eden, 1 mile north on Rt. 100, is good for swimming and boating; return on Rts. 100, 100C, and 15 via Johnson.

Jericho/Cambridge (38-mile loop). From Jeffersonville, drive southwest on Pleasant Valley Rd., a magnificent drive with the Green Mountains rising abruptly on your left. Go through Underhill Center to the junction with Rt. 15. At Rt. 15, either turn right to head back to Cambridge or continue south on Jericho Center Rd.; return via Jericho and Rt. 15 to Cambridge Village, then drive back along Rt. 15 to Jeffersonville.

Jeffersonville/Johnson (18-mile loop). From the junction of Rts. 15 and 108, head north on Rt. 108, but turn onto Rt. 109 (note the Poland Covered Bridge on your right). Take your first right, Hogback Rd., which shadows the north bank of the Lamoille River most of the way into Johnson. Return via Rt. 15.

HISTORIC HOUSE **The Noyes House Museum** (802-888-7617), 122 Main St (Rte. 100)., Morrisville. Open mid-June until Sep., Wed.–Sat. Guided tours 1–5 or by appointment. Admission by donation. Carlos Noyes was a 19th-century banker who spent much of his fortune expanding this 1820 Federal-style homestead. Its 18 rooms and carriage barn contain one of the state's best collections of Vermont memorabilia, including an 1,800-piece Cheney pitcher and Toby jug collection, and Indian Joe's canoe.

✳ To Do

BICYCLING *Rentals:* Mountain bike rentals are available in Jeffersonville at **Foot of the Notch Bicycles** (802-644-8182) and in Jeffersonville at **Pinnacle Ski & Sports** (877-445-1280), Rt. 108 at Smugglers' Notch.

Bicycle touring: **Smugglers Notch Inn** (802-644-6607). The owners can help with local bike routes.

The **Cambridge Greenway** recreation path runs 1.3 miles along the Lamoille River from Jeffersonville east.

Missisquoi Valley Rail Trail, a 26-mile-long recreation path, traverses the northern tier of this region, following the Missisquoi River from Enosburg Falls to Richford. For a map, call the Northwest Regional Planning Commission (802-524-5958; nrpcvt.com).

CANOEING AND KAYAKING The **Lamoille River** from Jeffersonville to Cambridge is considered good for novices in spring and early summer; two small sets of rapids.

Bert's Boats (802-644-8189; bertsboats.com), at 73 Smugglers View Rd. in Jeffersonville, rents canoes and kayaks and offers shuttle service and tours from 3 to 12 miles. Paddles are all flat and Class I water; tours to Peterson Gorge and Boyden Winery.

Green River Canoe & Kayaks (802-644-8336) operates from 155 Junction Hill Rd. in Jeffersonville. Guided canoe and kayaking trips, especially ecotours led by trained naturalists; also instruction and rentals, tours to Boyden Winery.

For Sterling Ridge Resort, see *Lodging*.

A MID-RIDE NOSH AT 158 MAIN RESTAU-
RANT & BAKERY, JEFFERSONVILLE
Diane E. Foulds

FISHING The stretch of the Lamoille River between Cambridge and Johnson reputedly offers great fly- and spin-fishing for brown trout.

Green Mountain Troutfitters (802-644-2214; gmtrout.com), 233 Mill St. (Rt. 108S), Jeffersonville. Fishing gear, clinics, and guided tours.

Smugglers' Notch Resort (800-451-8752) offers frequent fly-casting clinics, fly-fishing stream tours, and small-mouth bass fishing in-season.

T. J.'s Outdoors (802-888-6210), 81

Bridge St., Morrisville, offers year-round fishing, archery, and muzzle-loader supplies, and fishing guide service May–Sept.

Pleasant Valley Fly Fishing Guides (802-644-2813; pleasantvalleyflyfishing .com). Lawton Weber specializes in dry-fly wild trout fishing in his half- and full-day excursions. All expertise levels welcome; all equipment provided.

GOLF **Copley Country Club** (802-888-3013), Country Club Rd., Morrisville, is a nine-hole course open May–Oct.

HIKING **Prospect Rock**, Johnson. An easy hike yields an exceptional view of the Lamoille River Valley and the high mountains to the south. Look for a steel bridge to the Ithiel Falls Camp Meeting Ground. Hike north on the white-blazed Long Trail 0.7 mile to the summit.

Belvidere Mountain–Ritterbush Pond and **Devil's Gulch**. These are basically two stretches of the Long Trail; one heads north (three and a half hours round-trip) to the summit of Belvidere Mountain, the other south (two and three-quarter hours round-trip) to a gulch filled with rocks and ferns. Both are described in the Green Mountain Club's *Long Trail Guide*.

Sterling Pond, Jeffersonville. This is one our favorite hikes, accessible from the top of the Notch parking area, beginning across the road from the information booth. Look for the LONG TRAIL sign and register. Follow the white blazes to a T-intersection (about 35 to 45 minutes up). Turn left at the sign for Sterling Pond Shelter. It's a short walk to the "the highest trout pond in the state." For views, follow the trail around the end of the pond, through the woods, and turn left off the Long Trail, up a short rise to a clearing at the top of Sterling Lift. Return by the same route. We have fond memories of being able to ski from the Smuggs to Spruce Peak lifts via Sterling Pond but, alas, that's no longer an option.

HORSEBACK RIDING ♂ **Brewster River Horse Center** (802-644-8051), 480 Edwards Rd. off Rt. 108, Jeffersonville, 1.3 miles from Smugglers' Notch Resort, offers guided trail rides and pony rides for kids June–mid-Oct.

LaJoie Stables (802-644-5347; lajoiestables.com), 992 Pollander Rd. in Jeffersonville. Horseback riding offered all year, including trail rides, pony rides, and overnight treks.

LLAMA TREKS **Northern Vermont Llama Co.** (802-644-2257), 766 Lapland Rd., Waterville. Treks depart from the Smugglers' Notch Resort and head into the backcountry. Geoff and Lindsay Chandler offer half- and full-day treks, depending on the season. Snacks are provided with half-day treks, picnic and snack for full-day outings. Call for rates and to reserve. Family rates available.

Applecheek Farm (802-888-4482; applecheekfarm.com), 567 McFarlane Rd., Hyde Park. Trek on "wilderness trails"; picnic and farm tour included.

PICNICKING There are several outstanding roadside picnic areas: On Rt. 108, 0.2 mile north of the junction with Rt. 15 at Jeffersonville, four picnic tables (one covered) on the bank of the Lamoille; on Rt. 108 south of Jeffersonville Village on the east side of the highway; on Rt. 108 in Smugglers Notch itself (see *To See*); on Rt. 15, just 1.5 miles east of the Cambridge–Johnson line.

SWIMMING Brewster River Gorge, accessible from Rt. 108 south of Jeffersonville (turn off at the covered bridge).

Smugglers' Notch Resort (802-644-8851; 800-451-8752) features an elaborate water park with eight heated pools and four waterslides in summer, plus a winter pool.

Green River Reservoir State Park (802-888-1349; vtstateparks.com), off Rt. 15 east (Green River Dam Rd.), Morrisville, is an undeveloped, 653-acre reservoir with about 19 miles of shoreline. One of the largest unsullied ponds in Vermont.

TENNIS Courts at **Smugglers' Notch Resort** (800-451-8752), a summer program of clinics for adults and children, and daily instruction at the TenPro Tennis School.

WALKING The **Cambridge Greenway** recreation path runs 1.3 miles along the Lamoille River from Jeffersonville east.

Lamoille County Nature Center (802-888-4965), Cole Hill Rd., Morrisville. Two nature trails offer easy walking and the chance to see deer, bear, and a variety of birds, also lady's slippers in early summer. Inquire about programs offered in the outdoor amphitheater.

✳ Winter Sports

CROSS-COUNTRY SKIING Nordic Ski and Snowshoe Adventure Center (802-644-8851), Smugglers' Notch Resort. Narrow trails wind up and down through the trees, then climb meadows away from the resort complex, for a total of 34 km of cross-country trails and 24 km of snowshoe trails; rentals; also telemark, skate skiing, and snowshoe rentals; lessons and tours; a warming hut with cocoa and a woodstove.

Smugglers Notch. The steep, rocky stretch of Rt. 108 that is closed to traffic for snow season is open to cross-country skiers. Guided tours are offered by the Nordic Adventure Center (see above).

DOWNHILL SKIING ♂ **Smugglers' Notch Resort** (800-451-8752; smuggs .com), Jeffersonville. In 1956 a group of local residents organized Smugglers' Notch Ski Ways on Sterling Mountain, a western shoulder of 3,640-foot-high Madonna. In 1963 a high-powered group headed by IBM board chairman Tom Watson gained a controlling interest and began developing the area as Madonna Mountain, a self-contained, Aspen-style resort. Only two owners later, with 650 condominiums, Smugglers' is a major ski destination poised over a natural snow bowl with a satisfying variety of terrain spread over three interconnected mountains: beginner trails on Morse Mountain (2,250 feet), intermediate runs on mid-sized Sterling Mountain (3,010 feet), and expert and glade skiing on Madonna, the highest of the three, with its spectacular long-distance views. (A shuttle links the base areas.) You're greeted by a huge, muddy parking lot, but don't be put off: This is one of New England's best-run vacation spots, summer and winter both. Warm-up huts serve hot meals atop Sterling Peak, and a full range of restaurants lies at the base.

It soon becomes clear why many Vermont skiers bypass Stowe for "Smuggs": The crowds are thinner, the prices lower, and the trails as challenging. After all, this is the site of the only triple-black-diamond run in the East, a sheer drop halfway down Madonna known as The Black Hole. One trail goes 3.5 miles, making it northern Vermont's largest vertical descent, a whopping 2,610 feet. But you also find the opposite extreme: Sir Henry's Learning and Fun Park at the base of Morse Mountain is a mini slope with a half-speed chairlift, a great place for toddlers (and older beginners) to cut their teeth. Two attendants wait on each end to catch you; there's also a Magic Carpet lift on an electric conveyer belt that inches you along like a moving sidewalk.

Smugglers' Notch Resort

SKIING AT SMUGGLERS' NOTCH

Lifts: 6 double chairlifts, 2 surface.

Trails: 78, including two 3.5-mile trails; 25 percent expert, 56 percent intermediate, 19 percent beginner.

Vertical drop: 2,610 feet.

Snowmaking: 61 percent.

Facilities: Mountain Lodge, base lodge with ski shop, rentals, cafeteria, pub. The reception center/ski shop at Morse Mountain has a Village Center, source of rentals and tickets; the complex also includes a ski shop, deli, country store, and restaurant/snack bar. Top of the Notch warming hut is at the Sterling chair terminal. Snowboarding.

Ski school: Group and private lessons at Morse and Madonna, beginners at Morse. Children's ski and snowboarding camp.

For children: Day care for kids 6 weeks–3 years. Discovery Dynamos Ski Camp for 3- to 5-year-olds—all day with hot lunch and two lessons, games, and races. Adventure Rangers Ski and Snowboard Camps for 6- to 10-year-olds: all day with hot lunch and two lessons; games and races. The Notch Squad is for kids 11–15. Mountain Explorers Ski Program for 16- to 17-year-olds begins at noon daily; lesson and evening activities; 2 teen centers.

Rates: $62 for a 1-day, 3-mountain adult lift ticket; $46 ages 6–18. Kids 5 and seniors 70+ under ski free.

Note: See *Lodging* for packages that greatly reduce ski-week rates. A 5-day ski week, which automatically includes lessons for all children and beginners, is usually the best option.

March (bargain season) is a great time to come. This far north snow lingers long past midseason, augmenting the man-made base.

ICE SKATING Crew Arena (802-888-0166; crewarena.org), 704 Bridge St., Morrisville. A year-round indoor skating rink iced over June–Feb. Call for a public skating schedule.

SLEIGH RIDES 🖊 **Applecheek Farm** (802-888-4482; applecheekfarm.com), 567 McFarlane Rd., Hyde Park. John and Judy Clark's gentle Belgians, Sparky and Sam, take you through the woods by day or night. Hot beverage and farm tour included.

LaJoie Stables (802-644-5347), on Pollander Rd. in Cambridge. Sleigh rides offered all winter.

Charlie Horse Sleigh Rides (802-888-2220; charliehorserides.com), 421 N. Hyde Park Rd., Hyde Park, 13 miles from Stowe Village on Rt. 100. Anthony Godin offers 20- to 25-minute rides through the woods daily 10–6.

SNOWMOBILING **Smugglers' Notch Snowmobile Tours** (800-347-8266), Junction Hill Rd., Jefferson. Evening one-hour tours through Smugglers Notch. Customized day tours from two to four hours. Ride on new Polaris machines.

✳ Lodging

INNS AND BED & BREAKFASTS

🖊 **Nye's Green Valley Farm Bed & Breakfast** (802-644-1984; nyesgreen valleyfarm.com), 8976 Rt. 15 west, Jeffersonville 05464. A brick Colonial about 4 miles east of Jeffersonville on Rt. 15. As a child, Marsha Nye Lane played in this 1810 former stagecoach tavern that her great-grandfather had bought in 1867, that her uncle had farmed, and that her father was born in. It passed through several owners; when she learned that the bank had foreclosed on the property, she and her husband, David, bought and restored the farmhouse to look the way she remembered it. Now it accommodates

NYE'S GREEN VALLEY FARM BED & BREAK-FAST, JEFFERSONVILLE

Diane E. Foulds

guests in three air-conditioned rooms, one with private bath. All of them are light and cozy with quilts and comfy chairs. Breakfast, served family-style, includes freshly baked breads, fresh fruit, and two or three choices of entrées. Common rooms are beautifully furnished with rare antiques, including a collection of handblown inkwells. There's a steep, narrow staircase in the kitchen, and you notice square-headed nails in the floors and ceilings. Outdoors is a pond, the scene of summer campfires, a thriving garden with the tallest bee balm we've ever seen, and the Lanes' antiques shop, one of eight nearby. $75–95 includes breakfast; a new, fully equipped cottage across the road is $125.

◎ 🐾 🖊 "¶" **Sterling Ridge Resort** (802-644-8265; 800-347-8266; sterling ridgeresort.com), 155 Sterling Ridge Dr., Jeffersonville 05464. Sterling Ridge is a secluded log cabin village with a variety of attractively furnished accommodations scattered among fields, ponds, and flower beds. Pond House is a four-bedroom farmhouse that's great for families ($210–410 per night). The main lodge, built in 1988, has been divided into three- and four-bedroom suites ($180–275 per night; the whole building can be rented for

$340 per night). Back beyond the pond, Scott and Susan Peterson have built 18 one- and two-bedroom log cabins ($99–140 for standard log cabins, with a two-night minimum stay), each nicely designed with a fireplace, cathedral ceiling, fully equipped kitchen, and outdoor grill. The inn's 360 acres are webbed with 20 km of trails; facilities include a hot tub and outdoor pool. Mountain bikes, boats, and snowshoes are available.

Donomar Inn (802-644-2937; donomar.com), 916 Rt. 108 south, Jeffersonville 05464. The most popular spot in this handsome country home is the solarium, a tiled, sun-filled dining area off the kitchen with gorgeous mountain views. There's also a cozy library with a fireplace and Oriental carpets, a fieldstone fireplace in the great room, a six-person outdoor hot tub (bring your swimsuit), and a common room with a TV/VCR/DVD player. Mary Bouvier and Moira Donovan offer six rooms, four with private bath, some with fireplace and Jacuzzi. Rates range $75–175 per room double occupancy, which includes a full breakfast of fresh fruit, homemade breads, a hot entrée, and imported teas. Resident dog and cat.

Fitch Hill Inn (802-888-3834; 800-639-2903; fitchhillinn.com), 258 Fitch Hill Rd., Hyde Park 05655. Handy to many parts of the North Country, this 18th-century hilltop house owned by Julie and John Rohleder is nicely maintained. There are six air-conditioned guest rooms, each with private bath and most named for a state (our favorite is Vermont), all tastefully furnished and equipped with ceiling fans; two are able to accommodate more than two people. Two rooms, New Hampshire and Green Mountains, come with small kitchen, two-person whirlpool tub, and fireplace. Ample common space includes a sunny parlor with a woodstove. There are two covered porches for guest use and an impressive library of videos for the VCR. $150–210 in high season, $100–160 in low, includes a full hot breakfast and afternoon snack.

&. **The Governor's House in Hyde Park** (802-888-6888; 866-800-6888; onehundredmain.com), 100 Main St., Hyde Park 05655. Suzanne Boden has completely restored this sumptuous mansion to reflect the periods of 1893—when the house was erected—and 1759 when the Longfellow House, after which it was designed, was built in Cambridge, Massachusetts. There are eight guest rooms, six with private bath and one fully handicapped accessible, as is the entire first floor of the inn. Boden serves an elegant afternoon tea in the library on Thu. and Sun. and alfresco suppers when there is a production at Hyde Park Opera House across the street. Guests are invited to arrive early for lemonade and croquet on the expansive lawns, or simply to sit on the back portico and enjoy hors d'oeuvres (BYOB) as the sun sets behind the mountains. $115–235 (singles from $95) includes three-course breakfast, and tea. Inquire about the "Elope to Vermont" package.

 **Village Victorian** (802-888-8850; 866-266-4672; villagevictorian

THE GOVERNOR'S HOUSE IN HYDE PARK

Diane E. Foulds

RESORT

𝒹 ઇ **Smugglers' Notch Resort** (802-644-8851; U.S. and Canada 800-451-8752 ; UK 0800-169-8219; smuggs.com), 4323 Rt. 108 south, Smugglers' Notch 05464.

While "Smuggs" remains a serious ski resort throughout the winter season, year-round it's geared to families, clubs, and reunions and the atmosphere is that of a big family camp with endless things to do. In winter everyone trudges around pink-cheeked in oversized ski boots; in summer they're barefoot and towel-swathed, lapping ice cream while still dripping from one of the many pools. Free shuttle vans and canopied golf carts pick you up and taxi you wherever you want to go within the 100-acre core grounds of this 1,000-acre property.

Throughout the summer vacation season Smugglers' maintains, hands-down, the largest, best-organized, and most reasonably priced family program in New England. Treasures, the nursery for newborns and tots, is particularly impressive, as is the program for teens. Upward of 400 kids ages 3–17 participate in four age-appropriate camps, orchestrated by 180 college-aged counselors. The fun never stops: fishing, movies, nature and hiking, games, music and dance, arts and craft, disk golf, and more. Summer tennis and other packages are also available. Facilities include six different playgrounds, a nature center, a Ping-Pong/arcade room for rainy days, and a teen center with interactive video games. Despite the absence of a natural lake, there is water everywhere: eight pools, four with waterslides, plus elaborate creations like Little Smugglers Lagoon—a faux cave with a waterfall, fountains, spouts, and a shallow "river" that propels inner-tubed youngsters around one end of the

.com), 107 Union St., Morrisville 05661. Ellen and Philip Wolff are your hosts in an 1890s Victorian in the village of Morrisville, 7 miles north of Stowe Village. All five guest rooms have queen bed and private bath, with a TV/VCR combo and air conditioner in each; there are two rooms in the annex across the street. The Wolffs also offer a fully furnished, winterized lake cottage on Shadow Lake, about 30 miles northeast. $80–150 includes full breakfast. Discounts for longer stays.

TOWN HOUSES Notch Glen Rentals (802-644-5985; notchglen rentals.com), 150 Chez Lane (Rt. 108),

Jeffersonville 05464. Townhouse units with views of Smugglers Notch and Mount Mansfield. One-, two-, or three-bedroom units equipped with a full kitchen, dining and living room, TV. One bedroom is available as a separate efficiency with full bath, king-sized bed, and kitchenette, or included as a third bedroom. $115–130 per night for a studio, two-night minimum; cheaper by week, month.

MOTEL 🐾 𝒹 ઇ **Sunset Motor Inn** (802-888-4956; 800-544-2347; sunset motorinn.com), 160 Rt. 15 west, at the junction of Rts. 100 and 15, Morrisville 05661. Fifty-five comfortable units, pool. There's also Rum Runner's Hideaway, a pristine, 8-acre lake high up the mountain with canoes, paddleboats, and a water trampoline.

Most packages last five to seven days and include everything but meals so that parents can go off and do their own thing without worrying, be it tennis lessons, golf, guided mountain hikes, day trips to Montreal, art or yoga classes, cooking demonstrations, wine or chocolate tastings. There are also family-geared facilities and activities like mini golf, evening bonfires, and fireworks; Thursday is country fair day, with games, face painting, sack races, and pony rides.

Altogether there are more than 650 condominium units in a variety of shapes accommodating a total of 3,200 people. Condos are grouped into four "neighborhoods," each with its own central facilities. All offer full kitchen facilities, TV, phones, Internet access, and in-building access to laundry facilities. Units are all privately owned and vary widely from studios, to five-bedroom suites (all recently upgraded), to luxury units with Jacuzzis. Some are wheelchair accessible. Most are roadside but some are slope-side or up in the woods. Packages prices are based on number of people and services rather than on specific accommodations; guests choose on the Web site from what's available for their size party and desired time slot.

In winter a Club Smugglers' five-day ski week includes lodging, lift tickets, ski or snowboard camp for ages 3–5, lessons for youth–age 17, and learn-to-ski lessons for adults, plus use of the FunZone, pool, and tubing. Summer FamilyFest Camp Programs for youngsters begin at $1,575 per week for a two-child family. Add 14.5 percent for combined state tax and service charge.

some with whirlpool bath and refrigerator, several that are fully wheelchair accessible. There are three fully equipped three-bedroom houses, with easy access to several ski areas and an outdoor pool. The family-friendly **Sam's Charlmont Restaurant** (see *Eating Out*) is right next door. Rates $81–184, houses $172–330. Kids 12 and under stay free.

CAMPGROUND Brewster River Campground (802-644-2126; brewsterrivercampground.com), 110 Campground Dr., off Rt. 108, Jeffersonville 05464. Just 20 "low-tech" tent sites, a tepee, and several lean-tos on 20

secluded acres with a 40-foot waterfall and a river where you can pan for gold. There's a fire pit, picnic tables, and a modern bathhouse (free hot showers); no pets (but there's a local kennel). Tent sites are $25 per night, hookups $30; $40 for the lean-to or tepee. Not suitable for large vehicles with internal plumbing.

✳ Where to Eat

DINING OUT 158 Main (802-644-8100; 158main.com), 158 Main St., Jeffersonville. Serving breakfast, lunch, and dinner daily except Mon. and closing Sun. at 2. Jack Foley has introduced a menu of "innovative traditionalism" featuring organic vegetables from local farms, seafood chowders, big, fresh salads, and the usual steaks, seafood, and pizza. The high-ceilinged, hardwood-floored dining room, formerly a dry goods store, shares space with a bakery selling fudge-covered brownies, cookies, Italian- and French-style baguettes, and whole wheat loaves fresh from the oven. The lunch and dinner menus cover the basics, but the ingredients are fresh and locally grown and the soup homemade. Breakfast could be French toast made with baguettes and Grand Marnier, Florentine eggs Benedict with spinach, or a shrimp and Gorgonzola salad. Fully licensed. Dinner entrées $13–16 with soup and salad.

✒ **Three Mountain Lodge** (802-644-5736), Rt. 108, Smugglers' Notch Rd., Jeffersonville. Open 4–9 PM; Sunday brunch 9–3, closed just Mon. in peak season, Mon. and Tue. in low season. This old ski lodge has plenty of atmosphere and features fresh New England seafood, Black Angus beef, vegetarian entrées, homemade pasta, and homemade ice cream, daily specials. Sunday brunch is big. Daily and seasonal specials. Entrées $18.95–29.95, but you can always dine on "Light Fare," like hand-battered fresh fish-and-chips ($11.95).

Winding Brook Bistro (802-635-9950; windingbrookbistro.com), 933 Rt. 100C. Open for dinner except Mon., live music Thu. Chef-owner Chase Vanderveer has created the nicest kind of country bistro. The plank walls hung with paintings from the nearby Vermont Studio Center and undraped windows letting in a sense of the Gihon River out back are the setting for artfully prepared fresh produce. Dinner might begin with a choice of salads or maybe three-cheese spinach or sweet-sausage-stuffed por-

tobello. You can sup on sandwiches and pastas, maybe "Rasta Pasta" (Jamaican jerk spiced organic soy tofu with leeks, roasted red peppers, and spinach in a spicy tomato sauce over penne). A wide choice of entrées might include broiled blue crab stuffed fillet of sole, Piccata of pork loin, and (always) roast rack of lamb with mint Dijon and hazelnut crust. $18–28.

🍲 ♿ **Persico's Plum & Main** (802-635-7596), middle of Main St., Johnson. Open 6 AM–8 PM weekdays, until 9 Fri. and Sat., 8 AM–1 PM Sun. Closed Mon. Culinary Institute of America graduate Pat Persico could be writing his own ticket in Stowe, but this Vermont native would rather serve local folks along with the stray skier and leaf-peeper. The breakfast specials might include apple cinnamon griddle-cakes with home fries and syrup, or a bacon, cheddar, and onion omelet. The lunch menu covers the basics, but the ingredients are fresh and locally grown, and the soup homemade. The dinner menu changes nightly but could include baked fresh haddock with a spinach seafood stuffing, or prime rib of beef. BYOB. Inquire about specialty nights, like roast turkey or Italian. Pat's wife, Laurel, bakes the desserts, like coconut cream and maple oat nut pie. Entrées range $10.95–19.95.

Hearth & Candle (802-644-1260), Smugglers' Notch Resort, Jeffersonville. Open daily 4:30–9. This New England–style homestead was one of the first structures built in the condo village. It offers a choice of family dining or the adults-only Birch room. Moderately priced.

EATING OUT

In Jeffersonville
Stella Notte (802-644-8884), Rt. 108 across from Smuggs. Family-friendly Italian . . . pastas and seafood.

Cupboard Deli (802-644-2069), at the junction of Rts. 15 and 108. Open 5 AM–10 PM daily; from 6 AM weekends. A peerless choice of wraps, pizza, baked goods, beer and wine.

Pegg's Cookin' Roadhouse Café (802-644-2227), junction of Rts. 15 and 108. Open for all three meals, known for baked beans, sweet potato fries, onion rings, and pies.

In Johnson

♪ ♿ **Edelweiss Bakery and Kaffee Shop** (802-635-7946), 325 Lower Main St. west, Johnson. Breakfast, lunch, Sunday brunch. Closed Mon. The bakery is downstairs, the café up in this converted Victorian on the western edge of town. The European-style fare includes croissants, baguettes, whole-grain breads, and delectable fruit tarts. Lunches include fresh salads from the new salad bar, unusual sandwich combinations, and delicious soups.

"▼" **Loving Cup Café** (802-635-7423), 38 Main St., Johnson. Open weekdays 7–5, Sat. and Sun. 9–4. Laid-back student hangout with art on the walls and fresh-brewed java, plus frozen frappuccinos. You order in the kitchen of this 19th-century house and sit down in the mango-colored living room or in the former dining room, where online computers are available by the hour.

In Morrisville

♪ **The Bee's Knees** (802-888-7889; thebeesknees-vt.com), 82 Lower Main St., Morrisville. Open Tue.–Fri., 6:30 AM–10 PM, Sat. and Sun., 8 AM–10 PM. Sharon Deitz's recently expanded Caribbean- and African-accented bistro serves up stunning surprises in such a northern clime using local produce: quinoa feta soup with scallions, for example, along with curried tofu salad sandwiches, ginger-laced drinks, and the cool, spicy cucumber soup we had on a muggy day in June. Dine on

Portuguese kale and chicken potpie. The tables are mismatched, the decor artsy, the clientele laid-back, and children welcome to play with the toys. Fair-trade coffee, organic wine. Live music nearly every night. Local beer and organic wine.

🍴 ♪ **Sam's Charlmont Restaurant** (802-888-4242; 800-781-4626), 116 Rt. 100, Morrisville, at the junction of Rts. 100 and 15. Open daily, all three meals. This family restaurant has been around for 40 years and remains a fixture in Morrisville, hosting local banquets and special events and generally keeping its many faithful customers happy. Owner Sam Jadallah has improved upon the winning menu: meat loaf, lasagna, strawberry waffles, and large portions. Air-conditioned booths, pine tables. Reasonable.

Melben's Restaurant (802-888-3009), 10 Railroad St., Morrisville, down the street from the Bijoux Cinema. Moderately priced Italian specialties and fresh seafood. Open daily for lunch and dinner, Sunday for brunch.

♿ **Hilary's** (802-888-5352), Rt. 100, Northgate Plaza, Morrisville. Breakfast, lunch, dinner, and Sunday brunch are all served daily in this pleasant place that's good for everything from sandwiches to seafood, from vegetarian dishes to steak. Fully licensed.

✳ Entertainment

Lamoille County Players (802-888-4507); call for summer schedule of productions.

The Cambridge Arts Council stages theater, concerts, and coffeehouses in Jeffersonville. Check local bulletin boards.

Vermont Studio Center Lecture and Reading Series, **Vermont Studio Center** (802-635-2727; vermont studiocenter.org), Johnson. Over the past 30 years this nonprofit center has absorbed more than two dozen buildings in the village of Johnson. The lecture hall is a former meetinghouse, and the gallery, exhibiting the work of artists in residence, is in a former grain mill one street back from Main, down by the river. Billed as the largest artists' and writers' residency program in the United States, this unusual campus stages frequent gallery shows, readings, and lectures open to the public.

Burklyn Ballet and Theatre (802-635-0438), Dibden Center for the Arts, Johnson State College, Johnson. Weekly performances in July and August, Sat., 8 PM.

Bijoux Cineplex 4 (802-888-3293), Portland St. (Rt. 100), Morrisville. All shows $4 on Tue. and Thu.

✳ Selective Shopping

ANTIQUES Green Apple Antique Center (802-644-2989), 60 Main St., Jeffersonville. Daily 9–5, Sun. 11–4. Located in the old Noble Pearl Building, this center represents more than 30 dealers and consigners.

Smugglers' Notch Antiques (802-644-2100; smugglersnotchantiques .com), Rt. 108 south. Daily May–Oct., 10–5; Nov.–Apr., open Fri.–Sun. This dairy-barn-turned-antiques-center with 35 dealer booths specializes in custom-made and antique furniture.

The Buggyman Antiques Shop (802-635-2110), Rt. 15, Johnson. Open daily 10–5. A big old barn and 18th-century farmhouse filled with antiques, including wagons, buggies, and sleighs.

Victorian House Antiques (802-635-9549), Johnson. A multidealer and consignment shop.

Antiques By Vermont Hands (802-635-7664; byvermonthands.com), Rt. 15, Johnson (1 mile west of the village), carries fine European and early

American antiques and some locally made furniture. Open daily except Tue. 10–5, or by appointment.

Nye's Green Valley Farm Antiques (802-644-1984), Rt. 15 between Jeffersonville and Johnson. Open daily 10–5:30. Old Vermont farmhouse furnishings and a wide selection of American pressed glass.

ART AND CRAFTS GALLERIES
Milk Room Gallery (802-644-5122; milkroomgallery.com), 105 Main St., Jeffersonville, open year-round. A collection that started in the milk room of a nearby farm has blossomed into this midvillage gallery featuring some 50 painters, plus sculpture, pottery, rugs, and framing.

Visions of Vermont Gallery (802-644-8183), 94 Main St., Jeffersonville. Open Tue.–Sun. 10–4. Vermont landscapes, featuring the work of Eric Tobin.

Tegu Gallery (802-888-1261; riverarts vt.org), Portland St., Morrisville. Open Mon.–Fri. 8–4:30. A new gallery run by River Arts, the Tegu Gallery exhibits the work of regional artists as well as that created by participants in River Arts' workshops.

FARMS AND A WINERY ◯◯ **Boyden Valley Farm and Winery** (802-644-8151; boydenvalley.com), 64 Rt. 104, at the intersection of Rts. 15 and 104, just west of Cambridge Village. There's a lot going on here. This splendid former dairy farm bordering the Lamoille River, one that's been in the family for four generations, is now known for more than a dozen widely respected grape and fruit wines and for naturally raised beef as well as maple syrup. The former dairy barn now includes the Milk House Market (open year-round), selling Boyden Farm beef and other Vermont-raised meats, and a Scoop Shop. Most recently a portion of the barn has been transformed into a venue for weddings and events. The 1878 carriage barn houses the winery (open daily May–Dec., 10–5 with tours at 11:30 and 1; Fri.–Sun the rest of the year). A tour, wine tasting, and a sampling of artisanal cheeses, with prosciutto and bread with wine is $16.95; $5 for tasting any wine. See *Canoeing* for a guided paddle that includes a tasting. There are also seasonal attractions: the sugarhouse, hayrides, a corn maze, petting farm, a concert series, Harvest Festival (late Sept.), and more. However, we caution calling ahead from our own midafternoon midsummer experience.

Applecheek Farm (802-888-4482; applecheekfarm.com), 567 McFarlane Rd., Hyde Park. Call before coming. A dairy farm with a maple sugaring operation; other farm animals include llamas, emus, draft horses, and miniature horses. Llama treks with picnic, barbecue with horse and wagon rides.

SPECIALTY STORES **Johnson Woolen Mills** (802-635-7185; 877-635-WOOL; johnsonwoolenmills.com), 51 Lower Main St., Johnson. Open year-round, daily 10–5. Although wool is no longer loomed in this picturesque mill, the fine line of clothing for which Johnson Woolen Mills has been known since 1842 is made on the premises under ownership by the same family for four generations. This mill's label can still be found in shops throughout the country, and its famous, heavy green wool work pants and checked jackets, a uniform of Vermont farmers, are especially popular in Alaska. Although there are few discounts at the factory store, the selection of wool jackets and pants—for men, women, and children—is exceptional. The mail-order catalog is replete with

sweaters, wool ties, hunting jackets, blankets, and other staples available in the shop.

Three Mountain Outfitters (802-644-8563). Located at Smugglers' Notch Resort. Seasonal sports clothes, skis, snowboards, boots, helmets, as well as toys, shoes and boots, T-shirts, and accessories.

Marvin's Butternut Country Store (802-635-2329), 31 Main St., Johnson, is open Mon.–Sat. 9–5:30, Sun. 11–4. This is the retail outlet for the Marvin family's maple products, plus a variety of specialty foods and Vermont gifts.

🐾 ⑆ **Arthur's Department Store** (802-888-3125), 63 Main St., Morrisville. Arthur and Theresa Breault and their daughter, Adrienne, do their buying in New York, Boston, Dallas, and Las Vegas; they have created an unexpectedly fine and friendly source of clothing and footwear for men, women, juniors, and children. Genuine bargains in the basement.

Ebenezer Books (802-635-7472), 2 Lower Main St., Johnson. Formerly Ryan Books, this is an inviting independent book store specializing in children's books, fiction, and local authors. Stroll down from Plum & Main (good food) and stop in on your way to Johnson Woolen Mills (destination shopping).

Vermont Maple Outlet (802-644-5482; vermontmapleoutlet.com), 3929 Rt. 15 between Jefferson and Cambridge. A nice selection of cheese, syrup, handmade jams, and gift boxes. Open daily 9–5.

Forget-Me-Not Shop (802-635-2335), Rt. 15, 1.5 miles west of Johnson. This eclectic store carries international military surplus clothing and gear, gift items of all sorts, jewelry, and famous-label clothing at discounted prices. Open daily 9–9.

✳ Special Events

Last weekend of January:
Winterfest—a primitive biathlon with muzzle loaders and snowshoes.

First weekend of June: **Vermont Dairy Festival**—arts and crafts, horse pulling, stage shows, two-hour Saturday parade, country-and-western jamboree Sunday.

July 4: **Celebration**, Jeffersonville—an outstanding small-town parade at 10 AM followed by a chicken barbecue, games, crafts, cow-flop bingo, and a frog-jumping contest on the green behind the elementary school. Evening music and fireworks at Smugglers' Notch Resort, food.

Late July: **Lamoille County Field Days** (802-635-7113), Rt. 100C, Johnson—a classic small-town fair with family entertainment. Wheelchair accessible. **Morristown Community Festival** (802-888-1261)—art, food, music, sidewalk sale along Main Street in Morrisville.

Early August: **Blueberry Festival** (802-456-7012), Grand View Winery, Cambridge—pies, jams, wines, and plain old berries; live music; free.

Labor Day weekend: **Festivities** in Cambridge—barbecue on the green, flea market, family road run (3.1 miles) from Jeffersonville to Cambridge along back roads.

Mid-September: **Festival La Moelle** (802-888-4294), a celebration of French Canadian heritage in downtown Morrisville.

The Northeast Kingdom

6

ST. JOHNSBURY, CRAFTSBURY, AND
BURKE MOUNTAIN

THE LAKE COUNTRY, INCLUDING
NEWPORT, JAY PEAK, BARTON,
THE ISLAND POND AREA, AND THE
EASTERN TOWNSHIPS OF QUEBEC

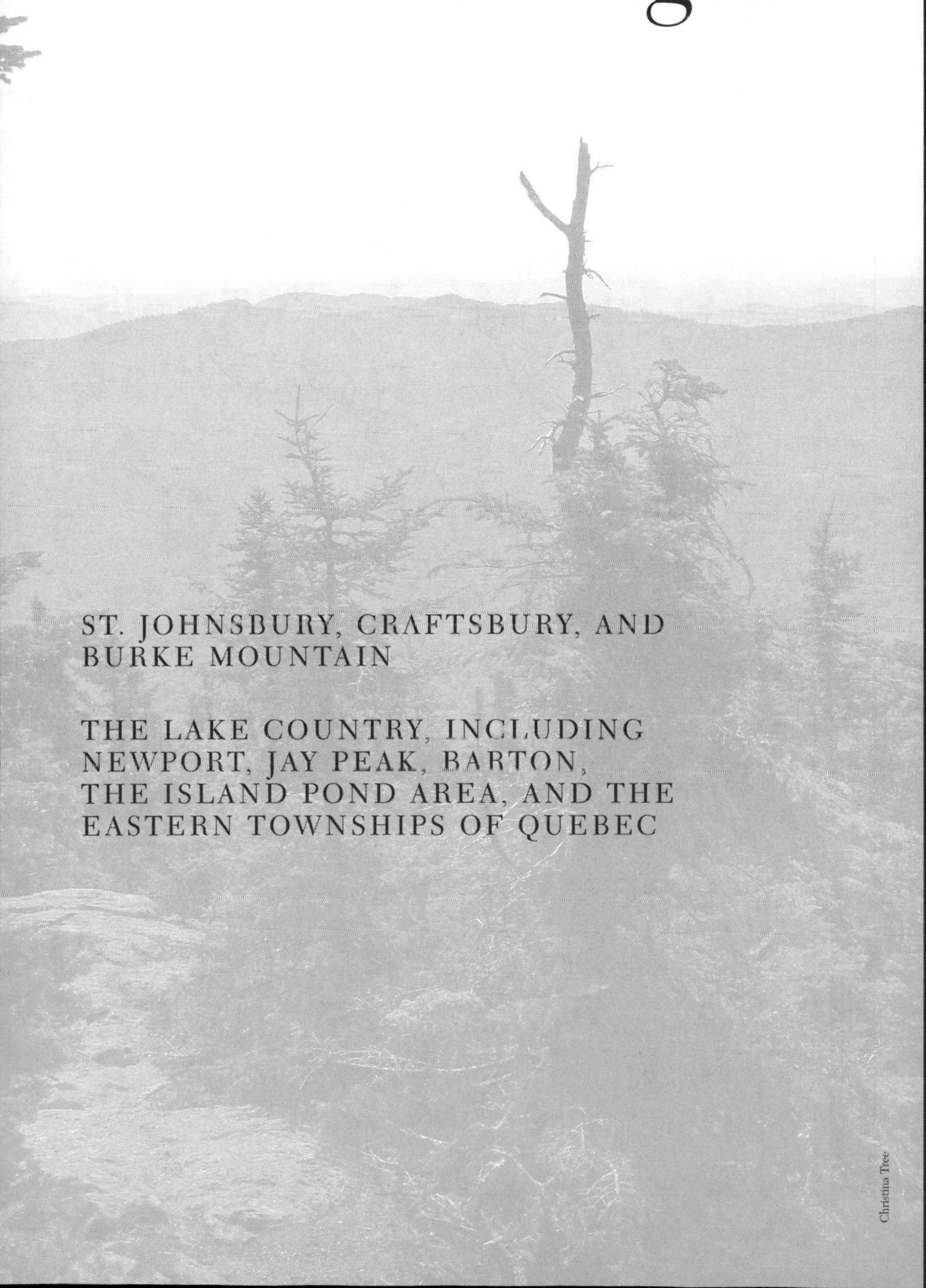

Christina Tree

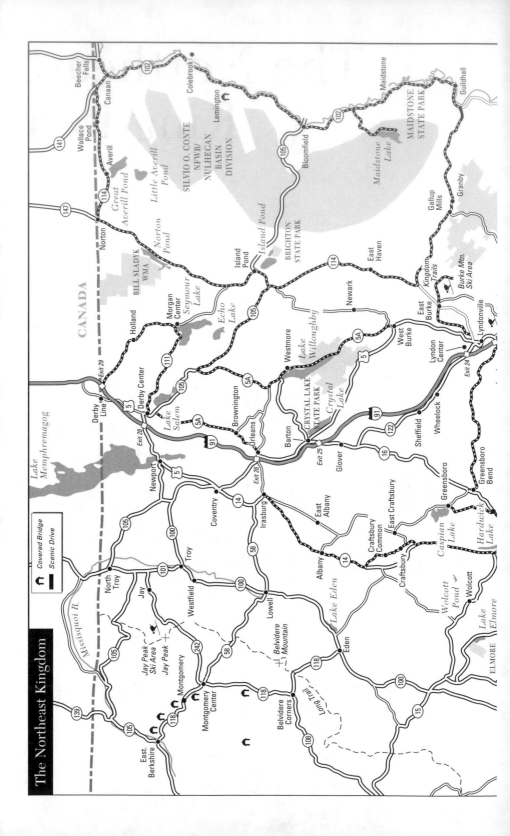

The Northeast Kingdom

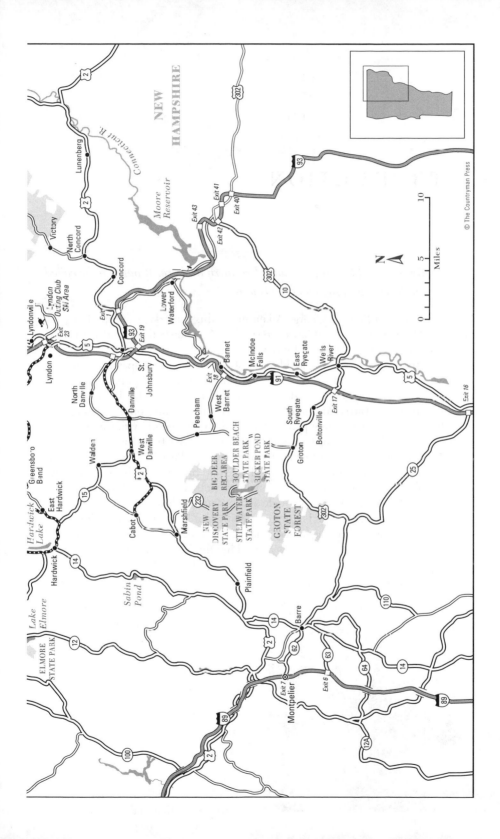

INTRODUCTION

You know, this is such beautiful country up here. It ought to be called the Northeast Kingdom of Vermont.

It was in 1949 that Senator George Aiken made this remark to a group in Lyndonville. The name he coined has since stuck to Vermont's three northeastern counties: Orleans, Caledonia, and Essex.

This is the state's most rural and lake-spotted corner, encompassing more than 2,000 square miles, including 37,575 acres of public lakes and ponds and 3,540 miles of rivers. Aside from a few dramatic elevations, such as Jay Peak on its northwestern fringe and Burke Mountain at its heart, this is a predominantly high, open, glacially carved plateau of humped hills and rolling farmland, with some lonely timber country along the northern reaches of the Connecticut River.

For many decades neither Burke Mountain nor Jay Peak had much impact on surrounding communities in summer and fall. That, however, is changing. Jay Peak's new 18-hole golf course is drawing patrons from both sides of the border, and the resort has embarked on a major upgrade and expansion. Burke's current owners have also made improvements. The big summer–fall magnet, though, is Kingdom Trails: more than 100 miles of mountain bike trails (used in winter for cross-country) webbing the high country surrounding the village of East Burke.

AIKEN COINED THE NAME *NORTHEAST KINGDOM*; MOSHER TELLS ITS STORY.

Still, the area attracts fewer summer visitors than it did in the era of trains and steamboats, when large hotels clustered on Lakes Memphremagog and Willoughby. Foliage season, which begins early here and is frequently over by Columbus Day, draws relatively few leaf-peepers, perhaps because of the way the roads run. I-93 puts St. Johnsbury within a three-hour drive of Boston but farther from New York than most of Vermont.

We have included some outstanding lodging and attractions in the Eastern Townships in the province of Quebec. Little more than half an hour's drive across the border, this is a totally different place, a lively resort area with French fare and ambience. Vermont and Canada mingle in the waters of Lake Memphremagog (which is mostly in Canada). There are four border crossings.

Within the Kingdom itself lodging options range from working farms to ski resorts and include inns, B&Bs, and plenty of summer rentals. All the amenities are here: golf, tennis, and horseback riding as well as hiking, biking, boating and fishing. Winter sports include ice fishing, tracking and snowshoeing, some of New England's best snowmobiling, and cross-country as well as superb downhill skiing.

The key to this Kingdom is following farm roads and—in the process of finding an isolated craftsperson, a maple producer, or a swimming hole—stumbling on breathtaking views and memorable people. Frequently you come across traces of the Kingdom's oldest thoroughfare, the 48-mile Bayley-Hazen Military Road, which runs diagonally across the region. It was begun at Wells River on the Connecticut River in 1776 by General Jacob Bayley, and continued in 1778–79 by General Moses Hazen as far as Hazen's Notch (a plaque on Rt. 58 tells the story). It was a flop as an invasion route but served settlers well after the Revolution when it came time to establish towns in this area.

The Northeast Kingdom has a story to tell. Listen at a lunch counter, in a general store, at a church supper, at a county fair, or during the peerless Northeast Kingdom Foliage Festival. Tune in with Howard Frank Mosher's beautifully written books—*Northern Borders*, *Where the Rivers Flow North*, *A Stranger in the Kingdom*, *Disappearances*, and *On Kingdom Mountain*. Kingdom-based filmmaker Jay Craven has turned three of these into films.

Like many of the world's most beautiful places, the Kingdom's preservation is fragile, a fact recognized by the National Geographic Society, which has chosen it as one of the few areas in this country to support through its "geotourism" plan, working with the Northeast Tourism Association (see *Guidance*).

While this is the single most distinctive corner of the entire state, 2,000 square miles is too large an area to describe without dividing it in two. If you have a particular passion such as canoeing, cross-country skiing, fishing, hiking, or mountain biking, check *To Do* in both.

GUIDANCE **The Northeast Kingdom Travel and Tourism Association** (802-626-8511; 800-884-8001; travelthekingdom.com), a nonprofit umbrella organization promoting the area, publishes the useful *Travel Planner*, *Geotourism Map Guide*, and excellent hiking, biking, and paddling guides to the region.

MEDICAL EMERGENCY Emergency service is available by calling **911**.

Northeastern Vermont Regional Hospital (802-748-8141), 1315 Hospital Dr., St. Johnsbury. **North Country Hospital** (802-334-7331), 189 Prouty Dr., Newport.

GEORGE AIKEN

Vermont History Center

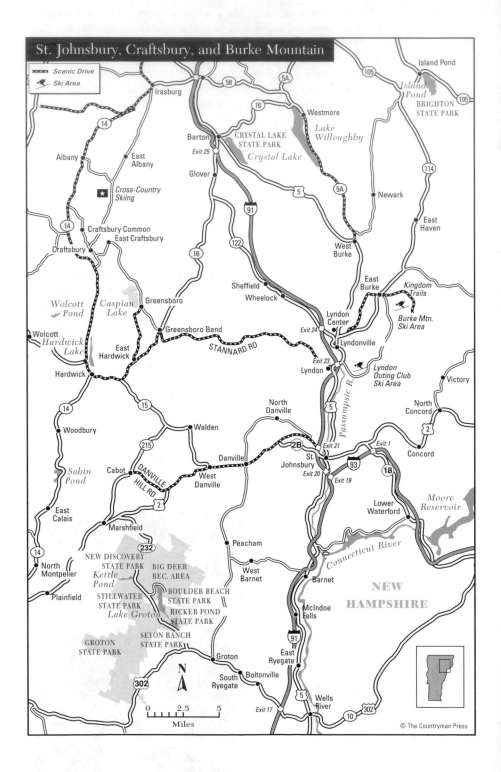

St. Johnsbury, Craftsbury, and Burke Mountain

Legend:
- ▬▬▬ Scenic Drive
- 🎿 Ski Area

Island Pond

Island Pond
BRIGHTON
STATE PARK

Irasburg

58

5A

105

105

16

14

Westmore

Lake Willoughby

Barton

CRYSTAL LAKE
STATE PARK

Exit 25

Crystal Lake

114

Albany

East Albany

Glover

5

5A

Newark

★ Cross-Country Skiing

91

East Haven

14

Craftsbury Common
East Craftsbury

122

West Burke

Craftsbury

16

East Burke

Kingdom Trails

Wolcott Pond

Caspian Lake

Greensboro

Sheffield
Wheelock

Lyndon Center

Exit 24

Burke Mtn. Ski Area

Hardwick Lake

Greensboro Bend

Lyndonville

East Hardwick

STANNARD RD.

Exit 23

Lyndon

Lyndon Outing Club Ski Area

Hardwick

15

Lyndon

Passumpsic R.

Victory

North Danville

14

North Concord

Woodbury

Walden

5

2

215

Danville

Exit 21

Exit 1

Concord

2B

St. Johnsbury

Sabin Pond

Cabot

DANVILLE HILL RD.

West Danville

Exit 20

Exit 19

93

18

2

East Calais

Marshfield

Moore Reservoir

Lower Waterford

14

North Montpelier

232

NEW DISCOVERY
STATE PARK
Kettle Pond

BIG DEER
REC. AREA

Peacham

West Barnet

Connecticut River

Barnet

NEW
HAMPSHIRE

Plainfield

STILLWATER
STATE PARK
Lake Groton

BOULDER BEACH
STATE PARK

RICKER POND
STATE PARK

McIndoe Falls

GROTON
STATE PARK

SEYON RANCH
STATE PARK

N

302

Groton

East Ryegate

South Ryegate

Boltonville

91

5

Wells River

Exit 17

10

302

0   2.5   5
Miles

© The Countryman Press

ST. JOHNSBURY, CRAFTSBURY, AND BURKE MOUNTAIN

With a population of about 6,500, St. Johnsbury is the largest community in the Northeast Kingdom. Thanks to members of the Fairbanks family, who began manufacturing their world-famous scale here in the 1830s, it is graced with a superb museum of natural and local history, a handsome athenaeum, and an outstanding public academy. The general late-19th-century affluence that St. J (as it is affectionately known) enjoyed as an active rail junction and industrial center has been commemorated in ornate brick along Railroad Street and in the fine mansions along Main Street, set high above the commercial downtown. In the 1960s, when Fairbanks became a division of a conglomerate—which threatened to move the scaleworks south—townspeople themselves raised the money to subsidize a new plant. This is a spirited community boasting one of the country's oldest town bands (performing Monday nights all summer in Courthouse Park), a busy calendar of concerts, lectures, and plays, and all the shops and services needed by residents of the picturesque villages along the Connecticut River to the south, the rolling hills to the southwest and northwest, and the lonely woodlands to the east. Less than a dozen miles north, the wide main street of Lyndonville is also lined with useful shops. Burke Mountain, a short way up Rt. 114, is accessible by car as well as by foot and bike in summer and draws skiers from throughout the Northeast in winter.

As Rt. 2 climbs steeply west from St. J to Danville, a spectacular panorama of the White Mountains unfolds to the east. The village of Danville itself is a beauty, and the back roads running south to Peacham and north to Walden follow ridges with long views. Continue on through Hardwick and north to Craftsbury, where fields roll away like waves to the mountains in the distance.

Craftsbury is a composite of scattered villages, most of which you drive through in a trice. It's Craftsbury Common, with its magnificent common surrounded by white homes, academy, and church, that compels you to stop. Get lost in the surrounding web of well-maintained dirt roads. Eventually you hit a paved, numbered road, and in the meantime you find some of Vermont's most breathtaking farmscape, spotted with small lakes and large ponds. Don't miss Greensboro, an early-20th-century summer compound on Caspian Lake.

GUIDANCE **Northeast Kingdom Chamber of Commerce** (802-748-3678; 800-639-6379; nekchamber.com), Suite 3, 51 Depot Square, St. Johnsbury 05819.

Christina Tree

ST. JOHNSBURY WELCOME CENTER

The chamber maintains the outstanding **St. Johnsbury Welcome Center** in its vintage railroad station, open year-round: in summer and fall Mon.–Sat. 9–6, Sun. 10–4; in winter Mon.–Sat. 9–5, Sat.–Sun. 10–2. A source for lodging, dining, and general information for the region.

GETTING THERE *By car:* I-93 makes the Northeast Kingdom far more accessible from the southeast than is still generally realized: Bostonians can be in St. Johnsbury in three hours. Note that I-91 works like a fireman's pole, a quick way to move north–south through the Kingdom. In snow, beware the high, open, 16-mile stretch of highway between Lyndon Center and Barton known as Sheffield Heights.

By bus: **Rural Community Transportation** (802-748-8170; riderct.org) offers service from White River Junction (linked by bus and train to New York City and Boston) to St. J.

✳ Towns and Villages

Barnet (population: 1,690). An old Scots settlement encompassing the villages of McIndoe Falls as well as East and West Barnet and Barnet Center. The village of Barnet itself is on a curve of the Connecticut River, almost lost today in a curious intertwining of I-91 and Rt. 5. **Goodwillie House** (802-633-2891) in Barnet Center, built in 1790 by a Scottish pastor, served as a stop on the Underground Railroad and now houses the collections of the Barnet Historical Society; unfortunately it's only open by request and on Fall Foliage Day. Drive to West Barnet to find **Harvey's Lake** (good for both fishing and swimming); along the way stop by the 1870s **Ben Thresher's Mill** (open Sat. 10–2 July–Sept., and daily during foliage season). The beautiful round red **Moore Barn** sits above the Passumpsic River in East Barnet (north on Rt. 5 from Barnet). Also see the Karmê Chöling Shambhala Meditation Center (karmecholing.org) under *Lodging*.

Burke (population 1,719; chamber of commerce 802-626-4124; burkevermont

.com). The town includes Burke Hollow and West Burke, but it's the village of East Burke that's home to Burke Mountain (see *Downhill Skiing and Snowboarding*) and Burke Mountain Academy. In summer and fall the big draw is Kingdom Trails (see *Biking*). Burke is a big but moderately developed ski mountain that weathered four bankruptcies in the 1980s and '90s. The current owner, Florida-based Ginn, is a developer with a 10-year plan that includes quadrupling the number of skiers, building more than 1,000 condominiums and homes, an 18-hole golf course and slope-side village and spa. At present East Burke is a sleepy gathering of restaurants and shops around a general store and gas station. **The Burke Mountain Clubhouse** (802-626-9823) is a library with paintings and a historical collection; it's open Mon., Tue., and Thu. 2–5, also by appointment.

Cabot (population: 1,090). Known during the War of 1812 for its distilleries (the whiskey was sold to Canadians), this distinctly upcountry village is now famed for its cheese. The Cabot Farmers Co-op Creamery is Vermont's major producer, and its visitor center is a popular attraction. Cabot is called the mother of the Winooski because the river rises in four of its ponds. Technically the town is in Washington County, but it's tightly bound into the network of Kingdom roads.

Concord (population: 1,205). Six miles east of St. Johnsbury on Rt. 2, Concord is a proudly built village with an unusual number of columned houses. The **Concord Museum** (802-695-330) is found upstairs in the tower-topped town hall; there's a picture of St. Johnsbury's Railroad Street, painted in the 1940s, on its stage curtain. A plaque declares this to be the site of the country's first "Normal School" (to train teachers) in 1823, founded by the Reverend Samuel R. Hall, who is also credited with inventing the blackboard. Photos of Concord in the 1890s line the walls in the Mooselook Restaurant east of the village on Rt. 2. A short way farther along, the 400-acre Miles Pond offers boat access, as does Shadow Lake in Concord Center.

Craftsbury (population: 1,200). Few places convey such a sense of tranquility and order as the village of **Craftsbury Common**. In summer, petunias bloom in window boxes, and the green of the grass contrasts crisply with the white fence. In

CRAFTSBURY COMMON

Christina Tree

Christina Tree

INSIDE THE JOHN WOODRUFF MEMORIAL
LIBRARY IN EAST CRAFTSBURY

winter, the general whitewash of this scene contrasts with the blue of the sky. Throughout the year there are nearby places to stay and books to check out at the desk in the new **Craftsbury Public Library** (802-586-9683) with its rockers on the porch, comfortable reading corners, WiFi, and imposing portraits of Samuel and Ebenezer Crafts (Yale, class of 1740). Due to war debts, he was forced to sell his tavern in Sturbridge, Massachusetts (the still-popular Publick House). He made his way here over the Bayley-Hazen Military Road, eventually bringing his family and 150 of his Sturbridge neighbors this way on sleds. Ebenezer was quick to establish a school. His son Samuel, a Harvard graduate who served two terms as Vermont's governor, founded Craftsbury Academy, which still serves as the public high school for the town. **Babcock House Museum** (802-586-2825), beside the library, houses the Craftsbury Historical Society collection; it's open June–mid-Oct., Wed. and Sat. 10–noon. The **Sterling College** campus adds to the variety and serves in summer as home for **Circus Smirkus**. In East Craftsbury the **John Woodruff Memorial Library** (802-586-9692) preserves the look of the general store (vintage 1840s) while offering its stock of 20,000 books, including many children's titles, to visitors as well as residents. Open Wed. and Sat. 9–noon, 2–5, and 7–9:30; also 12:15–1:30 on Sun. Many farmers welcome visitors to their sugarhouses during sugaring season in late March and early April and sell syrup from their farmhouses year-round. Inns and B&Bs offer year-round lodging, and **Craftsbury Outdoor Center** offers one of the most extensive and dependable cross-country ski networks in New England; its summer sculling program is also nationally recognized. An extensive web of well-surfaced dirt farm roads meander in all directions, beloved by bicyclists and horseback riders. In 1930 Craftsbury had close to 100 farms, each with an average of 10 cows. In 2006 there were just 15 dairy farms, but many had diversified. The barns survive, and John Broadhead of Craftsbury Outdoor Center offers guests a van tour.

Danville (population 2,336; danvillevt.com). Until 1855, Danville was the shire town of Caledonia County. Its village is set high on a plateau, with a bandstand and Civil War monument in the center of its large green. The town hall was built as the county courthouse, and the small, square Passumpsic Savings Bank is one of the safest strongholds around, thanks to devices installed after it was last held up, in 1935. Danville is headquarters for the American Society of Dowsers. **Dowser's Hall** (802-684-3417) is open weekdays 9–5; note the summer concerts on the green (see *Entertainment*) and the Danville Fair (see *Special Events*). **West Danville** is a crossroads (Rts. 15 and 2) cluster of two general stores and a major crafts shop (see *Selective Shopping*). One of the world's smallest libraries sits across the road at **Joe's Pond** (named for a Native American beloved by early settlers), beside a public beach with picnic facilities. The water from Joe's Pond is said to empty, eventually, into Long Island Sound, while that from Molly's Pond (a mile south, named for Joe's wife) presumably winds up in the Gulf of St. Lawrence.

Greensboro (population: 770). Shaped like an hourglass, **Caspian Lake** has a century-old following. The unusual purity of its water is checked three times weekly in-season by its association of cottage owners—who include noted authors, educators, and socialites—all of whom mingle in **Willey's Store**, one of Vermont's most genuine and extensive village emporiums, in the center of Greensboro. You'll also find a public beach in the village and walking trails east of the village, near Highland Lodge, which also maintains superb cross-country skiing trails in winter. Greensboro claims Vermont's oldest (nine-hole) golf course.

Hardwick (population: 3,174). The **Hardwick Chamber of Commerce** (802-472-5906; heartofvt.com) also serves surrounding towns (Stannard, Walden, Wolcott, Craftsbury, Greensboro, Cabot, and Woodbury). This hardscrabble little commercial center is making national news as a center for reinventing local agriculture. At this writing it's home to the Vermont Milk Co. (milk, cheese, ice cream) and Vermont Soy (produced from local beans) and the planned home for the non-profit Center for Agriculture Economy and a Vermont Food Venture, an incubator for businesses like the area's current success stories, Wolcott-based High Mowing Organic Seeds, Craftsbury-based Pete's Greens, and Greensboro-based Jasper Hill Cheese. At Claire's Restaurant and Bar, a cooperative effort opened in 2008 (see *Dining Out*), the motto is "Local ingredients open to the world." Interestingly, this isn't the first time Hardwick has channeled local resources to a wider world. Its Victorian architecture is a reminder of the town's heyday as one of the world's major granite processors. The granite was actually in Woodbury, 5 miles south, whence it arrived by rail. Thousands of skilled European craftsmen moved to town beginning in the 1870s and continuing into the 1920s; a number of French Canadians remain. The Lamoille River runs through town, good for fly-fishing, beneath the swinging (pedestrian) bridge linking Main Street with parking. East Hardwick is also worth finding. **The Hardwick Historical Society** (802-472-8555) is housed in the former Hardwick Depot. The neighboring **Hardwick Town House** (see *Entertainment*) is noted for its hand-painted stage curtains and frequent concerts, live productions, and lectures.

Lyndon (population: 5,713). An up-and-down roll of land encompasses the villages of Lyndonville, Lyndon Center, Lyndon Corner, Red Village, and East Lyndon, and the neighborhoods of Vail Hill, Pudding Hill, Darling Hill, and Squabble Hollow. Lyndon isn't a tourist town, but it offers real, down-home hospitality and **five covered bridges**. The village of Lyndonville was developed by the Passumpsic River Railroad Co. in the 1860s. Besides a handsome (long gone) station and a number of brick rail shops, the company laid out broad streets, planted elm trees, and landscaped Bandstand Park. **Lyndon State College** is on Vail Hill (T. N. Vail was the first president of AT&T; he came here to buy a horse and ended up buying a farm, which eventually turned into 20 farms, much of which is now occupied by the campus). Lyndonville's famous product is **Bag Balm**, manufactured since 1899 in the middle of Lyndonville. Band concerts are held Wednesday evenings during summer months in Bandstand Park, also Lyndonville. **Lyndon Area Chamber of Commerce** (802-626-9696; lyndonvermont.com) maintains an information center in the **Historic Lyndon Freight House** (see *Eating Out*), which also showcases the town's railroading history. The Caledonia County Fairgrounds are the site of frequent events; the **Caledonia County Fair** itself runs for five days in early August.

Peacham (population: 635). High on a ridge overlooking the White Mountains, this is a tiny but aristocratic village settled just after the Revolution, with a fine new library at the four-corners. Peacham's handsome homes and setting have attracted retired professors, literati, artistic luminaries, and ambassadors. All three Peachams (South, East, and Center) are worth exploring, as are the roads between. The **Peacham Historical House** (peachamhistorical.org) is open July–early Oct., Sun. 2–4, also on July 4 and Foliage Day. The latter is when the 1820s blacksmith shop operates and "Ghost Walks," with current residents impersonating long-deceased counterparts, are offered in hilltop **Peacham Cemetery**— which tells its own story and offers one of the best views in the Kingdom any day.

✷ Must-See

LOCAL ATTRACTIONS ✍ **Cabot Creamery Visitor Center** (802-563-3393; 800-837-4261; cabotcheese.com), Cabot Village (no way can you miss it). Open year-round: June–Oct., daily 9–5; the rest of the year, Mon.–Sat. 9–4, from 10 in Jan. Cabot has been judged "best cheddar in the world" at the industry's olympics.

PEACHAM

Christina Tree

Cooperatively owned by dairy farmers since 1919, the center showcases its history with a video and offers tours, every half hour, of "Cheddar Hall" to view the cheesemaking (token fee per person over age 12 includes samples). The store features all of Cabot's many dairy products, along with other Vermont products. Call ahead to check when cheese is being made and inquire about the week's specials.

Maple Grove Farms of Vermont (802-748-5141; maplegrove.com), 1052 Portland St. (Rt. 2 east), St. Johnsbury. May–Oct., guided tours offered daily 8–4:30 of "the world's oldest and largest maple candy factory." In business since 1915, this is an old-fashioned factory in which maple candy is made from molds. A film in the adjacent museum depicts maple production and displays tools of the trade. The gift store stocks many things besides maple.

The American Society of Dowsers (802-684-3417; dowsers.org) is head-

571

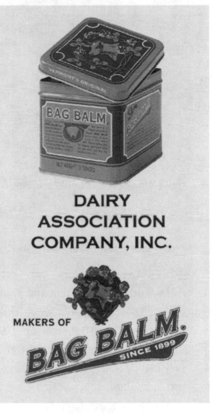

Bag Balm (802-626-3610; bag balm.com). Developed in 1899 as an antiseptic ointment for cattle, Bag Balm proved particularly effective for chapped udders and is still used by Vermont farmers. Its campy, old-fashioned green tins now appear in Madison Avenue pharmacies and ski resort boutiques, at far higher prices than they fetch locally. Inquire about weekday tours of the small factory on Lyndonville's Main St. (Rt. 5). The company, which has been owned by the same family since it opened its doors, still employs just four workers "on the floor." Bag Balm is sold here, also at the Lyndonville Pharmacy and Lyndonville Hardware.

DAIRY ASSOCIATION COMPANY, INC.

MAKERS OF *BAG BALM.* SINCE 1899

quartered in Dowser's Hall (open weekdays 9–5), Brainerd St., just off the common in Danville, the **American Society of Dowsers Bookstore** (800-711-9497), also here, is open Wed.–Sat. 9–6, selling books about dowsing, also books and tapes on healing, and dowsing equipment. Check out the labyrinth in the rear of the building. The ancient art of dowsing is the knack of finding water through the use of a forked stick, a pair of angle rods, or a pendulum. The society has thousands of members throughout the world.

Also see *Gardens* under *Selective Shopping*.

COVERED BRIDGES Five are in within the town of **Lyndon**—one 120-foot, 1865 bridge across the Passumpsic, 3 miles north of town off Rt. 114; one as you enter town, a genuine 1869 bridge moved from its original site; two in Lyndon Corner (one dating from 1879, the other from 1881, both west off Rt. 5); the fifth in Lyndon Center on Rt. 122. Pick up a map at the **Freight House** in Lyndonville. See *Scenic Drives* for directions to the recently restored **Greenbank's Hollow Bridge** in South Danville.

FOR FAMILIES *Note:* The Fairbanks Museum is number one in this category.

✐ **The Great Vermont Corn Maze** (802-748-1399; ww.vermontcornmaze.com), Patterson Farm, 1404 Wheelock Rd., North Danville. Open Aug. and Sept., 10–5; Oct., 10–4 (until the second to last Sunday). It takes from 40 minutes to two hours to thread the miles of pathways between walls of corn. "Cheater Poles" along the

Christina Tree

INSIDE THE ST. JOHNSBURY ANETHAEUM

MUSEUMS

✒ **The Fairbanks Museum and Planetarium** (802-748-2372; fairbanksmuseum
.org), 1302 Main, St. Johnsbury. Open year-round, Mon.–Sat. 9–5, Sun. 1–5
(closed Mon., mid-Oct.–mid-Apr.). $6 adults, $5 seniors and ages 5–17; $5 for
planetarium shows, which are Sat. and Sun. at 1:30 year-round, 11 and 1:30
daily in July and Aug. A wonderfully Victorian-style "Cabinet of Curiosities,"
said to be the oldest science education museum in the nation and the state's
only public planetarium, the Fairbanks is much more as well.

"I wish the museum to be the people's school . . . to teach the village the
meaning of nature and religion," explained Franklin Fairbanks at the museum's
1891 dedication.

The main hall is capped by a 30-foot-high, barrel-vaulted ceiling, its floor
lined with Victorian-style cabinets displaying thousands of stuffed animals:
from mice to a vintage 1898 moose, from bats to bears (including a superb
polar bear), birds galore (from hummingbirds to passenger pigeons), reptiles
and fish, insect nests. Founder Franklin Fairbanks was passionate about nature,
and the collection represents most native species of mammals and birds as
well as many gathered from around the world, a total of 3,000 specimens. The
Vermont State Geologic Collection is also displayed, along with an extensive
herbarium of New England plants. The balcony, which circles the entire hall
level, is lined with historical displays depicting local 19th-century life (including
the Civil War) and exhibits drawn from a 5,000-piece collection representing
most of the world's far corners—Malaysia, the Orient, the Middle East, and
Africa—by the Fairbanks family and their friends. Altogether the museum displays 160,000 objects.

In the planetarium, which seats just 50 people, you learn about the night
sky as it appears in the Northeast Kingdom. The museum is also a U.S. weather

observation station, and its daily "Eye on the Sky" forecasts are a fixture of Vermont Public Radio (VPR). The weather station is in the basement, worth a visit to see exhibits telling the story of the Fairbanks family and their scales and an interactive kids-geared

St. Johnsbury Anethaeum

HORACE AND FRANKLIN FAIRBANKS

exhibit. There is a fine little gift shop. The museum archives include a resource library for studies and information about the Northeast Kingdom. Ambitious exhibits in the main gallery change seasonally. The annual Fairbanks Festival of Traditional Crafts (late Sept.) features demonstrations of the Kingdom's tradition-al home industries.

St. Johnsbury Athenaeum and Art Gallery (802-748-8291; stjathenaeum.org), 1171 Main St., St. Johnsbury. Open Mon. and Wed. 10–8, Tue., Thu., Fri., 10–5:30, Sat. 8:30–4, closed Sun. Donation appreciated. Completed in 1871, the athenaeum was conceived and carefully creat-ed (not just donated) by Horace Fairbanks, who personally selected the paintings and leather-bound collection of 7,000 books. The art gallery, the big attraction, is said to be the old-est unaltered gallery in the country and has a distinctly 19th-century feel. Smaller canvases and sculptures are grouped around the out-sized painting *Domes of the Yosemite*, by Albert Bierstadt. Natural light through an arched skylight enhances the effect of looking into the Yosemite Valley. The gallery is at the rear of this fascinating public library, a Nation-al Historic Landmark, which has recently reopened after extensive renovations that included adding 18 feet to the former lecture hall (now open stacks), uncovering arched windows, subtly inserting an elevator, and gen-erally restoring the 1870s look of the galleried reading rooms.

THE FAIRBANKS MUSEUM
Courtesy of the Fairbanks Museum

way permit a quick exit. A barnyard nature center, gardens, and "Miney's Korny Kid Korn Maze" are geared to younger children. Call first if the weather is questionable. Everyone we've talked to who has found this place has been enthusiastic, but we've also spoken to people who never did find it. Begin at the blinking light on Rt. 2 in Danville and head north; it's best to download the map on the Web site.

♨ ✎ **Stephen Huneck's Gallery and Dog Chapel** (800-449-2580; dogmt.com), 143 Parks Rd., marked from Rt. 2 east of St. Johnsbury. Open Mon.–Sat. 10–5, Sun. 11–4. The full-scale wooden chapel "welcomes all creeds and breeds. No dogma allowed." Seven surrounding acres on "Dog Mountain" are planted in wildflowers, and visitors are welcome to bring (or e-mail) photos of their beloved animals to grace the chapel walls. The gallery, of course, showcases nationally known Huneck's stylish, carved wooden animals and bold, fanciful furniture, panels, and jewelry, and his children's books, featuring his black Lab Sally. Dogs welcome.

SCENIC DRIVES **Route 2 west from St. Johnsbury to Danville**. As the road climbs steadily, the White Mountains rise like a white wall in the distance. This actually works better if you are driving east from Danville. Either way, be sure to pull off (there's an eastbound pullout) to appreciate the panorama.

Danville Hill Road. Continue west on Rt. 2 from West Danville to East Cabot; after Molly's Pond, take the right-hand turn—Danville Hill Rd., marked for Cabot. This is a high road with long mountain views; note the Cabot Creamery Visitor Center in Cabot.

Burke Mountain. A 2.5-mile auto road leads to the summit of Burke Mountain (3,267 feet). From the parking lot it's just a few steps through the trees to one of the most sweeping views of the White Mountains and points east. From the top of the lifts (on the other side of the parking lot), another superlative view encompasses Lake Willoughby and the Green Mountains to the west. Bring a picnic. This preserve was formerly the 10,000-acre Darling State Forest, donated to the state in 1933. The road was constructed by the Civilian Conservation Corps. The toll road ($5) and campground are open May 25–Oct. 15.

Darling Hill Road from Rt. 114 in East Burke, 5 miles south to Rt. 114 in Lyndonville, follows a ridge past a magnificent former estate that once encompassed many old homesteads and still offers great views. The bright yellow 38-room mansion, on a private drive, has been beautifully restored.

Greensboro Village to East Hardwick. The road passes through Hardwick Street (that's the name of the hamlet) and a fine collection of Federal and Greek Revival houses; from Greensboro Village to Hardwick it makes a beeline through high and open farm country; and from Craftsbury Common north to Rt. 14 through Albany and Irasburg, it follows the rich farmland of the Black River Valley.

Danville to Peacham via Greenbanks Hollow. At the Danville green two divergent roads head south for Peacham. Follow the road posted for Dowser's Hall, rather than Peacham Road. This runs right through the covered bridge in Greenbanks Hollow, recently neatened up with picnic benches and a historic plaque describing this "forgotten village." In 1849 Benjamin Greenbank converted an existing mill into a five-story wooden textile factory, the centerpiece of a village that was completely destroyed by fire in 1885. Only the stone foundations of the mill, the rushing stream, and the bridge survive.

BIKING

Kingdom Trails Association (802-626-0737; kingdomtrails.org). The East Burke area is webbed by roughly 100 miles of trails, a composite of systems on Darling Hill, around the village, and on Burke Mountain itself, as well as the Burke cross-country trails. It's maintained by a nonprofit conservation organization that receives permission from 45 landowners. Trails thread pastures and woods and vary from narrow singletracks and double-diamond downhill trails on Burke Mountain itself to wide old logging and fire roads. Most offer glorious views. Rave reviews have positioned the network as a strong magnet for bicycle clubs from throughout the East, with roughly half its patrons now coming from Quebec. The association's office in the middle of the village is decorated with artworks fashioned from recycled bicycle parts and gear and offers changing rooms. Pick up a map and a pass (day passes are $10 adults, $5 ages 8–15; season passes are $40 per individual and $100 per family). Tickets are also available, along with bike rentals, across the road at **East Burke Sports** (802-626-3215; east burkesports.com). Owner John Worth is credited with kick-starting the formation of Kingdom Trails, which was incorporated in 1994. Check the Web site for trail updates and conditions, also for local lodging, including rentals and camping.

Craftsbury Outdoor Center (802-586-7767; craftsbury.com), Craftsbury Common, rents 21-speed fat-tire bikes and offers instruction and guide service on 200 miles of dirt roads through glorious farm country, also on 10 km of singletrack snowshoeing trails on its own 320 acres. Also see *Lodging.*

Village Sports Shop (802-626-8448), 511 Broad St. (Rt. 5) in Lyndonville also rents mountain bikes.

Biking the Kingdom, a map/guide to 15 road biking tours, is available from the Northeast Kingdom Travel & Tourism Association (802-626-8511; traveltheking dom.com), with an office in East Burke.

MOUNTAIN BIKING AT KINGDOM TRAILS, EAST BURKE

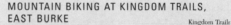

Kingdom Trails

Lyndon to Greensboro Bend. An old ridge road with splendid views, 17-mile **Stannard Mountain Road** is unpaved but usually well graveled most of the way, best traveled in summer and fall. Check locally, though, because there are occasional washouts. The views are best driving west.

✳ To Do

FISHING Fishing is huge here. The Kingdom is pocked with glacial lakes and laced with streams. For regulations, check under Fish & Game at nekchamber .com. Check out **Harvey's Lake** in West Barnet, the **Moore Reservoir**, **Shadow Lake**, and **Miles Pond** in Concord, **Ricker** and **Levi Ponds** in Groton State Forest, **Lake Eligo** and **Caspian Lake** in Greensboro, and **Little** and **Great Hosmer Ponds** in Craftsbury, as well as the **Lamoille**, **Passumpsic**, **Moose**, and **Connecticut Rivers**. Local lakes are also good for salmon, lake and rainbow trout, and perch. There are trout in the streams, too. A handicapped-accessible fishing platform has been constructed in **Passumpsic Village** on the Passumpsic River. The **Lamoille River** in Hardwick is good for trout and perch.

At **Seyon Ranch** in Groton State Park (see *Lodging*) there is squaretail trout fishing, with flies only, from boats rented at the site. George Willy at the **Village Inn in East Burke** (again, see *Lodging*) offers guiding and driftboats. Under *Campgrounds* see **Harvey's Lake Cabins and Campground**; also see **Quimby Country** and **Seymour Lake Lodge**, and *Fishing* in "The Lake Country."

FITNESS CENTER **The Club at Old Mill** (802-748-5313), Perkins St., St. Johnsbury. Indoor tennis, racquetball, aerobics, Nautilus, free weights, sauna, Jacuzzi. day passes.

GOLF **St. Johnsbury Country Club** (802-748-9894; 800-748-8899), off Rt. 5 north, open daily mid-May–Oct. This is an outstanding PGA-rated, 18-hole course, truly one of the Kingdom's gems. The original nine holes were designed in 1923; nine more were added by Geoffrey Cornish. Amenities include cart rentals and **Greenside Restaurant**, all renovated in 2005.

Mountain View Country Club (802-533-9294), Greensboro, nine holes. Established 1898; open to nonmembers midweek only. Use of carts permitted only for health reasons.

Kirby Country Club (802-748-9200), 5 miles east of St. Johnsbury on Rt. 2 in Kirby. Open daily Apr.–Nov. Marc Poulin's evolving, challenging nine-hole course and clubhouse offer great views. Reasonably priced.

HIKING AND WALKING TRAILS See *Green Space*, also Craftsbury Outdoor Center and Kingdom Trails Association under *Biking*. Request a copy of *Hiking in the Northeast Kingdom* (800-884-8001; travelthekingdom.com).

HORSEBACK RIDING **D-N-D Stables** (802-626-8237) in East Burke. Debby Newland guides riders 12 and older (unless they are experienced) of all abilities on trails that extend from her farm to local snowmobile and cross-country trails, as well as the Kingdom Trails system. Younger children are welcome to ride in the ring. Rides are tailored to the rider (maximum of four) and can be as long as desired.

PADDLING East of St. Johnsbury, the **Moore** and **Comerford reservoirs**, created by dams, are good for canoeing (there are two boat launches in Lower Waterford)—as we found out one evening, listening to birdcalls and watching a baby beaver swim steadily toward a beaver lodge beneath the pines. Below the Comerford Dam, the stretch of the **Connecticut River** south to McIndoe Falls (now the McIndoe Dam) is excellent, and the portage around the dam isn't difficult. Other rivers that invite canoeing are the **Passumpsic** and **Moose**, which join the Sleeper at St. Johnsbury. A boat launch on the Moose River can be accessed from Concord Avenue in St. J, and look for a boat launch on the Passumpsic in Passumpsic Village, 5 miles south of St. Johnsbury. Canoe and kayak rentals are available from **East Burke Sports** (802-626-3215; eastburkesports.com) in East Burke and from **Village Sport Shop** (802-626-8448), 511 Broad St., Lyndonville. **Craftsbury Outdoor Center** (see *Sculling*) rents canoes and kayaks for use on Great Hosmer Pond. **Highland Lodge** has canoes and kayaks for guest use on Caspian Lake. Boat rentals are available from **Injun Joe Court** (802-684-3430; injunjoecourt .net), Rt. 2, West Danville, and **Harvey's Lake Campground** (802-633-2213), West Barnet. This area is pocked with lakes, and launches are shown on the state map. Also see *Campgrounds*.

Request a free copy of the map/guide *Waterways of the Northeast Kingdom* (800-884-8001; travelthekingdom.com).

RUNNING **Craftsbury Outdoor Center** (802-586-7767; craftsbury.com), Craftsbury Common, offers five-, six-, and seven-day camps late June–July; different sessions focus on training for triathlons, marathons, road racing, Masters running, and just plain fun and fitness. Camps are open to all ages and abilities; the reasonably priced all-inclusive price covers coaching, lodging, and three daily meals.

SCULLING **Craftsbury Outdoor Center** (802 586 7767, craftsbury.com), Craftsbury Common, has offered nationally acclaimed summer sculling programs for 30 years. Weekend, four-day, and weeklong sessions run late May–mid-Sept.

SCULLING AT CRAFTSBURY OUTDOOR CENTER

Amy Wilton, Laughing Dog Photography

Open to all ages and skill levels. Sessions include tailored coaching, video analysis, demo equipment, and access to the swim beach, massage, nature trails, and mountain biking with lodging and three daily meals.

SWIMMING There are public beaches on **Harvey's Lake** in West Barnet; **Caspian Lake** in Greensboro Village; **Joe's Pond** in West Danville; **Molly's Pond** in Marshfield; **Shadow Lake Beach** (in Glover marked from Rt. 16); **Miles Pond** in Concord; and within **Groton State Forest**, notably at **Boulder Beach State Park** (802-584-3823; vtstateparks.com). If you can find it, also check out **Tickle-naked Pond** in Ryegate (off Rt. 302 west of Wells River). There are public pools in St. Johnsbury and in Lyndonville.

TREE CLIMBING **New England Tree Climbing** (802-684-9795; newengland treeclimbing.com), Danville. No joke. This is a serious skill, pitched to climbers ages 7–70. Inquire about the three-hour, basic "Tree Climbing Experience" ($50 adult, $25 for children under 12) and more extensive and expensive courses.

✳ Winter Sports

CROSS-COUNTRY SKIING AND SNOWSHOEING Two of New England's outstanding cross-country trail systems are found in this area. Unfortunately, you have to settle on one or the other—given the way the roads run, they're an hour's drive apart.

In the Craftsbury area
Craftsbury Outdoor Center Nordic Ski Center (802-586-7767; craftsbury .com), Craftsbury Common, grooms 85 km of its 130 km marked and maintained trail system; it offers rentals, instruction, and lodging packages. The system connects with **Highland Lodge** (see *Lodging*) in Greensboro, which offers a total of 60 km of trails, 15 of them well groomed. The only major New England cross-country system that's nowhere near an alpine ski hill, the Craftsbury Outdoor Center/Highland Lodge trails web the kind of red-barn-spotted farmscape that's equated with, but increasingly rare in, Vermont. They traverse rolling fields, woods, and maple and evergreen groves, with stunning views of the distant Green Mountains. Thanks to their elevation and Craftsbury's exceptional grooming, they also represent some of the most dependable cross-country skiing in the Northeast and usually remain skiable well into March and sugaring season. Home to the late-January Bankworth Craftsbury Ski Marathon, one of Vermont's standout winter events. Daily trail passes available.

In East Burke
Kingdom Trails Cross-Country Ski Area (802-535-5662; kingdomtrails.org). Two separate trail networks are maintained by the nonprofit Kingdom Trails Association (see *Biking*). A 20-km system with spectacular views on Darling Hill is best accessed from the Vermont Children's Theater on Darling Hill Rd., while a 30-km network begins at the touring center on Dashne Rd., marked from Rt. 114 just beyond the entrance to Burke Mountain (see *Downhill Skiing*). A $10 trail fee accesses both of these groomed systems and many more miles of backcountry. Rentals, lessons, and guided tours originate in both warming huts.

♿ **Seyon Ranch State Park** (802-584-3829; vtstateparks.com). This isolated

1890s hunting/fishing lodge deep in Groton State Forest has been winterized and caters to cross-country skiers with 5 miles of groomed trails.

DOGSLED TOURS **Hardscrabble Dogsled Tours** (802-626-9895), based in Sheffield, offers tours ranging in length from one to six hours, also guided snowshoeing.

DOWNHILL SKIING AND SNOWBOARDING **Burke Mountain** (888-BURKEVT; skiburke.com), East Burke. "The Vermonter's Mountain" is a big peak with a respectable vertical, known for excellent terrain and reasonable prices. After many ups and downs, it is currently owned by the Florida-based Ginn Company, which has made some substantive improvements in snowmaking (abetting a 232 inch annual snowfall), revamped the base lodge, and added a detachable high-speed quad lift to service the lower mountain. Plans call for the creation of a new, intermediate trail system with slope-side condos, homes, an 18-hole golf course, and more. This is the home of Burke Mountain Academy, a prep school for aspiring racers, known for the number of graduates who become Olympic contenders.

Lifts: 2 quad chairlifts (1 detachable), 2 surface lifts.

Trails and slopes: 45 trails, 10 glades (240 acres).

Elevation: 3,267 feet.

Vertical drop: 2,011 feet.

Snowmaking: 80 percent.

Snowboarding: 4 terrain parks, season-long freestyle program.

Facilities: Sherburne Base Lodge includes glass-walled Tamarack Grill as well as a cafeteria; a midslope lodge with its Bear Den Lounge serves the upper mountain. Trailside lodging is offered in dozens of privately owned condos (Burke Vacation

THE VIEW TOWARD THE WHITE MOUNTAINS FROM BURKE

Burke Mountain

Rentals: 802-626-1161; Burke Mountain Rentals: 888-282-2188, Burke Slopeside Lodging (burkeslopesidelodging.com; 802-626-3066). Also check with the Burke Area Chamber of Commerce (burkevermont.com), the best way to compare local lifts and lodging packages, including local motels and B&Bs.

Programs: Kids' programs during weekends and holiday periods; ski school, rentals.

Rates: Nonholidays $58 adults, $42 seniors and students; holidays $60 adults, $43 seniors and juniors, less for Vermonters, for multidays, and with lodging packages. *Note:* Students of all ages pay the same price, just as long as they're dependent.

SLEIGH RIDES **Wildflower Inn** (see *Lodging*) arranges sleigh rides for guests and will accommodate nonguests when possible. **Haden Tanner** (802-467-3639), a farrier in Sutton, also offers sleigh rides.

SNOWMOBILING Given the extent of the trail system, accessibility to the trail from local lodging places, and dependable snow cover, this area is becoming as well known among snowmobilers as it is to cross-country skiers. The trail systems, however, seldom cross. **The Northeast Kingdom Chamber of Commerce** (802-748-3678; 800-639-6379; nekchamber.com) publishes a map describing what's required to sled here and a list of the local clubs from which you must purchase a VAST membership in order to use the trails. Rentals are available from **All Around Power Equipment** (802-748-1413), Rt. 5 north, St. Johnsbury, which offers snowmobile storage as well as trail access. Also see *Snowmobiling* in "The Lake Country."

✳ Green Space

Barr Hill Nature Preserve, Greensboro. Turn right at the town hall and go about 0.5 mile to Barr Hill Rd. (another left). The trails at Barr Hill, managed by The Vermont Nature Conservancy, overlook Caspian Lake. Don't miss the view from the top. In winter ski and snowshoe trails are maintained by Highland Lodge.

Groton State Forest (802-584-3829; vtstateparks.com), off Rt. 232 (which runs north–south, connecting Rts. 2 and 302). This 25,600-plus-acre forest is the second largest contiguous landholding by the state of Vermont. It's a scenic and rugged place, best known for its five separate campgrounds (see *Campgrounds*) and fishing, but it also harbors Lake Groton and both Osmore and Ricker ponds. There's an extensive year-round trail system. The area was intensively logged, beginning in 1873 with the opening of the Montpelier & Wells Railroad that ran through the forest, ending in the 1920s when most of the timber had been cut. Subsequent fires further altered the landscape from evergreens to mostly maple and birch. The naturalist-staffed **Groton Nature Center** (802-584-3823) in **Boulder Beach State Park** (a day-use area featuring a swim beach on Lake Groton), marked from Rt. 232, is open June–early Sep. and serves as the information source for the forest and the trailhead for the 2.5-mile trail to Peacham Bog. Seyon Ranch State Park (see *Lodging*) is on Noyes Pond in another part of the forest, catering to groups, fishermen, and cross-country skiers. Favorite hikes in the **Groton State Forest Trail System** include the **Peacham Bog Natural Area** and two trails to the summit of **Owls Head Mountain** (there's a summer road as well as a trail), where a handsome old CCC wood-and-stone watchtower commands spectacular views.

Hardwick Trails, Hazen Union School, Hardwick. Six miles of nonmotorized nature and recreational trails wind through the woods behind the high school in the middle of the village.

Victory Basin, alias Victory Bog. This 4,970-acre preserve administered by the Vermont Fish and Wildlife Department includes a 25-acre boreal bog with rare plant life, 1,800 acres of wetlands, 1,084 acres of hardwoods, and 71 acres of clearings and old fields. The dirt road access is via Victory; there are three parking areas: Mitchell's Landing, Lee Hill, and Damons Crossing.

Waterford Dam at Moore Reservoir. New England Power offers guided tours of the huge complex of turbines. There are also picnic sites and a boat launch here. The approach is from the New Hampshire side of the Connecticut River, just below Lower Waterford, Vermont, off Rt. 135.

In St. Johnsbury
Fred Mold Park, near the confluence of the Passumpsic and Moose rivers, is a great picnic spot by a waterfall and old mill. **The Arlington Preserve**, accessible from Waterman Circle, is a 33-acre nature preserve with woods, meadows, and rock outcroppings.

See also *Biking, Hiking and Walking Trails,* and *Camping.*

✳ Lodging

In the St. Johnsbury area
⚭ "♈" **Rabbit Hill Inn** (802-748-5168; 800-76-BUNNY; rabbithillinn.com), Rt. 18, Lower Waterford 05848. Brian and Leslie Mulcahy welcome you to this pillared landmark, an inn since 1795. All 19 rooms and suites are romantic confections, with canopy beds, antiques, and "indulging" bathrooms. Many have a working fireplace, Jacuzzi for two, and private porch. All have been painstakingly furnished, complete with a "room diary." Children should be at least 14 years old. Summer swimming and fishing in a freshwater pond, canoeing, and golf privileges; winter cross-country skiing and snowshoeing. $195–355 per couple, higher in foliage season, includes breakfast, afternoon tea, a five-course candlelit dinner, and gratuities.

🌸 🐾 "♈" **Emergo Farm B&B** (802-684-2215; 888-383-1185), 261 Webster Hill, Danville 05828. Just north of the village, this strikingly handsome, prizewinning working dairy farm has been in the same family for six genera-

tions. Our stay in the upstairs front room, tastefully furnished with family antiques, and with private bath and view of the White Mountains, was one of the most pleasant of the summer. There is also a two-bedroom apartment with full kitchen and sitting room. Older children only, please. The farm's 230 acres include a hilltop with panoramic views of much of the Kingdom. Historical and present-day farm tours are offered, and livestock includes Nigerian dwarf goats as well as 140 head of cattle (90 milking cows). Lori Webster also manages nearby Good Fellas Tavern & Restaurant (see *Eating Out*). $80 per room single occupancy, $90 double includes an outstanding full breakfast, served downstairs in the dining room. The apartment is $150 per night.

"♈" **Estabrook House B&B** (802-751-8261; estabrookhouse.com), 1596 Main St., St. Johnsbury 05891. Maurine Hennings has painstakingly restored this handsome, vintage-1856 painted lady on the quiet, residential end of

EMERGO FARM IN DANVILLE

Main Street and within walking distance on the Fairbanks Museum and Atheneum. The house is spacious, comfortable, and uncluttered. Four antiques-furnished guest rooms share a bath. Guests are limited to six. In her former life Maurine was constantly on the road for her company, so she's especially sensitive to the needs of solo travelers. $90 for the smallish twin-bedded "Nook," $105 for the remaining rooms, full breakfast included.

🐾 ✿ **Broadview Farm B&B** (802-748-9902), 2627 McDowell Rd., North Danville 05828. Open Memorial

BROADVIEW B&B, NORTH DANVILLE

Day–Oct. This shingle-style country mansion has been in Molly Newell's family since 1901. It's 4 miles off Route 2, set on 300 acres with a panoramic view of mountains, on a farm road in North Danville. In the late 19th century, before its shingles and gables, this old farmhouse took in summer boarders, advertising its 2,000-foot elevation as a sure escape from malaria and hay fever. Molly has thoroughly renovated the old place, removing 4,000 pounds of radiators, replacing windows, and gutting and redesigning the kitchen while preserving the fine woodwork, detailing, and maple floors throughout the house. The three guest rooms are furnished with family antiques (check out the great oak set in the Yellow Room) and include a big room under the eaves, good for a family of four. Baths are private or shared; $100–120 double includes a full breakfast. Dogs $5 per night.

The Old Homestead (802-633-4016; 877-OLD-HOME; theoldhomestead .com), 157305 Rt. 5, Barnet 05821. Gail Warnaar plays the oboe and bassoon, sells music for double-reed instruments, and offers five rooms in her 1850s village home, which faces Rt. 5 and backs on gardens and meadow. Two second-floor rooms (private baths) feature porches overlooking the grounds, while a small first-floor single room with a spool bed (shared bath) is appealing. Common space is comfortable, and musical groups will find rehearsal space. $79–150 includes a breakfast of fruit and fresh-baked bread; reduced rates for weekdays and longer stays.

In the Burke Mountain Area
∞ 🐾 ♿ **The Inn at Mountain View Farm** (802-626-9924; innmtnview .com), 3383 Darling Hill Rd., East Burke 05832. Like the Wildflower Inn,

this is part of a onetime 9,000-acre hilltop estate owned by Elmer Darling, a Burke native who built the brick creamery in 1890 to supply dairy products to his Fifth Avenue Hotel (it used to churn out 600 pounds of butter a month and 70 pounds of cheese per day). The inn also includes the neighboring "Farm House" and the magnificent red barns and other outbuildings. Its 440 acres spread across a high ridge and are laced with paths, part of the Kingdom Trails network (see *Biking*) maintained for walking, mountain biking, and cross-country skiing. Marilyn Pastore has tastefully decorated the 14 guest rooms (private baths), which are divided between the Creamery and the Farm House with its three "luxury suites," each with gas fireplace and Jacuzzi. A sauna is accessible to all guests. The centrally air-conditioned Creamery houses the inn's sitting room and a dining room serving breakfast and dinner to guests. The inn is a favorite for weddings and reunions, given its renovated Morgan barn. $175–285 includes a full breakfast and tea. Inquire about special packages.

🦞 🐾 ✐ ¹⁷¹ᵘ **The Village Inn of East Burke** (802-626-3161; 802-793-4517; villageinnofeastburke.com), Box 186, East Burke 05832. This comfortable, affordable B&B offers genuine hospitality and many rarely found amenities, like a fully equipped guest kitchen; an inviting living room with a fireplace, books, games, and satellite TV; a weather-proofed Jacuzzi near the extensive gardens (guests are invited to pick what's in-season) and a streamside picnic/lounging area. All five rooms have private bath and are comfortably, tastefully decorated, each different and varying in size—one with a sleeping loft and large enough to accommodate families—but all are the same price. Innkeeper George Willy is also a fishing guide who offers driftboat tours,

while Lorraine Willy raises bees and maintains a large organic garden. Both are plugged in to the many ways of the area. $90 per couple, $25 per extra person includes a full breakfast. Inquire about reasonably priced packages for fishing, skiing, and biking, as well as about the apartment accommodating up to 12 people.

🦞 **Branch Brook Bed & Breakfast** (802-626-8316; 800-572-7712;), P.O. Box 217, Lyndon 05849. Ann Tolman's 1850 house is only minutes but seems many miles from the I-91 exit. It has long, graceful parlor windows and a front room with a pencil-post canopy bed, locally crafted from cherrywood and worthy of brides. Other inviting rooms are tucked under exposed beams along an el, furnished with antiques. All but two of the five have private bath. Prices are $85–110 per couple with a hearty breakfast prepared on Ann's English Aga cooker. Two of Lyndon's five covered bridges are within walking distance.

Moonlight Inn Vermont (802-626-0780), P.O. Box 1325, 801 Center St., Lyndonville 05851. Shirley Banks welcomes visitors with genuine western friendliness, while Dick Banks is the quiet, capable Vermonter. Their spacious Victorian house on a quiet side street offers comfortable common space and three second-floor guest rooms, one with twins, all with private bath. A serious quilter, Shirley offers lessons and quilting weekends. $105 includes a full breakfast.

In the Craftsbury area

∞ ✿ ¹⁷¹ᵘ **Inn on the Common** (802-586-9619; 800-521-2233; innonthe common.com), Craftsbury Common 05827. Jim and Judi Lamberti are the innkeepers at this elegant country inn, with 15 rooms divided among three Federal-style buildings, two facing each other and the third a short walk

✎ ᵔ "T" **The Wildflower Inn** (802-626-8310; 800-627-8310; wildflowerinn.com), 2059 Darling Hill Rd., Lyndonville 05851. One of Vermont's best family-geared resorts clusters around a 19th-century farmhouse set high on a ridge with a spectacular view across surrounding hills and valleys. It's surrounded by its own 530 acres, with extensive flower gardens and trails maintained for hiking, mountain biking, and cross-country skiing. Jim and Mary O'Reilly have eight children (five boys, three girls), and have fitted rooms and condo-style suites with child-geared amenities, such as small rockers and diaper-changing tables, but no TVs. The idea is to get children out of their rooms and let them find one another in

THE VIEW FROM WILDFLOWER INN, LYNDONVILLE

Christina Tree

away. Five rooms have a woodstove or wood-burning fireplace, and one has a Jacuzzi. The main inn also houses an attractive library and dining room (see *Dining Out*). In summer there's a solar-heated pool, perennial gardens, lawn croquet, and a tennis court. Nearby Craftsbury Outdoor Center is a destination for mountain biking, running, and sculling, and offers some of New England's best cross-country skiing. $195–375 per couple (low season $145–255) includes dinner and full breakfast. Pets are $25 by prior reservation. Children over age 9.

Whetstone Brook Bed & Breakfast (802-586-6916), 1037 South Craftsbury Rd., Craftsbury 05826-4220. An 1826 Vermont classic Cape that, with addi-

tions, has been home to six generations of the Wilson family is now Audrey and Bryce Wilson's retirement project, a pleasant B&B. There's a piano in the living room and an Aga stove in the kitchen; the small round tables in the dining room are positioned to view the meadow through the French doors. An upstairs room with a double and single has a private bath, while two more rooms share; the ground-floor Apple Blossom Room has a queen bed and private bath. $99–125, $10 per extra person, includes a full breakfast.

🐾 **The Kimball House** (802-472-6228; kimballhouse.com), 173 Glenside Ave., Hardwick 05843. Sue and Todd Holmes have lived in this big, handsome 1890s painted lady since

the playroom, the outdoor play structures, the petting barn, the pool (there's one for toddlers), or the Playbarn—hub of supervised morning art, crafts, and summer nature programs for ages 3–11. For older children a sports complex offers basketball, a batting cage, tennis court, playing field, and (also a big appeal for parents) the beckoning system of the Kingdom Trails (see *Biking*). For cross-country skiers, Burke Mountain's trails are minutes away. Adult spaces include a sauna and outdoor hot tub, an attractive parlor and library— stocked with games and the kind of books you really want to read. The land- scaped pool commands a spectacular view of rolling hills, and there are also lawn games and walking trails. Dinner is in Juniper's (see *Dining Out*), but for children there's the option of parent-free dining at Daisy's Diner, a 5:30–9:30 din- ner and activity program (summer only). Breakfast is a three-course produc- tion, and afternoon snacks are also served. Rates: Upstairs in the main house, two family suites have great views. A total of 24 units (10 rooms and 14 suites), some with and some without views, include a romantic hideaway with whirlpool bath in the old schoolhouse (with view). Grand Meadow ($290–475) is a two-bedroom retreat sleeping eight with two baths (a Jacuzzi in one), full kitchen, dining and lounging area, and view. $125–225 for rooms, $145–250 for one-room suites, $195–330 for two-room suites, $240–430 for three-room suites. Rates are per couple B&B plus $32 per child over age 3; $10 for ages 3 and under. Singles pay $32 less. Inquire about special packages.

1979 but have only recently (with their four children grown) converted it to a B&B. All three guest rooms are upstairs (one has twin iron beds) and share two full baths, one upstairs and one down. There's plenty of common space, plus a big wraparound porch and backyard. $89–99 per couple includes a full breakfast.

Elsewhere
Guildhall Country Inn & Restau- rant (802-676-3720), 7042 Rt. 102, Guildhall 05905. Open May–Oct. Set on the Connecticut River in one of the most isolated and beautiful villages in the North Country, this comfortable inn offers four rooms with shared bath. $75 with a full breakfast. The nearest town (7 miles) is actually Lancaster,

New Hampshire. Eleanor and Steve Degnan also operate an Italian restau- rant here; see *Eating Out*.

MOTOR LODGES ☀ ✿ **Fairbanks Inn** (802-748-5666; stjay.com), 401 Western Ave. (Rt. 2 east), St. Johns- bury 05819. This three-story, 45-unit, surprisingly luxurious motel on the outskirts of town has central air-condi- tioning, cable, dataports, outdoor heat- ed pool, and fitness center privileges.

✿ "¶" **Comfort Inn & Suites** (802- 748-1500; vtcomfortinnsuites.com), off I-91, Exit 20, Rt. 5 south. A 107-unit high-rise motel with an indoor heated pool, a fitness center, a video arcade, cable, dataports, direct VAST trail access.

✒ "𝗜" **Highland Lodge** (802-533-2647; highlandlodge.com), Greensboro 05841. Open Memorial Day weekend–mid-Oct. and Christmas week–mid-March. This rambling Victorian-era inn, set in 120 acres high above Caspian Lake, manages to be both airy in warm weather and cozy in winter. It's a vanishing breed: a genuine country inn, effortlessly hospitable to all who walk in. It's now managed by the third and fourth generation of Smiths (David and Wilhelmina, Alex and Yukiyo), hosts whose warmth is reflected in the atmosphere. Common space include a library with desks and armchairs, a game room, a living room with fireplace, and a sitting room with baby grand piano and a long, rocker-lined front porch. Upstairs are 11 crisp and comfortable guest rooms, all with private bath. There are also 11 cottages (4 remain open in winter). In summer, facilities include tennis courts and a pleasant beach with bathhouse and canoes, kayaks and sailboats, along with the nature trails on the property and in the adjacent Barr Hill Nature Preserve; in winter the draw is cross-country skiing on the extensive trail network radiating from the inn's touring center, rising to unusual elevations with superb views. Inside, there is an unusual amount of relaxing space. Outside, rockers line the expansive porch. For children, there's an organized summer program (ages 4–9) in the Play Barn with an outstanding art program; resulting artwork is nailed to nearby pine trees, a truly astonishing "Forest of Art." $265–340 per couple, $40–100 per child depending on age, includes dinner as well as breakfast; inquire about family rates. Less in May and weekdays in June, Sept., Oct., Jan., and Mar. Also see *Dining Out*.

✒ "𝗜" **Colonnade Inn** (802-626-9316; 877-435-5688), 28 Back Center Rd., Lyndonville 05851. A two-story, 40-unit motel just off I-91, Exit 23. Standard motel rooms, cable TV and phone, continental breakfast.

🐾 ✒ "𝗜" **Lynburke Lodge & Motel** (802-626-3346; lynburkemotel.com), 791 Main St., Lyndonville 05851; junction of Rts. 5 and 114. A family-run motel with an outdoor swimming pool, 6 miles from Burke Mountain, 0.5 mile from access to Kingdom Trails for bicycling and cross-county skiing. Standard rooms to family suites, $79 weekends in season, less off-season and midweek. The **Valley View Restaurant** across the road serves all three meals.

RENEWAL CENTERS FOR BODY AND SPIRIT Karmê Chöling Shambhala Meditation Center (802-633-2384; karmecholing.org), 369 Patneaude Lane, Barnet 05821. Receptionist: 9–5 weekdays, 1:30–5 weekends. The oldest (founded in 1970) and probably still the best of New England's Buddhist meditation centers, Karmê Chöling follows the Tibetan Buddhist path of understanding one's own mind through meditation. What began as a small center in an old farmhouse now includes 540 wooded, path-webbed acres, six meditation halls, a practice pavilion, an *azuchi* (Zen archery range), a large organic garden, private guest rooms, and dining facilities. The centerpiece remains the original, now expanded farmhouse with its beautiful Main Shrine Room. Casual visitors are welcome (call beforehand), but this is all about one to seven day retreats (many are geared to weekends) on a variety of themes but with the practice of "mindfulness meditation" at their heart. The daily routine begins with a 6:30 wakeup call and continues until 10:30 lights-out. Space to sleep in the Main Shrine Room is included in the cost of a program.

ℙ Stepping Stone Spa and Wellness Center (802-6263104; steppingstonespa.com), 1545 Darling Hill Rd., Lyndonville 05851. Sited in 570 acres along a high ridge with panoramic views and access to the Kingdom Trails system, this four-room inn was designed and built from scratch as a spa inn by Joan and Richard (Dick) Downing. Check the Web site for descriptions of the professional spa staff and spa menu. The inn is also a short walk to a ridgetop, medieval-style Catholic chapel with superlative views,

also built by the Downings. $125–250 per couple includes breakfast; dinner, featuring organic food and wine, is also offered to guests on weekends, year-round. June–Oct. lunch and dinner are available to outside guests by reservation. Inquire about bike, ski, and spa packages. This is also a day spa with massages and a menu of other spa options available to the public.

OTHER LODGING ♿ ℙ Seyon Ranch State Park (802-584-3829; vtstateparks.com). This isolated 1890s hunting/fishing lodge on Noyes Pond, deep in Groton State Forest, is staffed and open year-round, catering to fishermen and cross-country skiers, snowshoers, and snowmobilers in-season, offering retreats and courting groups in between. There's a living room with fireplace, a dining room, and a meeting space. Six rooms have double and queen beds, and there are bunk rooms with shared baths, accommodating a total of 16, and serving up to 50 for meals. Inquire about special programs like quilting and cooking. Managers

⊗ ♣ 🐾 **Craftsbury Outdoor Center** (802-586-7767; 800-729-7751; craftsbury.com), 535 Lost Nation Rd., Craftsbury Common 05827. Recreational programs are the big attractions here, with accommodations for 90 guests divided between two rustic lodges: 35 rooms sharing lavatory-style hall bathrooms, 7 with private bath, 2 efficiency apartments, and 4 housekeeping cottages sleeping four to eight. Three meals are served, buffet-style, in the dining hall. Guests come for the programs offered: running, sculling, walking, mountain biking, and cross-country skiing, along with winter Elderhostel programs; or they stay and enjoy the outdoors at their own pace. Facilities include swimming at Lake Hosmer, exercise rooms, sauna, tennis courts, 320 acres, and in winter, simply the best network of cross-country ski trails in the East. $86–175 per person/$140–273 per couple, including three plentiful meals with vegetarian options; family and multiday rates are available. Pets are allowed in two lakeside cottages ($50 cleaning fee). (See also *Biking, Sculling, Running*, and *Cross-Country Skiing*.)

Jessie Mae and Adam offer three meals daily. $69 per room, meals extra.

CAMPGROUNDS Groton State Forest (802-584-3829; vtstateparks .com) in Marshfield and Groton. This 25,623-acre preserve offers five separate campgrounds, each an individual state park, all accessed from Rt. 232. **New Discovery Campground** (802-584-3042) has a total of 47 campsites, 14 of them lean-tos; beach privileges and hiking trails; primitive camping. **Stillwater Campground** (802-584-3822), on the west side of Lake Groton, has a total of 63 tent sites, 16 lean-tos; campers' beach and boat launch; rental boats, dump station. **Ricker Pond Campground** (802-584-3821) has a total of 33 campsites, 22 of them lean-tos, on the south side of Ricker Pond; campers' beach, rental boats, nature trail, dump station. **Big Deer State Park** (802-584-3822) has 28 tent/trailer sites (no hookups) near Boulder Beach and Groton Nature Center with many miles of trails. **Kettle Pond** (802-426-3042), on the south side of the pond, has walk-in fishing, group camping, hiking, and snowmobiling. For an overview of Groton State Forest, see *Green Space*.

Burke Mountain Campground (888-287-5388; 802-626-7300), a small campground on Burke Mountain with five lean-tos and room for 19 tents, is geared to hikers and bikers

🐾 🎿 ✍ **Harvey's Lake Cabins and Campground** (802-633-2213; harveys lakecabins.com), 190 Camper's Lane, West Barnet 05821. Open mid-May–mid-Oct. Vermont's oldest private campground, owned by Marybeth Vereline's family since the 1950s: 10 lakefront, furnished (antique funk decor) cabins with kitchen, bath, living area, loft bedrooms ($400–895 per week, $60–135 daily), and 53 wooded

secluded sites for RVs, pop-ups, and tents on 35 acres. Swimming and fishing; also kayak and canoe rentals, camp store, a rec room with pool table and video games, and a children's play area.

Note: Reasonably priced rentals abound in this area; check listings on the Web sites listed under *Guidance* and Google "vacation rentals" + "Vermont."

✳ Where to Eat

DINING OUT

In the St. Johnsbury area

Elements (802-748-8400; elements food.com), 98 Mill St. (off Railroad St.), St. Johnsbury. Open for dinner Tue.–Sat. 5–9. A former water-powered woodworking mill with all its wheels and belts still intact makes a great space for this hip new hideaway just off the main drag. A long bar backed by blocks of glass divides the space into two distinct dining areas (we prefer the bar side); in summer a deck overhangs the Passumpsic River. Chef Ryan O'Malley and sous-chef Jeff Wilson combine local ingredients wherever possible in novel and delicious ways. The menu changes a bit every week but always includes the house pâté, Vermont cheese plate, smoked trout, steak *frite*, and apple cake; there are plenty of vegetarian selections. Check the Web site for the weekly chef's menu and a page of more focused plates—flatbreads, dinner salads, and light entrées—at lower prices. Entrées $15–23. The list of wines by the glass, as well as by the bottle, is extensive.

Rabbit Hill Inn (802-748-5168; rabbithillinn.com), Rt. 18 in Lower Waterford. Open to outside guests by reservation, space permitting. The elegant dining room holds just 15 tables, and both food and atmosphere are carefully orchestrated. There's candlelight, and music many nights, to complement three-course dinners with a $45 prix fixe. The choice of five entrées in autumn included seared farm-raised venison and a risotto-filled little pumpkin. Half a dozen desserts included a chocolate soufflé, homemade ice creams, and a sampler of local cheeses. Add 18 percent service.

Creamery Restaurant (802-684-3616), Danville. Open Tue.–Sat. for dinner only. A former creamery with a blackboard menu featuring homemade soups, curries, and pad Thais, along with salads, pies, and a choice of meat and seafood dishes. Breads and soups are homemade, and salad comes with all dinners. Marion Beattie has been owner-manager for 30 years. Entrées $14–20; there's a less expensive pub menu.

In the Lyndonville–Burke area

🍴 ♪ **Tamarack Grill** (802-626-7390; skiburke.com), upstairs in the ski base lodge at Burke Mountain, East Burke. Open for dinner Wed.–Sun., 4–10, also for lunch Dec.–Mar. Billed as "a modern American bistro," this is attractive dining spot is lively now pretty much year-round. The sports pub side features a vintage double chair and more than a dozen beers on draft, while the glass-walled restaurant overlooks the mountain. Local greens and other ingredients are featured in a large, varied, and reasonably priced menu that includes pastas, burgers, and St. Louis ribs as well as steaks. Children's menu. Reservations advised on weekends. Inquire about live music.

♪ **River Garden Café** (802-626-3514; rivergardencafe.com), Rt. 114, East Burke Village. Open Wed.–Sun. for lunch and dinner; Sunday brunch is 11–2. Reservations advised. A popular place with an attractive decor and wide-ranging menu. Lunch is a varied choice of sandwiches, wraps, and sal-

ads. Dinner entrées might include pepper-crusted lamb loin, roast salmon served with artichoke hearts, olives, and tomatoes on couscous, or Jamaican jerk chicken with eggplant Parmesan. The wine list is a point of pride. Breads and desserts are homemade. The café atmosphere is casually elegant, with a year-round back porch and summer patio dining within earshot of the river. There's a "just for kids" menu.

♪ **Juniper's at The Wildflower Inn** (802-626-8310; wildflowerinn.com), between Lyndonville and East Burke on Darling Hill Rd. Open (except Nov. and Apr.) Mon.–Sat. 5:30–9. Reservations advised if you want a table on the sunporch, overlooking a spread of hills and valleys. You can dine on filet mignon ($25), but entrées on an extensive menu average $15 and tend toward comfort foods like "slow cooked shepherd's pie," roast all-natural pork, and Vermont-raised lemon-herb chicken. There are "Junior Juniper" plates for kids. Entrées come with warm rolls and salad. Sandwiches

RIVER GARDEN CAFÉ, EAST BURKE

Christina Tree

and burgers are also available. Much of the beef served is from all-natural belted Galloway cattle raised here on Darling Hill. Salads and sandwiches are also served. Vermont beer featured.

In the Craftsbury area
Claire's Restaurant and Bar (802-472-7053; clairesvt.com), 41 S. Main St., Hardwick. Open daily except Wed., 5–9. Check for midday weekend hours. Reservations suggested. Many Vermont restaurants claim to feature locally gown ingredients, but this spot is all about eating locally. Greens, grains, cheese, poultry, fish, veggies, fruit, and more, much of it supplied within hours from some 35 farms within a matter of miles. A menu might include several "small plates"—perhaps a tomato tart with caramelized onions and tapenade; a choice of "bowls" like whole wheat fusilli, garlic scapes, feta, and pesto cream; and half a dozen entrées, maybe Moroccan chicken with olives, lemons, kohlrabi, and couscous, or grilled trout with roasted fennel and tomato confit. It's all as good as it sounds, reflecting the skilled efforts not just of chef Steve Obranovich and local farmers but the enterprise of local residents who banded together to launch this effort plus the faith of many others who contributed by buying $1,000 coupon books, good for meals. Designed and decorated cheerfully and simply by local architects and artists, Claire's fills two narrow, adjoining storefronts in the middle of Hardwick and is priced for local budgets. Entrées $12.50–22 (for the local sirloin with local blue cheese).

Highland Lodge (802-533-2647; highlandlodge.com), Greensboro. The inn is open late May–mid-Oct. and Christmas week–mid-Mar. Nonguests are welcome for breakfast, lunch, and dinner (by reservation); in winter lunch is served Thu.–Sun. The inn's old-fashioned dining room is attractive, and in summer there's also service, weather permitting, on the long front porch, overlooking the lakes and mountains. The dinner menu, which has long featured produce from local farms, changes daily and usually includes five entrées and four courses. Choices might range from linguine with saffron cream and julienned vegetables to roulade of pork tenderloin with shiitake sauce ($12–26). Dessert might be a walnut torte with chocolate ganache. You can also choose from a lighter burger, sandwich, and salad menu. There's a respectable wine list.

Inn on the Common (802-586-9619; 800-521-2233; innonthecommon.com), Craftsbury Common. Open to the public Fri.–Sat. evenings by reservation. The inn dining room has the feel of an elegant restaurant. The à la carte menu changes seasonally and offers several choices per course. On a summer evening you might begin with a lobster bisque, then dine on wild salmon with wild rice or beef tenderloin with béarnaise sauce. Dessert might be Vermont Green Mountain cheesecake or key lime pie. Innkeeper Jim Lamberti prides himself on the wine list; selections are available with each course. Entrées $19.50–29.50, plus 15 percent gratuity.

EATING OUT

In and around St. Johnsbury
The Wine Gate (802-748-3288), Railroad Street, St. Johnsbury. Open Mon.–Fri. 11–2, Thu.–Sat. 5–closing. Housed in a former rail warehouse beside the handsome station that's now the region's major welcome center, this is an attractive space with a lunch menu featuring a wide choice of paninis and salads. There are also reasonably priced entrées and a tapas menu.

☙ **Good Fellas Tavern & Restaurant** (802-748-4249), 59 Parker Rd., just off Rt. 2, east of Danville Village. Open Wed.–Sat. 4–9, Sun. 11:30–8. Known for homemade soups, seafood, steaks, and pasta, this is a reliable country restaurant with a sports bar, a separate dining area, and a seasonal deck that's great for families.

& **Anthony's Restaurant** (802-748-3613), 321 Railroad St. Open 6:30 AM–8 PM Tue.–Sat.; closing at 4 Sun.–Mon. Anthony and Judy Proia have run this cheerful family-geared diner since 1979, remodeling it several times to make it handicapped accessible and give it a homier feel. Regulars still gather around the counter, and there are booths as well. Breakfast is big: corned beef hash, specialty omelets, and about everything else you can think of. "Specials" at all three meals. The fries (try sweet potato) and onion rings are made fresh, along with the soups; pies are a point of pride.

Dylan's Café (802-748-6748), 378 Railroad St., St. Johnsbury. Open Mon.–Sat. for breakfast and lunch, this pleasant café is positioned in the middle of St. J's shopping block, good for baked onion soup, a tomato-Brie tart, or an in-house roast turkey club with green apples, bacon, Gouda, sun-dried tomatoes, and more.

Mooselook Restaurant (802-695-2950), Rt. 2, east of Concord. Open from 6 AM daily for all three meals— except Mon., when it's just breakfast and lunch. This is a better-than-average North Country kind of place: "Most" soups are homemade, and specialties include country-fried steak and Vermont-fried chicken; all meals include soup and choice of potato and vegetable. This is also "home of the slugger," a 7-ounce burger with all the fixings. For visitors the bonus is what's on the walls: dozens of vintage photos of what this area was all about more than a century ago.

Kham Thai Cuisine (802-758424), 1112 Memorial Dr. (Rt. 5 north), St. Johnsbury. Open daily 11–9, Sun. noon–8. A great addition to local dining options, known for fresh ingredients and spices, reasonably priced, reliable.

Goldie's Gathering (802-563-3377), 3075 Main St., Cabot Village. Open Wed.–Sat. for all three meals, Sun. 9–1. Visitors headed for the Cabot Creamery should be aware of this better-than-average restaurant, turning local ingredients into down-home meals. It's next to the hardware store in the middle of the village.

Upper Valley Grill (802-584-3101), junction of Rts. 302 and 232, Groton. Open 6 AM–9 PM daily. At the junction of two lonely stretches of road, this is a welcome oasis: a general store with a friendly, U-shaped counter in back, good for homemade soups, apple pie, and daily specials.

In the Lyndonville–Burke area
Miss Lyndonville Diner (802-626-9890), Rt. 5 south, Lyndonville. Open from 6 AM until supper, famed for breakfast, including strawberry pancakes with whipped cream, also pies, homemade French toast, and jumbo eggs. This is one of the best of Vermont's surviving vintage railroad car diners.

⚘ ☙ **Lyndon Freight House** (802-626-1174), 1000 Broad St., Lyndonville. Open daily 6:30 AM–9:30 PM. Local dairy farmers Eric and Cathy Paris have salvaged and restored this middle-of-town former freight station (1868), transforming it into a combination restaurant/railroad museum, information center, and ice cream parlor. The menu features local meats, fresh greens and veggies, fresh-baked breads, and the fluffiest of omelets plus Carmen's wildly popular ice cream (64 flavors). There's more: Starbucks coffee and a crafts gallery upstairs. This is one of two buildings left from the 22 built here by the Boston & Maine. This village sprang into existence with the 1860s arrival of the railroad and remained an important rail yard for the B&M until the 20th century. Most local families have railroad ties, and memorabilia has come pouring in. Note the original freight scale in the dining room and glass tabletops showcasing some of the 3,000 freight bills and letters found stashed in the walls during the renovations. Walls are hung with early-1900s photos, and a model train circles a diorama of a 1940s Lyndonville. Frequently, too, a real freight train still comes rumbling by.

Trout River Brewery (802-616-9396; troutriverbrewing.com), Rt. 5, Lyndonville. Fri. and Sat. 5–8:30, open for hand-tossed pizzas as well as the selection of ales and other draft brews, made on the premises. The three signature beers here are Rainbow Red

FAMILY AT FREIGHT HOUSE, LYNDONVILLE
Christina Tree

(medium bodied), Scottish Ale, and Hoppin' Mad Trout; also seasonal specials. Inquire about tours and tastings.

✍ **The Pub Outback** (802-626-1188; thepuboutback.com), East Burke, out back of the Bailey's & Burke General Store. Open daily 4–9, later Fri. and Sat. This former cow barn is now a cheerful pub with a full menu, from soups to pitas, veggies, burgers, sandwiches, steaks, pastas, great onion rings, the works. Children's menu. Full bar.

Café Sweet Basil (626-9713), 60 Depot St., Lyndonville. Open for lunch Wed.–Fri. 11:30–2, for dinner Wed.–Sat. 5:30–8:30. An appealing ambience with an interesting menu. We lunched on a grilled tomato soup and quesadilla—good, but service was painfully slow. Still, we would like to give it a try for dinner.

In the Craftsbury area

✍ **The Village Restaurant** (802-472-5701), 19 Main St., Hardwick. Open daily 6 AM–10 PM, but check on Mon. Sited at the junction of Rts. 14 and 15, this landmark little diner can fill the bill. Our family was heading for Claire's (see *Dining Out*), which was closed that evening. The back room with its view of the Lamoille River was a pleasant surprise, and the food was fine.

House of Pizza (802-472-3380), Wolcott St. (Rt. 14, north of the village), Hardwick. Open daily 10–9, until 10 Fri.–Sat. This can be a crucial roadfood stop if you are heading up to Craftsbury on a snowy evening. The pizzas are good, also salads, lasagna, calzones, grinders.

Buffalo Mountain Coop and Café (802-472-8800), upstairs in the co-op, Main St., Hardwick. Open Mon.–Sat. 9–6, Sun. 10–4. Soups, coffees, light food, grilled cheese with avocado.

Elsewhere

Guildhall Country Inn & Restaurant (802-676-3720), 7042 Rt. 102, Guildhall. Open May–Oct., Fri.–Sat. 4:30–8:30. Call ahead. Set on the Connecticut River in one of the most isolated and beautiful villages in the North Country, this is the only dining option within a fairly large radius (Lancaster, New Hampshire, is 7 miles away). Eleanor and Steve Degnan, who have operated this 1850s house for many years as a B&B, now serve up lasagna, eggplant, and veal dishes, among other Italian staples, all made from scratch.

For Warners Gallery, Happy Hours Restaurant, and P&H Truck Stop in Wells River, see "Lower Cohase."

TEA **The Brick House and Perennial Pleasures Nursery** (802-472-5104), East Hardwick (posted from Rt. 16). Open Memorial Day–Labor Day, noon–4; closed Mon. English-born Judith Kane serves a traditional "Cream Tea" (cucumber sandwiches, scones, and fresh cream) and offers an assortment of teas, cold drinks, and pastries. Reservations suggested, but patrons "are welcome to pop in." Many come just for the gift shop, known for its splendid summer hats as well as jewelry, clothing, books, gardening tools, and more. The 3 acres of perennial gardens (perennialpleasures.net, open 10–5) represent more than 900 varieties of plants, featuring heirloom flowers—lemon lilies, golden glow—and medicinal plants.

✹ Entertainment

Catamount Arts (802-748-2600; 888-757-5559; catamountarts.org), 115 Eastern Ave., St. Johnsbury. The new venue for this long-established, non-profit arts center features nightly screenings in two theaters, the larger Cinema 1, screening popular films, and the smaller Cinema 2 with regional premieres, mini series, and programs devoted to Vermont filmmakers. There's an extensive video library, a biweekly jazz-on-Sunday series, and a gallery showcasing local artists; also live performances and special events.

Star Theater 802-748-9511), 18 Eastern Ave., St. Johnsbury. Cinemas 1-2-3; first-run movies.

Craftsbury Chamber Players (800-639-3443; craftsburychamberplayers .org) has brought chamber music to northern Vermont for 40 years. The series runs mid-July–mid-Aug. Check the current schedule for performances at the Hardwick Town House, the Presbyterian Church in East Craftsbury, and Fellowship Hall in Greensboro. Most performers are faculty members at the Juilliard School of Music in New York City.

Hardwick Town House (802-472-8800; nekarts.org), 127 Church St., Hardwick. Home to the Northeast Kingdom Arts Council and the Craftsbury Chamber Players, this 1860 schoolhouse also hosts a variety of programs: film, drama, music, lectures, and other live performances. The stage features a vintage hand-painted curtain.

✐ **Vermont Children's Theater** (summer only: 802-626-5358), Darling Hill Rd., Lyndonville. Sited next to the Wildflower Inn, this is a genuine theater in a former hay barn. Local youngsters (some 120 are usually involved) perform amazingly well. Performances in July are by thespians ages 7–18. Tickets: $8 adult, $4–6 for youngsters.

✐ **Circus Smirkus** (802-533-7443; 800-532-7443; smirkus.org), based at Sterling College, Craftsbury Common. June–mid-Aug, this is a a nationally recognized program cultivating acrobatic and other circus skills for children—ranging from a "smirking weekend" for 6- to 8-year-olds to advanced sessions and performances in more than a dozen towns all over New England.

The Music Box (802-586-7533; the musicboxvt.org), 147 Creek Rd., Craftsbury. Built as a piano-tuning studio and offering exceptional acoustics, this is a venue for frequent concerts and performances.

Band concerts: **St. Johnsbury Town Band concerts**, weekly all summer at the bandstand in Town Hall Park, Mon. 8 PM. **Lyndonville Town Band concerts**, every Wed. in summer at 8 PM. **Danville** concerts on the green, Sun. at 7 in July and Aug. **Craftsbury band concerts** at the band shell on the common, Sun. at 7 in July and Aug. In **Greensboro**, concerts on the dock at Caspian Lake are sponsored by the Greensboro Association, summer Sun. at 7:30.

✳ Selective Shopping

ANTIQUES SHOPS Route 5 Antiques & Collectibles (802-626-5430), Rt. 5, Lyndonville. Open daily, except Tue., 10–5. A multidealer and consignment shop.

Antiques & Emporium (802-626-3500), 182 S. Wheelock Rd., Lyndonville. Open daily 10–5, except Tue. Housed in a former grade school, a multigroup shop with everything from rugs and clocks to furniture, pottery, and prints.

BOOKSTORES Galaxy Bookshop (802-472-5533; galaxybookshop.com), 7 Mill St., Hardwick. Linda Ramsdell's full-service shop fills a vintage-1910 bank building, complete with a drive-through window for rental audiotapes (call ahead). This is a full-service book-store specializing in Vermont writers and unusual titles. Armchairs invite lingering, and the frequent authors readings and special events attract a far-flung community. Satellite **Stardust Books** (802-586-2200) in the former library on Craftsbury Common is open Sat. 10–1 (coinciding with the farmer's market) and Wed. 3–6; its café is also open for morning coffee weekdays 8–10.

Green Mountain Books & Prints (802-626-5051), 1055 Broad St., Lyndonville (Rt. 5 on the corner of the common). Open Mon.–Sat. 9–5. This book lover's haven has recently been passed on from its second generation owner to longtime staffer Kim Crady-Smith. It's an unusual mix of new and used books; many new, discounted titles and rare books. Vermontiana, Native American, and children's books are specialties, but the range is wide and patrons are welcome to sit in a corner for as long as they wish. Bigger than it looks at first: There are separate children's and fiction rooms.

Boxcar & Caboose Bookshop (802-748-3551; 800-754-9830; boxcarand caboosee.com), 394 Railroad St., St. Johnsbury. St. Johnsbury Academy history teacher Scott Beck and wife Joelle own this bright, well-stocked downtown store, with a large children's section and café (coffees, bagels).

Antiquarian Muse (802-472-3536), 144 Main St., Hardwick. Call before coming. Hours vary. A brick house filled with 5,000 used and collectible books for adults and children.

Lilac Cottage Books (802-586-9971), at Mill Village Pottery, Craftsbury Common. See *Crafts Shops*. This extensive collection of used books is housed in the barn beside the pottery.

CHEESE For the **Cabot Creamery Visitor Center**, see *To See*.

Bonnie View Sheep Farm (802-755-6878), 2228 South Albany Rd., Craftsbury Common. Neil Urie produces his award-winning cheeses—Blue, Camembert, and feta, as well as a hard Vermont Shepherd–style cheese—on the 470-acre farm that's been in the family since 1890. He's not really set up for visitors but not averse to those who drop by, no easy feat given the maze of dirt roads leading to his farm. It's sublime backcountry, however, and 5 PM is the best time to come. Look for his cheese at local stores.

Jasper Hill Farm (802-533-2566), 884 Garvin Hill Rd., Greensboro. Mateo and Andy Kehler make Winnemere cheese (cloth-bound hard cheddar that needs to age for a year), Bayley-Hazen Blue, and Constant Bliss (named for a Union scout from Greensboro killed in the Civil War), all soft, washed-rind cheese, widely distributed.

Vermont Milk Company (802-472-5800), 85 Industrial Rd. (Rt. 15, across from the Grand Union), Hardwick. There's a visitor center, retail shop, and factory tours of this facility for processing milk, cheese, yogurt, and ice cream.

CRAFTS SHOPS

In the St. Johnsbury area
Northeast Kingdom Artisans Guild (802-748-0158), 430 Railroad St. Open Mon.–Sat.; closed Mon. off-season. This cooperative of close to 100 Vermont artists showcases some magnificent work in many media.

Joe's Pond Craft Shop (802-684-2192; joespondcrafts.com), 2748 Rt. 2 west, West Danville, adjoining Hastings Store at the junction with Rt. 15. Open May–Dec., Tue.–Sun. Deborah Stresing can usually be found at her loom behind the counter in the barn she has filled with well-chosen quilts,

baskets, block prints, woodworking, floorcloths and rag rugs (her own), cards, felted bags—the work of close to 40 craftspeople in all.

Bird Man (802-563-2877), Danville Hill Rd., Cabot. Open July–Oct., Mon.–Sat. 8–5. Edmond Menard whittles truly amazing birds from a single piece of green cedar. Given the intricately fanned tails of his iconic small birds, it's difficult not to come away with a reasonably priced Christmas ornament, a pelican (holding small fish in his beak), hummingbird, or chickadee.

Peacham Corner Guild (802-592-3332), 643 Bayley-Hazen Rd., Peacham Corner. Open June–mid-Oct daily 10–5, Sun. 11–5. A cooperative selling handcrafted gifts and small antiques.

In the Craftsbury–Greensboro area
Mill Village Pottery (802-586-9971), 6 Mill Village Rd. (on the way to Craftsbury Outdoor Center), Craftsbury Common. Open summer and fall 10–5 daily; usually open off-season, too, but call ahead. Lynn Flory specializes in one-of-a-kind vessels and unusual functional ware such as the "Yunan steamer," a lidded ceramic pot with a conical chimney in its center, designed to retain vitamins and minerals.

FARMS AND FARM STANDS
Stillmeadow Farm (802-755-6713), 158 Urie Rd., South Albany. Open May–July. The dairy cows are gone but the greenhouses at this handsome farm, one that's been in the same family since the 1830s, are well worth a visit. Elizabeth Urie sells a variety of vegetable plants and flowers; hanging baskets and planters are a specialty. We couldn't believe the reasonable prices for the flats and splendid planter we carried home.

Pete's Greens (petesgreens.com), Craftsbury Village. Pete Johnson's certified-organic vegetable farm supplies restaurants and stores through much of Vermont; the seasonal farmstand on the edge of this village is open most days, on the honor system.

Brigid's Farm (802-592-3062), 123 Slack St., Peacham. Call ahead. A small farm with sheep, Angora goats, and dairy goats with a weaving studio and mittens, hand-spun yarns, spinning wheels, natural dye extracts, and supplies sold.

Snowshoe Farm (802-592-3153; snowshoefarm.com), 520 The Great Rd., Peacham. Open year-round, but call. Ron and Terry Miller breed alpacas and process their fiber, selling it along with hand-knit or woven alpaca products.

Randall Stick Park (802-748-6203; randallstickparkplacealpacas.com), 521 Morrill Rd., Danville. Year-round, but call before coming. Huacaya alpacas are bred, also pet alpacas for sale. The store sells alpaca fiber produced at the farm.

Also see the listings under *Cheese*. At Emergo Farm (see *Lodging*) guests are invited to join in farm chores and visitors are welcome to tour the dairy barns.

GALLERIES *Note:* St. Johnsbury's most famous art gallery is the St. Johnsbury Athenaeum (see *To See*).

South Walden Schoolhouse Gallery (802-563-5600; schoolhouse.phozon .com), Rt. 15, South Walden, between Danville and Hardwick. Open Memorial Day–Christmas Eve, Wed.–Sun. 1–6. Katherine Koutulak's gallery showcases paintings, jewelry, and more by better than 20 local artists.

GRACE Gallery (802-472-6857), 13 Mill St., Hardwick. Open Tue.–Thu. 10–3. *GRACE* stands for "Grassroots Art and Community Effort," a 25-year-old program that offers art workshops and displays the rotating exhibits in the old firehouse.

GARDENS **Vermont Daylilies** (802-533-2438), behind Lakeview Inn, Main St., Greensboro. Over 500 varieties of daylilies with display gardens; also potted daylilies, hostas, and garden perennials on sale. The gardens are always open, while the store is open May–Sept. 10–5.

Perennial Pleasures Nursery (802-472-5104; perennialpleasures.net), East Hardwick. Open May–Sept. Sited at the Brick House (see *Brews*) and run by Rachel Kane, this unusual nursery specializes in authentic 17th-, 18th-, and 19th-century restoration gardens. There are 3 acres of flowering perennial and herb gardens, grassy walks, and arbors; more than 375 varieties of plants are available.

GENERAL STORES **Willey's Store** (802-533-2621), Greensboro Village. Open 6:30–6, Sun. 8–1. One of the biggest and best general stores in the state, in business over 100 years; an extensive grocery, produce, and meat section, local dairy products (check out Constant Bliss cheese, made in Greensboro), hardware, toys, and just about everything else you should have brought for a vacation but forgot. Don't miss the upstairs with its selection of everything from flannel shirts and buttons through yard cloth and boots . . . and then there's the large hardware wing. Helpful staff will help you find what you are looking for and occasionally sell you something you never thought of wanting.

Hastings Store (802-684-3398), West Danville. Jane Hastings is the third generation of her family to manage the store and post office serving "64 people in the village and the 300 cottages on the lake." Garey Larrabee, Jane's husband, is known locally for his homemade sausage and the doughnuts and blueberry cake he makes fresh each morning. Built as a 19th-century stagecoach stop, the rambling, double-porched store is positioned picturesquely across Rt. 2 from Joe's Pond. Jane Larrabee happens to be a justice of the peace and frequently performs waterside weddings; four couples have been married right at the counter. Hastings doesn't sell gas, beer, or wine, and there's no lunch counter, but you'll find all that next door at **Joe's Pond Country Store**. According to Deborah Stresing, owner of Joe's Pond Craft Store, housed in between the two, it's a symbiotic relationship.

Marty's First Stop (802-684-2574), Rt. 2, east of Danville. Open 5:30 AM–9 PM. Dedicated as we are to promoting classic old-time general stores, this is an exception we have to acknowledge, a Mobil station with an extensive grocery and deli, filling a real need for locals and for visitors headed for vacation rentals. It's also good for homemade soups, generous grinders, and more.

Bailey's & Burke General Store (802-626-9250; baileysandburke.com), Rt. 114, East Burke. Open weekdays 8–7, Sun. 8–8. This classic old general store has been nicely fancied up by longtime local residents Jody Fried and Bill Turner. The second-floor gallery has been restored and displays work by local craftsmen. Downstairs are breads, pies, cookies, and coffee cakes baked daily right here; also a deli featuring specialty pizzas, cheeses, cold cuts, soups, and salads with café tables to eat them at. A selection of wines, coffees, and teas.

Kerrigan's Market & Deli (802-467-8800), 4080 Rt. 5, West Burke. A gen-

Christina Tree

UPSTAIRS AT WILLEY'S STORE IN GREENSBORO

eral store with a full-service deli and pizzas.

Peacham Store (802-592-3310), Peacham Village. Open spring–New Year's, daily 8–6, hot food until 5. A picturesque red-clapboard store at a photogenic crossroads. Visitor-geared with crafts, collectibles, and specialty foods. The big attraction here are hot soups and other great meals-to-go, prepared in the adjoining kitchen.

SPECIAL SHOPS **Caplan's Army Store Work & Sportswear** (802-748-3236), 457 Railroad St., St. Johnsbury. It's getting harder and harder to find a genuine army & navy store, and this is the genuine article. Established in 1922 and still in the same family, a serious source of quilted jackets, skiwear, Woolrich sweaters, hunting boots, and such; good value and friendly service.

The Farmer's Daughter (802-748-3994), Rt. 2 east of St. Johnsbury. Open mid-Apr.–mid-Nov., daily 8–8. Billed as the country's oldest "Gift Barn"—not just because the barn is 180 years old but also because it's been under the same ownership for 43 years. A lot of stuff, much of it hokey but fun.

Kingdom Outdoors (802-748-3433; kingdomoutdoors.com), 452 Railroad

St., St. Johnsbury. This is a serious gear and outdoor clothing shop with the focus on backpacking, climbing, camping, and paddling in summer and on snowboarding and skating in winter.

Moose River Lake and Lodge Store (802-748-2423), 370 Railroad St., St. Johnsbury. Open except Sun. 10–5; in summer Sun., too (11–4). Antiques, rustic furniture, and accessories for the home, camp, or cabin: taxidermy specialties, deer antlers and skulls, prints, pack baskets, fishing creels and snowshoes, folk art, an extensive wine collection, and more.

Samadhi Store and Workshop (802-633-4440), 30 Church St., Barnet. Open Mon.–Fri. 9–5, Sat.10–4. An off-shoot of nearby Karmê Chöling, selling singing bowls and gongs, robes, teas, Vermont-made raku incense bowls, lacquerware from Japan and Korea, locally made meditation benches and tables, and meditation cushions and yoga mats made on-site.

Diamond Hill Store (802-684-9797), Rt. 2, Danville on the green. This former general store is now a sleek emporium specializing in handmade chocolates, wine, and gifts.

SUGARHOUSES Rowell Sugarhouse (802-563-2756), 4962 Rt. 15, Walden. Visitors are welcome year-round, 9–5. Maple cream and candy as well as sugar; also Vermont honey and sheepskins, crafts, paintings.

Gebbie's Maplehurst Farm (800-258-7699), 2183 Gebbie Rd., Greensboro. Peter and Sandra Gebbie are major local maple producers, perpetuating a business that's been welcoming visitors for generations.

Goodrich's Sugarhouse (802-563-9917; goodrichmaplefarm.com), just off Rt. 2 by Molly's Pond in East Cabot. A family tradition for seven generations, open to visitors Mar.–Dec. with a full line of award-winning maple products.

Goss's Sugar House (802-633-4743), 101 Maple Lane, Barnet. Gordon and Pat Goss have won a blue ribbon for their syrup at the Caledonia County Fair. They welcome visitors, sell year-round, and will ship.

High Meadow Farm (802-467-3621) East Burke. The sugarhouse is open in-season. Call for directions.

THE FARMER'S DAUGHTER

Christina Tree

✳ Special Events

January, last weekend: **TD Banknorth Craftsbury X-C Ski Marathon** (craftsbury.com)—a great classic technique event open to skiers of all skills; 25 and 50 km races for the true competitors, 10 for ordinary skiers. All begin and end at Craftsbury Common, traversing the network of high, dependably snow trails maintained by Craftsbury Outdoor Center and Highland Lodge. Food stops are a feature.

February: **Snowflake Festival Winter Carnival**, Lyndonville–Burke. Events include a crafts show, snow sculpture, ski races for all ages and abilities, sleigh rides, music, and art. **Burke Mountain Dog Sled Dash** (*last weekend*).

Last weekend of March: **Open sugarhouses** (vtmaple.org).

May: **Annual Vermont Open Studio Weekend** (vermontcrafts.com) on Memorial Day weekend. **Hardwick Spring Festival** (*last weekend*) includes a parade, crafts fair, and chicken BBQ.

June: **Tour de Kingdom** (*first weekend*; tourdekingdom.com), a competitive and recreational century ride from Burke through the Lake Region, 15, 25, 50, and 75 miles for all ages. **Cultural Heritage Festival** (*third week*) at Lyndon State College.

June through October: **Farmer's markets**, in downtown St. Johnsbury Sat. 9–1; in Craftsbury Sat. 10–1; in Danville Wed. 9–1; in Hardwick Fri. 3–6.

July: The **July 4 parade** in Cabot is the best around (802-563-2279). **Peacham Independence Day festivities** include a Ghost Walk in the cemetery, with past residents impersonated. **Burklyn Arts Council Summer Craft Fair** (*Saturday closest to July 4*) in Bandstand Park, Lyndonville. **Antiques and Uniques Fair** in Craftsbury Common. **Stars and Stripes Pageant** (*last weekend*), Lyndonville—big auction, parade featuring Bread and Puppet Uncle Sam, barbecue. The **Irasburg Church Fair** is the third Saturday.

♫ *July through August:* **Circus Smirkus** (802-533-7443), Greensboro. A children's circus camp stages frequent performances.

August: **Old Home Days**, Craftsbury Common—parade, games, crafts (802-586-7766). **Danville Fair** (*first weekend*) on the green features a parade with floats, more than 75 years of tradition. **Annual Kingdom Triathlon** (*midmonth*; kingdomtriathlon.org) at Lake Salem, a 500-yard swim, 13-mile bike ride, and 5-mile run. **Caledonia County Fair** (*third week*), Mountain View Park, Lyndonville—horse, pony, and ox pulling; cattle, sheep, alpaca, rabbit, and swine shows; midway, rides, demolition derby, music.

September: **Burke Mountain Bike Race** (*first weekend after Labor Day*) up the Toll Road. **Burke Fall Foliage Festival** (*last Saturday of September*). **Art on Main,** Newport (*last Sunday*).

September through October: **Northeast Kingdom Fall Foliage Festival**, the last week in September or first one in October. Seven towns take turns hosting visitors, feeding them breakfast, lunch, and dinner, and guiding them to beauty spots and points of interest within their borders. In Walden the specialty is Christmas wreath making; in Cabot there's a tour of the cheese factory; in Plainfield, farm tours; in Peacham, a Ghost Walk and crafts fair; in Barnet the exceptional historical society house is open, and guided tours of back roads are outstanding. The day in Groton includes a parade, lumberjack's breakfast, and chicken pie supper. The finale comes

NORTHEAST KINGDOM FALL FOLIAGE FESTIVAL

in St. Johnsbury, with a farmer's market and art and crafts fair. For details, contact the Northeast Kingdom Chamber (see *Guidance*).

Fall Foliage Train Rides (thelyndon freighthouse.comfor tickets and info).

First weekend of October: **Fall Foliage Craft Fair** in Hardwick.

First Sunday of October: **Autumn on the Green** in Danville includes the **Cabot Apple Pie and Cheese Festival**.

November: **Old Fashioned Game Supper** in Danville (since 1921). **Kirby Quilters Craft Fair** (*Saturday after Thanksgiving*; kirbyquilters.com) is huge—it fills two gyms at Lyndon State College.

First weekend of December: **Burklyn Christmas Crafts Market**—a major gathering of North Country craftspeople and artists in the Lyndon Town School.

THE LAKE COUNTRY

INCLUDING NEWPORT, JAY PEAK, BARTON, THE ISLAND POND AREA, AND THE EASTERN TOWNSHIPS OF QUEBEC

The border area between Vermont's Northeast Kingdom and Quebec's Eastern Townships is big-sky, gently rolling farm and logging country, spotted with stunning lakes. The largest of these is 32-mile-long Memphremagog with Newport at its foot.

At the height of railroad passenger service, large wooden hotels rose on the shores of several of these lakes. In Newport the 400-room Memphremagog House stood beside the railroad station, Newport House was across the street, and the New City Hotel was nearby. Guests came by train from Boston and Philadelphia. Lindbergh came with his *Spirit of Saint Louis*, and there was a racetrack and a paddle-wheeler.

THE NEWPORT WATERFRONT

Christina Tree

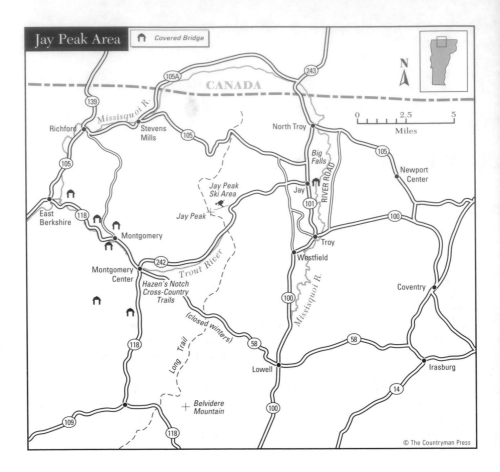

In recent years Newport has reclaimed its lakefront with an attractive boat-house and walkway, but it's quieter than it used to be. Drive east and you are quickly in little-trafficked lake country: Lakes Derby and Salem, Seymour and Echo all have good fishing, and dozens of smaller ponds have boat launches. Island Pond is a town as well as a lake, and for travelers it looms large on the map because you have to pass through it to get to access the surrounding empty (of people, but teeming with moose, black bear, and other wildlife) woodland, much of it now publicly owned. There's good fishing around Averill, where Quimby Country, the region's oldest and most unusual resort, is squirreled away. Beyond, this lonely stretch of the Connecticut River dwindles into a stream, and then widens into the Connecticut Lakes.

Southeast of this northern tier is Lake Willoughby, Vermont's most hauntingly beautiful lake. Mounts Hor and Pisgah rise abruptly from opposite shores, creating a fjordlike effect when viewed from the public beach at the southern tip of the lake. Mostly undeveloped, Willoughby is surrounded for much of its length by state forest, and the water is stocked with salmon and rainbow trout. A well-known resort area in the days of grand hotels and steamboats, it now has a limited but loyal following of sailors, sailboarders (there is always a breeze here), and year-round fishermen.

Barton, the area's southernmost commercial center, also boomed in the late 19th century, when six passenger trains a day stopped in summer, bringing guests to fill the town's big hotels (long gone) or the gingerbread "camps" (still there) on Crystal Lake. Between Barton and Willoughby Lake, don't miss the Stone House Museum; south of Barton look for the Bread and Puppet Museum and performances.

West of Newport, Jay Peak marks the northern march of the Green Mountains, towering like a sentinel above the border country. In summer and fall as well as in winter, a 60-passenger aerial tram hoists visitors to the 3,861-foot summit. The view sweeps from Mount Washington to Montreal, back across the lake, down the spine of the Green Mountains, and southwest across Lake Champlain to the Adirondacks. In winter this major ski mountain draws more than half its skiers from Montreal, only about an hour away.

The waters of Quebec and Vermont mingle in Lake Memphremagog, and the international line runs right through the Haskell Opera House in Derby Line—the audience in America attends concerts performed in Canada. Even the major border crossing (passports required) at Derby Line isn't especially busy. There are four more rural crossing along this border, which divides two very different cultures. As the French say, *"Vive la difference!"*

We include just a sampling of the Eastern Townships as an added enticement to come to the Kingdom, which it complements with its resort amenities, vineyards, and distinctly French ambience. Since 1974, when French was declared the official language in the province of Quebec, there's a sense that you have flown across the Atlantic when in fact you've driven little more than half an hour north of the border. Still, Americans are welcomed and understood.

IN THE LATE 19TH CENTURY TRAVELERS STEPPED OFF THE TRAIN ON ONE SIDE OF THE MEMPREHMAGOG HOUSE AND BOARDED BOARDED STEAMERS ON THE OTHER FOR A RIDE UP THE LAKE.

Vermont Historical Society

𝕸emphremagog 𝕳ouse, 𝕹ewport, 𝖁t.

D. A. Clifford, Photographer, St. Johnsbury, Vt.   (OVER.)

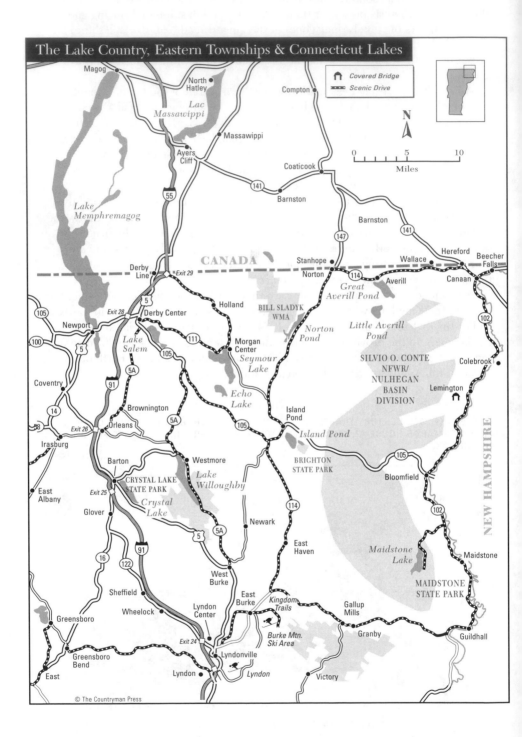

The Lake Country, Eastern Townships & Connecticut Lakes

Covered Bridge
Scenic Drive

N

0   5   10
Miles

Magog
North Hatley
Compton
Lac Massawippi
Massawippi
Ayers Cliff
Coaticook
55
141
Barnston
Barnston
Lake Memphremagog
147
141
Hereford
Beecher Falls
CANADA
Stanhope
Wallace
Derby Line
Exit 29
Norton
114
Averill
Canaan
Great Averill Pond
5
Holland
BILL SLADYK WMA
Little Averill Pond
102
105
Exit 28
Derby Center
111
Norton Pond
Newport
100
Morgan Center
SILVIO O. CONTE NFWR/ NULHEGAN BASIN DIVISION
Colebrook
Lake Salem
105
Seymour Lake
5
Coventry
91
5A
Echo Lake
Lemington
14
Brownington
Island Pond
18
Exit 26
Orleans
5A
Island Pond
Irasburg
Barton
Westmore
BRIGHTON STATE PARK
105
Bloomfield
East Albany
CRYSTAL LAKE STATE PARK
Exit 25
Lake Willoughby
102
Glover
Crystal Lake
Newark
114
NEW HAMPSHIRE
5
5A
East Haven
Maidstone Lake
Maidstone
16
91
West Burke
MAIDSTONE STATE PARK
122
Sheffield
Kingdom Trails
Wheelock
Lyndon Center
East Burke
Gallup Mills
Granby
Guildhall
Greensboro
Exit 24
Burke Mtn. Ski Area
Greensboro Bend
Lyndonville
Victory
East
Lyndon
Lyndon

© The Countryman Press

Web sites to check before you come

The Northeast Kingdom Travel & Tourism Association offers the area's best overall Web site: travelthekingdom.

Barton Area Chamber of Commerce (centerofthekingdom.com) serves the southern part of this region and has listings of summer lakeside cottages.

Also useful, specific to their regions: islandpond.org; vt.northcountry.org; and northcountrychamber.org (for the North Country Chamber of Commerce, serving the very northeastern corner of Vermont and the Connecticut Lakes in New Hampshire). For the Eastern Townships of Quebec, see easterntownships.org.

Welcome centers

Vermont North Country Chamber of Commerce (802-334-7782; vtnorth country.org) maintains a new walk-in visitor center on the causeway in Newport, theoretically open daily year-round but volunteer operated.

Island Pond (802-723-9889), Rt. 105 at the south end of Main St. Open daily 10–4 during snowmobiling season, otherwise Wed.–Sun., but volunteer dependent. A spiffy new welcome center with restrooms.

The Derby Line Welcome Center (802-873-3311) on I-91 south, with restrooms, at the border serves arriving Canadians.

North Country Chamber of Commerce (800-698-8939; northcountrychamber .org), Rt. 3, 1.5 miles north of Colebrook, New Hampshire, open year-round daily 9–7, is a gateway information center (with restrooms) for visitors approaching from the White Mountains.

Also see the region's gateway welcome center in St. Johnsbury.

GETTING AROUND Two pieces of advice: (1) Avoid driving lonely stretches after dark. If you must, do so slowly, watching for moose, which are difficult to spot at night and deadly if you collide at high speed. (2) Gas up. Pumps are few and far between, and tempting woods roads abound.

WHEN TO COME In winter skiers head for Jay Peak, snowmobilers converge on Island Pond, and ice fishers come to many of the lakes; anglers come in spring, hunters in fall. Otherwise this is summer lake and fall foliage country. Foliage comes early, usually peaking the last weekend in September and the first in October.

BORDER CROSSINGS AND REQUIREMENTS **Derby Line, Vermont, and Stanstead, Quebec**, represent a major border crossing (I-91 continues north as Hwy. 55), linking up with the major east–west highway between Montreal and Quebec City. Less busy crossings include: **North Troy** (Rt. 243), **Norton** (Rt. 114 to Canadian Rt. 147), and **Beecher Falls** (Rt. 3 to Rt. 253). While passports are not technically required at this writing for U.S. citizens reentering by car, they certainly will be within the life of this book. At this writing U.S. citizens are permitted to bring in Quebec cheese (except goat), apples, tinned meats (with the exception of goat and lamb), and one bottle of wine duty-free.

MEDICAL EMERGENCY Emergency service is available by calling **911**.

Christina Tree

LAKE MEMPHREMAGOG FROM MAGOG, QUEBEC

North Country Hospital & Medical Center (802-334-7331), Prouty Dr., Newport.

✳ Communities

Newport (population: 2,558) The city has reclaimed its lakefront with a marina and outstanding walkway. Its past splendor is recalled in archival photos mounted by the Memphremagog Historical Society of Newport in the State Office Building, where there's also a display on northern Vermont Abenaki people, from Paleolithic through current times.

Barton Village (population: 742). The hotels are gone, but Crystal Lake remains beautiful, with a clifflike promontory on one side and public beaches at its northern rim. There is golf here, and the town of Barton itself packs an astounding number of services into its small downtown. The Crystal Lake Falls Historical Association maintains the Pierce House Museum, 97 Water St. (open June–Aug., Sun. 1–5), next to the old-fashioned office of the *Barton Chronicle*, an excellent weekly covering much of Orleans and Essex counties.

Brownington Village is a crossroads full of outstanding, early-19th-century buildings, the core of a once proud hill town long since eclipsed by such valley centers as Barton, Orleans, and Newport. There are 19th-century flower and heirloom herb gardens behind the Eaton House and a spectacular panorama from the wooden observatory set up in a meadow behind the church. A descriptive walking tour booklet is available at the Old Stone House Museum (see *To See*).

Island Pond (population: 853; islandpondchamber.org). The crossroads of Vermont's lonely, northeasternmost corner, Island Pond has the look and feel of an outpost. It's home to a spiffy new welcome center and to Brighton State Park (see *Green Space*). A sign in front of the city-sized depot reads, *Pioneer railroad planner John A. Poor's dream of an international railroad connecting Montreal, Canada, with the ice-free harbor of Portland, Maine, became a reality on July 18, 1854, when the first through trains met at this great halfway point on the Grand Trunk railway.* During the late 19th century and into the 20th, Island Pond hummed with the business of servicing frequent passenger trains and freight trains trans-porting logs and wood pulp. No longer. Today it's a funky village on a pond with an island in its center. The Twelve Tribes, a religious community, has rooted here, buying and restoring many of the Victorian houses and operating the town's one big specialty store. In winter Island Pond is the region's snowmobiling capital. With its lakeside camping and easy access to hiking and fishing, this is a reasonably priced base for a family vacation.

Montgomery (population: 929) is known for its six covered bridges (see *To See*). It began as a lumbering center and was for a long time one of the world's major producers of timothy grass seed. The Montgomery Historical Society's collection is housed in an 1835 wooden church, open June–Sept. at stated hours; the society also sponsors Saturday-evening concerts on the common in July and Aug. Lunch and shopping can be found 2 miles east in **Montgomery Center**, crossroads for Rt. 242 (to Jay Peak), Rt. 118 (north to Richford and south to Stowe). It's also the terminus for Rt. 58, which angles back through **Hazen's Notch** over a high woods pass and down through fields into Lowell. An inviting drive in summer, it's open only for the first 4 miles in winter, just far enough to access the magnificent and dependably snowy trails at **Hazen's Notch Cross-country Ski and Snowshoe-ing Center**.

North Hatley, Quebec (population: 748). Some 20 miles north of Derby Line on Lake Massawippi, this village was founded in the 1770s by loyalists who moved north from New England during the Revolution. It became a fashionable resort for wealthy (American) southerners, who sold their summer homes in "Yankee land" after the Civil War. In 1900 there were 15 summer hotels here, one with 365 rooms. The village with its lakeside shops, cafés, and walkway, is charming, a mag-net for tourists from Montreal.

Magaog, Quebec (population: 23,880; 800-267-2744; tourisme-memphremagog .com). A 19th century textile town, Magog is now a resort center with a lively down-town, a lakeside walkway and bike path; it's a departure point for excursion boats.

✳ To See

LAKES Lake Memphremagog, Newport. Vermont's second largest lake stretch-es 32 miles north to Magog, Quebec. Only 5 miles are within the United States. The name is said to be Abenaki for "Beautiful Waters." On the western shore look for Owls Head, a distinctive monadnock that's also a ski area, and for **St. Benoit du Lac** (see *To See*). Also check listings under *Boating*, *Fishing*, and *Swimming*.

Lake Willoughby, Westmore. Vermont's most dramatic lake, nearly 5 miles long and more than 300 feet deep, shaped like a stocking with a foot toward the north and Mount Pisgah and Mount Hor rising to more than 2,500 feet on opposite sides at the southern end. See *Boating*, *Fishing*, *Swimming*, and *Lodging*.

Seymour Lake. There is a public beach in the tiny village of Morgan Center, also the spot to rent boats for fishing for landlocked salmon. In winter this lake is pep-pered with fishing shanties, and there is a system of cross-country trails (ungroomed).

Echo Lake. Much smaller than Seymour Lake and adjoining it on the south, this lake is circled by a dirt road and gently rolling hills. There is also public boat access. Good fishing for trout and landlocked salmon.

The Old Stone House Museum (802-754-2022; oldstonehousemuseum .org), off Rt. 58 east of Orleans in Brownington. Open May 15–Oct. 15, Wed.–Sun. 11–5. $5 adults, $4 county residents, $2 students. This striking, four-story, 30-room granite building with a clerestory, completed in 1836 as a dormitory for the Orleans County Grammar School, houses the collections of the Orleans County Historical Society Museum. The building is all the more dramatic,

OLD STONE HOUSE   Christina Tree

set among the village's scattering of early-19th-century houses and the surrounding 55 acres of farmland. Its story is compelling. The school's headmaster and the building's architect was Alexander Twilight (1795–1875), the first person of African parentage to attend an American college (Middlebury, 1823) or serve in a

Island Pond is actually a small lake with a 20-acre island off the sandy beach and a wooded campground in **Brighton State Park**. Boating and fishing are both easily accessible.

Crystal Lake, Barton. Roughly 3 miles long and about 1 mile wide, in places more than 100 feet deep, this glacial lake is beautifully sited between rough-hewn mountains. Crystal Lake State Park (see *Swimming*) is justly popular; summer rental cottages can be found through the Barton Area Chamber of Commerce. Also see *Fishing*.

Maidstone Lake, Guildhall. One of Vermont's cleanest, clearest, most remote lakes was designated a state park in 1938. This was wilderness, but the Civilian Conservation Corps built fireplaces for camping, along with the lodge and picnic shelter that are still in use (see *Green Space*). The lake offers good trout fishing but is best known as a loon nesting area.

The town of Glover also harbors three small, fish-stocked lakes: **Daniels Pond**, **Shadow Lake**, and **Lake Parker**.

state legislature (Vermont House of Representatives, 1836). The museum includes a visitor center in the circa-1839 Alexander Twilight House, from which guided tours depart to view the Old Stone House. Here, some rooms have been restored while others showcase special exhibits and historical collections from towns throughout Orleans County (including tools, paintings, furniture, and decorative arts). The Lawrence Barn features an exhibit titled A Hard Row to Hoe: Two Centuries of Farming in Orleans County. Inquire about special, year-round workshops. **Old Stone House Day**, second Sunday in August, represents one of the Kingdom's biggest annual events with a farmer's market, picnic, kids' activities, live music, crafts demonstrations, and more. Any day, pick up the walking tour guide to the Brownington Historic District—and don't miss the view from the observatory tower on Prospect Hill. This is one of the most magical places in Vermont. Check the Web site for year-round special events and workshops.

ALEXANDER TWILIGHT

Old Stone House Museum

MUSEUMS & ATTRACTIONS Bread and Puppet Theater Museum (802-525-3031; breadandpuppet.org), 753 Heights Rd. (Rt. 122), Glover. Open mid-May–Oct., 10–6. The internationally known Bread and Puppet Theater tours in winter, but much of the year the weathered, vintage-1863 dairy barn is open to anyone who stops (free, but donations welcome). It houses one of the biggest collections and some of the biggest puppets in the world: huge and haunting puppet dwarfs, giants, devils, and other fantastic figures of good and evil, the artistic expressions of German-born Peter Schumann, who founded the Bread and Puppet Theater in 1962 and moved it to Glover in 1974. Inquire about tours, but usually visitors wander and wonder. Publications, postcards, and "Cheap Art" are sold in the shop. Sat. and Sun. in July and Aug., performances are staged in the outdoor arena in the neighboring field and in the timber-frame theater.

Jay Peak summit. The spectacular view from the top is accessible via the 60-person tram at Jay Peak Resort (802-966-2611), Rt. 242, Jay. It operates daily during ski season and from the last weekend in June–Labor Day, then in foliage season, mid-Sept.–Columbus Day.

Montgomery and its covered bridges. Montgomery boasts a grand total of six Town lattice covered bridges: one right in Montgomery Village over Black Falls Creek; one south on Rt. 118; another nearby but 3 miles off Rt. 118 on West Hill on an abandoned side road over a waterfall; another northwest on Rt. 118 over the Trout River; and two in Montgomery Center, both a mile west of Rt. 118 over the Trout River (see our area map). Montgomery Village itself is picturesque.

Abbaye de St. Benoit du Lac (819-843-4080; st-benoit-du-lac.com), Austin, Quebec. Open daily. This French Benedictine monastery, founded in 1912, is sited on the west shore of Lake Memphremagog. It's an imposing building with a landmark tower. The resident monks welcome visitors for daily Mass and daily Eucharist (10:45 AM) and vespers (5 PM), at which Gregorian chant is sung. The big, popular shop sells monastery products

Christina Tree

BREAD AND PUPPET THEATER MUSEUM, GLOVER

such as cheese and hard cider, as well as books and recordings of Gregorian chant, vestments, and religious articles. In autumn the orchards are open for PYO. The easiest route from Newport is via the North Troy border crossing, then through Mansonville, South Bolton, and Austin. The shop is open Mon.–Sat. 9–10:45 and 11:45–4:30; until 6 in July and Aug. Retreats are offered for men in a guest house on the grounds and for women in a neighboring convent.

VIEW FROM THE TOWER AT ST. BENOIT-DU-LAC, QUEBEC

Christina Tree

✳ To Do

BIKING While the region's formal mountain biking meccas are described in the St. Johnsbury chapter, this pristine area offers hundreds of miles of dirt and logging roads. Request the excellent bike map for the Kingdom from the **Northeast Kingdom Travel and Tourism Association** (800-884-8001; travelthekingdom).

A time-honored and -tested 22.6- or 33.7-mile ride begins at the Montgomery House Inn (see *Lodging*) in

Montgomery Village, passes two covered bridges along Rt. 118 north, and takes you to East Berkshire; you can simply continue to Enosburg Falls, where Lake Carmi offers camping and swimming, or turn onto the Richford Rd., looping back to Montgomery or up into Canada. The **Missisquoi Valley Rail Trail** (see "The Northwest Corner") begins in Richford and runs 26.4 miles west to St. Albans.

BIRDING The most famous birds in the Kingdom are the peregrine falcons that nest on Mount Pisgah on Willoughby Lake. Falcons return in spring, nest during summer, and leave by August. Early morning and late afternoon are the best times to see them from the north end of the west-facing cliff.

Over 100 species of birds have been spotted around Lake Willoughby alone. Maidstone Lake is famed as a nesting area for loons, and the Nulhegan Basin is an important breeding habitat for migratory birds and nesting thrushes and warblers. Boreal forests in the basin support rare species such as spruce grouse, gray jay, Wilson's warbler, olive-sided flycatcher, rusty blackbird, black-backed woodpecker, and three-toed woodpecker. A splendid, free *Connecticut River Birding Trail/Northern Section* map/guide is available locally; also see birdtrail.org. **Siskin Ecological Adventures** (siskinea.org) offers tours to lesser-known spots like the bird sanctuary on the Barton River.

BOATING With thousands of miles of rivers and streams and the lion's share of the Kingdom's more than 37,000 acres of lakes and ponds, this area offers some of the best paddling in the Northeast. The DeLorme *Vermont Atlas and Gazetteer* shows put-ins.

North Woods Stewardship Center (802-723-6551; northwoodscenter.org), 10 Mile Square Rd., East Charleston (5 miles west of Island Pond), offers rental canoes on the Clyde River, also guided canoe expeditions on a variety of waters.

LAKE WILLOUGHBY

Christina Tree

White Caps Campgrounds (802-467-3345) at the southern end of Lake Willoughby rents canoes and kayaks. Aluminum boats (14 feet) with small motors, also pontoons, may be rented at **Newport Marine** (802-334-5911) at Farrants Point on Lake Memphremagog. Boats are also available at **Brighton State Park** in Island Pond (see *Green Space*), as well as **Anglin' Boat Rentals** on Crystal Lake in Barton (802-525-4544). **Clyde River Recreation** (802-895-4333; clyde riverrecreation.com), 0.25 mile east of the junction of Rts. 5A and 105 in West Charleston, rents kayaks, canoes, and small boats and offers drop-off and delivery.

On the **Connecticut River**, Canaan is a good place to put in, but there are several rapids at the start. Canoeing is also good below Colebrook, New Hampshire, for 3 miles but then rather fast for an equal distance. (See also *Fishing*.)

The 86-mile-long **Missisquoi River** makes a complete loop around Jay, passes briefly through Quebec, and continues across Vermont to empty into Lake Champlain. The upper half of the river near Jay offers fast water in spring; the lower reaches are gentle and broad, good spring and summer ground for beginners and those who enjoy traversing outstanding rural landscape. For canoes and boat rentals, contact the **Missisquoi Riverbend B&B** (802-744-9991), Rt. 100, Troy. For an overview of a 174-mile route through northern Vermont see northern forestcanoetrail.org.

FISHING This is a fly-fishing mecca, drawing serious fishermen to wilderness brooks and ponds as well as rivers and lakes. Most general stores sell three-day fishing licenses (see *Fishing* in "What's Where" for fishing regulations). Check in the *Vermont Atlas and Gazetteer* for local access points to ponds. Rental boats, bait, and tackle are available at the sites listed under *Boating*. The pamphlet *Vermont Guide to Fishing*, prepared by the Vermont Fish and Wildlife Department, available locally, tells where to find what. Biologist Ken Hastings of Colebrook, New Hampshire, and **Osprey Fishing Adventures** (603-922-3800; ospreyfishing adventures.com) is the fishing guru for this stretch of the river, offering one- and three-day fly-fishing trips on his driftboat. Guides can also be found through the **Vermont Outdoor Guide Association** (800-425-8747; voga.org) and through local fishing-geared lodging, listed below.

In May head for the **Willoughby Falls Wildlife Management Area**. From Orleans drive east on Rt. 58 for 0.2 mile. At the BROWNINGTON sign bear left and drive 0.1 mile to the Vermont Fish and Wildlife parking area. Between the last week in April and the second week in May, wild rainbow trout climb the falls here, jumping high to clear the whitewater to reach their spawning ground. **Willoughby** is known as the prime fishing lake; check out the **Clyde River** for brook trout and landlocked salmon, the **Barton River** for trout and perch. **Lake Memphremagog** is good for smelt, smallmouth bass, and walleye, in addition to salmon and trout, but also has plenty of milfoil. **Seymour Lake** is (at this writing) milfoil-free and known for bass and lake trout. **Holland Pond** and **Echo Lake** are known for rainbow trout, and **Norton Pond** is known for fighting pike. Ice fishing is particularly popular on Memphremagog and Seymour Lake. There is a state fish hatchery in Newark; **Newark Pond** has an access and is good for yellow perch along with trout. The **Willoughby River** is known, especially in early spring, for rainbow trout, as are the **Barton** and **Black Rivers**. The **Clyde River**, acclaimed as the first river in the country to have a dam removed for environmental reasons, is known for landlocked Atlantic salmon. Lodging geared to fishermen includes **Seymour Lake Lodge** in Morgan, which offers advice and free boats to its guests, and **Quimby Country**, a self-contained resort that includes 70-acre Forest Lake, 0.5 mile from 1,200-acre Great Averill Pond, both lonely and remote but good for trout and salmon; rowboats can be rented here by the day. Also see the **Village Inn** of East Burke in the St. Johnsbury chapter, and check out *Green Space* as well. The **Trout River** deserves its name, and brook trout can also be found in the **Missisquoi**.

GOLF The **Jay Peak Championship Golf Course** at Jay Peak Resort (jaypeak resort.com), Rt. 242, Jay. Designed by Graham Cooke, this 18-hole course empha-sizes natural features and offers some memorable views.

Newport Country Club (802-334-2391), off Mount Vernon St., overlooking the lake. Eighteen holes, rentals, instruction, restaurant; Apr.–Nov.

Dufferin Heights Golf Club (819-876-2113), Stanstead, Quebec. May–Nov. Nine holes, cart rentals, restaurant.

Orleans Country Club (802-754-2333), Rt. 58, near Lake Willoughby. Apr.–Nov.; 18 holes, rentals, instruction.

Barton Golf Course (802-525-1126), Telfer Hill Rd., Barton. Apr.–Sept., 18 holes, cart rentals, low fees.

Grandad's Invitational, Newark. This nine-hole course is a local legend. Ask around for directions and leave your fee in the mailbox.

HIKING AND WALKING **Mount Pisgah** and **Mount Hor**, Lake Willoughby. Named respectively for the place where the Lord sent Moses to view the Promised Land and for the place Moses' brother Aaron died after the Lord commanded him to go there, these twin mountains, separated by a narrow stretch of lake, form Willoughby Gap. Both are within the 7,000-acre Willoughby State Forest and offer well-maintained hiking trails. Mount Pisgah (2,751 feet) on the east side of the lake (access marked from Rt. 5A) has fairly short climbs yielding spectacular views of the White Mountains; trails up Mount Hor (2,648 feet) begin on the Civilian Conservation Corps road, 1.8 miles west of its junction with Rt. 5A, and also offer panoramic views of the Green Mountains to the west. For details, consult *50 Hikes in Vermont* (Backcountry Guides) and *Day Hiker's Guide to Vermont* (Green Mountain Club).

Wheeler Mountain. The trail begins on Wheeler Mountain Rd., which leaves the north side of Rt. 5, 8.3 miles north of West Burke and 5 miles south of Barton Vil-lage. From the highway, the unpaved road climbs 1.9 miles to the trailhead.

Bald Mountain. There are excellent views from the newly restored fire tower at the summit of this, the tallest peak in the Willoughby Lake area. Trails ascend to the summit from both the north (Lookout's Trail, 2.8 miles) and the south (Long Pond Trail, 2.1 miles). From the north side of Bald Mountain, you can hike on trails and wilderness roads all the way to the summit of Mount Hor; Haystack Mountain (a side trip) has excellent views and two trails. Details can be found in *Day Hiker's Guide to Vermont* (see *Hiking and Walking* in "What's Where").

Bluff Mountain (2,380 feet) looms over Island Pond to the north. It's a popular climb with spectacular views. The trail starts from Rt. 114, north of the village. Inquire locally for directions.

Monadnock Mountain (elevation: 3,140 feet), in Lemington, towers over the Connecticut River and Colebrook, New Hampshire. A trail runs west, beginning as a driveway off Rt. 102 near the bridge to Colebrook. An abandoned fire tower crowns the summit.

HIKING The **Long Trail** terminates its 262-mile route at the Canadian border, 10 miles north of Jay Peak, but the trek up Jay itself is what most hikers look for here. The most popular ascent is from Rt. 242, 1.2 miles west of the entrance to the ski area; the round-trip hike takes three hours. For details on this and the section of the trail between Hazen's Notch and Rt. 242, also for the final, fairly flat leg to the border, see the *Long Trail Guide*, published by the Green Mountain Club, which maintains the trail and four shelters in this area.

✔ **Hazen's Notch Association** (802-326-4799; hazensnotch.org), 1421 Hazen's Notch Rd. (Rt. 58), Montgomery Center. Open May 15–Nov. 15. No trail fee, but contributions appreciated. Twenty miles of this network are maintained for hiking, winding through 2,500 acres of privately owned woods and meadows; it's 15 minutes to Bear Paw Pond. The 2-mile-long Burnt Mountain Trail ascends to the 2,700-foot summit of Burnt Mountain, an open summit with 360-degree views that include Hazen's Notch, the Jay Mountains, Mount Mansfield, and Lake Champlain. Stop by the welcome center on Rt. 58. Dogs must be leashed. Inquire about frequent nature walks, fly-fishing workshops, and other special events. Sharon and Rolf Anderson offer nature and ecology day camps for children 6–9, Adventure Day and Overnight Camps for those 10–15.

HORSEBACK RIDING **Perry Farm** (802-754-2396) in Brownington offers sleigh and carriage rides drawn by Morgan horses through the Brownington Historic District.

Galloping Acres Riding Stable (802-754-2337), Ticehurst Rd., Brownington. Open year-round, 10–dusk. Horseback riding through woods and fields on back roads, also wagon pulled by Belgians. Pony rides, too.

SWIMMING In Newport try **Prouty Beach**, a public facility on Lake Memphremagog. On Seymour Lake there is a public beach in Morgan Center. There are state facilities at **Brighton State Park** (802-723-9702) in Island Pond, a large beach that is sandy and shallow for quite a way out, great for children. **Crystal Lake State Beach** (802-525-6205), 90 Bellwater Ave., Barton (just east of the village off Rt. 15), is open daily late May–Sept., with lifeguard, bathhouse (built of stones quarried on the lake and built in the late 1930s by the CCC), and picnic facilities; and **Pageant Park**, a mile farther east on Rt. 16, is a town-owned park open daily until 10 PM, also with a bathhouse and camping (primarily tenting). **May Pond**, also along Rt. 16 in Barton, is a great spot for swimming, canoeing, and kayaking. **Lake Willoughby** has small public beaches at both its northern and southern tips. **Boulder Beach Day Use Area** (802-584-3820) in Groton State Forest has a public beach, picnic area, snack bar, and bathhouse.

SCENIC DRIVES **Big Falls of the Missisquoi**. River Rd. hugs the river, paralleling Rt. 101 between Troy and North Troy. You can access the falls from either town or from Vielleux Rd. off Rt. 101 at its junction with Rt. 105. This last is the prettiest route, through farmland and through the covered bridge south of the falls. Look for the unmarked pull-off in a grove of pine trees. The falls, thundering through a deep gorge, are awe-inspiringly magnificent.

Hazen's Notch. From Montgomery Center an unpromising narrow road, Rt. 58, climbs steeply east, quickly changing to dirt. In winter it's open only for the first 4 miles and is a popular ski-touring spot. In summer it's a beautiful road, dappled with sunlight through the thick foliage. Look for a picnic spot near the height-of-land, close to a clear roadside spring. A historic site plaque says the road through the high pass was built by General Moses Hazen in 1778–79, commissioned by George Washington himself. The road was begun in 1776, 48 miles to the southeast at the town of Wells River on the Connecticut River, and was intended to reach St. John, Quebec. It was abandoned on this spot in April 1779 when the news that British patrols might use it as an invasion route (it was meant to work the other way) reached the camp at Hazen's Notch.

Christina Tree

BIG FALLS IN THE NORTH TROY AREA

West Burke to Westmore. The stretch of Rt. 5A along Lake Willoughby is one of the most breathtaking anywhere.

Island Pond–Lake Willoughby shortcut. An easy route to navigate from Westmore on Lake Willoughby: Turn north in the middle of the village on Hinton Ridge Rd. and follow it through high, rolling farmland and forest (never mind name changes) until it reaches a T intersection. Turn right and right again onto Rt. 105 into Island Pond. The reverse direction is even more beautiful but tricky at the beginning (left onto Hudson Rd. off Rt. 105 and then your second left onto Westmore Rd.).

Island Pond Loop

This 66-mile loop circles the northeastern corner of Vermont, beginning in Island Pond and heading north on Rt. 114. The Canadian National Railway's Grand Trunk line from Montreal to Portland, Maine, hugs the highway the full 16 miles to Norton. This railway was once Montreal's winter lifeline to Europe, as goods could not be shipped into or out of the frozen port of Montreal during the coldest months. About halfway to Norton, near the south end of long and slender Norton Pond (there's a boat launch on Rt. 114), a gravel road to the left leads into the Bill Sladyk Wildlife Management Area, frequented by hunters, fishermen, and loggers. Just before you reach the tiny village of Norton (opposite slightly larger Stanhope, Quebec), the forest thins out and farmland reappears. Norton was the site of the notorious Earth People's Park, a 1960s-style, loosely governed hippie commune that once numbered hundreds of residents but is now state owned; no one is allowed to live there. The road passes several farms, a school, and the Norton Country Store (open daily 7 AM–9 PM), then swings abruptly eastward to avoid the imposing Canadian port-of-entry.

Eastern Townships detour: Some 15 minutes north on Rt. 147 brings you to Coaticook with "the world's largest pedestrian suspension bridge" spanning Coaticook Gorge. Compton is another 10 minutes' drive north (see *Selective Shopping*). From Coaticook return on scenic Rt. 141 along Lake Wallace and into Canaan.

If you head eastward along the U.S. side of the border, Rt. 114 reenters the forest, passing a series of lakes, most of which are dotted with hunting and fishing camps. The largest of the lakes is Great Averill Pond. For directions to the boat launch, stop by the **Lakeview Store** (open daily 8–7), where owner Priscilla Roy sells the wool that she spins, also weaving supplies and locally handcrafted items. East of the store a road leads to **Quimby Country**, one of Vermont's oldest and most interesting resorts (see the boxed description in *Lodging*). Shortly after passing Big Averill, you leave the St. Lawrence watershed and begin a rapid descent into the Connecticut River Valley. Halfway from Averill to Canaan, the road skirts the south shore of sizable Wallace Pond, almost entirely within the province of Quebec.

Canaan, 14 miles east of Norton, is a pleasant pocket of civilization with a handsome green, Fletcher Park, that features a lovely Greek Revival building in its far corner. Built as a tavern in 1846 and said to have served for a while as the northernmost U.S. stop on the Underground Railroad, this is now the **Alice M. Ward Memorial Library** (802-266-7135), worth a stop to see the Canaan Historical Society's changing exhibits upstairs. A covered bridge once spanned the Connecticut River here, connecting it with West Stewartstown, New Hampshire. Today you barely notice the river, here just a fledgling stream spanned by a brief bridge. Turn north along this stream if you want to see the village of Beecher Falls, 2 miles north. The small, sagging village is dominated by the huge Ethan Allen Furniture plant (closed at this writing) and is a Canadian border crossing. Across another brief bridge is Stewartstown, New Hampshire.

In reality these far corners of Vermont and New Hampshire form a region of their own, a fishing, snowmobiling, and moose-watching mecca known by various names but most accurately as the **Connecticut Lakes**. You might want to detour north on Rt. 3 in New Hampshire (Vermont ends at Beecher Falls). A state-operated **Great North Woods Welcome Center**, open daily 9–7, weekends 8–8 (with restrooms), south of Pittsburg orients visitors to the series of four lakes strung along the 22 semi-wilderness miles north of town (greatnorthwoods.org). This stretch of Rt. 3 is known as "Moose Alley" for reasons easy to grasp if you drive it on a summer evening. Fishing lodges and rental camps, salted away around these lakes, far outnumber lodging options contained in the entire vast area of Vermont covered by this chapter, but you see few from the road. Die-hard Connecticut River buffs may want to hike in to its source, a small pond accessible via a path beside the Rt. 3 border station (restrooms).

From Canaan the loop turns south on Rt. 102, through river-bottom farmland, through Lemington, and past the impressively long **Columbia covered bridge**, which demands a photo stop. This stretch of the river valley alternately narrows and widens, and the road tunnels through forest, broken occasionally by farms, fields, and glimpses of impressive mountains. In Bloomfield (the store may or may not be open) the Grand Trunk railroad line angles east across the road, heading for Portland. Here our route turns west on Rt. 105 (it's 16 miles back to Island Pond).

For another rewarding detour, however, continue at least the mile down Rt. 102 to the wooded path (on the left) into **Brunswick Springs**, once the site of a mineral springs resort. At this sacred Abenaki site, the resort's buildings repeatedly burned; only their foundations and an eerie cement stairway leading down to the riverbank remain. Please be respectful of the property, now owned by a local Abenaki group. Water from the sulfur springs still runs from spigots. Park next to the white wooden former town hall (on your left, heading south). The road in is usually chained off. It's roughly a 15-minute walk.

Another 4 miles south on Rt. 102 (and 5 miles in on a dirt road) brings you to **Maidstone State Park**, offering camping and swimming as well as fishing. The Connecticut River widens noticeably the farther south you drive on Rt. 102, and views of the White Mountains are increasingly dramatic. If you continue another 7 miles south to Guildhall, you are informed by a billboard-sized sign that the town was "discovered" in 1754, chartered in 1761, and settled in 1764, making it the oldest town in northeastern Vermont (by contrast, Norton was not settled until 1860). An attractive, square green is flanked by historically interesting buildings: a tiny courthouse, church, town hall (the Guild Hall, 1798), and an ornate 1909 Classical Revival library with stained-glass windows. An unassuming white-clapboard house serves as a county lockup.

Two miles downriver from Guildhall, a town road marked GRANBY runs west off Rt. 102, beginning as a paved road but becoming gravel well before reaching the tiny hamlets of Granby and Gallup Mills, about 8 miles from Rt. 102. This is wild, wooded, and boggy country, good for spotting moose and bear. Lumber camps and sawmills once peppered this area, and there was even a steam railway. The road finally descends about 8 miles west of Granby to reach Rt. 114, joining it a couple of miles north of East Burke. Take Rt. 114 some 12 miles north through rolling, mixed farm- and forestland to its junction with Rt. 105, 2 miles west of Island Pond.

❄ Winter Sports

CROSS-COUNTRY SKIING **Hazen's Notch Association** (802-326-4799; hazensnotch.org), welcome center at 1423 Hazen's Notch Rd. (Rt. 58), Montgomery Center. One of the first nonprofit ski centers in Vermont, with 39 trails on 2,500 acres of private land, 40 km meticulously tracked for cross-country and snowshoeing (also see *Hiking*). Trails offer fine views of Jay Peak and the Cold Hollow Mountains and connect with the Catamount Trail. Early and late in the season, this tends to be one of half a dozen cross-country networks in New England that have snow (elevation: 900–2,800 feet). Ten miles of dedicated snowshoe trails include the path up Burnt Mountain. Lessons and rentals, also full-moon snowshoe tours. No dogs or walking please. *Note:* A trail fee is charged in winter.

Jay Peak Ski Touring Center (800-451-4449, 4850 Rte. 242, Jay. The resort maintains 20 km of groomed cross-country trails.

North Woods Stewardship Center (802-723-6551; northwoodscenter.org), 10 Mile Square Rd., East Charleston (5 miles west of Island Pond off Rt. 105), is a

1,700-acre preserve with 35 km of groomed skiing and snowshoeing trails. Rentals and guided tours are offered.

DOWNHILL SKIING ✏ **Jay Peak** (information and reservations 802-988-2611; 800-451-4449 including Canada; snow conditions 802-988-9601; jaypeakresort.com). In winter, storms sweep down from Canada or roll in from Lake Champlain, showering the clutch of mountains around Jay with dependable quantities of snow. Admittedly, given its exposed position, Jay can be windy and frigid in January and February (we try to visit in March), the reason—along with spectacular snowfall—that regulars are drawn by "off-piste" skiing through glades and into the backcountry beyond. In nearby Hazen's Notch, cross-country skiers also find some of the most dependably snowy and beautiful trails in New England.

While there's an easy-intermediate trail (Northway) off the summit, Jay Peak regulars duck into glades right off the top. Jay's 20 glades and extreme chutes are what draw many of its regulars, who like to strike out into 150 acres of backcountry terrain. Unlike regular runs, wooded trails ("glades") cannot be covered by human-made snow and so require a lot of the natural stuff, which is what Jay Peak has in spades: an average of 330 inches annually. That's twice the snow many New England areas receive.

For three decades the resort's owners were Montreal based, but in 2008 Jay's long-time president and CEO, Bill Stenger, acquired it and announced development plans totaling $96 million. At this writing a new base lodge, to include a 57-unit hotel, is due for completion this coming ski season. Plans then call for the demolition of the present (vintage-1970s) Hotel Jay, replacing it with a 120-unit hotel. (See also Jay Resort under *Lodging*).

The original trails here are stateside, on a shoulder of Jay Peak. Still considered some of the toughest runs in Vermont, they were carved 30 years ago by local residents. An enterprising Kiwanis group (it included the parish priest) convinced the Vermont Legislature to reroute existing roads up over the high ridge from which Jay's access road rises, thus linking it to northwestern Vermont as well as to the Northeast Kingdom. They imported an Austrian skimeister to create a true trail system and ski school. In the early 1960s Weyerhaeuser Corporation acquired the ski area and installed a Swiss-built tramway to Jay's Peak, which it topped with a Sky Haus tram station, a building that emphasizes the crest of the summit and gives it a distinctly Matterhorn-like cap.

Lifts: 60-passenger aerial tramway; 3 quad chairs, 1 triple, 1 double; 1 T-bar.

Vertical drop: 2,153 feet.

Trails and slopes: 76 trails, glades, and chutes totaling more than 50 miles of skiing, spread over 2 peaks, connected by a ridgeline; 100+ acres of gladed terrain.

Off-piste skiing: 200 acres.

Snowboarding: 4 terrain parks; board demo center, rentals, instruction.

Snowmaking: 80 percent of the total 385 acres.

Snowshoeing: Weekly snowshoeing walks led by a naturalist.

Facilities: Austria Haus and Tram Haus base lodges with cafeteria, pub, and ski and rental shop. Sky Haus cafeteria at the summit. Nursery and day care facilities. Rentals. A lighted skating rink and skate rentals. Van service is offered from

Burlington International Airport (80 miles away) and from the Amtrak station in St. Albans (a 45-minute drive).

Ski school: U.S.- and Canadian-certified instructors, adult and junior racing clinics, American Teaching Method (ATM). Telemarking instruction and rentals offered.

For children: Mountain Explorers for both skiing and snowboarding for 5- to 12-year-old group, kinderschool for ages 2–5. Day care for ages 2–7.

Rates: $65 adult, $45 junior (14 and under), but far cheaper for multidays and with lodging packages.

SLEIGH RIDES **Phil & Karen's Sleigh/Hayrides** (802-744-9928), 143 Kennison Rd., Westfield. Old-fashioned sleigh or hayrides drawn by Belgian horses are offered through meadows and along a quiet road.

Perry Farm (802-754-2396) in Brownington offers hay- and sleigh rides for groups of up to 10 people. At **Galloping Acres** (802-754-2337), Brownington Center, wagon and sleigh rides are offered.

SNOWMOBILING *Northeast Kingdom Snowmobile Map* is free from the **Northeast Kingdom Chamber of Commerce** (800-639-6379). Island Pond is the snowmobiling capital of the Kingdom, from which groomed VAST (**Vermont Association of Snow Travelers**; vtvast.org) trails radiate in all directions. The local Brighton Snowmobile Club maintains a snow phone: 802-723-4316. **Kingdom Cat Corp.** (802-723-9702; kingdomcat.com) on Cross St. in Island Pond is the snowmobile rental operation in the area, and offers guided tours.

❊ Green Space

Note: For more information on Vermont state parks, visit vtstateparks.com.

Brighton State Park (802-723-4360), Island Pond, 2 miles east on Rt. 105 to State Park Rd. Open mid-May–mid-Oct. Campsites are nestled in a stand of white birch trees on Spectacle Pond: 63 tent/trailer sites, 21 lean-tos, and a rental cabin. The park includes frontage on the south shore of Island Pond, where there's a day-use area that features a sandy beach (check to make sure it's open), a bathhouse with restrooms, and rental boats. Hiking trails include a leisurely trek to Indian Point and wildlife. Watch for moose and loons.

Maidstone State Park (802-676-3930), RR 1, Box 388, Brunswick 05905. Open Memorial Day–Labor Day. Five miles south of Bloomfield on Rt. 102, then 5 miles on dirt road, this is the most remote Vermont state park and retains much of its wilderness forest of maple, beech, and hemlock. The park's camping and day-use facilities are on Maidstone Lake, one of the most pristine in Vermont. It's home to lake trout, rainbow trout, and brookies. Moose sightings and the call of the loon are common. There's a beach, picnic area, picnic shelter, hiking trails, 45 tent/trailer sites, and 37 lean-tos.

North Woods Stewardship Center (802-723-6551; northwoodscenter.org), 10 Mile Square Rd., East Charleston (5 miles west of Island Pond), is a 1,700-acre preserve with 40 km of walking/skiing and snowshoeing trails. Aside from its formal nature hikes, guided canoeing, and frequent outreach programs, the center also serves as an informal clearinghouse for local canoe, fishing, tracking, and nature guides.

Bill Sladyk Wildlife Management Area, off Rt. 114, south of Norton Pond: 9,500 forested acres, also accessible via a gravel road past Holland Pond from Holland Village, 11 miles east of Derby. A detailed map is available from the **Fish and Wildlife Department** in Waterbury (802-241-3700).

& **Silvio O. Conte National Fish and Wildlife Refuge, Nulhegan Basin Division** (802-962-5240; nulhegan.com), 5360 Rt. 105, Brunswick. Mailing address: P.O. Box 2127, Island Pond 05846. In 1999 when the Champion International Corporation announced plans to sell its holdings in Essex County, the U.S. Fish and Wildlife Service purchased this 26,000-acre tract (roughly 10 miles in diameter) that's home to rare animals and migratory birds. The Vermont Agency of Natural Resources acquired some 22,000 adjoining acres to form the West Mountain Wildlife Management Area; another 84,000 acres surrounding these preserves continue to be logged but with easements to protect their development. Over 100 species of birds nest in the Nulhegan Basin, which is home to moose, black bear, beaver, fisher, white-tailed deer, and coyote. The Nulhegan River and its tributaries harbor brook trout, bullhead, chain pickerel, chub, and more. The refuge is open to hunting, fishing, trapping, bird-watching, and hiking. It includes 40 miles of gravel roads, 17 miles of wooded pathways, and the Mollie Beattie Bog interpretive boardwalk (handicapped accessible). No biking. Request a map.

✳ Lodging

RESORTS ❧ **Jay Peak Resort** (800-451-4449; jaypeakresort.com), Rt. 242, Jay 05859. For the 2009 ski season a new 57-unit slope-side hotel is slated to open, supplementing the Hotel Jay, a tired but adequate lodge with 48 big rooms, a pleasant public dining room, a game room, a family room, sauna and Jacuzzi, and an outdoor pool (summer only). A two-day package including lift, lodging, and dinner is $336.88 per person. Kids 14 and under stay and ski free; you're charged only for meals. Less off-season. *Condominiums:* **Jay Peak Condominiums**. A total of 263 condos and town houses have been constructed in clusters over the years and vary widely in look and size, studios to five-bedrooms; all have fireplace, living room, and fully equipped kitchen. Most are trailside.

Hovey Manor (800-661-2412; hoveymanor.com), 575 Hovey Rd., North Hatley, Quebec, Canada J0B 2C0. A pillared southern-style lakeside mansion built in 1900 by the president of Georgia Power, set in 25 acres with lovely English gardens on the shore of Lake Massawipi. Owned by the Stafford family since 1979, the resort is a member of Relais & Chateaux. The 36 guest rooms and five suites are divided among the original mansion, icehouse, pump house, electric house, and caretaker's residence; several of the most luxurious are squirreled away in the trees, atop a bluff above the hotel, with decks overlooking the lake. They vary in size and decor, but most have lake views, many with fireplace, Jacuzzi, and balcony. Amenities include two beaches, a lakeside pool, exercise room, access to kayaks and sailboats, massage, yoga, and cross-country ski trails. Dining is central to the experience here. In addition to the formal dining room, a fireside pub is the venue for lunch, served in-season on the lakeside terrace. $260–590 MAP per couple (Canadian) for rooms, $530–920 per couple MAP per suite. Inquire about packages. Also see *Dining Out.*

∞ **Auberge Ripplecove & Spa** (800-668-4296; ripplecove.com), 700 Ripplecove, Ayer's Cliff, Quebec, Canada JOB 1CO. Founded by members of the Stafford family as a rough-hewn fishing lodge back in the 1940s, this is now another romantic resort, rivaling Hovey Manor both in food and facilities. You'll find 26 rooms, five suites, two cottages, 12 acres, and a recently added rustic-style spa with a lake view. Every room is different. Eighty percent have fireplaces and a lake view, and many offer fireplace and whirlpool tub. There's also the original family-friendly log cabin (owned by the Staffords in 1945 when there was no electricity) and another three-bedroom cottage with a Jacuzzi, private pool, and water views. Here dining is also central to the experience, consciously a shade less "haute" than Hovey Manor. Owned by a different branch of the Stafford family, the two compete. It's literally in a cove near the southern end of Lake Massawipi. Heated pool, tennis court, bike path (bikes available). $266–584 (Canadian) per couple MAP per room, gratuity included, $520–630 per suite, more for the cabin and cottage.

INNS AND B&BS

Newport/Derby Line Area

🐾 🖊 ♿ "1" **Cliff Haven Farm Bed & Breakfast** (802-334-2401; cliffhaven farmbedandbreakfast.com), 5463 Lake Rd., Newport Center 05857. Jacques and Mim LeBlanc's 19th-century post-and-beam farmhouse is a real gem. Set in their 300 acres, it overlooks Lake Memphremagog from a rise—which continues to rise through meadows to a swim pond near the height of their land. Our ground-floor guest room was really a spacious suite, tastefully and comfortably decorated. All three guest rooms have private bath with whirlpool tub; they're also fitted with gas fireplace, antiques, TV/VCR, microwave, and small fridge. $135–175 includes a full breakfast and afternoon tea, less if you stay three nights.

Lake Salem Inn (802-766-5560; lake saleminn.com), 1273 Rt. 105, Derby 05829. This attractive inn with its columned porch is set on 7 acres overlooking Lake Salem. Joe and Mo Profera offer four guest rooms, all with private bath. The spacious first-floor "library" ($125) has a queen-sized sleigh bed and a sitting area, the Zen Room ($125) is airy and tranquil, and both the Wyoming Room and the Hideaway have lake views and private decks ($155). Common space includes a TV, books, and games; there's a back deck and boat dock. Rates include a full breakfast, and dinner (Joe used to own an Italian restaurant) is available on request. No children, please. A chef in his previous life, Joe is delighted to prepare dinner for his guests, even for nonguests on request (see *Dining Out*).

"1" **Water's Edge B&B** (802-334-7726; watersedgebnb.com), 324 Wishing Well Ave., Newport 05855. Several miles north of downtown Newport, Pat Bryan's contemporary house sits right on the edge of Lake Memphremagog. Common space is tasteful and includes a deck. The three guest rooms include a queen room with a lake view ($90), a splendid corner queen with two windows on the lake ($110), and a suite with a sitting area and gas stove ($145). All rooms have private bath and TV. In summer guests have use of the canoe, rowboat, and dock; in winter there's snowmobile and ice-fishing access right out the front door. Bird-watching year-round. Rates include a full breakfast. Residents include two gentle Saint Bernards.

Garden of Edie Bed & Breakfast (802-766-8116; gardenofedie.com),

◎ 🐾 ✎ **Quimby Country** (802-822-5533; quimby country.com), P.O. Box 20, Averill 05901. This is one of Vermont's most historic and most rustic resorts. Less than 3 miles from Canada and 10 miles from New Hampshire, Quimby first opened as a fishing lodge in 1894. It's set in literally thousands of acres of woodland, fac-ing Forest Lake and a

QUIMBY COUNTRY

Christina Tree

short walk in the woods from 1,200-acre Great Averill Pond. Each of the well-spaced 20 cottages is different, but all have woodstoves in their living rooms and are named for a fishing fly. In the lodge a big stone hearth is the focal point of the book-lined common room. Many of the Adirondack-style furnishings date back to the 1890s, as do the polished wooden tables in the spacious old-fashioned dining room and the rockers lining the porch, over-looking Forest Lake.

Under the management of Hortense Quimby (daughter of the founder), this evolved into a family-oriented resort, attracting an elite following so fiercely loyal that on Miss Quimby's death in the 1960s, a number of regulars formed a corporation to buy it and perpetuate its special ambience. Thanks to innkeeper Joanie Binns, who has been at Quimby's one way or another for more than 30 years, newcomers quickly feel as welcome as multi-generationers. When the place is in full operation, July–late Aug., the staff top two dozen and guests are limited to 70. All three meals are served.

2005 Herrick Rd., Derby 05819. High on a ridge that seems to define the border between Vermont and Quebec, with 90- to 100-mile views. This is a contemporary house with three com-fortable guest rooms (request one with a view), shared and private baths. The ebullient hostess serves a full break-fast, perhaps Swedish pancakes, and afternoon specialty cakes; she is a baker. $115–125 per couple.

The Birchwood B&B (802-873-9104;), 502 Main St., Derby Line 05830. Betty and Dick Fletcher's hand-some 1920s village house has three spacious, antiques-furnished (the cou-ple owns an antiques store), immacu-late bedrooms with private bath: the Double Bed Chamber (antique pineapple bed), the blue-and-white Queen Canopy Chamber, and the green-and-pink Twin Bed Room. The

There's a supervised children's program for ages 5–15, as well as a full program of family-inclusive happenings such as picnics on a remote beach and sunset cookouts and music at "The Rocks" on Big Averill. Amenities include kayaks, canoes and sailboats, a tennis court, playground, and rec hall. Rates are $164–199 per adult, $80–97 per child depending on age and week, including all three meals and the kids' program, which offers swimming, hiking, overnight camping, and rainy-day activities. Reasonable rates during spring fishing season (May 10–June 27), and again Aug. 30–foliage season, when cottages are available on a housekeeping basis ($97 single, $142 double, $56 per additional person, $34 per child 16 and under) and it's quiet enough to hear the lake ripple and leaves fall. This is a great place for birders and naturalists of all kinds (ask about the peat bog), for walkers, and for good conversation, weddings, and family reunions.

Christina Tree

fireplace in the formally furnished living room is frequently lit, and guests gather around the long formal dining table for full, candlelit breakfasts. $120–125 includes breakfast. Children 12 years and older please.

Jay Peak Area
Montgomery House B&B (802-326-3269; montgomeryhouseinn.com), 2057 N. Main St. (Rte. 118), Montgomery 05470. A white-pillared brick inn built in 1803 as the Montgomery Village stage stop, this is an appealing place to stay. Innkeepers Deb and Dr. Bob Winders offer eight attractive rooms (private baths) and seven suites (one with three bedrooms) divided between the main inn and neighboring Burdette House with its back deck (Adirondack chairs are also positioned behind the inn) with a view of Hazen's

Notch. Some have fireplace or wood-burning stove and steam shower or whirlpool bath. The inn itself also offers a small reading/talking area, warmed by a soapstone stove off a cozy taproom; there's a low-beamed, charming dining room (see *Dining Out*). This is not a place for children. Beyond the porch is the village with its six covered bridges, and from the back there is a hot tub under the gazebo with a view of Hazen's Notch, a venue for small weddings. Summer is low season: $135 per room, $185–215 per suite B&B. Ski season: $176 for rooms, from $225 for suites.

☼ "¶" Phineas Swann (802-326-4306; phineasswann.com), 195 Main St., Montgomery Center 05471. John Perkins and Jay Kerch have brought considerable skill, resources, and energy to this delightful village B&B. It's all about fantasy, fun—and dogs. Jay, a former New York City interior decorator, has created three rooms, four attractive suites, and two separate one-bedroom apartments with kitchens in the River House Annex right on the Trout River (out back). John is a former international banker and an enthusiastic chef. Rooms are elaborately decorated, and there's an exuberance to everything. "One-bedrooms" (with a sitting area) are $99–249; two-bedroom suites with a living room and sleep sofa are $119–299; weekly rates. B&B in the main inn is $89–249, depending on the room and size. Dogs, even more than one, are very welcome (no extra charge and hosted by two resident canines) in the Carriage House and River House suites, A four-course, candlelit dinner is available with 24-hour advance notice ($59 per person), and family-style meals are served to guests in the River House ($22–36). Check the Web site for a slew of special packages.

"¶" Jay Village Inn (802-988-2306; stayatjay.com), 1078 Rt. 242, Jay 05859. Three miles downhill from Jay Peak in Jay Four Corners, this classic log ski lodge is best known as a convivial restaurant and pub—but the rooms upstairs have been tastefully refurbished, all with private bath. There are seven double rooms, varying in size and shape, and four family suites (sleeping four to five). The quietest rooms are on the third floor and include our favorite, with a fireplace and sleigh bed. In summer there's a heated pool, and the outside hot tub gets year-round use. From $69 in summer and fall; during ski season from $80 weekdays; $95–225 for rooms, $200–300 for an apartment sleeping up to 12. No breakfast, but the Jay Country Store across the road serves a good one. Also see *Dining Out*.

∞ Inglenook Lodge (802-988-2880; 800-331-4346; inglenookvermont.com), Rt. 242, Jay 05859. This is a big, friendly, family-owned and -geared ski lodge just 2 miles from Jay Peak. The focal point is a sunken living room around an open, circular hearth; there's an indoor pool and Jacuzzi as well as game room and full-service restaurant and bar. The 18 guest rooms (private baths) include 6 with queen beds. Eight are family sized with double beds and bunks, and there are two suites. $89 per couple B&B in summer, $149 per person ski package. Inquire about condo rentals.

☼ ✍ Riverbend B&B (802-744-9991; riverbendvt.com), 6198 Rt. 100, Troy 05868. A Victorian farmhouse on the edge of the village offers 15 acres on the Missisquoi River. Innkeepers Paul Becker and Jim McKimm enjoy introducing guests to the delights of paddling (canoes available). The house offers three suites with private bath. This is a comfortable, casual place with fireplaces in the dining room and library. Birders are particularly welcome. $95 per couple weekends, $89 weekdays, $35 per extra adult, $15 per child over age 5, full breakfast included. $10 a night per (well-mannered) pet.

Couture's Maple Shop and Bed & Breakfast (802-744-2733; 800-845-2733; maplesyrupvermont.com), 560 Rt. 100, Westfield 05874-9197. Pauline and Jacques Couture raised six children in this 1892 farmhouse while also maintaining a dairy farm and sizable maple syrup business. Three guest rooms with queen-sized bed and pull-out couch share a bath; a family room (private bath) sleeps six. The cow barn is out the back door, and the sugarhouse is just up the hill. $90 per couple ($20 per extra person) includes a full breakfast served in the newly renovated farm kitchen.

In the Barton area

🎣 ⚔ "1" **Rodgers Country Inn** (802-525-6677; 800-729-1704; rodgers countryinn.com), 582 Rodgers Rd., West Glover 05875. Not far from Shadow Lake, this proud old farmhouse has been in Jim Rodgers's family since the 1800s. Far from any traffic, it's surrounded by its 350 acres, beckoning guests out for a walk down to the beaver pond or a bike along miles of hard-packed farm roads. Shadow Lake is good for swimming, boating, and fishing. There's plenty of common space—an enclosed porch, living rooms (flat-screen TV and VCR), and a game room with Ping-Pong table. We've stopped by over the years but it wasn't until we spent a night here this year that we realized what makes this place so special: Nancy Rodgers serves meals family-style in the bright dining room off her open kitchen. The food is farm fresh and delicious, and there's good conversation between guests and hosts. Dinner is, however, optional ($15 per adult, $7 per child), and guests can have as much privacy as they wish. Breakfast is full, included in B&B rates: $50 single, $70 per couple; MAP (dinner included) is $65 per adult MAP, $22.50 per child under 12 ($275/$135 per week). Snowmobilers and cross-country skiers (Craftsbury Outdoor Center is nearby) are both welcome. Inquire about a new, winterized cabin, sleeping six to eight with direct access to VAST trails ($600–700 per week) near the beaver pond and an older, seasonal one, sleeping seven, by a small pond ($500 per week) off by its own private pond. Weekend rentals are available.

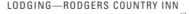 **Maple Manor B&B** (802-525-9591; maple-manor.com), 77 Maple Lane, West Glover 05875. This elaborate mansion with more than a touch of fantasy is an anomaly in the surrounding farmscape, a 250-acre estate specializing in elaborate weddings. The original farmhouse has been expanded

LODGING—RODGERS COUNTRY INN

Christina Tree

and fitted with French doors, a conservatory, and many large windows through which the light streams. Both the common rooms and three guest rooms are exuberantly decorated. $125–225 per night includes a three-course candlelit breakfast served at the formally set dining room table, overlooking the flower gardens and pool. The top floor of the equestrian barn can accommodate groups of up to 200 for wedding receptions. Sleigh rides are offered in winter.

🐾 ❧ **Angie's Haven** (802-754-6182), 2587 Schoolhouse Rd., Brownington 05860. This renovated 1890s farmhouse with a contemporary addition is sited on a back road, surrounded by rolling fields. Louise Evens offers three rooms, one on the ground floor that's handicapped accessible (including the bath) with twin beds and a view of Willoughby Gap ($120–140). Upstairs, a suite with twin beds (which can be a king) offers this same view and has a sitting area and Jacuzzi tub ($140). A smaller room with a double bed also has a private bath (with shower, $110). Add $25 for a third person; $10 less for single occupancy. Rates include a full breakfast. Inquire about special packages. Bicyclists especially welcome.

On Lake Willoughby
❧ **WilloughVale Inn on Lake Willoughby** (802-525-4123; 800-594-9102; willoughvale.com), RR 2, Box 403, Westmore 05860. This contemporary, traditionally designed inn and cottages now represent the only lodging to be had on Vermont's most dramatic lake. Windows maximize the view. Guest rooms in the inn itself include three "luxury suites" with fireside Jacuzzi and private porch, one with a living/dining room and kitchen, and seven attractive rooms with private bath, phone, and TV (one handicapped

accessible). There are four housekeeping cottages (one and two bedrooms) with fireplaces across the road, right on the lake and four new two-bedroom "lakeview" cottages up behind and above the inn. A taproom and light dinners are available; breakfast is also available for guests. Standard rooms with queen beds in the main inn begin at $125 midweek in winter and $153 in summer and fall; the Lupine Room, with four-poster and Jacuzzi, ranges $193–203; weekly rates are offered. The Pisgah Cottage with a Jacuzzi, living room with fireplace, pullout sofa bed, and eat-in kitchen as well as deck and private dock is $230 midweek in winter, $279–289 in high season. All rates are higher during holiday periods and lowest Mar.–June when, honestly, you would have to pay us to be here. This is a luxurious but lonely spot. WilloughVale is owned and operated by the Gameroff family, who also own the Green Mountain Inn in Stowe. There is an impersonal feel, and the restaurant (see *Dining Out*) is opened only for dinner and on a varying schedule (call ahead).

Island Pond
The Lakefront Inn & Motel (802-723-6507; lakefrontinn.com), 127 Cross St., Island Pond 05846. A two-story motel and a main building housing the lobby and suites with one or two bedrooms in the center of the village overlooking the lake. Six of the 20 units have built-in kitchenettes. A floating dock is reserved for motel guests only during summer months, and a heated multibay garage is available for guests to work on servicing their snowmobiles in winter. Just across the way are public tennis courts, a beach, a picnic area, a boat launch, a lighted ice hockey rink, and a children's playground. Rates range from $119 based on double occupancy to

$325 for a large family suite based on occupancy of six in winter (high season), $20 per extra person. Robert and Sharon Dexter are the innkeepers.

CAMPGROUNDS See Brighton State Park and Maidstone State Park in *Green Space.*

White Caps Campground (802-467-3345; whitecapscampground.com), 5659 Rt. 5A, is sited at the southern tip of Lake Willoughby, with electric, water, and sewer hookups, a camp store, laundry facilities, rental RV units, rental kayaks and canoes.

Note: Reasonably priced rentals abound in this area. See the Web sites listed under *Guidance* or Google "vacation rentals" + "Vermont."

✳ Where to Eat

DINING OUT *Note:* **Hovey Manor** (hoveymanor.com) in North Hatley, Quebec, and **Auberge Ripplecove** (ripplecove.com) in Ayer's Cliff (see *Lodging*) represent superb gastronomy, certainly this area's destination dining and in a class of their own. Check their Web sites for current menus. Admittedly, these inns are pricey, but Lake Massawippi offers a choice of lodging (see easterntownships.org). Serious foodies should dine at both of these inns at least once in their lifetime.

In the Newport and Lakes Area
WilloughVale Inn (802-525-2123; willoughvale.com), Rt. 5A, Westmore. Open nightly in July and Aug. and Labor Day–Columbus Day; Thu.–Sat. during the Christmas and ice-fishing seasons, but call to check. The Willoughby Room and less formal Tap Room both overlook Lake Willoughby. Entrées range from $15.95 (stuffed chicken breast) to $22.95 (New York strip sirloin). You can always also get a burger.

Lago Trattoria (802-334-8222; lago trattoria.com), 95 Main St., Newport. Open nightly from 5 PM. The decor is modern Italian and chef-owner Frank Richardi claims not to fry anything except calamari. The menu includes pastas and staples like chicken Marsala and cacciatore. Pizzas from $11, otherwise entrées $16–32.

⌇ **Eastside** (802-334-2340), 47 Landing St., Newport. Open for lunch and dinner weekdays, breakfast too on weekends. A large old landmark the best lake view of any restaurant in town, also a seasonal outdoor deck and dock. The reasonably priced lunch menu might include lamb stew and biscuits or grilled chicken salad. The salad bar can be a meal in itself. Many locals come just for dessert (try the pecan ribbon). Dinner entrées range from $12.95 for chicken 'n biscuits, to $26.95 for prime rib and crab legs. On our last visit two different kinds of fish were baked to death, but the limitless salad bar (mixed greens) saved the meal. Children's menu.

Derby Cow Palace (802-766-4724), Main St. (Rt. 5), Derby. Open at noon on weekends, from 3 PM weekdays. Doug Nelson, owner of the largest local dairy operation and of Cow Town Elk Ranch, operates this large, log restaurant specializing in beef, from burgers to prime rib. Fully licensed, with a bar menu.

Salem Lake Inn (802-766-5560), 1273 Rt. 105, Derby. Joe Profera was a restaurateur in his previous life. He offers a choice of four-course ($25) or seven-course ($75) Italian dinners in his gracious lakeside inn by reservation.

⌇ **Quimby Country** (802-822-5533; quimbycountry.com), off Rt. 114, Averill (see *Lodging*). Open by reservation to nonguests, last week of June–last week in Aug., serving a very full breakfast ($13) and a generous, delicious dinner (BYOB) featuring fresh, local produce, on-premises daily baking, and a limited menu as well as weekly lobster bakes ($35). Children's menu.

In the Jay Peak Area

Montgomery House B&B (802-326-3269), 2057 N. Main St. (Rt. 118), Montgomery Village. Dinner is served Fri.–Sun. by reservation, with orders placed by 1 PM. Closed Nov., May. The low-beamed dining room of this delightful old inn is a romantic setting for candlelit dinners. A choice of entrées ranges from fresh corn chowder and veal sausage sandwich ($10.50) to rack of lamb ($21) and includes beef burgundy ($15). Wine and beer are served.

Black Bear Restaurant at the Jay Village Inn (802-988-2306), 1078 Rt. 242, Jay. Open nightly from 4. The liveliest dining scene on the Jay side of the mountain. A warm, informal lodge atmosphere with a big stone fireplace at the center of the dining room and the pub tucked into its own space. From pastas, reasonably priced specials, and slow-smoked BBQ ribs to steak au poivre, lamb loin, and garlic sautéed shrimps and scallops.

The Belfry (802-326-4400), Rt. 242, between Montgomery Center and the Jay Peak access road. Open nightly 4–9, later on weekends. No reservations, and during ski season you'd better get here early (or late) if you want a booth. Built in 1902 as a schoolhouse, this is the area's most popular pub, and the food's good, thanks to longtime manager Chantal Pothier who now owns it, along with Marty Lumbra, who drives the local school bus. If you've been here a day or two, chances are you will recognize someone in the crowd around the mirrored oak-and-marble back bar. The soup is homemade, and the blackboard lists daily specials, like pan-blackened fish and grilled lamb chops. The set menu features "Belfry Steak" ("price depends on the chef's mood"), salads, burgers, and deep-fried mushrooms. Wednesday is Italian night. Inquire about music.

Inglenook Lodge (802-988-2880), Rt. 202, Jay. The menu changes frequently but this big, cheerful lodge dining room is always a good deal, specializing in complete dinners with a soup and salad bar.

North Troy Village Restaurant (802-988-4063), Main St., North Troy. Open Thu.–Sun. at 5 PM. Irene McDermott and chef Gary Birchard ("The Bear") have an enthusiastic following. The attractive dining room in this 1890s village hotel is the scene of memorable meals. The menu is extensive and features seafood, pastas, prime rib specials, and dinners for two such as rack of lamb and broiled seafood specialty dishes. There's a kids' menu and "mini-meals," like a five-ounce tournedo (why don't other restaurant do this?) as well as a burger. Warning: The "Little Bear Cut" is enormous. Entrées from $9.95 for pastas to $25.95 for rack of lamb. All come with soup and salad, homemade bread, and veggies.

Hidden Country Restaurant (802-744-6149), Rt. 100, Lowell. Open Wed.–Sat. 4:30–9 PM, Sun. 8–11 AM and noon–8. Begun in 1988 by Joe St. Onge, this restaurant draws diners from throughout the Kingdom. Plenty of atmosphere (must be seen to be appreciated). The specialties are old-fashioned pot roast ($13.95), homemade potpies ($14.95), and prime rib ($15.95–22.95). Rolls and desserts are homemade, and the specialty cocktails and Friday fish fry are famous. There's a trout pond for paid fishing and an eight-hole chip-and-putt golf course. No credit cards.

☞ **Paddington's** (802-326-3232), English Rose Inn, 195 Rt. 242, between Jay Peak and Montgomery Center. Open Thu.–Sun. 5–9:30. We have only breakfasted here, but chef-owners Gary and Mary Jane Bouchard-Pike both hold culinary school degrees and have spent their lives in the restaurant business. Children's menu available.

EATING OUT

For breakfast and lunch

The Brown Cow (802-334-7887), 350 E. Main St., Newport, open daily 5 AM–1 PM, Sun. 6–1. This is a great spot to linger over breakfast. Chef salads, steak dinners, homemade ice cream on homemade pie.

Newport Natural Foods Café (802-334-2626), 194 Main St., Newport. Open Mon.–Sat. 8–4, Sun. 10–4, longer hours in summer. This recently expanded café offers a choice of a regular menu as well as vegan and vegetarian, a variety of paninis, soups, and wraps, smoked tempeh, a good salad bar, and wholesome baked goods.

In the Jay area

🐾 ☞ **Bernie's Café** (802-326-4682), Main St., Montgomery Center. Open 6:30 AM–10 PM. Bigger than it looks from its greenhouse-style front, this is a genuine gathering spot for the area. Breakfast options include bagels and eggs any style, and the breads are baked daily, for sale separately as well as used in sandwiches. Soups are a luncheon specialty, and at dinner the menu ranges from sautéed scampi through pastas. Fully licensed with a pub in back. Chef-owner John Boucher frequently presides behind the counter.

ᵀ **Trout River Traders** (802-326-3058; troutrivertraders.com), Montgomery Center. Open 9–5 daily. This is a great lunch stop, good for soups from scratch, good chili, overstuffed sandwiches such as chicken with dill. All meats are roasted on the premises, and bread is fresh baked. Cappuccino, lattes, and espresso are served at the soda fountain, along with New York egg creams and Italian cream sodas. Some tables, overstuffed chairs, a woodstove in winter.

Junction 101 Restaurant (802-744-2700), 4278 Rt. 100, Troy. Open daily. Tina Farrell, chef-owner, offers good "affordable family dining": steak, seafood, and nightly specials, full-service bar, friendly service.

Jay Village Store (802-988-4040), Rt. 242, Jay Village. Grill operates daily 6 AM–3 PM, sandwiches until closing (9 PM); Sun. from 7:30. We can vouch for breakfast. Paninis are the house specialty. Request the "Lumberjack"

TROUT RIVER TRADERS

Christina Tree

(green onions, turkey, caramelized onions, maple mayo, and Vermont cheese). Seating at the counter and at tables in the solarium.

In the Lake Willoughby area

Restaurant at Robin's Roost (802-525-4347), 280 Rt. 5A, just north of Lake Willoughby. Open Thu.–Fri. 11–9, Sat.–Sun. 8–9. Chef-owner Ed Levie offers the basics and daily specials. Staples include pot roast, steak tips, and baked, broiled, or fried seafood.

Northern Exposure (802-525-3789), Rt. 5A, Westmore on Lake Willoughby. Open Mon.–Sat. 6 AM–8 PM, Sun. 8–8; in winter, 6–6, Sun. 8–6. A general store with a deli good for grinders, pizza, BBQ chicken, steak 'n' cheese, salads, chili, and soup of the day (great corn chowder.)

In the Seymour Lake area

Morgan Country Store (802-895-2726), Rt. 111, Morgan Center. A genuine general store with a pay phone (few cell phones work around here), post office, live bait, and an extensive breakfast, lunch (burgers, sandwiches, salads), and pizza menu.

Seymour Lake Market. Open daily Apr.–Oct. Famous breakfast pizza, salads, deli.

In Island Pond and beyond

🦞 🍴 **Jennifer's Restaurant** (802-723-6135), 18 Cross St. At this writing the town's gathering spot for all three meals is closed but is due to reopen. Check for hours.

Pickles Family Restaurant & Pub at the Clyde River Hotel (802-723-5663), 5 Cross St., Island Pond. Open for breakfast, lunch and dinner except Tues. in summer; also closed Mon. in Winter. The 48-seat restaurant in this mid 19th century hotel has taken on new life under current owners. Good for omelets and Belgian style waffles

through seafood platters and baby back ribs. Full liquor.

Friendly Pizza (802-723-4616), 31 Derby St. (Rt. 105). Closed Mon., otherwise open from 11 until at least 9 PM. John Koxarakis offers a variety of pizzas, also steaks, spaghetti, sandwiches, grinders, and Greek salad, in his small eatery on the southern fringe of the village.

DeBanville's General Store (802-962-3311), 47 Rt. 105, Bloomfield. Open Sun.–Wed. 8–8, Thu.–Sat. 8–9. A glorious big, new general store in this lonely junction (just above Brunswick Springs) is a source of subs, wraps, and deli items.

In Canaan

🦞 🍴 **Bessie's Diner**, 166 Gale St., under new ownership, due to reopen in snowmobiling season. Wine and beer. **Cow Licks**, an ice cream window, operates summers.

In the Barton area

🍴 **The Parker Pie Co.** (802-525-3366; parkerpie.com). West Glover Village. Open except Mon., 11–9. A totally delightful space in the back of the village store featuring thin-crust New York–style pizza with toppings that include local veggies and cheeses as well as Vermont smoked sausage and bacon and salads of local greens, plus four beers on tap and wine by the glass. Sandwiches and nachos are also available—but trust us, pizza doesn't get better than this. Live music Thu. evenings.

Parson's Corner (525-4500), 14 Glover Rd. (Rt. 16 on the southern edge of town). Open except Tue. 5–2:30. This cheerful, family-owned eatery serves breakfast all day and daily specials (Monday it's meat loaf). Soups, slaw, ice cream, and a lot more made from scratch.

"1" Barton Pharmacy. Open weekdays 5 AM–7 PM, Sat. 6 AM–7 PM., Sun. 7–3. This is a middle-of-town gathering spot, good for soup, salads, sandwiches, burgers, a fountain, and more.

Candlepin Restaurant (802-525-6513), Rt. 5 north of Barton. Open daily for all three meals. Just minutes off I-91. Under new ownership, a nicely refurbished space with booths, staples like Vermont roast turkey, fried seafood, pie; full liquor license.

Martha's Diner (802-754-6800), Rts. 5/14, Coventry. Open Mon.–Fri. 5 AM–2 PM, Sat. 5:30–1, Sun. 6–1. A classic chrome diner with classic diner food.

❋ Entertainment

&. **Haskell Opera House** (802-873-3020; haskellopera.org), Derby Line. This splendid vintage-1904 theater has perfect acoustics, three antique stage sets, a rare roll-up curtain depicting scenes of Venice, and a rococo interior. Its season runs late Apr.–mid-Oct. and includes performances by a resident theater company, opera, and dance, and a variety of outstanding concerts.

QNEK Productions (802-334-8145), the summer resident theater company at the Haskell, offers reasonably priced evening and matinee productions of musicals and other stock Broadway hits. Tickets for opera house performances are also available at the Woodknot Bookshop, Newport (802-334-6720).

Bread and Puppet Theater Museum (802-525-3031), Rt. 122, Glover. The internationally known Bread and Puppet Theater with its huge and haunting puppet dwarfs, giants, and devils perform Sun. in July and Aug. at 3 PM in the outdoors area and Fri. and Sat. nights in the timber-frame theater. Also see *To See*.

Waterfront Cinemas (802-334-6572), 137 Waterfront Plaza, Newport. First-run films on three screens.

The Piggery Theatre (819-842-2431; piggery.com), 25 Chemin Simard, North Hatley, Quebec. A long-established summer playhouse featuring plays, revues, and other performances, primarily in English.

Note: The **Tamarack Grill at Burke Mountain** is a frequent venue for well-known musical groups. **Parker Pie** on Lake Parker in West Glover (see *Eating Out*) and the **Newport Gateway building** (802-334-1005) on Lake Memphremagog are frequent venues for summer–fall music.

❋ Selective Shopping

Woodknot Books (802-334-6572), 137 Main St., Newport. Open 9–5 except Sun., Fri. until 6. A good selection of books and magazines.

The Great Outdoors (802-334-2831; greatourdoorsvermont.com). 59 Waterfront Plaza, Newport. In summer the store features an extensive array of fishing gear and sells fishing licenses; four-season sporting goods. Rental bikes, kayaks, and canoes, also rental in-line skates, snowshoes, cross-country skis, and snowboards.

Wider than the Sky (802-334-2322; widerthanthesky.com), 158 Main St., Newport. This big, bright combination children's book and toy store is a winner.

Country Thyme (802-766-2852; 800-334-7905; countrythymevermont.com), 60 Rt. 111, Derby (near the junction of Rts. 111 and 5). Every inch of the ground floor in Kay Courson's house is crammed with gifts, toys, specialty foods, Christmas decorations, and more.

In the Jay Area
Trout River Traders (802-326-3058; troutrivertraders.com), Montgomery

Center. Michael Savel and Mark Cellucci have reestablished this photogenic old country store as the village gathering place. Relax with a latte in an easy chair by the fire or on the back deck and browse the shelves for local crafts and products, gifts, antiques, specialty foods, and locally spun yarn and locally made hats and scarves.

Jay Country Store (802-988-4040), Jay Village. Open daily. The center of Jay Village, selling papers, gas, food, and wine basics, also a deli (see *Eating Out*), plus an interesting assortment of gift items and cards.

Couture's Maple Shop (802-744-733; 800-845-2733), 560 Rt. 100, Westfield. Open year-round, Mon.–Sat. 8–6. A long-established maple producer: maple candy, cream, granulated sugar, pancake mix, and salad dressing, as well as syrup; will ship anywhere.

Jed's Maple Products (802-744-2095; jedsmaple.com), 475 Carter Rd., Westfield. Syrup, candy, and frosted nuts. Inquire about the annual Mud Season Sugar On Snow Party.

In Island Pond

Simon the Tanner (802-723-4452), Cross and Main Sts. Open daily except Sat., closing at 3 on Fri., otherwise 9–5, until 8 on Thu. This is an unlikely spot for such a huge shoe store, but here it is selling a wide variety of name-brand shoes—Birkenstock and Clarks sandals, Dansko and Stegmann clogs, Doc Martens, work boots, winter boots, and a big selection of athletic shoes, all at below-usual prices. There is also a nice selection of men's, women's, and children's clothing, a bargain basement, and a line of natural soaps and body care products made by the Twelve Tribes. The store is owned and run by members of this international sect, which came to Island Pond several decades ago, restoring a number of houses and winning the respect of the community.

In the Barton–Glover–Lake Willoughby area

Currier's Quality Market (802-525-8822), Glover. Open year-round daily, Mon.–Sat. 6–9, Sun. 9–6. James and Gloria Currier's general store is a must-stop if just to see the 948-pound (stuffed) moose and variety of formerly live animals lurking in the aisles and festooned from the rafters of this old-style emporium. In addition to staples and a good deli counter with hot specials, this is a major sporting goods store, selling fishing and hunting licenses and stocking extensive gear.

Evansville Trading Post (802-754-6305), Rt. 58 between Orleans and Lake Willoughby. Open early May–Oct. A crafts cooperative for Clan of the Hawk, the local Abenaki Indian band. The 39-acre tribal grounds are the scene of a big powwow the first weekend in August and a crafts show the last week in July.

Willoughby Gap Farmstand (802-467-9847; willoughbygap.com), Rt. 5A just south of Lake Willoughby. Open June–foliage, Tue.–Sun. 11–6. MORE THAN A FARMSTAND, the sign proclaims, and this is true. There are farm-grown veggies, pickles, maple popcorn, plus handmade quilts and other crafted

CURRIER'S QUALITY MARKET, GLOVER

Christina Tree

items, picnic tables, goats, chickens, and a series of special events, like a sugar-on-snow party in July.

Steffi's Studio (802-754-6012), Irasburg green. Steffi Huess crafts gold and silver jewelry, and sells it along with other local arts and crafts right from the front room in her home.

Labour of Love Gardens (802-525-6695), Rt. 16, Glover Village. An acre of public gardens is behind the house, on the Barton River, mid-May until frost, plus antiques and crafts.

Sugarmill Farm (802-525-3701), Rt. 16 south of Barton Village. Mid-Mar.–mid-Nov. The Auger family sell their own syrup; sugar-on-snow in-season.

Sugarwoods Farm (802-525-3718), 2287) Rt. 16, Glover. Open May–Sept., 8–4:30; Feb.–Apr., Sat. 8–1. A major outlet for maple syrup, candy, and sugaring equipment.

In the Eastern Townships of Quebec

Fromagerie La Station (819-835-5301; fromagerielastation.com), 440 Chemin de Hatley, Compton. Open daily June–Nov.; Dec.–May, open Thu.–Sun. 10–5. Compton is less than 20 minutes north of the border, in the middle of rolling farmland. Carole Routhier and her son Simon-Pierre Bolduc make and sell exceptional raw-milk cheeses from the family herd of Holsteins. It's permissible to bring firm cheese back across the border, and we picnicked pleasurably on "Alfred le Fermier" for several days.

Savon des Cantons (877-868-0161; savondescantons.com), N1540 Chemin des Peres, Magog. Continue north on the road by St. Benoit du Lac and you come to this roadside shop (open daily June–Sept., 9–6; May and Oct., Thu.–Sun. 10–5; otherwise on weekends. The herbalist as well as the herbs and oils are from Provence, and the handmade results are therapeutic as well as pleasing.

Vignoble Le Cep d'Argent (877-864-4441; cepdargent.com), 1257 Chemin de la Rivière, Magog. This is a long-established winery on the shore of Lake Memphremagog. The vintners are French and tours are offered Apr.–Thanksgiving. A menu of fruit,

SAVONS DES CANTON, MAGOG, QUEBEC

Christina Tree

local cheese, and crudités or a full meal is also available, as are samplings of its close to 20 products, from champagne to ice wines with a variety of table wines.

Verger le Gros Pierre (819-835-5549; grospierre.com), 6335 Route Louis-St.-Laurent. This is a major orchard (8,000 apple trees, many varieties); also raspberries and strawberries in-season. About 20 minutes through farmland from the border at Norton. We visited on a September Sunday at the height of PYO season and feasted on crêpes stuffed with apples, ham, and cheese, served with sparking cider. Plates of local cheese were also available, along with hard cider. A great place for families with a playground and tractor rides.

✳ Special Events

Last Sunday of January: **Hazen's Notch Ski Race**.

February: **Newport Winter Carnival**. **Barton Snowmobile Races**. **Winter Festival**—varied events include a race from the summit of Jay Peak to Jay Village. **Mountain Mardi Gras** at Jay in late season.

March: **Sugaring** throughout the region.

May: **Open Studio Weekend** (vermontcrafts.com).

June: **Antique Gas/Steam Engine Show** at the Old Stone House Muse-

um in Brownington (oldstonehouse museum.org).

July–August: **Concerts on the common**, presented by the Montgomery Historical Society on Saturday evening (802-326-4404). **Harvest Day**, Montgomery.

August: **Orleans County Arts and Crafts Fair** (*first Saturday*; 802-334-7325) in Barton. **Northeast Kingdom Music Festival** (*first weekend*; nekmf .com) at the Chilly Ranch in Albany. **International Car Show** in Newport (802-334-6079). **Orleans County Fair** (*last week*) in Barton, an old-fashioned event at the extensive fairground—horse, pony, and ox pulling, harness racing, stage shows, demo derby, tractor pull, arts, crafts, and agricultural exhibits. **Clan of the Hawk Pow Wow** at the Evansville Trading Post (see *Selective Shopping*). **Old Stone House Day**—open house, picnic lunch, crafts demonstrations at the museum in Brownington Village (oldstonehousemuseum.org). **North Country Moose Festival** (*last week*)—based in Colebrook, New Hampshire, a series of colorful events on both sides of the Connecticut River.

Columbus Day weekend: **Octoberfest**, Jay Peak—big annual art and crafts fair.

New Year's Eve: **First Night** celebration in St. Johnsbury.

INDEX